The Works of John Owen

VOLUME II

The Works of
JOHN OWEN

EDITED BY
William H. Goold

VOLUME II

The Banner of Truth Trust

This Edition of
THE WORKS OF JOHN OWEN
first published by Johnstone & Hunter, 1850–53

Reprinted by
THE BANNER OF TRUTH TRUST
3 Murrayfield Road, Edinburgh EH12 6EL
PO Box 621, Carlisle, Pennsylvania 17013, USA

VOLUME II

1965
Second printing 1976
Third printing 1980
ISBN 0 85151 124 4

Printed and bound in Great Britain by
Fakenham Press Limited
Fakenham, Norfolk

CONTENTS OF VOL. II.

OF COMMUNION WITH GOD THE FATHER, SON, AND HOLY GHOST.

Page

PREFATORY NOTE BY THE EDITOR 2

Preface 3

Note to the Reader by D. Burgess 4

PART I.

CHAP. I.—That the saints have communion with God—1 John i. 3 considered to that purpose—Somewhat of the nature of communion in general . . . 5

CHAP. II.—That the saints have this communion distinctly with the Father, Son, and Spirit—1 John v. 7 opened to this purpose; also, 1 Cor. xii. 4-6, Eph. ii. 18 —Father and Son mentioned jointly in this communion; the Father solely, the Son also, and the Holy Ghost singly—The saints' respective regard in all worship to each person manifested—Faith in the Father, 1 John v. 9, 10; and love towards him, 1 John ii. 15, Mal. i. 6—So in prayer and praise—It is so likewise with the Son, John xiv. 1—Of our communion with the Holy Ghost—The truth farther confirmed 9

CHAP. III.—Of the peculiar and distinct communion which the saints have with the Father—Observations for the clearing of the whole premised—Our peculiar communion with the Father is in love—1 John iv. 7, 8; 2 Cor. xiii. 14; John xvi. 26, 27; Rom. v. 5; John iii. 16, xiv. 23; Tit. iii. 4, opened to this purpose—What is required of believers to hold communion with the Father in love—His love received by faith—Returns of love to him—God's love to us and ours to him— Wherein they agree—Wherein they differ 17

CHAP. IV.—Inferences on the former doctrine concerning communion with the Father in love 31

PART II.

CHAP. I.—Of the fellowship which the saints have with Jesus Christ the Son of God —That they have such a fellowship proved, 1 Cor. i. 9; Rev. iii. 20: Cant. ii. 1-7 opened; also Prov. ix. 1-5 40

VOL. II.

Page

CHAP. II.—What it is wherein we have peculiar fellowship with the Lord Christ—
This is in grace—This proved, John i. 14, 16, 17; 2 Cor. xiii. 14; 2 Thess. iii.
17, 18—Grace of various acceptations—Personal grace in Christ proposed to consideration—The grace of Christ as mediator intended, Ps. xlv. 2—Cant. v. 10,
Christ, how white and ruddy—His fitness to save, from the grace of union—His
fulness to save—His suitableness to endear—These considerations improved   .   46

CHAP. III.—Of the way and manner whereby the saints hold communion with the
Lord Christ as to personal grace—The conjugal relation between Christ and the
saints, Cant. ii. 16; Isa. liv. 5, etc.; Cant. iii. 11, opened—The way of communion
in conjugal relation, Hos. iii. 3; Cant. i. 15—On the part of Christ—On the part
of the saints   54

DIGRESSION I.

Some excellencies of Christ proposed to consideration, to endear our hearts unto
him—His description, Cant. v., opened   59

DIGRESSION II.

All solid wisdom laid up in Christ—True wisdom, wherein it consists—Knowledge
of God, in Christ only to be obtained—What of God may be known by his
works—Some properties of God not discovered but in Christ only; love, mercy
—Others not fully but in him; as vindictive justice, patience, wisdom, all-
sufficiency—No property of God savingly known but in Christ—What is required to a saving knowledge of the properties of God—No true knowledge
of ourselves but in Christ—Knowledge of ourselves, wherein it consisteth—
Knowledge of sin, how to be had in Christ; also of righteousness and of judgment—The wisdom of walking with God hid in Christ—What is required
thereunto—Other pretenders to the title of wisdom examined and rejected—
Christ alone exalted   79

CHAP. IV.—Of communion with Christ in a conjugal relation in respect of consequential affections—His delight in his saints first insisted on, Isa. lxii. 5; Cant.
iii. 11; Prov. viii. 31—Instance of Christ's delight in believers—He reveals his
whole heart to them, John xv. 14, 15; himself, John xiv. 21; his kingdom;
enables them to communicate their mind to him, giving them assistance, a way,
boldness, Rom. viii. 26, 27—The saints delight in Christ; this manifested Cant.
ii. 7, viii. 6—Cant. iii. 1-5, opened—Their delight in his servants and ordinances
of worship for his sake   117

CHAP. V.—Other consequential affections:—1. On the part of Christ—He values his
saints—Evidences of that valuation:—(1.) His incarnation; (2.) Exinanition,
2 Cor. viii. 9; Phil. ii. 6, 7; (3.) Obedience as a servant; (4.) In his death. His
valuation of them in comparison of others. 2. Believers' estimation of Christ:—
(1.) They value him above all other things and persons; (2.) Above their own
lives; (3.) All spiritual excellencies. The sum of all on the part of Christ—The
sum on the part of believers. The third conjugal affection—On the part of
Christ, pity or compassion—Wherein manifested—Suffering and supply, fruits
of compassion—Several ways whereby Christ relieves the saints under temptations—His compassion in their afflictions. Chastity, the third conjugal affection
in the saints. The fourth—On the part of Christ, bounty; on the part of the
saints, duty   133

CHAP. VI.—Of communion with Christ in purchased grace—Purchased grace considered in respect of its rise and fountain—The first rise of it, in the obedience
of Christ—Obedience properly ascribed to Christ—Two ways considered: what

Page

it was, and wherein it did consist—Of his obedience to the law in general—Of the law of the Mediator—His habitual righteousness, how necessary; as also his obedience to the law of the Mediator—Of his actual obedience or active righteousness—All Christ's obedience performed as he was Mediator—His active obedience for us—This proved at large, Gal. iv. 4, 5; Rom. v. 18, 19; Phil. iii. 9; Zech. iii. 3–5—One objection removed—Considerations of Christ's active righteousness closed—Of the death of Christ, and its influence into our acceptation with God—A price; redemption, what it is—A sacrifice; atonement made thereby—A punishment; satisfaction thereby—The intercession of Christ; with its influence into our acceptation with God 154

CHAP. VII.—The nature of purchased grace; referred to three heads:—1. Of our acceptation with God; two parts of it. 2. Of the grace of sanctification; the several parts of it 169

CHAP. VIII.—How the saints hold communion with Christ as to their acceptation with God—What is required on the part of Christ hereunto; in his intention; in the declaration thereof—The sum of our acceptation with God, wherein it consists—What is required on the part of believers to this communion, and how they hold it, with Christ—Some objections proposed to consideration, why the elect are not accepted immediately on the undertaking and the death of Christ—In what sense they are so—Christ a common or public person—How he came to be so—The way of our acceptation with God on that account—The second objection—The necessity of our obedience stated, Eph. ii. 8–10—The grounds, causes, and ends of it manifested—Its proper place in the new covenant—How the saints, in particular, hold communion with Christ in this purchased grace—They approve of this righteousness; the grounds thereof—Reject their own; the grounds thereof—The commutation of sin and righteousness between Christ and believers; some objections answered 173

CHAP. IX.—Of communion with Christ in holiness—The several acts ascribed unto the Lord Christ herein: 1. His intercession; 2. Sending of the Spirit; 3. Bestows habitual grace—What that is, and wherein it consists—This purchased by Christ; bestowed by him—Of actual grace—How the saints hold communion with Christ in these things; manifested in sundry particulars . . . 197

CHAP. X.—Of communion with Christ in privileges—Of adoption; the nature of it, the consequences of it—Peculiar privileges attending it; liberty, title, boldness, affliction—Communion with Christ hereby 207

PART III.

CHAP. I.—The foundation of our communion with the Holy Ghost (John xvi. 1–7) opened at large—Παράκλητος, a Comforter; who he is—The Holy Ghost; his own will in his coming to us; sent also by Christ—The Spirit sent as a sanctifier and as a comforter—The adjuncts of his mission considered—The foundation of his mission, John xv. 26—His procession from the Father twofold; as to personality, as to office—Things considerable in his procession as to office—The manner of his collation—He is given freely; sent authoritatively—The sin against the Holy Ghost, whence unpardonable—How we ask the Spirit of the Father—To grieve the Spirit, what—Poured out—How the Holy Ghost is received; by faith—Faith's actings in receiving the Holy Ghost—His abode with us, how declared—How we may lose our comfort whilst the Comforter abides with us . . 222

CHAP. II.—Of the actings of the Holy Ghost in us, being bestowed on us—He worketh effectually, distributeth, giveth 234

Page

CHAP. III.—Of the things wherein we have communion with the Holy Ghost—He brings to remembrance the things spoken by Christ, John xiv. 26—The manner how he doth it—The Spirit glorifies Christ in the hearts of believers, John xvi. 14, sheds abroad the love of God in them—The witness of the Spirit, what it is, Rom. viii. 16—The sealing of the Spirit, Eph. i. 13—The Spirit, how an earnest; on the part of God, on the part of the saints—Difference between the earnest of the Spirit and tasting of the powers of the world to come—Unction by the Spirit, Isa. xi. 2, 3—The various teachings of the Holy Ghost—How the Spirit of adoption and of supplication 236

CHAP. IV.—The general consequences in the hearts of believers of the effects of the Holy Ghost before mentioned—Consolation; its adjuncts, peace, joy—How it is wrought immediately, mediately 249

CHAP. V.—Some observations and inferences from discourses foregoing concerning the Spirit—The contempt of the whole administration of the Spirit by some—The vain pretence of the Spirit by others—The false spirit discovered . . 254

CHAP. VI.—Of particular communion with the Holy Ghost—Of preparation thereunto —Valuation of the benefits we receive by him—What it is he comforts us in and against; wherewith; how 259

CHAP. VII.—The general ways of the saints' acting in communion with the Holy Ghost 264

CHAP. VIII.—Particular directions for communion with the Holy Ghost . . 268

A VINDICATION OF SOME PASSAGES IN A DISCOURSE CONCERNING COMMUNION WITH GOD.

PREFATORY NOTE BY THE EDITOR 276
A Vindication of some Passages, &c. 277

A BRIEF DECLARATION AND VINDICATION OF THE DOCTRINE OF THE TRINITY.

PREFATORY NOTE BY THE EDITOR 366
To the Reader 367
Preface 371
The Doctrine of the Holy Trinity explained and vindicated . . . 377
Of the Person of Christ 413
Of the Satisfaction of Christ 419
Appendix 441

OF

COMMUNION

WITH

GOD THE FATHER, SON, AND HOLY GHOST,

EACH PERSON DISTINCTLY,

IN LOVE, GRACE, AND CONSOLATION;

OR,

THE SAINTS' FELLOWSHIP WITH THE FATHER, SON, AND HOLY GHOST UNFOLDED.

" God is love."—1 JOHN iv. 8.
" Tell me, O thou whom my soul loveth, where thou feedest."—CANT. i. 7.
" Make haste, my beloved."—CANT. viii. 14.
" Grieve not the Holy Spirit of God, whereby ye are sealed unto the day of redemption."—EPH. iv. 30.
" Now there are diversities of gifts, but the same Spirit. And there are differences of administrations, but the same Lord. And there are diversities of operations, but it is the same God."—1 COR. xii. 4-6.

PREFATORY NOTE.

THE reader may be referred to the Life of Dr Owen (vol. i. p. lxxii.) for a general criticism on the merits of the following treatise. It was published in 1657, shortly after he had ceased to be Vice-Chancellor in the University of Oxford. From the brief preface affixed to it, it appears that, for a period of more than six years, he had been under some engagement to publish the substance of the work. It has been inferred, accordingly, that it is the substance of some discourses which he had preached in Oxford; but, as he became Vice-Chancellor only in September 1652, there is more probability in the supposition that they are the discourses which refreshed and cheered his attached congregation at Coggeshall.

There are two peculiarities which deserve attention in the treatise. The oversight of one of them has created some misconception of the author's design, and led some to fancy that he was wandering from it, in various passages which are in strict harmony with his main and original purpose in the work. The term "Communion," as used by Owen, is used in a wider sense than is consistent with that which is now generally attached to it in religious phraseology. It denotes not merely the interchange of feeling between God in his gracious character and a soul in a gracious state, but the gracious relationship upon which this holy interchange is based. On the part of Christ, for example, all his work and its results are described, from the atonement till it takes effect in the actual justification of the sinner.

The grand peculiarity distinguishing the treatise is the fulness of illustration with which he dilates on the communion enjoyed by believers with each person of the Godhead respectively. Fully to comprehend his views on this point, it is needful to bear in mind the meaning under which the word Communion is employed by Owen.

ANALYSIS.

PART I.—The fact of communion with God is asserted, CHAP. I. Passages in Scripture are quoted to show that special mention is made of communion with all the persons of the Trinity, II. Communion with the FATHER is described, III.; and practical inferences deduced from it, IV.

PART II.—The reality of communion with CHRIST is proved, CHAP. I.; and the nature of it is subsequently considered, II. It is shown to consist in grace; and then the grace of Christ is exhibited under three divisions :—his *personal grace*, III.–VI.; and under this branch are two long digressions. designed to unfold the glory and loveliness of Christ;—*purchased grace*, VII.–X.; in which the mediatorial work of Christ is fully considered, in reference to our acceptance with God, VII., VIII.; sanctification, IX.; and the privileges of the covenant, X.;—and *grace* as *communicated* by the *Spirit*, and conspicuous in the fruits of personal holiness. This last division is illustrated under sanctification, as contained under the head of *purchased grace*.

PART III.—Communion with the HOLY GHOST is expounded in the eight following chapters ;—the foundation of it, CHAP. I.; his gracious and effectual influence in believers, II.; the elements in which it consists, III.; the effects in the hearts of believers, IV.; and general inferences and particular directions for communion with the Spirit, V.–VIII.

The arrangement of the treatise may seem involved and complicated, and the endless divisions and subdivisions may distract rather than assist the attention of the reader. The warm glow of sanctified emotion, however, and occasionally thoughts of singular power and originality, which are found throughout the treatise, sustain the interest, and more than reward perusal. Few passages in any theological writer are more thrilling than the reference to the spotless humanity of Christ, in terms full of sanctified genius, on page 64.

An account of the strange controversy to which this treatise gave rise, many years after its publication, will be found on page 276.—ED.

PREFACE.

IT is now six years past since I was brought under an engagement of promise for the publishing of some meditations on the subject which thou wilt find handled in the ensuing treatise. The reasons of this delay, being not of public concernment, I shall not need to mention. Those who have been in expectation of this duty from me, have, for the most part, been so far acquainted with my condition and employments, as to be able to satisfy themselves as to the deferring of their desires. That which I have to add at present is only this:—having had many opportunities, since the time I first delivered any thing in public on this subject (which was the means of bringing me under the engagements mentioned), to re-assume the consideration of what I had first fixed on, I have been enabled to give it that improvement, and to make those additions to the main of the design and matter treated on, that my first debt is come at length to be only the occasion of what is now tendered to the saints of God. I shall speak nothing of the subject here handled; it may, I hope, speak for itself, in that spiritual savour and relish which it will yield to them whose hearts are not so filled with other things as to render the sweet things of the gospel bitter to them. The design of the whole treatise thou wilt find, Christian reader, in the first chapters of the first part; and I shall not detain thee here with the perusal of any thing which in its proper place will offer itself unto thee: know only, that the whole of it hath been recommended to the grace of God in many supplications, for its usefulness unto them that are interested in the good things mentioned therein.

J. O.

OXON. CH. CH. COLL.,
 July 10, 1657.

TO THE READER.

ALPHONSUS, king of Spain, is said to have found food and physic in reading Livy; and Ferdinand, king of Sicily, in reading Quintus Curtius: but thou hast here nobler entertainments, vastly richer dainties, incomparably more sovereign medicines;—I had almost said, the very highest of angel's food is here set before thee; and, as Pliny speaks, " permista deliciis auxilia,"—things that minister unto grace and comfort, to holy life and liveliness.

Such is this treatise,—this, which is the only one extant upon its great and necessary subject,—this, whose praise hath been long in the churches, and hath gone enamelled with the honourable reproaches of more than one English Bolsec, —this, whose great author, like the sun, is well known to the world, by eminence of heavenly light and labours,—this, which, as his many other works, can be no other than manna unto sound Christians, though no better than stone and serpent to Socinians and their fellow-commoners.

Importunity hath drawn me to say thus much more than I could think needful to be said concerning any work of Dr Owen's;—needful in our day itself, a day wherein " pauci sacras Scripturas, plures nomina rerum, plurimi nomina magistrorum sequuntur;"—" few do cleave to the holy Scriptures ; many do rest in scholastic, senseless sounds; and most men do hang their faith upon their rabbi's sleeves."

This only I add:—of the swarms every day rising, there are few books but do want their readers ; yet, if I understand aright, there are not many readers but do want this book.

In which censure I think I am no tyrant, which the philosopher names the worst of wild beasts; and I am sure I am no flatterer, which he calls, as justly, the worst of tame beasts,—Καὶ ταῦτα μὲν δὴ ταῦτα.

Let the simple souls (the " paucissimæ lectionis mancipia") who take the doctrine of distinct communion with the Divine Persons to be a new-fangled one and uncouth, observe the words of the Rev. Mr Samuel Clarke (the annotator on the Bible), in his sermon on 1 John i. 7: " It is to be noted, that there is a distinct fellowship with each of the persons of the blessed Trinity." Let them attend what is said by Mr Lewis Stuckley, in his preface to Mr Polwheil's book of Quenching the Spirit: " It is a most glorious truth, though considered but by few, that believers have, or may have, distinct communion with the three persons, Father, Son, and Spirit. This is attested by the finger of God, and solemnly owned by the first and best age of Christianity." To name no more, let them read heedfully but the second chapter of this treatise, and it is hoped that then they shall no longer " contra antidotum insanire, "—no longer rage against God's holy medicinal truth, as St Austin saith he did while he was a Manichee; testifying, in so many words, [that] his error was his very god.

Reader, I am

Thy servant in Christ Jesus,

DANIEL BURGESS.[1]

[1] See vol ix. p. 2.

OF COMMUNION WITH GOD.

PART I.

CHAPTER I.

That the saints have communion with God—1 John i. 3 considered to that purpose—Somewhat of the nature of communion in general.

IN the First Epistle of John, chap. i., verse 3, the apostle assures them to whom he wrote that the fellowship of believers "is with the Father, and with his Son Jesus Christ:"[1] and this he doth with such an unusual kind of expression as bears the force of an asseveration; whence we have rendered it, "Truly our fellowship is with the Father, and with his Son Jesus Christ."

The outward appearance and condition of the saints in those days being very mean and contemptible,—their leaders being accounted as the filth of this world, and as the offscouring of all things,[2]—the inviting others unto fellowship with them, and a participation of the precious things which they did enjoy, seems to be exposed to many contrary reasonings and objections: "What benefit is there in *communion* with them? Is it any thing else but to be sharers in troubles, reproaches, scorns, and all manner of evils?" To prevent or remove these and the like exceptions, the apostle gives them to whom he wrote to know (and that with some earnestness of expression), that notwithstanding all the disadvantages their fellowship lay under, unto a carnal view, yet in truth it was, and would be found to be (in reference to *some* with whom they held it), very honourable, glorious, and desirable. For "truly," saith he, "our fellowship is with the Father, and with his Son Jesus Christ."

This being so earnestly and directly asserted by the apostle, we may boldly follow him with our affirmation,—namely, "*That the saints of God have communion with him.*" And *a holy and spiritual* communion it is, as shall be declared. How this is spoken

---

[1] Καὶ ἡ κοινωνία δὲ ἡ ἡμετέρα, etc.

[2] Ὡς περικαθάρματα τοῦ κόσμου.—1 Cor. iv. 8–13; Rom. viii. 35, 36; Heb. x. 32–34. "Christianos ad leones. Et puto, nos Deus apostolos novissimos elegit veluti bestiarios."—Tert. de Pud., Acts xvii. 18; Gal. vi. 12. "Semper casuris similes, nunquamque cadentes."

distinctly in reference to the Father and the Son, must afterward be fully opened and carried on.

By nature, since the entrance of sin, no man hath any communion with God. He is *light*,[1] we *darkness;* and what communion hath light with darkness? He is *life*, we are *dead*,—he is *love*, and we are *enmity;* and what agreement can there be between us? Men in such a condition have neither Christ,[2] nor hope, nor God in the world, Eph. ii. 12; "being alienated from the life of God through the ignorance that is in them," chap. iv. 18. Now, two cannot walk together, unless they be agreed, Amos iii. 3. Whilst there is this *distance* between God and man, there is no *walking together* for them in any fellowship or communion. Our first *interest* in God was so lost by sin,[3] as that there was left unto us (in ourselves) no possibility of a recovery. As we had deprived ourselves of all *power* for a returnal, so God had not revealed any way of *access* unto himself; or that he could, under any consideration, be approached unto by sinners in peace. Not any *work* that God had made, not any *attribute* that he had revealed, could give the least light into such a dispensation.

The manifestation of grace and pardoning mercy, which is the only door of entrance into any such communion, is not committed unto any but unto him alone[4] *in* whom it is, *by* whom that grace and mercy was purchased, *through* whom it is dispensed, who reveals it from the bosom of the Father. Hence this communion and fellowship with God is not in express terms mentioned in the Old Testament. The thing itself is found there; but the clear light of it, and the boldness of faith in it, is discovered in the gospel, and by the Spirit administered therein. By that Spirit we have this liberty, 2 Cor. iii. 17, 18. Abraham was the *friend* of God, Isa. xli. 8; David, a man after his own *heart;* Enoch *walked* with him, Gen. v. 22;—all enjoying this communion and fellowship for the substance of it. But the way into the holiest was not yet made manifest whilst the first tabernacle was standing, Heb. ix. 8. Though they had communion with God, yet they had not παῤῥησίαν,—a boldness and confidence in that communion. This follows the entrance of our High Priest into the most holy place, Heb. iv. 16, x. 19. The vail also was upon them, that they had not ἐλευθερίαν, freedom and liberty in their access

[1] 1 John i. 5; 2 Cor. vi. 14; Eph. v. 8; John v. 21; Matt. xxii. 32; Eph. ii. 1; 1 John iv. 8; Rom. viii. 7.

[2] "Magna hominis miseria est cum illo non esse, sine quo non potest esse."—August.

[3] Eccles. vii. 29; Jer. xiii. 23; Acts iv. 12; Isa. xxxiii. 14.

[4] John i. 18; Heb. x. 19–21. "Unus verusque Mediator per sacrificium pacis reconcilians nos Deo; unum cum illo manebat cui offerebat; unum in se fecit, pro quibus offerebat; unus ipse fuit, qui offerebat, et quod offerebat."—[Slightly changed from] August. de Trinit., iv. c. 14.

to God, 2 Cor. iii. 15, 16, etc. But now in Christ we have [1]bold-ness and access with confidence to God, Eph. iii. 12. This boldness and access with confidence the saints of old were not acquainted with. By Jesus Christ alone, then, on all considerations as to being and full manifestation, is this distance taken away. He hath con-secrated for us a new and living way (the old being quite shut up), "through the vail, that is to say, his flesh," Heb. x. 20; and " through him we have access by one Spirit unto the Father," Eph. ii. 18. " Ye who sometimes were far off, are made nigh by the blood of Christ, for he is our peace," etc., verses 13, 14. Of this foundation of all our communion with God, more afterward, and at large. Upon this new bottom and foundation, by this new and living way, are sinners admitted unto communion with God, and have fellowship with him. And truly, for sinners to have fellowship with God, the infinitely holy God, is an astonishing dispensation.[2] To speak a little of it in general:—Communion relates to things and persons. A joint participation in any thing whatever, good or evil,[3] duty or enjoy-ment, nature or actions, gives this denomination to them so partaking of it. A common interest in the same *nature* gives all men a fellow-ship or communion therein. Of the elect it is said, Τὰ παιδία κεκοι-νώνηκε σαρκὸς καὶ αἵματος, Heb. ii. 14, " Those children partook of " (or had fellowship in, with the rest of the world) " flesh and blood,"— the same common nature with the rest of mankind; and, therefore, Christ also came into the same fellowship: Καὶ αὐτὸς παραπλησίως μετέσχε τῶν αὐτῶν. There is also a communion as to *state* and *con-dition,* whether it be good or evil; and this, either in things *internal* and spiritual,—such as is the communion of saints among themselves; or in respect of *outward* things. So was it with Christ and the two thieves, as to one condition, and to one of them in respect of another. They were ἐν τῷ αὐτῷ κρίματι,—under the same sentence to the cross, Luke xxiii. 40, " ejusdem doloris socii." They had communion as to that evil condition whereunto they were adjudged; and one of them requested (which he also obtained) a participation in that blessed condition whereupon our Saviour was immediately to enter. There is also a communion or fellowship in *actions,* whether *good* or *evil.* In *good,* is that communion and fellowship in the gospel, or in the performance and celebration of that worship of God which in the gospel is instituted; which the saints do enjoy, Phil. i. 5; which, as to the general kind of it, David so rejoices in, Ps. xlii. 4. In *evil,* was

---

[1] Παῤῥησίαν καὶ τὴν προσαγωγὴν ἐν πεποιθήσει.

[2] 1 John iii. 1. Φίλων μὲν ὄντων, οὐδὲν δεῖ δικαιοσύνης· δίκαιοι δὲ ὄντες προσδέονται φιλίας.—Arist. Eth., lib. viii. cap. 1.

[3] " Quemadmodum enim nobis arrhabonem Spiritus reliquit, ita et a nobis arrhabonem carnis accepit, et vexit in cœlum, pignus totius summæ illuc quan-doque redigendæ."—Tertul. De Resur., c. li.

that wherein Simeon and Levi were brethren, Gen. xlix. 5. They had communion in that cruel act of revenge and murder. Our communion with God is not comprised in any one of these kinds; of some of them it is *exclusive*. It cannot be natural; it must be *voluntary* and by consent. It cannot be of state and conditions; but in actions. It cannot be in the same actions upon a third party; but in a return from one to another. The infinite disparity that is between God and man, made the great philosopher conclude that there could be no friendship between them.[1] Some distance in the persons holding friendship he could allow, nor could exactly determine the bounds and extent thereof; but that between God and man, in his apprehension, left no place for it. Another says, indeed, that there is "communitas homini cum Deo,"—a certain fellowship between God and man; but the general intercourse of providence is all he apprehended. Some arose to higher expressions; but they understood nothing whereof they spake. This knowledge is hid in Christ; as will afterward be made to appear. It is too wonderful for nature, as sinful and corrupted. Terror and apprehensions of death at the presence of God is all that it guides unto. But we have, as was said, a *new* foundation, and a *new* discovery of this privilege.

Now, communion is the mutual communication of such good things as wherein the persons holding that communion are delighted, bottomed upon some union between them. So it was with Jonathan and David; their souls clave to one another (1 Sam. xx. 17) *in love*.[2] There was the *union* of love between them; and then they really communicated all issues of love mutually.[3] In spiritual things this is more eminent: those who enjoy this communion have the most excellent union for the foundation of it; and the issues of that union, which they mutually communicate, are the most precious and eminent.

Of the union which is the foundation of all that communion we have with God I have spoken largely elsewhere, and have nothing farther to add thereunto.

Our communion, then, with God consisteth in his *communication of himself unto us, with our returnal unto him* of that which he requireth and accepteth, flowing from that *union*[4] which in Jesus Christ

---

[1] Ἀκριβὴς μὲν οὖν ἐν τοιούτοις οὐκ ἔστιν ὁρισμός, ἕως τίνος οἱ φίλοι πολλῶν γὰρ ἀφαιρουμένων, ἔτι μένει, πολὺ δὲ χωρισθέντος, οἷον τοῦ Θεοῦ οὐκ ἔτι.—Aristot. Eth., lib. viii. c. 7; Cicer. de Nat. Deor., lib. i.   [2] Πάντα τὰ τῶν φίλων κοινά.

[3] Καὶ ἡ παροιμία, κοινὰ τὰ φίλων, ὀρθῶς, ἐν κοινωνίᾳ γὰρ ἡ φιλία.—Arist. Eth., viii.

[4] "Nostra quippe et ipsius conjunctio, nec miscet personas, nec unit substantias, sed affectus consociat, et confœderat voluntates."—Cyp. de Cœn. Domini. [No treatise of Cyprian bears such a title. There is a treatise, " De Cœnâ Domini," ascribed to Cyprian, but on grounds so questionable and insufficient that it is sometimes not included among his supposititious works. A statement referring to the union between Christ and his people, as illustrated by the sacramental elements, occurs in his letter to Cœcilius, " De Sacramento Dominici Calicis ;" but the words of the above quotation are not contained in it.]

we have with him. And it is twofold:—1. *Perfect and complete*, in the full fruition of his glory and total giving up of ourselves to him, resting in him as our utmost end; which we shall enjoy when we see him as he is;—and, 2. *Initial and incomplete*, in the first-fruits and dawnings of that perfection which we have here in grace; which only I shall handle.

It is, then, I say, of that mutual communication[1] in giving and receiving, after a most holy and spiritual manner, which is between God and the saints while they walk together in a covenant of peace, ratified in the blood of Jesus, whereof we are to treat. And this we shall do, if God permit; in the meantime praying the God and Father of our Lord and Saviour Jesus Christ, who hath, of the riches of his grace, recovered us from a state of enmity into a condition of communion and fellowship with himself, that both he that writes, and they that read the words of his mercy, may have such a taste of his sweetness and excellencies therein, as to be stirred up to a farther longing after the fulness of his salvation, and the eternal fruition of him in glory.

CHAPTER II.

That the saints have this communion distinctly with the Father, Son, and Spirit— 1 John v. 7 opened to this purpose; also, 1 Cor. xii. 4-6, Eph. ii. 18—Father and Son mentioned jointly in this communion; the Father solely, the Son also, and the Holy Ghost singly—The saints' respective regard in all worship to each person manifested—Faith in the Father, John v. 9, 10; and love towards him, 1 John ii. 15, Mal. i. 6—So in prayer and praise—It is so likewise with the Son, John xiv. 1—Of our communion with the Holy Ghost—The truth farther confirmed.

THAT the saints have communion with God, and what communion in general is, was declared in the first chapter. The *manner* how this communion is carried on, and the *matter* wherein it doth consist, comes next under consideration. For the *first*, in respect of the distinct persons of the Godhead with whom they have this fellowship, it is either *distinct* and peculiar, or else obtained and exercised *jointly* and in common. That the saints have distinct communion with the Father, and the Son, and the Holy Spirit (that is, distinctly with the Father, and distinctly with the Son, and distinctly with the Holy Spirit), and in what the peculiar *appropriation* of this distinct com-

[1] " Magna etiam illa communitas est, quæ conficitur ex beneficiis ultro citro, datis acceptis."—Cic. Off., lib. i. c. 17.

munion unto the several persons doth consist, must, in the first place, be made manifest.[1]

1 John v. 7, the apostle tells us, "There are three that bear record in heaven, the Father, the Word, and the Holy Ghost." In heaven they are, and bear witness to us. And what is it that they bear witness unto? Unto the sonship of Christ, and the salvation of believers in his blood. Of the carrying on of that, both by blood and water, justification and sanctification, is he there treating. Now, how do they bear witness hereunto? even as three, as three distinct witnesses. When God witnesseth concerning our salvation, surely it is incumbent on us to receive his testimony. And *as* he beareth witness, *so* are we to receive it. Now this is done distinctly. The Father beareth witness, the Son beareth witness, and the Holy Spirit beareth witness; for they are three distinct witnesses. So, then, are we to receive their several testimonies: and in doing so we have communion with them severally; for in *this giving and receiving* of testimony consists no small part of our fellowship with God. Wherein their distinct witnessing consists will be afterward declared.

1 Cor. xii. 4–6, the apostle, speaking of the distribution of gifts and graces unto the saints, ascribes them distinctly, in respect of the fountain of their communication, unto the distinct persons. "There are diversities of gifts, but the same SPIRIT,"[2]—"that one and the self-same Spirit;" that is, the Holy Ghost, verse 11. "And there are differences of administrations, but the same Lord," the same Lord Jesus, verse 5. "And there are diversities of operations, but it is the same God," etc., even the Father, Eph. iv. 6. So graces and gifts are bestowed, and so are they received.

And not only in the *emanation* of grace from God, and the *illapses* of the Spirit on us, but also in all our approaches unto God, is the same distinction observed.[3] "For through Christ we have access by one Spirit unto the Father," Eph. ii. 18. Our access unto God (wherein we have communion with him) is διὰ Χριστοῦ, "through Christ," ἐν Πνεύματι, "in the Spirit," and πρὸς τὸν Πατέρα, "unto the Father;"—the persons being here considered as engaged *distinctly* unto the accomplishment of the counsel of the will of God revealed in the gospel.

Sometimes, indeed, there is express mention made only of the

---

[1] "Ecce dico alium esse patrem, et alium filium, non divisione alium, sed distinctione."—Tertul. adv. Prax.

Οὐ φθάνω τὸ ἓν νοῆσαι, καὶ τοῖς τρισὶ περιλάμπομαι, οὐ φθάνω τὰ τρία διελεῖν, καὶ εἰς τὸ ἓν ἀναφέρομαι.—Greg. Naz.

[2] Χαρίσματα, διακονίας, ἐνεργήματα.

[3] Πᾶσαν μὲν γὰρ δέησιν καὶ προσευχὴν καὶ ἔντευξιν, καὶ εὐχαριστίαν ἀναπεμπτέον τῷ ἐπὶ πᾶσι Θεῷ, διὰ τοῦ ἐπὶ πάντων ἀγγέλων ἀρχιερέως ἐμψύχου λόγου καὶ Θεοῦ.—Orig. cont. Cels., lib. v. [c. 4.]

Father and the Son, 1 John i. 3, " Our fellowship is with the Father, and with his Son Jesus Christ." The particle " and" is both distinguishing and uniting. Also John xiv. 23, " If a man love me, he will keep my words : and my Father will love him, and we will come unto him, and make our abode with him." It is in this communion wherein Father and Son do make their abode with the soul.

Sometimes the Son only is spoken of, as to this purpose. 1 Cor. i. 9, " God is faithful, by whom ye were called unto the fellowship of his Son Jesus Christ our Lord." And, Rev. iii. 20, " If any man hear my voice, and open the door, I will come in to him, and will sup with him, and he with me;"—of which place afterward.

Sometimes the Spirit alone is mentioned. 2 Cor. xiii. 14, " The grace of the Lord Jesus Christ, and the love of God, and the communion of the Holy Ghost be with you all." This distinct communion, then, of the saints with the Father, Son, and Spirit, is very plain in the Scripture; but yet it may admit of farther demonstration Only this caution I must lay in beforehand :—whatever is affirmed in the pursuit of this truth, it is done with relation to the explanation ensuing, in the beginning of the next chapter.

The way and means, then, on the part of the saints, whereby in Christ they enjoy communion with God, are all the spiritual and holy actings[1] and outgoings of their souls in those graces, and by those ways, wherein both the *moral* and *instituted* worship of God doth consist. Faith, love, trust, joy, etc., are the natural or moral worship of God, whereby those in whom they are have communion with him. Now, these are either *immediately* acted on God, and not tied to any ways or means outwardly manifesting themselves; or else they are farther drawn forth, in solemn prayer and praises, according unto that way which he hath appointed. That the Scripture doth distinctly assign all these unto the Father, Son, and Spirit,—manifesting that the saints do, in all of them, both as they are purely and nakedly moral, and as farther clothed with instituted worship, respect each person respectively,—is that which, to give light to the assertion in hand, I shall farther declare by particular instances :—

1. For the FATHER. Faith, love, obedience, etc., are peculiarly and distinctly yielded by the saints unto him; and he is peculiarly manifested in those ways as acting *peculiarly* towards them : which should draw them forth and stir them up thereunto. He gives *testimony* unto, and beareth witness of, his Son, 1 John v. 9, " This is the witness of God which he hath testified of his Son." In his bearing witness he is an object of belief. When he gives testimony (which he doth as the Father, because he doth it of the Son) he is to be received in it by faith. And this is affirmed, verse 10, " He that

[1] Hic tibi præcipuè sit purâ mente colendus.

believeth on the Son of God, hath the witness in himself." To believe on the Son of God in this place, is to receive the Lord Christ as the Son, the Son given unto us,[1] for all the ends of the Father's love, upon the credit of the Father's testimony; and, therefore, therein is faith immediately acted on the Father. So it follows in the next words, " He that believeth not God" (that is, the Father, who bears witness to the Son) " hath made him a liar." " Ye believe in God," saith our Saviour, John xiv. 1; that is, the Father as such, for he adds, " Believe also in me;" or, " Believe you in God; believe also in me." God, as the *prima Veritas*, upon whose authority is founded, and whereunto all divine faith is ultimately resolved, is not to be considered ὑποστατικῶς, as peculiarly expressive of any person, but οὐσιωδῶς, comprehending the whole Deity; which undividedly is the prime object thereof. But in this particular it is the testimony and authority of the Father (as such) therein, of which we speak, and whereupon faith is distinctly fixed on him;—which, if it were not so, the Son could not add, " Believe also in me."

The like also is said of love. 1 John ii. 15, " If any man love the world, the love of the Father is not in him;" that is, the love which we bear to him, not that which we receive from him. The Father is here placed as the object of our love, in opposition to the world, which takes up our affections ἡ ἀγάπη τοῦ Πατρός. The Father denotes the matter and object, not the efficient cause, of the love inquired after. And this love of him as a Father is that which he calls his " honour," Mal. i. 6.

Farther: these graces as acted in prayer and praises, and as clothed with instituted worship, are peculiarly directed unto him. " Ye call on the Father," 1 Pet. i. 17. Eph. iii. 14, 15, " For this cause I bow my knees unto the Father of our Lord Jesus Christ, of whom the whole family in heaven and earth is named." Bowing the knee compriseth the whole worship of God, both that which is moral, in the universal obedience he requireth, and those peculiar ways of carrying it on which are by him appointed, Isa. xlv. 23, " Unto me," saith the Lord, " every knee shall bow, every tongue shall swear." Which, verses 24, 25, he declareth to consist in their acknowledging of him for righteousness and strength. Yea, it seems sometimes to comprehend the *orderly* subjection of the whole creation unto his sovereignty.[2] In this place of the apostle it hath a far more restrained acceptation, and is but a figurative expression of prayer, taken from the most expressive *bodily* posture to be used in

---

[1] Isa. ix. 6; 1 Cor. i. 30; Matt. v. 16, 45, vi. 1, 4, 6, 8, vii. 21, xii. 50; Luke xxiv. 49; John iv. 23, vi. 45, xii. 26, xiv. 6, 21, 23, xv. 1, xvi. 25, 27, xx. 17; Gal. i. 1, 3; Eph. ii. 18, v. 20; 1 Thess. i. 1; James i. 17; 1 Pet. i. 17; 1 John ii. 13, etc.
[2] Rom. xiv. 10, 11; Phil. ii. 10.

that duty. This he farther manifests, Eph. iii. 16, 17, declaring at large what his aim was, and whereabouts his thoughts were exercised, in that bowing of his knees. The workings, then, of the Spirit of grace in that duty are distinctly directed to the Father as such, as the fountain of the Deity, and of all good things in Christ,—as the "Father of our Lord Jesus Christ." And therefore the same apostle doth, in another place, expressly *conjoin*, and yet as expressly *distinguish*, the Father and the Son in directing his supplications, 1 Thess. iii. 11, "God himself even our Father, and our Lord Jesus Christ, direct our way unto you." The like precedent, also, have you of thanksgiving, Eph. i. 3, 4, "Blessed be the God and Father of our Lord Jesus Christ," etc. I shall not add those very *many places* wherein the several particulars[1] that do concur unto that whole divine worship (not to be communicated unto any, by nature not God, without idolatry) wherein the saints do hold communion with God, are distinctly directed to the person of the Father.

2. It is so also in reference unto the SON. John xiv. 1, "Ye believe in God," saith Christ, "believe also in me;"—"Believe also, act faith distinctly on me; faith divine, supernatural,—that faith whereby you believe in God, that is, the Father." There is a believing of Christ, —namely, that he is the Son of God, the Saviour of the world. That is that whose neglect our Saviour so threatened unto the Pharisees, John viii. 24, "If ye believe not that I am he, ye shall die in your sins." In this sense faith is not immediately fixed on the Son, being only an owning of him (that is, the Christ to be the Son), by closing with the testimony of the Father concerning him. But there is also a believing on him, called "Believing on the name of the Son of God," 1 John v. 13; so also John ix. 36;—yea, the distinct affixing of faith, affiance, and confidence on the Lord Jesus Christ the Son of God, as the Son of God, is most frequently pressed. John iii. 16, "God" (that is, the Father) "so loved the world, ... that whosoever believeth in him" (that is, the Son) "should not perish." The Son, who is given of the Father, is believed on. "He that believeth on him is not condemned," verse 18. "He that believeth on the Son hath everlasting life," verse 36. "This is the work of God, that ye believe on him whom he hath sent," John vi. 29, 40; 1 John v. 10. The foundation of the whole is laid, John v. 23, "That all men should honour the Son, even as they honour the Father. He that honoureth not the Son honoureth not the Father which hath sent him." But of this honour and worship of the Son I have treated at large elsewhere;[2] and shall not in general insist upon it again. For *love*, I shall only add that solemn apostolical benediction, Eph. vi. 24, "Grace be with all them that love our Lord Jesus Christ in sincerity,"

---

[1] Jer. x. 10, xvii. 5, 6; Gal. iv. 8.   [2] Vind. Evan., cap. x. vol. xii.

—that is, with divine love, the love of religious worship; which is the only *incorrupt* love of the Lord Jesus.

Farther: that faith, hope, and love, acting themselves in all manner of obedience and appointed worship, are peculiarly due from the saints,[1] and distinctly directed unto the Son, is abundantly manifest from that solemn doxology, Rev. i. 5, 6, "Unto him that loved us, and washed us from our sins in his own blood, and hath made us kings and priests unto God and his Father; to him be glory and dominion for ever and ever. Amen." Which yet is set forth with more glory, chap. v. 8, "The four living creatures, and the four and twenty elders fell down before the Lamb, having every one of them harps, and golden vials full of odours, which are the prayers of saints:" and verses 13, 14, "Every creature which is in heaven, and on the earth, and under the earth, and such as are in the sea, and all that are in them, heard I saying, Blessing, and honour, and glory, and power, be unto him that sitteth upon the throne, and unto the Lamb for ever and ever." The Father and the Son (he that sits upon the throne, and the Lamb) are held out jointly, yet distinctly, as the adequate object of all divine worship and honour, for ever and ever. And therefore Stephen, in his solemn dying invocation, fixeth his faith and hope distinctly on him, Acts vii. 59, 60, "Lord Jesus, receive my spirit;" and, "Lord, lay not this sin to their charge;"—for he knew that the Son of man had power to forgive sins also. And this worship of the Lord Jesus, the apostle makes the discriminating character of the saints, 1 Cor. i. 2, "With all," saith he, "that in every place call upon the name of Jesus Christ our Lord, both theirs and ours;" that is, with all the saints of God. And invocation generally comprises the whole worship of God.[2] This, then, is the due of our Mediator, though as God, as the Son,—not as Mediator.

3. Thus also is it in reference unto the HOLY SPIRIT of grace. The closing of the great sin of unbelief[3] is still described as an opposition unto, and a resisting of that Holy Spirit. And you have distinct mention of the love of the Spirit, Rom. xv. 30. The apostle also peculiarly directs his supplication to him in that solemn benediction, 2 Cor. xiii. 14, "The grace of the Lord Jesus Christ, and the love of God, and the communion of the Holy Ghost, be with you all." And such benedictions are originally supplications. He is likewise entitled unto all instituted worship, from the appointment of the administration of baptism in his name, Matt. xxviii. 19. Of which things more afterward.

---

[1] Ps. ii. 7, 12; Dan. iii. 25; Matt. iii. 17, xvii. 5, xxii. 45; John iii. 36, v. 19-26, viii. 36; 1 Cor. i. 9; Gal. i. 16, iv. 6; 1 John ii. 22-24, v. 10-13; Heb. i. 6; Phil. ii. 10; John v. 23.

[2] Isa. lvi. 7; Rom. x. 12-14.   Acts vii. 51.

Now, of the things which have been delivered this is the sum:—there is no grace whereby our souls go forth unto God, no act of divine worship yielded unto him, no duty or obedience performed, but they are distinctly directed unto Father, Son, and Spirit. Now, by these and such like ways as these, do we hold communion with God; and therefore we have that communion distinctly, as hath been described.

This also may farther appear, if we consider how distinctly the persons of the Deity are revealed to act in the *communication* of those good things, wherein the saints have communion with God.[1] As all the spiritual *ascendings* of their souls are assigned unto them respectively, so all their internal receivings of the communications of God unto them are held out in such a distribution as points at distinct rises and fountains (though not of being in themselves, yet) of dispensations unto us. Now this is declared two ways:—

(1.) When the *same* thing is, at the *same* time, ascribed *jointly* and yet *distinctly* to all the persons in the Deity, and *respectively* to each of them. So are grace and peace, Rev. i. 4, 5, " Grace be unto you, and peace, from him which is, and which was, and which is to come; and from the seven Spirits which are before his throne; and from Jesus Christ, who is the faithful witness," etc. The seven Spirits before the throne, are the Holy Spirit of God, considered as the perfect fountain of every perfect gift and dispensation. All are here joined together, and yet all mentioned as distinguished in their communication of grace and peace unto the saints. " Grace and peace be unto you, from the Father, and from," etc.

(2.) When the *same* thing is attributed *severally* and singly unto each person. There is, indeed, no gracious influence from above, no illapse of light, life, love, or grace upon our hearts, but proceedeth in such a dispensation. I shall give only one instance, which is very comprehensive, and may be thought to comprise all other particulars; and this is TEACHING. The teaching of God is the real communication of all and every particular emanation from himself unto the saints whereof they are made partakers. That promise, " They shall be all taught of God," inwraps in itself the whole mystery of grace, as to its actual dispensation unto us, so far as we may be made real possessors of it. Now this is assigned,—

[1.] Unto the FATHER. The accomplishment of that promise is peculiarly referred to him, John vi. 45, " It is written in the prophets, And they shall be all taught of God. Every man therefore that hath heard, and hath learned of the Father, cometh unto me." This teaching, whereby we are translated from death unto life, brought

[1] "Tametsi omnia unus idemque Deus efficit, ut dicitur,—opera Trinitatis ad extra sunt indivisa, distinguuntur tamen personæ discrimine in istis operibus."—Matt. iii. 16; Acts iii. 13; Gen. xix. 24, i. 26; Matt. xxviii. 19; 2 Cor. xiii. 14.

unto Christ, unto a participation of life and love in him,—it is of and from the Father: him we hear, of him we learn,[1] by him are we brought unto union and communion with the Lord Jesus. This is his drawing us, his begetting us anew of his own will, by his own Spirit; and in which work he employs the ministers of the gospel, Acts xxvi. 17, 18.

[2.] Unto the SON. The Father proclaims him from heaven to be the great teacher, in that solemn charge to hear him, which came once [and] again from the excellent glory: " This is my beloved Son; hear him." The whole of his prophetical, and no small part of his kingly office, consists in this teaching; herein is he said to draw men unto him, as the Father is said to do in his teaching, John xii. 32; which he doth with such efficacy, that " the dead hear his voice and live."[2] The teaching of the Son is a life-giving, a spirit-breathing teaching;— an effectual influence of light, whereby he shines into darkness; a com- munication of life, quickening the dead; an opening of blind eyes, and changing of hard hearts; a pouring out of the Spirit, with all the fruits thereof. Hence he claims it as his privilege to be the sole master, Matt. xxiii. 10, " One is your Master, even Christ."

[3.] To the SPIRIT. John xiv. 26, " The Comforter, he shall teach you all things." " But the anointing which ye have received," saith the apostle, " abideth in you, and ye need not that any man teach you: but as the same anointing teacheth you of all things, and is truth, and is no lie, and even as it hath taught you, ye shall abide in him," 1 John ii. 27. That teaching unction which is not only true, but truth itself, is only the Holy Spirit of God: so that he teacheth also; being given unto us " that we might know the things that are freely given to us of God," 1 Cor. ii. 12. I have chosen this special instance because, as I told you, it is comprehensive, and comprises in itself most of the particulars that might be annumerated,—quicken- ing, preserving, etc.

This, then, farther drives on the truth that lies under demonstra- tion; there being such a distinct communication of grace from the several persons of the Deity, the saints must needs have distinct com- munion with them.

It remaineth only to intimate, in a word, *wherein this distinction* lies, and what is the ground thereof. Now, this is, that the Father doth it by the way of *original authority;* the Son by the way of com- municating from a *purchased treasury;* the Holy Spirit by the way of *immediate efficacy.*

1st. The Father communicates all grace by the way of *original*

---

[1] Matt. xi. 25; John i. 13; James i. 18.
[2] Matt. iii. 17, xvii. 5; 2 Pet. i. 17; Deut. xviii. 15-20, etc.; Acts iii. 22, 23; John v. 25; Isa. lxi. 1-3; Luke iv. 18, 19.

authority: " He quickeneth WHOM HE WILL," John v. 21.   " OF HIS OWN WILL begat he us," James i. 18.   Life-giving power is, in respect of original authority, invested in the Father by the way of eminency; and therefore, in sending of the quickening Spirit, Christ is said to do it from the Father, or the Father himself to do it. " But the Comforter, which is the Holy Ghost, whom the Father will send," John xiv. 26.   " But when the Comforter is come, whom I will send unto you from the Father," John xv. 26;—though he be also said to send him himself, on another account, John xvi. 7.

2*dly.* The Son, by the way of making out *a purchased treasury:* " Of his fulness have all we received, and grace for grace," John i. 16. And whence is this fulness?   " It pleased the Father that in him should all fulness dwell," Col. i. 19.   And upon what account he hath the dispensation of that fulness to him committed you may see, Phil. ii. 8–11.   " When thou shalt make his soul an offering for sin, he shall prolong his days, and the pleasure of the LORD shall prosper in his hand.   He shall see of the travail of his soul, and shall be satisfied: by his knowledge shall my righteous servant justify many; for he shall bear their iniquities," Isa. liii. 10,11. And with this fulness he hath also authority for the communication of it, John v. 25–27; Matt. xxviii. 18.

3*dly.* The Spirit doth it by the way of *immediate efficacy,* Rom. viii. 11, " But if the Spirit of him that raised up Jesus from the dead dwell in you, he that raised up Christ from the dead shall also quicken your mortal bodies by his Spirit that dwelleth in you."   Here are all three comprised, with their distinct concurrence unto our quickening. Here is the Father's authoritative quickening,—"He raised Christ from the dead, and he shall quicken you;" and the Son's mediatory quickening,—for it is done in " the death of Christ;" and the Spirit's immediate efficacy,—"He shall do it by the Spirit that dwelleth in you." He that desires to see this whole matter farther explained, may consult what I have elsewhere written on this subject.   And thus is the distinct communion whereof we treat both proved and demonstrated.

CHAPTER III.

Of the peculiar and distinct communion which the saints have with the Father— Observations for the clearing of the whole premised—Our peculiar communion with the Father is in love—1 John iv. 7, 8; 2 Cor. xiii. 14; John xvi. 26, 27; Rom. v. 5; John iii. 16, xiv. 23; Tit. iii. 4, opened to this purpose—What is required of believers to hold communion with the Father in love—His love received by faith—Returns of love to him—God's love to us and ours to him—Wherein they agree—Wherein they differ.

HAVING proved that there is such a distinct communion in respect of Father, Son, and Spirit, as whereof we speak, it remains that it be farther cleared up by an induction of instances, to manifest what [it is], and wherein the saints peculiarly hold this communion with the *several* persons respectively: which also I shall do, after the premising some observations, necessary to be previously considered, as was promised, for the clearing of what hath been spoken. And they are these that follow:—

1. When I assign any thing as *peculiar* wherein we distinctly hold communion with any person, I do not exclude the other persons from communion with the soul in the very same thing. Only this, I say, *principally*, immediately, and by the way of eminency, we have, in such a thing, or in such a way, communion with some one person; and therein with the others *secondarily*, and by the way of consequence on that foundation; for the person, as the person, of any one of them, is not the prime *object* of divine worship, but as it is *identified* with the nature or essence of God. Now, the works that outwardly are of God (called "Trinitatis ad extra"),[1] which are commonly said to be *common and undivided*, are either wholly so, and in all respects, as all works of common providence; or else, being common in respect of their acts, they are distinguished in respect of that principle, or next and immediate rise in the manner of operation: so creation is *appropriated* to the Father, redemption to the Son. In which sense we speak of these things.

2. There is a concurrence of the *actings* and operations of the whole Deity[2] in that *dispensation*, wherein each person concurs to the work of our salvation, unto every *act* of our communion with each singular person. Look, by what act soever we hold communion with any person, there is an *influence* from every person to the putting forth of that act.[3] As, suppose it to be the act of faith:—It is bestowed on us by the Father: " It is not of yourselves: it is the gift of God," Eph. ii. 8. It is the Father that revealeth the gospel, and Christ therein, Matt. xi. 25. And it is purchased for us by the Son: " Unto you it is given in the behalf of Christ, to believe on him," Phil. i. 29. In him are we " blessed with spiritual blessings," Eph. i. 3. He bestows on us, and increaseth faith in us, Luke xvii. 5. And it is wrought in us by the Spirit; he administers that " exceeding greatness of his power," which he exerciseth towards them who believe, " according to the working of his mighty power, which he wrought in Christ, when he raised him from the dead," Eph. i. 19, 20; Rom. viii. 11.

[1] Opera ad extra sunt indivisa.

[2] Πατὴρ σὺν υἱῷ καὶ πανάγνῳ πνεύματι
Τριὰς προσώποις εὐκρινής, μονὰς φύσει.
Μήτ' οὖν ἀριθμῷ συγχέῃς ὑποστάσεις,
Μήτ' ἂν Θεὸν σὺ προσκυνῶν τιμᾷς φύσιν·
Μία τριὰς γὰρ, εἷς Θεὸς παντοκράτωρ.—Greg. Naz. Iamb. Car. iii.

[3] Προσκυνῶμεν τὴν μίαν ἐν τοῖς τρισὶ θεότητα.—Idem. Orat., 24. See Thom. 22, q. 84, A. 3, q. 84, a. 1; Alexan. Ales. Sum. Theol., p. 3, q. 30, m. 1, a. 3.

3. When I assign any *particular* thing wherein we hold communion with any person, I do not do it *exclusively* unto other mediums of communion; but only by the way of inducing a special and eminent instance for the proof and manifestation of the former general assertion: otherwise there is no grace or duty wherein we have not communion with God in the way described. In every thing wherein we are made partakers of the divine nature, there is a communication and receiving between God and us; so near are we unto him in Christ.

4. By asserting this distinct communion, which merely respects that order in the dispensation of grace which God is pleased to hold out in the gospel, I intend not in the least to shut up all communion with God under these precincts (his ways being exceeding broad, containing a perfection whereof there is no end), nor to prejudice that holy fellowship we have with the whole Deity, in our walking before him in covenant-obedience; which also, God assisting, I shall handle hereafter.

These few observations being premised, I come now to declare what it is wherein peculiarly and eminently the saints have communion with the Father; and this is LOVE,—free, undeserved, and eternal love. This the Father peculiarly fixes upon the saints; this they are immediately to eye in him, to receive of him, and to make such returns thereof as he is delighted withal. This is the great *discovery* of the gospel: for whereas the Father, as the fountain of the Deity, is not known any other way but as full of wrath, anger, and indignation against sin, nor can the sons of men have any other thoughts of him (Rom. i. 18; Isa. xxxiii. 13, 14; Hab. i. 13; Ps. v. 4–6; Eph. ii. 3),—here he is now revealed peculiarly as love, as full of it unto us; the manifestation whereof is the peculiar work of the gospel, Tit. iii. 4.

1. 1 John iv. 8, "God is love." That the name of God is here taken personally,[1] and for the person of the Father, not essentially, is evident from verse 9, where he is distinguished from his only begotten Son whom he sends into the world. Now, saith he, "The Father is love;" that is, not only of an infinitely gracious, tender, compassionate, and loving nature, according as he hath proclaimed himself, Exod. xxxiv. 6, 7, but also one that eminently and peculiarly dispenseth himself unto us in free love." So the apostle sets it forth in the following verses: "This is love," verse 9;—"This is that which I would have you take notice of in him, that he makes out love unto

---

[1] Deut. xxxiii. 3; Jer. xxxi. 3; John iii. 16, v. 42, xiv. 21; Rom. v. 5, viii. 39; Eph. ii. 4; 1 John ii. 15, iv. 10, 11; Heb. xii. 6. "Multo ἐμφατικώτερον loquitur quam si Deum diceret summopere, atque adeo infinite nos amare, cum Deum dicit erga nos ipsam charitatem esse, cujus latissimum τεκμήριον profert."—Beza in loc.

you, in 'sending his only begotten Son into the world, that we might live through him.'" So also, verse 10, "He loved us, and sent his Son to be the propitiation for our sins." And that this is peculiarly to be eyed in him, the Holy Ghost plainly declares, in making it antecedent to the sending of Christ, and all mercies and benefits whatever by him received. This love, I say, in itself, is antecedent to the purchase of Christ, although the whole fruit thereof be made out alone thereby, Eph. i. 4–6.

2. So in that distribution made by the apostle in his solemn parting benediction, 2 Cor. xiii. 14, "The grace of the Lord Jesus Christ, THE LOVE OF GOD, and the fellowship of the Holy Ghost, be with you all." Ascribing sundry things unto the distinct persons, it is *love* that he peculiarly assigns to the Father. And the fellowship of the Spirit is mentioned with the grace of Christ and the love of God, because it is by the Spirit alone that we have fellowship with Christ in grace, and with the Father in love, although we have also peculiar fellowship with him; as shall be declared.

3. John xvi. 26, 27, saith our Saviour, "I say not unto you, that I will pray the Father for you; for the Father himself loveth you."[1] But how is this, that our Saviour saith, "I say not that I will pray the Father for you," when he saith plainly, chap. xiv. 16, "I will pray the Father for you?" The disciples, with all the gracious words, comfortable and faithful promises of their Master, with most heavenly discoveries of his heart unto them, were even fully convinced of HIS dear and tender affections towards them; as also of his continued care and kindness, that he would not forget them when bodily he was gone from them, as he was now upon his departure: but now all their thoughts are concerning the Father, how they should be accepted with him, what respect he had towards them. Saith our Saviour, "Take no care of that, nay, impose not that upon me, of procuring the Father's love for you; but know that this is his peculiar respect towards you, and which you are in him: 'He himself loves you.' It is true, indeed (and as I told you), that I will pray the Father to send you the Spirit, the Comforter, and with him all the gracious fruits of his love; but yet in the point of *love itself*, free love, eternal love, there is no need of any intercession for that: for eminently the Father himself loves you. Resolve of that, that you may hold com-

---

[1] " Quomodo igitur negat? negat secundum quid; hoc est, negat se ideo rogaturum patrem, ut patrem illis conciliet, et ad illos amandos et exaudiendos flectat; quasi non sit suapte sponte erga illos propensus. Voluit ergo Christus his verbis persuadere apostolis, non solum se, sed etiam ipsum patrem illos complecti amore maximo. Et ita patrem eos amare, ac promptum habere animum illis gratificandi, et benefaciendi, ut nullius, neque ipsius filii opus habeat tali intercessione, qua solent placari, et flecti homines non admodum erga aliquem bene affecti," etc.—Zanc. de trib. nom. Elo., lib. iv. cap. 9. Vid. Hilar de Trinit., lib. vi. p. 97., ed. Eras.

munion with him in it, and be no more troubled about it.   Yea, as your great trouble is about the Father's love, so you can no way more trouble or burden him, than by your unkindness in not believing of it."   So it must needs be where sincere love is questioned.

4. The apostle teaches the same, Rom. v. 5, "The love of God is shed abroad in our hearts by the Holy Ghost, which is given unto us."   God, whose love this is, is plainly distinguished from the Holy Ghost, who sheds abroad that love of his; and, verse 8, he is also distinguished from the Son, for it is from that love of his that the Son is sent: and therefore it is the Father of whom the apostle here specially speaketh.   And what is it that he ascribes to him?   Even love; which also, verse 8, he commendeth to us,—sets it forth in such a signal and eminent expression, that we may take notice of it, and close with him in it.   To carry this business to its height, there is not only most frequent peculiar mention of the love of God, where the Father is eminently intended, and of the love of the Father expressly, but he is also called "The God of love," 2 Cor. xiii. 11, and is said to be "love:" so that whoever will know him, 1 John iv. 8, or dwell in him by fellowship or communion, verse 16, must do it as "he is love."

5. Nay, whereas there is a twofold divine love, *beneplaciti* and *amicitiæ*, a love of good pleasure and destination, and a love of friendship and approbation, they are both peculiarly assigned to the Father in an eminent manner:—

(1.) John iii. 16, " God so loved the world, that he gave," etc.; that is, with the love of his purpose and good pleasure, his determinate will of doing good.   This is distinctly ascribed to him, being laid down as the cause of sending his Son.   So Rom. ix. 11, 12; Eph. i. 4, 5; 2 Thess. ii. 13, 14; 1 John iv. 8, 9.

(2.) John xiv. 23, there is[1] mention of that other kind of love whereof we speak.   " If a man love me," saith Christ, " he will keep my words: and my Father will love him, and we will come unto him, and make our abode with him."   The love of friendship and approbation is here eminently ascribed to him.   Says Christ, " We will come," even Father and Son, " to such a one, and dwell with him;" that is, by the Spirit: but yet he would have us take notice, that, in point of love, the Father hath a peculiar prerogative: " My Father will love him."

6. Yea, and as this love is peculiarly to be eyed in him, so it is to be looked on as the *fountain* of all following gracious dispensations. Christians walk oftentimes with exceedingly troubled hearts, concerning the thoughts of the Father towards them.   They are well per-

---

[1] " Diligi a patre, recipi in amicitiam summi Dei; a Deo foveri, adeoque Deo esse in deliciis."—Bucerus in loc.

suaded of the Lord Christ and his good-will; the difficulty lies in what is their acceptance with the Father,—what is his heart towards them?[1] " Show us the Father, and it sufficeth us," John xiv. 8. Now, this ought to be so far away, that his love ought to be looked on as the fountain from whence all other sweetnesses flow. Thus the apostle sets it out, Tit. iii. 4, " After that the kindness and love of God our Saviour toward man appeared." It is of the Father of whom he speaks; for, verse 6, he tells us that " he makes out unto us," or " sheds that love upon us abundantly, through Jesus Christ our Saviour." And this love he makes the hinge upon which the great alteration and translation of the saints doth turn; for, saith he, verse 3, " We ourselves also were sometimes foolish, disobedient, deceived, serving divers lusts and pleasures, living in malice and envy, hateful, and hating one another." All naught, all out of order, and vile. Whence, then, is our recovery? The whole rise of it is from this love of God, flowing out by the ways there described. For when the kindness and love of God appeared,—that is, in the fruits of it,—then did this alteration ensue. To secure us hereof, there is not any thing that hath a loving and tender nature in the world, and doth act suitably thereunto, which God hath not compared himself unto. Separate all weakness and imperfection which is in them, yet great impressions of love must abide. He is as a father, a mother, a shepherd, a hen over chickens, and the like, Ps. ciii. 13; Isa. lxiii. 16; Matt. vi. 6; Isa. lxvi. 13; Ps. xxiii. 1; Isa. xl. 11; Matt. xxiii. 37.

I shall not need to add any more proofs. This is that which is demonstrated:—*There is love in the person of the Father peculiarly held out unto the saints, as wherein he will and doth hold communion with them.*

Now, to complete communion with the Father *in love*, two things are required of believers:—(1.) *That they receive it of him.* (2.) *That they make suitable returns unto him.*

(1.) That *they do receive it.* Communion consists in *giving* and *receiving.* Until the love of the Father be received, we have no communion with him therein. How, then, is this love of the Father to be received, so as to hold fellowship with him? I answer, By *faith.* The receiving of it is the believing of it. God hath so fully, so eminently revealed his love, that it may be received by faith. " Ye believe in God," John xiv. 1; that is, the Father. And what is to be believed in him? His love; for he is "love," 1 John iv. 8.

It is true, there is not an *immediate* acting of faith upon the Father, but by the Son. " He is the way, the truth, and the life: no man cometh unto the Father but by him," John xiv. 6. He is the

---

[1] " Te quod attinet non sumus solliciti,—illud modo desideramus, ut patrem nobis vel semel intueri concedatur."—Cartwright Har. in John xiv. 8.

merciful high priest over the house of God, by whom we have[1] access
to the throne of grace: by him is our manuduction unto the Father;
by him we believe in God, 1 Pet. i. 21.   But this is that I say,—When
by and through Christ we have an access unto the Father, we then
behold his glory also, and see his love that he peculiarly bears unto
us, and act faith thereon.   We are then, I say, to eye it, to believe
it, to receive it, as in him; the issues and fruits thereof being made
out unto us through Christ alone.   Though there be no light for us
but in the beams, yet we may by beams see the sun, which is
the fountain of it.   Though all our refreshment actually lie in the
streams, yet by them we are led up unto the *fountain*.   Jesus
Christ, in respect of the love of the Father, is but the beam, the
stream; wherein though actually all our light, our refreshment lies,
yet by him we are led to the fountain, the sun of eternal love itself.
Would believers exercise themselves herein, they would find it a
matter of no small *spiritual* improvement in their walking with
God.

This is that which is aimed at.   Many dark and disturbing thoughts
are apt to arise in this thing.   Few can carry up their hearts and
minds to this height by faith, as to rest their souls in the love of the
Father; they live below it, in the troublesome region of hopes and
fears, storms and clouds.   All here is serene and quiet.   But how to
attain to this pitch they know not.   This is the will of God, that he
may always be eyed as benign, kind, tender, loving, and unchangeable therein; and that peculiarly as the Father, as the great fountain
and spring of all gracious communications and fruits of love.   This is
that which Christ came to reveal,—God as a Father, John i. 18; that
name which he declares to those who are given him out of the world,
John xvii. 6.   And this is that which he effectually leads us to by
himself, as he is the only way of going to God as a Father, John
xiv. 5, 6; that is, as love: and by doing so, gives us the rest which he
promiseth; for the love of the Father is the only rest of the soul.
It is true, as was said, we do not this *formally* in the first instant of
believing.   We believe in God through Christ, 1 Pet. i. 21; faith seeks
out rest for the soul.   This is presented to it by Christ, the mediator,
as the only procuring cause.   Here it abides not, but by Christ it
hath an access to the Father, Eph. ii. 18,—into his love; finds out
that he is love, as having a design, a purpose of love, a good pleasure
towards us from eternity,—a delight, a complacency, a good-will in
Christ,—all cause of anger and aversation being taken away.   The
soul being thus, by faith through Christ, and by him, brought into
the bosom of God, into a comfortable persuasion and spiritual perception and sense of his love, there reposes and rests itself.   And this

[1] Eph. ii. 18.

is the first thing the saints do, in their communion with the Father; of the due improvement whereof, more afterward.

(2.) For that suitable *return* which is required, this also (in a main part of it, beyond which I shall not now extend it) consisteth in love.[1] God loves, that he may be beloved.[2]   When he comes to command the return of his received love, to complete communion with him, he says, " My son, give me thine heart," Prov. xxiii. 26,—thy affections, thy love.   " Thou shalt love the Lord thy God with all thy heart, and with all thy soul, and with all thy strength, and with all thy mind," Luke x. 27; this is the return that he demandeth.   When the soul sees God, in his dispensation of love, to be love, to be infinitely lovely and loving, rests upon and delights in him as such, —then hath it communion with him in love.   This is love, that God loves us first, and then we love him again.   I shall not now go forth into a description of divine love.   Generally, love[3] is an affection of union and nearness, with complacency therein.   So long as the Father is looked on under any other apprehension, but only as acting love upon the soul, it breeds in the soul a dread and aversation.[4]   Hence the flying and hiding of sinners, in the Scriptures.   But when he who is the Father is considered as a father, acting love on the soul, this[5] raises it to love again.   This is, in faith, the ground of all acceptable obedience, Deut. v. 10; Exod. xx. 6; Deut. x. 12, xi. 1, 13, xiii. 3.

Thus is this whole business stated by the apostle, Eph. i. 4, " According as he hath chosen us in him before the foundation of the world, that we should be holy and without blame before him in love." It begins in the *love of God,* and ends in *our love to him.*   That is it which the eternal love of God aims at in us, and works us up unto. It is true, our universal obedience falls within the compass of our communion with God; but that is with him as God, our blessed sovereign, lawgiver, and rewarder: as he is the Father, our Father in Christ, as revealed unto us to be love, above and contrary to all the expectations of the natural man; so it is in love that we have this intercourse with him.   Nor do I intend only that love which is as the life and form of all moral obedience; but a peculiar delight and acquiescing in the Father, revealed effectually as love unto the soul.

That this communion with the Father in love may be made the more clear and evident, I shall show two things:—[1.] Wherein *this*

---

[1] Deut. vi. 4, 5.

[2] " Amor supernè descendens ad divinam pulchritudinem omnia convocat."— Proclus lib. de Anima. et Dæm.

[3] " Unio substantialis est causa amoris sui ipsius; similitudinis, est causa amoris alterius; sed unio realis quam amans quærit de re amata, est effectus amoris."— Thom. 12, q. 28, 1, 3.

[4] Josh. xxii. 5, xxiii. 11; Neh. i. 5.

[5] Ps. xviii. 1, xxxi. 23, xcvii. 10, cxvi. 1; 1 Cor. ii. 9; James i. 12; Isa. lvi. 6; Matt. xxii. 37; Rom. viii. 28.

love of God unto us and our love to him do agree, as to some manner of analogy and likeness.　[2.] *Wherein they[1] differ;* which will farther discover the nature of each of them.

[1.] They agree in two things:—

1*st.* That they are each a love of rest and complacency.

(1*st.*) The love of God is so.　Zeph. iii. 17, " The LORD thy God in the midst of thee is mighty; he will save, he will rejoice over thee with joy, he will rest in his love; he will joy over thee with singing." Both these things are here assigned unto God in his love,—[2]REST and DELIGHT.　The words are, יַחֲרִישׁ בְּאַהֲבָתוֹ,—" He shall be silent because of his love."　To rest with contentment is expressed by being silent; that is, without repining, without complaint.　This God doth upon the account of his own love, so full, so every way complete and absolute, that it will not allow him to complain of any thing in them whom he loves, but he is silent on the account thereof.　Or, "Rest in his love;" that is, he will not remove it,—he will not seek farther for another object.　It shall make its abode upon the soul where it is once fixed, for ever.　And COMPLACENCY or DELIGHT: " He rejoiceth with singing;" as one that is fully satisfied in that object he hath fixed his love on.　Here are two words used to express the delight and joy that God hath in his love,—יָשִׂישׂ and יָגִיל.　The first denotes the inward affection of the mind, joy of heart; and to set out the intenseness hereof, it is said he shall do it בְּשִׂמְחָה,—in gladness, or with joy.　To have joy of heart in gladness, is the highest expression of delight in love.　The latter word denotes not the inward affection, but the outward[3] demonstration of it: ἀγαλλιᾷν seems to be formed of it.　It is to exult in outward demonstration of internal delight and joy;—" Tripudiare," to leap, as men overcome with some joyful surprisal.　And therefore God is said to do this בְּרִנָּה,—with a joyful sound, or singing.　To rejoice with gladness of heart, to exult with singing and praise, argues the greatest delight and complacency possible.　When he would express the contrary of this love, he says οὐκ εὐδόκησε,—" he was not well pleased," 1 Cor. x. 5; he fixed not his delight nor rest on them.　And, " If any man draw back, the Lord's soul hath no pleasure in him," Heb. x. 38; Jer. xxii. 28; Hos. viii. 8; Mal. i. 10.　He takes pleasure in those that abide with him.　He sings to his church, " A vineyard of red wine: I the LORD do keep it," Isa. xxvii. 2, 3; Ps. cxlvii. 11, cxlix. 4.　There is rest and compla-

---

[1] 'Ανάλογον δ' ἐν ἁπάσαις ταῖς καθ' ὑπεροχὴν οὔσαις φιλίαις, καὶ τὴν φίλησιν δεῖ γίνεσθαι, etc.—Arist. Eth., lib. viii. cap. 7.

[2] " Effectus amoris quando habetur amatum, est delectatio."—Thom. 12, q. 25, a. 2, l.　" Amor est complacentia amantis in amato.　Amor est motus cordis, delectantis se in aliquo."—August.

[3] " Externum magis gaudii gestum, quam internam animi lætitiam significat, cum velut tripudiis et volutationibus gaudere se quis ostendit."—Pagnin.　גּיל; lætitiâ gestiit, animi lætitiam gestu corporis expressit, exilivit gaudio."—Calas.

cency in his love. There is in the Hebrew but a metathesis of a
letter between the word that signifies a love of will and desire (אָהַב
is so to love), and that which denotes a love of rest and acquiescency
(which is, אָבָה); and both are applied to God. He wills good to us,
that he may rest in that will. Some say, ἀγαπᾷν, "to love," is from
ἄγαν πόθεσθαι, perfectly to acquiesce in the thing loved. And when
God calls his Son ἀγαπητόν, "beloved," Matt. iii. 17, he adds, as an
exposition of it, ἐν ᾧ εὐδόκησα, "in whom I rest well pleased."

(2dly.) The return that the saints make unto him, to complete communion with him herein, holds some analogy with his love in this;
for it is a love also of[1] rest and delight. "Return unto thy rest, O
my soul," says David, Ps. cxvi. 7. He makes God his *rest;* that is,
he in whom his soul doth rest, without seeking farther for a more
suitable and desirable object. "Whom have I," saith he, "in heaven
but thee? and there is none upon earth that I desire beside thee,"
Ps. lxxiii. 25.[2] Thus the soul gathers itself from all its wanderings,
from all other beloveds, to rest in God alone,—to satiate and content
itself in him; choosing the Father for his present and eternal rest.
And this also with *delight.* "Thy loving-kindness," saith the psalmist,
"is better than life; therefore will I praise thee," Ps. lxiii. 3. "Than
life," מֵחַיִּים,—before lives. I will not deny but life in a single consideration sometimes is so expressed, but always emphatically; so
that the whole life, with all the concernments of it, which may render it considerable, are thereby intended. Austin, on this place,
reading it[3] "super vitas," extends it to the several courses of life that
men engage themselves in. Life, in the whole continuance of it,
with all its *advantages* whatever, is at least intended. Supposing
himself in the jaws of death, rolling into the grave through innumerable troubles, yet he found more sweetness in God than in a long
life, under its best and most noble considerations, attended with all
enjoyments that make it pleasant and comfortable. From both these
is that of the church, in Hos. xiv. 3, "Asshur shall not save us; we
will not ride upon horses: neither will we say any more to the work
of our hands, Ye are our gods: for in thee the fatherless findeth
mercy." They reject the most goodly appearances of rest and contentment, to make up all in God, on whom they cast themselves, as
otherwise helpless orphans.

2dly. The mutual love of God and the saints agrees in this,—that

---

[1] "Fecisti nos ad te, domine, et irrequietum est cor nostrum donec veniat ad
te."—Aug. Conf.

[2] Ps. xxxvii. 7; Isa. xxviii. 12; Heb. iv. 9.

[3] "Super vitas: quas vitas? Quas sibi homines eligunt; alius elegit sibi vitam
negociandi, alius vitam rusticandi; alius vitam fœnerandi, alius vitam militandi,
alius illam, alius illam. Diversæ sunt vitæ, sed melior est misericordia tua super
vitas nostras."—Aug. Enarrat. in Ps. lxii.

the way of communicating the issues and fruits of these loves is *only in Christ*. The Father communicates no issue of his love unto us but through Christ; and we make no return of love unto him but through Christ. He is the *treasury* wherein the Father disposeth all the riches of his grace, taken from the bottomless mine of his eternal love; and he is the *priest* into whose hand we put all the offerings that we return unto the Father. Thence he is first, and by way of eminency, said to love the Son; not only as his eternal Son,—as he was the delight of his soul before the foundation of the world, Prov. viii. 30,—but also as our mediator, and the means of conveying his love to us, Matt. iii. 17; John iii. 35, v. 20, x. 17, xv. 9, xvii. 24. And we are said through him to believe in and to have access to God.

(*1st.*) The Father loves us, and "chose us before the foundation of the world;" but in the pursuit of that love, he "blesseth us with all spiritual blessings in heavenly places in Christ," Eph. i. 3, 4. From his love, he sheds or pours out the Holy Spirit richly upon us, through Jesus Christ our Saviour, Tit. iii. 6. In the pouring out of his love, there is not one drop falls besides the Lord Christ. The holy anointing oil was all poured on the head of Aaron, Ps. cxxxiii. 2; and thence went down to the skirts of his clothing. Love is first poured out on Christ; and from him it drops as the dew of Hermon upon the souls of his saints. The Father will have him to have " in all things the pre-eminence," Col. i. 18; " it pleased him that in him all fulness should dwell," verse 19; that " of his fulness we might receive, and grace for grace," John i. 16. Though the love of the Father's purpose and good pleasure have its rise and foundation in his mere grace and will, yet the design of its accomplishment is only in Christ. All the fruits of it are first given to him; and it is in him only that they are dispensed to us. So that though the saints may, nay, do, see an infinite ocean of love unto them in the bosom of the Father, yet they are not to look for one drop from him but what comes through Christ. He is the only means of communication. Love in the Father is like *honey in the flower;*—it must be in the comb before it be for our use. Christ must extract and prepare this honey for us. He draws this water from the fountain through union and dispensation of fulness;—we by faith, from the wells of salvation that are in him. This was in part before discovered.

(*2dly.*) Our returns are all *in him*, and *by him* also. And well is it with us that it is so. What lame and blind sacrifices should we otherwise present unto God! He [1]bears the iniquity of our offerings, and he adds incense unto our prayers. Our love is fixed on the Father; but it is conveyed to him through the Son of his love. He is the only way for our *graces* as well as our *persons* to go unto God;

Exod. xxviii. 38; Rev. viii. 3; John xiv. 6; Heb. x. 19-22.

through him passeth all our desire, our delight, our complacency, our obedience. Of which more afterward.

Now, in these two things there is some resemblance between that mutual love of the Father and the saints wherein they hold communion.

[2.] There are sundry things wherein they differ:—

1*st.* The love of God is a love of *bounty;* our love unto him is a love of *duty.*

(1*st.*) The love of the Father is a love of *bounty,*—a descending love; such a love as carries him out to do good things to us, great things for us. His love lies at the bottom of all dispensations towards us; and we scarce anywhere find any mention of it, but it is held out as the cause and fountain of some free gift flowing from it. He [1]loves us, and sends his Son to die for us;—he loves us, and blesseth us with all spiritual blessings. Loving is choosing, Rom. ix. 11, 12. He loves us and chastiseth us. [It is] a [2]love like that of the heavens to the earth, when, being full of rain, they pour forth showers to make it fruitful; as the sea communicates its waters to the rivers by the way of bounty, out of its own fulness,—they return unto it only what they receive from it. It is the love of a spring, of a fountain,—always communicating;—[3]a love from whence proceeds every thing that is lovely in its object. It infuseth into, and creates goodness in, the persons beloved. And this answers the description of love given by the philosopher. "To love," saith he, "ἔστι βούλεσθαι τινί ἃ οἴεται ἀγαθά, καὶ κατὰ δύναμιν πρακτικὸν εἶναι τούτων." He that loves works out good to them he loveth, as he is able. God's power and will are commensurate;—what he willeth he worketh.

(2*dly.*) Our love unto God is a love of *duty,* the love of a child. His love descends upon us in bounty and fruitfulness;[4] our love ascends unto him in duty and thankfulness. He adds to us by his love; we nothing to him by ours. Our goodness extends not unto him. Though our love be fixed on him[5] immediately, yet no fruit of our love reacheth him immediately; though he requires our love, he is not benefited by it, Job xxxv. 5–8, Rom. xi. 35, Job xxii. 2, 3. It is indeed made up of these four things:—1. *Rest;* 2. *Delight;* 3. *Reverence;* 4. *Obedience.* By these do we hold communion with

[1] John iii. 16; Rom. v. 8; Eph. i. 3, 4; 1 John iv. 9, 10; Heb. xii. 6; Rev. iii. 19.

[2] Ἐραν δὲ σεμνὸν οὐρανὸν πληρούμενον ὄμβρου, πισεῖν εἰς γαῖαν.—Eurip., [as quoted by Aristotle, Eth. viii. 1. The quotation at large is :—

Ἐρᾷ δ' ὁ σεμνὸς οὐρανὸς πληρούμενος

Ὄμβρου, πισεῖν εἰς γαῖαν Ἀφροδίτης ὕπο.—Eurip. Frag.]

[3] "Amor Dei est infundens et creans bonitatem in amatis."—Thom. p. p. q. 20, A. 2, C.

[4] "Amor Dei causat bonitatem in rebus, sed amor noster causatur ab ea."

[5] "Dilectio quæ est appetitivæ virtutis actus, etiam in statum viæ tendit in Deum primo et immediate."—Thom. 22, q. 27, a. 4.

the Father in his love. Hence God calls that love which is due to him as a father, "honour," Mal. i. 6, "If I be a father, where is mine honour?" It is a deserved act of duty.

2*dly.* They differ in this:—The love of the Father unto us is an *antecedent* love; our love unto him is a *consequent* love.

(1*st.*) The love of the Father unto us is an *antecedent* love, and that in two respects:—

[1*st.*] It is antecedent in respect of our *love*, 1 John iv. 10, "Herein is love, not that we loved God, but that he loved us." His love goes before ours. The father loves the child, when the child knows not the father, much less loves him. Yea, we are by nature θεοστυγεῖς, Rom. i. 30,—haters of God. He is in his own nature φιλάνθρωπος,—a lover of men; and surely all mutual love between him and us must begin on his hand.

[2*dly.*] In respect of all other *causes* of love whatever. It goes not only before our love, but also any thing in us that is lovely.[1] Rom. v. 8, "God commendeth his love towards us, in that whilst we were yet sinners Christ died for us." Not only his love, but the eminent fruit thereof, is made out towards us as sinners. Sin holds out all of unloveliness and undesirableness that can be in a creature. The very mention of that removes all causes, all moving occasions of love whatever. Yet, as such, have we the commendation of the Father's love unto us, by a most signal testimony. Not only when we have done no good, but when we are in our blood, doth he love us;—not because we are better than others, but because himself is infinitely good. His kindness appears when we are foolish and disobedient. Hence he is said to "love the world;" that is, those who have nothing but what is in and of the world, whose whole [portion] lies in evil.

(2*dly.*) Our love is *consequential* in both these regards:—

[1*st.*] In respect of the *love of God.* Never did creature turn his affections towards God, if the heart of God were not first set upon him.

[2*dly.*] In respect of sufficient causes of love. God must be revealed unto us as lovely and desirable, as a fit and suitable object unto the soul to set up its rest upon, before we can bear any love unto him. The saints (in this sense) do not love God for nothing, but for that excellency, loveliness, and desirableness that is in him. As the psalmist says, in one particular, Ps. cxvi. 1, "I love the Lord, because!" so may we in general; we love the Lord, because! Or, as David in another case, "What have I now done? is there not a cause?" If any man inquire about our love to God, we may say, "What have we now done? is there not a *cause?*"

3*dly.* They differ in this also:—*The love of God is like himself,*—

[1] Ezek. xvi. 1–14, etc.; Rom. ix. 11, 12; Tit. iii. 3–6; Deut. vii. 6–8; Matt. xi. 25, 26; John iii. 16.

equal, constant, not capable of augmentation or diminution; our love is like ourselves,—unequal, increasing, waning, growing, declining. His, like the *sun*, always the same in its light, though a cloud may sometimes interpose; ours, as the *moon*, hath its enlargements and straitenings.

(1*st.*) The love of the Father is *equal*, etc.;[1] whom he loves, he loves unto the end, and he loves them always alike. "The Strength of Israel is not a man, that he should repent." On whom he fixes his love, it is immutable; it doth not grow to eternity, it is not diminished at any time. It is an eternal love, that had no beginning, that shall have no ending; that cannot be heightened by any act of ours, that cannot be lessened by any thing in us. I say, in itself it is thus; otherwise, in a twofold regard, it may admit of change:—

[1*st.*] In respect of its *fruits.* It is, as I said, a fruitful love, a love of bounty. In reference unto those fruits, it may sometimes be greater, sometimes less; its communications are various. Who among the saints finds it not [so]? What life, what light, what strength, sometimes! and again, how dead, how dark, how weak! as God is pleased to let out or to restrain the fruits of his love. All the graces of the Spirit in us, all sanctified enjoyments whatever, are fruits of his love. How variously these are dispensed, how differently at sundry seasons to the same persons, experience will abundantly testify.

[2*dly.*] In respect of its *discoveries* and manifestations. He "sheds abroad his love in our hearts by the Holy Ghost," Rom. v. 5,—gives us a sense of it, manifests it unto us. Now, this is[2] various and changeable, sometimes more, sometimes less; now he shines, anon hides his face, as it may be for our profit. Our Father will not always *chide*, lest we be cast down; he doth not always *smile*, lest we be full and neglect him: but yet, still his love in itself is the same. When for a little moment he hides his face, yet he gathers us with everlasting kindness.

Objection. But you will say, "This comes nigh to that blasphemy, *that God loves his people in their sinning* as well as in their strictest obedience; and, if so, who will care to serve him more, or to walk with him unto well-pleasing?"

Answer. There are few truths of Christ which, from some or other, have not received like entertainment with this. Terms and appellations are at the will of every imposer; things are not at all varied by them. The love of God in itself is the eternal purpose and act of his will. This is no more changeable than God himself: if it were, no flesh could be saved; but it[3] changeth not, and we are not con-

---

[1] 1 Sam. xv. 29; Isa. xlvi. 10; Jer. xxxi. 3; Mal. iii. 6; James i. 17; 2 Tim. ii. 19.
[2] Ps. xxxi. 16, lxvii. 1, cxix. 135, xiii. 1, xxvii. 9, xxx. 7, lxxxviii. 14; Isa. viii. 17.
[3] Mal. iii. 6.

sumed. What then? loves he his people in their sinning? Yes; his people,—not their sinning. Alters[1] he not his love towards them? Not the *purpose* of his will, but the *dispensations* of his grace. He *rebukes* them, he *chastens* them, he *hides* his face from them, he *smites* them, he *fills* them with a sense of [his] indignation; but woe, woe would it be to us, should he change in his love, or take away his kindness from us! Those very things which seem to be demonstrations of the change of his affections towards his, do as clearly proceed from love as those which seem to be the most genuine issues thereof. "But will not this encourage to sin?" He never tasted of the love of God that can seriously make this objection. The *doctrine* of grace may be turned into wantonness; the *principle* cannot. I shall not wrong the saints by giving another answer to this objection: Detestation of sin in any may well consist with the acceptation of their persons, and their designation to life eternal.

But now our love to God is ebbing and flowing, waning and increasing. We lose our first love, and we grow again in love;[2]—scarce a day at a stand. What poor creatures are we! How unlike the Lord and his love! "Unstable as water, we cannot excel." Now it is, "Though all men forsake thee, I will not;" anon, "I know not the man." One day, "I shall never be moved, my hill is so strong;" the next, "All men are liars, I shall perish." When ever was the time, where ever was the place, that our love was one day equal towards God?

And thus, these agreements and discrepancies do farther describe that mutual love of the Father and the saints, wherein they hold communion. Other instances as to the person of the Father I shall not give, but endeavour to make some improvement of this in the next chapter.

CHAPTER IV.

Inferences on the former doctrine concerning communion with the Father in love.

HAVING thus discovered the nature of that distinct communion which we have with the Father, it remaineth that we give some *exhortations* unto it, *directions* in it, and take some *observations* from it:—

1. First, then, this is a duty wherein it is most evident that Chris-

---

[1] Ps. xxxix. 11; Heb. xii. 7, 8; Rev. iii. 19; Isa. viii. 17, lvii. 17; Job vi. 4; Ps. vi. 6, xxxviii. 3–5, etc.
[2] Rev. ii. 4, iii. 2; Eph iii. 16–19.

tians are but little exercised,—namely, in holding immediate communion with the Father in love.   Unacquaintedness with our
mercies, our privileges, is our sin as well as our trouble.   We hearken
not to the voice of the Spirit,[1] which is given unto us, " that we may
know the things that are freely bestowed on us of God." This makes
us go heavily, when we might rejoice; and to be weak, where we
might be strong in the Lord.   How few of the saints are experimentally acquainted with this privilege of holding immediate communion with the Father in love!   With what anxious, doubtful
thoughts do they look upon him!   What fears, what questionings
are there, of his good-will and kindness!   At the best, many think
there is no sweetness at all in him towards us, but what is purchased
at the high price of the blood of Jesus.   It is true, that alone is the
way of communication; but the free fountain and spring of all is in
the bosom of the Father.[2] " Eternal life was with the Father, and is
manifested unto us."   Let us, then,—

(1.) *Eye the Father as love;* look not on him as an always lowering father, but as one most[3] kind and tender.   Let us look on him
by faith, as one that hath had thoughts of kindness towards us from
everlasting.   It is misapprehension of God that makes any run from
him, who have the least breathing wrought in them after him.   " They
that know thee will put their trust in thee."   Men cannot abide with
God in spiritual meditations.   He loseth *soul's company* by their
want of this insight into his love.   They fix their thoughts only on
his terrible majesty, severity, and greatness; and so their spirits are
not endeared.   Would a soul continually eye his everlasting tenderness and compassion, his thoughts of kindness that have been from
of old, his present gracious acceptance, it could not bear an hour's
absence from him; whereas now, perhaps, it cannot watch with him
one hour.   Let, then, this be the saints' first notion of the Father,—
as one full of eternal, free love towards them: let their hearts and
thoughts be filled with breaking through all discouragements that
lie in the way.   To raise them hereunto, let them consider,—

[1.] *Whose* love it is.   It is the love of him who is in himself all-
sufficient, infinitely satiated with himself and his own glorious excellencies and perfections; who hath no need to go forth with his love
unto others, nor to seek an object of it without himself.   There
might he rest with delight and complacency to eternity.   He is sufficient unto his own love.   He had his Son, also, his eternal[4] Wisdom,
to rejoice and delight himself in from all eternity, Prov. viii. 30.
This might take up and satiate the whole delight of the Father; but

---

[1] 1 Cor. ii. 12.   [2] Ζωὴ ἥτις ἦν πρὸς τὸν Πατέρα, καὶ ἐφανερώθη ἡμῖν.—1 John i. 2.
[3] Ps. ciii. 9 ; Mic. vii. 18.
[4] שַׁעֲשׁוּעִים יוֹם יוֹם.   "Optime in Dei Filium quadrat *patris delicias*."—Mer. in loc.

he will love his saints also. And it is such a love, as wherein he seeks not his own satisfaction only, but our good therein also;—the love of a God, the love of a Father, whose proper outgoings are *kindness* and *bounty.*

[2.] *What kind of love* it is. And it is,—

1*st. Eternal.* It was fixed on us before the[1] foundation of the world. Before we were, or had done the least good, then were his thoughts upon us,—then was his delight in us;—then did the Son rejoice in the thoughts of fulfilling his Father's delight in him, Prov. viii. 30. Yea, the delight of the Father in the Son, there mentioned, is not so much his absolute delight in him as the express image of his person and the brightness of his glory, wherein he might behold all his own excellencies and perfections; as with respect unto his love and his delight in the sons of men. So the order of the words require us to understand it: "I was daily his delight," and, "My delights were with the sons of men;"—that is, in the thoughts of kindness and redemption for them: and in that respect, also, was he his Father's delight. It was from eternity that he laid in his own bosom a design for our happiness. The very thought of this is enough to make all that is within us, like the babe in the womb of Elisabeth, to leap for joy. A sense of it cannot but prostrate our souls to the lowest abasement of a humble, holy reverence, and make us rejoice before him with trembling.

2*dly. Free.* He[2] loves us because he *will;* there *was,* there *is,* nothing in us for which we should be beloved. Did we deserve his love, it must go less in its valuation. Things of due debt are seldom the matter of thankfulness; but that which is *eternally antecedent* to our being, must needs be *absolutely free* in its respects to our well-being. This gives it life and being, is the reason of it, and sets a price upon it, Rom. ix. 11; Eph. i. 3, 4; Titus iii. 5; James i. 18.

3*dly.* [3]*Unchangeable.* Though we change every day, yet his love changeth not. Could any kind of provocation turn it away, it had long since ceased. Its unchangeableness is that which carrieth out the Father unto that infiniteness of patience and forbearance (without which we die, we perish), 2 Pet. iii. 9, which he exerciseth towards us. And it is,—

4*thly.* [4]*Distinguishing.* He hath not thus loved all the world: "Jacob have I loved, but Esau have I hated." Why should he fix

---

[1] Rom. ix. 11, 12; Acts xv. 18; 2 Tim. i. 9, ii. 19; Prov. viii. 31; Jer. xxxi. 3.

[2] Matt. xi. 25, 26. "Hoc tanto et tam ineffabili bono, nemo inventus est dignus; sordet natura sine gratia."—Pros. de lib. Arb. ad Ruff.

[3] Mal. iii. 6; James i. 17; Hos. xi. 9.

[4] Rom. ix. 12. "Omnia diligit Deus, quæ fecit; et inter ea magis diligit creaturas rationales, et de illis eas amplius quæ sunt membra unigeniti sui. Et multo magis ipsum unigenitum."—August.

his love on us, and pass by millions from whom we differ not by[1] nature,—that he should make us sharers in that, and all the fruits of it, which most of the great and[2] wise men of the world are excluded from? I name but the heads of things. Let them enlarge whose hearts are touched.

Let, I say, the soul frequently eye the love of the Father, and that under these considerations,—they are all soul-conquering and endearing.

(2.) So *eye* it as to *receive* it. Unless this be added, all is in vain as to any communion with God. We do not hold communion with him in any thing, until it be received by faith. This, then, is that which I would provoke the saints of God unto, even to[3] believe this love of God for themselves and their own part,—believe that such is the heart of the Father towards them,—accept of his witness herein. His love is not ours in the sweetness of it until it be so received. Continually, then, act thoughts of faith on God, as love to thee,—as embracing thee with the eternal free love before described. When the Lord is, by his word, presented as such unto thee, let thy mind know it, and assent that it is so; and thy will embrace it, in its being so; and all thy affections be filled with it. Set thy whole heart to it; let it be bound with the cords of this love.[4] If the King be bound in the galleries with thy love, shouldst thou not be bound in heaven with his?

(3.) Let it have its proper *fruit* and efficacy upon thy heart, in return of love to him again. So shall we walk in the light of God's countenance, and hold holy communion with our Father all the day long. Let us not deal unkindly with him, and return him slighting for his good-will. Let there not be such a heart in us as to deal so unthankfully with our God.

2. Now, to further us in this duty, and the daily constant practice of it, I shall add one or two considerations that may be of importance thereunto; as,—

(1.) It is exceeding *acceptable* unto God, even our Father, that we should thus hold communion with him in his love,—that he may be received into our souls as one full of love, tenderness, and kindness, towards us. Flesh and blood is apt to have very hard thoughts of him,—to think he is always angry, yea, implacable; that it is not for poor creatures to draw nigh to him; that nothing in the world is more desirable than never to come into his presence, or, as they say, where he hath any thing to do. "Who[5] among us shall dwell with the devouring fire? who among us shall dwell with everlasting burnings?" say the sinners in Zion. [6]And, "I knew thou wast an austere man," saith the evil servant in the gospel. Now, there is not any thing more

---

[1] Eph. ii. 3.   [2] Matt. xi. 25, 26; 1 Cor. i. 20.   [3] 1 John iv. 16.
[4] Cant. vii. 5.   [5] Isa. xxxiii. 14.   [6] Luke xix. 21.

grievous to the Lord, nor more subservient to the design of Satan upon the soul, than such thoughts as these. Satan claps his hands (if I may so say) when he can take up the soul with such thoughts of God: he hath enough,—all that he doth desire. This hath been his design and way from the beginning. The[1] first blood that murderer shed was by this means. He leads our first parents into hard thoughts of God: " Hath God said so? hath he threatened you with death? He knows well enough it will be better with you;"—with this engine did he batter and overthrow all mankind in[2] one; and being mindful of his ancient conquest, he readily useth the same weapons wherewith then he so successfully contended. Now, it is exceeding grievous to the Spirit of God to be so slandered in the hearts of those whom he dearly loves. How doth he expostulate this with Zion! " What iniquity[3] have ye seen in me?" saith he; " have I been a wilderness unto you, or a land of darkness?"[4] " Zion said, The LORD hath forsaken me, and my Lord hath forgotten me. Can a woman," etc. The Lord takes nothing worse at the hands of his, than such hard thoughts of him, knowing full well what fruit this bitter root is like to bear,—what alienations of heart,—what drawings back,—what unbelief and tergiversations in our walking with him. How unwilling is a child to come into the presence of an angry father! Consider, then, this in the first place,—receiving of the Father as he holds out love to the soul, gives him the honour he aims at, and is exceeding acceptable unto him. He often sets it out in an eminent manner, that it may be so received:—" He commendeth his love toward us," Rom. v. 8. " Behold, what manner of love the Father hath bestowed upon us!" 1 John iii. 1. Whence, then, is this folly? Men are afraid to have good thoughts of God. They think it a boldness to eye God as good, gracious, tender, kind, loving: I speak of saints; but for the other side, they can judge him hard, austere, severe, almost implacable, and fierce (the very worst affections of the very worst of men, and most hated of him, Rom. i. 31; 2 Tim. iii. 3), and think herein they do well. Is not this soul-deceit from Satan? Was it not his design from the beginning to inject such thoughts of God? Assure thyself, then, there is nothing more acceptable unto the Father, than for us to keep up our hearts unto him as the eternal fountain of all that rich grace which flows out to sinners in the blood of Jesus. And,—

(2.) This will be exceeding effectual to *endear* thy soul unto God, to cause thee to delight in him, and to make thy abode with him. Many saints have no greater burden in their lives, than that their hearts do not come clearly and fully up, constantly to delight and

---

[1] Gen. iii. 5.   [2] 'Εφ' ῷ πάντες ἥμαρτον, Rom. v. 12.
[3] Jer. ii. 5, 21.   [4] Isa. xl. 27–29, xlix. 15, 16.

rejoice in God;—that there is still an indisposedness of spirit unto close walking with him. What is at the bottom of this distemper? Is it not their unskilfulness in or neglect of this duty, even of holding communion with the Father in love? So much as we see of the love of God, so much shall we delight in him, and no more. Every other discovery of God, without this, will but make the soul fly from him; but if the heart be once much taken up with this the eminency of the Father's love, it cannot choose but be overpowered, conquered, and endeared unto him. This, if any thing, will work upon us to make our abode with him. If the love of a father will not make a child delight in him, what will? Put, then, this to the venture: exercise your thoughts upon this very thing, the eternal, free, and fruitful love of the Father, and see if your hearts be not wrought upon to delight in him. I dare boldly say, believers will find it as thriving a course as ever they pitched on in their lives. Sit down a little at the fountain, and you will quickly have a farther discovery of the sweetness of the streams. You who have run from him, will not be able, after a while, to keep at a distance for a moment.

Objection 1. But some may say, "Alas! how shall I hold communion with the Father in love? I know not at all whether he loves me or no; and shall I venture to cast myself upon it? How if I should not be accepted? should I not rather perish for my presumption, than find sweetness in his bosom? God seems to me only as a consuming fire and everlasting burnings; so that I dread to look up unto him."

Answer. I know not what may be understood by knowing of the love of God; though it be carried on by spiritual sense and experience, yet it is received purely by believing. Our knowing of it, is our believing of it as revealed. "We have known and believed the love that God hath to us. God is love," 1 John iv. 16. This is the assurance which, at the very entrance of walking with God, thou mayest have of this love. He who is truth hath said it; and whatever thy heart says, or Satan says, unless thou wilt take it up on this account, thou doest thy endeavour to make him a liar who hath spoken it, 1 John v. 10.

Obj. 2. "I can believe that God is love to others, for he hath said he is love; but that he will be so to me, I see no ground of persuasion; there is no cause, no reason in the world, why he should turn one thought of love or kindness towards me: and therefore I dare not cast myself upon it, to hold communion with him in his special love."

Ans. He hath spoken it as particularly to thee as to any one in the world. And for cause of love, he hath as much to fix it on thee as on any of the children of men; that is, none at all without himself. So that I shall make speedy work with this objection. Never any one from the foundation of the world, who believed such love in the

Father, and made returns of love to him again, was deceived; neither shall ever any to the world's end be so, in so doing. Thou art, then, in this, upon a most sure bottom. If thou believest and receivest the Father as love, he will infallibly be so to thee, though others may fall under his severity. But,—

Obj. 3. "I cannot find my heart making returns of love unto God. Could I find my soul set upon him, I could then believe his soul delighted in me."

Ans. This is the most *preposterous* course that possibly thy thoughts can pitch upon, a most ready way to rob God of his glory. "Herein is love," saith the Holy Ghost, "not that we loved God, but that he loved us" first, 1 John iv. 10, 11. Now, thou wouldst invert this order, and say, "Herein is love, not that God loved me, but that I love him first." This is to take the glory of God from him: that, whereas he loves us without a cause that is in ourselves, and we have all cause in the world to love him, thou wouldst have the contrary, —namely, that something should be in thee for which God should love thee, even thy love to him; and that thou shouldst love God, before thou knowest any thing lovely in him,—namely, whether he love thee or no. This is a course of flesh's finding out, that will never bring glory to God, nor peace to thy own soul. Lay down, then, *thy reasonings;* take up the love of the Father upon a *pure act of believing,* and that will open thy soul to let it out unto the Lord in the communion of love.

To make yet some farther improvement of this truth so opened and exhorted unto as before;—it will discover unto us *the eminency and privilege of the saints of God.* What low thoughts soever the sons of men may have of them, it will appear that they have meat to eat that the world knows not of. They have close communion and fellowship with the Father. They deal with him in the *interchange of love.* Men are generally esteemed according to the company they keep. It is an honour to stand in the presence of princes, though but as servants. What honour, then, have all the saints, to stand with boldness in the presence of the Father, and there to enjoy his bosom love! What a blessing did the queen of Sheba pronounce on the servants of Solomon, who stood before him, and heard his wisdom! How much more blessed, then, are they who stand continually before the God of Solomon, hearing his wisdom, enjoying his love! Whilst others have their fellowship with Satan and their own lusts, making provision for them, and receiving perishing refreshments from them, ("whose end is destruction, whose god is their belly, and whose glory is in their shame, who mind earthly things,") they have this sweet communion with the Father.

Moreover, what *a safe and sweet retreat* is here for the saints, in all the scorns, reproaches, scandals, misrepresentations, which they undergo in the world. When[1] a child is abused abroad in the streets by strangers, he runs with speed to the bosom of his father; there he makes his complaint, and is comforted. In all the hard[2] censures and tongue-persecutions which the saints meet withal in the streets of the world, they may run with their moanings unto their Father, and be comforted. " As one whom his mother comforteth, so will I comfort you," saith the Lord, Isa. lxvi. 13. So that the soul may say, " If I have hatred in the world, I will go where I am sure of love. Though all others are hard to me, yet my Father is tender and full of compassion : I will go to him, and satisfy myself in him. Here I am accounted vile, frowned on, and rejected; but I have honour and love with him, whose kindness is better than life itself. There I shall have all things in the fountain, which others have but in the drops. There is in my Father's love every thing desirable : there is the sweetness of all mercies in the abstract itself, and that fully and durably."

Evidently, then, *the saints are the most mistaken men* in the world. If they say,[3] " Come and have fellowship with us;" are not men ready to say, " Why, what are you ? a sorry company of[4] seditious, factious persons. Be it known unto you, that we despise your fellowship. When we intend to leave fellowship with all honest men, and men of worth, then will we come to you." But, alas ! how are men mistaken ! Truly their fellowship is with the Father : let men think of it as they please, they have close, spiritual, heavenly refreshings, in the mutual communication of love with the Father himself. How they are generally misconceived, the apostle declares, 2 Cor. vi. 8–10, " As deceivers, and yet true; as unknown, and yet well known; as dying, and, behold, we live; as chastened, and not killed; as sorrowful, yet always rejoicing; as poor, yet making many rich; as having nothing, and yet possessing all things." And as it is thus in general, so in no one thing more than this, that they are looked on as poor, low, despicable persons, when indeed they are the only great and noble personages in the world. Consider the company they keep : it is with the Father;—who so glorious ? The merchandise they trade in, it is love;—what so precious? Doubtless they are the excellent on the earth, Ps. xvi. 3.

Farther; this will *discover a main difference between the saints and empty professors :*—As to the performance of duties, and so the enjoyment of outward privileges, fruitless professors often walk hand in hand with them; but now come to their secret retirements, and

---

[1] Isa. xxvi. 20.
[2] Ἐμπαιγμῶν πεῖραν ἔλαβον, Heb. xi. 36. Ὀνειδισμοῖς θεατριζόμενοι, Heb. x. 33.
[3] 1 John i. 3.   [4] Acts xvii. 6, xxviii. 22.

what a difference is there! There the saints hold communion with God: hypocrites, for the most part, with the world and their own lusts;—with them they converse and communicate; they hearken what they will say to them, and make provision for them, when the saints are sweetly wrapt up in the bosom of their Father's love. It is oftentimes even almost impossible that believers should, in outward appearance, go beyond them who have very rotten hearts: but this meat they have, which others know not of; this refreshment in the banqueting house, wherein others have no share;—in the multitude of their thoughts, the comforts of God their Father refresh their souls.

Now, then (to draw towards a close of this discourse), if these things be so, " what manner of men ought we to be, in all manner of holy conversation?" Even " our God is a consuming fire." What communion is there between light and darkness? Shall sin and lust dwell in those thoughts which receive in and carry out love from and unto the Father? Holiness becometh his presence for ever. An unclean spirit cannot draw nigh unto him;—an unholy heart can make no abode with him. A lewd person will not desire to hold fellowship with a sober man; and will a man of vain and foolish imaginations hold communion and dwell with the most holy God? There is not any consideration of this love but is a powerful motive unto holiness, and leads thereunto. Ephraim says, " What have I to do any more with idols?" when in God he finds salvation. Communion with the Father is wholly inconsistent with `loose walking. " If we say that we have fellowship with him, and walk in darkness, we lie, and do not the truth," 1 John i. 6. " He that saith, I know him" (I have communion with him), "and keepeth not his commandments, is a liar, and the truth is not in him," chap. ii. 4. The most specious and glorious pretence made to an acquaintance with the Father, without holiness and obedience to his commandments, serves only to prove the pretenders to be liars. The love of the world and of the Father dwell not together.

And if this be so (to shut up all), how many that go under the name of Christians, come short of the truth of it! How unacquainted are the generality of professors with the mystery of this communion, and the fruits of it! Do not many very evidently hold communion with their lusts and with the world, and yet would be thought to have a portion and inheritance among them that are sanctified? They have neither new name nor white stone, and yet would be called the people of the Most High. May it not be said of many of them, rather, that God is not in all their thoughts, than that they have communion with him? The Lord open the eyes of men, that they may see and know that walking with God is a matter not of form, but power! And so far of peculiar communion with the Father, in the instance of love which we have insisted on. "He is also faithful who hath called us to the fellowship of his Son Jesus Christ our Lord;" —of which in the next place.

PART II.

CHAPTER I.

Of the fellowship which the saints have with Jesus Christ the Son of God— That they have such a fellowship proved, 1 Cor. i. 9; Rev. iii. 20; Cant. ii. 1–7 opened; also Prov. ix. 1–5.

OF that distinct communion which we have with the person of the Father we have treated in the foregoing chapters; we now proceed to the consideration of that which we have with his Son, Jesus Christ our Lord. Now the fellowship we have with the second person, is with him as Mediator,—in that office whereunto, by dispensation, he submitted himself for our sakes; being "made of a woman, made under the law, to redeem them that were under the law, that we might receive the adoption of sons," Gal. iv. 4, 5. And herein I shall do these two things:—I. Declare that we have such fellowship with the Son of God. II. Show wherein that fellowship or communion doth consist:—

I. For the first, I shall only produce some few places of Scripture to *confirm* it, that it is so:—1 Cor. i. 9, "God is faithful, by whom ye were called unto the fellowship of his Son Jesus Christ our Lord." This is that whereunto all the saints are called, and wherein, by the faithfulness of God, they shall be preserved, even fellowship with Jesus Christ our Lord. We are called of God the Father, as the Father, in pursuit of his love, to communion with the Son, as our Lord.

Rev. iii. 20, "Behold, I stand at the door, and knock: if any man hear my voice, and open the door, I will come in to him, and will sup with him, and he with me."[1] Certainly this is fellowship, or I know not what is. Christ will sup with believers: he refreshes himself with his own graces in them, by his Spirit bestowed on them. The Lord Christ is exceedingly delighted in tasting of the sweet fruits of the Spirit in the saints. Hence is that prayer of the spouse that she may have something for his entertainment when he cometh to her, Cant. iv. 16, "Awake, O north wind; and come, thou south; blow upon my garden, that the spices thereof may flow out. Let my

---

[1] John xiv. 23.

Beloved come into his garden, and eat his pleasant fruits." The souls of the saints are the garden of Jesus Christ, the good ground, Heb. vi. 7;—a garden for delight; he rejoices in them; "his delights are with the sons of men," Prov. viii. 31; and he "rejoices over them," Zeph. iii. 17;—and a garden for fruit, yea, pleasant fruit; so he describes it, Cant. iv. 12–14, "A garden inclosed is my sister, my spouse; a spring shut up, a fountain sealed. Thy plants are an orchard of pomegranates, with pleasant fruits; camphire, with spikenard, spikenard and saffron; calamus and cinnamon, with all trees of frankincense; myrrh and aloes, with all chief spices." Whatever is sweet and delicious for taste, whatever savoury and odoriferous, whatever is useful and medicinal, is in this garden. There is all manner of spiritual refreshments, of all kinds whatever, in the souls of the saints, for the Lord Jesus. On this account is the spouse so earnest in the prayer mentioned for an increase of these things, that her Beloved may sup with her, as he hath promised. "Awake, O north wind," etc.;—"O that the breathings and workings of the Spirit of all grace might stir up all his gifts and graces in me, that the Lord Jesus, the beloved of my soul, may have meet and acceptable entertainment from me!" God complains of want of fruit in his vineyard, Isa. v. 2; Hos. x. 1. Want of good food for Christ's entertainment is that the spouse feared, and labours to prevent. A barren heart is not fit to receive him. And the delight he takes in the fruit of the Spirit is unspeakable. This he expresses at large, Cant. v. 1, "I am come," saith he; "I have eaten, I am refreshed." He calls it פְּרִי מְגָדִים, "The fruit of his sweetnesses;" or most pleasant to him. Moreover, as Christ sups with his saints, so he hath promised they shall sup with him, to complete that fellowship they have with him. Christ provides for their entertainment in a most eminent manner. There are beasts killed, and wine is mingled, and a table furnished, Prov. ix. 2. He calls the spiritual dainties that he hath for them a "feast," a "wedding," [1] "a feast of fat things, wine on the lees," etc. The fatted calf is killed for their entertainment. Such is the communion, and such is the mutual entertainment of Christ and his saints in that communion.

Cant. ii. 1–7, "I am the rose of Sharon, and the lily of the valleys. As the lily among thorns, so is my love among the daughters. As the apple-tree among the trees of the wood, so is my Beloved among the sons. I sat down under his shadow with great delight, and his fruit was sweet to my taste," etc.

In the two first verses you have the description that Christ gives, first of himself, then of his church. Of himself, verse 1; that is, what he is to his spouse: "I am the rose of Sharon, and the lily of the

[1] Isa. xxv. 6; Matt. xxii. 8; Rev. xix. 7.

valleys." The Lord[1] Christ is, in the Scripture, compared to all things of eminency in the whole creation. He is in the heavens the *sun*, and the bright morning star: as the *lion* among the beasts, the lion of the tribe of Judah. Among the flowers of the field, here he is the *rose* and the *lily*. The two eminencies of flowers, sweetness of savour and beauty of colour, are divided between these. The rose for sweetness, and the lily for beauty ("Solomon in all his glory was not arrayed like one of these"), have the pre-eminence. Farther, he is "the rose of Sharon," a fruitful plain, where the choicest herds were fed, 1 Chron. xxvii. 29; so eminent, that it is promised to the church that there shall be given unto her the [2]excellency of Sharon, Isa. xxxv. 2. This fruitful place, doubtless, brought forth the most precious roses. Christ, in the savour of his love, and in his righteousness (which is as the garment wherein Jacob received his blessing, giving forth a smell as the smell of a pleasant field, Gen. xxvii. 27), is as this excellent rose, to draw and allure the hearts of his saints unto him. As God smelled a sweet savour from the blood of his atonement, Eph. v. 2; so from the graces wherewith for them he is anointed, his saints receive a refreshing, cherishing savour, Cant. i. 3. A sweet savour expresses that which is acceptable and delightful, Gen. viii. 21. He is also "the lily of the valleys;" that of all flowers is the most eminent in beauty, Matt. vi. 29. Most desirable is he, for the comeliness and perfection of his person; incomparably fairer than the children of men: of which afterward. He, then, being thus unto them (abundantly satiating all their spiritual senses) their refreshment, their ornament, their delight, their glory; in the next verse he tells us what they are to him: "As the lily among thorns, so is my beloved among the daughters." That Christ and his church are likened unto and termed the same thing (as here the lily), is, as from their union by the indwelling of the same Spirit, so from that [3]conformity and likeness that is between them, and whereunto the saints are appointed. Now she is a lily, very beautiful unto Christ; "as the lily among thorns:"—1. By the way of *eminency;* as the lily excelleth the thorns, so do the saints all others whatever, in the eye of Christ. Let comparison be made, so will it be found to be. And,—2. By the way of *trial;* the residue of the world being "pricking briers and grieving thorns to the house of Israel," Ezek. xxviii. 24. "The best of them is as a brier, the most upright is sharper than a thorn hedge," Mic. vii. 4. And thus are they among the daughters,—even the most eminent collections of the most improved professors, that are no more but so. There cannot be in any greater comparison, a greater exaltation of the ex-

---

[1] Mal. iv. 2; Rev. xii. 1; Luke i. 78, 'Ανατολὴ ἐξ ὕψους· Numb. xxiv. 17; 2 Pet. i. 19; Rev. xxii. 16; Gen. xlix. 9; Mic. v. 8; Rev. v. 5.

[2] Isa. xxxiii. 9, lxv 10.   [3] Rom. viii. 29.

cellency of any thing. So, then, is Christ to them indeed, verse 1;
so are they in his esteem, and indeed, verse 2. How he is in their
esteem and indeed, we have, verse 3.

" As the apple-tree among the trees of the wood, so is my Beloved
among the sons. I sat down under his shadow with great delight,
and his fruit was sweet to my taste." To carry on this intercourse,
the spouse begins to speak her thoughts of, and to show her delight
in, the Lord Christ; and as he compares her to the lily among the
thorns, so she him to the *apple-tree* among the trees of the wood.
And she adds this reason of it, even because he hath the two eminent things of trees, which the residue of them have not:—1. *Fruit*
for food; 2. *Shade* for refreshment. Of the one she eateth, under
the other she resteth; both with great delight. All other sons, either
angels, the sons of God by creation, Job i. 6, xxxviii. 7, or the sons
of Adam,—the best of his offspring, the leaders of those companies
which, verse 2, are called daughters, or sons of the old creation, the
top branches of all its desirable things,—are to an hungry, weary soul
(such alone seek for shade and fruit) but as the fruitless, leafless trees
of the forest, which will yield them neither food nor refreshment.
" In Christ," saith she, " there is fruit, fruit sweet to the taste; yea,
'his flesh is meat indeed, and his blood is drink indeed,' " John vi. 55.
"Moreover, he hath brought forth that everlasting righteousness which
will abundantly satisfy any hungry soul, after it hath gone to many
a barren tree for food, and hath found none.   Besides, he aboundeth
in precious and pleasant graces, whereof I may [1]eat; yea, he calls me
to do so, and that abundantly." These are the fruits that Christ
beareth. They speak of a tree that bringeth forth all things needful for life, in food and raiment.   Christ is that tree of life, which
hath brought forth all things that are needful unto life eternal.   In
him is that righteousness which we [2]hunger after;—in him is that
water of life, which whoso [3]drinketh of shall thirst no more.   Oh,
how sweet are the fruits of Christ's mediation to the faith of his saints!
He that can find no relief in mercy, pardon, grace, acceptation with
God, holiness, sanctification, etc., is an utter stranger to these things
([4]wine on the lees) that are prepared for believers.   Also, he hath
shades for refreshment and shelter;—shelter from wrath without, and
refreshment because of weariness from within.   The first use of the
[5]shade is to keep us from the *heat* of the sun, as did Jonah's gourd.
When the heat of wrath is ready to scorch the soul, Christ, interposing, bears it all.   Under the shadow of his wings we sit down constantly, quietly, safely, putting our trust in him; and all this with
great delight.   Yea, who can express the joy of a soul safe shadowed

[1] Cant. v. 1.   [2] Matt. v. 6.   [3] John iv. 14.   [4] Isa. xxv. 6; Prov. ix. 2.
[5] Jonah iv. 6; Isa. xxv. 4, xxxii. 2; 2 Cor. v. 21; Gal. iii. 13; Mal. iv. 2.

from wrath under the covert of the righteousness of the Lord Jesus!
There is also refreshment in a shade from *weariness*. He is "as the
shadow of a great rock in a weary land," Isa. xxxii. 2. From the
power of *corruptions*, trouble of temptations, distress of persecutions,
there is in him quiet, rest, and repose, Matt. xi. 27, 28.

Having thus mutually described each other, and so made it manifest that they cannot but be delighted in fellowship and communion,
in the next verses that communion of theirs is at large set forth
and described. I shall briefly observe four things therein:—(1.) *Sweetness*. (2.) *Delight*. (3.) *Safety*. (4.) *Comfort*.

(1.) *Sweetness:* " He brought me to the banqueting-house," or
" house of wine." It is all set forth under expressions of the greatest
sweetness and most delicious refreshment,—flagons, apples, wine, etc.
" HE entertains me," saith the spouse, " as some great personage.'
Great personages, at great entertainments, are had into the banqueting-house,—the house of wine and dainties. These are the preparations of grace and mercy,—love, kindness, supplies revealed in the
gospel, declared in the assemblies of the saints, exhibited by the Spirit.
This "love is better than wine," Cant. i. 2; it is "not meat and
drink, but righteousness, and[1] peace, and joy in the Holy Ghost."
Gospel dainties are sweet refreshments; whether these houses of wine
be the *Scriptures*, the *gospel*, or the *ordinances* dispensed in the
assemblies of the saints, or any eminent and signal manifestations of
special love (as banqueting is not every day's work, nor used at ordinary entertainments), it is all one. Wine, that cheereth the heart of
man, that makes him forget his misery, Prov. xxxi. 6, 7, that gives
him a cheerful look and countenance, Gen. xlix. 12, is that which is
promised. The grace exhibited by Christ in his ordinances is refreshing, strengthening, comforting, and full of sweetness to the souls
of the saints. Woe be to such full souls as loathe these honey-combs!
But thus Christ makes all his assemblies to be banqueting-houses;
and there he gives his saints entertainment.

(2.) *Delight*. The spouse is quite ravished with the sweetness of
this entertainment, finding love, and care, and kindness, bestowed by
Christ in the assemblies of the saints. Hence she cries out, verse 5,
" Stay me with flagons, comfort me with apples; for I am sick of
love." Upon the discovery of the excellency and sweetness of Christ
in the banqueting-house, the soul is instantly overpowered, and cries
out to be made partaker of the fulness of it. She is " *sick of love:*"
not (as some suppose) fainting for want of a sense of love, under the
apprehension of wrath; but made sick and faint, even overcome, with
the mighty actings of that divine affection, after she had once tasted
of the sweetness of Christ in the banqueting-house. Her desire de-

[1] Rom. xiv. 17; John vii. 37; Prov. xxvii. 7.

ferred, makes her heart sick; therefore she cries, " Stay me,"etc.;—" I
have seen a glimpse of the ' King in his beauty,'—tasted of the fruit
of his righteousness; my soul melteth in longing after him.   Oh!
support and sustain my spirit with his presence in his ordinances,—
those ' flagons and apples of his banqueting-house,'—or I shall quite
sink and faint!   Oh, what hast thou done, blessed Jesus!   I have seen
thee, and my soul is become as the chariots of Ammi-nadib.   Let me
have something from thee to support me, or I die."   When a person is
fainting on any occasion, these two things are to be done:—*strength*
is to be used to support him, that he sink not to the ground; and
comfortable things are to be applied, to refresh his spirits.   These
two the soul, overpowered and fainting with the force of its own
love, (raised by a sense of Christ's,) prayeth for.   It would have
strengthening grace to support it in that condition, that it may
be able to attend its duty; and consolations of the Holy Ghost, to
content, revive, and satiate it, until it come to a full enjoyment
of Christ.   And thus sweetly and with delight is this communion
carried on.

(3.) *Safety:* " His banner over me was love," verse 4.   The banner is an emblem of safety and protection,—a sign of the presence of
an host.   Persons belonging to an army do encamp under their
banner in security.   So did the children of Israel in the wilderness;
every tribe kept their camps under their own standard.   It is also a
token of success and victory, Ps. xx. 5.   Christ hath a banner for his
saints; and that is *love*.   All their protection is from his love; and
they shall have all the protection his love can give them.   This safe-
guards them from hell, death,—all their enemies.   Whatever presses
on them, it must pass through the banner of the love of the Lord
Jesus.   They have, then, great spiritual safety; which is another ornament or excellency of their communion with him.

(4.) *Supportment and consolation*, verse 6, " His left hand is
under my head, and his right hand doth embrace me."   Christ here
hath the posture of a most tender friend towards any one in sickness
and sadness.   The soul faints with love,—spiritual longings after the
enjoyment of his presence; and Christ comes in with his embraces.
He nourisheth and cherisheth his church, Eph. v. 29; Isa. lxiii. 9.
Now, " the hand under the head," is supportment, sustaining grace,
in pressures and difficulties; and " the hand that doth embrace," the
hand upon the heart, is joy and consolation;—in both, Christ rejoicing, as the " bridegroom rejoiceth over the bride," Isa. lxii. 5.
Now, thus to lie in the arms of Christ's love, under a perpetual
influence of supportment and refreshment, is certainly to hold communion with him.   And hereupon, verse 7, the spouse is most earnest for the continuance of his fellowship, charging all so to demean

themselves, that her Beloved be not disquieted, or provoked to depart.

In brief, this whole book is taken up in the description of the communion that is between the Lord Christ and his saints; and therefore, it is very needless to take from thence any more particular instances thereof.

I shall only add that of Prov. ix. 1–5, " Wisdom hath builded her house, she hath hewn out her seven pillars; she hath killed her beasts; she hath mingled her wine; she hath also furnished her table. She hath sent forth her maidens: she crieth upon the highest places of the city, Whoso is simple, let him turn in hither: as for him that wanteth understanding, she saith to him, Come, eat of my bread, and drink of the wine which I have mingled."

The Lord Christ, the eternal Wisdom of the Father, and who of God is made unto us wisdom, erects a *spiritual house*, wherein he makes provision for the entertainment of those guests whom he so freely invites. His church is the house which he hath built on a perfect number of pillars, that it might have a stable foundation: his slain beasts and mingled wine, wherewith his table is furnished, are those *spiritual fat things* of the gospel, which he hath prepared for those that come in upon his invitation. Surely, to eat of this bread, and drink of this wine, which he hath so graciously prepared, is to hold fellowship with him; for in what ways or things is there nearer communion than in such?

I might farther evince this truth, by a consideration of all *the relations* wherein Christ and his saints do stand; which necessarily require that there be a communion between them, if we do suppose they are faithful in those relations: but this is commonly treated on, and something will be spoken to it in one signal instance afterward.

CHAPTER II.

What it is wherein we have peculiar fellowship with the Lord Christ—This is in grace—This proved, John i. 14, 16, 17; 2 Cor. xiii. 14; 2 Thess. iii. 17, 18 —Grace of various acceptations—Personal grace in Christ proposed to consideration—The grace of Christ as Mediator intended, Ps. xlv. 2—Cant. v. 10, Christ, how white and ruddy—His fitness to save, from the grace of union—His fulness to save—His suitableness to endear—These considerations improved.

II. Having manifested that the saints hold peculiar fellowship with the Lord Jesus, it nextly follows that we show wherein it is that they have this peculiar communion with him.

Now, this is in GRACE. This is everywhere ascribed to him by the way of eminency. John i. 14, "He dwelt among us, full of grace and truth;"—grace in the truth and substance of it.[1] All that went before was but typical and in representation; in the truth and substance it comes only by Christ. "Grace and truth came by Jesus Christ," verse 17; "and of his fulness have all we received, and grace for grace," verse 16;—that is, we have communion with him in grace; we receive from him all manner of grace whatever; and therein have we fellowship with him.

So likewise in that *apostolical benediction,* wherein the communication of spiritual blessings from the several persons unto the saints is so exactly distinguished; it is grace that is ascribed to our Lord Jesus Christ, 2 Cor. xiii. 14, "The *grace* of the Lord Jesus Christ, and the love of God, and the communion of the Holy Ghost, be with you all." Yea, Paul is so delighted with this, that he makes it his motto, and the token whereby he would have his epistles known, 2 Thess. iii. 17, 18, "The salutation of Paul with mine own hand, which is the token in every epistle: so I write. The *grace* of our Lord Jesus Christ be with you all." Yea, he makes these two, "*Grace be with you,*" and, "The *Lord Jesus be with you,*" to be equivalent expressions; for whereas he affirmed the one to be the token in all his epistles, yet sometimes he useth the one only, sometimes the other of these, and sometimes puts them both together. This, then, is that which we are peculiarly to eye in the Lord Jesus, to receive it from him, even grace, gospel-grace, revealed in or exhibited by the gospel. He is the head-stone in the building of the temple of God, to whom "*Grace, grace,*" is to be cried, Zech. iv. 7.

Grace is a word of various acceptations. In its most eminent significations it may be referred unto one of these three heads:—

1. Grace of *personal presence* and comeliness. [2]So we say, "A graceful and comely person," either from himself or his ornaments. This in Christ (upon the matter) is the subject of near one-half of the book of Canticles; it is also mentioned, Ps. xlv. 2, "Thou art fairer than the children of men; grace is poured into thy lips." And unto this first head, in respect of Christ, do I refer also that acceptation of grace which, in respect of us, I fix in the third place. Those inconceivable gifts and fruits of the Spirit which were bestowed on him, and brought forth in him, concur to his personal excellency; as will afterward appear.

2. Grace of *free favour and acceptance.* [3]" By this grace we are

[1] Acts xv. 11; Rom. xvi. 24; 1 Cor. xvi. 23; 2 Cor. xiii. 14; Gal. vi. 18; Eph. vi. 24.   [2] Prov. i. 9, iii. 22, 34; Cant. iii. 6-11, v. 9-16, etc.
[3] Ezra ix. 8; Acts iv. 33; Luke ii. 40; Esther ii. 17; Ps. lxxxiv. 11; Eph. ii. 6; Acts xv. 40, xviii. 27; Rom. i. 7, iv. 4, 16, v. 2, 20, xi. 5, 6; 2 Thess. ii. 16; Tit. iii. 7; Rev. i. 4, etc.

saved;" that is, the free favour and gracious acceptation of God in
Christ. In this sense is it used in that frequent expression, "If I
have found grace in thy sight;" that is, if I be freely and favourably
accepted before thee. So he "giveth grace" (that is, favour) "unto
the humble," James iv. 6; Gen. xxxix. 21, xli. 37; Acts vii. 10;
1 Sam. ii. 26; 2 Kings xxv. 27, etc.

3. The *fruits of the Spirit*, sanctifying and renewing our natures,
enabling unto good, and preventing from evil, are so termed. Thus
the Lord tells Paul, "his grace was sufficient for him;" that is, the
assistance against temptation which he afforded him, Col. iii. 16;
2 Cor. viii. 6, 7; Heb. xii. 28.

These two latter, as relating unto Christ in respect of us who receive
them, I call *purchased grace*, being indeed purchased by him for us;
and our communion with him therein is termed a "fellowship in his
sufferings, and the power of his resurrection," Phil. iii. 10.

1. Let us begin with the first, which I call *personal grace;* and
concerning that do these two things:—(1.) Show *what it is*, and
wherein it consisteth; I mean the personal grace of Christ. And,—
(2.) Declare how the saints *hold immediate communion with him
therein.*

(1.) To the handling of the first, I shall only premise this observation:—It is Christ as mediator of whom we speak; and therefore,
by the "grace of his person," I understand not,—

[1.] The *glorious excellencies of his Deity* considered in itself,
abstracting from the office which for us, as God and man, he undertook.

[2.] Nor the outward appearance of his *numan nature*, neither
when he conversed here on earth, bearing our infirmities (whereof, by
reason of the charge that was laid upon him, the prophet gives quite
another character, Isa. lii. 14), concerning which some of the ancients
were very poetical in their expressions; nor yet as now exalted in
glory;—a vain imagination whereof makes many bear a false, a corrupted respect unto Christ, even upon carnal apprehensions of the
mighty exaltation of the human nature; which is but "to know Christ
after the flesh," 2 Cor. v. 16, a mischief much improved by the abomination of foolish imagery. But this is that which I intend,—the graces
of the person of Christ as he is vested with the office of mediation,
—his spiritual eminency, comeliness, and beauty, as appointed and
anointed by the Father unto the great work of bringing home all
his elect unto his bosom.

Now, in this respect the Scripture describes him as exceeding excellent, comely, and desirable,—far above comparison with the *chiefest*,
choicest created good, or any endearment imaginable.

Ps. xlv. 2, "Thou art fairer than the children of men: grace is poured into thy lips." [1]He is, beyond comparison, more beautiful and gracious than any here below,—יְפֵיפִיתָ, *(japhiaphitha);* the word is doubled, to increase its significancy, and to exalt its subject beyond all comparison. שׁוּפְרָךְ מַלְכָּא מְשִׁיחָא עֲדִיף מִבְּנֵי נְשָׁא, says the Chaldee paraphrast: " Thy fairness, O king Messiah, is more excellent than the sons of men." "Pulcher admodum præ filiis hominum;"—exceeding desirable. Inward beauty and glory is here expressed by that of outward shape, form, and appearance;[2] because that was so much esteemed in those who were to rule or govern. Isa. iv. 2, the prophet, terming of him "The branch of the Lord," and "The fruit of the earth," affirms that he shall be "beautiful and glorious, excellent and comely;" "for in him dwelleth all the fulness of the Godhead bodily," Col. ii. 9.

Cant. v. 9, the spouse is inquired of as to this very thing, even concerning the personal excellencies of the Lord Christ, her beloved: " What is thy Beloved" (say the daughters of Jerusalem) " more than another beloved, O thou fairest among women? what is thy Beloved more than another beloved ?" and she returns this answer, verse 10, " My Beloved is white and ruddy, the chiefest among ten thousand;" and so proceedeth to a particular description of him by his excellencies to the end of the chapter, and there concludeth that " he is altogether lovely," verse 16; whereof at large afterward. Particularly, he is here affirmed to be "white and ruddy;" a due mixture of which colours composes the most beautiful complexion.

1st. He is *white* in the glory of his *Deity,* and *ruddy* in the preciousness of his *humanity.* " His teeth are white with milk, and his eyes are red with wine," Gen. xlix. 12. Whiteness (if I may so say) is the complexion of glory. In that appearance of the Most High, the " Ancient of days," Dan. vii. 9, it is said, " His garment was white as snow, and the hair of his head like the pure wool;"—and of Christ in his transfiguration, when he had on him a mighty lustre of the Deity, "His face did shine as the sun, and his raiment was white as the light," Matt. xvii. 2; which, in the phrase of another evangelist, is, "White as snow, so as no fuller on earth can white them," Mark ix. 3. It was a divine, heavenly, surpassing glory that was upon him, Rev. i. 14. Hence the angels and glorified saints, that always behold him, and are fully translated into the image of the same glory, are still said to be in white robes.[3] His whiteness is his Deity, and the glory thereof.

---

[1] Isa. xi. 1; Jer. xxiii. 5, xxxiii. 15; Zech. iii. 8, vi. 12.

[2] 'Ὡς ἡδὺ καλὸς ὅταν ἔχῃ νοῦν σώφρονα, πρῶτον μὲν εἶδος ἄξιον τυραννίδος.—Porphyr. in Isag. Inde Suetonius de Domitiano. "Commendari se verecundiâ oris adeo sentiebat, ut apud senatum sic quondam jactaverit; usque adhuc certe animum meum probastis et vultum."—Sueton. Domit., cap. xviii. "Formæ elegantia in Rege laudatur, non quod per se decor oris magni æstimari debeat, sed quia in ipso vultu sæpe relu- ceat generosa indoles."—Calvin. in loc.

[3] Rev. iii. 4, 5, vi. 11, vii. 9, 13, xix. 14.

And on this account the Chaldee paraphrast ascribes this whole passage unto God. "They say," saith he, "to the house of Israel, 'Who is the God whom thou wilt serve?' etc. Then began the congregation of Israel to declare the praises of the Ruler of the world, and said, 'I will serve that God who is clothed in a garment white as snow, the splendour of the glory of whose countenance is as fire." He is also ruddy in the beauty of his humanity. Man was called Adam, from the red earth whereof he was made. The word here[1] used points him out as the second Adam, partaker of flesh and blood, because the children also partook of the same, Heb. ii. 14. The beauty and comeliness of the Lord Jesus in the union of both these in one person, shall afterward be declared.

2dly. He is white in the beauty of his innocency and holiness, and ruddy in the blood of his oblation. Whiteness is the badge of innocency and holiness. It is said of the Nazarites, for their typical holiness, "They were purer than snow, they were whiter than milk," Lam. iv. 7. And the prophet shows us that scarlet, red, and crimson, are the colours of sin and guilt; whiteness of innocency,[2] Isa. i. 18. Our Beloved was "a Lamb without blemish and without spot," 1 Pet. i. 19. "He did no sin, neither was guile found in his mouth," 1 Pet. ii. 22. He was "holy, harmless, undefiled, separate from sinners," Heb. vii. 26; as afterward will appear. And yet he who was so white in his innocency, was made ruddy in his own blood; and that two ways:—Naturally, in the pouring out of his blood, his precious blood, in that agony of his soul when thick drops of blood trickled to the ground, Luke xxii. 44; as also when the whips and thorns, nails and spears, poured it out abundantly: "There came forth blood and water," John xix. 34. He was ruddy by being drenched all over in his own blood. And morally, by the imputation of sin, whose colour is red and crimson. "God made him to be sin for us, who knew no sin," 2 Cor. v. 21. He who was white, became ruddy for our sakes, pouring out his blood an oblation for sin. This also renders him graceful: by his whiteness he fulfilled the law; by his redness he satisfied justice. "This is our Beloved, O ye daughters of Jerusalem."

3dly. His endearing excellency in the administration of his kingdom is hereby also expressed.[3] He is white in love and mercy unto his own; red with justice and revenge towards his enemies, Isa. lxiii. 3; Rev. xix. 13.

There are three things in general wherein this personal excellency

---

[1] דּוֹדִי צַח וְאָדוֹם   Cant. v. 10.

[2] "Alii candidum exponunt esse puris et probis, rubrum et cruentum reprobis ad eos puniendos ut Isaia, cap. lxiii. dicitur, מַדּוּעַ אָדֹם לִלְבוּשֶׁךָ Cur rubent vestimenta tua? quod nostri minus recte de Christi passione exponunt."—Mercer. in loc.

[3] Rev. vi. 2.

and grace of the Lord Christ doth consist:—(1*st.*) His *fitness* to save,
from the *grace of union,* and the proper necessary effects thereof.
(2*dly.*) His *fulness* to save, from the *grace of communion;* or the free
consequences of the grace of union.   (3*dly.*) His *excellency* to endear,
from his *complete suitableness* to all the wants of the souls of men:—

(1*st.*) His *fitness* to save,—his being ἱκανὸς, a fit Saviour, suited
to the work; and this, I say, is from his *grace of union.* The uniting
of the natures of God and man in one person made him fit to be a
Saviour to the uttermost. He lays his hand upon God, by partaking
of his nature, Zech. xiii. 7; and he lays his hand upon us, by being
partaker of our nature, Heb. ii. 14, 16: and so becomes a days-man,
or umpire between both. By this means he fills up all the distance
that was made by sin between God and us; and we who were far off
are made nigh in him. Upon this account it was that he had room
enough in his breast to receive, and power enough in his spirit to bear,
all the wrath that was prepared for us. Sin was *infinite* only in respect of the *object;* and punishment was *infinite* in respect of the
subject. This ariseth from his union.

Union is the conjunction of the two natures of God and man in
one person, John i. 14; Isa. ix. 6; Rom. i. 3, ix. 5. The necessary
consequences whereof are,—

[1*st.*] The *subsistence* of the human nature in the person of the
Son of God, having no subsistence of its own, Luke i. 35; 1 Tim.
iii. 16.

[2*dly.*] Κοινωνία ἰδιωμάτων,—that *communication* of *attributes* in
the person, whereby the properties of either nature are promiscuously
spoken of the person of Christ, under what name soever, of God or
man, he be spoken of, Acts xx. 28, iii. 21.

[3*dly.*] The *execution* of his office of mediation in his single person,
in respect of both natures: wherein is considerable, ὁ ἐνεργῶν,—the
agent, Christ himself, God and man. He is the *principium quo,*
ἐνεργητικὸν,—the principle that gives life and efficacy to the whole
work; and then, 2*dly,* The *principium quod,*—that which operates,
which is both natures distinctly considered. 3*dly.* The ἐνέργεια, or
δραστικὴ τῆς φύσεως κίνησις,—the effectual working itself of each nature.
And, *lastly,* the ἐνέργημα, or ἀποτέλεσμα,—the effect produced, which
ariseth from all, and relates to them all: so resolving the excellency
I speak of into his personal union.

(2*dly.*) His *fulness* to save, from the grace of communion or the
effects of his union, which are free; and consequences of it, which is
all the furniture that he received from the Father by the unction of
the Spirit, for the work of our salvation: " He is able also to save
them to the uttermost that come unto God by him," Heb. vii. 25;
having all fulness unto this end communicated unto him: " for it

pleased the Father that in him should all fulness dwell," Col. i. 19; and he received not " the Spirit by measure," John iii. 34. And from this fulness he makes out a suitable supply unto all that are his; " grace for grace," John i. 16. Had it been given to him by measure, we had exhausted it.

(3*dly*.) His *excellency* to endear, from his *complete suitableness* to all the wants of the souls of men. There is no man whatever, that hath any want in reference unto the things of God, but Christ will be unto him that which he wants: I speak of those who are given him of his Father. Is he *dead?* [1]Christ is *life*. Is he *weak?* Christ is the *power* of God, and the *wisdom* of God. Hath he the *sense of guilt* upon him? Christ is complete *righteousness*,—" The LORD our Righteousness." Many poor creatures are sensible of their wants, but know not where their remedy lies. Indeed, whether it be life or light, power or joy, all is wrapped up in him.

This, then, for the present, may suffice in general to be spoken of the personal grace of the Lord Christ:—He hath a fitness to save, having pity and ability, tenderness and power, to carry on that work to the uttermost; and a fulness to save, of redemption and sanctification, of righteousness and the Spirit; and a suitableness to the wants of all our souls: whereby he becomes exceedingly desirable, yea, altogether lovely; as afterward will appear in particular. And as to this, in the first place, the saints have distinct fellowship with the Lord Christ; the manner whereof shall be declared in the ensuing chapter.

Only, from this entrance that hath been made into the description of him with whom the saints have communion, some motives might be taken to stir us up thereunto; as also considerations to lay open the nakedness and insufficiency of all other ways and things unto which men engage their thoughts and desires, something may be now proposed. The daughters of Jerusalem, ordinary, common professors, having heard the spouse describing her Beloved, Cant. v. 10–16, etc., instantly are stirred up to seek him together with her; chap. vi. 1, " Whither is thy Beloved turned aside? that we may seek him with thee." What Paul says of them that crucified him, may be spoken of all that reject him, or refuse communion with him: " Had they known him, they would not have crucified the Lord of glory;"— Did men know him, were they acquainted in any measure with him, they would not so reject the Lord of glory. Himself calls them "simple ones," "fools," and "scorners," that despise his gracious invitation, Prov. i. 22. There are none who despise Christ, but only they that know him not; whose eyes the god of this world hath blinded, that they should not behold his glory. The souls of men do naturally seek something to rest and repose themselves upon,—something to satiate

---

[1] Col. iii. 4; 1 Cor. i. 24, 30; Jer. xxiii. 6.

and delight themselves withal, with which they [may] hold communion; and there are two ways whereby men proceed in the pursuit of what they so aim at. Some set before them some certain end,—perhaps pleasure, profit, or, in religion itself, acceptance with God; others seek after some end, but without any certainty, pleasing themselves now with one path, now with another, with various thoughts and ways, like them, Isa. lvii. 10,—because something comes in by the life of the hand, they give not over though weary. In what condition soever you may be (either in greediness pursuing some certain end, be it secular or religious; or wandering away in your own imaginations, wearying yourselves in the largeness of your ways), compare a little what you aim at, or what you do, with what you have already heard of Jesus Christ: if any thing you design be like to him, if any thing you desire be equal to him, let him be rejected as one that hath neither form nor comeliness in him; but if, indeed, all your ways be but vanity and vexation of spirit, in comparison of him, why do you spend your "money for that which is not bread, and your labour for that which satisfieth not?"

Use. 1. You that are yet in the *flower of your days*, full of health and strength, and, with all the vigour of your spirits, do pursue some one thing, some another, consider, I pray, what are all your beloveds to this Beloved? What have you gotten by them? Let us see the peace, quietness, assurance of everlasting blessedness that they have given you? Their paths are crooked paths, whoe'er goes in them shall not know peace. Behold here a fit object for your choicest affections,—one in whom you may find rest to your souls,—one in whom there is nothing will grieve and trouble you to eternity. Behold, he stands at the door of your souls, and knocks: O reject him not, lest you seek him and find him not! Pray study him a little; you love him not, because you know him not. Why doth one of you spend his time in idleness and folly, and wasting of precious time, —perhaps debauchedly? Why doth another associate and assemble himself with them that scoff at religion and the things of God? Merely because you know not our dear Lord Jesus. Oh, when he shall reveal himself to you, and tell you he is Jesus whom you have slighted and refused, how will it break your hearts, and make you mourn like a dove, that you have neglected him! and if you never come to know him, it had been better you had never been. Whilst it is called To-day, then, harden not your hearts.

Use 2. You that are, perhaps, seeking earnestly after a *righteousness, and are religious persons*, consider a little with yourselves,— hath Christ his due place in your hearts? is he your all? does he dwell in your thoughts? do you know him in his excellency and desirableness? do you indeed account all things "loss and dung" for his exceeding excellency? or rather, do you prefer almost any thing in the world before it? But more of these things afterward.

CHAPTER III.

Of the way and manner whereby the saints hold communion with the Lord Christ as to personal grace—The conjugal relation between Christ and the saints, Cant. ii. 16; Isa. liv. 5, etc.; Cant. iii. 11, opened—The way of communion in conjugal relation, Hos. iii. 3; Cant. i. 15—On the part of Christ—On the part of the saints.

(2.) THE next thing that comes under consideration is, the *way* whereby we hold communion with the Lord Christ, in respect of that personal grace whereof we have spoken. Now, this the Scripture manifests to be by the way of a *conjugal relation.* He is married unto us, and we unto him; which spiritual relation is attended with suitable conjugal affections. And this gives us fellowship with him as to his personal excellencies.

This the spouse expresseth, Cant. ii. 16, " My Beloved is mine, and I am his;"—" He is mine, I possess him, I have interest in him, as my head and my husband; and I am his, possessed of him, owned by him, given up unto him: and that as to my Beloved in a conjugal relation."

So Isa. liv. 5, " Thy Maker is thine husband; the LORD of hosts is his name; and thy Redeemer the Holy One of Israel; The God of the whole earth shall he be called." This is yielded as the reason why the church shall not be ashamed nor confounded, in the midst of her troubles and trials,—she is married unto her Maker, and her Redeemer is her husband. And Isaiah, chap. lxi. 10, setting out the mutual glory of Christ and his church in their walking together, he saith it is "as a bridegroom decketh himself with ornaments, and as a bride adorneth herself with jewels." Such is their condition, because such is their relation; which he also farther expresseth, chap. lxii. 5, " As the bridegroom rejoiceth over the bride, so shall thy God rejoice over thee." As it is with such persons in the day of their espousals, in the day of the gladness of their hearts, so is it with Christ and his saints in this relation. He is a husband to them, providing that it may be with them according to the state and condition whereinto he hath taken them.

To this purpose we have his faithful engagement, Hos. ii. 19, 20, " I will," saith he, "betroth thee unto me for ever; yea, I will betroth thee unto me in righteousness, and in judgment, and in loving-kindness, and in mercies. I will even betroth thee unto me in faithfulness." And it is the main design of the ministry of the gospel, to prevail with men to give up themselves unto the Lord Christ, as he reveals his kindness in this engagement. Hence Paul tells the Corinthians, 2 Cor. xi. 2, that he had "espoused them unto one husband, that he might present them as a chaste virgin unto Christ." This he had prevailed upon them for, by the preaching of the gospel, that they should give up themselves as a virgin, unto him who had betrothed them to himself as a husband.

And this is a *relation* wherein the Lord Jesus is exceedingly delighted, and inviteth others to behold him in this his glory, Cant. iii. 11, " Go forth," saith he, " O ye daughters of Jerusalem, and behold king Solomon with the crown wherewith his mother crowned him in the day of his espousals, and in the day of the gladness of his heart." He calls forth the daughters of Jerusalem (all sorts of professors) to consider him in the condition of betrothing and espousing his church unto himself. Moreover, he tells them that they shall find on him two things eminently upon this account:—1. *Honour.* It is the day of his coronation, and his spouse is the crown wherewith he is crowned. For as Christ is a diadem of beauty and a crown of glory unto Zion, Isa. xxviii. 5; so Zion also is a diadem and a crown unto him, Isa. lxii. 3. Christ makes this relation with his saints to be his glory and his honour. 2. *Delight.* The day of his espousals, of taking poor sinful souls into his bosom, is the day of the gladness of his heart. John was but the friend of the Bridegroom, that stood and heard his voice, when he was taking his bride unto himself; and he rejoiced greatly, John iii. 29: how much more, then, must be the joy and gladness of the Bridegroom himself! even that which is expressed, Zeph. iii. 17, " he rejoiceth with joy, he joys with singing."

It is the gladness of the heart of Christ, the joy of his soul, to take poor sinners into this relation with himself. He rejoiced in the thoughts of it from eternity, Prov. viii. 31; and always expresseth the greatest willingness to undergo the hard task required thereunto, Ps. xl. 7, 8; Heb. x. 7; yea, he was pained as a woman in travail, until he had accomplished it, Luke xii. 50. Because he loved his church, he gave himself for it, Eph. v. 25, despising the shame, and enduring the cross, Heb. xii. 2, that he might enjoy his bride,—that he might be for her, and she for him, and not for another, Hos. iii. 3. This is joy, when he is thus crowned by his mother. It is believers that are mother and brother of this Solomon, Matt. xii. 49, 50. They crown him in the day of his espousals, giving themselves to him, and becoming his glory, 2 Cor. viii. 23.

Thus he sets out his whole communion with his church under this

allusion, and that most frequently. The time of his taking the church
unto himself is the day of his marriage; and the church is his bride,
his wife, Rev. xix. 7, 8. The entertainment he makes for his saints
is a wedding supper, Matt. xxii. 3. The graces of his church are the
ornaments of his queen, Ps. xlv. 9–14; and the fellowship he hath
with his saints is as that which those who are mutually beloved in a
conjugal relation do hold, Cant. i. Hence Paul, in describing these
two, makes sudden and insensible transitions from one to the other,—
Eph. v., from verse 22 unto verse 32; concluding the whole with an
application unto Christ and the church.

It is now to be inquired, in the next place, how it is that we hold
communion with the person of Christ in respect of conjugal relations
and affections, and wherein this doth consist. Now, herein there are
some things that are common unto Christ and the saints, and some
things that are peculiar to each of them, as the nature of this relation
doth require. The whole may be reduced unto these two heads:—
[1.] *A mutual resignation of themselves one to the other;* [2.] *Mutual, consequential, conjugal affections.*

[1.] There is a *mutual resignation,* or making over of their persons
one to another. This is the first act of communion, as to the personal
grace of Christ. Christ makes himself over to the soul, to be his, as
to all the love, care, and tenderness of a husband; and the soul gives
up itself wholly unto the Lord Christ, to be his, as to all loving, tender obedience. And herein is the main of Christ's and the saints'
espousals. This, in the prophet, is set out under a parable of himself
and a harlot, Hos. iii. 3, "Thou shalt abide for me," saith he unto her,
"thou shalt not be for another, and I will be for thee."—"Poor harlot,"
saith the Lord Christ, "I have bought thee unto myself with the
price of mine own blood; and now, this is that which we will consent
unto,—I WILL BE FOR THEE, AND THOU SHALT BE FOR ME, and not
for another.

1st. Christ gives himself to the *soul,* with all his *excellencies,* righteousness, preciousness, graces, and eminencies, to be its Saviour,
head, and husband, for ever to dwell with it in this holy relation.
He looks upon the souls of his saints, likes them well, counts them
fair and beautiful, because he hath made them so. Cant. i. 15, "Behold, thou art fair, my companion; behold, thou art fair; thou hast
doves' eyes." Let others think what they please, Christ redoubles it,
that the souls of his saints are very beautiful, even perfect, through
his comeliness, which he puts upon them, Ezek. xvi. 14,—" Behold,
thou art fair, thou art fair:"[1] particularly, that their spiritual light is
very excellent and glorious; like the eyes of a dove, tender, discerning,
clear, and shining. Therefore he adds that pathetical wish of the

---

[1] " Repetit non citra πάθος, en tu pulchra es."—Mercer.

enjoyment of this his spouse, Cant. ii. 14, "O my dove," saith he, "that art in the clefts of the rock, in the secret places of the stairs, let me see thy countenance, let me hear thy voice; for sweet is thy voice, and thy countenance is comely;"—" Do not hide thyself, as one that flies to the clefts of the rocks; be not dejected, as one that hides herself behind the stairs, and is afraid to come forth to the company that inquires for her. Let not thy spirit be cast down at the weakness of thy supplications, let me yet hear thy sighs and groans, thy breathings and pantings to me; they are very sweet, very delightful: and thy spiritual countenance, thy appearance in heavenly things, is comely and delightful unto me." Neither doth he leave her thus, but, chap. iv. 8, presseth her hard to a closer [union] with him in this conjugal bond : " Come with me from Lebanon, my spouse, with me from Lebanon: look from the top of Amana, from the top of Shenir and Hermon, from the lions' dens, from the mountains of the leopards;"—" Thou art in a wandering condition (as the Israelites of old), among lions and leopards, sins and troubles; come from thence unto me, and I will give thee refreshment," Matt. xi. 28. Upon this invitation, the spouse boldly concludes, Cant. vii. 10, that the desire of Christ is towards her; that he doth indeed love her, and aim at taking her into this fellowship with himself. So, in carrying on this union, Christ freely bestoweth himself upon the soul. Precious and excellent as he is, he becometh ours. He makes himself to be so; and with him, all his graces. Hence saith the spouse, " 'My Beloved is mine;' in all that he is, he is mine." Because he is righteousness,[1] he is " The LORD our Righteousness," Jer. xxiii. 6. Because he is the wisdom of God, and the power of God, he is "made unto us wisdom," etc., 1 Cor. i. 30. Thus, " the branch of the LORD is beautiful and glorious, and the fruit of the earth is excellent and comely for them that are escaped of Israel," Isa. iv. 2. This is the first thing on the part of Christ,—*the free donation* and bestowing of himself upon us to be our Christ, our Beloved, as to all the ends and purposes of love, mercy, grace, and glory; whereunto in his mediation he is designed, in a marriage covenant never to be broken. This is the sum of what is intended:—The Lord Jesus Christ, fitted and prepared, by the accomplishment and furniture of his person as mediator, and the large purchase of grace and glory which he hath made, to be a husband to his saints, his church, tenders himself in the promises of the gospel to them in all his desirableness; convinces them of his good-will towards them, and his all-sufficiency for a supply of their wants; and upon their consent to accept of him,—which is all he requires or expects at their hands,—he engageth himself in a marriage covenant to be theirs for ever.

[1] Isa. xlv. 24, 25.

2dly. On the part of the *saints*, it is their *free, willing consent* to receive, embrace, and submit unto the Lord Jesus, as their husband, Lord, and Saviour,—to abide with him, subject their souls unto him, and to be ruled by him for ever.

Now, this in the soul is either initial, or the solemn consent at the first entrance of union; or consequential, in renewed acts of consent all our days. I speak of it especially in this latter sense, wherein it is proper unto communion; not in the former, wherein it primarily intendeth union.

There are two things that complete this *self-resignation* of the soul:—

(1*st.*) The *liking* of Christ, for his *excellency*, grace, and suitableness, far above all other beloveds whatever, preferring him in the judgment and mind above them all. In the place above mentioned, Cant. v. 9, the spouse being earnestly pressed, by professors at large, to give in her thoughts concerning the excellency of her Beloved in comparison of other endearments, answereth expressly, that he is "the chiefest of ten thousand, yea," verse 16, "altogether lovely,"—infinitely beyond comparison with the choicest created good or endearment imaginable. The soul takes a view of all that is in this world, "the lust of the flesh, the lust of the eyes, and the pride of life," and sees it all to be vanity,—that "the world passeth away, and the lust thereof," 1 John ii. 16, 17. These beloveds are no way to be compared unto him. It views also legal righteousness, blamelessness before men, uprightness of conversation, duties upon conviction, and concludes of all as Paul doth, Phil. iii. 8, "Doubtless, I count all these things loss for the excellency of the knowledge of Christ Jesus my Lord." So, also, doth the church, Hos. xiv. 3, reject all appearing assistances whatever,—as goodly as Asshur, as promising as idols,—that God alone may be preferred. And this is the soul's entrance into conjugal communion with Jesus Christ as to personal grace,—the constant preferring him above all pretenders to its affections, counting all loss and dung in comparison of him. Beloved peace, beloved natural relations, beloved wisdom and learning, beloved righteousness, beloved duties, [are] all loss, compared with Christ.

(2*dly.*) The *accepting* of Christ by the *will*, as its only husband, Lord, and Saviour. This is called "receiving" of Christ, John i. 12; and is not intended only for that solemn act whereby at first entrance we close with him, but also for the constant frame of the soul in abiding with him and owning of him as such. When the soul consents to take Christ on his own terms, to save him in his own way,[1] and says, "Lord, I would have had thee and salvation in my way, that it might

---

[1] Rom. ix. 31, 32, x. 3, 4.

have been partly of mine endeavours, and as it were by the works of
the law; I am now willing to receive thee and to be saved in thy way,
—merely by grace: and though I would have walked according to my
own mind, yet now I wholly give up myself to be ruled by thy Spirit;
for in thee have I righteousness and strength,[1] in thee am I justified
and do glory;"—then doth it carry on communion with Christ as to
the grace of his person. This it is to receive the Lord Jesus in his
comeliness and eminency. Let believers exercise their hearts abundantly unto this thing. This is choice communion with the Son Jesus
Christ. Let us receive him in all his excellencies, as he bestows himself upon us;—be frequent in thoughts of faith, comparing him with
other beloveds, sin, world, legal righteousness; and preferring him
before them, counting them all loss and dung in comparison of him.
And let our souls be persuaded of his sincerity and willingness in
giving himself, in all that he is, as mediator unto us, to be ours; and
let our hearts give up themselves unto him. Let us tell him that we
will be for him, and not for another: let him know it from us; he
delights to hear it, yea, he says, " Sweet is our voice, and our countenance is comely;"—and we shall not fail in the issue of sweet refreshment with him.

DIGRESSION I.

Some excellencies of Christ proposed to consideration, to endear our hearts unto
him—His description, Cant. v., opened.

To strengthen our hearts in the resignation mentioned of ourselves
unto the Lord Christ as our husband, as also to make way for the
stirring of us up to those consequential conjugal affections of which
mention shall afterward be made, I shall turn aside to a more full
description of some of the personal excellencies of the Lord Christ,
whereby the hearts of his saints are indeed endeared unto him.

In " The LORD our Righteousness," then, may these ensuing things
be considered; which are exceeding suitable to prevail upon our hearts
to give up themselves to be wholly his:—

1. He is exceeding excellent and desirable in his[2] *Deity*, and the
glory thereof. He is " *Jehovah our Righteousness*," Jer. xxiii. 6. In
the rejoicing of Zion at his coming to her, this is the bottom, " Be-

---

[1] Isa. xlv. 24.
[2] Numb. xxi. 5; 1 Cor. x. 9; Ps. lxviii. 18; Eph. iv. 8, 10; Ps. xcvii. 7; Heb.
i. 6; Ps. cii. 25; Isa. vii. 14; Luke ii. 34; Rom. ix. 5; 1 Pet. ii. 6; Isa. xl. 3,
xliv. 6, xlv. 22, xlviii. 12; Rom. xiv. 10; Rev. i. 11; Mal. iii. 1; Ps. ii. 12; Isa.
xxxv. 4, lii. 5, 6, xlv. 14, 15; Zech. ii. 8, 12, iii. 1, xii. 10; Matt. xvi. 16; Luke
i. 16, 17; John v. 18, 19, x. 30, i. 1, 3, 10, 14, vi. 62, viii. 23, 58; Col. i. 16; Heb.
i. 2, 10–12; John iii. 13, 31, xvi. 28; Mic. v. 2; Prov. viii. 23; John xvii. 5; Jer.

hold thy God!" Isa. xl. 9. "We have seen his glory," saith the apostle.
What glory is that? "The glory of the only-begotten Son of God,"
John i. 14. The choicest saints have been afraid and amazed at the
beauty of an angel; and the stoutest sinners have trembled at the
glory of one of those creatures in a low appearance, representing but
the back parts of their glory, who yet themselves, in their highest
advancement, do cover their faces at the presence of our Beloved, as
conscious to themselves of their utter disability to bear the rays of
his glory, Isa. vi. 2; John xii. 39–41. He is "*the fellow of the Lord
of hosts,*" Zech. xiii. 7. And though he once appeared in the form
of a servant, yet then "he thought it not robbery to be equal with
God," Phil. ii. 6. In the glory of this majesty he dwells in light
inaccessible. We "cannot by searching find out the Almighty unto
perfection: it is as high as heaven; what can we do? deeper than
hell; what can we know? the measure thereof is longer than the
earth, and broader than the sea," Job xi. 7–9. We may all say one
to another of this, "Surely we are more brutish than any man,
and have not the understanding of a man. We neither learned wisdom, nor have the knowledge of the holy. Who hath ascended up
into heaven, or descended? who hath gathered the wind in his fists?
who hath bound the waters in a garment? who hath established all
the ends of the earth? what is his name, and what is his Son's name,
if ye can tell," Prov. xxx. 2–4.

If any one should ask, now, with them in the Canticles, what is in
the Lord Jesus, our beloved, more than in other beloveds, that should
make him so desirable, and amiable, and worthy of acceptation?
what is he more than others? I ask, What is a *king* more than a
beggar? Much every way. Alas! this is nothing; they were born
alike, must die alike, and after that is the judgment. What is an
angel more than a *worm?* A worm is a creature, and an angel is
no more; he hath made the one to creep in the earth,—made also the
other to dwell in heaven. There is still a proportion between these,
they agree in something; but what are all the nothings of the world
to the God infinitely blessed for evermore? Shall the dust of the
balance, or the drop of the bucket be laid in the scale against him?
This is he of whom the sinners in Zion are afraid, and cry, "Who
amongst us shall dwell with the devouring fire, who amongst us
shall dwell with everlasting burnings?" I might now give you a
glimpse of his excellency in many of those properties and attributes
by which he discovers himself to the faith of poor sinners; but as

xxiii. 6; 1 John v. 20; Rev. i. 18, iv. 8; Acts xx. 28; 1 John iii. 16; Phil. ii. 6–8;
1 Tim. iii. 16; Heb. ii. 16; 1 John iv. 3; Heb. x. 5; John xx. 28; John x. 29–31;
Matt. xvi. 16; Rom. viii. 32; John iii. 16, 18; Col. i. 15; John xvii. 10; Isa. ix. 6;
Col. ii. 9; 1 Cor. viii. 6, ii. 8; Ps. lxviii. 17.

he that goes into a garden where there are innumerable flowers in great variety, gathers not all he sees, but crops here and there one, and another, I shall endeavour to open a door, and give an inlet into the infinite excellency of the graces of the Lord Jesus, as he is " God blessed for evermore,"—presenting the reader with one or two instances, leaving him to gather for his own use what farther he pleaseth.   Hence, then, observe,—

The *endless, bottomless, boundless grace* and compassion that is in him who is thus our husband, as he is the God of Zion. It is not the grace of a *creature*, nor all the grace that can possibly at once dwell in a created nature, that will serve our turn.   We are too indigent to be suited with such a supply.   There was a fulness of grace in the human nature of Christ,—he received not " the Spirit by measure," John iii. 34; a fulness like that of light in the sun, or of water in the sea (I speak not in respect of communication, but sufficiency); a fulness incomparably *above the measure of angels:* yet it was not properly an infinite fulness,—it was a created, and therefore a limited fulness.   If it could be conceived as separated from the Deity, surely so many thirsty, guilty souls, as every day drink deep and large draughts of grace and mercy from him, would (if I may so speak) sink him to the very bottom; nay, it could afford no supply at all, but only in a moral way.   But when the conduit of his humanity is inseparably united to the infinite, inexhaustible fountain of the Deity, who can look into the depths thereof? If, now, there be grace enough for sinners in an all-sufficient God, it is in Christ; and, indeed, in any other there cannot be enough.   The Lord gives this reason for the peace and confidence of sinners, Isa. liv. 4, 5, " Thou shalt not be ashamed, neither be thou confounded; for thou shalt not be put to shame."   But how shall this be? So much sin, and not ashamed! so much guilt, and not confounded! " Thy Maker," saith he, " is thine husband; the LORD of hosts is his name; and thy Redeemer the Holy One of Israel; The God of the whole earth shall he be called."   This is the bottom of all peace, confidence, and consolation,—the grace and mercy of our Maker, of the God of the whole earth. So are kindness and power tempered in him; he makes us, and mars us,—he is our God and our Göel, our Redeemer.   " Look unto me," saith he, " and be ye saved; for I am God, and none else," Isa. xlv. 22, " Surely, shall one say, In the LORD have I righteousness," verse 24.

And on this ground it is that if all the world should (if I may so say) set themselves to drink free grace, mercy, and pardon, drawing [1] water continually from the wells of salvation; if they should set themselves to draw from one single promise, an angel standing by and crying, " Drink, O my friends, yea, drink abundantly, take so

[1] Cant. v. 1; Isa. lv. 1; Rev. xxii. 17; John vii. 37, 38.

much grace and pardon as shall be abundantly sufficient for the world
of sin which is in every one of you;"—they would not be able to sink
the grace of the promise one hair's breadth. There is enough for
millions of worlds, if they were; because it flows into it from an infinite, bottomless fountain. "Fear not, O worm Jacob, I am God,
and not man," is the bottom of sinners' consolation. This is that
"head of gold" mentioned, Cant. v. 11, that most precious fountain of
grace and mercy. This infiniteness of grace, in respect of its spring
and fountain, will answer all objections that might hinder our souls
from drawing nigh to communion with him, and from a free embracing of him. Will not this suit us in all our distresses? What is
our finite guilt before it? Show me the sinner that can spread his
iniquities to the dimensions (if I may so say) of this grace. Here is
mercy enough for the greatest, the oldest, the stubbornest transgressor,—"Why will ye die, O house of Israel?" Take heed of them
who would rob you of the Deity of Christ. If there were no more
grace for me than what can be treasured up in a mere man, I should
rejoice [if] my portion might be under rocks and mountains.

Consider, hence, his *eternal, free, unchangeable love.* Were the
love of Christ unto us but the love of a mere man, though never so
excellent, innocent, and glorious, it must have a *beginning,* it must
have an *ending,* and perhaps be *fruitless.* The love of Christ in his
human nature towards his is exceeding, intense, tender, precious,
compassionate, abundantly heightened by a sense of our miseries, feeling of our wants, experience of our temptations; all flowing from that
rich stock of grace, pity, and compassion, which, on purpose for our
good and supply, was bestowed on him: but yet this love, as such,
cannot be infinite nor eternal, nor from itself absolutely unchangeable. Were it no more, though not to be paralleled nor fathomed,
yet our Saviour could not say of it, as he doth, "As the Father hath
loved me, so have I loved you," John xv. 9. His love could not be
compared with and equalled unto the divine love of the Father, in
those properties of eternity, fruitfulness, and unchangeableness, which
are the chief anchors of the soul, rolling itself on the bosom of Christ.
But now,—

(1.) It is *eternal:* "Come ye near unto me, hear ye this; I have
not," saith he, "spoken in secret from the beginning; from the time
that it was, there am I: and now the Lord GOD, and his Spirit, hath
sent me," Isa. xlviii. 16. He himself is "yesterday, to-day, and for
ever," Heb. xiii. 8; and so is his love, being his who is "Alpha and
Omega, the first and the last, the beginning and the ending, which
is, which was, and which is to come," Rev. i. 11.

(2.) *Unchangeable.* Our love is *like ourselves;* as we are, so are
all our affections: so is the love of Christ *like himself.* We love one,

one day, and hate him the next.   He changeth, and we change also: this day he is our right hand, our right eye; the next day, " Cut him off, pluck him out." [1]Jesus Christ is still the same; and so is his love. " In the beginning he laid the foundation of the earth; and the heavens are the works of his hands; they shall perish, but he remaineth: they all shall wax old as doth a garment; and as a vesture shall he fold them up, and they shall be changed: but he is the same, and his years fail not," Heb. i. 10–12.   He is the LORD, and he changeth not; and therefore we are not consumed.   Whom he loves, he loves unto the end.[2]   His love is such as never had beginning, and never shall have ending.

(3.) It is also *fruitful*,—fruitful in all gracious issues and effects. A man may love another as his own soul, yet perhaps that love of his cannot help him.   He may thereby pity him in prison, but not relieve him; bemoan him in misery, but not help him; suffer with him in trouble, but not ease him.   We cannot love grace into a child, nor mercy into a friend; we cannot love them into heaven, though it may be the great desire of our soul.   It was love that made Abraham cry, " O that Ishmael might live before thee!" but it might not be. But now the love of Christ, being the love of God, is *effectual and fruitful* in producing all the good things which he willeth unto his beloved.   He loves life, grace, and holiness into us; he loves us also into covenant, loves us into heaven.   Love in him is properly to will good to any one: whatever good Christ by his love wills to any, that willing is *operative* of that good.

These three qualifications of the love of Christ make it exceedingly eminent, and him exceeding desirable.   How many millions of sins, in every one of the elect, every one whereof were enough to condemn them all, hath this love overcome!   what mountains of unbelief doth it remove!   Look upon the conversation of any one saint, consider the frame of his heart, see the many stains and spots, the defilements and infirmities, wherewith his life is contaminated, and tell me whether the love that bears with all this be not to be admired.   And is it not the same towards thousands every day?   What streams of grace, purging, pardoning, quickening, assisting, do flow from it every day!   This is our Beloved, O ye daughters of Jerusalem.

2. He is desirable and worthy our acceptation, as considered in his *humanity;* even therein also, in reference to us, he is exceedingly desirable.   I shall only, in this, note unto you two things:—(1.) Its *freedom from sin;* (2.) It *fulness of grace;*—in both which regards the Scripture sets him out as exceedingly lovely and amiable.

(1.) He was *free from sin;*—the[3] Lamb of God, without spot, and without blemish; the male of the flock, to be offered unto God, the

---

[1] Gal. iv. 14, 15.   [2] Mal. iii. 6; John xiii. 1.   [3] 1 Pet. i. 19.

curse falling on all other oblations, and them that offer them, Mal.
i. 14. The purity of the snow is not to be compared with the whiteness of this lily, of this [1]rose of Sharon, even from the womb: "For
such an high priest became us, who is holy, harmless, undefiled, separate from sinners," Heb. vii. 26. Sanctified persons, whose stains are
in any measure washed away, are exceeding fair in the eye of Christ
himself. "Thou[2] art all fair," saith he, "my love, thou hast no spot
in thee." How fair, then, is he who never had the least spot or stain!

It is true, Adam at his creation had this spotless purity; so had
the angels: but they came immediately from the [3]hand of God,
without concurrence of any *secondary* cause. Jesus Christ[4] is a plant
and root out of a dry ground, a blossom from the stem of Jesse, a bud
from the loins of sinful man,—born of a sinner, after there had been
no innocent flesh in the world for four thousand years, every one upon
the roll of his genealogy being infected therewithal. To have a
flower of wonderful rarity to grow in *paradise,* a garden of God's own
planting, not sullied in the least, is not so strange; but, as the psalmist speaks (in another kind), to hear of it in a *wood,* to find it in a
forest, to have a spotless bud brought forth in the *wilderness* of corrupted nature, is a thing which angels may desire to look into. Nay,
more, this whole nature was not only defiled, but also accursed; not
only unclean, but also guilty,—guilty of Adam's transgression, in
whom we have all sinned. That the human nature of Christ should
be derived from hence free from guilt, free from pollution, this is to
be adored.

Objection. But you will say, " How can this be? who can bring a
clean thing from an unclean? How could Christ take our nature, and
not the defilements of it, and the guilt of it? If [5]Levi paid tithes in
the loins of Abraham, how is it that Christ did not sin in the loins
of Adam?"

Answer. There are two things in *original sin:*—

[1.] *Guilt of the first sin,* which is imputed to us. We all sinned in
him. Ἐφ᾽ ᾧ πάντες ἥμαρτον, Rom. v. 12, whether we render it relatively
"in whom," or illatively, "being all have sinned," all is one: that one
sin is the sin of us all,—" omnes eramus unus ille homo." We were
all in covenant with him; he was not only a natural head, but also a
federal head unto us. As Christ is to believers, Rom. v. 17; 1 Cor.
xv. 22, so was he to us all; and his transgression of that covenant is
reckoned to us.

[2.] There is the *derivation* of a polluted, corrupted nature from
him: [6]" Who can bring a clean thing out of an unclean?" " That

---

[1] Cant. ii. 1.   [2] Cant. i. 15, 16, iv. 1, 7, 10.   [3] Eccles. vii. 29.
[4] Isa. liii. 2.   [5] Heb. vii. 9, 10.
[6] Job xiv. 4; Φρόνημα τῆς σαρκός, Rom. viii. 7; John iii. 6. Νοὸς τῆς σαρκός, Col. ii. 18.

which is born of the flesh is flesh," and nothing else; whose wisdom and mind is corrupted also: a polluted fountain will have polluted streams. The *first person* corrupted *nature,* and that *nature* corrupts *all persons* following. Now, from both these was Christ most free:—

1st. He was *never federally in Adam,* and so not liable to the imputation of his sin on that account. It is true that sin was imputed to him when he was made sin;[1] thereby he took away the sin of the world, John i. 29: but it was imputed to him in the covenant of the Mediator, through his voluntary susception, and not in the covenant of Adam, by a legal imputation. Had it been reckoned to him as a descendant from Adam, he had not been a fit high priest to have offered sacrifices for us, as not being " separate from sinners," Heb. vii. 26. Had Adam stood in his innocency, Christ had not been incarnate, to have been a mediator for sinners; and therefore the counsel of his incarnation, morally, took not place[2] until after the fall. Though he was in Adam in a natural sense from his first creation, in respect of the purpose of God, Luke iii. 23, 38, yet he was not in him in a law sense until after the fall: so that, as to his own person, he had no more to do with the first sin of Adam, than with any personal sin of [any] one whose punishment he voluntarily took upon him; as we are not liable to the guilt of those progenitors who followed Adam, though naturally we were no less in them than in him. Therefore did he, all the days of his flesh, serve God in a covenant of works; and was therein accepted with him, having done nothing that should disannul the virtue of that covenant as to him. This doth not, then, in the least take off from his perfection.

2dly. For the *pollution of our nature,* it was prevented in him from the instant of conception, Luke i. 35, " The Holy Ghost shall come upon thee, and the power of the Highest shall overshadow thee: therefore also that holy thing that shall be born of thee shall be called the Son of God." He was " made of a woman," Gal. iv. 4; but that portion whereof he was made was sanctified by the Holy Ghost, that what was born thereof should be a holy thing. Not only the conjunction and union of soul and body, whereby a man becomes partaker of his whole nature, and therein of the pollution of sin, being a son of Adam, was prevented by the sanctification of the Holy Ghost, but it also accompanied the *very separation of his bodily substance* in the womb unto that sacred purpose whereunto it was set apart: so that upon all accounts he is " holy, harmless, undefiled." Add now hereunto, that he " did no sin, neither was guile found in his mouth," 1 Pet. ii. 22; that he "fulfilled all righteousness," Matt. iii. 15; his Father being always " well pleased " with him, verse 17, on the

---

[1] 2 Cor. v. 21.   [2] Gen. iii. 15.

account of his perfect obedience; yea, even in that sense wherein he chargeth his angels with folly, and those inhabitants of heaven are not clean in his sight; and his excellency and desirableness in this regard will lie before us. Such was he, such is he; and yet for our sakes was he contented not only to be esteemed by the vilest of men to be a transgressor, but to undergo from God the punishment due to the vilest sinners. Of which afterward.

(2.) The *fulness of grace* in Christ's *human nature* sets forth the *amiableness* and desirableness thereof. Should I make it my business to consider his perfections, as to this part of his excellency,—what he had from the womb, Luke i. 35, what received growth and improvement as to exercise in the days of his flesh, Luke ii. 52, with the complement of them all in glory,—the whole would tend to the purpose in hand. I am but taking a view of these things *in transitu.* These two things lie in open sight to all at the first consideration:—all grace was in him, for the *kinds* thereof; and all *degrees* of grace, for its perfections; and both of them make up that fulness that was in him. It is created grace that I intend; and therefore I speak of the kinds of it: it is grace inherent in a created nature, not infinite; and therefore I speak of the degrees of. it.

For the *fountain* of grace, the Holy Ghost, he received not him "by measure," John iii. 34; and for the communications of the Spirit, "it pleased the Father that in him should all fulness dwell," Col. i. 19,—"that in all things he might have the pre-eminence." But these things are commonly spoken unto.

This is the *Beloved* of our souls, "holy, harmless, undefiled;" "full of grace and truth;"—[1] full, to a sufficiency for every end of grace,—full, for practice, to be an example to men and angels as to obedience,—full, to a certainty of uninterrupted communion with God,—full, to a readiness of giving supply to others,—full, to suit him to all the occasions and necessities of the souls of men,—full, to a glory not unbecoming a subsistence in the person of the Son of God,—full, to a perfect victory, in trials, over all temptations,—full, to an exact correspondency to the whole law, every righteous and holy law of God, —full to the utmost capacity of a limited, created, finite nature,— full, to the greatest beauty and glory of a living temple of God,—full, to the full pleasure and delight of the soul of his Father,—full to an everlasting monument of the glory of God, in giving such inconceivable excellencies to the Son of man.

And this is the second thing considerable for the endearing of our souls to our Beloved.

3. Consider that he is *all this in one person.* We have not been

---

[1] John i. 14, 16; 1 Cor. xi. 1; Eph. v. 2; 1 Pet. ii. 21; Matt. iii. 17; Heb. ii. 18, vii. 25.

treating of *two*, a God and a man; but of[1] one who is God and man.
That Word that was with God in the beginning, and was God, John
i. 1, is also made flesh, verse 14;—not by a conversion of itself into
flesh; not by appearing in the outward shape and likeness of flesh;
but by assuming that holy thing that was born of the virgin, Luke
i. 35, into personal union with himself. So "The mighty God," Isa.
ix. 6, is a "child given" to us; that holy thing that was born of the
virgin is called "The Son of God," Luke i. 35. That which made
the man Christ Jesus to be *a man*, was the union of soul and body;
that which made him *that man*, and without which he was not *the
man*, was the subsistence of *both* united in the person of the Son of
God. As to the proof hereof, I have spoken of it [2]elsewhere at large;
I now propose it only in general, to show the amiableness of Christ
on this account. Here lies, hence arises, the grace, peace, life, and
security of the church,—of all believers; as by some few considerations
may be clearly evinced:—

(1.) Hence was he *fit*[3] to suffer and able to bear whatever was due
unto us, in that very action wherein the "Son of man gave his life
a ransom for many," Matt. xx. 28. "God redeemed his church with
his own blood," Acts xx. 28; and therein was the "love of God seen,
that he gave his life for us," 1 John iii. 16. On this account was there
room enough in his breast to receive the points of all the [4]*swords*
that were sharpened by the law against us; and *strength* enough in
his shoulders to bear the *burden* of that curse that was due to us.
Thence was he so *willing* to undertake the work of our redemption,
Heb. x. 7, 8, "Lo, I come to do thy will, O God,"—because he knew
his ability to go through with it. Had he not been man, he could
not have suffered;—had he not been God, his suffering could not
have availed either himself or us,—he had not satisfied; the suffering
of a mere man could not bear any proportion to that which in any
respect was infinite. Had the great and righteous God gathered
together all the sins that had been committed by his elect from the
foundation of the world, and searched the bosoms of all that were to
come to the end of the world, and taken them all, from the sin of
their nature to the least deviation from the rectitude of his most holy

[1] "Qui, propter homines liberandos ab æternâ morte, homo factus est, et ita ad
susceptionem humilitatis nostræ, sine suæ majestatis diminutione inclinans, ut
manens quod erat, assumensque quod non erat; veram servi formam, ei formæ,
in qua Deo patri est æqualis, adunaret, ut nec inferiorem absumeret glorificatio,
nec superiorem minueret assumptio; salvâ enim proprietate utriusque substantiæ,
et in unam coëunte personam, suscipitur a majestate humilitas, a virtute infirmi-
tas, a mortalitate æternitas, et ad rependendum nostræ conditionis debitum, natura inviolabilis naturæ est unita passibili," etc.—Leo. Serm. i. De Nat.

[2] Vind. Evan. c. vii. vol. xii.

[3] "Deus verus, et homo verus in unitatem Domini temperatur, ut, quod nostris
remediis congruebat, unus atque idem Dei hominumque mediator et mori possit ex
uno, et resurgere possit ex altero."—Leo. ubi sup. [4] Zech. xiii.7; Ps. lxxxix. 19.

law, and the highest provocation of their regenerate and unregenerate condition, and laid them on a mere holy, innocent, creature;—O how would they have overwhelmed him, and buried him for ever out of the presence of God's love! Therefore doth the apostle premise that glorious description of him to the purging of our sin: " He hath spoken unto us by his Son, whom he hath appointed heir of all things, by whom also he made the worlds; who being the brightness of his glory, and the express image of his person, and upholding all things by the word of his power," hath "purged our sins." Heb. i. 2, 3. It was he that purged our sins, who was the Son and heir of all things, by whom the world was made,—the brightness of his Father's glory, and express image of his person; he did it, he alone was able to do it. "God was manifested in the flesh," 1 Tim. iii. 16, for this work. The sword awaked against him that was the fellow of the Lord of hosts, Zech. xiii. 7; and by the wounds of that great shepherd are the sheep healed, 1 Pet. ii. 24, 25.

(2.) Hence doth he become an *endless*, bottomless fountain of grace to all them that believe. The fulness that it pleased the Father to commit to Christ, to be the great *treasury* and storehouse of the church, did not, doth not, lie in the human nature, considered in itself; but in the person of the mediator, God and man. Consider wherein his communication of grace doth consist, and this will be evident. The foundation of all is laid in his satisfaction, merit, and purchase; these are the morally procuring cause of all the grace we receive from Christ. Hence all grace becomes to be his;[1] all the things of the new covenant, the promises of God, all the mercy, love, grace, glory promised, became, I say, to be his. Not as though they were all actually invested, or did reside and were in the human nature, and were from thence *really* communicated to us by a participation of a portion of what did so inhere: but they are *morally* his, by a[2] compact, to be bestowed by him as he thinks good, as he is mediator, God and man; that is, the only begotten Son made flesh, John i. 14, " from whose fulness we receive, and grace for grace." The real communication of grace is by Christ sending the Holy Ghost to regenerate us, and to create all the habitual grace, with the daily supplies thereof, in our hearts, that we are made partakers of. Now the Holy Ghost is thus sent by Christ as mediator, God and man, as is at large declared, John xiv. xv. xvi.; of which more afterward. This, then, is that which I intend by this fulness of grace that is in Christ, from whence we have both our beginning and all our supplies; which makes him, as he is the Alpha and Omega of his church, the beginner and finisher of our faith, excellent and desirable to our souls:[3]—Upon

---

[1] John xvi. 14, 15.   [2] Isa. liii. 11, 12; John i. 16; Col. i. 19, 20.
[3] Heb. xii. 2; Rev. i. 11.

the payment of the great price of his blood, and full acquitment on the satisfaction he made, all grace whatever (of which at large afterward) becomes, in a moral sense, his, at his disposal; and he bestows it on, or works it in, the hearts of his by the Holy Ghost, according as, in his infinite wisdom, he sees it needful. How glorious is he to the soul on this consideration! That is most excellent to us which suits us in a wanting condition,—that which gives bread to the hungry, water to the thirsty, mercy to the perishing. All our reliefs are thus in our Beloved. Here is the *life* of our souls, the *joy* of our hearts, our *relief* against sin and *deliverance* from the wrath to come.

(3.) Thus is he *fitted* for a mediator, a days-man, an umpire between God and us,—being one with him, and one with us, and one in himself in this oneness, in the unity of one person. His ability and universal fitness for his office of mediator are hence usually demonstrated. And herein is he "Christ,[1] the power of God, and the wisdom of God." Herein shines out the infinitely glorious wisdom of God; which we may better admire than express. What soul that hath any acquaintance with these things falls not down with reverence and astonishment? How glorious is he that is the Beloved of our souls! What can be wanting that should encourage us to take up our rest and peace in his bosom? Unless all ways of relief and refreshment be so obstructed by unbelief, that no consideration can reach the heart to yield it the least assistance, it is impossible but that from hence the soul may gather that which will endear it unto him with whom we have to do. Let us dwell on the thoughts of it. This is the *hidden mystery;* great without controversy; admirable to eternity. What poor, low, perishing things do we spend our contemplations on! Were we to have no advantage by this astonishing dispensation, yet its excellency, glory, beauty, depths, deserve the flower of our inquiries, the vigour of our spirits, the substance of our time; but when, withal, our life, our peace, our joy, our inheritance, our eternity, our all, lies herein, shall not the thoughts of it always dwell in our hearts, always refresh and delight our souls?

(4.) He is excellent and glorious in this,—in that he is *exalted and invested with all authority.* When[2] Jacob heard of the exaltation of his son Joseph in Egypt, and saw the chariots that he had sent for him, his spirit fainted and recovered again, through abundance of joy and other overflowing affections. Is our Beloved lost, who for our sakes was upon the earth poor and persecuted, reviled, killed? No! he was dead, but he is alive, and, lo, he lives for ever and ever, and hath the keys of hell and of death.[3] Our Beloved is made a lord and ruler, Acts ii. 36. He is made a king; God sets

---

[1] 1 Cor. i. 24.   [2] Gen. xlv. 26, 27.   [3] Rev. i. 18.

him his king on his holy hill of Zion, Ps. ii. 6;[1] and he is crowned
with honour and dignity, after he had been "made a little lower than
the angels for the suffering of death," Heb. ii 7–9. And what is he
made king of? "All things are put in subjection under his feet,"
verse 8. And what power over them hath our Beloved? "All power
in heaven and earth," Matt. xxviii. 18. As for men, he hath power
given him "over all flesh," John xvii. 2. And in what glory doth he
exercise this power? He gives eternal life to his elect; ruling them
in the power of God, Micah v. 4, until he bring them to himself: and
for his enemies, his arrows are sharp in their hearts, Ps. xlv. 5; he
dips his vesture in their blood.[2] Oh, how glorious is he in his
authority over his enemies! In this world he terrifies, frightens,
awes, convinces, bruises their hearts and consciences,—fills them with
fear, terror, disquietment, until they yield him feigned obedience;
and sometimes with outward judgments bruises, breaks, turns the
wheel upon them,—stains all his vesture with their blood,—fills the
earth with their carcases: and at last will gather them all together,
beast, false prophet, nations, etc., and cast them into that lake that
burns with fire and brimstone.[3]

He is gloriously exalted above *angels* in this his authority, good
and bad, Eph. i. 20–22, "far above all principality, and power, and
might, and dominion, and every name that is named, not only in this
world, but also in that which is to come." They are all under his feet,
—at his command and absolute disposal. He is at the right hand of
God, in the highest exaltation possible, and in full possession of a kingdom over the whole creation; having received a "*name* above every
name," etc., Phil. ii. 9. Thus is he glorious in his *throne*, which is at
"the right hand of the ⁴Majesty on high;" glorious in his *commission*, which is "all power in heaven and earth;" glorious in his *name*,
a name above every name,—"Lord of lords, and King of kings;" glorious in his *sceptre*,—"a sceptre of righteousness is the sceptre of his
kingdom;" glorious in his *attendants*,—"his chariots are twenty thousand, even thousands of angels," among them he rideth on the heavens,
and sendeth out the voice of his strength, attended with ten thousand
times ten thousand of his holy ones; glorious in his *subjects*,—all
creatures in heaven and in earth, nothing is left that is not put in
subjection to him; glorious in his *way of rule*, and the administration of his kingdom,—full of sweetness, efficacy, power, serenity, holiness, righteousness, and grace, in and towards his elect,—of terror,

---

[1] Gen. xlix. 10; Numb. xxiv. 17, 19; Ps. ii. 1–9, lxxxix. 19–25, cx. 1–3; Isa.
xi. 1, 4, xxxii. 1, 2, liii. 12, lxiii. 1–3; Jer. xxiii. 5, 6; Dan. vii. 13, 14; Luke
ii. 11, xix. 38; John v. 22, 23; Acts ii. 34–36, v. 31; Phil. ii. 9–11; Eph. i. 20–22;
Rev. v. 12–14, xix. 16.   [2] Isa. lxiii. 3.   [3] Ps. cx. 6; Rev. xix. 20.
[4] Heb. i. 3; Eph. i. 22; Matt. xxviii. 18; Phil. ii. 10, 11; Rev. xix. 16; Ps. xlv.,
lxviii.; Dan. vii. 10

vengeance, and certain destruction towards the rebellious angels and men; glorious in the *issue of his kingdom*, when every knee shall bow before him, and all shall stand before his judgment-seat. And what a little portion of his glory is it that we have pointed to! This is the Beloved of the church,—its head, its husband; this is he with whom we have communion: but of the whole exaltation of Jesus Christ I am elsewhere to treat at large.

Having insisted on these generals, for the farther carrying on the motives to communion with Christ, in the relation mentioned, taken from his excellencies and perfections, I shall reflect on the description given of him by the spouse in the Canticles, to this very end and purpose. Cant. v. 10–16, "My Beloved is white and ruddy, the chiefest among ten thousand. His head is as the most fine gold, his locks are bushy, and black as a raven. His eyes are as the eyes of doves by the rivers of waters, washed with milk, and fitly set. His cheeks are as a bed of spices, as sweet flowers: his lips like lilies, dropping sweet-smelling myrrh. His hands are as gold rings, set with the beryl: his belly is as bright ivory overlaid with sapphires. His legs are as pillars of marble, set upon sockets of fine gold: his countenance is as Lebanon, excellent as the cedars. His mouth is most sweet: yea, he is altogether lovely. This is my Beloved, and this is my friend, O daughters of Jerusalem."

The general description given of him, verse 10, hath been before considered; the ensuing particulars are instances to make good the assertion that he is "the chiefest among ten thousand."

The spouse begins with his *head* and *face*, verses 11–13. In his head, she speaks first in general, unto the *substance* of it,—it is "fine gold;" and then in particular, as *to its ornaments*,—" his locks are bushy, and black as a raven."

1. "*His head is as the most fine gold,*" or, "His head gold, solid gold;" so some;—"made of pure gold;" so others;—χρυσίον κεφαλή, say the LXX., retaining part of both the Hebrew words, כֶּתֶם פָּז, —" massa auri."[1]

Two things are eminent in gold,—splendour or glory, and duration. This is that which the spouse speaks of the head of Christ. His head is his government, authority, and kingdom. Hence it is said, "A crown of pure gold was on his head," Ps. xxi. 3; and his head is here said to be gold, because of the crown of gold that adorns it,—

---

[1] So the words are quoted in all editions of this treatise. Fully to develop the meaning of the allusion, it seems necessary that the whole of the Septuagint rendering should be quoted,—Κιφαλὴ αὐτοῦ χρυσίον κιφάζ. It is the last word in which part of both the Hebrew words is said to be retained. There is some difficulty in fixing the import of פָּז. Gesenius refers us to Ps. xix. 10, in proof that it means *fine*, as distinguished from *common* gold; from פָּז, a root not used in Hebrew, but signifying, in the cognate dialect of the Arabic, to *separate*, to *purify metals*. Some

as the monarchy in Daniel that was most eminent for glory and
duration, is termed a "head of gold," Dan. ii. 38. And these two
things are eminent in the kingdom and authority of Christ:—

(1.) It is a *glorious* kingdom; he is full of glory and majesty, and
in his majesty he rides " prosperously," Ps. xlv. 3, 4. "His glory is
great in the salvation of God: honour and majesty are laid upon him:
he is made blessed for ever and ever," Ps. xxi. 5, 6. I might insist on
particulars, and show that there is not any thing that may render a
kingdom or government glorious, but it is in this of Christ in all its
excellencies. It is a *heavenly,* a *spiritual,* a *universal,* and *unshaken*
kingdom; all which render it glorious. But of this, somewhat before.

(2.) It is *durable,* yea, eternal,—solid gold. "His throne is for ever
and ever," Ps. xlv. 6; "of the increase of his government there shall
be no end, upon the throne of David, and upon his kingdom, to order
it, and to establish it with judgment and with justice from henceforth
even for ever," Isa. ix. 7. "His kingdom is an everlasting kingdom,"
Dan. vii. 27,—" a kingdom that shall never be destroyed," chap. ii. 44;
for he must reign until all his enemies be subdued. This is that head
of gold,—the splendour and eternity of his government.

And if you take the head in a natural sense, either the glory of
his Deity is here attended to, or the fulness and excellency of his
wisdom, which the head is the seat of. The allegory is not to be
straitened, whilst we keep to the analogy of faith.

2. For the *ornaments* of his head; his locks, they are said to be
"bushy," or curled, "black as a raven." His curled locks are black;
"as a raven," is added by way of illustration of the blackness, not
with any allusion to the nature of the raven. Take the head spoken
of in a *political* sense: his locks of hair—said to be *curled,* as seeming to be *entangled,* but really falling in perfect order and beauty,
as bushy locks—are his thoughts, and counsels, and ways, in the
administration of his kingdom. They are *black* or *dark,* because of
their *depth* and unsearchableness,—as God is said to dwell in thick
darkness; and *curled* or *bushy,* because of their exact *interweavings,*
from his infinite wisdom. His thoughts are many as the hairs of the
head, seeming to be perplexed and entangled, but really set in all
comely order, as curled bushy hair; deep and unsearchable, and

---

connect the term with Uphaz, a district from which gold was procured, Jer. x. 9.
Schultens derives the word from פָּז, to *leap,* to spring up into notice, in allusion
to the amount of gold discovered on the surface of the earth, through the previous
disintegration of the rock in which it was disseminated, and when a shower has
washed from it the soil by which it was covered. There is coincidence between
the etymology of the word suggested by the Dutch critic, and the fact that the
largest quantities of gold and gold ore have been discovered, not by excavation,
but by the washing of detritus in regions of primary and transition strata where
the eruption of igneous rocks has occurred : "As for the earth, ... it hath dust
of gold," Job xxviii. 5, 6.—Ed.

dreadful to his enemies, and full of beauty and comeliness to his be-loved. Such are, I say, the thoughts of his heart, the counsels of his wisdom, in reference to the administrations of his kingdom:—dark, perplexed, involved, to a carnal eye; in themselves, and to his saints, deep, manifold, ordered in all things, comely, desirable.

In a *natural* sense, black and curled locks denote comeliness, and vigour of youth. The strength and power of Christ, in the execution of his counsels, in all his ways, appears glorious and lovely.

The next thing described in him is his *eyes.* Verse 12, " His eyes are as the eyes of doves by the rivers of waters, washed with milk, and fitly set." The reason of this allusion is obvious:—doves are ten-der birds, not birds of prey; and of all others they have the most bright, shining, and piercing eye; their delight also in streams of water is known. Their being washed in milk, or clear, white, crystal water, adds to their beauty. And they are here said to be " fitly set;" that is, in due proportion for beauty and lustre,—as a precious stone in the foil or fulness of a ring, as the word signifies.

Eyes being for *sight*, discerning, knowledge, and acquaintance with the things that are to be seen; the knowledge, the understanding, the discerning Spirit of Christ Jesus, are here intended. In the allusion used four things are ascribed to them:—1. Tenderness; 2. Purity; 3. Discerning; and, 4. Glory:—

1. The *tenderness* and compassion of Christ towards his church is here intended. He looks on it with the eyes of galless doves; with tenderness and careful compassion; without anger, fury, or thoughts of revenge. So is the eye interpreted, Deut. xi. 12, " The eyes of the LORD thy God are upon that land." Why so? " It is a land that the LORD thy God careth for;"—careth for it in mercy. So are the eyes of Christ on us, as the eyes of one that in tenderness careth for us; that lays out his wisdom, knowledge, and understand-ing, in all tender love, in our behalf. He is the stone, that founda-tion-stone of the church, whereon " are seven eyes," Zech. iii. 9; wherein is a perfection of wisdom, knowledge, care, and kindness, for its guidance.

2. *Purity;*—as washed doves' eyes for purity. This may be taken either subjectively, for the excellency and immixed cleanness and purity of his sight and knowledge in himself; or objectively, for his delighting to behold purity in others. " He is of purer eyes than to behold iniquity," Hab. i. 13. " He hath no pleasure in wickedness; the foolish shall not stand in his sight," Ps. v. 4, 5. If the righteous soul of Lot was vexed with seeing the filthy deeds of wicked men, 2 Pet. ii. 8, who yet had eyes of flesh, in which there was a mixture of impurity; how much more do the pure eyes of our dear Lord Jesus abominate all the filthiness of sinners ! But herein lies the excel-

lency of his love to us, that he takes care to take away our filth and stains, that he may delight in us; and seeing we are so defiled, that it could no otherwise be done, he will do it by his own blood, Eph. v. 25–27, " Even as Christ also loved the church, and gave himself for it, that he might sanctify and cleanse it, with the washing of water by the word, that he might present it to himself a glorious church, not having spot, or wrinkle, or any such thing; but that it should be holy, and without blemish." The end of this undertaking is, that the church might be thus gloriously presented unto himself, because he is of purer eyes than to behold it with joy and delight in any other condition. He leaves not his spouse until he says of her, " Thou art all fair, my love; there is no spot in thee," Cant. iv. 7. Partly, he takes away our spots and stains, by the " renewing of the Holy Ghost;"[1] and wholly adorns us with his own righteousness: and that because of the purity of his own eyes, which " cannot behold iniquity,"—that he might present us to himself holy.

3. *Discerning.* He sees as doves, quickly, clearly, thoroughly,—to the bottom of that which he looks upon. Hence, in another place it is said that his " eyes are as a flame of fire," Rev. i. 14. And why so? That the churches might know that he is he which " searcheth the reins and hearts," Rev. ii. 23. He hath discerning eyes, nothing is hid from him; all things are open and naked before him with whom we have to do. It is said of him, whilst he was in this world, that " Jesus knew all men, and needed not that any should testify of man; for he knew what was in man," John ii. 24, 25. His piercing eyes look through all the thick coverings of hypocrites, and the snow [show] of pretences that is on them. He sees the inside of all; and what men are there, that they are to him. He sees not as we see, but ponders *the hidden man* of the heart. No humble, broken, contrite soul, shall lose one sigh or groan after him, and communion with him; no pant of love or desire is hid from him,—he sees in secret; no glorious performance of the most glorious hypocrite will avail with him,—his eyes look through all, and the filth of their hearts lies naked before him.

4. *Beauty* and glory are here intended also. Every thing of Christ is beautiful, for he is " altogether lovely," verse 16, but most glorious [is he] in his sight and wisdom: he is the wisdom of God's eternal wisdom itself; his understanding is infinite. What spots and stains are in all our knowledge ! When it is made perfect, yet it will still be finite and limited. His is without spot of darkness, without foil of limitedness.

Thus, then, is he beautiful and glorious:—his " head is of gold, his eyes are doves' eyes, washed in milk, and fitly set."

[1] Tit. iii. 5.

The next thing insisted on is his *cheeks.* Verse 13, "His cheeks are as a bed of spices; as sweet flowers," or "towers of perfumes" [marginal reading], or well-grown flowers. There are three things evidently pointed at in these words:—1. A sweet *savour,* as from *spices,* and *flowers,* and towers of perfume; 2. *Beauty* and order, as *spices* set in *rows or beds,* as the words import; 3. *Eminency* in that word, as *sweet* or *well-grown,* great flowers.

These things are in the cheeks of Christ. The Chaldeę paraphrast, who applies this whole song to God's dealings with the people of the Jews, makes these cheeks of the church's husband to be the two tables of stone, with the various lines drawn in them; but that allusion is strained, as are most of the conjectures of that scholiast.

The cheeks of a man are the seat of *comeliness* and manlike courage. The comeliness of Christ, as hath in part been declared, is from his fulness of grace in himself for us. His manly courage respects the administration of his rule and government, from his fulness of authority; as was before declared. This comeliness and courage the spouse, describing Christ as a beautiful, desirable personage, to show that spiritually he is so, calleth his cheeks; so to make up his parts, and proportion. And to them doth she ascribe,—

1. A sweet *savour,* order, and eminency. A sweet savour; as God is said to smell a sweet savour from the grace and obedience of his servants (Gen. viii. 21, the LORD smelled a savour of rest from the sacrifice of Noah), so do the saints smell a sweet savour from his grace laid up in Christ, Cant. i. 3. It is that which they rest in, which they delight in, which they are refreshed with. As the smell of aromatical spices and flowers pleases the natural sense, refreshes the spirits, and delights the person; so do the graces of Christ to his saints. They please their spiritual sense, they refresh their drooping spirits, and give delight to their souls. If he be nigh them, they smell his raiment, as Isaac the raiment of Jacob. They say, "It is as the smell of a field which the LORD hath blessed," Gen. xxvii. 27; and their souls are refreshed with it.

2. *Order* and *beauty* are as spices set in a garden bed. So are the graces of Christ. When spices are set in order, any one may know what is for his use, and take and gather it accordingly. Their answering, also, one to another makes them beautiful. So are the graces of Christ; in the gospel they are distinctly and in order set forth, that sinners by faith may view them, and take from him according to their necessity. They are ordered for the use of saints in the promises of the gospel. There is light in him, and life in him, and power in him, and all consolation in him;—a constellation of graces, shining with glory and beauty. Believers take a view of them all, see their glory and excellency, but fix especially on that

which, in the condition wherein they are, is most useful to them. One takes light and joy; another, life and power. By faith and prayer do they gather these things in this bed of spices. Not any that comes to him goes away unrefreshed. What may they not take, what may they not gather? what is it that the poor soul wants? Behold, it is here provided, set out in order in the promises of the gospel; which are as the beds wherein these spices are set for our use: and on the account hereof is the covenant said to be "ordered in all things," 2 Sam. xxiii. 5.

3. *Eminency.* His cheeks are "a tower of perfumes" held up, made conspicuous, visible, eminent. So it is with the graces of Christ, when held out and lifted up in the preaching of the gospel. They are a tower of perfumes,—a sweet savour to God and man.

The next clause of that verse is, "His lips are like lilies, dropping sweet-smelling myrrh." Two perfections in things natural are here alluded unto :—First, the glory of *colour* in the lilies, and the sweetness of *savour* in the myrrh. The glory and beauty of the lilies in those countries was such as that our Saviour tells us that "Solomon, in all his glory, was not arrayed like one of them," Matt. vi. 29; and the savour of myrrh such as, when the Scripture would set forth any thing to be an excellent savour, it compares it thereunto, Ps. xlv. 8; and thereof was the sweet and holy ointment chiefly made, Exod. xxx. 23–25: mention is also made frequently of it in other places, to the same purpose. It is said of Christ, that "grace was poured into his lips," Ps. xlv. 2; whence men wondered or were amazed—τοῖς λόγοις τῆς χάριτος [Luke iv. 22]—at the words of grace that proceeded out of his mouth. So that by the lips of Christ, and their dropping sweet-smelling myrrh, the word of Christ, its savour, excellency, and usefulness, is intended. Herein is he excellent and glorious indeed, surpassing the excellencies of those natural things which yet are most precious in their kind,—even in the glory, beauty, and usefulness of his word. Hence they that preach his word to the saving of the souls of men, are said to be a "sweet savour unto God," 2 Cor. ii. 15; and the savour of the knowledge of God is said to be manifested by them, verse 14. I might insist on the several properties of myrrh, whereto the word of Christ is here compared,—its bitterness in taste, its efficacy to preserve from putrefaction, its usefulness in perfumes and unctions,—and press the allegory in setting out the excellencies of the word in allusions to them; but I only insist on generals. This is that which the Holy Ghost here intends:—the word of Christ is sweet, savoury, precious unto believers; and they see him to be excellent, desirable, beautiful, in the precepts, promises, exhortations, and the most bitter threats thereof.

The spouse adds, "His hands are as gold rings set with the beryl" [verse 14]. The word "beryl," in the original, is "Tarshish;"[1] which the Septuagint have retained, not restraining it to any peculiar precious stone; the onyx, say some; the chrysolite, say others;—any precious stone shining with a sea-green colour, for the word signifies the sea also. Gold rings set with precious, glittering stones, are both valuable and desirable, for profit and ornament: so are the hands of Christ; that is, all his works,—the effects, by the cause. All his works are glorious; they are all fruits of wisdom, love, and bounty. "And his belly is as bright ivory, overlaid with sapphires." The smoothness and brightness of ivory, the preciousness and heavenly colour of the sapphires, are here called in, to give some lustre to the excellency of Christ." To these is his belly, or rather his bowels (which takes in the heart also), compared. It is the inward bowels, and not the outward bulk that is signified. Now, to show that by "bowels" in the Scripture, ascribed either to God or man, affections are intended, is needless. The tender love, unspeakable affections and kindness, of Christ to his church and people, is thus set out. What a beautiful sight is it to the eye, to see pure polished ivory set up and down with heaps of precious sapphires! How much more glorious are the tender affections, mercies, and compassion of the Lord Jesus unto believers!

Verse 15. The *strength* of his kingdom, the *faithfulness* and *stability* of his promises,—the height and glory of his person in his dominion,—the sweetness and excellency of communion with him, is set forth in these words: "His legs are as pillars of marble set upon sockets of fine gold; his countenance is as Lebanon, excellent as the cedars: his mouth is most sweet."

When the spouse hath gone thus far in the description of him, she concludes all in this general assertion: "He is wholly desirable,—altogether to be desired or beloved." As if she should have said,—" I have thus reckoned up some of the perfections of the creatures (things of most value, price, usefulness, beauty, glory, here below), and compared some of the excellencies of my Beloved unto them. In this way of allegory I can carry things no higher; I find nothing better or more desirable to shadow out and to present his loveliness and desirableness: but, alas! all this comes short of his perfections, beauty, and comeliness; ' he is *all wholly* to be desired, to be beloved;'"—

Lovely in his *person*,—in the glorious all-sufficiency of his Deity,

[1] As Ophir is taken for the *gold* of Ophir, in Job xxii. 24, so Tarshish, the name of a city, of which the locality is disputed, is used to denote a precious stone which was brought from it. It is translated "*beryl*" in the authorized version, though שֹׁהַם, in Exod. xxviii. 13, is also rendered by the same term. Some make תַּרְשִׁישׁ, the chrysolite or topaz of the moderns. The word has been thought to denote the *sea*, in Isa. xxiii. 10, but on slender ground.—ED.

gracious purity and holiness of his humanity, authority and majesty, love and power.

Lovely in his *birth* and incarnation; when he was rich, for our sakes becoming poor,—taking part of flesh and blood, because we partook of the same; being made of a woman, that for us he might be made under the law, even for our sakes.

Lovely in the whole *course* of his life, and the more than angelical holiness and obedience which, in the depth of poverty and persecution, he exercised therein;—doing good, receiving evil; blessing, and being cursed, reviled, reproached, all his days.

Lovely in his *death*; yea, therein most lovely to sinners;—never more glorious and desirable than when he came broken, dead, from the cross. Then had he carried all our sins into a land of forgetfulness; then had he made peace and reconciliation for us; then had he procured life and immortality for us.

Lovely in his whole *employment*, in his great undertaking,—in his *life, death, resurrection, ascension;* being a mediator between God and us, to recover the glory of God's justice, and to save our souls,—to bring us to an enjoyment of God, who were set at such an infinite distance from him by sin.

Lovely in the glory and majesty wherewith he is *crowned.* Now he is set down at the right hand of the Majesty on high; where, though he be terrible to his enemies, yet he is full of mercy, love, and compassion, towards his beloved ones.

Lovely in all those *supplies of grace and consolations*, in all the dispensations of his Holy Spirit, whereof his saints are made partakers.

Lovely in all the *tender care, power, and wisdom*, which he exercises in the protection, safe-guarding, and delivery of his church and people, in the midst of all the oppositions and persecutions whereunto they are exposed.

Lovely in all his *ordinances*, and the whole of that spiritually glorious worship which he hath appointed to his people, whereby they draw nigh and have communion with him and his Father.

Lovely and glorious in the *vengeance* he taketh, and will finally execute, upon the stubborn enemies of himself and his people.

Lovely in the *pardon* he hath purchased and doth dispense,—in the reconciliation he hath established,—in the grace he communicates,—in the consolations he doth administer,—in the peace and joy he gives his saints,—in his assured preservation of them unto glory.

What shall I say? there is no end of his excellencies and desirableness;—" He is altogether lovely. This is our beloved, and this is our friend, O daughters of Jerusalem."

DIGRESSION II.

All solid wisdom laid up in Christ—True wisdom, wherein it consists—Knowledge
of God, in Christ only to be obtained—What of God may be known by his
works—Some properties of God not discovered but in Christ only; love,
mercy—Others not fully but in him; as vindictive justice, patience, wisdom,
all-sufficiency—No property of God savingly known but in Christ—What is
required to a saving knowledge of the properties of God—No true knowledge
of ourselves but in Christ—Knowledge of ourselves, wherein it consisteth—
Knowledge of sin, how to be had in Christ; also of righteousness and of
judgment—The wisdom of walking with God hid in Christ—What is required
thereunto—Other pretenders to the title of wisdom examined and rejected—
Christ alone exalted.

A SECOND consideration of the excellencies of Christ, serving to
endear the hearts of them who stand with him in the relation insisted on, arises from that which, in the mistaken apprehension of it,
is the great darling of men, and in its true notion the great aim of
the saints; which is *wisdom and knowledge.* Let it be evinced that
all true and solid knowledge is laid up in, and is only to be attained
from and by, the Lord Jesus Christ; and the hearts of men, if they
are but true to themselves and their most predominate principles,
must needs be engaged to him. This is the great design of all men,
taken off from professed slavery to the world, and the pursuit of
sensual, licentious courses,—that they may be *wise:* and what ways the
generality of men engage in for the compassing of that end shall be
afterward considered. To the glory and honour of our dear Lord
Jesus Christ, and the establishment of our hearts in communion with
him, the design of this digression is to evince that all wisdom is laid
up in him, and that from him alone it is to be obtained.

1 Cor. i. 24, the Holy Ghost tells us that " Christ is the power
of God, and the wisdom of God:" not the *essential* Wisdom of God,
as he is the eternal Son of the Father (upon which account he is
called "Wisdom" in the Proverbs, chap. viii. 22, 23); but as he is *crucified,* verse 23. As he is crucified, so he is the wisdom of God; that
is, all that wisdom which God layeth forth for the discovery and
manifestation of himself, and for the saving of sinners, which makes
foolish all the wisdom of the world,—that is all in Christ crucified;
held out in him, by him, and to be obtained only from him. And
thereby in him do we see the glory of God, 2 Cor. iii. 18. For he
is not only said to be " the wisdom of God," but also to be "made
unto us wisdom," 1 Cor. i. 30. He is made, not by creation, but
ordination and appointment, wisdom unto us; not only by teaching
us wisdom (by a metonymy of the effect for the cause), as he is the

great prophet of his church, but also because by the knowing of him we become acquainted with the wisdom of God,—which is our wisdom; which is a metonymy of the adjunct. This, however verily promised, is thus only to be had. The sum of what is contended for is asserted in terms, Col. ii. 3, " In him are hid all the treasures of wisdom and knowledge."

There are two things that might seem to have some colour in claiming a title and interest in this business:—1. *Civil* wisdom and prudence, for the management of affairs; 2. *Ability* of learning and literature;—but God rejecteth both these, as of no use at all to the end and intent of true wisdom indeed. There is in the world that which is called " understanding;" but it comes to nothing. There is that which is called " wisdom;" but it is turned into folly, 1 Cor. i. 19, 20, " God brings to nothing the understanding of the prudent, and makes foolish this wisdom of the world." And if there be neither wisdom nor knowledge (as doubtless there is not), without the knowledge of God, Jer. viii. 9, it is all shut up in the Lord Jesus Christ: " No man hath seen God at any time; the only begotten Son, which is in the bosom of the Father, he hath revealed him." He is not seen at another time, John i. 18, nor known upon any other account, but only the revelation of the Son. He hath manifested him from his own bosom; and therefore, verse 9, it is said that he is "the true Light, which lighteth every man that cometh into the world,"—the true Light, which hath it in himself: and none hath any but from him; and all have it who come unto him. He who doth not so, is in darkness.

The sum of all true wisdom and knowledge may be reduced to these three heads:—I. The *knowledge of God*, his nature and his properties. II. The *knowledge of ourselves* in reference to the will of God concerning us. III. Skill to walk in *communion* with God:—

I. The knowledge of the works of God, and the chief end of all, doth necessarily attend these. 1. In these three is summed up all true wisdom and knowledge; and, 2,—Not any of them is to any purpose to be obtained, or is manifested, but only in and by the Lord Christ:—

1. God, by the work of the creation, by the creation itself, did reveal himself in many of his properties unto his creatures capable of his knowledge;—his power, his goodness, his wisdom, his all-sufficiency, are thereby known. This the apostle asserts, Rom. i. 19–21. Verse 19, he calls it τὸ γνωστὸν τοῦ Θεοῦ,—verse 20, that is, his eternal power and Godhead; and verse 21, a knowing of God: and [1] all this by the creation. But yet there are some properties of God which all the works of creation cannot in any measure reveal or make

---

[1] 'Επεὶ οὖν τὸ γενόμενον ὁ κόσμος ἐστὶν ὁ ξύμπας, ὁ τοῦτον θεωρῶν τάχα ἂν ἀκοῦσαι παρ' αὐτοῦ, ὡς ἐμὲ πεποίηκεν ὁ Θεός.—Plotin.

known;—as his *patience, long-suffering,* and *forbearance.*   For all things being made [1]good, there could be no place for the exercise of any of these properties, or manifestation of them.   The whole fabric of heaven and earth considered in itself, as at first created, will not discover any such thing as patience and forbearance in God;[2] which yet are eminent properties of his nature, as himself proclaims and declares, Exod. xxxiv. 6, 7.

Wherefore the Lord goes farther; and by the works of his *providence,* in preserving and ruling the world which he made, discovers and reveals these properties also.   For whereas by cursing the earth, and filling all the elements oftentimes with signs of his anger and indignation, he hath, as the apostle tells us, Rom. i. 18, "revealed from heaven his wrath against all ungodliness and unrighteousness of men;" yet not proceeding immediately to destroy all things, he hath manifested his patience and forbearance to all.   This Paul, Acts xiv. 16, 17, tells us: "He suffered all nations to walk in their own ways; yet he left not himself without witness, in that he did good, and gave rain from heaven and fruitful seasons, filling their hearts with food and gladness."   A large account of his goodness and wisdom herein the psalmist gives us, Ps. civ. throughout.   By these ways he bare witness to his own goodness and patience; and so it is said, "He endures with much long-suffering," etc., Rom. ix. 22.   But now, here all the world is at a stand; by all this they have but an obscure glimpse of God, and see not so much as his back parts.   Moses saw not that, until he was put into [3]the rock; and that rock was Christ.   There are some of the most eminent and glorious properties of God (I mean, in the manifestation whereof he will be most glorious; otherwise his properties are not to be compared) that there is not the least glimpse to be attained of out of the Lord Christ, but only by and in him; and some that comparatively we have no light of but in him; and of all the rest no *true* light but by him:—

(1.) Of the first sort, whereof not the least guess and imagination can enter into the heart of man but only by Christ, are *love* and *pardoning mercy:*—

[1.] Love; I mean *love unto sinners.*   Without this, man is of all creatures most miserable; and there is not the least glimpse of it that can possibly be discovered but in Christ.   The Holy Ghost says,

---

[1] Gen. i. 31.

[2] "Quamvis speciali cura atque indulgentia Dei, populum Israeliticum constat electum, omnesque alias nationes suas vias ingredi, hoc est, secundum propriam permissæ sunt vivere voluntatem, non ita tamen se æterna Creatoris bonitas ab illis hominibus avertit, ut eos ad cognoscendum atque metuendum nullis significationibus admoneret."—Prosp. de Vocat. Gent. 2, 4.   "Cœlum et terra, et omnia quæ in eis sunt, ecce undique mihi dicunt ut te amem, nec cessant dicere omnibus, ut sint inexcusabiles."—August. Confess., lib. x. cap. 6.

[3] Exod. xxxiii. 22; 1 Cor. x. 4.

1 John iv. 8, 16, "God is love;" that is, not only of a loving and
tender nature, but one that will exercise himself in a dispensation of
his love, eternal love, towards us,—one that hath purposes of love for
us from of old, and will fulfil them all towards us in due season. But
how is this demonstrated? how may we attain an acquaintance with it?
He tells us, verse 9, "In this was manifested the love of God, because
that God sent his only begotten Son into the world, that we might
live through him." This is the only discovery that God hath made
of any such property in his nature, or of any thought of exercising it
towards sinners,—in that he hath sent Jesus Christ into the world, that
we might live by him. Where now is the wise, where is the scribe,
where is the disputer of this world, with all their wisdom? Their
voice must be that of the hypocrites in Zion, Isa. xxxiii. 14, 15. That
wisdom which cannot teach me that God is love, shall ever pass for
folly. Let men go to the sun, moon, and stars, to showers of rain
and fruitful seasons, and answer truly what by them they learn
hereof. Let them not think themselves wiser or better than those
that went before them, who, to a man, got nothing by them, but
being left inexcusable.

[2.] *Pardoning mercy*, or grace. Without this, even his love would
be fruitless. What discovery may be made of this by a sinful man,
may be seen in the father of us all; who, when he had sinned, had
no reserve for mercy, but hid himself, Gen. iii. 8. He did it לְרוּחַ הַיּוֹם,
when the wind did but a little blow at the presence of God; and he
did it foolishly, thinking to "hide himself among trees!" Ps. cxxxix.
7, 8. "The law was given by Moses, but grace and truth came by Jesus
Christ," John i. 17,—grace in the truth and substance. Pardoning
mercy, that comes by Christ alone; that pardoning mercy which is
manifested in the gospel, and wherein God will be glorified to all
eternity, Eph. i. 6. I mean not that general mercy, that velleity of
acceptance which some put their hopes in:[1] that πάθος (which to ascribe
unto God is the greatest dishonour that can be done him) shines not
with one ray out of Christ; it is wholly treasured up in him, and revealed by him. Pardoning mercy is God's free, gracious acceptance
of a sinner upon satisfaction made to his justice in the blood of Jesus;
nor is any discovery of it, but as relating to the satisfaction of justice,
consistent with the glory of God. It is a mercy of inconceivable condescension in forgiveness, tempered with exact justice and severity. Rom.
iii. 25, God is said "to set forth Christ to be a propitiation through
faith in his blood, to declare his righteousness in the remission of sins;"

---

[1] Ἔστω δὴ ἔλεος, λύπη τις ἐπὶ φαινομένῳ κακῷ φθαρτικῷ καὶ λυπηρῷ τοῦ ἀναξίου συγχά-
νειν.—Arist. 2. Rhet. "Quid autem misericordia, nisi alienæ miseriæ quaedam in
nostro corde compassio; quâ alicui, si possumus, subvenire compellimur?"—August.
de Civit. Dei, lib. ix. cap. 5.

[1]his righteousness is also manifested in the business of forgiveness of sins: and therefore it is everywhere said to be wholly in Christ, Eph. i. 7. So that this gospel grace and pardoning mercy is alone purchased by him, and revealed in him. And this was the main end of all typical institutions,—to manifest that remission and forgiveness is wholly wrapped up in the Lord Christ, and that out of him there is not the least conjecture to be made of it, nor the least morsel to be tasted. Had not God set forth[2] the Lord Christ, all the angels in heaven and men on earth could not have apprehended that there had been any such thing in the nature of God as this grace of pardoning mercy. The apostle asserts the full manifestation as well as the exercise of this mercy to be in Christ only, Tit. iii. 4, 5, "After that the kindness and love of God our Saviour towards man appeared,"—namely, in the sending of Christ, and the declaration of him in the gospel. Then was this pardoning mercy and salvation not by works discovered.

And these are of those properties of God whereby he will be known, whereof there is not the least glimpse to be obtained but by and in Christ; and whoever knows him not by these, knows him not at all. They know an idol, and not the only true God. He that hath not the Son, the same hath not the Father, 1 John ii. 23; and not to have God as a Father, is not to have him at all; and he is known as a Father only as he is love, and full of pardoning mercy in Christ. How this is to be had the Holy Ghost tells us, 1 John v. 20, "The Son of God is come and hath given us an understanding, that we may know him that is true." By him alone we have our understanding to know him that is true. Now, these properties of God Christ revealeth in his doctrine, in the revelation he makes of God and his will, as the great prophet of the church, John xvii. 6. And on this account the knowledge of them is exposed to all, with an evidence unspeakably surmounting that which is given by the creation to his eternal power and Godhead. But the life of this knowledge lies in an acquaintance with his person, wherein the express image and beams of this glory of his Father do shine forth, Heb. i. 3; of which before.

(2.) There are other properties of God which, though also otherwise discovered, yet are so clearly, eminently, and savingly only in Jesus Christ; as,—[1.] His *vindictive justice* in punishing sin; [2.] His *patience, forbearance, and long-suffering* towards sinners; [3.] His *wisdom*, in managing things for his own glory; [4.] His *all-sufficiency*, in himself and unto others. All these, though they may receive some lower and inferior manifestations out of Christ, yet they clearly shine only in him; so as that it may be our wisdom to be acquainted with them.

---

[1] Κατακαυχᾶται ἔλιος κρίσιως, James ii. 13.   [2] Προέθετο.

[1.] His *vindictive justice.* God hath, indeed, many ways manifested his indignation and anger against sin; so that men cannot but
know that it is "the judgment of God, that they which commit such
things are worthy of death," Rom. i. 32.   He hath in the law threatened to kindle a fire in his anger that shall burn to the very heart
of hell.   And even in many providential dispensations, "his wrath is
revealed from heaven against all the ungodliness of men," Rom. i. 18.
So that men must say that he is a God of *judgment.*   And he that
shall but consider that the angels for sin were cast from heaven, shut
up under chains of everlasting darkness unto the judgment of the
great day (the[1] rumour whereof seems to have been spread among
the Gentiles, whence the poet makes his Jupiter threaten the inferior rebellious deities with that punishment); and how Sodom and
Gomorrah were condemned with an overthrow, and burned into ashes,
that they might be "examples unto those that should after live
ungodly," 2 Pet. ii. 6; cannot but discover much of God's vindictive
justice and his anger against sin.   But far more clear doth this shine
into us in the Lord Christ:—

1st. In him God hath manifested the *naturalness* of this righteousness unto him, in that it was impossible that it should be diverted
from sinners without the interposing of a propitiation.   Those who
lay the necessity of satisfaction merely upon the account of a free act
and determination of the will of God, leave, to my apprehension, no
just and indispensable[2] foundation for the death of Christ, but lay it
upon a supposition of that which might have been otherwise.   But
plainly, God, in that he[3] spared not his only Son, but made his soul
an offering for sin, and would admit of no atonement but in his blood,
hath abundantly manifested that it is of necessity to him (his holiness
and righteousness requiring it) to render indignation, wrath, tribulation, and anguish unto sin.   And the knowledge of this *naturalness*
of vindictive justice, with the *necessity* of its execution on supposition
of sin, is the only true and useful knowledge of it.   To look upon it
as that which God may exercise or forbear, makes his justice not a
property of his nature, but a free act of his *will;* and a *will to punish*
where one may do otherwise without injustice, is rather ill-will than
justice.

2dly. In the *penalty* inflicted on Christ for sin, this justice is far
more gloriously manifested than otherwise.   To see, indeed, a world,

---

[1] Ἦ μιν ἑλὼν ῥίψω ἐς Τάρταρον ἠερόεντα,

Τῆλε μάλ᾽, ἧχι βάθιστον ὑπὸ χθονός ἐστι βέρεθρον,

Ἔνθα σιδήρειαί τε πύλαι καὶ χάλκεος οὐδός,

Τόσσον ἔνερθ᾽ Ἀΐδεω, ὅσον οὐρανός ἐστ᾽ ἀπὸ γαίης.—Homer, Il. θ. 13-16.

[2] Vid. Diatrib. de Just. Divin. [A treatise by Owen, which will be found in
vol. x. of this edition of his works.]

[3] Rom. viii. 32; Isa. liii. 10; Heb. x. 7-9; Rom. i. 32; 2 Thess. i. 5, 6; Ps.
v. 5, 6; Hab. i. 13; Ps. cxix. 137.

made[1] good and beautiful, wrapped up in wrath and curses, clothed with thorns and briers; to see the whole beautiful creation made subject to vanity, given up to the bondage of corruption; to hear it groan in pain under that burden; to consider legions of angels, most glorious and immortal creatures, cast down into hell, bound with chains of darkness, and reserved for a more dreadful judgment for one sin; to view the ocean of the blood of souls spilt to eternity on this account,—will give some insight into this thing. But what is all this to that view of it which may be had by a spiritual eye in the Lord Christ? All these things are worms, and of no value in comparison of him. To see him who is the[2] wisdom of God, and the power of God, always[3] beloved of the Father; to see him, I say, fear,[4] and tremble, and bow, and sweat, and pray, and die; to see him lifted up upon the cross, the earth trembling under him, as if unable to bear his weight; and the heavens darkened over him, as if shut against his cry; and himself hanging between both, as if refused by both; and all this because our sins did meet upon him;—this of all things doth most abundantly manifest the severity of God's vindictive justice. Here, or nowhere, is it to be learned.

[2.] His *patience, forbearance, and long-suffering* towards sinners. There are many glimpses of the patience of God shining out in the works of his providence; but all exceedingly beneath that discovery of it which we have in Christ, especially in these three things:—

1st. The *manner* of its discovery. This, indeed, is evident to all, that God doth not ordinarily *immediately punish* men upon their offences. It may be learned from his constant way in governing the world: notwithstanding all provocations, yet he doth [5]good to men; causing his sun to shine upon them, sending them rain and fruitful seasons, filling their hearts with food and gladness. Whence it was easy for them to conclude that there was in him abundance of goodness and forbearance. But all this is yet in much darkness, being the exurgency of men's reasonings from their observations; yea, the management of it [God's patience] hath been such as that it hath proved a snare almost universally unto them towards whom it hath been exercised, Eccles. viii. 11, as well as a temptation to them who have looked on, Job xxi. 7; Ps. lxxiii. 2–4, etc.; Jer. xii. 1; Hab. i. 13. The discovery of it in Christ is utterly of another nature. In him the very nature of God is discovered to be love and kindness; and that he will exercise the same to sinners, he hath promised, sworn, and solemnly engaged himself by covenant. And that we may not hesitate about the aim

---

[1] Gen. iii. 17–19, viii. 21; Rom. viii. 21, 22; 2 Pet. ii. 4–6, iii. 6; Jude 6, 7.
[2] 1 Cor. i. 30.   [3] Matt. iii. 17.   [4] Matt. xxvi. 37, 38; Mark xiv. 33; Luke xxii. 43, 44; Heb. v. 7; Matt. xxvii. 51: Mark xv. 33, 34; Isa. liii. 6.
[5] Matt. v. 45; Acts xiv. 17, 18.

which he hath herein, there is a stable bottom and foundation of acting suitably to those gracious properties of his nature held forth,—
namely, the reconciliation and atonement that is made in the blood
of Christ.   Whatever discovery were made of the patience and lenity
of God unto us, yet if it were not withal revealed that the other properties of God, as his justice and revenge for sin, had their actings
also assigned to them to the full, there could be little consolation
gathered from the former.   And therefore, though God may teach
men his goodness and forbearance, by sending them rain and fruitful
seasons, yet withal at the same time, upon all occasions, " revealing
his wrath from heaven against the ungodliness of men," Rom. i. 18,
it is impossible that they should do any thing but miserably fluctuate
and tremble at the event of these dispensations; and yet this is the
best that men can have out of Christ, the utmost they can attain
unto.   With the present possession of good things administered in this
patience, men might, and did for a season, take up their thoughts and
satiate themselves; but yet they were not in the least delivered from
the[1] bondage they were in by reason of death, and the darkness
attending it.   The law reveals no patience or forbearance in God; it
speaks, as to the issue of transgressions, nothing but sword and fire,
had not God interposed by an act of sovereignty.   But now, as was
said, with that revelation of forbearance which we have in Christ,
there is also a discovery of the satisfaction of his justice and wrath
against sin; so that we need not fear any actings from them to interfere with the works of his patience, which are so sweet unto us.
Hence God is said to be " in Christ, reconciling the world to himself," 2 Cor. v. 19; manifesting himself in him as one that hath now
no more to do for the manifestation of all his attributes,—that is, for
the glorifying of himself,—but only to forbear, reconcile, and pardon
sin in him.

2*dly.* In the *nature* of it.   What is there in that forbearance which
out of Christ is revealed?   Merely a not immediate punishing upon
the[2] offence, and, withal, giving and continuing temporal mercies;
such things as men are prone to abuse, and may perish with their
bosoms full of them to eternity.   That which lies hid in Christ, and
is revealed from him, is full of love, sweetness, tenderness, kindness,
grace.   It is the Lord's waiting to be gracious to sinners; waiting for
an advantage to show love and kindness, for the most eminent endearing of a soul unto himself, Isa. xxx. 18, " Therefore will the

---

[1] " Animula vagula, blandula,
    Hospes comesque corporis,
    Quæ nunc abibis in loca
    Pallida, rigida, nudula ?
    Nec ut soles dabis jocos."—Had. Imp.
[2] Rom. ii. 4, 5, ix. 22.

LORD wait, that he may be gracious unto you; and therefore will he be exalted, that he may have mercy upon you." Neither is there any revelation of God that the soul finds more sweetness in than this. When it [one's soul] is experimentally convinced that God from time to time hath passed by many, innumerable iniquities, he is astonished to think that God should do so; and admires that he did not take the advantage of his provocations to cast him out of his presence. He finds that, with infinite wisdom, in all long-suffering, he hath managed all his dispensations towards him to recover him from the power of the devil, to rebuke and chasten his spirit for sin, to endear him unto himself;—there is, I say, nothing of greater sweetness to the soul than this: and therefore the apostle says, Rom. iii. 25, that all is "through the forbearance of God." God makes way for complete forgiveness of sins through this his forbearance; which the other doth not.

3dly. They differ in their *ends and aims.* What is the aim and design of God in the dispensation of that forbearance which is manifested and may be discovered out of Christ? The apostle tells us, Rom. ix. 22, "What if God, willing to show his wrath, and to make his power known, endured with much long-suffering the vessels of wrath fitted for destruction?" It was but to leave them inexcusable, that his power and wrath against sin might be manifested in their destruction. And therefore he calls it "a suffering of them to walk in their own ways," Acts xiv. 16; which elsewhere he holds out as a most dreadful judgment,—to wit, in respect of that issue whereto it will certainly come; as Ps. lxxxi. 12, "I gave them up unto their own hearts' lusts, and they walked in their own counsels:" which is as dreadful a[1] condition as a creature is capable of falling into in this world. And Acts xvii. 30, he calls it a "winking at the sins of their ignorance;" as it were taking no care nor thought of them in their dark condition, as it appears by the antithesis, "But now he commandeth all men everywhere to repent." He did not take so much notice of them then as to command them to repent, by any clear revelation of his mind and will. And therefore the exhortation of the apostle, Rom. ii. 4, "Despisest thou the riches of his goodness and forbearance and long-suffering, not knowing that the goodness of God leadeth thee to repentance?" is spoken to the Jews, who had advantages to learn the natural tendency of that goodness and forbearance which God exercises in Christ; which, indeed, leads to repentance: or else he doth in general intimate that, in very reason, men ought to make another use of those things than usually they do, and which he chargeth them

---

[1] " Eos, quibus indulgere videtur, quibus parcere, molles venturis malis (Deus) format."—Seneca, " De Providentiâ," cap. iv.—" Pro dii immortales! cur interdum in hominum sceleribus maximis, aut connivetis, aut præsentis fraudis pœnas in diem reservatis !"—Cic. pro Cæl. 24.

withal, verse 5, " But after thy hardness and impenitent heart," etc. At[1] best, then, the patience of God unto men out of Christ, by reason of their own incorrigible stubbornness, proves but like the waters of the river Phasis, that are sweet at the top and bitter in the bottom; they swim for a while in the sweet and good things of this life, Luke xvi. 25; wherewith being filled, they sink to the depth of all bitterness.

But now, evidently and directly, the end of that patience and forbearance of God which is exercised in Christ, and discovered in him to us, is the saving and bringing unto God those towards whom he is pleased to exercise them. And therefore Peter tells you, 2 Pet. iii. 9, that he is " long-suffering to us-ward, not willing that any should perish, but that all should come to repentance;"—that is, all us towards whom he exercises forbearance; for that is the end of it, that his will concerning our repentance and salvation may be accomplished. And the nature of it, with its end, is well expressed, Isa. liv. 9, " This is as the waters of Noah unto me: for as I have sworn that the waters of Noah should no more go over the earth, so have I sworn that I would not be wroth," etc. It is God's taking a course, in his infinite wisdom and goodness, that we shall not be destroyed notwithstanding our sins; and therefore, Rom. xv. 5, these two things are laid together in God, as coming together from him, " The God of patience and consolation:" his patience is a matter of the greatest consolation. And this is another property of God, which, though it may break forth in some rays, to some ends and purposes, in other things, yet the treasures of it are hid in Christ; and none is acquainted with it, unto any spiritual advantage, that learns it not in him.

[3.] His *wisdom*, his infinite wisdom, in managing things for his own glory, and the good of them towards whom he hath thoughts of love. The Lord, indeed, hath laid out and manifested infinite wisdom[2] in his works of creation, providence, and governing of his world: in wisdom hath he made all his creatures. " How manifold are his works! in wisdom hath he made them all; the earth is full of his riches," Ps. civ. 24. So in his providence, his supportment and guidance of all things, in order to one another, and his own glory, unto the ends appointed for them; for all these things " come forth from the LORD of hosts, who is wonderful in counsel, and excellent in working," Isa. xxviii. 29. His law also is for ever to be admired, for the excellency of the wisdom therein, Deut. iv. 7, 8. But yet there is that which Paul is astonished at, and wherein God will for ever be

---

[1] Κατὰ μὲν τοῦ ἐπιῤῥέοντος βάψαντα, γλυκὺ τὸ ὕδωρ ἀνιμήσασθαι· εἰ δὲ εἰς βάθος τὶς καθήκιν τὴν κάλπιν, ἀλμυρόν.—Arrian. περιπ. Εὐξείνου πόντου.

[2] " Si amabilis est sapientia cum cognitione rerum conditarum, quam amabilis est sapientia, quæ condidit omnia ex nihilo ? "—August. Lib. Meditat., c. xviii.

exalted, which he calls,. " The depth of the riches of the wisdom and knowledge of God," Rom. xi. 33;—that is only hid in and revealed by Christ. Hence, as he is said to be " the[1] wisdom of God," and to be "made unto us wisdom;" so the design of God, which is carried along in him, and revealed in the gospel, is called " the wisdom of God," and a "mystery; even the hidden wisdom which God ordained before the world was; which none of the princes of this world knew," 1 Cor. ii. 7, 8. Eph. iii. 10, it is called, " The manifold wisdom of God;" and to discover the depth and riches of this wisdom, he tells us in that verse that it is such, that principalities and powers, that very angels themselves, could not in the least measure get any acquaintance with it, until God, by gathering of a church of sinners, did actually discover it. Hence Peter informs us, that they who are so well acquainted with all the works of God, do yet bow down and desire with earnestness to look into these things (the things of the wisdom of God in the gospel), 1 Pet. i. 12. It asks a man much wisdom to make a curious work, fabric, and building; but if one shall come and deface it, to raise up the same building to more beauty and glory than ever, this is excellence of wisdom indeed. God in the beginning made all things good, glorious, and beautiful. When all things had an innocency and beauty, the clear[2] impress of his wisdom and goodness upon them, they were very glorious; especially man, who was made for his special glory. Now, all this beauty was defaced by sin, and the whole[3] creation rolled up in darkness, wrath, curses, confusion, and the great praise of God buried in the heaps of it. Man, especially, was utterly lost, and came short of the glory of God, for which he was created, Rom. iii. 23. Here, now, doth the depth of the riches of the wisdom and knowledge of God open itself. A design in Christ shines out from his bosom, that was lodged there from eternity, to recover things to such an estate as shall be exceedingly to the advantage of his glory, infinitely above what at first appeared, and for the putting of sinners into inconceivably a better condition than they were in before the entrance of sin. He appears now glorious; he is known to be a God [4]pardoning iniquity and sin, and *advances the riches of his grace:* which was his design, Eph. i. 6. He hath infinitely vindicated his justice also, in the face of men, angels, and devils, in setting forth his Son for a [5]propitiation. It is also to our advantage; we are more fully established in his favour, and are carried on towards a more exceeding [6]weight of glory than formerly was revealed. Hence was that ejaculation of one of the ancients, "O felix culpa, quæ talem meruit redemptorem!" Thus Paul tells us, " Great is the mystery of godliness," 1 Tim. iii. 16, and that " without controversy." We

---

[1] 1 Cor. i. 20, 30.   [2] Gen. i. 31.   [3] Gen. iii. 17, 18; Rom. i. 18.
[4] Exod. xxxiii. 18, 19, xxxiv. 6, 7.   [5] Rom. iii. 24, 25.   [6] 2 Cor. iv. 17.

receive " grace for grace;"[1]—for that grace lost in Adam, better grace in Christ. Confessedly, this is a depth of wisdom indeed. And of the love of Christ to his church, and his union with it, to carry on this business, " This is a great mystery," Eph. v. 32, says the apostle; great wisdom lies herein.

So, then, this also is hid in Christ,—the great and unspeakable riches of the wisdom of God, in *pardoning* sin, *saving* sinners, satisfying *justice*, fulfilling the *law*, repairing his own *honour*, and providing for us a more exceeding weight of glory; and all this out of such a condition as wherein it was impossible that it should enter into the hearts of angels or men how ever the glory of God should be repaired, and one sinning creature delivered from everlasting ruin. Hence it is said, that at the last day God " shall be glorified in his saints, and admired in all them that believe," 2 Thess. i. 10. It shall be an admirable thing, and God shall be for ever glorious in it, even in the bringing of believers to himself. To save sinners through believing, shall be found to be a far more admirable work than to create the world of nothing.

[4.] His *all-sufficiency* is the last of this sort that I shall name.

God's all-sufficiency in himself is his absolute and universal perfection, whereby nothing is wanting *in* him, nothing *to* him: no accession can be made to his fulness, no decrease or wasting can happen thereunto. There is also in him an all-sufficiency for others; which is his power to impart and communicate his goodness and himself so to them as to satisfy and fill them, in their utmost capacity, with whatever is good and desirable to them. For the first of these,—his all-sufficiency for the communication of his *goodness*, that is, in the outward effect of it,—God abundantly manifested in the creation, in that he made all things good, all things perfect; that is, to whom nothing was wanting in their own kind;—he put a stamp of his own goodness upon them all. But now for the latter,—his giving *himself* as an all-sufficient God, to be *enjoyed* by the creatures, to hold out all that is in him *for the satiating and making them blessed*,—that is alone discovered by and in Christ. In him he is a Father, a God in covenant, wherein he hath promised to lay out himself for them; in him hath he promised to give himself into their everlasting fruition, as their exceeding great reward.

And so I have insisted on the second sort of properties in God, whereof, though we have some obscure glimpse in other things, yet the clear knowledge of them, and acquaintance with them, is only to be had in the Lord Christ.

That which remaineth is, briefly to declare that not any of the properties of God whatever can be known, savingly and to consola-

[1] John i. 16.

tion, but only in him; and so, consequently, all the wisdom of the knowledge of God is hid in him alone, and from him to be obtained.

2. There is no *saving knowledge of any property of God*, nor such as brings *consolation*, but what alone is to be had in Christ Jesus, being laid up in him, and manifested by him. Some eye the justice of God, and know that this is his righteousness, "that they which do such things" (as sin) "are worthy of death," Rom. i. 32. But this is to no other end but to make them cry, "Who amongst us shall dwell with the devouring fire?" Isa. xxxiii. 14. Others fix upon his patience, goodness, mercy, forbearance; but it doth not at all lead them to repentance; but "they despise the riches of his goodness, and after their hardness and impenitent hearts treasure up unto themselves wrath against the day of wrath," Rom. ii. 4, 5. Others, by the very works of creation and providence, come to know "his eternal power and Godhead; but they glorify him not as God, nor are thankful, but become vain in their imagination, and their foolish hearts are darkened," Rom. i. 20. Whatever discovery men have of truth out of Christ, they "hold it captive under unrighteousness," verse 18. Hence Jude tells us, verse 10, that "in what they know naturally, as brute beasts, in those things they corrupt themselves."

That we may have a saving knowledge of the properties of God, attended with consolation, these three things are required:—(1.) That God hath *manifested* the glory of them all in a way of doing good unto us. (2.) That he will yet *exercise* and lay them out to the utmost in our behalf. (3.) That, being so *manifested* and *exercised*, they are fit and powerful to bring us *to the everlasting fruition of* himself; which is our blessedness. Now, all these three lie hid in Christ; and the least glimpse of them out of him is not to be attained.

(1.) This is to be received, that God hath actually *manifested* the glory of all his attributes in a way of doing us good. What will it avail our souls, what comfort will it bring unto us, what endearment will it put upon our hearts unto God, to know that he is infinitely righteous, just, and holy, unchangeably true and faithful, if we know not how he may preserve the glory of his justice and faithfulness in his comminations and threatenings, but only in our ruin and destruction? if we can from thence only say it is a righteous thing with him to recompense tribulation unto us for our iniquities? What fruit of this consideration had Adam in the garden? Gen. iii. What sweetness, what encouragement, is there in knowing that he is *patient* and *full of forbearance*, if the glory of these is to be exalted in enduring the vessels of wrath fitted for destruction? nay, what will it avail us to hear him proclaim himself "The LORD, The LORD God,[1] mer-

[1] Exod. xxxiv. 6, 7.

ciful and gracious, abundant in goodness and truth," yet, withal, that
he will "by no means clear the guilty,"—so shutting up the exercise
of all his other properties towards us, upon the account of our iniquity?
Doubtless, not at all. Under this naked consideration of the properties of God, justice will make men fly and hide, Gen. iii.; Isa. ii. 21,
xxxiii. 15, 16;—patience, render them obdurate, Eccles. viii. 11. Holiness utterly deters them from all thoughts of approach unto him,
John xxiv. 19. What relief have we from thoughts of his immensity
and omnipresence, if we have cause only to contrive how to fly from
him (Ps. cxxxix. 11, 12), if we have no pledge of his gracious presence
with us? This is that which brings salvation, when we shall see that
God hath glorified all his properties in a way of doing us good. Now,
this he hath done in Jesus Christ. In him hath he made his justice
glorious, in making all our iniquities to[1] meet upon him, causing him
to bear them all, as the scape-goat in the wilderness; not sparing
him, but giving him up to death for us all;—so exalting his justice
and indignation against sin in a way of freeing us from the condemnation of it, Rom. iii. 25, viii. 33, 34. In him hath he made his truth
glorious, and his faithfulness, in the exact accomplishment of all his
absolute threatenings and promises. That fountain-threat and commination whence all others flow, Gen. ii. 17, "In the day thou eatest
thereof thou shalt die the death;" seconded with a curse, Deut. xxvii.
26, "Cursed is every one that continueth not," etc. [Gal. iii. 10]—is
in him accomplished, fulfilled, and the truth of God in them laid in a
way to our good. He, by the grace of God, tasted death for us, Heb.
ii. 9; and so delivered us who were subject to death, verse 15; and he
hath fulfilled the curse, by being made a curse for us, Gal. iii. 13.
So that in his very threatenings his truth is made glorious in a way
to our good. And for his promises, "They are all yea, and in him
Amen, unto the glory of God by us," 2 Cor. i. 20. And for his
mercy, goodness, and the riches of his grace, how eminently are they
made glorious in Christ, and advanced for our good! God hath set
him forth to declare his righteousness for the forgiveness of sin; he
hath made way in him for ever to exalt the glory of his pardoning
mercy towards sinners. To manifest this is the great design of the
gospel, as Paul admirably sets it out, Eph. i. 5–8. There must our
souls come to an acquaintance with them, or for ever live in darkness.

Now, this is a *saving knowledge*, and full of consolation, when we
can see all the properties of God made glorious and exalted in
a way of doing us good. And this wisdom is hid only in Jesus
Christ. Hence, when he desired his Father to glorify his name,
John xii. 24,—to make in him his *name* (that is, his nature, his

---

[1] Isa. liii. 5, 6; Lev. xvi. 21; Rom. viii. 32.

properties, his will) all glorious in that work of redemption he had in hand,—he was instantly answered from heaven, "I have both glorified it and will glorify it again." He will give it its utmost glory in him.

(2.) That God will yet *exercise* and lay out those properties of his to the utmost in our behalf. Though he hath made them all glorious in a way that may tend to our good, yet it doth not absolutely follow that he will *use* them for our good; for do we not see innumerable persons perishing everlastingly, notwithstanding the manifestation of himself which God hath made in Christ? Wherefore farther, God hath committed all his properties into the hand of Christ if I may so say, to be managed in our behalf, and for our good. He[1] is "The power of God, and the wisdom of God;" he is "The LORD our Righteousness," and is "made unto us of God wisdom, and righteousness, sanctification, and redemption." Christ having glorified his Father in all his attributes, he hath now the exercise of them committed to him, that he might be the captain of salvation to them that do believe; so that if, in the righteousness, the goodness, the love, the mercy, the all-sufficiency of God, there be any thing that will do us good, the Lord Jesus is fully interested with the dispensing of it in our behalf. Hence God is said to be "in him, reconciling the world unto himself," 2 Cor. v. 18. Whatever is in him, he layeth it out for the reconciliation of the world, in and by the Lord Christ; and he becomes "The LORD our Righteousness," Isa. xlv. 24, 25. And this is the second thing required.

(3.) There remaineth only, then, that these attributes of God, so manifested and exercised, are *powerful and able* to bring us to the everlasting fruition of him. To evince this, the Lord wraps up the whole covenant of grace in *one* promise, signifying no less: "I will be your God." In the covenant, God becomes our God, and we are his people; and thereby all his attributes are ours also. And lest that we should doubt—when once our eyes are opened to see in any measure the inconceivable difficulty that is in this thing, what unimaginable obstacles on all hands there lie against us—that all is not enough to deliver and save us, God hath, I say, wrapped it up in this expression, Gen. xvii. 1, "I am," saith he,[2] "God Almighty" (all-sufficient);—"I am wholly able to perform all my undertakings, and to be thy exceeding great reward. I can remove all difficulties, answer all objections, pardon all sins, conquer all opposition: I am God all-sufficient." Now, you know in whom this covenant and all the promises thereof are ratified, and in whose blood it is confirmed,—

---

[1] 1 Cor. i. 20, 30; Jer. xxiii. 6.

[2] "Shaddai, Aquila interpretatur ἄλκιμον, quod nos robustum et ad omnia perpetranda sufficientem possumus dicere."—Hieron., Epist. cxxxvi.

to wit, in the Lord Christ alone; in him only is God an all-sufficient God to any, and an exceeding great reward. And hence Christ
himself is said to "save to the uttermost them that come to God
by him," Heb. vii. And these three things, I say, are required to
be known, that we may have a saving acquaintance, and such as
is attended with consolation, with any of the properties of God;
and all these being hid only in Christ, from him alone it is to be
obtained.

This, then, is the first part of our first demonstration,—that all true
and sound wisdom and knowledge is laid up in the Lord Christ, and
from him alone to be obtained; because our wisdom, consisting, in a
main part of it, in the knowledge of God, his nature, and his properties, this lies wholly hid in Christ, nor can possibly be obtained
but by him.

II. For the *knowledge of ourselves*, which is the SECOND part of
our[1] wisdom, this consists in these three things, which our Saviour
sends his Spirit to convince the world of,—even " sin, righteousness,
and judgment," John xvi. 8. To know ourselves in reference unto
these three, is a main part of true and sound wisdom; for they all
respect the supernatural and immortal end whereunto we are appointed; and there is none of these that we can attain unto but only
in Christ.

1. In respect of *sin*. There is a sense and knowledge of sin left
in the *consciences* of all men by nature. To tell them what is good
and evil in many things, to approve and disapprove of what they do,
in reference to a *judgment* to come, they need not go farther than
themselves, Rom. ii. 14, 15. But this is obscure, and relates mostly
to greater sins, and is in sum that which the apostle gives us, Rom.
i. 32, "They know the judgment of God, that they which do such
things are worthy of death." This he placeth among the common
presumptions and notions that are received by mankind,—namely,
that it is[2] "righteous with God, that they who do such things are
worthy of death." And if that be true, which is commonly received,
that no nation is so barbarous or rude, but it retaineth *some sense
of a Deity;* then this also is true, that there is no nation but hath *a
sense of sin,* and the displeasure of God for it. For this is the very
first[3] notion of God in the world, that he is the rewarder of good and

---

[1] ‘Η σοφία ἐστὶ τῶν τιμιωτάτων.—Arist.

[2] Τὸ δικαίωμα τοῦ Θεοῦ ἐπιγνόντες ὅτι οἱ τὰ τοιαῦτα πράσσοντες ἄξιοι θανάτου εἰσίν.—Rom.
i. 32. "Perfecto demum scelere, magnitudo ejus intellecta est."—Tacit.

Τί χρῆμα πάσχεις; τίς σ' ἀπόλλυσιν νόσος;
‘Η σύνεσις, ὅτι σύνοιδα δείν' εἰργασμένος.—Eurip. Orest. 395, 396.

[3] "Primus est deorum cultus, Deos credere : deinde reddere illis majestatem
suam, reddere bonitatem, sine qua nulla majestas est. Scire illos esse qui præsident
mundo : qui universa vi sua temperant : qui humani generis tutelam gerunt."—

evil. Hence were all the sacrifices, purgings, expiations, which were
so generally spread over the face of the earth. But this was and is
but very dark, in respect of that knowledge of sin with its appurte-
nances, which is to be obtained.

A farther knowledge of sin, upon all accounts whatever, is given
by the law; that law which was "added because of transgressions."
This[1] revives *doctrinally* all that sense of good and evil which was
at first implanted in man; and it is a glass, whereinto whosoever is
able *spiritually* to look, may see sin in all its ugliness and deformity.
The truth is, look upon the *law* in its purity, holiness, compass, and
perfection; its *manner of delivery*,[2] with dread, terror, thunder,
earthquakes, fire; the *sanction of it*, in death, curse, wrath; and it
makes a wonderful discovery of sin, upon every account: its pollution,
guilt, and exceeding sinfulness are seen by it. But yet all this doth
not suffice to give a man a true and thorough conviction of sin. Not
but that the glass is clear, but of ourselves we have not eyes to look
into it; the rule is straight, but we cannot apply it: and therefore
Christ sends his Spirit to convince the world of sin, John xvi. 8;
who, though, as to some ends and purposes, he makes use of the law,
yet the work of conviction, which alone is a useful knowledge of sin,
is his peculiar work. And so the discovery of sin may also be said
to be by Christ,—to be part of the wisdom that is hid in him. But
yet there is a twofold regard besides this, of his sending his Spirit to
convince us, wherein this wisdom appears to be hid in him:—First,
because there are some near *concernments* of sin, which are more
clearly held out in the Lord Christ's being made sin for us, than any
other way. Secondly, in that there is no knowledge to be had of

Senec., Epist. xcvi. "Neque honor ullus deberi potest Deo, si nihil præstat colenti;
nec ullus metus, si non irascitur non colenti."—Lactan.

"Raro antecedentem scelestum
Deseruit pede pæna claudo."—Horat., Od. iii. 2, 31, 32.

"Quo fugis Encelade? quascunque accesseris oras,
Sub Jove semper eris," etc.

——————— "Hos tu
Evasisse putes, quos diri conscia facti
Mens habet attonitos, et surdo verbere cædit?"—Juvenal, Sat. xiii. 192.

Οἴει σὺ τοὺς θανόντας, ὦ Νικόστρατι,
Τρυφῆς ἁπάσης μιταλαβόντας ἐν βίῳ,
Πιφευγίναι, τὸ θεῖον ὡς λιληθότας;
"Εστιν Δίκης ὀφθαλμός, ὃς τὰ πάνθ᾽ ὁρᾷ.
Καὶ γὰρ καθ᾽ ᾅδην δύο τρίβους νομίζομεν,
Μίαν δικαίων, ἑτέραν δ᾽ ἀσεβῶν εἶν᾽ ὁδόν.
Κ᾽ εἰ τοὺς δύο καλύψει ἡ γῆ, φασὶ, χρόνῳ
'Αρπάζ᾽, ἀπελθών, κλίπτ᾽, ἀποστέροι, κύκα.
Μηδὲν πλανηθῇς, ἔσται κἂν ᾅδου κρίσις.
"Ηνπερ ποιήσει Θεὸς ὁ πάντων δεσπότης,
Οὗ τοὔνομα φοβερὸν οὐδ᾽ ἂν ὀνομάσαιμ᾽ ᾽ἐγώ. κ. τ. λ.
—Philemon, juxta Justin. Martyr. seu Diphil. juxta Clement.

[1] Gal. iii. 19; Rom. vii. 13.
[2] Exod. xix. 18–20; Deut. iv. 11; Heb. xii. 18–21.

sin, so as to give it a *spiritual and saving improvement*, but only in
him.

For the first, there are four things in sin that clearly shine out in
the cross of Christ:—(1.) The *desert* of it.   (2.) Man's *impotency* by
reason of it.   (3.) The *death* of it.   (4.) A *new end put to it.*

(1.) The *desert* of sin doth clearly shine in the cross of Christ upon
a twofold account:—[1.] Of the *person* suffering for it.   [2.] Of the
penalty he underwent.

[1.] Of the person suffering for it.   This the Scripture oftentimes
very emphatically sets forth, and lays great weight upon: John iii.
16, " God so loved the world, that he gave his only begotten Son."
It was his only Son that God sent into the world to suffer for sin,
Rom. viii. 32.   " He spared not his own Son, but delivered him
up for us all."   To see a slave beaten and corrected, it argues a
fault committed; but yet perhaps the demerit of it was not very great.
The correction of a son argues a great provocation; that of an only
son, the greatest imaginable.   Never was sin seen to be more abo-
minably sinful and full of provocation, than when the burden of it
was upon the shoulders of the Son of God.   God having made his
Son, the Son of his love, his only begotten, full of grace and truth,[1]
sin for us, to manifest his indignation against it, and how utterly
impossible it is that he should let the least sin go unpunished, he
lays[2] hand on him, and spares him not.   If[3] sin be imputed to the
dear Son of his bosom, as upon his own voluntary assumption of it
it was (for he said to his Father, " Lo, I come to do thy will," and all
our iniquities did meet on him), [and] he will not spare him any thing
of the due desert of it; is it not most clear from hence, even from
the blood of the cross of Christ, that such is the demerit of sin, that
it is altogether impossible that God should pass by any, the least, unpunished?   If he would have done it for any, he would have done it in
reference to his only Son; but he spared him not.

Moreover, God is not at all delighted with, nor desirous of, the
blood, the tears, the cries, the inexpressible torments and sufferings,
of the Son of his love (for he delights not in the anguish of any,—
" he doth not[4] afflict willingly, nor grieve the children of men,"
much less the Son of his bosom); only he required that his law be
fulfilled, his justice satisfied, his wrath atoned for sin; and nothing
less than all this would bring it about.   If the debt of sin might
have been compounded for at a cheaper rate, it had never been held
up at the price of the blood of Christ.   Here, then, soul, take a view
of the desert of sin; behold it far more evident than in all the threatenings and curses of the law.   " I thought, indeed," mayest thou say
from thence, " that sin, being found on such a poor worm as I am,

[1] 2 Cor. v. 21.   [2] Zech. xiii. 7.   [3] Heb. x. 7; Isa. liii. 6.   [4] Lam. iii. 33.

was worthy of death; but that it should have this effect if charged on the Son of God,—*that* I never once imagined."

[2.] Consider also, farther, *what he suffered.* For though he was so excellent a one, yet perhaps it was but a light affliction and trial that he underwent, especially considering the strength he had to bear it. Why, whatever it were, it made this[1] "fellow of the LORD of hosts," this[2] "lion of the tribe of Judah," this[3] "mighty one," "the[4] wisdom and power of God," to tremble,[5] sweat, cry, pray, wrestle, and that with strong supplications. Some of the popish devotionists tell us that one drop, the least, of the blood of Christ, was abundantly enough to redeem all the world; but they err, not knowing the desert of sin, nor the severity of the justice of God. If one drop less than was shed, one pang less than was laid on, would have done it, those other drops had not been shed, nor those other pangs laid on. God did not cruciate the dearly-beloved of his soul for nought. But there is more than all this:—

It pleased God to [6] bruise him, to put him to grief, to make his soul an offering for sin, and to pour out his life unto death. He [7] hid himself from him,—was far from the voice of his cry, until he cried out, "My God, my God, why hast thou forsaken me?" He made him [8] sin and a [9] curse for us; executed on him the sentence of the law; brought him into an agony, wherein he sweat thick drops of blood, was grievously troubled, and his soul was heavy unto death. He that was the power of God, and the wisdom of God, went stooping under the burden, until the whole frame of nature seemed astonished at it. Now this, as I said before that it discovered the indignation of God against sin, so it clearly holds out the desert of it. Would you, then, see the true demerit of sin?—take the measure of it from the mediation of Christ, especially his cross. It brought him who was the Son of God, equal unto God, God blessed for ever, into the form of a [10] servant, who had not where to lay his head. It pursued him all his life with afflictions and persecutions; and lastly brought him under the rod of God; there bruised him and brake him,—[11] slew the Lord of life. Hence is deep humiliation for it, upon the account of him whom we [12] have pierced. And this is the first spiritual view of sin we have in Christ.

(2.) The wisdom of understanding our *impotency*, by reason of sin, is wrapped up in him. By our impotency, I understand two things:—[1.] Our *disability* to make any *atonement* with God for sin. [2.] Our *disability to answer* his mind and will, in all or any of the *obedience* that he requireth, by reason of sin.

---

[1] Zech. xiii. 7.   [2] Rev. v. 5.   [3] Ps. lxxxix. 19   [4] Prov. viii. 22; 1 Cor. i. 24.
[5] Matt. xxvi. 37, 38; Mark xiv. 33, 34; Luke xxii. 44; Heb. v. 7.
[6] Isa. liii. 5, 6.   [7] Ps. xxii. 1.   [8] 2 Cor. v. 21.   [9] Gal. iii. 13.
[10] Phil. ii. 8.   [11] 1 Cor. ii. 7.   [12] Zech. xii. 10.

[1.] For the first, that alone is discovered in Christ. Many inquiries have the sons of men made after an atonement,—many ways have they entered into to accomplish it. After this they inquire, Mic. vi. 6, 7, " Will any manner of sacrifices, though appointed of God, as burnt-offerings, and calves of a year old; though very costly, thousands of rams, and ten thousand rivers of oil; though dreadful and tremendous, offering violence to nature, as to give my children to the fire;"—will any of these things make an atonement? David doth positively, indeed,-determine this business, Ps. xlix. 7, 8, " None of them" (of the best or richest of men) " can by any means redeem his brother, nor give to God a ransom for him; for the redemption of their soul is precious, and it ceaseth for ever." It cannot be done,— no atonement can be made; yet men would still be doing, still attempting: hence did they heap up[1] sacrifices, some costly, some bloody and inhuman. The Jews, to this day, think that God was atoned for sin by the sacrifices of bulls and goats, and the like. And the Socinians acknowledge no atonement, but what consists in men's repentance and new obedience. In the cross of Christ are the mouths of all stopped as to this thing. For,—

1st. God hath there discovered that *no sacrifices for sin*, though of his own *appointment*, could ever make them *perfect* that offered them, Heb. x. 11. Those sacrifices could never take away sin;[2]—those services could never make them perfect that performed them, as to the conscience, Heb. ix. 9; as the apostle proves, chap. x. 1. And thence the Lord rejects all sacrifices and offerings whatever, as to any such end and purpose, verses 6–8, Christ, in their stead, saying, " Lo, I come;" and by him we are " justified from all things, from which we could not be justified by the law," Acts xiii. 39: God, I say, in Christ, hath condemned all sacrifices, as wholly insufficient in the least to make an atonement for sin. And how great a thing it was to instruct the sons of men in this wisdom, the event hath manifested.

2dly. He hath also written *vanity* on all other endeavours whatever, that have been undertaken for that purpose. Rom. iii. 24–26, by setting forth his only Son " to be a propitiation," he leaves no doubt upon the spirits of men that in themselves they could make no atonement; for " if righteousness were by the law, then were Christ dead in vain." To what purpose should he be made a propitiation, were not we ourselves weak and without strength to any such purpose? So the apostle argues, Rom. v. 6, when we had no power, then did he by death make an atonement; as verses 8, 9.

This, wisdom then, is also hid in Christ. Men may see by other helps, perhaps, far enough to fill them with dread and astonishment, as those in Isa. xxxiii. 14; but such a sight and view of it as may

---

[1] Vid. Diatr. de Just. Divin. cap. iii. vol. x.   [2] Ps. xl. 6, 7.

lead a soul to any comfortable settlement about it,—that only is discovered in this treasury of heaven, the Lord Jesus.

[2.] Our disability to answer the mind and will of God, in all or any of the *obedience* that he requireth, is in him only to be discovered. This, indeed, is a thing that many will not be acquainted with to this day. To teach a man that he cannot do what he ought to do, and for which he condemns himself if he do it not, is no easy task. Man rises up with all his power to plead against a conviction of impotency. Not to mention the proud[1] conceits and expressions of the philosophers, how many that would be called Christians do yet creep, by several degrees, in the persuasion of a power of fulfilling the law! And from whence, indeed, should men have this knowledge that we have not? *Nature* will not teach it,—that is[2] proud and conceited; and it is one part of its pride, weakness, and corruption, not to know it at all. The *law* will not teach it: for though that will show us *what we have done amiss*, yet it will not discover to us that *we could not do better;* yea, by requiring exact obedience of us, it takes for granted that such power is in us for that purpose: it takes no notice that we have *lost* it; nor doth it concern it so to do. This, then, also lies hid in the Lord Jesus. Rom. viii. 2–4, " The law of the Spirit of life in Christ Jesus hath made me free from the law of sin and death. For what the law could not do, in that it was weak through the flesh, God sending his own Son in the likeness of sinful flesh, and for sin, condemned sin in the flesh; that the righteousness of the law might be fulfilled in us." The law can bring forth no righteousness, no obedience; it is weak to any such purpose, by reason of the flesh, and that corruption that is come on us. These two things are done in Christ, and by him:—First, *Sin is condemned* as to its guilt, and we set free from that; the righteousness of the law by his obedience is fulfilled in us, who could never do it ourselves. And, secondly, That *obedience* which is required of us, *his Spirit works* it in us. So that that perfection of obedience which we have in him is imputed to us; and the sincerity that we have in obedience is from his Spirit bestowed on us. And this is the most excellent glass, wherein we see our impotency; for what need we his perfect obedience to be made ours, but that we have not, can not attain any? what need we his Spirit of life to quicken us, but that we are dead in trespasses and sins?

(3.) The *death* of sin;—sin dying in us now, in some measure, whilst we are alive. This is a third concernment of sin which it is our wisdom to be acquainted with; and it is hid only in Christ. There is a

---

[1] " Quia unusquisque sibi virtutem acquirit; nemo sapientum de ea gratias Deo egit."—Cicer.

[2] " Natura sic apparet vitiata, ut hoc majoris vitii sit non videre."—Aug.

twofold dying of sin:—as to the *exercise* of it in our mortal members; and as to the *root*, principle, and power of it in our souls. The first, indeed, may be learned in part out of Christ. Christless men may have sin dying in them, as to the outward exercise of it. Men's bodies may be disabled for the service of their lusts, or the practice of them may not consist with their interest. Sin is never *more alive*[1] than when it is thus dying. But there is a dying of it as to the root, the principle of it,—the daily decaying of the strength, power, and life of it; and this is to be had alone in Christ. Sin is a thing that of itself is not apt to die or to decay, but to get ground, and strength, and life, in the subject wherein it is, to eternity; prevent all its actual eruptions, yet its *original* enmity against God will still grow. In believers it is still dying and decaying, until it be utterly abolished. The opening of this treasury [mystery?] you have, Rom. vi. 3–6, etc. " Know ye not, that so many of us as were baptized into Jesus Christ were baptized into his death? Therefore we are buried with him by baptism into death, that like as Christ was raised from the dead by the glory of the Father, even so we also should walk in newness of life. For if we have been planted together in the likeness of his death, we shall be also in the likeness of his resurrection; knowing this, that our old man is crucified with him, that the body of sin might be destroyed, that henceforth we should not serve sin." This is the design of the apostle in the beginning of that chapter, not only to manifest whence is the principle and rise of our mortification and the death of sin, even from the death and blood of Christ; but also the manner of sin's continuance and dying in us, from the manner of Christ's dying for sin. He was crucified for us, and thereby sin was crucified in us; he died for us, and the body of sin is destroyed, that we should not serve sin; and as he was raised from the dead, that death should not have dominion over him, so also are we raised from sin, that it should not have dominion over us. This wisdom is hid in Christ only. Moses at his dying day had all his strength and vigour; so have sin and the law to all out of Jesus: at their dying day, sin is no way decayed. Now, next to the receiving of the righteousness prepared for us, to know this is the chiefest part of our wisdom. To be truly acquainted with the *principle* of the dying of sin, to feel virtue and power flowing from the cross of Christ to that purpose, to find sin crucified in us, as Christ was crucified for us,—this is wisdom indeed, that is in him alone.

(4.) There is a *glorious end* whereunto sin is appointed and ordained, and discovered in Christ, that others are unacquainted withal. Sin in its own nature tends merely to the dishonour of God, the debasement of his majesty, and the ruin of the creature in whom it is;

---

[1] See Treatise of Mortification. [Works, vol. vi.]

hell itself is but the filling of wretched creatures with the[1] fruit of their own devices.   The comminations and threats of God in the law do manifest one other end of it, even the demonstration of the vindictive justice of God, in measuring out unto it a meet[2] recompense of reward.   But here the law stays (and with it all other light) and discovers no other use or end of it at all.   In the Lord Jesus there is the *manifestation* of another and more glorious end; to wit, the praise of God's *glorious*[3] *grace* in the pardon and forgiveness of it;—God having taken order in Christ that that thing which tended merely to his dishonour should be managed to his infinite glory, and that which of all things he desireth to exalt,—even that he may be known and believed to be a[4] " God pardoning iniquity, transgression and sin."   To return, then, to this part of our demonstration:—

In the knowledge of ourselves, in reference to our eternal condition, doth much of our wisdom consist.   There is not any thing wherein, in this depraved condition of nature, we are more concerned than sin; without a knowledge of that, we know not ourselves.   " Fools make a mock of sin."   A true saving knowledge of sin is to be had only in the Lord Christ: in him may we see the desert of our iniquities, and their pollution, which could not be borne or expiated but by his blood; neither is there any wholesome view of these but in Christ.   In him and his cross is discovered our universal impotency, either of *atoning God's justice* or *living up to his will*.   The death of sin is procured by, and discovered in, the death of Christ; as also the manifestation of the riches of God's grace in the pardoning thereof. A real and experimental acquaintance, as to ourselves, with all which, is our wisdom; and it is that which is of more value than all the wisdom of the world.

2. *Righteousness* is a second thing whereof the Spirit of Christ convinces the world, and the main thing that it is our wisdom to be acquainted withal.   This all men are persuaded of, that God is a most righteous God; (that is a natural notion of God which Abraham insisted on, Gen. xviii. 25, " Shall not the Judge of all the earth do right?") they " know that this is the judgment of God, that they who commit such things are worthy of death," Rom. i. 32; that " it is a righteous thing with him to recompense tribulation unto offenders," 2 Thess. i. 6.   He is "a God of purer eyes than to behold evil," Hab. i. 13; and therefore, " the ungodly cannot stand in judgment," Ps. i. 5.   Hence the great inquiry of every one (who lies in any measure under the power of it), convinced of immortality and the judgment to come, is concerning the righteousness wherewith to appear in the presence of this righteous God.   This more or less they are solicitous about all their days; and so, as the apostle speaks, Heb.

---

[1] Prov. i. 31; Jer. xvii. 10.   [2] 2 Thess. i. 6.   [3] Eph. i. 6.   [4] Heb. viii. 6–13.

ii. 15, "through the fear of death they are all their lifetime subject to bondage,"—they are perplexed with fears about the issue of their righteousness, lest it should end in death and destruction.

(1.) Unto men set upon this inquiry, that which first and naturally presents itself, for their direction and assistance, assuredly promising them a righteousness that will abide the trial of God, provided they will follow its direction, is *the law.* The law hath many fair pleas to prevail with a soul to close with it for a righteousness before God. It was given out from God himself for that end and purpose; it contains the whole obedience that God requireth of any of the sons of men; it hath the promise of life annexed to it: "Do this, and live;" "The doers of the law are justified;" and, "If thou wilt enter into life, keep the commandments;"—yea, it is most certain that it must be wholly fulfilled, if we ever think to stand with boldness before God. This being some part of the plea of the law, there is no man that seeks after righteousness but doth, one time or another, attend to it, and attempt its direction. Many do it every day, who yet will not own that so they do. This, then, they set themselves about,—labouring to correct their lives, amend their ways, perform the duties required, and so follow after a righteousness according to the prescript of the law. And in this course do many men continue long with much perplexity;—sometimes hoping, oftener fearing; sometimes ready to *give quite over;* sometimes *vowing to continue* (their consciences being no way satisfied, nor righteousness in any measure attained) all their days. After they have wearied themselves perhaps for a long season, in the largeness of their ways, they come at length, with fear, trembling, and disappointment, to that conclusion of the apostle, "By the works of the law no flesh is justified;" and with dread cry that if God mark what is done amiss, there is no standing before him. That they have this issue, the apostle witnesseth, [1] Rom. ix. 31, 32, "Israel, who followed after the law of righteousness, hath not attained to the law of righteousness. Wherefore? Because they sought it not by faith, but as it were by the works of the law." It was not solely for want of endeavour in themselves that they were disappointed, for they earnestly followed after the law of righteousness; but from the nature of the thing itself,—it would not bear it. Righteousness was not to be obtained that way; "For," saith the apostle, "if they which are of the law be heirs, faith is made void, and the promise made of none effect; because the law worketh wrath," Rom. iv. 14, 15. The law itself is now such as that it cannot give life, Gal. iii. 21, "If there had been a law given which would have given life, verily righteousness should have been by the law." And he gives the reason in the next verse why it could not give life; be-

[1] Διώκων νόμον δικαιοσύνης εἰς νόμον δικαιοσύνης οὐκ ἔφθασε.

cause "the Scripture concludes all under sin;"—that is, it is very true, and the Scripture affirms it, that all men are sinners, and the law speaks not one word to sinners but death and destruction: therefore the apostle tells us plainly, that God himself found fault with this way of attaining righteousness, Heb. viii. 7, 8. [1]He complains of it; that is, he declares it insufficient for that end and purpose.

Now, there are two considerations that discover unto men the vanity and hopelessness of seeking righteousness in this path:—

[1.] That they have *already sinned:*[2] "For all have sinned, and come short of the glory of God," Rom. iii. 23. This they are sufficiently sensible of, that although they could for the time to come fulfil the whole law, yet there is a score, a reckoning, upon them already, that they know not how to answer for. Do they consult their guide, the [3]law itself, how they may be eased of the account that is past? it hath not one word of direction or consolation; but bids them prepare to *die.* The sentence is gone forth, and there is no escaping.

[2.] That if all *former debts* should be blotted out, yet they are no way able for the *future* to fulfil the law; they can as well move the earth with a finger, as answer the perfection thereof: and therefore, as I said, on this twofold account, they conclude that this labour is lost. [4]"By the works of the law shall no flesh be justified."

(2.) Wherefore, secondly, Being thus disappointed, by *the severity and inexorableness* of the law, men generally betake themselves to some other way, that may *satisfy* them as to those considerations which took them off from their former hopes; and this, for the most part, is by fixing themselves upon some ways of atonement to satisfy God, and helping out the rest with hopes of mercy. Not to insist on the ways of atonement and expiation which the Gentiles had pitched on; nor on the many ways and inventions—by works satisfactory of their own, supererogations of others, indulgences, and purgatory in the close—that the Papists have found out for this end and purpose; it is, I say, proper to all convinced persons, as above, to seek for a righteousness, partly by an endeavour to satisfy for what is past, and partly by hoping after general mercy. This the apostle calls a seeking for it "as it were by the works of the law," Rom. ix. 32; [5]not directly, " but as it were" by the works of the law, making up one thing with another. And he tells us what issue they have in this business, chap. x. 3, "Being ignorant of God's righteousness, and going about to establish their own righteousness, they have not submitted themselves unto the righteousness of God." They were by it enemies to the righteousness of God. The ground of this going about to establish their own righteousness was, that they were ignorant of the righteousness

---

[1] Μεμφόμενος.   [2] Πάντες ἥμαρτον, Rom. iii. 23, v. 12.
[3] Deut. xxvii. 26; Gal. iii. 10.   [4] Gal. iii. 11, 12.   [5] Ὡς ἐξ ἔργων νόμου.

of God. Had they known the righteousness of God, and what exact conformity to his will he requireth, they had never undertaken such a fruitless business as to have compassed it "as it were by the works of the law." Yet this many will stick on a long time. Something they do, something they hope for; some old faults they will buy off with new obedience. And this pacifies their consciences for a season; but when the Spirit comes to convince them of righteousness, neither will this hold. Wherefore,—

(3.) The matter comes at length to this issue,—they look upon themselves under this twofold qualification; as,—

[1.] *Sinners*, obnoxious to the law of God and the curse thereof; so that unless that be satisfied, that nothing from thence shall ever be laid to their charge, it is altogether in vain once to seek after an appearance in the presence of God.

[2.] As *creatures* made to a supernatural and eternal end; and therefore bound to answer the whole mind and will of God in the obedience required at their hands. Now, it being before discovered to them that both these are beyond the compass of their own endeavours, and the assistance which they have formerly rested on, if their eternal condition be of any concernment to them, their wisdom is, to find out a righteousness that may answer both these to the utmost.

Now, both these are to be had only in the Lord Christ, who is our righteousness. This wisdom, and all the treasures of it, are hid in him.

1st. He *expiates* former iniquities, he satisfies for sin, and procures remission of it. Rom. iii. 24, 25, "Being justified freely by his grace, through the redemption that is in Christ Jesus: whom God hath set forth to be a propitiation through faith in his blood, to declare his righteousness for the remission of sins that are past, through the forbearance of God." "All we like sheep," etc., Isa. liii. 6. "Through his blood we have redemption, the forgiveness of sins," Eph. i. 7. "God spared not his own Son, but delivered," etc., Rom. viii. 32. This, even this alone, is our righteousness; as to that first part of it which consists in the removal of the whole guilt of sin, whereby we are come short of the glory of God. On this account it is that we are assured that none shall ever lay any thing to our charge, or condemn us, Rom. viii. 33, 34,—there being "no condemnation to them that are in Christ Jesus," verse 1. We are purged by the sacrifice of Christ, so as to have "no more conscience of sin," Heb. x. 2; that is, troubles in conscience about it. This wisdom is hid only in the Lord Jesus; in him alone is there an atonement discovered: and give me the wisdom which shall cut all scores concerning sin, and let the world take what remains. But,—

2dly. There is yet something more *required;* it is not enough that

we are not *guilty*, we must also be *actually righteous;*—not only all
sin is to be answered for, but all righteousness is to be fulfilled. By
taking away the guilt of sin, we are as persons innocent; but something more is required to make us to be considered as persons obedient. I know nothing to teach me that an innocent person shall
go to heaven, be rewarded, if he be no more but so. Adam was
innocent at his first creation, but he was to " do this," to " keep the
commandments," before he entered into " life:" he had no title to life
by innocency. This, then, moreover, is required, that the whole law
be fulfilled, and all the obedience performed that God requires at our
hands. This is the soul's second inquiry; and it finds a resolution
only in the Lord Christ: " For if, when we were enemies, we were
reconciled to God by the death of his Son, much more, being reconciled, we shall be saved by his life," Rom v. 10. His death reconciled us; then are we saved by his life. The actual obedience which
he yielded to the whole law of God, is that righteousness whereby
we are saved; if so be we are found in him, not having on our own
righteousness which is of the law, but the righteousness which is of
God by faith, Phil. iii. 9. This I shall have occasion to handle more
at large hereafter.

   To return, then: It is not, I suppose, any difficult task to persuade
men, convinced of immortality and judgment to come, that the main
of their wisdom lies in this, even to find out such a righteousness as
will accompany them for ever, and abide the severe trial of God himself. Now, all the wisdom of the world is but folly, as to the discovery of this thing. The utmost that man's wisdom can do, is but
to find out most wretched, burdensome, and vexatious ways of perishing eternally. All the treasures of this wisdom are hid in Christ; he
" of God is made unto us wisdom and righteousness," 1 Cor. i. 30.

   3. Come we to the last thing, which I shall but touch upon; and that
is *judgment*. The true wisdom of this also is hid in the Lord Christ; I
mean, in particular, that judgment that is for to come: so at present I
take the word in that place, [John xvi. 8.] Of what concernment this
is to us to know, I shall not speak;—it is that whose [1]influence upon
the sons of men is the principle of their discriminating themselves
from the beasts that perish. Neither shall I insist on the [2]obscure
intimations of it which are given by the present proceedings of Providence in governing the world; nor that greater light of it which
shines in the threats and promises of the law. The wisdom of it is

---

   [1] " Bene et composìte C. Cæsar. . . . . . de vita et morte disseruit, falsa, credo,
existimans, ea quæ de inferis memorantur; diverso itinere malos a bonis loca tetra,
inculta, fœda atque formidolosa habere."—Cato. apud. Sallust. Bell. Catil. lii.
   Ἀλλ' ἔστι καὶ τῷ ὄντι τὸ ἀνεβιώσκεσθαι, καὶ ἐκ τῶν τεθνεώτων τοὺς ζῶντας γίγνεσθαι, καὶ
τὰς τῶν τεθνεώτων ψυχὰς εἶναι· καὶ ταῖς μὲν ἀγαθαῖς ἄμεινον εἶναι, ταῖς δὲ κακαῖς, κάκιον.—
Plat. in Phæd. 17.
   [2] " Devenêre locos lætos, et amœna vireta
      Fortunatorum nemorum, sedesque beatas," etc.—Virg., Æn. vi. 638.

in two regards hid in the Lord Jesus:—(1.) As to the *truth* of it. (2.) As to the *manner* of it:—

(1.) For the *truth* of it; and so in and by him it is confirmed, and that two ways:—[1.] By his *death.* [2.] By his *resurrection:*—

[1.] By his *death.* God, in the death of Christ, punishing and condemning sin in the flesh of his own Son, in the sight of men, angels, and devils, hath given an abundant assurance of a righteous and universal judgment to come; wherefore, or upon what account imaginable, could he be induced to lay such a load on him, but that he will certainly reckon one day with the sons of men for all their works, ways, and walkings before him. *The death of Christ is a most solemn exemplar of the last judgment.* Those who own him to be the Son of God, will not deny a judgment to come.

[2.] By his *resurrection.* Acts xvii. 31, Πίστιν παρασχὼν πᾶσιν,— he hath given faith and assurance of this thing to all, by raising Christ from the dead, having appointed him to be the judge of all; in whom and by whom he will judge the world in righteousness. And then,—

(2.) And, lastly, for the *manner* of it: that it shall be by him who hath loved us, and given himself for us,—who is himself the righteousness that he requires at our hands; and on the other side, by him who hath been, in his *person, grace, ways, worship, servants,* reviled, despised, contemned by the men of the world;—which holds out unspeakable consolation on the one hand, and terror on the other: so that the wisdom of this also is hid in Christ.

And this is the second part of our first demonstration. Thus the knowledge of ourselves, in reference to our supernatural end, is no small portion of our wisdom. The things of the greatest concernment hereunto are, sin, righteousness, and judgment; the wisdom of all which is alone hid in the Lord Jesus: which was to be proved.

III. The THIRD part of our wisdom is to walk with God. Now, that one may walk with another, six[1] things are required:—1. Agreement. 2. Acquaintance. 3. A way. 4. Strength. 5. Boldness. 6. An aiming at the same end. All these, with the wisdom of them, are hid in the Lord Jesus.

1. *Agreement.* The prophet tells us that two cannot walk together unless they be agreed, Amos iii. 3. Until agreement be made, there is no communion, no walking together. God and man by nature (or whilst man is in the state of nature) are at the greatest enmity. He declares nothing to us but wrath, Rom. i. 18; whence we are said to be children of it; that is, born obnoxious to it, Eph. ii. 3: and whilst we remain in that condition, "the wrath of God abideth on us," John

---

[1] In the previous editions it is stated that *five* things are required to walk with God, and then *five* things are immediately enumerated. It will be found, however, that, in the subsequent illustration, *six* particulars are specified. A particular, the *way,* (see p. 109,) had been omitted in the division stated above. We have, therefore, altered it in accordance with Owen's real treatment of his subject.—ED.

iii. 36.   All the discovery that God makes of himself unto us is, that he is inexpressibly provoked; and therefore preparing wrath against the day of wrath, and the revelation of his righteous judgment. The day of his and sinners' meeting, is called "The day of wrath," Rom. ii. 5, 6.   Neither do we come short in our enmity against him; yea, we first began it, and we continue longest in it.   To express this enmity, the apostle tells us, that our very minds, the best part of us, are "enmity against God," Rom. viii. 7, 8; and that we neither are, nor will, nor can be, subject to him; our enmity manifesting itself by universal rebellion against him: whatever we do that seems otherwise, is but hypocrisy or flattery; yea, it is a part of this enmity to lessen it.   In this state the wisdom of walking with God must needs be most remote from the soul.   He is [1] "light, and in him is no darkness at all;" we are darkness, and in us there is no light at all.   He is life, a "living God;" we are dead, dead sinners,—dead in trespasses and sin.   He is "holiness," and glorious in it; we wholly defiled,—an abominable thing.   He is "love;" we full of hatred,—hating and being hated.   Surely this is no foundation for agreement, or, upon that, of. walking together: nothing can be more remote than this frame from such a condition.   The foundation, then, of this, I say, is laid in Christ, hid in Christ.   "He," saith the apostle, "is our peace; he hath made peace" for us, Eph. ii. 14, 15.   He slew the enmity in his own body on the cross, verse 16.

(1.) He takes out of the way the *cause of the enmity* that was between God and us,—sin and the curse of the law.   He makes an end of sin, and that by making atonement for iniquity, Dan. ix. 24; and he blotteth out the hand-writing of ordinances, Col. ii. 14, redeeming us from the curse, by "being made a curse for us," Gal. iii. 13.

(2.) He destroys him who would *continue the enmity*, and make the breach wider, Heb. ii. 14, "Through death he destroyed him that had the power of death, that is, the devil;" and, Col. ii 15, "Spoiled principalities and powers."

(3.) He made "*reconciliation* for the sins of the people," Heb. ii. 17; he made by his blood an atonement with God, to turn away that wrath which was due to us, so making peace.   Hereupon God is said to be "in Christ, reconciling the world unto himself," 2 Cor. v. 19;—being reconciled himself, verse 18, he lays down the enmity on his part, and proceeds to what remains,—to slay the enmity on our part, that we also may be reconciled.   And this also,—

(4.) He doth; for, Rom. v. 11, "By our Lord Jesus Christ we do receive the atonement," accept of the peace made and tendered, laying down our enmity to God; and so confirming an agreement betwixt us in his blood.   So that "through him we have an access

[1] 1 John i. 5, Σκοτία ἐν αὐτῷ οὐκ ἔστιν οὐδεμία.   John i. 5; Eph. v. 8, ii. 1; Exod. xv. 11; 1 John iv. 8; Tit. iii. 3.

unto the Father," Eph. ii. 18. Now, the whole wisdom of this agreement, without which there is no walking with God, is hid in Christ; out of him God on his part is a consuming fire,—we are as stubble fully dry, yet setting ourselves in battle array against that fire: if we are brought together we are consumed. All our approachings to him out of Christ are but to our detriment; in his blood alone have we this agreement. And let not any of us once suppose that we have taken any step in the paths of God with him, that any one duty is accepted, that all is not lost as to eternity, if we have not done it upon the account hereof.

2. There is required *acquaintance*, also, to walking together. Two may *meet together* in the same way, and have no quarrel between them, no enmity; but if they are mere strangers one to another, they *pass by* without the least communion together. It doth not suffice that the enmity betwixt God and us be taken away; we must also have acquaintance given us with him. Our not knowing of him is a great cause and a great part of our enmity. Our understandings are " darkened," and we are " alienated from the life of God," etc., Eph. iv. 18. This also, then, must be added, if we ever come to walk with God, which is our wisdom. And this also is hid in the Lord Christ, and comes forth from him. It is true there are sundry other means, as his word and his works, that God hath given the sons of men, to make a discovery of himself unto them, and to give them some acquaintance with him, that, as the apostle speaks, Acts xvii. 27, " they should seek the Lord, if haply they might find him;" but yet, as that knowledge of God which we have by his works is but very weak and imperfect, so that which we have by the word, the letter of it, by reason of our blindness, is not saving to us if we have no other help; for though that be light as the sun in the firmament, yet if we have no eyes in our heads, what can it avail us?—no saving acquaintance with him, that may direct us to walk with him, can be obtained. This also is hid in the Lord Jesus, and comes forth from him, 1 John v. 20, " He hath given us an understanding, that we should know him that is true;"—all other light whatever without his giving us an understanding, will not do it. He is the true Light, which lighteth every one that is enlightened, John i. 9. He opens our understandings that we may understand the Scriptures, Luke xxiv. 45;—none hath known God at any time, " but he hath revealed him," John i. 18. God dwells in that " light which no man can approach unto," 1 Tim. vi. 16. None hath ever had any such acquaintance with him as to be said to have seen him, but by the revelation of Jesus Christ. Hence he tells the Pharisees, that notwithstanding all their great knowledge which they pretended, indeed they had " neither heard the voice of God at any time, nor seen his shape," John v. 37. They had no manner of spiritual acquaintance with

God, but he was unto them as a man whom they had never heard nor seen.   There is no acquaintance with God, as love, and full of kindness, patience, grace, and pardoning mercy (on which knowledge of him alone we can walk with him), but only in Christ; but of this fully before.   This, then, also is hid in him.

3. There must, moreover, be a *way* wherein we must walk with God.   God did at the beginning assign us a path to walk in with him, even the path of innocency and exact holiness, in a covenant of works.   This path, by sin, is so filled with thorns and briers, so stopped up by curses and wrath, that no flesh living can take one step in that path; a *new way* for us to walk in must be found out, if ever we think to hold communion with God.   And this also lies upon the former account.   It is hid in Christ.   All the world cannot, but *by and in him*, discover a path that a man may walk one step with God in.   And therefore the Holy Ghost tells us that Christ hath consecrated, dedicated, and set apart for that purpose, "a new and living way" into the holiest of all, Heb. x. 20; a new one, for the first, old one was useless; a living one, for the other is dead: therefore, saith he, verse 22, "Let us draw near;" having a way to walk in, let us draw near.   And this way that he hath prepared is no other but himself, John xiv. 6.   In answer to them who would go to the Father, and hold communion with him, he tells them, "I am the way; and no man cometh to the Father but by me."   He is *the medium of all communication* between God and us.   In him we meet, in him we walk.   All influences of love, kindness, mercy, from God to us, are through him; all our returns of love, delight, faith, obedience unto God, are all through him;—he being that "one way" God so often promiseth his people: and it is a glorious way, Isa. xxxv. 8,—a high way, a way of holiness, a way that none can err in that once enter it; which is farther set out, Isa. xlii. 16.   All other ways, all paths but this, go down to the chambers of death; they all lead to walk contrary to God.

4. But suppose all this,—that agreement be made, acquaintance given, and a way provided; yet if we have no *strength* to walk in that way, what will all this avail us?   This also, then, must be added; of ourselves we are of no strength, Rom. v. 6,—poor weaklings, not able to go a step in the ways of God.   When we are set in the way, either we throw ourselves down, or temptations cast us down, and we make no progress: and the Lord Jesus tells us plainly, that "without him we can do nothing," John xv. 5; not any thing at all that shall have the least acceptation with God.   Neither can all the creatures in heaven and earth yield us the least assistance.   Men's contending to do it in their own power, comes to nothing.   This part of this wisdom also is hid in Christ.   All strength to walk with God is from him.   "I can do all things through Christ, which strengtheneth me,"

saith St. Paul, Phil. iv. 13, who denies that of ourselves we have any sufficiency, 2 Cor. iii. 5. We that can do nothing in ourselves, we are such weaklings, can do all things in Jesus Christ, as giants; and therefore in him we are, against all oppositions in our way, "more than conquerors," Rom. viii. 37; and that because "from his fulness we receive grace for grace," John i. 16. From him have we the Spirit of life and power, whereby he bears, as on eagles' wings, swiftly, safely, in the paths of walking with God. Any step that is taken in any way, by strength that is not immediately from Christ, is one step towards hell. He first takes us by the arm and teaches us to go, until he leads us on to perfection. He hath milk and strong meat to feed us; he strengthens us with all might, and is with us in our running the race that is set before us. But yet,—

5. Whence should we take this *confidence* as to walk with God; even our God, who is "a consuming fire?" Heb. xii. 29. Was there not such a dread upon his people of old, that it was taken for granted among them that if they saw God at any time, it was not to be endured,—they must *die?* Can any, but with extreme horror, think of that dreadful appearance that he made unto them of old upon mount Sinai; until Moses himself, who was their mediator, said, "I exceedingly fear and quake?" Heb. xii. 21, and all the people said, "Let not God speak with us, lest we die?" Exod. xx. 19. Nay, though men have apprehensions of the goodness and kindness of God, yet upon any discovery of his glory, how do they tremble, and are filled with dread and astonishment! Hath it not been so with the "choicest of his saints?" Hab. iii. 16; Isa. vi. 5; Job xlii. 5, 6. Whence, then, should we take to ourselves this boldness, to walk with God? This the apostle will inform us in Heb. x. 19; it is "by the blood of Jesus:" so Eph. iii. 12, "In him we have boldness, and access with confidence;"—not standing afar off, like the people at the giving of the law, but drawing nigh to God with boldness; and that upon this account:—The dread and terror of God entered by sin; Adam had not the least thought of hiding himself until he had sinned. The *guilt* of sin being on the conscience, and this being *a common notion* left in the hearts of all, that God is a most righteous revenger thereof; this fills men with dread and horror at an apprehension of his presence, fearing that he is come to call their sins to remembrance. Now, the Lord Jesus, by the sacrifice and the atonement that he hath made, hath taken away this conscience of sin; that is, a dread of revenge from God upon the account of the guilt thereof. He hath removed the slaying sword of the law, and on that account gives us great boldness with God; discovering him unto us now, no longer as a revenging Judge, but as a tender, merciful, and reconciled Father. Moreover, whereas there is on us by nature a spirit of bondage, filling us with innumerable tormenting fears, he takes it away, and gives us

" the Spirit of adoption, whereby we cry Abba, Father," and behave ourselves with confidence and gracious boldness, as children: for "where the Spirit of the Lord is, there is liberty," 2 Cor. iii. 17; that is, a freedom from all that dread and terror which the administration of the law brought with it.   Now, as there is no sin that God will more severely revenge than any boldness that man takes with him out of Christ; so there is no grace more acceptable to him than that boldness which he is pleased to afford us in the blood of Jesus.   There is, then,—

6. But one thing more to add; and that is, that two cannot walk together unless they have the *same design* in hand, and aim at the same *end*.   This also, in a word, is given us in the Lord Jesus.   The end of God is the advancement of his own glory; none can aim at this end, but only in the Lord Jesus.   The sum of all is, that the whole wisdom of our walking with God is hid in Christ, and from him only to be obtained; as hath been manifest by an enumeration of particulars.

And so have I brought my first demonstration of what I intended unto a close, and manifested that all true wisdom and knowledge is laid up in, and laid out by, the Lord Jesus; and this by an induction of the chief particular heads of those things wherein confessedly our wisdom doth consist.   I have but one more to add, and therein I shall be brief.

SECONDLY,[1] then, I say this truth will be farther manifested by the consideration of the *insufficiency* and vanity of any thing else that may lay claim or pretend to a title to wisdom.

There be two things in the world that do pass under this account:—1. The one is *learning* or *literature;* skill and knowledge of arts, sciences, tongues, with the knowledge of the things that are past. 2. *Prudence and skill* for the management of ourselves in reference to others, in civil affairs, for public good; which is much the fairest flower within the border of nature's garden.   Now, concerning both these, I shall briefly evince,—(1.) That they are utterly *insufficient* for the compassing and obtaining of those *particular ends* whereunto they are designed.   (2.) That both of them *in conjunction*, with their utmost improvement, cannot reach the true general end of wisdom.   Both which considerations will set the crown, in the issue, upon the head of Jesus Christ:—

1. Begin we with the first of these, and that as to the first particular.   *Learning* itself, if it were all in one man, is not able to compass the particular end whereto it is designed; which writes " vanity and vexation" upon the forehead thereof.

The *particular end of literature* (though not observed by many,

! The division of which this indicates the second part, is implied, but not expressed, in p. 79, and the first paragraph of p. 80.—ED.

men's eyes being fixed on false ends, which compels them in their
progress " aberrare a scopo") is none other but to remove some part
of that curse which is come upon us by sin.   Learning is the product
of the soul's struggling with the curse for sin.   Adam, at his first
creation, was completely furnished with all that *knowledge* (excepting
only things not then in being, neither in themselves nor in any nátural
causes, as that which we now call *tongues*, and those things that are
the subject of *story*), as far as it lies in a needful tendency to the
utmost end of man, which we now press after.   There was no strait-
ness, much less darkness, upon his understanding, that should make
him sweat for a way to improve, and make out those general conceptions of things which he had.   For his knowledge of nature, it is
manifest, from his imposition of suitable names on all the creatures
(the particular reasons of the most of which to us are lost); wherein,
from the approbation given of his nomination of things in the Scripture, and the significancy of what yet remains evident, it is most
apparent it was done upon a clear acquaintance with their natures.
Hence Plato could observe,[1] that he was most wise that first imposed
names on things; yea, had more than human wisdom.   Were the
wisest man living, yea, a general collection of all the wise men in the
world, to make an experiment of their skill and learning, in giving
names to all living creatures, suitable to their natures and expressive
of their qualities, they would quickly perceive the loss they have incurred.   Adam was made *perfect*, for the whole end of ruling the
creatures and living to God, for which he was made; which, without
the knowledge of the nature of the one and the will of the other, he
could not be.   All this being lost by sin, a multiplication of tongues
also being brought in, as a curse for an after rebellion,[2] the whole
design of learning is but to *disentangle the soul from this issue of
sin.*   Ignorance, darkness, and blindness, is come upon the understanding; acquaintance with the works of God, spiritual and natural,
is lost; strangeness of communication is given, by multiplication of
tongues; tumultuating of passions and affections, with innumerable
darkening prejudices, are also come upon us.   To remove and take
this away—to disentangle the mind in its reasonings, to recover an
acquaintance with the works of God, to subduct the soul from under
the effects of the curse of division of tongues—is the aim and tendence
of literature.   This is the "aliquid quo tendit;" and he that hath
any other aim in it, " Passim sequitur corvum testâque lutoque."[3]
Now, not to insist upon that vanity and vexation of spirit, with the

---

[1] Οἶμαι μὲν ἐγὼ τὸν ἀληθέστατον λόγον περὶ τούτων εἶναι, ᾧ Σώκρατες, μείζω τινὰ δύναμιν
εἶναι ἢ ἀνθρωπείαν, τὴν θεμένην τὰ πρῶτα ὀνόματα τοῖς πράγμασιν.—Plato in Cratylo.

[2] Gen. xi. 3, etc.

[3] These words are borrowed from Pers., Sat. iii. 60, 61, in allusion to the fruitless pursuit of any object by the use of inadequate means.—ED.

innumerable evils wherewith this enterprise is attended, this is that I only say, it is in itself no way sufficient for the attainment of its end, which writes vanity upon its forehead with characters not to be obliterated. To this purpose I desire to observe these two things:—

(1.) That the *knowledge* aimed at to be recovered was given unto man in order to his *walking* with God, unto *that supernatural end* whereunto he was appointed. For after he was furnished with all his endowments, the law of life and death was given to him, that he might know wherefore he received them. Therefore, knowledge in him was spiritualized and sanctified: even that knowledge which he had by nature, in respect of its principle and end, was *spiritual*.

(2.) That the *loss* of it is part of that *curse* which was inflicted on us for sin. Whatever we come short in of the state of the first man in innocency, whether in loss of good or addition of evil, it is all of the curse for sin. Besides, that blindness, ignorance, darkness, deadness, which is everywhere ascribed to us in the state of nature, doth fully comprise that also whereof we speak.

On these two considerations it is most apparent that learning can no way of itself attain the end it aimeth at. For,—

[1.] That light which by it is discovered (which, the Lord knows, is very little, *weak, obscure, imperfect, uncertain, conjectural,* for a great part only enabling men to quarrel with and oppose one another, to the reproach of reason, yet I say, that which is attained by it) is not in the least measure by it *spiritualized,* or brought into that order of living to God, and with God, wherein at first it lay. This is wholly beyond its reach. As to this end, the apostle assures us that the utmost issue that men come to, is darkness and folly, Rom. i. 21, 22. Who knows not the profound inquiries, the subtile disputations, the acute reasonings, the admirable discoveries of Socrates, Plato, and Aristotle, and others? What, as to the purpose in hand, did they attain by all their studies and endeavours? Ἐμωράνθησαν, says the apostle,—" They became fools." He that, by general consent, bears the *crown* of reputation for wisdom from them all, with whom to have lived was counted an inestimable happiness,[1] died like a fool, sacrificing a cock to Æsculapius. And another [apostle assures us], that Jesus Christ alone is " the true Light," that lighteth us, John i. 9. And there is not any that hath any true light, but what is immediately from him. After all the learning of men, if they have nothing else, they are still natural men, and perceive not the things of God. Their light is still but darkness; and how great is that darkness! It is the Lord Jesus alone who is anointed to open the eyes of the blind. Men cannot spiritualize a notion, nor lay it in any order to the glori-

---

[1] Εἰ δέ τις τῶν ἀρετῆς ἐφιεμένων ὠφιλιμωτέρῳ τινὶ Σωκράτους συνεγίνετο, ἐκεῖνον ἐγὼ τὸν ἄνδρα ἀξιομακαριστότατον νομίζω.—Xenoph. apol. pro Socrat. ad finem.

fying of God. After all their endeavours, they are still blind and
dark, yea, darkness itself, knowing nothing as they should. I know
how the men of these attainments are apt to say, " Are we blind
also?" with great contempt of others; but God hath blasted all their
pride:[1] " Where," saith he, " is the wise? where is the scribe," etc.,
1 Cor i. 20. I shall not add what Paul hath farther cautioned us,
to the seeming condemning of philosophy as being fitted to make
spoil of souls; nor what [2] Tertullian with some other of the ancients
have spoken of it; being very confident that it was the *abuse*, and not
the true *use* and advantage of it, that they opposed. But,—

[2.] The *darkness and ignorance* that it strives to remove, being
come upon us as a curse, it is not in the least measure, as it is a
curse, able to remove it or take it away. He that hath attained to
the greatest height of literature, yet if he hath nothing else,—if he
have not Christ,—is as much under the curse of blindness, ignorance,
stupidity, dulness, as the poorest, silliest soul in the world. The curse
is only removed in him who was made a curse for us. Every thing
that is penal is taken away only by him on whom all our sins did
meet in a way of punishment; yea, upon this account. The *more
abilities* the mind is furnished withal, the more it *closes with the
curse*, and strengthens itself to act its enmity against God. All that
it receives doth but help it to set up high thoughts and imaginations against the Lord Christ. So that this knowledge comes short
of what in particular it is designed unto; and therefore cannot be that
solid wisdom we are inquiring after.

There be sundry other things whereby it were easy to blur the
countenance of this wisdom; and, from its intricacy, difficulty, uncertainty, unsatisfactoriness,—betraying its followers into that which they

---

[1] " O Sapientia superba irridens Christum crucifixum !"—August. Expos. in
Joh. Trac. 2, de cap. 1.

[2] " Hæreses a philosophiâ subornantur. Inde Æones, et formæ nescio quæ,
trinitas hominis apud Valentinum, Platonicus fuerat; inde Marcionis Deus melior
de tranquillitate, a Stoicis venerat. Et ut anima interire dicatur, ab Epicureis
observatur, et ut carnis restitutio negetur, de unâ omnium philosophorum scholâ
sumitur: . . . . . . Quid ergo Athenis et Hierosolymis? quid Academiæ et Ecclesiæ? quid hæreticis et Christianis? Nostra institutio de porticu Salomonis est.
Nobis curiositate opus non est post Jesum Christum; nec inquisitione post evan-
gelium. Cum credimus, nihil desideramus ultra credere. Hoc enim priùs credimus, non esse quod ultra credere debeamus."—Tertul. de Præscript. ad Hæret.
[cap. vii.]

—— Ἐπειδήπερ ἱκανῶς ἐκ τῶν προειρημένων τὰ τῶν φιλοσόφων ὑμῶν ἐλήλιγκται πράγματα
πάσης ἀγνοίας καὶ ἀπάτης φανέντα πλήρη. κ. τ. λ.—Just. Mart. ad Græc. Cohort. [c. xi.]

Μοῦνον ἐμοὶ φίλον ἔσκε λόγων κλέος, οὓς συνάγειραν
Ἀντολίη τι, δύσις τι, καὶ Ἑλλάδος εὖχος Αθῆναι,
Τοῖς ἔπι πολλ' ἐμόγησα πολὺν χρόνον, ἀλλὰ καὶ αὐτοὺς
Πρηνίας ἐν δαπέδῳ Χριστοῦ προπάροιθεν ἔθηκα,
Εἴξαντας μεγάλοιο Θεοῦ λόγῳ ὅς ῥα καλύπτει
Πάντα φρενὸς βροτέης στρεπτὸν πολυειδία μῦθον.——

Greg. Naz. Car. i. de Reb. Suis.

most profess to avoid, blindness and folly,—to write upon it "vanity and vexation of spirit." I hope I shall not need to add any thing to clear myself for not giving a due esteem and respect unto literature, my intendment being only to cast it down at the feet of Jesus Christ, and to set the crown upon his head.

2. Neither can the second part of the choicest wisdom out of Christ attain the peculiar end whereunto it is appointed; and that is *prudence in the management of civil affairs,*—than which no perishing thing is more glorious,—nothing more useful for the common good of human kind. Now, the immediate end of this prudence is to keep *the rational world* in bounds and order, to draw circles about the sons of men, and to keep them from passing their allotted bounds and limits, to the mutual disturbance and destruction of each other. All manner of trouble and disturbance ariseth from irregularity: one man breaking in upon the rights, usages, interests, relations of another, sets this world at variance. The sum and aim of all wisdom below is, to cause all things to move in their proper sphere, whereby it would be impossible there should be any more interfering than is in the celestial orbs, notwithstanding all their divers and various motions: to keep all to their own allotments, within the compass of the lines that are fallen unto them, is the special end of this wisdom.

Now, it will be a very easy task, to demonstrate that all civil prudence whatever[1] (besides the vexation of its attainment, and loss being attained) is no way able to compass this end. The present condition of affairs throughout the world, as also that of former ages, will abundantly testify it; but I shall farther discover the vanity of it for this end in some few observations. And the

(1.) First is, That, through the *righteous judgment* of God lopping off the top flowers of the pride of men, it frequently comes to pass that those who are furnished with the greatest abilities of this kind do lay them out to a direct contrary end unto that which is their natural tendency and aim. From whom, for the most part, are all the commotions in the world,—the breaking up of bounds, setting the whole frame of nature on fire? is it not from such men as these? Were not men so wise, the world, perhaps, would be more quiet, when the end of wisdom is to keep it in quietness. This seems to be a curse that God hath spread upon the wisdom of the world, in the most in whom it is, that it shall be employed in *direct opposition* to its proper end.

(2.) That God hath made this a *constant path* towards the advancement of his own glory, even to leaven the wisdom and the counsels of the wisest of the sons of men with folly and madness,

---

[1] Ὦ γῆρας ὡς ἐπαχθὲς ἀνθρώποισιν εἶ, καὶ πανταχῆ λυπηρόν, οὐ καθ᾽ ἓν μόνον, ἐν ᾧ γὰρ οὐδὲν δυνάμεθ᾽ οὐδ᾽ ἰσχύομεν, σὺ τηνικαῦθ᾽ ἡμᾶς διδάσκεις εὖ φρονεῖν.—Excerp. ex Nicostrat.

that they shall, in the depth of their policy, [1] advise things for the compassing of the ends they do propose as unsuitable as any thing that could proceed out of the mouth of a child or a fool, and as directly tending to their own disappointment and ruin as any thing that could be invented against them. " He destroys the wisdom of the wise, and brings to nothing the understanding of the prudent," 1 Cor. i. 19. This he largely describes, Isa. xix. 11–14. Drunkenness and staggering is the issue of all their wisdom; and that upon this account,—the Lord gives them the spirit of giddiness. So also Job v. 12–14. They meet with darkness in the day-time:[2] when all things seem clear about them, and a man would wonder how men should miss their way, then will God make it darkness to such as these. So Ps. xxxiii. 10. Hence God, as it were, sets them at work, and undertakes their disappointment, Isa. viii. 9, 10, " Go about your counsels," saith the Lord, " and I will take order that it shall come to nought." And, Ps. ii. 3, 4, when men are deep at their plots and contrivances, God is said to have them in derision, to laugh them to scorn, seeing the poor worms industriously working out their own ruin. Never was this made more clear than in the days wherein we live. Scarcely have any *wise* men been brought to destruction, but it hath evidently been through their own *folly;* neither hath the wisest counsel of most been one jot better than madness.

(3.) That this wisdom, which should tend to *universal quietness,* hath almost constantly given universal disquietness unto themselves in whom it hath been most eminent. " In much wisdom is much grief," Eccles. i. 18. And in the issue, some of them have made away with themselves, as Ahithophel; and the most of them have been violently despatched by others. There is, indeed, no end of the folly of this wisdom.[3] The great men of the world carry away the reputation of it;—really it is found in few of them. They are, for the most part, common events, whereunto they contribute not the least mite, which are ascribed to their care, vigilancy, and foresight. Mean men, that have learned to adore what is above them, reverence the meetings and conferences of those who are in greatness and esteem. Their weakness and folly is little known. Where this wisdom hath been most eminent, it hath dwelt so close upon the borders of atheism, been attended with such falseness and injustice, that it hath made its possessors wicked and infamous.

---

[1] " Isthuc est sapere, non quod ante pedes modò est,
    Videre; sed etiam illa quæ futura sunt,
    Prospicere."—Teren. Adelph. 3, 3, 33.
[2] Isa. xxix. 14, xlvii. 10; Jer. xlix. 7; Obad. 8.
[3] " Prudens futuri temporis exitum
    Caliginosa nocte premit Deus :
      Ridetque, si mortalis ultra
        Fas trepidat."—Horat., Od. iii. 29, 29.

I shall not need to give any more instances to manifest the insufficiency of this wisdom for the attaining of its own peculiar and
immediate end.   This is the vanity of any thing whatever,—that it
comes short of the mark it is directed unto.   It is far, then, from
being true and solid wisdom, seeing on the forehead thereof you may
read " Disappointment."

And this is the first reason why true wisdom cannot consist in
either of these,—because they come short even of the particular and
immediate ends they aim at.   But,—

Secondly, *Both these in conjunction*, with their utmost improvement, are not able to reach the true general end of wisdom.   This
assertion also falleth under an easy demonstration, and it were a
facile thing to discover their disability and unsuitableness for the
true end of wisdom; but it is so professedly done by him who had
the largest portion of both of any of the sons of men (Solomon in his
Preacher), that I shall not any farther insist upon it.

To draw, then, unto a close:—if true and *solid wisdom* is not in the
least to be found amongst these, if the *pearl* be not hid in this field, if
these two are but vanity and disappointment, it cannot but be to no
purpose to seek for it in any thing else below,—these being amongst
them incomparably the most excellent; and therefore, with one accord,
let us set the crown of this wisdom on the head of the Lord Jesus.

Let the reader, then, in a few words, take a view of the *tendency*
of this whole digression.   To draw our hearts to the more cheerful
entertainment of and delight in the Lord Jesus, is the aim thereof.
If all wisdom be laid up in him, and by an interest in him only to
be attained,—if all things beside him and without him that lay claim
thereto are folly and vanity,—let them that would be wise learn where
to repose their souls.

CHAPTER IV.

Of communion with Christ in a conjugal relation in respect of consequential affections—His delight in his saints first insisted on, Isa. lxii. 5 ; Cant. iii. 11 ;
Prov. viii. 21—Instance of Christ's delight in believers—He reveals his whole
heart to them, John xv. 14, 15 ; himself, 1 John xiv. 21 ; his kingdom ;
enables them to communicate their mind to him, giving them assistance, a
way, boldness, Rom. viii. 26, 27—The saints delight in Christ ; this manifested Cant. ii. 7, viii. 6—Cant. iii. 1-5, opened—Their delight in his servants
and ordinances of worship for his sake.

[1]THE communion begun, as before declared, between Christ and
the soul, is in the next place carried on by suitable *consequential*

------
[1] The division to which reference is here made will be found on page 56.   The
figure [2.] should have been inserted at the head of this chapter, to correspond

affections,—affections suiting such a relation. Christ having given himself to the soul, loves the soul; and the soul having given itself unto Christ, loveth him also. Christ loves his own, yea, " loves them to the end," John xiii. 1; and the saints they love Christ, they " love the Lord Jesus Christ in sincerity," Eph. vi. 24.

Now the love of Christ, wherewith he follows his saints, consists in these four things:—I. Delight. II. Valuation. III. Pity, or compassion. IV. Bounty. The love, also, of the saints unto Christ may be referred to these four heads:—Delight; Valuation; Chastity; Duty.

Two of these are of the *same kind,* and two *distinct;* as is required in this relation, wherein all things stand not on equal terms.

I. The first thing on the part of Christ is *delight.* Delight is the flowing of love and joy,—the[1] rest and complacence of the mind in a suitable, desirable good enjoyed. Now, Christ delights exceedingly in his saints: " As the bridegroom rejoiceth over the bride, so shall thy God rejoice over thee," Isa. lxii. 5. Hence he calleth the day of his espousals, the day of the " gladness of his heart," Cant. iii. 11. It is known that usually this is the most *unmixed* delight that the sons of men are in their pilgrimage made partakers of. The delight of the bridegroom in the day of his espousals is the height of what an expression of delight can be carried unto. This is in Christ answerable to the relation he takes us into. His heart is glad in us, without sorrow. And every day whilst we live is his *wedding-day.* It is said of him, Zeph. iii. 17, " The LORD thy God in the midst of thee" (that is, dwelling amongst us, taking our nature, John i. 14) " is mighty; he will save, he will rejoice over thee with joy; he will rest in his love, he will joy over thee with singing;" which is a full description of delight, in all the parts of it,—joy and exultation, rest and complacence. " I rejoiced," saith he, " in the habitable parts of the earth, and my delights were with the sons of men," Prov. viii. 31. The thoughts of communion with the saints were the joy of his heart from eternity. On the compact and agreement that was between his Father and him, that he should divide a portion with the strong, and save a remnant for his inheritance, his soul rejoiced in the thoughts of that pleasure and delight which he would take in them, when he should actually take them into communion with himself. Therefore in the preceding verse it is said he was by him as אָמוֹן; say we, " As one brought up with him," " alumnus;" the LXX render it ἁρμόζουσα· and the Latin, with most other translations, " cuncta componens," or " disponens." The word taken *actively,* signifies him whom another

with [1.] on that page. The insertion of it, however, would have required great changes, and rendered the subsequent numeration very obscure.—ED.

[1] Ἡδονὴ μᾶλλον ἐν ἠρεμίᾳ ἐστίν, ἢ ἐν κινήσει.—Arist. Eth., lib. vii., cap. 14. Τελειοῖ δὲ τὴν ἐνέργειαν ἡ ἡδονή.—Id. l. 10, c. 4.

takes into his care to breed up, and disposeth of things for his advantage. So did Christ take us then into his care, and rejoiced in the thoughts of the execution of his trust. Concerning them he saith, " Here will I dwell, and here will I make my habitation for ever." For them hath he chosen for his temple and his dwelling-place, because he delighteth in them. This makes him take them so nigh himself in every relation. As he is God, they are his temple; as he is a king, they are his subjects,—he is the king of saints; as he is a head, they are his body,—he is the head of the church; as he is a first-born, he makes them his brethren,—" he is not ashamed to call them brethren."

I shall choose out one particular from among many as an instance for the proof of this thing; and that is this:—Christ *reveals his secrets*, his mind, unto his saints, and enables them to reveal the secrets of their hearts to him;—an evident demonstration of great delight. It was Samson's carnal delight in Delilah that prevailed with him to reveal unto her those things which were of greatest concernment unto him; he will not hide his mind from her, though it cost him his life. It is only a bosom *friend* unto whom we will *unbosom* ourselves. Neither is there, possibly, a greater evidence of delight in close communion than this, that one will reveal his heart unto him whom he takes into society, and not entertain him with things common and vulgarly known. And therefore have I chose this instance, from amongst a thousand that might be given, of this delight of Christ in his saints.

He, then, communicates his mind unto his saints, and unto *them only;*—his mind, the counsel of his love, the thoughts of his heart, the purposes of his bosom, for our eternal good;—his mind, the ways of his grace, the workings of his Spirit, the rule of his sceptre, and the obedience of his gospel.[1] All *spiritual* revelation is by Christ. He is " the true Light, that lighteth every man that cometh into the world," John i. 9. He is the " Day-spring," the " Day-star," and the " Sun;" so that it is impossible any light should be but by him. From him it is that " the secret of the LORD is with them that fear him, and he shows them his covenant," Ps. xxv. 14; as he expresses it at large, John xv. 14, 15,[2] " Ye are my friends, if ye do whatsoever I command you. Henceforth I call you not servants; for the servant knoweth not what his lord doeth: but I have called you friends; for[3] all things that I have heard of my Father I have made known unto you." He makes them as his friends, and useth them as friends,—as

[1] Mal. iv. 2; Luke i. 78; 2 Pet. i. 19.

[2] " Voluntatem Dei nosse quisquam desiderat? fiat amicus Deo, quia si voluntatem hominis nosse vellet, cujus amicus non esset, omnes ejus impudentiam et stultitiam deriderent."—August. de Gen. Cont. Man., lib. i. cap. 2.

[3] " Vox πάντα ex subjecta materia, restrictionem ad doctrinam salutis requirit."—Tarnov. in loc.

bosom friends, in whom he is delighted. He makes known all his mind unto them; every thing that his Father hath committed to him as Mediator to be revealed, Acts xx. 24. And the apostle declares how this is done, 1 Cor. ii. 10, 11, " ' God hath revealed these things unto us by his Spirit;' for we have received him, 'that we might know the things that are freely given us of God.'" He sends us his Spirit, as he promised, to make known his mind unto his saints, and to lead them into all truth. And thence the apostle concludes, "We have known the mind of Christ," verse 16; "for he useth us as friends, and declareth it unto us," John i. 18. There is not any thing in the heart of Christ, wherein these his friends are concerned, that he doth not reveal to them. All his *love*, his *good-will*, the *secrets* of his cove- nant, the *paths* of obedience, the *mystery* of faith, is told them.

And all this is spoken in opposition to *unbelievers*, with whom he hath no *communion*. These know nothing of the mind of Christ as they ought: "The natural man receiveth not the things that are of God," 1 Cor. ii. 14. There is a wide difference between understand- ing *the doctrine of the Scripture* as in the letter, and a true knowing the mind of Christ. This we have by special unction from Christ, 1 John ii. 27, "We have an unction from the Holy One, and we know all things," 1 John ii. 20.

Now, the things which in this communion Christ reveals to them that *he delights in*, may be referred to these two heads:—1. Him- self. 2. His kingdom.

1. Himself. John xiv. 21, "He that loveth me shall be loved of my Father; and I will love him, and will manifest myself unto him;" —"manifest myself in all my graces, desirableness, and loveliness; he shall know me as I am, and such I will be unto him,—a Saviour, a Redeemer, the chiefest of ten thousand." He shall be acquainted with the true worth and value of the pearl of price; let others look upon him as having neither form nor comeliness, as no way desirable, he will manifest himself and his excellencies unto them in whom he is delighted, that they shall see him altogether lovely. He will vail himself to all the world; but the saints with open face shall behold his beauty and his glory, and so be translated into the image of the same glory, as by the Spirit of the Lord, 2 Cor. iii. 18.

2. His kingdom. They shall be acquainted with the *government of his Spirit* in their hearts; as also with his rule and the adminis- tration of authority in his word, and among his churches.

(1.) Thus, in the first place, doth he manifest his *delight* in his saints,—he communicates his *secrets* unto them. He gives them to know his person, his excellencies, his grace, his love, his kingdom, his will, the riches of his goodness, and the bowels of his mercy, more and more, when the world shall neither see nor know any such thing.

(2.) He enables his saints to *communicate* their mind, to reveal their souls, unto him, that so they may walk together as intimate friends. Christ knows *the minds of all.* He knows what is in man, and needs not that any man testify of him, John ii. 25. He searcheth the hearts and trieth the reins of all, Rev. ii. 23. But all know not how to communicate their mind to Christ. It will not avail a man at all that Christ knows his mind; for so he doth of every one, whether he will or no;—but that a man can make his heart known unto Christ, this is consolation. Hence the prayers of the saints are[1] incense, odours; and those of others are[2] howling, cutting off a dog's neck, offering of swine's blood,—an abomination unto the Lord. Now, three things are required to enable a man to communicate his heart unto the Lord Jesus:—

[1.] *Assistance for the work;* for of ourselves we cannot do it. And this the saints have by the Spirit of Jesus, Rom. viii. 26, 27, "Likewise the Spirit also helpeth our infirmities: for we know not what we should pray for as we ought; but the Spirit itself maketh intercession for us with groanings which cannot be uttered. And he that searcheth the hearts knoweth what is the mind of the Spirit, because he maketh intercession for the saints according to the will of God." All endeavours, all attempts for communion with God, without the supplies of the Spirit of supplications, without his effectual working in the heart, is of no value, nor to any purpose. And this *opening* of our hearts and bosoms to the Lord Jesus is that wherein he is exceedingly delighted. Hence is that affectionate call of his unto us, to be treating with him on this account, Cant. ii. 14, "O my dove, that art in the secret places of the stairs, let me see thy countenance, let me hear thy voice; for sweet is thy voice, and thy countenance is comely." When the soul on any account is driven to hide itself,—in any neglected condition, in the most unlikely place of abode,—then doth he call for this communication of itself by prayer to him; for which he gives the assistance of the Spirit mentioned.

[2.] A *way* whereby to approach unto God with our *desires.* This, also, we have by him provided for us, John xiv. 5, 6, "Thomas saith unto Jesus, Lord, we know not whither thou goest; and how can we know the way? Jesus saith unto him, I am the[3] way; no man cometh unto the Father, but by me." That way which we had of going unto God at our *creation* is quite shut up by *sin.* The sword of the law, which hath fire put into it by sin, turns every way, to stop all passages unto communion with God. Jesus Christ hath "consecrated a[4] new and living way" (for the saints) "through the vail,

---

[1] Rev. viii. 3. [2] Hos. vii. 14; Isa. lxvi. 3; Prov. xxviii. 9. [3] "Vera via vitæ."—Bez.
[4] "Via nullius ante trita solo. Πρόσφατον καὶ ζῶσαν, recens interfectam; tamen viventem."

that is to say, his flesh," Heb. x. 20. He hath consecrated and set it apart for believers, and for them alone. Others pretend to go to God with their prayers, but they come not nigh him. How can they possibly come to the end who go not in the way? Christ only is the way to the throne of grace; none comes to God but by him. "By him we have an access in one Spirit unto the Father," Eph. ii. 18. These two things, then, the saints have for the opening of their hearts at the throne of grace,—*assistance* and a *way.* The assistance of the Spirit, without which they are nothing; and the way of Christ's mediation, without which God is not to be approached unto.

[3.] *Boldness* to go unto God. The voice of sinners in themselves, if once acquainted with the terror of the Lord, is,—" Who among us shall dwell with the devouring fire? who among us shall dwell with everlasting burnings?" Isa. xxxiii. 14. And no marvel;[1] shame and trembling before God are the proper issues of sin. God will revenge that carnal, atheistical boldness which sinners out of Christ do use towards him. But we have now " boldness to enter into the holiest by the blood of Jesus, by a new and living way, which he hath consecrated for us, through the vail, that is to say, his flesh: and having an high priest over the house of God, we may draw near with a true heart, in full assurance of faith," Heb. x. 19, 20. The truth is, such is the glory and terror of the Lord, such the infinite perfection of his holiness, that, on clear sight of it, it will make the soul conclude that of itself it[2] cannot serve him; nor will it be to any advantage, but add to the fierceness of his destruction, once to draw nigh to him. It is in Christ alone, and on the account alone of his oblation and intercession, that we have any boldness to approach unto him. And these three advantages have the saints of communicating their minds unto the Lord Christ, which he hath provided for them, because he delights in them.

To touch a little by the way, because this is of great importance, I will instance in one of these, as I might in every one, that you may see the difference between a spiritual revealing of our minds unto Christ in this acceptable manner, and that praying upon conviction which others practise; and this shall be from the first,—namely, the assistance we have by the Spirit.

1st. The Spirit of Christ reveals to us *our own wants,* that we may reveal them unto him: " We know not what we should pray for as we ought," Rom. viii. 26; no [3]teachings under those of the Spirit of God are able to make our souls acquainted with their own wants,—its burdens, its temptations. For a soul to know its wants, its infirmities,

---

[1] Gen iii. 8, 9.
[2] Josh. xxiv. 19; Exod. xx. 19; Deut. v. 25, xviii. 16; Isa. xxxiii. 14; Mic. vi. 6, 7.
[3] Isa. xxxviii. 14.

is a heavenly discovery. He that hath this [1]assistance, his prayer is more than half made before he begins to pray. His conscience is affected with what he hath to do; his mind and spirit contend within him, there especially where he finds himself most straitened. He brings his burden on his shoulders, and unloads himself on the Lord Christ. He finds (not by a perplexing conviction, but a holy sense and weariness of sin) where he is dead, where dull and cold, wherein unbelieving, wherein tempted above all his strength, where the light of God's countenance is wanting. And all these the soul hath a sense of by the Spirit,—an inexpressible sense and experience. Without this, prayer is not prayer; [2]men's voices may be heard, but they speak not in their hearts. Sense of want is the spring of desire;—natural, of natural; spiritual, of spiritual. Without this sense given by the Holy Ghost, there is neither desire nor prayer.

2dly. The *expressions,* or the words of such persons, come exceeding *short of the labouring of* their hearts; and therefore, in and after their supplications, "the Spirit makes intercession with sighs and groans that cannot be [3]uttered." Some men's words go exceedingly beyond their hearts. Did their spirits come up to their expressions, it were well. He that hath this assistance can provide no clothing that is large and broad enough to set forth the desires of his heart; and therefore, in the close of his best and most fervent supplications, such a person finds a double dissatisfaction in them:—
1. That they are not *a righteousness* to be rested on; that if God should[4] mark what is in them amiss, they could not abide the trial.
2. That his heart in them is not *poured out,* nor delivered in any proportion to the holy desires and labourings that were conceived therein; though he may in Christ have great refreshment by them. The more they [saints] speak, the more they find they have left unspoken.

3dly. The intercession of the saints thus assisted *is according to the mind of God;* that is, they are guided by the Spirit to make requests for those things unto God which it is his will they should desire,—which he knows to be good for them, useful and suitable to them, in the condition wherein they are. There are many ways whereby we may know when we make our supplications according to the will of God. I shall instance only in one; that is, when we do it according to the promise: when our prayers are regulated by the promise, we make them according to the will of God. So David, Ps. cxix. 49, " Remember the word upon which thou hast caused me to hope." He prays, and regulates his desire by the word of promise

---

[1] " '*Υπερεντυγχάνειν*, est advocatorum qui clientibus desideria dictant."
[2] 1 Sam. i. 13.　　　　　　　　　　　[3] Isa. xxxviii. 14; Exod. xiv. 15.
[4] Isa. lxiv. 6; Ps. cxxx. 3.

wherein he had trusted. But yet, men may ask that which is in the promise, and yet not have their prayers regulated by the promise. They may pray for what is in the promise, but not as it is in the promise. So James says some "ask and receive not, because they ask amiss, that they may spend it on their lusts," chap. iv. 3. Though the things which God would have us ask be requested, yet if not according as he would have us do it, we ask amiss.

Two things are required, that we may pray for the things in the promise, as they are in the promise:—

(1st.) That we *look* upon them as *promised*, and promised in Christ; that is, that all the reason we have whence we hope for attaining the things we ask for, is from the mediation and purchase of Christ, in whom all the promises are yea and amen. This it is to ask the Father in Christ's name,—God as a father, the fountain; and Christ as the procurer of them.

(2dly.) That we ask for them for the *end* of the promise, not to spend on our lusts. When we ask pardon for sin, with secret[1] reserves in our hearts to continue in sin, we ask the choicest mercy of the covenant, to spend it on our lusts. The end of the promise the apostle tells us, 2 Cor. vii. 1, "Having these promises, let us cleanse ourselves from all pollution of the flesh and spirit, perfecting holiness in the fear of God." When we ask what is in the promise, as it is in the promise, to this end of the promise, our supplications are according to the will of God. And this is the first conjugal affection that Christ exerciseth towards believers,—*he delights in them;* which that he doth is evident, as upon other considerations innumerable, so from the instance given.

In return hereunto, for the carrying on of the communion between them, *the saints delight in Christ;* he is•their joy, their crown, their rejoicing, their life, food, health, strength, desire, righteousness, salvation, blessedness: without him they have nothing; in him they shall find all things. Gal. vi. 14, "God forbid that I should glory, save in the cross of our Lord Jesus Christ." He hath, from the foundation of the world, been the hope, expectation, desire, and delight of all believers. The promise of him was all (and it was enough) that God gave Adam in his inexpressible distress, to relieve and comfort him, Gen. iii. 15. Eve perhaps supposed that the promised seed had been born in her first-born, when she said, "I have gotten a man from[2] the LORD" (so most properly, אֵת denoting the fourth case); and this was the matter

---

[1] Ps. lxxviii. 35-37.

[2] According to the view to which Owen refers, the preposition should be dropped from the translation, and אֵת regarded as in apposition with Jehovah,—" I have gotten a man, Jehovah." The particle אֵת occurs in this sense, as simply demonstrative, forty times in the first four chapters of Genesis.—ED.

of her joy, Gen. iv. 1.   Lamech having Noah given to him as a type
of Christ and salvation by him, cries out, "This same shall comfort
us concerning our work and toil of our hands, because of the ground
which the LORD hath cursed," Gen. v. 29; he rejoices in him who
was to take away the curse, by being made a curse for us.   When
Abraham was in the height of his glory, returning from the conquest
of the kings of the east, that came against the confederate kings of
the vale of Sodom, God appears to him with a glorious promise, Gen.
xv. 1, "Fear not, Abram: I am thy shield, and thy exceeding great
reward."   What now could his soul more desire?   Alas! he cries (as
Reuben afterward, upon the loss of Joseph), "The child is not, and
whither shall I go?"   Verse 2, "Lord GOD, what wilt thou give me,
seeing I go childless?"   "Thou hast promised that in my seed shall
all the earth be blessed; if I have not that seed, ah! what good will all
other things do me?"   Thence it is said that he "rejoiced to see the
day of Christ; he saw it, and was glad," John viii. 56; the thoughts
of the coming of Christ, which he looked on at the distance of two
thousand years, was the joy and delight of his heart.   Jacob, blessing
his sons, lifted up his spirit when he comes to Judah, in whom he
considered the Shiloh to come, Gen. xlix. 8, 9; and a little after,
wearied with the foresight and consideration of the distresses of his
posterity, this he diverts to for his relief, as that great delight of his
soul: "I have waited for thy Salvation, O God;"—for him who was
to be the salvation of his people.   But it would be endless to instance
in particulars.   Old Simeon sums up the whole: Christ is God's
salvation, and Israel's glory, Luke ii. 30, 31; and whatever was called
the glory of old, it was either himself or a type of him.   The glory
of man is their delight.   Hence, Haggai ii. 7, he is called "The
Desire of all nations."   Him whom their soul loves and delights in,
[they] desire and long after.   So is the saints' delight in him made
a description of him, by way of eminence, Mal. iii. 1: "The Lord
whom ye seek shall suddenly come to his temple, even the messen-
ger of the covenant whom ye delight in."   "He whom ye seek,
whom ye delight in," is the description of Christ.   He is their delight
and desirable one, the person of their desire.   To fix on something in
particular:—

In that pattern of communion with Jesus Christ which we have
in the Canticles, this is abundantly insisted on.   The spouse tells us
that she sits down under his shadow with great delight, Cant. ii. 3.
And this delight to be vigorous and active, she manifests several ways;
wherein we should labour to find our hearts in like manner towards
him:—

1. By her exceeding *great care to keep his company* and society,
when once she had obtained it, chap. ii. 7, "I charge you, O ye

daughters of Jerusalem, by the roes, and by the hinds of the field, that ye stir not up, nor awake my love till he please." Having obtained sweet communion with Christ, described in the verses foregoing (of which before), here she expresseth her delight in it and desire of the continuance of it; and therefore, following on the allusion formerly insisted on, she speaks as one would do to her companion, [as one] that had rest with one she loved: "I charge you, by all that is dear to you,—by the things you most delight in, which among the creatures are most lovely, all the pleasant and desirable things that you can think of,—that you disturb him not." The sum of her aim and desire is, that nothing may fall out, nothing of sin or provocation happen, that may occasion Christ to depart from her, or to remove from that dispensation wherein he seemed to take that rest in her. " O stir him not up until he please!" that[1] is, never. הָאַהֲבָה,—love itself in the abstract, to express a πάθος, or earnest affection; for so that word is often used. When once the soul of a believer hath obtained sweet and real communion with Christ, it looks about him, watcheth all temptations, all ways whereby sin might approach, to disturb him in his enjoyment of his dear Lord and Saviour, his rest and desire. How doth it charge itself not to omit any thing, nor to do any thing that may interrupt the communion obtained! And because the common *entrance* of temptations, which tend to the *disturbance* of that rest and complacency which Christ takes in the soul, is from delightful diversions from actual communion with him; therefore is desire strong and active that the companions of such a soul, those with whom it doth converse, would not, by their proposals or allurements, divert it into any such frame as Christ cannot delight nor rest in. A believer that hath gotten Christ in his arms, is like one that hath found great spoils, or a pearl of price. He looks about him every way, and fears every thing that may deprive him of it. Riches make men watchful; and the actual sensible possession of him, in whom are all the riches and treasure of God, will make men look about them for the keeping of him. The line of *choicest communion*, is a line of the greatest *spiritual solicitousness: carelessness* in the enjoyment of Christ pretended, is a manifest evidence of a *false* heart.

2. The spouse manifests her delight in him, by the utmost impatience of his absence, with desires still of nearer communion with him.[2] Chap. viii. 6, " Set me as a seal upon thine heart, as a seal upon thine arm: for love is strong as death; jealousy is cruel as the grave: the coals thereof are coals of fire, which hath a most vehement flame." The allusion is doubtless from the high priest of the Jews, in his spi-

---

[1] " Æternitatem temporis juxta sensum mysticum in se includit, ut alias in Scriptura; quia nunquam a tali somno, id est, conjunctione cum sponso, excitari velit." —Mer. in loc.   [2] Hag. ii. 24; Jer. xxii. 24.

ritual representation of the church before God.   He had a breast-
plate which he is said to wear on his heart, Exod. xxviii. 29, wherein
the names of the children of Israel were engraven, after the manner
of seals or signets, and he bare them for a memorial before the Lord.
He had the like also upon his shoulders, or on his arms, verses 11, 12;
both representing the priesthood of Christ, who bears the names
of all his before his Father in the " holy of holies," Heb. ix. 24.
Now the seal on the heart, is near, inward, tender love and care,
which gives an impression and image on the heart of the thing so
loved.   " Set me," saith the spouse, " as a seal upon thine heart;"—
" Let me be constantly fixed in thy most tender and affectionate love;
let me always have a place in thine heart; let me have an engraving,
a mighty impression of love, upon thine heart, that shall never be obliterated."   The soul is never satisfied with thoughts of Christ's love
to it.   "O that it were more, that it were more! that I were as a ' seal
on his heart!' " is its language.   The soul knows, indeed, on serious
thoughts, that the love of Christ is inconceivable, and cannot be increased; but it would fain work up itself to an apprehension of it:
and therefore she adds here, " Set me as a seal upon thine arm."   The
heart is the *fountain*, but close and hidden; the arm is *manifestation
and power*.   " Let," saith the spouse, " thy love be manifested to me
in thy tender and powerful persuasion of me."   Two things are evident
in this request:—the continual mindfulness of Christ of the soul, as
having its condition still in his eye, engraven on his arm, Isa. xlix.
15, 16, with the exalting of his power for the preservation of it, suitable to the love of his heart unto it; and the manifestation of the
hidden love and care of the heart of Christ unto the soul, being made
visible on his arm, or evident by the fruit of it.   This is that which
she would be assured of; and without a sense whereof there is no
rest to be obtained.

The reason she gives of this earnestness in her supplications, is that
which principally evinces her delight in him: " Love is strong as
death, jealousy is cruel as the grave," or " hard as hell."   This is the
intendment of what is so loftily set out by so many metaphors in this
and the following verse:—" I am not able to bear the workings of my
love to thee, unless I may always have society and fellowship with
thee.   There is no satisfying of my love without it.   It is as the[1] grave,
that still says Give, give.   Death is not satisfied without its prey; if
it have not *all*, it hath *nothing*: let what will happen, if death hath
not its whole desire, it hath nothing at all.   Nor can it be withstood
in its appointed season; no ransom will be taken.   So is my love; if
I have thee not wholly, I have nothing.   Nor can all the world bribe
it to a diversion; it will be no more turned aside than death in its

[1] Prov. xxx. 16.

time. Also, I am not able to bear my jealous thoughts: I fear thou dost not love me, that thou hast forsaken me; because I know I deserve not to be beloved. These thoughts are hard as hell; they give no rest to my soul: if I find not myself on thy heart and arm, I am as one that lies down in *a bed of coals.*" This also argues a holy greediness of delight.

3. She farther manifests this by her solicitousness, trouble, and *perplexity,* in his loss and withdrawings. Men bewail the loss of that whose whole enjoyment they delight in; we easily bear the absence of that whose presence is not delightful. This state of the spouse is discovered, Cant. iii. 1–3, "By[1] night on my bed I sought him whom[2] my soul loveth: I sought him, but I found him not. I will rise now, and go about the city in the streets, and in the broad ways I will seek him whom my soul loveth: I sought him, but I found him not. The watchmen that go about the city found me: to whom I said, Saw ye him whom my soul loveth?" It is night now with the soul,—a time of darkness and trouble, or affliction. Whenever Christ is absent, it is night with a believer. He is the[3] *sun;* if he go down upon them, if his beams be eclipsed, if in his light they see no light, it is all darkness with them. Here, whether the coming of the night of any trouble on her made her discover Christ's absence, or the absence of Christ made it night with her, is not expressed. I rather think the latter; because, setting that aside, all things seem to be well with her. The absence of Christ will indeed make it night, dark as darkness itself, in the midst of all other glowing consolations. But is the spouse contented with this dispensation? She is upon her bed,—that is, of ease (the bed, indeed, sometimes signifies tribulation, Rev. ii. 22; but in this book, everywhere, rest and contentment: here is not the least intimation of any tribulation but what is in the want of Christ); but in the greatest peace and opportunity of ease and rest, a believer finds none in the absence of Christ: though he be on his bed, having nothing to disquiet him, he rests not, if Christ, his rest, be not there. She "sought him." Seeking of Christ by night, on the bed (that is, alone, in immediate inquest, and in the dark), hath two parts:—searching of our own souls for the cause of his *absence;* secondly, searching the promises for his *presence.*

(1.) The soul finding not Christ present in his *wonted* manner, *warming, cherishing, reviving it* with love, nigh to it, supping with it, always filling its thoughts with himself, dropping myrrh and sweet

---

[1] Isa. l. 10.

[2] " Eleganter periphrasi utitur loco nominis proprii, ut vim amoris sui exprimat." —Merc. " Ista repetitio assensum indicat et studium quo eum quærebat, et mœrorem quo angebatur, quod occurrere non posset."—Idem.

[3] Mal. iv. 2.

tastes of love into it; but, on the contrary, that other thoughts crowd in and perplex the heart, and Christ is not nigh when inquired after; it presently inquires into the cause of all this,[1] calls itself to an account what it hath *done*, how it hath *behaved itself*, that it is not with it as at other times,—that Christ hath withdrawn himself, and is not nigh to it in the wonted manner. Here it accomplisheth a diligent search; it considers the love, tenderness, and kindness of the Lord Jesus, what delight he takes in abiding with his saints, so that his departure is not without cause and provocation. " How," saith it, " have I demeaned myself, that I have lost my Beloved? where have I been wandering after other lovers?" And when the miscarriage is found out, it abounds in revenge and indignation.

(2.) Having driven this to some *issue*, the soul applieth itself to the promises of the covenant, wherein Christ is most graciously exhibited unto it; considers one, ponders another, to find a taste of him;— it considers diligently if it can see the delightful countenance and favour of Christ in them or no. But now, if (as it often falls out) the soul finds nothing but the *carcase*, but the bare *letter*, in the promise,—if it come to it as to the grave of Christ, of which it may be said (not in itself, but in respect of the seeking soul), " He is risen, he is not here,"—this amazes the soul, and it knows not what to do. As a man that hath a jewel of great price, having no occasion to use it, lays it aside, as he supposes, in a safe place; in an agony and extremity of want going to seek for his jewel, he finds it not in the place he expected, and is filled with amazement, and knows not what to do;—so is it with this pearl of the gospel. After a man hath sold all that he hath for it, and enjoyed it for a season, then to have it missing at a time of need, it must needs perplex him. So was it with the spouse here. " I sought him," saith she, " but I found him not;" a thing which not seldom befalls us in our communion with Christ.

But what doth she now do? doth she give over, and search no more? Nay; but says she, verse 2, " ' I will arise;' I will not so give over. I must have Christ, or die. I will now arise," (or, " let me arise,") " and go about this business."

[1.] She resolves to put herself upon *another course*, a more *vigorous inquest:* " I will arise and make use of other means besides those of private prayer, meditation, self-searching, and inquiring into the promises;" which she had insisted on before. It carries,—

1*st. Resolution*, and a zealous, violent casting off that frame wherein she had lost her love. " ' I [2] will arise;' I will not rest in this frame: I am undone if I do." So, sometimes God calls his church to arise and shake itself out of the dust. Abide not in that condition.

2*dly. Diligence.* " I will now take another course; I will leave

---

[1] 2 Cor. xiii. 5.　　　　　　　　[2] Isa. lii. 2, lx. 1.

no way unattempted, no means untried, whereby I may possibly recover communion with my Beloved."

This is the condition of a soul that finds not the wonted presence of Christ in its private and more retired inquiries,—dull in prayer, wandering in meditations, rare in thoughts of him,—" I will not bear this frame: whatever way God hath appointed, I will, in his strength, vigorously pursue, until this frame be altered, and I find my Beloved."

[2.] Then the way she puts herself upon, *is to go about the city.* Not to insist upon particulars, nor to strain the parts of the allegory too far, the city here intended is the city of God, the *church;* and the passing through the broad and narrow streets, is the diligent inquiry that the spouse makes in all the paths and ordinances given unto it. This, then, is the next thing the soul addresses itself unto in the want of Christ:—when it finds him not in any private endeavours, it makes vigorous application to the ordinances of public worship; in prayer, in preaching, in administration of the seals, doth it look after Christ. Indeed, the great inquiry the souls of believers make, in every ordinance, is after Christ. So much as they find of him, so much sweetness and refreshment have they, and no more. Especially when under any desertion, they rise up to this inquiry: they listen to every word, to every prayer, to find if any thing of Christ, any light from him, any life, any love, appears to them. " Oh, that Christ would at length meet me in this or that sermon, and recover my poor heart to some sight of his love,—to some taste of kindness!" The solicitousness of a believer in his inquest after Christ, when he finds not his presence, either for grace or consolation, as in former days, is indeed inexpressible. Much of the frame of such a heart is couched in the redoubling of the expression, " I sought him, I sought him;" setting out an inconceivable passion, and suitably industrious desire. Thus, being disappointed at home, the spouse proceeds.

But yet see the *event* of this also: " She sought him, but found him not." It doth sometimes so fall out, all will not do: " They shall seek him, and not find him;" they shall not come nigh him. Let them that enjoy any thing of the presence of Christ take heed what they do; if they provoke him to depart, if they lose him, it may cost them many a bitter inquiry before they find him again. When a soul prays and meditates, searches the promises in private; when it with earnestness and diligence attends all ordinances in public, and all to get one glimpse of the face of Jesus Christ, and all in vain, it is a sad condition.

What now follows in this estate? Verse 3, " The watchmen found me," etc. That these watchmen of the city of God are the watchmen and officers of the church, is confessed. And it is of sad consideration, that the Holy Ghost doth sometimes in this book take notice of them on no good account. Plainly, chap. v. 7, they turn persecutors. It was Luther's saying, "Nunquam periclitatur religio nisi inter reverendissimos." Here they are of a more gentle temper, and seeing the poor disconsolate soul, they seem to take notice of her condition.

It is the duty, indeed, of faithful watchmen, *to take notice of poor, troubled, deserted souls;*—not to keep at a distance, but to be willing to assist. And a truly pressed soul on the account of Christ's absence cannot cover its love, but must be inquiring after him: "Saw ye him whom my soul loveth?"—"This is my condition: I have had sweet enjoyment of my blessed Jesus,—he is now withdrawn from me. Can you help me? can you guide me to my consolation. What acquaintance have you with him? when saw you him? how did he manifest himself to you, and wherein?" All these labourings in his absence sufficiently discover the soul's delight in the presence of Christ. Go one step farther, to the discovery that it made of him once again, and it will yet be more evident. Verses 4, 5, "It was but a little that I passed from them, but I found him whom my soul loveth: I held him, and would not let him go, until I had brought him into my mother's house, and into the chamber of her that conceived me. I charge you, O ye daughters of Jerusalem," etc.

First, She tells you how she *came* to him: "She found him;"—what ways and by what means is not expressed. It often so falls out in our communion with Christ, when private and public means fail, and the soul hath nothing left but *waiting silently* and walking humbly, Christ appears; that his so doing may be evidently of grace. Let us not at any time give over in this condition. When all ways are past, the summer and harvest are gone without relief,—when neither bed nor watchmen can assist,—let us wait a little, and we shall see the Salvation of God. Christ honours his immediate absolute actings sometimes, though ordinarily he crowns his ordinances. Christ often manifests himself immediately, and out of ordinances, to them that wait for him in them;—that he will do so to them that despise them, I know not. Though he will meet men unexpectedly in his way, yet he will not meet them at all out of it. Let us wait as he hath appointed; let him appear as he pleaseth. How she deals with him when found is *nextly* declared: "She held him, and would not let him go," etc. They are all expressions of the greatest joy and delight imaginable. The sum is:—having at length come once more to an enjoyment of sweet communion with Christ, the soul lays fast hold on him by faith (κρατεῖν, "to hold fast," is an act of faith), refuses to part with him any more, in vehemency of love,—tries to keep him in ordinances in the house of its mother, the church of God; and so uses all means for the confirming of the mutual love between Christ and her: all the expressions, all the allusions used, evidencing delight to the utmost capacity of the soul. Should I pursue all the instances and testimonies that are given hereunto, in that one book of the Song of Solomon, I must enter upon an exposition of the greatest part of it; which is not my present business. Let the hearts of the saints that are acquainted with these things be allowed to make the close. What is it they long for, they rejoice in? what is it that satisfies them to the utmost, and gives sweet complacency to their spirits in every condition? what is it whose *loss* they fear, whose *absence* they cannot bear? Is it not this their Beloved, and he alone?

This, also, they farther manifest *by their delight in every thing that peculiarly belongs to Christ*, as his, in this world. This is an evidence of delight, when, for his sake whom we delight in, we also delight in every thing that belongs to him. Christ's great interest in this world lies in his people and his ordinances,—his household and their provision. Now in both these do the saints exceedingly delight, for his sake. Take an instance in both kinds in one man, namely, David, Ps. xvi. 3, "In the saints and the excellent" (or the noble) "of the earth is all my delight; my delight in them." Christ says of his church that she is "Hephzi-bah," Isa. lxii., "My delight in her." Here says David of the same, "Hephzi-bam,—"My delight in them." As Christ delights in his saints, so do they in one another, on his account. "Here," says David, "is all my delight." Whatever contentment he took in any other persons, it was nothing in comparison of the delight he took in them. Hence, mention is made of "laying down our lives for the brethren," or any common cause wherein the interest of the community of the brethren does lie.

Secondly, For the ordinances, consider the same person. Ps. xlii., lxxxiv., and xlviii., are such plentiful testimonies throughout, as we need no farther inquiring; nor shall I go forth to a new discourse on this particular.

And this is the first mutual consequential act of conjugal affection, in this communion between Christ and believers:—*he delights in them, and they delight in him.* He delights in their prosperity, hath pleasure in it; they delight in his honour and glory, and in his presence with them. For his sake they delight in his servants (though by the world contemned) as the most excellent in the world; and in his ordinances, as the wisdom of God;—which are foolishness to the world.

CHAPTER V.

Other consequential affections:—1. On the part of Christ—He values his saints—Evidences of that valuation:—(1.) His incarnation; (2.) Exinanition, 2 Cor. viii. 9; Phil. ii. 6, 7; (3.) Obedience as a servant; (4.) In his death. His valuation of them in comparison of others. 2. Believers' estimation of Christ:—(1.) They value him above all other things and persons; (2.) Above their own lives; (3.) All spiritual excellencies. The sum of all on the part of Christ—The sum on the part of believers. The third conjugal affection—On the part of Christ, pity or compassion—Wherein manifested—Suffering and supply, fruits of compassion—Several ways whereby Christ relieves the saints under temptations—His ·compassion in their afflictions. Chastity, the third conjugal affection in the saints. The fourth—On the part of Christ, bounty; on the part of the saints, duty.

II. CHRIST values his saints, values believers (which is the second branch of that conjugal affection he bears towards them), having taken them into the relation whereof we speak. I shall not need to insist long on the demonstration hereof; heaven and earth are full of evi-·dences of it. Some few considerations will give life to the assertion. Consider them, then,—1. *Absolutely;* 2. *In respect of others;* and you will see what a valuation he puts upon them:—

1. All that ever he did or doth, all that ever he underwent or suffered as mediator, was for their sakes. Now, these things were so great and grievous, that had he not esteemed them above all that can be expressed, he had never engaged to their performance and undergoing. Take a few instances:—

(1.) For their sakes was he "made[1] *flesh;*" "manifested in the flesh." Heb. ii. 14, " Forasmuch then as the children are partakers of flesh and blood, he also himself likewise took part of the same." And the height of this valuation of them the apostle aggravates. Verse 16, " Verily he took not on him the nature of angels, but he took on him the seed of Abraham;" he had no such esteem of angels. Whether you take ἐπιλαμβάνεσθαι, properly to " take," or to " take hold of," as our translators, and so supply the word " nature," and refer the whole unto Christ's incarnation, who therein took our nature on him, and not the nature of angels; or for ἀναλαμβάνεσθαι, to " help," (he did not help nor succour fallen angels; but he did help and[2] succour the seed of Abraham,) and so consider it as the fruit of Christ's incarnation,—it is all one, as to our present business: his preferring the-seed of Abraham before angels, his valuing them above the other, is plainly expressed. And observe, that he came to help the seed of Abraham,—that is,[3] *believers.* His esteem and valuation is of them only.

---

[1] John i. 14; 1 Tim. iii. 16.   [2] Vide Vind. Evan., cap. xiii. vol. xii.
[3] Rom. iv. 17; Gal. iii. 7.

(2.) For their sakes he was so made flesh, as that there was an *emptying*, an *exinanition* of himself, and an eclipsing of his glory, and a becoming poor for them, 2 Cor. viii. 9, "Ye know the grace of our Lord Jesus Christ, that, though he was rich, yet for our sakes he became poor." Being rich in eternal glory with his Father, John xvii. 5, he became poor for believers. The same person that was rich was also poor. That the riches here meant can be none but those of the Deity, is evident, by its opposition to the poverty which as man he undertook. This is also more fully expressed, Phil. ii. 6, 7, "Who being in the form of God, counted it no robbery to be equal to God, but he emptied himself, taking the form of a servant, and being made in the fashion of a man, and found in form as a man," etc. That the "form of God" is here the essence of the Deity, sundry things inevitably evince; as,—

[1.] That he was therein[1] *equal* to God; that is, his Father. Now, nothing but God is equal to God. Not[2] Christ as he is mediator, in his greatest glory,—nothing but that which is infinite, is equal to that which is infinite.

[2.] The *form of God* is opposed to the *form of a servant;* and that form of a servant is called the "fashion of a man," verse 8,—that fashion wherein he was found when he gave himself to death, wherein as a man he poured out his blood and died. Μορφὴν δούλου λαβὼν (he "took the form of a servant"), is expounded in the next words, ἐν ὁμοιώματι ἀνθρώπων γενόμενος,—an expression used to set out his incarnation, Rom. viii. 3. God sent him ἐν ὁμοιώματι σαρκὸς ἁμαρτίας· in taking true flesh, he was in the "likeness of sinful flesh." Now, in thus doing, it is said ἑαυτὸν ἐκένωσε,—"he humbled, emptied himself, made himself of no reputation." In the very taking of flesh, there was a condescension, a debasing of the person of the Son of God; it could not be without it. If God humbled himself to "behold the things that are in heaven, and in the earth," Ps. cxiii. 6, then certainly it was an inconceivable condescension and abasement, not only to *behold*, but *take upon him* (into personal union) our nature with himself. And though nothing could possibly be taken off from the essential glory of the Deity, yet that person appearing in the fashion of a man, and form of a servant, the glory of it, as to the manifestation, was eclipsed; and he appeared[3] quite another thing than what indeed he was, and had been from eternity. Hence he prays that his Father would "glorify him with the glory he had with him before the world was," John xvii. 5, as to the manifestation of it. And so, though the divine nature was not abased, the person was.

(3.) For their sakes he so humbled and emptied himself, in taking flesh, as to become therein a *servant*,—in the eyes of the world of no

---

[1] See Vind. Evan., cap. xiii. vol. xii.   [2] John xiv. 28.   [3] Isa. liii. 2.

esteem nor account; and a true and real servant[1] unto the Father. For their sakes he humbled himself, and became obedient. All that he did and suffered in his life comes under this consideration; all which may be referred to these three heads:—[2][1.] *Fulfilling all righteousness.* [2.] *Enduring all manner of persecutions* and hardships. [3.] *Doing all manner of good to men.* He took on him, for their sakes, a life and course pointed to, Heb. v. 7, 8,—a life of prayers, tears, fears, obedience, suffering; and all this with cheerfulness and delight, calling his employment his "meat and drink," and still professing that the law of this obedience was in his[3] heart,—that he was content to do this will of God. He that will sorely revenge the least opposition that is or shall be made to him by others, was content to undergo any thing, all things, for believers.

(4.) He stays not here, but (for the consummation of all that went before) for their sakes he becomes *obedient to death,* the death of the cross. So he professeth to his Father, John xvii. 19, "For their sakes I sanctify myself;"—"I dedicate myself as an offering, as a sacrifice, to be killed and slain." This was his aim in all the former, that he might die; he was born, and [4]lived, that he might die. He valued them above his life. And if we might stay to consider a little what was in this death that he underwent for them, we should perceive what a price indeed he put upon them. The *curse*[5] *of the law* was in it, the [6]*wrath of God* was in it, the *loss of God's* [7]*presence* was in it. It was a [8]fearful cup that he tasted of, and drank of, that they might never taste of it. A man would not for ten thousand worlds be willing to undergo that which Christ underwent for us in that one thing of desertion from God, were it attended with no more distress but what a mere creature might possibly emerge from under. And what thoughts we should have of this himself tells us, John xv. 13, "Greater love hath no man than this, that a man lay down his life for his friends." It is impossible there should be any greater demonstration or evidence of love than this. What can any one do more? And yet he tells us in another place, that it hath another aggravation and heightening, Rom. v. 8, "God commendeth his love toward us, in that, while we were yet sinners, Christ died for us." When he did this for us we were sinners, and enemies, whom he might justly have destroyed. What more can be done?—to die for us when we were sinners! Such a death, in such a manner, with such attendancies of wrath and curse,—a death accompanied with the worst that God had ever threatened to sinners,—argues as high a valuation of us as the heart of Christ himself was capable of.

---

[1] Isa. xlii. 1, 19; John xiv. 31.   [2] Matt. iii. 15.   [3] Heb. x. 7, 8.
[4] Heb. ii. 14, 15.   [5] Gal. iii. 13.   [6] 2 Cor. v. 21.   [7] Ps. xxii. 1.
[8] Matt. xxvi. 39.

For one to part with his glory, his riches, his ease, his life, his love from God, to undergo loss, shame, wrath, curse, death, for another, is an evidence of a dear valuation; and that it was all on this account, we are informed, Heb. xii. 2. Certainly Christ had a dear esteem of them, that, rather than they should perish,—that they should not be his, and be made partakers of his glory,—he would part with all he had for their sakes, Eph. v. 25, 26.

There would be no end, should I go through all the instances of Christ's valuation of believers, in all their deliverances, afflictions, in all conditions of *sinning and suffering*,—what he hath done, what he doth in his intercession, what he delivers them from, what he procures for them; all telling out this one thing,—they are the apple of his eye, his jewel, his diadem, his crown.

2. In comparison of others. All the *world* is nothing to him in comparison of them. They are his *garden;* the rest of the world, a *wilderness.* Cant. iv. 12, " A garden enclosed is my sister, my spouse; a spring shut up, a fountain sealed." They are his *inheritance;* the rest, his enemies, of no regard with him. So Isa. xliii. 3, 4, " I am the LORD thy God, the Holy One of Israel, thy Saviour: I gave Egypt for thy ransom, Ethiopia and Seba for thee. Since thou wast [1]precious in my sight, thou hast been honourable, and I have loved thee: therefore will I give men for thee, and people for thy life." The reason of this dealing of Christ with his church, in parting with all others for them, is, because he loves her. She is precious and honourable in his sight; thence he puts this great esteem upon her. Indeed, he disposeth of all nations and their interests according as is for the good of believers. Amos ix. 9, in all the siftings of the nations, the eye of God is upon the house of Israel; not a grain of them shall perish. Look to heaven; *angels* are appointed to minister for them, Heb. i. 14. Look into the world; the *nations* in general are either [2]blessed for their sakes, or [3]destroyed on their account,—preserved to try them, or rejected for their cruelty towards them; and will receive from Christ their [4]final doom according to their deportment towards these despised ones. On this account are the pillars of the earth borne up, and patience is exercised towards the perishing world. In a word, there is not the meanest, the weakest, the poorest believer on the earth, but Christ prizeth him more than all the world besides. Were our hearts filled much with thoughts hereof, it would tend much to our consolation.

To answer this, *believers also value* Jesus Christ; they have an esteem of him above all the world, and all things in the world. You

---

[1] " Amorem istum non esse vulgarem ostendit, dum nos pretiosos esse dicit."— Calv. in loc.

[2] Gen. xii. 3; Mic. v. 7, 8.

[3] Isa. xxxiv. 8, lxi. 2, lxiii. 4.

[4] Matt. xxv. 41-46.

have been in part acquainted with this before, in the account that was given of their delight in him, and inquiry after him. They say of him in their hearts continually, as David, "Whom have I in heaven but thee? and none upon earth I desire beside thee." Ps. lxxiii. 25. Neither heaven nor earth will yield them an object any way comparable to him, that they can delight in.

1. They value him *above all other things and persons.* " Mallem," said one,[1] "ruere cum Christo, quam regnare cum Cæsare. Pulchra terra, pulchrum cœlum, sed pulcherrimus dominus Jesus;"—Christ and a dungeon, Christ and a cross, is infinitely sweeter than a crown, a sceptre without him, to their souls. So was it with Moses, Heb. xi. 26, " He esteemed the reproach of Christ greater riches than the treasures in Egypt." The reproach of Christ is the worst consequent that the wickedness of the world or the malice of Satan can bring upon the followers of him. The treasures of Egypt were in those days the greatest in the world; Moses despised the very best of the world, for the worst of the cross of Christ. Indeed, himself hath told believers, that if they love any thing better than him, father or mother, they are not worthy of him. A despising of all things for Christ is the very first lesson of the gospel. " Give away all, take up the cross and follow me," was the way whereby he tried his disciples of old; and if there be not the same mind and heart in us, we are none of his.

2. They value him *above their lives.* Acts xx. 24, " My life is not dear, that I may perfect my course with joy, and the ministry I have received of the Lord Jesus;"—" Let life and all go, so that I may serve him; and, when all is done, enjoy him, and be made like to him." It is known what is reported of [2]Ignatius when he was led to martyrdom: " Let what will," said he, " come upon me, only so I may obtain Jesus Christ." Hence they of old rejoiced when whipped, scourged, put to shame, for his sake, Acts v. 41; Heb. xi. All is welcome that comes from him, or for him. The lives they have to live, the death they have to die, is little, is light, upon the thoughts of him who is the stay of their lives and the end of their death. Were it not for the refreshment which daily they receive by thoughts of him, they could not live,—their lives would be a burden to them; and the thoughts of enjoyment of him made them cry with Paul, " Oh that we were dissolved!" The stories of the martyrs of old and of late, the sufferers in giving witness to him under the dragon and under the false prophet, the neglect of life in women and children on his

---

[1] Luther.

[2] Νῦν ἄρχομαι εἶναι μαθητής, οὐδὲν τούτων τῶν ὁρωμένων ἐπιθυμῶ, ἵνα τὸν Ἰησοῦν Χριστὸν εὕρω. Πῦρ, σταυρός, θηρία, σύγκλασις ὀστέων, καὶ τῶν μελῶν διασπασμός, καὶ παντὸς τοῦ σώματος συντριβή, καὶ βάσανοι τοῦ διαβόλου εἰς ἐμὲ ἐλθωσιν, ἵνα Ἰησοῦ Χριστοῦ ἀπολαύσω.—Vit. Ignat. [Hieronymus, De Viris Illustribus, c. xvi.]

account, contempt of torments, whilst his name sweetened all, have rendered this truth clear to men and angels.

3. They value him *above all spiritual excellencies*, and all other righteousness whatever, Phil. iii. 7, 8, " Those things which were advantage to me, I esteemed loss for the excellency of the knowledge of Christ Jesus my Lord; for whose sake I have lost all things, and do esteem them common, that I may gain Christ, and be found in him." Having recounted the excellencies which he had, and the privileges which he enjoyed, in his Judaism,—which were all of a spiritual nature, and a participation wherein made the rest of his countrymen despise all the world, and look upon themselves as the only acceptable persons with God, resting on them for righteousness,—the apostle tells us what is his esteem of them, in comparison of the Lord Jesus. They are " loss and dung,"—things that for his sake he had really suffered the loss of; that is, whereas he had for many years been a zealot of the law,—seeking after a righteousness as it were by the works of it, Rom. ix. 32,—instantly serving God day and night, to obtain the promise, Acts xxvi. 7,—living in all good conscience from his youth, Acts xxiii.,—all the while very zealous for God and his institutions,—now [he] willingly casts away all these things, looks upon them as loss and dung, and could not only be contented to be without them, but, as for that end for which he sought after them, he abhorred them all. When men have been strongly convinced of their duty, and have laboured many years to keep a [1]good conscience,—have prayed, and heard, and done good, and denied themselves, and been [2]zealous for God, and laboured with all their might to [3]please him, and so at length to come to enjoy him; they had rather [4]part with all the world, life and all, than with this they have wrought. You know how unwilling we are to part with any thing we have laboured and beaten our heads about? How much more when the things are so excellent, as our duty to God, blamelessness of conversation, hope of heaven, and the like, which we have beaten our hearts about. But now, when once Christ appears to the soul, when he is known in his excellency, all these things, as without him, have their paint washed off, their beauty fades, their desirableness vanisheth, and the soul is not only contented to part with them all, but puts them away as a defiled thing, and cries, " In the Lord Jesus only is my righteousness[5] and glory." Prov. iii. 13–15, among innumerable testimonies, may be admitted to give witness hereunto, "Happy is the man that findeth wisdom, and the man that getteth understanding. For the merchandise of it is better than the merchandise of silver, and the gain thereof than fine gold. She is more precious than rubies: and all the

---

[1] Acts xxiii. 1.   [2] Rom. x 2, 3.   [3] Acts xxvi. 7.
[4] John ix. 40; Rom. ix. 30, 31.   [5] Isa. xlv. 24.

things that thou canst desire are not to be compared unto her." It is of Jesus Christ, the Wisdom of God, the eternal Wisdom of the Father, that the Holy Ghost speaks; as is evident from the description which is given hereof, chap. viii. He and his ways are better than silver and gold, rubies, and all desirable things; as in the gospel he likens himself to the[1] "pearl in the field," which when the merchantman finds, he sells all that he hath, to purchase. All goes for Christ;—all righteousness without him, all ways of religion, all goes for that one pearl. The glory of his Deity, the excellency of his person, his all-conquering desirableness, ineffable love, wonderful undertaking, unspeakable condescensions, effectual mediation, complete righteousness, lie in their eyes, ravish their hearts, fill their affections, and possess their souls. And this is the second mutual conjugal affection between Christ and believers; all which, on the part of Christ, may be referred unto two heads:—

1. All that he parted withal, all that he did, all that he suffered, all that he doth as mediator; he parted withal, did, suffered, doth, on the account *of his [2]love to and esteem of believers.* He parted with the greatest glory, he underwent the greatest misery, he doth the greatest works that ever were, because he loves his spouse,—because he values believers. What can more, what can farther be spoken? how little is the depth of that which is spoken fathomed! how unable are we to look into the mysterious recesses of it! He so loves, so values his saints, as that, having from eternity undertaken to bring them to God, he rejoices his soul in the thoughts of it; and pursues his design through heaven and hell, life and death, by suffering and doing, in mercy and with power; and ceaseth not until he bring it to perfection. For,—

2. He doth so value them, as that he will not *lose* any of them to *eternity*, though all the world should combine to take them out of his hand. When in the days of his flesh he foresaw what opposition, what danger, what rocks they should meet withal, he cried out, "Holy Father, keep them," John xvii. 11;—"Let not one of them be lost;" and tells us plainly, John x. 28, that no man shall take his sheep out of his hand. And because he was then in the form of a servant, and it might be supposed that he might not be able to hold them, he tells them true, as to his present condition of carrying on the work of mediation, his "Father was greater than he;"[3] and therefore to him he committed them, and none should take them out of his Father's hand, John x. 29. And whereas the world, afflictions, and

---

[1] Matt. xiii. 45, 46. "Principium culmenque omnium rerum pretii, margaritæ tenent."—Plin.

[2] Gal. ii. 20; John xiii. 34; Rev. i. 5, 6; Eph. v. 25, 26; Heb. x. 9, 10.

[3] John xiv. 28.

persecutions, which are without, may be conquered, and yet no security given but that sin from within, by the assistance of Satan, may prevail against them to their ruin; as he hath provided against Satan, in his promise that the gates of hell shall not prevail against them, so he hath taken care that sin itself shall not destroy them. Herein, indeed, is the depth of his love to be contemplated, that whereas his holy soul hates every sin (it is a burden, an abomination, a new wound to him), and his poor spouse is sinful (believers are full of sins, failings, and infirmities), he hides all, covers all, bears with all, rather than he will lose them; by his power preserving them from such sins as a remedy is not provided for in the covenant of grace. Oh, the world of sinful follies that our dear Lord Jesus bears withal on this account! Are not our own souls astonished with the thoughts of it? Infinite patience, infinite forbearance, infinite love, infinite grace, infinite mercy, are all set on work for this end, to answer this his valuation of us.

On our part it may also be referred to two heads:—

1. That, upon the discovery of him to our souls, they rejoice to [1]*part* with all things wherein they have delighted or reposed their confidence, *for him and his sake*, that they may enjoy him. Sin and lust, pleasure and profit, righteousness and duty, in their several conditions, all shall go, so they may have Christ.

2. That they are willing to part with all things rather than with [2] him, when they do enjoy him. To think of parting with peace, health, liberty, relations, wives, children; it is offensive, heavy, and grievous to the best of the saints: but their souls cannot bear the thoughts of parting with Jesus Christ; such a thought is cruel as the grave. The worst thoughts that, in any fear, [3]in desertions, they have of[4] hell, is, that they shall not enjoy Jesus Christ. So they may enjoy him here, hereafter be like him, be ever with him, stand in his presence; they can part with all things freely, cheerfully, be they never so beautiful, in reference to this life or that which is to come.

III. The third conjugal affection on the part of Christ is *pity and compassion*. As a man "nourisheth and cherisheth his [5]own flesh, so doth the Lord his church," Eph. v. 29. Christ hath a fellow feeling with his saints in all their troubles, as a man hath with his own flesh. This act of the conjugal love of Christ relates to the many trials and pressures of afflictions that his saints meet withal here below. He doth not deal with believers as the Samaritans with the Jews, that fawned on them in their prosperity, but despised them in

---

[1] Matt. xiii. 45, 46; Phil. iii. 8.   [2] Matt. x. 37.   [3] Cant. viii. 6.

[4] Καὶ τοῦτό μοι τῶν ἐν ᾅδου κολάσεων βαρύτερον ἂν εἴη.—Basil.

[5] "Fateor insitam esse nobis corporis nostri caritatem."—Senec. Epist. xiv. "Generi animantium omni est a natura tributum ut se, vitam, corpusque tueatur." —Cicer. Off. i. [iv.]

their trouble; he is as a tender [1]father, who, though perhaps he love all his children alike, yet he will take most pains with, and give most of his presence unto, one that is sick and weak, though therein and thereby he may be made most froward, and, as it should seem, hardest to be borne with. And (which is more than the pity of any father can extend to) he himself suffers with them, and takes share in all their troubles.

Now, all the sufferings of the saints in this world, wherein their head and husband exerciseth pity, tenderness, care, and compassion towards them, are of two sorts, or may be referred to two heads:— 1. Temptations. 2. Afflictions.

1. *Temptations* (under which head I comprise sin also, whereto they tend); as in, from, and by their own infirmities; as also from their adversaries without. The frame of the heart of Christ, and his deportment towards them in this condition, you have, Heb. iv. 15, "We have not an high priest which cannot be touched with the feeling of our infirmities." We have not such a one as cannot. The two negations do vehemently affirm that we have such an high priest as can be, or is, touched. The word "touched" comes exceedingly short of expressing the original word; it is [2]συμπαθῆσαι,—to "suffer together." "We have," saith the apostle, "such an high priest as can, and consequently doth, suffer with us,—endure our infirmities." And in what respect he suffers with us in regard of our infirmities, or hath a fellow-feeling with us in them, he declares in the next words, "He was tempted like as we are," verse 15. It is as to our [3]infirmities, our temptations, spiritual weakness; therein, in particular, hath he a compassionate sympathy and fellow-feeling with us. Whatever be our infirmities, so far as they are our temptations, he doth suffer with us under them, and compassionates us. Hence at the last [4]day he saith, "I was an hungered," etc. There are two ways of expressing a fellow-feeling and suffering with another:—(1.) *Per benevolam condolentiam,*—a "friendly grieving." (2.) *Per gratiosam opitulationem,*—a "gracious supply:" both are eminent in Christ:—

(1.) He [5]*grieves and labours* with us. Zech. i. 12, "The angel of the LORD answered and said, O LORD of hosts, how long wilt thou not have mercy on Jerusalem?" He speaks as one intimately affected

---

[1] Ps. ciii. 13.

[2] " Hoc quidem certum est, hoc vocabulo, summum illum consensum membrorum et capitis (id est, ecclesiæ et Christi) significari, de quo toties Paulus disserit. Deinde ut cum de Deo loquitur, ita, etiam de Christo glorioso disserens Scriptura, ad nostrum captum se demittit. Gloriosum autem ad dextram patris Christum sedere credimus; ubi dicitur nostris malis affici, quod sibi factum ducat quicquid nobis fit injuriæ, ideo clamans e cœlis, Saul cur me persequeris? Altiores speculationes scrutari, nec utile nec tutum existimo."—Bez. in loc.

[3] Rom. viii. 26; 1 Cor. xi. 32; 2 Cor. xi. 30, xii. 9, 10; Gal. iv. 13.

[4] Matt. xxv. 35.   [5] Acts ix. 4; Isa. lxiii. 9.

with the state and condition of poor Jerusalem; and therefore he hath bid all the world take notice that what is done to them is done to him, chap. ii. 8, 9; yea, to "the [1]apple of his eye."

(2.) In the second he abounds. Isa. xl. 11, "He shall feed his flock like a shepherd, he shall gather the lambs with his arm, and carry them in his bosom, and gently lead them that are with young." Yea, we have both here together,—*tender compassionateness and assistance.* The whole frame wherein he is here described is a [2]frame of the greatest [3]tenderness, compassion, condescension that can be imagined. His people are set forth under many infirmities; some are lambs, some great with young, some very tender, some burdened with temptations,—nothing in any of them all strong or comely. To them all Christ is [4]a shepherd, that feeds his own sheep, and drives them out to pleasant pasture; where, if he sees a poor weak lamb, [he] doth not thrust him on, but takes him into his bosom, where he both easeth and refresheth him: he leads him gently and tenderly. As did Jacob them that were burdened with [5]young, so doth our dear Lord Jesus with his flock, in the several ways and paths wherein he leads them. When he sees a poor soul, weak, tender, halting, ready to sink and perish, he takes him into his arms, by some gracious promise administered to him, carries him, bears him up when he is not able to go one step forward. Hence is his great quarrel with those shepherds, Ezek. xxxiv. 4, "Woe be to you shepherds! the diseased have ye not strengthened, neither have ye healed that which was sick, neither have ye bound up that which was broken, neither have ye brought again that which was driven away, neither have ye sought that which was lost." This is that which our careful, tender husband would have done.

So mention being made of his compassionateness and fellow-suffering with us, Heb. iv. 15, it is added, verse 16, that he administers χάριν εἰς εὔκαιρον βοήθειαν,—seasonable grace, grace for help in a time of need. This is an evidence of compassion, when, like the Samaritan, we afford seasonable help. To lament our troubles or miseries, without affording help, is to no purpose. Now, this Christ doth; he gives εὔκαιρον βοήθειαν,—seasonable help. Help being a thing that regards want, is always excellent; but its coming in season puts a crown

---

[1] Deut. xxxii. 10; Ps. xvii. 8.

[2]   "En ipse capellas
Protinus æger ago; hanc etiam vix Tityre duco," etc.
                                        —Virg. [Ec. i. 12.]

[3] "Quod frequenter in Scriptura, pastoris nomen Deus usurpat, personamque induit, non vulgare est teneri in nos amoris signum. Nam quum humilis et abjecta sit loquendi forma, singulariter erga nos affectus sit oportet, qui se nostrâ causa ita demittere non gravatur: mirum itaque nisi tam blanda et familiaris invitatio ad eum nos alliciat."—Calvin in Ps. xxiii. 1.

[4] Heb. xiii. 20; 1 Pet. ii. 25, v. 4; Ps. xxiii. 1; Zech. xiii. 7; Isa. xl. 11; Ezek. xxxiv. 23; John x. 11, 14, 16.   [5] Gen. xxxiii. 13.

upon it. A pardon to a malefactor when he is ready to be executed, is sweet and welcome. Such is the assistance given by Christ. All his saints may take this as a sure rule, both in their temptations and afflictions:—when they can want them, they shall not want relief; and when they can bear no longer, they shall be relieved, 1 Cor. x. 13.

So it is said *emphatically of him*, Heb. ii. 18, "In that he himself hath suffered being tempted, he is able to succour them that are tempted." It is true, there is something in all our temptations more than was in the temptation of Christ. There is something in ourselves to take part with every temptation; and there is enough in ourselves to [1]tempt us, though nothing else should appear against us. With Christ it was not so, John xiv. 30. But this is so far from taking off his compassion towards us, that, on all accounts whatever, it doth increase it; for if he will give us succour because we are tempted, the sorer our temptations are, the more ready will he be to succour us. Take some instances of Christ's giving εὔκαιρον βοήθειαν,— seasonable help in and under temptations unto sin. Now this he doth several ways:—

[1.] By keeping the soul which is liable to temptation and exposed to it, *in a strong habitual bent* against that sin that he is obnoxious to the assaults of. So it was in the case of Joseph: Christ knew that Joseph's great trial, and that whereon if he had been conquered he had been undone, would lie upon the hand of his mistress tempting him to lewdness; whereupon he kept his heart in a steady frame against that sin, as his answer without the least deliberation argues, Gen. xxxix. 9. In other things, wherein he was not so deeply concerned, Joseph's heart was not so fortified by habitual grace; as it appears by his swearing by the [2]life of Pharaoh. This is one way whereby Christ gives suitable help to his, in tenderness and compassion. The saints, in the course of their lives, by the company, society, business, they are cast upon, are liable and exposed to temptations great and violent, some in one kind, some in another. Herein is Christ exceedingly kind and tender to them, in fortifying their hearts with abundance of grace as to that sin unto temptations whereunto they are most exposed; when perhaps in other things they are very weak, and are often surprised.

[2.] Christ sometimes, by some strong *impulse* of actual grace, recovers the soul *from the very borders of sin.* So it was in the case of David, 1 Sam. xxiv. 4–6. "He was almost gone," as he speaks himself; "his feet had well-nigh slipped." The temptation was at the door of prevalency, when a mighty impulse of grace recovers him. To show his saints what they are, their own weakness and infirmity, he sometimes suffers them to go to the very edge and brow of the

[1] James i. 14, 15. [2] Gen. xlii. 15.

hill, and then causeth them to hear a word behind them saying, "This is the right way, walk in it,"—and that with power and efficacy; and so recovers them to himself.

[3.] By taking away the *temptation itself,* when it grows so strong and violent that the poor soul knows not what to do. ' This is called " delivering the godly out of temptation," 2 Pet. ii. 9, as a man is plucked out of the snare, and the snare left behind to hold another. This have I known to be the case of many, in sundry perplexing temptations. When they have been quite weary, have tried all means of help and assistance, and have not been able to come to a comfortable issue, on a sudden, unexpectedly, the Lord Christ, in his tenderness and compassion, rebukes Satan, that they hear not one word more of him as to their temptation. Christ comes in in the storm, and saith, " Peace, be still."

[4.] By giving in *fresh supplies of grace,* according as temptations do grow or increase. So was it in the case of Paul, 2 Cor. xii. 9, " My grace is sufficient for thee." The temptation, whatever it were, grew high; Paul was earnest for its removal; and receives only this answer, of the sufficiency of the grace of God for his supportment, notwithstanding all the growth and increase of the temptation.

[5.] By giving them *wisdom* to make a *right, holy, and spiritual improvement* of all temptations. James bids us " count it all joy when we fall into divers temptations," James i. 2: which could not be done were there not a holy and spiritual use to be made of them; which also himself manifests in the words following. There are manifold uses of temptations, which experienced Christians, with assistance suitable from Christ, may make of them. This is not the least, that by them we are brought to know ourselves. So Hezekiah was left to be tried, to know what was in him. By temptation, some bosom, hidden corruption is oftentimes discovered, that the soul knew not of before. As it was with[1] Hazael in respect of enormous crimes, so in lesser things with the saints. They would never have believed there had been such lusts and corruptions in them as they have discovered upon their temptations. Yea, divers having been tempted to one sin, have discovered another that they thought not of; as some, being tempted to pride, or worldliness, or looseness of conversation, have been startled by it, and led to a discovery of neglect of many duties and much communion with God, which before they thought not of. And this is from the tender care of Jesus Christ, giving them in suitable help; without which no man can possibly make use of or improve a temptation. And this is a suitable help indeed, whereby a temptation which otherwise, or to other persons, might be a deadly wound, proves the lancing of a festered sore, and

[1] 2 King viii. 13.

the letting out of corruption that otherwise might have endangered the life itself. So, 1 Pet. i. 6, " If need be ye are in heaviness through manifold temptations."

[6.] *When the soul is at any time more or less overcome by temptations, Christ in his tenderness relieves it with mercy and pardon;* so that his shall not sink utterly under their burden, 1 John ii. 1, 2.

By one, more, or all of these ways, doth the Lord Jesus manifest his conjugal tenderness and compassion towards the saints, in and under their temptations.

2. Christ is compassionate towards them in their *afflictions:* " In all their affliction he is afflicted," Isa. lxiii. 9; yea, it seems that all our afflictions (at least those of one sort,—namely, which consist in persecutions) are his in the first place, ours only by participation. Col. i. 24, We[1] " fill up the measure of the afflictions of Christ." Two things evidently manifest this compassionateness in Christ:—

(1.) *His interceding with his Father for their relief,* Zech. i. 12. Christ intercedeth on our behalf, not only in respect of our *sins,* but also our *sufferings;* and when the work of our afflictions is accomplished, we shall have the relief[2] he intercedes for. The Father always hears him; and we have not a deliverance from trouble, a recovering of health, ease of pain, freedom from any evil that ever laid hold upon us, but it is given us on the intercession of Jesus Christ. Believers are unacquainted with their own condition, if they look upon their mercies as dispensed in a way of common providence. And this may, indeed, be a cause why we esteem them no more, are no more thankful for them, nor fruitful in the enjoyment of them:— we see not how, by what means, nor on what account, they are dispensed to us. The generation of the people of God in the world are at this day alive, undevoured, merely on the account of the intercession of the Lord Jesus. His compassionateness hath been the fountain of their deliverances. Hence oftentimes he rebukes their sufferings and afflictions, that they shall not act to the utmost upon them when they are under them. He is with them when they pass through fire and water, Isa. xliii. 2, 3.

(2.) In that he doth and will, in the winding up of the matter, so sorely *revenge the quarrel* of their sufferings upon their enemies. He avenges his elect that cry unto him; yea, he doth it speedily. The controversy of Zion leads on the day of his vengeance, Isa. xxxiv. 8. He looks upon them sometimes in distress, and considers what is the state of the world in reference to them. Zech. i. 11, "We have walked to and fro through the earth, and, behold, all the earth sitteth still,

---

[1] " Τῶν παθημάτων Christi duo sunt genera: προτερήματα, quæ passus est in corpore suo, et ὑστερήματα, quæ in sanctis."—Zanc. in. loc.

[2] Heb. vii. 25.

and is at rest," say his messengers to him, whom he sent to consider the world and its condition during the affliction of his people. This commonly is the condition of the world in such a season, "They are at rest and quiet, their hearts are abundantly satiated;[1] they drink wine in bowls, and send gifts to one another." Then Christ looks to see who will come in for their succour, Isa. lix. 16, 17; and finding none engaging himself for their relief, by the destruction of their adversaries, himself undertakes it. Now, this vengeance he accomplishes two ways:—

[1.] Temporally, upon *persons, kingdoms, nations, and countries*; (a type whereof you have, Isa. lxiii. 1–6); as he did it upon the old Roman world, Rev. vi. 15, 16. And this also he doth two ways:—

1*st*. By *calling* out here and there an eminent *opposer*, and making him an example to all the world. So he dealt with Pharaoh: "For this cause have I raised thee up," Exod. ix. 16. So he doth to this day; he lays his hand upon eminent adversaries,—fills one with fury, another with folly, blasts a third, and makes another wither, or destroys them utterly and terribly. As a provoked lion, he lies not down without his prey.

2*dly*. In general, in the *vials of his wrath* which he will in these latter days pour out upon the antichristian world, and all that partake with them in their thoughts of vengeance and persecution. He will miserably destroy them, and make such work with them in the issue, that whosoever hears, both his ears shall tingle.

[2.] In eternal vengeance will he plead with the adversaries of his beloved, Matt. xxv. 41–46; 2 Thess. i. 6; Jude 15. It is hence evident that Christ abounds in pity and compassion towards his beloved. Instances might be multiplied, but these things are obvious, and occur to the thoughts of all.

In answer to this, I place in the saints chastity unto Christ, in every state and condition. That this might be the state of the church of Corinth, the apostle made it his endeavour. 2 Cor. xi. 2, 3, "I have espoused you to one husband, that I may present you as a chaste virgin to Christ. But I fear, lest by any means, as the serpent beguiled Eve through his subtilty, so your minds should be corrupted from the simplicity that is in Christ." And so is it said of the followers of the Lamb, on mount Sion, Rev. xiv. 4, "These are they which were not defiled with women, for they are virgins." What defilement that was they were free from, shall be afterward declared.

Now, there are three things wherein this chastity consists:—

1. The not taking any thing *into their affections and esteem* for those ends and purposes for which they have received Jesus Christ. Here the Galatians failed in their conjugal affection to Christ; they

---

[1] Amos vi. 3–6; Rev. xi. 10.

preserved not themselves chaste to him. They had received Christ
for life, and justification, and him only; but being after a while overcome with[1] charms, or bewitched, they took into the same place with
him the righteousness of the law. How Paul deals with them hereupon is known. How sorely, how pathetically doth he admonish them,
how severely reprove them, how clearly convince them of their madness and folly! This, then, is the first chaste affection believers bear
in their heart to Christ:—having received him for their righteousness
and salvation before God, for the fountain, spring, and well-head of
all their supplies, they will not now receive any other thing into his
room and in his stead. As to instance, in one particular:—We receive him for our[2] acceptance with God. All that here can stand in
competition with him for our affections, must be our own endeavours
for a [3] righteousness to commend us to God. Now, this must be either
before we receive him, or after. [As] for all duties and endeavours,
of what sort soever, for the pleasing of God before our receiving of
Christ, you know what was the apostle's frame, Phil. iii. 8–10. All
endeavours, all advantages, all privileges, he rejects with indignation,
as loss,—with abomination, as dung; and winds up all his aims and
desires in Christ alone and his righteousness, for those ends and purposes. But the works we do after we have received Christ are of another consideration. Indeed, they are acceptable to God; it pleaseth
him that we should walk in them. But as to that end for which we
receive Christ, [they are] of no other account than the former, Eph.
ii. 8–10. Even the works we do after believing,—those which we are
created unto in Christ Jesus, those that God hath ordained that believers "should walk in them,"—as to justification and acceptance with
God, (here called salvation), are excluded. It will one day appear
that Christ abhors the janglings of men about the place of their own
works and obedience, in the business of their acceptation with God;
nor will the saints find any peace in adulterous thoughts of that
kind. The chastity we owe unto him requires another frame. The
necessity, usefulness, and excellency of gospel obedience shall be afterward declared. It is marvellous to see how hard it is to keep some
professors to any faithfulness with Christ in this thing;—how many
disputes have been managed,[4] how many distinctions invented, how
many shifts and evasions studied, to keep up something, in some
place or other, to some purpose or other, that they may dally withal.
Those that love him indeed are otherwise minded.

Herein, then, of all things, do the saints endeavour to keep their
affections chaste and loyal to Jesus Christ. He is made unto them
of God "righteousness;" and they will own nothing else to that pur-

---

[1] Gal. iii 1.   [2] 1 Cor. i. 30.   [3] Rom. x. 4.
[4] " Perfice hoc precibus, pretio, ut hæream in parte aliqua tandem," etc.

pose: yea, sometimes they know not whether they have any interest in him or no,—he absents and withdraws himself; they still continue solitary, in a state of widowhood, refusing to be comforted, though many things offer themselves to that purpose, because he is not. When Christ is at any time absent from the soul, when it cannot see that it hath any interest in him, many lovers offer themselves to it, many woo its affections, to get it to rest on this or that thing for relief and succour; but though it go mourning never so long, it will have nothing but Christ to lean upon. Whenever the soul is in the wilderness, in the saddest condition, there it will stay until Christ come for to take it up, until it can come forth leaning upon him, Cant. viii. 5. The many instances of this that the book of Canticles affords us, we have in part spoken of before.

This doth he who hath communion with Christ:—he watcheth diligently over his own heart, that nothing creep into its affections, to give it any peace or establishment before God, but Christ only. Whenever that question is to be answered, " Wherewith shall I come before the LORD, and appear before the high God?" he doth not gather up, " This or that I will do;" or, " Here and there I will watch, and amend my ways;" but instantly he cries, " In the Lord Jesus have I [1] righteousness; all my desire is, to be found in him, not having on my own righteousness."

2. In *cherishing that Spirit, that holy Comforter, which Christ sends to us*, to abide with us in his room and stead. He tells us that he sends him to that purpose, John xvi. 7. He gives him to us, " vicariam navare operam," saith Tertullian,—to abide with us for ever, for all those ends and purposes which he hath to fulfil toward us and upon us; he gives him to dwell in us, to keep us, and preserve us blameless for himself. His name is in him, and with him: and it is upon this account that whatever is done to any of Christ's is done to him, because it is done to them in whom he is and dwells by his Spirit. Now, herein do the saints preserve their conjugal affections entire to Christ, that they labour by all means not to grieve his Holy Spirit, which he hath sent in his stead to abide with them. This the apostle puts them in mind of, Eph. iv. 30, " Grieve not the Holy Spirit."

There be two main ends for which Christ sends his Spirit to believers:—(1.) For their sanctification ; (2.) For their consolation : to which two all the particular acts of purging, teaching, anointing, and the rest that are ascribed to him, may be referred. So there be two ways whereby we may grieve him:—[1]. In respect of *sanctification;* [2.] In respect of *consolation:*—

(1.) In respect of *sanctification.* He is the Spirit of holiness,—holy

[1] Isa. xlv. 24; Phil. iii. 9; Hab. ii. 1–4

in himself, and the author of holiness in us: he works it in us, Tit.
iii. 5, and he persuades us to it, by those motions of his which are
not to be[1] quenched. Now, this, in the first place, grieves the Spirit,
—when he is carrying on in us and for us a work so infinitely for our
advantage, and without which we cannot see God, that we should run
cross to him, in ways of unholiness, pollution, and defilement. So the
connection of the words in the place before mentioned manifests, Eph.
iv. 28–31 ; and thence doth Paul bottom his powerful and most effectual persuasion unto holiness, even from the abode and indwelling of
this Holy Spirit with us, 1 Cor. iii. 16, 17.   Indeed, what can grieve
a loving and tender friend more than to oppose him and slight him
when he is most intent about our good,—and that a good of the
greatest consequence to us?   In this, then, believers make it their
business to keep their hearts loyal and their affections chaste to Jesus
Christ.   They labour instantly not to grieve the Holy Spirit by loose
and foolish, by careless and negligent walking, which he hath sent to
dwell and abide with them.   Therefore shall no anger, wrath, malice,
envy, dwell in their hearts; because they are contrary to the holy,
meek Spirit of Christ, which he hath given to dwell with them.
They attend to his motions, make use of his assistance, improve his
gifts, and nothing lies more upon their spirits, than that they may
walk worthy of the presence of this holy substitute of the Lord Jesus
Christ.

(2.) As to *consolation.* This is the second great end for which
Christ gives and sends his Spirit to us; who from thence, by the way
of eminency, is called " The Comforter."   To this end he seals us,
anoints us, establishes us, and gives us peace and joy.   Of all which
I shall afterward speak at large.   Now, there be two ways whereby
he may be grieved as to this end of his mission, and our chastity
to Jesus Christ thereby violated :—

[1.] *By placing our comforts and joys in other things,* and not
being filled with joy in the Holy Ghost.   When we make creatures
or creature comforts—any thing whatever but what we receive by the
Spirit of Christ—to be our joy and our delight, we are false with Christ.
So was it with Demas,[2] who loved the present world. When the ways
of the Spirit of God ̄are grievous and burdensome to us,—when we
say, " When will the Sabbath be past, that we may exact all our
labours?"—when our delight and refreshment lies in earthly things,
—we are unsuitable to Christ.   May not his Spirit say, " Why do I
still abide with these poor souls?   I provide them joys unspeakable
and glorious; but they refuse them, for perishing things.   I provide
them spiritual, eternal, abiding consolations, and it is all rejected for
a thing of nought."   This Christ cannot bear; wherefore, believers are

---

[1] 1 Thess. v. 19.   [2] 2 Tim. iv. 10.

exceeding careful in this, not to place their joy and consolation in any thing but what is administered by the Spirit. Their daily work is, to get their hearts crucified to the world and the things of it, and the world to their hearts; that they may not have living affections to dying things: they would fain look on the world as a crucified, dead thing, that hath neither form nor beauty; and if at any times they have been entangled with creatures and inferior contentment, and have lost their better joys, they cry out to Christ, " O restore to us the joys of thy Spirit!"

[2.] He is grieved when, through *darkness and unbelief*, we will not, do not, receive those consolations which he tenders to us, and which he is abundantly willing that we should receive. But of this I shall have occasion to speak afterward, in handling our communion with the Holy Ghost.

3. In [*keeping*] *his institutions*, or matter and manner of his worship. Christ marrying his church to himself, taking it to that relation, still expresseth the main of their chaste and choice affections to him to *lie in their keeping his institutions and his worship according to his appointment*. The breach of this he calls "adultery" everywhere, and "whoredom." He is a "jealous God;" and he gives himself that title only in respect of his institutions. And the whole apostasy of the Christian church unto false worship is called [1]"fornication;" and the church that leads the others to false worship, the "mother of harlots." On this account, those believers who really attend to communion with Jesus Christ, do labour to keep their hearts chaste to him in his ordinances, institutions, and worship; and that two ways:—

(1.) *They will receive nothing, practise nothing, own nothing, in his worship, but what is of his appointment.* They know that from the foundation of the world he never did allow, nor ever will, that in any thing the will of the creatures should be the measure of his honour or the principle of his worship, either as to matter or manner. It was a witty and true sense that one gave of the second commandment: "Non imago, non simulachrum prohibetur; sed non facies tibi;"—it is a making to ourselves, an inventing, a finding out, ways of worship, or means of honouring God, not by him appointed, that is so severely forbidden. Believers know what entertainment all will-worship finds with God: "Who hath required these things at your hand?" and, "In vain do you worship me, teaching for doctrines the traditions of men,"—is the best it meets with. I shall take leave to say what is upon my heart, and what (the Lord assisting) I shall willingly endeavour to make good against all the world,—namely, that that principle, *that the church hath power to institute and ap-*

[1] Rev. xvii. 5.

point any thing or ceremony belonging to the worship of God, either as to matter or to manner, beyond the orderly observance of such circumstances as necessarily attend such ordinances as Christ himself hath instituted, *lies at the bottom of all the horrible superstition and idolatry, of all the confusion, blood, persecution, and wars,* that have for so long a season spread themselves over the face of the Christian world; and that it is the design of a great part of the Revelation to make a discovery of this truth. And I doubt not but that the great controversy which God hath had with this nation for so many years, and which he hath pursued with so much anger and indignation, was upon this account:—that, contrary to that glorious light of the gospel which shone among us, the wills and fancies of men, under the name of order, decency, and the authority of the church (a chimera that none knew what it was, nor wherein the power of it did consist, nor in whom reside), were imposed on men in the ways and worship of God. Neither was all that pretence of glory, beauty, comeliness, and conformity, that then was pleaded, any thing more or less than what God doth so describe in the church of Israel, Ezek. xvi. 25, and forwards. Hence was the Spirit of God in prayer derided; hence was the powerful preaching of the gospel despised; hence was the Sabbath decried; hence was holiness stigmatized and persecuted;—to what end? That Jesus Christ might be deposed from the sole privilege and power of law-making in his church; that the true husband might be thrust aside, and adulterers of his spouse embraced; that taskmasters might be appointed in and over his house, which he never gave to his church, Eph. iv. 11; that a ceremonious, pompous, outward show worship, drawn from Pagan, Judaical, and Antichristian observations, might be introduced;—of all which there is not one word, tittle, or iota, in the whole book of God. This, then, they who hold communion with Christ are careful of:—they will admit of nothing, practise nothing, in the worship of God, private or public, but what they have his warrant for; unless it comes in his name, with "Thus saith the Lord Jesus," they will not hear an angel from heaven." They know the apostles themselves were to teach the saints only what Christ commanded them, Matt. xxviii. 20. You know how many in this very nation, in the days not long since past, yea, how many thousands, left their native soil, and went into a vast and howling wilderness in the utmost parts of the world, to keep their souls undefiled and chaste to their dear Lord Jesus, as to this of his worship and institutions.

(2.) They *readily embrace, receive, and practise every thing that the Lord Christ hath appointed.* They inquire diligently into his mind and will, that they may know it. They go to him for directions, and beg of him to lead them in the way they have not known.

The 119th Psalm may be a pattern for this. How doth the good, holy soul breathe after instruction in the ways and ordinances, the statutes and judgments, of God! This, I say, they are tender in: whatever is of Christ, they willingly submit unto, accept of, and give up themselves to the constant practice thereof; whatever comes on any other account they refuse.

IV. Christ manifests and evidences his love to his saints in a *way of bounty*,—in that rich, plentiful provision he makes for them. It hath "pleased the Father that in him should all fulness dwell," Col. i. 19; and that for this end, that "of his fulness we might all receive, and grace for grace," John i. 16. I shall not insist upon the particulars of that provision which Christ makes for his saints, with all those influences of the Spirit of life and grace that daily they receive from him,—that bread that he gives them to the full, the refreshment they have from him; I shall only observe this, that the Scripture affirms him to do all things for them in an abundant manner, or to do it richly, in a way of bounty. Whatever he gives us,—his grace to assist us, his presence to comfort us,—he doth it abundantly. You have the general assertion of it, Rom. v. 20, "Where sin abounded, grace did much more abound." If grace abound much more in comparison of sin, it is abundant grace indeed; as will easily be granted by any that shall consider how sin hath abounded, and doth, in every soul. Hence he is said to be able, and we are bid to expect that he should do for us "exceeding abundantly above all that we ask or think," Eph. iii. 20. Is it pardoning mercy we receive of him? why, he doth "*abundantly* pardon," Isa. lv. 7; he will multiply or add to pardon,— he will add pardon to pardon, that grace and mercy shall abound above all our sins and iniquities. Is it the Spirit he gives us? he sheds him upon us *richly* or "*abundantly*," Tit. iii. 6; not only bidding us drink of the water of life freely, but also bestowing him in such a plentiful measure, that rivers of water shall flow from them that receive him, John vii. 38, 39,—that they shall never thirst any more who have drank of him. Is it grace that we receive of him? he gives that also in a way of bounty; we receive "*abundance of grace*," Rom. v. 17; he "abounds toward us in all wisdom and prudence," Eph. i. 8. Hence is that invitation, Cant. v. 1. If in any things, then, we are straitened, it is in ourselves; Christ deals bountifully with us. Indeed, the great sin of believers is, that they make not use of Christ's bounty as they ought to do; that we do not every day take of him mercy in abundance. The oil never ceaseth till the vessels cease; supplies from Christ fail not but only when our faith fails in receiving them.

Then our return to Christ is in a way of duty. Unto this two things are required:—

1. That we *follow after* and practise holiness in the power of it,

as it is obedience unto Jesus Christ.   Under this formality, as obedience to him, all gospel obedience is called, " whatsoever Christ commands us," Matt. xxviii. 20; and saith he, John xv. 14, " Ye are my friends, if ye do whatsoever I command you;" and it is required of us that we live to him who died for us, 2 Cor. v. 15,—live to him in all holy obedience,—live to him as our Lord and King.   Not that I suppose there are peculiar precepts and a peculiar law of Jesus Christ, in the observance whereof we are justified, as the Socinians fancy; for surely the gospel requires of us no more, but " to love the Lord our God with all our hearts, and all our souls,"—which the law also required;—but that, the Lord Jesus having brought us into a condition of acceptance with God, wherein our obedience is well-pleasing to him, and we being to honour him as we honour the Father, that we have a respect and peculiar regard to him in all our obedience.   So Tit. ii. 14, he hath purchased us unto himself.   And thus believers do in their obedience; they eye Jesus Christ,—

(1.) As *the author of their faith and obedience,* for whose sake it is " given to them to believe," Phil. i. 29; and who by his Spirit works that obedience in them.   So the apostle, Heb. xii. 1, 2; in the course of our obedience we still look to Jesus, " the author of our faith." Faith is here both the grace of faith, and the fruit of it in obedience.

(2.) As him in, for, and by whom we have acceptance with God in our *obedience.*   They know all their duties are weak, imperfect, not able to abide the presence of God; and therefore they look to Christ as him who bears the iniquity of their holy things, who adds incense to their prayers, gathers out all the weeds of their duties, and makes them acceptable to God.

(3.) As one that hath *renewed the commands* of God unto them, with mighty obligations unto obedience.   So the apostle, 2 Cor. v. 14, 15, " The love of Christ constraineth us;" of which afterward.

(4.) They consider him as God, *equal with his Father,* to whom all honour and obedience is due.   So Rev. v. 13.   But these things I have, not long since, opened[1] in another treatise, dealing about the worship of Christ as mediator.   This, then, the saints do in all their obedience; they have a special regard to their dear Lord Jesus.   He is, on all these accounts, and innumerable others, continually in their thoughts.   His love to them, his life for them, his death for them,— all his kindness and mercy constrains them to live to him.

2. By labouring *to abound in fruits of holiness.*   As he deals with us in a way of bounty, and deals out unto us abundantly, so he requires that we abound in all grateful, obediential returns to him.   So we are exhorted to " be always abounding in the work of the Lord," 1 Cor. xv. 58.   This is that I intend:—the saints are not satisfied with

---

[1] Vindiciæ Evangel., chap. xiii. vol. xii.

that measure that at any time they have attained, but are still pressing, that they may be more dutiful, more fruitful to Christ.

And this is a little glimpse of some of that communion which we enjoy with Christ. It is but a little, from him who hath the least experience of it of all the saints of God; who yet hath found that in it which is better than ten thousand worlds; who desires to spend the residue of the few and evil days of his pilgrimage in pursuit hereof,—in the contemplation of the excellencies, desirableness, love, and grace of our dear Lord Jesus, and in making returns of obedience according to his will: to whose soul, in the midst of the perplexities of this wretched world, and cursed rebellions of his own heart, this is the great relief, that "He that shall come will come, and will not tarry." "The Spirit and the bride say, Come; and let him that readeth say, Come. Even so, come, Lord Jesus."

CHAPTER VI.

Of communion with Christ in purchased grace—Purchased grace considered in respect of its rise and fountain—The first rise of it, in the obedience of Christ—Obedience properly ascribed to Christ—Two ways considered: what it was, and wherein it did consist—Of his obedience to the law in general—Of the law of the Mediator—His habitual righteousness, how necessary; as also his obedience to the law of the Mediator—Of his actual obedience or active righteousness—All Christ's obedience performed as he was Mediator—His active obedience for us—This proved at large, Gal. iv. 4, 5; Rom. v. 19; Phil. iii. 10; Zech. iii. 3–5—One objection removed—Considerations of Christ's active righteousness closed—Of the death of Christ, and its influence into our acceptation with God—A price; redemption, what it is—A sacrifice; atonement made thereby—A punishment; satisfaction thereby—The intercession of Christ; with its influence into our acceptation with God.

OUR process[1] is now to communion with Christ in *purchased grace*, as it was before proposed: "That we may know him, and the power of his resurrection, and the fellowship of his sufferings, and be made conformable to his death," Phil. iii. 10.

By purchased grace, I understand all that righteousness and grace which Christ hath procured, or wrought out for us, or doth by any means make us partakers of, or bestows on us for our benefit, by any thing that he hath done or suffered, or by any thing he continueth to do as mediator:—First, *What this purchased grace is, and wherein it doth consist;* Secondly, *How we hold communion with Christ therein;* are the things that now come under consideration.

[1] [See beginning of chapter ii., for the leading divisions.]

The First may be considered two ways:—1. In respect of the *rise and fountain* of it; 2. Of its *nature*, or wherein it consisteth.

1. It hath a threefold rise, spring, or causality in Christ:—(1.) The *obedience* of his life.   (2.) The *suffering* of his death.   (3.) His continued *intercession*.   All the actions of Christ as mediator, leading to the communication of grace unto us, may be either referred to these heads, or to some things that are subservient to them or consequents of them.

2. For the nature of this grace wherein we have communion with Christ, flowing from these heads and fountains, it may be referred to these three:—(1.) Grace of *justification*, or acceptation with God; which makes a relative change in us, as to state and condition. (2.) Grace of *sanctification*, or holiness before God; which makes a real change in us, as to principle and operation.   (3.) Grace of *privilege;* which is mixed, as we shall show, if I go forth to the handling thereof.

Now, that we have communion with Christ in this purchased grace, is evident on this single consideration,—that there is almost nothing that Christ hath done, which is a spring of that grace whereof we speak, but we are said to do it with him.   We are "crucified" with him, Gal. ii. 20; we are "dead" with him, 2 Tim. ii. 11; Col. iii. 3; and "buried" with him, Rom. vi. 4; Col. ii. 12; we are "quickened together with him," Col. ii. 13; "risen" with him, Col. iii. 1.   "He hath quickened us together with Christ, and hath raised us up together, and made us sit together in heavenly places," Eph. ii. 5, 6.   In the actings of Christ, there is, by virtue of the compact between him as mediator, and the Father, such an assured foundation laid of the communication of the fruits of those actings unto those in whose stead he performed them, that they are said, in the participation of those fruits, to have done the same things with him.   The life and power of which truth we may have occasion hereafter to inquire into:—

(1.) The first fountain and spring of this grace, wherein we have our communion with Christ, is first to be considered; and that is the *obedience of his life:* concerning which it must be declared,— [1.] What it is that is intended thereby, and wherein it consisteth. [2.] What *influence* it hath into the grace whereof we speak.

To the handling of this I shall only premise this observation,— namely, that in the order of *procurement*, the life of Christ (as was necessary) precedeth his death; and therefore we shall handle it in the first place: but in the order of *application*, the benefits of his death are bestowed on us antecedently, in the nature of the things themselves, unto those of his life; as will appear, and that necessarily, from the state and condition wherein we are.

[1.] By the *obedience* of the life of Christ, I intend the universal conformity of the Lord Jesus Christ, as he was or is, in his being mediator, to the whole will of God; and his complete actual fulfilling of the whole of every law of God, or doing of all that God in them required. He might have been perfectly holy by obedience to the law of creation, the moral law, as the angels were; neither could any more, as a man walking with God, be required of him: but he submitted himself also to every law or ordinance that was introduced upon the occasion of sin, which, on his own account, he could not be subject to, it becoming him to " fulfil ¹all righteousness," Matt. iii. 15, as he spake in reference to a newly-instituted ceremony.

That obedience is properly ascribed unto Jesus Christ as mediator, the Scripture is witness, both as to name and thing. Heb. v. 8, " Though he were a Son, yet learned he obedience," etc.; yea, he was obedient in his sufferings, and it was that which gave life to his death, Phil. ii. 8. He was obedient to death: for therein " he did make his soul an offering for sin," Isa. liii. 10; or, " his soul made an offering for sin," as it is interpreted, verse 12, " he poured out his soul to death," or, " his soul poured out itself unto death." And he not only sanctified himself to be an offering, John xvii. 19, but he also " offered up himself," Heb. ix. 14, an " offering of a sweet savour to God," Eph. v. 2. Hence, as to the whole of his work, he is called the Father's " servant," Isa. xlii. 1, and verse 19: and he professes of himself that he " came into the world to do the will of God, the will of him that sent him;" for which he manifests " his great readiness," Heb. x. 7;—all which evince his obedience. But I suppose I need not insist on the proof of this, that Christ, in the work of mediation, and as mediator, was obedient, and did what he did willingly and cheerfully, in obedience to God.

Now, this obedience of Christ may be considered two ways:— 1*st.* As to the habitual root and fountain of it. 2*dly.* As to the actual parts or duties of it:—

1*st.* The *habitual righteousness* of Christ as mediator in his human nature, was the absolute, complete, exact conformity of the soul of Christ to the will, mind, or law of God; or his perfect habitually-inherent righteousness. This he had necessarily from the grace of union; from whence it is that that which was born of the virgin was a " holy thing," Luke i. 35. It was, I say, necessary consequentially,

---

¹ " Vox hæc δικαιοσύνη hoc quidem loco latissimè sumitur, ita ut significet non modo τὸ νόμιμον, sed et quicquid ullam æqui atque honesti habet rationem; nam lex Mosis de hoc baptismo nihil præscripserat."—Grot.

" Per δικαιοσύνη Christus hic non designat justitiam legalem, sed, ut ita loqui liceat, personalem; τὸ πρέπον personæ, et τὸ καθῆκον muneri."—Walæ.

'Εβαπτίσθη δὲ καὶ ἐνήστευσεν, οὐκ αὐτὸς ἀποῤῥύψεως ἢ νηστείας χρείαν ἔχων, ἢ καθάρσεως, ὁ τῇ φύσει καθαρὸς καὶ ἅγιος.—Clem.

that it should be so; though the effecting of it were by the free operations of the Spirit, Luke ii. 52. He had an all-fulness of grace on all accounts. This the apostle describes, Heb. vii. 26, " Such an high priest became us, holy, harmless, undefiled, separate from sinners." Every way separate and distant from sin and sinners he was to be; whence he is called " The Lamb of God, without spot or blemish," 1 Pet. i. 19. This habitual holiness of Christ was inconceivably above that of the angels. He who " [1]chargeth his angels with folly," Job iv. 18; " who putteth no trust in his saints; and in whose sight the heavens" (or their inhabitants) " are not clean," chap. xv. 15; always embraceth him in his bosom, and is always well pleased with him, Matt. iii. 17. And the reason of this is, because every other creature, though never so holy, hath the Spirit of God by measure; but he was not given to Christ " by measure," John iii. 34; and that because it pleased him that in him " should all fulness dwell," Col. i. 19. This habitual grace of Christ, though not absolutely infinite, yet, in respect of any other creature, it is as the water of the sea to the water of a pond or pool. All other creatures are depressed from perfection by this,—that they subsist in a created, dependent being; and so have the fountain of what is communicated to them without them. But the human nature of Christ subsists in the person of the Son of God; and so hath the bottom and fountain of its holiness in the strictest unity with itself.

2dly. The *actual* obedience of Christ, as was said, was his willing, cheerful, obediential performance of every thing, duty, or command, that God, by virtue of any law whereto we were subject and obnoxious, did require; and [his obedience], moreover, to the peculiar law of the mediator. Hereof, then, are two parts:—

(*1st.*) That whatever was *required* of us by virtue of any law,— that he did and fulfilled. Whatever was required of us by the law of nature, in our state of innocency; whatever kind of duty was added by morally positive or ceremonial institutions; whatever is required of us in way of obedience to righteous judicial laws,—he did it all. Hence he is said to be "made under the law," Gal. iv. 4; subject or obnoxious to it, to all the precepts or commands of it. So, Matt. iii 15, he said it became him to [2]"fulfil all righteousness,"—πᾶσαν δικαιοσύνην,—all manner of righteousness whatever; that is, everything that God required, as is evident from the application of that general axiom to the baptism of John. I shall not need, for this, to go to

---

[1] " Sensus est de angelis, qui si cum Deo conferantur, aut si eos secum Deus conferat, non habens rationem eorum quæ in illis posuit, et dotium ac donorum quæ in illos contulit, et quibus eos exornavit et illustravit, inveniat eos stolidos. Sanè quicquid habent angeli, a Deo habent."—Mercer. in loc.

[2] " Fuit legis servituti subjectus, ut eam implendo nos ab ea redimeret, et ab ejus servitute."—Bez.

particular instances, in the duties of the law of nature,—to God and his parents; of morally positive [duties], in the Sabbath, and other acts of worship; of the ceremonial law, in circumcision, and observation of all the rites of the Judaical church; of the judicial, in paying tribute to governors;—it will suffice, I presume, that on the one hand he "did no sin, neither was guile found in his mouth;" and on the other, that he "fulfilled all righteousness:" and thereupon the Father was always well pleased with him. This was that which he owned of himself, —that he came to do the will of God; and he did it.

(2dly.) There was a *peculiar law of the mediator*, which respected himself merely, and contained all those acts and duties of his which are not for our imitation. So that obedience which he showed in dying was peculiarly to this [1]law, John x. 18, " I have power to lay down my life: this commandment have I received of my Father." As mediator, he received this peculiar command of his Father, that he should lay down his life, and take it again; and he was obedient thereunto. Hence we say, he who is mediator did some things merely as a man, subject to the law of God in general; so he prayed for his persecutors,—those that put him to death, Luke xxiii. 34;— some things as mediator; so he prayed for his elect only, John xvii. 9. There were not worse in the world, really and evidently, than many of them that crucified him; yet, as a man, subject to the law, he forgave them, and prayed for them. When he prayed as mediator, his Father always heard him and answered him, John xi. 41; and in the other prayers he was accepted as one exactly performing his duty.

This, then, is the obedience of Christ; which was the first thing proposed to be considered. The next is,—

[2.] That it hath an influence into the grace of which we speak, wherein we hold communion with him,—namely, our *free acceptation* with God; what that influence is, must also follow in its order.

1st. For his *habitual righteousness*, I shall only propose it under these two considerations:—

(1st.) That upon this supposition, that it was *needful* that we should have a mediator that was God and man in one person, as it could not otherwise be, so it must needs be that he must be holy. For although there be but one primary necessary effect of the hypostatical union (which is the subsistence of the human nature in the person of the Son of God), yet that he that was so united to him should be a " holy thing," completely holy, was necessary also;—of which before.

(2dly.) That the *relation* which this righteousness of Christ hath to the grace we receive from him is only this,—that thereby he was

---

[1] " Proprium objectum obedientiæ est præceptum, tacitum vel expressum, id est, voluntas superioris quocunque modo innotescat."—Thom. 2, 2, q. 2, 5. Deut. xviii. 18; Acts iii. 22; John xii. 49, xiv. 31, vi. 38, v. 30.

ἱκανός,—fit to do all that he had to do for us. This is the intendment of the apostle, Heb. vii. 26. Such a one "became us;" it was needful he should be such a one, that he might do what he had to do. And the reasons hereof are two:—

[*1st.*] Had he not been completely furnished with habitual grace, he could never have *actually* fulfilled the righteousness which was required at his hands. It was therein that he was able to do all that he did. So himself lays down the presence of the Spirit with him as the bottom and foundation of his going forth to his work, Isa. lxi. 1.

[*2dly.*] He could not have been *a complete and perfect* sacrifice, nor have answered all the types and figures of him, that were[1] complete and without blemish. But now, Christ having this habitual righteousness, if he had never yielded any continued obedience to the law actively, but had suffered as soon after his incarnation as Adam sinned after his creation, he had been a fit sacrifice and offering; and therefore, doubtless, his following obedience hath another use besides to fit him for an oblation, for which he was most fit without it.

2dly. For Christ's obedience to the *law of mediation*, wherein it is not coincident with his passive obedience, as they speak (for I know that expression is improper); it was that which was requisite for the discharging of his office, and is not imputed unto us, as though we had done it, though the *ἀποτελέσματα* and fruits of it are; but is of the nature of his intercession, whereby he provides the good things we stand in need of, at least subserviently to his oblation and intercession;—of which more afterward.

3dly. About his *actual fulfilling* of the law, or doing all things that of us are required, there is some doubt and question; and about it there are three several opinions:—

(*1st.*) That this *active obedience* of Christ hath no farther influence into our justification and acceptation with God, but as it was *preparatory* to his blood-shedding and oblation; which is the sole cause of our justification, the whole righteousness which is imputed to us arising from thence.

(*2dly.*) That it may be considered two ways:—[*1st.*] As it is *purely obedience;* and so it hath no other state but that before mentioned. [*2dly.*] As it was accomplished with suffering, and joined with it, as it was part of his humiliation, so it is *imputed* to us, or is part of that upon the account whereof we are justified.

---

[1] "Præcipitur, Lev. xxii. 20, ne offeratur pecus in quo sit מום, mūm, id est corporis vitium : a מום efficitur *μῶμος* ' culpa:' unde Christus dicitur *ἄμωμος*, 'inculpatus:' opponitur autem מום τὸ תָּמִים, hoc est 'integrum.' Ibid., ver. 19, et sic Exod. xii. 5, præcipitur de agno paschali, ut sit תָּמִים, id est 'integer,' omnis scilicet vitii expers. Idem præcipitur de agnis jugis sacrificii, Numb. xxviii. 3, quibus ipsa nimirum sanctitas Christi tanquam victimæ præfigurata est."—Piscat., in 1 Pet. i. 19.

(3*dly.*) That this obedience of Christ, being done *for* us, is reckoned graciously of God *unto* us; and upon the account thereof are we accepted as righteous before him.   My intendment is not to handle this difference in the way of a controversy, but to give such an understanding of the whole as may speedily be reduced to the practice of godliness and consolation; and this I shall do in the ensuing observations:—

[1*st.*] That the obedience that Christ yielded to the law in general, is not only to the peculiar law of the mediator, though he yielded it *as mediator.*   He was incarnate as mediator, Heb. ii. 14; Gal. iv. 4; and all he afterward did, it was as our mediator.   For that cause " came he into the world," and did and suffered whatever he did or suffered in this world.   So that of this expression, *as mediator*, there is a twofold sense: for it may be taken strictly, as relating solely to the law of the mediator, and so Christ may be said to do as mediator only what he did in obedience to that law; but in the sense now insisted on, whatever Christ did as a man subject to any law, he did it as mediator, because he did it as part of the duty incumbent on him who undertook so to be.

[2*dly.*] That whatever *Christ did as mediator*, he did it for them whose mediator he was, or in whose stead and for whose good he executed the office of a mediator before God.   This the Holy Ghost witnesseth, Rom. viii. 3, 4, " What the law could not do, in that it was weak through the flesh, God sending his own Son in the likeness of sinful flesh, and for sin, condemned sin in the flesh, that the righteousness of the law might be fulfilled in us;" because that we could not in that condition of weakness whereinto we are cast by sin, come to God, and be freed from condemnation by the law, God sent Christ as a mediator, to do and suffer whatever the law required at our hands for that end and purpose, that we might not be condemned, but accepted of God.   It was all to this end,—" That the righteousness of the law might be fulfilled in us;" that is, which the law required of us, consisting in duties of obedience.   This Christ performed for us.   This expression of the apostle, " God sending his own Son in the likeness of sinful flesh, and for sin, condemned sin in the flesh;" if you will add to it, that of Gal. iv. 4, that he was so sent forth as that he was ὑπὸ νόμον γενόμενος, "made under the law," (that is, obnoxious to it, to·yield all the obedience that it doth require), comprises the whole of what Christ did or suffered ; and all this, the Holy Ghost tells us, was for us, verse 4.

[3*dly.*] That the end of this *active obedience* of Christ cannot be assigned to be, that he might be *fitted for his death and oblation.*   For he answered all types, and was every way ἱκανός (fit to be made an offering for sin), by his union and habitual grace.   So that if the obedience Christ performed be not reckoned to us, and done upon our account, there is no just cause to be assigned why he should live here in the world so long as he did, in perfect obedience to all the laws of God. Had he died before, there had been perfect innocence, and perfect holiness, by his habitual grace, and infinite virtue and worth from the dignity of his person; and surely he yielded not that long course of all manner of obedience, but for some great and special purpose in reference to our salvation.

[*4thly.*] That had not the obedience of Christ been for us (in what sense we shall see instantly), it might in his life have been required of him to yield obedience *to the law of nature*, the alone law which he could be liable to as a man; for an innocent man in a covenant of works, as he was, needs no other law, nor did God ever give any other law to any such person (the law of creation is all that an innocent creature is liable to, with what symbols of that law God is pleased to add). And yet to this law also was his subjection voluntary; and that not only consequentially, because he was born upon his own choice, not by any natural course, but also because as mediator, God and man, he was not by the institution of that law obliged unto it; being, as it were, exempted and lifted above that law by the hypostatical union: yet, when I say his subjection hereunto was voluntary, I do not intend that it was merely arbitrary and at choice whether he would yield obedience[1] unto it or no,—but on supposition of his undertaking to be a mediator, it was necessary it should be so,—but that he voluntarily and willingly submitted unto, and so became really subject to the commands of it. But now, moreover, Jesus Christ yielded perfect obedience to all those laws which came upon us by the occasion of sin, as the ceremonial law; yea, those very institutions that signified the washing away of sin, and repentance from sin, as the baptism of John, which he had no need of himself. This, therefore, must needs be for us.

[*5thly.*] That the obedience of Christ cannot be reckoned amongst his *sufferings*, but is clearly *distinct* from it, as to all formalities. Doing is one thing, suffering another; they are in diverse *predicaments*, and cannot be coincident.

See, then, briefly what we have obtained by those considerations; and then I shall intimate what is the stream issuing from this first spring or fountain of purchased grace, with what influence it hath thereinto:—

First, By the obedience of the life of Christ you see what is intended,—his willing submission unto, and perfect, complete fulfilling of, every law of God, that any of the saints of God were obliged unto. It is true, every act almost of Christ's obedience, from the blood of

---

[1] " Obedientia importat necessitatem respectu ejus quod præcipitur, et voluntatem respectu impletionis præcepti."—Thom. 3, q. 47, 2, 2.

his circumcision to the blood of his cross, was attended with suffering, —so that his whole life might, in that regard, be called a death; but yet, looking upon his willingness and obedience in it, it is distinguished from his sufferings peculiarly so called, and termed his[1] *active righteousness.* This is, then, I say, as was showed, that complete, absolutely perfect accomplishment of the whole law of God by Christ, our mediator; whereby he not only "did no sin, neither was there guile found in his mouth," but also most perfectly fulfilled all righteousness, as he affirmed it became him to do.

Secondly, That this obedience was performed by Christ not for himself, but for us, and in our stead. It is true, it must needs be, that whilst he had his conversation in the flesh he must be most perfectly and absolutely holy; but yet the prime intendment of his accomplishing of holiness,—which consists in the complete obedience of his whole life to any law of God,—that was no less for us than his suffering death. That this is so, the apostle tells us, Gal. iv. 4, 5, "God sent forth his Son, made of a woman, made under the law, to redeem them that were under the law." This Scripture, formerly named, must be a little farther insisted on. He was both made of a woman, and made under the law; that is, obedient to it for us. The end here, both of the incarnation and obedience of Christ to the law (for that must needs be understood here by the phrase ὑπὸ νόμον γενόμενος,—that is, disposed of in such a condition as that he must yield subjection and obedience to the law), was all to redeem us. In these two expressions, "Made of a woman, made under the law," the apostle doth not knit his incarnation and death together, with an exclusion of the obedience of his life. And he was so made under the law, as those were under the law whom he was to redeem. Now, we were under the law, not only as *obnoxious to its penalties,* but as *bound to all the duties of it.* That this is our being "under the law," the apostle informs us, Gal. iv. 21, "Tell me, ye that desire to be under the law." It was not the penalty of the law they desired to be under, but to be under it in respect of obedience. Take away, then, the end, and you destroy the means. If Christ were not incarnate nor made under the law for himself, he did not yield obedience for himself; it was all for us, *for our good.* Let us now look forward, and see what influence this hath into our acceptation.

Thirdly, Then, I say, this perfect, complete obedience of Christ to the law is reckoned unto us. As there is a truth in that, "The day thou eatest thou shalt die,"—death is the reward of sin, and so we cannot be freed from death but by the death of Christ, Heb. ii. 14, 15; so also is that no less true, "Do this, and live,"—that life is not to be ob-

---

[1] "In vita passivam habuit actionem; in morte passionem activam sustinuit; dum salutem operatur in medio terræ."—Bern. Ser. 4.

tained unless all be done that the law requires. That is still true, "If thou wilt enter into life, keep the commandments," Matt. xix. 17. They must, then, be kept by us, or our surety. Neither is it of any value which by some is objected, that if Christ yielded perfect obedience to the law for us, then are we no more bound to yield obedience; for by his undergoing death, the penalty of the law, we are freed from it. I answer, How did Christ undergo death? Merely as it was penal. How, then, are we delivered from death? Merely as it is penal. Yet we must die still; yea, as the last conflict with the effects of sin, as a passage to our Father, we must die. Well, then, Christ yielded perfect obedience to the law; but how did he do it? Purely as it stood in that *conditional* [*arrangement*], "Do this, and live." He did it in the strength of the grace he had received; he did it as a means of life, to procure life by it, as the tenor of a covenant. Are we, then, freed from this obedience? Yes; but how far? From doing it in our own strength; from doing it for this end, that we may obtain life everlasting. It is vain that some say confidently, that we must yet work for life; it is all one as to say we are yet under the old covenant, "Hoc fac, et vives:" we are not freed from obedience, as a way of walking with God, but we are, as a way of working to come to him: of which at large afterward.

Rom. v. 18, 19, "By the righteousness of one the free gift came upon all men unto justification of life: by the obedience of one shall many be made righteous," saith the Holy Ghost. By his obedience to the law are we made righteous; it is reckoned to us for righteousness. That the passive obedience of Christ is here only intended is false:—

First, It is opposed to the *disobedience* of Adam, which was *active.* The δικαίωμα is opposed παραπτώματι,—the righteousness to the fault. The fault was an active transgression of the law, and the obedience opposed to it must be an active accomplishment of it. Besides, obedience placed singly, in its own nature, denotes an action or actions conformable to the law; and therein came Christ, not to destroy but to fulfil the law, Matt. v. 17,—that was the design of his coming, and so for us; he came to fulfil the law for us, Isa. ix. 6, and [was] born to us, Luke ii. 11. This also was in that will of the Father which, out of his infinite love, he came to accomplish. *Secondly,* It cannot clearly be evinced that there is any such thing, in propriety of speech, as *passive obedience; obeying is doing,* to which passion or suffering cannot belong: I know it is commonly called so, when men obey until they suffer; but properly it is not so.

So also, Phil. iii. 9, "And be found in him, not having my own righteousness, which is of the law, but that which is through the faith of Christ, the righteousness which is of God by faith." The righteousness we receive is opposed to our own obedience to the law; opposed to it, not as something in another kind, but as something in the same kind excluding that from such an end which the other obtains. Now this is the obedience of Christ to the law,—himself thereby being "made to us righteousness," 1 Cor. i. 30.

Rom. v. 10, the issue of the death of Christ is placed upon reconciliation; that is, a slaying of the enmity and restoring us into that condition of peace and friendship wherein Adam was before his fall. But is there no more to be done? Notwithstanding that there was no wrath due to Adam, yet he was to obey, if he would enjoy eternal life. Something there is, moreover, to be done in respect of us, if, after the slaying of the enmity and reconciliation made, we shall enjoy life: "Being reconciled by his death," we are saved by that perfect obedience which in his life he yielded to the law of God. There is distinct mention made of reconciliation, through a non-imputation of sin, as Ps. xxxii. 1, Luke i. 77, Rom. iii. 25, 2 Cor. v. 19; and justification through an imputation of righteousness, Jer. xxiii. 6, Rom. iv. 5, 1 Cor. i. 30;—although these things are so far from being separated, that they are reciprocally affirmed of one another: which, as it doth not evince an identity, so it doth an eminent conjunction. And this last we have by the life of Christ.

This is fully expressed in that typical representation of our justification before the Lord, Zech. iii. 3–5. Two things are there expressed to belong to our free acceptation before God:—1. The taking away of the guilt of our sin, our filthy robes; this is done by the death of Christ. Remission of sin is the proper fruit thereof; but there is more also required, even a collation of righteousness, and thereby a right to life eternal. This is here called "Change of raiment;" so the Holy Ghost expresses it again, Isa. lxi. 10, where he calls it plainly "The garments of salvation," and "The robe of righteousness." Now this is only made ours by the obedience of Christ, as the other by his death.

Objection. "But if this be so, then are we as *righteous as Christ himself*, being righteous with his righteousness."

Answer. But first, here is a great difference,—if it were no more than that this righteousness was *inherent in* Christ, and properly his own, it is only reckoned or *imputed* to us, or freely bestowed on us, and we are made righteous with that which is not ours. But, secondly, the truth is, that Christ was not righteous with that righteousness for *himself*, but for *us;* so that here can be no comparison: only this we may say, we are righteous with his righteousness which he wrought for us, and that completely.

And this, now, is the rise of the purchased grace whereof we speak, —the obedience of Christ; and this is the influence of it into our acceptation with God.   Whereas the guilt of sin, and our obnoxiousness to punishment on that account, is removed and taken away (as shall farther be declared) by the death of Christ; and whereas, besides the taking away of sin, we have need of a complete righteousness, upon the account whereof we may be accepted with God; this obedience of Christ, through the free grace of God, is imputed unto us for that end and purpose.

This is all I shall for the present insist on to this purpose.   That the passive righteousness of Christ only is imputed to us in the non-imputation of sin, and that on the condition of our faith and new obedience, so exalting them into the room of the righteousness of Christ, is a thing which, in communion with the Lord Jesus, I have as yet no acquaintance withal.   What may be said in the way of argument on the one side or other must be elsewhere considered.

(2.) The second spring of our communion with Christ in purchased grace, is his death and oblation.   He lived for us, he died for us; he was ours in all he did, in all he suffered.[1]   I shall be the more brief in handling of this, because on another design I have [2]elsewhere at large treated of all the concernments of it.

Now, the death of Christ, as it is a spring of that purchased grace wherein we have communion with him, is in the Scripture proposed under a threefold consideration:—[1.] Of a price.   [2.] Of a sacrifice.   [3.] Of a penalty.

In the first regard, its proper effect is redemption; in the second, reconciliation or atonement; in the third, satisfaction; which are the great ingredients of that purchased grace whereby, in the first place, we have communion with Christ.

[1.] It is a *price*.   " We are bought with a price," 1 Cor. vi. 20; being " not redeemed with silver and gold, and corruptible things, but with the precious blood of Christ," 1 Pet. i. 18, 19 : which therein answers those things in other contracts.[3]   He came to " give his life a ransom for many," Matt. xx. 28,—a price of redemption, 1 Tim. ii. 6.   The proper use and energy of this expression in the Scripture, I have elsewhere declared.

Now, the proper effect and issue of the death of Christ as a price or ransom is, as I said, redemption.   Now, redemption is the deliverance of any one from bondage or captivity, and the miseries attending that condition, by the intervention or interposition of a price or

---

[1] " Tantane me tenuit vivendi, nate, voluptas,
　　Ut pro me hostili paterer succedere dextræ,
　　Quem genui ! tuane hæc genitor per vulnera servor,
　　Morte tua vivens?"—Virgil, Æneid. x. 846.

[2] Vindic. Evan., cap. xx.-xxii. vol. xii.

[3] " Nil quidem emitur nisi interveniente pretio; sed hoc tamen additum magnam emphasin habet."—Bez.

ransom, paid by the redeemer to him by whose authority the captive was detained:—

1*st.* In general, it is a deliverance. Hence Christ is called " The Deliverer," Rom. xi. 26; giving himself to " deliver us," Gal. i. 4. He is " Jesus, who delivers us from the wrath to come," 1 Thess. i. 10.

2*dly.* It is the delivery of one from *bondage* or captivity. We are, without him, all prisoners and captives, " bound in prison," Isa. lxi. 1; " sitting in darkness, in the prison house," Isa. xlii. 7, xlix. 9; " prisoners in the pit wherein there is no water," Zech. ix. 11; " the captives of the mighty, and the prey of the terrible," Isa. xlix. 25; under a " captivity that must be led captive," Ps. lxviii. 18: this puts us in "bondage," Heb. ii. 15.

3*dly.* The person committing thus to prison and into bondage, is *God himself.* To him we owe " our debts," Matt. vi. 12, xviii. 23–27; against him are our offences, Ps. li. 4; he is the judge and lawgiver, James iv. 12. To sin is to rebel against him. He shuts up men under disobedience, Rom. xi. 32; and he shall cast both body and soul of the impenitent into hell-fire, Matt. x. 28. To his wrath are men obnoxious, John iii. 36; and lie under it by the sentence of the law, which is their prison.

4*thly.* The *miseries* that attend this condition are innumerable. Bondage to Satan, sin, and the world, comprises the sum of them; from all which we are delivered by the death of Christ, as a price or ransom. " God hath delivered us from the power of darkness, and hath translated us into the kingdom of his dear Son; in whom we have redemption through his blood," Col. i. 13, 14. And he " redeems us from all iniquity," Tit. ii. 14; " from our vain conversation," 1 Pet. i. 18, 19; even from the guilt and power of our sin; purchasing us to himself " a peculiar people, zealous of good works," Tit ii. 14: so dying for the " redemption of transgressions," Heb. ix. 15; redeeming us also from the world, Gal. iv. 5.

5*thly.* And all this is by the *payment of the price mentioned into the hand of God,* by whose supreme authority we are detained captives, under the sentence of the law. The debt is due to the great householder, Matt. xviii. 23, 24; and the penalty, his curse and wrath: from which by it we are delivered, Rev. i. 5.

This the Holy Ghost frequently insists on. Rom. iii. 24, 25, " Being justified freely by his grace, through the redemption that is in Christ Jesus; whom God hath set forth to be a propitiation through faith in his blood, to declare his righteousness for the remission of sins:" so also, 1 Cor. vi. 20; 1 Pet. i. 18; Matt. xx. 28; 1 Tim. ii. 6; Eph. i. 7; Col. i. 13; Gal. iii. 13. And this is the first consideration of the death of Christ, as it hath an influence into the procurement of that grace wherein we hold communion with him.

[2.] It was a *sacrifice* also. He had a body prepared him, Heb. x. 5; wherein he was to accomplish what by the typical oblations and burnt-offerings of the law was prefigured. And that body he offered, Heb. x. 10;—that is, his whole human nature; for "his soul" also was made "an offering for sin," Isa. liii. 10: on which account he is said to offer himself, Eph. v. 2; Heb. i. 3, ix. 26. He gave himself a sacrifice to God of a sweet-smelling savour; and this he did willingly,[1] as became him who was to be a sacrifice,—the law of this obedience being written in his heart, Ps. xl. 8; that is, he had a readiness, willingness, desire for its performance.

Now, the end of sacrifices, such as his was, bloody and for sin, Rom. v. 10; Heb. ii. 17, was atonement and reconciliation. This is everywhere ascribed to them, that they were to make atonement; that is, in a way suitable to their nature. And this is the tendency of the death of Christ, as a sacrifice, atonement, and reconciliation with God. Sin had broken friendship between God and us, Isa. lxiii. 10; whence his wrath was on us, John iii. 36; and we are by nature obnoxious to it, Eph. ii. 3. This is taken away by the death of Christ, as it was a sacrifice, Dan. ix. 24. " When we were enemies, we were reconciled to God by the death of his Son," Rom. v. 10. And thereby do we " receive the atonement," verse 11; for " God was in Christ reconciling the world to himself, not imputing to them their sins and their iniquities," 2 Cor. v. 19–21: so also, Eph. ii. 12–16, and in sundry other places. And this is the second consideration of the death of Christ; which I do but name, having at large insisted on these things elsewhere.

[3.] It was also a *punishment*,—a punishment in our stead. " He was wounded for our transgressions, he was bruised for our iniquities: the chastisement of our peace was upon him," Isa. liii. 5. God made all our iniquities (that is, the punishment of them) " to meet upon him," verse 6. " He bare the sins of many," verse 12; " his own self bare our sins in his own body on the tree," 1 Pet. ii. 24; and therein he " who knew no sin, was made sin for us," 2 Cor. v. 21. What it is in the Scripture to bear sin, see Deut. xix. 15, xx. 17; Numb. xiv. 33; Ezek. xviii. 20. The nature, kind, matter, and manner of this punishment I have, as I said before, elsewhere discussed.

Now, bearing of punishment tends directly to the giving satisfaction to him who was offended, and on that account inflicted the punishment. Justice can desire no more than a proportional punishment,

---

[1] " Observatum est a sacrificantibus, ut si hostia quæ ad aras duceretur, fuisset vehementer reluctata, ostendtssetque se invitam altaribus admoveri, amoveretur, quia invito Deo eam offerri putabant; quæ vero stetisset oblata, hanc volenti numini dari existimabant."—Macrob. Saturnal. lib. iii. " Hoc quoque notandum, vitulos ad aras humeris hominum allatos non fere litare; sicut nec claudicante, nec aliena hostia placari deos; neque trahente se ab aris."—Plin. lib. viii. cap. 45.

due to the offence. And this, on his own voluntary taking of our persons, undertaking to be our mediator, was inflicted on our dear Lord Jesus. His substituting himself in our room being allowed of by the righteous Judge, satisfaction to him doth thence properly ensue.

And this is the threefold consideration of the death of Christ, as it is a principal spring and fountain of that grace wherein we have communion with him; for, as will appear in our process, the single and most eminent part of purchased grace, is nothing but the natural exurgency of the threefold effect of the death of Christ, intimated to flow from it on the account of the threefold consideration insisted on. This, then, is the second rise of purchased grace, which we are to eye, if we will hold communion with Christ in it,—his death and blood-shedding, under this threefold notion of a price, an offering, and punishment. But,—

(3.) This is not all: the Lord Christ goes farther yet; he doth not leave us so, but follows on the work to the utmost. [1] " He died for our sins, and rose again for our justification." He rose again to carry on the complete work of purchased grace,—that is, by his intercession; which is the third rise of it. In respect of this, he is said to be " able to save them to the uttermost that come unto God by him, seeing he ever liveth to make intercession for them," Heb. vii. 25.

Now, the intercession of Christ, in respect of its influence into purchased grace, is considered two ways:—

[1.] As a *continuance and carrying* on of his oblation, for the making out of all the fruits and effects thereof unto us. This is called his " appearing in the presence of God for us," Heb. ix. 24; that is, as the high priest, having offered the great offering for expiation of sin, carried in the blood thereof into the most holy place, where was the representation of the presence of God, so to perfect the atonement he made for himself and the people; so the Lord Christ, having offered himself as a sweet-smelling sacrifice to God, being sprinkled with his own blood, appears in the presence of God, as it were to mind him of the engagement made to him, for the redemption of sinners by his blood, and the making out the good things to them which were procured thereby. And so this appearance of his hath an influence into purchased grace, inasmuch as thereby he puts in his claim for it in our behalf.

[2.] He procureth *the Holy Spirit* for us, effectually to collate and bestow all this purchased grace upon us. That he would do this, and doth it, for us, we have his engagement, John xiv. 16. This is purchased grace, in respect of its fountain and spring;—of which I shall not speak farther at present, seeing I must handle it at large in the matter of the communion we have with the Holy Ghost.

[1] Rom. iv. 25.

CHAPTER VII.

The nature of purchased grace; referred to three heads:—1. Of our acceptation with God; two parts of it.   2. Of the grace of sanctification; the several parts of it.

THE fountain of that purchased grace wherein the saints have communion with Christ being discovered, in the next place the nature of this grace itself may be considered.   As was said, it may be referred unto three heads:—1. Grace of acceptation with God. 2. Grace of sanctification from God.   3. Grace of privileges with and before God.

1. Of *acceptation* with God.   Out of Christ, we are in a state of[1] alienation from God, accepted neither in our persons nor our services. Sin makes a separation between God and us:—that state, with all its consequences and attendancies, [it] is not my business to unfold.   The first issue of purchased grace is to restore us into a state of acceptation.   And this is done two ways:—(1.) By a removal of that for which we are refused,—the cause of the enmity.   (2.) By a bestowing of that for which we are accepted.

Not only all causes of quarrel were to be taken away, that so we should not be under displeasure, but also that was to be given unto us that makes us the objects of God's delight and pleasure, on the account of the want whereof we are distanced from God:—

(1.) It gives a removal of that for which we are refused.   This is *sin in the guilt,* and all the attendancies thereof.   The first issue of purchased grace tends to the taking away of sin in its guilt, that it shall not bind over the soul to the wages of it, which is death.

How this is accomplished and brought about by Christ, was evidenced in the close of the foregoing chapter.   It is the fruit and effect of his death for us.   Guilt of sin was the only cause of our separation and distance from God, as hath been said.   This made us obnoxious to wrath, punishment, and the whole displeasure of God; on the account hereof were we imprisoned under the curse of the law, and given up to the power of Satan.   This is the state of our unacceptation.   By his death, Christ—bearing the curse, undergoing the punishment that was due to us, paying the ransom that was due for us—delivers us from this condition.   And thus far the death of Christ is the sole cause of our acceptation with God,—that all cause of quarrel and rejection of us is thereby taken away.   And to that end are his sufferings reckoned to us; for, being " made sin for us," 2 Cor. v. 21, he is made " righteousness unto us," 1 Cor. i. 30.

[1] John iii. 36; Eph. ii. 12, 13.

But yet farther; this will not *complete* our acceptation with God. The old quarrel may be laid aside, and yet no new friendship begun; we may be not sinners, and yet not be so far righteous as to have a right to the kingdom of heaven. Adam had no right to life because he was innocent; he must, moreover, " do this," and then he shall " live." He must not only have a *negative* righteousness,—he was not guilty of any thing; but also a *positive* righteousness,—he must do all things.

(2.) This, then, is required, in the second place, to our complete acceptation, that we have not only the *not imputation of sin*, but also a *reckoning of righteousness.* Now, this we have in the obedience of the life of Christ. This also was discovered in the last chapter. The obedience of the life of Christ was for us, is imputed to us, and is our righteousness before God;—by his obedience are we "made righteous," Rom. v. 19. On what score the obedience of faith takes place, shall be afterward declared.

These two things, then, complete our grace of acceptation. Sin being removed, and righteousness bestowed, we have peace with God, —are continually accepted before him. There is not any thing to charge us withal: that which was, is taken out of the way by Christ, and nailed to his cross,—made fast there; yea, publicly and legally cancelled, that it can never be admitted again as an evidence. What court among men would admit of an evidence that hath been publicly cancelled, and nailed up for all to see it? So hath Christ dealt with that which was against us; and not only so, but also he puts that upon us for which we are received into favour. He makes us comely through his beauty; gives us white raiment to stand before the Lord. This is the first part of purchased grace wherein the saints have communion with Jesus Christ. In remission of sin and imputation of righteousness doth it consist; from the death of Christ, as a price, sacrifice, and a punishment,—from the life of Christ spent in obedience to the law, doth it arise. The great product it is of the Father's righteousness, wisdom, love, and grace;—the great and astonishable fruit of the love and condescension of the Son;—the great discovery of the Holy Ghost in the revelation of the mystery of the gospel.

2. The second is grace of *sanctification.* He makes us not only *accepted,* but also *acceptable.* He doth not only purchase love for his saints, but also makes them lovely. He came not by blood only, but by water and blood. He doth not only justify his saints from the guilt of sin, but also sanctify and wash them from the filth of sin. The first is from his life and death as a sacrifice of propitiation; this from his death as a purchase, and his life as an example. So the apostle, Heb. ix. 14; as also Eph. v. 26, 27. Two things are

eminent in this issue of purchased grace:—(1.) The removal of *defile-ment;* (2.) The bestowing of *cleanness* in actual grace.

(1.) For the first, it is also *threefold:*—

[1.] The *habitual* cleansing of our nature. We are naturally un-clean, defiled,—habitually so; for "Who can bring a clean thing out of an unclean?" Job xiv. 4; "That which is born of the flesh is flesh," John iii. 6. It is in the pollution of our blood that we are born, Ezek. xvi.,—wholly defiled and polluted. The grace of sanctifica-tion, purchased by the blood of Christ, removes this defilement of our nature. 1 Cor. vi. 11, "Such were some of you; but ye are washed, ye are sanctified." So also Tit. iii. 3-5, "He hath saved us by the washing of regeneration, and the renewing of the Holy Ghost." How far this original, habitual pollution is removed, need not be disputed; it is certain the soul is made fair and beautiful in the sight of God. Though the sin that doth defile remains, yet its habitual defilement is taken away. But the handling of this lies not in my aim.

[2.] Taking away the *pollutions of all our actual transgressions.* There is a defilement attending every actual sin. Our own clothes make us to be abhorred, Job ix. 31. A spot, a stain, rust, wrinkle, filth, blood, attends every sin. Now, 1 John i. 7, "The blood of Jesus Christ cleanseth us from all sin." Besides the defilement of our na-tures which he purgeth, Tit. iii. 5, he takes away the defilement of our persons by actual follies. "By one offering he perfected for ever them that are sanctified;" by himself he "purged our sins," before he sat down at the right hand of the Majesty on high, Heb. i. 3.

[3.] In our best duties we have defilement, Isa. lxiv. 6. Self, un-belief, form, drop themselves into all that we do. We may be ashamed of our choicest performances. God hath promised that the saints' good works shall follow them. Truly, were they to be measured by the rule as they come from us, and weighed in the balance of the sanctuary, it might be well for us that they might be buried for ever. But the Lord Christ first, as our high priest, bears the iniquity, the guilt, and provocation, which in severe justice doth attend them, Exod. xxviii. 38; and not only so, but he washes away all their filth and defilements. He is as a refiner's fire, to purge both the sons of Levi and their offerings; adding, moreover, sweet incense to them, that they may be accepted. Whatever is of the *Spirit*, of *himself*, of *grace*,—that remains; whatever is of *self, flesh, unbelief* (that is, hay and stubble),—that he consumes, wastes, takes away. So that the saints' good works shall meet them one day with a changed countenance, that they shall scarce know them: that which seemed to them to be black, deformed, defiled, shall appear beautiful and glorious; they shall not be afraid of them, but rejoice to see and follow them.

And this cleansing of our natures, persons, and duties, hath its whole foundation in the death of Christ. Hence our washing and purifying, our cleansing and purging, is ascribed to his blood and the sprinkling thereof. Meritoriously, this work is done, by the shedding of the blood of Christ; efficiently, by its sprinkling. The sprinkling of the blood of Christ proceedeth from the communication of the Holy Ghost; which he promiseth to us, as purchased by him for us. He is the pure water, wherewith we are sprinkled from all our sins, —that spirit of judgment and burning that takes away the filth and blood of the daughters of Zion. And this is the first thing in the grace of sanctification; of which more afterward.

(2.) By bestowing *cleanness* as to actual grace. The blood of Christ in this purchased grace doth not only take away defilement, but also it gives purity; and that also in a threefold gradation:—

[1.] It gives the *Spirit of holiness to dwell in us.* "He is made unto us sanctification," 1 Cor. i. 30, by procuring for us the Spirit of sanctification. Our renewing is of the Holy Ghost, who is shed on us through Christ alone, Tit. iii. 6. This the apostle mainly insists on, Rom. viii.,—to wit, that the prime and principal gift of sanctification that we receive from Christ, is the indwelling of the Spirit, and our following after the guidance hereof. But what concerns the Spirit in any kind, must be referred to that which I have to offer concerning our communion with him.

[2.] He gives us *habitual grace;*—a principle of grace, opposed to the principle of lust that is in us by nature. This is the grace that dwells in us, makes its abode with us; which, according to the distinct faculties of our souls wherein it is, or the distinct objects about which it is exercised, receiveth various appellations, being indeed all but one new principle of life. In the understanding, it is light; in the will, obedience; in the affections, love; in all, faith. So, also, it is differenced in respect of its operations. When it carries out the soul to rest on Christ, it is faith; when to delight in him, it is love; but still one and the same habit of grace. And this is the second thing.

[3.] *Actual influence for the performance* of every spiritual duty whatever. After the saints have both the former, yet Christ tells them that without him "they can do nothing," John xv. 5. They are still in dependence upon him for new influences of grace, or supplies of the Spirit. They cannot live and spend upon the old stock; for every new act they must have new grace. He must "work in us to will and to do of his good pleasure," Phil. ii. 13. And in these three, thus briefly named, consists that purchased grace in the point of sanctification, as to the collating of purity and cleanness, wherein we have communion with Christ.

3. This purchased grace consists in privileges to stand before God,

and these are of two sorts,—*primary* and *consequential*. Primary, is *adoption*,—the Spirit of adoption; consequential, are all the *favours* of the gospel, which the saints alone have right unto. But of this I shall speak when I come to the last branch,—of communion with the Holy Ghost.

These are the things wherein we have communion with Christ as to purchased grace in this life. Drive them up to perfection, and you have that which we call everlasting glory. Perfect acceptance, perfect holiness, perfect adoption, or inheritance of sons,—that is glory.

Our process now, in the next place, is to what I mainly intend, even the manner how we hold communion with Christ in these things; and that in the order laid down; as,—

I. How we hold communion with him in the obedience of his *life and merit* of his death, as to acceptance with God the Father.

II. How we hold communion with Christ in his *blood*, as to the Spirit of sanctification, the habits and acts of grace.

III. How we hold communion with him as to the privileges we enjoy. Of which in the ensuing chapters.

CHAPTER VIII.

How the saints hold communion with Christ as to their acceptation with God—
What is required on the part of Christ hereunto; in his intention; in the
declaration thereof—The sum of our acceptation with God, wherein it consists—What is required on the part of believers to this communion, and how
they hold it, with Christ—Some objections proposed to consideration, why the
elect are not accepted immediately on the undertaking and the death of
Christ—In what sense they are so—Christ a common or public person—How
he came to be so—The way of our acceptation with God on that account—
The second objection—The necessity of our obedience stated, Eph. ii. 8-10
—The grounds, causes, and ends of it manifested—Its proper place in the
new covenant—How the saints, in particular, hold communion with Christ in
this purchased grace—They approve of this righteousness; the grounds thereof—Reject their own; the grounds thereof—The commutation of sin and
righteousness between Christ and believers; some objections answered.

I. COMMUNION with Christ in purchased grace, as unto *acceptation with God*, from the obedience of his life and efficacy of his death, is the first thing we inquire into. The discovery of what on the part of Christ and what on our part is required thereunto (for our mutual actings, even his and ours, are necessary, that we may have fellowship and communion together herein), is that which herein I intend.

First, On the part of Christ there is no more required but these two things:—(1.) That what he did, he did not for himself, but for us.

(2.) What he suffered, he suffered not for himself, but for us. That is, that his intention from eternity, and when he was in the world, was, that all that he did and suffered was and should be for us and our advantage,· as to our acceptance with God; that he still continueth making use of what he so did and suffered for that end and purpose, and that only.   Now, this is most evident:—

(1.) What he *did*, he did for us, and not for himself: " He was made under the law, that we might receive the adoption of sons," Gal. iv. 4, 5.   He was made under the law; that is, in that condition that he was obnoxious to the will and commands of it.   And why was this? to what end? for himself?   No; but to redeem us is the aim of all that he did,—of all his obedience: and that he did.   This very intention in what he did he acquaints us with, John xvii. 19, " For their sakes I sanctify myself, that they may be sanctified through the truth."   " I sanctify myself,—dedicate and set myself apart to all that work I have to do.   I came not to do my own will; I came to save that which was lost; to minister, not to be ministered unto; and to give my life a ransom;"—it was the testimony he bare to all he did in the world.   This intendment of his is especially to be eyed.   From eternity he had thoughts of what he would do for us; and delighted himself therein.   And when he was in the world, in all he went about, he had still this thought, " This is for them, and this is for them,—my beloved."   When he went to be baptized, says John, " I have need to be baptized of thee, and comest thou to me?" Matt. iii. 14, 15; as if he had said, " Thou hast no need at all of it."   But says Christ, " Suffer it to be so, now; for thus it becometh us to fulfil all righteousness;"—" I do it for them who have none at all, and stand obliged unto all."

(2.) In what he *suffered*.   This is more clear, Dan. ix. 26, " Messiah shall be cut off, but not for himself."   And the apostle lays down this as a main difference between him and the high priests of the Jews, that when they made their solemn offerings, they offered first for themselves, and then for the people; but Jesus Christ offered only for others.   He had no sin, and could make no sacrifice for his own sin, which he had not, but only for others.   He " tasted death every man," Heb. ii. 9,—" gave his life a ransom for many," Matt. xx. 28.   The " iniquity of us all was made to meet on him," Isa. liii. 6;—" He bare our sins in his own body on the tree," 1 Pet. ii. 24;—" loved the church, and gave himself for it," Eph. v. 25; Gal. ii. 20; Rom. iv. 25; Rev. i. 5, 6; Tit. ii. 14; 1 Tim. ii. 6; Isa. liii. 12; John xvii. 19.   But this is exceeding clear and confessed, that Christ in his suffering and oblation, had his intention only upon the good of his elect, and their acceptation with God; suffering for us, " the just for the unjust, that he might bring us to God."

Secondly, To complete this communion on the part of Christ, it is required,—

(1.) That there be added to what he hath done, *the gospel tenders* of that complete righteousness and acceptation with God which ariseth from his perfect obedience and sufferings. Now, they are twofold:—

[1.] *Declaratory*, in the conditional promises of the gospel. Mark xvi. 15; Matt. xi. 28, "He that believeth shall be saved;" "Come unto me, and I will give you rest;" "As Moses lifted up the serpent," etc.; "Christ is the end of the law for righteousness to every one that believeth," Rom. x. 4; and innumerable others. Now, declaratory tenders are very precious, there is much kindness in them, and if they be rejected, they will be the "savour of death unto death;" but the Lord Christ knows that the outward letter, though never so effectually held out, will not enable any of his for that reception of his righteousness which is necessary to interest them therein; wherefore,—

[2.] In this tender of acceptation with God, on the account of what he hath done and suffered, a *law is established*, that whosoever receives it shall be so accepted. But Christ knows the condition and state of his in this world. This will not do; if he do not effectually invest them with it, all is lost. Therefore,—

(2.) He sends them *his Holy Spirit, to quicken them*, John vi. 63, —to cause them that are "dead to hear his voice," John v. 25; and to work in them whatever is required of them, to make them partakers of his righteousness and accepted with God.

Thus doth Christ deal with his:—he lives and dies with an intention to work out and complete righteousness for them; their enjoying of it, to a perfect acceptation before God, is all that in the one and other he aimed at. Then he tenders it unto them, declares the usefulness and preciousness of it to their souls, stirring them up to a desire and valuation of it; and lastly, effectually bestows it upon them, reckons it unto them as theirs, that they should by it, for it, with it, be perfectly accepted with his Father.

Thus, for our acceptation with God, two things are required:—

First, That *satisfaction be made for our disobedience,*—for whatever we had done which might damage the justice and honour of God; and that God be atoned towards us: which could no otherwise be, but by undergoing the penalty of the law. This, I have showed abundantly, is done by the death of Christ. God "made him to be sin for us," 2 Cor. v. 21,—a "curse," Gal. iii. 13. On this account we have our absolution,—our acquitment from the guilt of sin, the sentence of the law, the wrath of God, Rom. viii. 33, 34. We are justified, acquitted, freed from condemnation, because it was Christ that died; "he bare our sins in his own body on the tree," 1 Pet. ii. 24.

Second, That *the righteousness of the law be fulfilled,* and the obedience performed that is required at our hands. And this is done by the life of Christ, Rom. v. 18, 19. So that answerably hereunto, according to our state and the condition of our acceptation with God, there are two parts:—

Our *absolution from the guilt* of sin, that our disobedience be not charged upon us. This we have by the death of Christ; our sins being imputed to him, shall not be imputed to us, 2 Cor. v. 21; Rom. iv. 25; Isa. liii. 12.

Imputation of righteousness, that we may be accounted perfectly righteous before God; and this we have by the life of Christ. His righteousness in yielding obedience to the law is imputed to us. And thus is our acceptation with God completed. Being discharged from the guilt of our disobedience by the death of Christ, and having the righteousness of the life of Christ imputed to us, we have friendship and peace with God. And this is that which I call our grace of acceptation with God, wherein we have communion with Jesus Christ.

That which remains for me to do, is to show how believers hold distinct communion with Christ in this grace of acceptation, and how thereby they keep alive a sense of it,—the comfort and life of it being to be renewed every day. Without this, life is a hell; no peace, no joy can we be made partakers of, but what hath its rise from hence. Look what grounded persuasion we have of our acceptation with God, that he is at peace with us; thereunto is the revenue of our peace, comfort, joy, yea, and holiness itself, proportioned.

But yet, before I come in particular to handle our practical communion with the Lord Jesus in this thing, I must remove two considerable objections;—the one of them lying against the first part of our acceptation with God, the other against the latter.

Objection 1. For our *absolution by and upon the death of Christ*, it may be said, that "if the elect have their absolution, reconciliation, and freedom by the death, blood, and cross of Christ, whence is it, then, that they were not *all actually absolved* at the death of Christ, or at least so soon as they are born, but that many of them live a long while under the wrath of God in this world, as being unbelievers, under the sentence and condemning power of the law? John iii. 36. Why are they not immediately freed, upon the payment of the price and making reconciliation for them?"

Obj. 2. "If the obedience of the life of Christ be imputed unto us, and that is our righteousness before God, then what *need we yield any obedience ourselves?* Is not all our praying, labouring, watching, fasting, giving alms,—are not all fruits of holiness, in purity of heart and usefulness of conversation, all in vain and to no purpose? And who, then, will or need take care to be holy, humble, righteous, meek, temperate, patient, good, peaceable, or to abound in good works in the world?"

1. I shall, God assisting, briefly remove these two objections, and then proceed to carry on the design in hand, about our communion with Christ:—

(1.) Jesus Christ, in his undertaking of the work of our reconciliation with God,—for which cause he came into the world,—and the accomplishment of it by his death, was constituted and considered as a *common, public person,* in the stead of them for whose reconciliation to God he suffered. Hence he is the "mediator between God and man," 1 Tim. ii. 5,—that is, one who undertook to God for us, as the next words manifest, verse 6, "Who gave himself a ransom for all,"— and the "surety of the better covenant," Heb. vii. 22; undertaking for and on the behalf of them with whom that covenant was made. Hence he is said to be given "for a covenant of the people," Isa. xlii. 6; and a "leader," lv. 4. He was the second Adam, 1 Cor. xv. 45, 47, to all ends and purposes of righteousness, to his spiritual seed, as the first Adam was of sin to his natural seed, Rom. v. 15–19.

(2.) His being thus a *common person,* arose chiefly from these things:—

[1.] In general, from *the covenant* entered into by himself with his Father to this purpose. The terms of this covenant are at large insisted on, Isa. liii., summed up, Ps. xl. 7, 8; Heb. x. 8–10. Hence the Father became to be his God; which is a covenant expression, Ps. lxxxix. 26; Heb. i. 5; Ps. xxii. 1, xl. 8, xlv. 7; Rev. iii. 12; Mic. v. 4. So was he by his Father on this account designed to this work, Isa. xlii. 1, 6, xlix. 9; Mal. iii. 1; Zech. xiii. 7; John iii. 16; 1 Tim. i. 15. Thus the "counsel of peace" became to be "between them both," Zech. vi. 13; that is, the Father and Son. And the Son rejoices from eternity in the thought of this undertaking, Prov. viii. 22–30. The command given him to this purpose, the promises made to him thereon, the assistance afforded to him, I have elsewhere handled.

[2.] In *the sovereign grant,* appointment, and design of the Father, giving and delivering the elect to Jesus Christ in this covenant, to be redeemed and reconciled to himself. John xvii. 6, "Thine they were, and thou gavest them me." They were God's by eternal designation and election, and he gave them to Christ to be redeemed. Hence, before their calling or believing, he calls them his "sheep," John x. 15, 16, laying down his life for them as such; and hence are we said to be "chosen in Christ," Eph. i. 4, or designed to obtain all the fruits of the love of God by Christ, and committed into his hand for that end and purpose.

[3.] In his *undertaking to suffer* what was due to them, and to do what was to be done by them, that they might be delivered, recon-

ciled, and accepted with God.   And he undertakes to give in to the
Father, without loss or miscarriage, what he had so received of the
Father as above, John xvii. 2, 12, vi. 37, 39; as Jacob did the
cattle he received of Laban, Gen. xxxi. 39, 40.   Of both these I have
treated somewhat at large elsewhere, in handling the covenant between
the Father and the Son; so that I shall not need to take it up here
again.

[4.] They being *given* unto him, he undertaking for them to do
and suffer what was on their part required, he received, *on their behalf
and for them, all the promises* of all the mercies, grace, good things,
and privileges, which they were to receive upon the account of his
undertaking for them.   On this account eternal life is said to be
promised of God "before the world began," Tit. i. 2; that is, to the Son
of God for us, on his undertaking on our behalf.   And grace, also, is
said to be given unto us "before the world began," 2 Tim. i. 9; that
is, in Christ, our appointed head, mediator, and representative.

[5.] Christ being thus a common person, a mediator, surety, and
representative, of his church, upon his undertaking, as to efficacy and
merit, and upon his actual performance, as *to solemn declaration*, was
as such acquitted, absolved, justified, and freed, from all and every
thing that, on the behalf of the elect, as due to them, was charged
upon him, or could so be; I say, as to all the efficacy and merit of
his undertakings, he was immediately absolved upon his faithfulness,
in his first engagement: and thereby all the saints of the Old Testament were saved by his blood no less than we.   As to solemn declaration, he was so absolved when, the "pains of death being loosed,
he was "declared to be the Son of God with power, by the resurrection
from the dead;" Rom. i. 4, God saying to him, "Thou art my Son;
this day have I begotten thee," Ps. ii. 7.   And this his absolution doth
Christ express his confidence of, Isa. l. 5–9.   And he was "justified,"
1 Tim. iii. 16.   That which I intend by this absolution of Christ as
a public person is this:—God having made him under the law, for
them who were so, Gal. iv. 4; in their stead, obnoxious to the punishment due to sin, made him sin, 2 Cor. v. 21; and so gave justice,
and law, and all the consequents of the curse thereof, power against
him, Isa. liii. 6;—upon his undergoing of that which was required of
him, verse 12, God looses the pains and power of death, accepts him,
and is well pleased with him, as to the performance and discharge
of his work, John xvii. 3–6; pronounceth him free from the obligation that was on him, Acts xiii.; and gave him a promise of all good
things he aimed at, and which his soul desired.   Hereon are all the
promises of God made to Christ, and their accomplishment,—all the
encouragements given him to ask and make demand of the things
originally engaged for to him, Ps. ii. 8, (which he did accordingly, John

xvii.),—founded and built. And here lies the certain, stable foundation of our absolution, and acceptation with God. Christ in our stead, acting for us as our surety, being acquitted, absolved, solemnly declared to have answered the whole debt that was incumbent on him to pay, and made satisfaction for all the injury we had done, a general pardon is sealed for us all, to be sued out particularly in the way to be appointed. For,—

[6.] Christ as a public person being thus absolved, it became righteous with God, a righteous thing, from the covenant, compact, and convention, that was between him and the Mediator, that those in whose stead he was, *should obtain, and have bestowed on them, all the fruits of his death*, in reconciliation with God, Rom. v. 8–11; that as Christ received the general acquittance for them all, so they should every one of them enjoy it respectively. This is everywhere manifested in those expressions which express a commutation designed by God in this matter; as 2 Cor. v. 21; Gal. iii. 13; 1 Pet. ii. 21, 24;—of which afterward.

[7.] Being thus acquitted in the covenant of the Mediator (whence they are said to be circumcised with him, to die with him, to be buried with him, to rise with him, to sit with him in heavenly places,—namely, in the covenant of the Mediator), and it being righteous that they should be acquitted personally in the covenant of grace, it was determined by Father, Son, and Holy Ghost, that the way of their actual personal deliverance from the sentence and curse of the law should be in and by such a way and dispensation as might lead to the *praise of the glorious grace of God*, Eph. i. 5–7. The appointment of God is, that we shall have the adoption of children. The means of it, is by Jesus Christ; the peculiar way of bringing it about, is by the redemption that is in his blood; the end, is the praise of his glorious grace. And thence it is,—

[8.] That until the full time of their actual deliverance, determined and appointed to them in their several generations, be accomplished, they are *personally* under the curse of the law; and, on that account, are *legally* obnoxious to the wrath of God, from which they shall certainly be delivered;—I say, they are thus personally obnoxious to the law, and the curse thereof; but not at all with its primitive intention of execution upon them, but as it is a means appointed to help forward their acquaintance with Christ, and acceptance with God, on his account. When this is accomplished, that whole obligation ceases, being continued on them in a design of love; their last condition being such as that they cannot without it be brought to a participation of Christ, to the praise of the glorious grace of God.

[9.] The end of the dispensation of grace being to glorify the whole Trinity, the order fixed on and appointed wherein this is to be done, is, by *ascending to the Father's love through the work of the Spirit and blood of the Son.* The emanation of divine love to us begins with the Father, is carried on by the Son, and then communicated by the Spirit; the Father designing, the Son purchasing, the Spirit effectually working: which is their order. Our participation is first by the work of the Spirit, to an actual interest in the blood of the Son; whence we have acceptation with the Father.

This, then, is the order whereby we are brought to acceptation with the Father, for the glory of God through Christ:—

1st. That the *Spirit may be glorified,* he is given unto us, to quicken us, convert us, work faith in us, Rom. viii. 11; Eph. i. 19, 20; according to all the promises of the covenant, Isa. iv. 4, 5; Ezek. xi. 19, xxxvi. 26.

2dly. This being wrought in us, *for the glory of the Son,* we are actually interested, according to the tenor of the covenant, at the same instant of time, in the *blood of Christ,* as to the benefits which he hath procured for us thereby; yea, this very work of the Spirit itself is a fruit and part of the purchase of Christ. But we speak of our sense of this thing, whereunto the communication of the Spirit is antecedent. And,—

3dly. To the *glory of the Father,* we are accepted with him, justified, freed from guilt, pardoned, and have " peace with God," Rom. v. 1. Thus, " through Christ we have access by one Spirit unto the Father," Eph. ii. 17. And thus are both Father and Son and the Holy Spirit glorified in our justification and acceptation with God; the Father in his free love, the Son in his full purchase, and the Holy Spirit in his effectual working.

[10.] All this, in all the parts of it, is no less fully procured for us, nor less freely bestowed on us, for Christ's sake, on his account, as part of his purchase and merits, than if all of us *immediately* upon his death, had been translated into heaven; only this way of our deliverance and freedom is fixed on, that the whole Trinity may be glorified thereby. And this may suffice in answer to the first objection. Though our reconciliation with God be fully and completely procured by the death of Christ, and all the ways and means whereby it is accomplished; yet we are brought unto an actual enjoyment thereof, by the way and in the order mentioned, for the praise of the glorious grace of God.

2. The second objection is, " *That if the righteousness and obedience of Christ to the law be imputed unto us, then what need we yield obedience ourselves?*" To this, also, I shall return answer as briefly as I can in the ensuing observations:—

(1.) The placing of our gospel obedience on the right foot of account (that it may neither be *exalted into a state,* condition, use, or end, not given it of God; nor any *reason*, cause, motive, end, necessity of it, on the other hand, taken away, weakened, or impaired), is a matter of great importance. Some make our obedience, the works of faith, our works, the matter or cause of our justification; some, the condition of the imputation of the righteousness of Christ; some, the qualification of the person justified, on the one hand; some exclude all the necessity of them, and turn the grace of God into lasciviousness, on the other. To debate these differences is not my present business; only, I say, on this and other accounts, the right stating of our obedience is of great importance as to our walking with God.

(2.) We do by no means assign the *same place*, condition, state, and use to the *obedience of Christ imputed* to us, and our *obedience performed* to God. If we did, they were really inconsistent. And therefore those who affirm that our obedience is the condition or cause of our justification, do all of them deny the imputation of the obedience of Christ unto us. The righteousness of Christ is imputed to us, as that on the account whereof we are accepted and esteemed righteous before God, and are really so, though not inherently. We are as truly righteous with the obedience of Christ imputed to us as Adam was, or could have been, by a complete righteousness of his own performance. So Rom. v. 18, by his obedience we are made righteous,—made so truly, and so accepted; as by the disobedience of Adam we are truly made trespassers, and so accounted. And this is that which the apostle desires to be found in, in opposition to his own righteousness, Phil. iii. 9. But our own obedience is not the righteousness whereupon we are accepted and justified before God; although it be acceptable to God that we should abound therein. And this distinction the apostle doth evidently deliver and confirm, so as nothing can be more clearly revealed: Eph. ii. 8–10, " For by grace are ye saved through faith: and that not of yourselves: it is the gift of God: not of works, lest any man should boast. For we are his workmanship, created in Christ Jesus unto good works, which God hath prepared that we should walk in them." We are saved, or justified (for that it is whereof the apostle treats), "by grace through faith," which receives Jesus Christ and his obedience; " not of works, lest any man should boast." "But what works are they that the apostle intends?" The works of believers, as in the very beginning of the next words is manifest: " 'For we are,' we believers, with our obedience and our works, of whom I speak." " Yea; but what need, then, of works?" Need still there is: " We are his workmanship," etc.

Two things the apostle intimates in these words:—

[1.] A reason why we cannot be saved by works,—namely, because we do them not in or by *our own strength;* which is necessary we should do, if we will be saved by them, or justified by them. " But this is not so," saith the apostle; "for we are the workmanship of God," etc.;—all our works are wrought in us, by full and effectual, undeserved grace.

[2.] An assertion of the necessity of good works, notwithstanding that we are not saved by them; and that is, that God *has ordained* that we shall walk in them:·which is a sufficient ground of our obedience, whatever be the use of it.

If you will say, then, "What are the true and proper *gospel grounds, reasons,* uses, and motives of our obedience; whence the necessity thereof may be demonstrated, and our souls be stirred up to abound and be fruitful therein?" I say, they are so many, and lie so deep in the mystery of the gospel and dispensation of grace, spread themselves so throughout the whole revelation of the will of God unto us, that to handle them fully and distinctly, and to give them their due weight, is a thing that I cannot engage in, lest I should be turned aside from what I principally intend. I shall only give you some brief heads of what might at large be insisted on:—

1*st.* Our universal obedience and good works are indispensably necessary, from the sovereign appointment and *will* of God; Father, Son, and Holy Ghost.

In general. "This is the will of God, even your sanctification," or holiness, 1 Thess. iv. 3. This is that which God wills, which he requires of us,—that we be holy, that we be obedient, that we do his will as the angels do in heaven. The equity, necessity, profit, and advantage of this ground of our obedience might at large be insisted on; and, were there no more, this might suffice alone,—if it be the will of God, it is our duty:—

(1*st.*) The Father hath ordained or appointed it. It is the will of the Father, Eph. ii. 10. The Father is spoken of personally, Christ being mentioned as mediator.

(2*dly.*) The Son hath ordained and appointed it as mediator. John xv. 16, "'I have ordained you, that ye should bring forth fruit' of obedience, and that it should remain." And,—

(3*dly.*) The Holy Ghost appoints and ordains believers to works of obedience and holiness, and to work holiness in others. So, in particular, Acts xiii. 2, he appoints and designs men to the great work of obedience in preaching the gospel. And in sinning, men sin against him.

2*dly.* Our holiness, our obedience, work of righteousness, is one eminent and especial end of the peculiar dispensation of Father, Son, and Spirit, in the business of exalting the glory of God in our salvation,—of the electing love of the Father, the purchasing love of the Son, and the operative love of the Spirit:—

(1*st.*) It is a peculiar end of the *electing* love of the Father, Eph.

i. 4, "He hath chosen us, that we should be holy and without blame."
So Isa. iv. 3, 4. His aim and design in choosing of us was, that we
should be holy and unblamable before him in love. This he is to
accomplish, and will bring about in them that are his. "He chooses
us to salvation, through sanctification of the Spirit, and belief of the
truth," 2 Thess. ii. 13. This the Father designed as the first and
immediate end of electing love; and proposes the consideration of that
love as a motive to holiness, 1 John iv. 8–10.

(2dly.) It is so also of the *exceeding love* of the Son; whereof the
testimonies are innumerable. I shall give but one or two:—Tit. ii. 14,
"Who gave himself for us, that he might redeem us from all iniquity,
and purify unto himself a peculiar people, zealous of good works."
This was his aim, his design, in giving himself for us; as Eph. v. 25–27,
"Christ loved the church, and gave himself for it; that he might
sanctify and cleanse it with the washing of water by the word; that
he might present it to himself a glorious church, not having spot, or
wrinkle, or any such thing; but that it should be holy, and without
blemish." 2 Cor. v. 15; Rom. vi. 11.

(3dly.) It is the *very work of the love* of the Holy Ghost. His whole
work upon us, in us, for us, consists in preparing of us for obedience;
enabling of us thereunto, and bringing forth the fruits of it in us.
And this he doth in opposition to a righteousness of our own, either
before it or to be made up by it, Tit. iii. 5. I need not insist on this.
The fruits of the Spirit in us are known, Gal. v. 22, 23.

And thus have we a twofold bottom of the necessity of our obedience and personal holiness:—God hath appointed it, he requires it;
and it is an eminent immediate end of the distinct dispensation of
Father, Son, and Holy Ghost, in the work of our salvation. If God's
sovereignty over us is to be owned, if his love towards us be to be
regarded, if the whole work of the ever-blessed Trinity, for us, in us,
be of any moment, our obedience is necessary.

3dly. It is necessary in respect of the *end* thereof; and that whether
you consider God, ourselves, or the world:—

(1st.) The end of our obedience, in respect of God, is, his *glory and
honour*, Mal. i. 6. This is God's honour,—all that we give him. It
is true, he will take his honour from the stoutest and proudest rebel
in the world; but all we give him is in our obedience. The glorifying
of God by our obedience is all that we are or can be. Particularly,—

[1st.] It is the glory of the *Father*. Matt. v. 16, "Let your light
so shine before men, that they may see your good works, and glorify
your Father which is in heaven." By our walking in the light of
faith doth glory arise to the Father. The fruits of his love, of his
grace, of his kindness, are seen upon us; and God is glorified in our
behalf. And,—

[2*dly.*] The *Son is glorified thereby.* It is the will of God that as all men honour the Father, so should they honour the Son, John v. 23. And how is this done? By believing in him, John xiv. 1; obeying of him. Hence, John xvii. 10, he says he is glorified in believers; and prays for an increase of grace and union for them, that he may yet be more glorified, and all might know that, as mediator, he was sent of God.

[3*dly.*] The *Spirit is glorified also by it.* He is grieved by our disobedience, Eph. iv. 30; and therefore his glory is in our bringing forth fruit. He dwells in us, as in his temple; which is not to be defiled. Holiness becometh his habitation for ever.

Now, if this that hath been said be not sufficient to evince a necessity of our obedience, we must suppose ourselves to speak with a sort of men who regard neither the sovereignty, nor love, nor glory of God, Father, Son, or Holy Ghost. Let men say what they please, though our obedience should be all lost, and never regarded (which is impossible, for God is not unjust, to forget our labour of love), yet here is a sufficient bottom, ground, and reason of yielding more obedience unto God than ever we shall do whilst we live in this world. I speak also only of gospel grounds of obedience, and not of those that are natural and legal, which are indispensable to all mankind.

(2*dly.*) The end in respect of *ourselves* immediately is threefold:— [1*st.*] Honour. [2*dly.*] Peace. [3*dly.*] Usefulness.

[1*st.*] *Honour.* It is by holiness that we are made like unto God, and his image is renewed again in us. This was our honour at our creation, this exalted us above all our fellow-creatures here below,— we were made in the image of God. This we lost by sin, and became like the beasts that perish. To this honour, of conformity to God, of bearing his image, are we exalted again by holiness alone. " Be ye holy," says God, " for I am holy," 1 Pet. i. 16; and, " Be ye perfect" (that is, in doing good), "even as your Father which is in heaven is perfect," Matt. v. 48,—in a likeness and conformity to him. And herein is the image of God renewed; Eph. iv. 23, 24, therein we " put on the new man, which after God is created in righteousness and holiness of truth." This was that which originally was attended with power and dominion;—is still all that is beautiful or comely in the world. How it makes men honourable and precious in the sight of God, of angels, of men; how alone it is that which is not despised, which is of price before the Lord; what contempt and scorn he hath of them in whom it is not,—in what abomination he hath them and all their ways,—might easily be evinced.

[2*dly.*] *Peace.* By it we have communion with God, wherein peace alone is to be enjoyed. " The wicked are like the troubled sea, that cannot rest;" and, " There is no peace" to them, " saith my God," Isa.

lvii. 20, 21.   There is no peace, rest, or quietness, in a distance, separation, or alienation from God.   He is the rest of our souls.   In the light of his countenance is life and peace.   Now, "if we walk in the light, as he is in the light, we have fellowship one with another," 1 John i. 7; "and truly our fellowship is with the Father, and with his Son Jesus Christ," verse 3.   He that walks in the light of new obedience, he hath communion with God, and in his presence is fulness of joy for ever; without it, there is nothing but darkness, and wandering, and confusion.

[3dly.] Usefulness.   A man without holiness is good for nothing. "Ephraim," says the prophet, "is an empty vine, that brings forth fruit to itself."   And what is such a vine good for?   Nothing. Saith another prophet, "A man cannot make so much as a pin of it, to hang a vessel on."   A barren tree is good for nothing, but to be cut down for the fire.   Notwithstanding the seeming usefulness of men who serve the providence of God in their generations, I could easily manifest that the world and the church might want them, and that, indeed, in themselves they are good for nothing.   Only the holy man is *commune bonum.*

(3dly.) The end of it in respect of *others* in the world is manifold:—

[1st.] It serves to the *conviction* and stopping the mouths of some of the enemies of God, both here and hereafter:—1. *Here.* 1 Pet. iii. 16, "Having a good conscience; that, wherein they speak evil of you, as of evil-doers, they may be ashamed that falsely accuse your good conversation in Christ."   By our keeping of a good conscience men will be made ashamed of their false accusations; that whereas their malice and hatred of the ways of God hath provoked them to speak all manner of evil of the profession of them, by the holiness and righteousness of the saints, they are convinced and made ashamed, as a thief is when he is taken, and be driven to acknowledge that God is amongst them, and that they are wicked themselves, John xvii. 23. 2. *Hereafter.*   It is said that the saints shall judge the world.   It is on this, as well as upon other considerations:—their good works, their righteousness, their holiness, shall be brought forth, and manifested to all the world; and the righteousness of God's judgments against wicked men be thence evinced.   "See," says Christ, "these are they that I own, whom you so despised and abhorred; and see their works following them: this and that they have done, when you wallowed in your abominations," Matt. xxv. 42, 43.

[2dly] The *conversion of others.* 1 Pet. ii. 12, "Having your conversation honest among the Gentiles; that, wherein they speak against you as evil-doers, they may, by your good works, which they shall behold, glorify God in the day of visitation," Matt. v. 16.   Even

revilers, persecutors, evil-speakers, have been overcome by the constant holy walking of professors; and when their day of visitation hath come, have glorified God on that account, 1 Pet. iii. 1, 2.

[3dly.] The *benefit of all;* partly in keeping off judgments from the residue of men, as ten good men would have preserved Sodom:[1] partly by their real communication of good to them with whom they have to do in their generation. Holiness makes a man a good man, useful to all; and others eat of the fruits of the Spirit that he brings forth continually.

[4thly.] It is necessary in respect of the *state* and condition of *justified persons;* and that whether you consider their relative state of acceptation, or their state of sanctification:—

First. They are *accepted* and received into friendship with a holy God,—a God of purer eyes than to behold iniquity,—who hates every unclean thing. And is it not necessary that they should be holy who are admitted into his presence, walk in his sight,—yea, lie in his bosom? Should they not with all diligence cleanse themselves from all pollution of[2] flesh and spirit, and perfect holiness in the fear of the Lord?

Secondly. In respect of *sanctification.* We have in us a new creature, 2 Cor. v. 17. This new creature is fed, cherished, nourished, kept alive, by the fruits of holiness. To what end hath God given us new hearts, and new natures? Is it that we should kill them? stifle the creature that is found in us in the womb? that we should give him to the old man to be devoured?

[5thly.] It is necessary in respect of the *proper place of holiness* in the new covenant; and that is twofold:—

First. Of the *means* unto the end. God hath appointed that holiness shall be the means, [3]the way to that eternal life, which, as in itself and originally [it] is his gift by Jesus Christ, so, with regard to his constitution of our obedience, as the means of attaining it, [it] is a reward, and God in bestowing of it a rewarder. Though it be neither the cause, matter, nor condition of our justification, yet it is the way appointed of God for us to walk in for the obtaining of salvation. And therefore, he that hath hope of eternal life purifies himself, as he is pure: and none shall ever come to that end who walketh not in that way; for without holiness it is impossible to see God.

Secondly. It is a *testimony* and pledge of adoption,—a sign and evidence of grace; that is, of acceptation with God. And,—

Thirdly. The whole *expression* of our thankfulness.

Now, there is not one of all these causes and reasons of the neces-

---

[1] Gen. xviii. 32.   [2] 2 Cor. vii. 1.
[3] Rom. vi. 23; Heb. xi. 6; Gen. xvii. 1; Ps. xix. 11, lviii. 11; Matt. v. 12, x. 41; Rom. iv. 4; Col. ii. 18, iii. 24; Heb. x. 35, xi. 26; 2 Pet. ii. 13.

sity, the indispensable necessity of our obedience, good works, and personal righteousness, but would require a more large discourse to unfold and explain than I have allotted to the proposal of them all; and innumerable others there are of the same import, that I cannot name. He that upon these accounts doth not think universal holiness and obedience to be of indispensable necessity, unless also it be exalted into the room of the obedience and righteousness of Christ, let him be filthy still.

These objections being removed, and having, at the entrance of this chapter, declared what is done on the part of Christ, as to our fellowship with him in this purchased grace, as to our acceptance with God, it remains that I now show what also is required and performed on our part for the completing thereof. This, then, consists in the ensuing particulars:—

1. The *saints cordially approve* of this righteousness, as that alone which is absolutely complete, and able to make them acceptable before God. And this supposeth six things:—

(1.) Their clear and full *conviction* of the necessity of a righteousness wherewith to appear before God. This is always in their thoughts; this in their whole lives they take for granted. Many men spend their days in obstinacy and hardness, adding drunkenness unto thirst, never once inquiring what their condition shall be when they enter into eternity; others trifle away their time and their souls, sowing the wind of empty hopes, and preparing to reap a whirlwind of wrath; but this lies at the bottom of all the saints' communion with Christ,—a deep, fixed, resolved persuasion of an absolute and indispensable necessity of a righteousness wherewith to appear before God. The holiness of God's nature, the righteousness of his government, the severity of his law, the terror of his wrath, are always before them. They have been all convinced of sin, and have looked on themselves as ready to sink under the vengeance due to it. They have all cried, " Men and brethren, what shall we do to be saved?" " Wherewith shall we come before God?" and have all concluded, that it is in vain to flatter themselves with hopes of escaping as they are by nature. If God be holy and righteous, and of purer eyes than to behold iniquity, they must have a righteousness to stand before him; and they know what will be the cry one day of those who now bear up themselves, as if they were otherwise minded, Isa. liii. 1–5; Mic. vi. 6, 7.

(2.) They weigh their *own righteousness* in the balance, and find it wanting; and this two ways:—

[1.] In *general,* and upon the whole of the matter, at their first setting themselves before God. When men are convinced of the necessity of a righteousness, they catch at every thing that presents itself to them for relief. Like men ready to sink in deep waters, [they] catch at that which is next, to save them from drowning; which sometimes proves a rotten stick, that sinks with them. So did the Jews, Rom. ix. 31, 32; they caught hold of the law, and it would not relieve them; and how they perished with it the apostle declares, chap. x. 1–4. The law put them upon setting up a righteousness of their own. This kept them doing, and in hope; but kept them from submitting to the righteousness of God. Here many perish, and never get one step nearer God all their days. This the saints renounce; they have no confidence in the flesh: they know that all they can do, all that the law can do, which is weak through the flesh, will not avail them. See what judgment Paul makes of all a man's own righteousness, Phil. iii. 8–10. This they bear in their minds daily, this they fill their thoughts withal, that upon the account of what they have done, can do, ever shall do, they cannot be accepted with God, or justified thereby. This keeps their souls humble, full of a sense of their own vileness, all their days.

[2.] In *particular*. They daily weigh all their *particular actions* in the balance, and find them wanting, as to any such completeness as, upon their own account, to be accepted with God. " Oh!" says a saint, " if I had nothing to commend me unto God but this prayer, this duty, this conquest of a temptation, wherein I myself see so many failings, so much imperfection, could I appear with any boldness before him? Shall I, then, piece up a garment of righteousness out of my best duties? Ah! it is all as a defiled cloth," Isa. lxiv. 6. These thoughts accompany them in all their duties, in their best and most choice performances:—" Lord, what am I in my best estate? How little suitableness unto thy holiness is in my best duties! O spare me, in reference to the best thing that ever I did in my life!" Neh. xiii. 22. When a man who lives upon convictions hath got some enlargements in duties, some conquest over a sin or temptation, he hugs himself, like Micah when he had got a Levite to be his priest: now surely it shall be well with him, now God will bless him: his heart is now at ease; he hath peace in what he hath done. But he who has communion with Christ, when he is *highest in duties of sanctification and holiness, is clearest in the apprehension of his own unprofitableness,* and rejects every thought that might arise in his heart of setting his peace in them, or upon them. He says to his soul, " Do these things seem something to thee? Alas! thou hast to do with an infinitely righteous God, who looks through and through all that vanity, which thou art but little acquainted withal; and should he deal with thee according to thy best works, thou must perish."

(3.) They approve of, value, and rejoice in, *this righteousness*, for their acceptation, *which the Lord Jesus hath wrought out* and pro-

vided for them; this being discovered to them, they approve of it
with all their hearts, and rest in it. Isa. xlv. 24, "Surely, shall one say,
in the LORD have I righteousness and strength." This is their voice
and language, when once the righteousness of God in Christ is made
known unto them: "Here is righteousness indeed; here have I rest
for my soul. Like the merchantman in the gospel (Matt. xiii. 45, 46)
that finds the pearl of price, I had been searching up and down; I
looked this and that way for help, but it was far away; I spent my
strength for that which was not bread: here is that, indeed, which
makes me rich for ever!" When first the righteousness of Christ, for
acceptation with God, is revealed to a poor labouring soul, that hath
sought for rest and hath found none, he is surprised and amazed, and
is not able to contain himself: and such a one always in his heart
approves this righteousness on a twofold account:—

[1.] As full of *infinite wisdom.* "Unto them that believe," saith
the apostle, "Christ crucified is 'the wisdom of God,'" 1 Cor. i. 24.
They see infinite wisdom in this way of their acceptation with God.
"In what darkness," says such a one, "in what straits, in what entanglements, was my poor soul! How little able was I to look through
the clouds and perplexities wherewith I was encompassed! I looked
inwards, and there was nothing but sin, horror, fear, tremblings; I
looked upwards, and saw nothing but wrath, curses, and vengeance.
I knew that God was a holy and righteous God, and that no unclean
thing could abide before him; I knew that I was a poor, vile, unclean, and sinful creature; and how to bring these two together in
peace, I knew not. But in the *righteousness of Christ* doth a
world of wisdom open itself, dispelling all difficulties and darkness,
and manifesting a reconciliation of all this." "O the depth of the
riches both of the wisdom and knowledge of God!" Rom. xi. 33;
Col. ii. 3. But of this before.

[2.] As *full of grace.* He knows that sin had shut up the
whole way of grace towards him; and whereas God aims at nothing
so much as the manifestation of his grace, he was utterly cut short of
it. Now, to have a complete righteousness provided, and yet abundance of grace manifested, exceedingly delights the soul;—to have
God's dealing with his person all grace, and dealing with his righteousness all justice, takes up his thoughts. God everywhere assures
us that this righteousness is of grace. It is "by grace, and no more
of works," Rom xi. 6, as the apostle at large sets it out, Eph. ii. 7–9.
It is from riches of grace and kindness that the provision of this
righteousness is made. It is of mere grace that it is bestowed on us,
it is not at all of works; though it be in itself a righteousness of
works, yet to us it is of mere grace. So Tit. iii. 4–7, "But after that
the kindness and love of God our Saviour toward man appeared, not

by works of righteousness which we have done, but according to his
mercy he saved us, by the washing of regeneration, and renewing of
the Holy Ghost, which he shed on us abundantly through Jesus
Christ our Saviour, that being justified by his grace, we should be
made heirs according to the hope of eternal life." The rise of all this
dispensation is kindness and love; that is, *grace,* verse 4. The way
of communication, negatively, is not by works of righteousness that
we have done;—positively, by the communication of the Holy Ghost,
verse 5; the means of whose procurement is Jesus Christ, verse 6;—
and the work itself is by grace, verse 7. Here is use made of every
word almost, whereby the exceeding rich grace, kindness, mercy, and
goodness of God may be expressed, all concurring in this work. As:
1. Χρηστότης,—his goodness, benignity, readiness to communicate of
himself and his good things that may be profitable to us. 2. Φιλαν-
θρωπία,—mercy, love, and propensity of mind to help, assist, relieve
them of whom he speaks, towards whom he is so affected. 3. Ἔλεος,—
mercy, forgiveness, compassion, tenderness, to them that suffer; and
χάρις,—free pardoning bounty, undeserved love. And all this is said to
be τοῦ Θεοῦ σωτῆρος,—he exercises all these properties and attributes of
his nature towards us that he may save us; and in the bestowing of
it, giving us the Holy Ghost, it is said, ἐξέχεεν,—he poured him out as
water out of a vessel, without stop and hesitation; and that not in a
small measure, but πλουσίως,—richly and in abundance: whence, as to
the work itself, it is emphatically said, δικαιωθέντες τῇ ἐκείνου χάριτι,—
justified by the grace of him who is such a one. And this do the
saints of God, in their communion with Christ, exceedingly rejoice in
before him, that the way of their acceptation before God is a way of
grace, kindness, and mercy, that they might not boast in themselves,
but in the Lord and his goodness, crying, "How great is thy goodness! how great is thy bounty!"

(4.) They approve of it, and rejoice in it, as *a way of great peace
and security* to themselves and their own souls. They remember
what was their state and condition whilst they went about to set up a
righteousness of their own, and were not subject to the righteousness
of Christ,—how miserably they were tossed up and down with continual fluctuating thoughts. Sometimes they had hope, and sometimes
were full of fear; sometimes they thought themselves in some good
condition, and anon were at the very brink of hell, their consciences
being racked and torn with sin and fear: but now, " being justified
by faith, they have peace with God," Rom. v. 1. All is *quiet and
serene;* not only that *storm* is over, but they are in the *haven* where
they would be. They have abiding peace with God. Hence is that
description of Christ to a poor soul, Isa. xxxii. 2, " And a man shall
be as a hiding-place from the wind, and a covert from the tempest; as

rivers of water in a dry place, as the shadow of a great rock in a weary land." Wind and tempest, and drought and weariness,—nothing now troubles the soul that is in Christ; he hath a hiding-place, and a covert, and rivers of water, and the shadow of a great rock, for his security. This is the great mystery of faith in this business of our acceptation with God by Christ:—that whereas the soul of a believer finds enough in him and upon him to rend the very caul of the heart, to fill him with fears, terror, disquietments all his days, yet through Christ he is at perfect peace with God, Isa. xxvi. 3; Ps. iv. 6–8. Hence do the souls of believers exceedingly magnify Jesus Christ, that they can behold the face of God with boldness, confidence, peace, joy, assurance,—that they can call him Father, bear themselves on his love, walk up and down in quietness, and without fear. How glorious is the Son of God in this grace! They remember the wormwood and gall that they have eaten;—the vinegar and tears they have drunk;—the trembling of their souls, like an aspen leaf that is shaken with the wind. Whenever they thought of God, what contrivances have they had to hide, and fly, and escape! To be brought now to settlement and security, must needs greatly affect them.

(5.) They cordially *approve* of this righteousness, because it is a way and means of *exceeding exaltation* and honour of the Lord Jesus, whom their souls do love. Being once brought to an acquaintance with Jesus Christ, their hearts desire nothing more than that he may be honoured and glorified to the utmost, and in all things have the pre-eminence. Now, what can more tend to the advancing and honouring of him in our hearts, than to know that he is made of God unto us " wisdom and righteousness?" 1 Cor. i. 30. Not that he is this or that part of our acceptation with God; but he is all,—he is the whole. They know that on the account of his working out their acceptation with God, he is,—

[1.] Honoured of God *his Father*. Phil. ii. 7–11, " He made himself of no reputation, and took upon him the form of a servant, and was made in the likeness of men: and being found in fashion as a man, he humbled himself, and became obedient unto death, even the death of the cross. Wherefore God also hath highly exalted him, and given him a name which is above every name: that at the name of Jesus every knee should bow, of things in heaven, and things in earth, and things under the earth; and that every tongue should confess that Jesus Christ is Lord, to the glory of God the Father." Whether that word " wherefore " denotes a connection of causality or only a consequence, this is evident, that on the account of his suffering, and as the end of it, he was [1]honoured and exalted of God to an

---

[1] .Ps. cx. 1, 5, ii. 8, 9; Zech. ix. 10; Ps. lxxii. 8; Rom. xiv. 11; Isa. xlv. 23, Phil. ii. 10.

unspeakable pre-eminence, dignity, and authority; according as God had promised him on the same account, Isa. liii. 11, 12; Acts ii. 36, v. 30, 31. And therefore it is said, that when " he had by himself purged our sins, he sat down at the right hand of the Majesty on high," Heb. i. 3.

[2.] He is on this account honoured of all *the angels in heaven*, even because of this great work of bringing sinners unto God; for they do not only bow down and desire to look into the mystery of the cross, 1 Pet. i. 12, but worship and praise him always on this account: Rev. v. 11–14, " I heard the voice of many angels round about the throne, and the living creatures and the elders: and the number of them was ten thousand times ten thousand, and thousands of thousands; saying with a loud voice, Worthy is the Lamb that was slain to receive power, and riches, and wisdom, and strength, and honour, and glory, and blessing. And every creature which is in heaven and earth, and under the earth, and such as are in the sea, and all that are in them, heard I saying, Blessing, and honour, and glory, and power, be unto him that sitteth upon the throne, and unto the Lamb for ever and ever. And the living creatures said, Amen. And the four and twenty elders fell down and worshipped him that liveth for ever and ever." The reason given of this glorious and wonderful doxology, this attribution of honour and glory to Jesus Christ by the whole host of heaven, is, because he was the Lamb that was slain; that is, because of the work of our redemption and our bringing unto God. And it is not a little refreshment and rejoicing to the souls of the saints, to know that all the angels of God, the whole host of heaven, which never sinned, do yet continually rejoice and ascribe praise and honour to the Lord Jesus, for his bringing them to peace and favour with God.

[3.] He is honoured *by his saints all the world over;* and indeed, if they do not, who should? If they honour him not as they honour the Father, they are, of all men, the most unworthy. But see what they do, Rev. i. 5, 6, " Unto him that loved us, and washed us from our sins in his own blood, and hath made us kings and priests unto God and his Father; to him be glory and dominion for ever and ever. Amen." Chap. v. 8–10, " The four living creatures and four and twenty elders fell down before the Lamb, having every one of them harps, and golden vials full of odours, which are the prayers of saints. And they sung a new song, saying, Thou art worthy to take the book, and to open the seals thereof: for thou wast slain, and hast redeemed us to God by thy blood, out of every kindred, and tongue, and people, and nation; and hast made us unto our God kings and priests: and we shall reign on the earth." The great, solemn worship of the Christian church consists in this assignation of honour and glory to the Lord Jesus: therefore do they love him, honour him, delight in him; as Paul, Phil. iii. 8; and so the spouse, Cant. v. 9–16. And this is on this account,—

(6.) They cordially approve of this righteousness, this way of acceptation, as that which brings *glory to God as such*. When they were labouring under the guilt of sin, that which did most of all perplex their souls was, that their safety was inconsistent with the glory and honour of the great God,—[1]with his justice, faithfulness, and truth, all which were engaged for the destruction of sin; and how to come off from ruin without the loss of their honour [*i. e.*, the honour of the fore-mentioned attributes] they saw not. But now by the revelation of this righteousness from faith to faith, they plainly see that all the properties of God are exceedingly glorified in the pardon, justification, and acceptance of poor sinners; as before was manifested.

And this is the first way whereby the saints hold daily communion with the Lord Jesus in this purchased grace of acceptation with God: they consider, approve of, and rejoice in, the way, means, and thing itself.

2. They make an *actual commutation* with the Lord Jesus as to their sins and his righteousness. Of this there are also sundry parts:—

(1.) They continually keep alive upon their hearts a *sense of the guilt* and evil of sin; even then when they are under some comfortable persuasions of their personal acceptance with God. Sense of pardon takes away the horror and fear, but not a due sense of the guilt of sin. It is the daily exercise of the saints of God, to consider the great provocation that is in sin,—their sins, the sin of their nature and lives; to render themselves vile in their own hearts and thoughts on that account; to compare it with the terror of the Lord; and to judge themselves continually. This they do in general. "My sin is ever before me," says David. They set sin before them, not to terrify and affright their souls with it, but that a due sense of the evil of it may be kept alive upon their hearts.

(2.) They gather up in their thoughts the sins for which they have not made *a particular reckoning* with God in Christ; or if they have begun so to do, yet they have not made clear work of it, nor come to a clear and comfortable issue. There is nothing more dreadful than for a man to be able to digest his convictions;—to have sin look him in the face, and speak perhaps some words of terror to him, and to be able, by any charms of diversions or delays, to put it off, without coming to a full trial as to state and condition in reference thereunto. This the saints do:—they gather up their sins, lay them in the balance of the law, see and consider their weight and desert; and then,—

[1] Rom. i. 17, x. 3, 4.

(3.) They make this commutation I speak of with Jesus Christ; that is,—

[1.] They seriously consider, and by faith *conquer*, all objections to the contrary, that Jesus Christ, by *the will and appointment* of the Father, hath really undergone the punishment that was due to those sins that lie now under his eye and consideration, Isa. liii. 6; 2 Cor. v. 21. He hath as certainly and really answered the justice of God for them as, if he himself (the sinner) should at that instant be cast into hell, he could do.

[2.] They hearken to the voice of Christ calling them to *him* with their burden, " Come unto me, all ye that are weary and heavy laden;"—" Come with your burdens; come, thou poor soul, with thy guilt of sin." Why? what to do? " Why, this is mine," saith Christ; " this agreement I made with my Father, that I should come, and take thy sins, and bear them away: they were my lot. Give me thy *burden*, give me all thy *sins.* Thou knowest not what to do with them; I know how to dispose of them well enough, so that God shall be glorified, and thy soul delivered." Hereupon,—

[3.] They lay down *their sins at the cross of Christ,* upon his shoulders. This is faith's great and bold venture upon the grace, faithfulness, and truth of God, to stand by the cross and say, " Ah! he is bruised for my sins, and wounded for my transgressions, and the chastisement of my peace is upon him. He is thus made sin for me. Here I give up my sins to him that is able to bear them, to undergo them. He requires it of my hands, that I should be content that he should undertake for them; and that I heartily consent unto." This is every day's work; I know not how any peace can be maintained with God without it. If it be the work of souls to receive Christ, as made sin for us, we must receive him as one that takes our sins upon him. Not as though he died any more, or suffered any more; but as the faith of the saints of old made that present and done before their eyes [which had] not yet come to pass, Heb. xi. 1, so faith now makes that present which was accomplished and past many generations ago. This it is to know Christ crucified.

[4.] Having thus by faith given up their sins to Christ, and seen God laying them all on him, they draw nigh, and *take from him that righteousness* which he hath wrought out for them; so fulfilling the whole of that of the apostle, 2 Cor. v. 21, " He was made sin for us, that we might be made the righteousness of God in him." They consider him tendering himself and his righteousness, to be their righteousness before God; they take it, and accept of it, and complete this blessed bartering and exchange of faith. Anger, curse, wrath, death, sin as to its guilt, he took it all and takes it all away. With him we leave whatever of this nature belongs to us; and from him we receive love, life, righteousness, and peace.

Objection. But it may be said, "Surely this course of procedure can never be acceptable to Jesus Christ. What! shall we daily come to him with our filth, our guilt, our sins? May he not, will he not, bid us keep them to ourselves? they are our own. Shall we be always giving sins, and taking righteousness?"

Answer. There is not any thing that Jesus Christ is more delighted with, than that his saints should always hold communion with him as to this business of giving and receiving. For,—

1. This *exceedingly honours* him, and gives him the glory that is his due. Many, indeed, cry "Lord, Lord," and make mention of him, but honour him not at all. How so? They take his work out of his hands, and ascribe it unto other things; their repentance, their duties, shall bear their iniquities. They do not say so; but they do so. The commutation they make, if they make any, it is with themselves. All their bartering about sin is in and with their own souls The work that Christ came to do in the world, was to "bear our iniquities," and lay down his life a ransom for our sins. The cup he had to drink of was filled with our sins, as to the punishment due to them. What greater dishonour, then, can be done to the Lord Jesus, than to ascribe this work to any thing else,—to think to get rid of our sins [by] any other way or means? Herein, then, I say, is Christ honoured indeed, when we go to him with our sins by faith, and say unto him, "Lord, this is thy work; this is that for which thou camest into the world; this is that thou hast undertaken to do. Thou callest for my burden, which is too heavy for me to bear; take it, blessed Redeemer Thou tenderest thy righteousness; that is my portion." Then is Christ honoured, then is the glory of mediation ascribed to him, when we walk with him in this communion.

2. This *exceedingly endears the souls of the saints to him,* and constrains them to put a due valuation upon him, his love, his righteousness, and grace. When they find, and have the daily use of it, then they do it. Who would not love him? "I have been with the Lord Jesus," may the poor soul say: "I have left my sins, my burden, with him; and he hath given me his righteousness, wherewith I am going with boldness to God. I was *dead,* and am *alive;* for he *died* for me: I was *cursed,* and am *blessed;* for he was made a *curse for me:* I was *troubled,* but have *peace;* for the *chastisement of my peace* was upon him. I knew not what to do, nor whither to cause *my sorrow* to go; by him have I received *joy unspeakable and glorious.* If I do not love him, delight in him, obey him, live to him, die for him, I am worse than the devils in hell." Now the great aim of Christ in the world is, to have a high place and esteem in the

hearts of his people; to have there, as he hath in himself, the pre-eminence in all things,—not to be jostled up and down among other things,—to be all, and in all. And thus are the saints of God prepared to esteem him, upon the engaging themselves to this communion with him.

Obj. Yea, but you will say, "If this be so, what need we to *repent or amend our ways?* it is but going to Christ by faith, making this exchange with him: and so we may sin, that grace may abound."

Ans. I judge no man's person; but this I must needs say, that I do not understand how a man *that makes this objection in cold blood,* not under a temptation or accidental darkness, can have any *true or real acquaintance with Jesus Christ:* however, this I am certain of, that this communion in itself produces quite other effects than those supposed. For,—

1. For repentance; it is, I suppose, a *gospel repentance* that is intended. For a legal, bondage repentance, full of dread, amazement, terror, self-love, astonishment at the presence of God, I confess this communion takes it away, prevents it, casts it out, with its bondage and fear; but for gospel repentance, whose nature consists in godly sorrow for sin, with its relinquishment, proceeding from faith, love, and abhorrency of sin, on accounts of Father, Son, and Spirit, both law and love,—that this should be hindered by this communion, is not possible. I told you that the foundation of this communion is laid in a deep, serious, daily consideration of sin, its guilt, vileness, and abomination, and our own vileness on that account; that a sense hereof is to be kept alive in and upon the heart of every one that will enjoy this communion with Christ: without it Christ is of no value nor esteem to him. Now, is it possible that a man should daily fill his heart with the thoughts of the vileness of sin, on all considerations whatever,—of law, love, grace, gospel, life, and death,—and be filled with self-abhorrency on this account, and yet be a stranger to godly sorrow? Here is the mistake,—the foundation of this communion is laid in that which they suppose it overthrows.

2. But what shall we say for *obedience?* "If Christ be so glorified and honoured by taking our sins, the more we bring to him, the more will he be glorified." A man could not suppose that this objection would be made, but that the Holy Ghost, who knows what is in man and his heart, hath made it for them, and in their name, Rom. vi. 1–3. The very same doctrine that I have insisted on being delivered, chap. v. 18–20, the same objection is made to it: and for those who think it may have any weight, I refer them to the answer given in that chapter by the apostle; as also to what was said before to the necessity of our obedience, notwithstanding the imputation of the righteousness of Christ

But you will say, "How should we address ourselves to the performance of this duty? what path are we to walk in?"

Faith exercises itself in it, especially three ways:—

(1.) In *meditation.* The heart goes over, in its own thoughts, the part above insisted on, sometimes severally, sometimes jointly, sometimes fixing primarily on one thing, sometimes on another, and sometimes going over the whole. At one time, perhaps, the soul is most upon consideration of its own sinfulness, and filling itself with shame and self-abhorrency on that account; sometimes it is filled with the thoughts of the righteousness of Christ, and with joy unspeakable and glorious on that account. Especially on great occasions, when grieved and burdened by negligence, or eruption of corruption, then the soul goes over the whole work, and so drives things to an issue with God, and takes up the peace that Christ hath wrought out for him.

(2.) In considering and *inquiring into the promises* of the gospel, which hold out all these things:—the excellency, fulness, and suitableness of the righteousness of Christ, the rejection of all false righteousness, and the commutation made in the love of God; which was formerly insisted on.

(3.) In *prayer.* Herein do their souls go through this work day by day; and this communion have all the saints with the Lord Jesus, as to their acceptation with God: which was the first thing proposed to consideration.

———

CHAPTER IX.

Of communion with Christ in holiness—The several acts ascribed unto the Lord Christ herein: 1. His intercession; 2. Sending of the Spirit; 3. Bestows habitual grace—What that is, and wherein it consists—This purchased by Christ; bestowed by him—Of actual grace—How the saints hold communion with Christ in these things; manifested in sundry particulars.

II. Our communion with the Lord Jesus as to that grace of *sanctification* and purification whereof we have made mention, in the several distinctions and degrees thereof, formerly, is nextly to be considered. And herein the former method must be observed; and we must show,—1. What are the peculiar *actings* of the Lord Christ as to this communion; and, 2. What is the *duty* of the saints herein. The sum is,—How we hold communion with Christ in *holiness*, as well as in *righteousness;* and that very briefly:—

1. There are several acts ascribed unto the Lord Jesus in reference to this particular; as,—

(1.) His *interceding* with the Father, by virtue of his oblation in the behalf of his, that he would bestow the Holy Spirit on them. Here I choose to enter, because of the oblation of Christ itself I have spoken before; otherwise, every thing is to be run up to that head, that source and spring. There lies the foundation of all spiritual mercies whatever; as afterward also shall be manifested. Now the Spirit, as unto us a Spirit of grace, holiness, and consolation, is of the purchase of Christ. It is upon the matter, the great promise of the new covenant, Ezek. xi. 19, " I will put a new spirit within you;" so also, chap. xxxvi. 27; Jer. xxxii. 39, 40; and in sundry other places, whereof afterward. Christ is the mediator and "surety of this new covenant." Heb. vii. 22, " Jesus was made surety of a better testament," or rather covenant;—a testament needs no surety. He is the undertaker on the part of God and man also: of *man, to give satisfaction; of God, to bestow the whole grace of the promise;* as chap. ix. 15, " For this cause he is the mediator of the new testament, that by means of death, for the redemption of transgressions that were under the first testament, they which are called might receive the promise of eternal inheritance." He both satisfied for sin and procured the promise. He procures all the love and kindness which are the fruits of the covenant, being himself the original promise thereof, Gen. iii. 15; the whole being so " ordered in all things, and made sure," 2 Sam. xxiii. 5, that the residue of its effects should all be derived from him, depend upon him, and be procured by him,—" that he in all things might have the pre-eminence," Col. i. 18; according to the compact and agreement made with him, Isa. liii. 12. They are all the purchase of his blood; and therefore the Spirit also, as promised in that covenant, 1 Cor. i. 30. Now, the whole fruit and purchase of his death is made out from the Father upon his intercession. This (John xiv. 16–18) he promiseth his disciples, that he will pursue the work which he hath in hand in their behalf, and intercede with the Father for the Spirit, as a fruit of his purchase. Therefore he tells them that he will not pray the Father for his love unto them, because the eternal love of the Father is not the fruit but the fountain of his purchase: but the Spirit, that is a fruit; " That," saith he, " I will pray the Father for," etc. And what Christ asketh the Father as mediator to bestow on us, that is part of his purchase,[1] being promised unto him, upon his undertaking to do the will of God. And this is the first thing that is to be considered in the Lord Jesus, as to the communication of the Spirit of sanctification and purification, the first thing to be considered in this our communion with him,—*he intercedes* with his Father, that he may be bestowed on us as a fruit of his death and bloodshed in our behalf. This is the relation of the Spirit

[1] Ps. ii. 8; Isa. liii. 12; Ps. xl. 8–12.

of holiness, as bestowed on us, unto the mediation of Christ. He is the great [1]foundation of the covenant of grace; being himself ever-lastingly destinated and freely given to make a purchase of all the good things thereof. Receiving, according to promise, the Holy Ghost, Acts ii. 33, he sheds him abroad on his own. This faith considers, fixes on, dwells upon. For,—

(2.) His prayer being granted, as the [2] Father " hears him always," he *actually sends his Spirit* into the hearts of his saints, there to dwell in his stead, and to do all things for them and in them which he himself hath to do. This, secondly, is the Lord Christ by faith to be eyed in; and that not only in respect of the first enduing of our hearts with his Holy Spirit, but also of the continual supplies of it, drawing forth and exciting more effectual [3]operations and actings of that indwelling Spirit. Hence, though (John xiv. 16) he says the Father will give them the Comforter, because the original and sove-reign dispensation is in his hand, and it is by him made out, upon the intercession of Christ; yet, not being bestowed immediately on us, but, as it were, given into the hand of Christ for us, he affirms that (as to actual collation or bestowing) he sends him himself; chap. xv. 26, " I will send the Comforter to you, from the Father." He receives him from his Father, and actually sends him unto his saints. So, chap. xvi. 7, " I will send him." And, verses 14, 15, he manifests how he will send him. He will furnish him with that which is his to bestow upon them: " He shall take of mine (of that which is pro-perly and peculiarly so,—mine, as mediator,—the fruit of my life and death unto holiness), and give it unto you." But of these things more afterward. This, then, is the second thing that the Lord Christ doth, and which is to be eyed in him:—He sends his Holy Spirit into our hearts; which is the [4]efficient cause of all holiness and sanctifica-tion,—quickening, enlightening, purifying the souls of his saints. How our union with him, with all the benefit thereon depending, floweth from this his communication of the Spirit unto us, to abide with us, and to dwell in us, I have at large [5]elsewhere declared; where also this whole matter is more fully opened. And this is to be considered in him by faith, in reference to the Spirit itself.

(3.) There is that which we call *habitual grace;* that is, the fruits of the Spirit,—the spirit which is born of the Spirit, John iii. 6. That which is born of, or produced by, the Holy Ghost, in the heart or soul of a man when he is regenerate, that which makes him so, is spirit; in opposition to [6]the flesh, or that enmity which is in us by nature against God. It is faith, love, joy, hope, and the rest of the

---

[1] Gen. iii. 15; Isa. xlii. 6, xlix. 8; Dan. ix. 24.   [2] John xi. 42.
[3] " Vicariam navare operam."—Tertull., Prov. i. 23.
[4] Titus iii. 5, 6.   [5] Saints' Perseverance, chap. viii. vol. xi.   [6] Gal. v. 17.

graces of the gospel, in their root or common principle, concerning which these two things are to be observed:—

[1.] That though many particular graces are mentioned, yet there are *not different habits or qualities* in us,—not several or distinct principles to answer them; but only the same [1]habit or spiritual principle putting forth itself in various operations or ways of working, according to the variety of the objects which it goeth forth unto, is their common principle: so that it is called and distinguished, as above, rather in respect of *actual exercise*, with relation to its objects, than habitual inherence; it being one root which hath these many branches.

[2.] This is that which I intend by this habit of grace,—*a [2]new, gracious, spiritual [3]life, or principle, [4]created, and [5]bestowed on the soul, whereby it is [6]changed in all its faculties and affections, fitted and enabled to go forth in the way of obedience unto every divine object that is proposed unto it, according to the mind of God.* For instance, the mind can discern of [7]spiritual things in a spiritual manner; and therein it is light, *illumination.* The whole soul closeth with Christ, as held forth in the promises of the gospel for righteousness and salvation: that is *faith;* which being the main and principal work of it, it often gives denomination unto the whole. So when it rests in God, in Christ, with delight, desire, and complacency, it is called *love;* being, indeed, the principle suiting all the faculties of our souls for spiritual and living operations, according to their natural use. Now it differs,—

1st. From the *Spirit dwelling* in the saints; for it is a *created quality.* The Spirit dwells in us as a free agent in a holy habitation. This grace, as a quality, remains in us, as in its own proper subject, that hath not any subsistence but therein, and is capable of being intended[8] or restrained under great variety of degrees.

2dly. From *actual grace, which is transient;* this making its residence in the soul. [9]*Actual grace is an illapse of divine influence and assistance, working in and by the soul any spiritual act or duty whatsoever, without any pre-existence unto that act or continuance after it,* "God working in us, both to will and to do." But this habitual grace is always resident in us, causing the soul to be a

[1] 2 Cor. v. 17.

[2] Cor. v. 17; Ezek. xi. 19, xviii. 31, xxxvi. 26; Gal. vi. 15; Eph. ii. 15, iv. 24; Col. iii. 10; 1 Pet. ii. 2; John iii. 6.

[3] Col. iii. 3, 4; Eph. ii. 1, 5; Rom. viii. 11; John v. 21, vi. 63.

[4] Ps. li. 10; Eph ii. 10, iv. 24; Col. iii. 10; 2 Cor. v. 17.

[5] 2 Cor. iii. 5, iv. 6; Acts v. 31; Luke i. 79; John iv. 14, iii. 27; 1 Cor. ii. 12; Eph. iv. 7; Phil. i. 29.

[6] Acts xxvi. 18; Eph. v. 8; 2 Cor. v. 17; John v. 24.

[7] 1 Cor. ii. 12; Eph. i. 18; 2 Cor. iii. 18, iv. 6.

[8] *Intended* is here used in a sense now obsolete,—*stretched, increased.*—ED.

[9] 2 Cor. iii. 5; Ps. cxix. 36; Phil. ii. 13.

meet principle for all those holy and spiritual operations which by
actual grace are to be performed.   And,—

3dly. It is *capable of augmentation and diminution,* as was said.
In some it is more large and more effectual than in others; yea, in
some persons, more at one time than another.   Hence are those
[1]dyings, decays, ruins, recoveries, complaints, and rejoicings, whereof
so frequent mention is made in the Scripture.

These things being premised as to the nature of it, let us now
consider what we are to eye in the Lord Jesus in reference thereunto, to make an entrance into our communion with him therein,
as things by him or on his part performed:—

As I said of the Spirit, so, in the *first* place, I say of this, it
is of the *purchase of Christ,* and is so to be looked on.   "It is
given unto us for [2]his sake to believe on him," Phil. i. 29.   The
Lord, on the behalf of Christ, for his sake, because it is purchased
and procured by him for us, bestows faith, and (by same rule) all
grace upon us.   "We are blessed with all spiritual blessings in
heavenly places in him," Eph. i. 3.   "In him;"[3] that is, in and through
his mediation for us.   His oblation and intercession lie at the bottom
of this dispensation.   Were not grace by them procured, it would
never by any one soul be enjoyed.   All grace is from this fountain.
In our receiving it from Christ, we must still consider what it [4]cost
him.   Want of this weakens faith in its proper workings.   His whole
intercession is founded on his oblation, 1 John ii. 1, 2.   What he
purchased by his death, that—nor more nor less, as hath been often
said—he intercedeth may be bestowed.   And he prays that all his
saints may have this grace whereof we speak, John xvii. 17.   Did
we continually consider all grace as the fruit of the purchase of Christ,
it would be an exceeding endearment on our spirits: nor can we
without this consideration, according to the tenor of the gospel, ask
or expect any grace.   It is no prejudice to the free grace of the
Father, to look on any thing as the purchase of the Son; it was from
that grace that he made that purchase: and in the receiving of grace
from God, we have not communion with Christ, who is yet the treasury and storehouse of it, unless we look upon it as his purchase.   He
hath obtained that we should be [5]sanctified throughout, have life in
us, be humble, holy, believing, dividing the spoil with the mighty,
by destroying the works of the devil in us.

Secondly. The Lord Christ doth *actually communicate* this grace
unto his saints, and bestows it on them: "Of his fulness have all we
received, and grace for grace," John i. 16.   For,—

[1] Cant. v. 2; Rev. ii. 5, iii. 2, 3, 17, 19; Hos. xiv. 4; Ps. li., etc.
[2] Ὑπὲρ Χριστοῦ.   [3] 1 John ii. 1, 2.   [4] Rom. viii. 32.
[5] Eph. v. 25–27; Tit. ii. 14; Rom. vi. 4.

(1*st*.) The Father *actually invests* him with all the grace whereof, by *compact* and agreement, he hath made a purchase (as he received the promise of the Spirit); which is all that is of use for the bringing his many sons to glory. "It pleased the Father that in him should all fulness dwell," Col. i. 19,—that he should be invested with a fulness of that grace which is needful for his people. This himself calls the "power of giving eternal life to his elect," John xvii. 2; which power is not only his ability to do it, but also his right to do it. Hence this delivering of all things unto him by his Father, he lays as the bottom of his inviting sinners unto him for refreshment: "All things are delivered unto me of my Father," Matt. xi. 27. "Come unto me, all that labour and are heavy laden, and I will give you rest," verse 28. This being the covenant of the Father with him, and his promise unto him, that upon the making "his soul an offering for sin, he should see his seed, and the pleasure of the LORD should prosper in his hand," Isa. liii. 10, in the verses following, the "pouring out of his soul unto death, and bearing the sins of many," is laid as the bottom and procuring cause of these things:—1. Of justification: "By his knowledge he shall justify many." 2. Of sanctification; in "destroying the works of the devil," verses 11, 12. Thus comes our merciful high priest to be the great possessor of all grace, that he may give out to us according to his own pleasure, quickening whom he will. He hath it in him really as our head, in that he received not that Spirit by measure (John iii. 34) which is the bond of union between him and us, 1 Cor. vi. 17; whereby holding him, the head, we are filled with his fulness, Eph. i. 22, 23; Col. i. 19. He hath it as a common person, intrusted with it in our behalf, Rom. v. 14–17. "The last Adam is made" unto us "a quickening Spirit," 1 Cor. xv. 45. He is also a treasury of this grace in a moral and law sense: not only as "it pleased the Father that in him should all fulness dwell," Col. i. 19; but also because in his mediation, as hath been declared, is founded the whole dispensation of grace.

(2*dly*.) Being thus actually vested with this power, and privilege, and fulness, he designs the Spirit to take of this fulness, and to give it unto us: "He shall take of mine, and shall show it unto you," John xvi. 15. The Spirit takes of that fulness that is in Christ, and in the name of the Lord Jesus bestows it actually on them for whose sanctification he is sent. Concerning the manner and almighty efficacy of the Spirit of grace whereby this is done (I mean this actual collation of grace upon his peculiar ones), more will be spoken afterward.

(3*dly*.) For *actual grace*, or that influence or power whereby the saints are enabled to perform particular duties according to the mind of God, there is not any need of farther enlargement about it. What concerns our communion with the Lord Christ therein, holds proportion with what was spoken before.

There remaineth only one thing more to be observed concerning those things whereof mention hath been made, and I proceed to the way whereby we carry on communion with the Lord Jesus in all these; and that is, that these things may be considered two ways:—
1. In respect of their *first collation*, or bestowing on the soul.   2. In respect of their *continuance and increase*, as unto the degrees of them.

In the first sense, as to the real communicating of the Spirit of grace unto the soul, so raising it from death unto life, the saints have no kind of communion with Christ therein but only what consists in a passive reception of that life-giving, quickening Spirit and power. They are but as the dead bones in the prophet; the wind blows on them, and they live;—as Lazarus in the grave; Christ calls, and they come forth, the call being accompanied with life and power.   This, then, is not that whereof particularly I speak; but it is the second, in respect of farther efficacy of the Spirit and increase of grace, both habitual and actual, whereby we become more holy, and to be more powerful in walking with God,—have more fruit in obedience and success against temptations.   And in this,—

2. They hold communion with the Lord Christ.   And wherein and how they do it, shall now be declared.

They continually eye the Lord Jesus as the great Joseph, that hath the disposal of all the granaries of the kingdom of heaven committed unto him; as one in whom it hath pleased the Father to gather all things unto a head, Eph. i. 10, that from him all things might be dispensed unto them.   All treasures, all fulness, the Spirit not by measure, are in him.   And this fulness in this Joseph, in reference to their condition, they eye in these three particulars:—

(1.) In the preparation unto the dispensation mentioned, in the *expiating, purging, purifying efficacy of his blood*.   It was a sacrifice not only of atonement, as offered, but also of purification, as poured out.   This the apostle eminently sets forth, Heb. ix. 13, 14, " For if the blood of bulls and of goats, and the ashes of an heifer sprinkling the unclean, sanctifieth to the purifying of the flesh: how much more shall·the blood of Christ, who through the eternal Spirit offered himself without spot to God, purge your conscience from dead works to serve the living God?"   This blood of his is that which answers all typical institutions for carnal purification; and therefore hath a spiritually-purifying, cleansing, sanctifying virtue in itself, as offered and poured out.   Hence it is called, " A fountain for sin and for uncleanness," Zech. xiii. 1; that is, for their washing and taking away;
—" A fountain opened;" ready prepared, virtuous, efficacious in itself,

before any be put into it; because poured out, instituted, appointed
to that purpose. The saints see that in themselves they are still
exceedingly defiled; and, indeed, to have a sight of the defilements of
sin is a more spiritual discovery than to have only a sense of the
guilt of sin. *This* follows every conviction, and is commensurate unto
it; *that*, usually only such as reveal the purity and holiness of God
and all his ways. Hereupon they cry with shame, within themselves,
" Unclean, unclean,"—unclean in their natures, unclean in their persons, unclean in their conversations; all rolled in the [1]blood of their
defilements; their hearts by nature a very sink, and their lives a
dunghill. They know, also, that no unclean thing shall enter into
the kingdom of God, or have place in the new Jerusalem; that God
is of purer eyes than to behold iniquity. They cannot endure to look
on themselves; and how shall they dare to appear in his presence?
What remedies shall they now use? " Though they wash themselves
with nitre, and take them much soap, yet their iniquity will continue
marked," Jer. ii. 22. Wherewith, then, shall they come before the
Lord? For the removal of this, I say, they look, in the first place, to
the purifying virtue of the blood of Christ, which is able to cleanse
them from all their sins, 1 John i. 7; being the spring from whence
floweth all the purifying virtue, which in the issue will take away
all their spots and stains, " make them holy and without blemish.
and in the end present them glorious unto himself," Eph. v. 26, 27.
This they dwell upon with thoughts of faith; they roll it in their
minds and spirits. Here faith obtains new life, new vigour, when a
sense of vileness hath even overwhelmed it. Here is a fountain
opened: draw nigh, and see its beauty, purity, and efficacy. Here is
a foundation laid of that work whose accomplishment we long for.
One moment's communion with Christ by faith herein is more effectual to the purging of the soul, to the increasing of grace, than the
utmost self-endeavours of a thousand ages.

(2.) They eye the blood of Christ *as the blood of sprinkling*.
Coming to " Jesus, the mediator of the new covenant," they come to
the [2] " blood of sprinkling," Heb. xii. 24. The eyeing of the blood
of Christ as shed will not of itself take away pollution. There is not
only αἱματεκχυσία,—a " shedding of blood," without which there is no
remission, Heb. ix. 22; but there is also αἵματος ῥαντισμός,—a " sprinkling of blood," without which there is no actual purification. This
the apostle largely describes, Heb. ix. 19, " When Moses," saith he,
" had spoken every precept to all the people according to the law,
he took the blood of calves and of goats, with water, and scarlet wool,
and hyssop, and sprinkled both the book and all the people, saying,

---

[1] Ezek. xvi. 4, 6, etc.; John iii. 3, 5; Πᾶν κοινοῦν, Rev. xxi. 27; Hab. i. 13.
[2] Αἷμα ῥαντισμοῦ.

This is the blood of the testament which God hath enjoined unto you. Moreover he sprinkled likewise with blood both the tabernacle, and all the vessels of the ministry. And almost all things are by the law purged with blood. It was therefore necessary that the patterns of things in the heavens should be purified with these; but the heavenly things themselves with better sacrifices than these," verses 19–23. He had formerly compared the blood of Christ to the blood of sacrifices, as offered, in respect of the impetration and the purchase it made; now he doth it unto that blood as sprinkled, in respect of its application unto purification and holiness. And he tells us how this sprinkling was performed: it was by dipping hyssop in the blood of the sacrifice, and so dashing it out upon the things and persons to be purified; as the institution also was with the *paschal* lamb, Exod. xii. 7. Hence, David, in a sense of the pollution of sin, prays that he may be "purged with hyssop," Ps. li. 7. For that this peculiarly respected the uncleanness and defilement of sin, is evident, because there is no mention made, in the institution of any sacrifice (after that of the lamb before mentioned), of sprinkling blood with hyssop, but only in those which respected *purification* of uncleanness; as in the case of leprosy, Lev. xiv. 6; and all other defilements, Numb. xix. 18: which latter, indeed, is not of blood, but of the water of separation; this also being eminently typical of the blood of Christ, which is the fountain for separation for uncleanness, Zech. xiii. 1. Now, this *bunch* of hyssop, wherein the blood of purification was prepared for the sprinkling of the unclean, is (unto us) the free promises of Christ. The cleansing virtue of the blood of Christ lies in the promises, as the blood of sacrifices in the hyssop, ready to pass out unto them that draw nigh thereunto. Therefore the apostle argueth from receiving of the promise unto universal *holiness and purity:* "Having therefore these promises, dearly beloved, let us cleanse ourselves from all filthiness of the flesh and spirit, perfecting holiness in the fear of God," 2 Cor. vii. 1. This, then, the saints do:—they eye the blood of Christ as it is in the promise, ready to issue out upon the soul, for the purification thereof; and thence is purging and cleansing virtue to be communicated unto them, and by the blood of Christ are they to be purged from all their sins, 1 John i. 7. Thus far, as it were, this purifying blood, thus prepared and made ready, is at some distance to the soul. Though it be shed to this purpose, that it might purge, cleanse, and sanctify, though it be taken up with the bunch of hyssop in the promises, yet the soul may not partake of it. Wherefore,—

(3.) They look upon him as, in *his own* Spirit, he is the only *dispenser of the Spirit and of all grace* of sanctification and holiness. They consider that upon his intercession it is granted to him that he shall make effectual all the fruits of his purchase, to the sanctification, the purifying and making glorious in holiness, of his whole people. They know that this is actually to be accomplished by the Spirit, according to the innumerable promises given to that purpose. He is to *sprinkle* that blood upon their souls; he is to *create* the holiness in them that they long after; he is to be himself in them a *well* of water springing up to everlasting life. In this state they look to Jesus: here faith fixes itself, in expectation of his giving out the Spirit for all these ends and purposes; mixing the promises with faith, and so becoming actual partaker of all this grace. This is their way, this their communion with Christ; this is the life of faith, as to grace and holiness. Blessed is the soul that is exercised therein: " He shall be as a tree planted by the waters, and that spreadeth out her roots by the river, and shall not see when heat cometh, but her leaf shall be green; and shall not be careful in the year of drought, neither shall cease from yielding fruit," Jer. xvii. 8. Convinced persons who know not Christ, nor the fellowship of his sufferings, would spin a holiness out of their own bowels; they would work it out in their own strength. They begin it with[1] trying endeavours; and follow it with vows, duties, resolutions, engagements, sweating at it all the day long. Thus they continue for a season,—their hypocrisy, for the most part, ending in *apostasy.* The saints of God do, in the very entrance of their walking with him, reckon upon it that they have a threefold want:— [1.] Of the *Spirit of holiness* to dwell in them. [2.] Of a *habit of holiness* to be infused into them. [3.] Of *actual assistance* to work all their works for them; and that if these should continue to be wanting, they can never, with all their might, power, and endeavours, perform any one act of holiness before the Lord. They know that of themselves they have no sufficiency,—that[2] without Christ they can do nothing: therefore they look to him, who is intrusted with a fulness of all these in their behalf; and thereupon by faith derive from him an increase of that whereof they stand in need. Thus, I say, have the saints communion with Christ, as to their *sanctification* and holiness. From him do they receive the Spirit to dwell in them; from him the new *principle* of life, which is the root of all their obedience; from him have they actual *assistance* for every duty they are called unto. In waiting for, expectation and receiving of these blessings, on the accounts before mentioned, do they spend their lives and time with him. In vain is help looked for from other mountains; in vain do men spend their strength in following after righteousness, if this be wanting. Fix thy soul here; thou shalt not tarry until thou be ashamed. This is the way, the only way, to obtain full, effectual manifestations of the Spirit's dwelling in us; to have our hearts purified, our consciences

[1] Rom. x. 1-4.   [2] John xv. 5.

purged, our sins mortified, our graces increased, our souls made humble, holy, zealous, believing,—like to him; to have our lives fruitful, our deaths comfortable.   Let us herein abide, eyeing Christ by
faith, to attain that measure of conformity to him which is allotted
unto us in this world, that when we shall see him as he is, we may be
like unto him.

CHAPTER X.

Of communion with Christ in privileges—Of adoption; the nature of it, the consequences of it—Peculiar privileges attending it; liberty, title, boldness, affliction—Communion with Christ hereby.

III. THE third thing wherein we have communion with Christ, is
grace of privilege before God; I mean, as the *third head* of purchased
grace.   The privileges we enjoy by Christ are great and innumerable;
to insist on them in particular were work for a man's whole life, not a
design to be wrapped up in a few sheets.   I shall take a view of them
only in the head, the spring and fountain whence they all arise and
flow,—this is *our adoption:* " Beloved, now are we the sons of God,"
1 John iii. 2.   This is our great and fountain privilege.   Whence is it
that we are so?   It is from the love of the Father.   Verse 1, " Behold,
what manner of love the Father hath bestowed upon us, that we should
be called the sons of God!"   But by whom immediately do we receive this honour?   As many as believe on Christ, he gives them this
power, to become the sons of God, John i. 12.   Himself was appointed
to be the first-born among many brethren, Rom. viii. 29; and his
taking us to be brethren, Heb. ii. 11, makes us become the children
of God.   Now, that God is our Father, by being the Father of Christ,
and we his children by being the brethren of Christ, being the head
and sum of all the honour, privilege, right, and title we have, let us
a little consider the nature of that act whereby we are invested with
this state and title,—namely, our adoption.

*Now, adoption is the authoritative translation of a believer, by
Jesus Christ, from the family of the world and Satan into the
family of God, with his investiture in all the privileges and advantages of that family.*

To the complete adoption of any person, these five things are
required:—

1. That he be *actually*, and of his own right, of another family
than that whereinto he is adopted.   He must be the son of one
family or other, in his own right, as all persons are.

2. That there be a *family* unto which of himself he hath no right, whereinto he is to be grafted. If a man comes into a family upon a *personal* right, though originally at never so great a distance, that man is not adopted. If a man of a most remote consanguinity do come into the inheritance of any family by the death of the nearer heirs, though his right before were little better than nothing, yet he is a born son of that family,—he is not adopted. [In adoption] he is not to have the plea of the most remote *possibility* of succession.

3. That there be an *authoritative, legal translation* of him, by some that have power thereinto, from one family into another. It was not, by the *law* of old, in the power of particular persons to adopt when and whom they would. It was to be done by the *authority* of the sovereign power.

4. That the adopted person be freed from all the obligations that be upon him unto the family from whence he is translated; otherwise he can be no way useful or serviceable unto the family whereinto he is ingrafted. He cannot serve two masters, much less *two fathers*.

5. That, by virtue of his adoption, he be invested in all the rights, *privileges*, advantages, and title to the whole inheritance, of the family into which he is adopted, in as full and ample manner as if he had been born a son therein.

Now, all these things and circumstances do concur and are found in the adoption of believers:—

1. They are, by their own *original right*, of another family than that whereinto they are adopted. They are "by nature the children of wrath," Eph. ii. 3,—sons of wrath,—of that family whose inheritance is "wrath,"—called "the power of darkness," Col. i. 13; for from thence doth God "translate them into the kingdom of his dear Son." This is the family of the world and of Satan, of which by nature believers are. Whatever is to be inherited in that family,—as wrath, curse, death, hell,—they have a right thereunto. Neither can they of themselves, or by themselves, get free of this family: a strong man armed keeps them in subjection. Their natural estate is a family condition, attended with all the circumstances of a family,—family duties and services, rights and titles, relations and observances. They are of the black family of sin and Satan.

2. There is *another family whereinto* they are to be translated, and whereunto of themselves they have neither right nor title. This is that family in heaven and earth which is called after the name of Christ, Eph. iii. 15,—the great family of God. God hath a[1] house and family for his children; of whom some he maintains on the riches of his grace, and some he entertains with the fulness of his glory. This is that house whereof the Lord Christ is the great dispenser, it having

[1] Hab. iii. 6.

pleased the Father to "gather together in one all things in him, both which are in heaven, and which are on earth, even in him," Eph. i. 10. Herein live all the sons and daughters of God, spending largely on the riches of his grace. Unto this family of themselves they have no right nor title; they are wholly alienated from it, Eph. ii. 12, and can lay no claim to any thing in it. God driving fallen Adam out of the garden, and shutting up all ways of return with a flaming sword, ready to cut him off if he should attempt it, abundantly declares that he, and all in him, had lost all right of approaching unto God in any family relation. Corrupted, cursed nature is not vested with the least right to any thing of God. Therefore,—

3. They have an *authoritative translation* from one of these families to another. It is not done in a *private*, underhand way, but in the way of authority. John i. 12, "As many as received him, to them gave he power to become the sons of God,"—power or authority. This investing them with the power, excellency, and right of the sons of God, is a *forensical act*, and hath a legal proceeding in it. It is called the "making us meet to be partakers of the inheritance of the saints in light," Col. i. 12;—a judicial exalting us into membership in that family, where God is the Father, Christ the[1] elder brother, all saints and angels brethren and fellow-children, and the inheritance a crown immortal and incorruptible, that fades not away.

Now, this authoritative translation of believers from one family into another consisteth of these two parts:—

(1.) An *effectual proclamation* and declaration of such a person's immunity from all obligations to the former family, to which by nature he was related. And this declaration hath a threefold object:—

[1.] *Angels.* It is declared unto them; they are the sons of God. They are the[2] sons of God, and so of the family whereinto the adopted person is to be admitted; and therefore it concerns them to know who are invested with the rights of that family, that they may discharge their duty towards them. Unto them, then, it is declared that believers are freed from the family of sin and hell, to become fellow-sons and servants with them. And this is done two ways:—

1st. Generally, by *the doctrine of the gospel.* Eph. iii. 10, "Unto the principalities and powers in heavenly places is made known by the church the manifold wisdom of God."

By the church is this wisdom made known to the angels, either as the doctrine of the gospel is delivered unto it, or as it is gathered thereby. And what is this wisdom of God that is thus made known to principalities and powers? It is, that "the Gentiles should be fellow-heirs and of the same body with us," verse 6. The mystery of adopting sinners of the Gentiles, taking them from their slavery in the

[1] Rom. viii. 29; Heb. ii. 12.   [2] Job i. 6, xxxviii. 7; Heb. xii. 22–24; Rev. xxii. 9.

family of the world, that they might have a right of heirship, becoming sons in the family of God, is this wisdom, thus made known. And how was it primitively made known? It was " revealed by the Spirit unto the prophets and apostles," verse 5.

2dly. In particular, by *immediate revelation.* When any particular soul is freed from the family of this world, it is revealed to the angels. " There is joy in the presence of the angels of God" (that is, among the angels, and by them) " over one sinner that repenteth," Luke xv. 10. Now, the angels cannot of themselves absolutely know the true repentance of a sinner in itself; it is a work wrought in that cabinet which none hath a key unto but Jesus Christ; by him it is revealed to the angels, when the peculiar care and charge of such a one is committed to them. These things have their transaction before the angels, Luke xii. 8, 9. Christ owns the names of his brethren before the angels, Rev. iii. 5. When he gives them admittance into the family where they are, Heb. xii. 22, he declares to them that they are sons, that they may discharge their duty towards them, Heb. i. 14.

[2.] It is denounced in a judicial way *unto Satan,* the great master of the family whereunto they were in subjection. When the Lord Christ delivers a soul from under the power of that strong armed one, he binds him,—ties him from the exercise of that power and dominion which before he had over him. And by this means doth he know that such a one is delivered from his family; and all his future attempts upon him are encroachings upon the possession and inheritance of the Lord Christ.

[3.] Unto *the conscience of the person adopted.* The Spirit of Christ testifies to the heart and conscience of a believer that he is freed from all engagements unto the family of Satan, and is become the son of God, Rom. viii. 14, 15; and enables him to cry, " Abba, Father," Gal. iv. 6. Of the particulars of this testification of the Spirit, and of its absolving the soul from its old alliance, I shall speak afterward. And herein consists the first thing mentioned.

(2.) There is an *authoritative ingrafting* of a believer actually into the family of God, and investing him with the whole right of sonship. Now this, as unto us, hath sundry acts:—

[1.] The giving a believer *a new name* in a white stone, Rev. ii. 17. They that are adopted are to take new names; they change their names they had in their old families, to take the names of the families whereinto they are translated. This new name is, " A child of God." That is the new name given in adoption; and no man knoweth what is in that name, but only he that doth receive it. And this new name is given and written in a white stone;—that is the *tessera* of our admission into the house of God. It is a stone of judicial acquitment.

Our adoption by the Spirit is bottomed on our absolution in the blood of Jesus; and therefore is the new name in the white stone privilege grounded on discharge. The white stone quits the claim of the old family; the new name gives entrance to the other.

[2.] An enrolling of his name in the catalogue of the household of God, admitting him thereby into fellowship therein. This is called the "writing of the house of Israel," Ezek. xiii. 9; that is, the roll wherein all the names of the Israel, the family of God, are written. God hath a catalogue of his household; Christ knows his sheep by name. When God writeth up the people, he counts that "this man was born in Zion," Ps. lxxxvii. 6. This is an extract of the Lamb's book of life.

[3.] Testifying to his conscience his acceptation with God, enabling him to behave himself as a child, Rom. viii. 15; Gal. iv. 5, 6.

4. The two last things required to adoption are, that the adopted person be freed from all *obligations* to the family from whence he is translated, and invested with the *rights and privileges* of that whereinto he is translated. Now, because these two comprise the whole issue of adoption, wherein the saints have communion with Christ, I shall handle them together, referring the concernments of them unto these four heads:—(1.) *Liberty.* (2.) *Title*, or right. (3.) *Boldness.* (4.) *Correction* These are the four things, in reference to the family of the adopted person, that he doth receive by his adoption, wherein he holds communion with the Lord Jesus:—

(1.) *Liberty.* The Spirit of the Lord, that was upon the Lord Jesus, did anoint him to proclaim liberty to the captives, Isa. lxi. 1; and "where the Spirit of the Lord is" (that is, the Spirit of Christ, given to us by him because we are sons), "there is liberty," 2 Cor. iii. 17. All spiritual liberty is from the Spirit of adoption; whatever else is pretended, is licentiousness. So the apostle argues, Gal. iv. 6, 7, "He hath sent forth his Spirit into their hearts, crying, Abba, Father. Wherefore ye are no more servants,"—no more in bondage, but have the liberty of sons. And this liberty respects,—

[1.] In the first place, the family from whence the adopted person is translated. It is his setting free from all the obligations of that family. Now, in this sense, the liberty which the saints have by adoption is either from that which is *real* or that which is *pretended:*—

1*st.* That which is *real* respects a twofold issue of law and sin. The moral, unchangeable law of God, and sin, being in conjunction, meeting with reference to any persons, hath, and hath had, a twofold issue:—

(1*st.*) An *economical* institution of a new law of ordinances, keeping in bondage those to whom it was given, Col. ii. 14.

(2*dly.*) A natural (if I may so call it) pressing of those persons with its power and efficacy against sin; whereof there are these parts:—

[1*st.*] Its *rigour* and terror in commanding.

[2*dly.*] Its *impossibility* for accomplishment, and so insufficiency for its primitively appointed end.

[3*dly.*] The *issues* of its transgression; which are referred unto two heads:—1. Curse. 2. Death. I shall speak very briefly of these, because they are commonly handled, and granted by all.

2*dly.* That which is *pretended,* is the power of any whatever over *the conscience,* when once made free by Christ:—

(1*st.*) Believers are freed from *the instituted law of ordinances,* which, upon the testimony of the apostles, was a yoke which neither we nor our fathers (in the faith) could bear, Acts xv. 10; wherefore Christ "blotted out this hand-writing of ordinances that was against them, which was contrary to them, and took it out of the way, nailing it to his cross," Col. ii. 14: and thereupon the apostle, after a long dispute concerning the liberty that we have from that law, concludes with this instruction: Gal. v. 1, "Stand fast in the liberty wherewith Christ hath made us free."

(2*dly.*) In reference to the *moral law:*—

[1*st.*] The first thing we have liberty from, is its *rigour* and terror in commanding. Heb. xii. 18–22, "We are not come to the mount that might be touched, and that burned with fire, to the whirlwind, darkness, and tempest, to the sound of the trumpet, and the voice of words, which they that heard besought that they might hear it no more; but we are come to mount Sion," etc. As to that administration of the law wherein it was given out with dread and terror, and so exacted its obedience with rigour, we are freed from it, we are not called to that estate.

[2*dly.*] Its *impossibility* of accomplishment, and so insufficiency for its primitive end, by reason of sin; or, we are freed from the law as the instrument of righteousness, since, by the impossibility of its fulfilling as to us, it is become insufficient for any such purpose, Rom. viii. 2, 3; Gal. iii. 21–23. There being an impossibility of obtaining life by the law, we are exempted from it as to any such end, and that by the righteousness of Christ, Rom. viii. 3.

[3*dly.*] From *the issue of its transgression:*—

First. *Curse.* There is a solemn curse inwrapping the whole wrath annexed to the law, with reference to the transgression thereof; and from this are we wholly at liberty. Gal. iii. 13, "Christ hath redeemed us from the curse of the law by being made a curse for us."

Secondly. *Death,* Heb. ii. 15; and therewith from Satan, Heb. ii. 14, Col. i. 13; and sin, Rom. vi. 14, 1 Pet. i. 18; with the world, Gal. i. 4; with all the attendancies, advantages, and claims of them all, Gal. iv. 3–5, Col. ii. 20; without which we could not live one day.

That which is pretended and claimed by some (wherein in deed and in truth we were never in bondage, but are hereby eminently set free), is the power of binding conscience by any laws and constitutions not from God, Col. ii. 20–22.

[2.] [In the second place,] there is a *liberty in* the family of God, as well as a *liberty from* the family of Satan. Sons are free. Their obedience is a free obedience; they have the Spirit of the Lord: and where he is, there is liberty, 2 Cor. iii. 17. As a Spirit of adoption, he is opposed to the spirit of bondage, Rom. viii. 15. Now, this liberty of our Father's family, which we have as sons and children, being adopted by Christ through the Spirit, is a spiritual largeness of heart, whereby the children of God do freely, willingly, genuinely, without fear, terror, bondage, and constraint, go forth unto all holy obedience in Christ.

I say, this is our liberty in our Father's family: what we have liberty from, hath been already declared.

There are *Gibeonites* outwardly attending the family of God, that do the service of his house as the *drudgery* of their lives. The principle they yield obedience upon, is a *spirit of bondage* unto fear, Rom. viii. 15; the *rule* they do it by, is the law in its dread and rigour, exacting it of them to the utmost, without mercy and mitigation; the *end* they do it for, is to fly from the wrath to come, to pacify conscience, and seek righteousness as it were by the works of the law. Thus servilely, painfully, fruitlessly, they seek to serve their own conviction all their days.

The saints by adoption have a largeness of heart in all holy obedience. Saith David, " I will walk at liberty, for I seek thy precepts," Ps. cxix. 45; Isa. lxi. 1; Luke iv. 18; Rom. viii. 2, 21; Gal. iv. 7, v. 1, 13; James i. 25; John viii. 32, 33, 36; Rom. vi. 18; 1 Pet. ii. 16. Now, this amplitude, or son-like freedom of the Spirit in obedience, consists in sundry things:—

1*st.* In the principles of all spiritual service; which are *life* and *love;*—the one respecting the matter of their obedience, giving them power; the other respecting the manner of their obedience, giving them joy and sweetness in it:—

(1*st.*) It is from *life;* that gives them power as to the matter of obedience. Rom. viii. 2, " The law of the Spirit of life in Christ Jesus sets them free from the law of sin and death." It frees them, it carries them out to all obedience freely; so that " they walk after the Spirit," verse 1, that being the principle of their workings. Gal. ii. 20, " Christ liveth in me; and the life which I now live in the flesh, I live by the faith of the Son of God;"—" The life which I now live in the flesh (that is, the obedience which I yield unto God whilst I am in the flesh), it is from a principle of life, Christ living in me. There is, then, power for all living unto God, from Christ in them, the Spirit of life from Christ carrying them out thereto. The fruits of a dead root are but dead excrescences; living acts are from a principle of life.

Hence you may see the difference between the liberty that slaves assume, and the liberty which is due to children:—

[1st.] Slaves take liberty *from* duty; children have liberty *in* duty. There is not a greater mistake in the world, than that the liberty of sons in the house of God consists in this,—they can perform duties, or take the freedom to omit them; they can serve in the family of God (that is, they think they may if they will), and they can choose whether they will or no. This is a liberty stolen by slaves, not a liberty given by the Spirit unto sons.

The liberty of *sons* is in the inward spiritual freedom of their hearts, naturally and kindly going out in all the ways and worship of God. When they find themselves straitened and shut up in them, they wrestle with God for enlargement, and are never contented with the doing of a duty, unless it be done as in Christ, with free, genuine, and enlarged hearts. The liberty that servants have is *from duty;* the liberty given to sons is *in duty.*

[2dly.] The liberty of slaves or servants is from mistaken, *deceiving conclusions;* the liberty of sons is from the power of the indwelling Spirit of grace: or, the liberty of servants is from outward, dead conclusions; the liberty of sons, from an inward, living principle.

(2dly.) Love, as to the *manner* of their obedience, gives them delight and joy. John xiv. 15, " If ye love me," says Christ, " keep my commandments." Love is the bottom of all their duties; hence our Saviour resolves all obedience into the love of God and our neighbour; and Paul, upon the same ground, tells us " that love is the fulfilling of the law," Rom. xiii. 10. Where love is in any duty, it is complete in Christ. How often doth David, even with admiration, express this principle of his walking with God! " O," saith he, " how I love thy commandments!" This gives saints delight, that the commandments of Christ are not grievous to them. Jacob's hard service was not grievous to him, because of his love to Rachel. No duty of a saint is grievous to him, because of his love to Christ. They do from hence all things with delight and complacency. Hence do they long for advantages of walking with God,—pant after more ability; and this is a great share of their son-like freedom in obedience. It gives them joy in it. 1 John iv. 18, " There is no fear in love; but perfect love casteth out fear." When their soul is acted to obedience by love, it expels that fear which is the issue of bondage upon the spirit. Now, when there is a concurrence of these two (life and love), there is freedom, liberty, largeness of heart, exceedingly distanced from that strait and bondaged frame which many walk in all their days, that know not the adoption of sons.

2dly. The *object* of their obedience is represented to them as *desirable*, whereas to others it is *terrible*. In all their approaches to God, they eye him as a *Father;* they call him Father, Gal. iv. 6, not in the form of words, but in the spirit of sons. God in Christ is continually before them; not only as one deserving all the honours and obedience which he requires, but also as one exceedingly to be delighted in, as being all-sufficient to satisfy and satiate all the desires of the soul. When others napkin their talents, as having to deal with an austere master, they draw out their strength to the uttermost, as drawing nigh to a gracious rewarder. They go, from the principle of life and love, to the bosom of a living and loving Father; they do but return the strength they do receive unto the fountain, unto the ocean.

3dly. Their *motive* unto obedience is *love*, 2 Cor. v. 14. From an apprehension of love, they are effectually carried out by love to give up themselves unto him who is love. What a freedom is this! what a largeness of spirit is in them who walk according to this rule! Darkness, fear, bondage, conviction, hopes of righteousness, accompany others in their ways; the sons, by the Spirit of adoption, have light, love, with complacency, in all their walkings with God. The world is a universal stranger unto the frame of children in their Father's house.

4thly. The *manner* of their obedience is *willingness*. "They yield themselves unto God, as those that are alive from the dead," Rom. vi. 13; they yield themselves,—give up themselves willingly, cheerfully, freely. "With my whole heart," saith David. Rom. xii. 1, "They present themselves a living sacrifice," and a willing sacrifice.

5thly. The *rule* of their walking with God is the law of liberty, as divested of all its terrifying, threatening, killing, condemning, cursing power; and rendered, in the blood of Jesus, sweet, tender, useful, directing,—helpful as a rule of walking in the life they have received, not the way of working for the life they have not. I might give more instances. These may suffice to manifest that liberty of obedience in the family of God which his sons and daughters have, that the poor convinced Gibeonites are not acquainted withal.

(2.) The second thing which the children of God have by adoption is *title*. They have title and right to all the privileges and advantages of the family whereinto they are translated. This is the *pre-eminence* of the true sons of any family. The ground on which Sarah pleaded the ejection of Ishmael was, that he was the son of the bondwoman, Gen. xxi. 10, and so no genuine child of the family; and therefore could have no right of heirship with Isaac. The apostle's arguing is, "We are no more servants, but sons; and if sons, then heirs," Rom. viii. 14–17,—"then have we right and title: and being not born hereunto (for by nature we are the children of wrath), we have this right by our adoption."

Now, the saints hereby have a double right and title:—1st. *Proper* and direct, in respect of spirituals. 2dly. *Consequential*, in respect of temporals:—

[1.] The first, also, or the title, as adopted sons, unto spirituals, is, in respect of the object of it, twofold:—(1st.) Unto a *present place,* name, and room, in the house of God, and all the privileges and administrations thereof. (2dly.) To a *future fulness* of the great inheritance of glory,—of a kingdom purchased for that whole family whereof they are by Jesus Christ:—

1st. They have a title unto, and an interest in, the whole *administration* of the family of God here.

The supreme administration of the house of God in the hand of the Lord Christ, as to the institution of ordinances and dispensation of the Spirit, to enliven and make effectual those ordinances for the end of their institution, is the prime notion of this administration. And hereof they are the prime objects; all this is for them, and exercised towards them.   God hath given Jesus Christ to be the "head over all things unto the church, which is his body," Eph. i. 22, 23: he hath made him the head over all these spiritual things, committed the authoritative administration of them all unto him, to the use and behoof of the church; that is, the family of God. It is for the benefit and advantage of the many sons whom he will bring unto glory that he doth all these things, Heb. ii. 10; see Eph. iv. 8–13.   The aim of the Lord Jesus in establishing gospel administrations, and administrators, is "for the perfecting of the saints, the work of the ministry," etc.   All is for them, all is for the family.   In that is the faithfulness of Christ exercised; he is faithful in all the house of God, Heb. iii. 2. Hence the apostle tells the Corinthians, 1 Cor. iii. 22, 23, of all these gospel administrations and ordinances, they are all theirs, and all for them.   What benefit soever redoundeth to the world by the things of the gospel (as much doth every way), it is engaged for it to the children of this family.   This, then, is the aim and intendment of the Lord Christ in the institution of all gospel ordinances and administrations,—that they may be of use for the house and family of God, and all his children and servants therein.

It is true, the word is preached to all the world, to gather in the children of God's purpose that are scattered up and down in the world, and to leave the rest inexcusable; but the prime end and aim of the Lord Christ thereby is, to gather in those heirs of salvation unto the enjoyment of that feast of fat things which he hath prepared for them in his house.

Again: they, and they only, have right and title to gospel administrations, and the privileges of the family of God, as they are held out in his church according to his mind. The church is the " house of God," 1 Tim. iii. 15; Heb. iii. 6; herein he keeps and maintains his whole family, ordering them according to his mind and will. Now, who shall have any right in the house of God, but only his children? We will not allow a right to any but our own children in our houses: will God, think you, allow any right in his house but to his children? Is it meet, to "take the children's bread and cast it unto the dogs?" We shall see that none but children have any right or title to the privileges and advantages of the house of God, if we consider,—

(1st.) The *nature* of that house. It is made up of such persons as it is impossible that any but adopted children should have right unto a place in it. It is composed of "living stones," 1 Pet. ii. 5;—a " chosen generation, a royal priesthood, an holy nation, a peculiar people," verse 9;—" saints and faithful in Christ Jesus," Eph. i. 1;— "saints and faithful brethren," Col. i. 2;—a people that are " all righteous," Isa. lx. 21; and the whole fabric of it is glorious, chap. liv. 11–14,—the way of the house is " a way of holiness," which the unclean shall not pass through, chap. xxxv. 8; yea, expressly, they are the " sons and daughters of the Lord Almighty," and they only, 2 Cor. vi. 17, 18; all others are excluded, Rev. xxi. 27. It is true that oftentimes, at unawares, other persons creep into the great house of God; and so there become in it " not only vessels of gold and silver, but also of wood and of earth," etc., 2 Tim. ii. 20; but they only creep in, as Jude speaks, verse 4, they have no right nor title to it.

(2dly.) The *privileges* of the house are such as they will not suit nor profit any other. To what purpose is it to give food to a dead man? Will he grow strong by it? will he increase upon it? The things of the family and house of God are food for living souls. Now, children only are alive, all others are dead in trespasses and sins. What will outward signs avail, if life and power be away? Look upon what particular you please of the saints' enjoyments in the family of God, you shall find them all suited unto believers; and, being bestowed on the world, [they] would be a pearl in the snout of a swine.

It is, then, only the sons of the family that have this right; they have fellowship with one another, and *that* fellowship with the Father and the Son Jesus Christ; they set forth the Lord's death till he come; they are intrusted with all the ordinances of the house, and the administration of them. And who shall deny them the enjoyment of this right, or keep them from what Christ hath purchased for them? And the Lord will in the end give them hearts everywhere to make use of this title accordingly, and not to wander on the mountains, forgetting their resting-place.

2dly. They have a title to the future *fulness* of the inheritance
that is purchased for this whole family by Jesus Christ. So the
apostle argues, Rom. viii. 17, " If children, then heirs," etc. All
God's children are " first-born," Heb. xii. 23; and therefore are heirs:
hence the whole weight of glory that is prepared for them is called
the inheritance, Col. i. 12, " The inheritance of the saints in light."
" If ye be Christ's, then are ye Abraham's seed, and heirs according
to the promise," Gal. iii. 29. Heirs of the promise; that is, of all
things promised unto Abraham in and with Christ.

There are three things that in this regard the children of God are
said to be heirs unto:—

(*1st.*) The *promise;* as in that place of Gal. iii. 29 and Heb. vi. 17.
God shows to " the heirs of the promise the immutability of his
counsel;" as Abraham, Isaac, and Jacob, are said to be " heirs of the
same promise," Heb. xi. 9. God had from the foundation of the
world made a most excellent promise in Christ, containing a deliverance from all evil, and an engagement for the bestowing of all good
things upon them. It contains a deliverance from all the evil which
the guilt of sin and dominion of Satan had brought upon them, with
an investiture of them in all spiritual blessings in heavenly things in
Christ Jesus. Hence, Heb. ix. 15, the Holy Ghost calls it a " promise of the eternal inheritance." This, in the first place, are the
adopted children of God heirs unto. Look, whatever is in the promise which God made at the beginning to fallen man, and hath since
solemnly renewed and confirmed by his oath; they are heirs of it,
and are accepted in their claim for their inheritance in the courts of
heaven.

(*2dly.*) They are heirs of *righteousness,* Heb. xi. 7. Noah was an
heir of the righteousness which is by faith; which Peter calls a being
" heir of the grace of life," 1 Pet. iii. 7. And James puts both these
together, chap. ii. 5, " Heirs of the kingdom which God hath promised;" that is, of the kingdom of grace, and the righteousness
thereof. And in this respect it is that the apostle tells us, Eph. i. 11,
that " we have obtained an inheritance;" which he also places with
the righteousness of faith, Acts xxvi. 18. Now, by this righteousness, grace, and inheritance, is not only intended that righteousness
which we are here actually made partakers of, but also the end and
accomplishment of that righteousness in glory; which is also assured
in the next place,—

(*3dly.*) They are " heirs of *salvation,*" Heb. i. 14, and " heirs according to the hope of eternal life," Tit. iii. 7; which Peter calls an
" inheritance incorruptible," 1 Pet. i. 4; and Paul, the " reward of
the inheritance," Col. iii. 24,—that is, the issue of the inheritance of
light and holiness, which they already enjoy. Thus, then, distinguish

the full salvation by Christ into the foundation of it, the promises; and the means of it, righteousness and holiness; and the end of it, eternal glory. The sons of God have a right and title to all, in that they are made heirs with Christ.

And this is that which is the main of the saints' title and right, which they have by adoption; which in sum is, that the Lord is their portion and inheritance, and they are the inheritance of the Lord: and a large portion it is that they have; the lines are fallen to them in a goodly place.

[2.] Besides this *principal*, the adopted sons of God have a second *consequential* right,—a right unto the things of this world; that is, unto all the portions of it which God is pleased to intrust them here withal. Christ is the "heir of all things," Heb. i. 2; all right and title to the things of the creation was lost and forfeited by sin. The Lord, by his sovereignty, had made an original grant of all things here below for man's use; he had appointed the residue of the works of his hands, in their several stations, to be serviceable unto his behoof. Sin reversed this whole grant and institution,—all things were set at liberty from this subjection unto him; yet that liberty, being a taking them off from the end to which they were originally appointed, is a part of their vanity and curse. It is evil to any thing to be laid aside as to the end to which it was primitively appointed. By this means the whole creation is turned loose from any subordinate ruler; and man, having lost the whole title whereby he held his dominion over and possession of the creatures, hath not the least colour of interest in any of them, nor can lay any claim unto them. But now the Lord, intending to take a portion to himself out of the lump of fallen mankind, whom he appointed heirs of salvation, he doth not immediately destroy the works of creation, but reserve them for their use in their pilgrimage. To this end he invests the whole right and title of them in the second Adam, which the first had lost; he appoints him "heir of all things." And thereupon his adopted ones, being "fellow-heirs with Christ," become also to have a right and title unto the things of this creation. To clear up this right, what it is, I must give some few observations:—

1*st*. The right they have is not as the right that Christ hath; that is, sovereign and supreme, to do what he will with his own; but theirs is subordinate, and such as that they must be accountable for the use of those things whereunto they have a right and title. The right of Christ is the right of the *Lord* of the house; the right of the saints is the right of *servants*.

2*dly*. That the *whole number* of the children of God have a right unto the *whole earth*, which is the Lord's, and the fulness thereof, in these two regards:—

(*1st.*) He who is the sovereign Lord of it doth preserve it merely for their use, and upon their account; all others whatever being *malæ fidei possessores*, invading a portion of the Lord's territories, without grant or leave from him.

(*2dly.*) In that Christ hath promised to give them the kingdom and dominion of it, in such a way and manner as in his providence he shall dispose; that is, that the government of the earth shall be exercised to their advantage.

3*dly.* This right is a *spiritual right*, which doth not give a civil interest, but only sanctifies the right and interest bestowed. God hath providentially disposed of the civil bounds of the inheritance of men, Acts xvii. 26, suffering the men of the world to enjoy a portion here, and that oftentimes very full and plenteous; and that for his children's sake, that those beasts of the forest, which are made to be destroyed, may not break loose upon the whole possession. Hence,—

4*thly.* No *one particular adopted person* hath any right, by virtue thereof, to any portion of earthly things whereunto he hath not right and title upon a *civil interest*, given him by the providence of God. But,—

5*thly.* This they have by their adoption; that,—

(*1st.*) Look, what *portion soever* God is pleased to give them, they have a *right* unto it, as it is re-invested in Christ, and not as it lies wholly undèr the curse and vanity that is come upon the creation by sin; and therefore can never be called unto an account for usurping that which they have no right unto, as shall all the sons of men who violently grasp those things which God hath set at liberty from under their dominion because of sin.

(*2dly.*) By this their right, they are led unto a *sanctified use* of what thereby they do enjoy; inasmuch as the things themselves are to them *pledges* of the Father's love, washed in the blood of Christ, and endearments upon their spirits to live to his praise who gives them all things richly to enjoy.

And this is a second thing we have by our adoption; and hence I dare say of unbelievers, they have no true right unto any thing, of what kind soever, that they do possess.

They have no true, unquestionable right, I say, even unto the temporal things they do possess; it is true they have a civil right in respect of others, but they have not a sanctified right in respect of their own souls. They have a right and title that will hold plea in the courts of men, but not a right that will hold in the court of God, and in their own conscience. It will one day be sad with them, when they shall come to give an account of their enjoyments. They shall not only be reckoned withal for the abuse of that they have possessed, that they have not used and laid it out for the glory of him whose it is; but also, that they have even laid their hands upon the creatures of God, and kept them from them for whose sakes alone they are preserved from destruction. When the God of glory shall come home to any of them, either in their consciences here, or in the judgment that is for to come, and speak with the terror of a revengeful judge, " I have suffered you to enjoy corn, wine, and oil,—a great portion of my creatures; you have rolled yourselves in wealth and prosperity, when the right heirs of these things lived poor, and low, and mean, at the next doors;—give in now an answer what and how you have used these things. What have you laid out for the service and advancement of the gospel? What have you given unto them for whom nothing was provided ? what contribution have you made for the poor saints? Have you had a ready hand, and willing mind, to lay down all for my sake ?"—when they shall be compelled to answer, as the truth is, " Lord, we had, indeed, a large portion in the world; but we took it to be our own, and thought we might have done what we would with our own. We have ate the fat, and drank the sweet, and left the rest of our substance for our babes: we have spent somewhat upon our lusts, somewhat upon our friends; but the truth is, we cannot say that we made friends of this unrighteous mammon,—that we used it to the advancement of the gospel, or for ministering unto thy poor saints: and now, behold, we must die," etc.:—so also, when the Lord shall proceed farther, and question not only the *use* of these things, but also their *title* to them, and tell them, " The earth is mine, and the fulness thereof. I did, indeed, make an original grant of these things to man; but that is lost by sin: I have restored it only for my saints. Why have you laid, then, your fingers of prey upon that which was not yours? why have you compelled my creatures to serve you and your lusts, which I had set loose from under your dominion? Give me *my flax, my wine, and wool;* I will set you naked as in the day of your birth, and revenge upon you your rapine, and unjust possession of that which was not yours:"—I say, at such a time, what will men do?

(3.)[1] *Boldness* with God by Christ is another privilege of our adoption. But hereof I have spoken at large before, in treating of the excellency of Christ in respect of our approach to God by him; so that I shall not re-assume the consideration of it.

(4.) *Affliction,* also, as proceeding from love, as leading to spiritual advantages, as conforming unto Christ, as sweetened with his presence, is the privilege of children, Heb. xii. 3–6; but on these particulars I must not insist.

This, I say, is the *head* and source of all the privileges which Christ hath purchased for us, wherein also we have fellowship with

[1] See division, p. 211.

him: fellowship in *name;* we are (as he is) sons of God: fellowship
in *title* and right; we are heirs, co-heirs with Christ: fellowship in
likeness and conformity; we are predestinated to be like the first-
born of the family: fellowship in *honour;* he is not ashamed to call
us brethren: fellowship in *sufferings;* he learned obedience by what
he suffered, and every son is to be scourged that is received: fellowship in his *kingdom;* we shall reign with him. Of all which I must
speak peculiarly in another place, and so shall not here draw out the
discourse concerning them any farther.

PART III.

CHAPTER I.

OF COMMUNION WITH THE HOLY GHOST.

The foundation of our communion with the Holy Ghost (John xvi. 1–7) opened at
large—Παράκλητος, a Comforter; who he is—The Holy Ghost; his own will
in his coming to us; sent also by Christ—The Spirit sent as a sanctifier and
as a comforter—The adjuncts of his mission considered—The foundation of
his mission, John xv. 26—His procession from the Father twofold; as to
personality, or to office—Things considerable in his procession as to office
—The manner of his collation—He is given freely; sent authoritatively—
The sin against the Holy Ghost, whence unpardonable—How we ask the
Spirit of the Father—To grieve the Spirit, what—Poured out—How the
Holy Ghost is received; by faith—Faith's actings in receiving the Holy
Ghost—His abode with us, how declared—How we may lose our comfort
whilst the Comforter abides with us.

THE foundation of all our communion with the Holy Ghost consisting in his *mission,* or sending to be our comforter, by Jesus Christ,
the whole matter of that economy or dispensation is firstly to be proposed and considered, that so we may have a right understanding of
the truth inquired after. Now, the main promise hereof, and the
chief considerations of it, with the good received and evil prevented
thereby, being given and declared in the beginning of the 16th chapter
of John, I shall take a view of the state of it as there proposed.

Our blessed Saviour being to leave the world, having acquainted
his disciples, among other things, what entertainment in general they
were like to find in it and meet withal, gives the reason why he now
gave them the doleful tidings of it, considering how sad and dispirited
they were upon the mention of his departure from them. Verse 1,
"These things have I spoken unto you, that ye should not be of

fended."—" I have," saith he, " given you an acquaintance with these things (that is, the things which will come upon you, which you are to suffer) beforehand, lest you who, poor souls! have entertained expectations of another state of affairs, should be surprised, so as to be offended at me and my doctrine, and fall away from me.   You are now forewarned, and know what you have to look for.   Yea," saith he, verse 2, " having acquainted you in general that you shall be persecuted, I tell you plainly that there shall be a *combination* of all men against you, and all sorts of men will put forth their power for your ruin."—" They shall cast you out of the synagogues; yea, the time cometh that whosoever killeth you will think that he doeth God service."—" The *ecclesiastical* power shall *excommunicate* you,—they shall put you out of their synagogues: and that you may not expect relief from the power of the *magistrate* against their perversity, they will *kill* you: and that you may know that they will do it to the purpose, without check or control, they will think that in killing you they do God good service; which will cause them to act rigorously, and to the utmost."

" But this is a shaking trial," might they reply: " is our condition such, that men, in killing us, will think to approve their consciences to God?"   " Yea, they will," saith our Saviour; " but yet, that you be not mistaken, nor trouble your consciences about their confidences, know that their blind and desperate ignorance is the cause of their fury and persuasion," verse 3, " These things will they do unto you, because they have not known the Father, nor me."

This, then, was to be the state with the disciples.   But why did our Saviour tell it them at this season, to add fear and perplexities to their grief and sorrow? what advantage should they obtain thereby? Saith their blessed Master, verse 4, " There are *weighty reasons* why I should tell you these things; chiefly, that as you may be provided for them, so, when they do befall you, you may be supported with the consideration of my Deity and omniscience, who told you all these things before they came to pass," verse 4, " But these things have I told you, that when the time shall come, ye may remember that I told you of them."   " But if they be so *necessary*, whence is it that thou hast not acquainted us with it all this while? why not in the *beginning*,—at our first *calling?"*   " Even," saith our Saviour, " because there was no need of any such thing; for whilst I was with you, you had protection and direction at hand."—" 'And these things I said not at the beginning, because I was present with you:' but now the state of things is altered; I must leave you," verse 4.   " And for your parts, so are you astonished with sorrow, that you do not ask me ' whither I go;' the consideration whereof would certainly relieve you, seeing I go to take possession of my glory, and to carry on the work of your salvation: but your hearts are filled with sorrow and fears, and you do not so much as inquire after relief," verses 5, 6. Whereupon he adjoins that wonderful assertion, verse 7, "Nevertheless I tell you the truth; It is expedient for you that I go away: for if I go not away, the Comforter will not come unto you; but if I depart, I will send him unto you."

This verse, then, being *the peculiar foundation* of what shall afterward be declared, must particularly be considered, as to the words of it and their interpretation; and that both with respect to the preface of them and the asseveration in them, with the reason annexed thereunto.

1. The preface to them:—

(1.) The first word, ἀλλά, is an adversative, not excepting to any thing of what himself had spoken before, but to their apprehension: " I know you have sad thoughts of these things; but yet, nevertheless."

(2.) Ἐγὼ τὴν ἀλήθειαν λέγω ὑμῖν,—" I tell you the truth." The words are exceedingly emphatical, and denote some great thing to be ushered in by them. First, Ἐγώ,—"*I* tell it you, this that shall now be spoken; I who love you, who take care of you, who am now about to lay down my life for you; they are my dying words, that you may believe me; I who am truth itself, I tell you." And,—

Ἐγὼ τὴν ἀλήθειαν λέγω,—" I tell you the truth." " You have in your sad, misgiving hearts many misapprehensions of things. You think if I would abide with you, all these evils might be prevented; but, alas! you know not what is good for you, nor what is expedient. ' I tell you the truth;' this is truth itself, and quiet your hearts in it." There is need of a great deal of evidence of truth, to comfort their souls that are dejected and disconsolate under an apprehension of the absence of Christ from them, be the apprehension true or false.

And this is the first part of the words of our Saviour, the preface to what he was to deliver to them, by way of a weighty, convincing asseveration, to disentangle thereby the thoughts of his disciples from prejudice, and to prepare them for the receiving of that great truth which he was to deliver.

2. The assertion itself follows: Συμφέρει ὑμῖν, ἵνα ἐγὼ ἀπέλθω,—" It is expedient for you that I go away."

There are two things in the words:—Christ's *departure;* and the *usefulness* of it to his disciples:—

For his *departure*, it is known what is intended by it;—the withdrawing his bodily presence from the earth after his resurrection, the " heaven being to receive him, until the times of the restitution of all things," Acts iii. 21; for in respect of his Deity, and the exercise of love and care towards them, he promised to be with them to

the end of the world, Matt. xxviii. 20. Of this saith he, Συμφέρει ὑμῖν,
—" It conduceth to your good; it is *profitable* for you; it is for your
advantage; it will answer the end that you aim at." That is the sense
of the word which we have translated " expedient;"—" It is for your
profit and advantage." This, then, is that which our Saviour asserts,
and that with the earnestness before mentioned, desiring to convince
his sorrowful followers of the truth of it,—namely, that his departure,
which they so much feared and were troubled to think of, would turn
to their profit and advantage.

3. Now, although it might be expected that they should acquiesce
in this asseveration of truth itself, yet because they were generally
concerned in the *ground of the truth* of it, he acquaints them with
that also; and, that we may confess it to be a great matter, that gives
certainty and evidence to that proposition, he expresses it negatively
and positively: " If I go not away, he will not come; but if I depart,
I will send him." Concerning the going away of Christ I have
spoken before; of the Comforter, his coming and sending, I shall now
treat, as being the thing aimed at.

'Ο παράκλητος: the word being of sundry significations, many translations have thought fit not to restrain it, but do retain the original
word " paracletus;" so the Syriac also: and, as some think, it was a
word before in use among the Jews (whence the Chaldee paraphrast
makes use of it, Job xvi. 20[1]); and amongst them it signifies one that
so taught others as to delight them also in his teaching,—that is, to
be their comforter. In Scripture it hath two eminent significations,—
an " advocate" and a " comforter;" in the first sense our Saviour is
called παράκλητος, 1 John ii. 1. Whether it be better rendered here
an advocate or a comforter may be doubted.

Look into the foregoing occasion of the words, which is the disciples' sorrow and trouble, and it seems to require the Comforter:
" Sorrow hath filled your hearts; but I will send you the Comforter;"—
look into the next words following, which contain his peculiar work
for which he is now promised to be sent, and they require he should
be an Advocate, to plead the cause of Christ against the world, verse 8.
I shall choose rather to interpret the promise by the occasion of it,
which was the sorrow of his disciples, and to retain the name of the
Comforter.

Who this Comforter is, our blessed Saviour had before declared,
chap. xv. 26. He is Πνεῦμα τῆς ἀληθείας,—" the Spirit of truth;" that
is, the Holy Ghost, who revealeth all truth to the sons of men. Now,

---

[1] מְלִיצַי רֵעָי, rendered in our translation, " My friends scorn me," is in the Tar-
gum, to which Owen alludes, פְּרַקְלִיטַי חַבְרַי, " My advocates are my friends." The
word is the Greek παράκλητοι in Hebrew characters.—ED.

of this Comforter two things are affirmed:—(1.) That he shall *come*. (2.) That Christ shall *send* him.

(1.) That he shall come. The affirmative of his coming on the performance of that condition of it, of Christ going away, is included in the negation of his coming without its accomplishment: "If I go not away, he will not come;"—"If I do go (ἐλεύσεται), he will come." So that there is not only the mission of Christ, but the will of the Spirit, in his coming: "He will come,"—his own will is in his work.

(2.) Πέμψω αὐτόν,—"I will send him." The mystery of his sending the Spirit, our Saviour instructs his disciples in by degrees. Chap. xiv. 16, he saith, "I will *pray the Father*, and he shall give you another Comforter;" in the progress of his discourse he gets one step more upon their faith, verse 26, "But the Comforter, which is the Holy Ghost, *whom the Father will send in my name;*" but, chap. xv. 26, he saith, "*I will send him from the Father;*" and here, absolutely, "*I will send him.*" The business of sending the Holy Ghost by Christ—which argues his personal procession also from him, the Son —was a deep mystery, which at once they could not bear; and therefore he thus instructs them in it by degrees.

This is the sum:—the presence of the Holy Ghost with believers as a comforter, sent by Christ for those ends and purposes for which he is promised, is better and more profitable for believers than any *corporeal* presence of Christ can be, now he hath fulfilled the one sacrifice for sin which he was to offer.

Now, the Holy Spirit is promised under a twofold consideration:— [1.] As a *Spirit of sanctification* to the elect, to convert them and make them believers. [2.] As a *Spirit of consolation* to believers, to give them the privileges of the death and purchase of Christ: it is in the latter sense only wherein he is here spoken of. Now, as to his presence with us in this regard, and the end and purposes for which he is sent, for what is aimed at, observe,—1*st*. The *rise* and fountain of it; 2*dly*. The *manner* of his being given; 3*dly*. Our *manner of receiving him;* 4*thly*. His *abiding with us;* 5*thly*. His *acting in us;* 6*thly*. What are *the effects of his working* in us: and then how we hold communion with him will from all these appear.

What the Scripture speaketh to these particulars, shall briefly be considered:—

1*st*. For the fountain of his coming, it is mentioned, John xv. 26, Παρὰ τοῦ Πατρὸς ἐκπορεύεται,—"He proceedeth from the Father;" this is the fountain of this dispensation, he proceedeth from the Father. Now there is a twofold ἐκπόρευσις or "procession" of the Spirit:—

(1*st*.) Φυσική or ὑποστατική, in respect of *substance* and personality.

(2*dly*.) 'Οικονομική or *dispensatory*, in respect of the work of grace.

Of the first—in which respect he is the Spirit of the Father and the Son, proceeding from both eternally, so receiving his substance and personality—I speak not: it is a business of another nature than that I have now in hand. Therein, indeed, lies the first and most remote foundation of all our distinct communion with him and our worship of him; but because abiding in the naked consideration hereof, we can make no other progress than the *bare acquiescence of faith* in the mystery revealed, with the performance of that which is due to the person solely on the account of his participation of the essence, I shall not at present dwell upon it.

His ἐκπόρευσις or *proceeding*, mentioned in the place insisted on, is his *economical* or dispensatory proceeding, for the carrying on of the work of grace. It is spoken of him in reference to his being sent by Christ after his ascension: " I will send him which proceedeth,"— namely, "then when I send him." As God is said to "come out of his place," Isa. xxvi. 21, not in regard of any mutation in him, but of the new work which he would effect; so it follows, the Lord comes out of his place " to punish the inhabitants of the earth." And it is in reference to a peculiar work that he is said to proceed,—namely, to testify of Christ: which cannot be assigned to him in respect of his *eternal procession*, but of his *actual dispensation;* as it is said of Christ, " He came forth from God." The single mention of the Father in this place, and not of the Son, belongs to the gradation before mentioned, whereby our Saviour discovers this mystery to his disciples. He speaks as much concerning himself, John xvi. 7. And this relation *ad extra* (as they call it) of the Spirit unto the Father and the Son, in respect of operation, proves his relation *ad intra*, in respect of personal procession; whereof I spake before.

Three things are considerable in the foundation of this dispensation, in reference to our communion with the Holy Ghost :—

[1st.] That the will of the Spirit is in the *work:* Ἐκπορεύεται,— " He comes forth himself." Frequent mention is made (as we shall see afterward) of his being sent, his being given, and poured out; [but] that it might not be thus apprehended, either that this Spirit were altogether an *inferior, created* spirit, a mere servant, as some have blasphemed, nor yet merely and principally, as to his personality, the virtue of God, as some have fancied, he hath ἰδιώματα ὑποστατικά, personal properties, applied to him in this work, arguing his personality and liberty. Ἐκπορεύεται,—" He, of himself and of his own accord, proceedeth."

[2dly.] The *condescension* of the Holy Ghost in this order of working, this dispensation, to proceed from the Father and the Son, as to this work; to take upon him this work of a Comforter, as the Son did the work of a Redeemer: of which afterward.

[3dly.] The *fountain* of the whole is discovered to be the Father, that we may know his works in the pursuit of electing love, which everywhere is ascribed to the Father. This is the order here intimated:—First, there is the πρόθεσις of the Father, or the *purpose* of his love, the fountain of all; then the ἐρώτησις, the *asking* of the Son, John xiv. 16, which takes in his merit and purchase; whereunto follows ἐκπόρευσις, or willing *proceeding* of the Holy Ghost. And this gives testimony, also, to the foundation of this whole discourse,—namely, our peculiar communion with the Father in love, the Son in grace, and the Holy Ghost in consolation. This is the door and entrance of that fellowship of the Holy Ghost whereunto we are called. His gracious and blessed will, his infinite and ineffable condescension, being eyed by faith as the foundation of all those effects which he works in us, and privileges whereof by him we are made partakers, our souls are peculiarly conversant with him, and their desires, affections, and thankfulness, terminated on him: of which more afterward. This is the first thing considerable in our communion with the Holy Ghost.

2dly. The manner of his *collation* or bestowing, or the manner of his communication unto us from this fountain, is herein also considerable; and it is variously expressed, to denote three things:—

(*1st.*) The *freeness* of it: thus he is said to be GIVEN, John xiv. 16; "He shall give you another Comforter." I need not multiply places to this purpose. The most frequent adjunct of the communication of the Spirit is this, that he is given and received as of gift: "He will give his Holy Spirit to them that ask him." That which is of gift is free. The Spirit of grace is given of grace: and not only the Spirit of sanctification, or the Spirit to sanctify and convert us, is a gift of free grace, but in the sense whereof we speak, in respect of consolation, he is of gift also; he is promised to be given unto believers.[1] Hence the Spirit is said to be received by the gospel, not by the law, Gal. iii. 2; that is, of *mere grace*, and not of *our own procuring.* And all his workings are called χαρίσματα,—"free donations." He is freely bestowed, and freely works; and the different measures wherein he is received, for those ends and purposes of consolation which we shall consider, by believers, which are great, various, and inexpressible, arise from hence, that we have him by donation, or free gift. And this is the tenure whereby we hold and enjoy him, a tenure of *free donation.* So is he to be *eyed*, so to be *asked*, so to be *received.* And this, also, faith takes in and closeth withal, in our communion with the Comforter:—the conjunction and accord of his will with the gift of Father and Son; the one respecting the distinct operation of the Deity in the person of the Holy Ghost; the other, the economy of the whole Trinity in the work of our salvation by Jesus Christ. Here

[1] Neh. ix. 20; John xiv. 16, vii. 39, xx. 22; Acts ii. 28, v. 32, viii. 15, x. 47, xv. 8, xix. 2; Rom. v. 5; 1 Cor. ii. 12, vi. 19, xii. 7; 1 Thess. iv. 8; 1 John iv. 13.

the soul rejoiceth itself in the Comforter,—that he is willing to come to him, that he is willing to be given him.   And seeing all is will and gift, grace is magnified on this account.

(2dly.) The *authority* of it.   Thence he is said to be SENT.   Chap. xiv. 26, " The Father will send him in my name;" and, chap. xv. 26, "I will send him unto you from the Father;" and, " Him will I send unto you," chap. xvi. 7.   This mission of the Holy Ghost by the Father and the Son, as it answers the order of the persons' subsistence in the blessed Trinity, and his procession from them both, so the order voluntarily engaged in by them for the accomplishment, as was said, of the work of our salvation.   There is in it, in a most special manner, the condescension of the Holy Ghost, in his love to us, to the authoritative delegation of Father and Son in this business; which argues not a disparity, dissimilitude, or inequality of *essence*, but of *office*, in this work.   It is the office of the Holy Ghost to be an advocate for us, and a comforter to us; in which respect, not absolutely, he is thus sent authoritatively by Father and Son.   It is a known maxim, that " inæqualitas officii non tollit æqualitatem naturæ."   This subjection (if I may so call it), or inequality in respect of office, doth no ways prejudice the equality of nature which he hath with Father and Son; no more than the mission of the Son by the Father doth his.   And on this authoritative mission of the Spirit doth the right apprehension of many mysteries in the gospel, and the ordering of our hearts in communion with him, depend.

[*1st.*] Hence is the sin against the Holy Ghost (what it is I do not now dispute) unpardonable, and hath that adjunct of rebellion put upon it that no other sin hath,—namely, because he comes not, he acts not, in his own name only, though in his own also, but in the name and authority of the Father and Son, from and by whom he is sent; and therefore, to sin against him is to sin against all the authority of God, all the love of the Trinity, and the utmost condescension of each person to the work of our salvation.   It is, I say, from the authoritative mission of the Spirit that the sin against him is peculiarly unpardonable;—it is a sin against the recapitulation of the love of the Father, Son, and Spirit.   And from this consideration, were that our present business, might the true nature of the sin against the Holy Ghost be investigated.   Certainly it must consist in the contempt of some operation of his, as acting in the name and authority of the whole Trinity, and that in their ineffable condescension to the work of grace.   But this is of another consideration.

[*2dly.*] On this account we are to *pray the Father and the Son* to give the Spirit to us.   Luke xi. 13, " Your heavenly Father will give the Holy Spirit to them that ask him."   Now the Holy Ghost, being God, is no less to be invocated, prayed to, and called on, than the Father and Son; as elsewhere I have proved.   How, then, do we ask the Father for him, as we do in all our supplications, seeing that we also pray that he himself would come to us, visit us, and abide with us?   In our prayers that are directed to himself, we consider him as essentially God over all, blessed for evermore; we pray for him from the Father and Son, as under this mission and delegation from them.   And, indeed, God having most plentifully revealed himself in the order of this dispensation to us, we are (as Christians generally do) in our communion to abound in answerable addresses; that is, not only to the person of the Holy Ghost himself, but properly to the Father and Son for him, which refers to this dispensation.

[*3dly.*] Hence is that great weight, in particular, laid upon our *not grieving the Spirit*, Eph. iv. 30,—because he comes to us in the name, with the love, and upon the condescension, of the whole blessed Trinity.   To do that which might grieve him so sent, on such an account, for that end and purpose which shall afterward be mentioned, is a great aggravation of sin.   He expects cheerful entertainment with us, and may do so justly, upon his own account, and the account of the work which he comes about; but when this also is added, that he is sent of the Father and the Son, commissioned with their love and grace, to communicate them to their souls,—this is that which is, or ought to be, of unspeakable esteem with believers.   And this is that second thing expressed in the manner of his communication,— he is sent by authority.

(*3dly.*) He is said to be poured out or SHED on us, Tit. iii. 6, οὗ ἐξέχεεν ἐφ' ἡμᾶς πλουσίως,—that Holy Ghost which he hath richly poured out upon us, or shed on us abundantly.   And this was the chief expression of his communication under the Old Testament; the mystery of the Father and the Son, and the matter of commission and delegation being then not so clearly discovered.   Isa. xxxii. 15, "Until the Spirit be poured upon us from on high, and the wilderness be a fruitful field, and the fruitful field be counted for a forest;" that is, till the Gentiles be called, and the Jews rejected.   And chap. xliv. 3, "I will pour my Spirit upon thy seed, and my blessing upon thine offspring."   That eminent place of Zech. xii. 10 is always in our thoughts.   Now, this expression, as is known, is taken from the allusion of the Spirit unto water; and that in relation to all the uses of water, both natural and typical.   A particular relation of them I cannot now insist on; perhaps efficacy and plenty are chiefly intended.

Now, this threefold expression, of *giving*, *sending*, and *pouring* out, of the Spirit, gives us the three great properties of the covenant of grace:—*First*, That it is *free;* he is *given*.   *Secondly*, That it is orderly, ordered in all things, and sure, from the love of the Father, by the procurement of the Son; and thence is that variety of expression, of the *Father's sending* him, and *the Son's sending* him from the Father, he being the gift of the Father's love, and purchase of the blood of the Son. *Thirdly.* The efficacy of it, as was last observed. And this is the second thing considerable.

3dly. The third, which is our *receiving* him, I shall speak more briefly of. That which I first proposed of the Spirit, considered as a Spirit of *sanctification* and a Spirit of *consolation,* is here to be minded. Our receiving of him as a Spirit of sanctification is a mere passive reception, as a vessel receives water. He comes as the wind on Ezekiel's dead bones, and makes them live; he comes into dead hearts, and quickens them, by an act of his almighty power: but now, as he is the Spirit of consolation, it is otherwise. In this sense our Saviour tells us that the "world cannot receive him," John xiv. 17, "The world receiveth him not, because it seeth him not, neither knoweth him: but ye know him, for he dwelleth with you, and shall be in you." That it is the Spirit of consolation, or the Spirit for consolation, that here is promised, is evident from the close of the verse, where he is said then to be in them when he is promised to them. He was in them as a Spirit of quickening and sanctification when promised to them as a Spirit of comfort and consolation, to abide with them for that purpose. Now, the power that is here denied to be in the *world,* with the reason of it, that they cannot receive the Spirit, because they know him not, is ascribed to *believers;*—they can receive him, because they know him. So that there is an active power to be put forth in his reception for consolation, though not in his reception for regeneration and sanctification. And this is the power of faith. So Gal. iii. 2, they received the Spirit by the hearing of faith;—the preaching of the gospel, begetting faith in them, enabled them to receive the Spirit. Hence, believing is put as the qualification of all our receiving the Holy Ghost. John vii. 39, "This he spake of the Spirit, which they that believe on him should receive." It is believers that thus receive the Spirit; and they receive him by faith. Now, there are three special acts of faith, whereby it goes forth in the receiving of the Spirit. I shall but name them:—

(*1st.*) It considers the Spirit, in the *economy* before described, as promised. It is faith alone that makes profit of the benefit of the promises, Heb. iv. 2. Now he is called the Spirit of that promise, Eph. i. 13,—the Spirit that in the covenant is promised; and we receive the promise of the Spirit through faith, Gal. iii. 14: so that the receiving of the Spirit through faith, is the receiving of him as promised. Faith eyes the promise of God and of Jesus Christ, of sending the Spirit for all those ends that he is desired; thus it depends, waits, mixing the promise with itself, until it receive him.

(2dly.) By *prayer.* He is given as a Spirit of supplication, that we may ask him as a Spirit of consolation, Luke xi. 13; and, indeed, this asking of the Spirit of God, in the name of Christ, either directly or immediately, or under the name of some fruit and effect of him, is the chiefest work of faith in this world.

(3dly.) It cherisheth him, by *attending to his motions,* improving his actings according to his mind and will; which is all I shall say to this third thing, or our receiving of the Spirit, which is sent of Jesus Christ. We do it by faith, looking on him as purchased by Jesus Christ, and promised of the Father; we seek him at the hands of God, and do receive him.

4thly. The next considerable thing is, his *abode* with us. Now this is two ways expressed in the Scripture:—

(1st.) In *general.* As to the thing itself, it is said he shall abide with us.

(2dly.) In *particular.* As to the manner of its abiding, it is by *inhabitation* or indwelling. Of the inhabitation of the Spirit I have spoken fully[1] elsewhere, nor shall I now insist on it. Only whereas the Spirit, as hath been observed, is considered as a Spirit of sancti-fication, or a Spirit of consolation, he is said to dwell in us chiefly, or perhaps solely, as he is a Spirit of sanctification: which is evident from the work he doeth, as indwelling,—he quickeneth and sanctifieth, Rom. viii. 11; and the manner of his indwelling,—as in a temple, which he makes holy thereby, 1 Cor. vi. 19; and his permanency in his so doing,—which, as is evident, relates to sanctification only: but yet the general notion of it in abiding is ascribed to him as a comforter, John xiv. 16, "He shall abide with you for ever." Now, all the difficulty of this promise lies in this, that whereas the Spirit of sanctification dwells in us always, and it is therefore impossible that we should lose utterly our holiness, whence is it that, if the *Comforter* abide with us for ever, we may yet utterly lose *our comfort?* A little to clear this in our passage:—

[1st.] He is *promised* to abide with the disciples for *ever,* in op-position *to the abode of Christ.* Christ, in the flesh, had been with them for a little while, and now was leaving them, and going to his Father. He had been the comforter immediately himself for a season, but is now upon his departing; wherefore, promising them another comforter, they might fear that he would even but visit them for a little season also, and then their condition would be worse than ever. Nay, but saith our Saviour, "Fear it not: this is *the last dispensa-tion;* there is to be no alteration. When I am gone, the Comforter

---

[1] Perseverance of the Saints, chap. viii. vol. xi.

is to do all the remaining work: there is not another to be looked for, and I promise you him; nor shall he depart from you, but always abide with you."

[*2dly.*] The Comforter may always *abide* with us, though not always *comfort* us; he who is the Comforter may abide, though he do not always that work. For other ends and purposes he is always with us; as to sanctify and make us holy. So was the case with David, Ps. li. 11, 12, "Take not thy Holy Spirit from me." The Holy Spirit of sanctification was still with David; but saith he, "Restore unto me the joy of thy salvation;"—that is, the Spirit of consolation, that was lost, when the promise was made good in the abode of the other.

[*3dly.*] The Comforter may abide *as a comforter*, when he doth not *actually comfort* the soul. In truth, as to the essence of holiness, he cannot dwell in us but withal he must make us holy; for the temple of God is holy;—but as to his comforting, his actings therein are all of his sovereign will; so that he may abide, and yet not actually comfort us.

[*4thly.*] The Spirit often *works* for it, and *tenders* consolation to us, when we do not receive it; the well is nigh, and we see it not,—we refuse to be comforted. I told you that the Spirit as a sanctifier comes with power, to conquer an unbelieving heart; the Spirit as a comforter comes with sweetness, to be received in a believing heart. He speaks, and we believe not that it is his voice; he tenders the things of consolation, and we receive them not. "My sore ran," saith David, "and my soul refused to be comforted."

[*5thly.*] I deny that ever the Holy Spirit doth *absolutely* and *universally* leave a believing soul *without consolation.* A man may be darkened, clouded, refuse comfort,—actually find none, feel none; but radically he hath a foundation of consolation, which in due time will be drawn forth: and therefore, when God promises that he will heal sinners, and restore comfort to them, as Isa. lvii. 18, it is not that they were without any, but that they had not so much as they needed, that that promise is made. To insist on the several ways whereby men refuse comfort, and come short of the strong consolation which God is willing that we should receive, is not my purpose at present. Thus, then, the Spirit being sent and given, abideth with the souls of believers,—leaves them not, though he variously manifest himself in his operations: of which in the next place.

CHAPTER II.

Of the actings of the Holy Ghost in us, being bestowed on us—He worketh
effectually, distributeth, giveth.

HAVING thus declared from whence and how the Holy Ghost is
given unto us as a Spirit of consolation, I come, in the next place,—

5thly. To declare what are his *actings in us* and towards us, being
so bestowed on us and received by us. Now, here are two general
heads to be considered:—(*1st.*) The manner and kind of his actings
in us, which are variously expressed; and, (*2dly.*) The particular products of his actings in our souls, wherein we have communion with
him. The first is variously expressed; I shall pass through them
briefly:—

(*1st.*) He is said (ἐνεργεῖν) " to work effectually," 1 Cor. xii. 11, " All
these worketh " (or effecteth) " that one and the self-same Spirit." It
is spoken there, indeed, in respect of his distribution of gifts; but the
way is the same for the communication of graces and privileges. He
doth it by working: which, as it evinces his personality, especially
as considered with the words following, " Dividing to every man according to his will " (for to work according to will is the inseparable
property of a person, and is spoken expressly of God, Eph. i. 11); so
in relation to verse 6, foregoing, it makes no less evident his Deity.
What he is here said to do as the Spirit bestowed on us and given
unto us, there is he said as God himself to do: " There are diversities
of operations, but it is the same God which worketh all in all;" which
here, in other words, is, " All these worketh that one and the self-
same Spirit, dividing to every man severally as he will." What we
have, then, from him, we have by the way of his energetical working.
It is not by proposing this or that argument to us, persuading us by
these or those moral motives or inducements alone, leaving us to
make use of them as we can; but he works effectually himself, what
he communicates of grace or consolation to us.

[*2dly.*] In the same verse, as to the manner of his operation, he is
said διαιρεῖν,—he *divideth* or distributeth *to every one as he will.* This
of distribution adds to that of operation, choice, judgment, and freedom. He that distributes variously, doth it with choice, and judgment,
and freedom of will. Such are the proceedings of the Spirit in his
dispensations: to one, he giveth one thing eminently; to another,
another;—to one, in one degree; to another, in another. Thus are the
saints, in his *sovereignty*, kept in a constant *dependence* on him. He
distributes as he will;—who should not be content with his portion?

what claim can any lay to that which he distributeth as he will? which is farther manifested,—

[*3dly.*] By his being said to *give* when and what he bestows. They " spake with other tongues, as the Spirit gave them utterance," Acts ii. 4. He gave them to them; that is, freely: whatever he bestows upon us, is of his gift. And hence it is to be observed, that in the economy of our salvation, the acting of no one person doth prejudice the freedom and liberty of any other: so the love of the Father in sending the Son is free, and his sending doth no ways prejudice the liberty and love of the Son, but that he lays down his life freely also; so the satisfaction and purchase made by the Son doth no way prejudice the freedom of the Father's grace in pardoning and accepting us thereupon; so the Father's and Son's sending of the Spirit doth not derogate from his freedom in his workings, but he gives freely what he gives. And the reason of this is, because the will of the Father, Son, and Holy Ghost, is essentially the same; so that in the acting of one there is the counsel of all and each freely therein.

Thus, in general, is the manner and kind of his working in us and towards us, being bestowed upon us, described. Power, choice, freedom, are evidently denoted in the expressions insisted on. It is not any peculiar work of his towards us that is hereby declared, but the manner how he doth produce the *effects* that shall be insisted on.

(*2dly.*) That which remains, in the last place, for the explanation of the things proposed to be explained as *the foundation* of the communion which we have with the Holy Ghost, is,—

The *effects* that, being thus sent and thus working, he doth produce; which I shall do, not casting them into any artificial method, but taking them up as I find them lying scattered up and down in the Scripture, only descending from those which are more general to those which are more particular, neither aiming nor desiring to gather all the severals, but insisting on those which do most obviously occur.

Only as formerly, so now you must observe, that I speak of the Spirit principally (if not only) as a *comforter*, and not as a *sanctifier;* and therefore the great work of the Spirit towards us all our days, in the constant and continual supplies of new light, power, vigour, as to our receivings of grace from him, belonging to that head of sanctification, must be omitted.

Nor shall I insist on those things which the Comforter doth in believers effect towards others, in his testifying to them and convincing of the world, which are promised, John xv. 26, xvi. 8, wherein he is properly their advocate; but only on those which as a comforter he works in and towards them on whom he is bestowed.

CHAPTER III.

Of the things wherein we have communion with the Holy Ghost—He brings to remembrance the things spoken by Christ, John xiv. 26—The manner how he doth it—The Spirit glorifies Christ in the hearts of believers, John xvi. 14, sheds abroad the love of God in them—The witness of the Spirit, what it is, Rom. viii. 16—The sealing of the Spirit, Eph. i. 13—The Spirit, how an earnest; on the part of God, on the part of the saints—Difference between the earnest of the Spirit and tasting of the powers of the world to come—Unction by the Spirit, Isa. xi. 2, 3—The various teachings of the Holy Ghost—How the Spirit of adoption and of supplication.

THE things which, in the foregoing chapters, I called effects of the Holy Ghost in us, or towards us, are the subject-matter of our communion with him, or the things wherein we hold peculiar fellowship with him as our comforter. These are now proposed to consideration:—

1. The first and most general is that of John xiv. 26, " He shall teach you all things, and bring all things to your remembrance, whatsoever I have said unto you." There are two parts of this promise:— (1.) Of *teaching*. (2.) Of *bringing to remembrance*. Of his teaching I shall speak afterward, when I come to treat of his anointing us.

His bringing the things to remembrance that Christ spake is the first general promise of him as a comforter: 'Υπομνήσει ὑμᾶς πάντα,— " He shall make you mind all these things." Now, this also may be considered two ways:—

[1.] Merely in respect of *the things spoken themselves*. So our Saviour here promiseth his apostles that the Holy Ghost should bring to their minds, by an immediate efficacy, the things that he had spoken, that by *his inspiration* they might be enabled to write and preach them for the good and benefit of his church. So Peter tells us, 2 Epist. i. 21, " Holy men of God spake as they were moved by the Holy Ghost" (that is, in writing the Scripture); ὑπὸ Πνεύματος ἁγίου φερόμενοι,—borne up by him, carried beyond themselves, to speak his words, and what he indited to them. The apostles forgot much of what Christ had said to them, or might do so; and what they did retain, in a natural way of remembrance, was not a sufficient foundation to them to write what they so remembered for a rule of faith to the church. For the word of prophecy is not ἰδίας ἐπιλύσεως,—from any man's proper impulse; it comes not from any private conception, understanding, or remembrance. Wherefore, Christ promises that the Holy Ghost shall do this work; that they might infallibly give out what he had delivered to them. Hence that expression in Luke i. 3, Παρηκολουθηκότι ἄνωθεν, is better rendered, " Having obtained perfect knowledge of things from above,"—noting the rise and spring of his so understanding things as to be able infallibly to give them out in a rule of faith to the church, than the beginning of the things themselves spoken of; which the word itself will not easily allow of.

[2.] In respect of the *comfort* of what he had spoken, which seems to be a great part of the intendment of this promise. He had been speaking to them things suited for their consolation; giving them precious promises of the supplies they should have from him in this life,—of the love of the Father, of the glory he was providing for them, the sense and comfort whereof is unspeakable, and the joy arising from them full of glory. But saith he, " I know how unable you are to make use of these things for your own consolation; the Spirit, therefore, shall recover them upon your minds, in their full strength and vigour, for that end for which I speak them." And this is one cause why it was expedient for believers that Christ's *bodily absence* should be supplied by the presence of the Spirit. Whilst he was with them, how little efficacy on their hearts had any of the heavenly promises he gave them ! When the Spirit came, how full of joy did he make all things to them ! That which was his peculiar work, which belonged to him by virtue of his office, that he also might be glorified, was reserved for him. And this is his work to the end of the world,— to bring the promises of Christ to our minds and hearts, to give us the comfort of them, the joy and sweetness of them, much beyond that which the disciples found in them, when Christ in person spake them to them; their gracious influence being then restrained, that, as was said, the dispensation of the Spirit might be glorified. So are the next words to this promise, verse 27, " Peace I leave with you, my peace I give unto you." The Comforter being sent to bring what Christ said to remembrance, the consequent of it is peace, and freedom from trouble of heart;—whatever peace, relief, comfort, joy, supportment, we have at any time received from any work, promise, or thing done by Christ, it all belongs to this dispensation of the Comforter. In vain should we apply our natural abilities to remember, call to mind, consider, the promises of Christ; without success would it be,—it is so daily: but when the Comforter doth undertake the work, it is done to the purpose. How we have peculiar communion with him herein, in faith and obedience, in the consolation received in and by the promises of him brought to mind, shall be afterward declared. This, in general, is obtained:—our Saviour Jesus Christ, leaving the efficacy even of those promises which in person he gave to his apostles in their great distress, as to their consolation, unto the Holy Ghost, we may see the *immediate spring* of all the spiritual comfort we have in this world, and the fellowship which we have with the Holy Ghost therein.

Only here, as in all the particulars following, the manner of the

Spirit's working this thing is always to be borne in mind, and the interest of his power, will, and goodness in his working. He doth this,—1st. *Powerfully*, or *effectually;* 2dly. *Voluntarily;* 3dly. *Freely.*

1st. *Powerfully:* and therefore doth comfort from the words and promises of Christ sometimes break in through all opposition into the saddest and darkest condition imaginable; it comes and makes men sing in a dungeon, rejoice in flames, glory in tribulation; it will into prisons, racks, through temptations, and the greatest distresses imaginable. Whence is this? Τὸ Πνεῦμα ἐνεργεῖ,—the Spirit works effectually, his power is in it; he will work, and none shall let him. If he will bring to our remembrance the promises of Christ for our consolation, neither Satan nor man, sin nor world, nor death, shall interrupt our comfort. This the saints, who have communion with the Holy Ghost, know to their advantage. Sometimes the heavens are black over them, and the earth trembles under them; public, personal calamities and distresses appear so full of horror and darkness, that they are ready to faint with the apprehensions of them;— hence is their great relief, and the retrievement of their spirits; their consolation or trouble depends not on any outward condition or inward frame of their own hearts, but on the powerful and effectual workings of the Holy Ghost, which by faith they give themselves up unto.

2dly. *Voluntarily,*—distributing to every one as he will; and therefore is this work done in so great variety, both as to the same person and divers. For the same person, full of joy sometimes in a great distress, full of consolation,—every promise brings sweetness when his pressures are great and heavy; another time, in the least trial [he] seeks for comfort, searches the promise, and it is far away. The reason is, Πνεῦμα διαιρεῖ καθὼς βούλεται,—the Spirit distributes as he will. And so with divers persons: to some each promise is full of life and comfort; others taste little all their days;—all upon the same account. And this faith especially regards in the whole business of consolation:—it depends on the sovereign will of the Holy Ghost; and so is not tied unto any rules or course of procedure. Therefore doth it exercise itself in waiting upon him for the seasonable accomplishment of the good pleasure of his will.

3dly. *Freely.* Much of the variety of the dispensation of consolation by promises depends on this freedom of the Spirit's operation. Hence it is that comfort is given *unexpectedly*, when the heart hath all the reasons in the world to look for distress and sorrow; thus sometimes it is the first means of recovering a backsliding soul, who might justly expect to be utterly cast off. And these considerations are to be carried on in all the other effects and fruits of the Comforter: of which afterward. And in this first general effect or work of the Holy Ghost towards us have we communion and fellowship with him. The life and soul of all our comforts lie treasured up in the promises of Christ. They are the breasts of all our consolation. Who knows not how powerless they are in the bare letter, even when improved to the uttermost by our considerations of them, and meditation on them? as also how unexpectedly they sometimes break upon the soul with a conquering, endearing life and vigour? Here faith deals peculiarly with the Holy Ghost. It considers the promises themselves; looks up to him, waits for him, considers his appearances in the word depended on,—owns him in his work and efficacy. No sooner doth the soul begin to feel the life of a promise warming his heart, relieving, cherishing, supporting, delivering from fear, entanglements, or troubles, but it may, it ought, to know that the Holy Ghost is there; which will add to his joy, and lead him into fellowship with him.

2. The next general work seems to be that of John xvi. 14, " The Comforter shall glorify me; for he shall receive of mine, and shall show it unto you." The work of the Spirit is *to glorify Christ:* whence, by the way, we may see how far that spirit is from being the Comforter who sets up himself in the room of Christ; such a spirit as saith he is all himself: " for as for him that suffered at Jerusalem, it is no matter that we trouble ourselves about him. This spirit is now all. This is not the Comforter. His work is to glorify Christ,—him that sends him. And this is an evident sign of a false spirit, whatever its pretence be, if it glorify not that Christ who was now speaking to his apostles; and such are many that are gone abroad into the world. But what shall this Spirit do, that Christ may be glorified? " He shall," saith he, " take of mine,"—ἐκ τοῦ ἐμοῦ λήψεται. What these things are is declared in the next verse: " All things that the Father hath are mine; therefore I said he shall take of mine." It is not of the essence and essential properties of the Father and Son that our Saviour speaks; but of the grace which is communicated to us by them. This Christ calls, " My things," being the fruit of his purchase and mediation: on which account he saith all his Father's things are his; that is, the things that the Father, in his eternal love, hath provided to be dispensed in the blood of his Son,—all the fruits of election. " These," said he, " the Comforter shall receive; that is, they shall be committed unto him to dispose for your good and advantage, to the end before proposed." So it follows, ἀναγγελεῖ,— " He shall show, or declare and make them known to you." Thus, then, is he a comforter. He reveals to the souls of sinners the good things of the covenant of grace, which the Father hath provided, and the Son purchased. He shows to us mercy, grace, forgiveness, righteousness, acceptation with God; letteth us know that these are the

things of Christ, which he hath procured for us; shows them to us for our comfort and establishment.   These things, I say, he effectually declares to the souls of believers; and makes them know them for their own good;—know them as originally the things of the Father, prepared from eternity in his love and good-will; as purchased for them by Christ, and laid up in store in the covenant of grace for their use.   Then is Christ magnified and glorified in their hearts; then they know what a Saviour and Redeemer he is.   A soul doth never glorify or honour Christ upon a discovery or sense of the eternal redemption he hath purchased for him, but it is in him a peculiar effect of the Holy Ghost as our comforter.   "No man can say that Jesus is the Lord, but by the Holy Ghost," 1 Cor. xii. 3.

3. He "sheds the love of God abroad in our hearts," Rom. v. 5. That it is the *love of God to us*, not *our love to God*, which is here intended, the context is so clear as nothing can be added thereunto. Now, the love of God is either of *ordination* or of *acceptation*,—the love of his purpose to do us good, or the love of acceptation and approbation with him.   Both these are called the love of God frequently in Scripture, as I have declared.   Now, how can these be shed abroad in our hearts?   Not in themselves, but in a sense of them,—in a spiritual apprehension of them. 'Εκκέχυται, is "shed abroad;" the same word that is used concerning the Comforter being given us, Tit. iii. 6. God sheds him abundantly, or pours him on us; so he sheds abroad, or pours out the love of God in our hearts.   Not to insist on the expression, which is metaphorical, the business is, that the Comforter gives a sweet and plentiful evidence and persuasion of the love of God to us, such as the soul is taken, delighted, satiated withal.   This is his work, and he doth it effectually.   To give a poor sinful soul *a comfortable persuasion*, affecting it throughout, in all its faculties and affections, that God in Jesus Christ loves him, delights in him, is well pleased with him, hath thoughts of tenderness and kindness towards him; to give, I say, a soul an overflowing sense hereof, is an inexpressible mercy.

This we have in a peculiar manner by the Holy Ghost; it is his peculiar work.   As all his works are works of love and kindness, so this of communicating a sense of the love of the Father mixes itself with all the particulars of his actings.   And as we have herein peculiar communion with himself, so by him we have communion with the Father, even in his love, which is thus shed abroad in our hearts: so not only do we rejoice in, and glorify the Holy Ghost, which doth this work, but in him also whose love it is.   Thus is it also in respect of the Son, in his taking of his, and showing of it unto us, as was declared.   What we have of heaven in this world lies herein; and the manner of our fellowship with the Holy Ghost on this account falls in with what was spoken before.

4. Another effect we have of his, Rom. viii. 16, "The Spirit itself beareth witness with our spirit, that we are the children of God." You know whose children we are by nature;—children of Satan and of the curse, or of wrath. By the Spirit we are put into another capacity, and are *adopted to be the children of God,* inasmuch as by receiving the Spirit of our Father we become the children of our Father. Thence is he called, verse 15, "The Spirit of adoption." Now, sometimes the soul, because it hath somewhat remaining in it of the principle that it had in its old condition, is put to question whether it be a child of God or no; and thereupon, as in a thing of the greatest importance, puts in its claim, with all the evidences that it hath to make good its title. The Spirit comes and bears witness in this case. An allusion it is to judicial proceedings in point of titles and evidences. The judge being set, the person concerned lays his claim, produceth his evidences, and pleads them; his adversaries endeavouring all that in them lies to invalidate them, and disannul his plea, and to cast him in his claim. In the midst of the trial, a person of known and approved integrity comes into the court, and gives testimony fully and directly on the behalf of the claimer; which stops the mouths of all his adversaries, and fills the man that pleaded with joy and satisfaction. So is it in this case. The soul, by the power of its own conscience, is brought before the law of God. There a man puts in his plea,—that he is a child of God, that he belongs to God's family; and for this end produceth all his evidences, every thing whereby faith gives him an interest in God. Satan, in the meantime, opposeth with all his might; sin and law assist him; many flaws are found in his evidences; the truth of them all is questioned; and the soul hangs in suspense as to the issue. In the midst of the plea and contest the Comforter comes, and, by a word of promise or otherwise, overpowers the heart with a comfortable persuasion (and bears down all objections) that his plea is good, and that he is a child of God. And therefore it is said of him, Συμμαρτυρεῖ τῷ Πνεύματι ἡμῶν. When our spirits are pleading their right and title, he comes in and bears witness on our side; at the same time enabling us to put forth acts of filial obedience, kind and child-like; which is called "crying, Abba, Father," Gal. iv. 6. Remember still the manner of the Spirit's working, before mentioned,—that he doth it effectually, voluntarily, and freely. Hence sometimes the dispute hangs long,—the cause is pleading many years. The law seems sometimes to prevail, sin and Satan to rejoice; and the poor soul is filled with dread about its inheritance. Perhaps its own witness, from its faith, sanctification, former experience, keeps up the plea with some life and comfort;

but the work is not done, the conquest is not fully obtained, until the Spirit, who worketh freely and effectually, when and how he will, comes in with his testimony also; clothing his power with a word of promise, he makes all parties concerned to attend unto him, and puts an end to the controversy.

Herein he gives us holy communion with himself. The soul knows his voice when he speaks, " Nec hominem sonat." There is something too great in it to be the effect of a created power. When the Lord Jesus Christ at one word stilled the raging of the sea and wind, all that were with him knew there was divine power at hand, Matt. viii. 25–27. And when the Holy Ghost by one word stills the tumults and storms that are raised in the soul, giving it an immediate calm and security, it knows his divine power, and rejoices in his presence.

5. *He seals us.* " We are sealed by the Holy Spirit of promise, Eph. i. 13; and, " Grieve not the Holy Spirit, whereby ye are sealed unto the day of redemption," chap. iv. 30. I am not very clear in the certain peculiar intendment of this metaphor; what I am persuaded of the mind of God in it I shall briefly impart. In a seal two things are considered:—(1.) The *nature of it.* (2.) The *use of it.*

(1.) The *nature* of sealing consists in the imparting of the image or character of the seal to the thing sealed. This is to seal a thing, —to stamp the character of the seal on it. In this sense, the effectual communication of the image of God unto us should be our sealing. The Spirit in believers, really communicating the image of God, in righteousness and true holiness, unto the soul, sealeth us. To have this stamp of the Holy Ghost, so as to be an evidence unto the soul that it is accepted with God, is to be sealed by the Spirit; taking the metaphor from the nature of sealing.[1] And in this sense is our Saviour said to be sealed of God, John vi. 27, even from that impression of the power, wisdom, and majesty of God that he had upon him in the discharge of his office.

(2.) The *end* of sealing is twofold:—

[1.] To *confirm or ratify* any grant or conveyance made in writing. In such cases men set their seals to make good and confirm their grants; and when this is done they are irrevocable. Or to confirm the testimony that is given by any one of the truth of any thing. Such was the manner among the Jews:—when any one had given true witness unto any thing or matter, and it was received by the judges, they instantly set their seals to it, to confirm it in judgment. Hence it is said, that he who receives the testimony of Christ "sets to his seal that God is true," John iii. 33. The promise is the great grant and conveyance of life and salvation in Christ to the souls of believers. That we may have full assurance of the truth and irrevocableness of

---

[1] Rev. vii. 4.

the promise, God gives us the Spirit to satisfy our hearts of it; and thence is he said to seal us, by assuring our hearts of those promises and their stability. But, though many expositors go this way, I do not see how this can consist with the very meaning of the word. It is not said that the promise is sealed, but that we are sealed; and when we seal a deed or grant to any one, we do not say the man is sealed, but the deed or grant.

[2.] To *appropriate, distinguish*, or *keep safe*. This is the end of sealing. Men set their seals on that which they appropriate and desire to keep safe for themselves. So, evidently, in this sense are the servants of God said to be sealed, Rev. vii. 4; that is, marked with God's mark, as his peculiar ones,—for this sealing answers to the setting of a mark, Ezek. ix. 4. Then are believers sealed, when they are marked for God to be heirs of the purchased inheritance, and to be preserved to the day of redemption. Now, if this be the sealing intended, it denotes not an act of sense in the heart, but of security to the person. The Father gives the elect into the hands of Christ to be redeemed; having redeemed them, in due time they are called by the Spirit, and marked for God, and so give up themselves to the hands of the Father.

If you ask, now, "Which of these senses is chiefly intended in this expression of our being sealed by the Holy Ghost?" I answer, The first, not excluding the other. We are sealed to the day of redemption, when, from the stamp, image, and character of the Spirit upon our souls, we have a fresh sense of the love of God given to us, with a comfortable persuasion of our acceptation with him. But of this whole matter I have treated at large[1] elsewhere.

Thus, then, the Holy Ghost communicates unto us his own likeness; which is also the image of the Father and the Son. " We are changed into this image by the Lord the Spirit," 2 Cor. iii. 18; and herein he brings us into fellowship with himself. Our likeness to him gives us boldness with him. His work we look for, his fruits we pray for; and when any effect of grace, any discovery of the image of Christ implanted in us, gives us a persuasion of our being separated and set apart for God, we have a communion with him therein.

6. *He is an earnest unto us.* 2 Cor. i. 22, He hath "given the earnest of the Spirit in our hearts;" chap. v. 5, "Who also hath given unto us the earnest of the Spirit;" as also, Eph. i. 13, 14, "Ye are sealed with that Holy Spirit of promise, which is the earnest of our inheritance." In the two former places we are said to have the earnest of the Spirit; in the latter, the Spirit is said to be our earnest: "of the Spirit," then, in the first place, is, as we say, "genitivus materiæ;" denoting not the cause, but the thing itself,—not the author

[1] Perseverance of the Saints, chap. viii., vol. xi.

of the earnest, but the matter of it.   The Spirit is our earnest; as in the last place is expressed.   The consideration of what is meant by the "Spirit," here, and what is meant by an "earnest," will give some insight into this privilege, which we receive by the Comforter:—

(1.) What *grace*, what gift of the Spirit, is intended by this earnest, some have made inquiry; I suppose to no purpose.   It is the Spirit himself, *personally* considered, that is said to be this earnest, 2 Cor. i. 22.   It is God hath given the earnest of the Spirit in our hearts: an expression directly answering that of Gal. iv. 6, "God hath sent forth the Spirit of his Son into your hearts;"—that is, the person of the Spirit; for nothing else can be called the Spirit of his Son: and in Eph. i. 14, he hath given the Spirit (ὅς for ὅ); which is that earnest. The Spirit of promise himself is this earnest.   In giving us this Spirit he gives us this earnest.

(2.) An earnest it is,—ἀῤῥαϐών.   Neither the Greek nor the Latin has any word to express directly what is here intended.   The Latins have made words for it, from that expressed here in the Greek, "arrha" and "arrabo."   The Greek word is but the Hebrew "herabon" [עֵרָבוֹן] ; which, as some conceive, came amongst them by the Tyrian merchants, being a word of trade.   It is by some rendered, in Latin, "pignus," a "pledge;" but this cannot be here intended.   A *pledge* is that property which any one gives or leaves in the custody of another, to assure him that he will give him, or pay him, some other thing; in the nature of that which we call a "pawn."   Now, the thing that is here intended, is a part of that which is to come, and but a part of it, according to the trade use of the word, whence the metaphor is taken; it is excellently rendered in our language, an "earnest." An earnest is part of the price of any thing, or part of any grant, given beforehand to assure the person to whom it is given that at the appointed season he shall receive the whole that is promised him.

That a thing be an earnest, it is required,—

[1.] That it be part of the whole, *of the same kind* and nature with it; as we do give so much money in earnest to pay so much more.

[2.] That it be a *confirmation of a promise* and appointment; first the whole is promised, then the earnest is given for the good and true performance of that promise.

Thus the Spirit is this earnest.   God gives us the promise of eternal life.   To confirm this to us, he giveth us his Spirit; which is, as the first part of the promise, to secure us of the whole.   Hence he is said to be the earnest of the inheritance that is promised and purchased.

And it may be considered how it may be said to be an earnest on the part of God, who gives him; and on the part of believers, who receive him:—

1st. He is an earnest *on the part of God*, in that God gives him as a *choice part* of the inheritance itself, and of the same kind with the whole, as an earnest ought to be.   The full inheritance promised, is the fulness of the Spirit in the enjoyment of God.   When that Spirit which is given us in this world shall have perfectly taken away all sin and sorrow, and shall have made us able to enjoy the glory of God in his presence, that is the full inheritance promised.   So that the Spirit given us for the fitting of us for enjoyment of God in some measure, whilst we are here, is the earnest of the whole.

God doth it to this purpose, to assure us and secure us of the inheritance.   Having given us so many ¹securities without us,—his word, promises, covenant, oath, the revelation and discovery of his faithfulness and immutability in them all,—he is pleased also graciously to give us one within us, Isa. lix. 21, that we may have all the security we are capable of.   What can more be done?   He hath given us of the Holy Spirit;—in him the first-fruits of glory, the utmost pledge of his love, the earnest of all.

2dly. On *the part of believers* he is an earnest, in that he gives them an acquaintance with,—

(*1st.*) The *love of God.*   Their acceptation with him makes known to them their favour in his sight,—that he is their Father, and will deal with them as with children; and consequently, that the inheritance shall be theirs.   He sends his Spirit into our hearts, " crying, Abba, Father," Gal. iv. 6.   And what is the inference of believers from hence? Verse 7, "Then we are not servants, but sons; and if sons, then heirs of God."   The same apostle, again, Rom. viii. 17, " If children, then heirs; heirs of God, and joint heirs with Christ."   On that persuasion of the Spirit that we are children, the inference is, "Then heirs, heirs of God, and joint heirs with Christ."   We have, then, a right to an inheritance, and an eviction of it.   This is the use, then, we have of it,—even the Spirit persuading us of our sonship and acceptation with God our Father.   And what is this inheritance of glory?   "If we suffer with him, we shall be glorified together."   And that the Spirit is given for this end is attested, 1 John iii. 24, " Hereby we know that he abideth in us, by the Spirit which he hath given us."   The apostle is speaking of our union with God, which he expresseth in the words foregoing: " He that keepeth his commandments dwelleth in him, and he in him;"—of that union elsewhere.   Now, this we know from hence, even by the Spirit which he hath given us,—the Spirit acquaints us with it.   Not that we have such an acquaintance, but that the argument is good and conclusive in itself, " We have of the Spirit; therefore he dwells in us, and we in him:" because, indeed, his dwelling in us is by that Spirit, and our interest in him is from thence.   A sense of this he giveth as he pleaseth.

¹ Heb. vi. 17, 18.

(*2dly.*) The Spirit being given as an earnest, acquaints believers *with their inheritance*, 1 Cor. ii. 9, 10. As an earnest, being part of the whole, gives knowledge of it, so doth the Spirit; as in sundry particulars might be demonstrated.

So is he in all respects completely an earnest,—given of God, received by us, as the beginning of our inheritance, and the assurance of it. So much as we have of the Spirit, so much we have of heaven in perfect enjoyment, and so much evidence of its future fulness. Under this apprehension of him in the dispensation of grace do believers receive him and rejoice in him. Every gracious, self-evidencing act of his in their hearts they rejoice in, as a drop from heaven, and long for the ocean of it. Not to drive every effect of grace to this issue, is to neglect the work of the Holy Ghost in us and towards us.

There remains only that a difference be, in a few words, assigned between believers receiving the Spirit as an earnest of the whole inheritance, and hypocrites " tasting of the powers of the world to come," Heb. vi. 5. A taste of the powers of the world to come seems to be the same with the earnest of the inheritance. But,—

[*1st.*] That by " the powers of the world to come " in that place is intended the joys of heaven, there is, indeed, no ground to imagine. They are nowhere so called; nor doth it suitably express the glory that shall be revealed, which we shall be made partakers of. It is, doubtless, the powerful ministry of the ordinances and dispensations of the times of the gospel (there called to the Hebrews according to their own idiom), the powers or great effectual things of the world to come, that is intended. But,—

[*2dly.*] Suppose that by " the powers of the world to come " the glory of heaven is intended, there is a wide difference between taking a *vanishing taste* of it ourselves, and receiving *an abiding earnest* from God. To take a taste of the things of heaven, and to have them assured of God as from his love, differ greatly. A hypocrite may have his thoughts raised to a great deal of joy and contentment in the consideration of the good things of the kingdom of God for a season, considering the things in themselves; but the Spirit, as he is an earnest, gives us a pledge of them as provided for us in the love of God and purchase of his Son Jesus Christ. This by the way.

7. The Spirit *anoints believers*. We are " anointed" by the Spirit, 2 Cor. i. 21. We have " an unction from the Holy One, and we know all things," 1 John ii. 20, 27. I cannot intend to run this expression up into its rise and original; also, I have done it elsewhere. The use of unctions in the Judaical church, the meaning and intendment of the types attended therewith, the offices that men were consecrated unto thereby, are at the bottom of this expression; nearer

the unction of Jesus Christ (from whence he is called Messiah, and the Christ, the whole performance of his office of mediatorship being called also his anointing, Dan. ix. 24, as to his furnishment for it), concurs hereunto. Christ is said to be "anointed with the oil of gladness above his fellows," Heb. i. 9; which is the same with that of John iii. 34, "God giveth not the Spirit by measure unto him." We, who have the Spirit by measure, are anointed with the "oil of gladness;" Christ hath the fulness of the Spirit, whence our measure is communicated: so he is anointed above us, "that in all things he may have the pre-eminence." How Christ was anointed with the Spirit to his threefold office of king, priest, and prophet; how, by virtue of an unction, with the same Spirit dwelling in him and us, we become to be interested in these offices of his, and are made also kings, priests, and prophets to God, is known, and would be matter of a long discourse to handle; and my design is only to communicate the things treated of.

I shall only, therefore, fix on one place, where the communications of the Spirit in this unction of Christ are enumerated,—of which, in our measure, from him and with him, by this unction, we are made partakers,—and that is, Isa. xi. 2, 3, "The Spirit of the LORD shall rest upon him, the Spirit of wisdom and understanding, the Spirit of counsel and might, the Spirit of knowledge, and of the fear of the LORD," etc. Many of *the endowments* of Christ, from the Spirit wherewith he was abundantly anointed, are here recounted. Principally those of wisdom, counsel, and understanding, are insisted on; on the account whereof all the treasures of wisdom and knowledge are said to be in him, Col. ii. 3. And though this be but some part of the furniture of Jesus Christ for the discharge of his office, yet it is such, as, where our anointing to the same purpose is mentioned, it is said peculiarly on effecting of such qualifications as these: so 1 John ii. 20, 27, the work of the anointing is to teach us; the Spirit therein is a Spirit of wisdom and understanding, of counsel, knowledge, and quick understanding in the fear of the Lord. So was the great promise of the Comforter, that he should "teach us," John xiv. 26,—that he should "guide us into all truth," chap. xvi. 13. This of teaching us the mind and will of God, in the manner wherein we are taught it by the Spirit, our comforter, is an eminent part of our unction by him; which only I shall instance in. Give me leave to say, there is a threefold teaching by the Spirit:—

(1.) A teaching by the Spirit of *conviction* and illumination. So the Spirit teacheth the world (that is, many in it) by the preaching of the word; as he is promised to do, John xvi. 8.

(2.) A teaching by the Spirit of *sanctification;* opening blind eyes, giving a new understanding, shining into our hearts, to give us a knowledge of the glory of God in the face of Jesus Christ; enabling us to receive spiritual things in a spiritual light, 1 Cor. ii. 13; giving a saving knowledge of the mystery of the gospel: and this in several degrees is common to believers.

(3.) A teaching by the Spirit of *consolation;*—making sweet, useful, and joyful to the soul, the discoveries that are made of the mind and will of God in the light of the Spirit of sanctification. Here the oil of the Spirit is called the "oil of gladness,"—that which brings joy and gladness with it; and the name of Christ thereby discovered is a sweet "ointment poured forth," that causeth souls to run after him with joy and delight, Cant. i. 3. We see it by daily experience, that very many have little taste and sweetness and relish in their souls of those truths which yet they savingly know and believe; but when we are taught by this unction, oh, how sweet is every thing we know of God! As we may see in the place of John where mention is made of the teaching of this unction, it respects peculiarly the Spirit teaching of us the love of God in Christ, the shining of his countenance; which, as David speaks, puts gladness into our hearts, Ps. iv. 6, 7.

We have this, then, by the Spirit:—he teacheth us of the love of God in Christ; he makes every gospel truth as wine well refined to our souls, and the good things of it to be a feast of fat things;—gives us joy and gladness of heart with all that we know of God; which is the great preservative of the soul to keep it close to truth. The apostle speaks of our teaching by this unction, as the means whereby we are preserved from seduction. Indeed, to know any truth in the power, sweetness, joy, and gladness of it, is that great security of the soul's constancy in the preservation and retaining of it. They will readily change truth for error, who find no more sweetness in the one than in the other. I must crave the reader's pardon for my brief passing over these great things of the gospel; my present design is rather to *enumerate* than to *unfold* them. This one work of the Holy Ghost, might it be pursued, would require a fuller discourse than I can allot unto the whole matter in hand. All the privileges we enjoy, all the dignity and honour we are invested withal, our whole dedication unto God, our nobility and royalty, our interest in all church advantages and approaches to God in worship, our separation from the world, the name whereby we are called, the liberty we enjoy,—all flow from this head, all are branches of this effect of the Holy Ghost. I have mentioned only our teaching by this unction,—a teaching that brings joy and gladness with it, by giving the heart a sense of the truth wherein we are instructed. When we find any of the good truths of the gospel come home to our souls with life, vigour, and power, giving us gladness of heart, transforming us into the image and likeness of it,—the Holy Ghost is then at his work, is pouring out of his oil.

8. We have *adoption also* by the Spirit; hence he is called the "Spirit of adoption;" that is, either he who is given to adopted ones, to secure them of it, to beget in their hearts a sense and persuasion of the Father's adopting love; or else to give them the privilege itself, as is intimated, John i. 12. Neither is that opposite hereunto which we have, Gal. iv. 6; for God may send the Spirit of supplication into our hearts, because we are sons, and yet adopted by his Spirit. But of this elsewhere.

9. He is also called the *"Spirit of supplication;"* under which notion he is promised, Zech. xii. 10; and how he effects that in us is declared, Rom. viii. 26, 27, Gal. iv. 6; and we are thence said to "pray in the Holy Ghost." Our prayers may be considered two ways:—

(1.) First, as a *spiritual duty* required of us by God; and so they are wrought in us by the Spirit of sanctification, which helps us to perform all our duties, by exalting all the faculties of the soul for the spiritual discharge of their respective offices in them.

(2.) As *a means of retaining communion* with God, whereby we sweetly ease our hearts in the bosom of the Father, and receive in refreshing tastes of his love. The soul is never more raised with the love of God than when by the Spirit taken into intimate communion with him in the discharge of this duty; and therein it belongs to the Spirit of consolation, to the Spirit promised as a comforter. And this is the next thing to be considered in our communion with the Holy Ghost,—namely, what are the peculiar effects which he worketh in us, and towards us, being so bestowed on us as was declared, and working in the way and manner insisted on. Now, these are,—his bringing the promises of Christ to remembrance, glorifying him in our hearts, shedding abroad the love of God in us, witnessing with us as to our spiritual estate and condition, sealing us to the day of redemption (being the earnest of our inheritance), anointing us with privileges as to their consolation, confirming our adoption, and being present with us in our supplications. Here is the wisdom of faith,— to find out and meet with the Comforter in all these things; not to lose their sweetness, by lying in the dark [as] to their author, nor coming short of the returns which are required of us.

CHAPTER IV.

The general consequences in the hearts of believers of the effects of the Holy Ghost before mentioned—Consolation; its adjuncts, peace, joy—How it is wrought immediately, mediately.

HAVING proceeded thus far in discovering the way of our communion with the Holy Ghost, and insisted on the most noble and known effects that he produceth, it remains that it be declared what *general consequences* of these effects there are brought forth in the hearts of believers; and so we shall at least have made mention of the main heads of his dispensation and work in the economy of grace. Now, these (as with the former) I shall do little more than name; it being not at all in my design to handle the natures of them, but only to show what respects they bear to the business in hand:—

1. *Consolation* is the first of these: "The disciples walked in the fear of the Lord, and in the consolation of the Holy Ghost," Acts ix. 31, Τῇ παρακλήσει τοῦ ἁγίου Πνεύματος. He is ὁ παράκλητος, and he gives παράκλησιν: from his work towards us, and in us, we have comfort and consolation. This is the first general consequent of his dispensation and work. Whenever there is mention made of comfort and consolation in the Scripture given to the saints (as there is most frequently), it is the proper consequent of the work of the Holy Ghost towards them. Comfort or consolation in general, is the setting and composing of the soul in rest and contentedness in the midst of or from troubles, by the consideration or presence of some good, wherein it is interested, outweighing the evil, trouble, or perplexity that it hath to wrestle withal. Where mention is made of comfort and consolation, properly so called, there is relation to trouble or perplexity; so the apostle, 2 Cor. i. 5, 6, "As the sufferings of Christ abound in us, so our consolation also aboundeth by Christ." Suffering and consolation are opposed, the latter being a relief against the former; so are all the promises of comfort, and all the expressions of it, in the Old and New Testament still proposed as reliefs against trouble.

And, as I said, consolation ariseth from the presence or consideration of a greater good, that outbalances the evil or perplexity wherewith we are to contend. Now, in the effects or acts of the Holy Ghost before mentioned lie all the springs of our consolation. There is no comfort but from them; and there is no trouble that we may not have comfort in and against by them. That a man may have consolation in any condition, nothing is required but the presence of a good, rendering the evil wherewith he is pressed inconsiderable to him. Suppose a man under the greatest calamity that can possibly befall a child of God, or a confluence of all those evils numbered by Paul, Rom. viii. 35, etc.; let this man have the Holy Ghost performing the works mentioned before towards him, and, in despite of all his evils, his consolations will abound. Suppose him to have a sense of the love of God all the while shed abroad in his heart, a clear witness within that he is a child of God, accepted with him, that he is sealed and marked of God for his own, that he is an heir of all the promises of God, and the like; it is impossible that man should not triumph in all his tribulations.

From this rise of all our consolation are those descriptions which we have of it in the Scripture, from its properties and adjuncts; as,—

(1.) It is *abiding.* Thence it is called "Everlasting consolation," 2 Thess. ii. 16, "God, even our Father, which hath loved us, and given us everlasting consolation;"—that is, comfort that vanisheth not; and that because it riseth from everlasting things. There may be some perishing comfort given for a little season by perishing things; but abiding consolation, which we have by the Holy Ghost, is from things everlasting:—everlasting love, eternal redemption, an everlasting inheritance.

(2.) *Strong.* Heb. vi. 18, "That the heirs of the promise should receive strong consolation." As strong opposition lies sometimes against us, and trouble, whose bands are strong, so is our consolation strong; it abounds, and is unconquerable,—*ἰσχυρὰ παράκλησις.* It is such as will make its way through all opposition; it confirms, corroborates, and strengthens the heart under any evil; it fortifies the soul, and makes it able cheerfully to undergo any thing that it is called unto: and that because it is from him who is strong.

(3.) It is *precious.* Hence the apostle makes it the great motive unto obedience, which he exhorts the Philippians unto, chap. ii. 1, "If there be any consolation in Christ;"—"If you set any esteem and valuation upon this precious mercy of consolation in Christ, by those comforts, let it be so with you."

And this is the first general consequent in the hearts of believers of those great effects of the Holy Ghost before mentioned. Now, this is so large and comprehensive, comprising so many of our concernments in our walking with God, that the Holy Ghost receives his denomination, as to the whole work he hath to perform for us, from hence,—he is the Comforter; as Jesus Christ, from the work of redemption and salvation, is the Redeemer and Saviour of his church. Now, as we have no consolation but from the Holy Ghost, so all his effects towards us have certainly this consequent more or less in us. Yea, I dare say, whatever we have in the kinds of the things before mentioned that brings not consolation with it, in the root at least, if not in the ripe fruit, is not of the Holy Ghost. The way whereby comfort issues out from those works of his, belongs to particular cases. The fellowship we have with him consists, in no small portion of it, in the consolation we receive from him. This gives us a valuation of his love; teacheth whither to make applications in our distress,—whom to pray for, to pray to,—whom to wait upon, in perplexities.

2. *Peace* ariseth hence also. Rom. xv. 13, "The God of hope fill you with all peace in believing, that you may abound in hope through the power of the Holy Ghost." The power of the Holy Ghost is not

only extended to hope, but to our peace also in believing.   So is it in the connection of those promises, John xiv. 26, 27, "I will give you the Comforter:" and what then? what follows that grant? "Peace," saith he, "I leave with you; my peace I give unto you." Nor doth Christ otherwise leave his peace, or give his peace unto them, but by bestowing the Comforter on them.   The peace of Christ consists in the soul's sense of its acceptation with God in friendship.   So is Christ said to be "our peace," Eph. ii. 14, by slaying the enmity between God and us, and in taking away the handwriting that was against us. Rom. v. 1, "Being justified by faith, we have peace with God."   A comfortable persuasion of our acceptation with God in Christ is the bottom of this peace; it inwraps deliverance from eternal wrath, hatred, curse, condemnation,—all sweetly affecting the soul and conscience.

And this is a *branch* from the same *root* with that foregoing,—a consequent of the effects of the Holy Ghost before mentioned.   Suppose a man chosen in the eternal love of the Father, redeemed by the blood of the Son, and justified freely by the grace of God, so that he hath a right to all the promises of the gospel; yet this person can by no reasonings nor arguings of his own heart, by no considerations of the promises themselves, nor of the love of God or grace of Christ in them, be brought to any establishment in peace, until it be produced in him as a fruit and consequent of the work of the Holy Ghost in him and towards him.   "Peace" is the fruit of the Spirit, Gal. v. 22.   The savour of the Spirit is "life and peace," Rom. viii. 6. All we have is from him and by him.

3. *Joy*, also, is of this number.   The Spirit, as was showed, is called "The oil of gladness," Heb. i. 9.   His anointing brings gladness with it, Isa. lxi. 3, "The oil of joy for mourning."   "The kingdom of God is righteousness, and peace, and joy in the Holy Ghost," Rom. xiv. 17; "Received the word with joy in the Holy Ghost," 1 Thess. i. 6,— "with joy," as Peter tells believers, "unspeakable and full of glory," 1 Epist. i. 8.   To give joy to the hearts of believers is eminently the work of the Comforter; and this he doth by the particulars before instanced in.   That "rejoicing in hope of the glory of God," mentioned Rom. v. 2, which carries the soul through any tribulation, even with glorying, hath its rise in the Spirit's "shedding abroad the love of God in our hearts," verse 5.   Now, there are two ways whereby the Spirit worketh this joy in the hearts of believers:—

(1.) He doth it *immediately* by himself; without the consideration of any other acts or works of his, or the interposition of any reasonings, or deductions and conclusions.   As in *sanctification* he is a well of water springing up in the soul, immediately exerting his efficacy and refreshment; so in *consolation*, he immediately works the soul and minds of men to a joyful, rejoicing, and spiritual frame, filling them with exultation and gladness;—not that this arises from our reflex consideration of the love of God, but rather gives occasion thereunto.   When he so sheds abroad the love of God in our hearts, and so fills them with gladness by an immediate act and operation (as he caused John Baptist to leap for joy in the womb upon the approach of the mother of Jesus),—then doth the soul, even from hence, raise itself to a consideration of the love of God, whence joy and rejoicing doth also flow.   Of this joy there is no account to be given, but that the Spirit worketh it when and how he will.   He secretly infuseth and distils it into the soul, prevailing against all fears and sorrows, filling it with gladness, exultations; and sometimes with unspeakable raptures of mind.

(2.) *Mediately.*   By his other works towards us, he gives a sense of the love of God, with our adoption and acceptation with him; and on the consideration thereof enables us to receive it.   Let what hath been spoken of his operations towards us be considered,—what assurance he gives us of the love of God; what life, power, and security; what pledge of our eternal welfare,—and it will be easily perceived that he lays a sufficient foundation of this joy and gladness.   Not that we are able, upon any rational consideration, deduction, or conclusion, that we can make from the things mentioned, to affect our hearts with the joy and gladness intended; it is left no less the proper work of the Spirit to do it from hence, and by the intervenience of these considerations, than to do it immediately without them.   This process of producing joy in the heart, we have, Ps. xxiii. 5, 6, " Thou anointest my head with oil."   Hence is the conclusion, as in the way of exultation, " Surely goodness and mercy shall follow me."   Of this effect of the Comforter, see Isa. xxxv. throughout.

4. *Hope,* also, is an effect of those workings of the Holy Ghost in us and towards us, Rom. xv. 13.   These, I say, are the general consequents of the effects of the Holy Ghost upon the hearts of believers; which, if we might consider them in their offspring, with all the branches that shoot out from them, in exultation, assurance, boldness, confidence, expectation, glorying, and the like, it would appear how far our whole communion with God is influenced by them.   But I only name the heads of things, and hasten to what remains.   It is the general and particular way of our communion with the Holy Ghost that should nextly ensue, but that some other considerations necessarily do here interpose themselves.

CHAPTER V.

Some observations and inferences from discourses foregoing concerning the Spirit
—The contempt of the whole administration of the Spirit by some—The vain
pretence of the Spirit by others—The false spirit discovered.

THIS process being made, I should now show immediately, how we
hold the communion proposed with the Holy Ghost, in the things
laid down and manifested to contain his peculiar work towards us;
but there are some miscarriages in the world in reference unto this
dispensation of the Holy Ghost, both on the one hand and the other,
in contempt of his true work and pretence of that which is not, that
I cannot but remark in my passage: which to do shall be the business of this chapter.

Take a view, then, of the state and condition of them who, professing to believe the gospel of Jesus Christ, do yet contemn and
despise his Spirit, as to all its operations, gifts, graces, and dispensations to his churches and saints. Whilst Christ was in the world with
his disciples, he made them no greater promise, neither in respect of
their own good nor of carrying on the work which he had committed
to them, than this of giving them the Holy Ghost. Him he instructeth them to pray for of the Father, as that which is needful for them,
as bread for children, Luke xi. 13. Him he promiseth them, as a
well of water springing up in them, for their refreshment, strengthening, and consolation unto everlasting life, John vii. 37–39; as also
to carry on and accomplish the whole work of the ministry to them
committed, John xvi. 8–11; with all those eminent works and privileges before mentioned. And upon his ascension, this is laid as the
bottom of that glorious communication of gifts and graces in his plentiful effusion mentioned, Eph. iv. 8, 11, 12,—namely, that he had
received of the Father the promise of the Holy Ghost, Act ii. 33;
and that in such an eminent manner as thereby to make the greatest
and most glorious difference between the administration of the new
covenant and old. Especially doth the whole work of the ministry
relate to the Holy Ghost; though that be not my present business to
evince. He calls men to that work, and they are separated unto him,
Acts xiii. 2; he furnisheth them with gifts and abilities for that employment, 1 Cor. xii. 7–10. So that the whole religion we profess,
without this administration of the Spirit, is nothing; nor is there any
fruit without it of the resurrection of Christ from the dead.

This being the state of things,—that in our worship of and obedience to God, in our own consolation, sanctification, and ministerial employment, the Spirit is the principle, the life, soul, the all of the
whole; yet so desperate hath been the malice of Satan, and wicked-

ness of men, that their great endeavour hath been to shut him quite out of all gospel administrations.

First, his *gifts* and graces were not only decried, but almost *excluded* from the public worship of the church, by the imposition of an operose form of service, to be read by the minister; which to do is neither a peculiar gift of the Holy Ghost to any, nor of the ministry at all. It is marvellous to consider what pleas and pretences were invented and used by learned men,—from its *antiquity*, its *composure* and approbation by *martyrs*, the beauty of uniformity in the worship of God, established and pressed thereby, etc.,—for the defence and maintenance of it. But the main argument they insisted on, and the chief field wherein they expatiated and laid out all their eloquence, was the vain babbling repetitions and folly of men praying by the Spirit. When once this was fallen upon, all (at least as they supposed) was carried away before them, and their adversaries rendered sufficiently ridiculous: so great is the cunning of Satan, and so unsearchable are the follies of the hearts of men. The sum of all these reasonings amounts to no more but this,—" Though the Lord Jesus Christ hath promised the Holy Ghost to be with his church to the end of the world, to fit and furnish men with gifts and abilities for the carrying on of that worship which he requires and accepteth at our hands, yet the work is not done to the purpose; the gifts he bestows are not sufficient to that end, neither as to invocation nor doctrine: and, therefore, we will not only help men by our directions, but exclude them from their exercise." This, I say, was the sum of all, as I could undeniably evidence, were that my present business. What innumerable evils ensue on this principle, in a formal setting apart of men to the ministry who had never once "tasted of the powers of the world to come," nor received any gifts from the Holy Ghost to that purpose; of crying up and growing in an outside pompous worship, wholly foreign to the power and simplicity of the gospel; of silencing, destroying, banishing, men whose ministry was accompanied with the evidence and demonstration of the Spirit,—I shall not need to declare. This is that I aim at, to point out the public contempt of the Holy Ghost, his gifts and graces, with their administration in the church of God, that hath been found even where the gospel hath been professed.

Again: it is a thing of most sad consideration, once to call to mind the improvement of that principle of contempt of the Spirit in private men and their ways. The name of the Spirit was grown a term of reproach. To plead for, or pretend to pray by, the Spirit, was enough to render a man the object of scorn and reproach from all sorts of men, from the pulpit to the stage. "What! you are full of the Spirit; you will pray by the Spirit; you have the gift: let us hear your non-

sense;"—and yet, perhaps, these men would think themselves wronged
not to be accounted Christians.   Christians! yea, have not some pretending themselves to be leaders of the flock,—yea, mounted a storey
or two above their brethren, and claiming a rule and government
over them,—made it their business to scoff at and reproach the gifts
of the Spirit of God?   And if this were the frame of their spirit,
what might be expected from others of professed profaneness?   It is
not imaginable to what height of blasphemy the process in this kind
amounted.   The Lord grant there be nothing of this cursed leaven
still remaining amongst us!   Some bleatings of ill importance[1] are
sometimes heard.   Is this the fellowship of the Holy Ghost that believers are called unto?   Is this the due entertainment of him whom
our Saviour promised to send for the supply of his bodily absence, so
as we might be no losers thereby?   Is it not enough that men should
be contented with such a stupid blindness, as, being called Christians,
to look no farther for their comfort and consolation than moral considerations common to heathens would lead them, when one infinitely
holy and blessed person of the Trinity hath taken this office upon
him to be our comforter, but they must oppose and despise him
also?   Nothing more discovers how few there are in the world that
have interest in that blessed name whereby we are all called.   But
this is no place to pursue this discourse.   The aim of this discourse
is, to evince the folly and madness of men in general, who profess to
own the gospel of Christ, and yet condemn and despise his Spirit, in
whomsoever he is manifested.   Let us be zealous of the gifts of the
Spirit, not envious at them.

From what hath been discoursed we may also *try the spirits* that
are gone abroad in the world, and which have been exercising themselves, at several seasons, ever since the ascension of Christ.   The
iniquity of the generation that is past and passing away lay in open,
cursed opposition to the Holy Ghost.   God hath been above them,
wherein they behaved themselves presumptuously.   Satan, whose
design, as he is god of this world, is to be uppermost, not to dwell
wholly in any form cast down by the providence of God, hath now
transformed himself into an angel of light; and he will pretend the
Spirit also and only.   But there are " seducing spirits," 1 Tim. iv. 1;
and we have a " command not to believe every spirit, but try the
spirits," 1 John iv. 1: and the reason added is, " Because many false
prophets are gone out into the world;"—that is, men pretending to the
revelation of new doctrines by the Spirit; whose deceits in the first
church Paul intimateth, 2 Thess. ii. 2; calling on men not to be
"shaken in mind by spirit." The truth is, the spirits of these days are
so gross, that a man of a very easy discerning may find them out

---

[1] *Importance,* in an obsolete sense of the word, *import* or meaning.—ED.

and yet their delusion so strong, that not a few are deceived. This is one thing that lies evident to every eye,—that, according to his wonted course, Satan, with his delusions, is run into an extreme to his former actings.

Not long since, his great design, as I manifested, was to cry up ordinances without the Spirit, casting all the reproach that he could upon him;—now, to cry up a spirit without and against ordinances, casting all reproach and contempt possible upon them. Then, he would have a *ministry* without the *Spirit;*—now, a *Spirit* without a *ministry.* Then, the *reading* of the word might suffice, without either preaching or praying by the Spirit;—now, the *Spirit* is enough, without reading or studying the word at all. Then, he allowed a literal embracing of what Christ had done in the flesh;—now, he talks of Christ in the Spirit only, and denies him to be come in the flesh,—the proper character of the false spirit we are warned of, 1 John iv. 1. Now, because it is most certain that the Spirit which we are to hear and embrace is the Spirit promised by Christ (which is so clear, that him the Montanists' paraclete, yea, and Mohammed, pretended himself to be, and those of our days affirm, who pretend the same), let us briefly try them by some of the effects mentioned, which Christ hath promised to give the Holy Ghost for:—

The first general effect, as was observed, was this,—that he should bring to remembrance the things that Christ spake, for our guidance and consolation. This was to be the work of the Holy Ghost towards the apostles, who were to be the penmen of the Scriptures: this is to be his work towards believers to the end of the world. Now, the things that Christ hath spoken and done are "written that we might believe, and believing, have life through his name," John xx. 31; they are written in the Scripture. This, then, is the work of the Spirit which Christ hath promised;—he shall bring to our remembrance, and give us understanding of the words of Christ in the Scripture, for our guidance and consolation. Is this, now, the work of the spirit which is abroad in the world, and perverteth many? Nothing less. His business is, to decry the things that Christ hath spoken which are written in the word; to pretend *new revelations* of his own; to lead men from the written word, wherein the whole work of God and all the promises of Christ are recorded.

Again: the work of the Spirit promised by Christ is to glorify him: "He shall glorify me; for he shall receive of mine, and shall show it unto you," John xvi. 14. Him who was to suffer at Jerusalem, who then spake to his disciples, it was to make him glorious, honourable, and of high esteem in the hearts of believers; and that by showing his things (his love, kindness, grace, and purchase) unto them. This is the work of the Spirit. The work of the spirit that is gone abroad, is to glorify itself, to decry and render contemptible Christ that suffered for us, under the name of a Christ without us; which it slights and despiseth, and that professedly. Its own glory, its own honour, is all that it aims at; wholly inverting the order of the divine dispensations. The fountain of all being and lying in the Father's love, the Son came to glorify the Father. He still says, " I seek not mine own glory, but the glory of him that sent me." The Son having carried on the work of redemption, was now to be glorified with the Father. So he prays that it might be, John xvii. 1, " The hour is come, glorify thy Son;" and that with the glory which he had before the world was, when his joint counsel was in the carrying on the Father's love. Wherefore the Holy Ghost is sent, and his work is to glorify the Son. But now, as I said, we have a spirit come forth whose whole business is to glorify himself; whereby we may easily know whence he is.

Furthermore: the Holy Ghost sheds abroad the love of God in our hearts, as was declared, and thence fills them with joy, peace, and hope; quieting and refreshing the hearts of them in whom he dwells; giving them liberty and rest, confidence, and the boldness of children. This spirit whereof men now boast is a spirit of bondage, whose utmost work is to make men quake and tremble; casting them into an un-son-like frame of spirit, driving them up and down with horror and bondage, and drinking up their *very natural spirits*, and making their whole man wither away. There is scarce any one thing that more evidently manifesteth the spirit whereby some are now acted not to be the Comforter promised by Christ, than this,—that he is a spirit of bondage and slavery in them in whom he is, and a spirit of cruelty and reproach towards others; in a direct opposition to the Holy Ghost in believers, and all the ends and purposes for which, as a spirit of adoption and consolation, he is bestowed on them.

To give one instance more: the Holy Ghost bestowed on believers is a Spirit of prayer and supplication; as was manifested. The spirit wherewith we have to do, pretends the carrying men above such low and contemptible means of communion with God. In a word, it were a very easy and facile task, to pass through all of the eminent effects of the Holy Ghost in and towards believers, and to manifest that the pretending spirit of our days comes in a direct opposition and contradiction to every one of them. Thus hath Satan passed .from one extreme to another,—from a bitter, wretched opposition to the Spirit of Christ, unto a cursed pretending to the Spirit; still to the same end and purpose.

I might give sundry other instances of the contempt or abuse of the dispensation of the Spirit. Those mentioned are the extremes whereunto all other are or may be reduced; and I will not farther divert from that which lies directly in my aim.

CHAPTER VI.

Of particular communion with the Holy Ghost—Of preparation thereunto—Valuation of the benefits we receive by him—What it is he comforts, us in and against; wherewith; how.

THE way being thus made plain for us, I come to show how we hold particular communion with the Holy Ghost, as he is promised of Christ to be our comforter, and as working out our consolation by the means formerly insisted on. Now, the first thing I shall do herein, is the proposal of that which may be some preparation to the duty under consideration; and this by leading the souls of believers to a due valuation of this work of his towards us, whence he is called our Comforter.

To raise up our hearts to this frame, and fit us for the duty intended, let us consider these three things:—

FIRST, *What it is he comforts us against.*

SECONDLY, *Wherewith he comforts us.*

THIRDLY, *The principle of all his actings and operations in us for our consolation.*

FIRST. There are but three things in the whole course of our pilgrimage that the consolations of the Holy Ghost are useful and necessary in:—

1. In our *afflictions.* Affliction is part of the *provision* that God hath made in his house for his children, Heb. xii. 5, 6. The great variety of its causes, means, uses, and effects, is generally known. There is a measure of them appointed for every one. To be wholly without them is a temptation; and so in some measure an affliction. That which I am to speak unto is, that in all our afflictions we need the consolations of the Holy Ghost. It is the nature of man to relieve himself, when he is entangled, by all ways and means. According as men's natural spirits are, so do they manage themselves under pressures. "The spirit of a man will bear his infirmity;" at least, will struggle with it.

There are two great evils, one of which does generally seize on men under their afflictions, and keep them from a due management of them. The apostle mentioneth them both, Heb. xii. 5, Μὴ ὀλιγώρει παιδείας Κυρίου, μηδὲ ἐκλύου, ὑπ᾽ αὐτοῦ ἐλεγχόμενος,—" Despise not the chastisement of the Lord; neither faint when thou art reproved." One of these extremes do men usually fall into; either they despise the Lord's correction, or sink under it

(1.) Men *despise it.* They account that which befalls them to be *a light or common thing;* they take no notice of God in it; they can shift with it well enough: they look on instruments, second causes; provide for their own defence and vindication with little regard to God or his hand in their affliction. And the ground of this is, because they take in succours, in their trouble, that God will not mix his grace withal; they fix on other remedies than what he hath appointed, and utterly lose all the benefits and advantage of their affliction. And so shall every man do that relieves himself from any thing but the consolations of the Holy Ghost.

(2.) Men *faint and sink* under their trials and afflictions; which the apostle farther reproves, verse 12. The first despise the assistance of the Holy Ghost through pride of heart; the latter refuse it through dejectedness of spirit, and sink under the weight of their troubles. And who, almost, is there that offends not on one of these hands? Had we not learned to count light of the chastisements of the Lord, and to take little notice of his dealings with us, we should find the season of our afflictions to comprise no small portion of our pilgrimage.

Now, there is no due management of our souls under any affliction, so that God may have the glory of it, and ourselves any spiritual benefit or improvement thereby, but by the consolations of the Holy Ghost. All that our Saviour promiseth his disciples, when he tells them of the great trials and tribulations they were to undergo, is, "I will send you the Spirit, the Comforter; he shall give you peace in me, when in the world you shall have trouble. He shall guide and direct, and keep you in all your trials." And so, the apostle tells us, it came to pass, 2 Cor. i. 4–6; yea, and this, under the greatest afflictions, will carry the soul to the highest joy, peace, rest, and contentment. So the same apostle, Rom. v. 3, "We glory in tribulations." It is a great expression. He had said before, "We rejoice in hope of the glory of God," verse 2. Yea, but what if manifold afflictions and tribulations befall us? "Why, even in them also we glory," saith he; "we glory in our tribulations." But whence is it that our spirits are so borne up to a due management of afflictions, as to glory in them in the Lord? He tells us, verse 5, it is from the "shedding abroad of the love of God in our hearts by the Holy Ghost." And thence are believers said to "receive the word in much affliction, with joy of the Holy Ghost," 1 Thess. i. 6; and to "take joyfully the spoiling of their goods." This is that I aim at:—there is no management nor improvement of any affliction, but merely and solely by the *consolations of the Holy Ghost*. Is it, then, of any esteem or value unto you that you lose not all your trials, temptations, and afflictions?—learn to value that whereby alone they are rendered useful.

2. *Sin* is the *second burden* of our lives, and much the greatest.

Unto this is this consolation peculiarly suited.   So Heb. vi. 17, 18, an allusion is taken from the manslayer under the law, who, having killed a man unawares, and brought the guilt of his blood upon himself, fled with speed for his deliverance to the city of refuge.   Our great and only refuge from the guilt of sin is the Lord Jesus Christ; in our flying to him, doth the Spirit administer consolation to us. *A sense of sin* fills the heart with troubles and disquietness; it is *the Holy Ghost* which gives us peace in Christ;—that gives an apprehension of wrath; the Holy Ghost sheds abroad the love of God in our hearts;—from thence doth Satan and the law accuse us, as objects of God's hatred; the Spirit bears witness with our spirits that we are the children of God.   There is not any one engine or instrument that sin useth or sets up against our peace, but one effect or other of the Holy Ghost towards us is suited and fitted to the casting of it down.

3. In *the whole course of our obedience* are his consolations necessary also, that we may go through with it cheerfully, willingly, patiently to the end.   This will afterward be more fully discovered, as to particulars, when I come to give directions for our communion with this blessed Comforter.   In a word, in all the concernments of this life, and in our whole expectation of another, we stand in need of the consolations of the Holy Ghost.

Without them, we shall either despise afflictions or faint under them, and God be neglected as to his intendments in them.

Without them, *sin* will either harden us to a contempt of it, or cast us down to a neglect of the remedies graciously provided against it.

Without them, *duties* will either puff us up with pride, or leave us without that sweetness which is in new obedience.

Without them, *prosperity* will make us carnal, sensual, and to take up our contentment in these things, and utterly weaken us for the trials of adversity.

Without them, the *comforts of our relations* will separate us from God, and the loss of them make our hearts as Nabal's.

Without them, the *calamity* of the church will overwhelm us, and the prosperity of the church will not concern us.

Without them, we shall have *wisdom* for no work, *peace* in no condition, *strength* for no duty, *success* in no trial, *joy* in no state,— no *comfort* in life, no *light* in death.

Now, our afflictions, our sins, and our obedience, with the attendancies of them respectively, are the great concernments of our lives. What we are in reference unto God is comprised in them, and the due management of them, with their contraries, which come under the same rule; through all these doth there run a line of consolation from the Holy Ghost, that gives us a joyful issue throughout.   How sad is the condition of poor souls destitute of these consolations! What poor shifts are they forced to betake themselves unto! what giants have they to encounter in their own strength! and whether they are conquered or seem to conquer, they have nothing but the misery of their trials!

The SECOND thing considerable, to teach us to put a due valuation on the consolations of the Holy Ghost, is the matter of them, or that wherewith he comforts us. Now, this may be referred to the two heads that I have formerly treated of,—the love of the Father, and the grace of the Son. All the consolations of the Holy Ghost consist in his acquainting us with, and communicating unto us, the love of the Father and the grace of the Son; nor is there any thing in the one or the other but he makes it a matter of consolation to us: so that, indeed, we have our communion with the Father in his love, and the Son in his grace, by the operation of the Holy Ghost.

1. He *communicates* to us, and acquaints us with, the *love* of the Father. Having informed his disciples with that ground and foundation of their consolation which by the Comforter they should receive, our blessed Saviour (John xvi. 27) shuts up all in this, " The Father himself loveth you." This is that which the Comforter is given to acquaint us withal,—even that God is the Father, and that he loves us. In particular, that the Father, the first person in the Trinity, considered so distinctly, loves us. On this account is he said so often to come forth from the Father, because he comes in pursuit of his love, and to acquaint the hearts of believers therewith, that they may be comforted and established. By persuading us of the eternal and unchangeable love of the Father, he fills us with consolation. And, indeed, all the effects of the Holy Ghost before mentioned have their tendency this way. Of this love and its transcendent excellency you heard at large before. Whatever is desirable in it is thus communicated to us by the Holy Ghost. A sense of this is able not only to relieve us, but to make us in every condition to rejoice with joy unspeakable and glorious. It is not with an increase of corn, and wine, and oil, but with the shining of the countenance of God upon us, that he comforts our souls, Ps. iv. 6, 7. " The *world* hateth me," may such a soul as hath the Spirit say; " but my *Father* loves me. Men despise me as a *hypocrite;* but my Father loves me as a *child.* I am *poor* in this world; but I have a *rich* inheritance in the love of my Father. I am *straitened* in all things; but there is *bread enough* in my Father's house. I *mourn* in secret under the power of my lusts and sin, where no eyes see me; but the Father sees me, and is full of compassion. With a sense of his kindness, which is better than life, I rejoice in tribulation, glory in affliction, triumph as a conqueror. Though I am killed all the day long, all my sorrows

have a *bottom* that may be fathomed,—my trials, *bounds* that may be compassed; but *the breadth,* and *depth,* and *height* of the love of the Father, who can express?" I might render glorious this way of the Spirit's comforting us with the love of the Father, by comparing it with all other causes and means of joy and consolation whatever; and so discover their emptiness, its fulness,—their nothingness, its being all; as also by revealing the properties of it before rehearsed.

2. Again: he doth it by *communicating* to us, and acquainting us with, the *grace of Christ,*—all the fruits of his purchase, all the desireableness of his person, as we are interested in him. The grace of Christ, as I formerly discoursed of at large, is referred to two heads,— the grace of his person, and of his office and work. By both these doth the Holy Ghost administer consolation to us, John xvi. 14. He glorifies Christ by revealing his excellencies and desirableness to believers, as the " chiefest of ten thousand,—altogether lovely;" and then he shows them of the things of Christ,—his love, grace, all the fruits of his death, suffering, resurrection, and intercession: and with these supports their hearts and souls. And here, whatever is of refreshment in the pardon of sin, deliverance from the curse, and wrath to come, in justification and adoption, with the innumerable privileges attending them in the hope of glory given unto us, comes in on this head of account.

THIRDLY. The *principle* and fountain of all his actings for our consolation comes next under consideration, to the same end; and this leads us a little nearer to the communion intended to be directed in. Now, this is his own great love and infinite condescension. He willingly proceedeth or comes forth from the Father to be our comforter. He knew what we were, and what we could do, and what would be our dealings with him,—he knew we would grieve him, provoke him, quench his motions, defile his dwelling-place; and yet he would come to be our comforter. Want of a due consideration of this great love of the Holy Ghost weakens all the principles of our obedience. Did this dwell and abide upon our hearts, what a dear valuation must we needs put upon all his operations and actings towards us! Nothing, indeed, is valuable but what comes from love and good-will. This is the way the Scripture takes to raise up our hearts to a right and due estimation of our redemption by Jesus Christ. It tells us that he did it freely; that of his own will he hath laid down his life; that he did it out of love.[1] " In this was manifested the love of God, that he laid down his life for us;" " He loved us, and gave himself for us;" " He loved us, and washed us from our sins in his own blood." Hereunto it adds our state and condition, considered as he undertook for us,—sinners, enemies, dead, alienated; then he loved us, and died

[1] 1 John iv. 9, iii. 16; Gal. ii. 20; Rev. i. 5.

for us, and washed us with his blood.   May we not hence, also, have a valuation of the dispensation of the Spirit for our consolation? He proceeds to that end from the Father; he distributes as he will, works as he pleaseth.   And what are we, towards whom he carrieth on this work?   Froward, perverse, unthankful; grieving, vexing, provoking him.   Yet in his love and tenderness doth he continue to do us good. Let us by faith consider this love of the Holy Ghost.   It is the head and source of all the communion we have with him in this life.   This is, as I said, spoken only to prepare our hearts to the communion proposed; and what a little portion is it of what might be spoken! How might all these considerations be aggravated! what a number-less number might be added !   It suffices that, from what is spoken, it appears that the work in hand is amongst the greatest duties and most excellent privileges of the gospel.

CHAPTER VII.

The general ways of the saints' acting in communion with the Holy Ghost.

As in the account given of the actings of the Holy Ghost in us, we manifested first the general adjuncts of his actings, or the manner thereof; so now, in the description of the returns of our souls to him, I shall, in the first place, propose the general actings of faith in refer-ence to this work of the Holy Ghost, and then descend unto parti-culars.   Now, there are three general ways of the soul's deportment in this communion, expressed all negatively in the Scripture, but all including positive duties.   Now these are,—First, *Not to grieve him.* Secondly, *Not to quench his motions.*   Thirdly, *Not to resist him.*

There are three things considerable in the Holy Ghost:—1. His *person*, as dwelling in us; 2. His *actings by grace*, or his motions; 3. His *working* in the ordinances of the word, and the sacraments;— all for the same end and purpose.

To these three are the three cautions before suited:—1. Not to *grieve* him, in respect of his *person* dwelling in us.   2. Not to *quench* him, in respect of the *actings* and motions of his grace. 3. Not to *resist* him, in respect of *the ordinances* of Christ, and his gifts for their administration.   Now, because the whole general duty of believers, in their communion with the Holy Ghost, is com-prised in these three things, I shall handle them severally:—

1. The first *caution* concerns his *person* immediately, as dwell-ing in us.   It is given, Eph. iv. 30, " Grieve not the Holy Spirit of

God." There is a complaint, Isa. lxiii. 10, of them who vexed or grieved the Spirit of God; and from thence doth this caution seem to be taken. That it is the person of the Holy Ghost which is here intended, is evident,—

(1.) From the *phrase*, or manner of expression, with a double article, Τὸ Πνεῦμα τὸ ἅγιον,—"That Holy Spirit;" and also,—

(2.) From the work assigned to him in the following words, of "sealing to the day of redemption;" which, as hath been manifested, is the work of the Holy Ghost. Now, whereas this may be understood of the Spirit in others, or in ourselves, it is evident that the apostle intends it in the latter sense, by his addition of that signal and eminent privilege which we ourselves enjoy by him: he seals us to the day of redemption.

Let us see, then, the tendency of this expression, as comprising the first general rule of our communion with the Holy Ghost,—"Grieve not the Spirit."

The term of "grieving," or affecting with sorrow, may be considered either *actively*, in respect of the persons grieving; or *passively*, in respect of the persons grieved. In the latter sense the expression is metaphorical. The Spirit cannot be grieved, or affected with sorrow; which infers alteration, disappointment, weakness,—all incompatible with his infinite perfections; yet men may actively do that which is fit and able to grieve any one that stands affected towards them as doth the Holy Ghost. If he be not grieved, it is no thanks to us, but to his own unchangeable nature. So that there are two things denoted in this expression:—

First, That the Holy Ghost is affected towards us as one that is loving, careful, tender, *concerned in our good and well-doing;* and therefore upon our miscarriages is said to be grieved: as a good friend of a kind and loving nature is apt to be on the miscarriage of him whom he doth affect. And this is that we are principally to regard in this caution, as the ground and foundation of it,—the love, kindness, and tenderness of the Holy Ghost unto us. "Grieve him not."

Secondly, That we may do those things *that are proper to grieve him,* though he be not passively grieved; our sin being no less therein than if he were grieved as we are. Now, how this is done, how the Spirit is grieved, the apostle declareth in the contexture of that discourse, verses 21–24. He presseth to a progress in sanctification, and all the fruits of regeneration, verses 25–29. He dehorts from sundry particular evils that were contrary thereto, and then gives the general enforcement of the one and the other, "And grieve not the Holy Spirit of God;" that is, by coming short of that universal sanctification which our planting into Christ doth require. The *positive duty* included in this caution, of not grieving the Holy Spirit, is this,—

that we pursue universal holiness with regard unto, and upon the account of, the love, kindness, and tenderness, of the Holy Ghost. This is the foundation of our communion we have in general. When the soul considers the love, kindness, and tenderness of the Holy Ghost unto him; when he considers all the fruits and acts of his love and good-will towards him; and on that account, and under that consideration, because he is so concerned in our ways and walkings, to abstain from evils, and to walk in all duties of holiness,—this is to have communion with him. This consideration, that the Holy Ghost, who is our comforter, is delighted with our obedience, grieved at our evils and follies, being made a continual motive to, and reason of, our close walking with God in all holiness, is, I say, the first general way of our communion with him.

Here let us fix a little. We lose both *the power and pleasure* of our obedience for want of this consideration. We see on what account the Holy Ghost undertakes to be our comforter, by what ways and means he performs that office towards us; what an unworthy thing it is to grieve him, who comes to us on purpose to give us consolation! Let the soul, in the whole course of its obedience, exercise itself by faith to thoughts hereof, and lay due weight upon it: "The Holy Ghost, in his infinite love and kindness towards me, hath condescended to be my comforter; he doth it willingly, freely, powerfully. What have I received from him! in the multitude of my perplexities how hath he refreshed my soul! Can I live one day without his consolations? And shall I be regardless of him in that wherein he is concerned? Shall I grieve him by negligence, sin, and folly? Shall not his love constrain me to walk before him to all well-pleasing?" So have we in general fellowship with him.

2. The second is that of 1 Thess. v. 19, "Quench not the Spirit." There are various thoughts about the sense of these words. "The Spirit in others, that is, their spiritual gifts," say some; but then it falls in with what follows, verse 20, "Despise not prophesyings." "The light that God hath set up in our hearts," say others; but where is that called absolutely Τὸ Πνεῦμα,—"The Spirit?" It is the Holy Ghost himself that is here intended, not immediately, in respect of his *person* (in which regard he is said to be grieved, which is a personal affection); but in respect of his *motions, actings, and operations.* The Holy Ghost was typified by the fire that was always kept alive on the altar. He is also called a "Spirit of burning." The reasons of that allusion are manifold; not now to be insisted on. Now, the opposition that is made to fire in its actings, is by quenching. Hence the opposition made to the actings of the Holy Ghost are called "quenching of the Spirit," as some kind of wet wood will do, when it is cast into the fire. Thence are we said, in pursuance

of the same metaphor, ἀναζωπυρεῖν,—to "stir up with new fire," the gifts that are in us. The Holy Ghost is striving with us, acting in us, moving variously for our growth in grace, and bringing forth fruit meet for the principle he hath endued us withal. "Take heed," saith the apostle, "lest, by the power of your lusts and temptations, you attend not to his workings, but hinder him in his good-will towards you; that is, what in you lieth."

This, then, is the second general rule for our communion with the Holy Ghost. It respects his gracious *operations* in us and by us. There are several and various ways whereby the Holy Ghost is said to act, exert, and put forth his power in us; partly by moving upon and stirring up the grace we have received; partly by new supplies of grace from Jesus Christ, falling in with occasions for their exercise, raising good motions immediately or occasionally within us;—all tending to our furtherance in obedience and walking with God. All these are we carefully to observe and take notice of,—consider the fountain whence they come, and the end which they lead us unto. Hence have we communion with the Holy Ghost, when we can consider him by faith as the immediate author of all supplies, assistances, and the whole relief we have by grace; of all good actings, risings, motions in our hearts; of all strivings and contendings against sin. When we consider, I say, all these his actings and workings in their tendency to our consolation, and on that account are careful and watchful to improve them all to the end aimed at, as coming from him who is so loving, and kind, and tender to us, we have communion with him.

This is that which is intended,—every gracious acting of the blessed Spirit in and towards our souls, is constantly by faith to be considered as *coming* from him in a peculiar manner; his mind, his good-will is to be observed therein. Hence, care and diligence for the improvement of every motion of his will arise; thence reverence of his presence with us, with due spiritual regard to his holiness, doth ensue, and our souls are wonted to intercourse with him.

3. The third caution concerns him and his *work*, in the dispensation of that great *ordinance of the word*. Stephen tells the Jews, Acts vii. 51, that they "resisted the Holy Ghost." How did they do it? Why, as their fathers did it: "As your fathers did, so do ye." How did their fathers resist the Holy Ghost? Verse 52, "They persecuted the prophets, and slew them;" their opposition to the prophets in preaching the gospel, or their showing of the coming of the Just One, was their resisting of the Holy Ghost. Now, the Holy Ghost is said to be resisted in the contempt of the preaching of the word; because the gift of preaching of it is from him. [1] "The manifestation of the Spirit is given to profit." Hence, when our Saviour

promiseth the Spirit to his disciples, to be present with them for the conviction of the world, he tells them he will give them a mouth and wisdom, which their adversaries shall not be able to gainsay nor resist, Luke xxi. 15; concerning which, in the accomplishment of it in Stephen, it is said that they "were not able to resist the Spirit by which he spake," Acts vi. 10. The Holy Ghost then setting up a ministry in the church, separating men thereto, furnishing them with gifts and abilities for the dispensation of the word; the not obeying of that word, opposing of it, not falling down before it, is called resisting of the Holy Ghost. This, in the examples of the wickedness of others, are we cautioned against. And this inwraps the third general rule of our communion with the Holy Ghost:—in the dispensation of the word of the gospel, the authority, wisdom, and goodness of the Holy Ghost, in furnishing men with gifts for that end and purpose, and his presence with them, as to the virtue thereof, is to be eyed, and subjection given unto it on that account. On this reason, I say, on this ground, is obedience to be yielded to the word, in the *ministerial dispensation thereof,*—because the Holy Ghost, and he alone, doth furnish with gifts to that end and purpose. When this consideration causeth us to fall low before the word, then have we communion with the Holy Ghost in that ordinance. But this is commonly spoken unto.

CHAPTER VIII.

Particular directions for communion with the Holy Ghost.

BEFORE I name particular directions for our communion with the Holy Ghost, I must premise some *cautions,* as far as the *directions* to be given, concerning his worship.

First. The *divine nature* is the reason and cause of all worship; so that it is impossible to *worship any one* person, and not worship the *whole* Trinity. It is, and that not without ground, denied by the schoolmen, that the *formal reason* and object of divine worship is in the persons *precisely* considered; that is, under the formally-constitutive reason of their personality, which is their relation to each other. But this belongs to the divine nature and essence, and to their *distinct* persons as they are *identified* with the essence itself. Hence is that way of praying to the Trinity, by the repetition of the same petition to the several persons (as in the Litany), groundless, if not impious. It supposeth that one person is worshipped, and not another, when each person is worshipped as God, and each person is so;—as though we first should desire one thing of the Father, and be heard and granted by him, then ask the same thing of the Son, and so of the Holy Ghost; and so act as to the same thing three distinct acts of worship, and expect to be heard and have the same thing granted three times distinctly, when all the works of the Trinity, *ad extra*, are indivisible.

The proper and peculiar object of divine worship and invocation is *the essence of God*, in its infinite excellency, dignity, majesty, and its causality, as the first sovereign cause of all things. Now, this is common to all the three persons, and is proper to each of them; not formally as a person, but as God blessed for ever. All adoration respects that which is common to all; so that in each act of adoration and worship, all are adored and worshipped. The creatures worship their Creator; and a man, him in whose image he was created,—namely,·him "from whom descendeth every good and perfect gift:" all this describing God as God. Hence,—

Secondly. When we begin our *prayers* to God the Father, and end them in the name of Jesus Christ, yet the Son is no less invocated and worshipped in the beginning than the Father, though he be peculiarly mentioned as mediator in the close,—not as Son to himself, but as *mediator to the whole Trinity*, or God in Trinity. But in the invocation of God the Father we invocate every person; because we invocate the Father as God, every person being so.

Thirdly. In that *heavenly directory* which we have, Eph. ii. 18, this whole business is declared. Our access in our worship is said to be "to the Father;" and this "through Christ," or his mediation; "by the Spirit," or his assistance. Here is a distinction of the persons, as to their operations, but not at all as to their being the object of our worship. For the Son and the Holy Ghost are no less worshipped in our access to God than the Father himself; only, the grace of the Father, which we obtain by the mediation of the Son and the assistance of the Spirit, is that which we draw nigh to God for. So that when, by the distinct dispensation of the Trinity, and every person, we are led to worship (that is, to act faith on or invocate) any person, we do herein worship the whole Trinity; and every person, by what name soever, of Father, Son, or Holy Ghost, we invocate him. So that this is to be observed in this whole matter,—that when any work of the Holy Ghost (or any other person), which is appropriated to him (we never exclude the concurrence of other persons), draws us to the worship of him, yet he is not worshipped exclusively, but the whole Godhead is worshipped.

Fourthly. These cautions being premised, I say that we are *distinctly to worship* the Holy Ghost. As it is in the case of faith in respect of the Father and the Son, John xiv. 1, "Believe in God, believe also in me,"—this extends itself no less to the Holy Ghost. Christ called the disciples for the acting of faith on him, he being upon the accomplishment of the great work of his mediation; and the Holy Ghost, now carrying on the work of his delegation, requireth the same. And to the same purpose are their distinct operations mentioned: " My Father worketh hitherto, and I work." Now, as the formal reason of the worship of the Son is not his mediation, but his being God (his mediation being a powerful motive thereto), so *the formal reason* of our worshipping the Holy Ghost is not his *being our comforter*, but his *being God;* yet his being our comforter is a powerful motive thereunto.

This is the sum of the first direction:—the grace, actings, love, effects of the Holy Ghost, as he is our comforter, ought to stir us up and provoke us to love, worship, believe in, and invocate him;—though all this, being directed to him as God, is no less directed, on that account, to the other persons than to him. Only by the fruits of his love towards us are we stirred up unto it.

These things being presupposed, let the saints learn to act faith distinctly on the Holy Ghost, as the immediate efficient cause of all the good things mentioned;—faith, I say, to believe in him; and faith in all things to believe him and to yield obedience to him; faith, not imagination. The distinction of the persons in the Trinity is not to be fancied, but believed. So, then, the Scripture so fully, frequently, clearly, distinctly ascribing the things we have been speaking of to the immediate efficiency of the Holy Ghost, faith closeth with him in the truth revealed, and peculiarly regards him, worships him, serves him, waits for him, prayeth to him, praiseth him;—all these things, I say, the saints do in faith. The person of the Holy Ghost, revealing itself in these operations and effects, is the peculiar object of our worship. Therefore, when he ought to be peculiarly honoured, and is not, he is peculiarly sinned against. Acts v. 3, Ananias is said to lie to the Holy Ghost,—not to God; which being taken essentially, would denote the whole Trinity, but peculiarly to the Holy Ghost. Him he was to have honoured peculiarly in that especial gift of his which he made profession of;—not doing it, he sinned peculiarly against him. But this must be a little farther branched into particulars :—

Let us, then, lay weight on every effect of the Holy Ghost in any of the particulars before mentioned, on this account, that they are acts of his love and power towards us. This faith will do, that takes notice of his *kindness in all things.* Frequently he performs, in sundry particulars, the office of a comforter towards us, and we are not thoroughly comforted,—we take no notice at all of what he doth. Then is he grieved. Of those who do receive and own the consolation he tenders and administers, how few are there that consider him as the Comforter, and rejoice in him as they ought! Upon every work of consolation that the believer receives, this ought his faith to resolve upon,—" This is from the Holy Ghost; he is the Comforter, the God of all consolation; I know there is no joy, peace, hope, nor comfort, but what he works, gives, and bestows; and, that he might give me this consolation, he hath willingly condescended to this office of a comforter. His love was in it, and on that account doth he continue it. Also, he is sent by the Father and Son for that end and purpose. By this means come I to be partaker of my joy,—it is in the Holy Ghost; of consolation,—he is the Comforter. What price, now, shall I set upon his love! how shall I value the mercy that I have received!"

This, I say, is applicable to every particular effect of the Holy Ghost towards us; and herein have we communion and fellowship with him, as was in part discovered in our handling the particulars. Doth he shed abroad the love of God in our hearts? doth he witness unto our adoption? The soul considers his presence, ponders his love, his condescension, goodness, and kindness; is filled with reverence of him, and cares [takes care] not to grieve him, and labours to preserve his temple, his habitation, pure and holy.

Again: our communion with him causeth in us *returning praise*, and thanks, and honour, and glory, and blessing to him, on the account of the mercies and privileges which we receive from him; which are many. Herein consists our next direction. So do we with the Son of God on the account of our redemption: " Unto him that loved us, and washed us from our sins in his own blood, to him be glory and dominion for ever and ever," Rev. i. 5, 6. And are not the like praises and blessings due to him by whom the work of redemption is made effectual to us? who with no less infinite love undertook our consolation than the Son our redemption. When we feel our hearts warmed with joy, supported in peace, established in our obedience, let us ascribe to him the praise that is due to him, bless his name, and rejoice in him.

And this glorifying of the Holy Ghost in thanksgivings, *on a spiritual sense* of his consolations, is no small part of our communion with him. Considering his free engagement in this work, his coming forth from the Father to this purpose, his mission by the Son, and condescension therein, his love and kindness, the soul of a believer is poured out in thankful praises to him, and is sweetly affected with the duty. There is no duty that leaves a more heavenly savour in the soul than this doth.

Also, in our prayers to him for the carrying on the work of our consolation, which he hath undertaken, lies our communion with him. John prays for grace and peace from the *seven Spirits* that are before the throne, or the Holy Ghost, whose operations are perfect and complete. This part of his worship is expressly mentioned frequently in Scripture; and all others do necessarily attend it. Let the saints consider what need they stand in of these effects of the Holy Ghost before mentioned, with many such others as might be insisted on; weigh all the privileges which we are made partakers of; remember that he distributes them as he will, that he hath the sovereign disposal of them; and they will be prepared for this duty.

How and in what sense it is to be performed hath been already declared: what is the *formal* reason of this worship, and *ultimate* object of it, I have also manifested. In the duty itself is put forth no small part of the life, efficacy, and vigour of faith; and we come short of that enlargedness of spirit in dealing with God, and are straitened from walking in the breadth of his ways, which we are called unto, if we learn not ourselves to meet him with his worship in every way he is pleased to communicate himself unto us. In these things he does so in the person of the Holy Ghost. In that person do we meet him, his love, grace, and authority, by our prayers and supplications.

Again : consider him as he *condescends to this delegation* of the Father and the Son to be our comforter, and ask him daily of the Father in the name of Jesus Christ. This is the daily work of believers. They look upon, and by faith consider, the Holy Ghost as promised to be sent. In this promise, they know, lies all their grace, peace, mercy, joy, and hope. For by him so promised, and him alone, are these things communicated to them. If, therefore, our life to God, or the joy of that life, be considerable, in this we are to abound,— to ask him of the Father, as children do of their parents daily bread. And as, in this asking and receiving of the Holy Ghost, we have communion with the Father in his love, whence he is sent; and with the Son in his grace, whereby he is obtained for us; so with himself, on the account of his voluntary condescension to this dispensation.. Every request for the Holy Ghost implies our closing with all these. O the riches of the grace of God!

Humbling ourselves for our miscarriages in reference to him is another part of our communion with him. That we have *grieved* him as to his person, *quenched* him as to the motion of his grace, or *resisted* him in his ordinances, is to be mourned for; as hath been declared. Let our souls be humbled before him on this account. This one considerable ingredient of godly sorrow, and the thoughts of it, are as suitable to the affecting of our hearts with humiliation, and indignation against sin, as any other whatever. I might proceed in the like considerations; as also make application of them to the particular effects of the Holy Ghost enumerated; but my design is only to point out the heads of things, and to leave them to the improvement of others.

I shall shut up this whole discourse with some considerations of the sad estate and condition of men not interested in this promise of the Spirit, nor made partakers of his consolation :—

1. They have no *true consolation* or comfort, be their estate and condition what it will. Are they under affliction or in trouble?— they must bear their own burden; and how much too weak they are for it, if God be pleased to lay on his hand with more weight than ordinary, is easily known. Men may have stoutness of spirit, and put on great resolutions to wrestle with their troubles; but when this is merely from the natural spirit of a man,—

(1.) For the most part it is but an outside. It is done with respect to others, that they may not appear low-spirited or dejected. Their hearts are eaten up and devoured with troubles and anxiety of mind. Their thoughts are perplexed, and they are still striving, but never come to a conquest. Every new trouble, every little alteration in their trials, puts them to new vexation. It is an ungrounded resolution that bears them up, and they are easily shaken.

(2.) What is the best of their resolves and enduring? .It is but a contending with God, who hath entangled them,—the struggling of a flea under a mountain. Yea, though, on outward considerations and principles, they endeavour after patience and tolerance, yet all is but a contending with God,—a striving to be quiet under that which God hath sent on purpose to disturb them. God doth not afflict men without the Spirit, to exercise their patience; but to disturb their peace and security. All their arming themselves with patience and resolution, is but to keep the hold that God will cast them out of, or else make them the nearer to ruin. This is the best of their consolation in the time of their trouble.

(3.) If they do promise themselves any thing of the care of God towards them, and relieve themselves thereby,—as they often do, on one account or another, especially when they are driven from other holds,—all their relief is but like the dreaming of an hungry man, who supposeth that he eateth and drinketh, and is refreshed; but when he awaketh, he is empty and disappointed. So are they as to all their relief that they promise to receive from God, and the support which they seem to have from him. When they are awaked at the latter day, and see all things clearly, they will find that God was their enemy, laughing at their calamity, and mocking when their fear was on them.

So is it with them in trouble. Is it any better with them in their prosperity? This, indeed, is often great, and is marvellously described in Scripture, as to their lives, and oftentimes quiet, peaceable ends. But have they any true consolation all their days? They eat, drink, sleep, and make merry, and perhaps heap up to themselves; but how little do these things make them to differ from the beasts that perish! Solomon's advantage, to have the use and know the utmost of these things, much beyond any of the sons of men of our generation, is commonly taken notice of. The account also that he gives of them is known: "They are all vanity and vexation of spirit." This is their consolation:—a crackling of thorns under the pot, a sudden flash and blaze, that begins but to perish. So that both adversity and prosperity slayeth them; and whether they are laughing or crying, they are still dying.

2. They have *no peace*,—no peace with God, nor in their own souls. I know that many of them, upon false bottoms, grounds, and expectations, do make a shift to keep things in some quietness, neither is it my business at present to discover the falseness and unsoundness of it; but this is their state. True and solid peace being an effect of the Holy Ghost in the hearts of believers (as hath been declared), they who are not made partakers of him have no such peace. They may cry, "Peace, peace," indeed, when sudden destruction is at hand. The *principles* of their peace (as may be easily evinced) are, darkness or ignorance, treachery of conscience, self-righteousness, and vain hope. To these heads may all the principles of their peace be reduced; and what will these avail them in the day when the Lord shall deal with them?

3. I might say the same concerning their *joy* and *hope;*—they are false and perishing. Let them, then, consider this, who have satisfied themselves with a persuasion of their interest in the good things of the gospel, and yet have despised the Spirit of Christ. I know there are many that may pretend to him, and yet are strangers from his grace; but if they perish who in profession use him kindly, and honour him, if he dwell not in them with power, where shall they appear who oppose and affront him? The Scripture tells us, that unless the Spirit of Christ be in us, we are dead, we are reprobates, —we are none of Christ's. Without him you can have none of those *glorious effects* of his towards believers before mentioned; and you are so far from inquiring whether he be in you or no, as that you are ready to deride them in whom he is. Are there none who profess the gospel, who have never once seriously inquired whether they are made partakers of the Holy Ghost or no? You that almost account it a ridiculous thing to be put upon any such question, who look on all men as vain pretenders that talk of the Spirit, the Lord awake such men to a sight of their condition before it be too late! If the Spirit dwell not in you, if he be not your Comforter, neither is God your Father, nor the Son your Advocate, nor have you any portion in the gospel. O that God would awake some poor soul to the consideration of this thing, before the neglect and contempt of the Holy Ghost come to that despising of him from which there is no recovery! —that the Lord would spread before them all the folly of their hearts, that they may be *ashamed* and confounded, and do no more presumptuously!

A

VINDICATION

OF

SOME PASSAGES IN A DISCOURSE CONCERNING

COMMUNION WITH GOD,

FROM

THE EXCEPTIONS OF WILLIAM SHERLOCK,

RECTOR OF ST GEORGE, BOTOLPH LANE.

PREFATORY NOTE.

WILLIAM SHERLOCK, father of Dr Thomas Sherlock, an eminent bishop of London, was himself distinguished as an author, and mingled deeply in the controversies of his day. His strictures on Owen's work on Communion with God appeared in 1674, after that work had been seventeen years before the public. It seems to have been Sherlock's first appearance in authorship; and some of his subsequent treatises, such as those on Providence and on Death, afford a better specimen of his abilities. They are destitute of evangelical principle and feeling, and imbued throughout with a freezing rationalism of tone; but, nevertheless, contain some views of the Divine administration, acutely conceived and ably stated. He became rector of St George, Botolph Lane, received a prebend in St Paul's, and was appointed Master of the Temple about 1684. His conduct at the Revolution was not straightforward, and laid him open to the reproaches of the Jacobites, who blamed him for deserting their party. There was a controversy of some importance between him and Dr South. The latter, on the ground of some expressions in the work by the former on the Trinity (1690), accused him of *Tritheism.* Sherlock retorted by accusing his critic of *Sabellianism.* He died in 1707, at the age of sixty-six.

Sherlock's work against Owen was entitled, " A Discourse concerning the Knowledge of Jesus Christ, and on Union and Communion with Him," etc. Owen confines himself, in his reply, to an exposure of the misrepresentations in which Sherlock had indulged. The latter, for example, sought to fix on the Puritan divine the doctrine, that the knowledge of divine things was to be obtained from the person of Christ, apart from the truth as revealed in the Scriptures. Our author successfully vindicates himself from this charge, and repudiates other sentiments equally mystical, and ascribed to him with equal injustice. The views of Sherlock, on the points at issue, have been termed, " a confused mass of Socinianized Arminianism." Owen evinces a strength of feeling, in some parts of his " Vindication," which may be accounted for on the ground that he resented the attack as part of a systematic effort made at this time to destroy his standing and reputation as an author. In the main, there is a dignity in his statements which contrasts well with the wayward petulance of his antagonist; and occasionally the reader will find a vein of quiet and skilful irony, in the way in which he disposes of the crude views of Sherlock.

Such was the beginning of the Communion Controversy, which soon embraced a wider range of topics, and points of more importance, than the merits of Owen's book. Besides the original disputants, others entered the field. Robert Ferguson, in 1675, wrote against Sherlock a volume entitled, " The Interest of Reason in Religion," etc. Edward Polhill followed, in " An Answer to the Discourse of Mr William Sherlock," etc. Vincent Alsop first displayed in this controversy his powers of wit and acumen as an author, in his " Antisozzo, or Sherlocismus Enervatus." Henry Hickman, a man of considerable gifts, and pastor of an English congregation at Leyden, wrote the " Speculum Sherlockianum," etc. Samuel Rollè, a nonconformist, wrote the " Prodromus, or the Character of Mr Sherlock's Book;" and also, in the same controversy, " Justification Justified." Thomas Danson, who had been ejected from Sibton, and author of several works against the Quakers, wrote " The Friendly Debate between Satan and Sherlock," and afterwards he published again in defence of it. Sherlock, in 1675, replied to Owen and Ferguson in his " Defence and Continuation of the Discourse concerning the Knowledge of Jesus Christ." He was supported by Thomas Hotchkis, Rector of Staunton, in a " Discourse concerning the Imputation of Christ's Righteousness," etc. The singular diligence of Mr Orme has compiled this full list of the works published in this controversy; but he is not quite correct in affirming that it was closed by the replies of Sherlock and Hotchkis in 1675. A second part of the work by Hotchkis appeared in 1678; and Sherlock was the author of two other works, " An Answer to Thomas Danson's scandalous pamphlet, entitled ' A Friendly Conference,'" etc., which appeared in 1677, and was followed by a " Vindication of Mr Sherlock against the Cavils of Mr Danson."—ED.

A VINDICATION

OF

SOME PASSAGES IN A DISCOURSE CONCERNING
COMMUNION WITH GOD.

It is now near twenty years since I wrote and published a Discourse concerning Communion with God. Of what use and advantage it hath been to any, as to their furtherance in the design aimed at therein, is left unto them to judge by whom it hath been perused with any candid diligence; and I do know that multitudes of persons fearing God, and desiring to walk before him in sincerity, are ready, if occasion require, to give testimony unto the benefit which they have received thereby;—as I can also at any time produce the testimonies of [as] learned and holy persons, it may be, as any I know living, both in England and out of it, who, owning the truth contained in it, have highly avowed its usefulness, and are ready yet so to do. With all other persons, so far as ever I heard, it passed at the rate of a tolerable acceptation with discourses of the same kind and nature. And however any thing or passage in it might not, possibly, suit the apprehensions of some, yet, being wholly practical, designed for popular edification, without any direct engagement into things controversial, I looked for no opposition unto it or exception against it; but that it would at least be suffered to pass at that rate of allowance which is universally granted unto that sort of writings, both of ancient and modern authors. Accordingly it so fell out, and continued for many years; until some persons began to judge it their interest, and to make it their business, to cavil at my writings, and to load my person with reproaches. With what little success, as to their avowed designs, they have laboured therein,—how openly their endeavours are sunk into contempt with all sorts of persons pretending unto the least sobriety or modesty,—I suppose they are not themselves altogether insensible. Among the things which this sort of men sought to make an advantage of against me, I found that two or three of them began to reflect on that discourse; though it appeared they had not satisfied themselves what as yet to fix upon, their nibbling cavils being exceedingly ridiculous.

But yet, from those intimations of some men's good-will towards it,—sufficient to provoke the industry of such as either needed their assistance or valued their favour,—I was in expectation that one or other would possess that province, and attempt the whole discourse or some parts of it. Nor was I dissatisfied in my apprehensions of that design; for, being earnestly solicited to suffer it to be reprinted, I was very willing to see what either could or would be objected against it before it received another impression. For whereas it was written now near twenty years ago, when there was the deepest peace in the minds of all men about the things treated of therein, and when I had no apprehension of any dissent from the principal design, scope, and parts of it by any called Christians in the world, the Socinians only excepted (whom I had therein no regard unto), I thought it highly probable that some things might have been so expressed as to render a review and amendment to them more than ordinarily necessary. And I reckoned it not improbable, but that from one malevolent adversary I might receive a more instructive information of such escapes of diligence than I could do in so long a time from all the more impartial readers of it; for as unto the substance of the doctrine declared in it, I was sufficiently secure, not only of its truth, but that it would immovably endure the rudest assaults of such oppositions as I did expect. I was therefore very well satisfied when I heard of the publishing of this treatise of Mr Sherlock's,—which, as I was informed, and since have found true, was principally intended against myself, and that discourse (that is, that book), because I was the author of it, which will at last prove it to be its only guilt and crime;—for I thought I should be at once now satisfied, both what it was which was so long contriving against it (whereof I could give no conjecture), as also be directed unto any such mistakes as might have befallen me in matter or manner of expression, which I would or might rectify before the book received another edition. But, upon a view and perusal of this discourse, I found myself under a double surprisal. For, first, in reference to my own, I could not find any thing, any doctrine, any expressions, any words reflected on, which the exceptions of this man do give me the least occasion to alter, or to desire that they had been otherwise either expressed or delivered;—not any thing which now, after near twenty years, I do not still equally approve of, and which I am not yet ready to justify. The other part of my surprisal was somewhat particular, though, in truth, it ought to have been none at all; and this was with respect unto those doctrinal principles which he manageth his oppositions upon. A surprisal they were unto me, because wild, uncouth, extravagant, and contrary to the common faith of Christians,—being all of them traduced,[1] and some of them transcribed, from the writings of the Socinians; [while] yet [they] ought not to have been so, because I was assured that an opposition unto that discourse could be managed on no other [ground]. But, however, the doctrine maintained by this man, and those opposed or scorned by him, are not my special concernment; for what is it to me what the Rector of etc., preacheth or publisheth, beyond my common interest in the truths of the gospel, with other men as great strangers unto him as myself, who to my knowledge never saw him, nor heard of his name till infamed by his book? Only, I shall take leave to say, that the doctrine here published, and licensed so to be, is either the doctrine of the present church of England, or it is not. If it be so, I shall be forced to declare that I neither have, nor will have, any communion therein; and that, as for other reasons, so in particular, because I will not renounce or depart from that which I know to be the true, ancient, and catholic doctrine of this church. If it be not so,—as I am assured, with respect unto many bishops and other learned men, that it is not,—it is certainly the concernment of them who preside therein to take care that such kind of discourses be not countenanced with the stamp of their public authority, lest they and the church be represented unto a great disadvantage with many.

It was some months after the publishing of this discourse, before I entertained any thoughts of taking the least notice of it,—yea, I was resolved to the contrary, and declared those resolutions as I had occasion; neither was it until very lately that my second thoughts came to a compliance with the desires of some others, to consider my own peculiar concernment therein. And this is all which I now design; for the examination of the opinions which this author hath vented under the countenance of public licence, whatever they may think, I know to be more the concernment of other men than mine. Nor yet do I enter into the consideration of what is written by this author with the least respect unto myself, or my own reputation, which I have the satisfaction to conceive not to be prejudiced by such pitiful attempts; nor have I the least desire to preserve it in the minds of such persons as wherein it can suffer on this occasion. But the vindication of some sacred truths, petulantly traduced by this author, seems to be cast on me in an especial manner; because he hath opposed them, and endeavoured to expose them to scorn, as declared in my book; whence others, more meet for this work, might think themselves discharged from taking notice of them. Setting aside this consideration, I can freely give this sort of men leave to go on with their revilings and scoffings until they are weary or ashamed;

[1] [Brought over, borrowed.]

which, as far as I can discern, upon consideration of their ability for
such a work, and their confidence therein, is not like to be in haste;—
at least, they can change their course, and when they are out of breath
in pursuit of one sort of calumnies, betake themselves unto another.
Witness the late malicious, and yet withal ridiculous, reports that
they have divulged concerning me, even with respect unto civil affairs,
and their industry therein; for although they were such as had not
any thing of the least probability or likelihood to give them countenance, yet were they so impetuously divulged, and so readily entertained by many, as made me think there was more than the common
artifices of calumny employed in their raising and improvement,
especially considering what persons I can justly charge those reports
upon.   But in this course they may proceed whilst they please and
think convenient: I find myself no more concerned in what they
write or say of this nature than if it were no more but,—

$$—\text{ἐπεὶ ἤτε κακῷ οὔτ' ἄφρονι φωτὶ ἔοικας.}^{1}$$
$$\text{Οὐλέ τε, καὶ μέγα χαῖρε, Θεοὶ δέ τοι ὄλᾶια δοῖεν.}^{2}$$

It is the doctrine traduced only that I am concerned about, and that
as it hath been the doctrine of the church of England.

It may be it will be said (for there is no security against confidence
and immodesty, backed with secular advantages), that the doctrinal
principles asserted in this book are agreeable with the doctrine of the
church in former times; and therefore those opposed in it, such as
are condemned thereby.   Hereabout I shall make no long contest
with them who once discover that their minds are by any means
emboldened to undertake the defence of such shameless untruths;
nor shall I multiply testimonies to prove the contrary, which others
are more concerned to do, if they intend not to betray the religion
of that church with whose preservation and defence they are intrusted.
Only, because there are ancient divines of this church, who, I am
persuaded, will be allowed with the most to have known as well the
doctrine of it, and as firmly to have adhered thereunto, as this author,
who have particularly spoken unto most of the things which he hath
opposed, or rather reproached, I shall transcribe the words of one of
them, whereby he, and those who employ him, may be minded with
whom they have to do in those things.   For, as to the writers of the
ancient church, there is herein no regard had unto them.   He whom
I shall name is Mr. Hooker, and that in his famous book of " Ecclesiastical Polity;" who, in the fifth book thereof, and 56th paragraph,
thus discourseth:—

    "We have hitherto spoken of the person and of the presence of
Christ.   Participation is that mutual inward hold which Christ hath
of us, and we of him, in such sort that each possesseth other by way

---

[1] Od. ζ. 187.   [2] Od. ω. 401.

of special interest, property, and inherent copulation." And after the interposition of some things concerning the mutual in-being and love of the Father and the Son, he thus proceedeth:—" We are by nature the sons of Adam. When God created Adam, he created us; and as many as are descended from Adam have in themselves the root out of which they spring. The sons of God we neither are all nor any one of us, otherwise than only by grace and favour. The sons of God have God's own natural Son as a second Adam from heaven; whose race and progeny they are by spiritual and heavenly birth. God therefore loving eternally his Son, he must needs eternally in him have loved, and preferred before all others, them which are spiritually since descended and sprung out of him. These were in God as in their Saviour, and not as in their Creator only. It was the purpose of his saving goodness, his saving wisdom, and his saving power, which inclined itself towards them. They which thus were in God eternally by their intended admission to life, have, by vocation or adoption, God actually now in them, as the artificer is in the work which his hand doth presently frame. Life, as all other gifts and benefits, groweth originally from the Father, and cometh not to us but by the Son, nor by the Son to any of us in particular, but through the Spirit. For this cause the apostle wisheth to the church of Corinth, ' the grace of our Lord Jesus Christ, and the love of God, and the fellowship of the Holy Ghost;' which three St Peter comprehendeth in one,—*the participation of the divine nature.* We are, therefore, in God through Christ eternally, according to that intent and purpose whereby we are chosen to be made his in this present world before the world itself was made. We are in God through the knowledge which is had of us, and the love which is borne towards us from everlasting; but in God we actually are no longer than only from the time of our actual adoption into the body of his true church, —into the fellowship of his children. For his church he knoweth and loveth; so that they which are in the church are thereby known to be in him. Our being in Christ by eternal foreknowledge saveth us not, without our actual and real adoption into the fellowship of his saints in this present world. For in him we actually are by our actual incorporation into that society which hath him for their head, and doth make together with him one body (he and they in that respect having one name); for which cause, by virtue of this mystical conjunction, we are of him, and in him, even as though our very flesh and bones should be made continuate with his. We are in Christ, because he knoweth and loveth us, even as parts of himself. No man is actually in him but they in whom he actually is; for he which hath not the Son of God hath not life. 'I am the vine, ye are the branches: he that abideth in me, and I in him, the same bringeth forth much fruit;' but the branch severed from the vine withereth. We are, therefore, adopted sons of God to eternal life by participation of the only begotten Son of God, whose life is the well-spring and cause of ours. It is too cold an interpretation, whereby some men expound our being· in Christ to import nothing else but only that the self-same nature which maketh us to be men is in him, and maketh him man as we are. For what man in the world is there which hath not so far forth communion with Jesus Christ? It is not this that can sustain the weight of such sentences as speak of the mystery of our coherence with Jesus Christ. The church is in Christ, as Eve was in Adam. Yea, by grace we are every [one] of us in Christ and in his church, as by nature we were in those, our first parents. God made Eve of the rib of Adam; and his church he frameth out of the very flesh, the very wounded and bleeding side, of the Son of man. His body crucified, and his blood shed for the life of the world, are the true elements of that heavenly being which maketh us such as himself is of whom we come. For which cause the words of Adam may be fitly the words of Christ concerning his church, ' Flesh of my flesh, and bone of my bones;'—'A true nature, extract out of mine own body.' So that in him, even according to his manhood, we, according to our heavenly being, are as branches in that root out of which they grow. To all things he is life, and to men light, as the Son of God; to the church, both life and light eternal, by being made the Son of man for us, and by being in us a Saviour, whether we respect him as God or as man. Adam is in us as an original cause of our nature, and of that corruption of nature which causeth death; Christ as the cause original of restoration to life. The person of Adam is not in us, but his nature, and the corruption of his nature, derived into all men by propagation. Christ having Adam's nature, as we have, but incorrupt, deriveth not nature but incorruption, and that immediately from his own person, into all that belong unto him. As, therefore, we are really partakers of the body of sin and death received from Adam; so, except we be truly partakers of Christ, and as really possessed of his Spirit, all we speak of eternal life is but a dream. That which quickeneth us is the Spirit of the second Adam, and his flesh that wherewith he quickeneth. That which in him made our nature uncorrupt was the union of his Deity with our nature. And in that respect the sentence of death and condemnation, which only taketh hold upon sinful flesh, could no way possibly extend unto him. This caused his voluntary death for others to prevail with God, and to have the force of an expiatory sacrifice. The blood of Christ, as the apostle witnesseth, doth, therefore, take away sin; because, ' Through the eternal Spirit he offered himself unto God without spot.' That which sanctified our nature in Christ,

—that which made it a sacrifice available to take away sin, is the same which quickened it, raised it out of the grave after death, and exalted it unto glory. Seeing, therefore, that Christ is in us a quickening Spirit, the first degree of communion with Christ must needs consist in the participation of his Spirit, which Cyprian in that respect termeth 'germanissimam societatem,'—the highest and truest society that can be between man and him, which is both God and man in one. These things St Cyril duly considering, reproveth their speeches which taught that only the Deity of Christ is the vine whereupon we by faith do depend as branches, and that neither his flesh nor our bodies are comprised in this resemblance. For doth any man doubt but that even from the flesh of Christ our very bodies do receive that life which shall make them glorious at the latter day; and for which they are already accounted parts of his blessed body? Our corruptible bodies could never live the life they shall live, were it not that here they are joined with his body, which is incorruptible; and that his is in ours as a cause of immortality,—a cause, by removing, through the death and merit of his own flesh, that which hindered the life of ours. Christ is, therefore, both as God and as man, that true vine whereof we both spiritually and corporally are branches. The mixture of his bodily substance with ours is a thing which the ancient fathers disclaim. Yet the mixture of his flesh with ours they speak of, to signify what our very bodies, through mystical conjunction, receive from that vital efficacy which we know to be in his; and from bodily mixtures they borrow divers similitudes, rather to declare the truth than the manner of coherence between his sacred [body] and the sanctified bodies of saints. Thus much no Christian man will deny, that when Christ sanctified his own flesh, giving as God, and taking as man, the Holy Ghost, he did not this for himself only, but for our sakes, that the grace of sanctification and life, which was first received in him, might pass from him to his whole race, as malediction came from Adam unto all mankind. Howbeit, because the work of his Spirit to those effects is in us prevented by sin and death possessing us before, it is of necessity that as well our present sanctification into newness of life, as the future restoration of our bodies, should presuppose a participation of the grace, efficacy, merit, or virtue of his body and blood;— without which foundation first laid, there is no place for those other operations of the Spirit of Christ to ensue. So that Christ imparteth plainly himself by degrees. It pleaseth him, in mercy, to account himself incomplete and maimed without us. But most assured we are, that we all receive of his fulness, because he is in us as a moving and working cause; from which many blessed effects are really found to ensue, and that in sundry both kinds and degrees, all tend-

ing to eternal happiness. It must be confessed, that of Christ working
as a creator and a governor of the world, by providence all are partakers;—not all partakers of that grace whereby he inhabiteth whom
he saveth. Again: as he dwelleth not by grace in all, so neither
doth he equally work in all them in whom he dwelleth. 'Whence
is it,' saith St Augustine, 'that some be holier than others are, but
because God doth dwell in some more plentifully than in others?'
And because the divine substance of Christ is equally in all, his
human substance equally distant from all, it appeareth that the participation of Christ, wherein there are many degrees and differences,
must needs consist in such effects as, being derived from both natures
of Christ really into us, are made our own: and we, by having them
in us, are truly said to have him from whom they come ; Christ also,
more or less, to inhabit and impart himself, as the graces are fewer
or more, greater or smaller, which really flow into us from Christ.
Christ is whole with the whole church, and whole with every part of
the church, as touching his person, which can no way divide itself, or
be possessed by degrees and portions. But the participation of Christ
importeth, besides the presence of Christ's person, and besides the
mystical copulation thereof with the parts and members of his whole
church, a true actual influence of grace, whereby the life which we
live according to godliness is his; and from him we receive those
perfections wherein our eternal happiness consisteth. Thus we par-
ticipate Christ:—partly by imputation; as when those things which
he did and suffered for us are imputed unto us for righteousness;—
partly by habitual and real infusion; as when grace is inwardly bestowed while we are on earth;—and afterward more fully, both our
souls and bodies made like unto his in glory. The first thing of his
so infused into our hearts in this life is the Spirit of Christ; whereupon, because the rest, of what kind soever, do all both necessarily
depend and infallibly also ensue, therefore the apostles term it sometimes the seed of God, sometimes the pledge of our heavenly inheritance, sometimes the hansel or earnest of that which is to come. From
whence it is that they which belong to the mystical body of our Saviour Christ, and be in number as the stars of heaven,—divided successively, by reason of their mortal condition, into many generations,
—are, notwithstanding, coupled every one to Christ their head, and
all unto every particular person amongst themselves; inasmuch as
the same Spirit which anointed the blessed soul of our Saviour Christ
doth so formalize, unite, and actuate his whole race, as if both he and
they were so many limbs compacted into one body, by being quickened all with one and the same soul. That wherein we are partakers
of Jesus Christ by imputation, agreeth equally unto all that have it;
for it consisteth in such acts and deeds of his as could not have longer

continuance than while they were in doing, nor at that very time belong unto any other but to him from whom they come: and therefore, how men, either then, or before, or since, should be made partakers of them, there can be no way imagined but only by imputation. Again: a deed must either not be imputed to any, but rest altogether in him whose it is; or, if at all it be imputed, they which have it by imputation must have it such as it is,—whole. So that degrees being neither in the personal presence of Christ, nor in the participation of those effects which are ours by imputation only, it resteth that we wholly apply them to the participation of Christ's infused grace; although, even in this kind also, the first beginning of life, the seed of God, the first-fruits of Christ's Spirit, be without latitude. For we have hereby only the being of the sons of God: in which number, how far soever one may seem to excel another, yet touching this, that all are sons, they are all equals; some, happily, better sons than the rest are, but none any more a son than another. Thus, therefore, we see how the Father is in the Son, and the Son in the Father; how they both are in all things, and all things in them: what communion Christ hath with his church; how his church, and every member thereof, is in him by original derivation, and he personally in them, by way of mystical association, wrought through the gift of the Holy Ghost; which they that are his receive from him, and, together with the same, what benefit soever the vital force of his body and blood may yield;—yea, by steps and degrees they receive the complete measure of all such divine grace as doth sanctify and save throughout, till the day of their final exaltation to a state of fellowship in glory with him, whose partakers they are now in those things that tend to glory."

This one testimony ought to be enough unto this sort of men, whilst they are at any consistency with their own reputation; for it is evident that there is nothing concerning personal election, effectual vocation, justification by the imputation of the righteousness of Christ, participation of him, union of believers unto and with his person, derivation of grace from him, etc., which are so reproached by our present author, but they are asserted by this great champion of the church of England, who undoubtedly knew the doctrine which it owned, and in his days approved, and that in such words and expressions, as remote from the sentiments, or at least as unsavoury to the palates, of these men, as any they except against in others.

And what themselves so severely charge on us in point of discipline, that nothing be spoken about it until all is answered that is written by Mr Hooker in its defence, may, I hope, not immodestly be so far returned, as to desire them that in point of doctrine they will grant us truce, until they have moved out of the way what is written to the same purpose by Mr Hooker. Why do not they speak

to him to leave fooling, and to speak sense, as they do to others?
But let these things be as they are; I have no especial concernment
in them, nor shall take any farther notice of them, but only as they
influence the exceptions which this author makes unto some passages
in that book of mine. And in what I shall do herein, I shall take
as little notice as may be of those scurrilous and reproachful expressions, which either his inclination or his circumstances induced
him to make use of. If he be pleased with such a course of procedure, I can only assure him, that as to my concernment, I am not
displeased; and so he is left unto his full liberty for the future.

The first thing he quarrels about, is my asserting the necessity of
acquaintance with the person of Christ; which expression he frequently makes use of afterward in a way of reproach. The use of
the word "acquaintance," in this matter, is warranted by our translation of the Scripture, and that properly, where it is required of us
to acquaint ourselves with God. And that I intended nothing
thereby but the knowledge of Jesus Christ, is evident beyond any
pretence to the contrary to be suggested by the most subtle or inventive malice. The crime, therefore, wherewith I am here charged,
is my assertion that it is necessary that Christians should know Jesus
Christ; which I have afterward increased, by affirming also that they
ought to love him: for by Jesus Christ all the world of Christians
intend the person of Christ; and the most of them, all of them,—the
Socinians only excepted,—by his person, "the Word made flesh," or
the Son of God incarnate, the mediator between God and man. For
because the name Christ is sometimes used metonymically, to conclude thence that Jesus Christ is not Jesus Christ, or that it is not
the person of Christ that is firstly and properly intended by that
name in the gospel, is a lewd and impious imagination; and we may
as well make Christ to be only a light within us, as to be the doctrine
of the gospel without us. This knowledge of Jesus Christ I aver to
be the only fountain of all saving knowledge: which is farther reflected
on by this author; and he adds (no doubt out of respect unto me),
"that he will not envy the glory of this discovery unto its author;"
and therefore honestly confesseth that he met with it in my book.
But what doth he intend? Whither will prejudice and corrupt designs carry and transport the minds of men? Is it possible that he
should be ignorant that it is the duty of all Christians to know Jesus
Christ, to be acquainted with the person of Christ, and that this is
the fountain of all saving knowledge, until he met with it in my book
about communion with God; which I dare say he looked not into,
but only to find what he might except against? It is the Holy
Ghost himself that is the author of this discovery; and it is the great
fundamental principle of the gospel. Wherefore, surely, this cannot

be the man's intention; and therefore we must look a little farther, to see what it is that he aimeth at. After, then, the repetition of some words of mine, he adds, as his sense upon them, p. 39, " So that it seems the gospel of Christ makes a very imperfect and obscure discovery of the nature, attributes, and the will of God, and the methods of our recovery. We may thoroughly understand whatever is revealed in the gospel, and yet not have a clear and saving knowledge of these things, until we get a more intimate acquaintance with the person of Christ." And again, p. 40: " I shall show you what additions these men make to the gospel of Christ by an acquaintance with his person; and I confess I am very much beholden to this author, for acknowledging whence they fetch all their orthodox and gospel mysteries, for I had almost pored my eyes out with seeking for them in the gospel, but could never find them; but I learn now, that indeed they are not to be found there, unless we be first acquainted with the person of Christ." So far as I can gather up the sense of these loose expressions, it is, that I assert a knowledge of the person of Jesus Christ which is not revealed in the gospel, which is not taught us in the writings of Moses, the prophets, or apostles, but must be had some other way. He tells me afterward, p. 41, that I put in a word fallaciously, which expresseth the contrary; as though I intended another knowledge of Christ than what is declared in the gospel. Now, he either thought that this was not my design or intention, but would make use of a pretence of it for his advantage unto an end aimed at (which what it was I know well enough); or he thought, indeed, that I did assert and maintain such a knowledge of the person of Christ as was not received by Scripture revelation. If it was the first, we have an instance of that new morality which these new doctrines are accompanied withal; if the latter, he discovers how meet a person he is to treat of things of this nature. Wherefore, to prevent such scandalous miscarriages, or futilous imaginations for the future, I here tell him, that if he can find in that book, or any other of my writings, any expression, or word, or syllable, intimating any knowledge of. Christ, or any acquaintance with the person of Christ, but what is revealed and declared in the gospel, in the writings of Moses, the prophets, and apostles, and as it is so revealed and declared, and learned from thence, I will publicly burn that book with my own hands, to give him and all the world satisfaction. Nay, I say more: if an angel from heaven pretend to give any other knowledge of the person of Christ, but what is revealed in the gospel, let him be accursed. And here I leave this author to consider with himself, what was the true occasion why he should first thus represent himself unto the world in print, by the avowing of so unworthy and notorious a calumny.

Whereas, therefore, by an acquaintance with the person of Christ, it is undeniably evident that I intended nothing but that knowledge of Christ which it is the duty of every Christian to labour after,—no other but what is revealed, declared, and delivered in the Scripture, as almost every page of my book doth manifest where I treat of these things; I do here again, with the good leave of this author, assert, that this knowledge of Christ is very necessary unto Christians, and the fountain of all saving knowledge whatever. And as he may, if he please, review the honesty and truth of that passage, p. 38, "So that our acquaintance with Christ's person, in this man's divinity, signifies such a knowledge of what Christ is, hath done, and suffered for us, from whence we may learn those greater, deeper, and more saving mysteries of the gospel, which Christ hath not expressly revealed to us;" so I will not so far suspect the Christianity of them with whom we have to do, as to think it necessary to confirm by texts of Scripture either of these assertions; which whoever denies is an open apostate from the gospel.

Having laid this foundation in an equal mixture of that truth and sobriety wherewith sundry late writings of this nature and to the same purpose have been stuffed, he proceeds to declare what desperate consequences ensue upon the necessity of that knowledge of Jesus Christ which I have asserted, addressing himself thereunto, p. 40.

-Many instances of such dealings will make me apt to think that some men, whatever they pretend to the contrary, have but little knowledge of Jesus Christ indeed. But whatever this man thinks of him, an account must one day be given before and unto him of such false calumnies as his lines are stuffed withal. Those who will believe him, that he hath almost "pored out his eyes" in reading the gospel, with a design to find out mysteries that are not in it, are left by me to their liberty; only I cannot but say, that his way of expressing the study of the Scripture, is [not?] such as becometh a man of his wisdom, gravity, and principles. He will, I hope, one day be better acquainted with what belongs unto the due investigation of sacred truth in the Scripture, than to suppose it represented by such childish expressions. What he hath learned from me I know not; but that I have anywhere taught that there are mysteries of religion that are not to be found in the gospel, unless we are first acquainted with the person of Christ, is a frontless and impudent falsehood. I own no other, never taught other knowledge of Christ, or acquaintance with his person, but what is revealed and declared in the gospel; and therefore, no mysteries of religion can be thence known and received, before we are acquainted with the gospel itself. Yet I will mind this author of that, whereof if he be ignorant, he is unfit to be a teacher of others, and which if he deny, he is unworthy the name of a Christian,—namely, that by the knowledge of the person of Christ, the great mystery of God manifest in the flesh, as revealed and declared in the gospel, we are led into a clear and full understanding of many other mysteries of grace and truth; which are all centred in his person, and without which we can have no true nor sound understanding of them. I shall speak it yet again, that this author, if it be possible, may understand it; or, however, that he and his co-partners in design may know that I neither am nor ever will be ashamed of it:—that without the knowledge of the person of Christ, which is our acquaintance with him (as we are commanded to acquaint ourselves with God) as he is the eternal Son of God incarnate, the mediator between God and man, with the mystery of the love, grace, and truth of God therein, as revealed and declared in the Scripture, there is no true, useful, saving knowledge of any other mysteries or truths of the gospel to be attained. This being the substance of what is asserted in my discourse, I challenge this man, or any to whose pleasure and favour his endeavours in this kind are sacrificed, to assert and maintain the contrary, if so be they are indeed armed with such a confidence as to impugn the foundations of Christianity.

But to evince his intention, he transcribeth the ensuing passages out of my discourse:—P. 41, " The sum of all true wisdom and knowledge may be reduced to these three heads:—1. The knowledge of God; his nature and properties. 2. The knowledge of ourselves with reference to the will of God concerning us. 3. Skill to walk in communion with God. In these three is summed up all true wisdom and knowledge, and not any of them is to any purpose to be obtained, or is manifested, but only in and by the Lord Christ."

This whole passage I am far from disliking, upon this representation of it, or any expression in it. Those who are not pleased with this distribution of spiritual wisdom, may make use of any such of their own wherewith they are better satisfied. This of mine was sufficient unto my purpose. Hereon this censure is passed by him:— " Where *by* is fallaciously added to include the revelations Christ hath made; whereas his first undertaking was, to show how impossible it is to understand these things savingly and clearly, notwithstanding all those revelations God hath made of himself and his will by Moses and the prophets, and by Christ himself, without an acquaintance with his person." The fallacy pretended is merely of his own coining; my words are plain, and suited unto my own purpose, and to declare my mind in what I intend; which he openly corrupting, or not at all understanding, frames an end never thought of by me, and then feigns fallacious means of attaining it. The knowledge I mean is to be learned by Christ; neither is any thing to be learned in him but what is learned by him. I do say, indeed, now, whatever I have said

before, that it is impossible to understand any sacred truth savingly
and clearly, without the knowledge of the person of Christ; and shall
say so still, let this man and his companions say what they will to
the contrary: but that in my so saying I exclude the consideration
of the revelations which Christ hath made, or that God hath made
of himself by Moses and the prophets, and Christ himself, the principal whereof concern his person, and whence alone we come to know
him, is an assertion becoming the modesty and ingenuity of this author.
But hereon he proceeds, and says, that as to the first head he will
take notice of those peculiar discoveries of the nature of God of which
the world was ignorant before, and of which revelation is wholly silent,
but are now clearly and savingly learned from an acquaintance with
Christ's person. But what, in the meantime, is become of modesty,
truth, and honesty? Do men reckon that there is no account to be
given of such falsifications? Is there any one word or tittle in my
discourse of any such knowledge of the nature or properties of God
as whereof revelation is wholly silent? What doth this man intend?
Doth he either not at all understand what I say; or doth he not care
what he says himself? What have I done to him? wherein have I
injured him? how have I provoked him, that he should sacrifice his
conscience and reputation unto such a revenge? Must he yet hear
it again? I never thought, I never owned, I never wrote, that there
was any acquaintance to be obtained with any property of the nature
of God by the knowledge of the person of Christ, but what is taught
and revealed in the gospel; from whence alone all knowledge of
Christ, his person, and his doctrine, is to be learned. And yet I
will say again, if we learn not thence to know the Lord Christ,—that
is, his person,—we shall never know any thing of God, ourselves, or
our duty, clearly and savingly (I use the words again, notwithstanding the reflections on them, as more proper in this matter than any
used by our author in his eloquent discourse), and as we ought to do.
From hence he proceeds unto weak and confused discourses about
the knowledge of God and his properties without any knowledge of
Christ; for he not only tells us " what reason we had to believe such
and such things of God, if Christ had never appeared in the world,"
(take care, I pray, that we be thought as little beholden to Him as
may be), " but that God's readiness to pardon, and the like, are plainly
revealed in the Scripture, without any farther acquaintance with the
person of Christ," p. 43. What this farther acquaintance with the
person of Christ should mean, I do not well understand: it may be,
any more acquaintance with respect unto some that is necessary;—
it may be, without any more ado as to an acquaintance with him.
And if this be his intention,—as it must be, if there be sense in his
words,—that God's readiness to pardon sinners is revealed in the Scrip-

ture without respect unto the person of Jesus Christ, it is a piece of dull Socinianism; which, because I have sufficiently confuted elsewhere, I shall not here farther discover the folly of. [As] for a knowledge of God's essential properties by the light of nature, it was never denied by me; yea, I have written and contended for it in another way than can be impeached by such trifling declamations. But yet, with his good leave, I do believe that there is no saving knowledge of, or acquaintance with God or his properties, to be attained, but in and through Jesus Christ, as revealed unto us in the gospel. And this I can confirm with testimonies of the Scripture, fathers, schoolmen, and divines of all sorts, with reasons and arguments, such as I know this author cannot answer. And whatever great apprehensions he may have of his skill and abilities to know God and his properties by the light of nature, now that he neither knows nor is able to distinguish what he learns from thence, and what he hath imbibed in his education from an emanation of divine revelation; yet I believe there were as wise men as himself amongst those ancient philosophers, concerning whom and their inquiries into the nature of God our apostle pronounces those censures, Rom. i.; 1 Cor. i.

But on this goodly foundation he proceeds unto a particular inference, p. 44, saying, " And is not this a confident man, to tell us that the love of God to sinners, and his pardoning mercy, could never have entered into the heart of man but by Christ, when the experience of the whole world confutes him? For, whatever becomes of his new theories, both Jews and heathens, who understood nothing at all of what Christ was to do in order to our recovery, did believe God to be gracious and merciful to sinners, and had reason to do so; because God himself had assured the Jews that he was a gracious and merciful God, pardoning iniquity, transgressions, and sins. And those natural notions heathens had of God, and all those discoveries God had made of himself in the works of creation and providence, did assure them that God is very good: and it is not possible to understand what goodness is, without pardoning grace."

I beg his excuse: truth and good company will give a modest man a little confidence sometimes; and against his experience of the whole world, falsely pretended, I can oppose the testimonies of the Scripture, and all the ancient writers of the church, very few excepted. We can know of God only what he hath, one way or other, revealed of himself, and nothing else; and I say again, that God hath not revealed his love unto sinners, and his pardoning mercy, any other way but in and by Jesus Christ. For what he adds as to the knowledge which the Jews had of these things by God's revelation in the Scripture, when he can prove that all those revelations, or any of them, had not respect unto the promised seed,—the Son of

God,—to be exhibited in the flesh to destroy the works of the devil, he will speak somewhat unto his purpose. In the meantime, this insertion of the consideration of them who enjoyed that revelation of Christ which God was pleased to build his church upon under the Old Testament, is weak and impertinent. Their apprehensions, I acknowledge, concerning the person of Christ, and the speciality of the work of his mediation, were dark and obscure; but so, also, proportionably was their knowledge of all other sacred truths, which yet with all diligence they inquired into. That which I intended is expressed by the apostle, 1 Cor. ii. 9, 10, " It is written, Eye hath not seen, nor ear heard, neither have entered into the heart of man, the things which God hath prepared for them that love him. But God hath revealed them unto us by his Spirit." What a confident man was this apostle, as to affirm that the things of the grace and mercy of God did never enter into the heart of man to conceive, nor would so have done, had they not been revealed'by the Spirit of God in the gospel through Jesus Christ!

But this is only a transient charge. There ensues that which is much more severe, p. 45; as, for instance, "He tells us, ' that in Christ' (that is, in his death and sufferings for our sins) 'God hath manifested the naturalness of this righteousness' (that is, vindictive justice in punishing sin), ' that it was impossible that it should be diverted from sinners without the interposing of a propitiation; that is, that God is so just and righteous, that he cannot pardon sin without satisfaction to his justice.' Now, this indeed is such a notion of justice as is perfectly new, which neither Scripture nor nature acquaints us with; for all mankind have accounted it an act of goodness, without the least suspicion of injustice in it, to remit injuries and offences without exacting any punishment,—that he is so far from being just, that he is cruel and savage, who will remit no offence till he hath satisfied his revenge." The reader who is in any measure or degree acquainted with these things, knows full well what is intended by that which I have asserted. It is no more but this,—that such is the essential holiness and righteousness of the nature of God, that, considering him as the supreme governor and ruler of all mankind, it was inconsistent with the holiness and rectitude of his rule, and the glory of his government, to pass by sin absolutely, or to pardon it without satisfaction, propitiation, or atonement. This, I said, was made evident in the death and sufferings of Christ, wherein God made all our iniquities to meet upon him, and spared him not, that we might obtain mercy and grace. This is here now called out by our author as a very dangerous or foolish passage in my discourse, which he thought he might highly advantage his reputation by reflecting upon. But as the orator said to his adversary, " Equidem vehementer lætor eum esse me, in quem tu cum cuperes, nullam contumeliam jacere potueris, quæ non ad maximam partem civium convenerit,"—so it is here fallen out. If this man knows not that this is the judgment of the generality of the most learned divines of Europe upon the matter, of all who have engaged with any success against the Socinians, one or two only excepted, I can pity him, but not relieve him in his unhappiness, unless he will be pleased to take more pains in reading good books than as yet he appeareth to have done. But for the thing itself, and his reflections upon it, I shall observe yet some few things, and so pass on;—as first, the opposition that he makes unto my position is nothing but a crude assertion of one of the meanest and most absurd sophisms which the Socinians use in this cause,—namely, that every one may remit injuries and offences as he pleaseth, without exacting any punishment: which, as it is true in most cases of injuries and offences against private persons, wherein no others are concerned but themselves, nor are they obliged by any law of the community to pursue their own right; so, with respect unto public rulers of the community, and unto such injuries and offences as are done against supreme rule, tending directly unto the dissolution of the society centring in it, to suppose that such rulers are not obliged to inflict those punishments which justice and the preservation of the community doth require, is a fond and ridiculous imagination,—destructive, if pursued, unto all human society, and rendering government a useless thing in the world. Therefore, what this author (who seems to understand very little of these things) adds, " that governors may spare or punish as they see reason for it;" if the rule of that reason and judgment be not that justice which respects the good and benefit of the society or community, they do amiss, and sin, in sparing and punishing: which I suppose he will not ascribe unto the government of God. But I have fully debated these things in sundry writings against the Socinians; so that I will not again enlarge upon them without a more important occasion. It is not improbable but he knows where to find those discourses; and he may, when he please, exercise his skill upon them. Again: I cannot but remark upon the consequences that he chargeth this position withal; and yet I cannot do it without begging pardon for repeating such horrid and desperate blasphemies. P. 46, " The account," saith he, " of this is very plain; because the justice of God hath glutted itself with revenge on sin in the death of Christ, and so henceforward we may be sure he will be very kind, as a revengeful man is when his passion is over." P. 47, " The sum of which is, that God is all love and patience when he hath taken his fill of revenge; as others use to say that the devil is very good when he is pleased." P. 59, " The justice and vengeance of God, having their actings assigned them to the full, being glutted and satiated with the blood of Christ, God may," etc. I desire the reader to remember that the supposition whereon all these inferences are built, is only that of the necessity of the satisfaction of Christ with respect unto the holiness and righteousness of God as the author of the law, and the supreme governor of mankind. And is this language becoming a son of the church of England? Might it not be more justly expected from a Jew or a Mohammedan,—from Servetus or Socinus, from whom it is borrowed,—than from a son of this church, in a book published by licence and authority? But it is to no purpose to complain: those who are pleased with these things, let them be so. But what if, after all, these impious, blasphemous consequences do follow as much upon this author's opinion as upon mine, and that with a greater show of probability? and what if, forgetting himself, within a few leaves he says the very same thing that I do, and casts himself under his own severest condemnation?

For the first: I presume he owns the satisfaction of Christ, and I will suppose it until he directly denies it; therefore, also, he owns and grants that God would not pardon any sin, but upon a supposition of a previous satisfaction made by Jesus Christ. Here, then, lies all the difference between us;—that I say God could not, with respect unto his holiness and justice, as the author of the law and governor of the world, pardon sin absolutely without satisfaction: he says, that although he might have done so without the least diminution of his glory, yet he would not, but would have his Son by his death and suffering to make satisfaction for sin. I leave it now, not only to every learned and impartial reader, but to every man in his wits who understands common sense, whether the blasphemous consequences, which I will not again defile ink and paper with the expression of, do not seem to follow more directly upon his opinion than mine. For whereas I say not that God requireth any thing unto the exercise of grace and mercy, but what he grants that he doth so also;—only I say he doth it because requisite unto his justice; he, because he chose it by a free act of his will and wisdom, when he might have done otherwise, without the least disadvantage unto his righteousness or rule, or the least impeachment to the glory of his holiness. The odious blasphemies mentioned do apparently seem to make a nearer approach unto his assertion than unto mine. I cannot proceed unto a farther declaration of it, because I abhor the rehearsal of such horrid profaneness. The truth is, they follow not in the least (if there be any thing in them but odious satanical exprobrations of the truth of the satisfaction of Christ) on either opinion; though I say this author knows not well how to discharge himself of them.

But what if he be all this while only roving in his discourse about the things that he hath no due comprehension of, merely out of a transporting desire to gratify himself and others, in traducing and making exceptions against my writings? What if, when he comes a little to himself, and expresseth the notions that have been instilled into him, he saith expressly as much as I do, or have done in any place of my writings? It is plain he does so, p. 49, in these words: —" As for sin, the gospel assures us that God is an irreconcilable enemy to all wickedness, it being so contrary to his own most holy nature, that if he have any love for himself, and any esteem for his own perfections and works, he must hate sin, which is so unlike himself, and which destroys the beauty and perfection of his workmanship. For this end he sent his Son into the world to destroy the works of the devil," etc. Here is the substance of what at any time on this subject I have pleaded for:—" God is an irreconcilable enemy to all wickedness,"—that it " is contrary to his holy nature, so that he must hate it; and therefore sends his Son," etc. If sin be contrary to God's holy nature,—if he must hate it, unless he will not love himself, nor value his own perfections, and therefore sent his Son to make satisfaction, we are absolutely agreed in this matter, and our author hath lost " operam et oleum" in his attempt. But for the matter itself, if he be able to come unto any consistency in his thoughts, or to know what is his own mind therein, I do hereby acquaint him that I have written one entire discourse[1] on that subject, and have lately reinforced the same argument in my Exercitations on the Epistle to the Hebrews, wherein my judgment on this point is declared and maintained. Let him attempt an answer, if he please, unto them, or do it if he can. What he farther discourseth on this subject, pp. 46, 47, consisteth only in odious representations and vile reflections on the principal doctrines of the gospel, not to be mentioned without offence and horror. But as to me, he proceeds to except, after his scoffing manner, against another passage, pp. 47, 48, —" But, however, sinners have great reasons to rejoice in it, when they consider the nature and end of God's patience and forbearance towards them,—viz., That it is God's taking a course, in his infinite wisdom and goodness, that we should not be destroyed notwithstanding our sins; that as before, the least sin could not escape without punishment, justice being so natural to God that he cannot forgive without punishing; so the justice of God being now satisfied by the death of Christ, the greatest sins can do us no hurt, but we shall escape with a ' notwithstanding our sins.' This, it seems, we learn from an acquaintance with Christ's person, though his gospel instructs us otherwise, that ' without holiness no man shall see God.'" But he is here again at a loss, and understands not what he is about. That

---

[1] Owen, in all probability, alludes to his " Diatriba de Justitiâ Divinâ." See vol. x. of his Works.—Ed.

whereof he was discoursing is the necessity of the satisfaction of Christ, and that must be it which he maketh his inference from; but the passage he insists on, he lays down as expressive of the end of God's patience and forbearance towards sinners, which here is of no place nor consideration. But so it falls out, that he is seldom at any agreement with himself in any parts of his discourse; the reason whereof I do somewhat more than guess at. However, for the passage which he cites out of my discourse, I like it so well, as that I shall not trouble myself to inquire whether it be there or no, or on what occasion it is introduced. The words are,—" That God hath, in his justice, wisdom, and goodness, taken a course that we should not be destroyed, notwithstanding our sins" (that is, to save sinners); " for he that believeth, although he be a sinner, shall be saved; and he that believeth not shall be damned," as one hath assured us, whom I desire to believe and trust unto. If this be not so, what will become of this man and myself, with all our writings? for I know that we are both sinners; and if God will not save us, or deliver us from destruction, notwithstanding our sins,—that is, pardon them through the bloodshedding of Jesus Christ, wherein we have redemption, even the forgiveness of sins,—it had been better for us that we had never been born. And I do yet again say, that God doth not, that he will not, pardon the least sin, without respect unto the satisfaction of Christ, according as the apostle declares, 2 Cor. v. 18–21; and the expression which must be set on the other side, on the supposition whereof the greatest sin can do us no harm, is this man's addition, which his usual respect unto truth hath produced. But, withal, I never said, I never wrote, that the only supposition of the satisfaction of Christ is sufficient of itself to free us from destruction by sin.

There is, moreover, required on our part, faith and repentance; without which we can have no advantage by it, or interest in it. But he seems to understand by that expression, " notwithstanding our sins," though we should live and die in our sins without faith, repentance, or new obedience; for he supposeth it sufficient to manifest the folly of this assertion, to mention that declaration of the mind of Christ in the gospel, that " without holiness no man shall see God." I wonder whether he thinks that those who believe the satisfaction of Christ, and the necessity thereof, wherein God " made him to be sin who knew no sin, that we might be made the righteousness of God in him," do believe that the personal holiness of men is [not] indispensably necessary unto the pleasing and enjoyment of God. If he suppose that the satisfaction of Christ and the necessity of our personal holiness are really inconsistent, he must be treated in another manner: if he suppose that although they are consistent, yet those whom he opposeth do so trust to the satisfaction of Christ, as to judge that faith, repentance, and holiness, are not indispensably necessary to salvation, he manifests how well skilled he is in their principles and practices. I have always looked on it as a piece of the highest disingenuity among the Quakers, that when any one pleads for the satisfaction of Christ or the imputation of his righteousness, they will clamorously cry out, and hear nothing to the contrary, " Yea, you are for the saving of polluted, defiled sinners; let men live in their sins and be all foul within, it is no matter, so long as they have a righteousness and a Christ without them." I have, I say, always looked upon it as a most disingenuous procedure in them, seeing no one is catechised amongst us, who knoweth not that we press a necessity of sanctification and holiness, equal with that of justification and righteousness. And yet this very course is here steered by this author, contrary to the constant declaration of the judgments of them with whom he hath to do,—contrary to the common evidence of their writings, preaching, praying, disputing unto another purpose; and that without relieving or countenancing himself by any one word or expression used or uttered by them. He chargeth [them] as though they made holiness a very indifferent thing, and such as it doth not much concern any man whether he have an interest in or no; and I know not whether is more marvellous unto me, that some men can so far concoct all principles of conscience and modesty as to publish such slanderous untruths, or that others can take contentment and satisfaction therein, who cannot but understand their disingenuity and falsehood.

His proceed in the same page is to except against that revelation of the wisdom of God which I affirm to have been made in the person and sufferings of Christ, which I thought I might have asserted without offence. But this man will have it, that " there is no wisdom therein, if justice be so natural to God, that nothing could satisfy him but the death of his own Son." That any thing else could satisfy divine justice but the sufferings and death of the Son of God, so far as I know, he is the first that found out or discovered, if he hath yet found it out. Some have imagined that God will pardon sin, and doth so, without any satisfaction at all; and some have thought that other ways of the reparation of lost mankind were possible, without this satisfaction of divine justice, which yet God in his wisdom determined on; but that satisfaction could be any otherwise made to divine justice, but by the death of the Son of God incarnate, none have used to say who know what they say in these things. " But wisdom," he saith, " consists in the choice of the best and fittest means to attain an end, when there were more ways than one of doing it; but it requires no great wisdom to choose when there is but one possible way." Yea, this it is to measure God,—things infinite and divine, by our-

selves. Doth this man think that God's ends, as ours, have an existence in themselves out of him, antecedent unto any acts of his divine
wisdom? Doth he imagine that he balanceth probable means for
the attaining of an end, choosing some and rejecting others? Doth
he surmise that the acts of divine wisdom with respect unto the end
and means are so really distinct, as the one to have a priority in time
before the others? Alas, that men should have the confidence to
publish such slight and crude imaginations! Again: the Scripture,
which so often expresseth the incarnation of the Son of God, and the
whole work of his mediation thereon, as the effect of the infinite
wisdom of God,—as that wherein the stores, riches, and treasures of it
are laid forth,—doth nowhere so speak of it in comparison with other
means not so suited unto the same end, but absolutely, and as it is
in its own nature; unless it be when it is compared with those typical
institutions which, being appointed to resemble it, some did rest in.
And lastly, whereas there was but this one way for the redemption
of mankind, and the restoration of the honour of God's justice and
holiness, as he is the supreme lawgiver and governor of the universe;
and whereas this one way was not in the least pervious unto any
created understanding, angelical or human, nor could the least of its
concerns have ever entered into the hearts of any (nor, it may be, shall
they ever know or be able to find it out unto perfection, but it will
be left the object of their admiration unto eternity);—if this author
can see no wisdom, or no great wisdom, in the finding out and ap-
pointing of this way, who can help it? I wish he would more diligently attend unto their teachings who are able to instruct him better;
and from whom, as having no prejudice against them, he may be
willing to learn.

But this is the least part of what this worthy censurer of theological discourses rebukes and corrects. For whereas I had said, that
we " might learn our disability to answer the mind and will of God
in all or any part of the obedience he requireth,"—that is, without
Christ or out of him; he adds, " That is, that it is impossible for us
to do any thing that is good, but we must be acted, like machines,
by an external force,—by the irresistible power of the grace and Spirit
of God. This, I am sure, is a new discovery; we learn no such thing
from the gospel, and I do not see how he proves it from an acquaintance with Christ." But if he intends what he speaks, " we can do
no good, but must be acted, like machines, by an external force," and
chargeth this on me, it is a false accusation, proceeding from malice
or ignorance, or a mixture of both. If he intend, that we can of
ourselves do any thing that is spiritually good and acceptable before
God, without the efficacious work of the Spirit and grace of God in
us, which I only deny, he is a Pelagian, and stands anathematized

by many councils of the ancient church. And [as] for what is my judgment about the impotency that is in us by nature unto any spiritual good,—the necessity of the effectual operation of the Spirit of God in and to our conversion, with his aids and assistances of actual grace in our whole course of obedience, which is no other but that of the ancient church, the most learned fathers, and the church of England itself in former days,—I have now sufficiently declared and confirmed it in another discourse; whither this author is remitted, either to learn to speak honestly of what he opposeth, or to understand it better, or answer it if he can.

He adds, " But still there is a more glorious discovery than this behind; and that is, the glorious end whereunto sin is appointed and ordained (I suppose he means by God) is discovered in Christ,— namely, for the demonstration of God's vindictive justice, in measuring out to it a meet recompense of reward, and for the praise of God's glorious grace in the pardon and forgiveness of it;—that is, that it could not be known how just and severe God is, but by punishing sin, nor how good and gracious God is, but by pardoning of it; and, therefore, lest his justice and mercy should never be known to the world, he appoints and ordains sin to this end,—that is, decrees that men shall sin that he may make some of them the vessels of his wrath, and the examples of his fierce vengeance and displeasure, and others the vessels of his mercy, to the praise and glory of his free grace in Christ. This, indeed, is such a discovery as nature and revelation could not make," p. 51; which, in the next page, he calls God's " truckling and bartering with sin and the devil for his glory."

Although there is nothing in the words here reported as mine which is not capable of a fair defence, seeing it is expressly affirmed that " God set forth his Son to be a propitiation to declare his righteousness," yet I know not how it came to pass that I had a mind to turn unto the passage itself in my discourse, which I had not done before on any occasion, as not supposing that he would falsify my words, with whom it was so easy to pervert my meaning at any time, and to reproach what he could not confute. But, that I may give a specimen of this man's honesty and ingenuity, I shall transcribe the passage which he excepts against, because I confess it gave me some surprisal upon its first perusal. My words are these: " There is a glorious end whereunto sin is appointed and ordained discovered in Christ, that others are unacquainted withal. Sin, in its own nature, tends merely to the dishonour of God, the debasement of his majesty, and the ruin of the creature in whom it is. Hell itself is but the filling of wretched creatures with the fruit of their own devices. The comminations and threats of God in the law do manifest one other end of it,—even the demonstration of the vindictive justice of God in measuring out unto it a meet recompense of reward. But here the law stays, and with it all other light, and discovers no other use or end of it at all. In the Lord Jesus Christ there is the manifestation of another and more glorious end, to wit, the praise of God's glorious grace in the pardon and forgiveness of it;—God having taken order in Christ, that that thing which tended merely to his dishonour should be managed to his infinite glory, and that which of all things he desired to exalt,—even that he may be known and believed to be a God pardoning iniquity, transgression, and sin." Such was my ignorance, that I did not think that any Christian, unless he were a professed Socinian, would ever have made exceptions against any thing in this discourse; the whole of it being openly proclaimed in the gospel, and confirmed in the particulars by sundry texts of Scripture, quoted in the margin of my book, which this man took no notice of. For the advantage he would make from the expression about the end whereunto sin is appointed and ordained, it is childish and ridiculous; for every one who is not wilfully blind must see, that, by " ordained," I intended, not any ordination as to the futurition of sin, but to the disposal of sin to its proper end being committed, or to ordain it unto its end upon a supposition of its being; which quite spoils this author's ensuing harangue. But my judgment in this matter is better expressed by another than I am able to do it myself, and, therefore, in his words I shall represent it. It is Augustine: saith he, " Saluberrime confitemur quod rectissime credimus, Deum Dominumque rerum omnium qui creavit omnia bona valde, et mala ex bonis exortura esse præscivit, et scivit magis ad suam omnipotentissimam bonitatem pertinere, etiam de malis benefacere, quam mala esse non sinere; sic ordinasse angelorum et hominum vitam, ut in ea prius ostenderet quid posset eorum liberum arbitrium, deinde quid posset suæ gratiæ beneficium, justitiæque judicium."

This, our author would have to be God's " bartering with sin and the devil for his glory;" the bold impiety of which expression, among many others, for whose necessary repetition I crave pardon, manifests with what frame of spirit, with what reverence of God himself and all holy things, this discourse is managed.

But it seems I add, that "the demonstration of God's justice in measuring out unto sin a meet recompense of reward is discovered in Christ, as this author says." Let him read again, "The comminations and threatenings of God in the law," etc. If this man were acquainted with Christ, he could not but learn somewhat more of truth and modesty, unless he be wilfully stupid. But what is the crime of this paragraph? That which it teacheth is, that sin, in its own nature, hath no end but the dishonour of God and the eternal ruin of the sinner; that, by the sentence and curse of the law, God hath manifested that he will glorify his justice in the punishing of it; as also, that, in and through Jesus Christ, he will glorify grace and mercy in its pardon, on the terms of the gospel. What would he be at? If he have a mind to quarrel with the Bible, and to conflict the fundamental principles of Christianity, to what purpose doth he cavil at my obscure discourses, when the proper object of his displeasure lies plainly before him?

Let us proceed yet a little farther with our author, although I confess myself to be already utterly wearied with the perusal of such vain and frivolous imaginations. Yet thus he goes on, p. 53, "Thus much for the knowledge of ourselves with respect to sin, which is hid only in the Lord Christ. But then we learn what our righteousness is, wherewith we must appear before God, from an acquaintance with Christ. We have already learned how unable we are to make atonement for our sins, without which they can never be forgiven, and how unable we are to do any thing that is good;—and yet nothing can deliver us from the justice and wrath of God, but a full satisfaction for our sins; and nothing can give us a title to a reward, but a perfect and unsinning righteousness. What should we do in this case? How shall we escape hell, or get to heaven, when we can neither expiate for our past sins, nor do any good for the time to come? Why, here we are relieved again by an acquaintance with Christ. His death expiates former iniquities, and removes the whole guilt of sin. But this is not enough, that we are not guilty, we must also be actually righteous; not only all sin is to be answered for, but all righteousness is to be fulfilled. Now, this righteousness we find only in Christ; we are reconciled to God by his death, and saved by his life. That actual obedience he yielded to the whole law of God, is that righteousness whereby we are saved; we are innocent by virtue of his sacrifice and expiation, and righteous with his righteousness."

What is here interposed,—that we cannot do any good for the time to come,—must be interpreted of ourselves, without the aid or assistance of the grace of God. And the things here reported by this author, are so expressed and represented, to expose them to reproach and scorn, to have them esteemed not only false, but ridiculous. But whether he be in his wits or no, or what he intends, so to traduce and scoff at the fundamental doctrines of the gospel, I profess I know not. What is it he would deny? what is it he would assert? Are we able to make an atonement for our sins? Can we be forgiven without an atonement? Can we of ourselves do any good without the aid and assistance of grace? Can any thing we do be a full satisfaction for our sins, or deliver us from the wrath of God; that is, the punishment due to our sins? Doth not the death of Christ expiate former iniquities, and remove the whole guilt of sin? Is the contrary to these things the doctrine of the church of England? Is this the religion which is authorized to be preached? and are these the opinions that are licensed to be published unto all the world? But, as I observed before, these things are other men's concernment more than mine, and with them I leave them. But I have said, as he quotes the place, " that we are reconciled to God by the death of Christ, and saved by his life, that actual obedience which he yielded to the whole law of God." As the former part of these words are expressly the apostle's, Rom. v. 10, and so produced by me; so the next words I add are these of the same apostle, " If so be we are found in him, not having on our own righteousness which is of the law, but the righteousness which is of God by faith;" which he may do well to consider, and answer when he can.

Once more, and I shall be beholden to this author for a little respite of severity, whilst he diverts to the magisterial reproof of some other persons. Thus, then, he proceeds, p. 55:—" The third part of our wisdom is, to walk with God: and to that is required agreement, acquaintance, a way, strength, boldness, and aiming at the same end; and all these, with the wisdom of them, are hid in Jesus Christ." So far are my words, to which he adds: " The sum of which, in short, is this:—that Christ having expiated our sins, and fulfilled all righteousness for us, though we have no personal righteousness of our own, but are as contrary unto God as darkness is to light, and death to life, and a universal pollution and defilement to a universal and glorious holiness, and hatred to love; yet the righteousness of Christ is a sufficient, nay, the only foundation of our agreement, and, upon that, of our walking with God: though St John tells us, ' If we say that we have fellowship with him, and walk in darkness, we lie, and do not the truth; but if we walk in the light, as God is in the light, we have fellowship one with another, and the blood of Jesus Christ his Son cleanseth us from all sin,' 1 John i. 6, 7. And our only acquaintance with God and knowledge of him is hid in Christ, which his word and works could not discover, as you heard above. And he is the only way wherein we must walk with God; and we receive all our strength from him; and he makes us bold and confident too, having removed the guilt of sin, so that now we may look justice in the face, and whet our knife at the counter door, all our debts being discharged by Christ, as these bold acquaintances and familiars of Christ use to speak. And in Christ we design the same end that God doth, which is the advancement of his own glory; that is, I suppose, by trusting unto the expiation and righteousness of Christ for salvation, without doing any thing ourselves, we take care that

God shall not be wronged of the glory of his free grace, by a competition of any merits and deserts of our own."

What the author affirms to be the sum of my discourse in that place, which, indeed, he doth not transcribe, is, as to his affirmation of it, as contrary to God as darkness is to light, or death to life, or falsehood to the truth; that is, it is flagitiously false. That there is any agreement with God, or walking with God, for any men who have no personal righteousness of their own, but are contrary to God, etc., I never thought, I never wrote, nor any thing that should give the least countenance unto a suspicion to that purpose. The necessity of an habitual and actual personal, inherent righteousness, of sanctification and holiness, of gospel obedience, of fruitfulness in good works, unto all who intend to walk with God, or come to the enjoyment of him, I have asserted and proved, with other manner of arguments than this author is acquainted withal. The remainder of his discourse in this place is composed of immorality and profaneness. To the first I must refer his charge, that " our only acquaintance with God and knowledge of him is hid in Christ, which his word could not discover," as he again expresseth it, pp. 98, 99, " But that the reverend doctor confessed the plain truth, that their religion is wholly owing to an acquaintance with the person of Christ, and could never have been clearly and savingly learned from his gospel had they not first grown acquainted with his person;" which is plainly false. I own no knowledge of God, nor of Christ, but what is revealed in the word, as was before declared. And unto the other head belongs the most of what ensues; for what is the intendment of those reproaches which are cast on my supposed assertions? Christ is the only way wherein or whereby we must walk with God. Yes, so he says, " I am the way;" " There is no coming to God but by me;" he having consecrated for us in himself " a new and living way" of drawing nigh to God. We receive all our strength from him; yes, for he says, " Without me ye can do nothing." He makes us bold and confident also, having removed the guilt of sin. So the apostle tells us, Heb. x. 19–22. What then? what follows upon these plain, positive, divine assertions of the Scripture? Why, then " we may look justice in the face, and whet our knife at the counter door." Goodly son of the church of England! Not that I impute these profane scoffings unto the church itself,—which I shall never do until it be discovered that the rulers of it do give approbation to such abominations; but I would mind the man of his relation to that church, which, to my knowledge, teacheth better learning and manners.

From p. 57 to the end of his second section, p. 75, he giveth us a scheme of religion, which, in his scoffing language, he says, " men learn from an acquaintance with the person of Christ; and affirms, "that there needs no more to expose it to scorn with considering men than his proposal of it;" which therein he owns to be his design. I know not any peculiar concernment of mine therein, until he comes towards the close of it; which I shall particularly consider. But the substance of the religion which he thus avowedly attempts to expose to scorn, is the doctrine of God's eternal election;—of his infinite wisdom in sending his Son to declare his righteousness for the forgiveness of sins, or in satisfying his justice, that sin might be pardoned, to the praise of the glory of his grace;—of the imputation of the righteousness of Christ unto them that do believe;—of a sense of sin, humiliation for it, looking unto Christ for life and salvation, as the Israelites looked up to the brazen serpent in the wilderness;—of going to Christ by faith for healing our natures and cleansing our sins; with some other doctrines of the same importance. These are the principles which, according to his ability, he sarcastically traduceth and endeavoureth to reflect scorn upon, by the false representation of some of them, and debasing others with an intermixture of vile and profane expressions. It is not impossible but that some or other may judge it their duty to rebuke this horrible (and yet were it not for the ignorance and profaneness of some men's minds, every way contemptible) petulancy. For my part I have other things to do, and shall only add, that I know no other Christian state in the world wherein such discourses would be allowed to pass under the signature of public authority. Only I wish the author more modesty and sobriety than to attempt, or suppose he shall succeed, in exposing to scorn the avowed doctrine in general of the church wherein he lives; and which hath in the parts of it been asserted and defended by the greatest and most learned prelates thereof in the foregoing ages, such as Jewell, Whitgift, Abbot, Morton, Usher, Hall, Davenant, Prideaux, etc., with the most learned persons of its communion, as Reynolds, Whitaker, Hooker, Sutcliffe, etc., and others innumerable; —testified unto in the name of this church by the divines, sent by public authority to the synod of Dort;—taught by the principal practical divines of this nation; and maintained by the most learned of the dignified clergy at this day. He is no doubt at liberty to dissent from the doctrine of the church, and of all the learned men thereof; but for a young man to suppose that, with a few loose, idle words, he shall expose to scorn that doctrine which the persons mentioned, and others innumerable, have not only explained, confirmed, and defended, with pains indefatigable, all kind of learning and skill, ecclesiastical, philosophical, and theological, in books and volumes, which the Christian world as yet knoweth, peruseth, and prizeth, but also lived long in fervent prayers to God for the revelation of his mind and truth unto them, and in the holy practice of obedience suited unto the doctrines they professed,—is somewhat remote from that Christian humility which he ought not only to exercise in himself, but to give an example of unto others. But if this be the fruit of despising the knowledge of the person of Christ,—of the necessity of his satisfaction, —of the imputation of his righteousness,—of union unto his person as our head,—of a sense of the displeasure of God due to sin,—of the spirit of bondage and adoption,—of the corruption of nature, and our disability to do any thing that is spiritually good without the effectual aids of grace;—if these, I say, and the like issues of appearing pride and elation of mind, be the fruit and consequent of rejecting these principles of the doctrine of the gospel, it manifests that there is, and will be, a proportion between the errors of men's minds and the depravation of their affections. It were a most easy task to go over all the particulars mentioned by him, and to manifest how foully he hath prevaricated in their representation,—how he hath cast contempt on some duties of religion indispensably necessary unto salvation; and brought in the very words of the Scripture,—and that in the true proper sense and intendment of them, according to the judgment of all Christians, ancient and modern (as that of looking to Christ, as the Israelites looked to the brazen serpent in the wilderness),—to bear a share and part in his scorn and contempt: as also, to defend and vindicate, not his odious, disingenuous expressions, but what he invidiously designeth to expose, beyond his ability to gainsay, or with any pretence of sober learning to reply unto. But I give it up into the hands of those who are more concerned in the chastisement of such imaginations. Only, I cannot but tell this author what I have learned by long observation,—namely, that those who, in opposing others, make it their design to [publish] and place their confidence in false representations, and invidious expressions of their judgments and opinions, waiving a true stating of the things in difference, and weighing of the arguments wherewith they are confirmed,—whatever pretence they may make of confidence, and contempt of them with whom they have to do, yet this way of writing proceeds from a secret sense of their disability to maintain their own opinions, or to reply to the reasonings of their adversaries in a fair and lawful disputation; or from such depraved affections as are sufficient to deter any sober person from the least communication in those principles which are so pleaded for. And the same I must say of that kind of writing (which in some late authors fills up almost every page in their books) which, beyond a design to load the persons of men with reproaches and calumnies, consists only in the collecting of passages here and there, up and down, out of the writings of others; which, as cut off from the body of their discourses, and design of the places which they belong unto, may, with a little artifice, either of addition or detrac-

tion, with some false glosses, whereof we shall have an immediate
instance, be represented weak, or untrue, or improper, or some way
or other obnoxious to censure. When diligence, modesty, love of
truth, sobriety, true use of learning, shall again visit the world in a
more plentiful manner; though differences should continue amongst
us, yet men will be enabled to manage them honestly, without contracting so much guilt on themselves, or giving such fearful offence
and scandal unto others. But I return.

That wherein I am particularly concerned, is the close wherewith
he winds up this candid, ingenious discourse, p. 74. He quotes my
words, " That 'the soul consents to take Christ on his own terms, to
save him in his own way; and saith, Lord, I would have had thee
and salvation in my way, that it might have been partly of mine
endeavours, and as it were by the works of the law' (that is, by obeying the laws of the gospel); 'but I am now willing to receive thee, and
to be saved in thy way, merely by grace' (that is, without doing any
thing, without obeying thee). The most contented spouse, certainly,
that ever was in the world, to submit to such hard conditions as to
be saved for nothing. But what a pretty compliment doth the soul
make to Christ after all this, when she adds, 'And though I would
have walked according to my own mind, yet now I wholly give up
myself to be ruled by thy Spirit.'"

If the reader will be at the pains to look on the discourse whence
these passages are taken, I shall desire no more of his favour but
that he profess himself to be a Christian, and then let him freely
pronounce whether he find any thing in it obnoxious to censure. Or,
I desire that any man, who hath not forfeited all reason and ingenuity
unto faction and party, if he differ from me, truly to state wherein,
and oppose what I have said with an answer unto the testimonies
wherewith it is confirmed, referred unto in the margin of my discourse.
But the way of this author's proceeding, if there be no plea to be
made for it from his ignorance and unacquaintedness not only with
the person of Christ, but with most of the other things he undertakes
to write about, is altogether inexcusable. The way whereby I have
expressed the consent of the soul in the receiving of Jesus Christ, to be
justified, sanctified, saved by him, I still avow, as suited unto the mind
of the Holy Ghost, and the experience of them that really believe.
And whereas I added, that before believing, the soul did seek for salvation by the works of the law, as it is natural unto all, and as the
Holy Ghost affirms of some (whose words alone I used, and expressly
quoted that place from whence I took them,—namely, Rom. ix. 31,
32;)—this man adds, as an exposition of that expression, " That is,
by obeying the laws of the gospel." But he knew that these were
the words of the apostle, or he did not; if he did not, nor would take

notice of them so to be, although directed to the place from whence they are taken, it is evident how meet he is to debate matters of this nature and concernment, and how far he is yet from being in danger to "pore out his eyes" in reading the Scripture, as he pretends. If he did know them to be his words, why doth he put such a sense upon them as, in his own apprehension, is derogatory to gospel obedience? Whatever he thought of beforehand, it is likely he will now say that it is my sense, and not the apostle's, which he intends. But how will he prove that I intended any other sense than that of the apostle? how should this appear? Let him, if he can, produce any word in my whole discourse intimating any other sense. Nay, it is evident that I had no other intention but only to refer unto that place of the apostle, and the proper sense of it; which is to express the mind and actings of those who, being ignorant of the righteousness of God, go about to establish their own righteousness; as he farther explains himself, Rom. x. 3, 4. That I could not intend obedience unto the laws of the gospel is so evident, that nothing but abominable prejudice or ignorance could hinder any man from discerning it. For that faith which I expressed by the soul's consent to take Christ as a saviour and a ruler, is the very first act of obedience unto the gospel: so that therein or thereon to exclude obedience unto the gospel, is to deny what I assert; which, under the favour of this author, I understand myself better than to do. And as to all other acts of obedience unto the laws of the gospel, following and proceeding from sincere believing, it is openly evident that I could not understand them, when I spake only of what was antecedent unto them. And if this man knows not what transactions are in the minds of many before they do come unto the acceptance of Christ on his own terms, or believe in him according to the tenor of the gospel, there is reason to pity the people that are committed unto his care and instruction, what regard soever ought to be had unto himself. And his pitiful trifling in the exposition he adds of this passage, "To be saved without doing any thing, without obeying thee, and the law," doth but increase the guilt of his prevarications; for the words immediately added in my discourse are,—"And although I have walked according unto mine own mind, yet now I wholly give up myself to be ruled by thy Spirit;" which, unto the understanding of all men who understand any thing in these matters, signify no less than an engagement unto the universal relinquishment of sin, and entire obedience unto Jesus Christ in all things. "But this," saith he, "is a pretty compliment that the soul makes to Christ after all." But why is this to be esteemed only a "pretty compliment?" It is spoken at the same time, and, as it were, with the same breath, there being in the discourse no period between this passage and that before; and why must it be esteemed quite of another nature, so that herein the soul should only compliment, and be real in what is before expressed? What if one should say, it was real only in this latter expression and engagement, —that the former was only a "pretty compliment?" May it not, with respect unto my sense and intention (from any thing in my words, or that can be gathered from them, or any circumstances of the place), be spoken with as much regard unto truth and honesty? What religion these men are of I know not. If it be such as teacheth them these practices, and countenanceth them in them, I openly declare that I am not of it, nor would be so for all that this world can afford. I shall have done, when I have desired him to take notice, that I not only believe and maintain the necessity of obedience unto all the laws, precepts, commands, and institutions of the gospel,—of universal holiness, the mortification of all sin, fruitfulness in good works, in all that intend or design salvation by Jesus Christ; but also have proved and confirmed my persuasion and assertions by better and more cogent arguments than any which, by his writings, he seems as yet to be acquainted withal. And unless he can prove that I have spoken or written any thing to the contrary, or he can disprove the arguments whereby I have confirmed it, I do here declare him a person altogether unfit to be dealt withal about things of this nature, his ignorance or malice being invincible; nor shall I, on any provocation, ever hereafter take notice of him until he hath mended his manners.

His third section, p. 76, consists of three parts:—First, "That some" (wherein it is apparent that I am chiefly, if not only, intended) "do found a religion upon a pretended acquaintance with Christ's person, without and besides the gospel;" whereunto he opposeth his running title of "No acquaintance with Christ but by revelation." Secondly, A supposition of a scheme of religion drawn from the knowledge of Christ's person; whereunto he opposeth another, which he judgeth better. Thirdly, An essay to draw up the whole plot and design of Christianity, with the method of the recovery of sinners unto God. In the first of these, I suppose that I am, if not solely, yet principally, intended; especially considering what he affirms, pp. 98, 99, —namely, that "I plainly confess our religion is wholly owing unto acquaintance with the person of Christ, and could never have been clearly and savingly learned from the gospel, had we not first grown acquainted with his person." Now, herein there is an especial instance of that truth and honesty wherewith my writings are entertained by this sort of men. It is true, I have asserted that it is necessary for Christians to know Jesus Christ,—to be acquainted with his person; that is (as I have fully and largely declared it in the discourse excepted against), the glory of his divine nature, the purity of his human, the infinite condescension of his person in the assumption of our nature, his love and grace, etc., as is at large there declared: and now I add, that he by whom this is denied is no Christian. Secondly, I have taught, that by this knowledge of the person of Christ, or an understanding of the great mystery of godliness, God manifested in the flesh, which we ought to pray for and labour after, we come more fully and clearly to understand sundry other important mysteries of heavenly truth; which without the knowledge of Christ we cannot attain unto. And how impertinent this man's exceptions are against this assertion, we have seen already. But, thirdly, That this knowledge of Christ, or acquaintance with him, is to be attained before we come to know the gospel, or by any other means than the gospel, or is any other but the declaration that is made thereof in and by the gospel, was never thought, spoken, or written by me, and is here falsely supposed by this author, as elsewhere falsely charged on me. And I again challenge him to produce any one letter or tittle out of any of my writings to give countenance unto this frontless calumny. And therefore, although I do not like his expression, p. 77, "Whoever would understand the religion of our Saviour, must learn it from his doctrine, and not from his person," for many reasons I could give; yet I believe no less than he, that the efficacy of Christ's mediation depending on God's appointment can be known only by revelation, and that no man can draw any one conclusion from the person of Christ which the gospel hath not expressly taught; because we can know no more of its excellency, worth, and works, than what is there revealed: whereby he may see how miserably ill-will, malice, or ignorance has betrayed him into the futilous pains of writing this section upon a contrary supposition falsely imputed unto me. And as for his drawing schemes of religion, I must tell him, and let him disprove it if he be able, I own no religion, no article of faith, but what is taught expressly in the Scripture, mostly confirmed by the ancient general councils of the primitive church, and the writings of the most learned fathers, against all sorts of heretics, especially the Gnostics, Photinians, and Pelagians, consonant to the articles of the church of England, and the doctrine of all the reformed churches of Europe. And if in the exposition of any place of Scripture I dissent from any that, for the substance of it, own the religion I do, I do it not without cogent reasons from the Scripture itself; and where, in any opinions which learned men have (and, it may be, always had) different apprehensions about, which hath not been thought to prejudice the unity of faith amongst them, I hope I do endeavour to manage that dissent with that modesty and sobriety which becometh me. And as for the schemes, plots, or designs of religion or Christianity, given us by this author and owned by him (it being taken pretendedly from the person of Christ, when it is hoped that he may have a better to give us from the gospel, seeing he hath told us we must learn our religion from his doctrine and not from his person); besides that it is liable unto innumerable exceptions in particular, which may easily be given in against it by such as have nothing else to do, whereas it makes no mention of the effectual grace of Christ and the gospel for the conversion and sanctification of sinners, and the necessity thereof unto all acts of holy obedience,—it is merely Pelagianism, and stands anathematized by sundry councils of the ancient church. I shall not, therefore, concern myself farther in any passages of this section, most of them wherein it reflects on others standing in competition for truth and ingenuity with the foundation and design of the whole; only I shall say, that the passage of pp. 88, 89,—" This made the divine goodness so restlessly zealous and concerned for the recovery of mankind; various ways he attempted in former ages, but with little success, as I observed before; but at last God sent his Son, our Lord Jesus Christ, into the world,"—without a very cautious explanation and charitable construction, is false, scandalous, and blasphemous. For allow this author, who contends so severely for propriety of expressions, against allusions and metaphors, to say that the divine goodness was "restlessly zealous and concerned" (for, indeed, such is our weakness, that, whether we will or no, we must sometimes learn and teach divine things in such words as are suited to convey an apprehension of them unto our minds, though, in their application unto the divine nature, they are incapable of being understood in the propriety of their signification, though this be as untowardly expressed as any thing I have of late met withal); yet what colour can be put upon, what excuse can be made for, this doctrine, that " God in former ages, by various ways, attempted the recovery of mankind, but with little success," I know not. Various attempts in God for any end without success, do not lead the mind into right notions of his infinite wisdom and omnipotency; and that God, by any way, at any time, attempted the recovery of mankind distinctly and separately from the sending of his Son, is lewdly false.

In the greatest part of his fourth section, entitled, " How men pervert the Scripture to make it comply with their fancy," I am not much concerned; save that the foundation of the whole, and that which animates his discourse from first to last, is laid in an impudent calumny,—namely, that I declare that " our religion is wholly owing to an acquaintance with the person of Christ, and could never have been clearly and savingly learned from his gospel, had we not first grown acquainted with his person." This shameless falsehood is that alone whence he takes occasion and confidence to reproach myself and others, to condemn the doctrine of all the reformed churches, and openly to traduce and vilify the Scripture itself. I shall only briefly touch on some of the impotent dictates of this great corrector of divinity and religion. His discourse of accommodating Scripture expressions to men's own dreams, pp. 99–101, being such as any man may use concerning any other men on the like occasion, if they have a mind unto it, and intend to have no more regard to their consciences than some others seem to have, may be passed by. P. 102, he falls upon the ways of expounding Scripture among those whom he sets himself against, and positively affirms, " that there are two ways of it in great vogue among them:—First, By the sound and clink of the words and phrases; which, as he says, is all some men understand by keeping a form of sound words. Secondly, When this will not do, they reason about the sense of them from their own preconceived notions and opinions, and prove that this must be the meaning of Scripture, because otherwise it is not reconcilable to their dreams; which is called expounding Scripture by the analogy of faith."

Thus far he; and yet we shall have the same man not long hence pleading for the necessity of holiness. But I wish, for my part, he would take notice that I despise that holiness, and the principles of it, which will allow men to coin, invent, and publish such notorious untruths against any sort of men whatever. And whereas, by what immediately follows, I seem to be principally intended in this charge, as I know the untruth of it, so I have published some expositions on some parts of the Scripture to the judgment of the Christian world; to which I appeal from the censures of this man and his companions, as also for those which, if I live and God will, I shall yet publish; and do declare, that, for reasons very satisfactory to my mind, I will not come to him nor them to learn how to expound the Scripture.

But he will justify his charge by particular instances, telling us, p. 102, " Thus when men are possessed with a fancy of an acquaintance with Christ's person, then to know Christ can signify nothing else but to know his person and all his personal excellencies, and beauties, fulness, and preciousness, etc. And when Christ is said to be made wisdom to us, this is a plain proof that we must learn all our spiritual wisdom from an acquaintance with his person; though some duller men can understand no more by it than the wisdom of those revelations Christ hath made of God's will to the world." I would beg of this man, that if he hath any regard unto the honour of Christian religion, or care of his own soul, he would be tender in this matter, and not reflect with his usual disdain upon the knowledge of the person of Christ. I must tell him again, what all Christians believe,—Jesus Christ is Jesus Christ, the eternal Son of God incarnate. The person of Christ is Christ himself, and nothing else; his personal excellencies are the properties of his person, as his two natures are united therein, and as he was thereby made meet to be the mediator between God and man. To know Christ in the language of the Scripture, [of] the whole church of God ancient and present, in common sense and understanding, is to know the person of Christ as revealed and declared in the gospel, with respect unto the ends for which he is proposed and made known therein. And this knowledge of him, as it is accompanied with, and cannot be without, the knowledge of his mind and will, declared in his precepts, promises, and institutions, is effectual to work and produce, in the souls of them who so know him, that faith in him, and obedience unto him, which he doth require. And what would this man have? He who is otherwise minded hath renounced his Christianity, if ever he had any; and if he be thus persuaded, to what purpose is it to set up and combat the mormos and chimeras of his own imagination? Well, then, I do maintain, that to know Christ according to the gospel, is to know the person of Christ; for Christ and his person are the same. Would he now have me to prove this by testimonies or arguments, or the consent of the ancient church? I must beg his excuse at present; and so for the future, unless I have occasion to deal with Gnostics, Familists, or Quakers. And as for the latter clause, wherein Christ is said to be made wisdom unto us, he says, "Some duller men can understand no more by it than the wisdom of those revelations Christ hath made of God's will to the world,"—who are dull men indeed, and so let them pass.

His ensuing discourses, in pp. 103–105, contain the boldest reflections on, and openest derisions of, the expressions and way of teaching spiritual things warranted in and by the Scripture, that to my knowledge I ever read in a book licensed to be printed by public authority: as, in particular, the expressions of faith in Christ, by " coming unto him," and " receiving of him,"—which are the words of the Holy Ghost, and used by him in his wisdom to instruct us in the nature of this duty,—are, amongst others, the subjects of his scorn. The first part of it, though I remember not to have given any occasion to be particularly concerned in it, I shall briefly consider. P. 103, " Thus when men have first learned, from an acquaintance with Christ, to place all their hopes of salvation in a personal union with Christ, from whom they receive the free communications of pardon and grace, righteousness and salvation, what more plain proof can any man who is resolved to believe this, desire of it, than 1 John v. 12, ' He that hath the Son hath life, and he that hath not the Son hath not life?' And what can having the Son signify, but having an interest in him, being made one with him? though some will be so perverse as to understand it of believing, and having his gospel. But the phrase of ' having the Son,' confutes that dull and moral interpretation, especially when we remember it is called, ' being in Christ, and abiding in him;' which must signify a very near union between Christ's person and us."

I suppose that expression of "personal union" sprung out of design, and not out of ignorance; for, if I mistake not, he doth somewhere in his book'take notice that it is disclaimed, and only a union of believers with or unto the person of Christ asserted; or, if it be his mistake, all comes to the same issue. Personal, or hypostatical union, is that of different natures in the same person, giving them the same singular subsistence. This none pretend unto with Jesus Christ. But it is the union of believers unto the person of Christ which is spiritual and mystical, whereby they are in him and he in them, and so are one with him, their head, as members of his mystical body, which is pleaded for herein, with the free communications of grace, righteousness, and salvation, in the several and distinct ways whereby we are capable to receive them from him, or be made partakers of them; [in this] we place all hopes of salvation. And we do judge, moreover, that he who is otherwise minded must betake himself unto another gospel; for he completely renounceth that in our Bibles. Is this our crime,—that which we are thus charged with, and traduced for? Is the contrary hereunto the doctrine that the present church of England approveth and instructs her children in? Or doth any man think that we will be scared from our faith and hope by such weak and frivolous attempts against them? Yea, but it may be it is not so much the thing itself, as the miserable proof which we produce from the Scripture in the confirmation of it; for we do it from that of the apostle, 1 John v. 12. If he think that we prove these things only by this testimony, he is mistaken at his wonted rate. Our faith herein is built upon innumerable express testimonies of the Scripture,—indeed the whole revelation of the will of God and the way of salvation by Jesus Christ in the gospel. Those who prove it, also, from this text, have sufficient ground and reason for what they plead. And, notwithstanding the pleasant scoffing humour of this author, we yet say that it is perverse folly for any one to say that the having of the Son or Christ expressed in the text, doth intend either the having an interest in him and union with him, or the obeying of his gospel, exclusively to the other,—these being inseparable, and included in the same expression. And as to what he adds about being in Christ, and abiding in him,—which are the greatest privileges of believers, and that as expressed in words taught by the Holy Ghost,—it is of the same strain of profaneness with much of what ensues; which I shall not farther inquire into.

I find not myself concerned in his ensuing talk, but only in one reflection on the words of the Scripture, and the repetition of his old, putid, and shameless calumny, p. 108, until we come to p. 126, where

he arraigns an occasional discourse of mine about the necessity of
holiness and good works; wherein he hath only filched out of the
whole what he thought he could wrest unto his end, and scoffingly
descant upon. I shall, therefore, for once, transcribe the whole passage as it lies in my book, and refer it to the judgment of the reader,
p. 206:[1]—

" 2. The second objection is, ' *That if the righteousness and obedience of Christ to the law be imputed unto us, then what need we
yield obedience ourselves?*' To this, also, I shall return answer as
briefly as I can in the ensuing observations:—

" (1.) The placing of our gospel obedience on the right foot of
account (that it may neither be *exalted into a state*, condition, use,
or end, not given it of God; nor any *reason*, cause, motive, end, necessity of it, on the other hand, taken away, weakened, or impaired),
is a matter of great importance. Some make our obedience, the
works of faith, our works, the matter or cause of our justification;
some, the condition of the imputation of the righteousness of Christ;
some, the qualification of the person justified, on the one hand; some
exclude all the necessity of them, and turn the grace of God into
lasciviousness, on the other. To debate these differences is not my present business; only, I say, on this and other accounts, the right stating
of our obedience is of great importance as to our walking with God.

" (2.) We do by no means assign the *same place*, condition, state,
and use to the *obedience of Christ imputed* to us, and our *obedience
performed* to God. If we did, they were really inconsistent. And
therefore those who affirm that our obedience is the condition or
cause of our justification, do all of them deny the imputation of the
obedience of Christ unto us. The righteousness of Christ is imputed
to us, as that on the account whereof we are accepted and esteemed
righteous before God, and are really so, though not inherently. We
are as truly righteous with the obedience of Christ imputed to us as
Adam was, or could have been, by a complete righteousness of his
own performance. So Rom. v. 18, by his obedience we are made
righteous,—made so truly, and so accepted; as by the disobedience of
Adam we are truly made trespassers, and so accounted. And this is
that which the apostle desires to be found in, in opposition to his own
righteousness, Phil. iii. 9. But our own obedience is not the righteousness whereupon we are accepted and justified before God; although
it be acceptable to God that we should abound therein. And this
distinction the apostle doth evidently deliver and confirm, so as nothing can be more clearly revealed: Eph. ii. 8–10, ' For by grace are
ye saved through faith: and that not of yourselves: it is the gift of

---

[1] In the present edition of Owen's Works, the passage will be found in p. 180
of this volume.

God: not of works, lest any man should boast. For we are his workmanship, created in Christ Jesus unto good works, which God hath prepared that we should walk in them.' We are saved, or justified (for that it is whereof the apostle treats), 'by grace through faith,' which receives Jesus Christ and his obedience; ' not of works, lest any man should boast.' 'But what works are they that the apostle intends?' The works of believers, as in the very beginning of the next words is manifest: ' " For we are," we believers, with our obedience and our works, of whom I speak.' 'Yea; but what need, then, of works?' Need still there is: 'We are his workmanship,' etc.

" Two things the apostle intimates in these words:—

" [1.] A reason why we cannot be saved by works,—namely, because we do them not in or by *our own strength;* which is necessary we should do, if we will be saved by them, or justified by them. 'But this is not so,' saith the apostle; 'for we are the workmanship of God,' etc.;—all our works are wrought in us, by full and effectual, undeserved grace.

" [2.] An assertion of the necessity of good works, notwithstanding that we are not saved by them; and that is, that God *has ordained* that we shall walk in them: which is a sufficient ground of our obedience, whatever be the use of it.

"If you will say, then, 'What are the true and proper *gospel grounds, reasons,* uses, and motives of our obedience; whence the necessity thereof may be demonstrated, and our souls be stirred up to abound and be fruitful therein?' I say, they are so many, and lie so deep in the mystery of the gospel and dispensation of grace, spread themselves so throughout the whole revelation of the will of God unto us, that to handle them fully and distinctly, and to give them their due weight, is a thing that I cannot engage in, lest I should be turned aside from what I principally intend. I shall only give you some brief heads of what might at large be insisted on:—

" 1*st.* Our universal obedience and good works are indispensably necessary, from the sovereign appointment and *will* of God; Father, Son, and Holy Ghost.

" In general. 'This is the will of God, even your sanctification,' or holiness, 1 Thess. iv. 3. This is that which God wills, which he requires of us,—that we be holy, that we be obedient, that we do his will as the angels do in heaven. The equity, necessity, profit, and advantage of this ground of our obedience might at large be insisted on; and, were there no more, this might suffice alone,—if it be the will of God, it is our duty:—

" (1*st.*) The Father hath ordained or appointed it. It is the will of the Father, Eph. ii. 10. The Father is spoken of personally, Christ being mentioned as mediator.

" (*2dly.*) The Son hath ordained and appointed it as mediator. John xv. 16, 'I have ordained you, that ye should bring forth fruit' of obedience, and that it should remain.' And,—

" (*3dly.*) The Holy Ghost appoints and ordains believers to works of obedience and holiness, and to work holiness in others. So, in particular, Acts xiii. 2, he appoints and designs men to the great work of obedience in preaching the gospel. And in sinning, men sin against him.

" *2dly.* Our holiness, our obedience, work of righteousness, is one eminent and especial end of the peculiar dispensation of Father, Son, and Spirit, in the business of exalting the glory of God in our salvation,—of the electing love of the Father, the purchasing love of the Son, and the operative love of the Spirit:—

" (*1st.*) It is a peculiar end of the *electing* love of the Father, Eph. i. 4, 'He hath chosen us, that we should be holy and without blame.' So Isa. iv. 3, 4. His aim and design in choosing of us was, that we should be holy and unblamable before him in love. This he is to accomplish, and will bring about in them that are his. 'He chooses us to salvation, through sanctification of the Spirit, and belief of the truth,' 2 Thess. ii. 13. This the Father designed as the first and immediate end of electing love; and proposes the consideration of that love as a motive to holiness, 1 John iv. 8–10.

" (*2dly.*) It is so also of the *exceeding love* of the Son; whereof the testimonies are innumerable. I shall give but one or two:—Tit. ii. 14, 'Who gave himself for us, that he might redeem us from all iniquity, and purify unto himself a peculiar people, zealous of good works.' This was his aim, his design, in giving himself for us; as Eph. v. 25–27, 'Christ loved the church, and gave himself for it; that he might sanctify and cleanse it with the washing of water by the word; that he might present it to himself a glorious church, not having spot, or wrinkle, or any such thing; but that it should be holy, and without blemish.' 2 Cor. v. 15; Rom. vi. 11.

" (*3dly.*) It is the *very work of the love* of the Holy Ghost. His whole work upon us, in us, for us, consists in preparing of us for obedience; enabling of us thereunto, and bringing forth the fruits of it in us. And this he doth in opposition to a righteousness of our own, either before it or to be made up by it, Tit. iii. 5. I need not insist on this. The fruits of the Spirit in us are known, Gal. v. 22, 23.

" And thus have we a twofold bottom of the necessity of our obedience and personal holiness:—God hath appointed it, he requires it; and it is an eminent immediate end of the distinct dispensation of Father, Son, and Holy Ghost, in the work of our salvation. If God's sovereignty over us is to be owned, if his love towards us be to be regarded, if the whole work of the ever-blessed Trinity, for us, in us, be of any moment, our obedience is necessary.

" *3dly.* It is necessary in respect of the *end* thereof; and that whether you consider God, ourselves, or the world:—

" (*1st.*) The end of our obedience, in respect of God, is, his *glory and honour*, Mal. i. 6. This is God's honour,—all that we give him. It is true, he will take his honour from the stoutest and proudest rebel in the world; but all we give him is in our obedience. The glorifying of God by our obedience is all that we are or can be. Particularly,—

" [*1st.*] It is the glory of the *Father*. Matt. v. 16, ' Let your light so shine before men, that they may see your good works, and glorify your Father which is in heaven.' By our walking in the light of faith doth glory arise to the Father. The fruits of his love, of his grace, of his kindness, are seen upon us; and God is glorified in our behalf. . And,—

" [*2dly.*] The *Son is glorified thereby.* It is the will of God that as all men honour the Father, so should they honour the Son, John v. 23. And how is this done? By believing in him, John xiv. 1; obeying of him. Hence, John xvii. 10, he says he is glorified in believers; and prays for an increase of grace and union for them, that he may yet be more glorified, and all might know that, as mediator, he was sent of God.

" [*3dly.*] The *Spirit is glorified also by it.* He is grieved by our disobedience, Eph. iv. 30; and therefore his glory is in our bringing forth fruit. He dwells in us, as in his temple; which is not to be defiled. Holiness becometh his habitation for ever.

" Now, if this that hath been said be not sufficient to evince a necessity of our obedience, we must suppose ourselves to speak with a sort of men who regard neither the sovereignty, nor love, nor glory of God, Father, Son, or Holy Ghost. Let men say what they please, though our obedience should be all lost, and never regarded (which is impossible, for God is not unjust, to forget our labour of love), yet here is a sufficient bottom, ground, and reason of yielding more obedience unto God than ever we shall do whilst we live in this world. I speak also only of gospel grounds of obedience, and not of those that are natural and legal, which are indispensable to all mankind.

" (*2dly.*) The end in respect of *ourselves* immediately is threefold: —[*1st.*] Honour. [*2dly.*] Peace. [*3dly.*] Usefulness.

" [*1st.*] *Honour.* It is by holiness that we are made like unto God, and his image is renewed again in us. This was our honour at our creation, this exalted us above all our fellow-creatures here below,— we were made in the image of God. This we lost by sin, and became like the beasts that perish. To this honour, of conformity to God, of bearing his image, are we exalted again by holiness alone. ' Be ye holy,' says God, ' for I am holy,' 1 Pet. i. 16; and, ' Be ye perfect' (that is, in doing good), 'even as your Father which is in heaven is perfect,' Matt. v. 48,—in a likeness and conformity to him. And herein is the image of God renewed; Eph. iv. 23, 24, therein we 'put on the new man, which after God is created in righteousness and holiness of truth.' This was that which originally was attended with power and dominion;—is still all that is beautiful or comely in the world. How it makes men honourable and precious in the sight of God, of angels, of men; how alone it is that which is not despised, which is of price before the Lord; what contempt and scorn he hath of them in whom it is not,—in what abomination he hath them and all their ways,—might easily be evinced.

"[2dly.] Peace. By it we have communion with God, wherein peace alone is to be enjoyed. 'The wicked are like the troubled sea, that cannot rest;' and, 'There is no peace' to them, 'saith my God,' Isa. lvii. 20, 21. There is no peace, rest, or quietness, in a distance, separation, or alienation from God. He is the rest of our souls. In the light of his countenance is life and peace. Now, 'if we walk in the light, as he is in the light, we have fellowship one with another,' 1 John i. 7; 'and truly our fellowship is with the Father, and with his Son Jesus Christ,' verse 3. He that walks in the light of new obedience, he hath communion with God, and in his presence is fulness of joy for ever; without it, there is nothing but darkness, and wandering, and confusion.

"[3dly.] Usefulness. A man without holiness is good for nothing. 'Ephraim,' says the prophet, 'is an empty vine, that brings forth fruit to itself.' And what is such a vine good for? Nothing. Saith another prophet, 'A man cannot make so much as a pin of it, to hang a vessel on.' A barren tree is good for nothing, but to be cut down for the fire. Notwithstanding the seeming usefulness of men who serve the providence of God in their generations, I could easily manifest that the world and the church might want them, and that, indeed, in themselves they are good for nothing. Only the holy man is commune bonum.

"(3dly.) The end of it in respect of others in the world is manifold:—

"[1st.] It serves to the conviction and stopping the mouths of some of the enemies of God, both here and hereafter:—1. Here. 1 Pet. iii. 16, 'Having a good conscience; that, wherein they speak evil of you, as of evil-doers, they may be ashamed that falsely accuse your good conversation in Christ.' By our keeping of a good conscience men will be made ashamed of their false accusations; that whereas their malice and hatred of the ways of God hath provoked them to speak all manner of evil of the profession of them, by the holiness and righteousness of the saints, they are convinced and made ashamed, as a thief is when he is taken, and be driven to acknowledge that God is

amongst them, and that they are wicked themselves, John xvii. 23.
2. *Hereafter.* It is said that the saints shall judge the world. It
is on this, as well as upon other considerations:—their good works,
their righteousness, their holiness, shall be brought forth, and manifested to all the world; and the righteousness of God's judgments
against wicked men be thence evinced. 'See,' says Christ, 'these
are they that I own, whom you so despised and abhorred; and see
their works following them: this and that they have done, when you
wallowed in your abominations,' Matt. xxv. 42, 43.

" [*2dly.*] The *conversion of others.* 1 Pet. ii. 12, ' Having your conversation honest among the Gentiles; that, wherein they speak against
you as evil-doers, they may, by your good works, which they shall
behold, glorify God in the day of visitation,' Matt. v. 16. Even
revilers, persecutors, evil-speakers, have been overcome by the constant holy walking of professors; and when their day of visitation
hath come, have glorified God on that account, 1 Pet. iii. 1, 2.

" [*3dly.*] The *benefit of all;* partly in keeping off judgments from
the residue of men, as ten good men would have preserved Sodom:[1]
partly by their real communication of good to them with whom they
have to do in their generation. Holiness makes a man a good man,
useful to all; and others eat of the fruits of the Spirit that he brings
forth continually.

" [*4thly.*] It is necessary in respect of the *state* and condition of
justified persons; and that whether you consider their relative state
of acceptation, or their state of sanctification:—

" *First.* They are *accepted* and received into friendship with a holy
God,—a God of purer eyes than to behold iniquity,—who hates every
unclean thing. And is it not necessary that they should be holy who
are admitted into his presence, walk in his sight,—yea, lie in his
bosom? Should they not with all diligence cleanse themselves from all
pollution of [2] flesh and spirit, and perfect holiness in the fear of the Lord?

" *Secondly.* In respect of *sanctification.* We have in us a new creature, 2 Cor. v. 17. This new creature is fed, cherished, nourished, kept
alive, by the fruits of holiness. To what end hath God given us new
hearts, and new natures? Is it that we should kill them? stifle the
creature that is found in us in the womb? that we should give him
to the old man to be devoured?

" [*5thly.*] It is necessary in respect of the *proper place of holiness*
in the new covenant; and that is twofold:—

" *First.* Of the *means* unto the end. God hath appointed that holiness shall be the means, [3] the way to that eternal life, which, as in it-

[1] Gen. xviii. 32.   [2] 2 Cor. vii. 1.
[3] Rom. vi. 23; Heb. xi. 6; Gen. xvii. 1; Ps. xix. 11, lviii. 11; Matt. v. 12, x. 41;
Rom. iv. 4; Col. ii. 18, iii. 24; Heb. x. 35, xi. 26; 2 Pet. ii. 13.

self and originally [it] is his gift by Jesus Christ, so, with regard to his constitution of our obedience, as the means of attaining it, [it] is a reward, and God in bestowing of it a rewarder. Though it be neither the cause, matter, nor condition of our justification, yet it is the way appointed of God for us to walk in for the obtaining of salvation. And therefore, he that hath hope of eternal life purifies himself, as he is pure: and none shall ever come to that end who walketh not in that way; for without holiness it is impossible to see God.

" *Secondly.* It is a *testimony* and pledge of adoption,—a sign and evidence of grace; that is, of acceptation with God. And,—

" *Thirdly.* The whole *expression* of our thankfulness.

" Now, there is not one of all these causes and reasons of the necessity, the indispensable necessity of our obedience, good works, and personal righteousness, but would require a more large discourse to unfold and explain than I have allotted to the proposal of them all; and innumerable others there are of the same import, that I cannot name. He that upon these accounts doth not think universal holiness and obedience to be of indispensable necessity, unless also it be exalted into the room of the obedience and righteousness of Christ, let him be filthy still."

I confess this whole discourse proceedeth on the supposition of the imputation of the righteousness of Christ unto us for our justification. And herein I have as good company as the prelacy and whole church of England can afford; sundry from among them having written large discourses in its confirmation, and the rest having, till of late, approved of it in others. I wish this man, or any of his companions in design, would undertake the answering of Bishop Downham on this subject. No man ever carried this matter higher than Luther; nor did he, in all his writings, more positively and plainly contend for it than in his comment on the Epistle to the Galatians;—yet was that book translated into English by the approbation of the then bishop of London, who also prefixed himself a commendatory epistle unto it. The judgment of Hooker we have heard before. But what need I mention in particular any of the rest of those great and learned names who have made famous the profession of the church of England by their writings throughout the world? Had this man, in their days, treated this doctrine with his present scoffing petulancy, he had scarce been rector of St George, Botolph Lane, much less filled with such hopes and expectations of future advancements, as it is not impossible that he is now possessed with, upon his memorable achievements. But, on this supposition, I do, first, appeal to the judgment of the church of England itself as to the truth of the doctrine delivered in my discourse, and the principles which this man proceedeth on in his exceptions against it. 2. Though it be but a part of a popular discourse, and never intended for scholastic accuracy, yet, as to the assertions contained in it, I challenge this author to take and allow the ordinary, usual sense of the words, with the open design of them, and to answer them when he can. And, 3. In the meantime I appeal unto every indifferent reader whether the mere perusal of this whole passage do not cast this man's futilous cavils out of all consideration? So that I shall only content myself with very few remarks upon them:—

1. Upon my asserting the necessity of good works, he adds, "A very suspicious word; which, methinks, these men should be afraid to name." And why so? We do acknowledge that we do not seek for righteousness by the works of the law; we design not our personal justification by them, nor to merit life or salvation; but betake ourselves unto what even Bellarmine himself came to at last as the safest retreat,—namely, the merits and righteousness of Christ: but for attendance unto them, performance of them, and fruitfulness in them, we are not afraid nor ashamed at any time to enter into judgment with them by whom we are traduced. And as I have nothing to say unto this author, who is known unto me only by that portraiture and character which he hath given of himself in this book; which I could have wished, for his own sake, had been drawn with a mixture of more lines of truth and modesty: so I know there are not a few who, in the course of a vain, worldly conversation, whilst there is scarce a back or belly of a disciple of Christ that blesseth God upon the account of their bounty or charity (the footsteps of levity, vanity, scurrility, and profaneness, being, moreover, left upon all the paths of their haunt), are wont to declaim about holiness, good works, and justification by them; which is a ready way to instruct men to atheism, or the scorn of every thing that is professed in religion. But yet,

2. He shows how impotent and impertinent our arguments are for the proof of the necessity of holiness. And as to the first of them, from the commands of God, he saith, "That if, after all these commands, God hath left it indifferent whether we obey him or no, I hope such commands cannot make obedience necessary." Wonderful divinity! A man must needs be well acquainted with God and himself who can suppose that any of his commands shall leave it indifferent, whether we will obey them or no. Yea, "But will he damn men if they do not obey his commands for holiness?" Yes, yes; no doubt he will do so. Yea, "But we may be, notwithstanding this command, justified and saved without this holiness." False and impertinent: we are neither justified nor saved without them, though we are not justified by them, nor saved for them.

Unto my enforcement of the necessity of holiness from the ends of God in election and redemption, he replies, p. 127, "The Father hath elected us to be holy, and the Son redeemed us to be holy; but will the Father elect and the Son redeem none but those who are holy, and reject and reprobate all others? Doth this election and redemption suppose holiness in us, or is it without any regard to it? For if we be elected and redeemed without any regard unto our own being holy, our election and redemption is secure, whether we be holy or not." Wonderful divinity again! Election and redemption suppose holiness in us! We are elected and redeemed with regard unto our own holiness! that is, antecedently unto our election and redemption; for holiness being the effect and fruit of them, is that which he opposeth. Not many pages after this, he falls into a great admiration of the catechism of the church of England, which none blamed that I know of, as to what is contained in it. But it were to be wished that he had been well instructed in some others, that he might not have divulged and obtruded on the world such crude and palpable mistakes. For this respect of redemption, at least, unto an antecedent holiness in us (that is, antecedent unto it), is such a piece of foppery in religion, as a man would wonder how any one could be guilty of, who hath almost "pored out his eyes" in reading the Scripture. All the remaining cavils of this chapter are but the effects of the like fulsome ignorance; for out of some passages, scraped together from several parts of my discourse (and those not only cut off from their proper scope and end, which is not mentioned by him at all, but also mangled in their representation), he would frame the appearance of a contradiction between what I say on the one hand, that there is no peace with God to be obtained by and for sinners but by the atonement that is made for them in the blood of Jesus Christ, with the remission of sin and justification by faith which ensue thereon (which I hope I shall not live to hear denied by the church of England), and the necessity of holiness and fruitfulness in obedience, to maintain in our own souls a sense of that peace with God which we have, being justified by faith. And he who understands not the consistency of those things, hath little reason to despise good catechisms, whatever thoughts he hath had of his own sufficiency.

The whole design of what remains of this section, is to insinuate that there can be no necessity of holiness or obedience unto God, unless we are justified and saved thereby; which I knew not before to have been, nor indeed do yet know it to be, the doctrine of the church of England. But be it whose it will, I am sure it is not that of the Scripture, and I have so disproved it in other discourses, which this man may now see if he please, as that I shall not here again reassume the same argument; and although I am weary of consulting this woful mixture of disingenuity and ignorance, yet I shall remark somewhat on one or two passages more, and leave him, if he please, unto a due apprehension, that what remains is unanswerable scoffing.

The first is that of p. 131. " But, however, holiness is necessary with respect to sanctification: ' We have in us a new creature, 2 Cor. v. 17. This new creature is fed, cherished, nourished, and kept alive, by the fruits of holiness. To what end hath God given us new hearts, and new natures ? Is it that we should kill them, stifle the creature that is found in us in the womb ? that we should give him to the old man to be devoured ?' The phrase of this is admirable, and the reasoning unanswerable; for if men be new creatures, they will certainly live new lives, and this makes holiness absolutely necessary, by the same reason that every thing necessarily is what it is: but still we inquire after a necessary obligation to the practice of holiness, and that we cannot yet discover."

The reader will see easily how this is picked out of the whole discourse, as that which he imagined would yield some advantage to reflect upon; for, let him pretend what he please to the contrary, he hath laid this end too open to be denied; and I am no way solicitous what will be his success therein. Had he aimed at the discovery of truth, he ought to have examined the whole of the discourse, and not thus have rent one piece of it from the other. As to the phrase of speech which I use, it is, I acknowledge, metaphorical; but yet, being used only in a popular way of instruction, is sufficiently warranted from the Scripture, which administers occasion and gives countenance unto every expression in it, the whole being full well understood by those who are exercised in the life of God. And for the reasoning of it, it is such as I know this man cannot answer: for the new creature, however he may fancy, is not a new conversation, nor a living holily; but it is the principle, and spiritual ability, produced in believers by the power and grace of the Holy Ghost, enabling them to walk in newness of life and holiness of conversation. And this principle being bestowed on us, wrought in us, for that very end, it is necessary for us, unless we will neglect and despise the grace which we have received, that we walk in holiness, and abound in the fruits of righteousness, whereunto it leads and tends. Let him answer this if he can, and when he hath done so, answer the apostle in like manner; or scoff not only at me, but at him also.

The last passage I shall remark upon in this section is what he gives us as the sum of the whole. P. 135, "The sum of all is, that to know Christ is not to be thus acquainted with his person, but to understand his gospel in its full latitude and extent; it is not the person, but the gospel of Christ which is the way, the truth, and the life, which directs us in the way to life and happiness. And again, this acquaintance with Christ's person, which these men pretend to, is only a work of fancy, and teaches men the arts of hypocrisy," etc.

I do not know that ever I met with any thing thus crudely asserted among the Quakers, in contempt of the person of Christ; for whereas he says of himself expressly, "I am the way, the truth, and the life," to say he is not so (for Jesus Christ is his person, and nothing else), carries in it a bold contradiction, both parts of which cannot be true. When the subject of a proposition is owned, there may be great controversy about the sense of the predicate; as when Christ says he is the vine: there may be so also about the subject of a proposition, when the expression is of a third thing, and dubious; as where Christ says, "This is my body:" but when the person speaking is the subject, and speaks of himself, to deny what he says, is to give him the lie. "I am the way, the truth, and the life," saith Christ;—"He is not," saith our author, "but the gospel is so." If he had allowed our Lord Jesus Christ to have spoken the truth, but only to have added, "Though he was so, yet he was so no otherwise but by the gospel," there had been somewhat of modesty in the expression; but this saying, that the "person of Christ is not,—the gospel is so," is intolerable. It is so, however, that this young man, without consulting or despising the exposition of all divines, ancient or modern, and the common sense of all Christians, should dare to obtrude his crude and undigested conceptions upon so great a word of Christ himself, countenanced only by the corrupt and false glosses of some obscure Socinians: which some or other may possibly in due time mind him of; I have other work to do.

But according to his exposition of this heavenly oracle, what shall any one imagine to be the sense of the context, where "I," and "me," spoken of Christ, do so often occur? Suppose that the words of that whole verse, "I am the way, the truth, and the life, no man cometh to the Father but by me," have this sense,—not Christ himself is the way, the truth, and the life, but the gospel; "No man cometh to the Father but by me;" that is, not by me, but by "the gospel,"—must not all the expressions of the same nature in the context have the same exposition? as namely, verse 1, "Ye believe in God, believe also in me;" that is, not in me but in "the gospel;"—"I go to prepare a place for you;" that is, not I do so, but "the gospel;" verse 3, "I will come again and receive you to myself;" that is, not I, but "the gospel" will do so; and so of all other things which Christ in that place seems to speak of himself. If this be his way of interpreting Scripture, I wonder not that he blames others for their defect and miscarriages therein.

When I first considered these two last sections, I did not suspect but that he had at least truly represented my words, which he thought meet to reflect upon and scoff at; as knowing how easy it was for any one whose conscience would give him a dispensation for such an undertaking, to pick out sayings and expressions from the most innocent discourse, and odiously to propose them, as cut off from their proper coherence, and under a concealment of the end and the principal sense designed in them. Wherefore I did not so much as read over the discourse excepted against; only, once or twice observing my words, as quoted by him, not directly to comply with what I knew to be my sense and intention, I turned unto the particular places to discover his prevarication. But having gone through this ungrateful task, I took the pains to read over the whole digression in my book, which his exceptions are levelled against; and, upon my review of it, my admiration of his dealing was not a little increased. I cannot, therefore, but desire of the most partial adherers unto this censurer of other men's labours, judgments, and expressions, but once to read over that discourse, and if they own themselves to be Christians, I shall submit the whole of it, with the consideration of his reflections upon it, unto their judgments. If they refuse so to do, I let them know I despise their censures, and do look on the satisfaction they take in this man's scoffing reflections as the laughter of fools, or the crackling of thorns under a pot. For those who will be at so much pains to undeceive themselves, they will find that that expression of the "person of Christ" is but once or twice used in all that long discourse, and that occasionally; which, by the outcries here made against it, any one would suppose to have filled up almost all the pages of it. He will find, also, that I have owned and declared the revelation that God hath made of himself, the properties of his nature, and his will, in his works of creation and providence, in its full extent and efficacy; and that by the knowledge of God in Christ, which I so much insist upon, I openly, plainly, and declaredly, intend nothing but the declaration that God hath made of himself in Jesus Christ by the gospel: whereof the knowledge of his person, the great mystery of godliness, God manifested in the flesh, with what he did and suffered as the mediator between God and man, is the chiefest instance; in which knowledge consisteth all our wisdom of living unto God. Hereon I have no more to add, but that he by whom these things are denied or derided, doth openly renounce his Christianity. And that I do not lay this unto the charge of this doughty writer, is because I am satisfied that he hath not done it out of any such design, but partly out of ignorance of the things which he undertakes to write about, and partly to satisfy the malevolence of himself and some others against my person: which sort of depraved affections, where men give up themselves unto their prevalency, will blind the eyes and pervert the judgments of persons as wise as he.

In the first section of his fourth chapter I am not particularly concerned; and whilst he only vents his own conceits, be they never so idle or atheological, I shall never trouble myself, either with their examination or confutation. So many as he can persuade to be of his mind,—that we have no union with Christ but by virtue of union with the church (the contrary whereof is absolutely true); that Christ is so a head of rule and government unto the church, as that he is not a head of influence and supplies of spiritual life (contrary to the faith of the catholic church in all ages); that these assertions of his have any countenance from antiquity, or the least from the passages quoted out of Chrysostom by himself; that his glosses upon many texts of Scripture (which have an admirable coincidence with those of two other persons whom I shall name when occasion requires it) are sufficient to affix upon them the sense which he pleads for, with many other things of an equal falsehood and impertinency wherewith this section is stuffed,—shall, without any farther trouble from me, be left to follow their own inclinations. But yet, notwithstanding all the great pains he hath taken to instruct us in the nature of the union between Christ and believers, I shall take leave to prefer that given by Mr Hooker before it, not only as more true and agreeable unto the Scripture, but also as better expressing the doctrine of the church of England in this matter. And if these things please the present rulers of the church,—wherein upon the matter Christ is shuffled off, and the whole of our spiritual union is resolved into the doctrine of the gospel, and the rule of the church by bishops and pastors, let it imply what contradiction it will, as it doth the highest, seeing it is by the doctrine of the gospel that we are taught our union with Christ, and his rule of the church by his laws and Spirit,—I have only the advantage to know somewhat more than I did formerly, though not much to my satisfaction.

But he that shall consider what reflections are cast in this discourse on the necessity of satisfaction to be made unto divine justice, and from whom they are borrowed; the miserable, weak attempt that is made therein to reduce all Christ's mediatory actings unto his kingly office, and, in particular, his intercession; the faint mention that is made of the satisfaction of Christ, clogged with the addition of ignorance of the philosophy of it, as it is called, well enough complying with them who grant that the Lord Christ did what God was satisfied withal, with sundry other things of the like nature; will not be to seek whence these things come, nor whither they are going, nor to whom our author is beholden for most of his rare notions; which it is an easy thing at any time to acquaint him withal.

The second section of this chapter is filled principally with exceptions against my discourse about the personal excellencies of Christ as mediator; if I may not rather say, with the reflections on the glory of Christ himself. [As] for my own discourse upon it, I acknowledge it to be weak, and not only inconceivably beneath the dignity and merit of the subject, but also far short of what is taught and delivered by many ancient writers of the church unto that purpose; and [as] for his exceptions, they are such a composition of ignorance and spite as is hardly to be paralleled. His entrance upon his work is (p. 200) as followeth:—" Secondly, Let us inquire what they mean by the person of Christ, to which believers must be united. And here they have outdone all the metaphysical subtilties of Suarez, and have found out a person for Christ distinct from his Godhead and manhood; for there can be no other sense made of what Dr Owen tells us,—that by the ' graces of his person' he doth not mean the ' glorious excellencies of his Deity considered in itself, abstracting from the office which for us, as God and man, he undertook; nor the outward appearance of his human nature, when he conversed here on earth, nor yet as now exalted in glory: but the graces of the person of Christ, as he is vested with the office of mediation,—his spiritual eminency, comeliness, beauty, as appointed and anointed by the Father unto that great work of bringing home all his elect into his bosom.' Now, unless the person of Christ as mediator be distinct from his person as God-man, all this is idle talk; for what personal graces are there in Christ as mediator which do not belong to him either as God or man? There are some things, indeed, which our Saviour did and suffered, which he was not obliged to, either as God or man, but as mediator; but surely he will not call the peculiar duties and actions of an office personal graces."—

I have now learned not to trust unto the honesty and ingenuity of our author, as to his quotations out of my book; which I find that he hath here mangled and altered, as in other places, and shall therefore transcribe the whole passage in my own words, p. 51:[1] " It is Christ as mediator of whom we speak; and therefore, by the ' grace of his person,' I understand not, first, The glorious excellencies of his Deity considered in itself, abstracting from the office which for us, as God and man, he undertook; nor, secondly, The outward appearance of his human nature, neither when he conversed here on earth, bearing our infirmities (whereof, by reason of the charge that was laid upon him, the prophet gives quite another character, Isa. lii. 14), concerning which some of the ancients are very poetical in their expressions; nor yet as now exalted in glory;—a vain imagination whereof makes many bear a false, a corrupted respect unto Christ, even upon carnal apprehensions of the mighty exaltation of the human nature; which is but to ' know Christ after the flesh,'—a mischief much improved by the abomination of foolish imagery. But this is that which I in-

[1] Page 48 of this volume.

tend,—the graces of the person of Christ as he is vested with the office of mediation, his spiritual eminency, comeliness, and beauty, etc. Now, in this respect the Scripture describes him as exceeding excellent, comely, and desirable,—far above comparison with the chiefest, choicest created good, or any endearment imaginable;" which I prove at large from Ps. xlv. 2; Isa. iv. 2; Cant. v. 9, adding an explanation of the whole.

In the digression, some passages whereof he carps at in this section, my design was to declare, as was said, somewhat of the glory of the person of Christ. To this end I considered both the glory of his divine and the many excellencies of his human nature; but that which I principally insisted on was the excellency of his person as God and man in one, whereby he was meet and able to be the mediator between God and man, and to effect all the great and blessed ends of his mediation. That our Lord Jesus Christ was God, and that there were, on that account, in his person the essential excellencies and properties of the divine nature, I suppose he will not deny; nor will he do so that he was truly man, and that his human nature was endowed with many glorious graces and excellencies which are peculiar thereunto. That there is a distinct consideration of his person as both these natures are united therein, is that which he seems to have a mind to except against. And is it meet that any one who hath aught else to do should spend any moments of that time which he knows how better to improve, in the pursuit of a man's impertinencies, who is so bewildered in his own ignorance and confidence, that he knows neither where he is nor what he says? Did not the Son of God, by assuming our human nature, continuing what he was, become what he was not? Was not the person of Christ, by the communication of the properties of each nature in it and to it, a principle of such operations as he could not have wrought either as God or man, separately considered? How else did God "redeem his church with his own blood?" or how is that true which he says, John iii. 13, "And no man hath ascended up to heaven, but he that came down from heaven, even the Son of man, which is in heaven?" Was not the union of the two natures in the same person (which was a property neither of the divine nor human nature, but a distinct ineffable effect of divine condescension, wisdom, and grace, which the ancients unanimously call the " grace of union," whose subject is the person of Christ) that whereby he was fit, meet, and able, for all the works of his mediation? Doth not the Scripture, moreover, propose unto our faith and consolation the glory, power, and grace of the person of Christ as he is " God over all, blessed for ever;" and his love, sympathy, care and compassion as man; yet all acting themselves in the one and selfsame person of the Son of God? Let him read the first chapter of the Epiṣtle to the Hebrews, and see what account he can give thereof. And are not these such principles of Christian religion as no man ought to be ignorant of, or can deny, without the guilt of the heresies condemned in the first general councils? And they are no other principles which my whole discourse excepted against doth proceed upon. But saith our author, "Unless the person of Christ as mediator be distinct from his person as God-man, all this is idle talk." Very good! and why so? Why, "What personal graces are there in Christ as mediator, which do not belong unto him either as God or man?" But is he not ashamed of this ignorance? Is it not a personal grace and excellency that he is God and man in one person? which belongs not to him either as God or man. And are there not personal operations innumerable depending hereon, which could not have been wrought by him either as God or man; as raising himself from the dead by his own power, and redeeming the church with his blood? Are not most of the descriptions that are given us of Christ in the Scripture, most of the operations which are assigned unto him, such as neither belong unto nor proceed from the divine or human nature, separately considered, but from the person of Christ, as both these natures are united in it? That which seems to have led him into the maze wherein he is bewildered in his ensuing discourse, is, that considering there are but two natures in Christ, the divine and the human,—and nature is the principle of all operations,—he supposed that nothing could be said of Christ, nothing ascribed to his person, but what was directly, formally predicated of one of his natures, distinctly considered. But he might have easily inquired of himself,—that seeing all the properties and acts of the divine nature are absolutely divine, and all those of the human nature absolutely human, whence it came to pass that all the operations and works of Christ, as mediator, are *theandrical?*[1] Although there be nothing in the person of Christ but his divine and human nature, yet the person of Christ is neither his divine nature nor his human; for the human nature is, and ever was, of itself, ἀνυπόστατος; and the divine, to the complete constitution of the person of the Mediator, in and unto its own *hypostasis* assumed the human: so that, although every energy or operation be δραστικὴ τῆς φύσεως κίνησις, and so the distinct natures are distinct principles of Christ's operations, yet his person is the principal or only agent; which being God-man, all the actions thereof, by virtue of the communication of the properties of both natures therein, are *theandrical.* And the excellency of this person of Christ, wherein he was every way fitted for the work of mediation, I call sometimes his personal grace, and will not go to him to learn to speak and express myself in these things. And

---

[1] Proceeding from the divine and human natures in personal union.—FD.

it is most false which he affirms, p. 203, "That I distinguish the graces of Christ's person as mediator from the graces of his person as God and man." Neither could any man have run into such an imagination who had competently understood the things which he speaks about; and the bare proposal of these things is enough to defeat the design of all his ensuing cavils and exceptions.

And as to what he closeth withal, that "Surely I will not call the peculiar duties and actions of an office personal graces;" I suppose that he knoweth not well what he intends thereby. Whatever he hath fancied about Christ being the name of an office, Jesus Christ, of whom we speak, is a person, and not an office; and there are no such things *in rerum natura* as the actions of an office. And if by them he intends the actions of a person in the discharge of an office, whatever he calls them, I will call the habits in Christ, from whence all his actions in the performance of his office do proceed, "personal graces," and that whether he will or no. So he is a "merciful, faithful, and compassionate high priest," Heb. ii. 17, iv. 15, v. 2. And all his actions, in the discharge of his office of priesthood, being principled and regulated by those qualifications, I do call them his personal graces, and do hope that, for the future, I may obtain his leave so to do. The like may be said of his other offices.

The discourse which he thus raves against is didactical, and accommodated unto a popular way of instruction; and it hath been hitherto the common ingenuity of all learned men to give an allowance unto such discourses, so as not to exact from them an accuracy and propriety in expressions, such as is required in those that are scholastical or polemical. It is that which, by common consent, is allowed to the tractates of the ancients of that nature,—especially where nothing is taught but what, for the substance of it, is consonant unto the truth. But this man attempts not only a severity in nibbling at all expressions which he fancieth liable unto his censures, but, with a disingenuous artifice, waiving the tenor and process of the discourse, which I presume he found not himself able to oppose, he takes out, sometimes here, sometimes there, up and down, backward and forward, at his pleasure, what he will, to put, if it be possible, an ill sense upon the whole. And, if he have not hereby given a sufficient discovery of his good-will towards the doing of somewhat to my disadvantage, he hath failed in his whole endeavour; for there is no expression which he hath fixed on as the subject of his reflections, which is truly mine, but that as it is used by me, and with respect unto its end, I will defend it against him and all his co-partners, whilst the Scripture may be allowed to be the rule and measure of our conceptions and expressions about sacred things. And although at present I am utterly wearied with the consideration of such sad triflings, I shall accept from him the kindness of an obligation to so much patience as is necessary unto the perusal of the ensuing leaves, wherein I am concerned.

First, p. 202, he would pick something, if he knew what, out of my quotations of Cant. v. 9, to express or illustrate the excellency of Christ; which first he calls an "excellent proof," by way of scorn. But as it is far from being the only proof produced in the confirmation of the same truth, and is applied rather to illustrate what was spoken, than to prove it, yet, by his favour, I shall make bold to continue my apprehensions of the occasional exposition of the words which I have given in that place, until he is pleased to acquaint me with a better; which, I suppose, will be long enough. For what he adds,— "But, however, white and ruddy belong to his divine and human nature, and that without regard to his mediatory office; for he had been white in the glory of his Deity, and ruddy with the red earth of his humanity, whether he had been considered as mediator or not," —it comes from the same spring of skill and benevolence with those afore. For what wise talk is it, of Christ's being God and man, without the consideration of his being mediator! as though he were ever, or ever should have been, God and man, but with respect unto his mediation? His scoff at the red earth of Christ's humanity, represented as my words, is grounded upon a palpable falsification; for my words are, "He was also ruddy in the beauty of his humanity. Man was called Adam, from the red earth whereof he was made. The word here used points him out as the second Adam, partaker of flesh and blood, because the children also partook of the same." And if he be displeased with these expressions, let him take his own time to be pleased again; it is that wherein I am not concerned. But my fault, which so highly deserved his correction, is, that I apply that to the person of Christ which belongs unto his natures. But what if I say no such thing, or had no such design in that place? For although I do maintain a distinct consideration of the excellency of Christ's person, as comprising both his natures united,—though every real thing in his person belongs formally and radically unto one [or other] of the natures (those other excellencies being the exurgency of their union), whereby his person was fitted and suited unto his mediatory operations, which in neither nature, singly considered, he could have performed,—and shall continue to maintain it against whosoever dares directly to oppose it; yet in this place I intended it not, which this man knew well enough,—the very next words unto what he pretends to prove it [by], being, "The beauty and comeliness of the Lord Jesus Christ, in the union of both these in one person, shall afterward be declared." And so we have an equality in judgment and ingenuity throughout this censure.

Hence he leaps to p. 64 of my book, thence backwards to p. 53, and then up and down, I know not how nor whither. He begins with p. 64:[1]—" And in his first digression concerning the excellency of Christ Jesus, to invite us to communion with him in a conjugal relation, he tells us that Christ is exceeding excellent and desirable in his Deity, and the glory thereof; he is desirable and worthy our acceptation as considered in his humanity, in his freedom from sin, fulness of grace, etc. Now, though this looks very like a contradiction, that by the graces of his person, he meant neither the excellencies of his divine nor human nature; yet he hath a salvo which will deliver him both from contradiction and from nonsense,—that he doth not consider these excellencies of his Deity or humanity as abstracted from his office of mediator, though he might if he pleased: for he considers those excellencies which are not peculiar to the office of mediation, but which would have belonged unto him as God and man, whether he had been mediator or not. But what becomes of his distinction of the graces of Christ's person as mediator from the graces of his person as God and man, when there are no personal graces in Christ but what belong to his Deity or his humanity?"

I am sufficiently satisfied that he neither knows where he is nor what he doth, or hath no due comprehension of the things he treats about. That which he opposeth, if he intend to oppose any thing by me asserted, is, that whereas Christ is God, the essential properties of his divine nature are to be considered as the formal motive unto, and object of, faith, love, and obedience; and whereas he is man also, his excellencies, in the glorious endowment of his human nature, with his alliance unto us therein, and his furniture of grace for the discharge of his office, are proposed unto our faith and love in the Scripture. And of these things we ought to take a distinct consideration; our faith concerning them being not only taught in the Scripture, but fully confirmed in the confessions and determinations of the primitive church. But the person of Christ, wherein these two natures are united, is of another distinct consideration; and such things are spoken thereof as cannot, under any single enunciation, be ascribed unto either nature, though nothing be so but what formally belongs unto one of them, or is the necessary consequent and exurgency of their union. See Isa. ix. 6; 1 Tim. iii. 16; John i. 14. It is of the "glory of the Word of God made flesh" that I discourse. But this man talks of what would have belonged to Christ as God-man, whether he had been mediator or not; as though the Son of God either was, or was ever designed to be, or can be, considered as God-man, and not as mediator. And thence he would

---

[1] Page 59 of present volume.

relieve himself by the calumny of assigning a distinction unto me between the graces of Christ's person as mediator, and the graces of his person as God and man (that is, one person); which is a mere figment of his own misunderstanding. Upon the whole, he comes to that accurate thesis of his own,—that there are no personal graces in Christ but what belong to his Deity or humanity. Personal graces belonging unto the humanity, or human nature of Christ,—that nature being ἀνυπόστατος, or such as hath no personal subsistence of its own,—is a notion that those may thank him for who have a mind to do it. And he may do well to consider what his thoughts are of the grace of our Lord Jesus Christ, mentioned Phil. ii. 6–11.

But he will now discover the design of all these things, and afterward make it good by quotations out of my book. The first he doth, p. 203, and onwards: " But whatever becomes of the sense of the distinction, there is a very deep fetch in it, the observing of which will discover the whole mystery of the person of Christ and our union to him. For these men consider that Christ saves us as he is our mediator, and not merely considered as God or man; and they imagine that we receive grace and salvation from Christ's person just as we do water out of a conduit, or a gift and largess from a prince,—that it flows to us from our union to his person; and therefore they dress up the person of the Mediator with all those personal excellencies and graces which may make him a fit Saviour, that those who are thus united to his person (of which more in the next section) need not fear missing of salvation. Hence they ransack all the boundless perfections of the Deity, and whatever they can find or fancy speaks any comfort to sinners, this is presently a personal grace of the Mediator;—they consider all the glorious effects of his mediation; and whatever great things are spoken of his gospel, or religion, or intercession for us, these serve as personal graces: so that all our hopes may be built, not on the gospel covenant, but on the person of Christ. So that the dispute now lies between the person of Christ and his gospel,—which must be the foundation of our hope,—which is the way to life and happiness."

First, We do consider and believe that Christ saves as a mediator; that is, as God and man in one person, exercising the office of a mediator, and not merely as God or man. This we believe with all the catholic church of Christ, and can with boldness say, He that doth not so, let him be *anathema maran-atha*. Secondly, We do not imagine, but believe from the Scripture, and with the whole church of God, that we receive grace and salvation from the person of Christ in those distinct ways wherein they are capable of being received; and let him be *anathema* who believes otherwise. Only, whether his putting of grace and salvation into the same way of reception belong unto his accuracy in expressing his own sentiments, or his ingenuity in the representation of other men's words, I leave undetermined. The similitudes he useth to express our faith in these things, show his good-will towards·scoffing and profaneness. We say, there is real communication of grace from the person of Christ, as the head of the church, unto all the members of his mystical body by his Spirit, whereby they are quickened, sanctified, and enabled unto all holy obedience; and, if it be denied by him, he stands anathematized by sundry councils of the ancient church. We say not, that we receive it as " water out of a conduit," which is of a limited, determined capacity; whereas we say, the person of Christ, by reason of his Deity, is an immense, eternal, living spring or fountain of all grace. And when God calls himself a " fountain of living water;" and the Lord Christ calls his Spirit communicated to believers " living water" (under which appellations he was frequently promised in the Old Testament); as also the grace and mercy of the gospel, the "water of life,"—inviting us to receive them, and to drink of them, —this author may be advised to take heed of profane scoffing at these things. Whether any have said, that we receive grace and salvation from Christ, as " a gift or largess from a prince," I know not; if they have, the sole defect therein is, that the allusion doth no way sufficiently set forth the freedom and bounty of Christ in the communication of them unto sinners; and wherein else it offends, let him soberly declare, if he can. This is the charge upon us in point of faith and judgment; which, in one word, amounts to no more but this,—that we are Christians: and so, by the grace of God, we intend to continue, let this man deride us whilst he pleaseth. Thirdly, His next charge concerns our practice in the pursuit of these dreadful principles, which, by their repetition, he hath exposed to scorn: " And therefore they dress up," etc. What doth this poor man intend? what is the design of all this profaneness? The declaration of the natures and person of Christ,—of his grace and work,—the ascribing unto him what is directly and expressly in terms ascribed unto him in the Scripture, or relating, as we are able, the description it gives of him,—is here called, " Dressing up the person of the Mediator with all those personal graces that may make him a fit Saviour." The preparation of the person of Christ to be a fit and meet Saviour for sinners, which he profanely compares to the dressing up of ——, is the greatest, most glorious, and admirable effect that ever infinite wisdom, goodness, power, and love wrought and produced, or will do so unto eternity. And those on whom he reflects design nothing, do nothing in this matter, but only endeavour, according to the measure of the gift of Christ which they have received, to declare and explain what is revealed and taught in the Scripture thereof; and those who exceed the bounds of Scripture revelation herein (if any do so) we do abhor. And as for those who are united unto Christ, although we say not that they need not fear missing of salvation, seeing they are to be brought unto it, not only through the exercise of all graces, whereof fear is one, but also through such trials and temptations as will always give them a fear of heed and diligence, and sometimes such a fear of the event of things as shall combat their faith, and shake its firmest resolves; yet we fear not to say, that those who are really united unto Jesus Christ shall be assuredly saved; which I have proved elsewhere beyond the fear of any opposition from this author, or others like minded. Fourthly, He adds "Hence they ransack," etc. But what is the meaning of these expressions? Doth not the Scripture declare that Christ is God as well as man? Doth it not build all our faith, obedience, and salvation on that consideration? Are not the properties of the divine nature everywhere in the Scripture declared and proposed unto us for the ingenerating and establishing faith in us, and to be the object of, and exercise of, all grace and obedience? And is it now become a crime that any should seek to declare and instruct others in these things from the Scripture, and to the same end for which they are therein revealed? Is this, with any evidence of sobriety, to be traduced as a "ransacking the boundless perfections of the divine nature, to dress up the person of the Mediator"? Is he a Christian, or doth he deserve that name, who contemns or despiseth the consideration of the properties of the divine nature in the person of Christ (see Isa. vi. 1–4; John xii. 41; Isa. ix. 6; John i. 14; Phil. ii. 6, etc.), or shall think that the grace or excellencies of his person do not principally consist in them, as the human nature is united thereunto? Fifthly, "They consider all the glorious effects of his mediation." All the effects of Christ's mediation,—all the things that are spoken of the gospel, etc., do all of them declare the excellency of the person of Christ, as effects declare their cause, and may and ought to be considered unto that end, as occasion doth require; and no otherwise are they considered by those whom he doth oppose. Sixthly, But the end of these strange principles and practices, he tells us, is, "That all our hopes may be built, not on the gospel covenant, but on the person of Christ." But I say again, What is it that this man intends? What is become of a common regard to God and man? Who do so build their hopes on Christ as to reject or despise the gospel covenant, as he calls it?—though I am afraid, should he come to explain himself, he will be at a loss about the true nature of the gospel covenant, as I find him to be about the person and grace of Christ. He telleth us, indeed, that "Not the person of Christ, but the gospel, is the way." Did we ever say, "Not the covenant of grace, but the person of Christ is all we regard?" But whence comes this causeless fear and jealousy,—or rather, this evil surmise, that if any endeavour to exalt the person of Christ, immediately the covenant of the gospel (that is, in truth, the covenant which is declared in the gospel) must be discarded? Is there an inconsistency between Christ and the covenant? I never met with any who was so fearful and jealous lest too much should be ascribed in the matter of our salvation to Jesus Christ; and when there is no more so, but what the Scripture doth expressly and in words assign unto him and affirm of him, instantly we have an outcry that the gospel and the covenant are rejected, and that a " dispute lies between the person of Christ and his gospel." But let him not trouble himself; for as he cannot, and as he knows he cannot, produce any one word or one syllable out of any writings of mine, that should derogate any thing from the excellency, nature, necessity, or use of the new covenant; so, though it may be he do not, and doth therefore fancy and dream of disputes between Christ and the gospel, we do know how to respect both the person of Christ and the covenant,—both Jesus Christ and the gospel, in their proper places. And in particular, we do know, that as it is the person of Christ who is the author of the gospel, and who as mediator in his work of mediation gives life, and efficacy, and establishment unto the covenant of grace; so both the gospel and that covenant do declare the glory and design the exaltation of Jesus Christ himself. Speaking, therefore, comparatively, all our hopes are built on Jesus Christ, who alone filleth all things; yet also we have our hopes in God, through the covenant declared in the gospel, as the way designing the rule of our obedience, securing our acceptance and reward. And to deal as gently as I can warrant myself to do with this writer, the dispute he mentions between the person of Christ and the gospel, which shall be the foundation of our hope, is only in his own fond imagination, distempered by disingenuity and malevolence. For, if I should charge what the appearance of his expressions will well bear, what he says seems to be out of a design, influenced by ignorance or heresy, to exclude Jesus Christ, God and man, from being the principal foundation of the church, and which all its hopes are built upon. This being the sum ˉof his charge, I hope he will fully prove it in the quotations from my discourse, which he now sets himself to produce; assuring him that if he do not, but come short therein, setting aside his odious and foppish, profane deductions, I do aver them all in plain terms, that he may, on his next occasion of writing, save his labour in searching after what he may oppose. Thus, therefore, he proceeds, p. 205:—

" To make this appear, I shall consider that account which Dr Owen gives us of the personal graces and excellencies of Christ, which in general consist in three things:—First, His fitness to save, from the grace of union, and the proper and necessary effects thereof. Secondly, His fulness to save, from the grace of communion, or the free consequences of the grace of union. And, thirdly, His excellency to endear, from his complete suitableness to all the wants of the souls of men. First, That he is fit to be a Saviour, from the grace of union. And if you will understand what this strange grace of union is, it is the uniting the nature of God and man in one person, which makes him fit to be a Saviour to the uttermost. He lays his hand upon God, by partaking of his nature; and he lays his hand on us, by partaking of our nature: and so becomes a days-man or umpire between both. Now, though this be a great truth, that the union of the divine and human nature in Christ did excellently qualify him for the office of a mediator, yet this is the unhappiest man in expressing and proving it that I have met with. For what an untoward representation is this of Christ's mediation, that he came to make peace by laying his hands on God and men, as if he came to part a fray or scuffle: and he might as well have named Gen. i. 1, or Matt. i. 1, or any other place of Scripture, for the proof of it, as those he mentions."

To what end it is that he cites these passages out of my discourse is somewhat difficult to divine. Himself confesseth that what is asserted (at least in one of them) is a great truth, only, I am " the unhappiest man in expressing and proving it that ever he met with." It is evident enough to me, that he hath not met with many who have treated of this subject, or hath little understood those he hath met withal; so that there may be yet some behind as unhappy as myself. And seeing he hath so good a leisure from other occasions, as to spend his time in telling the world how unhappy I am in my proving and expressing of what himself acknowledgeth to be true, he may be pleased to take notice, that I am now sensible of my own unhappiness also, in having fallen under a diversion from better employments by such sad and woful impertinencies. But being at once charged with both these misadventures,—untowardness in expression, and weakness in the proof of a plain truth, I shall willingly admit of information, to mend my way of writing for the future. And the first reflection he casts on my expressions, is my calling the union of the two natures in Christ in the same person, the " grace of union;" for so he says, " If you would understand what this strange grace of union is." But I crave his pardon in not complying with his directions, for my company's sake. No man, who hath once consulted the writings of the ancients on this subject, can be a stranger unto χάρις ἑνώσεως, and " gratia unionis," they so continually occur in the writings of all sorts of divines, both ancient and modern. Yea, but there is yet worse behind; for, " What an untoward representation

is this of Christ's mediation, that he came to make peace by laying
his hands on God and men, as if he came to part a fray or scuffle."
My words are, "The uniting of the natures of God and man in one
person, made him fit to be a Saviour to the uttermost. He laid his
hand upon God, by partaking of his nature, Zech. xiii. 7; and he lays
his hand upon us, by partaking of our nature, Heb. ii. 14, 16: and so
becomes a days-man or umpire between both." See what it is to be
adventurous. I doubt not but that he thought that I had invented
that expression, or at least, that I was the first who ever applied it
unto this interposition of Christ between God and man; but as I took
the words, and so my warranty for the expression from the Scripture,
Job ix. 33, so it hath commonly been applied by divines in the same
manner, particularly by Bishop Usher (in his "Immanuel," pp. 8, 9,
as I remember); whose unhappiness in expressing himself in divinity
this man needs not much to bewail. But let my expressions be what
they will, I shall not escape the unhappiness and weakness of my
proofs; for " I might," he says, "as well have quoted Gen. i. 1, and
Matt. i. 1, for the proof of the unity of the divine and human nature
in the person of Christ, and his fitness thence to be a Saviour, as
those I named,"—namely, Zech. xiii. 7; Heb. ii. 14, 16. Say you
so? Why, then, I do here undertake to maintain the personal union,
and the fitness of Christ from thence to be a Saviour, from these two
texts, against this man and all his fraternity in design. And at
present I cannot but wonder at his confidence, seeing I am sure he
cannot be ignorant that one of these places, at least,—namely, that of
Heb. ii. 16,—is as much, as frequently, as vehemently pleaded by all
sorts of divines, ancient and modern, to prove the assumption of our
human nature into personal subsistence with the Son of God, that so
he might be ἱκανός (fit and able to save us), as any one testimony in
the whole Scripture. And the same truth is as evidently contained
and expressed in the former, seeing no man could be the "fellow of
the LORD of hosts" but he that was partaker of the same nature with
him; and no one could have the sword of God upon him to smite
him, which was needful unto our salvation, but he that was partaker
of our nature, or man also. And the mere recital of these testimonies was sufficient unto my purpose in that place, where I designed
only to declare, and not dispute the truth. If he yet think that I
cannot prove what I assert from these testimonies, let him consult
my "Vindiciæ Evangelicæ," where, according as that work required,
I have directly pleaded these scriptures to the same purpose, insisting at large on the vindication of one of them; and let him answer
what I have there pleaded, if he be able. And I shall allow him to
make his advantage unto that purpose, if he please, of whatever
evasions the Socinians have found out to escape the force of that tes-

timony. For there is none of them of any note but have attempted by various artifices to shield their opinion, in denying the assumption of our human nature into personal union with the Son of God, and therewithal his pre-existence unto his nativity of the blessed Virgin, from the divine evidence given against it in that place of Heb. ii. 16; which yet, if this author may be believed, doth make no more against them than Gen. i. 1. Wherefore, this severe censure, together with the modesty of the expression, wherein Christ making peace between God and man is compared to the parting of a fray or scuffle, may pass at the same rate and value with those which are gone before.

His ensuing pages are taken up, for the most part, with the transcription of passages out of my discourse, raked together from several places at his pleasure. I shall not impose the needless labour on the reader of a third perusal of them: nor shall I take the pains to restore the several passages to their proper place and coherence, which he hath rent them from, to try his skill and strength upon them separately and apart; for I see not that they stand in need of using the least of their own circumstantial evidence in their vindication. I shall therefore only take notice of his exceptions against them. And, p. 207, whereas I had said on some occasion, that on such a supposition we could have supplies of grace only in a moral way, it falls under his derision in his parenthesis; and that is a very pitiful way indeed. But I must yet tell him, by the way, that if he allow of no supplies of grace but in a moral way, he is a Pelagian, and as such, stands condemned by the catholic church. And when his occasions will permit it, I desire he would answer what is written by myself in another discourse, in the refutation of this sole moral operation of grace, and the assertion of another way of the communication of it unto us. Leave fooling, and "the unhappiest man in expressing himself that ever I met with" will not do it; he must betake himself to another course, if he intend to engage into the handling of things of this nature. He adds, whereas I had said, " 'The grace of the promises' (of the person of Christ you mean):" I know well enough what I mean; but the truth is, I know not well what he means; nor whether it be out of ignorance that he doth indeed fancy an opposition between Christ and the promises, that what is ascribed unto the one must needs be derogated from the other, when the promise is but the means and instrument of conveying the grace of Christ unto us; or whether it proceeds from a real dislike that the person of Christ—that is, Jesus Christ himself—should be esteemed of any use or consideration in religion, that he talks at this rate. But from whence ever it proceeds, this cavilling humour is unworthy of any man of ingenuity or learning. By his following parenthesis ("a world of sin is something") I suppose I have somewhere used that expression, whence it is reflected on; but he quotes not the place, and I cannot find it. I shall therefore only at present tell him, as (if I remember aright) I have done already, that I will not come to him nor any of his companions to learn to express myself in these things; and, moreover, that I despise their censures. The discourses he is carping at in particular in this place are neither doctrinal nor argumentative, but consist in the application of truths before proved unto the minds and affections of men. And, as I said, I will not come to him nor his fraternity to learn how to manage such a subject, much less a logical and argumentative way of reasoning; nor have I any inducement thereunto from any thing that as yet I have seen in their writings. It also troubles him, p. 208, that whereas I know how unsuited the best and most accurate of our expressions are unto the true nature and being of divine things, as they are in themselves, and what need we have to make use of allusions, and sometimes less proper expressions, to convey a sense of them unto the minds and affections of men, I had once or twice used that ἐπανόρθωσις, "if I may so say;" which yet if he had not known used in other good authors, treating of things of the same nature, he knew I could take protection against his severity under the example of the apostle, using words to the same purpose upon an alike occasion, Heb. vii. But at length he intends to be serious, and from those words of mine, "Here is mercy enough for the greatest, the oldest, the stubbornest transgressor;" he adds, "Enough, in all reason, this: what a comfort is it to sinners to have such a God for their Saviour, whose grace is boundless and bottomless, and exceeds the largest dimensions of their sins, though there be a world of sin in them. But what, now, if the divine nature itself have not such an endless, boundless, bottomless grace and compassion as the doctor now talks of? For at other times, when it serves his turn better, we can hear nothing from him but the 'naturalness of God's vindictive justice.' Though God be rich in mercy, he never told us that his mercy was so boundless and bottomless; he had given a great many demonstrations of the severity of his anger against sinners, who could not be much worse than the 'greatest, the oldest, and the stubbornest transgressors.'"

Let the reader take notice, that I propose no grace in Christ unto or for such sinners, but only that which may invite all sorts of them, though under the most discouraging qualifications, to come unto him for grace and mercy by faith and repentance. And on supposition that this was my sense, as he cannot deny it to be, I add only, in answer, that this his profane scoffing at it, is that which reflects on Christ and his gospel, and God himself and his word; which must be accounted for. See Isa. lv. 7. Secondly, For the opposition which he childishly frames between God's vindictive justice and his mercy and grace, it is answered already. Thirdly, It is false that God hath not told us that his grace is boundless and bottomless, in the sense wherein I use those words, sufficient to pardon the greatest, the oldest, the stubbornest of sinners,—namely, that turn unto him by faith and repentance; and he who knows not how this consists with severity and anger against impenitent sinners, is yet to learn his catechism. But yet he adds farther, pp. 208, 209, " Supposing the divine nature were such a bottomless fountain of grace, how comes this to be a personal grace of the Mediator? For a mediator, as mediator, ought not to be considered as the fountain, but as the minister of grace. God the Father certainly ought to come in for a share, at least, in being the fountain of grace, though the doctor is pleased to take no notice of him. But how excellent is the grace of Christ's person above the grace of the gospel; for that is a bounded and limited thing, a strait gate and narrow way, that leadeth unto life. There is no such boundless mercy as all the sins in the world cannot equal its dimensions, as will save the greatest, the oldest, and the stubbornest transgressors."

I beg the reader to believe that I am now so utterly weary with the repetition of these impertinencies, that I can hardly prevail with myself to fill my pen once more with ink about them; and I see no reason now to go on, but only that I have begun; and, on all accounts, I shall be as brief as possible. I say, then, first, I did not consider this boundless grace in Christ as mediator, but considered it as in him who is mediator; and so the divine nature, with all its properties, are greatly to be considered in him, if the gospel be true. But, secondly, It is untrue that Christ, as mediator, is only the minister of grace, and not the fountain of it; for he is mediator as God and man in one person. Thirdly, To suppose an exemption of the person of the Father from being the fountain of grace absolutely, in the order of the divine subsistence of the persons in the Trinity, and of their operations suited thereunto, upon the ascription of it unto the Son, is a fond imagination, which could befall no man who understands any thing of things of this nature. It doth as well follow, that if the Son created the world, the Father did not; if the Son uphold all things by the word of his power, the Father doth not;—that is, that the Son is not in the Father, nor the Father in the Son. The acts, indeed, of Christ's mediation respect the ministration of grace, being the procuring and communicating causes thereof; but the person of Christ the mediator is the fountain of grace. So they thought who beheld his glory,—" The glory as of the only begotten of the Father, full of grace and truth." But the especial relation of grace unto the Father, as sending the Son; unto the Son, as sent by him and incarnate; and unto the Holy Spirit, as proceeding from and sent by them both, I have elsewhere fully declared, and shall not in this place (which, indeed, will scarce give admittance unto any thing of so serious a nature) again insist thereon. Fourthly, The opposition which he would again set between Christ and the gospel is impious in itself; and, if he thinks to charge it on me, openly false. I challenge him and all his accomplices to produce any one word out of any writing of mine that, from a plea or pretence of grace in Christ, should give countenance unto any in the neglect of the least precept given or duty required in the gospel. And notwithstanding all that I have said or taught concerning the boundless, bottomless grace and mercy of Christ towards believing, humble, penitent sinners, I do believe the way of gospel obedience, indispensably required to be walked in by all that will come to the enjoyment of God, to be so narrow, that no revilers, nor false accusers, nor scoffers, nor despisers of gospel mysteries, continuing so to be, can walk therein;—but that there is not grace and mercy declared and tendered in the gospel also unto all sorts of sinners, under any qualifications whatever, who, upon its invitation, will come to God through Jesus Christ by faith and repentance, is an impious imagination.

A discourse much of the same nature follows, concerning the love of Christ, after he hath treated his person and grace at his pleasure. And this he takes occasion for from some passages in my book (as formerly), scraped together from several places, so as he thought fit and convenient unto his purpose. P. 209, " Thus the love of Christ is an eternal love, because his divine nature is eternal; and it is an unchangeable love, because his divine nature is unchangeable; and his love is fruitful, for it being the love of God, it must be effectual and fruitful in producing all the things which he willeth unto his beloved. He loves life, grace, holiness into us, loves us into covenant, loves us into heaven. This is an excellent love, indeed, which doth all for us, and leaves nothing for us to do. We owe this discovery to an acquaintance with Christ's person, or rather with his divine nature; for the gospel is very silent in this matter. All that the gospel tells us is, that Christ loveth sinners, so as to die for them; that he loves good men, who believe and obey his gospel, so as to save them; that he continues to love them while they continue to be good, but hates them when they return to their old vices: and therefore, I say, there is great reason for sinners to fetch their comforts not from the gospel, but from the person of Christ, which as far excels the gospel as the gospel excels the law."

I do suppose the expressions mentioned are, for the substance of them, in my book; and shall, therefore, only inquire what it is in them which he excepteth against, and for which I am reproached, as one that hath an acquaintance with Christ's person; which is now grown so common and trite an expression, that were it not condited unto some men's palates by its profaneness, it would argue a great barrenness in this author's invention, that can vary no more in the topic of reviling. It had been well if his licenser had accommodated him with some part of his talent herein. But what is it that is excepted against? Is it that the love of Christ, as he is God, is eternal? or is it that it is unchangeable? or is it that it is fruitful or effective of good things unto the persons beloved? The philosopher tells us, that to [have] love for any one, is, Βούλεσθαί τινι ἃ οἴεται ἀγαθά, καὶ τὸ κατὰ δύναμιν πρακτικὸν εἶναι τούτων. It is this efficacy of the love of Christ which must bear all the present charge. The meaning of my words, therefore, is, that the love of Christ is unto us the cause of life, grace, holiness, and the reward of heaven. And because it is in the nature of love to be effective, according unto the ability of the person loving, of the good which it wills unto the object beloved, I expressed it as I thought meet, by loving these things to us. And I am so far on this occasion, and [on account of] the severe reflection on me for an acquaintance with Christ, from altering my thoughts, that I say still with confidence, he who is otherwise minded is no Christian. And if this man knows not how the love of Christ is the cause of grace and glory, how it is effective of them, and that in a perfect consistency with all other causes and means of them, and the necessity of our obedience, he may do well to abstain a little from writing, until he is better informed. But saith he, "This is an excellent love, indeed, which doth all for us, and leaves us nothing to do." But who told him so? who ever said so? Doth he think that if our life, grace, holiness, glory, be from the love of Christ originally, causally, by virtue of his divine, gracious operations in us and towards us, that there is no duty incumbent on them who would be made partakers of them, or use or improve them unto their proper ends? Shall we, then, to please him, say that we have neither life, nor grace, nor holiness, nor glory, from the love of Christ; but whereas most of them are our own duties, we have them wholly from ourselves? Let them do so who have a mind to renounce Christ and his gospel; I shall come into no partnership with them. [As] for what he adds, "All that the gospel teaches us," etc., he should have done well to have said, as far as he knows; which is a limitation with a witness. If this be all the gospel which the man knows and preaches, I pity them whom he hath taken under his instruction. Doth Christ in his love do nothing unto the quickening and conversion of men? nothing to the purification and sanctification of believers? nothing as to their consolation and establishment? nothing as to the administration of strength against temptations? nothing as to supplies of grace, in the increase of faith, love, and obedience, etc.? This ignorance or profaneness is greatly to be bewailed, as his ensuing scoff, repeated now *usque ad nauseam*, about an opposition between Christ and his gospel, is to be despised. And if the Lord Christ hath no other love but what this man will allow, the state of the church in this world depends on a very slender thread. But attempts of this nature will fall short enough of prevailing with sober Christians to forego their faith and persuasion,—that it is from the love of Christ that believers are preserved in that condition wherein he doth and will approve of them. Yea, to suppose that this is all the grace of the gospel, that whilst men are good Christ loves them, and when they are bad he hates them (both which are true); and farther, that he doth by his grace neither make them good, nor preserve them that are so made,—is to renounce all that is properly so called.

He yet proceeds, first to evert this love which I asserted, and then to declare his own apprehensions concerning the love of Christ. The first in the ensuing words, p. 210, " But, methinks this is a very odd way of arguing from the divine nature; for if the love of Christ as God be so infinite, eternal, unchangeable, fruitful, I would willingly understand how sin, death, and misery came into the world. For if this love be so eternal and unchangeable, because the divine nature is so, then it was always so; for God always was what he is, and that which is eternal could never be other than it is now: and why could not this eternal, and unchangeable, and fruitful love, as well preserve us from falling into sin, and misery, and death, as love life and holiness into us? For it is a little odd, first to love us into sin and death, that then he may love us into life and holiness: which, indeed, could not be, if this love of God were always so unchangeable and fruitful as this author persuades us it is now; for if this love had always loved life and holiness into us, I cannot conceive how it should happen that we should sin and die."

It is well if he know what it is that he aims at in these words; I am sure what he says doth not in the least impeach the truth which he designs to oppose. The name and nature of God are everywhere in the Scripture proposed unto us as the object of, and encouragement unto, our faith, and his love in particular is therein represented unchangeable, because he himself is so; but it doth not hence follow that God loveth any one naturally, or necessarily. His love is a free act of his will; and therefore, though it be like himself, such as becomes his nature, yet it is not necessarily determined on any object, nor limited as unto the nature, degrees, and effects of it. He loves whom he pleaseth, and as unto what end he pleaseth. Jacob he loved, and Esau he hated; and those effects which, from his love or out of it, he will communicate unto them, are various, according to the counsel of his will. Some he loves only as to temporal and common mercies, some as to spiritual grace and glory; for he hath mercy on whom he will have mercy. Wherefore it is no way contrary unto, and inconsistent with, the eternity, the immutability, and fruitfulness of the love of God, that he suffered sin to enter into the world, or that he doth dispense more grace in Jesus Christ under the New Testament than he did under the Old. God is always the same that he was; love in God is always of the same nature that it was; but the objects, acts, and effects of this love, with the measures and degrees of them, are the issues of the counsel or free purposes of his will. Want of the understanding hereof makes this man imagine, that if God's love in Christ, wherewith he loveth us, be eternal and fruitful, then must God necessarily always—in or out of Christ, under the old or new covenant—love all persons, elect or not elect, with the same love as to the effects and fruits of it; which is a wondrous profound apprehension. The reader, therefore, if he please, may take notice, that the love which I intend, and whereunto I ascribe those properties, is the especial love of God in Christ unto the elect. Concerning this himself says, that he loves them with an everlasting love, and therefore "draws them with loving-kindness," Jer. xxxi. 3; which love, I shall be bold to say, is eternal and fruitful. And hence, as he changeth not, whereon the sons of Jacob are not consumed, Mal. iii. 6, there being with him "neither variableness, nor shadow of turning," James i. 17; so accordingly he hath in this matter, by his promise and oath, declared the immutability of his counsel, Heb. vi. 17, 18,—which seems to intimate that his love is unchangeable. And whereas this eternal love is in Christ Jesus as the way and means of making it certain in all its effects, and with respect unto its whole design, it is fruitful in all grace and glory, Eph. i. 3–5. And if he cannot understand how, notwithstanding all this, sin so entered into the world under the law of creation and the first covenant as to defeat in us all the benefits thereof, at present I cannot help him; for, as I am sure enough he would scorn to learn any thing of me, so I am not at leisure to put it to the trial.

His own account of the love of God succeeds. P. 211, "Not that I deny that the love of God is eternal, unchangeable, fruitful; that is, that God was always good, and always continues good, and manifesteth his love and goodness in such ways as are suitable to his nature, which is the fruitfulness of it: but then, the unchangeableness of God's love doth not consist in being always determined to the same object, but that he always loves for the same reason; that is, that he always loves true virtue and goodness, wherever he sees it, and never ceases to love any person till he ceases to be good: and then the immutability of his love is the reason why he loves no longer; for should he love a wicked man, the reason and nature of his love would change. And the fruitfulness of God's love, with respect to the methods of his grace and providence, doth not consist in procuring what he loves by an omnipotent and irresistible power; for then sin and death could never have entered into the world: but he governs and doth good to his creatures, in such ways as are most suitable to their natures. He governs reasonable creatures by principles of reason, as he doth the material world by the necessary laws of matter, and brute creatures by the instincts and propensities of nature."

This may pass for a system of his divinity, which how he will reconcile unto the doctrine of the church of England in her articles, she and he may do well to consider. But, whatever he means by the love of God always determined unto the same object, it were an easy thing to prove, beyond the reach of his contradiction, that persons are the objects of God's eternal love, as well as things and qualifications are of his approbation; or, that he loves some persons with an everlasting and unchangeable love, so as to preserve them from all ruining evils, and so as they may be always meet objects of his approving love, unto his glory: and whereas these things have been debated and disputed on all hands with much learning and diligence, our author is a very happy man if, with a few such loose expressions as these repeated, he thinks to determine all the controversies about election and effectual grace, with perseverance, on the Pelagian side. The hypothesis here maintained, that because God always and unchangeably approves of what is good in any, or of the obedience of his creatures, and disapproves or hates sin, condemning it in his law, [and] that therefore he may love the same person one day and hate him another, notwithstanding his pretences that he is constant unto the reason of his love, will inevitably fall into one of these conclusions:— either, that God indeed never loveth any man, be he who he will; or, that he is changeable in his love, upon outward, external reasons, as we are: and let him choose which he will own. In the meantime, such a love of God towards believers as shall always effectually preserve them meet objects of his love and approbation, is not to be baffled by such trifling impertinencies. His next reflection is on the manner of God's operations in the communication of grace and holiness; which, he says, is "not by omnipotent and irresistible power,"— confirming his assertion by that consideration, that then sin and death could never have entered into the world; which is resolved into another sweet supposition, that God must needs act the same power of grace towards all men, at all times, under each covenant, whether he will or no. But this it is to be a happy disputant,—all things succeed well with such persons which they undertake. And as to the manner of the operation of grace, how far grace itself may be said to be omnipotent, and in its operations irresistible, I have fully declared there; where he may oppose and refute it, if he have any mind thereunto. His present attempt against it in those words, that God "governs reasonable creatures by principles of reason," is so weak in this case, and impertinent, that it deserves no consideration; for all the operations of divine grace are suited unto the rational constitution of our beings, neither was ever man so wild as to fancy any of them such as are inconsistent with, or do offer force unto, the faculties of our souls in their operations. Yea, that which elevates, aids, and assists our rational faculties in their operations on and towards their proper objects, which is the work of efficacious grace, is the principal preservative of their power and liberty, and can be no way to their prejudice. And we do, moreover, acknowledge that those proposals which are made in the gospel unto our reason, are eminently suited to excite and prevail with it unto its proper use and exercise in compliance with them. Hence, although the habit of faith, or power of believing, be wrought in us by the Holy Ghost, yet the word of the gospel is the cause and means of all its acts, and the whole obedience which it produceth. But if by " governing reasonable creatures by principles of reason," he intends that God deals no otherwise by his grace with the souls of men, but only by proposing objective arguments and motives unto a compliance with his will, without internal aids and assistances of grace, it is a gross piece of Pelagianism, destructive of the gospel, sufficiently confuted elsewhere; and he may explain himself as he pleaseth.

His proceed is, to transcribe some other passages, taken out of my book here and there, in whose repetition he inserts some impertinent exceptions; but the design of the whole is to " state a controversy," as he calls it, between us and them, or those whom he calleth "they" and " we," whoever they be. And this, upon the occasion of my mentioning the fulness of grace, life, and righteousness that is in Christ, he doth in these words:—P. 215, " They say that these are the personal graces of Christ as mediator, which are inherent in him, and must be derived from his person; we say, they signify the perfection and excellency of his religion, as being the most perfect and complete declaration of the will of God, and the most powerful method of the divine wisdom for the reforming of the world, as it prescribes the only righteousness which is acceptable to God, and directs us in the only way to life and immortality."

I shall not absolutely accept of the terms of this controversy, as to the state of it on our part, proposed by him; and yet I shall not much vary from them. We say, therefore, that " Jesus Christ being full of all grace, excellencies, and perfections, he communicates them unto us in that degree as is necessary for us, and in proportion unto his abundant charity and goodness towards us; and we Christians, as his body, or fellow-members of his human nature, receive grace and mercy, flowing from him to us." This state of the controversy on our side I suppose he will not refuse, nor the terms of it; but will own them to be ours, though he will not, it may be, allow some of them to be proper or convenient. And that he may know who his "they" are, who are at this end of the difference, he may be pleased to take notice that these words are the whole and entire paraphrase of Dr Hammond on John i. 16; the first testimony he undertakes to answer. And when this author hath replied to Mr Hooker, Dr Jackson, and him, and such other pillars of the church of England as concur with them, it will be time enough for me to consider how I shall defend myself against him. Or, if he will take the controversy on our part in terms more directly expressive of my mind, it is the person of Christ is the fountain of all grace to the church (as he well observes my judgment to be), and that from him all grace and mercy is derived unto us; and then I do maintain, that the "they" whom he opposeth, are not only the church of England, but the whole catholic church in all ages. Who the "we" are, on the other hand, who reject this assertion, and believe that all the testimonies concerning the fulness of grace in Christ, and the communication thereof unto us, do only declare the excellency of his religion, is not easy to be conjectured;—for unless it be the people of Racow, I know not who are his associates. And let him but name three divines of any reputation in the church of England since the Reformation, who have given the least countenance unto his assertions, negative or positive, and I will acknowledge that he hath better associates in his profession than as yet I believe he hath. But that Jesus Christ himself, God and man in one person, the mediator between God and man, is not a fountain of grace and mercy to his church; that there is no real internal grace communicated by him, or derived from him unto his mystical body; that the fulness which is in him, or said to be in him, of grace and truth, of unsearchable riches of grace, etc., is nothing but the doctrine which he taught, as the most complete and perfect declaration of the will of God,—are opinions that cannot be divulged, under pretence of authority, without the most pernicious scandal to the present church of England. And if this be the man's religion, that this is all the fulness we receive from Christ,—"a perfect revelation of the divine will concerning the salvation of mankind; which contains so many excellent promises that it may well be called 'grace;' and prescribes such a plain and simple religion, so agreeable to the natural notions of good and evil, that it may well be called 'truth;'"—and complying with its doctrine, or yielding obedience unto its precepts and believing the promises which it gives, in our own strength, without any real aid, assistance, or communication of internal saving grace from the person of Jesus Christ, is our righteousness before God, whereon and for which we are justified,—I know as well as he whence it came, and perhaps better than he whither it will go.

The remaining discourse of this chapter consisteth of two parts:— First, An attempt to disprove any communication of real internal grace from the Lord Christ unto believers for their sanctification; Secondly, An endeavour to refute the imputation of his righteousness unto us for our justification. In the first he contends that all the fulness of grace and truth said to be in Christ consists either in the doctrine of the gospel or in the largeness of his church. In the latter, that faith in Christ is nothing but believing the gospel, and the authority of Christ who revealed it; and by yielding obedience whereunto, we are justified before God, on the account of an internal inherent righteousness in ourselves. Now, these are no small undertakings; the first of them being expressly contrary to the sense of the catholic church in all ages (for the Pelagians and the Socinians are by common agreement excluded from an interest therein); and the latter of them, contrary to the plain confessions of all the reformed churches, with the constant doctrine of this church of England: and therefore we may justly expect that they should be managed with much strength of argument, and evident demonstration. But the unhappiness of it is (I will not say his, but ours), that these are not things which our author as yet hath accustomed himself unto; and I cannot but say, that to my knowledge I never read a more weak, loose, and impertinent discourse, upon so weighty subjects, in my whole life before: he must have little to do, who can afford to spend his time in a particular examination of it, unless it be in the exposition of those places which are almost *verbatim* transcribed out of Schlichtingius.[1] Besides, for the first truth which he opposeth, I have confirmed it in a discourse which I suppose may be made public before this come to view, beyond what I expect any sober reply unto from him. Some texts of Scripture that mention a fulness in Christ he chooseth out, to manifest (to spéak a word by the way) that indeed they do not intend any such fulness in Christ himself. And the first is John i. 16; the exposition whereof which he gives is that of Schlichtingius, who yet extends the import of the words beyond what he will allow. The enforcement which he gives unto his exposition, by comparing the 14th and 17th verses with the 16th, is both weak and contradictory

---

[1] Jonas Schlichtingius was a Socinian author. He wrote "A Confession of Christian Faith, published in the name of the Churches which in Poland acknowledge one God, and his only begotten Son Jesus Christ, and the Holy Spirit." It appeared in the year 1642.—ED.

of itself; for the words of the 14th verse are, "The Word was made flesh, and dwelt among us (and we beheld his glory, the glory as of the only begotten of the Father), full of grace and truth." It is evident beyond contradiction, that the expression, "full of grace and truth," is exegetical of his glory as the only begotten of the Father, which was the glory of his person, and not the doctrine of the gospel. And for the opposition that is made between the law given by Moses, and the grace and truth which came by Jesus Christ, I shall yet rather adhere to the sense of the ancient church, and the most eminent doctors of it, which, if he knows not it to be concerning the effectual communication of real, renewing, sanctifying grace by Jesus Christ, there are enow who can inform him; rather than that woful gloss upon them,—"His doctrine is called 'grace,' because accompanied with such excellent promises; and may well be called 'truth,' because so agreeable to the natural notions of good and evil,"—which is the confession of the Pelagian unbelief: but these things are not my present concernment. For the latter part of his discourse, in his opposition unto the imputation of the righteousness of Christ, as he doth not go about once to state or declare the sense wherein it is pleaded for, nor produceth any one of the arguments wherewith it is confirmed, and omitteth the mention of most of the particular testimonies which declare and establish it; so, as unto those few which he takes notice of, he expressly founds his answers unto them on that woful subterfuge, that if they are capable of another interpretation, or having another sense given unto them, then nothing can be concluded from them to that purpose,—by which the Socinians seek to shelter themselves from all the testimonies that are given to his Deity and satisfaction. But I have no concernment, as I said, either in his opinions or his way of reasoning; and do know that those who have so, need not desire a better cause nor an easier adversary to deal withal.

In his third section, p. 279, he enters upon his exceptions unto the union of believers unto Jesus Christ, and with great modesty, at the entrance of his discourse, tells us, first, "how these men," with whom he hath to do, "have fitted the person of Christ unto all the wants and necessities of the sinner;" which yet, if he denies God himself to have done, he is openly injurious unto his wisdom and grace. The very first promise that was given concerning him was, that he should save sinners from all their wants, evils, and miseries, that might, did, or could befall them by the entrance of sin. But thus it falls out, when men will be talking of what they do not understand. Again, he adds how he hath "explained the Scripture metaphors whereby the union between Christ and Christians is represented; but that these men, instead of explaining of those metaphors, turn all religion into an allegory." But what if one should now tell him, that his explanation of these metaphors is the most absurd and irrational, and argues the most fulsome ignorance of the mystery of the gospel, that can be imagined; and that, on the other side, those whom he traduceth do explain them unto the understanding and experience of all that believe, and that in a way suited and directed unto by the Holy Ghost himself, to farther their faith, obedience, and consolation? As far as I perceive, he would be at no small loss how to relieve himself under this censure. The first thing he begins withal, and wherein, in the first place, I fall under his displeasure, is about the conjugal relation between Christ and believers, which he treats of, p. 280. "As for example," saith he, "Christ is called a husband, the church his spouse; and now all the invitations of the gospel are Christ's wooing and making love to his spouse;—and what other men call believing the gospel of Christ, whereby we devote ourselves to his service, these men call that consent and contract, which make up the marriage betwixt Christ and believers. Christ takes us for his spouse, and we take Christ for our husband, and that with all the solemnities of marriage, except the ring, which is left out as an antichristian ceremony; Christ saying thus, 'This is that we will consent unto, that I will be for thee, and thou shalt be for me, and not for another.' Christ gives himself to the soul, with all his excellencies, righteousness, preciousness, graces, and eminencies, to be its saviour, head, and husband,—to dwell with it in this holy relation; and the soul likes Christ for his excellencies, graces, suitableness, far above all other beloveds whatsoever, and accepts of Christ by the will for its husband, lord, and saviour. And thus the marriage is completed; and this is the day of Christ's espousals, and of the gladness of his heart. And now follow all mutual conjugal affections; which, on Christ's part, consist in delight, valuation, pity, compassion, bounty; on the saints' part, in delight, valuation, chastity, duty. But I have already corrected this fooling with Scripture metaphors and phrases."

It might, perhaps, not unbecome this author to be a little more sparing of his correction, unless his authority were more than it is, and his skill, also, in the management of it; for at present those whom he attempts upon are altogether insensible of any effects of his severity. But whereas he seems much at a loss how to evidence his own wisdom any other way than by calling them fools with whom he hath to do, it is sufficient to plead his excuse. But what is it that he is here so displeased at, as unfit for a man of his wisdom to bear withal, and therefore calls it "fooling?" Is it that there is a conjugal relation between Christ and the church?—that he is the bridegroom and husband of the church, and that the church is his bride and spouse?—that he becomes so unto it by a voluntarily, gracious act of his love, and that the church enters into that relation with him by their acceptance of him in that relation, and voluntarily giving up themselves unto him in faith, love, and obedience, suited thereunto? Is it that he loveth his church and cherisheth it as a husband? or that the church gives up itself in chaste and holy obedience unto him as her spouse? or is it my way and manner of expressing these things wherewith he is so provoked? If it be the latter, I desire he would, for his own satisfaction, take notice that I contemn his censures, and appeal to the judgment of those who have more understanding and experience in these things than, for aught I can discern by his writings, he hath yet attained unto. If it be the former, they are all of them so proved and confirmed from the Scripture in that very discourse which he excepteth against, as that he is not able to answer or reply one serious word thereunto. Indeed, to deny it, is to renounce the gospel and the catholic faith. It is, therefore, to no purpose for me here to go over again the nature of this relation between Christ and the church,—wherein really and truly it doth consist; what it is the Scripture instructeth us in thereby; what is that love, care, and tenderness of Christ, which it would have us thence to learn; and what is our own duty with respect thereunto, together with the consolation thence arising: the whole of this work is already discharged in that discourse which these impertinent cavils are raised against, and that suitably to the sense of the church in all ages, and of all sound expositors of those very many places of Scripture which I have urged and insisted on to that purpose. Let him, if he please, a little lay aside the severity of his corrections and befooling of men, and answer any material passage in the whole discourse, if he be able; or discover any thing in it not agreeable to the analogy of faith, or the sense of the ancient church, if he can. And though he seem, both here and in some of his ensuing pages, to have a particular contempt of what is cited or improved out of the book of Canticles to this purpose; yet, if he either deny that that whole book doth mystically express the conjugal relation that is between Christ and his church, with their mutual affections and delight in each other, or that the places particularly insisted on by me are not duly applied unto their proper intention, I can, at least, confirm them both by the authority of such persons as whose antiquity and learning will exercise the utmost of his confidence in calling them fools for their pains.

From hence for sundry pages he is pleased to give me a little respite, whilst he diverts his severity unto another; unto whose will and choice what to do in it I shall leave his peculiar concern, as knowing full well how easy it is for him to vindicate what he hath written on this subject from his impertinent exceptions, if he please.

In the meantime, if this author supposeth to add unto the reputation of his ingenuity and modesty by assaulting with a few pitiful cavils a book written with so much learning, judgment, and moderation, as that is which he excepts against, not daring in the meantime to contend with it in any thing of the expository or the argumentative part of it, but only to discover a malevolent desire to obstruct the use which it hath been of, and may yet farther be, to the church of God,—I hope he will not find many rivals in such a design. For my part, I do suppose it more becoming Christian modesty and sobriety, where men have laboured according to their ability in the explication of the mysteries of Christian religion, and that with an avowed intention to promote holiness and gospel obedience, to accept of what they have attained, wherein we can come unto a compliance with them; than, passing by whatever we cannot but approve of, or are not able to disprove, to make it our business to cavil at such expressions as either we do not like, or hope to pervert and abuse to their disadvantage.

P. 296, he returns again to my discourse, and fiercely pursues it for sundry leaves, in such a manner as becomes him, and is usual with him. That part of my book which he deals withal, is from p. 176[1] unto p. 187; and if any person of ingenuity and judgment will be pleased but to peruse it, and to compare it with this man's exceptions, I am secure it will need no farther vindication. But as it is represented in his cavilling way, it is impossible for any man either to conceive what is the true design of my discourse, or what the arguments wherewith what I assert is confirmed; which he doth most unduly pretend to give an account of: for he so chops, and changes, and alters at his pleasure, going backwards and forwards, and that from one thing to another, without any regard unto a scholastic or ingenuous debate of any thing that might be called a controversy, merely to seek out an appearance of advantage to vent his cavilling exceptions, as no judgment can rationally be made of his whole discourse, but only that he had a mind to have cast aspersions on mine, if he had known how. But such stuff as it is, we must now take the measure of it, and consider of what use it may be. And first he quotes those words from my book, "That Christ fulfilled all righteousness as he was mediator; and that whatever he did as mediator, he did it for them whose mediator he was, or in whose stead and for whose good he executed the office of a mediator before God: and hence it is that his complete and perfect obedience to the law is reckoned to us." He adds, "This is well said, if it were as well proved. And because this is a matter of great consequence, I shall first examine those reasons the doctor alleges to prove that Christ

[1] From p. 154 to p. 164 of this volume.

fulfilled all righteousness, as he was mediator, in their stead whose mediator he was."

These assertions are gathered up from several places in my discourse, though p. 182[1] is cited for them all. And if any one find himself concerned in these things, I may demand of him the labour of their perusal in my book itself; and for those who shall refuse a compliance with so reasonable a request, I do not esteem myself obliged to tender them any farther satisfaction. However, I say again, that the Lord Christ fulfilled all righteousness as mediator; and that what he did as mediator, he did it for them whose mediator he was, or in whose stead and for whose good he executed the office of a mediator before God. He says, "It is well said, if it were as well proved." I say, it is all proved in the places where it is asserted, and that with such testimonies and arguments as he dares not touch upon. And although he pretends to examine the reasons that I allege to prove that Christ fulfilled all righteousness, as he was mediator, in their stead whose mediator he was, yet indeed he doth not do so. For, first, I say no such thing as he here feigns me to say,— namely, that "Christ as mediator fulfilled all righteousness in our stead;" but only, that "Christ being the mediator, in our stead fulfilled all righteousness:" which is another thing, though perhaps he understands not the difference. Nor doth he so much as take notice of that testimony which is immediately subjoined unto the words he cites in the confirmation of them; but he will disprove this assertion, or at least manifest that it cannot be proved. And this he enters upon, p 297, "As for the first, we have some reason to require good proof of this, since the notion of a mediator includes no such thing. A mediator is one who interposeth between two differing parties, to accommodate the difference; but it was never heard of yet, that it was the office of a mediator to perform the terms and conditions himself. Moses was the mediator of the first covenant, Gal. iii. 19; and his office was to receive the law from God, to deliver it to the people, to command them to observe those rites, and sacrifices, and expiations which God had ordained: but he was not to fulfil the righteousness of the law for the whole congregation. Thus Christ is now the mediator of a better covenant; and his office required that he should preach the gospel, which contains the terms of peace and reconciliation beween God and men; and since God would not enter into covenant with sinners without the intervention of a sacrifice, he dies too, as a sacrifice and propitiation for the sins of the world."

I yet suppose that he observed not the inconsistencies of this discourse, and therefore shall a little mind him of them, although I am no way concerned in it or them. For, first, He tells us, that "a

---

[1] Pp. 162, 163, of this volume.

mediator is one who interposeth between two differing parties, to accommodate the difference;" and then gives us an instance in Moses, who is called a mediator in receiving the law, but did therein no way interpose himself between differing parties, to reconcile them. Secondly, From the nature of the mediation of Moses, he would describe the nature of the mediation of Christ; which Socinian fiction I could direct him to a sufficient confutation of, but that, thirdly, He rejects it himself in his next words,—that Christ as a mediator was to die as a sacrifice and propitiation for the sins of the world; which renders his mediation utterly of another kind and nature than that of Moses. The mistake of this discourse is, that he supposeth that men do argue from the general nature of the office of a mediator the work of mediation in this matter; when that which they do intend hence to prove, and what he intends to oppose, is the special nature of the mediatory office and work of Christ; which is peculiar, and hath sundry things essentially belonging unto it, that belong not unto any other kind of mediation whatever; whereof himself gives one signal instance.

In his ensuing pages he wonderfully perplexeth himself in gathering up sayings, backward and forward in my discourse, to make some advantage to his purpose, and hopes that he is arrived at no less success than a discovery of I know not what contradictions in what I have asserted. As I said before, so I say again, that I refer the determination and judgment of this whole matter unto any one who will but once read over the discourse excepted against. But for his part, I greatly pity him, as really supposing him at a loss in the sense of what is yet plainly delivered; and I had rather continue to think so, than to be relieved by supposing him guilty of such gross prevarications as he must be if he understands what he treats about. Plainly, I have showed that there was an especial law of mediation, which Christ was subject unto, at the commandment of the Father: that he should be incarnate; that he should be the king, priest, and prophet of his church; that he should bear our iniquities, make his soul an offering for sin, and give his life a ransom for many, were the principal parts of this law. The whole of it I have lately explained, in my exercitations unto the second part of the Exposition of the Epistle to the Hebrews; whereon, if he please, he may exercise and try his skill in a way of opposition. This law our Lord Jesus Christ did not yield obedience to in our stead, as though we had been obliged originally unto the duties of it, which we neither were nor could be; although what he suffered penally in any of them was in our stead; without which consideration he could not have righteously suffered in any kind. And the following trivial exception of this author, about the obligation on us to lay down our lives for the brethren, is meet for him to put in, seeing we are not obliged so to die for any one as Christ died for us. Was Paul crucified for you? But, secondly, Christ our mediator, and as mediator, was obliged unto all that obedience unto the moral, and all other laws of God, that the church was obliged unto; and that which I have asserted hereon is, that the effects of the former obedience of Christ are communicated unto us, but the latter obedience itself is imputed unto us; and [I] have proved it by those arguments which this man does not touch upon. All this is more fully, clearly, and plainly declared in the discourse itself; and I have only represented so much of it here again, that it might be evident unto all how frivolous are his exceptions. It is therefore to no purpose for me to transcribe again the quotations out of my book which he filleth up his pages with, seeing it is but little in them which he excepteth against; and whoever pleaseth, may consult them at large in the places from whence they are taken; or, because it is not easy to find them out singly, they are so picked up and down, backwards and forwards, curtailed and added to at pleasure, any one may, in a very little space of time, read over the whole unto his full satisfaction. I shall, therefore, only consider his exceptions, and haste unto an end of this fruitless trouble, wherein I am most unwillingly engaged by this man's unsuspected disingenuity and ignorance.

After the citation of some passages, he adds, p. 301, "This, methinks, is very strange, that what he did as mediator is not imputed unto us; but what he did, not as our mediator, but as a man subject to the law, that is imputed to us, and reckoned as if we had done it, by reason of his being our mediator. And it is as strange to the full, that Christ should do whatever was required of us by virtue of any law, when he was neither husband, nor wife, nor father, merchant nor tradesman, seaman nor soldier, captain nor lieutenant, much less a temporal prince and monarch. And how he should discharge the duties of these relations for us, which are required of us by certain laws, when he never was in any of these relations, and could not possibly be in all, is an argument which may exercise the subtilty of schoolmen, and to them I leave it."

It were greatly to be desired that he would be a little more heedful, and with attention read the writings of other men, that he might understand them before he comes to make such a bluster in his opposition to them: for I had told him plainly, that though there was a peculiar law of mediation, whose acts and duties we had no obligation unto, yet the Lord Christ, even as mediator, was obliged unto, and did personally perform, all the duties of obedience unto the law of God whereunto we were subject and obliged, p. 181,[1] sec. 14. And

[1] P. 159 of this volume.

it is strange to apprehend how he came to imagine that I said he did it not as our mediator, but as a private man. That which, possibly, might cast his thoughts into this disorder was, that he knew not that Christ was made a private man as mediator; which yet the Scripture is sufficiently express in. [As] for the following objections, that the Lord Christ was neither " husband nor wife, father nor tradesman," etc. (wherein yet possibly he is out in his account), I have frequently smiled at it when I have met with it in the Socinians, who are perking with it at every turn; but here it ought to be admired. But yet, without troubling those bugbears the schoolmen, he may be pleased to take notice, that the grace of duty and obedience in all relations is the same,—the relations administering only an external occasion unto its peculiar exercise; and what our Lord Jesus Christ did in the fulfilling of all righteousness in the circumstances and relations wherein he stood, may be imputed to us for our righteousness in all our relations, every act of duty and sin in them respecting the same law and principle. And hereon all his following exceptions for sundry pages, wherein he seems much to have pleased himself, do fall to nothing, as being resolved into his own mistakes, if he doth not prevaricate against his science and conscience; for the sum of them all he gives us in these words, p. 204, " That Christ did those things as mediator which did not belong to the laws of his mediation;" which, in what sense he did so, is fully explained in my discourse. And I am apt to guess, that either he is deceived or doth design to deceive, in expressing it by the " laws of his mediation;" which may comprise all the laws which as mediator he was subject unto. And so it is most true, that he did nothing as mediator but what belonged unto the laws of his mediation; but most false, that I have affirmed that he did: for I did distinguish between that peculiar law which required the public acts of his mediation, and those other laws which, as mediator, he was made subject unto. And if he neither doth nor will understand these things when he is told them, and they are proved unto him beyond what he can contradict, I know no reason why I should trouble myself with one that contends with his own mormos, though he never so lewdly or loudly call my name upon them. And whereas I know myself sufficiently subject unto mistakes and slips, so when I actually fall into them, as I shall not desire this man's forgiveness, but leave him to exercise the utmost of his severity, so I despise his ridiculous attempts to represent contradictions in my discourse, p. 306; all pretences whereunto are taken from his own ignorance, or feigned in his imagination. Of the like nature are all his ensuing cavils. I desire no more of any reader, but to peruse the places in my discourse which he carpeth at, and if he be a person of ordinary understanding in these things, I declare that I will stand to his censure and judgment, without giving him the least farther intimation of the sense and intendment of what I have written, or vindication of its truth. Thus, whereas I had plainly declared that the way whereby the Lord Christ, in his own person, became obnoxious and subject unto the law of creation, was by his own voluntary antecedent choice, otherwise than it is with those who are inevitably subject unto it by natural generation under it; as also, that the hypostatical union, in the first instant whereof the human nature was fitted for glory, might have exempted him from the obligation of any outward law whatever,—whence it appears that his consequential obedience, though necessary to himself, when he had submitted himself unto the law (as, " Lo, I come to do thy will, O God"), was designedly for us;—he miserably perplexeth himself to abuse his credulous readers with an apprehension that I had talked, like himself, at such a rate of nonsense as any one in his wits must needs despise. The meaning and sum of my discourse he would have to be this, p. 308, " That Christ had not been bound to live like a man, had he not been a man," with I know not what futilous cavils of the like nature; when all that I insisted on was the reason why Christ would be a man, and live like a man; which was, that we might receive the benefit and profit of his obedience, as he was our mediator. So in the close of the same wise harangue, from my saying, " That the Lord Christ, by virtue of the hypostatical union, might be exempted, as it were, and lifted above the law, which yet he willingly submitted unto, and in the same instant wherein he was made of a woman, was made also under the law, whence obedience unto it became necessary unto him,"—the man feigns I know not what contradictions in his fancy, whereof there is not the least appearance in the words unto any one who understands the matter expressed in them. And that the assumption of the human nature into union with the Son of God, with submission unto the law thereon to be performed in that nature, are distinct parts of the humiliation of Christ, I shall prove when more serious occasion is administered unto me.

In like manner he proceeds to put in his exceptions unto what I discoursed about the laws that an innocent man is liable unto. For I said, that God never gave any other law to an innocent person, but only the law of his creation, with such symbolical precepts as might be instances of his obedience thereunto. Something he would find fault with, but knows not well what; and therefore turmoils himself to give countenance unto a putid cavil. He tells us, " That it is a great favour that I acknowledge, p. 310, that God might add what symbols he pleased unto the law of creation." But the childishness of these impertinencies is shameful. To whom, I pray, is it a favour, or what doth the man intend by such a senseless scoff? Is there any word in my whole discourse intimating that God might not in a state of innocency give what positive laws he pleased unto innocent persons, as means and ways to express that obedience which they owed unto the law of creation? The task wherein I am engaged is so fruitless, so barren of any good use, in contending with such impertinent effects of malice and ignorance, that I am weary of every word I am forced to add in the pursuit of it; but he will yet have it, that " an innocent person, such as Christ was absolutely, may be obliged for his own sake to the observation of such laws and institutions as were introduced by the occasion of sin, and respected all of them the personal sins of them that were obliged by them;" which if he can believe, he is at liberty, for me, to persuade as many as he can to be of his mind, whilst I may be left unto my own liberty and choice, yea, to the necessity of my mind, in not believing contradictions. And for what he adds, that I " know those who conceit themselves above all forms of external worship," I must say to him that at present personally I know none that do so, but fear that some such there are; as also others who, despising not only the ways of external worship appointed by God himself, but also the laws of internal faith and grace, do satisfy themselves in a customary observance of forms of worship of their own devising.

In his next attempt he had been singular, and had spoken something which had looked like an answer to an argument, had he well laid the foundation of his procedure: for that position which he designeth the confutation of is thus laid down by him as mine, " There can be no reason assigned of Christ's obedience unto the law, but only this, that he did it in our stead;" whereas my words are, " That the end of the active obedience of Christ cannot be assigned to be that he might be fit for his death and oblation." And hereon what is afterward said against this particular end, he interprets as spoken against all other ends whatever, instancing in such as are every way consistent with the imputation of his obedience unto us; which could not be, had the only end of it been for himself, to fit him for his death and oblation. And this wilful mistake is sufficient to give occasion to combat his own imaginations for two or three pages together. P. 314, he pretends unto the recital of an argument of mine for the imputation of the righteousness of Christ, with the like pretence of attempting an answer unto it; but his design is not to manage any controversy with me, or against me, but, as he phraseth it, to expose my mistakes. I cannot, therefore, justly expect from him so much as common honesty will require, in case the real handling of a controversy in religion had been intended. But his way of procedure, so far as I know and understand, may be best suited unto his design. In this place, he doth neither fairly nor truly report my words, nor

take the least notice of the confirmation of my argument by the
removal of objections whereunto it seemed liable, nor of the reasons
and testimonies whereby it is farther proved; but, taking out of my
discourse what expressions he pleaseth, putting them together with
the same rule, he thinks he hath sufficiently exposed my mistakes,—
the thing he aimed at.   I have no more concernment in this matter
but to refer both him and the reader to the places in my discourse
reflected on;—him, truly to report and answer my arguments, if he
be able; and the reader, to judge as he pleaseth between us.   And I
would for this once desire of him, that if he indeed be concerned in
these things, he would peruse my discourse here raved at, and determine in his own mind whether I confidently affirm what is in dispute,
(that is, what I had then in dispute; for who could divine so long
ago what a doughty disputant this author would by this time sprout
up into?) and that this goes for an argument, or that he impudently
affirms me so to do, contrary unto his science and conscience, if he
had not quite "pored out his eyes" before he came to the end of a page
or two in my book.   And for the state of the question here proposed
by him, let none expect that upon so slight an occasion I shall divert
unto the discussion of it.   When this author, or any of his consorts
in design, shall soberly and candidly, without scoffing or railing, in a
way of argument or reasoning, becoming divines and men of learning,
answer any of those many writings which are extant against that
Socinian justification which he here approves and contends for, or
those written by the divines of the church of England on the same
subject, in the proof of what he denies, and confutation of what he
affirms, they may deserve to be taken notice of in the same rank and
order with those with whom they associate themselves.   And yet I
will not say but that these cavilling exceptions, giving a sufficient
intimation of what some men would be at, if ability and opportunity
did occur, may give occasion also unto a renewed vindication of the
truths opposed by them, in a way suited unto the use and edification
of the church, in due time and season.

From p. 185[1] of my book he retires, upon his new triumph, unto
p. 176,[2] as hoping to hook something from thence that might contribute unto the furtherance of his ingenious design, although my discourse in that place have no concernment in what he treateth about.
But let him be heard to what purpose he pleaseth.   Thus, therefore,
he proceeds, p. 315, "The doctor makes a great flourish with some
Scripture phrases, that there is almost nothing that Christ hath done
but what we are said to do it with him; we are crucified with him,
we are dead with him, buried with him, quickened together with
him.   In the actings of Christ there is, by virtue of the compact

---

[1] P. 162.   [2] P. 154 of this volume.

between him, as mediator, and the Father, such an assured foundation laid, that by communication of the fruit of these actings unto those in whose stead he performed them, they are said, in the participation of these fruits, to have done the same things with him. But he is quite out in the reason of these expressions, which is not that we are accounted to do the same things which Christ did,—for the things here mentioned belong to the peculiar office of his mediation, which he told us before were not reckoned as done by us,—but because we do some things like them. Our dying to sin is a conformity to the death of Christ; and our walking in newness of life is our conformity to his resurrection: and the consideration of the death and resurrection of Christ is very powerful to engage us to die to sin, and to rise unto a new life. And this is the true reason of these phrases."

Any man may perceive, from what he is pleased here himself to report of my words, that I was not treating about the imputation of the righteousness of Christ, which he is now inveighing against; and it will be much more evident unto every one that shall cast an eye on that discourse. But the design of this confused rambling I have been forced now frequently to give an account of, and shall, if it be possible, trouble the reader with it no more. The present difference between us, which he was ambitious to represent, is only this, that whereas it seems he will allow that those expressions of our being " crucified with Christ, dead with him, buried with him, quickened with him," do intend nothing but only our doing of something like unto that which Christ did; I do add, moreover, that we do those things by the virtue and efficacy of the grace which is communicated unto us from what the Lord Christ so did and acted for us, as the mediator of the new covenant, whereby alone we partake of their power, communicate in their virtue, and are conformed unto him as our head; wherein I know I have, as the testimony of the Scripture, so the judgment of the catholic church of Christ on my side, and am very little concerned in the censure of this person, that I am " quite out in the reason of these expressions."

For what remains of his discourse, so far as I am concerned in it, it is made up of such expositions of some texts of Scripture as issue, for the most part, in a direct contradiction to the text itself, or some express passages of the context. So doth that of Gal. iv. 4, 5, which he first undertakes to speak unto, giving us nothing but what was first invented by Crellius, in his book against Grotius, and is almost translated verbatim out of the comment of Schlichtingius upon the place; the remainder of them corruptly Socinianizing against the sense of the church of God. Hereunto are added such pitiful mistakes, with reflections on me for distinguishing between obeying and suffering (which conceit he most profoundly disproves by showing that one may obey in suffering, and that Christ did so, against him who hath written more about the obedience of Christ in dying, or laying down his life for us, than he seems to have read on the same subject, as also concerning the ends and uses of his death; which I challenge him and all his companions to answer and disprove, if they can), as I cannot satisfy myself in the farther consideration of; no, not with that speed and haste of writing now used: which nothing could give countenance unto but the meanness of the occasion, and unprofitableness of the argument in hand. Wherefore, this being the manner of the man, I am not able to give an account unto myself or the reader of the misspense of more time in the review of such impertinencies. I shall add a few things, and conclude.

First. I desire to know whether this author will abide by what he asserts, as his own judgment, in opposition unto what he puts in his exception against in my discourse:—P. 320, " All the influence which the sacrifice of Christ's death, and the righteousness of his life have, that I can find in the Scripture, is, that to this we owe the covenant of grace;" that is, as he afterward explains himself, "That God would for the sake of Christ enter into a new covenant with mankind, wherein he promiseth pardon of sin and eternal life to them that believe and obey the gospel." I leave him herein to his second thoughts; for as he hath now expressed himself, there is no reconciliation of his assertion to common sense, or the fundamental principles of Christian religion. That God entered into the new covenant originally only for the sake of those things whereby that covenant was ratified and confirmed, and that Christ was so the mediator of the new covenant, that he died not for the redemption of transgressions under the first covenant, whereby the whole consideration of his satisfaction and of redemption, properly so called, is excluded; that there is no consideration to be had of his purchase of the inheritance of grace and glory, with many other things of the same importance; and that the gospel, or the doctrine of the gospel, is the new covenant (which is only a perspicuous declaration of it), are things that may become these new sons of the church of England, which the elder church would not have borne withal.

Secondly. The reader may take notice, that in some other discourses of mine now[1] published, which were all of them finished before I had the advantage to peruse the friendly and judicious animadversions of this author, he will find most of the matters which

---

[1] In the course of the same year in which this reply to Sherlock appeared, Owen's " Discourse on the Holy Spirit," and the second volume of his "Exposition of the Epistle to the Hebrews" were published. There is much in both of them on the points at issue between Owen and Sherlock.—Ed.

he excepts against both cleared, proved, and vindicated, and that those principles which he directs his opposition against are so established, as that I neither expect nor fear any such assault upon them, from this sort of men, as becometh a serious debate on things of this nature.

Thirdly. That I have confined myself, in the consideration of this author's discourse, unto what I was personally concerned in, without looking at or accepting of the advantages which offered themselves of reflecting upon him, either as unto the matter of his discourse, or unto the manner of expressing himself in its delivery. For, besides that I have no mind, and that for many reasons, to enter voluntarily into any contest with this man, the mistakes which he hath apparently been led into by ignorance or prejudice, his fulsome errors against the Scripture, the doctrine of the ancient church, and the church of England, are so multiplied and scattered throughout the whole, that a discovery and confutation of them will scarce deserve the expense of time that must be wasted therein, until a more plausible countenance or strenuous defence be given unto them. And as for what he aimeth at, I know well enough where to find the whole of it, handled with more civility and appearance of reason; and therefore, when I am free, or resolved to treat concerning them, I shall do so in the consideration of what is taught by his authors and masters, and not of what he hath borrowed from them.

Fourthly. I shall assure the reader, that as a thousand of such trifling cavillers or revilers, as I have had some to deal withal, shall neither discourage nor hinder me in the remaining service which I may have yet to fulfil, in the patience of God, for the church of Christ and truth of the gospel; nor, it may be, occasion me any more to divert in the least unto the consideration of what they whisper or clamour, unless they are able to betake themselves unto a more sober and Christian way of handling things in controversy: so if they will not, or dare not, forego this supposed advantage of reproaching the doctrine of nonconformists (under which pretence they openly, and as yet securely, scorn and deride them, when they are all of them the avowed doctrines of all the reformed churches, and of this of England in particular); and if they think it not meet to oppose themselves and endeavours unto those writings which have been composed and published professedly in the declaration and defence of the truth scoffed at and impugned by them, but choose rather to exercise their skill and anger on passages rent out of practical discourses, accommodated in the manner of their delivery unto the capacity of the community of believers, as it is fit they should be; I do suppose that, at one time or other, from one hand or another, they may meet with some such discourse, concerning justification and the imputation of the righteousness of Christ, as may give them occasion to be quiet, or to exercise the best of their skill and industry in an opposition unto it,—as many such there are already extant, which they wisely take no notice of, but only rave against occasional passages in discourses of another nature,—unless they resolve on no occasion to forego the shelter they have betaken themselves unto.

A BRIEF

DECLARATION AND VINDICATION

OF

THE DOCTRINE OF THE TRINITY:

AS ALSO OF

THE PERSON AND SATISFACTION OF CHRIST:

ACCOMMODATED TO THE CAPACITY AND USE OF SUCH AS MAY BE IN DANGER TO BE SEDUCED;
AND THE ESTABLISHMENT OF THE TRUTH.

" Search the Scriptures."—JOHN v. 39.

Imprimatur,

ROB. GROVE, R. P. D.

Episcop. Lond. a Sac. Dom.

Feb. 3, 1668–9.

PREFATORY NOTE.

FEW of Owen's treatises have been more extensively circulated and generally useful than his "Brief Declaration and Vindication of the Doctrine of the Trinity," etc. It was published in 1669; and the author of the anonymous memoir of Owen, prefixed to an edition of his Sermons in 1720, informs us, "This small piece hath met with such an universal acceptance by true Christians of all denominations, that the *seventh edition* of it was lately published." An edition printed in Glasgow was published in 1798, and professes to be the *eighth*. A translation of the work appeared in the Dutch language (Vitringa, Doct. Christ., pars vi. p. 6, edit. 1776).

At the time when the treatise was published, the momentous doctrines of the Trinity and the Atonement were violently assailed; but it was not so much for the refutation of opponents as for " the edification and establishment of the plain Christian," that our author composed the following little work. The reader will find in it traces of that deep and familiar acquaintance with opposing views, and with the highest theology involved in the question, which might be expected from Dr Owen on a subject which he seems to have studied with peculiar industry and research. Reference may be made to his " Vindiciæ Evangelicæ," and his "Exposition of the Epistle to the Hebrews," in proof how thoroughly he had mastered the whole controversy in regard to the divinity and satisfaction of Christ, so far as the discussion had extended in his day. His controversy with Biddle, in which he wrote his " Vindiciæ Evangelicæ," took place in 1655; and the first volume of the "Exposition" was published only the year before the "Brief Declaration," etc., appeared. The latter may be regarded, accordingly, as the substance of these important works, condensed and adapted to popular use and comprehension, in all that relates to the proper Godhead of the Son, and the nature of the work which he accomplished in the redemption of his people.

Notes have been supplied, in the course of the treatise, explanatory of some allusions to various writers, whose names are now almost unknown, and in one or two instances, we have briefly indicated to what extent passages quoted by Owen have been affected by the results and discoveries of modern criticism. For the special object which he had in view, he adopts the course which has since been generally approved of and pursued, as obviously the wisest and safest in defending and expounding the doctrine of the Trinity. He appeals to the broad mass of Scripture evidence in favour of the doctrine, and after proving the divine unity, together with the divinity of Father, Son, and Holy Ghost respectively, is careful not to enter on any discussion in regard to the unrevealed mysteries involved in the relations of the Trinity, beyond what was necessary for the refutation of those who argue, that whatever in this high doctrine is incomprehensible by *reason*, must be incompatible with *revelation*. This little work is farther remarkable for the almost total absence of the tedious digressions, which abound in the other works of Owen. Such logical unity and concentration of thought is the more remarkable, when we find that the treatise was written, as he tells us, " in a few hours." But it was a subject on which his mind was fully stored, and his whole heart was interested. The treatise which follows, therefore, was not the spark struck in some moment of collision, and serving only a temporary purpose, but a steady flame nourished from the beaten oil of the sanctuary.—ED.

TO THE READER.

————

CHRISTIAN READER,

THIS small treatise háth no other design but thy good, and establishment in the truth. And therefore, as laying aside that consideration alone, I·could desirously have been excused from the labour of those hours which were spent in its composure; so in the work itself I admitted no one thought, but how the things treated of in it might and ought to be managed unto thy spiritual benefit and advantage. Other designs most men have in writing what is to be exposed to public view, and lawfully may have so; in this I have nothing but merely thy good. I have neither been particularly provoked nor opposed by the adversaries of the truth here pleaded for, nor have any need, from any self-respect, to publish such a small, plain discourse as this. Love alone to the truth, and the welfare of thy soul, has given efficacy to their importunity who pressed me to this small service.

The matters here treated of are on all hands confessed to be of the greatest moment, such as the eternal welfare of the souls of men is immediately and directly concerned in. This all those who believe the sacred truths here proposed and explained do unanimously profess and contend for; nor is it denied by those by whom they are opposed. There is no need, therefore, to give thee any especial reasons to evince thy concernment in these things, nor the greatness of that concernment, thereby to induce thee unto their serious consideration. It were well, indeed, that these great, sacred, and mysterious truths might, without contention or controversies about them, be left unto the faith of believers, as proposed in the Scripture, with that explanation of them which, in the ordinary ministry and dispensation of the gospel, is necessary and required.

Certainly, these tremendous mysteries are not by us willingly to be exposed, or prostituted to the cavils of every perverse querist and disputer;—those συζητηταὶ τοῦ αἰῶνος τούτου, whose pretended wisdom (indeed ignorance, darkness, and folly) God hath designed to confound and destroy in them and by them. For my part, I can assure thee, reader, I have no mind to contend and dispute about these things, which I humbly adore and believe as they are revealed. It is the importunity of adversaries, in their attempts to draw and seduce the souls of men from the truth and simplicity of the gospel in these great fundamentals of it, that alone can justify any to debate upon, or eristically [in the form of controversy] to handle these awful mysteries. This renders it our duty, and that indispensably, inasmuch as we are required to " contend earnestly for the faith once delivered unto the saints." But yet, also, when this necessity is imposed on us, we are by no means discharged from that humble reverence of mind wherewith we ought always to be conversant about them; nor from that regard unto the way and manner of their revelation in the Scripture which may preserve us from all unnecessary intermixture of litigious or exotic phrases and expressions in their assertion and declaration. I know our adversaries could, upon the matter, decry any thing peculiarly mysterious in these things, although they are frequently and emphatically in the Scriptures affirmed so to be. But, whilst they deny the mysteries of the things themselves,—which are

such as every way become the glorious being and wisdom of God,—they are forced
to assign such an enigmatical sense unto the words, expressions, and propositions
wherein they are revealed and declared in the Scripture, as to turn almost the
whole gospel into an allegory, wherein nothing is properly expressed but in some
kind of allusion unto what is so elsewhere: which irrational way of proceeding,
leaving nothing certain in what is or may be expressed by word or writing, is
covered over with a pretence of *right reason;* which utterly refuseth to be so employed. These things the reader will find afterward made manifest, so far as the
nature of this brief discourse will bear. And I shall only desire these few things
of him that intends its perusal:—First, That he would not look on the subject here
treated of as the matter of an ordinary controversy in religion,—

> —— " Neque enim hic levia aut ludicra petuntur
> Præmia; lectoris de vita animæque salute
> Certatur."[1]

They are things which immediately and directly in themselves concern the eternal
salvation of the souls of men; and their consideration ought always to be attended
with a due sense of their weight and importance. Secondly, Let him bring with
him a due reverence of the majesty, and infinite, incomprehensible nature of God,
as that which is not to be prostituted to the captious and sophistical scanning of
men of corrupt minds, but to be humbly adored, according to the revelation that
he hath made of himself. Thirdly, That he be willing to submit his soul and
conscience to the plain and obvious sense of Scripture propositions and testimonies,
without seeking out evasions and pretences for unbelief. These requests I cannot
but judge equal, and fear not the success where they are sincerely complied withal.

I have only to add, that in handling the doctrine of the satisfaction of Christ, I
have proceeded on that principle which, as it is fully confirmed in the Scripture,
so it hath been constantly maintained and adhered unto by the most of those who
with judgment and success have managed these controversies against the Socinians:
and this is, that the essential holiness of God, with his justice or righteousness,
as the supreme governor of all, did indispensably require that sin should not absolutely go unpunished; and that it should do so, stands in a repugnancy to those
holy properties of his nature. This, I say, hath been always constantly maintained
by far the greatest number of them who have thoroughly understood the contra-
versy in this matter, and have successfully engaged in it. And as their arguments
for their assertion are plainly unanswerable, so the neglect of abiding by it is causelessly to forego one of the most fundamental and invincible principles in our cause.
He who first laboured in the defence of the doctrine of the satisfaction of Christ,
after Socinus had formed his imaginations about the salvation that he wrought, and
began to dispute about it, was Covetus,[2] a learned man, who laid the foundation of
his whole disputation in the justice of God, necessarily requiring, and indispensably,
the punishment of sin. And, indeed, the state of the controversy as it is laid down
by Socinus, in his book " De Jesu Christo Servatore," which is an answer to this
Covetus, is genuine, and that which ought not to be receded from, as having been
the direct ground of all the controversial writings on that subject which have since
been published in Europe. And it is in these words laid down by Socinus himself:

---

[1] —— " Nec enim levia aut ludicra petuntur
Præmia, sed Turni de vita et sanguine certant."—Virg. Æn. xii. 764.
[2] The only notice of this divine we can discover will be found in the Bibliotheca of Konigius
(1678).   All the information he communicates respecting him is in these words:—" Covetus
(Jacobus) Parisiensis Theologus.   An. 1608 obiit.   Reliquit Apologiam de Justificatione."   Socinus, in a curious preface to his work, mentioned above, " De Jesu Christo Servatore," narrates in
what manner Covetus and he first happened to meet.   They subsequently exchanged communications on the points in dispute between them.   It was in reply to the arguments of Covetus in
this correspondence, that Socinus wrote the work to which Dr Owen alludes.   It is matter of re-
gret that so little is known of one whom Owen mentions so respectfully, and who had the honour
of supplying the first antidote and check to the heresies of Socinus.—Ed.

" Communis et orthodoxa (ut asseris) sententia est, Jesum Christum ideo servatorem nostrum esse, quia divinæ justitiæ per quam peccatores damnari merebamur,
pro peccatis nostris plene satisfecerit; quæ satisfactio, per fidem, imputatur nobis
ex dono Dei credentibus." This he ascribes to Covetus: " The common and
orthodox judgment is, that Jesus Christ is therefore our Saviour, because he hath
satisfied the justice of God, by which we, being sinners, deserved to be condemned
for all our sins" [which satisfaction, through faith, is imputed to us who through
the grace of God believe.] In opposition whereunto he thus expresseth his own
opinion: " Ego vero censeo, et orthodoxam sententiam esse arbitror, Jesum Christum ideo servatorem nostrum esse, quia salutis æternæ viam nobis annuntia-
verit, confirmaverit, et in sua ipsius persona, cum vitæ exemplo, tum ex mortuis
resurgendo, manifestè ostenderit; vitamque æternam nobis ei fidem habentibus ipse
daturus sit. Divinæ autem justitiæ, per quam peccatores damnari meremur, pro
peccatis nostris neque illum satisfecisse, neque ut satisfaceret, opus fuisse arbitror;"—
" I judge and suppose it to be the orthodox opinion, that Jesus Christ is therefore
our Saviour, because he hath declared unto us the way of eternal salvation, and
confirmed it in his own person; manifestly showing it, both by the example of his
life and by rising from the dead; and in that he will give eternal life unto us,
believing in him. And I affirm, that he neither made satisfaction to the justice of
God, whereby we deserved to be damned for our sins, nor was there any need that
he should so do." This is the true state of the question; and the principal subtlety
of Crellius, the great defender of this part of the doctrine of Socinus, in his book
of the " Causes of the Death of Christ," and the defence of this book, " De Jesu
Christo Servatore," consists in speaking almost the same words with those whom
he doth oppose, but still intending the same things with Socinus himself. This
opinion, as was said of Socinus, Covetus opposed and everted on the principle
before mentioned.

The same truth was confirmed also by Zarnovitius, who first wrote against
Socinus' book; as also by Otto Casmannus, who engaged in the same work; and
by Abraham Salinarius. Upon the same foundation do proceed Paræus, Piscator,
Lubbertus, Lucius, Camero, Voetius, Amyraldus, Placæus, Rivetus, Walæus,
Thysius, Altingius, Maresius, Essenius, Arnoldus, Turretinus, Baxter, with many
others. The Lutherans who have managed these controversies, as Tarnovius,
Meisnerus, Calovius, Stegmannus, Martinius, Franzius, with all others of their
way, have constantly maintained the same great fundamental principle of this
doctrine of the satisfaction of Christ; and it hath well and solidly been of late
asserted among ourselves on the same foundation. And as many of these authors
do expressly blame some of the schoolmen, as Aquinas, Durandus, Biel, Tataretus,
for granting a possibility of pardon without satisfaction, as opening a way to the
Socinian error in this matter; so also they fear not to affirm, that the foregoing
of this principle of God's vindictive justice indispensably requiring the punishment
of sin, doth not only weaken the cause of the truth, but indeed leave it indefensible.
However, I suppose men ought to be wary how they censure the authors mentioned, as such who expose the cause they undertook to defend unto contempt;
for greater, more able, and learned defenders, this truth hath not as yet found,
nor doth stand in need of.   J. O.

THE PREFACE.

The disciples of our Lord Jesus Christ having made that great confession of him, in distinction and opposition unto them who accounted him only as a prophet, "Thou art the Christ, the Son of the living God," Matt. xvi. 14, 16, he doth, on the occasion thereof, give out unto them that great charter of the church's stability and continuance, "Upon this rock I will build my church; and the gates of hell shall not prevail against it," verse 18. He is himself the rock upon which his church is built,—as God is called the rock of his people, on the account of his eternal power and immutability, Deut. xxxii. 4, 18, 31, Isa. xxvi. 4; and himself the *spiritual* rock which gave out supplies of mercy and assistance to the people in the wilderness, 1 Cor. x. 4.

The relation of the *professing church* unto this rock consists in the faith of this confession, that he is "the Christ, the Son of the living God." This our Lord Jesus Christ hath promised to secure against all attempts; yet so as plainly to declare, that there should be great and severe opposition made thereunto. For whereas the *prevalency* of the gates of hell in an enmity unto this confession is denied, a great and vigorous attempt to prevail therein is no less certainly *foretold.* Neither hath it otherwise fallen out. In all ages, from the first solemn foundation of the church of the New Testament, it hath, one way or other, been fiercely attempted by the "gates of hell." For some time after the resurrection of Christ from the dead, the principal endeavours of Satan, and men acting under him, or acted by him, were pointed against the very foundation of the church, as laid in the expression before mentioned. Almost all the errors and heresies wherewith for three or four centuries of years it was perplexed, were principally against the person of Christ himself; and, consequently, the nature and being of the holy and blessed Trinity. But being disappointed in his design herein, through the watchful care of the Lord Christ over his promise, in the following ages Satan turned his craft and violence against sundry parts of the superstructure, and, by the assistance of the Papacy, cast them into confusion,—nothing, as it were, remaining firm, stable, and in order, but only this one confession, which in a particular manner the Lord Christ hath taken upon himself to secure.

In these latter ages of the world, the power and care of Jesus Christ reviving towards his church, in the reformation of it, even the ruined heaps of its building have been again reduced into some tolerable order and beauty. The old enemy of its peace and welfare falling hereby under a disappointment, and finding his travail and labour for many generations in a great part frustrate, he is returned again to his old work of attacking *the foundation* itself; as he is unweary and restless, and can be quiet neither conqueror nor conquered,—nor will be so, until he is bound and cast into the lake that burneth with fire. For no sooner had the reformation of religion firmed itself in some of the European provinces, but immediately, in a proportion of distance not unanswerable unto what fell out from the first foundation of the church, sundry persons, by the instigation of Satan, attempted the disturbance and ruin of it, by the very same errors and heresies about the Trinity, the person of Christ and his offices, the person of the Holy Ghost and his grace, wherewith its first trouble and ruin was endeavoured. And hereof we have of late an instance given among ourselves, and that so notoriously known, through a mixture of imprudence and impudence in the managers of it, that a very brief reflection upon it will suffice unto our present design.

It was always supposed, and known to some, that there are sundry persons in this nation, who, having been themselves seduced into Socinianism, did make it their business, under various pretences, to draw others into a compliance with them in the same way and persuasion. Neither hath this, for sundry years, been so secretly carried, but that the design of it hath variously discovered itself by *overt acts* of conferences, disputations, and publishing of books; which last way of late hath been sedulously pursued. Unto these three is now a *visible accession* made, by that sort of people whom men will call Quakers, from their deportment at the first erection of their way (long since deserted by them), until, by some new revolutions of opinions, they cast themselves under a more proper denomination. That there is a conjunction issued between both these sorts of men, in an opposition to the holy Trinity, with the person and grace of Christ, the pamphlets of late published by the one and the other do sufficiently evince. For however they may seem in sundry things as yet to look diverse ways, yet, like Samson's foxes, they are knit together by the tail of consent in these fire-brand opinions, and jointly endeavour to consume the standing corn of the church of God. And their joint management of their business of late hath been as though it were their design to give as great a vogue and report to their opinions as by any ways they are able. Hence, besides their attempts to be proclaiming their opinions, under various pretences, in all assemblies whereinto they may intrude themselves (as they know) without trouble, they are exceeding sedulous in scattering and giving away, yea, imposing *gratis* (and, as to some, *ingratiis*), their small books which they publish, upon all sorts of persons promiscuously, as they have advantage so to do. By this means their opinions being of late become the talk and discourse of *the common sort of Christians*, and the exercise of many,—amongst whom are not a few that, on sundry accounts, which I shall not mention, may possibly be exposed unto disadvantage and prejudice thereby,—it hath been thought meet by some that the sacred truths which these men oppose should be plainly and briefly asserted and confirmed from the Scripture; that those of *the meanest sort of professors*, who are sincere and upright, exercising themselves to keep a good conscience in matters of faith and obedience to God, may have somewhat in a readiness, both to guide them in their farther inquiry into the truth, as also to confirm their faith in what they have already received, when at any time it is shaken or opposed by the "cunning sleight of men that lie in wait to deceive."

And this compriseth the design of the ensuing discourse. It may possibly be judged needless by some, as it was in its first proposal by him by whom it is written; and that because this matter at present is, by an especial providence, cast on other hands, who both have, and doubtless, as occasion shall require, will well acquit themselves in the defence of the truths opposed. Not to give any other account of the reasons of this small undertaking, it may suffice, that "in publico discrimine omnis homo miles est,"—"every man's concernment lying in a common danger,"—it is free for every one to manage it as he thinks best, and is able, so it be without prejudice to the whole or the particular concerns of others. If a city be on fire, whose bucket that brings water to quench it ought to be refused? The attempt to cast fire into the city of God by the opinions mentioned, is open and plain; and a timely stop being to be put unto it, the more hands that are orderly employed in its quenching, the more speedy and secure is the effect like to be.

Now, because the assertors of the opinions mentioned do seem to set out themselves to be *some great ones*, above the ordinary rate of men, as having found out, and being able publicly to maintain, such things as never would have entered into the minds of others to have thought on or conceived; and also that they seem with many to be thought worthy of their consideration because they now are new, and such as they have not been acquainted withal; I shall, in this prefatory entrance, briefly manifest that those who have amongst us undertaken the management of these opinions have brought nothing new unto them, but either a little contemptible sophistry and caption of words, on the one hand, or futilous, affected, unintelligible expressions, on the other,—the opinions themselves being no other but such as the church of God, having been opposed by and troubled with from the beginning, hath prevailed against and triumphed over in all generations. And were it not that confidence is the only relief which enraged impotency adheres unto and expects supplies from, I should greatly admire that those amongst us who have undertaken an enforcement of these old exploded errors, whose weakness doth so openly discover and proclaim itself in all their endeavours, should judge themselves competent to give a new spirit of life to the dead carcase of these rotten heresies, which the faith of the saints in all ages hath triumphed over, and which truth and learning have, under the care and watchfulness of Christ, so often baffled out of the world.

The Jews, in the time of our Saviour's converse on the earth, being fallen greatly from the faith and worship of their forefathers, and ready to sink into their last and utmost apostasy from God, seem, amongst many other truths, to have much lost that of the doctrine of the holy Trinity, and of the person of the Messiah. It was, indeed, suited, in the dispensation of God, unto the work that the Lord Jesus had to fulfil in the world, that, before his passion and resurrection, the knowledge of his divine nature, as unto his individual person, should be concealed from the most of men. For this cause, although he was " in the form of God, and thought it not robbery to be equal with God, yet he made himself of no reputation, by taking on him the form of a servant, and being made in the likeness of men, that being found in the fashion of a man, he might be obedient unto death," Phil. ii. 6–8; whereby his divine glory was vailed for a season, until he was " declared to be the Son of God with power, according to the Spirit of holiness, by the resurrection from the dead," Rom. i. 4; and then " was glorified with that glory which he had with the Father before the world was," John xvii. 5. And as this dispensation was needful unto the accomplishment of the whole work which, as our mediator, he had undertaken, so, in particular, he who was in himself the Lord of hosts, a sanctuary to them that feared him, became hereby " a stone of stumbling and a rock of offence to both the houses of Israel, for a gin and for a snare to the inhabitants of Jerusalem," Isa. viii. 13, 14. See Luke ii. 34; Rom. ix. 33; 1 Pet. ii. 8; Isa. xxviii. 16. But yet, notwithstanding, as occasions required, suitably unto his own holy ends and designs, he forbare not to give plain and open testimony to his own divine nature and eternal pre-existence unto his incarnation. And this was it which, of all other things, most provoked the carnal Jews with whom he had to do; for having, as was said, lost the doctrine of the Trinity and person of the Messiah, in a great measure, whenever he asserted his Deity, they were immediately enraged, and endeavoured to destroy him. So was it, plainly, John viii. 56–59. Saith he, " Your father Abraham rejoiced to see my day: and he saw it, and was glad. Then said the Jews unto him, Thou art not yet fifty years old, and hast thou seen Abraham? Jesus said unto them, Verily, verily, I say unto you, Before Abraham was, I am. Then took they up stones to cast at him." So, also, John x. 30–33, " I and my Father are one. Then the Jews took up stones again to stone him. Jesus answered them, Many good works have I showed you from my Father; for which of those works do ye stone me? The Jews answered him, saying, For a good work we stone thee not; but for blasphemy; and because that thou, being a man, makest thyself God." They understood well enough the meaning of those words, " I and my Father are one," —namely, that they were a plain assertion of his being God. This caused their rage. And this the Jews all abide by to this day,—namely, that he declared himself to be God, and therefore they slew him. Whereas, therefore, the first discovery of a plurality of persons in the divine essence consists in the revelation of the divine nature and personality of the Son, this being opposed, persecuted, and blasphemed by these Jews, they may be justly looked upon and esteemed as the *first assertors of that misbelief* which now some seek again so earnestly to promote. The Jews persecuted the Lord Christ, because he, being a man, declared himself also to be God; and others are ready to revile and reproach them who believe and teach what he declared.

After the resurrection and ascension of the Lord Jesus, all things being filled with tokens, evidences, and effects of his divine nature and power (Rom. i. 4), the church that began to be gathered in his name, and according to his doctrine, being, by his especial institution, to be initiated into the express profession of·the doctrine of the holy Trinity, as being to be *baptized in the name of the Father, and the Son, and the Holy Ghost,*—which confession compriseth the whole of the truth contended for, and by the indispensable placing of it at the first entrance into all obedience unto him, is made the doctrinal foundation of the church,—it continued for a season in the quiet and undisturbed possession of this sacred treasure.

The first who gave disquietment unto the disciples of Christ, by perverting the doctrine of the Trinity, was Simon Magus, with his followers;—an account of whose monstrous figments and unintelligible imaginations, with their coincidence with what some men dream in these latter days, shall elsewhere be given. Nor shall I need here to mention the colluvies of Gnostics, Valentinians, Marcionites, and Manichees; the foundation of all whose abominations lay in their misapprehensions of the being of God, their unbelief of the Trinity and person of Christ, as do those of some others also.

In especial, there was one Cerinthus, who was more active than others in his opposition to the doctrine of the person of Christ, and therein of the holy Trinity. To put a stop unto his abominations, all authors agree that John, writing his Gospel, prefixed unto it that plain declaration of the eternal Deity of Christ which it is prefaced withal. And the story is well attested by Irenæus, Eusebius, and others, from Polycarpus, who was his disciple, that this Cerinthus coming into the place where the apostle was, he left it, adding, as a reason of his departure, lest the building, through the just judgment of God, should fall upon them. And it was of the holy, wise providence of God to suffer some impious persons to oppose this doctrine before the death of that apostle, that he might, by infallible inspiration, farther reveal, manifest, and declare it, to the establishment of the church in future ages. For what can farther be desired to satisfy the minds of men who in any sense own the Lord Jesus Christ and the Scriptures, than that this controversy about the Trinity and person of Christ (for they stand and fall together) should be so eminently and expressly determined, as it were, immediately from heaven?

But he with whom we have to deal in this matter neither ever did, nor ever will, nor can, acquiesce or rest in the divine determination of any thing which he hath stirred up strife and controversy about: for as Cerinthus and the Ebionites persisted in the heresy of the Jews, who would have slain our Saviour for bearing witness to his own Deity, notwithstanding the evidence of that testimony, and the right apprehension which the Jews had of his mind therein; so he excited others to engage and persist in their opposition to the truth, notwithstanding this second particular determination of it from heaven, for their confutation or confusion. For after the more weak and confused oppositions made unto it by Theodotus Coriarius [*i.e.*, the tanner], Artemon, and some others, at length a stout champion appears visibly and expressly engaged against these fundamentals of our faith. This was Paulus Samosatenus, bishop of the church of Antioch, about the year 272;—a man of most intolerable pride, passion, and folly,—the greatest that hath left a name upon ecclesiastical records. This man openly and avowedly denied the doctrine of the Trinity, and the Deity of Christ in an especial manner. For although he endeavoured for a while to cloud his impious sentiments in ambiguous expressions, as others also have done (Euseb., lib. vii. cap. 27), yet being pressed by the professors of the truth, and supposing his party was somewhat confirmed, he plainly defended his heresy, and was cast out of the church wherein he presided. Some sixty years after, Photinus, bishop of Sirmium, with a pretence of more sobriety in life and conversation, undertook the management of the same design, with the same success.

What ensued afterward among the churches of God in this matter is of too large and diffused a nature to be here reported. These instances I have fixed on only to intimate, unto persons whose condition or occasions afford them not ability or leisure of themselves to inquire into the memorials of times past amongst the professors of the gospel of Christ, that these oppositions which are made at present amongst us unto these fundamental truths, and derived immediately from the late renewed enforcement of them made by Faustus Socinus and his followers, are nothing but old baffled attempts of Satan against the rock of the church and the building thereon, in the confession of the Son of the living God.

Now, as all men who have aught of a due reverence of God or his truth remaining with them, cannot but be wary how they give the least admittance to such opinions as have from the beginning been witnessed against and condemned by Christ himself, his apostles, and all that followed them in their faith and ways in all generations; so others, whose hearts may tremble for the danger they apprehend which these sacred truths may be in of being corrupted or defamed by the present opposition against them, may know that it is no other but what the church and faith of professors hath already been exercised with, and, through the power of Him that enables them, have constantly triumphed over. And, for my part, I look upon it as a blessed effect of the holy, wise providence of God, that those who have long harboured these abominations of denying the holy Trinity, and the person and satisfaction of Christ, in their minds, but yet have sheltered themselves from common observation under the shades of dark, obscure, and uncouth expressions, with many other specious pretences, should be given up to join themselves with such persons (and to profess a community of persuasion with them in those opinions, as have rendered themselves infamous from the first foundation of Christianity), and wherein they will assuredly meet with the same success as those have done who have gone before them.

For the other head of opposition, made by these persons unto the truth in reference unto the satisfaction of Christ, and the imputation of his righteousness thereon unto our justification, I have not much to say as to the time past. In general, the doctrine wherein they boast, being first brought forth in a rude misshapen manner by the Pelagian heretics, was afterward improved by one Abelardus, a sophistical scholar in France; but owes its principal form and poison unto the endeavours of Faustus Socinus, and those who have followed him in his subtle attempt to corrupt the whole doctrine of the gospel. Of these men are those amongst us who at this day so busily dispute and write about the Trinity, the Deity of Christ, and his satisfaction,—the followers and disciples. And it is much more from their masters, who were some of them men learned, diligent, and subtle, than from themselves, that they are judged to be of any great consideration. For I can truly say, that, upon the sedate examination of all that I could ever yet hear or get a sight of, either spoken or written by them,—that is, any amongst us,—I never yet observed an undertaking of so great importance managed with a greater evidence of incompetency and inability, to give any tolerable countenance unto it. If any of them shall for the future attempt to give any new countenance or props to their tottering errors, it will doubtless be attended unto by some of those many who cannot but know that it is incumbent on them " to contend earnestly for the faith once delivered unto the saints." This present brief endeavour is only to assist and direct those who are less exercised in the ways of managing controversies in religion, that they may have a brief comprehension of the truths opposed, with the firm foundations whereon they are built, and be in a readiness to shield their faith both against the fiery darts of Satan, and secure their minds against the " cunning sleight of men, who lie in wait to deceive." And wherein this discourse seems in any thing to be too brief or concise, the author is not to be blamed who was confined unto these strait bounds by those whose requests enjoined him this service.

DOCTRINE OF THE HOLY TRINITY

EXPLAINED AND VINDICATED.

THE doctrine of the blessed Trinity may be considered two ways: First, In respect unto the revelation and proposal of it in the Scripture, to direct us unto the author, object, and end of our faith, in our worship and obedience. Secondly, As it is farther declared and explained, in terms, expressions, and propositions, reduced from the original revelation of it, suited thereunto, and meet to direct and keep the mind from undue apprehensions of the things it believes, and to declare them, unto farther edification.

In the first way, it consists merely in the *propositions* wherein the revelation of God is expressed in the Scripture; and in this regard two things are required of us. First, To *understand* the terms of the propositions, as they are enunciations of truth; and, Secondly, To *believe* the things taught, revealed, and declared in them.

In the first instance, no more, I say, is required of us, but that we assent unto the assertions and testimonies of God concerning himself, according to their natural and genuine sense, as he will be known, believed in, feared, and worshipped by us, as he is our Creator, Lord, and Rewarder; and that because he himself hath, by his revelation, not only warranted us so to do, but also made it our *duty*, necessary and indispensable. Now, the sum of this revelation in this matter is, that *God is one;*—that this one God is *Father, Son, and Holy Ghost;*—that *the Father is the Father of the Son;* and *the Son, the Son of the Father;* and *the Holy Ghost, the Spirit of the Father and the Son;* and that, in respect of this their mutual relation, they are distinct from each other.

This is the *substance* of the doctrine of the Trinity, as to the first direct concernment of faith therein. The first intention of the Scripture, in the revelation of God towards us, is, as was said, that we might fear him, believe, worship, obey him, and live unto him, as God. That we may do this in a due manner, and worship *the only true God*, and not adore the false imaginations of our own minds, it declares, as was said, that this *God is one*, the Father, Son, and Holy Ghost;—that the *Father is this one God;* and therefore is to be believed in, worshipped, obeyed, lived unto, and in all things considered by us as the first cause, sovereign Lord, and last end of all;—that the *Son is the one true God;* and therefore is to be believed in, worshipped, obeyed, lived unto, and in all things considered by us as the first cause, sovereign Lord, and last end of all;—and so, also, of the Holy Ghost. This is the whole of faith's concernment in this matter, as it respects the direct revelation of God made by himself in the Scripture, and the first proper general end thereof. Let this be clearly confirmed by direct and *positive divine testimonies*, containing the declaration and revelation of God concerning himself, and faith is secured as to all it concerns; for it hath both its proper *formal object*, and is sufficiently enabled to be *directive* of divine worship and obedience.

The explication of this doctrine unto edification, suitable unto the revelation mentioned, is of another consideration; and two things are incumbent on us to take care of therein:—First, That what is affirmed and taught do directly tend unto the ends of the revelation itself, by informing and enlightening of the mind in the knowledge of the mystery of it, so far as in this life we are, by *divine assistance*, capable to comprehend it; that is, that faith may be increased, strengthened, and confirmed against temptations and oppositions of Satan, and men of corrupt minds; and that we may be distinctly directed unto, and encouraged in, the obedience unto, and worship of God, that are required of us. Secondly, That nothing be affirmed or taught herein that may beget or occasion any *undue apprehensions* concerning God, or our obedience unto him, with respect unto the best, highest, securest revelations that we have of him and our duty. These things being done and secured, the end of the declaration of this doctrine concerning God is attained.

In the declaration, then, of this doctrine unto the edification of the church, there is contained a farther explanation of the things before asserted, as proposed directly and in themselves as the object of our faith,—namely, *how God is one*, in respect of his *nature, substance, essence,* Godhead, or divine being; how, being Father, Son, and Holy Ghost, he subsisteth in these three distinct persons or *hypostases;* and what are their mutual respects to each other, by which, as their peculiar properties, giving them the manner of their subsistence, they are distinguished one from another; with sundry other things of the like necessary consequence unto the revelation mentioned.   And herein, as in the application of all other divine truths and mysteries whatever, yea, of *all moral commanded duties*, use is to be made of such words and expressions as, it may be, are not literally and formally contained in the Scripture; but only are, unto our conceptions and apprehensions, expository of what is so contained.   And to deny the liberty, yea, the necessity hereof, is to deny all interpretation of the Scripture,—all endeavours to express the sense of the words of it unto the understandings of one another; which is, in a word, to render the Scripture itself altogether useless. For if it be *unlawful* for me to speak or write what I conceive to be the sense of the words of the Scripture, and the nature of the thing signified and expressed by them, it is unlawful for me, also, to think or conceive in my mind what is the sense of the words or nature of the things; which to say, is to make brutes of ourselves, and to frustrate the whole design of God in giving unto us the great privilege of his word.

Wherefore, in the declaration of the doctrine of the Trinity, we may *lawfully*, nay, we must *necessarily*, make use of other words, phrases, and expressions, than what are literally and syllabically contained in the Scripture, but teach no other things.

Moreover, whatever is so revealed in the Scripture is no less *true* and divine as to whatever necessarily followeth thereon, than it is as unto that which is principally revealed and directly expressed.   For how far soever the lines be drawn and extended, from truth nothing can follow and ensue but what is true also; and that in the same kind of truth with that which it is derived and deduced from.   For if the principal assertion be a truth of divine revelation, so is also whatever is included therein, and which may be rightly from thence collected.   Hence it follows, that when the Scripture revealeth the Father, Son, and Holy Ghost to be one God, seeing it necessarily and unavoidably follows thereon that they are one in essence (wherein alone it is possible they can be one), and three in their distinct subsistences (wherein alone it is possible they can be three),—this is no less of divine revelation than the first principle from whence these things follow.

These being the *respects* which the doctrine of the Trinity falls under, the necessary method of faith and reason, in the believing and declaring of it, is plain and evident:—

FIRST. The *revelation* of it is to be asserted and vindicated, as it is proposed to be believed, for the ends mentioned.   Now, this is, as was declared, that *there is one God;* that *this God is Father, Son, and Holy Ghost;* and so, that the Father is God, so is the Son, so is the Holy Ghost.

This being received and admitted by faith, the *explication* of it is,—

SECONDLY, To be insisted on, and not taken into consideration until the others be admitted. And herein lies the preposterous course of those who fallaciously and captiously go about to oppose this sacred truth:—they will always begin their opposition, not unto the *revelation* of it, but unto the *explanation* of it; which is used only for farther edification. Their disputes and cavils shall be against the *Trinity, essence, substance, persons, personality, respects, properties* of the divine persons, with the *modes* of expressing these things; whilst the plain *scriptural revelation* of the things themselves from whence they are but explanatory deductions, is not spoken to, nor admitted into confirmation. By this means have they entangled many weak, unstable souls, who, when they have met with things too high, hard, and difficult for them (which in divine mysteries they may quickly do), in the explication of this doctrine, have suffered themselves to be taken off from a due consideration of the full and plain revelation of the thing itself in Scripture; until, their temptations being made strong, and their darkness increased, it was too late for them to return unto it; as bringing along with them the cavils wherewith they were prepossessed, rather than that faith and obedience which is required. But yet all this while these explanations, so excepted against, are indeed not of any *original consideration* in this matter. Let the direct, express revelations of the doctrine be confirmed, they will follow of themselves, nor will be excepted against by those who believe and receive it. Let that be rejected, and they will *fall of themselves*, and never be contended for by those who did make use of them. But of these things we shall treat again afterward.

This, therefore, is the way, the only way that we *rationally* can, and that which in *duty* we ought to proceed in and by, for the asserting and confirming of the doctrine of the holy Trinity under consideration,—namely, that we produce divine revelations or testimonies, wherein faith may safely rest and acquiesce, that *God is one;* that *this one God is Father, Son, and Holy Ghost;* so that the Father is God, so also is the Son, and the Holy Ghost likewise, and, as such, are to be believed in, obeyed, worshipped, acknowledged, as the first cause and last end of all,—our Lord and reward. If this be not admitted, if somewhat of it be not, particularly [if it be] denied, we need not, we have no warrant or ground to proceed any farther, or at all to discourse about the unity of the divine essence, or the distinction of the persons.

We have not, therefore, any *original contest* in this matter with any, but such as deny either *God to be one*, or the *Father to be God*, or the *Son to be God*, or the *Holy Ghost so to be*. If any deny either of these in particular, we are ready to confirm it by sufficient testimonies of Scripture, or clear and undeniable divine revelation. When this is evinced and vindicated, we shall willingly proceed to manifest that the explications used of this doctrine unto the edification of the church are according to truth, and such as necessarily are required by the nature of the things themselves. And this gives us the method of the ensuing small discourse, with the reasons of it:—

I. The first thing which we affirm to be delivered unto us by divine revelation as the object of our faith, is, that *God is one.* I know that this may be uncontrollably evinced by the light of reason itself, unto as good and quiet an assurance as the mind of man is capable of in any of its apprehensions whatever; but I speak of it now as it is confirmed unto us by divine revelation. How this assertion of one God respects the nature, essence, or divine being of God, shall be declared afterward. At present it is enough to represent the testimonies that he is one,—only one. And because we have no difference with our adversaries distinctly about this matter, I shall only name some few of them. Deut. vi. 4, " Hear, O Israel; The LORD our God is one LORD." A most pregnant testimony; and yet, notwithstanding, as I shall elsewhere manifest, the Trinity itself; in that one divine essence, is here asserted. Isa. xliv. 6, 8, " Thus saith the LORD the King of Israel, and his Redeemer the LORD of hosts; I am the first, and I am the last; and beside me there is no God. Is there a God beside me? yea, there is no God; I know not any." In which also we may manifest that a plurality of persons is included and expressed. And although there be no more absolute and sacred truth than this, that God is one, yet it may be evinced that it is nowhere mentioned in the Scripture, but that, either in the words themselves or the context of the place, a *plurality of persons* in that one sense is intimated.

II. Secondly, It is proposed as the object of our faith, that *the Father is God.* And herein, as is pretended, there is also an agreement between us and those who oppose the doctrine of the Trinity. But there is a mistake in this matter. Their hypothesis, as they call it, or, indeed, presumptuous error, casts all the conceptions that are given us concerning God in the Scripture into disorder and confusion. For the Father, as he whom we worship, is often called so only with reference unto his Son; as the Son is so with reference to the Father. He is the " only begotten of the Father," John i. 14. But now, if this Son had no pre-existence in his divine nature before he was born of the Virgin, there was no God the Father seventeen hundred years ago, because there was no Son. And on this ground did the Marcionites[1] of old plainly deny *the Father* (whom, under

---

[1] Marcion was a native of Pontus, and a celebrated heretic, who lived and propagated his errors in the middle of the second century. He seems to have been

the New Testament, we worship) to be the God of the Old Testament, who made the world, and was worshipped from the foundation of it. For it seems to follow, that he whom we worship being the Father, and on this supposition that the Son had no pre-existence unto his incarnation, he was not the Father under the Old Testament; he is some other from him that was so revealed. I know the folly of that inference; yet how, on this opinion of the sole existence of the Son in time, men can prove the Father to be God, let others determine. "He that abideth in the doctrine of Christ, he hath both the Father and the Son;" but "whosoever transgresseth and abideth not in the doctrine of Christ, hath not God," 2 John 9. Whoever denies Christ the Son, as the Son, that is, the eternal Son of God, he loses the Father also, and the true God; he hath not God. For that God which is not the Father, and which ever was, and was not the Father, is not the true God. Hence many of the fathers, even of the first writers of the church, were forced unto great pains in the confirmation of this truth, that the Father of Jesus Christ was he who made the world, gave the law, spake by the prophets, and was the author of the Old Testament; and that against men who professed themselves to be Christians. And this brutish apprehension of theirs arose from no other principle but this, that the Son had only a temporal existence, and was not the eternal Son of God.

But that I may not in this brief discourse digress unto other controversies than what lies directly before us, and seeing the adversaries of the truth we contend for do, in words at least, grant that the Father of our Lord Jesus Christ is the true God, or the only true God, I shall not farther show the inconsistency of their hypothesis with this confession, but take it for granted that to us "there is one God, the Father," 1 Cor. viii. 6; see John xvii. 3. So that he who is not the Father, who was not so from eternity, whose paternity is not equally co-existent unto his Deity, is not God unto us.

III. Thirdly, It is asserted and believed by the church *that Jesus Christ is God, the eternal Son of God;*—that is, he is proposed, declared, and revealed unto us in the Scripture to be God, that is to be served, worshipped, believed in, obeyed as God, upon the account of his *own divine excellencies.* And whereas we believe and know that

---

engaged in teaching his heretical views at Rome in A.D. 139. He held two original and seminal principles,—the invisible and nameless one, "the Good;" and the visible God, "the Creator." Epiphanius ascribes to him a third,—"the Devil." The second, according to his system, was the God of the Old Testament, the author of evil; and Christ was the Son of the first, sent by him to overthrow the dominion of God the Creator. He held that there was an irreconcilable opposition between God the Creator revealed in the Old Testament Scriptures, and the Christian God revealed in the New. One ground on which he maintained this preposterous notion is mentioned and explained above by Dr Owen. Tertullian devotes five books to the refutation of the errors of Marcion.—ED.

he was man, that he was born, lived, and died as a man, it is declared that he is God also; and that, as God, he did pre-exist in the form of God before his incarnation, which was effected by voluntary actings of his own,—which could not be without a pre-existence in another nature. This is proposed unto us to be believed upon divine testimony and by divine revelation. And the sole inquiry in this matter is, whether this be proposed in the Scripture as an object of faith, and that which is indispensably necessary for us to believe? Let us, then, nakedly attend unto what the Scripture asserts in this matter, and that in the order of the books of it, in some particular instances which at present occur to mind; as these that follow:—

Ps. xlv. 6, "Thy throne, O God, is for ever and ever." Applied unto Christ, Heb. i. 8, "But unto the Son he saith, Thy throne, O God, is for ever and ever."

Ps. lxviii. 17, 18, "The chariots of God are twenty thousand, even thousands of angels: the LORD is among them, as in Sinai, in the holy place. Thou hast ascended on high, thou hast led captivity captive: thou hast received gifts for men; yea, for the rebellious also, that the LORD God might dwell among them." Applied unto the Son, Eph. iv. 8–10, "Wherefore he saith, When he ascended up on high, he led captivity captive, and gave gifts unto men. Now that he ascended, what is it but that he also descended first into the lower parts of the earth? He that descended is the same also that ascended up far above all heavens, that he might fill all things."

Ps. cx. 1, "The LORD said unto my Lord, Sit thou at my right hand." Applied unto Christ by himself, Matt. xxii. 44.

Ps. cii. 25–27, "Of old hast thou laid the foundation of the earth; and the heavens are the work of thy hands. They shall perish, but thou shalt endure: yea, all of them shall wax old like a garment; as a vesture shalt thou change them, and they shall be changed: but thou art the same, and thy years shall have no end." Declared by the apostle to be meant of the Son, Heb. i. 10–12.

Prov. viii. 22–31, "The LORD possessed me in the beginning of his way, before his works of old. I was set up from everlasting, from the beginning, or ever the earth was. When there were no depths, I was brought forth; when there were no fountains abounding with water. Before the mountains were settled, before the hills was I brought forth: while as yet he had not made the earth, nor the fields, nor the highest part of the dust of the world. When he prepared the heavens, I was there: when he set a compass upon the face of the depth: when he established the clouds above: when he strengthened the fountains of the deep: when he gave to the sea his decree, that the waters should not pass his commandment: when he appointed the foundations of the earth: then I was by him, as one brought up with him: and I was daily his delight, rejoicing always before him; rejoicing in the habitable part of his earth; and my delights were with the sons of men."

Isa. vi. 1–3, 'I saw also the LORD sitting upon a throne, high and lifted up, and his train filled the temple. Above it stood the seraphims: each one had six wings; with twain he covered his face, and with twain he covered his feet, and with twain he did fly. And one cried unto another, and said, Holy, holy, holy, is the LORD of hosts: the whole earth is full of his glory." Applied unto the Son, John xii. 41.

Isa. viii. 13, 14, " Sanctify the LORD of hosts himself; and let him be your fear, and let him be your dread. And he shall be for a sanctuary; but for a stone of stumbling and for a rock of offence to both the houses of Israel, for a gin and for a snare to the inhabitants of Jerusalem." Applied unto the Son, Luke ii. 34; Rom. ix. 33; 1 Pet. ii. 8.

Isa. ix. 6, " For unto us a child is born, unto us a son is given; and the government shall be upon his shoulder: and his name shall be called Wonderful, Counsellor, The mighty God, The everlasting Father, The Prince of Peace. Of the increase of his government and peace there shall be no end."

Jer. xxiii. 5, 6, " Behold, the days come, saith the LORD, that I will raise unto David a righteous Branch; and this is his name whereby he shall be called, Jehovah our Righteousness."

Hos. xii. 3–5, " He took his brother by the heel in the womb, and by his strength he had power with God: yea, he had power over the angel, and prevailed: he wept, and made supplication unto him: he found him in Bethel, and there he spake with us; even the LORD God of hosts; the LORD is his memorial."

Zech. ii. 8, 9, " For thus saith the LORD of hosts, After the glory hath he sent me unto the nations which spoiled you: and ye shall know that the LORD of hosts hath sent me."

Matt. xvi. 16, " Thou art the Christ, the Son of the living God."

Luke i. 35, " The Holy Ghost shall come upon thee, and the power of the Highest shall overshadow thee: therefore also that holy thing which shall be born of thee shall be called the Son of God."

John i. 1–3. " In the beginning was the Word, and the Word was with God, and the Word was God. The same was in the beginning with God. All things were made by him; and without him was not any thing made that was made."

Verse 14, " And we beheld his glory, the glory as of the only be-gotten of the Father."

John iii. 13, " And no man hath ascended up to heaven, but he that came down from heaven, even the Son of man, which is in heaven."

John viii. 57, 58, " Then said the Jews unto him, Thou art not yet fifty years old, and hast thou seen Abraham? Jesus said unto them, Verily, verily, I say unto you, Before Abraham was, I am."

John x. 30, " I and my Father are one."

John xvii. 5, " And now, O Father, glorify thou me with thine own self with the glory which I had with thee before the world was."

John xx. 28, " And Thomas answered and said unto him, My Lord and my God."

Acts xx. 28, " Feed the church of God, which he hath purchased with his own blood."

Rom. i. 3, 4, "Concerning his Son Jesus Christ our Lord, which was made of the seed of David according to the flesh; and declared to be the Son of God with power, according to the spirit of holiness, by the resurrection from the dead."

Rom. ix. 5, " Of whom as concerning the flesh Christ came, who is over all, God blessed for ever. Amen."

Rom. xiv. 10–12, " For we shall all stand before the judgment-seat of Christ. For it is written, As I live, saith the Lord, every knee shall bow to me, and every tongue shall confess to God. So then every one of us shall give account of himself to God."

1 Cor. viii. 6, " And one Lord Jesus, by whom are all things, and we by him."

1 Cor. x. 9, "Neither let us tempt Christ, as some of them also tempted, and were destroyed of serpents;" compared with Numb. xxi. 6.

Phil. ii. 5, 6, " Let this mind be in you, which was also in Christ Jesus: who, being in the form of God, thought it not robbery to be equal with God."

Col. i. 15–17, " Who is the image of the invisible God, the first-born of every creature: for by him were all things created, that are in heaven, and that are in earth, visible and invisible, whether they be thrones, or dominions, or principalities, or powers; all things were created by him, and for him: and he is before all things, and by him all things consist."

1 Tim. iii. 16, " Without controversy great is the mystery of godliness: God was manifest in the flesh."

Tit. ii. 13, 14, " Looking for that blessed hope, and the glorious appearing of the great God and our Saviour Jesus Christ; who gave himself for us."

Heb. i. throughout.

Chap. iii. 4, " For every house is builded by some man; but he that built all things is God."

1 Pet. i. 11, " Searching what, or what manner of time, the Spirit of Christ which was in them did signify."

Chap. iii. 18–20, " For Christ also hath once suffered for sins, being put to death in the flesh, but quickened by the Spirit: by which also he went and preached unto the spirits in prison; which sometime were disobedient, when once the long-suffering of God waited in the days of Noah."

1 John iii. 16, " Hereby perceive we the love of God, because he laid down his life for us."

Chap. v. 20, " And we are in him that is true, even in his Son Jesus Christ. This is the true God, and eternal life."

Rev. i. 8, " I am Alpha and Omega, the beginning and the ending, saith the Lord, which is, and which was, and which is to come, the Almighty."

Verses 11–13, " I am Alpha and Omega, the first and the last: and, What thou seest, write in a book. . . . . And I turned to see the voice that spake with me. And, being turned, I saw seven golden candlesticks; and in the midst of the seven candlesticks one like unto the Son of man."

Verse 17, " And when I saw him, I fell at his feet as dead. And he laid his right hand upon me, saying unto me, Fear not; I am the first and the last."

Chap. ii. 23, " I am he which searcheth the reins and hearts: and I will give unto every one of you according to your works."

These are *some* of the places wherein the truth under consideration is revealed and declared,—some of the divine testimonies whereby it is confirmed and established, which I have not at present inquired after, but suddenly repeated as they came to mind. Many *more* of the like nature and importance may be added unto them, and shall be so as occasion doth require.

Let, now, any one who owns the Scripture to be the word of God, —to contain an infallible revelation of the things proposed in it to be believed,—and who hath any conscience exercised towards God for the receiving and submitting unto what he declares and reveals, take a view of these testimonies, and consider whether they do not sufficiently propose this object of our faith. Shall a few poor trifling sophisms, whose terms are scarcely understood by the most that amongst us make use of them, according as they have found them framed by others, be thought meet to be set up in opposition unto these multiplied testimonies of the Holy Ghost, and to cast the truth confirmed by them down from its credit and reputation in the consciences of men ? For my part, I do not see in any thing, but that the testimonies given to the Godhead of Christ, the eternal Son of God, are every way as clear and unquestionable as those are which testify to the being of God, or that there is any God at all. Were men acquainted with the Scriptures as they ought to be, and as the most, considering the means and advantages they have had, might have been; did they ponder and believe on what they read, or had they any tenderness in their consciences as to that reverence, obedience, and subjection of soul which God requires unto his word; it were utterly impossible that their faith in this matter should ever in the least be shaken by a few *lewd sophisms* or *loud clamours* of men destitute of the truth, and of the spirit of it.

That we may now improve these testimonies unto the end under design, as the nature of this brief discourse will bear, I shall first remove the general answers which the Socinians give unto them, and then manifest farther how uncontrollable they are, by giving an instance in the frivolous exceptions of the same persons to *one* of them in particular. And we are ready, God assisting, to maintain that there is not any one of them which doth not give a sufficient ground for faith to rest on in this matter concerning the Deity of Christ, and that against all the Socinians in the world.

They say, therefore, commonly, that we prove not by these testimonies what is by them denied. For they acknowledge *Christ to be God*, and that because he is exalted unto that glory and authority that all creatures are put into subjection unto him, and all, both men and angels, are commanded to worship and adore him. So that he is God by office, though he be not God by nature. He is God, but he is not the most high God. And this last expression they have almost continually in their mouths, "He is not the most high God." And commonly, with great contempt and scorn, they are ready to reproach them who have solidly confirmed the doctrine of the Deity of Christ as ignorant of the state of the controversy, in that they have not proved him to be *the most high God*, in subordination unto whom they acknowledge Christ to be God, and that he ought to be worshipped with divine and religious worship.

But there cannot be any thing more empty and vain than these pretences; and, besides, they accumulate in them their former errors, with the addition of new ones. For,—

First. The name of *the most high God* is first ascribed unto God in Gen. xiv. 18, 19, 22, denoting his sovereignty and dominion. Now, as other attributes of God, it is not *distinctive* of the subject, but only *descriptive* of it. So are all other excellencies of the nature of God. It doth not intimate that there are other gods, only he is the most high, or one over them all; but only that the true God is most high,—that is, endued with sovereign power, dominion, and authority over all. To say, then, that Christ indeed is God, but not the *most high* God, is all one as to say he is God, but not the *most holy* God, or not the *true* God; and so they have brought their Christ into the number of false gods, whilst they deny the true Christ, who, in his divine nature, is "over all, God blessed for ever," Rom. ix. 5; a phrase of speech perfectly expressing this attribute of the *most high God*.

Secondly. This answer is suited only unto those testimonies which express the *name of God* with a corresponding power and authority unto that name; for in reference unto these alone can it be pleaded, with any pretence of reason, that he is a God by office,—though that also be done very futilously and impertinently. But most of the testimonies produced speak directly unto his divine excellencies and properties, which belong unto his nature necessarily and absolutely. That he is eternal, omnipotent, immense, omniscient, infinitely wise; and that he is, and worketh, and produceth effects suitable unto all these properties, and such as nothing but they can enable him for; is abundantly proved by the foregoing testimonies. Now, all these concern a *divine nature*, a natural essence, a Godhead, and not such power or authority as a man may be exalted unto; yea, the ascribing any of them to such a one, implies the highest contradiction expressible.

Thirdly. This God in authority and office, and not by nature, that should be the object of divine worship, is a new abomination. For they are divine, essential excellencies that are *the formal reason* and *object* of worship, religious and divine; and to ascribe it unto any one that is *not God by nature*, is idolatry. By making, therefore, their Christ such a God as they describe, they bring him under the severe commination of the true God. Jer. x. 11, "The gods that have not made the heavens and the earth, even they shall perish from the earth, and from under these heavens." That Christ they worship they say is a God; but they deny that he is "that God that made the heavens and the earth:" and so leave him exposed to the threatenings of him, who will accomplish it to the uttermost.

Some other general exceptions sometimes they make use of, which the reader may free himself from the entanglement of, if he do but heed these ensuing rules:—

First. Distinction of persons (of which afterwards), it being in an infinite substance, doth no way prove a difference of *essence* between the Father and the Son. Where, therefore, Christ, as the Son, is said to be *another* from the Father, or God, spoken personally of the Father, it argues not in the least that he is not partaker of the same nature with him. That in one essence there can be but one person, may be true where the substance is finite and limited, but hath no place in that which is infinite.

Secondly. Distinction and inequality in respect of *office* in Christ, doth not in the least take away his equality and sameness with the Father in respect of nature and essence, Phil. ii. 7, 8. A son, of the same nature with his father, and therein equal to him, may in office be his inferior,—his subject.

Thirdly. The *advancement* and exaltation of Christ as mediator to any dignity whatever, upon or in reference to the work of our redemption and salvation, is not at all inconsistent with the essential honour, dignity, and worth, which he hath in himself as God blessed for ever. Though he humbled himself, and was exalted in *office*, yet in *nature* he was one and the same; he changed not.

Fourthly. The Scriptures, asserting the *humanity* of Christ, with the concernments thereof, as his birth, life, and death, do no more thereby deny his Deity than, by asserting his *Deity*, with the essential properties thereof, they deny his humanity.

Fifthly. God working in and by Christ as he was mediator, denotes the Father's sovereign appointment of the things mentioned to be done,—not his *immediate efficiency* in the doing of the things themselves.

These rules are proposed a little before their due place in the method which we pursue. But I thought meet to interpose them here, as containing a sufficient ground for the resolution and answering of all the sophisms and objections which the adversaries use in this cause.

From the cloud of witnesses before produced, every one whereof is singly sufficient to evert the Socinian infidelity, I shall in one of them give an instance, both of the clearness of the evidence and the weakness of the exceptions which are wont to be put in against them, as was promised; and this is John i. 1–3, " In the beginning was the Word, and the Word was with God, and the Word was God. The same was in the beginning with God. All things were made by him; and without him was not any thing made that was made."

By the Word, here, or ὁ Λόγος, on what account soever he be so called, either as being the eternal Word and Wisdom of the Father, or as the great Revealer of the will of God unto us, Jesus Christ the Son of God is intended. This is on all hands acknowledged; and the context will admit of no hesitation about it. For of this Word it is said, that " he came" into the world, verse 10; " was rejected by his own," verse 11; " was made flesh and dwelt among us, whose glory was the glory as of the only begotten Son of the Father," verse 14; called expressly " Jesus Christ," verse 17; " the only begotten Son of the Father," verse 18. The subject, then, treated of, is here agreed upon; and it is no less evident that it is the design of the apostle to declare both who and what he was of whom he treateth. Here, then, if any where, we may learn what we are to believe concerning the person of Christ; which also we may certainly do, if our minds are not perverted through prejudice, " whereby the god of this world doth blind the minds of them which believe not, lest the light of the glorious gospel of Christ, who is the image of God, should shine unto them," 2 Cor. iv. 4. Of this Word, then, this Son of God, it is affirmed, that he " was in the beginning." And this word, if it doth not absolutely and formally express eternity, yet it doth a *pre-exist-ence* unto the whole creation; which amounts to the same: for nothing can pre-exist unto all creatures, but in the nature of God, which is eternal; unless we shall suppose a creature before the crea-tion of any. But what is meant by this expression the Scripture doth elsewhere declare. Prov. viii. 23, " I was set up from everlast-ing, from the beginning, or ever the earth was." John xvii. 5, " Glorify thou me with thine own self, with the glory which I had with thee before the world was." Both which places, as they explain this phrase, so also do they undeniably testify unto the *eternal pre-existence* of Christ the Son of God. And in this case we prevail against our adversaries, if we prove any pre-existence of Christ unto his incarnation; which, as they absolutely deny, so to grant it would overthrow their whole heresy in this matter. And therefore they know that the testimony of our Saviour concerning himself, if under-stood in a proper, intelligible sense, is perfectly destructive of their pretensions, John viii. 58, " Before Abraham *was*, I *am*." For although there be no proper sense in the words, but a gross equivo-cation, if the existence of Christ before Abraham was born be not asserted in them (seeing he spake in answer to that objection of the Jews, that he was not yet fifty years old, and so could not have seen Abraham, nor Abraham him; and the Jews that were present, under-stood well enough that he asserted a divine pre-existence unto his being born, so long ago, as that hereon, after their manner, they took up stones to stone him, as supposing him to have blasphemed in as-serting his Deity, as others now do in the denying of it); yet they [Socinians], seeing how fatal this pre-existence, though not here absolutely asserted to be eternal, would be to their cause, contend that the meaning of the words is, that " Christ was to be the light of the world before Abraham was made the father of many nations;"— an interpretation so absurd and sottish, as never any man not infatu-ated by the god of this world could once admit and give counte-nance unto.

But " in the beginning," as absolutely used, is the same with " from everlasting," as it is expounded, Prov. viii. 23, and denoteth an eternal existence; which is here affirmed of the Word, the Son of God. But let the word " beginning," be restrained unto the subject-matter treated of (which is the creation of all things), and the pre-existence of Christ in his divine nature unto the creation of all things is plainly revealed, and inevitably asserted. And indeed, not only the word, but the discourse of these verses, doth plainly relate unto, and is expository of, the first verse in the Bible, Gen. i. 1, "In the beginning God created the heaven and the earth." There it is asserted that in the beginning God created all things; here, that the Word was in the beginning, and made all things. This, then, is the least that we have obtained from this first word of our testimony,—namely, that the Word or *Son of God had a personal pre-existence unto the whole creation.* In what nature this must be, let these men of reason satisfy themselves, who know that Creator and creatures take up the whole nature of beings. One of them he must be; and it may be well supposed that he was not a creature before the creation of any.

But, secondly, Where, or with whom, was this Word in the beginning? "It was," saith the Holy Ghost, "with God." There being no creature then existing, he could be nowhere but with God; that is, the Father, as it is expressed in one of the testimonies before going, Prov. viii. 22, "The LORD possessed me in the beginning of his way, before his works of old;" verse 30, "Then was I by him as one brought up with him, and I was daily his delight, rejoicing always before him;" that is, in the beginning this Word, or Wisdom of God, was with God.

And this is the same which our Lord Jesus asserts concerning himself, John iii. 13, "And no man," saith he, "hath ascended up to heaven, but he that came down from heaven, even the Son of man which is in heaven." And so in other places he affirms his being in heaven,—that is, with God,—at the same time when he was on the earth; whereby he declares the immensity of his nature, and the distinction of his person; and his coming down from heaven before he was incarnate on the earth, declaring his pre-existence; by both manifesting the meaning of this expression, that "in the beginning he was with God." But hereunto they have invented a notable evasion. For although they know not well what to make of the last clause of the words, that says, then he was in heaven when he spake on earth,—"The Son of man which is in heaven," answerable to the description of God's immensity, "Do not I fill heaven and earth? saith the Lord," Jer. xxiii. 24, but say that he was there by *heavenly meditation,* as another man may be; yet they give a very clear answer to what must of necessity be included in his descending from heaven, —namely, his pre-existence to his incarnation: for they tell us that, before his public ministry, he was in his human nature (which is all they allow unto him) taken up into heaven, and there taught the gospel, as the great impostor Mohammed pretended he was taught his Alkoran. If you ask them who told them so, they cannot tell; but they can tell when it was,—namely, when he was led by the Spirit into the wilderness for forty days after his baptism. But yet this instance is subject to another misadventure; in that one of the evangelists plainly affirms that he was "those forty days in the wilderness with the wild beasts," Mark i. 13, and so, surely, not in heaven in the same nature, by his bodily presence, with God and his holy angels.

And let me add this, by the way, that the interpretation of this place, John i. 1, to be mentioned afterward, and those of the two places before mentioned, John viii. 58, iii. 13, Faustus Socinus[1] learned out of his uncle Lælius' papers, as he confesseth; and doth more than intimate that he believed he had them as it were by revelation. And it may be so; they are indeed so forced, absurd, and irrational, that no man could ever fix upon them by any reasonable investigation; but the author of this revelation, if we may judge of the parent by the child, could be no other but the spirit of error and darkness. I suppose, therefore, that notwithstanding these exceptions, Christians will believe "that in the beginning the Word was with God;" that is, that the Son was with the Father, as is frequently elsewhere declared.

But *who* was this Word? Saith the apostle, *He was God.* He was so *with God* (that is, the Father), as that he himself was God also;— God, in that notion of God which both nature and the Scripture do represent; not a god by office, one exalted to that dignity (which cannot well be pretended before the creation of the world), but as Thomas confessed him, " Our Lord and our God," John xx. 28; or as Paul expresses it, " Over all, God blessed for ever;" or *the most high God;*

---

[1] The two Sozzini were descended from an honourable family, and were both born at Siena,—Lælius, the uncle, in 1525, and his nephew, Faustus, in 1539. The former became addicted to the careful study of the Scriptures, forsaking the legal profession, for which he had undergone some training; and acquiring, in furtherance of his favourite pursuit, the Greek, Hebrew, and Arabic languages. He is said to have been one of forty individuals who held meetings for conference on religious topics, chiefly at Vicenza, and who sought to establish a purer creed, by the rejection of certain doctrines on which all the divines of the Reformation strenuously insisted. To these Vicentine " colleges," as the meetings were termed, Socinians have been accustomed to trace the origin of their peculiar tenets. Dr M'Crie, in his " History of the Reformation in Italy" (p. 154), assigns strong reasons for discarding this account of the origin of Socinianism as unworthy of credit. Lælius never committed himself during his life to a direct avowal of his sentiments, and was on terms of intercourse and correspondence with the leading Reformers; intimating, however, his scruples and doubts to such an extent, that his soundness in the faith was questioned, and he received an admonition from Calvin. He left Italy in 1547, travelled extensively, and at length settled in Zurich, where he died in 1562, leaving behind him some manuscripts, to which Dr Owen alludes, and of which his nephew availed himself, in reducing the errors held in common by uncle and nephew to the form of a theological system.

The nephew, Faustus, had rather a chequered life. Tainted at an early age with the heresy of his uncle, he was under the necessity of quitting Siena; and after having held for twelve years some honourable offices in the court of the Duke of Tuscany, he repaired to Bâsle, and for three years devoted himself to theological study. The doubts of the uncle rose to the importance of convictions in the mind of the nephew. In consequence of divisions among the reformers of

which these men love to deny. Let not the infidelity of men, excited by the craft and malice of Satan, seek for blind occasions, and this matter is determined; if the word and testimony of God be able to umpire a difference amongst the children of men. Here is the sum of our creed in this matter, " In the beginning the Word was God," and so continues unto eternity, being Alpha and Omega, the first and the last, the Lord God Almighty.

And to show that he was so God in the beginning, as that he was *one* distinct, in something, from God the Father, by whom afterward he was sent into the world, he adds, verse 2, " The same was in the beginning with God." Farther, also, to evince what he hath asserted and revealed for us to believe, the Holy Ghost adds, both as a firm declaration of his eternal Deity, and also his immediate care of the world (which how he variously exercised, both in a way of providence and grace, he afterward declares), verse 3, " All things were made by him." He was so in the beginning, before all things, as that he made them all. And that it may not be supposed that the " all" that he is said to make or create was to be limited unto any certain sort of things, he adds, that " without him nothing was made that was made;" which gives the first assertion an absolute universality as to its subject.

And this he farther describes, verse 10, " He was in the world, and the world was made by him." The world that was made, hath a usual distribution, in the Scripture, into the " heavens and the earth,

---

Transylvania, who had become Antitrinitarians, he was sent for by Blandrata, one of their leaders, to reason Francis David out of some views he held regarding the adoration due to Christ. The result was, that David was cast into prison, where he died,—Socinus using no influence to restrain the Prince of Transylvania from such cruel intolerance; a fact too often forgotten by some who delight in reproaching Calvin for the death of Servetus. He visited Poland in 1579; but before his visit, the Antitrinitarians of that country had, by resolutions of their synods in 1563 and 1565, withdrawn from the communion of other churches, and published a Bible and a Catechism,—commonly known, from Rakau, the town in which it was published, as the " Racovian Catechism." Faustus Socinus was not at first well received by his Polish brethren; but he overcame their aversion to him, which at one time was so strong that he was nearly torn to pieces by a mob. He acquired considerable influence amongst them; managed to compose their differences, and became so popular, that his co-religionists adopted the name of Socinians, in preference to their old name of Unitarians. He died in 1604. His tracts were collected into two folio volumes of the " Bibliotheca Fratrum Polonorum." Starting with mistaken views of private judgment, he inferred, from the right to the exercise of individual belief on the authority of Scripture, the competency of reason to determine the credibility of doctrine; but his views differed from modern Rationalism, inasmuch as he adhered more to historical Christianity as the basis of his principles, and was by no means so free in impugning the authenticity of Scripture, when it bore against his system. His heresies assumed a shape more positive and definite than is generally fancied, and affected the doctrines of the Trinity, the divinity of Christ (on which his views were somewhat akin to Arianism), the necessity of an atonement, the nature of repentance, the efficacy of grace, the sacraments, and the eternity of future punishments. —ED.

and all things contained in them;"—as Acts iv. 24, " Lord, thou art God, which hast made heaven, and earth, and the sea, and all that in them is;" that is, the world, the making whereof is expressly assigned unto the Son, Heb. i. 10, " Thou, Lord, in the beginning hast laid the foundation of the earth; and the heavens are the works of thine hands." And the apostle Paul, to secure our understandings in this matter, instanceth in the most noble parts of the creation, and which, if any, might seem to be excepted from being made by him, Col. i. 16, " For by him were all things created, that are in heaven, and that are in earth, visible and invisible, whether they be thrones, or dominions, or principalities, or powers; all things were created by him, and for him." The Socinians say, indeed, that he made angels to be thrones and principalities; that is, he gave them their *order*, but not their *being:* which is expressly contrary to the words of the text; so that a man knows not well what to say to these persons, who, at their pleasure, cast off the authority of God in his word: " By him were all things created, that are in heaven, and that are in earth."

What now can be required to secure our faith in this matter? In what words possible could a divine revelation of the eternal power and Godhead of the Son of God be made more plain and clear unto the sons of men? or how could the truth of any thing more evidently be represented unto their minds? If we understand not the mind of God and intention of the Holy Ghost in this matter, we may utterly despair ever to come to an acquaintance with any thing that God reveals unto us; or, indeed, with any thing else that is expressed or is to be expressed, by words. It is directly said that the Word (that is Christ, as is acknowledged by all) " was with God," distinct from him; and " was God," one with him; that he was so " in the beginning," before the creation, that he " made all things,"—the world, all things in heaven and in earth: and if he be not God, who is? The sum is,—all the ways whereby we may know God are, his name, his properties, and his works; but they are all here ascribed by the Holy Ghost to the Son, to the Word: and he therefore is God, or we know neither who nor what God is.

But say the Socinians, " These things are quite otherwise, and the words have another sense in them than you imagine." What is it, I pray? We bring none to them, we impose no sense upon them, we strain not any word in them, from, beside, or beyond its native, genuine signification, its constant application in the Scripture, and common use amongst men. What, then, is this latent sense that is intended, and is discoverable only by themselves? Let us hear them coining and stamping this sense of theirs.

First, they say that by " In the beginning," is not meant of *the beginning of all things,* or the creation of them, but the beginning of the preaching of the gospel. But why so, I pray? Wherever these words are else used in the Scripture, they denote the beginning of all things, or eternity absolutely, or an existence preceding their creation. " In the beginning God created the heaven and the earth," Gen. i. 1. " I was set up from everlasting, from the beginning, or ever the earth was," Prov. viii. 23. " Thou, Lord, in the beginning hast laid the foundation of the earth," Heb. i. 10. And besides, these words are never used absolutely anywhere for the beginning of the gospel. There is mention made, indeed, of the " beginning of the gospel of Jesus Christ," Mark i. 1, which is referred to the preaching of John Baptist: but " In the beginning," absolutely, is never so used or applied; and they must meet with men of no small inclination unto them, who will, upon their desire, in a matter of so great importance, forego the sense of words which is natural and proper, fixed by its constant use in the Scripture, when applied in the same kind, for that which is forced and strained, and not once exemplified in the whole book of God. But the words, they say, are to be restrained to the subject-matter treated of. Well, what is that subject-matter? " *The new creation, by the preaching of the gospel.*" But this is plainly false; nor will the words allow any such sense, nor the context, nor is any thing offered to give evidence unto this corrupt perverting of the words, unless it be a farther perverting of other testimonies no less clear than this.

For what is, according to this interpretation, the meaning of these words, " In the beginning was the Word?" "That is, when John Baptist preached, and said, ' This is the Lamb of God,' which was signally the beginning of the gospel,—then he was." That is, he was when he was,—no doubt of it! And is not this a notable way of interpreting of Scripture which these great pretenders to a dictatorship in reason, indeed hucksters in sophistry, do make use of? But to go on with them in this supposition, How was he then with God,—" The Word was with God?" "That is," say they, " he was then known only to God, before John Baptist preached him in the beginning." But what shall compel us to admit of this uncouth sense and exposition,—" ' He was with God;' that is, he was known to God alone?" What is there singular herein? concerning how many things may the same be affirmed? Besides, it is absolutely *false.* He was known to the *angel* Gabriel, who came to his mother with the message of his incarnation, Luke i. 35. He was known to the *two angels* which appeared to the shepherds upon his birth, Luke ii. 9,—to all the *heavenly host* assembled to give praise and glory to God on the account of his nativity, as those who came to worship him, and to pay him the homage due unto him, Luke ii. 10, 13, 14. He was known to his *mother,* the blessed Virgin, and to *Joseph*, and *Zacharias*, and to *Elisabeth*, to *Simeon* and *Anna*, to *John Baptist*, and probably to many more to whom Simeon and Anna spake of him, Luke ii. 38. So that the sense pretended to be wrung out and extorted from these words, against their proper meaning and intendment, is indeed false and frivolous, and belongs not at all unto them.

But let this pass. What shall we say to the next words, "And the Word was God?" Give us leave, without disturbance from you, but to believe this expression, which compriseth a revelation of God, proposed to us on purpose that we should believe it, and there will be, as was said, an end of this difference and debate. Yea, but say they, "These words have another sense also." Strange! they seem to be so plain and positive, that it is impossible any other sense should be fixed on them but only this, that the Word was in the beginning, and was God; and therefore is so still, unless he who is once God can cease so to be. "But the meaning is, that afterwards God exalted him, and made him God, as to *rule, authority, and power.*" This *making of him God* is an expression very offensive to the ears of all sober Christians; and was therefore before exploded. And these things here, as all other figments, hang together like a rope of sand. In the beginning of the gospel he was God, before any knew him but only God; that is, after he had preached the gospel, and died, and rose again, and was exalted at the right hand of God, he was made God, and that not properly, which is absolutely impossible, but in an improper sense! How prove they, then, this perverse nonsense to be the sense of these plain words? They say it must needs be so. Let them believe them who are willing to perish with them.

Thus far, then, we have their sense:—" In the beginning," that is, about sixteen or seventeen hundred years ago, " the Word," that is, the human nature of Christ before it was made flesh, which it was in its being, " was with God," that is, known to God alone; and " in the beginning," that is afterwards, not in the beginning, was made God!—which is the sum of their exposition of this place.

But what shall we say to what is affirmed concerning his making of all things, so as that without him, that is, without his making of it, nothing was made that was made; especially seeing that these " all things" are expressly said to be the world, verse 10, and all things therein contained, even in heaven and earth? Col. i. 16. An ordinary man would think that they should now be taken hold of, and that there is no way of escape left unto them; but they have it in a readiness. By the " all things" here, are intended all things of the gospel,—the preaching of it, the sending of the apostles to preach it, and to declare the will of God; and by the " world," is intended the world to come, or the new state of things under the gospel. This is the substance of what is pleaded by the greatest masters amongst them in this matter, and they are not ashamed thus to plead.

And the reader, in this instance, may easily discern what a desperate cause they are engaged in, and how bold and desperate they are in the management of it. For,—

First, The words are a plain illustration of the *divine nature* of the Word, by his divine power and works, as the very series of them declares. He was God, and he made all things: "He that built all things is God," Heb. iii. 4.

Secondly, There is no one word spoken concerning the gospel, nor the preaching of it, nor any effects of that preaching; which the apostle expressly insists upon and declares afterward, verse 15, and so onwards.

Thirdly, The making of all things, here ascribed unto the Word, was done *in the beginning;* but that making of all things which they intend, in erecting the church by the preaching of the word, was not done in the beginning, but afterwards,—most of it, as themselves confess, after the ascension of Christ into heaven.

Fourthly, In this gloss, what is the meaning of "All things?" "Only some things," say the Socinians. What is the meaning of "Were made?" "That is, were *mended.*" "By him?" "That is, the apostles, principally preaching the gospel." And this "In the beginning?" "*After it was past;*"—for so they say expressly, that the prinnipal things here intended were effected by the apostles afterwards.

I think, since the *beginning*, place it when you will,—the beginning of the world or the beginning of the gospel,—there was never such an exposition of the words of God or man contended for.

Fifthly, It is said, "He made the world," and he "came" into it,—namely, the world which he made; and "the world," or the inhabitants of it "knew him not." But the world they intend did know him: for the church knew him, and acknowledged him to be the Son of God; for that was the foundation that it was built upon.

I have instanced directly in this *only testimony*, to give the reader a pledge of the full confirmation which may be given unto this great fundamental truth, by a due improvement of those other testimonies, or distinct revelations, which speak no less expressly to the same purpose. And of them there is not any one but we are ready to vindicate it, if called thereunto, from the exceptions of these men; which how bold and sophistical they are we may, in these now considered, also learn and know.

It appeareth, then, that there is a full, sufficient revelation made in the Scripture of the eternal Deity of the Son of God; and that he is so, as is the Father also. More particular testimonies I shall not at present insist upon, referring the full discussion and vindication of these truths to another season.

IV. Fourthly, We are, therefore, in the next place, to manifest that the same, or the like testimony, is given unto the Deity of the Holy Spirit; that is, that he is revealed and declared in the Scripture as the object of our faith, worship, and obedience, on the account and for the reason of those divine excellencies which are the sole reason of our yielding religious worship unto any, or expecting from any the reward that is promised unto us, or to be brought by them to the end for which we are. And herein lies, as was showed, the concernment of faith. When that knows what it is to believe as on divine revelation, and is enabled thereby to regulate the soul in its present obedience and future expectation, seeing it is its nature to work by love and hope, there it rests. Now, this is done to the utmost satisfaction in the revelation that is made of the divine existence, divine excellencies, and divine operations of the Spirit; as shall be briefly manifested.

But before we proceed, we may, in our way, observe a great congruency of success in those who have denied the Deity of the Son and those who have denied that of the Holy Spirit. For as to the Son, after some men began once to disbelieve the revelation concerning him, and would not acknowledge him to be God and man in one person, they could never settle nor agree, either what or who he was, or who was his Father, or why he was the Son. Some said he was a phantasm or appearance, and that he had no real subsistence in this world; and that all that was done by him was an appearance, he himself being they know not what elsewhere. That proud beast, Paulus Samosatenus,[1] whose flagitious life contended for a pre-eminence in wickedness with his prodigious heresies, was one of the first, after the Jews, that positively contended for his being a man, and no more; who was followed by Photinus and others. The Arians perceiving the folly of this opinion, with the odium of it amongst all that bare the name of Christians, and that they had as good deny the whole Scripture as not grant unto him a pre-existence in a divine nature antecedent to his incarnation, they framed a new Deity, which God should make before the world, in all things like himself, but not the same with him in essence and substance, but to be so like him that, by the writings of some of them, ye can scarce know the one from the other; and that this was the Son of God, also, who was afterward incarnate. Others, in the meantime, had more monstrous imaginations: some, that he was an *angel;* some, that he was the *sun;* some, that he was the *soul of the world;* some, the *light within men.*

---

[1] A heresiarch of the third century, elevated to the bishopric of Antioch about A.D. 260. He is said to have indulged in haughty pomp and licentious practices, and was deposed by a council held in 269, chiefly for his heretical doctrines;— amongst which he held, that while the Father, Son, and Holy Ghost are one God, they are not respectively distinct persons, and that the Son in particular had no distinct personality, but existed in God, and came to dwell in the man Jesus.

Departing from their proper rest, so have they hovered about, and so have they continued to do until this day.

In the same manner it is come to pass with them who have denied the Deity of the Holy Ghost. They could never find where to stand or abide; but one hath cried up one thing, another another. At first they observed that such things were everywhere ascribed unto him in the Scripture as uncontrollably evidence him to be an *intelligent, voluntary agent.* This they found so plain and evident, that they could not deny but that he was a *person*, or an intelligent subsistence. Wherefore, seeing they were resolved not to assent unto the revelation of his being God, they made him a created spirit, chief and above all others; but still, whatever else he were, he was only a creature. And this course some of late also have steered.

The Socinians, on the other hand, observing that such things are assigned and ascribed unto him, as that, if they acknowledge him to be a person, or a substance, they must, upon necessity, admit him to be God, though they seemed not, at first, at all agreed what to think or say concerning him positively, yet they all concurred peremptorily in denying his personality. Hereon, some of them said he was the gospel, which others of them have confuted; some, that he was Christ. Neither could they agree whether there was one Holy Ghost or more;—whether the Spirit of God, and the good Spirit of God, and the Holy Spirit, be the same or no. In general, now they conclude that he is " vis Dei," or " virtus Dei," or " efficacia Dei;"— no substance, but a quality,·that may be considered either as being in God, and then they say it is the Spirit of God; or as sanctifying and conforming men unto God, and then they say it is the Holy Ghost. Whether these things do answer the revelation made in the Scripture concerning the eternal Spirit of God, will be immediately manifested. Our Quakers, who have for a long season hovered up and down like a swarm of flies, with a confused noise and humming, begin now to settle in the opinions lately by them declared for. But what their thoughts will fall in to be concerning the Holy Ghost, when they shall be contented to speak intelligibly, and according to the usage of other men, or the pattern of Scripture the great rule of speaking or treating about spiritual things, I know not, and am uncertain whether they do so themselves or no. Whether he may be the light within them, or an infallible afflatus, is uncertain. In the meantime, what is revealed unto us in the Scripture to be believed concerning the Holy Ghost, his Deity and personality, may be seen in the ensuing testimonies.

The sum of this revelation is,—that the Holy Spirit is an eternally existing divine substance, the author of divine operations, and the object of divine and religious worship; that is, "Over all, God blessed for ever," as the ensuing testimonies evince:—

Gen. i. 2, "The Spirit of God moved upon the face of the waters"

Ps. xxxiii. 6, "By the word of the LORD were the heavens made; and all the host of them by the Spirit of his mouth."

Job xxvi. 13, "By his Spirit he hath garnished the heavens."

Job xxxiii. 4, "The Spirit of God hath made me."

Ps. civ. 30, "Thou sendest forth thy Spirit, they are created."

Matt. xxviii. 19, "Baptizing them in the name of the Father, and of the Son, and of the Holy Ghost."

Acts i. 16, "That scripture must needs have been fulfilled, which the Holy Ghost by the mouth of David spake."

Acts v. 3, "Peter said, Ananias, why hath Satan filled thine heart to lie to the Holy Ghost?" verse 4, "Thou hast not lied unto men, but unto God."

Acts xxviii. 25, 26, "Well spake the Holy Ghost by Esaias the prophet unto our fathers, saying, Go unto this people, and say," etc.

1 Cor. iii. 16, "Know ye not that ye are the temple of God, and that the Spirit of God dwelleth in you?"

1 Cor. xii. 11, "All these worketh that one and the self-same Spirit, dividing to every man severally as he will." Verse 6, "And there are diversities of operations, but it is the same God which worketh all in all."

2 Cor. xiii. 14, "The grace of the Lord Jesus Christ, and the love of God, and the communion of the Holy Ghost, be with you all."

Acts xx. 28, "Take heed to the flock over the which the Holy Ghost hath made you overseers."

Matt. xii. 31, "All manner of sin and blasphemy shall be forgiven unto men; but the blasphemy against the Holy Ghost shall not be forgiven unto men."

Ps. cxxxix. 7, "Whither shall I go from thy Spirit?"

John xiv. 26, "But the Comforter, which is the Holy Ghost, whom the Father will send in my name, he shall teach you all things."

Luke xii. 12, "The Holy Ghost shall teach you in the same hour what ye ought to say."

Acts xiii. 2, "As they ministered to the Lord, and fasted, the Holy Ghost said, Separate me Barnabas and Saul for the work whereunto I have called them."

Verse 4, "So they, being sent forth by the Holy Ghost, departed unto Seleucia," etc.

2 Pet. i. 21, "For the prophecy came not in old time by the will of man, but holy men of God spake as they were moved by the Holy Ghost."

It is evident, upon the first consideration, that there is not any thing which we believe concerning the Holy Ghost, but that it is plainly revealed and declared in these testimonies. He is directly affirmed to be, and is called, "God," Acts v. 3, 4; which the Socinians will not say is by virtue of an exaltation unto an office or authority, as they say of the Son. He is an *intelligent, voluntary, divine agent;* he knoweth, he worketh as he will: which things, if, in their frequent repetition, they are not sufficient to evince an intelligent agent, a personal subsistence, that hath being, life, and will, we must confess that the Scripture was written on purpose to lead us into mistakes and misapprehensions of what we are, under penalty of eternal ruin, rightly to apprehend and believe. It declareth, also, that he is the author and worker of all sorts of divine operations, requiring immensity, omnipotency, omniscience, and all other divine excellencies, unto their working and effecting. Moreover, it is *revealed* that he is peculiarly to be *believed in*, and may peculiarly be *sinned against*, [as] the great author of all grace in believers and order in the church. This is the sum of what we believe, of what is revealed in the Scripture concerning the Holy Ghost.

As, in the consideration of the preceding head, we vindicated *one testimony* in particular from the exceptions of the adversaries of the truth, so on this we may briefly sum up the evidence that is given us in the testimonies before produced, that the reader may the more easily understand their intendment, and what, in particular, they bear witness unto.

The sum is, that the Holy Ghost is a *divine, distinct person*, and neither merely the power or virtue of God, nor any created spirit whatever. This plainly appears, from what is revealed concerning him. For he who is placed in the same series or order with other divine persons, without the least note of difference or distinction from them, as to an interest in personality; who hath the names proper to a divine person only, and is frequently and directly called by them; who also hath personal properties, and is the voluntary author of personal, divine operations, and the proper object of divine worship,— he is a distinct divine person. And if these things be not a sufficient evidence and demonstration of a divine, intelligent substance, I shall, as was said before, despair to understand any thing that is expressed and declared by words. But now thus it is with the Holy Ghost, according to the revelation made concerning him in the Scripture. For,—

First. He is placed in the *same rank and order*, without any note of difference or distinction as to a distinct interest in the divine nature (that is, as we shall see, personality) with the other divine persons. Matt. xxviii. 19, "Baptizing them in the name of the Father, and of the Son, and of the Holy Ghost." 1 John v. 7, "There are three that bear record in heaven, the Father, the Word, and the Holy Ghost; and these three are one." 1 Cor. xii. 3–6, "No man can say that Jesus is the Lord, but by the Holy Ghost. Now, there are diversities of gifts, but the same Spirit. And there are differences of administrations, but the same Lord. And there are diversities of operations, but it is the same God which worketh all in all." Neither doth a denial of his divine being and distinct existence leave any tolerable sense unto these expressions. For read the words of the first place from the mind of the Socinians, and see what is it that can be gathered from them, "Baptizing them in the name of the Father, and of the Son, and of the virtue or efficacy of the Father." Can any thing be more absonant from faith and reason than this absurd expression? and yet it is the direct sense, if it be any, that these men put upon the words. To join a *quality* with acknowledged persons, and that in such things and cases as wherein they are proposed under a personal consideration, is a strange kind of mystery. And the like may be manifested concerning the other places.

Secondly. He also hath the *names* proper to a divine person only; for he is expressly called " God," Acts v. He who is termed the " Holy Ghost," verse 3, and the " Spirit of the Lord," verse 9, is called also " God," verse 4. Now, this is the name of a divine person, on one account or other. The Socinians would not allow Christ to be called God were he not a divine person, though not by nature, yet by office and authority. And I suppose they will not find out an office for the Holy Ghost, whereunto he might be exalted, on the account whereof he might become God, seeing this would acknowledge him to be a person, which they deny. So he is called the "Comforter," John xvi. 7. A *personal appellation* this is also; and because he is the Comforter of all God's people, it can be the name of none but a divine person. In the same place, also, it is frequently affirmed, that he shall come, that he shall and will do such and such things; all of them declaring him to be a person.

Thirdly. He hath *personal properties* assigned unto him; as a will, 1 Cor. xii. 11, " He divideth to every man severally as he will;" and understanding, 1 Cor. ii. 10, "The Spirit searcheth all things, yea, the deep things of God;"—as also, all the actings that are ascribed unto him are all of them such as undeniably affirm personal properties in their principal and agent. For,—

Fourthly. He is the *voluntary author* of divine operations. He of old cherished the creation, Gen. i. 2, "The Spirit of God moved upon the face of the waters." He formed and garnished the heavens. He inspired, acted, and spake, in and by the prophets, Acts xxviii. 25, "Well spake the Holy Ghost by Esaias the prophet unto our fathers;" 2 Pet. i. 21, "The prophecy came not in old time by the will of man; but holy men of God spake as they were moved by the Holy Ghost." He regenerateth, enlighteneth, sanctifieth, comforteth, instructeth, leadeth, guideth, all the disciples of Christ, as the Scriptures everywhere testify. Now, all these are *personal operations,* and cannot, with any pretence of sobriety or consistency with reason, be constantly and uniformly assigned unto a quality or virtue. He is, as the Father and Son, God, with the properties of omniscience and omnipotency, of life, understanding, and will; and by these properties, works, acts, and produceth effects, according to wisdom, choice, and power.

Fifthly. The *same regard is had to him in faith,* worship, and obedience, as unto the other persons of the Father and Son. For our being baptized into his name, is our solemn engagement to believe in him, to yield obedience to him, and to worship him, as it puts the same obligation upon us to the Father and the Son. So also, in reference unto the worship of the church, he commands that the ministers of it be separated unto himself; Acts xiii. 2, "The Holy Ghost said, Separate me Barnabas and Saul for the work whereunto I have called them;" verse 4, "So they, being sent forth by the Holy Ghost, departed;"—which is comprehensive of all the religious worship of the church.

And on the same account is he sinned against, as Acts v. 3, 4, 9; for there is the same reason of sin and obedience. Against whom a man may sin formally and ultimately, him he is bound to obey, worship, and believe in. And this can be no quality, but God himself. For what may be the sense of this expression, "Thou hast lied to the efficacy of God in his operations?" or how can we be formally obliged unto obedience to a quality? There must, then, an antecedent obligation unto faith, trust, and religious obedience be supposed, as the ground of rendering a person capable of being guilty of sin towards any; for sin is but a failure in faith, obedience, or worship. These, therefore, are due unto the Holy Ghost; or a man could not sin against him so signally and fatally as some are said to do in the foregoing testimonies.

I say, therefore, unto this part of our cause, as unto the other, that unless we will cast off all reverence of God, and, in a kind of atheism which, as I suppose, the prevailing wickedness of this age hath not yet arrived unto, say that the Scriptures were written on purpose to deceive us, and to lead us into mistakes about, and misapprehensions of, what it proposeth unto us, we must acknowledge the Holy Ghost to be a substance, a person, God; yet distinct from the Father and the Son. For to tell us, that he will come unto us, that he will be our comforter, that he will teach us, lead us, guide us; that he spake of old in and by the prophets,—that they were moved by him, acted by him; that he "searcheth the deep things of God," works as he will; that he appointeth to himself ministers in the church;—in a word, to declare, in places innumerable, what he hath done, what he doth, what he will do, what he says and speaks, how he acts and proceeds, what his will is, and to warn us that we grieve him not, sin not against him, with things innumerable of the like nature; and all this while to oblige us to believe that he is not a person, a helper, a comforter, a searcher, a willer, but a quality in some especial operations of God, or his power and virtue in them, were to distract men, not to instruct them, and leave them no certain conclusion but this, that there is nothing certain in the whole book of God. And of no other tendency are these and the like imaginations of our adversaries in this matter.

But let us briefly consider what is objected in general unto the truth we have confirmed:—

They say, then, "The Holy Spirit is said to be *given*, to be *sent*, to be *bestowed* on men, and to be promised unto them: and therefore it cannot be that he should be God; for how can any of these things be spoken of God?"

I answer, First, As the expressions do not prove him to be God (nor did ever any produce them to that purpose), yet they undeniably prove him to be a person, or an intelligent, voluntary agent, concerning whom they are spoken and affirmed. For how can the power of God, or a quality, as they speak, be said to be sent, to be given, to be bestowed on men? So that these very expressions are destructive to their imaginations.

Secondly. He who is God, equal in nature and being with the Father, may be promised, sent, and given, with respect unto the holy dispensation and condescension wherein he hath undertaken the office of being our comforter and sanctifier.

Thirdly. The communications, distributions, impartings, divisions of the Spirit, which they mention, as they respect the *object* of them, or those on whom they were or are bestowed, denote only works, gifts, operations, and effects of the Spirit; the rule whereof is expressed, 1 Cor. xii. 11. He worketh them in whom he will, and as he will. And whether these and the like exceptions, taken from actings and operations which are plainly interpreted and explained in sundry places of Scripture, and evidently enough in the particular places where they are used, are sufficient to impeach the truth of the revelation before declared, all who have a due reverence of God, his word, and truths, will easily understand and discern.

These things being declared in the Scripture concerning the Father, the Son, and the Holy Ghost, it is, moreover, revealed, "And these three are one;" that is, one God, jointly to be worshipped, feared, adored, believed in, and obeyed, in order unto eternal life. For although this doth absolutely and necessarily follow from what is declared and hath been spoken concerning the one God, or oneness of the Deity, yet, for the confirmation of our faith, and that we may not, by the distinct consideration of the three be taken off from the one, it is particularly declared that "these three are one;" that one, the one and same God. But whereas, as was said before, this can no otherwise be, the testimonies given thereunto are not so frequently multiplied as they are unto those other heads of this truth, which, through the craft of Satan, and the pride of men, might be more liable to exceptions. But yet they are clear, full, and distinctly sufficient for faith to acquiesce in immediately, without any other expositions, interpretations, or arguments, beyond our understanding of the naked importance of the words. Such are they, of the Father [and] the Son, John x. 30, "I and my Father are one;"—Father, Son, and Spirit, 1 John v. 7, "There are three that bear record in heaven, the Father, the Word, and the Holy Ghost; and these three are one." Matt. xxviii. 19, "Baptizing them in the name of the Father, and of the Son, and of the Holy Ghost." For if those into whose name we are baptized be not one in nature, we are by our baptism engaged into the service and worship of more gods than one. For, as being baptized, or sacredly initiated, into or in the name of any one, doth *sacramentally* bind us unto a holy and religious obedience unto him, and in all things to the avowing of him as the God whose we are, and whom we serve, as here we are in the name of the Father, Son, and Spirit; so if they are not one God, the blasphemous consequence before mentioned must unavoidably be admitted: which it also must upon the Socinian principle; who, whilst of all others they seem to contend most for one God, are indeed direct polytheists, by owning others with religious respect, due to God alone, which are not so.

Once more: it is revealed, also, that these three are *distinct* among themselves, by certain peculiar *relative properties*, if I may yet use these terms. So that they are distinct, living, divine, intelligent, voluntary principles of operation or working, and that in and by internal acts one towards another, and in acts that outwardly respect the creation and the several parts of it. Now, this distinction *originally* lieth in this,—that the Father begetteth the Son, and the Son is begotten of the Father, and the Holy Spirit proceedeth from both of them. The manner of these things, so far as they may be expressed unto our edification, shall afterwards be spoken to. At present it sufficeth, for the satisfaction and confirmation of our faith, that the distinctions named are clearly revealed in the Scripture, and are proposed to be its proper object in this matter:—Ps. ii. 7, "Thou art my Son, this day have I begotten thee." Matt. xvi. 16, "Thou art the Christ, the Son of the living God." John i. 14, " We beheld his glory, the glory as of the only begotten of the Father." Verse 18, " No man hath seen God at any time; the only begotten Son, which is in the bosom of the Father, he hath declared him." John v. 26, " For as the Father hath life in himself, so hath he given to the Son to have life in himself." 1 John v. 20, " The Son of God is come, and hath given us an understanding." John xv. 26, " But when the Comforter is come, whom I will send unto you from the Father, even the Spirit of truth, which proceedeth from the Father, he shall testify of me."

Now, as the nature of this distinction lies in their mutual relation one to another, so it is the foundation of those distinct actings and operations whereby the distinction itself is clearly manifested and confirmed. And these actings, as was said, are either such as where one of them is the object of another's actings, or such as have the creature for their object. The first sort are testified unto, Ps. cx. 1; John i. 18, v. 20, xvii. 5; 1 Cor. ii. 10, 11; Prov. viii. 22; most of which places have been before recited. They which thus *know* each other, *love* each other, *delight* in each other, must needs be distinct; and so are they represented unto our faith. And for the other sort of actings, the Scripture is full of the expressions of them. See Gen. xix. 24; Zech. ii. 8; John v. 17; 1 Cor. xii. 7–11; 2 Cor. viii. 9.

Our conclusion from the whole is,—that there is nothing more fully expressed in the Scripture than this sacred truth, that there is one God, Father, Son, and Holy Ghost; which are divine, distinct, intelligent, voluntary, omnipotent principles of operation and working: which whosoever thinks himself obliged to believe the Scripture must believe; and concerning others, in this discourse, we are not solicitous.

This is that which was first proposed,—namely, to manifest what is expressly revealed in the Scripture concerning God the Father, Son, and Holy Ghost; so as that we may duly believe in him, yield obedience unto him, enjoy communion with him, walk in his love and fear, and so come at length to be blessed with him for evermore. Nor doth faith, for its security, establishment, and direction, absolutely stand in need of any farther exposition or explanation of these things, or the use of any terms not consecrated to the present service by the Holy Ghost. But whereas it may be variously assaulted by the temptations of Satan, and opposed by the subtle sophisms of men of corrupt minds; and whereas it is the duty of the disciples of Christ to grow in the knowledge of God, and our Lord and Saviour Jesus Christ, by an explicit apprehension of the things they do believe, so far as they are capable of them; this doctrine hath in all ages of the church been explained and taught in and by such expressions, terms, and propositions, as farther declare what is necessarily included in it, or consequent unto it; with an exclusion of such things, notions, and apprehensions, as are neither the one nor the other. This I shall briefly manifest, and then vindicate the whole from some exceptions, and so close this dissertation.

[First.] That God is *one*, was declared and proved. Now this *oneness* can respect nothing but the nature, being, substance, or essence of God. God is one in this respect. Some of these words, indeed, are not used in the Scripture; but whereas they are of the same importance and signification, and none of them include any thing of imperfection, they are properly used in the declaration of the *unity* of the Godhead. There is mention in the Scripture of the *Godhead* of God, Rom. i. 20, " His eternal power and Godhead;" and of his *nature*, by excluding them from being objects of our worship who are not God by nature, Gal. iv. 8. Now, this natural Godhead of God is his substance or essence, with all the holy, divine excellencies which naturally and necessarily appertain thereunto. Such are eternity, immensity, omnipotency, life, infinite holiness, goodness, and the like. This one nature, substance, or essence, being the nature, substance, or essence of God, as God, is the nature, essence, and substance of the Father, Son, and Spirit; one and the same absolutely in and unto each of them: for none can be God, as they are revealed to be, but by virtue of this·divine nature or being. Herein consists the *unity of the Godhead*.

Secondly. The *distinction* which the Scripture reveals between Father, Son, and Spirit, is that whereby they are three hypostases or persons, distinctly subsisting in the same divine essence or being. Now, a divine person is nothing but *the divine essence, upon the account of an especial property, subsisting in an especial manner*. As in the person of the Father there is the divine essence and being, with its property of *begetting the Son*, subsisting in an especial manner as the Father, and because this person hath the whole divine nature, all the essential properties of that nature are in that person. The wisdom, the understanding of God, the will of God, the immensity of God, is in that person, not as that person, but as the person is God. The like is to be said of the persons of the Son and of the Holy Ghost. Hereby each person having the understanding, the will, and power of God, becomes a distinct principle of operation; and yet all their actings *ad extra* being the actings of God, they are *undivided*, and are all the works of one, of the self-same God. And these things do not only necessarily follow, but are directly included, in the revelation made concerning God and his subsistence in the Scriptures.

[Thirdly.] There are, indeed, very many other things that are taught and disputed about this doctrine of the Trinity; as, the manner of the eternal generation of the Son,—of the essence of the Father.—of the procession of the Holy Ghost, and the difference of it from the generation of the Son,—of the mutual in-being of the persons, by reason of their unity in the same substance or essence,—the nature of their personal subsistence, with respect unto the properties whereby they are mutually distinguished;—all which are true and defensible against all the sophisms of the adversaries of this truth. Yet, because the distinct apprehension of them, and their accurate expression, is not necessary unto faith, as it is our guide and principle in and unto religious worship and obedience, they need not here be insisted on. Nor are those brief explications themselves before mentioned so proposed as to be placed immediately in the same rank or order with the original revelations before insisted on, but only are pressed as proper expressions of what is revealed, to increase our light and farther our edification. And although they cannot rationally be opposed or denied, nor ever were by any, but such as deny and oppose the things themselves as revealed, yet they that do so deny or oppose them, are to be required positively, in the first place, to deny or disapprove the oneness of the Deity, or to prove that the Father, or Son, or Holy Ghost, in particular, are not God, before they be allowed to speak one word against the manner of the explication of the truth concerning them. For either they grant the revelation declared and contended for, or they do not. If they do, let that concession be first laid down, namely,—that the Father, Son, and Spirit, are one God; and then let it be debated, whether they are one in substance and three in persons, or how else the matter is to be stated. If they deny it, it is a plain madness to dispute of the manner of any thing, and the way of expressing it, whilst the thing itself is denied to have a being; for of that which is not, there is neither manner, property, adjunct, nor effect. Let, then, such persons as this sort of men are ready to attempt with their sophistry, and to amuse with cavils about persons, substances, subsistences, and the like, desire to know of them what it is that they would be at. What would they deny? what would they disapprove? Is it that God is one? or that the Father is God, or the Son, or the Holy Ghost is so? If they deny or oppose either of these, they have testimonies and instances of divine revelation, or may have, in a readiness, to confound the devil and all his emissaries. If they will not do so, if they refuse it, then let them know that it is most foolish and unreasonable to contend about expressions and explanations of any thing, or doctrine, about the manner, respects, or relations of any thing, until the thing itself, or doctrine, be plainly confessed or denied. If this they refuse, as generally they do and will (which I speak upon sufficient experience), and will not be induced to deal openly, properly, and rationally, but will keep to their cavils and sophisms about terms and expressions, all farther debate or conference with them may justly, and ought, both conscientiously and rationally, to be refused and rejected. For these sacred mysteries of God and the gospel are not lightly to be made the subject of men's contests and disputations.

But as we dealt before in particular, so here I shall give instances of the sophistical exceptions that are used against the whole of this doctrine, and that with respect unto some late collections and representations of them; from whence they are taken up and used by many who seem not to understand the words, phrases, and expressions themselves, which they make use of.

The sum of what they say in general is,—1. *"How can these things be? how can three be one, and one be three? Every person hath its own substance; and, therefore, if there be three persons, there must be three substances, and so three Gods."*

Answer. Every person hath distinctly its *own substance*, for the one substance of the Deity is the substance of each person, so it is still but one; but each person hath not its own distinct substance, because the substance of them all is the same, as hath been proved.

2. They say, *"That if each person be God, then each person is infinite, and there being three persons, there must be three infinites."*

Ans. This follows not in the least; for each person is infinite as he is God. *All divine properties*, such as to be infinite is, belong not to the persons on the account of their personality, but on the account of their nature, which is one, for they are all natural properties.

3. But they say, *"If each person be God, and that God subsist in three persons, then in each person there are three persons or Gods."*

Ans. The collusion of this sophism consists in that expression, *"be God,"* and *"that God."* In the first place the nature of God is intended; in the latter, a singular person. Place the words intelligibly, and they are thus:—If each person be God, and the nature of God subsists in three persons, then in each person there are three persons; and then the folly of it will be evident.

4. But they farther infer, *"That if we deny the persons to be infinite, then an infinite being hath a finite mode of subsisting, and so I know not what supposition they make hence; that seeing there are not three infinites, then the Father, Son, and Spirit are three finites, that make up an infinite."*

The pitiful weakness of this cavil is open to all; for finite and infinite are properties and adjuncts of *beings*, and not of the *manner* of the subsistence of any thing. The nature of each person is infinite, and so is each person because of that nature. Of the manner of their subsistence, finite and infinite cannot be predicated or spoken, no farther than to say, an infinite being doth so subsist.

5. " But you grant," say they, " *that the only true God is the Father, and then if Christ be the only true God, he is the Father.*"

Ans. We say, the only true God is Father, Son, and Holy Ghost. We never say, the Scripture never says, that *the Father only is the true God ;* whence it would follow, that he that is the true God is the Father. But we grant the Father to be the only true God; and so we say is the Son also. And it doth not at all thence follow that the Son is the Father; because, in saying the Father is the true God, we respect not his paternity, or his paternal relation to his Son, but his nature, essence, and being. And the same we affirm concerning the other persons. And to say, that because each person is God, one person must be another, is to crave leave to disbelieve what God hath revealed, without giving any reason at all for their so doing.

But this sophism being borrowed from another, namely, Crellius,[1] who insisted much upon it, I shall upon his account, and not on theirs, who, as far as I can apprehend, understand little of the intendment of it, remove it more fully out of the way. It is proposed by him in way of syllogism, thus, " *The only true God is the Father; Christ is the only true God : therefore he is the Father.*" Now, this syllogism is ridiculously sophistical. For, in a categorical syllogism the major proposition is not to be particular, or equipollent to a particular ; for, from such a proposition, when any thing communicable to more is the subject of it, and is restrained unto one particular, nothing can be inferred in the conclusion. But such is this proposition here, *The only true God is the Father.* It is a particular proposition, wherein the subject is restrained unto a singular or individual predicate, though in itself communicable to more. Now, the proposition being so made particular, the terms of the subject or predicate are supposed reciprocal,—namely, that one God, and the Father, are the same; which is false, unless it be first proved that the name God is communicable to no more, or no other, than is the other term of Father : which to suppose, is to beg the whole question; for *the only true God* hath a larger signification than the term of Father or Son. So that, though the only true God be the Father, yet every one who is true God is not the Father. Seeing, then, that the name of God here supplies the place of a species, though it be singular ab-

---

[1] John Crell is not to be confounded with Samuel Crell, also a Socinian writer, who lived about a century later, and who seems to have been converted to the faith of our Lord's divinity. The former was born in Franconia in 1590. He was rector of the University of Rakau in 1616. He had a controversy with Grotius, and was recognised as a leader among the Socinians. He died 1633, leaving behind him works that occupy four volumes in the " Bibliotheca Fratrum Polonorum."—ED.

solutely, as it respects the divine nature, which is absolutely singular and one, and cannot be multiplied, yet in respect of communication it is otherwise; it is communicated unto more,—namely, to the Father, Son, and Holy Ghost. And, therefore, if any thing be intended to be concluded from hence, the proposition must be expressed according to what the subject requires, as capable of communication or attribution to more than one, as thus: Whoever is the only true God is the Father;—which proposition these persons and their masters shall never be able to prove.

I have given, in particular, these strictures thus briefly upon these empty sophisms; partly because they are well removed already, and partly because they are mere exscriptions out of an author not long since translated into English, unto whom an entire answer may ere long be returned.

That which at present shall suffice, is to give a general answer unto all these cavils, with all of the same kind which the men of these principles do usually insist upon.

1. " *The things,*" they say, " *which we teach concerning the Trinity, are contrary to reason;*" and thereof they endeavour to give sundry instances, wherein the sum of the opposition which they make unto this truth doth consist. But first, I ask, What reason is it that they intend? It is their own, the carnal reason of men. By that they will judge of these divine mysteries. The Scripture tells us, indeed, that the "spirit of a man which is in him knows the things of a man,"—a man's spirit, by natural reason, may judge of natural things;—" but the things of God knoweth no man, but the Spirit of God," 1 Cor. ii. 11. So that what we know of these things, we must receive upon the revelation of the Spirit of God merely, if the apostle may be believed. And it is given unto men to know the mysteries of the kingdom of God,—to some, and not to others; and unless it be so given them, they cannot know them. In particular, none can know the Father unless the Son reveal him. Nor will, or doth, or can, flesh and blood reveal or understand Jesus Christ to be the Son of the living God, unless the Father reveal him, and instruct us in the truth of it, Matt. xvi. 17. The way to come to the acknowledgment of these things, is that described by the apostle, Eph. iii. 14–19, " For this cause I bow my knees unto the Father of our Lord Jesus Christ, of whom the whole family in heaven and earth is named, that he would grant you, according to the riches of his glory, to be strengthened with might by his Spirit in the inner man; that Christ may dwell in your hearts by faith; that ye, being rooted and grounded in love, may be able to comprehend with all saints," etc. As also, Col. ii. 2, 3, That ye might come " unto all riches of the full assurance of understanding, to the acknowledgment of the mystery of God,

and of the Father, and of Christ, in whom are hid all the treasures of wisdom and knowledge." It is by faith and prayer, and through the revelation of God, that we may come to the acknowledgment of these things, and not by the carnal reasonings of men of corrupt minds.

2. *What reason* do they intend? If reason absolutely, the reason of things, we grant that nothing contrary unto it is to be admitted. But reason as it is in this or that man, particularly in themselves, we know to be weak, maimed, and imperfect; and that they are, and all other men, extremely remote from a just and full comprehension of the whole reason of things. Are they in such an estate as that their apprehension shall pass for the measure of the nature of all things? We know they are far from it. So that though we will not admit of any thing that is contrary to reason, yet the least intimation of a truth by divine revelation will make me embrace it, although it should be *contrary to the reason of all the Socinians in the world*. Reason in the abstract, or the just measure of the answering of one thing unto another, is of great moment: but reason—that is, what is pretended to be so, or appears to be so unto this or that man, especially in and about things of divine revelation—is of very small importance (of none at all) where it riseth up against the express testimonies of Scripture, and these multiplied, to their mutual confirmation and explanation.

3. Many things are *above reason,*—that is, as considered in this or that subject, as men,—which are not at all *against it.* It is an easy thing to compel the most curious inquirers of these days to a ready confession hereof, by multitudes of instances in things finite and temporary; and shall any dare to deny but it may be so in things heavenly, divine, and spiritual? Nay, there is no concernment of the being of God, or his properties, but is absolutely above the comprehension of our reason. We cannot by searching find out God, we cannot find out the Almighty to perfection.

4. The very foundation of all their objections and cavils against this truth, is destructive of as fundamental principles of reason as are in the world. They are all, at best, reduced to this: It cannot be thus in things finite; the same being cannot in one respect be *one,* in another *three,* and the like: and therefore it is so in things infinite. All these reasonings are built upon this supposition, that that which is *finite* can perfectly comprehend that which is *infinite,*—an assertion absurd, foolish, and contradictory unto itself. Again; it is the highest reason in things of pure revelation to captivate our understandings to the authority of the Revealer; which here is rejected. So that by a loud, specious, pretence of reason, these men, by a little captious sophistry, endeavour not only to countenance their unbelief, but to evert the greatest principles of reason itself.

5. The objections these men principally insist upon, are merely against the explanations we use of this doctrine,—not against the primitive revelation of it, which is the principal object of our faith ; which, how preposterous and irrational a course of proceeding it is, hath been declared.

6. It is a rule among philosophers, that if a man, on just grounds and reasons, have embraced any opinion or persuasion, he is not to desert it merely because he cannot answer every objection against it. For if the objections wherewith we may be entangled be not of the same weight and importance with the reason on which we embraced the opinion, it is a madness to forego it on the account thereof. And much more must this hold amongst the common sort of Christians, in things spiritual and divine. If they will let go and part with their faith in any truth, because they are not able to answer distinctly some objections that may be made against it, they may quickly find themselves disputed into atheism.

7. There is so great an intimation made of such an expression and resemblance of a Trinity in unity in the very works of the creation, as learned men have manifested by various instances, that it is most unreasonable to suppose that to be contrary to reason which many objects of rational consideration do more or less present unto our minds.

8. To add no more considerations of this nature, let any of the adversaries produce any one argument or grounds of reason, or those pretended to be such, against that that hath been asserted, that hath not already been baffled a thousand times, and it shall receive an answer, or a public acknowledgment, that it is indissoluble.

OF THE PERSON OF CHRIST.

The next head of opposition made by the men of this conspiracy against this sacred truth, is against the head of all truth, the person of our Lord Jesus Christ. The Socinians, indeed, would willingly put a better face or colour upon their error about the person of Christ than it will bear or endure to lie on it. For in their catechism, unto this question, " Is the Lord Jesus Christ *purus homo*, a mere man?" they answer, " By no means." " How then? hath he a divine nature also?" which is their next question. To this they say, " By no means; for this is contrary to right reason." How, then, will these pretended masters of reason reconcile these things? for to us it seems, that if Christ have no other nature but that of man, he is as to his nature *purus homo*, a mere man, and no more. Why, they answer, that " he is not a mere man, because he was born of a virgin." Strange!

that that should be an argument to prove him more than a man, which the Scripture, and all men in their right wits, grant to be an invincible reason to prove him to be a man, and, as he was born of her, no more. Rom. i. 3, " Concerning his Son Jesus Christ our Lord, which was made of the seed of David according to the flesh." Rom. ix. 5, " Whose are the fathers, and of whom, as concerning the flesh, Christ came." Gal. iv. 4, " God sent forth his Son, made of a woman, made under the law." But, say they, " He was endowed with the Spirit, wrought miracles, was raised from the dead, had all power given [him] in heaven and earth; for by these degrees he became to be God." But all men see that the inquiry is about the nature of Christ, and this answer is about his state and condition. Now this changeth not his nature on the one hand, no more than his being humbled, poor, and dying, did on the other. This is the right reason we have to deal withal in these men ! If a man should have inquired of some of them of old, whether Melchizedek were *purus homo*, a mere man, some of them would have said, " No, because he was the Holy Ghost;" some, " No, because he was the Son of God himself;" and some, " No, because he was an angel;"—for such foolish opinions have men fallen into. But how sottish soever their conceptions were, their answer to that inquiry would have been regular, because the question and answer respect the same subject in the same respect; but never any was so stupid as to answer, " He was not a mere man, (that is, by nature,) *because he was a priest of the high God,*"—which respects his office and condition. Yet, such is the pretence of these men about the person of Christ, to incrustate and give some colour unto their foul misbelief ; as supposing that it would be much to their disadvantage to own Christ only as a mere man,—though the most part of their disputes that they have troubled the Christian world withal have had no other design nor aim but to prove him so to be, and nothing else. I shall briefly, according to the method insisted on, first lay down what is the direct revelation which is the object of our faith in this matter, then express the revelation itself in the Scripture testimonies wherein it is recorded; and having vindicated some one or other of them from their exceptions, manifest how the doctrine hereof is farther explained, unto the edification of them that believe.

That there is a second person, the Son of God, in the holy *trin-unity* of the Godhead, we have proved before. That this person did, of his infinite love and grace, take upon him our nature,—human nature, —so as that the divine and human nature should become one person, one Christ, God and man in one, so that whatever he doth in and about our salvation, it is done by that one person, God and man, is revealed unto us in the Scripture as the object of our faith: and this is that which we believe concerning the person of Christ. Whatever acts are ascribed unto him, however immediately performed, in or by the human nature, or in and by his divine nature, they are all the acts of that one person, in whom are both these natures. That this Christ, God and man, is, because he is God, and on the account of what he hath done for us as man, to be believed in, worshipped with worship religious and divine, to be trusted and obeyed, this also is asserted in the Scripture. And these things are, as it were, the common notions of Christian religion,—the common principles of our profession, which the Scriptures also abundantly testify unto.

Isa. vii. 14, " Behold, a virgin shall conceive, and bear a son, and shall call his name Immanuel;" that is, he shall be God with us, or God in our nature. Not that *that* should be his name whereby he should be *called* in this world; but that this should be the condition of his person,—he should be " God with us," God in our nature. So are the words expounded, Matt. i. 20–23, " That which is conceived in her is of the Holy Ghost. And she shall bring forth a son, and thou shalt call his name Jesus; for he shall save his people from their sins. Now all this was done, that it might be fulfilled which was spoken of the Lord by the prophet, saying, Behold, a virgin shall be with child, and shall bring forth a son, and they shall call his name Emmanuel ; which, being interpreted, is, God with us." His name whereby he was to be called, was Jesus; that is, a Saviour. And thereby was accomplished the prediction of the prophet, that he should be Immanuel; which, being interpreted, is, " God with us." Now, a child born to be " God with us," is God in that child taking our nature upon him; and no otherwise can the words be understood.

Isa. ix. 6, " Unto us a child is born, unto us a son is given : and his name shall be called The mighty God." The child that is born, the son that is given, is the mighty God; and as the mighty God, and a child born, or son given, he is the Prince of Peace, as he is there called, or our Saviour.

John i. 14, " The Word was made flesh." That the Word was God, who made all things, he had before declared. Now, he affirms that this Word was made flesh. How? converted into flesh, into a man, so that he who was God ceased so to be, and was turned or changed into flesh,—that is, a man? Besides that this is utterly impossible, it is not affirmed. For the Word continued the Word still, although he was " made flesh," or " made of a woman," as it is elsewhere expressed,—or made of the seed of David,—or took our flesh or nature to be his own. Himself continuing God, as he was, became man also, which before he was not. " The Word was made flesh;" this is that which we believe and assert in this matter.

See John iii. 13, 31, vi. 62, xvi. 28. All which places assert the person of Christ to have descended from heaven in the assumption of human nature, and ascended into heaven therein [in that nature] being assumed ; and to have been in heaven as to his divine nature, when he was on the earth in the flesh that he had assumed.

Acts xx. 28, " Feed the church of God,[1] which he hath purchased with his own blood." The person spoken of is said to be God absolutely,—" the church of *God.*" And this God is said to have blood of his own;—the blood of Jesus Christ, being the blood of him that was God, though not the blood of him as God; for God is a spirit. And this undeniably testifies to the unity of his person as God and man.

Rom. i. 3, 4, " Concerning his Son Jesus Christ our Lord, who was made of the seed of David according to the flesh; and declared to be the Son of God with power, according to the spirit of holiness, by the resurrection from the dead." Rom. ix. 5, " Whose are the fathers, and of whom, as concerning the flesh, Christ came, who is over all, God blessed for ever. Amen." This is all we desire that we may believe without disturbance from the clamours of these men,—namely, that the same Christ, as concerning the flesh, came of the fathers, of David, and, in himself, is over all, God blessed for ever. This the Scripture asserts plainly; and why we should not believe it firmly, let these men give a reason when they are able.

Gal. iv. 4, " God sent forth his Son made of a woman." He was his Son, and was made of a woman, according as he expresses it, Heb. x. 5, " A body hast thou prepared me;" as also, Rom. viii. 3.

Phil. ii. 5-7, " Let this mind be in you, which was also in Christ Jesus: who, being in the form of God, thought it not robbery to be equal with God: but made himself of no reputation, and took upon him the form of a servant, and was made in the likeness of men." It is the same Christ that is spoken of. And it is here affirmed of him, that he was " in the form of God, and thought it not robbery to be equal with God." But is this all? Is this Jesus Christ God only? doth he subsist only in the form or nature of God? No; saith the apostle, " He took upon him the form of a servant, was made in the likeness of men, and was found in fashion as a man." That his being truly a man is expressed in these words our adversaries deny not; and we therefore believe that the same Jesus Christ is God also, because that is no less plainly expressed.

1 Tim. iii. 16, " And without controversy great is the mystery of godliness: God[2] was manifest in the flesh, justified in the Spirit, seen

---

[1] It involves a critical discussion of long standing, whether Κυρίου or Θεοῦ is the proper reading in this passage. By some recent editors of critical editions of the Greek Testament—Scholz, for instance—Θεοῦ is retained. Adhuc sub judice lis est.—Ed.

[2] Since the days of Owen, this reading has been the subject of protracted and sifting discussion. At one time the current of opinion had set in against Θεός

of angels." It is a mystery, indeed; under which name it is despised now and reproached; nor are we allowed so to call it, but are reflected on as flying to mysteries for our defence. But we must take leave to speak in this matter according to His directions without whom we cannot speak at all. A mystery it is, and that a great mystery; and that confessedly so, by all that do believe. And this is, that " God was manifested in the flesh." That it is the Lord Christ who is spoken of, every one of the ensuing expressions do evince: " Justified in the Spirit, seen of angels, preached unto the Gentiles, believed on in the world, received up into glory." And this, also, is the substance of what we believe in this matter,—namely, that Christ is God manifest in the flesh; which we acknowledge, own, and believe to be true, but a great mystery,—yet no less great and sacred a truth notwithstanding.

Heb. ii. 14, " Forasmuch then as the children are partakers of flesh and blood, he also himself likewise took part of the same." Verse 16, " For verily he took not on him the nature of angels; but he took on him the seed of Abraham." And this plainly affirms his pre-existence unto that assumption of our nature, and the unity of his person in it being so assumed.

1 John iii. 16, " Hereby perceive we the love of God, because he laid down his life for us." He who was God laid down for a season and parted with that life which was his own, in that nature of ours which he had assumed. And that taking of our nature is called his " coming in the flesh;" which whoso denies, is " not of God, but is the spirit of Antichrist," chap. iv. 3.

These are some of the places wherein the person of Christ is revealed unto our faith, that we may believe on the Son of God, and have eternal life.

The method formerly proposed would require that I should take off the general objections of the *adversaries* against this divine revelation, as also vindicate some peculiar testimonies from their exceptions; but because a particular opposition unto this truth hath not, as yet, publicly and directly been maintained and managed by any that I know of among ourselves, though the denial of it be expressly included in what they do affirm, I shall leave the farther confirmation thereof unto some other occasion, if it be offered, and it be judged necessary.

And this is that which the faith of believers rests in, as that which is plainly revealed unto them,—namely, that Jesus Christ is God and man in one person; and that all his actings in their behalf are the

as the reading, and the preference was given to ὅς. The results of later criticism decidedly converge in proof that the text as it stands in the received version is correct.—ED.

actings of him who is God and man; and that this Son of God, God and man, is to be believed in by them, and obeyed, that they [may] have eternal life.

What is farther added unto these express testimonies, and the full revelation of the truth contained in them in this matter, in way of explication educed from them, and suitable unto them, to the edification of the church, or information of the minds of believers in the right apprehension of this great mystery of God manifested in the flesh, may be reduced to these heads:—

1. That the person of the Son of God did not, in his assuming human nature to be his own, take *an individual person* of any one into a near conjunction with himself, but preventing the personal subsistence of human nature in that flesh which he assumed, he gave it its subsistence in his own person; whence it hath its *individuation* and distinction from all other persons whatever. This is the personal union. The divine and human nature in Christ have but one *personal subsistence;* and so are but one Christ, one distinct personal principle of all operations, of all that he did or doth as mediator. And this undeniably follows from what is declared in the testimonies mentioned. For the Word could not be made flesh, nor could he take on him the seed of Abraham, nor could the mighty God be a child born and given unto us, nor could God shed his blood for his church, but that the two natures so directly expressed must be united in one person; for otherwise, as they are two natures still, they would be two persons also.

2. Each nature thus united in Christ is entire, and preserves unto itself its own natural properties. For he is no less *perfect God* for being made *man;* nor no less a true, *perfect man*, consisting of soul and body, with all their essential parts, by that nature's being taken into subsistence with the *Son of God.* His divine nature still continues immense, omniscient, omnipotent, infinite in holiness, etc.; his human nature, finite, limited, and, before its glorification, subject to all infirmities of life and death that the same nature in others, absolutely considered, is obnoxious unto.

3. In each of these natures he acts suitably unto the essential properties and principles of that nature. As God, he made all things, upholds all things by the word of his power, fills heaven and earth, etc.; as man, he lived, hungered, suffered, died, rose, ascended into heaven: yet, by reason of the union of both these natures in the same person, not only his own person is said to do all these things, but the person expressed by the name which he hath on the account of one nature, is said to do that which he did only in the other. So God is said to "redeem his church with his own blood," and to "lay down his life for us," and the Son of man to be in heaven when he

was on the earth; all because of the unity of his person, as was declared. And these things do all of them directly and undeniably flow from what is revealed concerning his person, as before is declared.

OF THE SATISFACTION OF CHRIST.

The last thing to be inquired into, upon occasion of the late opposition to the great fundamental truths of the gospel, is the *satisfaction of Christ.* And the doctrine hereof is such as, I conceive, needs rather to be *explained* than vindicated. For it being the centre wherein most, if not all, the lines of gospel promises and precepts do meet, and the great medium of all our communion with God in faith and obedience, the great distinction between the religion of Christians and that of all others in the world, it will easily, on a due proposal, be assented unto by all who would be esteemed disciples of Jesus Christ. And whether a parcel of insipid cavils may be thought sufficient to obliterate the revelation of it, men of sober minds will judge and discern.

For the term of *satisfaction,* we contend not about it. It doth, indeed, properly express and connote that great *effect of the death of Christ* which, in the cause before us, we plead for. But yet, because it belongs rather to the explanation of the truth contended for, than is used expressly in the revelation of it, and because the right understanding of the word itself depends on some notions of law that as yet we need not take into consideration, I shall not, in this entrance of our discourse, insist precisely upon it, but leave it as the natural conclusion of what we shall find expressly declared in the Scripture. Neither do I say this as though I did decline the word, or the right use of it, or what is properly signified by it, but do only cast it into its proper place, answerable unto our method and design in the whole of this brief discourse.

I know some have taken a new way of expressing and declaring the doctrine concerning *the mediation of Christ,* with the causes and ends of his death, which they think more rational than that usually insisted on: but, as what I have yet heard of or seen in that kind, hath been not only unscriptural, but also very irrational, and most remote from that accuracy whereunto they pretend who make use of it; so, if they should publish their conceptions, it is not improbable but that they may meet with a *scholastical examination* by some hand or other.

Our present work, as hath been often declared, is for the establishment of the faith of them who may be attempted, if not brought into danger, to be seduced by the sleights of some who lie in wait to deceive, and the clamours of others who openly drive the same design. What, therefore, the Scripture plainly and clearly reveals in this matter, is the subject of our present inquiry. And either in so doing, as occasion shall be offered, we shall obviate, or, in the close of it remove, those sophisms that the sacred truth now proposed to consideration hath been attempted withal.

The sum of what the Scripture reveals about this great truth, commonly called the "satisfaction of Christ," may be reduced unto these ensuing heads:—

First. That *Adam, being made upright, sinned against God;* and all mankind, all his posterity, in him:—Gen. i. 27, "So God created man in his own image, in the image of God created he him; male and female created he them." Chap. iii. 11, "And he said, Who told thee that thou wast naked? hast thou eaten of the tree whereof I commanded thee that thou shouldest not eat?" Eccles. vii. 29, "Lo, this only have I found, that God made man upright; but they have sought out many inventions." Rom. v. 12, "Wherefore, as by one man sin entered into the world, and death by sin; and so death passed upon all men, for that all have sinned." Verse 18, "Therefore, as by the offence of one judgment came upon all men to condemnation." Verse 19, "By one man's disobedience many were made sinners."

Secondly. That, by this sin of our first parents, *all men are brought into an estate of sin and apostasy from God, and of enmity unto him:*—Gen. vi. 5, "God saw that the wickedness of man was great in the earth, and that every imagination of the thoughts of his heart was only evil continually." Ps. li. 5, "Behold, I was shapen in iniquity; and in sin did my mother conceive me." Rom. iii. 23, "For all have sinned, and come short of the glory of God." Chap. viii. 7, "The carnal mind is enmity against God: for it is not subject to the law of God, neither indeed can be." Eph. iv. 18, "Having the understanding darkened, being alienated from the life of God, through the ignorance that is in them, because of the blindness of their heart," chap. ii. 1; Col. ii. 13.

Thirdly. That in this state *all men continue in sin against God,* nor of themselves can do otherwise:—Rom. iii. 10–12, "There is none righteous, no, not one: there is none that understandeth, there is none that seeketh after God. They are all gone out of the way, they are together become unprofitable; there is none that doeth good, no, not one."

Fourthly. That the *justice and holiness of God, as he is the supreme governor and judge of all the world, require that sin be punished:*—Exod. xxxiv. 7, "That will by no means clear the guilty." Josh. xxiv. 19, "He is a holy God; he is a jealous God; he will not forgive your transgressions nor your sins." Ps. v. 4–6, "For thou art not a God that hath pleasure in wickedness: neither shall evil dwell with thee. The foolish shall not stand in thy sight: thou hatest all workers of iniquity. Thou shalt destroy them that speak leasing." Hab. i. 13, " Thou art of purer eyes than to behold evil, and canst not look upon iniquity." Isa. xxxiii. 14, " Who among us shall dwell with the devouring fire? who among us shall dwell with everlasting burnings?" Rom. i. 32, " Who knowing the judgment of God, that they which commit such things are worthy of death." Chap. iii. 5, 6, " Is God unrighteous who taketh vengeance? (I speak as a man) God forbid: for then how shall God judge the world?" 2 Thess. i. 6, " It is a righteous thing with God to recompense tribulation to them that trouble you." Heb. xii. 29, " For our God is a consuming fire;" from Deut. iv. 24.

Fifthly. That God, *hath also engaged his veracity and faithfulness in the sanction of the law,* not to leave sin unpunished:—Gen. ii. 17, " In the day thou eatest thereof thou shalt surely die." Deut. xxvii. 26, " Cursed be he that confirmeth not all the words of this law to do them." In this state and condition, mankind, had they been left without divine aid and help, must have perished eternally.

Sixthly. That God *out of his infinite goodness, grace, and love to mankind, sent his only Son to save and deliver them out of this condition:*—Matt. i. 21, " Thou shalt call his name Jesus; for he shall save his people from their sins." John iii. 16, 17, " God so loved the world, that he gave his only begotten Son, that whosoever believeth in him should not perish, but have everlasting life. For God sent not his Son into the world to condemn the world, but that the world through him might be saved." Rom. v. 8, " God commendeth his love toward us, in that, while we were yet sinners, Christ died for us." 1 John iv. 9, " In this was manifested the love of God toward us, because God sent his only begotten Son into the world, that we might live through him." Verse 10, " Herein is love, not that we loved God, but that he loved us, and sent his Son to be the propitiation for our sins." 1 Thess. i. 10, " Even Jesus, which delivered us from the wrath to come."

Seventhly. That *this love was the same in Father and Son,* acted distinctly in the manner that shall be afterward declared; so, vain are the pretences of men, who, from the love of the Father in this matter, would argue against the love of the Son, or on the contrary.

Eighthly. That the way, in general, whereby the Son of God, being incarnate, was to save lost sinners, *was by a substitution of himself, according to the design and appointment of God,* in the room of those whom he was to save:—2 Cor. v. 21, " He hath made him to be sin for us, who knew no sin; that we might become the righteousness of God in him." Gal. iii. 13, " Christ hath redeemed us from the curse of the law, being made a curse for us." Rom. v. 7, 8, " For scarcely for a righteous man will one die; yet peradventure for a good man some would even dare to die. But God commendeth his love toward us, in that, while we were yet sinners, Christ died for us." Chap. viii. 3, " For what the law could not do, in that it was weak through the flesh, God sending his own Son in the likeness of sinful flesh, and for sin, condemned sin in the flesh; that the righteousness of the law might be fulfilled in us." 1 Pet. ii. 24, " Who his own self bare our sins in his own body on the tree." Chap. iii. 18, " For Christ also hath once suffered for sins, the just for the unjust, that he might bring us to God." All these expressions undeniably evince a substitution of Christ as to suffering in the stead of them whom he was to save; which, in general, is all that we intend by his satisfaction, —namely, that he was made " sin for us," a " curse for us," " died for us," that is, in our stead, that we might be saved from the wrath to come. And all these expressions, as to their true, genuine importance, shall be vindicated as occasion shall require.

Ninthly. This way of his saving sinners is, in particular, several ways expressed in the Scripture. As,—

1. That *he offered himself a sacrifice to God*, to make atonement for our sins; and that in his death and sufferings:—Isa. liii. 10, " When thou shalt make his soul an offering for sin." John i. 29, " Behold the Lamb of God, who taketh away the sin of the world." Eph. v. 2, " Christ hath loved us, and hath given himself for us an offering and a sacrifice to God for a sweet-smelling savour." Heb. ii. 17, Was " a merciful high priest in things pertaining to God, to make reconciliation for the sins of the people." Chap. ix. 11–14, " But Christ being come an high priest of good things to come, by a greater and more perfect tabernacle, not made with hands, that is to say, not of this building; neither by the blood of goats and calves, but by his own blood, he entered in once into the holy place, having obtained eternal redemption for us. For if the blood of bulls," etc., " how much more shall the blood of Christ, who through the eternal Spirit offered himself without spot to God, purge your consciences from dead works ?"

2. That *he redeemed us by paying a price, a ransom*, for our redemption:—Mark x. 45, " The Son of man came to give his life a ransom for many." 1 Cor. vi. 20, vii. 23, " For ye are bought with a price." 1 Tim. ii. 6, " Who gave himself a ransom for all, to be testified in due time." Tit. ii. 14, " Who gave himself for us, that he might redeem us from all iniquity." 1 Pet. i. 18, 19, " For ye were not redeemed with corruptible things, as silver and gold; but with the precious blood of Christ, as of a lamb without blemish and without spot."

3. That *he bare our sins*, or the punishment due unto them:—Isa. liii. 5, 6, " He was wounded for our transgressions, he was bruised for our iniquities; the chastisement of our peace was upon him, and with his stripes we are healed. All we like sheep have gone astray; we have turned every one to his own way; and the LORD hath laid on him the iniquity of us all." Verse 11, " For he shall bear their iniquities." 1 Pet. ii. 24, " Who his own self bare our sins in his own body on the tree."

4. That *he answered the law and the penalty of it:*—Rom. viii. 3, 4, " God sending his own Son in the likeness of sinful flesh, and for sin, condemned sin in the flesh; that the righteousness of the law might be fulfilled in us." Gal. iii. 13, " Christ hath redeemed us from the curse of the law, being made a curse for us." Chap. iv. 4, 5, " God sent forth his Son, made of a woman, made under the law, to redeem them that were under the law."

5. That *he died for sin, and sinners*, to expiate the one, and in the stead of the other:—Rom. iv. 25, " He was delivered for our offences." Chap. v. 10, " When we were enemies, we were reconciled to God by the death of his Son." 1 Cor. xv. 3, " Christ died for our sins according to the Scriptures." 2 Cor. v. 14, " For the love of Christ constraineth us; because we thus judge, that if one died for all, then were all dead," 1 Thess. v. 9, 10.

6. Hence, on the part of God it is affirmed, that " he spared him not, but delivered him up for us all," Rom. viii. 32; and caused " all our iniquities to meet upon him," Isa. liii. 6.

7. The effect hereof was,—

(1.) That the *righteousness of God was glorified.* Rom. iii. 25, 26, " Whom God hath set forth to be a propitiation through faith in his blood, to declare his righteousness for the remission of sins." (2.) The *law fulfilled and satisfied*, as in the places before quoted, chap. viii. 3, 4; Gal. iii. 13, iv. 4, 5. (3.) *God reconciled.* 2 Cor. v. 18, 19, " God was in Christ reconciling the world unto himself, not imputing their trespasses unto them." Heb. ii. 17, " He made reconciliation for the sins of the people." (4.) *Atonement was made for sin.* Rom. v. 11, "By whom we have now received the atonement;" and peace was made with God. Eph. ii. 14, 16, " For he is our peace, who hath made both one, ... that he might reconcile both unto God in one body by the cross, having slain the enmity thereby." (5.) [*He*] *made an end of sin.* Dan. ix. 24, " To finish the transgression, and to make an end of sins, and to make reconciliation for iniquity, and to bring in everlasting righteousness." The glory of God in all these things being exalted, himself was well pleased, righteousness and everlasting redemption, or salvation, purchased for sinners. Heb. ix. 14, For in that " the chastisement of our peace was upon him," and that

" by his stripes we are healed," he being punished that we might go free, himself became a captain of salvation unto all that do obey him.

I have fixed on these particulars, to give every ordinary reader an instance how fully and plainly what he is to believe in this matter is revealed in the Scripture. And should I produce all the testimonies which expressly give witness unto these positions, it is known how great a part of the Bible must be transcribed. And these are the things which are indispensably required of us to believe, that we may be able to direct and regulate our obedience according to the mind and will of God. In the explanation of this doctrine unto farther edification, sundry things are usually insisted on, which necessarily and infallibly ensue upon the propositions of Scripture before laid down, and serve to beget in the minds of believers a due apprehension and right understanding of them; as,—

1. That God in this matter is to be considered as the chief, supreme, absolute rector and governor of all,—as the *Lord of the law*, and of sinners; but yet so as an offended ruler: not as an offended person, but as an offended ruler, who hath right to exact punishment upon transgressors, and whose righteousness of rule requires that he should so do

2. That because he is righteous and holy, as he is the supreme Judge of all the world, it is necessary that he do right in the punishing of sin; without which the order of the creation cannot be preserved. For sin being the creature's deduction of itself from the order of its dependence upon, and obedience unto, the Creator and supreme Lord of all, without a reduction of it by punishment, confusion would be brought into the whole creation.

3. That whereas the *law*, and the *sanction* of it, is the moral or declarative cause of the punishment of sin, and it directly obligeth the sinner himself unto punishment; God, as the supreme ruler, dispenseth, not with the act of the law, but the immediate object, and substitutes *another sufferer* in the room of them who are principally liable unto the sentence of it, and are now to be acquitted or freed;— that so the law may be satisfied, requiring the punishment of sin; justice exalted, whereof the law is an effect; and yet the sinner saved.

4. That the person thus substituted was *the Son of God incarnate*, who had power so to dispose of himself, with will and readiness for it; and was, upon the account of the dignity of his person, able to answer the penalty which all others had incurred and deserved.

5. That God, upon his *voluntary susception of* this office, and condescension to this work, did so lay our sins, in and by the sentence of the law, upon him, that he made therein *full satisfaction* for whatever legally could be charged on them for whom he died or suffered.

6. That the special way, terms, and conditions, whereby and

wherein sinners may be interested in this satisfaction made by Christ, are determined by the will of God, and declared in the Scripture.

These, and the like things, are usually insisted on in the explication or declaration of this head of our confession; and there is not any of them but may be sufficiently confirmed by divine testimonies. It may also be farther evinced, that there is nothing asserted in them, but what is excellently suited unto the common notions which mankind hath of God and his righteousness; and that in their practice they answer the light of nature and common reason, exemplified in sundry instances among the nations of the world.

I shall therefore take one argument from some of the testimonies before produced in the confirmation of this sacred truth, and proceed to remove the objections that are commonly bandied against it.

If the Lord Christ, according to the will of the Father, and by his own counsel and choice, was *substituted*, and did *substitute* himself, as the mediator of the covenant, in the room and in the stead of sinners, that they might be saved, and therein bare their sins, or the punishment due unto their sins, by undergoing the curse and penalty of the law, and therein also, according to the will of God, offered up himself for a propitiatory, expiatory sacrifice, to make atonement for sin, and reconciliation for sinners, that the justice of God being appeased, and the law fulfilled, they might go free, or be delivered from the wrath to come; and if therein, also, he paid a real satisfactory price for their redemption; then he made satisfaction to God for sin: for these are the things that we intend by that expression of satisfaction. But now all these things are openly and fully witnessed unto in the testimonies before produced, as may be observed by suiting some of them unto the several particulars here asserted:—

As, 1. What was done in this matter, was from the will, purpose, and love of God the Father, Ps. xl. 6–8; Heb. x. 5–7; Acts iv. 28; John iii. 16; Rom. viii. 3.

2. It was also done by his own voluntary consent, Phil. ii. 6–8.

3. He was substituted, and did substitute himself, as the mediator of the covenant, in the room and stead of sinners, that they may be saved, Heb. x. 5–7, vii. 22; Rom. iii. 25, 26, v. 7, 8.

4. And he did therein bear their sins, or the punishment due to their sins, Isa. liii. 6, 11; 1 Pet. ii. 24. And this,—

5. By undergoing the curse and penalty of the law, Gal. iii. 13; or the punishment of sin required by the law, 2 Cor. v. 21; Rom. viii. 3.

6. Herein, also, according to the will of God, he offered up himself a propitiatory and expiatory sacrifice, to make atonement for sin and reconciliation for sinners, Eph. v. 6; Rom. v. 6; Heb. ix. 11–14;—which he did, that the justice of God being satisfied, and

the law fulfilled, sinners might be freed from the wrath to come, Rom. iii. 25; 1 Thess. i. 10.

7. And hereby also he paid a real price of redemption for sin and sinners, 1 Pet. i. 18, 19; 1 Cor. vi. 20. These are the things which we are to believe concerning the satisfaction of Christ. And our explication of this doctrine we are ready to defend when called thereunto.

The consideration of the objections which are raised against this great fundamental truth shall close this discourse. And they are of two sorts:—First, In general, to the whole doctrine, as declared, or some of the more signal heads or parts of it. Secondly, Particular instances in this or that supposal, as consequences of the doctrine asserted. And, in general,—

First, they say, "*This is contrary to, and inconsistent with, the love, grace, mercy, and goodness of God, which are so celebrated in the Scripture as the principal properties of his nature and acts of his will wherein he will be glorified;—especially contrary to the freedom of forgiveness, which we are encouraged to expect, and commanded to believe.*" And this exception they endeavour to firm by testimonies that the Lord is good and gracious, and that he doth freely forgive us our sins and trespasses.

Ans. 1. I readily grant that whatever is really contrary to the grace, goodness, and mercy of God, whatever is inconsistent with the free forgiveness of sin, is not to be admitted; for these things are fully revealed in the Scripture, and must have a consistency with whatever else is therein revealed of God or his will.

2. As God is good, and gracious, and merciful, so also he is holy, righteous, true, and faithful. And these things are no less revealed concerning him than the others; and are no less essential properties of his nature than his goodness and grace. And as they are all essentially the same in him, and considered only under a different habitude or respect, as they are exerted by acts of his will; so it belongs to his infinite wisdom, that the effects of them, though divers, and produced by divers ways and means, may no way be contrary one to the other, but that mercy be exercised without the prejudice of justice or holiness, and justice be preserved entire, without any obstruction to the exercise of mercy.

3. The grace and love of God, that in this matter the Scripture reveals to be exercised in order unto the forgiveness of sinners, consists principally in two things:—(1.) In his holy eternal purpose of providing a relief for lost sinners. He hath done it, "to the praise of the glory of his grace," Eph. i. 6. (2.) In the sending his Son in the pursuit and for the accomplishment of the holy purpose of his will and grace. Herein most eminently doth the Scripture celebrate the

love, goodness, and kindness of God, as that whereby, in infinite and for ever to be adored wisdom and grace, he made way for the forgiveness of our sins. John iii. 16, "God so loved the world, that he gave his only begotten Son." Rom. iii. 25, "Whom God hath set forth to be a propitiation through 'faith in his blood." Rom. v. 8, "God commendeth his love toward us, in that, while we were yet sinners, Christ died for us." Tit. iii. 4; 1 John iv. 9, 10. Herein consists that ever to be adored love, goodness, grace, mercy, and condescension of God. Add hereunto, that, in the act of causing our iniquities to meet on Christ, wherein he immediately intended the declaration of his justice, Rom iii. 25,—"not sparing him, in delivering him up to death for us all," Rom. viii. 32,—there was a blessed harmony in the highest justice and most excellent grace and mercy. This grace, this goodness, this love of God towards mankind, towards sinners, our adversaries in this matter neither know nor understand; and so, indeed, what lies in them, remove the foundation of the whole gospel, and of all that faith and obedience which God requires at our hands.

4. Forgiveness, or the actual condonation of sinners, the pardon and forgiveness of sins, is *free;* but yet so as it is everywhere restrained unto a respect unto Christ, unto his death and blood-shedding. Eph. i. 7, "We have redemption through his blood, the forgiveness of sins." Chap. iv. 32. "God for Christ's sake hath forgiven you." Rom. iii. 25, 26, "God hath set him forth to be a propitiation through faith in his blood, to declare his righteousness for the remission of sins." It is absolutely free in respect of all immediate transactions between God and sinners.

(1.) Free on the part of God.

[1.] In the *eternal purpose* of it, when he might justly have suffered all men to have perished under the guilt of their sins. [2.] Free in the *means* that he used to effect it, unto his glory. 1*st.* In the sending of his Son; and, 2*dly.* In laying the punishment of our sin upon him. 3*dly.* In his covenant with him, that it should be accepted on our behalf. 4*thly.* In his tender and proposal of it by the gospel unto sinners, to be received without money or without price. 5*thly.* In the actual condonation and pardon of them that do believe.

(2.) It is free on the part of the persons that are forgiven; in that, [1.] It is given and granted to them, without any satisfaction made by them for their former transgressions. [2.] Without any merit to purchase or procure it. [3.] Without any penal, satisfactory suffering here, or in a purgatory hereafter. [4.] Without any expectation of a future recompense; or that, being pardoned, they should then make or give any satisfaction for what they had done before. And as any of these things would, so nothing else can, impeach the *freedom* of pardon and forgiveness. Whether, then, we respect the pardoner or the pardoned, pardon is every way free,—namely, on the part of God who forgives, and on the part of sinners that are forgiven. If God now hath, besides all this, provided himself a lamb for a sacrifice; if he hath, in infinite wisdom and grace, found out a way thus freely to forgive us our sins, to the praise and glory of his own holiness, righteousness, and severity against sin, as well as unto the unspeakable advancement of that grace, goodness, and bounty which he immediately exerciseth in the pardon of sin; are these men's eyes evil, because he is good? Will they not be contented to be pardoned, unless they may have it at the rate of despoiling God of his holiness, truth, righteousness, and faithfulness? And as this is certainly done by that way of pardon which these men propose, no reserve in the least being made for the glory of God in those holy properties of his nature which are immediately injured and opposed by sin; so that pardon itself, which they pretend so to magnify, having nothing to influence it but a mere arbitrary act of God's will, is utterly debased from its own proper worth and excellency. And I shall willingly undertake to manifest that they derogate no less from grace and mercy in pardon, than they do from the righteousness and holiness of God, by the forgiveness which they have feigned; and that in it both of them are perverted and despoiled of all their glory.

But they yet say, "*If God can freely pardon sin, why doth he not do it without satisfaction? If he cannot, he is weaker and more imperfect than man, who can do so.*"

Ans. 1. God cannot do many things that men can do;—not that he is *more imperfect* than they, but he cannot do them on the account of his perfection. He *cannot lie*, he cannot deny himself, he cannot change; which men can do, and do every day.

2. To pardon sin without satisfaction, in him who is absolutely holy, righteous, true, and faithful,—the absolute, necessary, supreme Governor of all sinners,—the author of the law, and sanction of it, wherein punishment is threatened and declared,—is to deny himself, and to do what *one infinitely perfect* cannot do.

3. I ask of these men, why God doth not pardon sins *freely*, without requiring faith, repentance, and obedience in them that are pardoned; yea, as the conditions on which they may be pardoned? For, seeing he is so infinitely good and gracious, cannot he pardon men without prescribing such terms and conditions unto them as he knoweth that men, and that incomparably the greatest number of them, will never come up unto, and so must of necessity perish for ever? Yea, but they say, "This cannot be: neither doth this impeach the freedom of pardon; for it is certain that God doth prescribe these things, and

yet he pardoneth *freely;* and it would altogether unbecome the holy God to pardon sinners that continue so to live and die in their sins." But do not these men see that they have hereby given away their cause which they contend for? For, if a prescription of sundry things to the sinner himself, without which he shall not be pardoned, do not at all impeach, as they say, the freedom of pardon, but God may be said freely to pardon sin notwithstanding it; how shall the receiving of satisfaction by another, nothing at all being required of the sinner, have the least appearance of any such thing? If the freedom of forgiveness consists in such a boundless notion as these men imagine, it is certain that the prescribing of faith and repentance in and unto sinners, antecedently to their participation of it, is much more evidently contrary unto it, than the receiving of satisfaction from another who is not to be pardoned can to any appear to be. Secondly, if it be contrary to the holiness of God to pardon any without requiring faith, repentance, and obedience in them (as it is indeed), let not these persons be offended if we believe him when he so frequently declares it, that it was so to remit sin, without the fulfilling of his law and satisfaction of his justice.

Secondly, they say, " *There is no such thing as justice in God requiring the punishment of sin; but that that which in him requireth and calleth for the punishment of sin is his anger and wrath; which expressions denote free acts of his will, and not any essential properties of his nature.*" So that God may punish sin or not punish it, at his pleasure; therefore there is no reason that he should require any satisfaction for sin, seeing he may pass it by absolutely as he pleaseth.

Ans. 1. Is it not strange, that the great Governor, the Judge of all the world, which, on the supposition of the creation of it, God is naturally and necessarily, should not also naturally be so righteous as to do right, in rendering unto every one according to his works?

2. The *sanction* and penalty of the law, which is the rule of punishment, was, I suppose, an effect of justice,—of God's natural and essential justice, and not of his anger or wrath. Certainly, never did any man make a law for the government of a people in anger. Draco's laws were not made in wrath, but according to the best apprehension of right and justice that he had, though said to be written in blood; and shall we think otherwise of the law of God?

3. Anger and wrath in God express the effects of justice, and so are not merely free acts of his will. This, therefore, is a tottering cause, that is built on the denial of God's essential righteousness. But it was proved before, and it is so elsewhere.

Thirdly, they say, " *That the sacrifice of Christ was only metaphorically so,*"—that he was a metaphorical priest, not one properly so called; and, therefore, that his sacrifice did not consist in his death and blood-shedding, but in his appearing in heaven upon his ascension, presenting himself unto God in the most holy place not made with hands as the mediator of the new covenant.

Ans. 1. When once these men come to this *evasion,* they think themselves safe, and that they may go whither they will without control. For they say it is true, Christ was a priest; but only he was a *metaphorical* one. He offered sacrifice; but it was a *metaphorical* one. He redeemed us; but with a *metaphorical* redemption. And so we are justified thereon; but with a *metaphorical* justification. And so, for aught I know, they are like to be saved with a *metaphorical salvation.* This is the substance of their plea in this matter:—Christ was not really a priest; but did somewhat like a priest. He offered not sacrifice really; but did somewhat that was like a sacrifice. He redeemed us not really; but did somewhat that looked like redemption. And what these things are, wherein their analogy consisteth, what proportion the things that Christ hath done bear to the things that are really so, from whence they receive their denomination, it is meet it should be wholly in the power of these persons to declare. But,—

2. What should hinder the death of Christ to be a *sacrifice,* a *proper sacrifice,* and, according to the nature, end, and use of sacrifices, to have made atonement and satisfaction for sin? (1.) It is expressly called so in the Scripture; wherein he is said to "offer himself, to make his soul an offering, to offer himself a sacrifice," Eph. v. 2; Heb. i. 3, ix. 14, 25, 26, vii. 27. And he is himself directly said to be a "priest," or a sacrificer, Heb. ii. 17. And it is nowhere intimated, much less expressed, that these things are not spoken properly, but metaphorically only. (2.) The legal sacrifices of the old law were instituted on purpose to represent and prepare the way for the bringing in of the sacrifice of the Lamb of God, so to take away the sin of the world; and is it not strange, that true and real sacrifices should be types and representations of that which was not so? On this supposition, all those sacrifices are but so many seductions from the right understanding of things between God and sinners. (3.) Nothing is wanting to render it a proper propitiatory sacrifice. For,—[1.] There was *the person offering,* and that was Christ himself, Heb. ix. 14, "He offered himself unto God." "He," that is, the sacrificer, denotes the person of Christ, God and man; and "himself," as the sacrifice, denotes his human nature · whence God is said to "purchase his church with his own blood," Acts xx. 28; for he offered himself through the eternal Spirit: so that,—[2.] There was *the matter of the sacrifice,* which was the human nature of Christ, soul and body. "His soul was made an offering for sin,"

Isa. liii. 10; and his body, " The offering of the body of Jesus Christ," Heb. x. 10,—his blood especially, which is often synecdochically mentioned for the whole. (4.) His death had the *nature* of a sacrifice: for,—[1.] Therein were the sins of men laid upon him, and not in his entrance into heaven; for "he bare our sins in his own body on the tree," 1 Pet. ii. 24. God made our sins then "to meet upon him," Isa. liii. 6; which gives the formality unto any sacrifices. "Quod in ejus caput sit," is the formal reason of all propitiatory sacrifices, and ever was so, as is expressly declared, Lev. xvi. 21, 22; and the phrase of "bearing sin," of "bearing iniquity," is constantly used for the undergoing of the punishment due to sin. [2.] It had the *end* of a proper sacrifice; it made expiation of sin, propitiation and atonement for sin, with reconciliation with God; and so took away that enmity that was between God and sinners, Heb. i. 3; Rom. iii. 25, 26; Heb. ii. 17, 18, v. 10; Rom. viii. 3; 2 Cor. v. 18, 19. And although God himself designed, appointed, and contrived, in wisdom, this way of reconciliation, as he did the means for the atoning of his own anger towards the friends of Job, commanding them to go unto him, and with him offer sacrifices for themselves, which he would accept, chap. xlii. 7, 8; yet, as he was the supreme Governor, the Lord of all, attended with infinite justice and holiness, atonement was made with him, and satisfaction to him thereby.

What hath been spoken may suffice to discover the emptiness and weakness of those exceptions which in general these men make against the truth before laid down from the Scripture. A brief examination of some particular instances, wherein they seek not so much to oppose as to reproach the revelation of this mystery of the gospel, shall put a close to this discourse. It is said, then,—

First, " *That if this be so, then it will follow that God is gracious to forgive, and yet [it is] impossible for him, unless the debt be fully satisfied.*"

Ans. 1. I suppose the confused and abrupt expression of things here, in words scarcely affording a tolerable sense, is rather from weakness than captiousness; and so I shall let the manner of the proposal pass. 2. What if this should follow, that God is gracious to forgive sinners, and yet will not, cannot, on the account of his own holiness and righteousness, actually forgive any, without satisfaction and atonement made for sin? the worst that can be hence concluded is, that the Scripture is true, which affirms both these in many places. 3. This sets out the exceeding greatness of the grace of God in forgiveness, that when sin could not be forgiven without satisfaction, and the sinner himself could no way make any such satisfaction, he provided himself a sacrifice of atonement, that the sinner might be discharged and pardoned. 4. Sin is not properly a debt, for then it might be paid in kind, by sin itself; but is called so only because it binds over the sinner to *punishment*, which is the satisfaction to be made for that which is properly a transgression, and improperly only a debt. It is added,—

Secondly, " *Hence it follows, that the finite and impotent creature is more capable of extending mercy and forgiveness than the infinite and omnipotent Creator.*"

Ans. 1. God being essentially holy and righteous, having engaged his *faithfulness* in the sanction of the law, and being naturally and necessarily the governor and ruler of the world, the forgiving of sin without satisfaction would be no perfection in him, but an effect of impotency and imperfection,—a thing which God cannot do, as he cannot lie, nor deny himself. 2. The direct contrary of what is insinuated is asserted by this doctrine; for, on the supposition of the satisfaction and atonement insisted on, not only doth God freely forgive, but that in such a way of righteousness and goodness, as no creature is able to conceive or express the glory and excellency of it. And to speak of the poor having pardons of private men, upon particular offences against themselves, who are commanded so to do, and have no right nor authority to require or exact punishment, nor is any due upon the mere account of their own concernment, in comparison with the forgiveness of God, ariseth out of a *deep ignorance* of the whole matter under consideration.

Thirdly. It is added by them, that hence it follows, " *That God so loved the world, that he gave his only Son to save it; and yet that God stood off in high displeasure, and Christ gave himself as a complete satisfaction to offended justice.*"

Ans. Something these men would say, if they knew what or how; for,—1. That God so loved the world as to give his only Son to save it, is the expression of the Scripture, and the foundation of the doctrine whose truth we contend for. 2. That Christ offered himself to make atonement for sinners, and therein made satisfaction to the justice of God, is the doctrine itself which these men oppose, and not any consequent of it. 3. That God stood off in high displeasure, is an expression which neither the Scripture useth, nor those who declare this doctrine from thence, nor is suited unto divine perfections, or the manner of divine operations. That intended seems to be, that the righteousness and law of God required the punishment due to sin to be undergone, and thereby satisfaction to be made unto God; which is no consequent of the doctrine, but the doctrine itself.

Fourthly. It is yet farther objected, " *That if Christ made satisfaction for sin, then he did it either as God or as man, or as God and man.*"

Ans. 1. *As God and man.* Acts xx. 28, " God redeemed his church with his own blood." 1 John iii. 16, "Hereby perceive we the love of God, because he laid down his life for us." Heb. ix. 14. 2. This dilemma is proposed, as that which proceeds on a supposition of *our own principles*, that Christ is God and man in one person: which, indeed, makes the pretended difficulty to be vain, and a mere effect of ignorance; for all the mediatory acts of Christ being the acts of his person, must of necessity be the acts of him as God and man. 3. There is yet another mistake in this inquiry; for satisfaction is in it looked on as a real act or operation of one or the other nature in Christ, when it is the *apotelesma* or effect of the actings, the doing and suffering of Christ—the dignity of what he did in reference unto the end for which he did it. For the two natures are so united in Christ as not to have a third compound principle of physical acts and operations thence arising; but each nature acts distinctly, according to its own being and properties, yet so as what is the immediate act of either nature is the act of him who is one in both; from whence it hath its dignity. 4. The sum is, that in all the mediatory actions of Christ we are to consider,—(1.) The *agent;* and that is the person of Christ. (2.) The *immediate principle* by which and from which the agent worketh; and that is the natures in the person. (3.) The *actions;* which are the effectual operations of either nature. (4.) The *effect* or work with respect to God and us; and this relates unto the person of the agent, the Lord Christ, God and man. A blending of the natures into one common principle of operation, as the compounding of mediums unto one end, is ridiculously supposed in this matter.

But yet, again; it is pretended that sundry consequences, *irreligious* and *irrational*, do ensue upon a supposition of the satisfaction pleaded for. What, then, are they?

First. " *That it is unlawful and impossible for God Almighty to be gracious and merciful, or to pardon transgressors.*"

Ans. The miserable, confused misapprehension of things which the proposal of this and the like consequences doth evidence, manifests sufficiently how unfit the makers of them are to manage controversies of this nature. For,—1. It is supposed that for God to be *gracious and merciful*, or to *pardon sinners*, are the same; which is to confound the essential properties of his nature with the free acts of his will. 2. Lawful or unlawful, are terms that can with no tolerable sense be used concerning any properties of God, all which are natural and necessary unto his being; as goodness, grace, and mercy, in particular, are. 3. That it is *impossible for God to pardon transgressors, according to this doctrine*, is a fond imagination; for it is only a declaration of the manner how he doth it. 4. As God is gracious and merciful, so also he is holy, and righteous, and true; and it became him, or was every way meet for him, in his way of exercising grace and mercy towards sinners, to order all things so, as that it might be done without the impeachment of his holiness, righteousness, and truth. It is said, again,—

Secondly, " *That God was inevitably compelled to this way of saving men;—the highest affront to his uncontrollable nature.*"

Ans. 1. Were the authors of these exceptions put to declare what they mean by God's " uncontrollable nature," they would hardly disentangle themselves with common sense; such masters of reason are they, indeed, whatever they would fain pretend to be. Controllable or uncontrollable, respects actings and operations, not beings or natures. 2. That, upon the principle opposed by these men, God was inevitably compelled to this way of saving men, is a fond and childish imagination. The whole business of the salvation of men, according unto this doctrine, depends on a mere free, sovereign act of God's will, exerting itself in a way of infinite wisdom, holiness, and grace. 3. The meaning of this objection (if it hath either sense or meaning in it) is, that God, freely purposing to save lost sinners, did it in a way becoming his holy nature and righteous law. What other course Infinite Wisdom could have taken for the satisfaction of his justice we know not;—that justice was to be satisfied, and that this way it is done we know and believe.

Thirdly. They say it hence follows, " *That it is unworthy of God to pardon, but not to inflict punishment on the innocent, or require a satisfaction where there was nothing due.*"

Ans. 1. What is *worthy* or *unworthy of God*, himself alone knows, and of men not any, but according to what he is pleased to declare and reveal; but, certainly, it is unworthy any person, pretending to the least interest in ingenuity or use of reason, to use such frivolous instances in any case of importance, which have not the least pretence of argument in them, but what ariseth from a gross misapprehension or misrepresentation of a doctrine designed to opposition. 2. To pardon sinners, is a thing becoming the goodness and grace of God; to do it by Christ, that which becometh them, and his holiness and righteousness also, Eph. i. 6, 7; Rom. iii. 25. 3. The Lord Christ was *personally innocent;* but " he who knew no sin was made sin for us," 2 Cor. v. 21. And as the mediator and surety of the covenant, he was to answer for the sins of them whom he undertook to save from the wrath to come, by giving himself a ransom for them, and making his soul an offering for their sin. 4. That nothing is due to the justice of God for sin,—that is, that sin doth not in the justice of God deserve punishment,—is a good, comfortable doctrine for men that are resolved to continue in their sins whilst they live in this world. The Scripture tells us that Christ *paid* what he took not; that all *our iniquities* were caused to meet upon him; that *he bare them* in his own body on the tree; that his *soul was made an offering* for sin, and thereby made reconciliation or atonement for the sins of the people. If these persons be otherwise minded, we cannot help it.

Fourthly. It is added, that "*This doctrine doth not only disadvantage the true virtue and real intent of Christ's life and death, but entirely deprives God of that praise which is owing to his greatest love and goodness.*"

Ans. 1. I suppose that this is the first time that this doctrine fell under this imputation; nor could it possibly be liable unto this charge from any who did either understand it or the grounds on which it is commonly opposed. For there is no end of the life or death of Christ which the Socinians themselves admit of, but it is also allowed and asserted in the doctrine new called in question. Do they say, that he taught the truth, or revealed the whole mind and will of God concerning his worship and our obedience? we say the same. Do they say, that by his death he bare testimony unto and confirmed the truth which he had taught? it is also owned by us. Do they say, that in what he did and suffered he set us an example that we should labour after conformity unto? it is what we acknowledge and teach : only, we say that all these things belong principally to his *prophetical office.* But we, moreover, affirm and believe, that as a priest, or in the discharge of his *sacerdotal office,* he did, in his death and sufferings, offer himself a sacrifice to God, to make atonement for our sins,—which they deny; and that he died for us, or in our stead, that we might go free: without the faith and acknowledgment whereof no part of the gospel can be rightly understood. All the ends, then, which they themselves assign of the life and death of Christ are by us granted; and the principal one, which gives life and efficacy to the rest, is by them denied. Neither,—2. Doth it fall under any possible imagination, that the *praise due unto God* should be eclipsed hereby. The love and kindness of God towards us is in the Scripture fixed principally and fundamentally on his " sending of his only begotten Son to die for us." And, certainly, the greater the work was that he had to do, the greater ought our acknowledgment of his love and kindness to be. But it is said,—

Fifthly, "*That it represents the Son as more kind and compassionate than the Father; whereas if both be the same God, then either the Father is as loving as the Son, or the Son as angry as the Father.*"

Ans. 1. The Scripture referreth the love of the Father unto two heads:—(1.) *The sending of his Son* to die for us, John iii. 16; Rom. v. 8; 1 John iv. 9, 10. (2.) *In choosing sinners unto a participation of the fruits of his love,* Eph. i. 3–6. The love of the Son is fixed signally on his actual giving himself to die for us, Gal. ii. 20; Eph. v. 25; Rev. i. 5. What balances these persons have got to weigh these loves in, and to conclude which is the greatest or most weighty, I know not. 2. Although only the actual discharge of his office be directly assigned to the love of Christ, yet his condescension in taking our nature upon him,—expressed by his mind, Phil. ii. 5-8, and the readiness of his will, Ps. xl. 8,—doth eminently comprise love in it also. 3. The love of the Father in sending of the Son was an *act of his will;* which being a natural and essential property of God, it was so far the act of the Son also, as he is partaker of the same nature, though eminently, and in respect of order, it was peculiarly the act of the Father. 4. The anger of God against sin is an effect of his essential righteousness and holiness, which belong to him as God; which yet hinders not but that both Father, and Son, and Spirit, acted love towards sinners. They say again,—

Sixthly, " *It robs God of the gift of his Son for our redemption, which the Scriptures attribute to the unmerited love he had for the world, in affirming the Son purchased that redemption from the Father, by the gift of himself to God as our complete satisfaction.*"

Ans. 1. It were endless to consider the improper and absurd expressions which are made use of in these exceptions, as here; the last words have no tolerable sense in them, according to any principles whatever. 2. If the Son's purchasing redemption for us, procuring, obtaining it, do rob God of the gift of his Son for our redemption, the Holy Ghost must answer for it; for, having " obtained" for us, or procured, or purchased, "eternal redemption," is the word used by himself, Heb. ix. 12; and to deny that he hath laid down his life a "ransom" for us, and hath " bought us with a price," is openly to deny the gospel. 3. In a word, the great gift of God consisted in giving his Son to obtain redemption for us. 4. Herein he " offered himself unto God," and " gave himself for us;" and if these persons are offended herewithal, what are we, that we should withstand God? They say,—

Seventhly, " *Since Christ could not pay what was not his own, it follows, that in the payment of his own the case still remains equally grievous; since the debt is not hereby absolved or forgiven, but transferred only; and, by consequence, we are no better provided for salvation than before, owing that now to the Son which was once owing to the Father.*"

Ans. The looseness and dubiousness of the expressions here used makes an appearance that there is something in them, when indeed there is not. There is an allusion in them to a debt and a payment, which is the most improper expression that is used in this matter; and the interpretation thereof is to be regulated by other proper expressions of the same thing. But to keep to the allusion:—1. Christ *paid his own,* but not for himself, Dan. ix. 26. 2. Paying it for us, the *debt* is discharged; and our actual discharge is to be given out according to the ways and means, and upon the conditions, appointed and constituted by the Father and Son. 3. When a debt is so transferred as that one is accepted in the room and obliged to payment in the stead of another, and that payment is made and accepted accordingly, all law and reason require that the original debtor be discharged. 4. What on this account we owe to the Son, is praise, thankfulness, and obedience, and not the debt which he took upon himself and discharged for us, when we were nonsolvent, by his love. So that this matter is plain enough, and not to be involved by such cloudy expressions and incoherent discourse, following the metaphor of a debt. For if God be considered as the creditor, we all as debtors, and being insolvent, Christ undertook, out of his love, to pay the debt for us, and did so accordingly, which was accepted with God; it follows that we are to be discharged upon God's terms, and under a new obligation unto his love who hath made this satisfaction for us: which we shall eternally acknowledge. It is said,—

Eighthly, " *It no way renders men beholden or in the least obliged to God, since by their doctrine he would not have abated us, nor did he Christ, the least farthing; so that the acknowledgments are peculiarly the Son's: which destroys the whole current of Scripture testimony for his good-will towards men. O the infamous portraiture this doctrine draws of the infinite goodness! Is this your retribution, O injurious satisfactionists?*"

Ans. This is but a bold repetition of what, in other words, was mentioned before over and over. Wherein the love of God in this matter consisted, and what is the obligation on us unto thankfulness and obedience, hath been before also declared; and we are not to be moved in fundamental truths by vain exclamations of weak and unstable men. It is said,—

Ninthly, " *That God's justice is satisfied for sins past, present, and to come, whereby God and Christ have lost both their power of enjoining godliness and prerogative of punishing disobedience; for what is once paid, is not revocable, and if punishment should arrest any for their debts, it argues a breach on God or Christ's part, or else that it hath not been sufficiently solved, and the penalty complete sustained by another.*"

Ans. The intention of this pretended consequence of our doctrine is, that, upon a supposition of satisfaction made by Christ, there is no solid foundation remaining for the prescription of faith, repentance, and obedience, on the one hand; or of punishing them who refuse so to obey, believe, or repent, on the other. The reason of this inference insinuated seems to be this,—that sin being satisfied for, cannot be called again to an account. For the former part of the pretended consequence,—namely, that on this supposition there is no foundation left for the prescription of godliness,—I cannot discern any thing in the least looking towards the confirmation of it in the words of the objection laid down. But these things are quite otherwise; as is manifest unto them that read and obey the gospel. For,—1. Christ's satisfaction for sins acquits not the creature of that dependence *on* God, and duty which he owes *to* God, which (notwithstanding *that*) God may justly, and doth prescribe unto him, suitable to his own nature, holiness, and will. The whole of our regard unto God doth not lie in an acquitment from sin. It is, moreover, required of us, as a necessary and indispensable consequence of the relation wherein we stand unto him, that we live to him and obey him, whether sin be satisfied for or no. The manner and measure hereof are to be regulated by his prescriptions, which are suited to his own wisdom and our condition; and they are now referred to the heads mentioned, of *faith, repentance,* and *new obedience.* 2. The satisfaction made for sin being not made by the sinner himself, there must of necessity be a rule, order, and law-constitution, how the sinner may come to be interested in it, and made partaker of it. For the consequent of the freedom of one by the suffering of another is not natural or necessary, but must proceed and arise from a law-constitution, compact, and agreement. Now, the *way* constituted and appointed is that of faith, or believing, as explained in the Scripture. If men believe not, they are no less liable to the punishment due to their sins than if no satisfaction at all were made for sinners. And whereas it is added, " *Forgetting that every one must appear before the judgment-seat of Christ, to receive according to the things done in the body, yea, and every one must give an account of himself to God;*" closing all with this, " *But many more are the gross absurdities and blasphemies that are the genuine fruits of this so confidently-believed doctrine of satisfaction :*" I say it is,—3. Certain that we must all appear before the judgment-seat of Christ, to receive according to the things done in the body; and therefore, woe will be unto them at the great day who are not able to plead the atonement made for their sins by the blood of Christ, and an evidence of their interest therein by their faith and obedience, or the things done and wrought in them and by them whilst they were in the body here in this world. And this it would better become these persons to betake themselves unto the consideration of, than to exercise themselves unto an unparalleled confidence in reproaching those with absurdities and blasphemies who believe the Deity and satisfaction of Jesus Christ, the Son of the living God, who died for us; which is the ground and bottom of all our expectation of a blessed life and immortality to come.

The removal of these objections against the truth, scattered of late up and down in the hands of all sorts of men, may suffice for our present purpose. If any amongst these men judge that they have an ability to manage the opposition against the truth as declared by us, with such pleas, arguments, and exceptions, as may pretend an interest in appearing reason, they shall, God assisting, be attended unto. With men given up to a spirit of railing or reviling,—though it be no small honour to be reproached by them who reject with scorn the eternal Deity of the Son of God, and the satisfactory atonement that he made for the sins of men,—no person of sobriety will contend. And I shall farther only desire the reader to take notice, that though these few sheets were written in a few hours, upon the desire and for the satisfaction of some private friends, and therefore contain merely an expression of present thoughts, without the least design or diversion of mind towards accuracy or ornament; yet the author is so far confident that the truth, and nothing else, is proposed and confirmed in them, that he fears not but that an opposition to what is here declared will be removed, and the truth reinforced in such a way and manner as may not be to its disadvantage.

AN APPENDIX.

———

THE preceding discourse, as hath been declared, was written for the use of *ordinary Christians,* or such as might be in danger to be seduced, or any way entangled in their minds, by the late attempts against the truths pleaded for: for those to whom the dispensation of the gospel is committed, are "debtors both to the Greeks and to the Barbarians; both to the wise and to the unwise," Rom. i. 14. It was therefore thought meet to insist only on things necessary, and such as their faith is immediately concerned in; and not to immix therewithal any such arguments or considerations as might not, by reason of the terms wherein they are expressed, be obvious to their capacity and understanding. Unto *plainness and perspicuity, brevity* was also required, by such as judged this work necessary. That design, we hope, is answered, and now discharged in some useful measure. But yet, because many of our arguments on the head of the satisfaction of Christ depend upon the genuine signification and notion of the words and terms wherein the doctrine of it is delivered,—which, for the reasons before mentioned, could not conveniently be discussed in the foregoing discourse,—I shall here, in some few instances, give an account of what farther confirmation the truth might receive by a due explanation of them. And I shall mention here but few of them, because a large dissertation concerning them all is intended[1] in another way.

First. For the term of *satisfaction* itself, it is granted that in this matter it is not found in the Scripture,—that is, it is not so ῥητῶς, or syllabically,—but it is κατὰ τὸ πρᾶγμα ἀναντιρρήτως; the thing itself intended is asserted in it, beyond all modest contradiction. Neither, indeed, is there in the Hebrew language any word that doth adequately answer unto it; no, nor yet in the Greek. As it is used in this cause, ἐγγύη, which is properly "sponsio," or "fide-jussio," in

———

[1] The "Vindiciæ Evangelicæ" of Owen, in reply to Biddle, had appeared fourteen years before the publication of this treatise. The probability is, therefore, that our author alludes above to the copious and elaborate refutation of Socinian errors in his "Exposition of the Epistle to the Hebrews."—ED.

its actual discharge, maketh the nearest approach unto it: *Ἱκανον ποιεῖν* is used to the same purpose. But there are words and phrases, both in the Old Testament and in the New, that are equipollent unto it, and express the matter or thing intended by it: as in the Old are, פִּדְיוֹן פָּדָה [Ps. xlix. 9], and כֹּפֶר. This last word we render "satisfaction," Numb. xxxv. 32, 33, where God denies that any *compensation*, sacred or civil, shall be received to free a murderer from the punishment due unto him; which properly expresseth what we intend: "Thou shalt admit of no satisfaction for the life of a murderer."

In the New Testament: *Λύτρον, ἀντίλυτρον, ἀπολύτρωσις, τιμή, ἱλασμός·* and the verbs, *λυτροῦν, ἀπολυτροῦν, ἐξαγοράζειν, ἱλάσκεσθαι*, are of the same importance, and some of them accommodated to express the thing intended, beyond that which hath obtained in vulgar use. For that which we intended hereby is, *the voluntary obedience unto death, and the passion or suffering, of our Lord Jesus Christ, God and man, whereby and wherein he offered himself, through the eternal Spirit, for a propitiatory sacrifice, that he might fulfil the law, or answer all its universal postulata; and as our sponsor, undertaking our cause, when we were under the sentence of condemnation, underwent the punishment due to us from the justice of God, being transferred on him; whereby having made a perfect and absolute propitiation or atonement for our sins, he procured for us deliverance from death and the curse, and a right unto life everlasting.* Now, this is more properly expressed by some of the words before mentioned than by that of satisfaction; which yet, nevertheless, as usually explained, is comprehensive, and no way unsuited to the matter intended by it.

In general, men by this word understand either "*reparationem offensæ*," or "*solutionem debiti*,"—either "reparation made for offence given unto any," or "the payment of a debt." "Debitum" is either "criminale" or "pecuniarium;" that is, either the obnoxiousness of a man to punishment for crimes or the guilt of them, in answer to that justice and law which he is necessarily liable and subject unto; or unto a payment or compensation by and of money, or what is valued by it;—which last consideration, neither in itself nor in any reasonings from an analogy unto it, can in this matter have any proper place. Satisfaction is the effect of the doing or suffering what is required for the answering of his charge against faults or sins, who hath right, authority, and power to require, exact, and inflict punishment for them. Some of the schoolmen define it by "Voluntaria redditio æquivalentis indebiti;" of which more elsewhere. The true meaning of, "to satisfy, or make satisfaction," is "tantum facere aut pati, quantum satis sit justè irato ad vindictam." This satisfaction is impleaded as inconsistent with free remission of sins,—how causelessly we have seen. It is so far from it, that it is necessary to make way for it, in case of a righteous law transgressed, and the public order of the universal Governor and government of all disturbed. And this God directs unto, Lev. iv. 31, "The priest shall make an atonement for him, and it shall be forgiven him." This atonement was a legal satisfaction, and it is by God himself premised to remission or pardon. And Paul prays Philemon to forgive Onesimus, though he took upon himself to make satisfaction for all the wrong or damage that he had sustained, Epist. verses 18, 19. And when God was displeased with the friends of Job, he prescribes a way to them, or what they shall do, and what they shall get done for them, that they might be accepted and pardoned, Job xlii. 7, 8, "The LORD said unto Eliphaz, My wrath is kindled against thee, and against thy two friends: therefore take unto you now seven bullocks and seven rams, and go to my servant Job, and offer up for yourselves a burnt-offering; and my servant Job shall pray for you: for him will I accept: lest I deal with you after your folly." He plainly enjoineth an atonement, that he might freely pardon them. And both these,—namely, satisfaction and pardon, with their order and consistency,—were solemnly represented by the great institution of the sacrifice of the scape-goat. For after all the sins of the people were put upon him, or the punishment of them transferred unto him in a type and representation, with " Quod in ejus caput sit," the formal reason of all sacrifices propitiatory, he was sent away with them; denoting the oblation or forgiveness of sin, after a translation made of its punishment, Lev. xvi. 21, 22. And whereas it is not expressly said that that goat suffered, or was slain, but was either עֲזָאזֵל, "hircus," ἀποπομπαῖος, "a goat sent away," or was sent to a rock called Azazel, in the wilderness, as Vatablus[1] and Oleaster,[2] with some others, think (which is not probable, seeing, though it might then be done whilst the people were in the wilderness of Sinai, yet could not, by reason of its distance, when the people were settled in Canaan, be annually observed), it was from the poverty of the types, whereof no one could fully represent that grace which it had particular respect unto. What, therefore, was wanting in that goat was supplied in the other, which was slain as a sin-offering, verses 15, 16.

Neither doth it follow, that, on the supposition of the satisfaction pleaded for, the freedom, pardon, or acquitment of the person originally guilty and liable to punishment must immediately and " ipso

[1] A celebrated Hebrew scholar. He was born in Picardy, and died 1547. His Notes on the Old Testament Scriptures, taken by his scholars from his observations, and arranged by Robert Stephens, were published 1557.

[2] A Portuguese Dominican and able scholar. He died in 1563, and left behind him Commentaries on the Pentateuch.—ED.

facto" ensue. It is not of the nature of every solution or satisfaction, that deliverance must "ipso facto" follow. And the reason of it is, because this satisfaction, by a succedaneous substitution of one to undergo punishment for another, must be founded in a voluntary compact and agreement. For there is required unto it a *relaxation of the law,* though not as unto the *punishment* to be inflicted, yet as unto the *person* to be punished. And it is otherwise in personal guilt than in pecuniary debts. In these, the debt itself is solely intended, the person only obliged with reference thereunto. In the other, the person is firstly and principally under the obligation. And therefore, when a pecuniary debt is paid, by whomsoever it be paid, the obligation of the person himself unto payment ceaseth "ipso facto." But in things criminal, the guilty person himself being firstly, immediately, and intentionally under the obligation unto punishment, when there is introduced by compact a vicarious solution, in the substitution of another to suffer, though he suffer the same absolutely which those should have done for whom he suffers, yet, because of the acceptation of his person to suffer, which might have been refused, and could not be admitted without some relaxation of the law, deliverance of the guilty persons cannot ensue "ipso facto," but by the intervention of the terms fixed on in the covenant or agreement for an admittance of the substitution.

It appears, from what hath been spoken, that, in this matter of satisfaction, God is not considered as a *creditor*, and sin as a *debt;* and the law as an obligation to the payment of that debt, and the Lord Christ as paying it;—though these notions may have been used by some for the illustration of the whole matter, and that not without countenance from sundry expressions in the Scripture to the same purpose. But God is considered as the infinitely holy and righteous author of the law, and supreme governor of all mankind, according to the tenor and sanction of it. Man is considered as a sinner, a transgressor of that law, and thereby obnoxious and liable to the punishment constituted in it and by it,—answerably unto the justice and holiness of its author. The substitution of Christ was merely *voluntary* on the part of God, and of himself, undertaking to be a sponsor, to answer for the sins of men by undergoing the punishment due unto them. To this end there was a relaxation of the law as to the persons that were to suffer, though not as to what was to be suffered Without the former, the substitution mentioned could not have been admitted; and on supposition of the latter, the suffering of Christ could not have had the nature of punishment, properly so called: for punishment relates to the *justice* and *righteousness* in government of him that exacts it and inflicts it; and this the justice of God doth not but by the law. Nor could the law be any way satisfied or fulfilled by the suffering of Christ, if, antecedently there-unto, its obligation, or power of obliging unto the penalty constituted in its sanction unto sin, was relaxed, dissolved, or dispensed withal. Nor was it agreeable to justice, nor would the nature of the things themselves admit of it, that another punishment should be inflicted on Christ than what we had deserved; nor could our sin be the impulsive cause of his death; nor could we have had any benefit thereby. And this may suffice to be added unto what was spoken before as to the nature of satisfaction, so far as the brevity of the discourse whereunto we are confined will bear, or the use whereunto it is designed doth require.

Secondly. The nature of the doctrine contended for being declared and cleared, we may, in one or two instances, manifest how evidently it is revealed, and how fully it may be confirmed or vindicated. It is, then, in the Scripture declared, that " Christ died for us,"—that he " died for our sins;" and that *we are thereby delivered.* This is the foundation of Christian religion as such. Without the faith and acknowledgment of it, we are not Christians. Neither is it, in these general terms, at all denied by the Socinians. It remains, therefore, that we consider,—1. How this is revealed and affirmed in the Scripture; and, 2. What is the true meaning of the expressions and propositions wherein it is revealed and affirmed;—for in them, as in sundry others, we affirm that the satisfaction pleaded for is con-tained.

1. Christ is said to *die,* to *give himself,* to *be delivered,* ὑπὲρ ἡμῶν, etc., for us, for his sheep, for the life of the world, for sinners, John vi. 51, x. 15; Rom. v. 6; 2 Cor. v. 14, 15; Gal. ii. 20; Heb. ii. 9. Moreover, he is said to die ὑπὲρ ἁμαρτιῶν, for sins, 1 Cor. xv. 3; Gal. i. 4. The end whereof, everywhere expressed in the gospel, is, that we might be *freed, delivered,* and *saved.* These things, as was said, are agreed unto and acknowledged.

2. The meaning and importance, we say, of these expressions is, that Christ died in our room, place, or stead, undergoing the death or punishment which we should have undergone in the way and manner before declared. _ And this is the satisfaction we plead for. It remains, therefore, that from the Scripture, the nature of the things treated of, the proper signification and constant use of the expressions mentioned, the exemplification of them in the customs and usages of the nations of the world, we do evince and manifest that what we have laid down is the true and proper sense of the words wherein this revelation of Christ's dying for us is expressed; so that they who deny Christ to have died for us in this sense do indeed deny that he properly died for us at all,—whatever benefits they grant that by his death we may obtain.

First. We may consider the use of this expression in the Scripture either indefinitely or in particular instances.

Only we must take this along with us, that dying for sins and transgressions, being added unto *dying for sinners* or persons, maketh the substitution of one in the room and stead of another more evident than when the dying of one for another only is mentioned. For whereas all predicates are regulated by their subjects, and it is ridiculous to say that one dieth in the stead of sins, the meaning can be no other but the bearing or answering of the sins of the sinner in whose stead any one dieth. And this is, in the Scripture, declared to be the sense of that expression, as we shall see afterward. Let us, therefore, consider some instances:—

John xi. 50, The words of Caiaphas' counsel are, Συμφέρει ἡμῖν, ἵνα εἷς ἄνθρωπος ἀποθάνῃ ὑπὲρ τοῦ λαοῦ, καὶ μὴ ὅλον τὸ ἔθνος ἀπόληται—" It is expedient for us, that one man should die for the people, and that the whole nation perish not:" which is expressed again, chap. xviii. 14, ἀπολέσθαι ὑπὲρ τοῦ λαοῦ, "perish for the people." Caiaphas feared that if Christ were spared, the people would be destroyed by the Romans. The way to free them, he thought, was by the destruction of Christ; him, therefore, he devoted to death, in lieu of the people. As he,—

> " Unum pro multis dabitur caput;"—
> " One head shall be given for many."

Not unlike the speech of Otho the emperor in Xiphilin,[1] when he slew himself to preserve his army; for when they would have persuaded him to renew the war after the defeat of some of his forces, and offered to lay down their lives to secure him, he replied, that he would not, adding this reason, Πολὺ γάρ που καὶ κρεῖττον, καὶ δικαιότερόν ἐστιν, ἕνα ὑπὲρ πάντων ἢ πολλοὺς ὑπὲρ ἑνὸς ἀπολέσθαι—" It is far better, and more just, that one should perish or die for all, than that many should perish for one;" that is, one in the stead of many, that they may go free; or as another speaks,—

> Ἐξὸν πρὸ πάντων μίαν ὑπερδοῦναι θανεῖν.—Eurip. Frag. Erech.
> " Let one be given up to die in the stead of all."

John xiii. 37, Τὴν ψυχήν μοῦ ὑπὲρ σοῦ θήσω. They are the words of St Peter unto Christ, " I will lay down my life for thee;"—"To free thee, I will expose my own head to danger, my life to death,—that thou mayest live, and I die." It is plain that he intended the same thing with the celebrated ἀντίψυχοι of old, who exposed their own lives (ψυχὴν ἀντὶ ψυχῆς) for one another. Such were Damon and

---

[1] A monk of Constantinople, who wrote an epitome of Dion Cassius, A.D. 1071-1078.—Ed.

Pythias, Orestes and Pylades, Nisus and Euryalus. Whence is that saying of Seneca, " Succurram perituro, sed ut ipse non peream; nisi si futurus ero magni hominis, aut magnæ rei merces;"—" I will relieve or succour one that is ready to perish; yet so as that I perish not myself,—unless thereby I be taken in lieu of some great man, or great matter;"—" For a great man, a man of great worth and usefulness, I could perish or die in his stead, that he might live and go free."

We have a great example, also, of the importance of this expression in these words of David concerning Absalom, 2 Sam. xviii. 33, מִי־יִתֵּן מוּתִי אֲנִי תַחְתֶּיךָ,—" Who will grant me to die, I for thee," or in thy stead, " my son Absalom?" [Literal rendering of the Hebrew.] It was never doubted but that David wished that he had died in the stead of his son, and to have undergone the death which he did, to have preserved him alive. As to the same purpose, though in another sense, Mezentius in Virgil expresses himself, when his son Lausus, interposing between him and danger in battle, was slain by Æneas:—

" Tantane me tenuit vivendi, nate, voluptas,
Ut pro me hostili paterer succedere dextræ
Quem genui? tuane hæc genitor per vulnera servor,
Morte tua vivens?"—Æn. x. 846.

" Hast thou, O son, fallen under the enemies' hand in my stead? am I saved by thy wounds? do I live by thy death?"

And the word תַּחַת, used by David, doth signify, when applied unto persons, either a *succession* or a *substitution;* still the coming of one into the place and room of another. When one *succeeded* to another in government, it is expressed by that word, 2 Sam. x. 1; 1 Kings i. 35, xix. 16. In other cases it denotes a *substitution.* So Jehu tells his guard, that if any one of them let any of Baal's priests escape, נַפְשׁוֹ תַּחַת נַפְשׁוֹ, 2 Kings x. 24,—his life should go in the stead of the life that he had suffered to escape.

And this answereth unto ἀντί in the Greek; which is also used in this matter, and ever denotes either equality, contrariety, or substitution. The two former senses can here have no place; the latter alone hath. So it is said, that Archelaus reigned ἀντὶ Ἡρώδου τοῦ πατρὸς αὐτοῦ, Matt. ii. 22,—" in the room" or stead " of his father Herod." So ὀφθαλμὸς ἀντὶ ὀφθαλμοῦ, ὀδοὺς ἀντὶ ὀδόντος, Matt. v. 38, is " an eye for an eye, and a tooth for a tooth." And this word also is used in expressing the death of Christ for us. He came δοῦναι τὴν ψυχὴν αὐτοῦ λύτρον ἀντὶ πολλῶν, Matt. xx. 28,—" to give his life a ransom for many;" that is, in their stead to die. So the words are used again, Mark x. 45. And both these notes of a succedaneous substitution are joined together, 1 Tim. ii. 6, Ὁ δοὺς ἑαυτὸν ἀντίλυτρον ὑπὲρ πάντων. And this the Greeks call τῆς ψυχῆς πρίασθαι,—to buy any thing, to purchase or procure any thing, with the price of one's life. So Tigranes in Xenophon, when Cyrus asked him what he would give or do for the liberty of his wife, whom he had taken prisoner, answered, Κἂν τῆς ψυχῆς πριαίμην ὥστε μήποτε λατρεῦσαι ταύτην·—" I will purchase her liberty with my life," or " the price of my soul." Whereon the woman being freed, affirmed afterward, that she considered none in the company, but him who said, ὡς τῆς ψυχῆς ἂν πρίαιτο ὥστε μή με δουλεύειν, " that he would purchase my liberty with his own life," [Cyrop. lib. iii.]

And these things are added on the occasion of the instances mentioned in the Scripture; whence it appears, that this expression of " dying for another" hath no other sense or meaning, but only dying instead of another, undergoing the death that he should undergo, that he might go free. And in this matter of Christ's dying for us, add that he so died for us as that he also died for our sins; that is, either to *bear their punishment* or to *expiate their guilt* (for other sense the words cannot admit); and he that pretends to give any other sense of them than that contended for, which implies the whole of what lies in the doctrine of satisfaction, " erit mihi magnus Apollo," even he who was the author of *all ambiguous oracles of old.*

And this is the common sense of " mori pro alio," and " pati pro alio," or " pro alio discrimen capitis subire;" a *substitution* is still denoted by that expression: which sufficeth us in this whole cause, for we know both into whose room he came, and what they were to suffer. Thus Entellus, killing and sacrificing an ox to Eryx in the stead of Dares, whom he was ready to have slain, when he was taken from him, expresseth himself,—

> " Hanc tibi, Eryx, meliorem animam pro morte Daretis
> Persolvo."—Æn. v. 483.

He offered the ox, a *better sacrifice, in the stead of Dares*, taken from him. So,—

> " Fratrem Pollux alterna morte redemit."—Æn. vi. 121.

And they speak so not only with respect unto death, but wherever any thing of durance or suffering is intended. So the angry master in the comedian:—

> " Verberibus cæsum te in pistrinum, Dave, dedam usque ad necem;
> Ea lege atque omine, ut, si te inde exemerim, ego pro te molam."—
> Ter. And., i. 2, 28.

He threatened his servant, to cast him into prison, to be macerated to death with labour; and that with this engagement, that if he ever let him out he would *grind for* him;—that is, in his stead. Wherefore, without offering violence to the common means of understanding things amongst men, another sense cannot be affixed to these words.

The *nature of the thing* itself will admit of no other exposition than that given unto it; and it hath been manifoldly exemplified among the nations of the world. For suppose a man guilty of any crime, and on the account thereof to be exposed unto danger from God or man, in a way of justice, wrath, or vengeance, and when he is ready to be given up unto suffering according unto his demerit, another should tender himself to die for him, that he might be freed; let an appeal be made to the common reason and understandings of all men, whether the intention of this his dying for another be not, that he substitutes himself in his stead, to undergo what he should have done, however the translation of punishment from one to another may be brought about and asserted; for at present we treat not of the *right*, but of the *fact*, or the thing itself. And to deny this to be the case as to the sufferings of Christ, is, as far as I can understand, to subvert the whole gospel.

Moreover, as was said, this hath been variously exemplified among the nations of the world; whose actings in such cases, because they excellently shadow out the general notion of the death of Christ for others, for sinners, and are appealed unto directly by the apostle to this purpose, Rom. v. 7, 8, I shall in a few instances reflect upon.

Not to insist on the voluntary surrogations of private persons, one into the *room* of another, mutually to undergo dangers and death for one another, as before mentioned, I shall only remember some public transactions, in reference unto communities, in nations, cities, or armies. Nothing is more celebrated amongst the ancients than this, that when they supposed themselves in danger, from the anger and displeasure of their gods, by reason of any guilt or crimes among them, some one person should either devote himself or be devoted by the people, to die for them; and therein to be made, as it were, an expiatory sacrifice. For where sin is the cause, and God is the object respected, the making of satisfaction by undergoing punishment, and expiating of sin by a propitiatory sacrifice, are but various expressions of the same thing. Now, those who so devoted themselves, as was said, to die in the stead of others, or to expiate their sins, and turn away the anger of God they feared, by their death, designed two things in what they did. First, That the *evils* which were impendent on the people, and feared, might fall on themselves, so that the people might go free. Secondly, That all good things which themselves desired, might be conferred on the people. Which things have a notable shadow in them of the great expiatory sacrifice, concerning which we treat, and expound the expressions wherein it is declared. The instance of the Decii is known; of whom the poet,—

> "Plebeiæ Deciorum animæ, plebeia fuerunt
> Nomina; pro totis legionibus Hi tamen, et pro
> Omnibus auxiliis, atque omni plebe Latina,
> Sufficiunt Diis infernis."

The two Decii, father and son, in imminent dangers of the people, devoted themselves, at several times, unto death and destruction. And saith he, "Sufficiunt Diis infernis,"—they satisfied for the whole people; adding the reason whence so it might be:—

> "Pluris enim Decii quam qui servantur ab illis."—Juv., Sat. vii. 254-8.

They were *more to be valued than all that were saved by them.* And the great historian doth excellently describe both the actions and expectations of the one and the other in what they did. The father, when the Roman army, commanded by himself and Titus Manlius, was near a total ruin by the Latins, called for the public priest, and caused him, with the usual solemn ceremonies, to devote him to death for the deliverance and safety of the army; after which, making his requests to his gods, ("dii quorum est potestas nostrorum hostiumque,") "the gods that had power over them and their adversaries," as he supposed, he cast himself into death by the swords of the enemy. "Conspectus ab utrâque acie aliquanto augustior humano visu, sicut cœlo missus piaculum omnis deorum iræ, qui pestem ab suis aversam in hostes ferret;"—"He was looked on by both armies as one more august than a man, as one sent from heaven, to be a piacular sacrifice, to appease the anger of the gods, and to transfer destruction from their own army to the enemies," Liv., Hist. viii. 9. His son, in like manner, in a great and dangerous battle against the Gauls and Samnites, wherein he commanded in chief, devoting himself, as his father had done, added unto the former solemn deprecations:—"Præ se agere sese formidinem ac fugam, cædemque ac cruorem, cœlestium, inferorum iras," lib. x. 28;—"That he carried away before him, from those for whom he devoted himself, 'fear and flight, slaughter and blood, the anger of the celestial and infernal gods.'" And as they did, in this devoting of themselves, design "averruncare malum, deûm iras, lustrare populum, aut exercitum, piaculum fieri," or περίψημα, ἀνάθημα, ἀποκάθαρμα,—"expiare crimina, scelus, reatum," or to remove all evil from others, by taking it on themselves in their stead; so also they thought they might, and intended in what they did, to covenant and contract for the good things they desired. So did these Decii; and so is Menœceus reported to have done, when he devoted himself for the city of Thebes, in danger to be destroyed by the Argives. So Papinius [Statius] introduceth him treating [with] his gods:—

> " Armorum superi, tuque ô qui funere tanto
> Indulges mihi, Phœbe, mori, date gaudia Thebis,
> Quæ pepigi, et toto quæ sanguine prodigus emi."—[Theb. x. 757.]

He reckoned that he had not only repelled all death and danger from Thebes, by his own, but that he had purchased joy, in peace and liberty, for the people.

And where there was none in public calamities that did voluntarily devote themselves, the people were wont to take some obnoxious person, to make him execrable, and to lay on him, according to their superstition, all the wrath of their gods, and so give him up to destruction. Such the apostle alludes unto, Rom. ix. 3; 1 Cor. iv. 9, 13. So the Massilians were wont to expiate their city by taking a person devoted, imprecating on his head all the evil that the city was obnoxious unto, casting him into the sea with these words, Περίψημα ἡμῶν γένου·—" Be thou our expiatory sacrifice." To which purpose were the solemn words that many used in their expiatory sacrifices, as Herodotus [lib. ii. 39] testifieth of the Egyptians, bringing their offerings. Saith he, Καταρέονται δὲ, τάδε λέγοντες, τῇσι κεφαλῇσιν· εἴ τι μέλλοι ἢ σφισι τοῖσι θύουσι, ἢ Αἰγύπτῳ τῇ συναπάσῃ κακὸν γενέσθαι ἐς κεφαλὴν ταύτην τραπέσθαι·—" They laid these imprecations on their heads, that if any evil were happening towards the sacrificer, or all Egypt, let it be all turned and laid on this devoted head."

And the persons whom they thus dealt withal, and made *execrate*, were commonly of the vilest of the people, or such as had rendered themselves detestable by their own crimes; whence was the complaint of the mother of Menœceus upon her son's devoting himself:—

> " Lustralemne feris, ego te puer inclyte Thebis,
> Devotumque caput, vilis seu mater alebam?"—
>   [Statius, Theb. x. 788, 789.]

I have recounted these instances to evince the common intention, sense, and understanding of that expression, of one dying for another, and to manifest by examples what is the sense of mankind about any one's being devoted and substituted in the room of others, to deliver them from death and danger; the consideration whereof, added to the constant use of the words mentioned in the Scripture, is sufficient to found and confirm this conclusion:—

"That whereas it is frequently affirmed in the Scripture, that 'Christ died for us, and for our sins,' etc., to deny that he died and suffered in our stead, undergoing the death whereunto we were obnoxious, and the punishment due to our sins, is,—if we respect in what we say or believe the constant use of those words in the Scripture, the nature of the thing itself concerning which they are used, the uncontrolled use of that expression in all sorts of writers in expressing the same thing, with the instances and examples of its meaning and intention among the nations of the world,—to deny that he died for us at all."

Neither will his *dying for our good* or advantage only, in what way or sense soever, answer or make good or true the assertion of his dying for us and our sins. And this is evident in the death of the apostles and martyrs. They all died for our good; our advantage and benefit was one end of their sufferings, in the will and appointment of God: and yet it cannot be said that they died *for us, or our sins.*

And if Christ died only for our good, though in a more effectual manner than they did, yet this altereth not the kind of his dying for us; nor can he thence be said, properly, according to the only due sense of that expression, so to do.

I shall, in this brief and hasty discourse, add only one consideration more about the death of Christ, to confirm the truth pleaded for; and that is, that he is said, in dying for sinners, " to bear their sins." Isa. liii. 11, " He shall bear their iniquities;" verse 12, " He bare the sin of many;" explained, verse 5, " He was wounded for our transgressions, he was bruised for our iniquities; the chastisement of our peace was upon him." 1 Pet. ii. 24, " Who his own self bare our sins in his own body on the tree," etc.

This expression is purely sacred. It occurreth not directly in other authors, though the sense of it in other words do frequently. They call it " luere peccata;" that is, " delictorum supplicium ferre,"—" to bear the punishment of sins." The meaning, therefore, of this phrase of speech is to be taken from the Scripture alone, and principally from the Old Testament, where it is originally used; and from whence it is transferred into the New Testament, in the same sense, and no other. Let us consider some of the places:—

Isa. liii. 11, עֲוֹנֹתָם הוּא יִסְבֹּל. The same word, סָבַל, is used verse 4, וּמַכְאֹבֵינוּ סְבָלָם,—" And our griefs, he hath borne them." The word signifies, properly, to bear a weight or a burden, as a man bears it on his shoulders,—" bajulo, porto." And it is never used with respect unto sin, but openly and plainly it signifies the undergoing of the punishment due unto it. So it occurs directly to our purpose, Lam. v. 7, אֲבֹתֵינוּ חָטְאוּ אֵינָם אֲנַחְנוּ עֲוֹנֹתֵיהֶם סָבָלְנוּ—" Our fathers have sinned, and are not; and we have borne their iniquities;" the punishment due to their sins. And why a new sense should be forged for these words when they are spoken concerning Christ, who can give a just reason?

Again; נָשָׂא is used to the same purpose, וְהוּא חֵטְא־רַבִּים נָשָׂא, Isa. liii.

12, " And he bare the sin of many." נָשָׂא is often used with respect unto sin; sometimes with reference unto God's actings about it, and sometimes with reference unto men's concerns in it. In the first way, or when it denotes an act of God, it signifies to lift up, to take away or pardon sin; and leaves the word עָוֹן, wherewith it is joined under its first signification, of iniquity, or the guilt of sin, with respect unto punishment ensuing as its consequent; for God pardoning the guilt of sin, the removal of the punishment doth necessarily ensue, guilt containing an obligation unto punishment. In the latter way, as it respects men or sinners, it constantly denotes the bearing of the punishment of sin, and gives that sense unto עָוֹן, with respect unto the guilt of sin as its cause. And hence ariseth the ambiguity of these words of Cain, Gen. iv. 13, גָּדוֹל עֲוֹנִי מִנְּשׂוֹא. If נָשָׂא denotes an act of God, if the words be spoken with reference, in the first place, to any acting of his towards Cain, עָוֹן retains the sense of iniquity, and the words are rightly rendered, " My sin is greater than to be forgiven." If it respect Cain himself firstly, עָוֹן assumes the signification of punishment, and the words are to be rendered, " My punishment is greater than I can bear," or " is to be borne by me."

This, I say, is the constant sense of this expression, nor can any instance to the contrary be produced. Some may be mentioned in the confirmation of it. Numb. xiv. 33, " Your children shall wander in the wilderness forty years," וְנָשְׂאוּ אֶת־זְנוּתֵיכֶם " and shall bear your whoredoms." Verse 34, תִּשְׂאוּ אֶת־עֲוֹנֹתֵיכֶם אַרְבָּעִים שָׁנָה,—" Ye shall bear your iniquities forty years;" that is, the punishment due to your whoredoms and iniquities, according to God's providential dealings with them at that time. Lev. xix. 8, " He that eateth it עֲוֹנוֹ יִשָּׂא shall bear his iniquity." How? נִכְרְתָה הַנֶּפֶשׁ הַהִוא,—" That soul shall be cut off." To be cut off for sin, by the punishment of it, and for its guilt, is to bear iniquity. So chap. xx. 16–18, for a man to bear his iniquity, and to be killed, slain, or put to death for it, are the same.

Ezek. xviii. 20, הַנֶּפֶשׁ הַחֹטֵאת הִיא תָמוּת בֵּן לֹא־יִשָּׂא בַּעֲוֹן הָאָב,—" The soul that sinneth, it shall die. The son shall not bear the sin of the father." To bear sin, and to die for sin, are the same. More instances might be added, all uniformly speaking the same sense of the words.

And as this sense is sufficiently, indeed invincibly, established by the invariable use of that expression in the Scripture so the manner whereby it is affirmed that the Lord Christ bare our iniquities, sets it absolutely free from all danger by opposition. For he bare our iniquities when וַיהוָה הִפְגִּיעַ בּוֹ אֵת עֲוֹן כֻּלָּנוּ,—" the LORD made to meet on him, or laid on him, the iniquity of us all," Isa. liii. 6; which words

the LXX. render, Καὶ Κύριος παρέδωκεν αὐτὸν ταῖς ἁμαρτίαις ἡμῶν·—
"The LORD gave him up, or delivered him unto our sins;" that is, to
be punished for them, for other sense the words can have none. "He
made him sin for us," 2 Cor. v. 21. So "he bare our sins," Isa. liii. 12.
How? "In his own body on the tree," 1 Pet. ii. 24; that when he
was, and in his being stricken, smitten, afflicted, wounded, bruised,
slain, so was the chastisement of our peace upon him.

Wherefore, to deny that the Lord Christ, in his death and suffering for us, underwent the punishment due to our sins, what we had
deserved, that we might be delivered, as it everts the great foundation of the gospel, so, by an open perverting of the plain words of the
Scripture, because not suited in their sense and importance to the
vain imaginations of men, it gives no small countenance to infidelity
and atheism.

END OF VOL II.

CONTENTS OF THE SIXTEEN VOLUMES

DIVISION 1: DOCTRINAL

Vol. 1   Life of Owen, by Andrew Thomson.
On the Person of Christ.
Meditations and Discourses on the Glory of Christ.
Meditations and Discourses on the Glory of Christ applied to
Sinners and Saints.
Two Short Catechisms.

Vol. 2   On Communion with God.
Vindication of the Preceding Discourse.
Vindication of the Doctrine of the Trinity.

Vol. 3   Discourse on the Holy Spirit: His Name, Nature, Personality,
Dispensation, Operations, and Effect – His Work in the Old
and New Creation explained, and the Doctrines Vindicated.
The Nature and Necessity of Gospel Holiness; the difference
between Grace and Morality, or a Spiritual Life unto God in
Evangelical Obedience, and a course of Moral Virtues, stated
and declared.

Vol. 4   The Reason of Faith.
Causes, Ways, and Means, of understanding the Mind of God,
as revealed in His Word, with assurance therein. And a
declaration of the perspicuity of the Scriptures, with the external
means of the interpretation of them.
On the Work of the Holy Spirit in Prayer; with a brief inquiry
into the nature and use of Mental Prayer and forms.
Of the Holy Spirit and His Work, as a Comforter and as the
Author of Spiritual Gifts.

Vol. 5   The Doctrine of Justification by Faith.
Evidences of the Faith of God's Elect.

DIVISION 2: PRACTICAL

Vol. 6   On the Mortification of Sin.
On Temptation.
On Indwelling Sin in Believers.
Exposition of Psalm 130.

SCIENCE IN ARCHAEOLOGY

SCIENCE
IN ARCHAEOLOGY

A Survey of Progress and Research

REVISED AND ENLARGED EDITION

Edited by
DON BROTHWELL
and ERIC HIGGS

With a Foreword by
GRAHAME CLARK

142 photographs,
139 line drawings
and 74 tables

PRAEGER PUBLISHERS
New York · Washington

BOOKS THAT MATTER

Published in the United States of America in 1970
by Praeger Publishers, Inc.
111 Fourth Avenue, New York, N.Y. 10003
Second edition revised and enlarged 1969
First published in the United States in 1963 by Basic Books, Inc.
© in London, England, by Thames and Hudson Ltd in 1963, 1969
All rights reserved
Library of Congress Catalog Card Number: 76-92580
Printed in Great Britain

Contents

LIST OF PLATES   10

LIST OF TEXT FIGURES   13

PREFACE TO THE SECOND EDITION   18

FOREWORD   19
     GRAHAME CLARK, F.B.A., *Disney Professor of Archaeology, University of Cambridge*

Scientific Studies in Archaeology   23
     DON BROTHWELL and ERIC HIGGS

SECTION I: DATING

1   Analytical Methods of Dating Bones   35
     KENNETH P. OAKLEY, F.B.A., *British Museum (Natural History), London*

2   Radiocarbon Dating   46
     E. H. WILLIS, *Director of Research, Isotypes Inc., Westwood, New Jersey*

3   Quaternary Dating by the Fission Track Technique   58
     ROBERT L. FLEISCHER, P. BURFORD PRICE and ROBERT M. WALKER, *General Electric Research and Development Centre, Schenactady, New York*

4   Obsidian Dating   62
     IRVING FRIEDMAN, ROBERT L. SMITH, *U.S. Geological Survey*
     DONOVAN CLARK, *Smithsonian Institution, Washington, D.C.*

5   Archaeomagnetism   76
     R. M. COOK, *Laurence Professor of Classical Archaeology, University of Cambridge*

6   The Potassium-Argon Dating of Upper Tertiary and Pleistocene Deposits   88
     W. GENTNER, *Director, Max-Planck Institute for Nuclear Physics, Heidelberg*
     H. J. LIPPOLT, *Max-Planck Institute for Nuclear Physics, Heidelberg*

7   Dating by the Potassium-Argon Method—Some Advances in Technique   101
     J. A. MILLER, *Department of Geodesy and Geophysics, University of Cambridge*

8   Dating Pottery by Thermoluminescence   106
     E. T. HALL, *Director, Research Laboratory for Archaeology and the History of Art, Oxford*

SECTION II: ENVIRONMENT

Climate

9   The Significance of Deep-Sea Cores   109
     CESARE EMILIANI, *Marine Laboratory, Institute of Marine Science, University of Miami*

Soils

10　Soil Silhouettes　　　　　　　　　　　　　　　　　　　　　　　118
　　L. BIEK, *Ancient Monuments Laboratory, Ministry of Public Building and Works,*
　　London

11　Soil, Stratification and Environment　　　　　　　　　　　　　　120
　　I. W. CORNWALL, *Institute of Archaeology, University of London*

12　Fluvial Geology　　　　　　　　　　　　　　　　　　　　　　　135
　　CLAUDIO VITA-FINZI, *Department of Geography, University College, London*

13　Cave Sediments and Prehistory　　　　　　　　　　　　　　　　151
　　ELISABETH SCHMID, *Professor of Early Prehistory and Director of the Laboratory for*
　　Prehistory, Faculty of Philosophy and Natural Sciences, University of Basle

Plants

14　Pollen Analysis　　　　　　　　　　　　　　　　　　　　　　　167
　　G. W. DIMBLEBY, *Professor of Environmental Archaeology, Institute of Archaeology,*
　　University of London

15　Wood and Charcoal in Archaeology　　　　　　　　　　　　　　178
　　A. CECILIA WESTERN, *Department of Antiquities, Ashmolean Museum, Oxford*

16　The Condition of 'Wood' from Archaeological Sites　　　　　　　188
　　J. W. LEVY, *Botany Department, Imperial College, London*

17　Dendrochronology　　　　　　　　　　　　　　　　　　　　　191
　　BRYANT BANNISTER, *Laboratory of Tree-Ring Research, University of Arizona,*
　　Tucson

18　Palaeo-Ethnobotany　　　　　　　　　　　　　　　　　　　　206
　　HANS HELBAEK, *National Museum, Copenhagen*

19　Palaeo-Ethnobotany in America　　　　　　　　　　　　　　　215
　　RICHARD A. YARNELL, *Department of Sociology and Anthropology, Emory*
　　University, Atlanta, Georgia

20　The Domestication of Yams: a Multi-disciplinary Problem　　　　229
　　JOHN ALEXANDER, *Staff Tutor in Archaeology, Department of Extra-mural*
　　Studies, University of London

21　Diet as revealed by Coprolites　　　　　　　　　　　　　　　　235
　　E. O. CALLEN, *Department of Entomology and Plant Pathology, Macdonald College,*
　　McGill University, Quebec

22　The Anthropology of Prehistoric Great Basin Human Coprolites　244
　　ROBERT F. HEIZER, *Department of Anthropology, University of California, Los*
　　Angeles

Animals

23　Pleistocene Mammals and the Origin of Species　　　　　　　　251
　　BJÖRN KURTÉN, *Museum of Zoology, University of Helsinki*

24　The Science and History of Domestic Animals　　　　　　　　　257
　　WOLF HERRE, *Director, Institute for Domestic Animal Research, Professor of the*
　　Anatomy and Physiology of Domestic Animals and of Zoology, University of Kiel

25 Social Organization as a Population Regulator   273
    V. C. WYNNE-EDWARDS, *Regius Professor of Natural History, University of Aberdeen*

26 The Ageing of Domestic Animals   283
    I. A. SILVER, *Sub-Department of Veterinary Anatomy, University of Cambridge*

27 The Origins of the Dog   303
    JULIET CLUTTON-BROCK, *Department of Zoology, British Museum (Natural History), London*

28 The Palaeopathology of Pleistocene and More Recent Mammals   310
    DON BROTHWELL

29 An Assessment of a Prehistoric Technique of Bovine Husbandry   315
    C. F. W. HIGHAM, *Professor of Anthropology, University of Otago*
    M. A. MESSAGE, *Lecturer in Anatomy, University of Cambridge*

30 Osteological Differences Between Sheep (*Ovis aries Linné*) and Goats (*Capra hircus Linné*)   331
    J. BOESSNECK, *Director, Institute for Palaeoanatomy and Research into Domestication and the History of Veterinary Medicine, University of Munich*

31 Bird Remains in Archaeology   359
    ELLIOT W. DAWSON, *New Zealand Oceanographic Institute, Department of Scientific and Industrial Research, Wellington*

32 Remains of Fishes and Other Aquatic Animals   376
    M. L. RYDER, *Agricultural Research Council, Animal Breeding Research Organization, Edinburgh 9*

33 Non-Marine Mollusca and Archaeology   395
    B. W. SPARKS, *Department of Geography, University of Cambridge*

34 Marine Mollusca in Archaeology   407
    N. J. SHACKLETON, *Sub-Department of Quaternary Research, University of Cambridge*

35 Molluscs as Food Remains in Archaeological Sites   415
    CLEMENT E. MEIGHAN, *Professor of Anthropology, University of California, Los Angeles*

36 Molluscs from Human Habitation Sites and the Problem of Ethnological Interpretation   423
    E. J. BIGGS, *Department of Zoology, British Museum (Natural History), London*

SECTION III: MAN

37 Sex Determination in Earlier Man   429
    SANTIAGO GENOVÉS, *Historical Institute, University of Mexico*

38 Estimation of Age and Mortality   440
    SANTIAGO GENOVÉS

39 Stature in Earlier Races of Mankind   453
    L. H. WELLS, *Professor of Anatomy, University of Capetown*

40 Cremations 468
NILS-GUSTAF GEJVALL, *Osteological Research Laboratory, Royal Castle, Ulriksdal, Solna*

41 The Palaeopathology of Human Skeletal Remains 480
MARCUS S. GOLDSTEIN, *Department of Health, Education and Welfare, Washington, D.C.*

42 The Study of Mummified and Dried Human Tissues 490
A. T. SANDISON, *Department of Pathology, University of Glasgow*

43 Buried Bone 503
J. D. GARLICK, *Faculty of Archaeology and Anthropology, University of Cambridge*

SECTION IV: MICROSCOPY AND RADIOGRAPHY

44 The Application of X-rays to the Study of Archaeological Materials 513
DON BROTHWELL, THEYA MOLLESON, RALPH HARCOURT, *British Museum (Natural History), London,* and P. H. K. GRAY, *Consultant Radiologist, S.W. Metropolitan R.H.B. (Guildford and Godalming Group of Hospitals)*

45 Microscopy and Prehistoric Bone 526
ANTONIO ASCENZI, *Professor of Morbid Anatomy, University of Pisa; Professor of Human Palaentology, University of Rome*

46 Remains Derived from Skin 539
M. L. RYDER, *Agricultural Research Council, Animal Breeding Research Organization, Edinburgh 9*

47 Microscopic Studies of Ancient Metals 555
F. C. THOMPSON, *Emeritus Professor of Metallurgy, University of Manchester*

48 The Study of Archaeological Materials by Means of the Scanning Electron Microscope: An Important New Field 564
DON BROTHWELL, *British Museum (Natural History), London*

SECTION V: ARTIFACTS

49 Artifacts 567
L. BIEK, *Ancient Monuments Laboratory, Ministry of Public Buildings and Works, London*

50 Petrological Examination 571
F. W. SHOTTON, F.R.S., *Professor of Geology, University of Birmingham*

51 Obsidian Analysis and the Obsidian Trade 578
J. R. CANN, *Department of Mineralogy, British Museum (Natural History), London*
J. E. DIXON, *Department of Mineralogy and Petrology, University of Cambridge*
COLIN RENFREW, *Department of Ancient History, University of Sheffield*

52 Some Aspects of Ceramic Technology 592
FREDERICK R. MATSON, *Professor of Archaeology, Pennsylvania State University*

53 Optical Emission Spectroscopy and the Study of Metallurgy in the European
Bronze Age 603
DENNIS BRITTON, *Pitt Rivers Museum, University of Oxford*
EVA E. RICHARDS, *Research Laboratory for Archaeology and the History of Art,
Oxford*

54 The Analytical Study of Glass in Archaeology 614
RAY W. SMITH, *International Committee on Ancient Glass, Oak Hill, Dublin, New
Hampshire*

55 Fibres of Archaeological Interest: Their Examination and Identification 624
H. M. APPLEYARD and A. B. WILDMAN, *Wool Industries Research Assoc., Leeds*

SECTION VI: STATISTICS

56 Archaeology and Statistics 635
DONALD J. TUGBY, *Department of Anthropology and Sociology, University of
Queensland*

57 Classification by Computer 649
F. R. HODSON, *Department of Prehistoric European Archaeology, Institute of
Archaeology, University of London*

58 Evolution at the Population Level: a Statistical Approach 661
BJÖRN KURTÉN, *Museum of Zoology, University of Helsinki*

59 Stones, Pots and People 669
DON BROTHWELL, *British Museum (Natural History), London*

SECTION VII: PROSPECTING

60 Magnetic Location 681
MARTIN AITKEN, *Research Laboratory for Archaeology and the History of Art,
Oxford*

61 Resistivity Surveying 695
ANTHONY CLARK, *Ancient Monuments Laboratory, Ministry of Public Buildings
and Works, London*

INDEX OF SITES 709

GENERAL INDEX 712

List of Plates

I Collagen fibres in fossil ivory from Siberia. Amino-acids in hydro-lysate from ulna of woolly rhinoceros from Lloyd's site, City of London *between pages* 64–5

II Femur and skull of Galley Hill Man. The Swanscombe skull. Molars of man, orang-utan and *Gigantopithecus* ,,

III The Radiocarbon Dating Laboratory, Cambridge. Punched card published by Radiocarbon Dates Inc. ,,

IV, V Etched fossil tracks in natural materials ,,

VI Hydration layers on obsidian artifacts under ordinary and crossed polarized lights, and on a reworked artifact ,,

VII Silhouette skeleton at Elp, Drenthe, Netherlands ,,

VIII Silhouette skeleton at Staines, Middlesex ,,

IX Alluvial stratification 160–61

X Section of peat, Cook's Study, and section of a topsoil mound, Bickley Moor Barrow ,,

XI Transverse sections of oak, ash, willow and pine 176–7

XII Types of tree-ring series ,,

XIII Impression and remains of ancient grains and seeds from Iraq and from Denmark 216–17

XIV Wild food items from Tonto National Monument, Arizona. Sunflower remains from Newt Kash Hollow Shelter, Kentucky ,,

XV Salts Cave, Kentucky ,,

XVI Palatal views of skulls of *Canis lupus lupus*. Dog jaws from Bronze Age Chios, Greece ,,

XVII Otoliths (ear-stones) from the tiger flathead 400–401

XVIII Shells from Near Eastern sites ,,

XIX Samples of cremated bone from prehistoric and recent cremations ,,

XX, XXI Specimens of mummified human tissue ,,

XXII   Mandible and humerus from an ewe. Femur from an Iron Age
        dog   *between pages* 400–401

XXIII   Samples of decalcified bone from mandibles Circeo IIa and IIIb   „

XXIV   Ancient specimens of wool and of follicle groups   „

XXV, XXVI   Structures of different metals and alloys at various stages of
            working   544–5

XXVII   Stereoscan microscope enlargements   „

XXVIII–XXXI   X-ray examination of artifacts   „

XXXII   Sections of axe-hammer, Herefordshire, and pictrite outcrop,
        Montgomeryshire, and of metamorphosed laterite, Co. Antrim   „

XXXIII Obsidians seen in both direct and transmitted light   592–3

XXXIV   Obsidians from various sources   „

XXXV   Scale for estimating amount of crushed shell in American
        Indian pottery, Rates of oxidation during firing of sandy and
        fine Tigris River clays   608–9

XXXVI   Axes of copper and of bronze from Britain and Ireland.
        Spectrum of a bronze in the near ultra-violet region   „

XXXVII Pneumatic tubes at Brookhaven reactor, Connecticut. Laminar
        structure of a small piece of weathering crust on glass   632–3

XXXVIII, XXXIX   Ancient specimens of fibres   „

XL   Taking readings with the proton magnetometer   „

Illustrations in the Text

Fig. 1	Summary of the major dating methods	*page* 24
2	Major cemeteries excavated in England for skeletal material	29
3	Fluctuation of the atmospheric radiocarbon content	48
4	Fission track ages compared with 'known' dates by other methods	59
5	Uranium concentration needed for dating	60
6	Thickness of obsidian hydration layer plotted against time	64
7	Variation in obsidian hydration rate in different climatic regions	66
8	Thickness of obsidian hydration layers at temperate sites	72
9	Thickness of obsidian hydration layer at Chorrera, Ecuador	73
10	Obsidian dating curve	74
11	Secular variation of the direction of the earth's magnetic field	83
12	Use of magnetic direction to determine the origin of potsherds	85
13	Decay scheme of K^{40}	89
14	An apparatus for measuring small amounts of argon	91
15	Ratio of the Rb–Sr age to the K–A age for a number of micas	93
16	Loss of radiogenic argon as a function of atmospheric argon loss	95
17	Isotopic temperatures from an equatorial Atlantic core	111
18	Isotopic temperatures from an equatorial Pacific core	112
19	Isotopic temperatures from Atlantic and Caribbean cores	113
20	Generalized chronology for the glacial Pleistocene	114
21	Gullying resulting in increased drainage density	136
22	Dams in Wadi Lebda, Libya	143
23	Development stages of alluvial formations in the Jordan trough	145
24	Concept of stream order	146
25	Source and distribution of different cave sediments	154
26, 27	The Alps and Jura: altitudes of caves, and of snow and forest lines since the Riss–Wurm interglacial	164, 165
28	Postglacial pollen sequence in Jutland	169
29	Pollen analysis of Cook's Study	174

Fig. 30 Pollen analysis of Portesham   *page* 175

31 Pollen analysis of Bickley Moor Barrow   176

32 Sections and main features of wood   179

33 Tree-ring chronology building   194

34 Comparison of skeleton plots of different tree-ring series   197

35 Comparison of measured curves of different tree-ring series   198

36 Grasses and seed from the stomach of Grauballe Man   209

37 Distribution of prehistoric archaeological corn in the Mid-West   220

38 Bone formation and fracture   284

39 Incisors of horse   292

40 Change of angle of profile of horse's incisors   294

41 'Bishoping' of horse's teeth   295

42 Relationship between length of upper carnassial and combined lengths of first
and second molars in dogs, wolves, jackals and the Natufian canids   305

43 Scatter diagram of Troldebjerg bovine metacarpals   319

44 Scatter diagram of Troldebjerg bovine radii   320

45 Skulls of Capra hircus ♀ and Ovis aries ♀   332

46 Occipital, nuchal plane   333

47 Atlas, dorsal aspect   334

48 Atlas, dorsal aspect   335

49 Horn development in the epistropheus   336

50 Epistropheus, side view   336

51, 52 Scapula, lateral and medial aspects   338

53 Humerus, dorsal aspect   339

54 Humerus, distal end   340

55 Humerus, distal end, lateral aspect   341

56 Ossa antebrachii, dorsal proximal end   342

57 Ossa antebrachii, distal aspect   343

58 Olecranon, proximal aspect   343

59 Pelvis, ventral aspect   344, 345

60 Pelvis, ventral aspect   346, 347

61, 62 Femur, proximal end, dorsal and lateral aspect   349

Fig. 63   Tibia, proximal end   *page* 350

64–68   Aspects of the talus   351

69   Calcaneus, lateral aspect   352

70   Calcaneus, dorsal aspect   353

71   Metapodia distal epiphysis   354

72, 73   Metacarpus distal aspect   355

74, 75   Phalanges primae anterior   356

76, 77   Phalanges secundae anterior   357

78, 79   Phalanges tertiae   358

80   External features of cartilaginous and bony fishes   377

81   Spines, scales, fins and vertebrae of various fishes   380

82   Skull of bony fish (salmon)   382

83   Skeleton of bony fish (perch)   383

84   Cold Quaternary mollusca   396

85, 86   Interglacial mollusca   398, 401

87   Relationship between known and predicted skeletal ages   450

88   Morphological changes in humerus due to ageing   451

89   Diagram of measurements of cremated bone   475

90   Pathological skeletal remains from different periods   482

91   Pathological cranial remains from different periods   484

92   Bone changes in leprosy   485

93   Examples of tumour in earlier man   487

94   Kjeldahl nitrogen content of animal bones   507

95   Birefringence curves, highly calcified normal bone and bone deprived of ossein   529

96   Refractive index of a series of fossil bones   531

97   Vertical section of skin   541

98   Section of primary wool follicle   543

99   Section of follicle group from domestic sheep   546

100   Double coat of wild sheep   546

101   Follicle groups from domestic goat and wild and domestic sheep   547

102   Follicle groups from the Dead Sea Scrolls   547

103   Microscope with vertical illuminator   557

104   Refractive index range of obsidians of known trace element   581

Fig. 105   Known obsidian sources of the world   *page* 584–5

106   Barium and zirconium content of Old World obsidians   587

107   Obsidian trade in the Near East   589

108   Layout of a large quartz spectrograph   605

109   Significant elements in British Bronze Age artifacts   612

110   Concentration of metal oxides in types of western ancient glass   615

111   Types of medulla   627

112   Some cuticular scale patterns   628

113, 114   Matrices showing archaeological units and situations   638

115   Analytical possibilities in three dimensions   639

116   La Tène bronze fibulae from Münsingen   650

117   Intuitive classification of thirty fibulae   652

118   Intuitive and computed classification of thirty fibulae   653

119   Average-link Cluster Analysis of seventy La Tène brooches   656–7

120, 121   'Best' two- and one-dimensional configuration of sixteen Mousterian
           assemblages   659

122   Left upper and lower cheek teeth of spotted hyena   662

123   Lengths of second and third lower premolars in specimens of cave hyena   664

124   Dimensions of third upper premolar in specimens of cave hyena   665

125   Nineteenth- and twentieth-century English grave-stone types distribution 674

126   Mean volume of Indian cooking jars, bowls and ladles   676

127   Log total floor space relative to log mean population   678

128   Sample readings from a proton magnetometer survey (at Water Newton)   683

129   Acquisition of thermoremanent magnetism   683

130   Magnetism of some archaeological materials   685

131   Magnetic anomalies from kilns   687

132   Proton magnetometer readings   688

133   Proton gradiometer readings   689

134   Flux gate gradiometer readings   689

135   Magnetic anomalies from pit and from iron   693

136   The Wenner four-probe arrangement   697

137   Distortion of current paths by high resistance feature   697

138   The Martin-Clark Resistivity Meter   699

139   Location of wall bastions at Mildenhall-Cunetio   705

PREFACE TO THE
SECOND EDITION

JUDGING FROM THE CIRCULATION and encouraging reviews of the first edition of this volume, it has clearly proved of some use to a range of people—both to other 'specialists' as well as to the general archaeologist wishing to become more familiar with some of the subjects covered.

Because the position as regards scientific studies is not the same as it was six years ago, and in view of the willingness on the part of the publishers to have a second edition, we have attempted this further selection of essays. In so doing, we have had to emerge through a complex of questions and problems related to the production of a second volume of this type. New studies have appeared, and had to be represented. Indeed, the application of statistical methods to archaeology is becoming such an important matter for consideration, that we have considered the subject worthy of an entirely new section. Scientific work has increased at different rates in different fields, and books not review studies are really the only way to cope with some of the growing mass of data. For instance, Leo Biek has drawn attention to the importance of microscopy in his *Archaeology and the Microscope* (1963), and Geoffrey Dimbleby has very usefully surveyed *Plants and Archaeology* (1967). Similarly, a short survey of palaeopathology could no longer hope to abbreviate the growing work in this field (as shown by the recent studies in: S. Jarcho (ed.), *Palaeopathology* (1967); and D. R. Brothwell and A. T. Sandison (eds), *Diseases in Antiquity* (1967).

Our task has been considerably complicated by the need, not only to revise previous texts and assemble new work, but to keep the size of the work and its cost within realistic limits. Our special concern in this new edition has been not only to continue to show the breadth of scientific work in archaeology, but also to emphasize new and expanding fields.

Editors are not the nicest of people to know and, in the hope that it will be some slight consolation, we should like to thank sincerely all the contributors to both editions, for their patience as well as their excellent co-operation.

FOREWORD

GRAHAME CLARK

IN HIS MODE OF WORK and in his general approach the archaeologist resembles in several significant respects the detective. Like the disciples of Sherlock Holmes he seeks to recover the activities of men in past time from clues which compensate for their incomplete and often vestigial character by abundance and diversity. Most of this evidence is necessarily circumstantial—it can only be made to speak by bringing upon it the resources of natural science; and the more effectively these can be harnessed the more complete the information likely to be won from traces, which in themselves may appear to the layman to be almost as slight as the bloodstains and finger-prints used by skilled detectives to reconstruct crimes. The correct interpretation of the data wrung by scientific means from material that may at first sight appear unpromising still depends on the genius, perspicacity and breadth of sympathy of the investigator; but the range of information on which his conclusions are based will be limited by the technical means at his disposal. What the archaeologist is able to learn about the past depends to a great extent on the completeness and discrimination with which he avails himself of the resources being made available on an ever more generous scale by his colleagues in a growing range of scientific disciplines.

It is a prime object of this book to provide a systematic conspectus of the bearing of the natural sciences on archaeological investigation. The book is addressed not merely to students of archaeology and of the various branches of natural science, but to all those who follow with growing fascination the unfolding of new and ever-widening perspectives of human history. It aims to show precisely how the different branches and techniques of natural science, many of them quite recently developed, are able to make their own peculiar contributions to our understanding of the past, allowing us to view the achievements of our forebears in altogether greater depth and detail than was possible only a few years ago.

It is logical for such a book to open with the scientific methods and techniques concerned with chronology, since without an ordered frame of reference the reconstruction of human history can hardly begin. Although both are concerned with past events, the archaeologist is as a rule concerned with a much greater depth in time. It is true that archaeology is capable of throwing important light on quite recent periods of history even in highly literate societies, particularly in spheres which for one reason or another have not been adequately recorded in writing; but the fact remains that many of the most important and exciting discoveries made by archaeologists relate to the vast and

in many respects decisive phases of human history entirely or almost entirely unillumina-
ted by the written word. Although this does not alter in any fundamental way the
essential process of detection, it does affect the emphasis placed on chronology and for
the remoter periods of prehistory in particular it implies the deployment of numerous
scientific techniques, some of them only recently brought into use or still in process of
development.

Like all other forms of life, man exists in a physical environment and we have to take
full account of this if we are to understand how he lived. This is very far from saying
that human life even at a material level can be explained in terms of external circumstances: environment certainly does not determine, but it does impose limits to the
possibilities open to people at any particular stage of culture; and by the same token the
stage of cultural development can itself be measured, at least in economic terms, by the
use made of the environment. In studying societies that flourished long ago the archaeologist—and more particularly the prehistoric archaeologist—has to consider the ecological conditions that prevailed at the relevant time and place. He can only do so by the
help of scientific colleagues technically equipped on the one hand to reconstitute the
climate and soil that together form the habitat and on the other to recover vegetation
and animals that constitute the biome and provide man in the most literal sense with the
basis of his subsistence.

Since the archaeologist, like the criminal detective with whom we have compared
him, is concerned with human activities, it follows that his interest centres more on man
and his culture than on his environment. He wants to know as much as he can about the
biological aspects of men, as individuals and as populations, and to obtain this he turns
to experts in various branches of human anatomy and physiology. The knowledge to be
won by investigating the physical remains of early man far transcends the biological
level, important though this undoubtedly is: in sometimes unexpected ways it throws
light on economic, social and even spiritual aspects of life. This only goes to show how
important it is to subject human burials—still after all among the most abundant finds
made by the archaeologist—to the scrutiny of those best equipped to extract the fullest
information from them.

When all is said, the archaeologist is primarily and specifically concerned with artifacts—the structures, tools, weapons, utensils, ornaments and gear that form his traditional stock-in-trade and provide him with his own insight into the life of earlier days.
All too commonly these have been studied from a merely morphological point of view,
as a means of distinguishing one culture from another and successive stages of development within each. Such methods of analysis, proper to art history, while sure of a place
in the archaeologist's armoury, are no longer his principal weapon even in the most
backward areas. Today the emphasis falls more on the effort to understand how the
various peoples of antiquity in fact lived and artifacts are being studied more and more
as sources of information about such broad topics as economy, technology, warfare,
settlement, social organization and religion. The effect of this shift of emphasis has once
more been to draw archaeology and the natural sciences closer together: whereas stylistic
analysis requires no more than intuitive appreciation, it requires a wide range of more or

less highly specialized scientific techniques and procedures to elicit full information about such things as the precise character and sources of raw materials, the techniques used to convert these into artifacts and the uses to which finished objects were put.

✓The growing involvement of archaeologists with colleagues in a wide range of sciences, whether in relation to dating, environment, man or material culture, does more than complicate their task of liaison: it is subtly changing their whole outlook. This can be illustrated in two ways, each exemplified in this book. First, there is a growing tendency to supplement qualitative by quantitative assessment and measurement. Secondly, and in some ways more fundamentally, there is a notable change of attitude towards the process of discovery on which archaeologists depend for their basic clues. Modern archaeologists have taken on something of the questing spirit of science: they no longer dig merely to accumulate data but to solve problems. For this reason they are not content to wait on accidental discoveries or even to dig into monuments merely because they happen to be visible: instead they strive to recover the precise evidence they need wherever this may exist. For this as well as for more prosaic reasons, archaeologists are eagerly availing themselves of new techniques of detection, techniques which have commonly been brought to an advanced stage of development in the course of prospecting for oil or for military purposes. As archaeologists learn to share in the great adventure of purposive research, they are coming to appreciate proton magnetometer and resistivity surveys not merely as useful accessories but as tools of fundamental importance.

To sum up, the archaeologist, despite all his triumphs, remains almost at the beginning of his task: immense fields of knowledge remain to be opened up, not merely in remote parts of the world, but even in the lands where archaeology passed through its initial primitive stages of development; and in gaining the deeper insights which only fresh data will make possible, he depends increasingly on harnessing the resources of modern science and technology. By drawing attention to some of the scientific methods and procedures now available to archaeology, the editors and authors of this book point the way to further progress in unfolding the common past of mankind.

Science, like the course of civilization itself, advances at an accelerating pace. So also does the application of science to the task of unfolding the unwritten history of man's changing relation to his environment, his advance towards a more complete and rational exploitation of natural resources in the interests of a fuller and more complex social life. The first edition of this book was rapidly exhausted. Yet already it is possible to add new and important scientific weapons to the already complicated armoury of archaeology. One may hope that the necessary means will be made more fully available so that these weapons, and others still in course of development, can be used to further man's understanding of his unrecorded past.

Scientific Studies in Archaeology

DON BROTHWELL and ERIC HIGGS

IT WILL BE MANY years before the impact of scientific applications in archaeology are fully appreciated in all parts of this multifarious discipline. Within the past three or four decades, very great changes have taken place, and this reorientation towards a more scientific attitude in archaeological research continues at a surprising pace. Pre-war attitudes to archaeology—considering archaeology as strictly an 'Arts' subject—are still voiced,[4] but can hardly be taken seriously by those wishing to see an ever fuller bio-cultural reconstruction of human populations in the past. Archaeology is not merely a matter of excavating numerous trenches (and publishing interminable sections of them), or reports on sherds or robber trenches or mosaics. The archaeologist is committed to attempt to piece together for earlier peoples, what the social anthropologist, ethnographer and physical anthropologist is similarly trying to achieve for living groups. Although it is increasingly necessary for many excavators to draw into their projects 'specialist' help, the archaeologist must not lose sight of the fact that he must be in full control of the coordination and general interpretation of all the results. To survive, the archaeologist can no longer afford to be parochial, either as regards techniques or in the great range of data to be derived from ancient sites. The essays which follow in this book are an attempt to show, somewhat briefly, the range of scientific techniques and information which are applied to, or derived from excavations and excavated material. There is no doubt that, in terms of training, this places a considerable burden on the archaeologist. However, as in a number of the science subjects which have undergone considerable transformation in the last few decades, there must be new attitudes to what are basic essentials. It may be argued that in archaeology, there is now a long established recourse to 'specialists' in other fields for a considerable proportion of the scientific data. Even supposing that there was an infinite supply of such people to assist and take over material, it would be very debatable whether this was an ideal state of affairs. But this question, we feel, does not really arise, for there are not—and never have been—enough of these tame 'specialists' to go around. Moreover, the situation looks like deteriorating and not improving. In the fields of zoology and physical anthropology, for instance, interest has swung away from osteological work and is unlikely ever again to occupy the attention of workers in these disciplines to more than a small degree. The answer, whether archaeologists like it or not, is that they (and the departments and institutions which they may govern) must adapt to the need for scientific research within their own discipline. Whether this is achieved by Parkinsonian expansion or a gradual re-allocation of some posts to the broader scientific research problems crying out for attention, is not a matter for our comment. What we wish to stress, here and by the following essays, is that scientific studies are now fully entrenched in archaeology, and that from these 'first beginnings' we must hope that a mature science of the human past will evolve. This transformation, without any doubt, is critical to the survival of archaeology in the twentieth century.

DATING PROBLEMS

The question of the reliability of dating claims is one which has dogged so many interpretations of human culture history and palaeontology. The battery of techniques which can now assist has even increased since the first edition of this volume, and is beginning to look quite formidable. A general assessment of these, one with another, is seen in Fig. 1, and it will be seen that the majority are relative dating methods. These latter techniques vary in precision, and at best only allow a tentative placing of a particular object or assemblage in a time sequence. Most are concerned with dating during human prehistory, and indeed there is a great need for an internationally applicable dating technique which can provide fairly exact dates on materials of the last thousand years. In the case of absolute chronometric methods, radiocarbon dating is likely to remain the queen of techniques for many years to come. However, in terms of human emergence

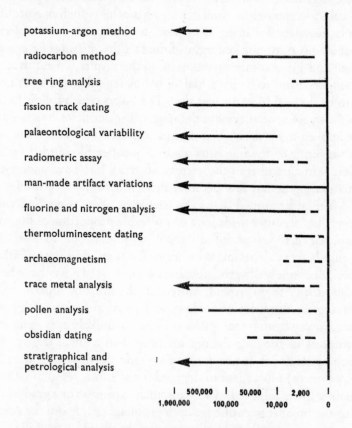

potassium-argon method

radiocarbon method

tree ring analysis

fission track dating

palaeontological variability

radiometric assay

man-made artifact variations

fluorine and nitrogen analysis

thermoluminescent dating

archaeomagnetism

trace metal analysis

pollen analysis

obsidian dating

stratigraphical and petrological analysis

| 500,000 | 50,000 | 2,000 |
| 1,000,000 | 100,000 | 10,000 | 0 |

Fig. 1 Summary of the major dating methods (relative and absolute) which are available to archaeology, and the approximate time zones which they cover. The years are before present.

and the beginnings of hominid cultures, potassium-argon dating has established itself as of special importance. Indeed, this technique has forced palaeontologists and pre-historians to push back hominid history from the original 'base-line' of about one million years to perhaps well over one and three quarter millions.

THE ENVIRONMENT

Human populations do not exist *in vacuo*, but are 'keyed' into the world around them in a variety of ways. They are part of an eco-system. Hunting and collecting economies depend upon the ecological patterns of the edible fauna and flora. Agricultural groups are critically dependent on the productivity of the soils available. All these factors in turn rely on a wide range of climates, and the fluctuation which may occur (annually, or over longer periods of time). This continually changing relationship between climate and world natural history produces various relative dating 'clocks' of local or broad regional significance. In particular, this has permitted the development of pollen analyses (still useful as dating evidence for deposits as early as Middle Pleistocene times), and studies of faunal change and micro-evolution. It has also meant that detailed research on various sedimentary deposits can fruitfully be extrapolated to the study of early human population chronology and environments. Environmental archaeology is therefore by no means marginal to other archaeological studies, but is of major and wide-ranging importance. The environments enveloping earlier peoples, though variable, were nevertheless a complex shared by all. Availability of food, soil fertility, temperature, humidity, and so on, have been some of the primary determinants of type of economy, form of habitation, and even complexity of society.

Without doubt, environmental studies are some of the most exciting and least ex-plored of any aspects of archaeology. If this discipline is to finally break away from the nineteenth-century antiquarianism which still pervades much work in this field, far more research must be undertaken on the broad question of environment in relation to culture. This, of course, has been a two-way relationship, and whereas earlier hominids were greatly influenced by the world around them, cultural progress during the past ten thousand years has seen a swing towards an ever increasing dominance over, and use of the natural environment by human communities. This has resulted in great changes in plant and animal distributions and in the 'perversion' of micro-evolution (domestication) in some species. It has also resulted in changes which are still little studied or appreciated. In particular, the spectrum of animal diseases (including those in man) have probably changed greatly during Neolithic and more recent periods, and at times have clearly been critical to cultural progress and to settlement.

The phenomenon of domestication is one which all of us are aware of to some extent; but exactly what it means, and how it can be identified in its earlier stages, are questions which are still far from resolved. This was very clear at a recent international sym-posium on domestication, held at the Institute of Archaeology in London.[8] These various problems may perhaps be summed up in the following way. We are still far from sure what variation was present in various domesticable species in Mesolithic/early Neolithic times. Also, in the case of animal groups, we do not know to what extent micro-evolutionary change may have occurred merely by restricting the breeding size (by artificial barriers) or selective killing of wild stocks, thus accentuating drift and founder effects.

In the case of plants, there is the related problem of to what extent early selection was truly intentional, from a domestication point of view, and to what extent it was inherent in a developing man/plant relationship—or for that matter man/animal relationship. Nor do we really have any idea of how far back in time such symbiotic relationships began, or how far at any time they had developed. One might even ask whether we are yet sure what value earlier peoples placed on a particular plant. Was the banana, for instance, initially selected and cultivated for its culturally useful leaves and fibrous material, or for the small incipient fruit?

To cross-examine the present position a little further, can we really believe—without far more data—that there was really an agricultural revolution? Have we sufficient information to place special significance on the Mesolithic/Neolithic hinterland? Recently, it has been argued that the concept of a well defined agricultural revolution might be misleading and oversimplified.[6] Certainly the time is ripe to reconsider this difficult question of when these symbiotic relationships began, and whether one can usefully believe in a simple ladder of progress from hunter-gatherer to incipient domestication to full domestication. Is it possible that where eclectic hunting-gathering was most profitable it existed, but where a closer man-plant/animal relationship was more useful, then that form of exploitation occurred as far back as Palaeolithic times? Clearly, it is only by more intensive study of palethnobotanical and palethnozoological data, and critical assessment of these findings, that we shall solve these complex questions.

HUMAN BIOLOGY OF THE PAST

Perhaps the oldest of all 'specialist' fields associated with archaeology is that concerned with the analysis of the remains of man himself. Oddly enough, however, it is a field which seems to cause more unhappiness to the excavator than interest, especially to those who are unfortunate enough (they think) to come across the remains of many bodies. In the Mediterranean area, Egyptologists have shown themselves to be the most calm and collected in the face of large numbers of burials, and as early as 1910 large and detailed monographs were appearing on East African material.[3] Excavators in Britain have certainly not behaved so commendably, and many skeletons have been lost, badly stored or partly thrown away.

The various articles concerned with the remains of man included in this book show clearly that the biology of earlier populations is by no means purely a matter of measuring skulls and computing indices. Even in death, there is a considerable range of data which can be obtained from the close study of parts of the human body, including the determination of the morphological affinities of a group by means of measurement, relative frequencies of age groupings, sex ratios, variations in height and robustness, the general health of the people, and even the variability of soft tissue traits.

Measurement is principally of value to demonstrate variability rather than close affinity. Long bone measurements—by their relative proportions and the stature estimates which can be calculated from them—may also provide evidence of group differences, although it seems likely that overall body length may be modified by climatic and, especially, nutritional factors. Certain diameters of these post-cranial bones are, incidentally, also of considerable value in sexing skeletons.

More recently, investigations on the frequencies of certain discontinuous traits of the skull offer to provide very useful additional information about earlier groups. A number of these traits are already being studied from a genetic point of view, the findings so far suggesting that at least some are likely to be controlled by a simple genetic background. Data of this kind have already been employed in the differentiation of both modern and ancient populations.[2,7]

Bones need not, however, be complete to yield information about an individual. Fragments may indicate with some certainty the number of individuals represented and even their possible sex, although great caution is needed, and sex determinations are especially questionable in remains antedating Upper Palaeolithic man. Cremated remains present even greater problems than unburnt pieces for there is often considerable fissuring and distortion which may obscure some features, and evidence of attrition—of use in age estimations—is usually destroyed by the splintering off of dental enamel under heat. Much information may however be gleaned from such uninspiring material. Yet again, pieces of bone (unburnt) may give an idea of the original histology of the bone, or be suitable for blood-typing research.

Because of the chemical nature of bones and teeth, there is obviously far more likelihood of these remaining than any of the soft tissues. Nevertheless, ancient soft tissues have been found at a variety of sites, and especially Egypt, Peru, and the bogs of Denmark and Schleswig-Holstein. Many of these bodies have been submitted to extensive examination, and of the recently discovered ones, those found in peat at Grauballe in Denmark and Windeby in Schleswig-Holstein have resulted in exhaustive analysis. Even the fingerprints, features which show considerable variability in modern peoples, were studied for possible deviations from modern norms!

An important and revealing aspect of the study of early peoples is that of mortality. As is evident from modern populations, age at death is highly correlated with living standards in a community, economic status, and pressure of disease.

The biological study of earlier human remains is thus a multi-faceted discipline which can tell us far more than that population A had shorter heads or longer faces than population B. Indeed it is vital to the complete understanding of man's cultural and social development.

ARTIFACTS

The material culture of earlier peoples is the 'stronghold' of traditional archaeology. Indeed, early 'cultures' are defined on assemblages or spacial man-made objects which have been judged to be critical to the identity of a particular community at a particular time.

Even artifacts, however, are being submitted to a range of scientific investigatory techniques not known or used a few decades ago. Emphasis is more on precision of quantitative and qualitative data, and although the significance of such results is variable, it is notable that the pre-war 'art appreciation' of archaeological objects has given way to a more mature and broad-based approach to human artifacts.

SOME PROMISING TECHNIQUES

A major change which has been made in this new edition is to emphasize the potential importance of certain methods, and in particular, statistics, in the full assessment of archaeological materials (biological as well as cultural). Simple statistical methods have in fact been applied to some archaeological finds since the late nineteenth century, but it is only with the advent of the larger computers that some detailed statistical treatment has become practicable. With the increasing availability of such machines, we can look forward to large-scale comparative studies which could not be envisaged before. But this brings its problems and pitfalls. To begin with, there is a need to be more 'computer oriented' in the collection of data. One must also face up to the question of what types of data might have long-term reference value in the computer's 'cold storage'. It is also important to realize right at the beginning that if the archaeological data fed into the computer is crude, no amount of statistical refinement will make the results other than very tentative. Finally, after all such work, the individual who initiated the analysis may well be called upon to 'judge' the results for what they are worth. Human conclusions, not machine-made ones, are going to be essential for many more years yet!

Although in the previous edition, microscopy and radiography of objects have been represented, we have given them somewhat different sectional emphasis in this volume because they are techniques deserving consideration in so many different branches of archaeological investigation. And new methods are still being developed here also; for instance, as in microradiography and scanning electron microscopy.

THE ORGANIZATION OF SCIENTIFIC STUDIES AND DATA

It seems important to emphasize that in compiling the series of essays in this volume, our primary wish has been to demonstrate the wide and fundamental importance of scientific studies in archaeology. It would be wrong, however, to assume that all is well in the marriage between scientific research and the traditional day-to-day business of archaeology. We shall have more to say about this shortly.

In various ways, it seems to us, the situation has got to change, although it varies from country to country. The position can perhaps be summed up in a few words, namely, that departments and institutions having a major interest in archaeological research must be prepared to undertake a range of scientific studies *themselves*. If proof is needed of the wisdom of this statement, one might give as an example the severely limited biological work of archaeological significance in Britain today. It is nothing less than farcical that there are no more than three of four full-time posts in this huge and critical research field, and there is no great hope of extended alliances with biology departments to combat this situation. This is even a two-way disaster, for not only is the information lacking on excavated materials, but all too often the specimens are abandoned (completely or in part) or retained in a jumbled state through lack of interest. The answer is not simply to pile the blame on the Inspectorate of Ancient Monuments, although recent criticisms of the lack of financial and staff balance in this department between excavation and conservation (and study) are justified.[1] Individual excavators, regional museums, and archaeology departments need to be far more aware of the need to conserve and properly curate material. This raises other problems, of what material should be saved, how it should be curated, and how data collected on the specimens

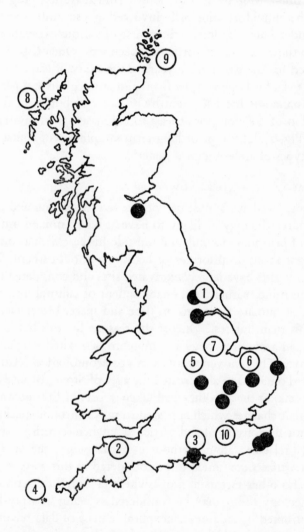

Fig. 2 Some major cemeteries excavated within the past two decades, which have yielded important skeletal material. Those indicated by a number are sites where special attention was given to the skeletons, or where these were the principal reasons for excavating. 1 Wharram Percy. 2 Cannington. 3 Winchester. 4 Tean. 5 Breedon-on-the-Hill. 6 Sedgeford. 7 Ancaster. 8 Ensay. 9 Newark Bay, 10 Nonsuch Palace.

should best be filed in this computer age. It is not unusual in these times to have international meetings and agreements on the standardization of techniques, analyses of materials, and data. Archaeology is in dire need of such a thing.

There is a final important question. To what extent should those who are involved in a particular line of scientific enquiry influence or advise on excavation policy in the future? It seems to us that gone are the days when excavators can call in 'specialist' colleagues *after* the field work is completed—although there is no doubt this still happens far too often. Moreover, some long-term excavation programmes might best be initiated by the individual principally involved in a scientific research project—or at least he might endeavour to influence the course of various excavations and the amount of time given to the collection of particular specimens. One of us (DRB), for instance, has been involved for the past twelve years in the study of early British skeletal series, where there is a need for large samples from as many regions and periods as possible. In a number of instances it has been worthwhile to collaborate in field-work, to urge further excavation of skeletons, or at least to emphasize the importance of statistically useful samples (Fig. 2). This type of long term sampling is of course equally applicable to many other types of archaeological material.

THE 'NEW ARCHAEOLOGY'—WHERE NOW?

The archaeologist, faced as he must be with an overwhelming and impossible task, far beyond the resources he may be likely to have at his command, must dig and analyse with a number of priorities in mind, and must do his best with a complex situation. He may have thought about his priorities, or he may not, but certainly he will have them.

So far, archaeologists have largely excavated sites and considered their data with one major priority in mind, namely, the establishment of cultural history, art history, and the distribution of human 'traditions' in time and space. Other factors have remained peripheral to this main interest. One of the reasons for this lies in the history of the subject. More than a hundred years ago museum orientated scholars sought a chronology for prehistory. They moved away from a palaeontological relative chronology to a chronology based on artifacts and created the ages of Stone, Bronze and Iron. It was an advance in that, taking the area they had taken, a part of Europe, there was apparently a series of coherent changes which appeared to make chronological sense. When wider areas were eventually considered and particularly when scientific dating methods began to replace other relative dating methods in archaeology, the later form was largely outmoded. But artifacts continued to be considered in this way.

There were also other factors at work which favoured this concentration upon the artifacts. Archaeology today may be considered as being in a pre-Darwinian stage of evolution. Confronted by an almost inexplicable mass of data relating to living things, such as the situation with which we are confronted in archaeology today, Darwin had made sense of them. He helped to emphasize laws or principles which ran through this complex of variation. They also included man, but man and the principles associated with him were overlain by a vast body of evidence for advanced human behaviour. The distinctive behaviour patterns of man were obviously different from and more complex than animal behaviour, and there was a reluctance to put man wholly back with the animals. Underlying this was a belief that human behaviour was an expression of 'free will', a little affected perhaps from time to time, by other factors in the biotope. Thus the history of man, interpreted through his artifacts considered more or less in isolation, became the main preoccupation of prehistory. *It suited the climate of thought of the time.*

Human behaviour can be studied in many ways, from animal behaviour studies to anthropology to history. While each of these disciplines is able to bring to the study of human behaviour its own expertise and its own form of evidence, they have a serious handicap, *a short perspective in time.* Some are confined to animal or human behaviour as it is now, or as with the social anthropologist to very recent times, or with the historian to within only 1 per cent of the lifetime of man upon earth. They must include in their concern the accidents of a moment, the accidents of history which may last for only a brief period perhaps only as long as a thousand years. With history one has only a few terminal millennia with which to deal. Human behaviour, as with all the other factors in the biotope or ecosystem is a dynamic and changing thing and by such methods we have snapshots towards the end of a long term dynamic process of two or three million years. Meagre, inadequate and fragmentary as it is, the archaeological record has a perspective in time which can iron out the short period occurrences and perceive the long-term trends which are lost in the short-term multitudinous variables of the terminal millennia. If the study of human behaviour is as important as it is said to be, then archaeology offers one of the most significant ways of studying it.

A generation which is now passing found that a great deal of its resources and therefore the direction of its researches was directed by the demand of museums for artifacts for purposes of exhibition. The 'newer archaeology' is more critical of hypothesis, more given to techniques rather than to discriminating, but can slip into wildly subjective evaluations within its own discipline and within the allied natural sciences. Statistical archaeology has brought with it a keener appreciation of definitions and values as its major contribution in recent years. But it is tiring already of destruction and is anxious to build a new framework for further research with a different objective.

The foundation of archaeological work in recent times then has been based largely upon the pursuit of archaeological 'cultures' and the consideration of culture has been largely based on the artifact or artifactual assemblages within a defined geographical area. The study of the assemblages had been by various methods, from a simple discriminating subjective analysis based on a few attributes to multivariate computer analyses, similarly based on the subjective selection of many attributes to form groups or clusters of artifacts and assemblages on the basis of similarities. It has then been the business of archaeologists to interpret such groups.

The customary hypothesis then made has been that a 'culture' represents a 'people'. What a 'people' might mean, whether or not it is a group of people speaking the same language or under the same jurisdiction or simply a long standing tradition held by many tribes or nations, is left unsaid. It has been translated into contemporary groups but it is difficult to believe in a Gravettien empire which stretched from the Russian steppes to the Pyrenees *c.* 20,000 years ago, or in peoples isolated by this approach on the tops of the Pennine range throughout the severities of a pre-Boreal winter, or in the adjacent Maglemose who, when they were not in the lowlands have been projected out into the swamps of the North Sea on the basis of a harpoon brought up by a trawler's net. Or that the early farmers of Denmark never exploited the sea shores which were left to a different group, the Ertebølle, who took no interest in the adjacent hinterland, or in fact that, on the basis of the present artifactual clusters, a single people were never responsible for the making of two different 'cultures'. It is also a picture drawn from our knowledge of primitive peoples being in recent times in 'cultural slums' and isolated by circumstance. Nor is it possible to believe easily that when artifacts dispersed, they did so because a people migrated. But by such a hypothesis, which is an attempt to trace tradition in time and space, one gets a prehistoric picture of invasions and mass movements of peoples, of wars and by a pyramid of hypotheses all the trappings of the historical picture. The tail of history wags the prehistoric dog. This hypothesis has resulted in considerations of the most devious and subtle intellectual complexity. It is a hypothesis which can still be made. But more can come out of archaeology than a faded history. It is not in accord with, nor does it satisfy the climate of thought of the present time, which asks not 'what happened in history?' but 'why?'

The fact that an archaeological site is a mine of information relevant to many disciplines is coming more into view in the minds of many, and one reviewer has even written that archaeological sites may be too important to be left to the archaeologist! There has been growing in recent decades what has been called the interdisciplinary approach, which, although basically a good trend, may at times lead to as much chaos as archaeological enlightenment.

Not a few workers in other fields will join the archaeologist and by a little labour turn the handle of well established techniques within his discipline and produce 'results'. Unfortunately, following this, it is by no means always easy to establish what is relevant to archaeology and what is only of interest to the related sciences. Indeed, it is a true but unhappy fact that the proper significance of some scientific findings may not be realized for years to come. One of the great distinctions of J. B. S. Haldane was that he could tackle facts from various disciplines and emerge with new views on the relevance of particular data. Archaeology could make good use of a few Haldanes at this moment!

But there has been a further serious problem affecting scientific research in archaeology. There was the tendency for each discipline, having snatched off its special research piece, to consider it in the light of its own core concept. Its own core concept was based on the consideration of its data in isolation, a hypothesis as to what tended to happen and what might happen if by good fortune its own material had been left to a more or less un-interrupted course unaffected by other factors in the biotope such as man. A hardened belief in restrictive practices, the worst kind of professional trade unionism, grew up and became an article of faith. Only a rash and perhaps untrustworthy scientist or archaeologist would dare to cross a disciplinary territorial boundary, for if he did, he could expect it to be defended fiercely and in the ensuing contest he would have little chance of survival. This is an example of true animal behaviour in the defence of territorial rights, which it is as well to remember. The result of all this was that the data from archaeological sites became fragmented away into a variety of separate enquiries which overlapped occasionally and fortuitously at the peripheries. A horrid porridge with little meaning was created of anthropocentric, phytocentric and zoocentric disciplines and indeed who can blame the few who have resisted such an approach, if they declare that there is indeed no meaning to it? But ignoring the situation doesn't really help. From the chaos must evolve an integrated and critical discipline, and before maturity one must inevitably expect a period of growth and adjustment. The essays presented here at least show that the growth is healthy, and if changes to adulthood are likely to be considerable, this does not mean that infancy shows other than normal progress.

A recent approach which is influencing archaeological thought is that of ecology and the eco-system. The idea inherent in this is that archaeological data should be taken and fitted into the core hypothesis arising from ecological considerations. This has the attraction that it gives a much broader basis to the consideration of archaeological data and the man/plant/animal relationship may be studied instead of man, plant and animal in separate compartments. It has the disadvantage that the data must be squeezed into an existing framework.

Whether this will or will not fit future archaeological needs as a basal complex will soon become clear. What is already obvious is that the re-ordering of priorities in archaeology is essential, and that the primary world-wide activities of man are very basic bio-social ones.

TABLE A

A tentative tripartite division of major human activities, experiences, and needs, relevant to the study of earlier human populations.

Tertiary	Myth, ritual, religion Art diversity (including building design) Transport Medicine and Surgery Metal, glass, and ceramic technology Culture 'crazes' (clothing styles etc.) Political and legal systems
Secondary	Territoriality (nomadic/sedentary behaviour) Group security (feuds, warfare etc.) Population movement and concentration Communication (language, writing) Agricultural techniques
Primary	Food quest (and alimentary functions) Availability of water Climatic adaptation (clothing, fire, habitation) Reproduction (and family structure) Disease Death

Table A attempts to list some of the phenomena which are important in the life and behaviour of human populations. A tripartite division of these topics has been attempted, and it will be seen that the primary factors are all concerned with ecology and demography. It is only in the tertiary category that most of the classic preoccupations of archaeology can be placed. Of course these factors can vary considerably in importance from culture to culture, but considering world wide variation, both temporally and spacially, the divisions given seem to offer the 'best fit'. In the past, most archaeological activity has been directed towards the tertiary category, partly because it is easier to find the materials of this group and partly because pure art history and the history of architecture have found it convenient to go under the name of archaeology. In Palaeontology, this situation would be rather like overactivity in the study of giant reptiles and mammals, but with little attention to molluscs, trilobites, or the actual general mechanisms of evolution.

We have purposely dwelt at length with the uncertainties and problems of archaeology today. Optimism is one of the commoner features of human behaviour, and no harm can be derived from a little hard pessimism for a change! However, we hope that the following contributions will help to show that all is not lost.

REFERENCES

1 ANON. 1968. *Nature*, *221*, 206–7
2 BROTHWELL, D. R. 1959. In *Bericht über die 6 Tangung der Deutschen Gesellschaft für Anthropologie in Kiel*, Gottingen, 103–9
3 ELLIOT SMITH, G. and WOOD JONES, F. 1910. Report on the human remains. *Archaeological survey of Nubia. Report of 1907–08*. Cairo
4 HAWKES, J. 1968. *Antiquity*, *42*, 255–62
5 HEYERDAHL, T. 1952. *American Indians in the Pacific*, London, 427–98
6 HIGGS, E. and JARMAN, M. 1969. *Antiquity*, *43*, 31–41
7 LAUGHLIN, W. S. and JØRGENSEN, J. B. 1956. *Acta Genet. 6*, 3–12
8 DIMBLEBY, G. W. and UCKO, P. J. 1969. (eds) *The Domestication and Exploitation of Plants and Animals* London. In the press

SECTION I DATING

1 *Analytical Methods of Dating Bones*

KENNETH P. OAKLEY

A CONSIDERABLE AMOUNT OF PROGRESS has been made during the last decade in the dating of bones, and a number of new techniques for this purpose have been developed. In briefly surveying them in this chapter it is important at the outset to distinguish two main types of dating, for a technique applicable in one type of dating may be quite inappropriate in another. The first type of dating is *relative dating*. This places a specimen, event or deposit in relation to an established sequence. Of course one may know the relative age of a specimen and yet have very little or no idea of its age in years (e.g. the Swanscombe skull). Where it is possible to measure actual age of a specimen, or of the contemporaneous matrix, the procedure is now usually referred to as *chronometric dating*.*

There is an ageing process inherent in organic materials which was discovered about 1947 by Professor W. F. Libby, then at the Institute of Nuclear Studies, Chicago, and within certain limits this makes it possible to determine the exact antiquity of some specimens in years. All living matter contains a small but practically constant proportion of the radioactive isotope of carbon, C^{14}, which is produced by cosmic-ray bombardment of nitrogen atoms in the outer atmosphere. When an animal or plant dies, the radioactive carbon in its tissues is no longer replenished from the atmosphere, and it disintegrates at a constant rate—the quantity is halved in 5,570 years. This figure is the Libby value of the half-life of C-14 or radiocarbon. Thus by measuring the radioactivity of the carbon extracted from an ancient specimen of organic material, its age can be calculated. After a certain lapse of time the radioactivity is too weak to be measured.

With existing techniques the backward limit of the radiocarbon method is between 60,000 and 70,000 years, but the range is gradually being increased with the development of the device known as isotopic enrichment in a diffusion column, having converted the carbon first into carbon dioxide.

---

* Some authors have used 'absolute dating' as synonymous with 'dating in years', but this usage makes no distinction between placing a specimen in a time bracket (e.g. determining its age as 40,000 ±2,000 years) and placing it on a time-line. Where it is possible to establish that two deposits in widely separated areas were formed contemporaneously (e.g. if they both contain the same fall of volcanic ash), they could be said to be of the same 'absolute' age even if their antiquity in *years* is unknown.

Another very practical limitation of radiocarbon dating is the fact that a certain minimum quantity of organic carbon must be available in the specimen or sample. Thus calcined bone is undatable whereas charred bone is potentially datable. The amount required depends partly on the level of age—the older the material the more the carbon required for an accurate dating—but the techniques are being improved in this as in other respects. Thus in 1953 when the antiquity of the Piltdown jawbone was doubted on the score of its fluorine and nitrogen content (*infra*), it would have been impossible to date it by C[14] because at that time about 6 grams of carbon were demanded by the laboratories using the method, and as this is approximately its total carbon content, the exercise would have involved the total destruction of this 'historic' specimen, suspected by then to have been probably fabricated out of a modern orang-utan jawbone. By 1959, however, the late Professor H. de Vries in the Groningen Laboratory undertook at the author's request to date it by C[14], and he was able to do so closely enough to confirm that it was geologically Recent.[1] This was on the basis of testing one gram of the bone, cut out of the corpus mandibulae, which yielded, after grinding and treatment in the Government Laboratory for the purpose of removing all possible traces of preservative, and after decalcification in Groningen, 0·1 gram of organic carbon. Measurement of its radioactivity showed that the jaw was a few centuries old, perhaps not so surprising when one recalls that the modern Dyaks preserve trophy orang-utan skulls for centuries in their longhouses and in ritual deposits in caves.

The absolute age of a skull or mandible is usually obtained indirectly, as when it comes from a deposit containing other material more suitable for radiocarbon dating, or other bones more easily expended. Thus the Palaeolithic skull found in spring-deposits at Florisbad, in the Orange Free State, has been dated as about 37,000 years old on the basis of radiocarbon dating of a seam of peat within the same deposit.[2]

Dating a specimen by the age of the containing deposit of course makes the assumption that they are contemporaneous and obviously this is not always justifiable, particularly where human remains are concerned, because of man's long-established practice of burying the dead.

The fluorine test (and other tests working on the same principle described below) was mainly devised for the purpose of checking the age-relation between bones and the deposit in which they have been found or to which they are attributed. Frequently it has been misunderstood. Thus, when it was stated a few years ago in a newspaper report that 'the fluorine test indicated that the Swanscombe skull was more than 100,000 years old', this was merely a way of saying that the test had confirmed its contemporaneity with the gravel in which it was found, and that geologists' current assessment of the antiquity of the gravel was 'more than 100,000 years old'.

The relative age of a fossil bone can be determined by comparing its chemical composition with that of other fossil bones of known ages from the same site or from the same area if they have been preserved under comparable conditions. As soon as bones are buried their composition is subject to chemical changes, some rapid, others much slower. The organic matter in bone consists mainly of fats and protein (collagen). The fatty matter of bone is lost quite rapidly after burial, but the protein disappears much more slowly, and under some conditions, where the soil is permanently frozen or where bacteria and air are excluded, it may persist for tens of thousands of years. Collagen fibres have been demonstrated in fossil ivory (Plate Ia) from Siberia, and in the humerus of a woolly rhinoceros excavated from Pleistocene clay on the site of the Lloyd's Building in Leadenhall Street in the City of London (Plate Ib).

The appearance or texture of a bone is not a reliable guide to how much organic matter it contains. During excavations at Gibraltar in the last century, the skeleton of a horse was encountered a few feet below the surface. It was taken at first to be the remains of a fossil horse, for the bones appeared to have lost the greater part of their organic matter; but, when the foot bones were exhumed, the shoes with which the animal had been shod were found still in position. It was in fact the remains of an Arab charger buried only 25 years earlier.

With such cases in mind the organic content of fossil bones had become widely regarded as an unreliable criterion of their antiquity, but extensive analytical studies carried out since the Second World War[3] have shown that some bones which appear to be well fossilized have in fact retained considerable amounts of protein. As bones lose their protein at a slow and, under the same conditions, fairly uniform rate, the relative ages of bones at some sites can be determined by comparing their organic contents—nitrogen, carbon, and chemically-bound water—or the quantity of mineral ash after burning, which becomes greater with age.

It is usually found most convenient to assess the residual organic matter in fossil bone or dentine by determining its nitrogen content by the method of chemical analysis known as micro-kjeldahl. As bone protein or collagen decays in course of fossilization, it is broken down into the various component amino-acids which are leached out or retained for varying lengths of time depending on the local conditions.[4,5] Some amino-acids were found surviving even in the bones of fossil fishes embedded in hard shales of a Devonian formation nearly 300 million years old in Ohio. In order to assess the degree of degradation of collagen in fossil bone, a sample is first dissolved in a suitable acid, and the amino-acids present in the resulting hydrolysate are then determined by means of paper-chromatography. A chromatogram (Plate Ib) prepared from a sample of the ulna of woolly rhinoceros in clay from the Lloyd's site showed strongly all the amino-acids composing collagen; whereas the Galley Hill skeleton, although only Bronze Age, preserved in gravelly matrix showed these amino-acids in reduced strength.

Changes in the mineral matter of buried bones and teeth depend on the composition of the percolating ground-water. They are of two kinds: (1) alteration of the phosphatic material of which bones are mainly composed (hydroxy-apatite), and (2) addition of new mineral matter (e.g. lime or iron oxide) in the pores of the bone. Changes of the latter kind involving an increase in weight are what people usually mean by 'fossilization', but they are often misleading as a means of relative dating. For this purpose, the more valuable change is the slow, invisible, weightless alteration which occurs through the irreversible substitution of one element for another in the hydroxy-apatite. The two elements which accumulate in this way are fluorine and uranium.

Of these elements fluorine is widely distributed in the form of soluble fluorides which occur in trace quantities in almost all ground-waters. When fluorine ions come into contact with bones and teeth, they are adsorbed and become locked in through replacing the hydroxyl ions in the ultramicroscopic crystals of hydroxy-apatite. Fluor-apatite is less soluble than hydroxy-apatite, so that when fluorine atoms have once been fixed in bone, they are not readily dissolved out. With the passage of time, bones and teeth in permeable deposits accumulate fluorine progressively. The rate at which the fluorine content increases varies from place to place, but bones which have lain for the same period of time in a particular deposit will have approximately the same fluorine content. As the fluorine fixed in bone is not readily removed, a specimen which has been washed out of a more ancient deposit and redeposited in another at a later date will show a much higher fluorine content than bones contemporaneous with the bed. Bones artificially interred in the same deposit at a later date may have come to resemble the fossils of the bed in appearance, but will have accumulated substantially less fluorine. This is the basis of the fluorine-dating method,[6,7] the usefulness of which was demonstrated in 1948 when it was applied to the Galley Hill skeleton[8] and the Swanscombe skull.

The Galley Hill skeleton is that of a man of modern type but with certain allegedly primitive traits. It was discovered in 1888 at a depth (it was said) of 8 ft in the river terrace gravels near Swanscombe, which contain Lower Palaeolithic hand-axes together with remains of extinct elephant and which certainly date from before the time of Neanderthal man. In these same gravels the bones of the Swanscombe skull were found in 1935–36 at a depth of 24 ft. The fluorine content of the Galley Hill skeleton, of the Swanscombe skull, and of fossil animal bones from the same gravels was determined by chemical analysis in the Government Chemist's Department. The results confirmed the antiquity of the Swanscombe skull and indicated that the Galley Hill skeleton was an intrusive burial considerably later than the Middle Pleistocene gravels in which it lay.

These fluorine results were later cross-checked by measurements of the nitrogen content of the same bones. The two sets of results are shown together in Table A.

TABLE A
Fluorine and nitrogen contents of the Galley Hill skeleton and the Swanscombe skull.

	Fluorine	Nitrogen
	%	%
Neolithic skull, Coldrum, Kent	0·3	1·9
Galley Hill skeleton	0·5	1·6
Swanscombe skull	1·7	traces
Bones of fossil mammals from Swanscombe gravels	1·5	traces

It will be seen that bones which have accumulated little fluorine have retained much nitrogen, and vice versa. Although the Galley Hill skeleton was clearly much later than the gravel in which it lay, the question of how much later, even in general terms, could not be solved by the fluorine or nitrogen methods of relative dating, because no bones in a similar matrix known to be Late Palaeolithic, Mesolithic, Neolithic, Bronze Age or of precise later date were available in the locality for comparison. However, the nitrogen tests showed that sufficient degraded collagen occurred in the skeleton to enable its age to be determined directly by the radiocarbon method if a portion of this famous specimen were sacrificed to this end. As the ratio C/N in collagen is approximately $2 \cdot 5 : 1$, it was estimated that 100 grams of the skeleton would yield about 4 grams of carbon. Accordingly in 1959 it was decided to make an accurate cast of one of the limb-bones, and then to drill out of it about 100 grams of tissue.

The bone powder was repeatedly washed in warm water and acetone (by Mr E. J. Johnson of the Government Chemist's Department) to remove any possible traces of celluloid or glue which might have been applied to the skeleton after excavation, and then it was submitted to the Research Laboratory of the British Museum, where Mr H. Barker[9] determined its age as $3,310 \pm 150$ years old, indicating that it was most probably an Early Bronze Age burial. This is probably the first instance in which an allegedly 'fossil' human skeleton has been dated directly by the radiocarbon method.

The solving of another outstanding problem, that of 'Piltdown Man', was also begun by means of relative dating techniques,[10] and was completed by the chronometric method of radiocarbon (p. 46). The unravelling of this complicated problem[11] (described by one distinguished scholar in 1950 as one that would probably never be solved) began in 1949 with the application of the fluorine-dating method to all the vertebrate specimens from the Piltdown gravel. In addition to the jawbone, canine or eye tooth, and fragments of human braincase, 17 fossil mammalian specimens had been recorded from the pit. These appeared to be of two ages: an older group originally called Pliocene, including pieces of the grinding teeth of a rare type of elephant which died out early in the Pleistocene—that is, more than 600,000 years ago according to conventional geological estimates; and a much later group including remains of beaver, red deer, and perhaps hippopotamus, dating from just before the last glaciation of about 60,000 years ago. It appeared that fossils of two formations had been washed together, through some strange chance. Those authorities who could not believe that the jawbone belonged to the skull held the view that the jaw belonged to the 'Pliocene' group, and the skull to the later.

Samples of all these specimens were submitted to the Government Chemist's Department, where they were analysed by Dr C. R. Hoskins. The fossils of the older group proved to contain a great deal of fluorine, 2 to 3% ($3 \cdot 8\%$ is the theoretical maximum). In striking contrast the amount of fluorine in small samples of the famous skull, jawbone, and canine tooth proved to be only between $0 \cdot 1$ and $0 \cdot 4\%$. It was not immediately obvious that these remains were bogus, because there did not appear to be any significant difference in fluorine content between the jawbone and skull, or between the skull and an associated molar tooth of hippopotamus (extinct in Britain since before the last glaciation).

In 1953, in order to test Professor J. S. Weiner's hypothesis that the jawbone and canine tooth were modern specimens faked to match fossilized human skull bones, larger samples were removed and submitted to the Government Chemist's Department, where they were analysed by Mr C. F. M. Fryd, who devised a way of measuring smaller amounts of fluorine than could be measured in 1949.[12] The jawbone and canine tooth proved to contain no more fluorine than fresh bones and teeth, whereas the human skull bones contained just enough to indicate that they were ancient. The nitrogen content of the jawbone and teeth was also determined, and proved to be the same as in fresh specimens.

The nitrogen content would not have proved the modernity of the jawbone conclusively without the cross-check provided by fluorine. The woolly rhinoceros bone from clay below the Lloyd's site (in which collagen fibres have been detected—p. 25) has the same nitrogen content as the Piltdown jawbone, yet it is undoubtedly fossil. The reason for its remarkable preservation is that it was embedded in clay which has provided an anaerobic and sterile environment since the Late Pleistocene. A fragment of mammoth bone from the same site, but from a layer of sand, contains almost no nitrogen. Fortunately the fluorine content of buried bones increases at about the same rate in sand (or gravel) and in clay. Thus these rhinoceros and mammoth bones both contain about 1% fluorine, as expected in alluvial deposits of Upper Pleistocene age in southern England. Thus if for the sake of argument it were supposed that the Piltdown jawbone had been encased in clay since Pleistocene times, and that this had prevented its organic content from being degraded, its fluorine content should nevertheless be higher than in modern bone. In fact, the matrix was said to be gravel.

The fluorine content of the Piltdown skull bones is lower than that of fossils from any other Pleistocene gravels in Britain. But so long as the hippopotamus tooth with the same low fluorine content was accepted as a local fossil it could be argued that the ground-water at Piltdown had been exceptionally deficient in fluorine since the Ice Age; the exposed dentine of a tooth and compact bone absorb fluorine at about the same rate. When evidence came to light that the hippopotamus tooth had been artificially stained, and therefore was a fraudulent introduction, the provisional dating of the Piltdown cranium as Late Pleistocene lost its foundation.

Further chemical studies of the Piltdown hippopotamus molar showed that its organic content is almost negligible, indicating that it is a fossil of considerable antiquity—whereas its low fluorine content suggested that it was not very ancient. It has now been found that in limestone cave deposits passage of fluorine ions is inhibited but that decay of organic matter proceeds at normal rates. Hippopotamus remains are rare in cave deposits, except in Mediterranean islands, for example Malta—which may be where the 'Piltdown' specimen came from originally.

A new method of relative dating of bones and teeth was tried with considerable success on the Piltdown specimens: the method of radiometric assay developed by the late Professor C. F. Davidson and Mr S. H. U. Bowie while working together in the Atomic Energy Division of the Geological Survey. It was established by Lord Rayleigh in 1908 that mineral phosphates, including fossil bones, contain uranium. Recent medical researches have shown that uranium circulating in the blood stream is fixed in the mineral matter of bones, probably through replacement of the calcium ions in the hydroxy-apatite. The same process of replacement occurs in bones buried in deposits through which ground-water percolates with traces of uranium. The longer a bone has lain in that deposit the more uranium it will have adsorbed. Uranium is radioactive, and consequently it is possible to estimate the uranium content of a fossil by making a count, under suitable conditions, of the amount of radioactive breakdown that is proceeding. Radiometric assays of fossil bones carried out at the Geological Survey showed that, although there is a wide variation in the radioactivity of fossils of the same age from different sites, there is a progressive build-up in the average radioactivity of fossils with increasing geological age. Moreover, contemporaneous bones and teeth from a single site show only a small range of radioactivity (although the radioactivity of the enamel of a tooth is generally less than that of dentine or cementum, which are more absorptive). Fossil bones and teeth from limestone formations and clays contain less uranium than specimens of the same age from gravels and sands. The radiometric assay can sometimes serve in the same way as fluorine analysis to distinguish between specimens which, for whatever reasons, are older or younger than the bed they are found in and those which are contemporaneous. It has an advantage over the fluorine method of dating in that it does not involve destruction of material.

TABLE B

Fluorine, nitrogen and uranium contents of human and mammal remains from Europe and North Africa.

	Fluorine	Nitrogen	'Uranium' (e.U$_3$O$_8$)
	%	%	p.p.m.*
Fresh bone	0·03	4·0	0
Piltdown jawbone	<0·03	3·9	0
Neolithic skull, Kent	0·3	1·9	–
Piltdown skull	0·1	1·4	1
Piltdown hippopotamus molar†	<0·1	<0·1	3
Malta hippopotamus molar†	0·1	<0·1	7
Swanscombe skull	1·7	trace	27
Suffolk Red Crag *Mastodon* molar†	1·9	trace	46
Piltdown '*Elephas* cf. *planifrons*' molar†	2·7	nil	610
Ichkeul '*Elephas* cf. *planifrons*' molar†	2·7	trace	580

* Equivalent uranium oxide content, estimated in parts per million on basis of beta-radiations per minute. That all this radiation is due to uranium is an assumption; in fact some is undoubtedly due to uranium 'daughter elements'. However, chemical analysis of the dentine of the Piltdown molar of *E.* cf. *planifrons* showed that it contained *c.* 1,000 p.p.m. of uranium oxide according to A. D. Baynes-Cope (*Bull. B.M. (N.H.), Geol.* vol. 2, no. 6, 1955, pp. 283–4).

† Samples of dentine or cementum.

When Bowie and Davidson carried out a radiometric assay of the Piltdown specimens[13] the results agreed with those obtained by fluorine analysis, indicating that the cranium is post-Pleistocene, and that the animal remains have been derived from very varied geological sources. The most striking additional information concerned the fragments of molar teeth of an extinct elephant—similar to *Elephas planifrons*, which lived early in the Pleistocene, and has been rarely if ever recorded elsewhere in Britain. These fragments proved to have a radioactivity far higher than that of any Tertiary or Pleistocene fossils from Britain that have been tested, and higher than that of fossil elephant teeth of the same age from foreign localities, with the exception only of a specimen of '*Elephas* cf. *planifrons*' from Ichkeul, in Tunisia, now referred to as *Archidiskodon africanavus*, an African member of the *Elephas planifrons* group.

Some summarized results obtained by the fluorine, nitrogen, and uranium methods are shown in Table B.

There are so many variables affecting the composition of fossil bones and teeth that it is usually impossible to use either fluorine content or radioactivity as more than a rough guide to the geological age of an isolated specimen. However, these methods, combined where necessary with nitrogen analysis, are useful in (a) establishing the relative ages of a variety of vertebrate remains occurring in comparable circumstances at the same or neighbouring sites, and (b) tracing the most likely origin of specimens derived from several possible sources. The usefulness of the combined techniques is well illustrated by the results obtained through applying them to the problem of the relative age and origin of remains of 'sabre-tooth tiger'—strictly speaking, they should be termed sabre-tooth *cats*—reported from British cave deposits.

In 1876 a canine tooth of *Machairodus* (*Epimachairodus*) was found in an Upper Palaeolithic layer at Robin Hood Cave, Cresswell Crags, Derbyshire. Some authorities have doubted whether this was a genuine find, suspecting that it had been fraudulently planted at the site, and that it had really originated in alluvial deposits of earliest

TABLE C

Fluorine, nitrogen and uranium contents of Epimachairodus *teeth from Creswell Crags and other European sites.*

Source of Epimachairodus dentine tested	Nitrogen	Fluorine	%F/ %P₂O₅ (× 100)	'Uranium' (e.U₃O₈)*
	%	%		p.p.m.
Val d'Arno, Italy	0·2	1·6	5·3	35
Mt Perrier, France	nil	1·9	6·3	30
Doveholes, Derbyshire	nil	2·5	8·6	68
Creswell, Derbyshire	2·1	0·2	0·8	<1
Kent's Cavern, Devon	1·2	<0·01	<0·1	5

* Equivalent uranium oxide content (estimated on basis of net β-radiations per minute).

Pleistocene (Villafranchian) age in France or Italy, where specimens of this genus are not uncommon. Comparison of the fluorine content of the Creswell tooth with that of Villafranchian specimens from the main Continental localities appears to dispel this suggestion (Table C). Other possibilities had to be considered. Was the Creswell canine derived from a Lower Pleistocene deposit in Derbyshire and brought into the Robin Hood's Cave by prehistoric man? There are many instances of fossils having been treasured during the Stone Age and transported many miles from their natural source—the most famous example is the Silurian trilobite found in a Magdalenian layer in Grotte du Trilobite at Arcy-sur-Cure (Yonne). Moreover, *Epimachairodus* canines (but specifically different from the Creswell specimen) have been found in association with Villafranchian fossils in a fissure deposit at Doveholes, which is also in Derbyshire. Yet their lack of organic matter, high fluorine content and high radioactivity contrast sharply with the Creswell specimen, whose composition agrees with that of local Upper Pleistocene cave mammals.

If it were still to be maintained that the Creswell canine had been fraudulently planted in the cave, its composition could only be accounted for by supposing that it had been obtained from some other similar *cave* deposit elsewhere; for in our experience it is only in limestone cave deposits that Pleistocene vertebrate specimens are so deficient in fluorine as this one is. Teeth of *Epimachairodus* (a genus widespread in the Old World) have in fact been reported from Upper Pleistocene ('Mousterian') cave-earth in Kent's Cavern, Torquay. It has generally been assumed by vertebrate palaeontologists in recent years that these specimens were residues from some much older deposit in the Torquay Cave system. The composition of one of the Kent's Cavern canines was therefore tested. The fluorine content of the dentine proved to be negligible, and the uranium content very low. The failure of these elements to circulate in calcareous cave deposits is of course recognized, but if these specimens were considerably older than the undoubtedly Upper Pleistocene mammoth teeth found in the same cave-earth they should contain substantially less organic matter. In fact they prove to contain just as much (*see* Table D).

TABLE D

Fluorine and nitrogen content of mammalian teeth from Kent's Cavern.

Specimens of dentine from Kent's Cavern	Nitrogen	$\%F/\%P_2O_5$ (× 100)
Epimachairodus canine (BMNH. Pal. 14954); cave-earth	% 1·2*	< 0·1
Mammoth molar; cave-earth	0·8	< 0.1
Bear molar; basal breccia	0·2	< 0·1

* Washing the sample in warm water and then in acetone to remove any possible traces of nitrogenous preservative effected no reduction in the nitrogen content.

Thus it may be inferred provisionally that sabre-tooth cats survived as rarities in some areas in Britain until Upper Pleistocene times, and that the last of them were contemporary with Middle Palaeolithic and possibly even with the earliest Upper Palaeolithic men. Surprising as this may seem, it should be recalled that the survival of *Epimachairodus* into late Middle Pleistocene times on the Continent is already well established.[14]

Some years ago I suggested[15] that it might be possible to solve the question of the relative antiquity of the enormous hominoid teeth (*Gigantopithecus*) bought by Professor G. H. R. von Koenigswald from Chinese drugstores along with other so-called dragons' teeth which are in fact recognizably the teeth of various fossil mammalia in three main age-groups, Lower Pliocene and Lower and Middle Pleistocene, and obtainable only from certain limited areas in China. The type-specimens (Plate IIc) of *Gigantopithecus* have been regarded as too precious to drill for the purpose of applying the full range of the F-U-N relative dating techniques (fluorine, uranium and nitrogen analyses); but their uranium content at least could be assessed by the method of radiometric assay since it involves no destruction of material. This has now been done through Professor von Koenigswald's courtesy in bringing two of the type specimens to the British Museum (Nat. Hist.) for the purpose. In each case the base of the tooth (largely dentine/cementum) was assayed. The results considered in conjunction with assays on drugstore specimens of known geological ages left no reasonable doubt that the type-specimens of *Gigantopithecus* belong to the Middle Pleistocene group of drugstore fossils.

TABLE E

Uranium content of Gigantopithecus *teeth and other Drugstore and Chinese Fossils of known ages.*

	$e.U_3O_8$ p.p.m.
Drugstore Fossils	
Lower Pliocene group	
Hipparion dentine	130
Hipparion dentine (second specimen)	90
Lower Pleistocene group	
Equus sanamensis dentine*	30
Middle Pleistocene group	
Ailuropoda dentine	$<$1
Gigantopithecus	
Type specimens (from Drugstores)	
Lower molar	1
Upper molar	10
Liucheng Cave molar	$<$1
Liucheng Cave-earth fauna (including	
Mastodon) early Middle Pleistocene	$<$1—10

* Made available through the courtesy of Mr Tom Harrisson, Curator of the Sarawak Museum. Further analyses are required in this and in other groups before the ranges of fluctuation will be known.

This conclusion agrees well with the recent discovery by Pei-Wen-Chung of examples of *Gigantopithecus* in a cave deposit with Middle Pleistocene fauna at Liucheng in the Kwangsi Province of southern China.[16] The Chinese scientists generously sent one of the original Liucheng molars of *Gigantopithecus* together with eight associated fossil mammalian specimens for testing in our laboratories in London, and a summary of the results is included in Table E.

Thus the new relative dating techniques both by supplementing the methods of 'absolute' (chronometric) dating, and by helping to establish the stratigraphical origins of specimens of doubtful provenance, are bringing a new element of certainty where previously much has been so uncertain.

REFERENCES AND NOTES

1 DE VRIES, H. and OAKLEY, K. P. 1959. *Nature 184*, 224–6
2 ZINDEREN BAKKER, E. M. VAN 1957. *Proc. 3rd Pan-Afr. Congr. Prehist. 1955*, London, 237
3 For example, COOK, S. F. and HEIZER, R. F. 1947. *Am. J. Phys. Anth. 5*, 201–20
4 ABELSON, P. H. 1955. *Yearbook Carnegie Inst., Washington 54*, 107–9
5 —— 1956. *Scientific American 195* (1), 83
6 MIDDLETON, J. 1844. *Proc. Geol. Soc. Lond. 4*, 431–3
7 CARNOT, A. 1893. *Ann. de Mines. Mémoires* 9ème sér., *3*, 155–95
8 OAKLEY, K. P. and MONTAGU, M.F.A. 1949. *Bull. Brit. Mus. (Nat. Hist.) Geol. 1* (2), 25–48
9 BARKER, H. and MACKEY, J. 1961. *Radiocarbon 3*, 41
10 The application of fluorine dating to 'Piltdown Man' was proposed in OAKLEY, K. P. 1948. *Advancement of Science 16*, 336–7. The first results were described in OAKLEY, K. P. and HOSKINS, C. R. 1950. *Nature 165*, 379–82, and further results leading to exposure of the forgery in WEINER, J. S., OAKLEY, K. P. and LE GROS CLARK, W. E. 1953. *Bull. Brit. Mus. (Nat. Hist.) Geol. 2* (3), 139–46; and the final relative dating by these and nine other authors in 1955. *Ibid. 2* (6), 225–87
11 For a convenient summary in 1955 see *American Scientist 43* (4), 573–83
12 FRYD, C. F. M. 1955. *Bull. Brit. Mus. (Nat. Hist.) Geol. 2* (6), 266–7
13 DAVIDSON, C. F. and BOWIE, S. H. U. 1955. *Ibid. 2* (6), 276–82
14 ADAM, K. D. 1961. *Stuttgarter Beiträge z. Naturkunde 78*, 29
15 OAKLEY, K. P. 1954. *The Times Sci. Rev. 13*, 16
16 PEI, W. C. 1957. *Vertebrata Palasiatica 1* (2), 65–70

2 Radiocarbon Dating

E. H. WILLIS

FEW AIDS TO ARCHAEOLOGICAL INVESTIGATIONS can have contributed as much to our knowledge of the time scale of past events as the radiocarbon dating method. Its global and universal application coupled with the relatively high degree of accuracy on samples of known age makes it the paramount dating method in the age range over which it is practical to use it. Scientific imagination was stirred by the first tentative measurements of Willard Libby, then of the Institute of Nuclear Studies, Chicago, who predicted the existence of radiocarbon in the atmosphere on purely theoretical grounds.[1] The early experiments were quick to be exploited, and the value of the method and the theoretical perception behind it were recognized in 1960 by the award to Professor Libby of the Nobel Prize for Chemistry.

The method relies on certain fundamental assumptions and these, as described below, may be criticized on the grounds that their validity might either be incorrect or might need serious modification. From time to time, notably when the radiocarbon chronology has been at variance with previously conceived chronologies, such criticism has aroused a certain amount of support. The physicists for their part have been most sensitive to the possibility of variations in the fundamental parameters of the method, and have devoted a considerable amount of their research effort to establish the validity of the prime assumptions. As frequently occurs in research of this nature, the by-products have themselves had considerable significance, particularly in the fields of isotopic fractionation of plant material, the turnover times of the stratosphere, troposphere and the oceans; and the past behaviour of the cosmic ray flux. It is therefore pertinent at the outset of this account to examine the validity of the assumptions that Libby first made, and to see under what circumstances it might be necessary to modify them to avoid serious errors in the estimation of the age of an unknown sample. It is perhaps a testimonial to Libby's original notion that the modifications, although important, detract little from the positive value of the method as a dating device.

THE FUNDAMENTAL ASSUMPTIONS

Libby,[2] in postulating the idea that the cosmic ray-produced radiocarbon might provide a valuable means of age determination, supposed that the C^{14} atoms would be readily oxidized to carbon dioxide and would mix freely with the atmospheric carbon dioxide. As a consequence of the rapid turnover of the earth's atmosphere, radiocarbon-labelled carbon dioxide would achieve a uniform global distribution, and might be expected to be taken up in the same proportion by all plant life during the process of photosynthesis. All animal life, derived directly or indirectly from plant material, would also be expected to contain the same universal specific activity. Sea life would be similarly affected, since the carbon dioxide of the atmosphere is in exchange equilibrium with the oceans which in turn reach equilibrium with the atmospheric carbon dioxide. He argued that these equilibria are reached quickly compared with the half-life of C^{14}. Upon the death of an organism, further uptake or exchange of radiocarbon would cease, leaving the trapped radiocarbon to decay exponentially with time.

If the specific activity of organic material has been constant over many thousands of years, then ancient organic material would have exhibited the same specific activity at the time of its death as organic material at the present time. If, then, it were possible to measure the activity of such an ancient sample and compare it with the activity of a modern sample, it would be possible, knowing the half-life of radiocarbon, to calculate the time that has elapsed since the ancient sample was in isotopic exchange equilibrium with the carbon reservoir.

The time t since the death of the organism would be given by

$$t = \frac{1}{\lambda} \log_e \frac{I_o}{I} \quad \dots\dots\dots\dots\dots\dots\dots\dots\dots (1)$$

where λ is the decay constant of radiocarbon; I is the measured activity of the ancient sample; and I_o is the measured activity of modern organic material.

As we have said, criticisms of the method have been made on the ground that one or another of the fundamental assumptions is either not valid, or required serious modification. The more controversial assumptions are:

(1) That the specific activity of living organic material has been constant over a very long period, and further that the contemporary assay is universal.

(2) That the biological materials which are to be assayed have retained their true original composition and ceased exchanging with reservoir carbon at the time of death.

(3) That the half-life of radiocarbon has been accurately determined.

1. *The constancy of the contemporary specific activity*. The specific activity of contemporary plant carbon will depend upon the concentration of radiocarbon in the atmosphere and also the extent of any isotopic fractionation which occurs during photosynthesis, and subsequent metabolism. The constancy of the atmospheric activity will depend in turn on the constancy of radiocarbon production and the rates of isotopic equilibrium within the components of the carbon reservoir.

To the first approximation the dates obtained using the method have been shown to be empirically correct. Nevertheless, with the refinement of the technique, de Vries [3] has shown that variations of the order of $\pm 1\%$ have occurred since AD 1500. This conclusion was reached by measuring the initial activity of carefully dated tree rings taking into account the radioactive decay. Following a similar technique, Willis, Münnich and Tauber,[4] conducting parallel measurement on the same sequoia tree in three separate laboratories, have extended the pattern of variations back to AD 600 with good agreement, and have observed the order of variations described by de Vries. Such variations would lead to errors, independent of the error due to counting statistics, of ± 100 years. Thus it could be that materials of one, three, or even five, finite ages could exhibit the same radiocarbon activity and then be ascribed to one common radiocarbon date. The implications are particularly troublesome for the archaeologist, who often requires a more precise age for his samples.

The variation in the specific activity might imply that the production rate of atmospheric radiocarbon has varied with time and thus the cosmic ray flux likewise, or, that in some way the equilibrium of the carbon reservoir has been disturbed. Stuiver [5] has correlated the variations described above with sunspot activity and has shown a distinct correlation between the two. Whether this is in fact a case of cause and effect still remains to be established.

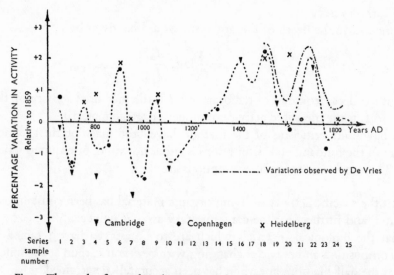

Fig. 3 The result of a combined experiment by the Copenhagen, Heidelberg and Cambridge dating laboratories on the fluctuation of the atmospheric radiocarbon content in the past 1,300 years using the tree rings of a Giant Sequoia as an index

(a) *Equilibrium between the parts of the reservoir.* Craig,[6] Broecker[7] and others have postulated a dynamic model to describe the equilibrium of the radiocarbon reservoir. This model represents a considerable simplification of the natural processes, but nevertheless affords an assessment to be made of the turnover times of the various phases of the reservoir.

The reservoir is continually being replenished by the radiocarbon production from cosmic radiation, and depleted by radioactive decay and sedimentation in the oceans. If the system has reached isotopic equilibrium, the rate of loss will equal the replenishment. The phases are represented by the atmosphere, the biosphere, the upper ocean above the thermocline, and the deep sea. A certain amount of radiocarbon will leak out of the exchange reservoir by becoming entombed in the ocean sediment. This description is known as the chain model. A refinement of this interpretation, known as the cyclic model, has been made to include the direct exchange between deep ocean water and the atmosphere when the former rises to the surface in polar regions. De Vries [8] has described an electrical analogy of Craig's model by considering the phases to constitute an interconnected network of condensers with parallel resistance leak paths.

The specific activity of the contemporary carbon in the different phases will depend largely on the mean residence time of a radiocarbon atom in each phase. As the exchange between growing plant life and the atmosphere is rapid, the contemporary activity of the biosphere will reflect the activity of the atmosphere almost exactly. The two activities will not, however, be identical since an isotopic enrichment in C^{12} is observed during the process of photosynthesis. The mean age of a radiocarbon atom in the surface ocean layers will be much larger than in the atmosphere, since it may have exchanged once or twice with the deep sea. This will mean that the specific activity of the upper ocean would be lower than the atmosphere if there were no isotopic fractionation. Because the latter effect enriches the ocean in radiocarbon, the activity is in fact nearly the same as that found in modern wood.

Similarly, the deep sea will exhibit a specific activity of an even lower value, since its large bulk means that the mean time spent by a radiocarbon atom in this phase is relatively large. Broecker [9] and colleagues at the Lamont Geological Observatory have utilized the apparent age of ocean water to extend our knowledge of the simple turnover model referred to earlier, and in particular to throw some light upon the turnover processes of the oceans themselves.

Isotopic fractionation. The accuracy of the solid carbon method for the contemporary assay was $\pm 2\%$. Kulp [10] found that in practice even this accuracy was difficult to obtain. The effects of isotopic fractionation, which had been demonstrated for several natural processes by Craig [11] for C^{13}, and predicted by extrapolation for C^{14}, were masked by this large error in the assay. The increased efficiency of gas proportional counting has led to the quantitative detection of these effects, especially by Suess,[12] Rafter [13] and Brannon et al.[14]

Craig had already shown by mass spectrometric measurements that the atmospheric carbon dioxide showed an enrichment of C^{13} with respect to modern wood of $1\cdot84\%$. On this basis Craig predicted that the C^{14} enrichment would be twice the value, namely $3\cdot6\%$. Rafter has measured the specific activity of air from Makaia, New Zealand, and obtained results in good agreement with the predicted figure of Craig. Brannon et al. have confirmed this figure, which seems well established.

Besides the natural isotopic fractionation that occurs during the growth of the organism, fractionation may also be introduced during the combustion and subsequent processing of the sample for counting. This fractionation is nearly always present if the overall yield of carbon from the original sample is less than 100%. As a consequence, corrections for this effect must be always taken into account during the calculation of the age of a sample. The fractionation of C^{14} with respect to C^{12} is almost exactly twice that of C^{13}, and since this stable isotope of carbon occurs naturally with an abundance of about 1% of C^{12}, the ratio between the two may be determined directly with a suitable mass spectrometer using double beam collection.

(b) *The fossil fuel effect.* These natural processes are further complicated by the large amounts of fossil fuel, containing no residual radiocarbon, which have been burned during the past century. This addition to the carbon reservoir has diluted the atmosphere with C^{12}. A corresponding lowering of the specific activity of modern wood has been observed,[12] but much of the effect has been buffered by exchange with the sea; there, however, the effect has been quite small.

The effect of the fossil fuel dilution influences dating considerably, since samples older than 100 years would exhibit a greater contemporary specific activity than 1950 wood. Moreover, the effect could conceivably be greater in some industrial areas, and dates published by different laboratories may be based on significantly different values for the specific contemporary activity. Before the recognition of this effect, such variations did in fact exist and the need for amending date lists was recognized by de Vries.[15]

Brannon[16] *et al.* have estimated a total combustion of $3\cdot3 \times 10^{17}$ gm of fossil fuel since 1860, from Putnam's [17] figures for world coal production, cumulative petroleum production, and natural gas (from the ratio of gas to oil production). This sum is equivalent to 14% of the total amount of carbon dioxide in the atmosphere, which would have exhibited a similar percentage increase in C^{12} in the absence of exchange with the other phases. In fact, as has been shown, this exchange does exist, and the observed dilution was only of the order of 3%.

(c) *Weapon testing effects.* The high neutron flux which occurs during the detonation of a thermonuclear bomb has a similar effect to the naturally occurring neutrons produced by cosmic radiation. Radiocarbon has been added to the atmosphere to such an extent that the dilution effect of the fossil fuel has been far more than compensated.

The cessation of weapon testing after the conclusion of a very intense series by all three interested nations has allowed the fate of a relatively large stratospheric injection of radiocarbon to be observed by samples taken over wide areas. The immediate response was a sharp rise in the spring of 1959 corresponding to the annual flushing of stratospheric air through the tropopause gap. This effect had been demonstrated in previous years by Münnich and Vogel [18] for radiocarbon and by other workers for other fall-out products. The rise of 1959 came to a peak at midsummer with a level in NW. Europe of about 32% above 1953 values,[19, 20] the Northern Hemisphere average being slightly less at around 26%.[21] In 1960, a continuous sampling programme at Cambridge showed no pronounced seasonal variation, and the midsummer level had dropped to 22% above 1953 values, and in 1961 a further drop of 2% was observed. The violation of the moratorium in the autumn of 1961, however, must inevitably lead to a reversal of this trend.

The effects of recent additions of both active and inactive carbon to the reservoir can largely be overcome for dating purposes by using a piece of wood over 100 years old as a standard for the contemporary activity, and this procedure is now common practice.

Standards. To offset any possible variation in the activity of contemporary samples used by different dating laboratories, the National Bureau of Standards, Washington,

D.C., now holds a batch of oxalic acid which is available as a universal reference against which laboratory standards may be checked. Similarly a standard is required for carbon 13/12 determinations, and the sample established by custom for this purpose is the belemnite sample used by Craig. There is an NBS C^{13}/C^{12} standard, however, and Craig [22] has shown a variation of 1·1 per mil between this and the belemnite standard.

The difference between the C^{13}/C^{12} ratio of a counting sample and that of the standard may be expressed by δC^{13}, thus:[23]

$$\delta C^{13} = \left(\frac{C^{13}/C^{12}\ \text{sample} - C^{13}/C^{12}\ \text{standard}}{C^{13}/C^{12}\ \text{standard}}\right) \times 1,000 \quad \dots\dots\dots (2)$$

The oxalic acid C^{14}/C^{12} standard is itself affected by the rise in activity due to nuclear weapon testing and is therefore higher than an 'ideal' contemporary sample might be. It transpires however from experience that wood of AD 1890, that is just prior to the industrial revolution, exhibits an activity equal to approximately 95% of the activity of the oxalic acid. This activity, designated in literature as 0·95 A_{ox}, is the accepted standard.

The oxalic acid standard must always be used with due reference to the C^{13}/C^{12} standard mentioned above. Craig [24] has measured about 20 samples of carbon dioxide gas made from the oxalic acid by a number of laboratories and the average C^{13}/C^{12} deviation from the standard is close to $-19\cdot0\ ^{o}/_{oo}$, and by agreement, this value is the established ratio for the oxalic acid. Since the oxidation, either wet or dry, is very prone to introduce further fractionation in the laboratory, it is essential that each batch of gas prepared from the NBS standard be assayed for C^{13}/C^{12} and due allowance made before using it as a reference for dating.

The corrected value for the oxalic acid standard activity, 0·95 A_{ox}, will be given by

$$0\cdot95\ A_{ox} = 0\cdot95\ A^{1}_{ox}\left(1 - \frac{2(19\cdot0 + \delta C^{13}_{ox})}{1,000}\right) \quad \dots\dots\dots\dots\dots (3)$$

where A^{1}_{ox} is the observed radiocarbon activity.[23]

19.0 is the average per millage C^{13}/C^{12} deviation of oxalic acid from the Chicago standard.

δC^{13}_{ox} is the measured C^{13}/C^{12} deviation of the sample of gas prepared from the oxalic acid.

It thus follows that if the measured value of the laboratory sample is -19%, then 0·95 $A_{ox} = 0.95\ A^{1}_{ox}$, and there is no correction.

Calculation of the activity of an unknown sample with respect to the standard. If δC^{14} is the measured deviation between the radiocarbon activity of the unknown sample and that of the standard as computed above, and expressed by

$$\delta C^{14} = \left(\frac{A\ \text{sample} - 0\cdot95\ A_{ox}}{0\cdot95\ A_{ox}}\right) \times 1,000 \dots\dots\dots\dots (4)$$

then the true deviation of the activity of the unknown sample when isotopic fractionation is taken into account may be expressed as Δ, given by

$$\Delta = \delta C^{14} - \left(2\delta C^{13} + 50\right)\left(1 + \frac{\delta C^{14}}{1,000}\right) \quad \ldots\ldots\ldots\ldots (5)$$

This value is then equivalent to $\left(\dfrac{I-I_0}{I_0}\right) \times 1,000$ using the symbols of equation (1),

and the age of the sample may be computed directly, since

$$\frac{I}{I_0} = \frac{\Delta + 1,000}{1,000}$$

$$\text{and } t = \frac{1}{\lambda} \log_e \frac{1,000}{\Delta + 1,000} \quad \ldots\ldots\ldots\ldots\ldots (6)$$

2. *Absence of exchange: the retention by biological materials of their original compositions.*
Barghorn[25] has shown that under anaerobic conditions there are no known bacteria
which will attack lignin. The cellulose fraction of plant material, however, can be the
subject of degradative processes. Unfortunately, the more resistant lignin fraction is
appreciably soluble and material of similar chemical composition may migrate and be
redeposited in another place. Since the more chemically stable cellulose fraction is
depleted by degradation processes, the situation can easily arise where redeposited material forms a major source of contamination. Where such a contamination is suspected,
the intrusive colloidal material may be extracted with alkali, and this material when
assayed invariably yields a much younger age than the residue.

The intrusion of secondary material into a sample can be seen readily in many stratigraphic sections where growing roots have penetrated many feet below the contemporary horizon.[26] Where such intrusion is recognized by fresh rootlets, these can be largely
mechanically removed, but perhaps the case is more serious where the secondary intrusion has itself been humified and is indistinguishable from the primary material.
Errors of this nature have the greater significance the greater the age of the deposit,
and may prove to be one of the limiting factors of the method.

Intrusions do not necessarily have to be of younger origin. In areas such as Britain
where there are large outcrops of Palaeozoic or Mesozoic coal, the boulder clays can be
shown to contain much comminuted material derived from them,[27] and lake deposits,
such as are often employed in dating the Late Glacial period, may contain enough inactive carbon from this source to increase the true dates appreciably.

It has been clearly shown by Deevey *et al.*[28] and Münnich[29] that when the prime
source of organic lake mud is by the photosynthesis of submerged plants in hard water,
the ancient carbon brought into lakes from limestone formations as soluble bicarbonate
may be incorporated into the carbohydrates made by green plants. If this were the only
source of carbon for the photosynthetic fixation of submerged aquatic plants in hard
water lakes, the dating of their remains might be expected to yield a spurious activity
of one half-life of radiocarbon, namely, about 5,000 years. In practice, however, this

figure is rarely realized since there is a constant exchange of carbon dioxide in the lake with the atmosphere, especially if it is shallow; this exchange will tend to restore a fraction of the C^{14} deficit.

3. *The half-life of radiocarbon.* The half-life of radiocarbon has been variously determined at values ranging from 7,200 to 4,700 yr. The evaluation of this quantity is essential to the method if radiocarbon ages are to be truly identified with solar years. The present internationally accepted half-life is 5,568 ± 30 yr, and is derived from the weighted average of three determinations. They are 5,580 ± 45 yr (Engelkeimer, Hammil, Inghram, and Libby[30]), 5,589 ± 75 yr (Jones[31]), and 5,513 ± 165 yr (Miller, Ballentine, Bernstein, Friedman, Nier, and Evans[32]). Each of these three values was derived from absolute gas counting methods and considerable trouble was taken to evaluate the efficiency of the counters used. In all three cases, mass spectrometric methods were used for the isotopic composition of the sample.

Later values (Caswell et al.,[33] Manor and Curtiss[34]) gave 5,900 ± 250 and 5,370 ± 210 yr, respectively, although the higher probable error signifies the lower accuracy of the measurements.

Since the three estimations from which the weighted average was taken were made on three different sets of apparatus, it seems probable that the accepted value for the half-life has a real error greater than the ± 30 yr quoted, which is based on statistics. Ralph [35] drew attention to the fact that measurements made on samples of known age back to 2000 BC indicated that the half-life of 5,568 years was not the best fit for the distribution of the points obtained when known age was plotted against measured age. Crowe [36] had earlier observed that samples of known age plotted on Libby's exponential decay curve in his book *Radiocarbon Dating* [37] tended to fall to one side of the curve. Indeed, a recent announcement by the U.S. National Bureau of Standards indicates that this value of 5,568, accepted universally for the past 10 years, is probably incorrect. Since several physical laboratories are known to be working on the same redetermination, it has been agreed to suspend a recalculation of existing published dates until international agreement has been reached. The redetermination is not likely to entail more than a few per cent alteration, and recalculation of previously published dates would be quite simple.

COUNTING METHODS

The process of establishing the activity of an ancient sample, comparing it with that of a contemporary sample, and thus computing the age in accordance with the formula quoted, should in theory be extremely simple. It is, however, far from simple, for radiocarbon is a weak β particle emitter and even the most energetic of its particles are easily stopped by a metal foil. Furthermore, the amount of radiation involved is extremely small, even for a modern sample. These two factors make it impossible to measure by the simplest form of radioactive measurement, namely by placing the sample on a tray under an end window Geiger counter, but in some circumstances it is possible to place a liquid, synthesized from the sample, in front of a scintillation counter. This technique has achieved comparatively little success until recently because of the difficult chemistry, but at the time of writing a substantial advance seems to have been made, and the technique holds much for the future. In general, however, the sample has to be introduced inside the counting chamber itself, and in one form or another the majority of dates produced so far have been obtained in this way.

Libby's original solution to the counting problems was the most direct way possible. He introduced the sample as elementary carbon into a specially constructed screen wall Geiger counter.[39] The carbon was spread evenly over the inner surface of a brass cylinder, and inserted into the counter. The ends were sealed in place, the counter evacuated, and then filled with a normal filling mixture of argon and ethylene. The filling mixture provides a Geiger counter with good counting characteristics, but although reliable from this point of view, the counting efficiency proved extremely low and counting errors correspondingly large. Twenty thousand years was consequently a generous upper limit to this technique. Furthermore, a source of error which soon became sufficiently large to cause the abandonment of solid carbon counting was the liability to contamination by both naturally occurring atmospheric radioactivities and to the ever-increasing fission products from nuclear tests. The need for higher accuracy with smaller sample requirement and freedom from outside contamination led to the examination of other methods of counting.

The most obvious course to take was the conversion of the sample carbon into the gas phase, and introducing it into a counting chamber as the filling gas. Since it is desirable to get as much sample into the counter as possible to achieve the maximum count rate, higher filling pressures than are normally used in Geiger counting are necessary and counting is generally carried out in the proportional region. The difference between the two is simply that in the Geiger counter the discharge resulting from the ionization of the gas spreads throughout the chamber and results in a large pulse no matter what energy the initial ionizing radiation possessed, whilst in a proportional counter, as its name implies, the final pulse obtained is proportional to the initial energy expended by the ionizing radiation. Weak ionizations produce weak pulses and strong ionizations produce strong pulses.

The choice of gas which is to be used as the counting medium will be influenced by the factors of ease of synthesis of the gas from the raw sample, the manner in which it behaves as a counting gas and how many atoms of carbon each molecule of the gas contains.

The Michigan laboratory [40] uses a mixture of carbon disulphide and carbon dioxide at relatively low gas pressures and is able to use this arrangement as a Geiger counter. It has proved very reliable and simple to operate but the efficiency of this method is, however, somewhat low since the operating pressure is limited.

Carbon dioxide is by far the easiest gas to synthesize, since it is obtained by direct combustion of the sample in a stream of oxygen. It would have few challengers but for the stringent purity requirements for reliable counting characteristics. It had long been held that carbon dioxide was useless as a counting medium, but by rigorous purification of all electronegative impurities it has been demonstrated to be completely reliable.[41] Fergusson [42] has estimated that one part of chlorine in ten million parts of carbon dioxide is sufficient to affect the counting characteristics appreciably. The greater number of laboratories at present producing dates rely on this method.

Methane is more tolerant to impurities and therefore satisfies the second requirement admirably. Its synthesis from carbon dioxide requires additional chemical processes which to some extent detract from its obvious counting qualities. It has one particular advantage over other gases, however, since it requires a much lower working voltage and can be operated at high pressures. At similar pressure with carbon dioxide, high voltage corona discharges become increasingly apparent.

Both acetylene and ethylene are diatomic in carbon and thus have an immediate advantage over both carbon dioxide and methane.[43-45] Syntheses are again more complex, but acetylene in particular has proved popular with a number of laboratories, and is more tolerant to impurities than carbon dioxide.

In practice, the size of counters and hence the amount of gas to fill them is limited largely by the availability of carbon from the sample. Archaeologists are naturally reluctant to part with quantities of precious samples, and the carbon content of geological samples, such as lake muds, is often in small supply. A small counter filled to a high pressure with a relatively low background will best meet the need for small sample size and accuracy of counting. The overall sensitivity of the counter is dependent upon the square of its contemporary count rate divided by its background.

Scintillation counting offers the attractive possibility of introducing much larger quantities of carbon into the counting system than with either of the two previous methods; again supposing sufficient sample to be available.

Routine measurements of natural radiocarbon have been successfully carried out by McAulay and associates [46] at Trinity College, Dublin, using methanol as a solvent. The decision to use scintillation counting in this case was influenced by the non-availability of liquid nitrogen supplies, which makes the use of gaseous systems involving vacuum line technique quite impossible. One of the limiting factors in the scintillation technique has hitherto been the synthesis of a suitable solvent. In most solvents prepared for radiocarbon dating, only one atom in the final molecule originates from the sample, but recently the synthesis of benzene has been reported [47] which derives all its carbon atoms from the raw sample. The syntheses in most forms of scintillation counting are more complex than gas proportional counting, but with the pressing need for age determinations greater than the 70,000 years obtained by the late Hessel de Vries by isotopic enrichment,[48] this method might promise a significant advance.

PUBLICATION OF DATES

The growing number of dates produced by the thirty or more laboratories now in operation presents a formidable amount of data to assimilate. There has thus been a great need for a medium through which dates may be published quickly and in a uniform manner. Two organizations have been created for this specific purpose, the one being complementary to the other.

The first is an offshoot from the *American Journal of Science*, formerly issued as a Supplement to that journal, but now published under the title of 'Radiocarbon'.

Published annually, this journal is supported by nearly every working laboratory, and serves as a source book for all radiocarbon dates. Each sample and its date is accompanied by a brief description of its provenance and significance, and is designated by the sample number and laboratory prefix letter.

The other medium is 'Radiocarbon Dates Inc.', a non-profit-making organization concerned with the distribution of dates on a punched card system. Each card, an example of which is shown in Plate III, contains all the relevant information, and may be sorted under a wide range of headings. Inquiries should be addressed to Radiocarbon Dates Inc., R. S. Peabody Museum for Archaeology, Andover, Mass., U.S.A., and for the journal, Sterling Tower, Yale University, New Haven, Conn., U.S.A.

Both organizations provide an excellent service, and by their very existence demonstrate the contribution that the method has made to the advancement of our knowledge of man's past history.

REFERENCES
1 LIBBY, W. F. 1946. *Phys. Rev. 69*, 671
2 —— 1955. *Radiocarbon Dating*, Chicago
3 DE VRIES, H. L. 1958. *Proc. Koninkl. Ned. Akad. Wetenschap. 61 no. 2*, 1
4 WILLIS, E. H., MÜNNICH, K. O. and TAUBER, H. 1960. *Am. J. Sci. Radiocarbon Suppl. 2*, 1–4
5 STUIVER, M. 1961. *J. Geophys. Res. 66*, 273
6 CRAIG, H. 1957. *Tellus 9*, 1.
7 BROECKER, W. S. and OLSON, E. A. 1960. *Science 132*, 712
8 DE VRIES, H. L. 1958. *Proc. Koninkl. Ned. Akad. Wetenschap. 61, no. 2*, 1
9 BROECKER, W. S., GERARD, R., EWING, M. and HEEZEN, B. C. 1960. *J. Geophys. Res. 65*, 2903
10 KULP, J. L. *et al.* 1958. *Natl. Acad. Sci.—Natl. Research Council 573*, Nuclear Science Series no. 24
11 CRAIG, H. 1953. *Geochim. et Cosmochim. Acta 3*, 53
12 SUESS, H. 1954. *Science 120*, 5
13 RAFTER, T. A. 1954. *New Zealand J. Sci. Technol. 36*, 363
14 BRANNON, H. R., WILLIAMS, M., SIMONS, L. H., PERRY, D., DAUGHTY, A. C. and McFARLAN, E. 1957. *Science 125*, 919
15 DE VRIES, H. L., BARENDSEN, G. W. and WATERBOLK, H. T. 1958. *Science 127*, 129
16 BRANNON, H. R. *et al., op. cit.*
17 PUTNAM, P. C. 1953. *Energy in the Future*, New York
18 MÜNNICH, K. O. and VOGEL, J. C. 1950. In Godwin, H. *Nature 184*, 1365
19 WILLIS, E. H. 1960. *Nature 188*, 552
20 TAUBER, H. 1960. *Science 131*, 921
21 BROECKER, W. C. and WALTON, A. 1959. *Science 130*, 273
22 CRAIG, H. 1957. *Geochim. et Cosmochim. Acta 12*, 133
23 BROECKER, W. C. and OLSEN, E. 1961. *Radiocarbon 3*
24 CRAIG, H. 1961 *Radiocarbon 3*
25 BARGHORN, E. S. 1961. *J. Sediment. Petroc. 22*
26 GODWIN, H. 1951. *Am. J. Sci. 249*, 301
27 —— and WILLIS, E. H. 1959. *Proc. Roy. Soc. B. 150*, 199
28 DEEVEY, E. S., GROSS, M. S., HUTCHINSON, G. E., and KRAYBILL, H. L. 1954. *Proc. Natl. Acad. Sci. U.S. 40*, 285
29 MÜNNICH, K. O. 1957. *Naturwissenschaften. 44*, 32
30 ENGELKEIMER, A. G., HAMMIL, W. H., INGHRAM, M. G. and LIBBY, W. F. 1949. *Phys. Rev. 75*, 1825
31 JONES, W. M. 1949. *Phys. Rev. 76*, 885
32 MILLER, W. W., BALLENTINE, R., BERNSTEIN, W., FRIEDMAN, L., NIER, A. O. and EVANS, R. D. 1950. *Phys. Rev. 77*, 714
33 CASWELL, R. S., BRABANT, J. M. and SCHWEBEL, A. 1954. *J. Res. Natl. Bur. Standards 53*, 27

34 MANOR, G. G. and CURTISS, L. F. 1951. *Ibid.*, *46*, 328
35 RALPH, E. K. and STUCKENRATH, R. 1960. *Nature 188*, 185
36 CROWE, C. 1958. *Nature 182*, 470
37 LIBBY, W. 1955. *Radiocarbon Dating*, Chicago, 2nd ed.
38 EDITORIAL, *Radiocarbon 3*
39 LIBBY, W. F. 1952. *Phys. Rev. 86*, 128
40 CRANE, H. *Radiocarbon 3*
41 DE VRIES, H. L. and BARENDSEN, E. 1953. *Physica 19*, 987
42 FERGUSSON, G. J. 1955. *Nucleonics 13*, 18
43 BARKER, H. 1953. *Nature 172*, 631
44 CRATHORNE, A. R. 1953. *Nature 172*, 634
45 SUESS, H. E. 1954. *Science 120*, 5
46 McAULAY, I. R. and DELANEY, C. F. G. 1959. *Proc. Roy. Dublin Soc.* Series A, *1*, 1
47 TAMERS, M. A. 1960. *Science 132*, 668
48 DE VRIES, H. L., DE VRIES, A. E. and HARRIS, A. 1958. *Science 128*, 472

3 Quaternary Dating by the Fission Track Technique

ROBERT L. FLEISCHER   P. BURFORD PRICE

ROBERT M. WALKER

AMONG DATING METHODS which make use of radioactive decay a uniquely awkward time span has been the period from 70,000 years ago back to nearly the beginning of the Pleistocene epoch, two or three million years ago. For ages greater than 70,000 years the short half-life (5,660 years) of carbon-14 makes carbon dating inapplicable; and although potassium-argon dates in the range 70,000 to 3,000,000 years can be determined, the long half-life (1,300 million years) of potassium-40 makes measuring such ages experimentally laborious, since great care must be paid to selection of suitable materials and to their processing. In contrast the new technique of fission track dating has been used to date materials of ages ranging from 20 years to more than 1,000,000,000 years before the present—the controlling factor being the presence of uranium impurities, usually in trace amounts such as are commonly found in nature.

Fission track dating makes use of the fact that over geological time spontaneous fission of uranium-238 impurities produces minute, sub-microscopic damage trails in most insulating solids, both crystalline and glassy. During the long periods involved, a large number of these damage trails can be created in many materials. If these damage sites are permanent, a simple count of their number allows an age to be measured.

The density of tracks depends on the uranium content as well as the age of the sample, and it is therefore necessary to measure the uranium concentration in each sample for which the 'fossil' tracks have been counted. The simplest way to make this measurement is to expose the sample to a known number of low energy (thermal) neutrons, which induce fission of a small fraction of the uranium atoms in the sample. Since the density of newly-produced tracks is proportional to the uranium concentration, a second track count allows this quantity to be measured and the age to be calculated. Fig. 4 indicates that a wide time span is accessible by this technique.

We have noted that the fission tracks are sub-microscopic in size. How then are they to be counted? The simple, general technique which is used depends on these damage tracks being chemically more reactive than is the surrounding undamaged material. Immersion of a sample in the proper chemical reagent allows rapid attack of the narrow regions of damage and slower dissolution of the adjacent undamaged material. Such treatments are used to create etch pits of optical size, each one marking a single fission site. Plates IV and V show examples of etched fossil tracks in natural materials.

Two of the considerations which decide whether a sample is suitable for fission track dating have already been mentioned. One requirement is that the particular crystalline or glassy material used must be able to retain tracks over long periods of time. Heating

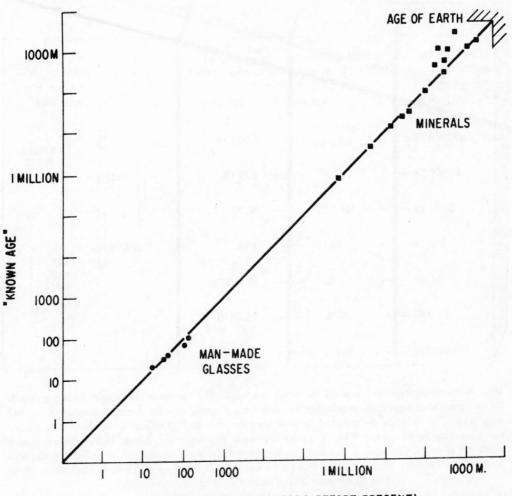

Fig. 4 Comparison of fission track ages with those 'known' by other methods, either (as in the case of man-made glasses) actually known dates or dates estimated from artistic style or, as in the case of natural minerals, dates measured by means of other radio-active decay schemes. Agreement between these ages has been found for periods of greater than 1,000,000,000 years.

will cause tracks to fade, and it follows that materials which will retain tracks to the highest temperatures are best for storing tracks over long times. Table A lists materials and their track fading temperatures determined by laboratory experiments. Empirically we know that those materials whose fading temperatures lie above 400°C can retain tracks over geological times. Others, such as feldspar glass (225°C) and autunite (50°C) are known to be unreliable dating materials.

A second need for fission track dating is sufficient uranium to produce a track density which can be counted within a reasonable time. Fig. 5 includes a graph of the minimum

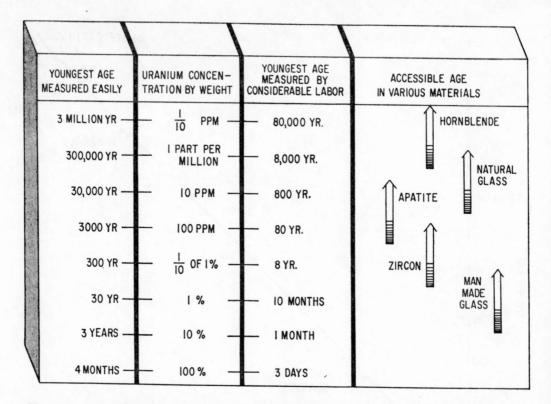

YOUNGEST AGE MEASURED EASILY	URANIUM CONCENTRATION BY WEIGHT	YOUNGEST AGE MEASURED BY CONSIDERABLE LABOR	ACCESSIBLE AGE IN VARIOUS MATERIALS
3 MILLION YR	$\frac{1}{10}$ PPM	80,000 YR.	HORNBLENDE
300,000 YR	1 PART PER MILLION	8,000 YR.	NATURAL GLASS
30,000 YR	10 PPM	800 YR.	APATITE
3000 YR	100 PPM	80 YR.	
300 YR	$\frac{1}{10}$ OF 1%	8 YR.	ZIRCON
30 YR	1 %	10 MONTHS	MAN MADE GLASS
3 YEARS	10 %	1 MONTH	
4 MONTHS	100 %	3 DAYS	

Fig. 5 Uranium concentration needed for dating as a function of the age of the sample. Values are given for two conditions depending on whether the observer is planning on a short, easy experiment or a more tedious one. For an 'easily' measured age it is assumed that the observer will spend one hour at his microscope counting fission-track etch pits. For a determination 'by considerable labour' nearly 40 hours of such work are assumed. Glass that is free from inclusions and bubbles is considered for estimating the time necessary for counting tracks. On the right are indicated the lowest ages which should be measurable in various minerals on the basis of their uranium contents.

values needed for measuring various ages and also indicates some materials which are often appropriate for various Quaternary times. Although glasses such as obsidian or pumice have been used most frequently, materials which typically have higher uranium content—zircon or apatite—would provide track densities that are conveniently high.

A third problem, which is often the most difficult to solve is not connected with the particular dating technique used but rather with assuring that a given material is of the same age as the event which one is trying to date. For example, although it is the age of the fossil remains of *Homo habilis* which is of interest, we must content ourselves with measuring the age of the volcanic deposit in which these remains were found. To establish that the volcanic deposit has the same age as the bones requires the combined efforts of archaeology, geology, and geochronology; and no one of these disciplines has sufficient power to resolve such a question alone. If crystalline material such as fossil tooth enamel were to prove suitable for dating, then the geologist's role would be less vital; but as yet no such material has proved usable.

One obvious case where archaeology, geology, and geochronology have all been brought to bear, and where now there is confidence in the age and its appropriateness, is in the dating of Bed I, Olduvai Gorge, Tanzania. The age of $1\frac{3}{4}$ million years found by potassium-argon dating has been checked and rechecked, correlated consistently with detailed stratigraphy, and confirmed independently by fission track dating. [See October 1965, Current Anthropology.]

TABLE A

Track fading temperatures for various materials (1 hour heating).

Material	Temperature (°C)	
Quartz	1025°	
Diopside	850°	
Bytownite	750°	Materials
Zircon	700°	in
Silica Glass	650°	which
Hornblende	575°	tracks
Tektite Glass	525°	are
Pigeonite	525°	likely
Muscovite	525°	to
Hypersthene	500°	be
Olivine	500°	'permanent'
Apatite	450°	
Soda Glass	375°	
Calcite	350°	Tracks
Feldspar Glass	225°	unlikely
Aragonite	125°	to be
Autunite	50°	'permanent'

REFERENCES

Fission Track Dating and its application to Quaternary Dating has been described in the following articles:

1 FLEISCHER, R. L., PRICE, P. B. and WALKER, R. M., 1965. *7th International Congress on Glass, Brussels, June–July,* vol. II, paper 224, pp. 1–8, New York
2 —— 1965. *Science* 149, 383–93
3 —— 1965. *Ann. Rev. Nuc. Sci.* 15, 1–28

4 *Obsidian Dating*

IRVING FRIEDMAN   ROBERT L. SMITH

DONOVAN CLARK

THE DATING OF OBSIDIAN ARTIFACTS is based upon the fact that a freshly made surface of obsidian, a variety of volcanic glass, will absorb water from its surroundings to form a measurable hydration layer.[1] This layer is not visible to the unaided eye and should not be confused with the patina that develops on many materials as a result of alteration or chemical weathering. The hydration begins the moment the surface is exposed by chipping or flaking and the penetration of water into the artifact continues at a known rate until the present time. Thus, when ancient man chipped or flaked a piece of obsidian he exposed fresh surfaces on which hydration then commenced. Measurement of the depth of penetration of hydration on the artifact should, then, provide a measure of the time that elapsed since the manufacture of the artifact.

This hydration process appears to be restricted to obsidian, and does not occur on other natural materials such as flint, jasper, quartz, chert, chalcedony and quartzite.

The development of this dating technique is very recent,[2] and although problems still remain to be worked out, the measurement of several thousand artifacts from archaeological sites all over the world has proven the method to be useful within the limitations to be discussed.[3]

The discovery that the hydration of obsidian was related, in part, to time, suggested that this fact could be utilized as a dating method. To accomplish this, however, required the following:

(1) Development of a technique for measuring hydration layers, that may vary from only a few tenths to perhaps 20 microns (10 to 1,000 millionths of an inch), and with a precision of about $\pm$ 0·2 micron (8 millionths of an inch).

(2) Determination of the rate at which the hydrated layer increased in thickness.

(3) Analysis of the factors that influence the rate of hydration.

(4) Analysis of the variability caused by alteration of the hydration layer by wear, etc.

(5) A determination of the archaeological factors that affect the correlation of the age of the artifact with the stratigraphic position in which it is found.

These factors will be considered in some detail in the sections to follow.

THE TECHNIQUE OF MEASUREMENT

The technique of measurement is fairly simple and quick. A thin platelike sample, which may be as small as 2 mm × 4 mm by 0·5 mm thick, is sawed from the artifact at right angles to the surface to be examined. This cutting is carried out, with the aid of an especially thin diamond-loaded metal saw blade, in a manner that causes little damage to the specimen. The cut slice is then cemented to a glass microscope slide and ground down, first with the aid of a motor-driven lap charged with a slurry of fine abrasive and water, and later by hand on a glass plate charged with the same abrasive, until the slice is about 0·05 mm (0·0025 in.) thick. The cutting and grinding of a typical sample requires about fifteen minutes.

This thin section is then examined under the microscope. Because the hydrated obsidian has a higher refractive index than does the non-hydrated obsidian and the interface between the hydrated and non-hydrated material is sharp, the division between the two can be seen under the microscope as a relatively sharp dividing line. Plate IVa is a photomicrograph of a typical sample taken with a 45 × objective and a 10 × ocular. The addition of water to the obsidian causes a change in volume that creates mechanical strain in the hydrated layer. This strain causes the hydrated layer to be seen as a bright band (strain birefringence) when viewed under crossed polarized light (Plate IVb). Strain birefringence is useful in detecting the hydrated layer, but the measurements to be described are usually made in plain light.

The measurements are made with the aid of a filar micrometer ocular, a special eye-piece containing a movable scale or hairline, the movement of which can be read on a drum on the side of the eyepiece. Layers thicker than 2 microns are measured using the 10 × or 12·5 × filar micrometer ocular and a 45 × objective (approx. 500 ×). Thinner layers are measured with a 100 × oil immersion objective with the filar micrometer eyepiece (approx. 1,000×). Examination and measurement under the microscope require about ten minutes per slide.

In our first paper on the method[2] we assigned an error of ± 0·2 micron to our measurements. We found that on duplicate thin sections made from the same artifact, 90% of the time our repeat measurements would fall within this assigned error.

Recently one of us (D. Clark) has made a careful statistical analysis of the measuring technique. In a test involving four different persons, each measuring an identical series of slides, the results showed a standard error of the mean of ± 0·2 micron. However, since people differ somewhat in their placing of the hairline, it is suggested that future users of the method calibrate themselves by measuring a set of standard slides.

RATE OF HYDRATION OF OBSIDIAN

In order for the measurements of hydration layer thickness to be translatable into an age, it is necessary that the rate of increase in thickness of the hydrated layer with time be known. Because the rate is too slow to allow direct measurement in the laboratory, it was necessary to secure artifacts of known age and to use the thickness of the hydrated layer of these specimens to determine the hydration rate. The difficulty has been in securing obsidian artifacts of really 'known' and reliable age. The ideal sample for our use would be one made 2,000 or more years ago, inscribed with the date of manufacture, and kept in a known environment from date of manufacture to present. Since no such pieces are available, we are forced to approximate this ideal. One source of old well-dated material is to be found in obsidian used to decorate Egyptian mummies and burial containers. This material can be dated with sufficient accuracy both historically and by radiocarbon. Unfortunately few such samples have been available to us. Of the Egyptian samples that we have obtained, many are of a rather rare form of volcanic glass called trachytic obsidian that differs chemically from the usual rhyolitic obsidian. This chemical difference results in a more rapid rate of hydration than occurs with rhyolitic obsidian. The rate determined with the trachytic obsidian cannot therefore be applied to rhyolitic obsidian artifacts.

Another source is obsidian associated with material which can be dated by radiocarbon. The problems here are that not only must account be taken of the errors possible in C^{14} dating, but the material dated by C^{14}, because of uncertain stratigraphic correspondences, may prove to be of an age quite different from that of the obsidian. Thus, attempts were made to secure dated obsidian from stratigraphic horizons in excavations where the obsidian is associated with cultural material datable either historically, or by tree ring dating of associated wood, C^{14} dating of associated charcoal, etc. The correlations are not always valid. Even burials, where the obsidian artifacts were interred with the body, present problems of older obsidian being buried long after it was originally chipped.

However, bearing in mind these problems inherent in securing accurately dated obsidian in order to establish hydration rates, it was still possible to establish tentative hydration rates and to assess many of the factors that influence the rate of hydration. Work now in progress and proposed should help make the hydration rate data more precise.

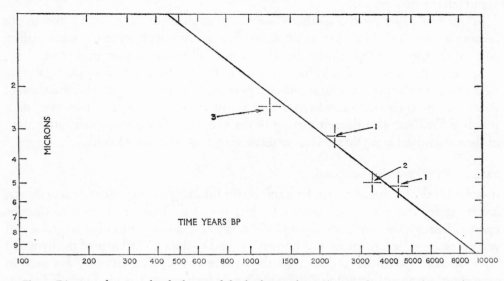

Fig. 6 Diagram showing the thickness of the hydration layer (microns) *vs.* time (years BP) on artifacts from Central California. From Clark[4]

On theoretical grounds it was thought that the penetration of water into the obsidian should follow the diffusion law $D = kt^{1/2}$, where $D =$ thickness of hydration layer in microns, $k =$ constant, $t =$ time in years. The data first presented [5] fitted this equation within the precision of the data. Recent work by Clark [4] on a carefully selected group of obsidians from burial sites in Central California, where the relative dates of the burials

(a) Collagen fibres in fossil ivory from Siberia.

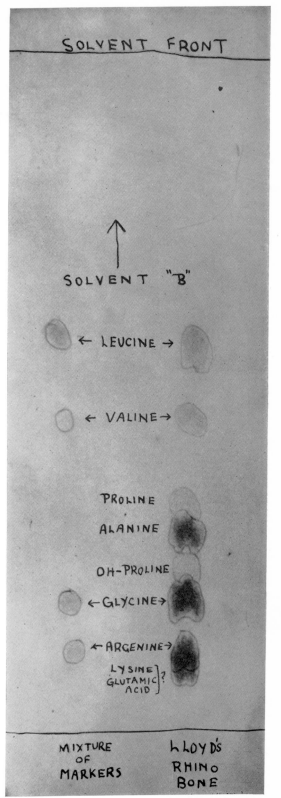

SOLVENT FRONT

SOLVENT "B"

← LEUCINE →

← VALINE →

PROLINE

ALANINE

OH-PROLINE

←GLYCINE→

←ARGENINE→

LYSINE ⎱?
GLUTAMIC ⎰
ACID

MIXTURE
OF
MARKERS

LLOYD'S
RHINO
BONE

(b) Chromatogram of amino-acids in hydrolysate from the ulna of a woolly rhinoceros found on the site of the Lloyd's Building, City of London. (Preparation by A. E. Rixon.)

(see page 35) PLATE I

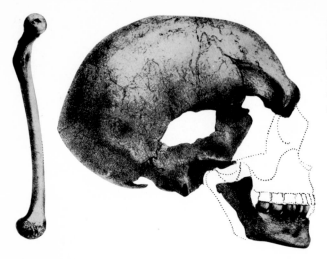

(a) Femur and skull of Galley Hill Man found in the Swanscombe Gravels in 1888. Fluorine and nitrogen tests indicated that this skeleton was an intrusive (post-Pleistocene) burial, that is, less than 10,000 years old. Radiocarbon dating of the residual collagen confirmed this, showing that the skeleton had an antiquity of between 3,000 and 4,000 years.

(b) The Swanscombe skull: the three known bones (found in 1935, 1936 and 1955) articulated and shown from behind. Fluorine, nitrogen and uranium analyses confirmed the contemporaneity of the skull with the Second Interglacial fauna in these gravels, indicating an antiquity of about a quarter of a million years. Photo courtesy Trustees of the British Museum (Natural History).

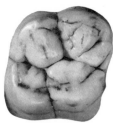

(c) Upper and lower molars of (left to right) man, orang-utan and *Gigantopithecus* ($\times\frac{3}{2}$), the last bought with a prescription for 'Dragon's Teeth' at Chinese drugstores. The Middle Pleistocene date of *Gigantopithecus* has been confirmed by radiometric assays. Photo courtesy Professor G. H. R. von Koenigswald.

PLATE II (see page 35)

(a) The Radiocarbon Dating Laboratory, Cambridge University. The glass vacuum line is used in the purification of carbon dioxide gas for proportional counting.

Nevada, Pyramid Lake Shell Lamont Laboratory L-364CS 17,500±600 yrs.
Astor Pass Region

Lat. 40°10'N x Long. 119°35'W Geology Gas proportional-counting, CO_2

Lake Lahontan area, Nev. The following measurements were made as part of a program designed to reconstruct the pattern of the climatic variations in the western part of the Great Basin (A detailed discussion of the results is being prepared by P. C. Orr and W. S. Broecker). Since a large majority of the measurements were made on carbonate materials, a study has been made of the validity of such materials as indicators of radiocarbon age (W. S. Broecker, in preparation). The samples were collected as part of a joint project by P. C. Orr and W. S. Broecker. Shell taken from sample L-364CR.

Broecker, W. S. and J. L. Kulp, 1957, Lamont Natural Radiocarbon Measurements, IV: Science, 126, p. 1333.

® 1958 Radiocarbon Dates Association, Inc. Serial no. 480

(b) A specimen of the punched-card index system published by 'Radiocarbon Dates Inc.' as a service to archaeology.

(see page 46) PLATE III

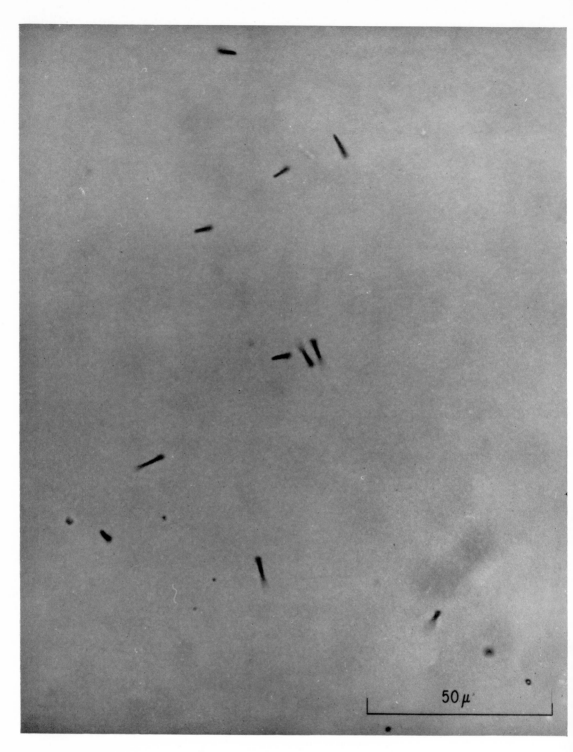

Examples of etched fossil tracks in natural materials.

PLATE IV (see page 58)

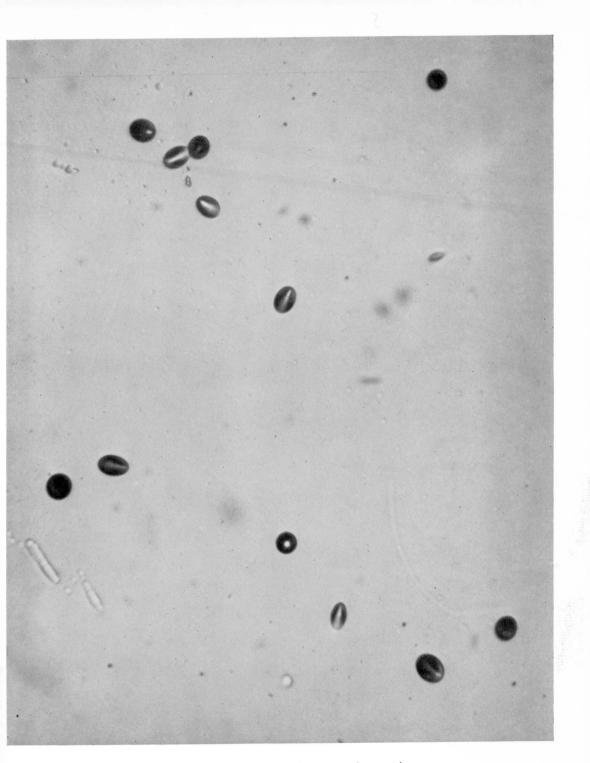

Examples of etched fossil tracks in natural materials.

(see page 58) PLATE V

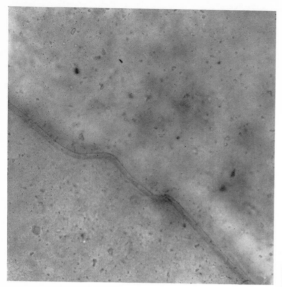

(a) Photomicrograph of a thin section of an obsidian artifact showing the hydration layer, as viewed in ordinary light. From Friedman and Smith.[2]

(b) Photomicrograph of the specimen shown in (a) viewed under crossed polarized light. The hydrated layer is bright because of strain birefringence. From Friedman and Smith.[2]

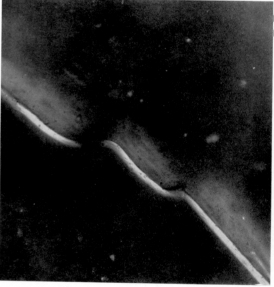

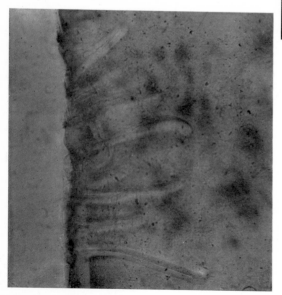

(c) Photomicrograph of a thin section of an obsidian artifact from Ecuador, showing a thick hydration layer along an original unworked surface (lower left) adjacent to a flaked area. Blows struck on the artifact introduced a series of short percussion cracks. The thickness of the hydration layer formed along these cracks is the same as on the remainder of the worked surfaces of the artifact. From Friedman and Smith.[2]

PLATE VI (see page 62)

Silhouette skeleton in Tumulus II, Elp (municipality of Westerbolk), Drenthe, Netherlands. Excavated by A. E. van Giffen, 1932.[23] Photo courtesy Institute for Biological Archaeology, State University, Groningen

(see page 118) PLATE VII

Iron manganese stain replacement of body in acid
gravel. Stain passes into 'bony' base of skull below.
C.1 500 years old. Mucking, Essex; p. 118.[39] (Photo
W. T. Jones.)

Humic residue of 'wooden post' in chalk. C. 3500
years old. Farncombe Down, Berks.; pp. 118, 121.
(Berks. Arch. J. 60, 1962, 8, Pl. IV—Photo P. A. Rahtz.)

PLATE VIII (see page 118)

are fairly well established and where there are several C^{14} dates in sequence, suggest a hydration rate that may follow $D = kt^{3/4}$. Again, further work may help establish the equation of the hydration rate. We need more well-dated obsidian artifacts to settle this point. Whether the hydration follows $D = kt^{3/4}$ is not important for most artifacts under 4,000 years old. The differences become important when dating artifacts of much greater age, say 20,000 years old.

FACTORS THAT INFLUENCE THE RATE OF HYDRATION

Early in the research we recognized that while all surficially exposed obsidian hydrates, the rate at which a layer of hydration will thicken depends primarily on the temperature at which it has been exposed while hydrating. Thus, like most diffusion processes, the rate is faster in warmer, and slower in colder environments. Translated to specific examples, we have found that artifacts buried in coastal Ecuador will hydrate ten times as fast as those buried in the frozen arctic of the northern Alaska Arctic Coast. Therefore, dating material of a given site or area will ideally require a knowledge of the local climatology, past and present. This may mean data on the soil temperature at the depth where the sample was buried. Where this is lacking, approximations based on air temperature and soil conductivity estimates will usually suffice. The accuracy of these temperature estimates need not be great, and this information is now being collected for archaeological sites containing obsidian artifacts. In many cases the change of climate since the obsidian artifacts were made is small, and can be approximated from geological and climatological data.

The temperature coefficient of the rate of hydration, although probably the largest variable, does seem to be the easiest of the variables to assess and to correct for. We need but to construct hydration curves for different climatic zones as was done in Fig. 3. More closely defined zones will ultimately allow closer control of this variable. Indeed, we should soon know the temperature dependence of the 'constant' k in the hydration rate equations, and this will allow us to calculate a hydration rate curve for any given site.

It might appear that another possible variable would be the relative dryness of the environment where the obsidian is buried. We have shown that obsidian of the same chemical composition buried in wet tropical coastal Ecuador hydrates at about the same rate as does material buried in a tomb in Egypt. The relative humidity of the environment has no apparent effect, probably because in any natural environment there is enough water to saturate the outer surface of the obsidian with a molecular film of water, and keep it saturated throughout the hydration history of the obsidian, and it is this saturated outer surface that helps determine the rate of penetration of water into the interior of the obsidian.

The chemical composition of the obsidian also influences the hydration rate, and we know that gross differences in chemistry, such as that existing between rhyolitic and trachytic obsidian, will cause a major change in hydration rate. Fortunately, most obsidian used for artifacts does not differ very much in chemical composition. Little is known about the specific chemical differences that exist between obsidians obtained from different outcrops or quarries in one small area. Even less is known about the influence of such minor chemical differences, if they exist, on the rates of hydration of such obsidian. In the course of our research, we have found small anomalies in sets of data, that may be related to minor chemical differences among the artifacts.

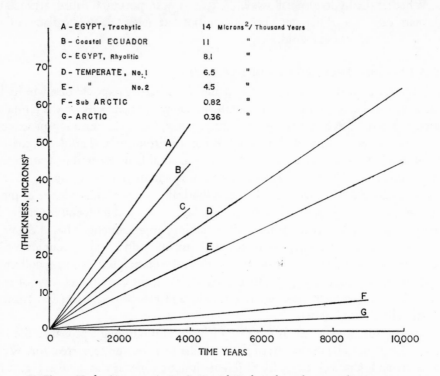

Fig. 7 Hydration rates A, B, C, D and E plotted on the same diagram to show the variation in the rate in different climatic regions. The rate of hydration of each scale is also stated as a mathematical expression of the slope of the corresponding line. From Friedman and Smith[2]

The Yayahuala site in the state of Hidalgo, Mexico furnishes us with such an anomalous set of data. Here artifacts made from grey obsidian are found mixed with artifacts made from a clear green obsidian. The two types of obsidian came from different quarries, and probably differ slightly chemically. The green objects have hydration rims greater than 3 microns, while the objects made from the grey obsidian all have rims less than 3 microns. Is this difference due to a variability in chemical composition between the obsidians, or is it a true age difference? In the latter case we may have a situation where the site was occupied for a time by people using obsidian and then abandoned. The people of a later occupancy then used obsidian from another quarry. In other words the two magnitudes of hydration in this site correlate with different coloured obsidian, and may reflect either a chemical difference in contemporary material, or the differences may express a change in cultural habits over time. Further work, both archaeological and chemical, will be necessary to further elucidate this problem.

CHANGES IN THICKNESS OF THE HYDRATION LAYER
BY MECHANICAL AND CHEMICAL PROCESSES

The hydration layer is extremely thin, and because it forms the outermost surface of the artifact it is subject to alteration by physical and chemical processes. For example, an artifact exposed to running water, wind, or sand for any length of time may lose part or all of the layer, at various locations, through abrasion. Commonly the abrasion will be obvious by inspection of the artifact. The edges, formerly sharp, are now rounded and the surface has a dull, matt appearance. However, it is unlikely that mechanical erosion can remove a uniform layer on all surfaces of the artifact. Often thin spots and chipped areas are seen on the thin sections. However, such effects can be caused during the grinding of the thin section, and may not be the result of natural abrasion. For these reasons, it is necessary to search the edges of the thin section thoroughly to locate the maximum and culturally representative thickness of hydration. We may stress, however, that typical thin section specimens present no measurement problems.

The hydrated layer consists of a glass containing about 3·5% water by weight, compared to less than 0·3% of water present in the main body of the non-hydrated obsidian. Diffusion of alkalis and other ions is very rapid in the high water content layer. Consequently, alteration and solution are speeded up in this layer as compared to the non-hydrated obsidian. Conceivably the chemical environment present in certain soils will speed up this chemical attack. Obsidian in areas of hydrothermal activity would seem especially prone to this vicissitude. Artifacts from sites near hot spring localities in Central California show a high degree of this form of alteration. This could account for the lack of any hydration on many of the artifacts examined from Jarmo, Iraq. However, except for a few sites, we have found little evidence for pronounced alteration of the hydrated layer by physical or chemical agents.

Because mechanical strain increases as the hydration layer becomes thicker a point is finally reached where the hydrated layer spalls off, and hydration begins again on the fresh surface that is created. Such spalling is not always complete and on some very old pieces of obsidian traces of a thicker layer can be found. We believe that spallation may occur when the layer is greater than about 40 microns. Therefore, on artifacts of supposedly great antiquity (over 50,000 years), it is well to cut several sections to look for such remnant layers.

Exposure of the artifact to fire, as, for example, when the obsidian is found in a cremation, affects the surface of the obsidian and makes it unsuitable for age determination. Such 'burned' artifacts are easily recognized by the fine, cross-hatched cracking or blistering of the surface.

CULTURAL FACTORS THAT AFFECT THE ARCHAEOLOGICAL
INTERPRETATION OF OBSIDIAN HYDRATION RESULTS

During the course of measuring and evaluating the results from thousands of obsidian artifacts, we have encountered occasional anomalous measurements, clearly not due to environmental factors or to laboratory error. The magnitude of the variability often indicates that these specimens are not contemporaneous with the provenience from which they were collected. For example, in a lot of ten specimens from a given strati-graphic level, typically six or seven may yield measurements which cluster rather well about the mode and mean. Three or four, however, may have a hydration layer obviously too thin or too thick. Usually these erratic measurements may be explained logically. Often, however, the archaeological grounds for so doing are less clear. Attention has recently been drawn to the re-use of obsidian artifacts of an old culture by peoples of a more recent culture. It is not, therefore, difficult to provide a plausible reason for the presence in a given cultural level of specimens which are too thickly hydrated, hence too old. It is rather the occasional presence of those specimens whose hydration is too thin that is somewhat less amenable to simple explanation. We may consider such factors as slight petrologic differences, post-cultural fracturing (thus exposing fresh surfaces for hydration), or even differential wear on these specimens. More plausible, perhaps, would be the chances of contamination of a given archaeo-logical stratum by peoples of a later horizon and the intrusion of later obsidian artifacts into this level. It seems equally possible that such a level can also be contaminated by overlying material during excavation. Another, if less likely source of error could derive from museum or laboratory mislabelling. Stratigraphic mixing is, of course, a chronic problem in archaeology, and the problems encountered in obsidian dating will not pro-vide us with the final solution. On the other hand, as we acquire more evidence, parti-cularly typological, we can better explain the occurrence of anomalous measurements. Meanwhile, we find it most feasible to measure five specimens or, if available, even ten specimens from each burial, stratigraphic level or other cultural component to be dated. We do not believe that reliance can be placed upon only one or two specimens with any assurance of precise dating. In passing we can, however, note one rather special excep-tion to this rule. In cases where the antiquity of manufacture is in question, it is a simple matter by this method to test whether a single artifact or work of art made of obsidian is authentically archaeological or a modern forgery. A lack of hydration safely implies manufacture within the twentieth century, and we have had occasion to make this test as a service to a few museums and collectors in the past few years.

We have discussed the method in some detail, and have stated that it is both reliable and precise. It remains to support this claim with results. While this publication is not a suitable medium for a detailed listing of hydration values, we hope that the following three fairly typical examples will serve dual ends. First, to demonstrate the approaches we have used in our research; and, secondly, to show the degree of confidence one may place in the method when unfavourable conditions, such as cultural and stratigraphic mixing, are not excessive.

The first illustration involves a study of fifty well-documented artifacts. These derived from ten different burials in seven representative sites in Central California. For the most part, associated artifacts, such as typological shell beads, permitted good relative place-ment of each burial lot. Since the obsidian artifacts in each lot clearly were associated with the burial, it was assumed, *a priori*, that the members of each lot were contempor-aneous. We shall observe that this assumption did not hold in a few cases because of re-use and other factors which we have described. Incidentally, one aspect of the procedure, we believe, added rigour to the test. This was the practice of making all the measurements on this series 'blind', that is, without the analysts making prior reference to the proveniences or assumed ages of the specimens. Table A lists the results of measurement on the entire series. The California sites represented are as follows:

(1) Kingsley Cave: A Late horizon (1,500 years BP to eighteenth-century site).
(2) Peterson 2: Another Late horizon site; two burials examined.
(3) Hotchkiss: A Late horizon site; two burials examined.
(4) Bodega Bay: A primarily Middle horizon (4,000 to 1,500 years BP) context, but containing an overlying Late horizon stratum.
(5) McClure: A Late horizon site.
(6) Goddard: A Late horizon site.
(7) Blossom: An Early horizon (c. 4,000 years BP) site; two burials examined.

It will be seen from these figures that, except for occasional anomalies, the within-burial variances are not great, and more importantly, the method readily discriminates between burials of different archaeological ages. It is unfortunate that a greater number of specimens for each burial were not available for testing; but we believe that, as they stand, the data are adequate.

A second example is that of Shanidar Cave, Iraq. The floor of the cave was partially excavated by Professor Ralph Solecki of Columbia University who submitted the obsidian samples for investigation. In excavating the cave, Professor Solecki made various cuts into the floor. Charcoal was found at certain depths in several of the cuts, and C^{14} dates were obtained on this charcoal. The obsidian was not usually associated with the charcoal and the correlation between the C^{14} dated layers and the obsidian was based on a comparison of cultural material found in the various strata. In Fig. 8 the thickness of the hydrated layer squared ($D = kt^{1/2}$) is plotted against the estimated age of the artifacts, as determined by the correlations mentioned above. In general there is good agreement between the thickness of the hydration layer and the estimated age of the artifacts. Additional samples secured by further excavation may clear up the few discrepancies.

The Chorrera site on the coast of Ecuador is an example of an archaeological site where obsidian artifacts made by an earlier culture have been re-used by later occupants of the site. The site consists of a habitation refuse deposit on the Rio Babahoyo, Guayas Province. Drs Clifford Evans and Betty Meggers[5] of the Smithsonian Institution excavated the site and studied the pottery found in the refuse deposit. Measurement of 62 obsidian pieces (see Fig. 9) from the site permitted us to group the artifacts into four groups as follows: (1) Hydration layers less than 2·0 microns. These, in view of their thinness and therefore late age, were classed as 'modern'. This checks with the fact that the site has been cultivated since the Spanish occupation and a banana plantation now occupies the site. (2) and (3). Two groups of artifacts found above the 285 cm layer. One group with hydration thickness from 2·9 to 3·9 microns and another from 3·9 to 4·9 microns. (4) Below 285 cm we find no artifacts with a hydration layer less than 5 microns. We conclude that artifacts having layers from 2·9 to 4·9 microns were made by

TABLE A

Thickness of hydration layer and approximate hydration age of artifacts associated with ten different burials from seven different sites in Central California.

Site and Burial	Measurements*	Hydration age approx.	Remarks
	μ	yrs BP	
Kingsley	1·4	700	Burial average 1·5±0·10 microns
Cave	1·5	750	Variance slight
Burial	1·6	850	Good agreement with archaeological
No. 93	1·6	850	estimate of age
	1·6	850	
Peterson 2	1·4	700	5th specimen contained two rims
Burial No.	1·5	750	of hydration. This condition
12/7697	1·5	750	ascribed to a case of reworking of
	1·7	900	an older artifact
	1·7/3·4	(omitted)	Burial average 1·5 ± 0·13
Peterson 2	1·6	850	6th specimen possibly reworked
Burial no.	1·6	850	Burial average: 1·7±0·13 microns
12/7696	1·7	900	
	1·8	1,000	
	1·9	1,050	
	2·0/4·1	omitted	
Hotchkiss	1·9	1,050	Burial average 2·1±0·14
Burial 52	2·0	1,100	Variance slight
	2·0	1,100	
	2·2	1,250	
	2·2	1,250	
Hotchkiss	2·1	1,150	Burial average 2·4±0·26 microns
Burial 22	2·5	1,500	
	2·5	1,500	
Bodega Bay	1·9	1,050	Burial average 2·5±0·50 microns
Burial 17	2·7	1,650	
	2·8	1,750	
McClure	2·3	1,300	Burial average 2·6±0·18 microns
Burial 13	2·6	1,550	
	2·6	1,550	
Goddard	2·6	1,550	4th and 5th specimens appear to be
Burial 7	2·9	1,800	cases of re-use
	3·0	1,850	Burial average 2·8±0·21 microns
	4·4	omitted	
	4·6	omitted	

TABLE A continued:

Site and Burial	Measurements*	Hydration age approx.	Remarks
	μ	yrs BP	
Blossom	4·3	3,100	Variance unexplained at present.
Burial 33	4·5	3,300	Burial av. 5·2±0·70 μ; av. of
	5·5	4,300	1st and 2nd, 4·6, of 3rd and 4th, 5·7.
	5·9	4,700	C¹⁴ composite dates on this site were
			4052±160, and 4100±250 BP
Blossom	4·8	3,600	Burial average 5·0±0·26 microns.
Burial 23	4·9	3,700	See remarks above
	5·3	4,000	

* Average of two analysts.
Hydration age estimates are based on the rate $D = kt^{3/4}$ (see Fig. 6, p. 64); samples submitted by Prof. R. F. Heizer, Univ. of California, Berkeley.

people who occupied the site subsequent to the first occupation. All the obsidian in the upper levels having hydration layers thicker than 5 microns could be interpreted as re-use and redeposition of older material.

On the basis of changes in pottery types Evans and Meggers [3] subdivided the Chorrera deposit into three parts:

'The Milagro period from 0 to 135 cm, the Tejar period from 135 to 300 cm; the Chorrera period from 300 cm to the bottom of the stratigraphic cut. The Chorrera period refuse coincides almost exactly with the earliest period distinguished on the basis of hydration thickness (greater than 5 microns). There is no clear demarcation in the thickness of the hydration layers at 135 cm that correlates with the Tejar-Milagro period subdivisions. However, the intermediate grouping of artifacts with hydration layers of 3·9 to 4·9 microns thickness gives a date that would be acceptable for the Tejar period, and the third group, with thicknesses of 2·9 to 3·9 microns, undoubtedly represents the Milagro period. If this interpretation is valid, then the artifacts, flakes, and chips of obsidian with hydration layers less than 3·9 microns in thickness in levels below 135 cm may be explained as mechanical mixture, either during occupation of the site, afterwards by rodent and small animal burrowing, or a specimen from an upper level in the walls of the stratigraphic cut accidentally falling into the excavation.

'The frequency of re-used material, which associates early objects with late levels; and the possibility of disturbance, which can move late material into earlier levels in habitation refuse, are two problems that the Chorrera stratigraphic excavation illustrates in an extreme way. The fact that the artifacts are chips or prismatic flakes used as blades or scrapers without shaping beyond the initial blows striking them from a

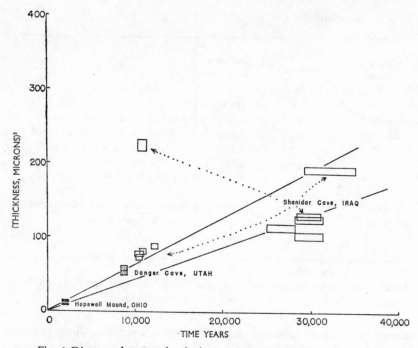

Fig. 8 Diagram showing the thickness of the hydration layer in microns squared on objects from Shanidar Cave, Iraq as well as from other sites in temperate zones. From Friedman and Smith[2]

core, rather than projectile points or carefully shaped artifacts, probably accounts for this extensive re-use. Comparable re-use might be predicted in other areas with similar rudimentary obsidian tools. However, with adequate knowledge of the cultural sequence and a sufficient number of samples per level, re-used objects can be readily distinguished from those of contemporary manufacture. Artifacts of too recent date can be recognized if a series of samples is secured for several sites of the same cultural period, and if the cultural sequence in the area is sufficiently well known. A good relative chronology is essential for evaluation of any absolute dates, whether they are derived from obsidian, radiocarbon, dendrochronology, or some other method.

CONCLUSIONS

The obsidian dating method is still in the developmental stage. In common with all dating techniques, it contains sources of error inherent in the technique. The authors have attempted to outline some of these sources of error. In addition to the technical errors, every dating technique contains archaeological problems related to the material used for dating. The re-use and stratigraphic mixing of obsidian is such a problem. In applying the obsidian dating technique, one must always keep in mind that the hydration thickness or 'date' represents the time from the moment of manufacture of the surface examined to the present time. This date may have little relationship to the time at

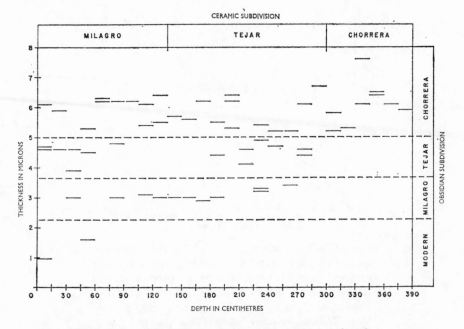

Fig. 9 The thickness of the hydration layers of the obsidian artifacts from various levels in Cut I, Site R–B–I, Chorrera, on the coast of Ecuador. The cultural divisions derive from pottery classification and the levels at which they subdivide are shown at the top. The divisions suggested by differences in thickness of the hydration layers of the obsidian artifacts are shown at the right. From Evans and Meggers[3]

which it was buried, or to the provenience in which it is ultimately found. We have examined several thousand samples from archaeological sites which range geographically through most of the world areas where obsidian is known naturally or culturally, and which range in time from European contact to the Lower Palaeolithic. Some of our results, for one or more of the reasons outlined above, show disagreement with archaeological age estimates ascertained by other archaeological or geochronological methods. On the whole, the obsidian hydration results are quite concordant with chronological expectations. In not a few cases of apparent disagreement the reason has not been difficult to find. A large portion of these results has been published, and several series of obsidian dates from major excavations will accompany the respective excavation reports when these monographs are eventually published.

APPENDIX

Since the publication of the first edition of *Science in Archaeology* the technique of obsidian dating has been applied to practical problems of archaeological chronology and seriation. Further research has been carried out on the method itself and the advances in the technique are discussed briefly in this appendix.

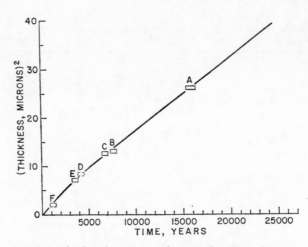

Fig. 10 Obsidian dating curve showing the relation between the radiocarbon (C–14) date in years before present and the thickness of the hydration layer in microns squared (ordinate). A = Shirataki, Loc. 31, 15,820 ± 400; B = Kojohama, 7,700 ± 200; C = Misato, 6,800 ± 225; D = Wakoto (compared with Tokoro, 4,150 ± 400); E = Nakazawa, 3,825 ± 175; F = Chikapunotsu (compared with Chikapunotsu, 920 ± 100; Sakaeura, 1070 ± 800 and Tanaka, 1100 ± 160). After Katsui and Kondo.[8]

Katsui and Kondo[8] applied obsidian dating to artifacts from six sites of non-ceramic to post-Jomon cultures in Hokkaido, Japan, and have determined rates of hydration in northern Japan over the past 20,000 years (Fig. 10). They have shown a change in hydration rate from the present rate of $2 \cdot 0 \, \mu^2/1,000$ years to a rate of $1 \cdot 6 \, \mu^2/1,000$ years. The change in rate occurred about 4,000 years ago, and is related to the warmer climate of the present as compared to the late Pleistocene climate of Hokkaido.

Friedman has determined hydration rates of $3 \cdot 4 \, \mu^2/1,000$ years for artifacts from north central Montana, and a rate of $5 \cdot 1 \, \mu^2/1,000$ years for artifacts 5,000 years old buried at a site just north of Yellowstone Park, in south central Montana (Rigler Buttes site).

In order to determine whether the hydration followed the $D = kt^{1/2}$ or $D = kt^{3/4}$ relations discussed earlier (p. 64), a series of laboratory experiments were undertaken by Friedman, Smith and Long.[6] Obsidian was hydrated at 100°C, and the hydration was shown to follow the relation $D = kt^{1/2}$.

The influence of the temperature of hydration on the rate of hydration can be calculated from the data given in the above paper. Bell has measured ground temperatures at an archaeological site in the highlands of Ecuador, and it is hoped that such measurements of ground temperature, when combined with the data referred to above (Friedman, Smith, and Long) will enable us to compute a hydration rate that will be sufficiently accurate to use for chronometric calculations.

REFERENCES

1 Ross, C. S. and Smith, R. L. 1955. *American Mineralogist 40*, 1071–89
   Friedman, I. and Smith, R. L. 1958. *Geochim. et Cosmochim. Acta 15*, 218–28
2 ——— 1960. *Am. Antiq. 25*, 476–522
3 Evans, C. and Meggers, B. J. 1960. *Ibid. 25*, 523–37
   Clark, D. L. 1961a. *Curr. Anth. 2*, 111–14
4 ——— 1961b. *The Obsidian Dating Method Applied to Central California Archaeology*. Ph.D. dissertation, Dept. of Anthropology, Stanford University
5 Evans, C. and Meggers, B. J. 1957. *Am. Antiq. 22*, 235–47
6 Friedman, I., Smith, R. L. and Long, W. 1966. *Bull. G.S.A. 77*, 323–8
7 Evans, C. 1965. Report No. 18 in *Reports of the Norwegian Archaeological Expedition to Easter Island and the East Pacific, Volume II—Miscellaneous Reports*. Santa Fe, New Mexico
8 Katsui, Y. and Kondo, Y. 1965. *Japanese Jour. Geol. and Geography, vol. XXXVI, nos. 2–4*, 45–60, pl. I
9 Michels, J. W. 1965. *Lithic serial chronology through obsidian hydration dating*. Doctoral Dissertation, Department of Anthropology, University of California, Los Angeles
10 Bell, Personal communication

5 Archaeomagnetism

R. M. COOK

ARCHAEOMAGNETISM—a term invented by its pioneer, Professor E. Thellier—is the study of the remanent magnetism of archaeological remains. It is distinguished from palaeomagnetism, which is the corresponding study of geological material, more for convenience than from principle. Both archaeomagnetism and palaeomagnetism are based on the facts that the magnetic field of the earth (of which the magnetic north of the compass presents the most familiar effect) is changing continually in direction and intensity and that these changes can leave natural records. Such records are said to have been observed in sedimentary rocks, where they result from the process of geological formation; but for archaeomagnetic studies it is the remanent magnetism caused through heat—and so named in full thermo-remanent magnetism—that is relevant.

GENERAL THEORY

General Statement. The process of thermo-remanent magnetization is, very simply, this. Many rocks contain magnetic oxides of iron. Above a certain temperature, known as the Curie point, the particles of these oxides lose their ability to retain magnetism; over a range of a few degrees between the Curie point and the so-called blocking temperature they are susceptible immediately to whatever magnetic field surrounds them—that is, they tend to acquire its direction and proportionately its intensity; below the blocking temperature they retain any magnetism they have acquired and are no longer affected by magnetic fields of low intensity, as in particular that of the earth. This general description needs some comments.

Curie Points. Different magnetic oxides have different Curie points. The highest, at 670°C, is that of haematite (α-Fe_2O_3). For magnetite (Fe_3O_4) it is 580°C. There are other oxides with lower Curie points, some within the range of ordinary atmospheric temperatures. It follows from the difference in Curie points that the different oxides in a rock may have different remanent magnetizations. If, for example, a rock containing magnetite and haematite is first heated to 670° and allowed to cool down and later is heated to 580° and again allowed to cool, the remanent magnetism of the haematite particles is that acquired during the first cooling and of the magnetite particles that acquired during the second cooling; if the surrounding fields during the first and second coolings were different, so too will be the remanent magnetisms of the two kinds of particles.

When a rock has two or more such magnetizations, its composite magnetization will be their mean. The components can be disentangled by reheating progressively to the appropriate Curie points, so that the magnetizations acquired at lower temperatures (and so more recently) are eliminated. In the example of the last paragraph, reheating to 580° would eliminate the later magnetization acquired by the particles of magnetite, but leave the haematite particles still undisturbed.

The magnetic constituents of rocks vary widely, but the proportion of oxides with low Curie points is inconsiderable in most of the well-fired clays encountered in archaeology.

Stability of Remanent Magnetism. Generally the remanent magnetism of a particle remains stable till it is heated beyond its blocking temperature. There are, though, some disturbing factors:

(1) Some rocks, because of their crystal structure, are unstable magnetically. This instability is very low in the commoner baked clays, but considerable in many volcanic rocks.

(2) In any rock some magnetic particles are likely to acquire a temporary magnetization from a low surrounding field. This viscous temporary magnetism seems to occur at temperatures in general not much below the blocking temperature, and so normally it affects only those particles which have a Curie point near atmospheric temperatures. Though the incidence of viscous magnetism increases with time, the rate of increase falls off quickly: as the Thelliers have shown, the number of particles affected after exposure of from 10 minutes to 14 days is as great as the number affected between 14 days and 90 years. So viscous magnetism can be detected and even calculated by reversing the position of a specimen for a few weeks and noting any changes in the magnetization. It can, of course, be eliminated by reheating to a convenient temperature, say 60°C.

(3) At temperatures below their blocking temperature the magnetic particles are not affected, viscosity apart, by other weak magnetic fields, such as that of the earth. But if the surrounding field is of higher intensity—for magnetite the resistance or coercive force is 20 oersted, for haematite 7,000 oersted—it can produce a new remanent magnetization. Such magnetization is described as isothermal or anhysteretic, according to the process by which it is induced. The only natural cause that is at all common is lightning. If isothermal or anhysteretic magnetization has not been complete and the particles of the more resistant oxides are unaffected, it can be eliminated or separated for calculation either by reheating to the temperature at which remagnetization took place or else by applying an alternating field equal in intensity to that which caused the new magnetization.

(4) After a rock has acquired a remanent magnetization chemical changes may occur, which convert a magnetic into a non-magnetic oxide or—more misleadingly—form new magnetic oxides. Such new oxides may acquire their remanent magnetism from the field surrounding them at the time of formation. Well-fired clays are not much subject to chemical changes, though experience suggests that prolonged waterlogging may have a considerable effect.

(5) Careless treatment in a laboratory may cause chemical changes or new magnetizations. If, for example, a sample is reheated to eliminate any remanent magnetism acquired at a low Curie point, it is obvious that, when the sample cools again through the critical range of temperature and is susceptible to remagnetization, cooling must be in a zero field (that is, in the absence of any effective magnetic field) or in a field of which the direction and intensity are known exactly.

Magnetic Fields. In normal conditions, when a rock is acquiring remanent magnetization, the principal field determining the magnetization is that of the earth. This field has several components, each of which varies more or less irregularly. The secular or long-term variation (that marked on the maps of the Ordnance Survey) is thought to be compounded of the main field of the earth, which has its North pole to the north of Hudson Bay and—at least for direction—is static over long periods, and of several regional disturbances, which are disposed erratically and have ranges of up to a thousand miles: these regional disturbances, recognized since the late seventeenth century, have a limited period of growth and decay (or of fluctuation) and move from east to west at a rate of about 1° in 5 years. For this reason the direction and intensity of the earth's field at one place does not necessarily (as far as is known) have a completely systematic relation to its direction and intensity at another place some hundreds of miles away, and so extrapolation for latitude and longitude is hazardous.

Besides the secular variation there are some minor, short-term variations, which fluctuate erratically in cycles of different lengths. Their contribution to the total field is small, very rarely exceeding 1° in direction and 1% in intensity and, considering the practicable limits of accuracy in archaeomagnetic work, they can usually be ignored.

Some other magnetic disturbances too must be considered. Deposits of magnetic minerals may produce local fields; usually these are already known and so can be discounted. A much more narrowly localized deflection may result from the proximity of some magnetized object, as for instance an iron crowbar leaning against the side of a cooling kiln; here with luck the investigator might be suspicious of his results, since the influence of a magnetic field decreases with the cube of its distance and so the further parts of the kiln would be noticeably less affected than the nearer. Further, when a potentially magnetic subject is cooling, those parts which first acquire a remanent magnetism may exert a weak magnetic effect on other parts as they in turn pass through their critical range of temperature; but since the magnetic intensity of archaeomagnetic subjects does not often exceed 10^{-2} e.m.u./cc or about one-fiftieth of the intensity of the earth's field, any errors so caused are not likely to be serious and may even be averaged out in the subject as a whole.

Unexplained Anomalies. Whenever specimens are taken from any sizeable archaeomagnetic subject, there are always appreciable differences between them in the direction and intensity of their remanent magnetism. If, for instance, ten samples are taken from a well-preserved kiln, the range in their respective declinations is rarely less than 5° (Table A). These differences, which do not seem to follow any logical pattern, are too great to be due to faults in collection or measurement; they are not regularly caused by accidental shifting of position; nor does it appear that they are completely explicable by any of the disturbing factors already mentioned. Whatever the reason or reasons, it is assumed that these differences can be discounted by taking a mean between them, and this assumption gives credible results.

Summary. The theory of remanent magnetism has not been worked out in complete detail, and the explanations of some phenomena are still tentative. For the practice of archaeomagnetism, what is most important is that most of the fired clays encountered have a very stable remanent magnetism, which records with fair accuracy the magnetic field of the earth at the time of magnetization: stones, unfortunately, are in general less stable, especially if they are of volcanic origin.

PURPOSES

The direction and intensity of the earth's magnetic field are, as has been said, changing continually, but observational records of these changes are very incomplete. For direction the first known observations of both inclination and declination were made in Rome in AD 1540, in London in 1586, and in some parts of the world not till the present century; the earlier of these observations made no allowance for short-term or local variations and are not precisely reliable. For intensity the first observations were made about 1830. So remanent magnetism offers geophysicists important evidence for the recent history of the earth's field, especially when the date of magnetization can be supplied by archaeological context, historical records, or (less accurately) by radio-carbon or some other natural chronometer. In this way it is practicable to plot approximately the variations of the magnetic field of the earth for a few thousand years in a few parts of the world. As such plots are constructed, they become useful to archaeologists for dating structures or objects of which the remanent magnetism is known but not the date: if, for example, a kiln of Roman-British type was found in London and the direction of its remanent magnetism gave values of 57° for declination and 1°E for inclination, its probable date (as Fig. 11 shows) would be in the region of AD 200. These are the major aims of archaeomagnetic study. There are also some minor applications for archaeology, as regards both direction and intensity.

DIRECTION

No simple connection has yet been detected between the secular variations in direction and intensity of the earth's magnetic field and, since also the practical procedures of measuring them are different, it is easier to discuss them separately.

Definitions. The direction of a magnetic field is expressed most conveniently in terms of horizontal and vertical planes. For the horizontal component or declination (D), which is the direction shown by the ordinary compass, true North serves as the point of reference. The inclination or dip (I) is reckoned as the vertical angle between the direction of the field and the horizontal plane (that is, at a point of the earth's surface, the tangent plane). At London in 1956 the mean value of the earth's field for D was 8°36·8′W and for I 66°37·4′, and in recent years the annual variation in D has been about 10′E.

Specimens. In any archaeomagnetic specimen, if the direction of its remanent magnetism is to be intelligible, it must have a known external point of reference. In other words, the specimen's orientation (relative, if not absolute) at the time when it was magnetized must be ascertained. Archaeologists who find this concept hard to grasp may consider the analogy of a map or plan without any geographic bearing marked on it.

This means in the case of burnt structures that, to be useful, they must be strictly *in situ* and not have collapsed or shifted. Movable objects are generally worthless for the study of the direction of the earth's field, except under two conditions for inclination. The first condition is that the place of firing should be known to a hundred miles or so, since latitude and longitude partly determine the local direction of the earth's field. The second condition is that the position of the object during firing should be given; in particular, bricks are normally stacked level in kilns and some pots (especially if of glazed ware) set upright, so that in the first instance one of the faces and in the other the foot should be fairly horizontal and so allow an approximate measurement of dip (though not, of course, of declination).

Other requirements of archaeomagnetic specimens (which cannot be judged safely by eye) are that they contain a sufficient proportion of magnetic oxides—for present apparatus the minimum is about 10^{-6} e.m.u./cc³—and that they have been fired well. It is an advantage too if they have not been exposed for long to weathering or water, and if they are not very fragmentary.

In practice the structures which provide the best material are kilns. They were generally sunk in the ground in open spaces, so that their lower part had an unusually good chance of surviving; more often than not their walls were made of clay or else lined with it, and they were fired to temperatures of not less than 800°C, that is well above the maximum Curie point. Hearths and cremation places as a rule were not so highly fired and the depth of magnetization is usually much less; further they are more liable than kilns to subsidence. The walls and floors of buildings that were burnt down can also give good results. Of structural materials clay (unfired at the time of construction) is best, stone more chancy, baked brick or tile difficult. In Roman hypocaust flues, for instance, the brick or tile already had a remanent magnetism when it was put in place and the subsequent heating may not have been high enough or penetrated far enough to replace that first magnetism completely.

For pots and other movable objects, if they are being considered for measurements of dip, there is a possible danger that they may have been remagnetized, whether wholly or partially, by accidental burning, during cooking or in a funeral pyre. This can sometimes be decided by discoloration or the circumstances of finding.

Collecting Samples. Since a portable magnetometer has not yet been produced to measure an archaeomagnetic structure *in situ*, samples must be removed for measurement in a fixed magnetometer in a laboratory. To compensate anomalies a number of samples—eight or more—should be taken, preferably from different parts of the structure and in a symmetrical pattern. What is essential is that each sample should be marked with its present (that is, its original) orientation, to serve as a reference for the direction of its own remanent magnetism. The most satisfactory method, where it is practicable, is—before detaching the sample—to cap it with plaster, taking care that the top surface is horizontal; this gives a plane of reference for the dip. On this horizontal surface is inscribed a known horizontal bearing, to which the sample's declination can be related. For the magnetometers which are used at present it is convenient to have samples mounted in the form of cubes. Again it is convenient, though not necessary, to prepare the cube at the time of collection. This is done by first cutting round the sample, so that it projects as a boss, and next a collapsible form—4½ in. square has proved a convenient size—is set round the boss, levelled with a spirit level, and filled with plaster. The horizontal bearing is taken best from a theodolite sighted on the sample as well as on some known fixed point; failing that, a box compass can be laid on the sample and its position and bearing marked. After this the sample is cut away from below, and its bottom too may be plastered over. Since many specimens are fragile or friable, plastering has the advantage also of conserving them.

Measuring Apparatus. The magnetic fields of archaeomagnetic specimens are relatively very weak, and so when they are measured it is necessary to exclude the effects of the earth's field and of any local disturbances. Two types of measuring apparatus are in use.

The astatic magnetometer adapts the principle of the compass needle. Two bar magnets are fixed one above the other on a vertical rod, which is suspended so that it can revolve freely. The two magnets are of equal strength and set in diametrically opposite directions. Since the pull on the two parts of the magnet system is equal and opposite, the effect of the earth's field is cancelled. But if a magnetized sample is put a little below the magnet system, it will affect the lower magnet more strongly than the upper and the magnet system will swing towards the direction of the sample. The reason is that the strength of a field decreases according to the cube of the distance; with the earth's field and even quite local disturbances the difference in distance of the two magnets from the centre of the field is infinitesimal or anyhow unimportant, but with the sample the difference is considerable. To reduce interference and disturbance the magnet system and sample should be enclosed in Helmholz coils. By setting the sample on its top and bottom, its declination is measured directly; the dip is calculated from readings taken when the sample is set on each of its four sides. This large number of measurements is necessary to compensate for any eccentricity of the sample's field in relation to the axis of the magnet system. The astatic magnetometer is simple and sensitive to fields as low as 10^{-7} e.m.u./cc: on the other hand measuring and calculating are slowish, and it is liable to disturbance by, for instance, passing traffic. Versions of this apparatus have been used in Tokyo, Prague and Cambridge.

The other type of magnetometer applies the principle of electromagnetic induction, that if a magnet (in this case an archaeomagnetic sample) is brought close to a coil of wire and there moved, an electrical voltage is set up between the ends of the coil. The voltage is greatest when the direction of the magnet's field is in alignment with the plane of the coil. The integrated voltage can be measured by attaching the coil to a galvanometer. Again disturbing fields are excluded by a system of Helmholz coils. For practical reasons samples are measured in three positions at right angles to each other, and their magnetic direction is ascertained from the three readings. The so-called ballistic magnetometer works by turning the sample quickly through half a circle, so producing a direct current. In the spinning magnetometer the sample is rotated continuously to produce an alternating current; unfortunately, the speed of rotation (on which the range of sensitivity depends) is often limited by the centrifugal momentum of the sample. The advantages of this type of magnetometer are that it is quicker in measuring and relatively immune to local disturbances; but it is more complex and less sensitive than the astatic type. Both the ballistic and the spinning magnetometers are used in Paris and Oxford.

Naturally each operator prefers his own type of apparatus; but if one compares the measurements of the same samples made in Paris, Oxford and Cambridge (Table A), it appears that in practice both rotating and astatic magnetometers can give on average satisfactory results.

TABLE A

Measurements made in Paris, Oxford and Cambridge of samples from a kiln at Grimstone End, Suffolk.

Sample No.	Declination			Inclination			Viscosity
	Paris	Oxford	Cambridge	Paris	Oxford	Cambridge	Paris
1	5·5W	1·2W	1·7W	66·4	65·6	63·5	0·9
2	6·0W	4·2W	4·0W	65·7	66·2	66·0	1·3
3	5·7W	3·2E	4·0W	67·9	67·5	67·0	0·7
4	4·25W	3·8W	3·0W	61·3	61·6	63·0	1·4
5	4·0W	2·8W	1·0W	62·7	60·7	65·0	0·4
6	2·6W	2·1W	2·5W	66·2	63·9	65·5	1·2
7	5·0W	1·9W	9·0W	66·4	65·4	68·0	0·4
8	1·8E	1·0W	0·0	67·9	68·4	67·0	0·6
9	9·5E	8·6E	10·5E	67·2	67·5	67·5	2·5
10	7·9W	5·5W	3·0W	63·9	63·6	65·5	1·1
average	3·0W	1·1W	1·8W	65·6	65·0	65·8	

Declination and inclination are given in degrees, the figure for viscosity is the percentage decrease in the vertical component after inversion.

Treatment of Measurements. The directions obtained by the magnetometer must first be related to the original orientation of the sample. If the sample has been made up into a cube in the way described on pp. 80–81, the reference for dip is to the top of the cube and for declination to the bearing marked on it. The result for dip is correct immediately; but the declination bearing must itself be related to true North.

The mean between the results from several samples of one structure may be plotted on a stereograph or computed. Fisher has developed a useful statistical treatment for the dispersion of the vectors. Where one sample of a set is very divergent from the others, it is probably fair to discard it, since few structures are completely homogeneous or perfectly preserved: in such cases it helps to have noted the position and state of each sample before collecting it.

Results for the Direction of the Earth's Field. For the past direction of the earth's field the present results are very limited in time and place. This is because good archaeo-magnetic material is not too easy to come by and little work has been done on it. Nor are the results in general precisely accurate, since most archaeomagnetic structures are not dated precisely; for kilns, which have provided so many of the specimens, the chronological evidence has usually been coarse pottery, on the dating of which archaeologists are not yet consistent with each other nor (I would guess) reliable to within fifty years.

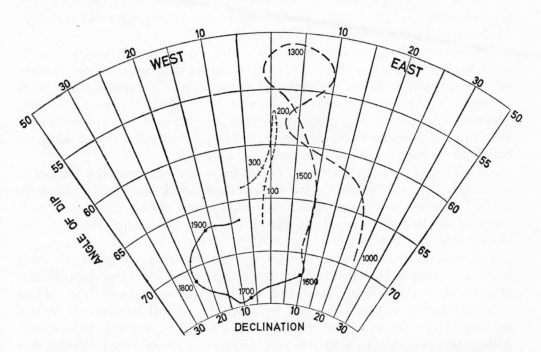

Fig. 11 Secular variation of the direction of the earth's magnetic field in England. The unbroken line gives the observed variation in London. Dates are all AD. (By courtesy of the Research Laboratory for Archaeology, Oxford.)

Even so, the provisional values for declination and inclination are already useful. For Britain we have a fair idea of the direction of the earth's field from the first to the fourth century AD and for northern France and the Rhineland indications for a rather longer period. There is a little evidence for Tunisia in the second century BC and the third century AD. In Britain, France and the Rhineland the earlier medieval period is almost blank, the later is now clearer in Britain. A scattered series of bricks offers further inclinations for France. There is also for Greece an unevenly distributed series of inclinations and declinations from the third millennium BC to the eighth century AD, for western Turkey inclinations from the second to the fourteenth centuries AD, and for the Caucasus inclinations particularly for the sixth to the twelfth centuries AD. With time and patience these sets of results could be extended, linked and refined, and a reasonable basis for limited extrapolation might be secured. Fig. 11 offers directional curves for Britain in the Roman and later medieval periods.

In the Far East a directional curve has been compiled from a long series of hearths and kilns in Japan, dating probably from a little before 3000 BC to the fifteenth century AD. Here it seems that viscous effects may have been strong and, if so, the measurements should be checked. For Shanghai in China reasonably coherent values for inclination were obtained in Oxford from porcelain vases of the third and second centuries BC and the tenth century AD. The Orient, like other regions where civilization is old, must have a sufficiency of useful archaeomagnetic material.

Archaeological Applications. The curves shown in Fig. 11, though not precisely accurate, are already serviceable to archaeology; in particular burnt structures of the Roman-British period may be datable by their remanent magnetism alone to within fifty years. Eventually it might be practicable to halve that margin. Archaeomagnetism has one inherent advantage over radiocarbon and thermoluminescence and other chronological indices dependent on automatic physical changes; the dates it offers are not calculated back from the present day, but from the nearest fixed point.

For this reason archaeomagnetism can be useful in relative dating also, whether or not there is any absolute chronological framework. It should, for example, be possible to decide whether the burning of the Mycenaean palaces of Greece occurred simultaneously (that is, within a period of twenty-five years) or over a longer time and, if so, in what order they were burnt.

Two minor uses of archaeomagnetic direction can sometimes be helpful in the study of broken pottery and clay figures. In such objects, fired well and in one piece, the lines of direction should, of course, be parallel in every part. Now many of these objects have wheelmarks or other indications by which the original horizontal or vertical relation of fragments can be determined. So first, if in two fragments the inclination or declination, as measured from their known horizontal or vertical plane, is similar, they can be from the same object; and if not, they cannot. Secondly, where two fragments come from the same object and agree in one component of the direction, their relative positions in the other plane can be obtained from the other component (Fig. 12).

INTENSITY

The intensity (*F*) of the earth's magnetic field differs with latitude, as does its direction, and it too is subject to regional disturbances. Its secular variation, though, seems to be independent of that of direction, and the rate of its change is markedly less. Present values for the intensity of the earth's field, measured on the surface of the earth, range from about 0·40 oersted at the magnetic equator to about 0·61 oersted at the magnetic poles.

Specimens. Specimens should, of course, be well fired and preferably, because of the methods of measurement, well oxidized and quite free from unfired or partially fired accretions. Since comparison is of intensity and not of direction, the orientation at the time of magnetization has no relevance here and so specimens can be taken freely from movable objects, such as pottery, as well as from structures. This means that there is available already a very large supply of usefully dated specimens which cover many parts of the world as far back as their Neolithic periods, when the making of pottery began. The main proviso is that, because of latitudinal and regional differences in the intensity of the earth's magnetic field, the place of firing (and not of finding) should be known. It is also worth repeating that if specimens have been reheated—in cooking, accidental fires or cremations—the original remanent magnetism may have been replaced in whole or part.

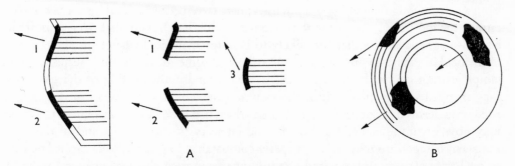

Fig. 12 Simplified diagram showing use of magnetic direction to determine (A) if sherds can be from the same pot, (B) the relative positions radially of sherds from the same pot. (In A, which is sectional, the horizontal lines represent wheelmarks and the arrows the magnetic inclination: so 1 and 2 can be from the same pot, but 3 cannot. In B, which is a schematic view from above, the arrows represent the magnetic declination.)

Measurement. The intensity of the remanent magnetism of a specimen depends on two factors. One is its magnetic constitution—what magnetic oxides it contains and in what abundance; this sets a limit to the maximum possible intensity, though in practice the limit is irrelevant for a field as weak as that of the earth. The other factor is the intensity of the field which caused the magnetization; the effect, up to the possible maximum, is proportionate to the cause. Since the aim of measuring is to determine the intensity of the magnetizing field, it is this proportion that must be determined. The one practicable method is first to measure the original remanent intensity of the specimen, then to eliminate that intensity by heat and remagnetize the specimen in some magnetic field of known intensity (for instance, the present field of the earth) and finally to measure the new remanent intensity. The ratio of the new to the old remanent intensity of the specimen should be the same as the ratio between the surrounding field now and at the time of the original magnetization: this statement is perhaps more clearly expressed by

the formula $\dfrac{M_L}{M_o} = \dfrac{F_L}{F_o}$, where M_L is the sample's new and M_o its original remanent

intensity and F_L and F_o the intensity of the surrounding field at the times of the second and the original magnetization. It is here assumed that the surrounding field at the time of original magnetization was that of the earth; for archaeomagnetic specimens the assumption is in general likely.

Both the types of magnetometer described on pp. 81–2 measure intensity as well as direction. In the rotating type readings are taken directly from the galvanometer.

With the astatic type it is anyhow convenient to restrict the swing of the magnet system by suspending it on a torsion fibre, and so the intensity of a specimen can be calculated from the degree to which it can deflect the magnet system when at a given distance from the specimen.

Remagnetization is more troublesome. The specimen must be heated to eliminate its original remanent magnetism and then let cool to acquire a new remanent magnetism from a surrounding field of known intensity; here two special precautions are necessary. First, if the specimen is to cool in the oven in which it was heated, that oven must itself be non-magnetic or else there are likely to be unpremeditated changes in the intensity of the field immediately surrounding the sample: if some such accident is suspected, the sample can, of course, be remagnetized again. Secondly, the heating of the specimen may change its magnetic constitution—new magnetic oxides may be formed, and un-fired or underfired portions of the specimen which had little or no remanent magnetism may now become magnetized—so that the intensity of the original and of the new remanent magnetisms may not be properly comparable. In general, well-cleaned objects of well-fired clay, if well oxidized, are immune from such chemical changes; reduced specimens may need to be remagnetized in an atmosphere of nitrogen, to prevent oxidation and its magnetic consequences.

TABLE B
Intensity of the remanent magnetism of French and other specimens.

Place	Date	Intensity (actual)	Intensity (adjusted)
		oersteds	oersteds
Paris	AD 1955	0·464	0·466
Paris	1930	0·459	0·461
Paris	1885	0·463	0·462
Paris	1848	0·471	0·460
Versailles	1750	> 0·48	> 0·43
Lille	1460	0·56	0·57
Paris	c. 300	0·70	0·73
Basle	c. 175	0·73	0·74
Fréjus	c. 0	0·65	0·69
Carthage	BC 146	0·71	0·78

The adjusted figures in the fourth column are based on the assumption that intensity is related to inclination; a value of 65°, close to the present value for Paris, has been taken as a norm.

Results for the Intensity of the Earth's Field. Measurements of intensity have been made for France (Table B), Czechoslovakia (4400 BC–AD 900), the Caucasus (from 3000 BC) and Japan (from 200 BC). In France the intensity of the earth's field has decreased by about a third in the last 1750 years, and results elsewhere seem to give a maximum in the late first millennium BC and a minimum about 2000 years earlier.

Archaeological Applications. For obtaining dates the intensity of remanent magnetism is much less exact than is its direction, perhaps eight or ten times less. Even so, it may be helpful in distinguishing between two dates at which the direction was the same. An application that might be important is the detection of forgeries of terracotta figures and pottery, if it proves that there was an appreciable difference between ancient and modern intensities. Here, though, there is another complication; ancient kilns were of clay or stone, but since the adoption of the electric kiln very recent forgeries may have intensities markedly different from those of the contemporary field of the earth. Again, if regional variations are large enough, it may be practicable to suggest the place of firing (or manufacture) for objects of which the date is known approximately. The ingenious reader can no doubt discover other applications.

CONCLUSION

The study of archaeomagnetism has not advanced far, more from shortage of students than of materials. There are still important theoretical problems to solve and very many more routine measurements must be made before a reasonably complete set of plots of variation can be produced. But it offers both geophysicists and archaeologists some information of kinds they cannot, anyhow yet, obtain elsewhere.

ACKNOWLEDGMENT

I am very grateful to my geophysical colleague Dr J. C. Belshé for reading and improving this account, and to Dr M. J. Aitken for advice on recent publications.

REFERENCES

1 THELLIER, E. 1938. *Annales de l'Inst. de Phys. du Globe 16*, 157–302. (A detailed general study of methods and principles.)
2 THELLIER, E. and O. 1959. *Annales de Géophysique 15*, 285–376. (A comprehensive account of the study of intensity.)
3 AITKEN, M. J. 1961. *Physics and Archaeology*. London and New York, pp. 8–11, 18–19, 121–55. (A good general account with long bibliography.)
4 THELLIER, E. 1966. *Nucleus 7*, 1–35. (Critical summary of work to date.)
5 AITKEN, M. J., WEAVER, G. H. and HAWLEY, H. N. 1962–7. *Archaeometry 5*, 14–19; *6*, 76–80; *9*, 187–97; *10*, 129–35. (Results for direction in Britain.)
6 BUCHA, V. 1967. *Archaeometry 10*, 12–22. (Results for intensity in Czechoslovakia.)
7 BELSHÉ, J. C., COOK, K. and R. M. 1963. *Annual of the British School at Athens 58*, 8–13. (Results for direction in Greece)
8 BAMMER, A. 1968. *Jahreshefte des oesterreichischen archäologischen Institutes 47*, Beiblatt, 1964–5. (Results for inclination from west Turkey.)
9 WATANABE, N. 1959. *Journal of the Faculty of Science, University of Tokyo*, sec. 5, *2*, 1–188. (Results for direction in Japan.)
10 SASAJIMA, A. and MAENAKA, K. 1966. *Mem. of College of Science, Kyoto*, B, *33.2*, 53–67. (Results for intensity in Japan.)
11 CLARKE, D. L. and CONNAH, G. 1962. *Antiquity 36*, 206–9. (An attempt to use inclination for the relative chronology of British 'beakers'.)

6 The Potassium–Argon Dating of Upper Tertiary and Pleistocene Deposits

W. GENTNER and H. J. LIPPOLT

AFTER THE DISCOVERY OF RADIOACTIVITY, Rutherford proved the possibility of dating geological events by showing that at least 500 million years must have elapsed since the formation of a fergusonite crystal which contained 7% uranium and 1·8 cc helium. By measuring the ratio of U/Pb in uranium minerals and the ratio of U/He, Boltwood[15] and Strutt[55] respectively put geological chronology on an absolute basis which was especially important for the Pre-Cambrian.

In the last decade all long-life isotopes have been examined for their suitability for absolute age determination, the Rb–Sr method and the K–A method becoming ever more important. The K–A method can be applied particularly for the dating of lower geological ages by virtue of the abundance of potassium and the improvements in high vacuum technique and sensitivity for measuring very small quantities of rare gases. However, there is at present considerable interest in applying the method to Quaternary problems. The following comments deal with this development.

THE DECAY OF K^{40}

Potassium as we find it in nature contains 93·2% K^{39}, 6·8% K^{41} and 0·0118% radioactive K^{40}. At the time of the formation of the earth the abundance of K^{40} was about 0·2%. Most of the K^{40} decayed into the isotopes Ca^{40} and A^{40}. Since the high half-life, of K^{40}, $1·30\pm0·04 . 10^9$y, is comparable to the age of earth, a small amount of K^{40} is still present, whereas the nuclides palladium 107 and iodine 129, with shorter half-lives, have decayed some billion years ago.

For each 100 K^{40} atoms which decay, 89% become Ca^{40} by β decay and 11% become A^{40} by K-capture. This branching ratio of $0·123\pm0·004$ is usually mentioned in addition to the half-life when giving age data. The K-capture of K^{40} is the reason for the large abundance of A^{40} in the atmosphere. The atmosphere con-

TABLE A

Amounts of rare gases in the atmosphere.

Rare gas	Volume %
Helium	$5·2 . 10^{-4}$
Argon $^{38+36}$	$3·7 . 10^{-3}$
Argon^{40}	$0·93$
Neon	$1·8 . 10^{-3}$
Krypton	$1·1 . 10^{-4}$
Xenon	$8·6 . 10^{-6}$

tains about 1% argon which is 100 times more abundant than the other rare gases. This explanation of the A^{40} in the atmosphere was made in 1937 by von Weizsäcker; it was proved to be the case by the measurement of A^{40} in minerals by Aldrich and Nier.[12] Fig. 13 shows the decay scheme of K^{40} as it has been confirmed by extensive investigations of various authors in the field of nuclear physics.

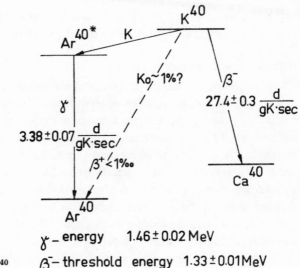

γ – energy 1.46 ± 0.02 MeV

Fig. 13 Decay scheme of K^{40} β^- – threshold energy 1.33 ± 0.01 MeV

Ever since it was discovered that A^{40} is produced by the decay of K^{40} the use of this method has found ever more applications for the following reasons:

(1) Potassium with about 2·8 weight per cent is one of the most abundant elements in the earth's crust and is contained in practically all minerals.

(2) A^{40} can be measured more easily than most other elements even in very small concentrations.

(3) The half-life of potassium $^{-40}$, $1·30 . 10^9$y, is long enough for appreciable A^{40} to be formed in potassium minerals within geologically interesting periods. By measuring the radiogenic A^{40}-concentration and the total content of potassium of a mineral one may determine the time which is necessary to produce the radiogenic A^{40}-concentration by radioactive decay.

$$A^{40}/K^{40} = (R/1+R) . (e^{\lambda t} - 1) \qquad \begin{array}{l} R = \text{branching ratio} \\ \lambda = \text{decay . constant} \end{array}$$

This period is designated as the potassium–argon age of the sample under the following assumptions:

(1) At time $t = 0$ the crystal contains only argon with an isotopic ratio the same as atmospheric argon, that is, no radiogenic argon is present ($[Ar^{41}] = 296 \times [Ar^{36}]$).

(2) During the measured time the K–A ratio is not changed by any chemical or physical process except by the radioactive decay of K^{40}.

(3) The period of the formation of the mineral must be much shorter than the age of the mineral.

These prerequisites however are not always completely fulfilled. There are two difficulties that require discussion:

(1) The losses of argon and potassium by diffusion and metamorphic changes.
(2) The isotopic composition of the argon in the mineral when it was formed.

POTASSIUM AND ARGON ANALYSIS

The content of potassium is usually determined by a flame-photometer. For small concentrations isotopic dilution analysis is used ($< 10^{-3}$ g/g). For even smaller potassium contents ($< 10^{-5}$ g/g), neutron activation analysis is required. An interesting survey of the reproducibility and accuracy of the different methods was made by Pinson.[50] He concluded that the flame-photometric method is very reliable. For example the results agree with gravimetric determinations by the J. L. Smith method. Systematic errors of about 6% are encountered while the reproducibility is about 2%. Further work revealed that flame photometric K determinations within 1% are feasible.[17, 57].

The determination of the concentration of argon is made in three steps: melting of the samples for the extraction of gases, purification of the extracted rare gases and determination of the quantities by an isotopic analysis.

The last step is carried out by a mass-spectrometer. The measurement of the argon by a McLeod manometer without the isotopic analysis gives reliable values only for concentrations over 10^{-4} cc A/g material, that is very old material. Measurements with neutron activation become unreliable for high atmospheric argon content.

Of the possible extraction methods, it is preferable to extract the gas by direct heating without the addition of auxiliary material to lower the melting point. The material can be melted in high vacuum by induction or by resistance heating in either a graphite or molybdenum crucible. In this way one can obtain temperatures considerably above the melting point of the minerals being investigated (mica $1,000°$, feldspar $1,200°$, quartz $1,700°$C). All of the impurities which one obtains by such a melting procedure can be removed by getter-materials (Ca–Cu–CuO, Zr, Ti-sponge).

In addition to the radiogenic A^{40} the material to be dated also contains argon from the atmosphere with an isotopic ratio $A^{40} : A^{38} : A^{36} = 296 : 0.19 : 1$. During the measurement atmospheric argon is added from small leaks, from diffusion through the walls of the apparatus, from the getter-materials and from the hot crucible and its surroundings. By measurement of the A^{36} and A^{38} concentrations one can determine the radiogenic A^{40}. If one has for example 1% atmospheric argon in addition to the radiogenic argon, the amount of A^{36} is quite small, only about 3.4×10^{-5} of the A^{40}. The mass-spectrometer used must therefore have sufficient resolution and with the tendency to smaller and smaller samples be suitable for high and ultra-high vacuum. A $60°$ glass sector spectrometer has proved successful for this application.[51] The cycloidal spectrometer and the omegatron can also be used in this way. Mass spectrometer and extraction line have to be bakeable up to 350°C.

In general the potassium and the radiogenic argon are not distributed homogeneously through the sample. The ideal solution is to determine argon and potassium in the same sample but this is only useful in special cases, as then it is only possible to make one determination. If one wished to measure several samples one after the other, it is better to use pulverized homogeneous material. The argon and potassium determination can then be made independently. If the grain size is too large one obtains a large variation from sample to sample. By the use of a grain size from 0·6 to 1·0 mm one has in a 0·5 to 1·0 g sample approximately 300 to 600 grains and therefore a representative sample. If one uses substantially smaller samples, then one must make the grain size still smaller. Gentner and Kley[33] have shown however that it is not advisable to have a grain size less than 100μ as then one must contend with substantial loss of argon.

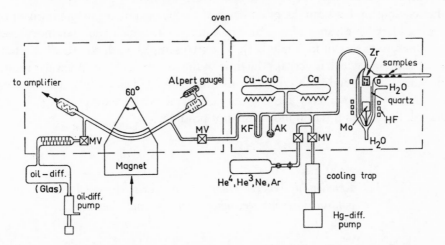

Fig. 14 Schematic diagram of an apparatus for measuring small amounts of argon

MINERALS SUITABLE FOR DATING

Potassium–argon ages have been determined for the igneous minerals muscovite, biotite, phlogopite, orthoclase, sanidine, microcline, and leucite, as well as volcanic glass and the sedimentary minerals glauconite, illite, carnallite and sylvite.

A number of these minerals are easily altered by metamorphism or can lose argon through diffusion. As a result one usually restricts the dating to biotite, muscovite and sanidine.

In addition to these minerals, because of the increased sensitivity of the procedures for determining argon and potassium, it is possible to use minerals which only have trace amounts of potassium. Indeed good results have been obtained for anorthoclase, oligoclase, augite, calcite and hornblende.

It is possible to have processes which alter the argon-40 to potassium ratio in the dated material. For example one can have a recrystallization of a potassium salt, or alteration of a feldspar into kaolin and sericite or chloritization of pyroxene; deposition of calcite or chlorite in the pores, or anion–exchange in clay minerals which alters the potassium content. A number of these changes can be recognized microscopically and the corresponding samples left aside. The loss of argon through diffusion from the crystal lattice is usually not recognizable.

From the standpoint of the measurements one prefers to date unaltered minerals. In view of the geological or archaeological problems however it is often desirable to date whole rock samples, which are easier to obtain and for which one does not require the labour of separating the minerals.

One must consider that whole rock samples contain in addition to large biotite and sanidine crystals other minerals which lose argon. Very small biotite and sanidine crystals lose argon too because of diffusion from the small grains. For this reason in dating complicated strata one rarely uses whole rock samples alone. On the other hand such samples can be used for relative age determinations.

The relationship between the grain size and the potassium argon age is given by two examples. Hart[36] measured a Pre-Cambrian muscovite which was metamorphosed and found the results shown in Table B(i). The two samples with the smallest grain sizes give the same age which is perhaps the time of the metamorphism. A similar result (here recalculated) was found with sylvite by Gentner et al.[32] (Table B(ii)). The true age was taken as the age for a very large grain size obtained by extrapolating the samples measured. For stones this is in most cases not possible.

TABLE B

Relationship between grain sizes of rock samples and potassium–argon age, after Hart (i) and Gentner et al. (ii).

(i) Radius	K–A Age
muscovite μ	million yrs.
1,000	700
690	555
250	440
110	350
55	360

(ii) Radius	K–A Age
sylvite *mm*	million yrs
2·0	17·5
1·3	16·3
0·8	14·3
0·4	11·3

COMPARISON OF POTASSIUM–ARGON AGES WITH OTHER METHODS

The different ways in which the radioactive ages of minerals are altered by metamorphic processes make it desirable to use two independent methods such as the K^{40}–A^{40} and the Rb^{87}–Sr^{87}. Age-determinations obtained from both methods for mica have about the same reliability as concordant lead ages. The results of the Rb–Sr and K–A methods agree well except for the cases of metamorphic rocks. This is shown by the histogram of Aldrich and Wetherill.[2] In Fig. 15 the abscisa has been changed to correspond to the newly determined half-life of Rb^{87} of $4 \cdot 7.10^{10}$y. Armstrong, Jäger and Eberhardt compared Rb–Sr and K–A– ages of 13 biotites from the Alps with ages between 20 and 10 million years and found excellent agreement within the limits of error, for ten age pairs within 10%.[13] Basset et al.[14] found a potassium–argon age of $13 \cdot 5.10^{6}$y for a sericite from a lead-zinc-silver-mine while Miller[48] found a uranium-lead age of 13.10^{6}y for a cogenetic uraninite. This is an example of the agreement of these two methods in the low age range.

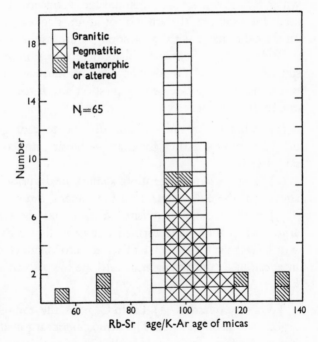

Fig. 15 Histogram of the ratio of the Rb–Sr age to the K–A age for micas from a number of rocks

THE POSSIBILITY OF DATING MORE RECENT PERIODS

The absolute age-determination of Tertiary and Pleistocene samples is difficult since the half-lives for the isotopes available are either too long or too short for the time involved. The lowest lead ages and the lowest Rb–Sr ages are about 10 million years while the highest C^{14} ages are some 70,000 years. Only the ionium and the Th^{230}–Pa^{231} methods have a higher range. They are, however, restricted to deep-sea sediments and corals. There remains a long time between $5 \cdot 10^{5}$y and 10^{7}y which can nowadays only be dated by the potassium–argon method and the new fission track dating method, preferably applied to volcanic glass. Judging from Rb–Sr results of Jäger 1962 on biotites and whole rock samples from the Alps it should be possible to expand this method down to Pleistocene ages.[38]

In this connection it is interesting to remember that one of the first potassium–argon determinations was made on a sample whose mineral age was Lower Miocene, namely 20 ± 1 million years, but for this determination 200g of potassium-rich sylvite was used.[32]

For ages in the Lower Tertiary the radioactive formula for potassium decay can be simplified to the form:

$$A^{40} = (\lambda . R/1 + R) . t . K^{40}$$

It can be clearly seen that with comparatively young ages the amount of measured argon also becomes small, so that in order to extend the method to recent periods it is necessary, as was also the case for very small samples, to develop the technique of the mass-spectrometric determination of small amounts of rare gases. One must find out which factors restrict the method. One is concerned on the one hand with the apparatus used, for example, the amount of argon degassed during a blank determination, and on the other hand with the amount of atmospheric argon in the sample material.

With modern apparatus a blank determination yield of approximately 10^{-8}cc atmospheric argon (STP) is possible. This amount can probably be made smaller so that it is not necessary to discuss this question any further. For the second question however one must consider:

(1) What is the ratio of atmospheric to radiogenic argon in the potassium-rich material used for dating, for example biotite, muscovite or sanidine, as well as the rock samples?

(2) Must the same precautions against the diffusion loss of argon be used for the young ages as for the older ages? That the mineral must be fresh is out of question.

(3) Is the basic prerequisite satisfied that the samples did not contain radiogenic argon when they were formed but that all was expelled through melting? In other words: was the K–A clock set back to zero? Connected with this is the question whether in addition to the young minerals one has also trace amounts of older minerals with higher A^{40}.

To clarify question (1) Table C gives the radiogenic and atmospheric content of argon in several biotites. The atmospheric argon does not come from the apparatus but comes from the sample itself. One sees that the ratios are unfavourable for young ages because the atmospheric argon requires a large correction. A small error, 1%, in the determination of argon-36 causes a 10% error in the radiogenic A^{40} when one has 90% atmospheric argon. From these results we conclude that it is not advisable to use tuff biotite for ages less than 1 million years. But it is easier to obtain results from rock biotites.

Reynolds[52] attempted to separate the air argon under the assumption that it was all adsorbed on the surface. In this case heating at 300–400°C should improve the ratio, in the same way that the inside walls of the high vacuum system are outgassed. As

TABLE C

Radiogenic and atmospheric content of argon in different biotites.

Sample	Age	Material	A^{rad}	A^{at}	ratio A^{rad}/A^{at}
	million yrs		$10^{-7}cc/g$ Mat	$10^{-7}cc/g$ Mat	
Katzenbuckel	66 ± 3	biotite	97·6	9·9	10
Fornicher Kopf	$0·27 \pm 0·10$	biotite	0·77	10·2	0·08
Bürzeln	$20·4 \pm 0·8$	tuff biotite	48·3	24·8	2
Leilenkopf	$1·5 \pm 0·3$	tuff biotite	4·4	62·4	0·07

Fig. 16 shows, however, only a fraction of the atmospheric argon is on the surface of the grains and easily released, most of it is within the crystal near the surface. One sees that in all cases when 60% of the argon is removed by heating also 10% of the radiogenic gas is lost. This is not a favourable situation. If the atmospheric argon is contained in a thin layer under the surface, the distribution is changed by heating so that only a part is pumped away. The loss of radiogenic argon during baking may be controlled by Ar³⁹ produced in the crystals by neutron activation.[31] Evernden and Curtis discovered that a large portion of the atmospheric argon is removed by etching the crystals in HF.[23] A second consequence of this acid treatment is that the grains become clean and freed from altered adhering minerals.

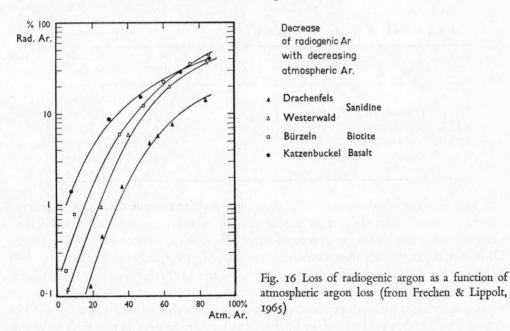

Decrease of radiogenic Ar with decreasing atmospheric Ar.

▲ Drachenfels   Sanidine
△ Westerwald
□ Bürzeln   Biotite
● Katzenbuckel   Basalt

Fig. 16 Loss of radiogenic argon as a function of atmospheric argon loss (from Frechen & Lippolt, 1965)

One therefore requires minerals with a high potassium content and with a small content of atmospheric argon. Gentner and Zähringer[59] found this to be the case for the

Australian-Indonesian tektites. They were able to determine an average age of 720,000 years. Sanidine, a volcanic glassy feldspar found in tuff, bentonite or other volcanic rocks, behaves similar to tektites. J. Frechen (Bonn) together with Gentner and Lippolt[31] has investigated sanidine crystals from different locations in the Pleistocene volcanic region of Germany. Table D shows several results which illustrate question (3).

Sample D was obtained from a large sanidine bomb. Samples E, M and O were sanidine grains of mm size obtained from tuffs. The percentage of atmospheric argon is quite low so that the ages are reliable. Unfortunately the ages from M and O do not agree with the stratigraphy. Geologically the ages should decrease in the sequence E, M, O, however the potassium–argon ages show the inverse tendency.

For biotites similar errors can be shown. It follows that these ages which should be under 300,000 years are not usable. The question arises whether one must contend with excess argon in all tuff minerals, as was also the case for one of the biotite samples obtained from Hegau tuffs. According to the results obtained by Curtis and Evernden this is not the case in all regions. These authors state that their volcanic sanidines of historic, Post- or Late-Pleistocene age yielded ages consistent with the concept of zero radiogenic argon content at the time of eruption.[18]

The danger that the age is too high because of the presence of old minerals is illustrated by the following example. The potassium–argon age of a sanidine and biotite sample obtained from the bentonite of Bischofszell in Hegau should show a sarmat–torton age in the Upper Miocene. As they show ages of 14·6 and 18·4 million years respectively the

TABLE D

Argon contents of Pleistocene sanidines.

Sample		Potassium	A^{rad}	A^{atm}	Age
		%	cc	%	million yrs
Eifel D	Leilenkopf II	10·85	1·66	27	0·39
Eifel E	Leilenkopf I	10·69	1·71	16	0·40
Eifel M	Leubsdorf	10·00	2·48	23	0·63
Eifel O	Kärlich	5·66	5·68	13	2·54

first may be right but the second 25% too old. It is quite possible that the fine-grained material contains tiny sanidine or biotite crystals of older age. Evernden and Curtis cited several examples for this source of error (Dighton's Cliff Extension, Olorgesailie, Olduvai Gorge).[23] They therefore made out a set of prerequisites to be fulfilled when dating tuffs. The main points are the primary nature of the tuff and age concordance of various mineral types and concentrates.

As it is certainly not always easy to separate the minerals completely, the question of dating whole rock samples needs to be discussed further. In general one finds an atmospheric argon content of about 10^7 to 10^6 cc argon/g of rock so that if one has a sample with a high potassium content it is still possible to obtain dates of less than 1 million years. If the samples have not been altered by metamorphic processes one can certainly use them for dating as the loss of gas by volume diffusion for young ages is lessening.

DATES OF YOUNG SAMPLES

The potassium argon dates in the Quaternary period contribute to three main problems, the establishment of a reliable time scale, the constancy of the earth's magnetic field, and the origin of tektites. The problem of the Plio-Pleistocene time scale is tied to the question of the coincidence in time of fossils in the different continents, the meaning of glacial deposits and the history of the emergence of man. These problems are usually interrelated and their solution gives additional information concerning special geological questions.

There may be perhaps about ten laboratories equipped for measuring such young ages but at present only a small number of dates is available.

Evernden et al.[26] in their paper on the utilization of glauconite and illites gave some biotite ages from which the border between the Miocene and Pliocene can be estimated. An age of 12·0 million years was found for the Coal Valley tuff in Nevada which should be close to this boundary. Lippolt et al. measured 12·5 million years for a sanidine from a Sarmat Hegau tuff which also lies close to the Miocene-Pliocene boundary.[45] More critical points have been given by Curtis et al.,[20] for example 9·1 million years for a biotite from the lower Hemphillian. Evernden et al.[24] devoted a special paper to a Cenozoic K-A- time scale of North America controlled by fossil mammals. Twenty-eight dates out of this paper belong in the Pliocene-Pleistocene period. According to this Clarendonian starts at about 12 million years and ends at 10 million years. The following Hemphillian lasted to 4–5 million years and the succeeding Blancan to 1·5 million years. An Irvingtonian fauna with mammuthus has an age of 1·36 million years. The Villafranchian is supposed to overlap with the younger Blancan and the Irvingtonian.

In their most recent publication Evernden and Curtis[23] present a large number of quaternary results. The central theme is the age of Bed I from Olduvai Gorge in Tanganyika, in which the Zinjanthropus was found by Leakey. An age of 1·75 million years for minerals from these Olduvai tuffs had been given[43] but von Koenigswald et al. urged the necessity for caution with regard to this new result. They based this opinion upon their unreliable determinations from tuffs in the Eifel area, from the stratigraphic record at that time on the Olduvai site and from a date of 1·3 million years for a basalt sample underlying Bed I. This basalt age appeared to be too young because of changes in the whole rock sample. Hay[37] mapped the critical strata more thoroughly and Evernden and Curtis[33] continued their measurements, and tried to exclude the possibilities of contamination and inherited argon concentrations. One-third out of about fifty measurements confirm the early result of 1·75 million years for this fossil-bearing layer. The time span between the basalt and Marker Bed I may be about 0·35 million years. Another important result for anthropology is 0·50 million years for an anorthoclase from a young Olduvai tuff, which overlies sediments with Chellian tools and which is overlain by those with Chellian-Acheulian tools. One date from Italy of 0·43 million years refers to an Abbevillian-Acheulian culture. The Olduvai results suggest that a correlation of the African pluvials with the European standard glaciations may be invalid. The difficulty in determining the stratigraphic position of the dated minerals seems to underly the discussion on so-called Stillbay and pseudo-Stillbay sites and this has led to a discrepancy of about a factor of ten between K–A– and C^{14} dates.

Kretzoi elucidated the stratigraphic complications for the Plio-Pleistocene period. In Europe the same name may be used for three different though overlapping time spans. Such drawbacks exist not only for the faunal definitions but also for the glacial correlations. In the Sierra Nevada six glaciations have been traced of which three should be younger than 150,000 years and two older than 0·7 and 0·94 million years respectively (Dalrymple 1964). The maximum age from K–A– measurements on young volcanics for these older glaciations is 2·6 and 3·2 million years. The two early glaciations in Kilimanjaro, however, are dated by Evernden and Curtis to 0·50 and 0·35 million years. According to the astronomical hypothesis the main European glaciations did not start at all before 0·6 million years.

Frechen and Lippolt[31] dated sanidines and basalts from the Eifel area. The sequence of this volcanism is well known by the intercalation of its products in the terraces of the middle Rhine river. The ages for the upper Main terrace are 0·40 to 0·42, for the lower Main terrace 0·34 to 0·35, for the upper Middle terrace 0·30, and for the middle Middle terrace 0·22 million years. Frechen and Lippolt adhere to the correlation of Rhine river terraces and ice ages given by Woldstedt (1958, pp. 70 and 212).[58] Accordingly the two middle terraces correspond to two phases of Mindel and the two main terraces to two phases of Günz (Eburon and Menap). This contradicts the results from the Sierra Nevada, if the correlation McGee = Nebraskan = Günz is correct, and the dates from Italy found by Evernden and Curtis for two samples 0·43 and 0·27 million years old, which are supposed to belong to the Flaminian–Nomentanan interglacial which is correlated by Blanc with the Holstein interglacial.

Another field for K–A– age determinations has been initiated by the students of palaeomagnetism. The polarity of the terrestrial magnetic field at a given time is recorded by the volcanics produced at this time. Therefore K–Ar– measurements were used to date many basalts on Hawaii, California, etc. Geomagnetic polarity epochs have been established lasting between 0·5 and 1 million years. The polarity was reversed between 0·85 million years and 2·5 million years (Matuyama zone) and before 3·4 million years (Gilbert zone), Gromme and Hay showed by investigating the Olduvai basalts that within the Matuyama epoch the field was normally polarized for a time. Cox et al.[16] found also normally polarized rocks of this age on St George Island in Alaska. A similar change in the direction of the field may have occurred on Hawaii and in the Sierra Nevada (Cox et al. 1964, McDougall 1964).

Tektites, strange natural glassy objects which are found at different places on the earth and are apparently not of volcanic origin have been divided in groups by K–Ar– measurements. Zähringer and Gentner[59, 60] showed that two out of the four groups have Quaternary ages. The tektites from Indochina, Indonesia and Australia are 0·72 million years old and those from the Ivory Coast 1·3 million years old. One hypothesis for the origin of tektites is the impact of a large meteorite on the earth. In Ghana adjacent to the Ivory Coast the Bosumtwi crater contains breccia and natural glasses, very similar geochemically to the Ivory coast tektites and with the same age, a fact which suggests a common origin of both.[35] The tektites on Java are found in the Trinil beds. Samples from the Muriah volcano on Java which are also found in the Trinil beds have been dated by von Koenigswald *et al.* and Evernden and Curtis to be 0·50 million years old. These two dates bracket the age of Pithecanthropus of Central Java. K–A– measurements have been used to date the basalts of the mid-Atlantic ridges. Kulp[4] and Miller[48] got ages between 3 and 8 million years.

Most of the dates can be seen to be generally related. They also give information with regard to local geologic problems and often change stratigraphic relationships. Kawano and Ueda for instance and Eberhardt and Ferrara give pertinent examples from the Quaternary.[39, 21]

CONCLUSIONS

The errors given with the potassium–argon dates are usually the statistical errors, denoting the reproducibility of the potassium and argon determinations. Possible systematic errors are often not considered. In addition the errors introduced by the decay constants are not included, but these are noted in the text and tables.

Errors introduced by diffusion or metamorphic processes which alter the potassium and argon contents of the samples are not considered so long as one cannot discern a change by microscopic examination of the samples.

The selection of suitable material for dating is indeed the main problem before undertaking potassium–argon measurements on a comparatively recent period. By the use of large samples it is possible to overlap with C^{14} results. It is only necessary to have a substance with little atmospheric argon and which meets the conditions outlined above. The method can be extended if the accuracy of the isotopic measurements of argon is improved.

In this connection it is interesting to ask if it is possible to measure the potassium–argon age directly on fossil materials. The authors have tried to date early Tertiary bones and teeth.[34] Their material had considerable air argon and because of the low potassium content ($< 1\%$) the small amount of radiogenic argon was not measurable. Furthermore a high diffusion rate was found. So for this reason it does not seem possible to date young fossil material.

REFERENCES

A: Review articles

1 AHRENS, L. H. 1956. Radioactive methods for determining geological age. *Reports on Progress in Physics 19*, 80

2 ALDRICH, L. T. and WETHERILL, G. W. 1958. *Ann. Rev. Nuclear Sci. 8*, 257

3 CARR, D. R. and KULP, J. L. 1957. *Bull. Geol. Soc. Am. 68*, 763

4 KULP, J. L. 1963. *Bull. Volcano. de l'Assoc. de Volcanologie XXVI*, 247

5 BAADSGAARD, H. and DODSON, M. H. 1964. *Quarterly Journal Geol. Soc. London. 120 S, 119*

6 MILLER, J. A. and FITCH, F. J. 1964. *Quarterly Journal Geol. Soc. London. 120 S, 101*

7 TILTON, G. R. and DAVIS, G. L. 1959. Geochronology. *Researches in Geochemistry*, New York, 190

8 WASSERBURG, G. J. 1954. Potassium-argon dating in FAUL, H. (ed.) *Nuclear Geology*, New York,

9 WETHERILL, G. W. 1957. *Science 126*, 545
10 ZÄHRINGER, J. 1960. *Geologische Rundschau 49* (1), 224
11 SCHAEFFER, O. A. and ZÄHRINGER, J. (*editors*). 1966. *Potassium argon dating*. Heidelberg

B: General references and notes

12 ALDRICH, L. T. and NIER, A. O. 1948. *Phys. Rev. 74*, 876
13 ARMSTRONG, R. L., JÄGER, E. and EBERHARDT, P. 1966. *Earth and Planetary Sci. Letters 1*, 13
14 BASSET, W. A., KERR, P. F., SCHAEFFER, O. A. and STOENNER, R. W. 1962. In *Bull. Geol. Soc. Am.*
15 BOLTWOOD, B. B. 1904. *Am. J. Sci. 23*, 77
16 COX, A., DOELL, R. R. and DALRYMPLE, G. B. 1965. *The Quaternary of the United States*. Princeton,817
17 COOPER, J. A. 1962. *Geochim. et Cosmochim. Acta 27*, 546
18 CURTIS, G. H. and EVERNDEN, J. F. 1962. *Nature 194*, 611
19 —— LIPSON, J. and EVERNDEN, J. F. 1956. *Nature 178*, 1360
20 —— SAVAGE, D. E. and EVERNDEN, J. F. 1960. *Ann. N.Y. Acad. Sci. 91*, 342
21 EBERHARDT, P. and FERRARA, G. 1962. *Nature 196*, 665
22 EMILIANI, C. 1955. *J. Geol. 63*, 538
23 EVERNDEN, J. F. and CURTIS, H. G. 1965. *Current Anthropology Oct. 65, Vol. 6, No. 4*, 341
24 —— SAVAGE, D. E., CURTIS, G. H. and JAMES, G. T. 1964. *Amer. Jour. of Sci. 262*, 145
25 —— CURTIS, G. H. and KISTLER, R. 1957. *Quarternaria 4*, 1
26 —— —— OBRADOVICH, J. and KISTLER, R. 1961. *Geochim. et Cosmochim. Acta 23*, 78
27 DALRYMPLE, G. B. 1963. *Geol. Soc. Amer. Bull. 74*, 379
28 —— 1964. *Geol. Soc. Amer. Bull. 75*, 753
29 —— COX, A. and DOELL, R. R. 1965. *Geol. Soc. Amer. Bull. 76*, 665
30 FRECHEN, J. and v.d. BOOM, G. 1959. *Fortschr. Geol. Rheinland u. Westf. 4*, 89
31 FRECHEN, J. and LIPPOLT, H. J. 1965. *Eiszeitalter und Gegenwart 16*, 5–30
32 GENTNER, W., PRÄG, R. and SMITS, F. 1953. *Geochim. et Cosmochim. Acta, 4*, 11
33 —— and KLEY, W. 1958. *Ibid. 14*, 98
34 —— and LIPPOLT, H. J. 1962. *Geochim. et Cosmochim. Acta, 26*, 1247
35 —— LIPPOLT, H. J. and MÜLLER, O. 1964. *Z.f. Naturforschg. 19a*, 150
36 HART, S. R. 1960. *Ann. N.Y. Acad. Sci. 91*, 192
37 HAY, R. L. 1963. *Science 139*, 829
38 JÄGER, E. 1962. *Jour. of Geophys. Res. 67*, 5293
39 KAWANO, Y. and UEDA, Y. 1964. *Science Reports III, Vol. IX*, 99. Tokoku Univ. Sendai, Japan
40 KOENIGSWALD, G. H. R. VON 1962. In KURTH, G. *Evolution und Hominisation*, Stuttgart, 112
41 —— GENTNER, W. and LIPPOLT, H. J. 1961. *Nature 192*, 720
42 KRETZOI, M. 1965. *Current Anthropology 6, No. 4*, 373
43 LEAKEY, L. S. B., EVERNDEN, J. F. and CURTIS, G. H. 1961. *Nature 191*, 478
44 LIPPOLT, H. J. 1961. Title Thesis, Univ. of Heidelberg
45 —— GENTNER, W. and WIMMENAUER, W. 1963. *Jh. geol. Landesamt Baden-Württemberg 6*, 507
46 McDOUGALL, I. 1964. *Geol. Soc. Amer. Bull. 75*, 107
47 —— and TARLING, D. H. 1964. *Nature 202*, 171
48 MILLER, D. 1959. Title Thesis, Columbia Univ.
49 MILLER, J. A. 1963. *Science in Archaeology*, 1st ed. 85
50 PINSON, W. H. JR 1960. *Ann. N.Y. Acad. Sci. 91*, 221
51 REYNOLDS, J. H. 1956. *Rev. Sci. Instrum. 27*, 928
52 —— 1957. *Geochim. et Cosmochim. Acta 12*, 177
53 —— 1960. *Ibid. 20*, 101
54 SMITS, F. and GENTNER, W. 1950. *Ibid. 1*, 22
55 STRUTT, R. J. 1910. *Proc. Roy. Soc. Lond. 83* (A), 298
56 WEIZSÄCKER, C. F. V. 1937. *Phys. Z. 38*, 623
57 WASSERBURG, G. J., ZARTMAN, R. E. and WEN, T. Y. 1962. *J. geophys. Res. 67*, 3607
58 WOLSTEDT, P. *Das Eiszeitalter*, Stuttgart, Vol. 1 1961, Vol. 2 1958, Vol. 3 1965
59 ZÄHRINGER, J. and GENTNER, W. 1963. *Nature 199*, 583
60 ZÄHRINGER, J. 1963. *Radioactive Dating, IAEA, Vienna*, 289

7 Dating by the Potassium–Argon Method—Some Advances in Technique

JOHN A. MILLER

IN APPLYING THE POTASSIUM–ARGON TECHNIQUE to archaeology there are two main problems to be considered. The first is to obtain physically accurate isotopic age measurements and the second is to place the correct interpretation upon them. Methods of increasing the accuracy of potassium-argon age determinations at young ages will be considered and problems of sample selection and evaluation will also be mentioned briefly, for as the archaeologist knows, it is not uncommon to find discordance between archaeological and geochronological evidence which may lead either to an erroneous re-interpretation of the archaeological evidence, or to a rejection of isotopic data in general. Though the utmost analytical precision may be achieved, it is rarely advisable to apply the results without first making a careful assessment of the material upon which measurements were made. A proper mineralogical investigation is essential.

The air of precision that surrounds the making of accurate physical observations should not detract from the awareness of the imperfections which condition the whole process.

ARGON EXTRACTION

The physical principles upon which the method is based and the experimental procedure are outlined elsewhere in this volume (p. 88). Radiogenic argon-40 is produced by the decay of potassium-40 by K-electron capture. Radiogenic argon is released in the laboratory by the fusion of rocks or minerals under high vacuum in an apparatus known as an argon line.

Air also contains argon-40 (total argon 0·937%), and is always present occluded onto the surface of the apparatus, crucible and sample, and in the residual gases in the argon line, for no vacuum pump can achieve a perfect vacuum. Atmospheric argon also contains argon-36 (and some argon-38), an isotope that is not produced in the sample as a result of radioactive decay. The ratio $^{40}Ar/^{36}Ar$ for atmospheric argon is known,[8] consequently by making isotopic ratio measurements on the argon yielded by fusion of the sample, that argon-40 which is of atmospheric origin can be estimated and subtracted from the total argon-40 present. Difficulties present themselves when the volume of atmospheric argon-40 is large compared with that of the radiogenic argon-40. Methods of reducing the atmospheric argon content of the gas samples must be devised.

It is possible to remove virtually all the atmospheric argon from the crucible and furnace unit by employing an 'automatic loader'. In this device the samples are contained in a glass tube protruding vertically from the top of the furnace unit and are held in place by horizontal steel rods. After assembling the furnace and reaching the required vacuum, the apparatus is baked, and then the crucible is heated strongly. This results in the desorption of occluded gases from both the crucible and furnace unit parts which become heated by conduction and radiation. After allowing the crucible to cool, the lowest steel rod is retracted by means of a magnet and the first sample dropped into the crucible. By using this method no air reaches the inner surface of the apparatus between determinations, and the atmospheric argon contamination of the sample is markedly reduced. At present ten samples are loaded at once and provided that complete fusion is achieved during each determination, no cross contamination of argon samples arises.

Air occluded onto the surface of the sample is often reduced by baking under vacuum in the argon line. This process is widely used, though there is always the possibility of removing some radiogenic argon as well. A further comment on this method is given on p. 105.

It has been shown[2] that the atmospheric argon contamination of feldspars can be reduced by washing them in 7–10% hydrofluoric acid at 50°C for 20–30 minutes. It is suggested that air exists in near surface sites in the crystal lattice and concluded that if these sites were removed, the atmospheric argon would be removed along with them. Furthermore, it was discovered that if the samples were cleaned then left for several days, the atmospheric argon would return. It is not clear why the surfaces do not readsorb air immediately, but it may be that the hydrofluoric acid treatment in some way blocks the surface sites against readsorption for some time. Nevertheless this procedure has a dramatic influence upon the atmospheric argon content of a sample of feldspar. The effect upon whole basic rock samples is not so pronounced.

MASS SPECTROMETRY OF YOUNG SAMPLES—THE OMEGATRON

In determining the potassium–argon age of a young rock or mineral it is essential to make very precise measurements of the ^{40}Ar/^{36}Ar ratio. The issue is further complicated by the fact that 'spike' argon-38 (mentioned in Chapter 6) contains small amounts of both argon-36 and argon-40. With present-day 'spike' argon-38 these constituents are small, but the argon-36 content must be especially taken into account for any error would introduce a magnified error in the estimation of the volume of radiogenic argon-40. A precise knowledge of the isotopic composition of the spike is therefore necessary.

When measuring young samples it would be advantageous to dispense with the spike altogether. If this is to be possible, it is essential to use some type of mass spectrometer that has a linear response with gas pressure and that has an ion beam output that is constant for a given gas sample volume over a period of time. A satisfactory way of achieving this is to have a mass spectrometer that operates with low energy source conditions that will not remove the sample by ion pumping and in which virtually every ion produced reaches the collector. Such an instrument would be less likely to suffer from random changes in sensitivity.

If an accurate determination of the ^{40}Ar/^{36}Ar ratio of the sample is to be made, it is essential that the measured ratio bears a constant and known relationship to the true ratio. This raises the question of mass discrimination, which is an effect introduced by the deviation of conditions in the mass spectrometer source from the ideal. In many modern instruments this deviation is constant and can be determined by isotopic analysis of argon of known isotopic composition. It is more satisfactory to eliminate the effect altogether.

Linear response, stable peak heights, high sensitivity and freedom from mass discrimination are features of certain kinds of omegatron-type mass spectrometer. Such an instrument has been described by Grasty and Miller.[3]

The omegatron device was first described by Sommer *et al.*[9] and later modified to a simpler design by Alpert and Buritz.[1] Ions formed in a magnetic field by electron bombardment will describe circles, the natural frequency of which is given by the cyclotron frequency, which is dependent upon magnetic field strength and ionic mass. A radiofrequency field applied perpendicularly to the magnetic field will accelerate ions that have a resonant frequency equal to the frequency of the applied field Their path will become an Archimedes spiral. Resonant ions can be trapped by a suitably placed collector and detected by a standard mass spectrometer amplifier. Non-resonant ions will describe circular paths with pulsing radii and will not reach the collector.

In the manner outlined above it is possible to produce argon samples containing reduced amounts of atmospheric argon and to make accurate isotope ratio measurements on small volumes ($<10^{-7}$ cc N.T.P. of gas).

SAMPLE EVALUATION

Inhomogeneity and alteration in basalts and basic rocks gives rise to poor results. In general it is the basic rocks that are likely to be of use to the archaeologists, hence the factors influencing the reliability of their isotopic ages are of importance. In the Cambridge laboratory initial investigations into dating basic rocks were carried out on samples of dolerite from the Whin Sill. Experiments showed that the retentivities of the rocks were not related to grain size or chemistry. A mineralogical study showed that there is a relationship between the argon retentivity and degree of alteration of the material. Subsequent investigations showed that serpentinization, mineralization, and kaolinization will reduce the true age of a basic rock. The presence of pyroxenes in ultra basic rocks, zeolites and inclusions of older material can cause discrepantly high ages. Mechanical effects such as flexuring and cleavage, or mechanically produced thermal effects will produce a lowering of the apparent age. Thermal effects, such as contact metamorphism have a like effect. The importance of a careful mineralogical investigation cannot be over-emphasized.[6]

THE ^{40}Ar/^{39}Ar METHOD

In the standard technique of potassium-argon dating a number of fundamental problems remain. Among these are (a) the difficulty of removing all the atmospheric argon-40 without losing some radiogenic argon-40, (b) inhomogeneity of material resulting in non-representative samples being used for potassium and argon analyses, which are carried out separately, (c) amounts of sample required; about 0·1 gm of mica is required for each potash determination by flame photometry, usually six are made, (d) small amounts of ^{40}Ar and ^{36}Ar in the ^{38}Ar 'spike' can introduce errors in determinations on very young materials.

A solution to these problems may be found in the ^{40}Ar/^{39}Ar methods.[5] Extensive investigations have been carried out in the Cambridge laboratory.[4, 7]

Potassium-39 when irradiated with fast neutrons produces argon-39. Argon-40 is generated in the sample by the natural decay of potassium-40 by K-electron capture.

For a sample of age t

$$^{40}\mathrm{Ar} = \frac{\lambda_e}{\lambda_e + \lambda_\beta}\ ^{40}\mathrm{K}(e^{t/\gamma} - 1) \qquad\qquad \mathrm{I}$$

where ^{40}K, ^{40}Ar are the amounts of the isotopes present, and $\gamma = 1$/total decay constant for potassium-40. λ_e, λ_β denote the decay constants for ^{40}K by K-electron capture and β-decay respectively. The amount of ^{39}Ar produced when this sample is irradiated is given by

$$^{39}\mathrm{Ar} = {}^{39}\mathrm{K}\!\int\!\phi(E)\sigma(E)dE \qquad\qquad 2$$

where $\phi(E)$ is the neutron flux at energy E and $\sigma(E)$ the cross-section of potassium-39 for such neutrons. The integration is performed over all incident neutron energies. It follows that

$$^{40}\mathrm{Ar}/^{39}\mathrm{Ar} = {}^{40}\mathrm{K}/^{39}\mathrm{K}\ \frac{\lambda_e}{(\lambda_e + \lambda_\beta)}\ \frac{(e^{t/\gamma} - 1)}{\int\!\phi(E)\,\sigma(E)dE} \qquad\qquad 3$$

$$\mathrm{Let}\ J = \mathrm{I}\ \frac{\lambda_e + \lambda_\beta}{\lambda_e}\!\int\!\phi(E)\sigma(E)dE \qquad\qquad 4$$

where I is the relative abundance of the potassium isotopes ^{39}K/^{40}K, J is a measure of the neutron absorption and is a constant at a given point in the can in which the sample is irradiated. From 3 and 4,

$$J = \frac{e^{t/\gamma} - \mathrm{I}}{^{40}\mathrm{Ar}/^{39}\mathrm{Ar}}$$

Using samples of known age, J can be determined. Samples and standards are irradiated alongside each other enclosed in quartz phials loaded in a cadmium shielded reactor can. The flux intensity used in the Cambridge experiments was about 10^{19} neutrons per square centimetre. The relative abundances of the isotopes ^{40}Ar, ^{39}Ar and ^{36}Ar were afterwards determined using a small argon line in conjunction with an omegatron type mass spectrometer.

The method requires that no argon isotopes are produced or destroyed in appreciable quantity during irradiation except for the production of ^{39}Ar. A study of the extensive literature indicates that this condition is satisfied in most instances.

This method of potassium–argon age determination has the following advantages over the conventional method. (1) the sample weight is orders of magnitude smaller than that required for a complete determination by conventional means, (2) a knowledge of the precise weight of the sample is not required, (3) inhomogeneities in the distribution of potassium within the sample are of no consequence and (4) no argon-38 'spike' is required.

Improved precision of age measurement on young samples may be achieved by using an extension of the method. If a sample is heated in stages beginning with very gentle heating and finishing with complete fusion the first argon to be released will be mainly atmospheric argon. If the ratio $^{40}Ar/^{36}Ar$ is plotted against the $^{39}Ar/^{36}Ar$ ratio, the result will be a straight line, the slope of which will be related to the age and having an intercept on the $^{40}Ar/^{36}Ar$ axis at a value equal to the $^{40}Ar/^{36}Ar$ ratio of atmospheric argon. The question of loss of radiogenic argon-40 during preliminary heating no longer arises, as the radiogenic argon-40 and the argon-39 will be released in constant ratio to one another. If a sample is a single mineral or a number of minerals all having the same age, a straight line will result. If two or more minerals are present having different ages and different activation energies of argon loss, then the slope of the line will change as heating progresses. It may prove possible to arrive at an indication of the different ages of the separate mineral constituents. Minerals having different ages and very similar activation energies will give an intermediate age.

The method is at present under intensive investigation.

EXPERIMENTAL ERRORS

Experimental errors, as distinct from those caused by gain or loss of argon due to geological factors, arise from errors in the measurement of potassium and argon contents of rocks or minerals. Though the magnitude of such variations can and has been estimated in a general way by making repeat measurements on the same material and upon standard samples, it is better practice to evaluate the actual experimental error for each individual determination. The apparent age of a sample is derived from a number of separate analytical results, the individual errors of which can be determined. A procedure of error evaluation is described in Miller and Fitch.[6] Results given without their associated errors are difficult to assess.

REFERENCES

1 ALPERT, D. and BURITZ, R. S. 1954. *App. Phys. 25*, 202
2 EVERNDEN, J. F., CURTIS, G. H., KISTLER, R. W. and OBRADOVICH, J. 1960. *Amer. Jour. Sci. 258*, 583
3 GRASTY, R. L. and MILLER, J. A. 1965. *Nature 207*, 1146
4 —— and MITCHELL, J. G. 1966. *Earth and Planetary Science Letters 1*, 121
5 MERRIHUE, C. M. 1965. *Trans. Amer. Geophys. Union 46*, 125
6 MILLER, J. A. and FITCH, F. J. 1964. *Q.J.G.S. Lond. 120S*, 101
7 MITCHELL, J. G. 1968. *Geochim et Cosmochim Acta 32*, 781
8 NIER, A. O. 1950. *Phys. Rev. 77*, 789
9 SOMMER, H., THOMAS, H. A. and HIPPLE, J. A. 1951. *Phys. Rev. 82*, 697

8 Dating Pottery by Thermoluminescence

ONE OF THE ARCHAEOLOGIST'S most important sources of information is his pottery. On this much of his stratigraphy and conclusions depend. Perhaps the most valuable contribution the scientist can make to the archaeologist is to develop a reliable and universal dating method for pottery sherds. Thermoremanent magnetic dating provides us potentially with a direct method of dating kilns which have remained unmoved since the time when they were last heated; but this method does not help us with the dating of pottery, the orientation of which at the time it was fired cannot possibly be known, except in exceptional instances. The technique of thermoluminescence has, however, given us more hope that we may be able to date isolated finds of pottery found in all places and conditions.[1, 2, 3]

A word of warning must at once be given; although research in this dating technique has been partially successful it is by no means a *routine* method which can provide indisputable results. This note is intended to give a brief outline of some of the principles involved as far as they are at present understood.

PRINCIPLES

The materials from which pottery is made, like so many of the natural minerals, contain a property of storing energy by trapping of electrons as atomic defects or impurity sites. This stored energy may be released by heating the material, when visible light will be emitted; this is known as thermoluminescence. The effect has often been observed and several workers have attempted to use the method for dating rocks, in particular at the University of Wisconsin.[4, 5, 6]

All pottery and ceramics contain certain amounts of radioactive impurities (e.g. uranium and thorium) to a concentration of a few parts per million. These materials emit alpha-particles at a known rate depending upon their concentration in the sample. When an alpha-particle is absorbed by the pottery minerals surrounding the radioactive impurity, it causes ionization of the mineral atoms: electrons are released from their tight natural binding to the nucleii and may settle at a later time at metastable states of higher energy. Thus energy is stored. At ordinary temperatures these electrons remain in these metastable states or traps. If at any time the material is heated, for example during the firing of a pot, to a sufficiently high temperature, the trapped electrons will be released, with the emission of light.

From the time when the pottery was fired, when all the traps were emptied, up to the present time, a process of filling will occur as the alpha-particles are absorbed by the material, and the longer this time the more will have been filled, thus the greater will be the thermoluminescence.

To date a piece of pottery, therefore, we must make the following measurements:

(i) measure the light output when the sample is heated up;
(ii) measure the alpha-radioactivity of the sample;
(iii) measure the susceptibility of the sample to the production of thermoluminescence by an artificial known irradiation from a radioactive source.

By a combination of these results it is possible to derive the absolute age, or time since firing, or to compare the result with those of pottery of known age in order to date the sample.

ACCURACY

There are many disturbing factors which may reduce the accuracy of the results obtained, although for pottery these are less than for geological specimens. The archaeological samples have not been subject to unknown conditions of temperature and pressure which may cause chemical changes or recrystallization: effects which disturb geological results.[6, 7] Moreover, measurement of a large number of samples from the same source can provide some variations against which the errors can be assessed. For comparative dating the accuracy of the standards used must be assumed. At this stage results indicate a possible error of ± 10 to 15%, although new techniques of mineral separation from the pottery sherds indicates that this uncertainty can be reduced. In good circumstances the date may be obtained to $\pm 3\%$. It must be emphasized that the physical process of thermoluminescence in pottery is very complicated and not completely understood and that research is aimed at obtaining the best experimental technique.

APPARATUS

The effect of thermoluminescence may be observed easily in materials that have a large number of trapping sites which contain trapped electrons; these materials when heated in a dark room will give out sufficient light to read a newspaper. Unfortunately the pottery and ceramic samples are considerably less efficient, nor do they contain a high radioactive content, so that the light levels obtained are very small—invisible to the human eye. The material used is powdered and spread evenly on a graphite plate which is heated in an atmosphere of nitrogen at a controlled rate so that the temperature rises as fast as $100°C/sec$. The light output is measured by a highly sensitive photomultiplier and both temperature and light output are plotted on a recorder. The recorded curve is compared with that produced during a second heating to about $500°C$ when all the thermoluminescence has been emitted and only the background emission from the heated plate is measured. The difference of the two traces will be the thermoluminscence light output of the sample. The alpha-activity of the specimen is measured with standard low level alpha-counting equipment.

The estimation of the susceptibility to the alpha-radiation for the production of thermoluminescence is more difficult since it is required to simulate the effect of thousands of years of radiation from the small inherent uranium and thorium activity in a few minutes. This is achieved at present by either alpha- or beta-radiation from comparatively strong sources. When beta-radiation is used the susceptibility is lower than for alpha-particles, but by a reasonably constant factor so that this may be allowed for.

CONCLUSION

Archaeologically the possibilities of this technique are exciting and have far-reaching consequences. Scientifically the problems are intriguing and create an interesting challenge. Time will tell us whether we have a dating method which may surpass in accuracy and convenience the existing time-honoured stratigraphic methods.

REFERENCES

1 KENNEDY, G. 1960. *Arch. News. 13,* 147
2 Research Laboratory for Archaeology and the History of Art, Oxford University, *Archaeometry 4*
3 HOUTERMANS, F. G. 1961. *Helv. Phys. Act. 33, vi/vii, 595*
4 FAUL, H. (*ed.*) 1954. *Nuclear Geology.* New York
5 ZELLER, E. J. 1957. *Bull. Am. Ass. Pet. Geol. 41,* 121
6 DANIELS, F., BOYD, C. A. and SAUNDERS, D. F. 1953. *Science 117,* 343
7 ARGINO, E. E. 1959. *J. Geophys. Res. 64,* 1638

SECTION II   ENVIRONMENT

CLIMATE

9 *The Significance of Deep-sea Cores*

CESARE EMILIANI

THE UNUSUAL IMPORTANCE AND INTEREST of deep-sea cores among Pleistocene studies stems from the fact that by using such cores it is possible to reconstruct a continuous, time-calibrated record of the temperature variations of the surface water of the ocean during the Pleistocene. The surface temperature of the ocean, especially in the Atlantic and adjacent seas, is known or inferred to be closely related to the amount of ice on the northern lands. The oceanic temperature curve obtained from the deep-sea cores is thus a representation of continental glaciation, with temperature valleys and peaks corresponding, respectively, to glacial and interglacial ages. It is therefore possible, by correlation, to estimate the ages and durations of continental Pleistocene stages beyond the range of C^{14} dating. Deep-sea cores consisting of undisturbed sections of *Globigerina*-ooze sediment are most useful for this type of studies.

Globigerina-ooze, covering approximately 40% of the ocean floor, consists essentially of clay and a substantial amount (from 30% to more than 90%) of calcium carbonate. The clay component consists of the finest detritus brought to the ocean by rivers and winds and distributed widely by ocean currents. The carbonate component consists largely of shells of pelagic Foraminifera living in the euphotic zone. These shells are emptied upon reproduction and fall to the bottom. Other elements of the carbonate component are coccoliths and the shells of benthonic Foraminifera. Accessory elements in the sediment include shells of Radiolaria and diatoms, Fe-Ni spherules of cosmic origin, volcanic ash, water-, wind- and ice-borne mineral particles of terrestrial origin, fish teeth and otoliths, holothurian sclerites, and some precipitates (largely Fe and Mn compounds).

Calcium carbonate elements are dissolved to varying extents both during sinking through the water and on the ocean floor. The dimensionally smaller elements, such as foraminiferal spines and coccoliths, are especially affected. Solution becomes conspicuous at depths greater than about 5,300 m. in the Atlantic and 4,400 m. in the Pacific, leaving red clay as the predominant sediment.

Mechanically, accumulation of deep-sea sediments occurs mainly in two ways: (a) by settling of particles from the water column above, and (b) by lateral influx of material along the ocean floor. Lateral influx ranges from the addition of micron-sized particles (clay and coccoliths) reworked from adjacent areas by gentle bottom currents, to catastrophic floods introduced by turbidity currents originating on continental and island slopes, sometimes hundreds of miles away. In addition, sections of deep-sea sediments ranging in thickness from centimetres to perhaps tens of metres may be removed by sudden slumps caused by earthquake waves or other natural agencies.

Bottom topography exerts an important effect on the pattern of deep-sea sedimentation. Thus, little or no sediment may accumulate on the tops of seamounts; elisions are frequent on the slopes bordering continents, islands and seamounts; and lateral influx of sediments by turbidity currents is common in basins draining slopes on which sufficient sediment accumulation occurs. As a result of the great amount of sediments contributed from land and the strong erosion of shelf sediments by the sea during times of low sea level, the deposition of sediment layers transported by turbidity currents has been conspicuous and widespread during the glacial ages in both the North Atlantic and the North Pacific. Indeed, the majority of the 221 deep-sea cores recently surveyed by Ericson et al.[20] contain sediment layers deposited by turbidity currents.

Deep-sea sediments are easily sampled using the piston corer, a device invented by Kullenberg [29] and further developed by Ewing and associates.[21] This device permits the recovery of cylindrical sedimentary sections 5 cm. in diameter and up to 25 m. long. A few thousand deep-sea cores of various lengths have been recovered during the past 15 years by various expeditions at sea, notably the Swedish Deep-Sea Expedition of 1947–1948 and the numerous expeditions of the Lamont Geological Observatory, the Scripps Institution of Oceanography, the Institute of Marine Sciences, University of Miami, and the Soviet Institute of Oceanology. Only a small minority of these cores have been found free of both elisions by slumping and additions by turbidity current deposition. These undisturbed cores provide continuous stratigraphic records, covering in continuity the time during which the sediments were deposited.

Globigerina-ooze accumulates at rates ranging from one to several centimetres per thousand years, depending upon geographic location, depth of the water, and the local topography of the ocean floor. Thus, undisturbed *Globigerina*-ooze cores 10 m. to 20 m. in length may contain continuous stratigraphic records ranging in time from the present to more than a million years ago.

Probably the most significant geophysical parameter of the Pleistocene is temperature. In fact, temperature is known to have changed markedly, repeatedly, and on a world-wide basis, in response to the various continental glaciations. The temperature variations of the surface waters of the oceans can be reconstructed from suitable deep-sea cores of *Globigerina*-ooze facies by using a variety of methods. Most important among these are the studies of relative abundances of different species of pelagic Foraminifera which have different temperature tolerances, and the measurement of the ratio of the two stable oxygen isotopes, O^{18} and O^{16}, in the calcium carbonate of the foraminiferal shells. The former method was first proposed by Philippi[32] while the latter was proposed by Urey[47] and developed by Urey, Epstein, and associates.[48, 14, 15] The percentage of $CaCO_3$ and the weight percentage of the foraminiferal shells are two additional parameters which have been found to be temperature dependent under special conditions.

Globigerina-ooze is commonly reworked by bottom animals to a depth of several centimetres below the sediment surface. Consequently, the time resolution of the deep-sea cores of Globigerina-ooze facies is generally not better than a few thousand years, and events closely spaced in time cannot be recognized as separate in the cores. As an example,

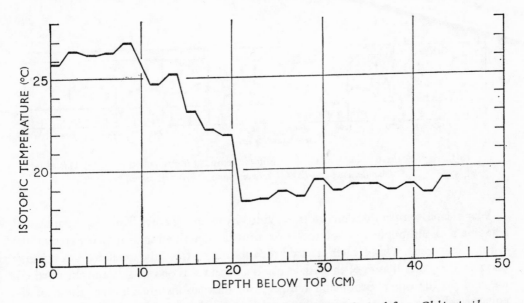

Fig. 17 Core 234A (equatorial Atlantic): isotopic temperatures obtained from Globigerinoides sacculifera. From Emiliani.[6]

the temperature fluctuations which are likely to have accompanied the various pulsations of the continental glaciers during the last deglaciation are represented in the deep-sea cores by a relatively smoothly rising temperature curve (Fig. 17). Globigerina-ooze cores, therefore, are most useful in the reconstruction of the major temperature variations of the Pleistocene, but are of little use for the study of the minor ones.

The stratigraphically longest deep-sea core of Globigerina-ooze facies so far described is core 58 of the Swedish Deep-Sea Expedition of 1947–1948, raised in the eastern equatorial Pacific from a depth of 4,400 m. This core is believed to contain an essentially continuous sedimentary section extending from the present to about 1·2 million years ago. Chemical analyses on this and other cores from the same general area[1] have revealed numerous, approximately periodical variations of the carbonate percentages, which are believed to have occurred in response to climatic changes. O^{18}/O^{16} analysis of core 58 (Fig. 18) showed a temperature decrease from the bottom of the core to its midpoint, followed by small temperature fluctuations in the upper half. Although the core may well penetrate the Pliocene, the position of the Plio-Pleistocene boundary cannot be established as this boundary is defined on the basis of the Plio-Pleistocene section at Le Castella, Calabria, southern Italy,[28] and no correlation between the two stratigraphies has yet been made.[13]

The temperature fluctuations in the upper portion of core 58 are of only 2° to 3°C. This small amplitude is probably due to the geographic location, the local pattern of vertical circulation of the ocean water, and the fact that only pelagic foraminiferal species of the relatively deeper growth habitats were available for isotopic analysis.[6] The temperature record is therefore not very clear.

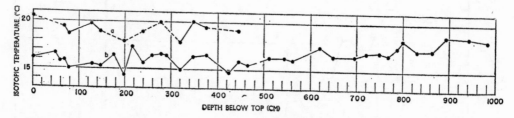

Fig. 18 Core 58 (eastern equatorial Pacific): isotopic temperatures obtained from (a) *Pulleniatina obliquiloculata* and (b) *Globorotalia tumida*. From Emiliani.[6]

A far clearer temperature record is provided by deep-sea cores from the Atlantic and adjacent seas, although none of the cores thus far described appears to represent the whole Pleistocene. This greater clarity probably results from the greater heat exchange between the water masses of the Atlantic and adjacent seas on one side and the northern ice caps on the other, producing temperature fluctuations greater than those of the equatorial Pacific. The more recent fluctuations were already rather clearly shown by the early works of Schott,[45] Bramlette and Bradley,[3] Cushman and Henbest,[5] Cushman,[4] Phleger[33, 34] and Phleger and Hamilton.[37] These investigations were based on the distribution of pelagic Foraminifera through relatively short cores from the equatorial and North Atlantic and the Caribbean. Similar work on the longer cores which have become available since the invention of the piston corer[35, 36, 38, 17, 21, 26, 31, 37, 46, 16, 42, 11, 12] has confirmed the early observations and extended the temperature record further back in time.

Estimates of temperature variation through deep-sea cores which are based on the relative abundances of pelagic Foraminifera are dependent upon the significance of different species as temperature indicators. Since the present latitudinal distribution is reasonably well known, especially in the Atlantic, the method is well founded in principle. In practice, however, different species may give different temperature estimates, as shown by Emiliani.[8, 11] In fact, temperature may not be the only factor controlling the relative abundances of pelagic Foraminifera, and temperature estimates based exclusively or predominantly on a single species are open to question. Furthermore, the relative abundances of pelagic Foraminifera in *Globerigerina*-ooze, which characteristically includes a large number of specimens belonging to a few common species and fewer specimens belonging to a number of less common species, form a close statistical system in which the relative abundance of any given common species is affected or controlled by the abundances of the other common species. Thus the relative abundance of *Globorotalia menardii*, extensively used by Ericson,[17] Ericson and Wollin,[21, 22] Ewing *et al.*[26] and Ericson *et al.*,[20] is controlled not only by temperature and other ecological factors but also by the relative abundances of other common species, some of which are markedly eurythermal. If the relative abundances of less common species are chosen for temperature estimates, the restriction imposed by the close statistical system is reduced. Indeed, the relative abundances of *Pulleniatina obliquiloculata* and *Sphaeroidinella dehiscens* in two Caribbean cores, as determined by Ericson and Wollin,[21] give temperature estimates which are in much closer agreement with the isotopic temperature determinations than similar estimates based on *Globorotalia menardii*.[8] If groups of

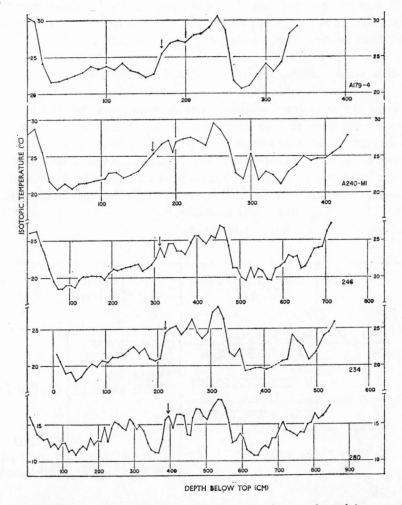

Fig. 19 Isotopic temperature curves of various cores (core numbers to the right); core 280: North Atlantic; cores 234 and 246: equatorial Atlantic; cores A240–M1 and A179–4: Caribbean. Arrows indicate the last occurrence of the subspecies *Globorotalia menardii flexuosa*. From Rosholt *et al.*[41]

species rather than single species are used for temperature estimates, a close agreement with the isotopic temperatures is also observed (Parker,[31] p. 236 and Fig. 2). The questionable micropaleontological method used by Ericson and associates, coupled with the almost complete lack of correlations among the deep-sea cores presumed to represent sediments older than about 500,000 years (Fig. 3 in [19], Fig. 20 in [23]) invalidates the sweeping stratigraphic, climatological, and chronological conclusions proposed by these authors.

A number of deep-sea cores from the Atlantic and adjacent seas have been analysed by the oxygen isotopic method (Fig. 19). [6, 9, 11, 12, 41, 42] The isotopic temperatures thus obtained are not unequivocally determined because the O^{18}/O^{16} ratio in carbonates deposited from water solutions is dependent upon not only the environmental temperature at the time of deposition but also the oxygen isotopic composition of the water. The present oxygen isotopic composition of the open oceanic water is reasonably well known or may be closely estimated from salinity data.[16] The assumption made in working with deep-sea cores is that the present oxygen isotopic composition of the open oceanic waters obtains also for the past. Corrections have been made for the isotopic effects caused by formation of the ice sheets during glacial ages.[6] While the oxygen isotopic temperatures obtained from deep-sea cores may not be identical to the natural temperatures, they are believed to be a fairly close representation.

The temperature curves of various cores (Fig. 19) show an appreciable background noise, which can be estimated at about 2°C. This noise arises from imperfect mixing of the sediment by bottom animals, sampling statistics, and an analytical error of $\pm 0.5°C$. The various temperature curves can be correlated easily and may be combined into a single, generalized temperature curve extending back to 425,000 years ago.[12] The more recent portion of this curve is shown in Fig. 20.

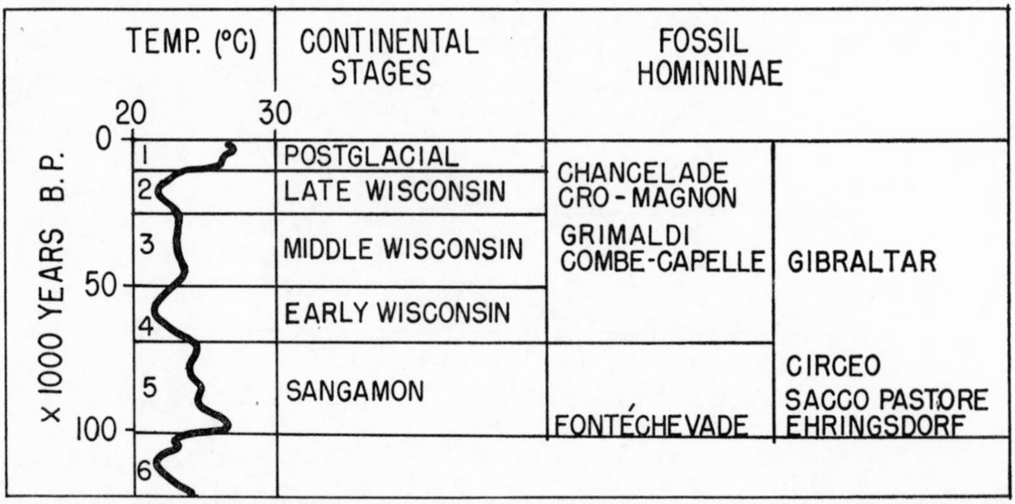

TEMP. (°C)	CONTINENTAL STAGES	FOSSIL HOMININAE	
20 30			
1	POSTGLACIAL	CHANCELADE CRO-MAGNON	
2	LATE WISCONSIN		
3	MIDDLE WISCONSIN	GRIMALDI COMBE-CAPELLE	GIBRALTAR
4	EARLY WISCONSIN		
5	SANGAMON		CIRCEO SACCO PASTORE EHRINGSDORF
6		FONTÉCHEVADE	

(× 1000 YEARS B.P.: 0, 50, 100)

Fig. 20 The Late Pleistocene: generalized chronology by absolute dating; temperature variations in the low latitudes; the standard stratigraphy of North America; and selected fossil hominids.

The time scale shown in Fig. 20 has been obtained by absolute dating of deep-sea cores to 150,000 years by the C^{14} and Pa^{231}/Th^{230} methods,[18, 41, 42, 43, 44] and by a simple extrapolation beyond that point. It is of interest to note that a similar chronology was obtained twenty-five years ago by Piggott and Urry[39, 40] using the Th^{230} method on cores which were studied stratigraphically by Bramlette and Bradley,[3] Cushman and Henbest[5] and Cushman.[4] The estimates of Emiliani[6] and Ericson et al.[20] are also in close agreement with the C^{14}-Pa^{231}/Th^{230} time scale.

The warm and cold temperature stages of the generalized temperature curve are identified by, respectively, odd and even integers increasing with age (Fig. 20). Correlations between these oceanic stages and the recognized glacial and interglacial stages of the continental stratigraphy can be assured only by absolute dating. Thus, stages 1 to 4 are seen to correlate, respectively, with the Postglacial, Late Wisconsin, Middle Wisconsin, and Early Wisconsin. Only a few pre-Wisconsin deposits in glacial and periglacial areas have been dated by absolute methods with sufficient accuracy to allow a correlation with the oceanic stages. These are the Worozonfian, Pelukian, Kotzebuan, and Middletonian interglacial stages of Alaska, which have been dated by the Th^{230}/U^{238} method.[2] The ages of these stages are very close to the ages of the temperature maxima of the oceanic stages 3, 5, 7, and 9 (Table A).

TABLE A

Continental Stages			Oceanic Stages	
Name	Age (years B.P.)	No.	Age (years B.P.)	
Late Wisconsin	10,000–25,000	2	10,000–25,000	
Middle Wisconsin (Port Talbot–Plum Point, Worozonfian)	25,000–55,000	3	25,000–50,000	
Early Wisconsin	55,000–70,000	4	50,000–70,000	
Pelukian	100,000	5	96,500	
Kotzebuan	172,500	7	171,500	
Middletonian	217,500	9	218,000	

Ages of continental stages (Late, Middle, and Early Wisconsin by C^{14}; Pelukian, Kotzebuan, and Middletonian, by Th^{230}/U^{238}) and ages of the corresponding temperature stages of the deep-sea cores (by C^{14} and Pa^{231}/Th^{230}). Ages of oceanic stages 5, 7, and 9 refer to the temperature maxima. Data from 6, 12, 41, 42, 2, 27.

The K^{40}/Ar^{40} ages so far published for materials from glacial and periglacial areas[24] are not yet sufficiently accurate, either because of sampling uncertainties or because of the analytical error, to allow unequivocal correlations with the oceanic stages. In particular, the age of 350–370,000 years determined for the deposits of the Jüngere Hauptterrasse of the Rhine[25, 30] falling, as it does, within the warm oceanic stage no. 15, suggests that either the deposits in question are interglacial rather than glacial, or that the material used for K^{40}/Ar^{40} analysis included some inherited argon.

In consideration of the fact that the continental deposits which have been dated accurately appear to correlate very closely with the oceanic temperature curve, there is little doubt that close correlations will also be obtained for the continental deposits which have not yet been dated or which have been dated with insufficient accuracy. In this context, it appears almost certain that the simple scheme of four or five major glaciations, still widely accepted, will have to be abandoned. In its place, is apparently emerging a picture of many alternating high and low temperature stages. At least some of these are probably the 'interstadials' within the classic glacial and interglacial stages of the Pleistocene.

The absolute ages of those fossil Hominidae whose stratigraphic position is clearly known and correlatable with the oceanic temperature curve, can be obtained by using the time scale of Fig. 20. Of particular interest is the observation that if, as is likely, the oceanic stage 5 is the last interglacial (Sangamon) and if the Fontéchevade remains date from that interglacial and are assigned to an early type of *Homo sapiens sapiens*, then modern man is about 100,000 years old.

SUMMARY

Deep-sea cores have provided a continuous, time-calibrated record of the temperature variations of the surface water of the ocean during the Pleistocene. This record is believed to reflect closely the continental glaciations, making it possible to estimate, by correlation, the ages and durations of continental Pleistocene stages too old to be dated by C^{14}. As a result, estimates for the ages of fossil hominids found in deposits of known stratigraphic position are also obtained. These estimates rest on the validity of the correlations between oceanic temperatures and continental stages, and between the source beds of the fossils and the standard continental stratigraphy.

REFERENCES

1 ARRHENIUS, G. 1952. *Swedish Deep-Sea Exped. 1947–1948, Repts. 5* (1)
2 BLANCHARD, R. L. 1963. *Uranium decay series disequilibrium in age determination of marine calcium carbonates.* Ph.D. Thesis, Dept. of Chemistry, Washington Univ., St. Louis, Missouri
3 BRAMLETTE, M. N. and BRADLEY, W. H. 1940. *US Geol. Survey Prof. Paper 196,* 1–34
4 CUSHMAN, J. A. 1941. *Am. J. Sci. 239,* 128–47
5 —— and HENBEST L. G. 1940. *US Geol. Survey Prof. Paper 196,* 35–50
6 EMILIANI, C. 1955. *J. Geol. 63,* 538–78
7 —— 1956. *Science 123,* 924–6
8 —— 1957. *Ibid. 125,* 383–7
9 —— 1958 *J. Geol. 66,* 264–75
10 —— 1960. Dating human evolution, in TAX, S. (ed.), *Evolution after Darwin,* Chicago, vol. 2, 57–66
11 —— 1964. *Bull. Geol. Soc. Am. 75,* 129–44
12 —— 1966. *Jour. Geology 74,* 109–26
13 —— MAYEDA, T. and SELLI, R. 1961. *Bull. Geol. Soc. Am. 72,* 679–88
14 EPSTEIN, S., BUCHSBAUM, R., LOWENSTAM, H. and UREY, H. C. 1951. *Ibid. 62,* 417–25
15 —— —— —— —— 1953. *Ibid. 64,* 1315–25
16 —— and MAYEDA, T. 1953. *Geochim. et Cosmochim. Acta 4,* 213–24
17 ERICSON, D. B. 1953. *Columbia University, Lamont Geol. Observatory Tech. Rept. on Submarine Geology,* no. 1

18 —— BROECKER, W. S., KULP, J. L. and WOLLIN, G. 1956. *Science 124*, 385–9
19 —— EWING, M. and WOLLIN, G. 1964. *Science 146*, 723, 732
20 —— —— —— and HEEZEN, B. C. 1961. *Bull. Geol. Soc. Am. 72*, 193–286
21 —— and WOLLIN, G. 1956. *Deep-Sea Research 3*, 104–25
22 —— —— 1956a. *Micropaleontology 2*, 257–70
23 —— —— 1964. *The Deep and the Past.* New York, 292 pp.
24 EVERNDEN, J. F. and CURTIS, G. H. 1965. *Current Anthropology 6*, 343–64
25 —— —— —— and KISTLER, R. 1957. *Quaternaria 4*, 13–17
26 EWING, M., ERICSON, D. B. and HEEZEN, B. C. 1958. Sediments and topography of the Gulf of Mexico in 'Habitat of Oil', *Am. Assoc. Petrol. Geol.* 995–1053
27 FLINT, R. F. and BRANDTNER, F. 1961. *Am. J. Sci. 259*, 321–8
28 *Seventh INQUA Congress*, Denver, Colorado, 1965.
29 KULLENBERG, B. 1947. *Svenska Hydr.-biol. Komm., Skr., Tredje Ser., Hydr. 1*, H. 2
30 LIPPOLT, H. J. 1961. *Alterbestimmungen nach der K-Ar-Methode bei kleinen Argon- und Kalium-konzentrationen.* Ph.D. Thesis, Heidelberg University, 82 pp.
31 PARKER, F. L. 1958. *Swedish Deep-Sea Exped. 1947–1948, Repts. 8* (4), 217–83
32 PHILIPPI, E. 1910. *Die Grundproben der deutschen Südpolar-Expedition, 1901–1903. II, Geographie und Geologie 6*, 411–616
33 PHLEGER, F. B. JR. 1939. *Bull. Geol. Soc. Am. 50*, 1395–1422
34 ——1942. *Ibid., 53*, 1073–98
35 —— 1947. *Göteborgs K. Vetensk. Vit. Samh. Handl., Sjätte Földen, Ser. B, 5*, 5
36 —— 1948. *Ibid.,* 14
37 —— and HAMILTON, W. A. 1946. *Bull. Geol. Soc. Am. 57*, 951–66
38 —— PARKER, F. L. and PEIRSON, J. F. 1953. *Swedish Deep-Sea Exped. 1947–1948, Repts. 7*, no. 1
39 PIGGOTT, C. S. and URRY, W. D. 1942a. *Am. J. Sci. 240*, 1–12
40 —— —— 1942b. *Bull. Geol. Soc. Am. 53*, 1187–1210
41 ROSHOLT, J. N., EMILIANI, C., GEISS, J., KOCZY, F. F. and WANGERSKY, P. J. 1961. *J. Geol. 69*, 162–85
42 —— —— —— —— —— 1962. *J. Geophys. Res. 67*, 2907–911
43 RUBIN, M. and SUESS, H. E. 1955. *Science 121*, 481–88
44 —— —— 1956. *Ibid. 123*, 442–48
45 SCHOTT, W. 1935. *Wiss. Ergeb. deutsch. Atlant. Exped. Forsch. u. Verm. 'Meteor' 1925–1927 3*, no. 3, 43–134
46 TODD, R. 1958. *Swedish Deep-Sea Exped. 1947–1948, Repts. 8*, no. 3, 167–215
47 UREY, H. C. 1947. *J. Chem. Soc.* 562–81
48 —— LOWENSTAM, H. A., EPSTEIN, S. and McKINNEY, C. R. 1951. *Bull. Geol. Soc. Am. 62*, 399–416

SOILS

10 Soil Silhouettes

L. BIEK

FOR EVERY MATERIAL and environment there is a (different) range between what is scientifically just recognizable and an apparent 'total absence' of indications. Over this range, evidence persists in soils in a reflected or even refracted form—usually as a colour contrast ('stain') with the ambient medium ('soil'), or sometimes by retaining some textural quality ('grain'), with or without staining. 'Silhouette' usefully describes this phenomenon as a whole, especially when (as often) there is a dark stain against a lighter background, and as it appears in a given plan or section. But the word has a two-dimensional connotation which may be misleading, and better designations might be 'altered feature', and, where appropriate, perhaps 'pseudomorph'.

During burial there is interaction between any man-deposited assemblage and the 'natural' environment, tending towards thermodynamical equilibrium. Strictly speaking, matter is always conserved, but in practice the results will vary widely. The significant criterion for archaeological work is persistence of either material or organization 'close enough' in nature or space for confidence in relating it back to the original. This approach is theoretically insecure because one cannot make comparisons except with better-preserved material elsewhere on typological grounds; and in the limit, when infinite dilution of significant characters has been reached, there can clearly be no certainty in *any* conceivable instance (for the next three or four millennia after the first experimental earthwork)[31] that anything prehistoric was in fact ever buried at the given spot (e.g. bone[1]).

Nevertheless, a given single feature (skeleton,[35] wooden pile[32]) sometimes passes from chalk or clay into sand or gravel in adjacent layers. At other times the same kind of features (coffins, skeletons[39]) are differently preserved on the same site in the same soil. The accompanying changes from original material into stain obviously make the interpretation of similar stains elsewhere more reliable. Occasionally a stain is found to grade downwards into the eroded but still bony remains of a skull[39] (Plate VIIIa).

One should distinguish between 'typed' and 'untyped' altered features, on the one hand, and between 'pragmatic' and 'supported' ones on the other. Clearly, where such a feature 'fits' into some preconceived typological pattern it must for the moment be accepted on that basis alone—as a pragmatic feature, such as a 'post hole', for which there may be no material proof (Plate VIIIb, but cf. above). Where opportunity offered, some scientific work may have been done to support a hypothesis, such as a 'skeleton in coffin'.

The most difficult and important cases arise with untyped features, where scientific examination must suggest an origin for a stain, or even develop some pattern where none may be visible. Clearly the experimental earthworks will provide increasingly useful evidence.[36]

The study ranges over the whole spectrum of materials; yet by definition the appropriate specialists are not normally equipped to deal with their own materials owing to the alteration. It thus usually falls to the soil scientist or surface geologist to attempt an interpretation of the altered remains, mainly by contrast with what they know could be 'natural'. At the same time it is clearly important that contact should be maintained as closely as possible with the specialist concerned.

For example, it is conceivable that a calcareous sandstone buried in acid soil might leave only an amorphous mass of the siliceous particles, petrologically characteristic in the same way as windblown deposits.[2] A collapsed cob-type wall built of gravel and sand strengthened with lime, from which the lime had been leached completely during burial, might be indistinguishable from the subsoil unless it contained 'foreign' material or showed an anomalous oxidation state.[3] Lightly burnt clay, perhaps completely rehydrated during burial, might nevertheless show some significant difference from the unburnt state, both structurally[4] and (hence) magnetically.[5] Indeed, changes in magnetic properties have been shown to occur without application of heat, presumably owing to oxidation-reduction phenomena in presence of much residual organic matter,[6] and hence relevant in connection with occupational altered features.[7]

Other silhouettes may appear as a regular pattern of ferruginous concretions resulting from iron nails in wood that has itself been completely altered;[8] a trail or jumble of green spots due to copper or copper alloy working;[9] or some white or (on exposure) pale violet spreads of lead[34] or silver[33] salts, respectively.

But by far the most numerous and important altered features result (presumably) from the decay of organic material. 'Wood' in the form of 'post holes', 'timber slots', 'sleeper trenches' and other 'structural members' is too common to deserve more than a mention, except in two respects: First, interaction may be fairly rapid and intense, so that a presumably permanent 'micropodzol' may be produced even horizontally around a ship[10] or coffin[11-13] in acid, sandy subsoil; or extensive 'shadowing' in blue-grey (? *vivianite*) may occur around even medieval 'trellis paths' under anaerobic, water-logged conditions[14]—here the wood itself is also preserved, but the shadows might remain even if the wood were subsequently removed. Secondly, extensive mineralization may occur quite rapidly, too—both by calcium[15] under neutral or alkaline conditions, and by iron and manganese[11, 13, 16-18] in more acid soils although here a very similar appearance may be due largely to organic residues.[19] This in itself does not affect the interpretation of a feature. But great care is necessary in working back from supported but untyped deposits: even a regular feature 'in manganese' may be misleading until full excavation shows, for instance, that accumulation must have resulted from impedance of drainage—as at the bottom of a silted ditch.[20]

Smaller fragments, and parts of the lower plants, are similarly affected[15, 16, 21, 22] but are less obvious unless present in quantity or as buried turf lines[11] or mounds,[36] or

(?deliberately) limed.[22] Pollen husks (p. 167) or silica bodies,[37] though 'altered' by the decay of associated tissue, are themselves little changed in acid soils and can add valuable direct information. Throughout, calcium-rich pseudomorphs are more likely to be interpretable than others. Evidence on buried leather from experimental earthworks suggests that careful excavation may recover, for example, imprints formed like squeezes in chalk slurry which has set—under pressure and/or with some solubilization—in contact with vegetable matter since decayed.[36] Misleading shapes can be produced in the presence of wood by the growth of iron corrosion products into solid chalk during burial in (e.g. constantly spring-fed?) aerobic waterlogged well deposits.[49] Extractives present in wood found anaerobically waterlogged after burial for 3,300 years apparently can be so aggressive that they will destroy wet polyurethane foam padding, though not tissue wrapping paper, in a relatively short time.[50] Animal remains, being more varied, give more complex results. Skeletal iron manganese silhouettes (Plate VII)[39] are the most common,[12, 16, 23] the mineral component of bone having the greatest resistance under most conditions, as might be expected, although such resistance is often modified by the close juxtaposition of organic matter which is subject to rapid biological attack. Attempts to intensify or even reveal residual bone concentrations with the aid of ultraviolet light have sometimes been successful.[47,48] Keratinous material such as horn or animal hair in its natural state, comes next in resistance, followed by leather, dressed and undressed skin, and finally textiles.[36, 51] In all these cases coherent persistence is relatively shortlived (p. 539) although there may be refracted evidence of fleece (in matted 'fibres'), wool (characteristic red-brown stain, recently noted after only two years' burial in chalk[36]), leather tyres (even after some six millennia) in the form of alum residues from the tawing.[24]

The position becomes really complex when in a typed feature all kinds of material are presumed to occur together. Phosphate analysis had been found useful in some cases in the characterization of 'body stains'[25] and was thus employed in another case[16] in an attempt to localize a 'skeleton' in a 'coffin' but failed to reveal significant differences. Instead, the visible stains appeared to be due mainly to manganese, exceeding ambient 'grave fill' controls by *one* order of magnitude in the 'skeleton', and by up to *two* in the 'wooden coffin', where closer examination further deduced remains of cereal or grass. Mineral accumulation in cellular tissue—preferentially on vegetable material, and possibly in the main an adsorption phenomenon, although polyphenolic and other complexes[38, 41] may play an intermediate part in the fixation—had evidently formed fair pseudomorphs before the organic structure was destroyed. 'Micropodzols' have been seen around an extant cremation bundle in a presumed 'cloth bag'.[26] Recently a simple spray[38] has been used for the rapid characterization of such features in the field, developing or intensifying (originally) 'organic' stains by reacting with their residual (humic) iron content.

Similar mineralization is, of course, common for both vegetable and animal remains in contact with corroding iron objects;[41] and a related but different mechanism acts even better by inhibiting microbiological activity to 'preserve' such material buried near enough to corroding copper (alloy) artifacts (Plate XXXb[31]).[42, 53] Both types are sometimes present side by side (Plate XXXI, p. 567[35]). In one case pseudomorphism was virtually complete, the weave of a textile fragment being preserved but the fibre altered beyond scientific recognition. In another, exactly comparable, case the fibre was just determinable as animal, probably wool, though part of it was found encased in a (recent) root.[27] Roots have been observed growing through leather after only a few years' burial[36, 43] and in up to $\frac{3}{4}$ in. thickness through the whole length of a 2-in. thick wooden piling plate (presumably) after the softening of its core.[52] Altered roots and root mats, much as solution holes,[44] can thus be difficult to distinguish from post holes and other man-made features or deposits.[40]

Throughout, only unburnt material has been considered; and the states described are implicit evidence that unburnt material was buried. Remains of 'hollow' logs, case-charred to a depth of up to an inch and their cores (presumably) silted up following decay, are occasionally found.[45] Contrary to popular belief, mere surface charring has no protective effect.[36] If not too distorted by firing or burial, organic matter is normally more useful charred rather than altered. Chemically, the residual carbon is virtually indestructible and the pseudomorphs so formed are usually faithful enough for quite close, though often not quantitative,[46] interpretation. Similar considerations apply to charred, and even calcined, bone—presumably because viable organic matter is removed from the sphere of microbiological attack which normally will not affect very seriously what amounts to the 'mineral ash'.

In general, it will be clear that a detailed knowledge of the basic geological and pedological background is essential if uncertainty is to be reduced to the minimum. If the specialist cannot visit the site, adequate control samples of such background material must be taken, if necessary on his instructions, to ensure that differentiation is statistically significant. This type of alteration takes place in moist and aerated soils and would appear to produce more important evidence from acid, sandy environments. Such an impression may be due partly to the better preservation of bone in chalky soils, and to the greater clarity of dark organic residues in them, making the establishment of prag-matic features a commonplace (Plate VIIIb). On the other hand, the marked prominence of iron and manganese movement draws attention to both natural and altered features in siliceous sandy and gravelly soils; yet differentiation is more difficult, and hence there are more cases of supported, typed features, even though support must remain ambivalent.

Almost the only examples of systematic surveys of untyped features have come in the search for limits of occupation;[28] geochemical reconnaissance[29] should, however, rank with aerial and geophysical surveys, in due course, wherever it can usefully complement them, as, for example, in developing features where no physical contrast shows.[38, 54] One might envisage the spraying of selected sections, or even large areas of scraped ground from helicopters (as with weedkillers), with suitable reagents, followed by aerial or other photographic survey. Alternatively, comparatively rapid 'statistical gridding' surveys are now a definite possibility, thanks to X-ray fluorescence spectro-metry.[30] But underlying all this work, as in other geo-surveys, the subsoil drainage pattern is decisive and, if very irregular, may produce anomalous or spurious effects that will obscure any altered feature unless they are properly taken into account.

From the specialist angle, all such evidence is inclined to be patchy and makes total investigation of the suspected area or section necessary. Research is needed into the exact material state of the just recognizable, coupled with the study of successively degraded material, to make extrapolation safer and to delimit the area within which altered features can usefully be supported by scientific analysis. If the present review is largely chemical in outlook, that is mainly because hardly any physical data—for instance, on the effects of compression and distortion, and other changes in morphological or even electrical properties—exist as yet. The British Association Committee's experimental earthworks[31, 36] are providing many valuable pointers, but only much detailed specialist study and increased interest on the part of the excavator will accelerate development in this field. Ultimately, a new kind of specialism, primarily concerned with subsoil pedology and/or subsurface geomorphology, will have to be recognized and take its proper place alongside the others. (See following article, p. 124.)

REFERENCES

 1 THOMPSON, M. W. and DIMBLEBY, G. W. 1957. *Proc. Prehist. Soc. 23*, 126
   PIGGOTT, C. M. 1943. *Proc. Prehist. Soc. 9*, 3; also in[13] p. 6
   E.g., at Sutton Hoo: ZEUNER, F. E. 1940. *Ant. J. 20*, 201–2, describes the environment, and the point was argued in detail at a later lecture (private communication); here, only c. 1300 years of burial are involved.
 2 E.g., PERRIN, R. M. S. 1956. *Nature 178*, 31–2: heavy-mineral assemblage in windblown sand
 3 BIEK, L. 1967. In HURST, D. G. and J. G., *J. Arch. Assoc. XXX*, 64
 4 BROWN, D. W. 196–. In GREENFIELD, E. *Excavations at Holbeach St. John's, Lincs., 1961* (forthcoming)
 5 LE BORGNE, E. 1960. *Ann. Géophys. 16*, 159–95
 6 —— 1955. *Ibid. 11*, 399–419
   HAIGH, G. 1958. *Phil. Mag. 3*, 267–86
 7 AITKEN, M. J. 1961. *Physics and Archaeology*, London and New York, 25–30; 1966. *Nature 212*, 1446–47
 8 E.g., at Sutton Hoo: PHILLIPS, C. W. 1956. In BRUCE-MITFORD, R. L. S. (ed.) *Recent Archaeological Excavations in Britain*, London, 162–3 and Pl. XXIX. Also see [39].
 9 BIEK, L. 196–. In WACHER, J. S. *Excavations at Catterick, Yorks., 1958–9*
10 PHILLIPS, C. W. 1940. *Ant. J. 20*, 101 and Fig. 5
11 BIEK, L. 196–. In RAHTZ, P. A. *Excavations at Little Ouseburn, Yorks., 1959* (forthcoming)
12 VAN GIFFEN, A. E. 1945. *Nieuwe Drentsche Volksalmanak 63*, Pl. 7⎱ visual appraisal only;
   KRAMER, W. 1951. *Germania 29*, 135–6 and Fig. 2; 137 and Fig. 4⎰ no details given.
13 BIEK, L. 1956. (Unpublished field notes on feature described) in GREENFIELD, E. 1960. *J. Derbys. Arch. N.H. Soc. 80*, 4–6 and Fig. 4
14 THOMPSON, M. W. 1956. *Arch. Cant. 70*, 52
15 LEVY, J. F. 196–. In MACKAY, R. R. *Excavations at Winklebury Camp, Hants., 1959* (forthcoming)
16 BASCOMB, C. L. and LEVY, J. F. 1957. In ASHBEE, P.: *Proc. Prehist. Soc. 23*, 162–3 and Fig. 7
17 FARMER, R. H. 1958. In RAHTZ, P. A., *Arch. Cant. 72*, 135
18 GOVERNMENT CHEMIST'S LABORATORY. 196–. In BIDDLE, M. *Nonsuch Palace*, Soc. Antiqs. Res. Rept. (forthcoming)
19 —— —— ——. 196–. In BIDDLE, M. *Excavations at Dover Castle, 1961–3, Arch. J.* (forthcoming)
20 BIEK, L. 196–. In RAHTZ, P. A. *Excavations at Cheddar, 1960–2* (forthcoming)
21 FARMER, R. H. 1957 (unpublished). *Report on wooden remains in iron pick head from White Castle, Mon.*
   —— 1960. In Greenfield, E., *Arch. Cant. 74*, 67–8
   —— 1961 (unpublished). *Report on charred wooden fragment from Downing Street site.* (A.M. no. 610141)
22 MONTGOMERY, W. 196–. In WEBSTER, G. *Excavations in Chesterton-on-Fosse, 1961* (forthcoming)
   METCALFE, C. R. 196–. In BIDDLE, M. *Excavations in Winchester, 1961ff.* (forthcoming); also in ADDYMAN, P. V. 196–. *Excavations at Ludgershall Castle, Wilts.* (forthcoming)

23 VAN GIFFEN, A. E. 1941. *Nieuwe Drentsche Volksalmanak 59*, 7–12 and Pl. 5
—— 1943. *Ibid. 61*, 9–10 and Pl. 14
24 WOOLLEY, SIR LEONARD. 1929. *Ur of the Chaldees*, London, 50 and 55; additional information kindly supplied by J. W. Waterer.
25 JOHNSON, A. 1954. In PIGGOTT, S. *Proc. Soc. Ant. Scot. 88*, 200–4
—— 1955. In SCOTT, J. G. *Ibid. 89*, 53
McALLISTER, J. S. V. 1965. In WATERMAN, D. M. *Ulster J. Arch. XXVIII*, 45
26 BIEK, L. 1959. (Unpublished field notes on feature described in) DUDLEY, D. 1964. *J. Roy. Inst., Cornwall, IV*, 428
27 HAIGH, D. 196–. In GILYARD BEER, R., and KNOCKER, G. M. *Excavations on the site o f Chertsey Abbey, Surrey, 1954* (forthcoming)
28 DAUNCEY, K. D. M. 1952. *Adv. Sci. 9*, 33–6
LUTZ, H. G. 1951. *Am. J. Sci. 249*, 925–8
SOKOLOFF, V. P. and CARTER, G. F. 1952. *Science 116*, 1–5
GAY, D. 196–. In ADDYMAN, P. V. and SAUNDERS, A. D. *Lydford, Devon, 1965–7* (forthcoming)
SCHWARTZ, G. T. 1967. *Archaeometry 10*, 57–63
29 NORTH, A. A. and WELLS, R. A. 1959. *Symposium de Exploración Geoquimica II*, 347–62
30 BELFORD, D. S. 1961. *Record of Brit. Wood Pres. Assocn. Convention*
31 JEWELL, P. A. 1963. *The Experimental Earthwork on Overton Down, Wilts., 1960*; a second earthwork was built on sandy heathland near Wareham, Dorset, in 1963. See also [36].
32 BIEK, L. 1963. *Archaeology and the Microscope*, London, 61, and Pl. 5
33 *Ibid.*, 131
34 ROBSON, W. W. and READ, T. A. 1959. (Unpublished analyses of objects (A.M. 5202) related to features (e.g. Pit Hut 2) described) in BARTON, K. J. 1962. *Trans. Essex Arch. Soc. I*, 17, 100
35 PIZER, N. H. 1966. In HUTCHINSON, P. *Proc. Camb. Ant. Soc. LIX*, 17–21
36 JEWELL, P. A. and DIMBLEBY, G. W. (eds.). 1966. *Proc. Prehist. Soc. XXXII*, 313–42
37 TAYLOR, G. 1958. (Reporting METCALFE, C. R.) in Fox, Lady (A.) *Med. Arch. II*, 156
38 BRONGERS, J. A. 1962–3. *Berichten R.O.B.*, *12–13*, 590
STAMBOLOV, T. 1968. *The Corrosion and Conservation of Metallic Antiquities and Works of Art: A Preliminary Survey*, Amsterdam, 34 ff.
39 JONES, M. U. and T. W. 196–. *Excavations at Mucking, Thurrock, Essex, 1965–7* (forthcoming)
40 See [32], pp. 62, 106, 123, 187
41 CUTLER, D. F. 1967. In STEAD, I. M., *Archaeologia CI*, 31ff.: see also [32], pp. 103, 128
42 HAINES, B., *et al.*, 196–. In ASHBEE, P. *Excavations at Amesbury, 1956* (forthcoming): see also [32], pp. 106, 118–26: and [22], [23], p. 570 below
43 GANSSER, A. 1950. *Ciba Review 81*, 2938–62
44 See [32], p. 75 and Pl. I.
45 E.g. GREENFIELD, E. 1960. See [13], p. 7 and Pl. III.
46 BOWMAN, A. R. A. 1966. *Studies on the Heat-induced Carbonization of Cereal Grains*. Thesis, Reading
47 RITCHIE, P. R. and PUGH, J. 1963. *Antiquity XXXVII*, 259–63
48 BRONGERS, A. J. 1965–6. *Berichten R.O.B. 15–16*, 227–8
49 BIEK, L. 196–. In STEAD, I. M. *Excavation of a Roman Well at Rudston, Yorks., 1967* (forthcoming); see also p. 569 below
50 MORGAN, G. C. and BIEK, L. 196–. In ASHBEE, P., *The Wilsford Shaft, 1961–2* (forthcoming)
51 See [32], p. 123
52 BIEK, L. 196–. In CURNOW, P., *et al.*, *Excavations at the Tower of London, 1957–9* (forthcoming)
53 VOGT. E. 1947. *Ciba Review, 54*, 1938–43
54 UNIVERSITY OF MICHIGAN. Infrared Physics Laboratory (ed.). 1968. *Fifth Symposium on Remote Sensing of Environment*. Also previous four symposia.
ANSON, A., McLERRAN, J. H. and PARKER, D. C. 1968. *Mater Res. Stand. 8*, 8–29

11 Soil, Stratification and Environment

I. W. CORNWALL

THE TERM 'UNSTRATIFIED', as applied to archaeological finds, has today become an epithet of opprobrium in the vocabulary of trained excavators, the implication being that any object, to be of much service in adding to our knowledge, should be relatable to the context in which it lay buried, so that no relevant information may be overlooked. Without this authentication, it is just another object, which, unless unique, or at least unusual among its kind, has nothing new to tell us.

Stratification, then, is the key to interpretation of a sequence of long-past events, whether affecting buildings with walls and floors, repairs, replannings, destructions and additions of different periods of occupation, or the substantially contemporaneous successive stages in the construction of a simple earthen barrow over a burial in open country. In the one case, the excavator is, most of the time, concerned with purposeful artifacts and modifications of them, which he, as an archaeologist, has been taught to recognize. In the other, the work, originally composed of natural materials, has frequently been left, ever since the time of its erection, to the forces of Nature, without further human interference, so that the sequence of events in the filling of the ditch, for instance, demands rather the eye of the natural scientist than of an archaeologist for its elucidation. The distinctions, here, between 'natural' and 'artificial' become rather fine, so that an excavator is often glad to seek the advice of a specialist to help in the explanation of his stratigraphy.

This is, perhaps, the prime function of the 'soil'-investigator from the prehistorian's point of view—to answer detailed questions such as: 'Is this black layer due to burning?', 'How was this pit-filling formed?' and so on. The consultant, for his part, has to be somewhat conversant not only with the science of the soil, in the narrow sense of pedology, but to some extent also with geology, geomorphology, climatology, mineralogy and petrology—the study, in fact, of the whole inanimate environment of the site, from the atmosphere above it to the geological 'solid' beneath and around it, both today and in times past, and of the materials at all periods available to the ancient inhabitants.

This aspect of the investigation of archaeological deposits is chiefly a matter of exercising the techniques of the sedimentary petrographer, combined with some fairly simple inorganic chemical procedures for the identification of common mineral substances, some of them perhaps artificial.

An approach of rather wider interest, however, is that of the environmentalist, the student of the natural settings of human cultures and of the relation of communities to their surroundings. The biological environment of early man has received considerable attention—as witness the important advances made through the study of floras and faunas of various periods. Of the inanimate environment, the important climatic part has mainly attracted interest, its direct influence on flora, fauna and human communities being obvious. The mineral environment ('mineral' being taken in the widest sense of the word, to include earth, air and water) has been studied mainly as the source of supply of industrial materials: stone, metals and building materials. This is certainly an important aspect of ancient economy, but scarcely touches the main theme.

Natural soils of today reflect the effects of climate on the local geological deposits and where, as beneath barrow-mounds and other earthworks, soils of earlier times have been preserved, their study may yield information about past climates to compare with that obtained (say) from pollen-analysis. Not only buried soils, but sediments in general, as, for example, those forming part of ditch-fillings or the overall mantling of a site, probably consist largely of redeposited contemporary soil-materials, so that even these 'colluvial' deposits may be of considerable interest.

Combining these two functions—helping to explain archaeological stratification and independently inquiring into the details of contemporary environment—the soil-investigator has become a recognized collaborator, so that such information as can be gained from the deposits themselves, which contain and cover archaeological finds and structures, is nowadays frequently with advantage added to that obtained by the study of the archaeological material proper. Recognition is thus practically accorded to the idea that archaeology is only one part of the whole study of ancient communities, in which the natural sciences also have a large role to play.

The further back in time that we carry our inquiry into the ways of life of ancient man, the more important become the relevant environmental studies. From Palaeolithic times we have, for the most part, only the worked stone and bone implements and the rare human fossils to guide us. Environmental evidences—animal bones, shells and plant-remains, geology, geomorphology, spelaeology, soil-studies—all can give us some glimpses of the climate and conditions of life of the time. They are necessary tools in the armoury of the Palaeolithic archaeologist, for without them he is relatively helpless, a mere typologist and technologist, bereft of any natural frame within which to comprehend the lives of the makers of his finds.

Glacial, river and lake deposits, marine and desert sediments, cave-fillings, volcanic ashes, dune-sands and, especially on the continent of Europe, the fossil soils represented by loess-loams, give to the student of archaeological deposits and soils an enormous variety of chiefly mineral materials with which to work out the environments of remote times past, which often differed enormously from those of today. Beyond the sand-grains or the soil thin-section under the narrow circle of his microscope-objective, he needs wide-angle geological and geographical insight to visualize landscapes unrecognizable now, owing to sea-level changes and later valley-cutting which have resulted in our existing topography. How did the beach-pebbles on the Chalk summits of the North Downs [1] come to be formed, seeing that the present watercourses and sea-beaches lie at so comparatively low a level? Evidently, when they were laid down the present Wealden basin did not exist. A long-enduring warm-temperate climate has rendered almost unrecognizable a once almost certainly chalky boulder-clay overlying the Hertfordshire Pebble Gravel [2] on the 400-foot contour, far above the Vale of St Albans, on the floor of which the later Chalky Boulder-Clay glaciation advanced. On this land-surface perhaps walked the contemporaries of Swanscombe Man, but of it remain only a few patches, capping what are now hill-tops, dissected remains of the wide, level forest floor of 200,000 years ago. Thin sections of the material show parabraunerde,*[3] or even braunlehm, soil-types, indicating much warmer summers than we have today.

The late S. Hazzledine Warren, reinterpreting the Clacton flint industry in 1951,[4] made an obvious, but all too often forgotten, observation: that though we find the tools of Lower Palaeolithic man in the former channel-deposits of the river, he did not live in the river-bed, but on its banks! One may straightway conclude from this that *none* of the river-gravel implements is archaeologically *in situ*. The living floors may once have resembled those of Olorgesailie[5] or Olduvai,[6] more fortunately preserved in East Africa, but here the meandering river has re-worked its own old flood-plain materials, sorting out the hand-axes and flakes with the coarser ballast and washing away the rest of the evidence. One must visualize the Great-Interglacial Thames flood-plain extending at about the 100-foot level above the present river, from Boyn Hill and far upstream down to Swanscombe, and a North Sea much more extensive than it is at present, the existing coasts being at about the 15-fathom line of soundings! Small wonder that we have not yet chanced on any 'floors' in the few vestiges left of that almost-vanished landscape!

Volcanic deposits present both problems and facilities unknown to British pre-historians, seeing that none as late in date as the Pleistocene exists here. Having had the opportunity, recently, to visit Mexico, this branch of sedimentary investigation is fresh in mind. The centre of that country is traversed from east to west by a major axis of crustal weakness, known as the Clarion Line, from its connection, to the west, with Clarion Island, far out in the Pacific. It appears to have originated in the later part of the Tertiary, but is still active today, as witness the first outburst of a new volcano, Parícutin, in the late 1940's, while Popocatépetl is still in the fumarolic stage and hot mineral springs are not uncommon. During the Pleistocene and Postglacial there were repeated eruptions, which mantled whole countrysides with pumice and ashes, chiefly andesitic in character. Between these, there were longish quiet phases, when the surface of such fresh deposits underwent some chemical weathering and soil-formation. Each soil formed was sometimes perfectly preserved in its entirety by the succeeding fall of freshly-ejected ash.

Thus, near the town of Puebla, a single gully, eroded under modern semi-arid conditions, with torrential downpours during a short wet season, exposed more than half a dozen such weatherings, some of considerable thickness, within a vertical compass of some 70 feet. The accumulation of andesite ashes overlay a fluviatile bone-bed, yielding a Pleistocene fauna. This gully, therefore, showing alternating vulcanism and soil-formation, exposes the entire local environmental sequence from some point in the later Pleistocene to the present day, as far as can be seen without a break. A later

* Some account of the principal soil-types and their environmental significance may be found in Corn-wall,[3] pp. 85–112.

visit has provided confirmatory detailed stratigraphical evidence the publication of which is in hand.[20]

The importance to Mexican prehistory of this discovery lies in the fact that several archaeological horizons in the Basin of Mexico occur in Pleistocene and Recent lake-deposits, or are correlatable with them by their relation to fossil beaches, indicating former higher levels of Lake Texcoco. Among these is the hitherto not firmly datable Tepexpan[7] human skeleton, with fossil pollen, mammoth-bones and implements of Palaeo-eastern type, as found in the south-western United States, occurring at the same horizon nearby. These same lake-deposits contain, at frequent intervals, layers of volcanic pumice, marking a series of ash-explosions which took place during their formation. It is now certain that these correspond to, and are petrologically correlatable with, some of the various terrestrial ash-layers, elsewhere surmounted by soils, so that eventually the lacustrine sequence with pollen, the volcanic sequence and the included soil-sequence may be inter-correlatable with the archaeological sequence over the wide area affected by the volcanoes.

It can be seen that this problem involves the close co-operation of several scientific specialists. All stand to gain by working out a joint system of relative dates. Though archaeology may seem to be the principal beneficiary, the most recent lava-flow from the Xitli volcano in the Mexico Basin took place at about the beginning of the Christian Era and the vulcanologists have been glad enough to accept the *terminus post quem* given by the radiocarbon date of the Late Pre-Classic cemetery which it covered at Copilco,[8] in the Federal District of Mexico.

Environmentally, the buried soils of central Mexico promise to be extremely interesting. The high colours suggest intensive weathering reached only in fully moist conditions completely different from the only sub-arid climate of modern times. Such a prominent feature should readily be recognizable everywhere in the region and so afford a valuable stratigraphical datum.

Stratified Mesolithic sites in north-western Europe, save those discovered in peat-bogs and lake-deposits, are not very numerous. Where there is peat, pollen-analysis obviously provides the best environmental and stratigraphical tool. Since the mineral content of such humic materials is generally low, the evidence from it in these circumstances is relatively unimportant.

One recent exception was a thick calcareous marl seen in sections at a prolific site at Thatcham, Berkshire.[9] This certainly indicated a lake and a long phase of open water with a minimum of vegetation, for the material often contained very little organic matter. This indicates deep water, 6 ft to 8 ft at least, for plants with floating leaves, such as water-lilies, will crowd lesser depths and give rise to a muddy or peaty bottom. Marls consist, in part, of chemically-precipitated calcium carbonate with such other mineral sediment, mainly of the finest silt and clay grades, as may be available. Limy crusts, formed on growing submerged weeds by withdrawal of CO_2 from the lime-bearing water, shells and the skeletons of planktonic plants and animals account for the rest.

Now, a mere study of the map will suggest that water of this depth covering the marl at Thatcham would drown the present Kennet floodplain, perhaps as far upstream as

Newbury racecourse, so that the lake, at that stage, must have been very extensive. The extent of the former deep water could probably be mapped without great difficulty by numbers of auger-holes of no great depth, strategically sited with regard to the present contours, to locate the shoreward margins of the marl deposit. Archaeologically speaking, this conclusion is not without significance, for it suggests that the Thatcham site is perhaps only one of many such in the vicinity, of which the remainder still await discovery.

The reason for the very existence of a Thatcham Lake has not yet been fully explained. At such a comparatively late date, any major geomorphological difference in the drainage-pattern of the Kennet valley from that of today can probably be discounted. Zeuner has suggested that a beaver-dam some way downstream towards Reading may have been responsible, for beavers figured in a small way in the Thatcham fauna. If so, prospecting for the likeliest site, and even for preserved remains, of such a dam might be rewarding.

With the arrival of Neolithic farmers and herdsmen, archaeology becomes at once more concerned with settlement-sites, communal tombs and other evidence of man-made structures. Clearance of forest or scrub for the establishment of fields and pastures represented man's first major intervention in Nature, not merely accepting the natural environment as he found it, but adapting it to his own purposes. Slash-and-burn with hoe-culture and the maintenance of clearings as grassland by grazing and browsing domestic stock are not now reflected with any clarity in our more recently disturbed soils. The best hope of discerning something of such activities is in soils of the period buried under earthworks—banks and barrow-mounds.

Especially on chalk, and other limestones, any long period without mechanical disturbance of the surface results in the formation of a more or less thick layer of stone-less humic soil. Cast-forming earthworms are chiefly responsible for this, for their activities in throwing up fine material at the surface result in the gradual sinking of stones and other solid bodies too large for them to swallow. The uppermost few inches, where they are chiefly active, consist of distinct crumbs composed largely of broken castings (rendsina). On silicate-soils of adequate base-status (e.g. the richer brownearths) this is also often the case, though the crumb-structure may be less marked. It is clear, therefore, that if the ancient soil beneath a Neolithic structure shows this typical 'worm-layer', it was not cultivated for some time before the erection of the earthwork, save, perhaps, by the most superficial scratching. If, however, the buried soil is not excessively acid (precluding habitation by cast-forming worms) and is found to be uniformly chalky or stony, it must have been disturbed, possibly by primitive tillage, at most within a decade or so before being covered. This was found to be the case in the buried land-surface beneath the Wayland's Smithy (Berks) megalithic tomb. This consideration of course applies also to suitable buried soils of any age, though with the introduction of improved tools and deeper cultivation, an even longer period of quiescence is needed, after disturbance, to re-establish the 'worm-layer' so that land even intermittently occupied is unlikely to show it.

Ploughing, as such, is very difficult to prove, unless the bedrock, as possibly in shallow soils on chalk, retains clear marks of the share. This is a question regularly posed to the soil-consultant, but no unmistakable affirmative case is known to the writer in this country. Flints, especially those with a white patina, and other hard stones are sometimes found spotted and streaked with rust. These are a permanent mark of cultivation with iron tools. Most must be attributed to contact with comparatively modern farm implements.

The fillings of ditches have, from time to time, provided interesting environmental evidence. The cursus-ditches covered by the bank of the Thornborough Middle Rings [10] showed such a concentration of organic matter that it seems likely that the area was forested while they were open. Similar evidence of forest environments has been adduced for earthworks (round barrows and hill-forts) of later periods also. It may well be that when many such structures were originally erected the country was wooded, so that they would not have been seen in the comparatively open situations which they now occupy. It is known from Roman sources, of course, that some Iron Age peoples deliberately chose wooded sites for their defensive earthworks. Missile weapons of the time having only a comparatively short effective range, a clear field of fire, such as has been desirable to static defence in later times, was not then so necessary. We tend to regard these things too much through modern eyes and to make unnecessary difficulties for ourselves in comprehending the ancients. Doubtless thick cover for attackers was not allowed to develop too close to the ramparts, but forest not only conceals defensive works and puzzles the stranger; it makes impossible any assault in formation and favours guerrilla tactics by the defenders.

The ditch of a Neolithic long barrow at Nutbane [11] showed a lens of distinctly wind-sorted sediment well up in the filling, that is formed some longish time after the erection of the monument, when it was already grassed over. The stratigraphical discontinuity of this lens with any body of material on the banks, from which it could have been washed in, led to a closer examination and, though somewhat cemented with calcium carbonate since its deposition, the well-graded quartz-grains suggested wind as the depositing agency. The insolubles, after acid-treatment, gave a mechanical analysis typical of wind-sorted sediment.

This material might have been deposited at the same time as the filling of one of the Y-Holes at Stonehenge,[12] previously shown to have a similar grading and probable mode of accumulation.

The same phenomenon was observed in some natural soils in Oxfordshire, buried under round barrows near Cassington,[13] of presumed Early Bronze Age date, the wind-action (if the same event) therefore having taken place *since* the building of the Nutbane long mound and *before* that of the round barrows at Cassington. No appreciable accumulation of wind-blown dust could happen in Wessex under present-day conditions of moisture all the year round and close vegetation-cover. Its occurrence during prehistoric times, therefore, is likely to be due to a period of somewhat warmer and drier summers (that is, a more continental climate), with at least seasonally and locally bare soil to provide a source of airborne dust. The palaeoclimatologists, on pollen evidence, have recognized such a phase, called the Sub-boreal, coincident in Britain with some part of the Early Bronze Age. If such wind-sorted sediments are attributable to the Sub-boreal climatic oscillation, they should be widespread in the southern counties in suitable situations and a watch is being kept for further examples.

Not long since, samples were examined from the section of a ditch associated with a Neolithic long mortuary enclosure at Normanton Down.[14, 15] Nothing resembling the Nutbane silt-lens was found, though this site was regarded as approximately of the same age as Nutbane. The only disturbance in the section was the modern ploughing of the surface, extending no more than 8 or 9 inches in depth. If a windborne silt had ever existed there, it could only have been obliterated by the plough if it lay high enough in the ditch-filling, that is, having been formed at a late enough stage, after the ditch had been almost completely filled. Without abandoning the above conclusions about wind-action, which seem to be justifiable in their own context, since the evidence is hard to explain by any other theory, one is inclined to suggest that the mortuary enclosure was perhaps distinctly earlier in date than the Nutbane barrow, so that any silty wind-blown deposit was either never accumulated in the already only shallow ditch-depression, or has since been ploughed up. It is perhaps risky to suggest even a relative date on such merely negative evidence. It must be added here that more recently discovered evidence of snail-shells from the Nutbane silt, studied by Dr Michael Kerney, pointed to a con-temporary moist-shady microclimate, certainly not one markedly dry. This does not necessarily invalidate the whole of the above argument, though demanding reconsidera-tion of the Nutbane case. The contradictory result may be due only to the presence of a local patch of scrub and undergrowth at the relevant time. It gave rise, however, to some heart-searchings and further experimentation, as a result of which a far more fundamental possible cause for the wind-sorted character of the sediment presented itself.

The parent-material of almost any siliceous sediment on the chalk is most likely to be the chalk itself, which is dissolved in time by weathering and leaves no more than 1% of siliceous and aluminous insolubles. These must themselves have been wind transported in Cretaceous times and have been deposited with the calcareous ooze then forming the sea-bottom, far from the contemporary land. When again released in recent times, by solution of the weathering chalk, such residues *already* display the wind-sorted grading observed, whatever the agency responsible for their final transport and deposition in a man-made ditch!

As more sophisticated cultures than those of semi-sedentary Neolithic cultivators and Bronze Age stockmen developed or intruded, structures due to man's activities become larger and more complex. Since the climate of the Early Iron Age apparently differed scarcely at all from that of the present day, the environmental aspect of soil-investiga-tions becomes less important than the purely stratigraphical. Buried soils under ramparts of hill-forts are almost invariably identical in type with their modern counterparts on the same bedrock. Nevertheless, a knowledge of soils sometimes enables a consultant to assist materially in the interpretation of stratification. Defensive earthworks and their ditches, for example, include evidences of natural denudation, silting and soil-formation along with the artificial features of their structures and fillings.

At Caesar's Camp, Holwood Park, Keston,[16] it was possible, from soil-evidence, to distinguish two clear phases of building of the inner bank, separated by a period long enough for natural weathering to have formed an immature soil on the sandy material of the first construction, before it was covered by the freshly-dug ditch-spoil of the second. Three podzol-soils clearly appeared in the rampart-section—the original soil before there was any occupation of the site, that formed on the first bank before its reconstruction, and the modern profile, developed since the abandonment of the site on the make-up of the enlarged rampart.

The relative immaturity of the second suggested that not more than a few decades had elapsed between the phases. This last not very precise conclusion was borne out by the archaeological material of the two phases, which, when fully studied, will probably yield more exact limiting dates for the intervening lapse of time. This, added to similar information from other sites, will eventually enable us to make better estimates of soil-maturity in future cases, under similar soil-conditions, where corroboration from external evidence may be lacking. Much more work on well-dated sites will be needed before any useful degree of precision can be expected in this sort of comparative dating.

A further extremely immature buried soil was detected within a single phase of addition to the rampart in another section at Keston, but was unsupported by any archaeological evidence for a break in the reconstruction. A possible explanation suggested for this was that the enlargement of the bank took place in partial stages over a considerable number of years. In view of the large area enclosed by the defences and the imposing dimensions of the rampart, this reconstruction represented a very considerable undertaking of earth-moving. Using only the primitive methods then available, this would either have involved literally thousands of full-time workers or, with a lesser labour-force, a proportionately longer time. The soil-evidence suggested that a number of years passed, at this particular point, between the beginning of enlargement of the rampart and its completion to the desired height.

While on sites of the Roman and later periods, up to quite late historical times, the stratigraphical method of excavation remains a valid tool to investigate those aspects of the life of societies which are incompletely, or not at all, known from literary sources, opportunities to use soil-investigations proper to supplement them become fewer and fewer. The consultant is, on the other hand, more and more called on to explain the nature and, if possible, to suggest the provenance of artifacts, in the shape of building materials, imported stones (such as tesserae), pigments, ornamental substances and evidences of technological activities such as tanning, metal- and glass-working, from floors, pits, hearths and drainage-gullies. A few instances may be quoted by way of illustration.

A sample from Verulamium formed part of a deposit found on the floor of a building. Black in colour, it was seen under the microscope to contain numerous small, dull-black, heavy, scale-like bodies, together with the usual debris of fallen buildings—quartz sand, lime-plaster or mortar, chips of flint, tile or pottery, bone and charcoal. The visual aspect of the scales not being very informative, save that they were clearly not natural objects, a qualitative analysis of a washed portion showed only iron present in quantity, among the metals, and no corresponding cations such as sulphide, which might have accounted for the black appearance. The material was evidently black iron oxide. A test with a magnet proved it to be, mineralogically, magnetite and its occurrence was thus easily explained as an accumulation of 'blacksmith's scales', the flakes of oxide forming on red-hot iron exposed to the air and falling from the anvil under the hammer. The room was thus shown to have been a smithy.

Charred grain and Purbeck 'Marble' from Dorset, used as an ornamental stone in buildings, were other interesting finds recorded from this site.

Anglo-Saxon Thetford [17] yielded a lump of crude glass, still retaining the form of the crucible in which it had been melted, bronze- and iron-slag, masses of wood-ash from industrial furnaces and fragments of Niedermendig (Eifel, Germany) lava, imported as quern-stones.

In every department of this work, though a beginning has been made, it is evident that we still have far to go. One of the most frequently recurring (and so far, generally insoluble) problems concerns organic matter. The humus of soils and archaeological deposits is an amorphous nitrogen-containing acidic complex of, at present, almost unknown composition and chemical constitution. Though, in most cases, obviously predominantly vegetable in origin, it must nearly always contain animal residues also, but we have as yet no way, certainly no simple, practical way, of distinguishing the one from the other, or of estimating their proportions.

Archaeologists submitting samples often want to know, specifically: 'Was this wood or leather?' Unless some recognizable microscopic structure survives, this is, so far, unanswerable in most cases. Other typical queries are: 'Is this deposit in a pot remains of food? If so, what sort of food?', 'Did this vessel contain milk or beer?' Search for surviving fats, starch-grains, proteins or yeast-cells has not yet been successful in the case of most British samples, or for tannins in supposed leather, though interesting and suggestive results have been obtained from Egyptian and other samples from arid climates.

It seems, however, that possibility of advance in these directions must exist could only specialist organic chemists be found having the skill, the time and the interest to devote to such problems. Little attention seems, as yet, to have been directed to them, perhaps because the results seem not to be economically valuable. It is, however, known [18] on the environmental side, for instance, that, today, holly (*Ilex aquifolia*), marching before the edge of a wood, is able, by the humus formed from its fallen leaves, so to improve podzolic heath-soils that deciduous trees, such as oak, may eventually spread in its wake and regenerate forest brownearth on relatively barren sands. Exactly how holly-humus differs from that of any other broad-leaved tree seems to be unknown, but the knowledge should be worth gaining for the forester.

On the chronological side, soils have been scientifically observed and investigated for little more than half a century. Their formation and growth are, on the other hand, extremely slow—a matter of thousands, rather than hundreds, of years in attaining a degree of maturity. Their rates of development under the infinitely variable conditions of Nature in different situations can only roughly and precariously be estimated. Here, archaeology, by affording evidence of soil-development on monuments and works well dated by other means, may, in due course, provide some sort of a time-scale, which could later be applied in its own favour, where other dating evidence was lacking. We have, so far, scarcely laid the foundations of this work.

There are, at the time of writing, two long-term experiments under way with just this object (among others of archaeological interest) in view. In the summer of 1960, a British Association Sub-Committee on Field Experiments,[19] set up in the Nature Reserve on the Chalk of Overton Down, Wiltshire, a 100-foot length of earthwork (linear bank and ditch) to investigate practically, over the next century or so, the processes and rates of denudation, ditch-filling, compaction, slumping, soil-formation, etc., in and on this 'monument' and the preservation of various materials incorporated in its structure during erection. The work was carried out by volunteer labour to exact specifications and dimensions, planned in advance and duly recorded. It is intended to section the bank and ditch at increasingly long intervals in the future, to determine, by the techniques of archaeological excavation, exactly how the original structures and materials have been altered or displaced during the known passage of time. Another similar experiment has been set up on a different soil in Dorset, to afford information on the influence of particular, varied environments on the processes and rates. These, and possibly others to follow, may be studied. Several branches of Natural Science, as well as archaeology, are expected to benefit from the exact quantitative knowledge gained. All have co-operated closely in the planning and will continue to do so at each future 'sampling'.

REFERENCES

1 WOOLDRIDGE, S. W. 1927. *Proc. Geol. Assoc. 38*, 49–132
2 —— 1960. *Proc. Geol. Assoc. 71*, 119
3 CORNWALL, I. W. 1958. *Soils for the Archaeologist*, London
4 WARREN, S. H. 1951. *Proc. Geol. Assoc. 62*, 107–35
5 LEAKEY, L. S. B. 1952. *Proc. 1st Pan-Afr. Cong. Prehist.*, Oxford
   COLE, S. 1954. *Prehistory of E. Africa*, London, 138
6 LEAKEY, L. S. B. 1961. *Nature 189*, 649
7 DE TERRA, M., ROMERO, J. and STEWART, T. 1949. Tepexpan Man. *Viking Fund publications in Anthropology*, no. 11, New York.
8 GAMIO, M. *c.* 1917. Las excavaciones del Pedregal de San Angel y la cultura arcáica del Valle de México, quoted in MARQUINA I., 1951, *Arquitectura prehispánica*, Inst. Nac. de Antr. e Hist. Mexico D.F., 20–21
9 WYMER, J. 1958, 1960. *Berks. Arch. J. 57*, 1–33; *Proc. Prehist. Soc. 26*, 342
10 THOMAS, N. 1956. *Yorks. Arch. J. 38*, 425–45
   CORNWALL, I. W. 1954. *Proc. Prehist. Soc.* (1953) *19*, 144 ff.
11 VACHER (*née* MORGAN), F. DE M. 1959. *Proc. Prehist. Soc. 25*, 15–51
12 CORNWALL, I. W. 1954. *Ibid.*
13 *Ibid.*
14 VACHER, F. DE M. 1960. *Proc. Prehist. Soc. 26*, 342
15 —— 1961. *Ibid. 27*, 160–73
16 PIERCY FOX, E. V. 1951. *Arch. Cant. 71*, 243–5
17 DUNNING, G. C. 1949. *Arch. J. 106*, 72 ff.
18 DIMBLEBY, G. W. and GILL, J. M. 1955. *Forestry 28*, 95–106

19 JEWELL, P. (ed.) 1963. *The Experimental Earthwork on Overton Down, Wiltshire, 1960*. Brit. Assoc. for the Advancement of Science, 100 pp.
—— and DIMBLEBY, G. W. (eds.) 1966. The experimental earthwork on Overton Down, Wiltshire, England: the first four years. *Proc. Prehist. Soc. 32*, 313–43
20 CORNWALL, I.W. 1969. *Bulletin of the Institute of Archaeology*, University of London, no. 8.

CLAUDIO VITA-FINZI

RIVER-LAID DEPOSITS are commonly used as the basis of climatic chronologies in areas which lay beyond the Pleistocene ice-sheets and glaciers. The precedent was set by Penck and Brückner in their classic Alpine studies; it is an approach which, in recent years, has received widest application in semi-arid areas, where stream action appears to be most sensitive to climatic changes. But, in spite of recent advances in the understanding of fluvial processes,[1] or perhaps because of them, the interpretation of alluvial successions in terms of climate has remained a tentative affair; the many physical and biological factors that influence stream behaviour are interrelated in such complex fashion that one can rarely speak of cause and effect. Hence prolonged controversies like that over the origin of arroyos in the American southwest. Before it will yield unequivocal climatic conclusions, the evidence of fluvial geology needs to be complemented with that of other lines of investigation.

There are two ways in which alluvial successions can be of immediate value in the study of past environments. First, they make it possible to reconstruct the topography and physical nature of the valley at different stages in its development. Second, they indicate the character of the streams by which erosion or deposition was performed. These aspects of palaeography and palaeohydrology are of obvious interest to the archaeologist concerned with ancient landscapes on a regional scale or with the conditions that typified an individual riverine site; they are discussed in this chapter with examples which relate both to prehistoric and historic times and consequently to both the Pleistocene and Holocene periods, but which are necessarily limited in scope by the writer's own experience.

ALLUVIAL SUCCESSIONS

A stream may be scouring its bed at one moment and aggrading it the next in response to its discharge and to a multiplicity of other variables; but in time an overall trend in one or the other direction will be manifested. Ultimately this may come to affect the entire catchment; or it may be found that, for example, the headwaters are engaged in downcutting while the trunk stream is aggrading (Fig. 21). It may be more helpful to think in terms of stream gradients: the collective outcome of what happens in individual reaches may ultimately be that the stream has either steepened or flattened its longitudinal profile, and thus increased or decreased its transporting power, presumably in order to restore an equilibrium which had been disturbed.[2] Provided the erosive phases do not accomplish their work too thoroughly, the valley will eventually inherit a suite of formations[3] separated by erosional breaks, soils, or tufaceous and other chemically-precipitated deposits. Clearly the record has to be read at various points in the drainage basin.

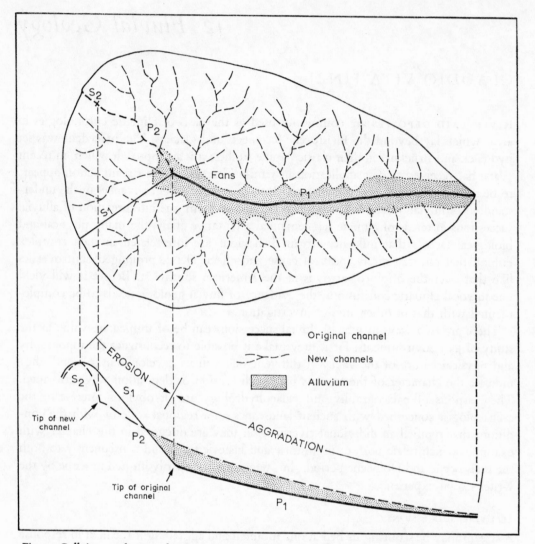

Fig. 21 Gullying on slopes and concomitant aggradation in main valley, resulting in increased drainage density and channel gradient. (After Strahler,[2] 1956, p. 635.)

Alluvial deposits generally survive as alluvial fans, as flat-topped infillings hemmed in by the valley sides, or as deltas and other features associated with deposition in standing water. A particular situation may be found to recur; thus, an alluvial fan is present at the mouth of most of the valleys that breach the Gebel Akhdar on the Cyrenaican coast,[4] the hills on the Algerian littoral, and the margins of the Dead Sea Rift.[5] Such patterns are frequently reflected in the distribution of different soils and consequently find their echo in the archaeological map. This kind of gross morphological analysis is an essential preliminary to sampling of all kinds, including the choice of stratigraphic sections and the collection of actual geological specimens. It is also a guide to the mode of deposition;

alluvial fans, for example, may usually be taken to signify intermittent stream flow during deposition.

The next step is to distinguish the individual formations. Sediments on the valley floor, representing various phases of cutting and filling, may give rise to a series of terraces each underlain by a different deposit (as distinct from terraces cut into a single deposit by an eroding stream); alluvial fans of different ages may nestle within one another (French: *emboité*). The importance of the break between two successive deposits must be gauged: too often, in the writer's opinion, intricate sequences have been described from exposures which have local, and not regional, significance. The countless Tyrrhenian transgressions and regressions that have been recognized on the Algerian coast[6] exemplify this point, for—if viewed in perspective—they are seen to be simply minor breaks in the regression that accompanied the Last Glaciation.

In alluvial deposits, disconformities denote interruptions in the course of deposition during which the land surface was at most affected by soil-forming agencies; unconformities are breaks during which erosion took place, perhaps with a concomitant increase in the density of the drainage network. An instance of the former has been described by prehistorians working in Epirus and the Peloponnese where what appears, on morphological grounds, to be a single deposit, may be subdivided into two or more portions by an abrupt change in colour[7] which coincides with a break in the archaeological record. The latter is well illustrated by an erosional break which separates two alluvial fills in the wadis of north-eastern Tripolitania and which was characterized by a sharp increase in the number of tributary gullies.[8]

The order in which the successive members of an alluvial succession were laid down is a problem to be tackled by conventional stratigraphic principles. Their actual dating employs a variety of techniques some of which are described elsewhere in this book; they include the C-14 method when suitable organic matter is found within the deposit, and the use of associated faunal or floral remains when a dated type sequence is available nearby. It is also often possible to make use of archaeological remains, for man has always been attracted by valleys in his search for water, game, soil, defensive sites, crossing points and navigable waterways, there to strew the ground with his implements and ruins.

ARCHAEOLOGICAL DATING

The triumph of the Uniformitarian Fluvialists over the Catastrophic Diluvialists in the middle of the last century made acceptable Boucher de Perthes' discovery of artefacts in association with the bones of extinct animals in the river gravels of the Somme, and helped to establish the antiquity of man.[9] Since then, archaeology has amply repaid its debt by supplying geologists with relative or approximate dates for the artefacts which they find in their deposits; at the same time the geological dating of archaeological sites, in certain situations, remains a valuable practice.[10]

The main criticism of archaeological dating in geology has been that it involves circular argument whereby artefacts whose relative age had been determined geologically at one place are used to date geological deposits somewhere else; indeed

Zeuner set out to show that Quaternary stratigraphy could stand without the help of archaeology.[11] Oakley has rebutted this criticism with regard to Palaeolithic remains.[12] Pottery, ruins and other remains including those of historical age allow the extension of the technique up to the present day. Indeed, Lyell, the champion of the Uniformitarian school, was already referring to potsherds and buried cities, as well as stone implements, to estimate the amount of silting, stream incision and tectonic uplift that had taken place since their burial.[13]

The term 'fossil earthenware', used by Darwin to describe the potsherds which he found in a loam deposit on the Peruvian coast,[14] epitomizes the merits and limitations of this approach. Sherds or flints merely give a minimum date to the host deposit, for they could have been washed in or buried at any time after their manufacture or loss. This evidently does not apply to a hearth or a camp site occupying what was the floor of an ephemeral stream. There is the additional problem that artefacts may have been worked into the deposit by worms, burrowing animals, cracking by desiccation or puddling by heavy rains. In semi-arid areas the development of superficial crusts provides another source of error. Coque has now shown[15] that the Acheulean artefacts whose discovery within a series of folded gravels near Gafsa had for long been quoted as evidence of late Quaternary earth movement, in fact came from a calcareous *croûte* capping the folded beds.

The second prerequisite is that the traditions and styles embodied in the archaeological finds should have spread rapidly. The rate at which they 'evolved' is, clearly, what controls the closeness with which the time-scale can be subdivided. Ideally, a stratified cave or settlement whose occupation lasted long enough to include all the cultural periods in question, and for which several C-14 dates are available, provides a standard reference succession. Haua Fteah does this for northern Cyrenaica.[16]

The above points may be illustrated with examples from Algeria. Here, the coastal *couches rouges*, an alluvial series formed during the low sea-level of the Last Glaciation, are rich in Aterian artefacts, which include a distinctive tanged point—*le fossile directeur le plus parfait qui se puisse souhaiter*.[17] The discovery of an Aterian point within the Mazouna formation, at the type exposure in the upper Ouarizane valley,[18] helped to support the writer's contention (based on lithology and morphology) that this deposit, which had been attributed by Anderson to a rise in sea-level during the Last Interglacial, could be correlated with the *couches rouges* of the Last Glaciation. When it came to dating this common phase of aggradation, however, Aterian implements were of less value, since they span a period lasting from over 30,000 to about 15,000 years ago.[12] Fortunately another industry with distinctive elements, known in the literature either as Oranian or Ibero–Maurusian, is found on the surface of the *couches rouges* and occasionally within their upper horizons.[6, 17] As it has been dated by C-14 to about 10,000–12,000 years ago,[19] this can be regarded as the period during which deposition of the red alluvial beds drew to a close.

Potsherds may permit the dating of successive alluvial formations to within a few hundred years. Several examples of this are to be found in the geological literature of the American southwest. In Chaco Canyon, for example, the main fill contains pottery dated to AD 500–700; that in the 'channel deposit' is a type made between AD 1100 and 1300.[20] Other remains can give even greater precision to the chronology. In Etruria the onset of aggradation has been dated by reference to a buried road, a mausoleum, a bath, and a coin of Roman age;[21] and the ruins of a fifth-century Byzantine fortress in Olympia have served the same purpose.[22] The alluvial Plain of Arta in Greece accumulated in historical times, but (at least in its north-western portion) not after the Turkish period, for a midden of this date at the foot of Kastro Orovon developed on the surface of the plain.[23] In the Gornalunga valley of Sicily, the 8–10 metre terrace had been laid down by about 325 BC when it served for a burial.[24]

Finally, charcoal and other organic material within the deposit itself can supply C-14 dates; these evidently apply only to a particular instant in the course of deposition, but nonetheless serve to check the validity of the proposed chronology. An alluvial deposit which had yielded Roman and Arab sherds in Tripolitania contained charcoal with a radiocarbon age of 610±100 years;[25] charcoal from a similar deposit near Rabat, in which nondescript sherds had been found, was dated to 800±200 years ago.[26] In the upper reaches of Wadi Hasa, Jordan, the alluvial fill that underlies much of the valley floor contains artefacts of a type associated with the Kebaran stage, which is thought to have persisted until the ninth millennium BC.[27] Roman remains on the surface of the deposit show that aggradation had ended by Classical times; and radiocarbon dating of a lens of charcoal within the alluvium demonstrates that deposition was in progress 3,950 years ago.[28]

The analogy that has been drawn between archaeological and organic fossils sometimes goes beyond the chronological aspect. Ancient remains, and in particular structures with a hydraulic function, reflect the nature of their environment; and, like fossils, they can be misleading. Some of the Roman dams of North Africa have been described as water reservoirs when in fact they are soil-retention dams;[29] the same applies to the *Gabarbands* of Baluchistan.[30] Interestingly, the former were invoked to show that aridity also typified North Africa in classical times, the latter to support the view that prehistoric Baluchistan was wetter than it is now. The 'ecological' approach gains from being applied to specific aspects of the environment. If there was a need to build a dam in order to divert Wadi Lebda away from the ancient harbour of Lepcis Magna,[31] the stream must have carried a heavy silt load. More precisely, it has been estimated that some of the larger spillways in the ancient diversion-canal walls in the Nahal Lavan Negev) were capable of handling flood flows of up to 100,000 cubic metres per hour.[32]

STREAM CHANNELS

Workers in Mesopotamia have often had to invoke shifts in the position of rivers to account for the character of some of their sites—as with the 'buried riverside quay' of Nimrud[33]—and sometimes for their very existence away from a perennial watercourse when the settlement is of a size that could not be supported by nearby wells, cisterns or *karezes*.[34] Roman dams in North Africa are found either perched above the present stream bed or lying away from it; repeated reconstruction and drastic rebuilding show that the streams were as mobile during the lifetime of the dams as they are today. Other ancient barrages in the Negev, and the Marib dam in Arabia,[35] reflect changes in the character of the watercourses for which damming was only partly responsible.

ESTUARIES AND DELTAS

In coastal areas, ancient harbours indicate the extent to which rivers have silted up their estuaries. Richborough, a Roman port on the River Stour (Kent), now lies inland.[36] At Ostia the growth of the Tiber delta at the beginning of the Christian Era was rapid enough to require raising the level of the streets and houses at least twice during two centuries;[37] ancient Ostia is now about 3 km away from the coast. The position of Utica shows that the Medjerda delta has been extended by 12 km since early Classical times;[38] its harbour had already been abandoned by the seventh century AD.[39] The extent of silting in historical times in lower Mesopotamia is less easily determined, for the archaeological evidence is not conclusive and the relative importance of earth movements is not clear.[40] Estuarine and deltaic sedimentation, to be more than curiosities, must be viewed in relation to what was happening inland. In the Mediterranean basin, for instance, rapid growth of deltas accompanied valley erosion and was inhibited during channel aggradation; in other words it contributed to the steepening and flattening of stream gradients.

CORRELATION

Events which are synchronous in the time-scale of geology may appear to be 'time-transgressive' in that of the historian. Arroyo cutting operated throughout the American southwest around AD 1300, but it did not begin or end everywhere simultaneously.[41] Aggradation affected the valleys of a large area bordering the Mediterranean at some period between late Classical times and the present day,[42] when downcutting and headward erosion prevail; but its precise duration is not everywhere known. Was it a universal event, or a case of analogous but independent events which happened to take place at roughly the same time? The issue is crucial when it comes to choosing between the two rival explanations for aggradation: climatic change and man-induced erosion.[43]

The correlation of formations and erosional phases within a single drainage basin presents similar difficulties. Although the various parts of a catchment make up a geomorphic system,[2, 44] this in turn consists (especially in streams which are not perennial) of sub-units which can at times behave in discrete fashion. There might be grounds for basing alluvial chronologies not on deposits but on unconformities, for the progress of erosion is commonly faster than that of widespread alluviation in the same basin.[45] But the overriding consideration is the need for maximum environmental evidence. The form of channels is still a poor guide to the nature of the agency that produced them. Deposits are more informative, and they also serve as the repository of organic remains.

PALAEOGEOGRAPHY

This somewhat grandiloquent term is here used for the reconstruction of the form and surface geology of the valley from palaeosols, unconformities and other discontinuities in the sedimentary record.

The ancient valley floor and slopes may be partly or totally buried by alluvium, or preserved by a duricrust veneer. When exposures are few it may be possible to fill in the gaps by boring or by reference to well records. The 'pedocalic paleosol' which is exposed between the Ucross and Kaycee formations on the banks of several streams in eastern Wyoming can be traced laterally away from the channel of Clear Creek by noting the depth at which the calcium carbonate content of the alluvia exhibits a sharp rise.[46] In the same way a fossil channel, filled with younger alluvium, which was observed on the side of an arroyo in Chaco Canyon, was followed upstream by judicious excavation.[47] Greater depths require drilling; the pre-Harappan floodplain of the Indus has been located by boring down until potsherds and brick fragments were no longer encountered.[48]

Perhaps the most important lesson learnt from the study of former channels is that gullying of the kind illustrated in tracts denouncing man's abuse of the soil has operated in times past when noble savages were innocuously picking berries. Some of those ancient gullies, still open to the sky, survive in the present landscape.[46]

Fluvial geology provides the essential background to the interpretation of ancient soil and water conservation schemes. In Tripolitania, the wadis, whose unstable courses have already been mentioned, now flow in deep trenches excavated in a generally incoherent alluvium which buried a limestone landscape in Late Pleistocene times;[49] the limestone is veiled by a calcareous crust (the *croûte zonaire* of French geologists) which also lines the former valley floors. The wadis are engaged in exhuming the fossil surface; when they have cut down far enough to encounter the relatively resistant crust their courses gradually shift downslope towards the original drainage axes. This was the general situation in Roman times, when the many soil-retention dams of Tripolitania were built; since then the wadis have continued to move, and, where the crust was thin and underlain by alluvium (rather than bedrock) they have breached it. In the example illustrated in Fig. 22, dam II now lies 7 m above the modern channel. The situation 2000 years ago favoured the erection of simple gravity dams, for it provided an impermeable floor and near-vertical banks (either bedrock spurs or alluvial terrace fronts) to which the masonry could be keyed. Today the crust at many of the best sites has been breached to expose permeable gravels, and the diagonal migration of the channels has produced asymmetrical cross-sections. Breaching of the valley-floor crust has also meant that the inlets to cisterns excavated in the valley floor to trap the water of ephemeral floods now lie above the reach of all but the highest flows.[50]

In parts of the Negev, a somewhat similar sequence of changes in channel form has to be postulated[32] in order to explain a complex sequence of ancient irrigation works. During the first stage (900–800 BC) the major wadis were wide, shallow depressions, and walls were used to stabilize the fields and spread the flood waters. The second stage (probably the Roman period) was initiated by gullying of the floodplains; diversion structures had to be built to raise the water. Floods or silting may have ultimately rendered this system unmanageable; the third stage saw the use of much more modest 'runoff farms'. Today cultivation is hampered by active gullying.

The presence of dams should put the investigator on his guard lest he confuse silt

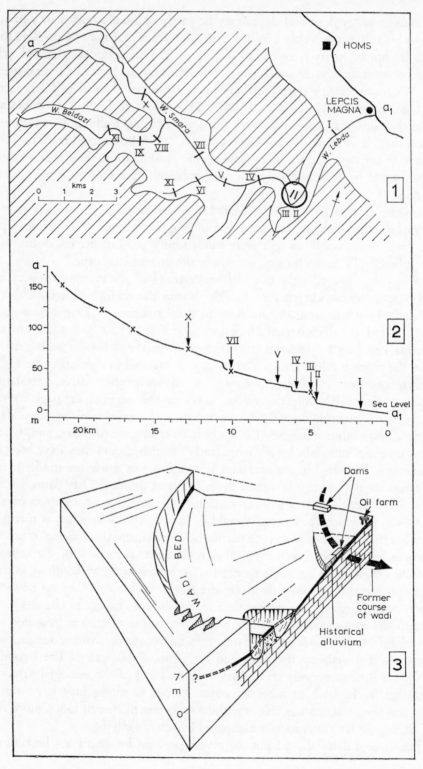

which has accumulated as a consequence of flood-irrigation with natural alluvial deposits, as some workers have done in Hadhramaut.[35] The converse appears to be true of some of the deposits in the Tafilalt oasis of southern Morocco which have been classified as *limons de palmeraies*, but which lie beyond the range of ancient irrigation works and are, furthermore, identical in lithology with a natural wadi fill found throughout Morocco. It is worth noting in this context that the *tell* of ancient Sigilmasa —an extensive mound of mud-brick and pottery—makes up the bulk of a feature depicted on a geological map of Tafilalt[52] as the *cailloutis inférieurs* of the Soltanian series.

When we move into the historical period a check on the geological findings may be available in the accounts of early travellers and perhaps even in their photographs and sketches. The geological evidence shows that in the Middle Ages the Chelif River in Algeria was aggrading its channel; the alluvium that accumulated reflects floodplain deposition by successive floods. It is agreeable to find that the Arab geographer Ibn Said, citing Abbou el Feddah, stated that, like the Nile, the Chelif renewed the fertility of its banks by regular flooding, a comparison which would not hold for the deeply entrenched channel of the modern stream.[53] The phase of alluviation which characterized many of the streams in the American southwest roughly between the fourteenth century and 1850 would seem to be the work of sluggish flat-floored streams with courses interrupted by marshy depressions; and this is what the 'old-timers' have described and depicted.[54] If there is no documentary corroboration, the alluvial record has to suffice, to be interpreted by analogy with present-day examples.

Students of agricultural history (and prehistory) often regard the environment as a relatively unchanging background against which was enacted the drama of evolving technology,[55] although they may concede that climate has fluctuated. The 'constant' of available land has sometimes changed even more drastically. In Epirus (north-western Greece) there have been two major periods of alluviation since the Last Interglacial.[23] (Plate IX.) During the first, tributary valleys built up coalescing alluvial fans whose material was reworked by the trunk streams. The resulting topography consisted of steep triangular facets bordering the flat floors of the major valleys; the fill was composed predominantly of soil washed down from the limestone hills. A drastic redistribution of the available soil thus occurred during the Palaeolithic occupation of the area. By Classical times, the fill had been trenched to bedrock along many reaches; after the Roman period, flood-plain deposition built up flat-topped strips of fine silty sand along the watercourses and also filled the estuaries. This makes up the bulk of the land in Epirus suitable for irrigation by virtue of its topography, its propinquity to streams, and its texture. The Jordan trough has been affected by a similar sequence of events with equally momentous agricultural consequences[5] (Fig. 23). The soils of the Chelif valley

Fig. 22 Wadi Lebda, Libya. (1) location of Roman dams; (2) longitudinal profile showing headwalls by whose retreat the dams have been left hanging; (3) dams II and III; since Roman times the wadi has shifted down a sloping surface capped by a calcareous crust and subsequently breached it.

bear a close relationship to the alluvial succession.[53] In Egypt, the development of the *terre végétale* has been ascribed to the aggradation that followed an early postglacial rise in sea-level.[56]

PALAEOHYDROLOGY

The combined evidence of form and lithology, in the present state of knowledge, rarely yields unequivocal information on stream discharges and regimes; the findings have to be couched in a special brand of *communiquese*. It is not solely a question of not knowing how particular deposits and forms are produced; often there is little or no information on the rate and operation of current processes. This is especially true of many of the areas where archaeologists have been most active, notably the Near East. There is no quick remedy; the value of hydrological observations, like the wisdom of patriarchs, is measured in years, even though refined statistical techniques make any record better than none.

Spring-laid calcareous deposits—tufa and travertine—have long served as a guide to fluctuations in the vigour of spring discharge in limestone areas.[57] Although the precipitation of calcium carbonate is influenced to varying degrees by plants and other living organisms, the degree of turbulence (and therefore the volume of discharge) is a major controlling factor in the rate of deposition. The topography of the valley floor formed by aggradation may perpetuate the process after the conditions that triggered it have ceased to operate. If the modern springs are known to respond with little delay to changes in the incidence of rainfall, it is reasonable to speak of wetter or drier periods where episodes of tufa formation have occurred simultaneously in several valleys, particularly if the various springs are not supplied by a single aquifer.[58] At any event, the question of local availability of water (and game) may be uppermost in the mind of the archaeologist faced with a prehistoric site with faunal remains.

If there are no figures for present-day discharge, the extent of tufaceous deposition in the bed of the watercourse or in irrigation canals will serve as a useful source of comparison. Near 'Ain Fasayil in Wadi Rashshash, Jordan, the rate at which a modern aqueduct is being blocked by scaling is comparable with that which afflicted a nearby Roman canal whose sides were repeatedly raised in order to maintain its capacity.

The origin of the extensive calcareous *croûtes zonaires* of North Africa, some of which contain artefacts, is still a matter of dispute.[59] In some areas their form, laminar structure and relationship to the underlying geology favours the view that they were formed at the surface by precipitation from sheetfloods,[60] and are thus the areal equivalent of valley tufas. The precise nature of the conditions involved remains difficult to visualize. As Butzer has stressed, their occurrence may indicate either moister or drier conditions, depending on the present situation.

The hydrological interpretation of alluvial (as opposed to chemical) deposits hinges on the analysis of their texture, structure and composition, their form, their relationship to other deposits in the catchment, their association with organic remains, supplemented by indirect evidence from outside the catchment.

Although climatic considerations are not central to the theme of this paper, it is

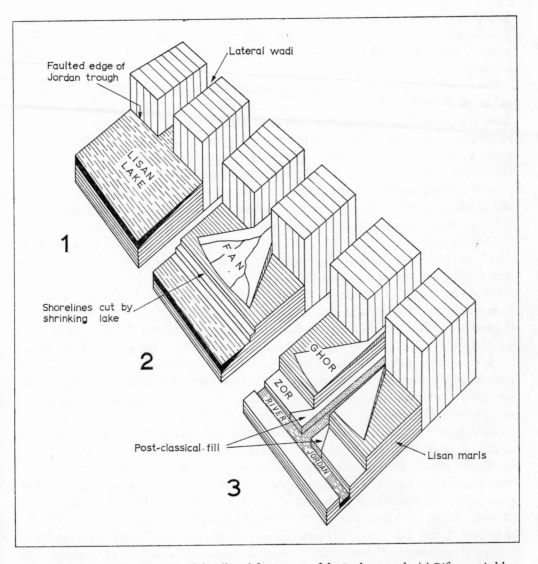

Fig. 23 Stages in the development of the alluvial formations of the Jordan trough. (1) Rift occupied by Pleistocene Lisan lake; (2) alluvial fans deposited on floor exposed by shrinking lake; (3) fans and Lisan Marls trenched by wadis; aggradation in post-Classical times; renewed downcutting.

helpful to visualize the environmental setting in general terms before tackling the individual streams. For this, the alluvial formations need to be followed laterally across the valley and also up- and downstream, outside the sphere of influence of fluvial processes. In this way it is found that in Morocco, for instance, the Soltanian deposits pass upvalley into periglacial material;[61] in Cyrenaica the Younger Gravels interfinger with fossil dunes on the coast and extend below present sea-level;[58] in Epirus the main valley fill passes into the lacustrine deposits of a formerly swollen Lake of Ioannina.

Unless they can be dated, climatic indicators which are not physically contiguous with the alluvial sequence, such as evidence that the snow line was formerly lower, are less reliable. The pollen and O^{18} record of lake and ocean cores suffers from the same limitation.

Floral and faunal remains within the alluvial formation, on the contrary, are useful guides to alluvial conditions. Snails may suggest a change from seasonal to perennial flow, as in Wadi Kofrein (Jordan) during the Middle Ages,[5] and from estuarine to fluvial conditions, as at Amri (on the lower Indus) since pre-Harappan times.[48] Plant impressions in the tufas of Wadi Derna (Cyrenaica), which contain Middle Palaeolithic artefacts, include laurel (*Laurus canariensis*) and aleppo pine (*Pinus halepensis*), which suggest a warm subhumid or humid environment.[58] The possibility that the nature of the plant and animal population may have been determined by strictly local factors limits their value as climatic indicators, but is particularly advantageous in the present context.

Tectonic deformation may have affected stream gradients or blocked their outlets during the period in question. Movement along faults looms large in Quennell's reconstruction of the history of drainage in Jordan;[62] uplift in the lower Indus valley is favoured by Raikes to explain silt deposition in Harappan times.[48] The demise of the Acheulean cataclysm at Gafsa does not invalidate the belief that alluvial deposits, even if poorly consolidated, can retain evidence of folding and faulting. In conjunction with geophysical evidence they may, by their exceptional thickness, betray crustal subsidence in the zone of greatest deposition.[53] Sites which were buried by alluvium will, as a result, now lie below their original elevation. Earth movements are attractive substitutes for the more traditional reasons adduced by archaeologists for sudden changes in the fortunes of valley sites, and a Catastrophist revival is already making itself felt.

Techniques of sedimentological and morphological analysis and their application in specific climatic areas are discussed in several accessible texts.[57, 64] The only point to be stressed here is that, although the measurement of a single attribute may suffice to distinguish, say, fluvial from marine deposits,[65] it is of limited value in palaeohydrological work. The debate over the origin of 'red beds' has for long hinged on the question of their colour, which may in fact be inherited from the source area or acquired by diagenesis during deposition.[66] Heavy mineral analysis can be of help in the correlation of separate successions,[67] but it cannot altogether supplant other lines of evidence. The same goes for mechanical analysis of sediments or mapping of terrace gradients.[68]

Butzer[57] cites a number of instances where the application of field and laboratory analysis of sediments at what he terms *alluvial sites* has yielded interesting results. Salzgitter-Lebenstedt, near Braunschweig, lay on the banks of a Late Pleistocene tundra stream; the Middle Pleistocene site of Markkleeberg, near Leipzig, occupied the periglacial gravels of a northward flowing stream; the twin sites of Torralba and Ambrona,

Fig. 24 A The concept of stream order, as first proposed by R. E. Horton in 1945; B two alluvial fills separated by an episode of downcutting. (After Leopold, Wolman and Miller,[46] 1964, pp. 135 and 459); C cross-section of alluvial fill; D assumed average cross-section in the same reach; E relation of computed cross-sectional area to stream order. (Simplified, after Leopold and Miller,[46] 1954, p. 70.)

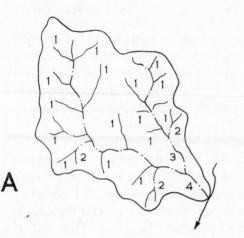

A

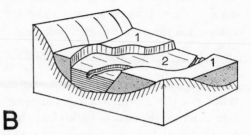

B

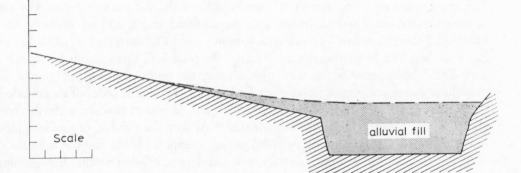

Scale

C

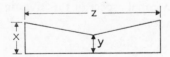

D

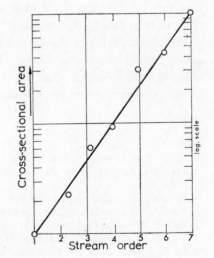

E

in Spain, 'were situated on the marshy floodplain margins of a stream valley during a moist, cold phase of the Lower Pleistocene'; Swanscombe was associated with downstream valley alluviation during a high sea-level. More specifically, morphometric gravel analysis has led Butzer to conclude that, during the early Würm, Mediterranean valleys which now carry only seasonal or episodic flow were characterized by more frequent or more powerful floods, although a pronounced dry season persisted.[60]

The volume of sediment composing successive alluvial fills whose duration is known, when compared with current sediment movement, have been used to compute the rate at which deposition took place. In their work on the Powder River (Wyoming), Leopold and Miller[46] estimated average cross-sections of distinct alluvial bodies in tributaries of different orders. (Fig. 24.) Plotting the cross-sectional areas for the Kaycee fill against stream order showed that they bear a consistent relationship. This made it possible to estimate the total volume of each alluvial formation by multiplying the different average cross-sections by the total length of the various tributaries. The rate at which the Kaycee and Lightning fills accumulated was found by dividing their volume by their 'duration'. The resulting figures had to be corrected to allow for the fact that there is a large discrepancy between the total load carried and that which is deposited. Though admittedly very approximate, the results are of great interest, for they show that deposition went on at rates which are of the same order of magnitude as those measured in the modern streams. Miller and Wendorf reached a similar conclusion in the Tesuque valley of New Mexico.[69] As with the survival of ancient gullies referred to earlier, this finding is opposed to the widespread belief that the activities of man, especially in the last few centuries, have accelerated erosion beyond the 'geologic norm'.[70] Here is a field of enquiry to which both archaeologists and conservationists can contribute.

Miller and Wendorf also suggested that the floodplain of the Rio Tesuque, during deposition of its high-terrace alluvium, would have been ideally suited to floodwater farming of the kind described by Bryan among the Navaho of New Mexico.[71] The lithology of the Hasa Formation in Jordan prompts a similar line of thought,[28] of obvious relevance to the origins of agriculture.

The above examples should suffice to show that, in the study of valley sites, fluvial geology should not be regarded as a specialist service to be consulted by the archaeologist when specific problems arise, but rather as an essential aspect of the investigation from its earliest stages; symbiosis, not mere collaboration.

REFERENCES

1 ALLEN, J. R. L. 1965. *Sedimentology* 5, 89–191
2 STRAHLER, A. N. 1956. In THOMAS, W. L. (*ed.*), *Man's role in changing the face of the earth*, Chicago, 621–38
3 The formation is the fundamental unit of stratigraphic classification, defined as a body of rock characterized by some internal lithologic homogeneity
4 HEY, R. W. 1962. *Quaternaria* 6, 435–49
5 VITA-FINZI, C. 1964. *Palestine Expl. Q.*95, 19–33
6 HILLY, J. 1962. *Bull. Serv. Carte géol. Alg. (n.s.)* 19

7 LEROI-GOURHAN, A., CHAVAILLON, A. and H. 1963. *Bull. Soc. préhist. fr. 60*, 249–65: DAKARIS, S. I., HIGGS, E. S. and HEY, R. W. 1964. *Proc. Prehist. Soc. 30*, 199–244

8 VITA-FINZI, C. 1960. *Ass. Int. Hydrol. Scient. 53*, 61–4

9 DANIEL, G. E. 1950. *A hundred years of archaeology*, London

10 PÉWÉ, T. L. 1954. *Amer. Antiquity 20*, 51–61

11 ZEUNER, F. E. 1959. *The Pleistocene Period*, London

12 OAKLEY, K. P. 1964. *Frameworks for dating fossil man*, London

13 LYELL, C. 1872. *Principles of geology* (11th ed.), London, 2 vols

14 DARWIN, C. 1890. *Journal of Researches* (9th ed.), London

15 COQUE, R. 1962. *La Tunisie Présaharienne*, Paris

16 McBURNEY, C. B. M. 1967. *The Haua Fteah (Cyrenaica)*, Cambridge

17 BALOUT, L. 1955. *Préhistoire de l'Afrique du Nord*, Paris

18 ANDERSON, R. van W. 1936. *Mem. geol. Soc. Amer. 4*, Washington; VITA-FINZI, C. 1967. *Man 2*, 205–15

19 CHOUBERT, G. 1962. *Quaternaria 6*, 137–75

20 BRYAN, K. 1941. *Assoc. Am. Geogr. Annals. 31*, 219–42

21 JUDSON, S. 1963. *Science 140*, 898–9

22 VITA-FINZI, C. 1966. *Amer. J. Arch. 70*, 175–78

23 HIGGS, E. S. and VITA-FINZI, C. 1966. *Proc. Prehist. Soc.* 1–29

24 JUDSON, S. 1963. *Amer. J. Arch. 67*, 287–9

25 VITA-FINZI, C. 1963. *Nature 198*, 880

26 GIGOUT, M. 1960. *Trav. Lab. géol. Univ. Lyon (n.s.) 6*

27 ALBRIGHT, W. F. 1956. In EHRICH, R. W. (ed.) *Chronologies in Old World Archaeology*, Chicago, 49

28 VITA-FINZI, C. 1966. *Man 1*, 386–90

29 OATES, D. 1953. *Pap. Brit. Sch. Rome 21*, 81–117; VITA-FINZI, C. 1961. *Antiquity 35*, 14–20

30 RAIKES, R. L. 1965. *East and West (n.s.) 15*, 3–12

31 ROMANELLI, P. 1925. *Leptis Magna*, Rome

32 EVENARI, M., *et al.*, 1961. *Science 133*, 979–96

33 BRADFORD, J. 1957. *Ancient Landscapes*, London, pl. 19

34 MACKAY, D. 1945. *Antiquity 19*, 135–44

35 BOWEN, R. L. B. JR. and ALBRIGHT, F. P. 1958. *Archaeological Discoveries in South Arabia*. Baltimore

36 PYDDOKE, E. 1961. *Stratification for the Archaeologist*, London

37 WARD-PERKINS, J. B. 1962. *Geog. J. 128*, 398–405

38 BUROLLET, P. F. 1952. Notes to *Porto Farina* geological map, Tunis

39 NAVAL INTELLIGENCE. 1945. *Tunisia*, London

40 LEES, G. M. and FALCON, N. L. 1952. *Geog. J. 118*, 24–39

41 JUDSON, S. 1953. *Bull. Bureau Amer. Ethnol. 154*, 285–302

42 VITA-FINZI, C. 1969. *The Mediterranean Valleys*, Cambridge

43 EISMA, D. 1964. *Nature 202*

44 CHORLEY, R. J. 1962. *U.S. Geol. Survey Prof. Paper 500–B*

45 LEOPOLD, L. B., WOLMAN, M. G. and MILLER, J. P. 1964. *Fluvial Processes in Geomorphology*, San Francisco and London

46 —— and MILLER, J. P. 1954. *U.S. Geol. Survey Water-Supply Paper 1261*

47 BRYAN, K. 1954. *Smithsonian Misc. Coll. 122*

48 RAIKES, R. L. 1965. *Antiquity 39*, 196–203; 1967. *Water, Weather and Prehistory*, London

49 LIPPARINI, T. 1940. *Boll. Soc. geol. ital. 59*, 221–301

50 VITA-FINZI, C. and BROGAN, O. 1966. *Libya Antiqua 2*, 65–71

51 MARGAT, J. 1960. *Notes et Mém. Serv. géol. Maroc. 150 bis*

52 —— 1960. *Publ. Serv. géol. Maroc. No. 150*

53 BOULAINE, J. 1957. *Étude des sols des plaines du Chélif*. Algiers

54 LEOPOLD, L. B. 1951. *Geog. Rev, 41*, 299–316

55 E.g. SLICHER VAN BATH, B. H. 1963. *The Agrarian history of Western Europe A.D. 500–1850*, London

56 FOURTAU, R. 1915, cited by HAYES, W. C. 1964. *J. Near Eastern Studies 23*, 73–114

57 BUTZER, K. W. 1964. *Environment and Archeology*, London; BRANNER, J. C. 1911. *Bull. geol. Soc. Amer. 22*, 187–206

58 McBurney, C. B. M. and Hey, R. W. 1955. *Prehistory and Pleistocene Geology in Cyrenaican Libya*, Cambridge

59 Durand, J. 1959. *Les sols rouges et les croûtes en Algérie*, Algiers

60 Butzer, K. W. 1963. In Howell, F. C. and Bourlière, F. (eds.). *African Ecology and Human Evolution*, Chicago, 1–27

61 Dresch, J. and Raynal, R. 1953. *Notes et Mem. Serv. géol. Maroc, No. 117*

62 Quennell, A. M. 1958. Q. *Jour. Geol. Soc. London. 114*, 1–24

63 Bernard, H. A. and Le Blanc, R. J. 1965. In Wright, H. E. Jr. and Frey, D. G. (eds.). *The Quaternary of the United States*, Princeton

64 Krumbein, W. C. and Sloss, L. L. 1951. *Stratigraphy and Sedimentation*, San Francisco and London

65 McCann, S. B. 1961. *Geol. Mag. 98*, 131–42

66 van Houten, F. B. 1961. In Nairn, A. E. M. (ed.) *Descriptive Palaeoclimatology*, New York, 89–139

67 Nossin, J. J. 1959. *Geomorphological aspects of the Pisuerga drainage area in the Cantabrian Mountains (Spain)*, Leiden

68 See, for example, Melton, M. A. 1965. *Jour. Geol. 73*, 181–9, and discussion by Lustig, L. K. 1966. *Jour. Geol. 74*, 95–101

69 Miller, J. P. and Wendorf, F. 1958. *Jour. Geol. 66*, 177–94

70 Leopold, L. B. 1956. In Thomas, W. L. (ed.) *Man's Role in Changing the Face of the Earth*, Chicago, 639–47

71 Bryan, K. 1929. *Geog. Rev. 19*, 444–56

13 Cave Sediments and Prehistory

ELISABETH SCHMID

CAVE EXCAVATIONS DEMAND not only a knowledge of prehistory, but a considerable amount of geological observation and research. This is because caves are places of manifold geological occurrences, the results of which are preserved in and as sediments. Where these sediments are sheltered inside a mountain they are more easily preserved than those at the surface. From an exact analysis of sedimentary accumulation in a cave it is possible to deduce the sequence and causes of the geological events, which are due mostly to climatic change and its consequences. As nearly all caves and cave sediments date from the later Quaternary period (the Upper Pleistocene and Holocene) their study comprises the most recent history of the earth. At the beginning of this period man was already in existence and during it he developed into his modern form.

Man has frequented caves and rock shelters at all times and in many areas of the world. In the earlier cultural periods caves were commonly used as living sites just as in later times; in addition they served as burial sites or places of ritual.

So long as the evidence of human activity lies directly on the surface of a cave floor, a straight study can be made of the individual objects. But geological questions arise with the excavation of cultural evidence when stony layers, earth or cave travertine have been deposited during or after the appearance of man. The sediments should be closely examined not merely for the purpose of answering geological questions: their analysis helps to answer many questions to do with culture. For instance an assessment can be made of the date of a cultural layer, the time interval between two excavated layers and contemporary conditions of landscape and climate. Moreover a detailed knowledge of the natural phenomena associated with caves allows conclusions to be drawn about the degree of human influence on the cave deposits.

Caves and shelters have provided refuge to animals as well as men. Wild and domestic animals like to escape from the sun into the shade of caves and to take shelter there from rain, snow and storms. Frequent visits of large groups of animals over a prolonged time may change the floor with their droppings and trampling. But as these animals use only the entrance, the floor in the interior of deep caves will remain undisturbed by them.

Carnivores like to use caves in order to devour their prey in peace. Gnawed bones often bear witness to this, and the eating places of the Ice Age cave hyena are spectacular examples.

The caves of cave bears were of special significance in the Pleistocene. In the mountain interior the bear hibernated in the uniform, though often low temperature. The female bore her young in the middle of winter and suckled them through the first months of their lives. Individuals died there—newly born weaklings, young animals which had not gained sufficient strength during the summer to stand the lack of food during the long hibernation, female bears at whelping time and wounded or aged adults. The carcasses having rotted, the skeletons, covered by stone rubble and earth, remained preserved in the caves of calcareous hills.

Thus there are two natural ways to account for animal bones found in cave sediments: as the remains of prey and as the remains of animals that died a natural death. Bones of small mammals are also found at the roosting places of birds of prey. Bat bones occur underneath their own sleeping places.

There is a third important cause of animal bones being found in cave sediments— the remains of human meals. However, the association of cultural remains and animal bones in one layer is not sufficient proof that the animal remains are due to human activity. For the occupation of the cave by man could have been followed by intervals during which animals frequented the cave, bearing their own traces. Short periods of time between these various visits are often undefined in cave sediments. It is thus all the more important to distinguish natural and 'artificial' deposits. The only way to accomplish this is with the help of the natural sciences.

All these aspects of cave excavation emphasize how closely linked prehistoric problems are with those of mammalian palaeontology and with geology.

CAVES AND CAVE SEDIMENTS

The character of a cave sediment is dependent on various influences, which must be discussed systematically. It is impossible to enter into every aspect, but any classification should consider the manifold geological and morphological conditions. These enable a recognition of contemporary events within one cave and provide correlations between different ones.

Origins and forms of caves. The processes of sedimentation are to a marked degree determined by the shape of the cave. Rather than give a detailed classification of caves we will confine ourselves to a division relative to sedimentary conditions, since these are important especially in relation to prehistory.

From the shape of a cave we can often deduce what material we can expect to find in it. From the sediments two types of caves can be distinguished:

> inner ('endogene') caves—mostly passages and chambers;
> outer ('exogene') caves—mostly shallow caves, shelters and niches.

Endogene caves are those which penetrate deep into a hill. Varied causes may produce such a cave formation. It may be the remains of a subterranean river course which ran through the hill before the valleys were carved into the present landscape, that is, a *karst* cave. Owing to the intensive subterranean activity of water a hill can be sponge-like, intersected by passages meeting in a chamber. Then follows an enlargement of the rounded passages by erosion. The water running in them deposits locally derived material and also some from greater distances. These local and foreign materials, carried along for deposition, have been moved on in a more or less horizontal direction. As soon as water ceases to flow through the passage, corrosion (solution processes of percolating water) sets in on the walls.

Long passages can also be formed by corrosion along lines of tectonic disturbance—the enlargement of a crack. This may occur at a particular depth when a constriction or the damming up of sediment prevents further downward erosion, so that this type of cave is often shaped like a horizontal tube. The ceiling is vaulted like an inverted 'V', and generally stretches up to a scarcely visible crack. Into such caves the water carries either fine material from the surface or dissolved calcium carbonate and freed residue from the rock in which the cave is situated. Often materials of both kinds are deposited together. The transportation of the descending material occurs in a more or less vertical direction. In smaller folds and faults dams also occur, occasionally initiating corrosion and cave formation. Here the percolating water transports dissolved calcium carbonate and freed residue along the line of the tectonic disturbance.

Endogene caves can also form at the contact surfaces of distinct rocks, where an underlying rock forms an impermeable dam. The combination of a vertical crack above a horizontally bedded rock of different composition is the most favourable condition for the formation of endogene caves. The most active process here is corrosion.

If endogene caves do not open onto a clear hillside or rock face, but onto the top edge of a rubble slope cloaking the foot of a hillside, then a damming of the water is caused by this material, which is mainly earthy. Groundwater overflows at the top edge of the rubble slope and can thus form caves by corrosion at the varying water levels.

Thermal waters and waters charged with minerals ascending from a considerable depth dissolve out many a cave passage by their corrosive activity.

Many endogene caves originally had no exits to the outside, until they were exposed by erosion from outside, or until the wall between the cave and the hillside got thinner and thinner, owing to internal corrosion, and then collapsed. Both processes can take place simultaneously. Only after such an exposure of the cave passage can the outside climate work directly on the cave walls and thereby on sedimentation.

Exogene caves are all those that do not penetrate into a hill as deep passages but which are formed from outside in the nature of niches, shallow caves and shelters. They are often eroded out either by a river, or on a lake- or sea-shore. They are situated at the height of a past water level, singly or side by side along a cliff. If they contain water-laid sediments these must have been carried into the cave from outside.

Similar caves can also be formed on isolated rock walls by the corrosion of less resistant parts of the stone. The floor of these corrosion caves generally slopes down towards the outside. The broken-off rubble falls outside in the initial stage. When the cavity has reached a sufficient depth the rubble accumulates at the entrance. In the case of rock shelters on a less sheer slope it piles up in front of the cave, so that a more horizontal floor is gradually formed. At this stage man has a use for the cave. In the course of time the floor at the back of the cave also gets covered. As soon as this happens the rock floor is protected against weathering and sedimentation takes its course as in any other cave with an originally horizontal floor.

Exogene caves do not penetrate deep into a hill. Only when several causes combine in cave formation do other forms arise, for example angular or displaced passage caves, which open out in front with a wide mouth.

Topographical positions of caves. Caves can occur in various positions on a hill, mountain or mountain range and show the processes of formation discussed in the previous section. Their topographical position is of importance with regard to sedimentation, because the effect of daily, seasonal or long-term changes in temperature and precipitation can vary considerably in different places.

If a cave is situated just beneath the surface on the slopes of a mountain, then daily precipitation has a direct effect on the cave climate. Seasonal changes of climate can also influence processes in the inner part of the cave. It is however essential that there should be a link with the surface by means of crevices, passages or chimneys.

But if a mountain range is high over the cave such a direct influence is not to be expected. Only in the case of low-lying caves can much decomposed rubble from the hill accumulate, enough sometimes to block up the entrance from the outside. In caves situated high up a mountain there tends to be a steady decomposition of the entrance area and thus a retreat of the mouth of the cave.

When a cave lies at the bottom of a valley, or a one-time valley, sediments are usually carried there by a river or stream either at the time when the stream channel is being shaped or by later flooding. These deposits can assist in the dating of the cave. The same holds with caves on lake- and sea-shores.

The direction in which a cave faces is important to the effect of the outer climate on sedimentation, especially at the entrance. Some situations can be quoted to illustrate this. If a cave faces south the sun can shine on the mouth for a long time and thereby have a direct effect on the front part of the cave's climate; but in a shaded position facing north only the air temperature has any effect. If it faces east a cave receives the warmth of the sun directly after the cool of the night, whereas if it faces west it catches the sun's rays after the air has warmed up for many hours.

Position of sediments within the cave. To interpret a cave sediment it is vital to examine the position within the cave where deposition has taken place (Fig. 25).

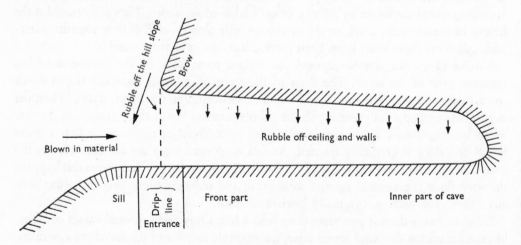

Fig. 25 Sources and distribution of the various sediments in a cave.

In a cave which does not lie in the flooding area of a stream, lake or the sea and cannot be flooded by water from inside the hill, we can expect the various parts of the cave to have accumulated the following materials:

Caves possessing a *sill* will collect there scree material from the brow of the cave. The scree can contain stones, soil and plants and animal remains from the entire area of the hill above the cave. In times of strong winds, during loess formation for example, there will also be present a considerable amount of aeolian deposit. The sediment, in other words scree plus material blown in, is then subjected to immediate processes of soil formation, to which plants contribute. Animal life appears, most clearly evidenced by snails. The swifter the process of deposition, the less the intensity of soil formation. Marked accumulation of scree, which in itself has been exposed to several processes of decomposition, prejudices a direct climatic interpretation of the sequence of layers. Another difficulty is the likelihood of part of the sediments having been washed away.

The area under the brow of the cave is called the *entrance*. At the entrance is the drip-line of rain or melted water running off the brow of the cave. Scree from above falls on this entrance area, as well as on the sill, in varying amounts. Material is also blown in this far. To these items are added decomposition products from the front of the roof of the cave. Since this area is under the unimpeded influence of climate, we can, by means of the deposited material, directly deduce the climatic causes of decomposition. During undisturbed sedimentation, material is in the main accumulated in the entrance area, because here scree plus blown-in material and decomposition products unite, and above all the influence of the weather is most active. In the event of sedimentation being not too rapid, plant and animal life develops as well. Inclusion of soil particles and organic remains from the scree is also a possibility.

Sediments thus reveal the climatic influences which create decomposition, together with those influences which produce soil formation. This being a contemporary occurrence, we are provided with a basis for reading climatic conditions by means of sedimentary processes and thereby both deducing relative dates and reconstructing environment.

A *drip-line* is only formed when the brow of the cave is of such a shape that rain and melted water can run along it. The drip starts where the brow meets the roof of the cave. Most caves possess such a drip-line. The water which drips or sometimes pours onto the floor of the cave loosens all fine particles and carries them away. This results in a strip of washed-off coarse material being exposed. If loosely packed stone material lies underneath then the water carries the fine material into the interstices. Thereby coarse and splintered rubble lower down receives 'secondary' earth. More frequently, however, the fine materials are deposited in front of and behind the drip-line. If the water dripping from the brow of the hill contains calcium carbonate, which it most commonly does, then this is deposited on the floor as sinter. On the other hand water containing CO_2 can also dissolve calcium carbonate, which it deposits immediately adjacent to or underneath as sinter; the more hollow spaces the percolating water finds, the deeper the calcification of the sediments. Both processes generally occur together. In caves whose brow is eroded back we can deduce the one-time position of the entrance from a similar calcification of sediments in front of the present brow of the cave.

In short, wherever the structure of a sediment makes washing a possibility we must examine minutely whether earth and travertine are primarily or secondarily deposited. On the sill, washing of this kind is caused by rainfall; at the entrance and further inside by dripping water.

In the *front part of the cave* sedimentation is directly influenced by the weather outside. But little light enters. There is a lack of vegetation, snails and soil formation. The rubble from the roof and walls settles down on the cave floor and is subjected to the same climatic influences as at the entrance, though the effect is less. There is, however, no extraneous material. For that reason the climatic conditions of sedimentation can generally be easily read in the front part of the cave.

In the *interior of the cave* sedimentation is subject to different laws. Daily and seasonal changes in climate do not penetrate or at least not directly. Therefore only important long-term changes can alter the mode of sedimentation. Earth and rubble can be included here, as evidence of marked changes in the course of major climatic events.

If we find materials in the lower sediments of the cave entrance which could only have been created in the front part, or even the interior of the cave, then they must have been secondarily carried to the entrance, in which case we must examine whether water activity or solifluction is responsible. Alternatively, if their creation can be proved as autochthonous, then we have proof that the mouth of the cave has been shifted back by weathering of the hillside. Thus we are now looking at what was once an inner section of a longer cave.

The nature of cave rock. The cave rock will play an important part in the process of sedimentation and in the type of sediments produced. If the cave lies in compact limestone the pieces that break off are different from those in the case of lumpy, shattered, laminated or fissile limestone. Also the mineral composition of the cave rock and the included substances must be considered in an examination of cave sediments—for example parts with a high content of quartz sand, oolite or fossils. An exact knowledge of cave rock allows a recognition of alien constituents in the sediments. Observation of the geological conditions in the neighbourhood of the cave enables one to judge from where and how alien substances got into the cave: because a cave impinged upon another rock formation inside the hill or because particles reached the cave floor through crevices and in percolating water from an overlying rock formation, or when gravel, erratic pieces, loess or soil were washed in from the hillside through cracks in the walls of the cave. In addition, a layer which once covered the hillside but is now weathered away may be represented in cave sediments.

Only if all natural explanations fail can foreign stone testify to the past presence of man.

Non-geological contributions to sediments. Many sediments contain inclusions which cannot be put down to any geological cause. They are brought in by either man or animals.

Material imported by man can be: tools and waste pieces of stone, bone, and in later cultures baked clay and metal. Stones can be included here which served as pot-boilers, hearths, punches, hammer-stones, anvils, grindstones and paving-stones, etc. In addition there are the minerals and fossils used by man as ornaments, and above all animal bones and their fragments with or without traces of cutting and burning. Often charcoal from wood fuel proves human activity. Collected foliage, plants and earth clinging to feet and clothes were likewise imported. Fire in a hearth affected by its heat the character of the cultural layer in the area. The climatic significance of the sediments is strongly prejudiced by human influence, if a direct interpretation cannot be made from the plant and animal remains themselves.

When a burial is made in the cave the layers, at least around the skeleton, are jumbled up by the digging and filling of the grave. We thus have a later disturbance.

The influences on a sediment which are attributed to man can be wiped out in the course of time after deposition. The older the layer the more the small distinguishing features disappear; this must also be taken into consideration when assessing sediments.

Caves are often visited by *animals*. The material brought in by them can be small stones, sand and soil stuck to their feet and fur. Deposited faeces also introduce foreign matter into the sediment, as does the decomposition of carcasses. The various origins of animal bones were mentioned on pp. 151–2. Great masses of almost homogeneous snail shells are brought in by rodents and birds and in Mesolithic stations by man as well.

In order to imply by nomenclature the mode of formation of a layer, I consider the following definitions useful:

geological layer	a natural accumulation of stones, earth, clay, etc., defined in more detail according to predominating components
fossil layer	animal remains included naturally in a sediment
archaeological layer	the occurrence of individual proofs of human presence, with or without fossil remains, and no noticeable alteration in the sediment
cultural layer	a sediment strongly influenced by human activity (fire, tool production, etc.), with many imported objects (stones, earth, bones, mollusc shells, plants, etc.)

Types of sediment and methods of interpretation. The most important cave sediments are limestone rubble, earth and cave travertine (sinter).

(a) Limestone rubble. There are two causes of limestone rubble breaking off from the walls and roof of a cave: one cause is water escaping through cracks, clefts and breakages in the limestone and carrying with it calcium carbonate together with loosened clay and sandy substances, which limestone contains in varying quantities; these are deposited on the floor of the cave. In this way the stone pieces surrounded by cracks lose their adhesion and fall to the floor. Evidence of corrosion, leaching of superficial alkalis, eroded and rounded edges are the indication of this on stone fragments of all sizes, which are embedded in an earth or travertine matrix. Such weathering is only possible in a temperate or warm climate with considerable precipitation.

A second cause of the formation of coarse limestone rubble is freezing and thawing. The increase in volume of water in the cracks during freezing loosens the stone pieces from their matrix, but the ice for the time being acts as a bond. It is only after thawing that the fragments fall out. Only a little water is necessary for this, but what is very necessary is frequent freezing and thawing, that is, temperature oscillations round about freezing point. Thus in the entrance and front part of the cave daily and seasonal variations influence sedimentation, which is also affected by rubble from the slopes of the hill above.

The inner part of the cave however is only affected by long-term changes of temperature. In cold times, that is in an ice age, such regular happenings occur in the great periglacial areas, their influence penetrating into caves. Above all, the times of transition, representing the advance and retreat stages of the ice sheets, bring fluctuating temperatures around freezing point deep into the inner cave. Deep perma-frost prevalent at peak phases of glaciation meant a cessation of sedimentation. In proportion to the penetration of the stone by water, which above all depends on the porosity of the rock, and in proportion to the frequency of freezing and thawing, coarse or fine-grained rubble is fractured off and deposited on the floor. The fact that this frost-fractured rubble shows marked variations in the various parts of the cave, even in contemporary deposits, is explained by the different degrees of influence by the outside climate. We can also expect that at the same place in the cave during different phases of a cold period the material will be reduced to different sizes. Therefore the course of an Ice Age can be inferred from the change in rubble size and stratified animal or archaeological objects can be more narrowly dated. The frost-fractured fragments are weathered a little or not at all in most cases. The edges exhibit a fresh surface. Earth and travertine only play a small part in such sediments. However in the entrance or where water percolates an admixture with small loess particles or earth is possible.

The larger the stone fragments in the frost rubble are, the greater are the interstices likely to be. In these the earth masses remain mostly loose because the blocks continue to support one another afterwards by a diagenetic clinging together of the sediments and by the pressure of more recent layers above the blocks. Therefore in layers with large tabular stones and blocks the fossil remains can be larger and less compressed than in layers with small stones. Sometimes fine material trickles down later into the interstices, so in sediments with large stones we must consider whether the earth is contemporary or later than the stones. In small stony layers large bones can be broken up by pressure of the sediments.

Such considerations are therefore very important as on them must be decided whether bones occurring between large stones are intrusive or indigenous and whether fractures in the bones are due to human or other processes.

(b) Earth. Silt and clay-like components are almost exclusively blown or washed into the front part of the cave during cold periods. In warm times however there is an important addition of earth washed by rainwater from the brow of the cave or the hill rising above. Fine material can also run off the rubble cone on the sill. In addition the atmosphere and plants in the entrance area make an additional attack on the rubble by a soil-forming process. Here also the loosening power of percolating water can be increased by the outer climate, so that more residues are freed from the stone.

With the separating of the calcium carbonate content from dripping water by evaporation, the newly created travertine often receives all the components of the cave stone which had remained stuck together up till then. In this process only the material from the native stone is laid down on the floor of the cave, without the earth content being increased.

Earthy deposits in cave interiors have neither blown in, nor in there turned to soil. But the trickling in of fine materials from the surface (loess, soil, etc.) particularly in caves very near a summit is highly likely. Then a sediment can survive in a cave, which has long ago been eroded from the surface or been recently weathered. Besides these fine components derived from the surface there are, in particular, residues freed from the native stone which can be piled up on the cave floor and form a complete earth coverage. Change of intensity in the water flow can cause bands varying between coarse and fine-grained sands and clays. A difference in mineral content can likewise cause banding which is in the main evidenced by fine layers of clay, iron or mineral efflorescences in the sequence of sedimentation. A yellow or brown colour in an earth complex depends primarily on iron content.

In the interior of the cave, sediments can change if there is a frequent occurrence of faeces and the decomposition of animal carcasses. The phosphate of bat guano is mostly coloured red or red-brown, without climate or soil development having had any share in this. Those cave bear layers which contain bones in a good quantity are mostly red-brown. Phosphate and the products of the decomposition of animal material cause the brown colour, or varying shades of red, yellow or black.

The earth carried in by cave bears on their fur and paws can never make a decisive contribution to accumulation in the interior of caves. A direct climatic interpretation of warm climate cannot be made from this red-brown colour of a cave bear layer, which always contains stone rubble. All that can be said about climate is that at the time of the formation of the sediment cave bear life was possible within reach of the cave and that ceiling rubble was being fractured off. A warm climate during the formation of a red-brown cave bear layer is therefore not an essential postulate.

(c) Travertine. In nearly all caves travertine plays a great part. It can have varied appearances: hard, crystalline and translucent, or a soft, crumbly, chalky or clay-like accumulation. With a heavy intake of water, this last type of travertine can become a slippery dough-like mass (*Montmilch*). Compact travertine masses mixed with earth can also occur in the caves.

In the *interior* of caves a clay-like travertine sinter is deposited by the percolating water. Evaporation and temperature oscillations play only a subordinate part. The decisive factor is the CO_2 content of the percolating water. This is originally rainwater which by trickling through soil on the hill absorbs CO_2 with which it can dissolve considerable quantities of calcium carbonate in the cracks of the stone. By means of the differential pressure when the water reaches the open cave large quantities of calcium carbonate are precipitated as stalactites. Therefore a high travertine content in a cave layer can only give a climatic clue in so far as during the time of its formation the hill must have carried vegetation. In the *entrance area* of the cave, however, the conditions resemble those of the surface. Here a warm climate encourages travertine formation, while strong air movement can also increase evaporation.

A special formation is 'clay travertine', consisting of dissolved cave stone; the dissolved components of the stone are transported by water and redeposited in a fine-grained form. In most cases this material with a high carbonate content is uniformly distributed throughout the clay, so that one can speak of a *white clay*. This does not demand an extremely warm climate, merely vegetation on the mountain surface.

(d) Humus content. The humus content in cave sediments is formed by vegetation or the decay of plant parts (grass, leaves and ferns) carried in by man or animals for the purpose of bedding or litter. If this humus content is once included in the soil it rarely disappears, so it can even be traced in very old layers. Washed-in soil can also be added to this. From the humus content the only deduction concerning the climate that can be made is that vegetation must have existed in the vicinity of the cave.

Acid humus can also be formed of disintegrated animal excreta and carcasses. The mineral arising from this is *Scharizerit*, related to phosphate earths. Thus a humus content may well be found in much frequented cave bear layers. All we can say about climate from this is that animal life was possible.

(e) Phosphate content. Stone and soil possess a natural amount of phosphate, which is not removed by circulating water. Also the phosphate contributions, which arise from decay of human meals (kitchen refuse) or of the excreta of cave bears as well as their carcasses, are preserved for tens of thousands of years in sediments. This observation has given rise to the 'phosphate method'. This is an analysis of the distribution of the phosphate content on a surface in order to discover the past presence of settlements, paths, burials, animal folds and such-like, which are indicated by high phosphate values. The measuring of phosphate content in a layered sequence can also help to trace the presence of man or animals at a particular horizon. Of course it must be borne in mind that while there is a concentration of phosphate on the surface, percolating water absorbs a certain amount and infiltrates the layers. It then happens that the phosphate content decreases uniformly downwards, until it reaches the permanent value of the sediments which are free from organic influences. In such layers nothing can be said about the measure of indigenous or infiltrated phosphate content. But a sudden decrease of the phosphate content in overlying strata indicates that then man or animals no longer frequented the cave.

But phosphates supply no evidence of climatic conditions. Their appearance is possible in cold as well as warm times. However in a cave bear layer, in the case of a uniform occupation, the phosphate content is higher if the breaking off of the ceiling rubble and the washing in of fine material decrease; this is because the changing ratio of intensity of sedimentation to the number of dead animals causes changes in phosphate content. Therefore the composition of a sequence must be examined in this light, because few bears plus little sediment can supply the same phosphate content as many bears plus much sediment. But likewise fewer bears and more sediment can cause a lessening of phosphate content. Therefore conclusions on climate must come much more readily from stone rubble or earth than from the strength of phosphate content.

The two Quaternary alluvial fills of Epirus, Greece, displayed in section in the Lazinia valley, a tributary of the Louros River. The older fill (below hammer) consists of angular and subrounded limestone gravel in a *terra rossa* matrix, and contains Middle and Advanced Palaeolithic artifacts; it forms alluvial fans where tributary streams debouch into major valleys or plains. The younger fill consists of clayey silt, with bands of fine gravel emphasizing the well-developed bedding, and contains sherds of Roman pottery; it forms a flat-topped terrace that borders the streams. The archaeology of Epirus cannot be interpreted without reference to the topographic, pedological and hydrological changes indicated by these two deposits.

(see page 135) PLATE IX

(a) Cook's Study. The zone of greater fissuring at the base of the peat marks the raw humus layer overlying the Mesolithic artifacts (see Fig. 29, p. 174).

(b) Bickley Moor Barrow. Section of the topsoil mound. The thin dark line below the pale zone in the centre of the photograph is shown by pollen analysis to be the primary surface. The present soil contrasts markedly in type with that of the Bronze Age (see Fig. 31, p. 176).

PLATE X (see page 167)

(f) Disturbances. All these physical and chemical phenomena only supply indications of the primary sedimentation process if no later events have caused disturbances, such as that made by an intrusive stream of water, rolling or transporting bodily the assorted particles; distinct layers can also be mixed, while percolating and dripping water may carry clay down into a loosely packed rubble so that in hollow places travertine especially develops (secondary travertine on the undersides of stones). Clay particles can swell up so much when saturated with water that at a slight inclination of the layer the material can start flowing gradually, and at the cave entrance this phenomenon can be enhanced by cryoturbation during cold times. Prehistoric man was also able to cause considerable disturbance by digging in caves, and burrowing animals may do likewise. Thus in the study of sediments in a cave we must first examine whether any sort of disturbance has subsequently altered the deposits.

RESEARCH METHODS

To recognize the various characteristics of the sediments described and to compare them quantitatively, they must not only be closely examined by excavation on the spot but a succession of analytical tests on the material must be made in the laboratory. When the samples are collected the following rules must be observed.

A series of samples should be taken if possible at various places in the cave—sill, entrance, front part of the cave, interior of the cave—from the rock floor right up to the surface of the deposits. The sedimentary process under the varied action of daily, seasonal or long-term changes of climate can be better followed using this method than if these influences are reconstructed only at one place.

The samples should be cut out of the section in a compact area and in a vertical line one on top of the other. By doing this the distance between the individual samples in fine-grained layers is narrowed; in layers with coarse stones however the distance apart can be very much greater. This is not only a requirement of technique but is more in keeping with the sedimentary process, since coarse material raises a sediment quicker than fine earth. It is advisable to take several samples even out of thicker layers which look homogeneous because experience has shown in many cases that important differences are only brought out by analysis.

Furthermore it is advisable, on a clean-cut section, to begin the extraction of the samples at the bottom. In this way only the portions that have already been sampled are contaminated by the loosened particles which are bound to fall down during the work. For analyses in the laboratory nothing must be removed in the way of artifacts, bones, stones and charcoal, otherwise the character of the deposits would be altered. Only where especially large stones or artifacts make the sample unnecessarily heavy can one leave them out, but this must be noted on the label of the samples. For any other technical details in the collection of samples reference can be made to a detailed account by the author (1958; pp. 26-29).

The object of analysis in the laboratory is to express the make-up of the scree by the distribution of grain-size in a sieving analysis, to discover the character of the fine material by its grain-size distribution in a washing analysis, and to define the most important chemical characteristics such as calcium carbonate content, humus content, and phosphate content. For techniques see the above-mentioned account, pp. 29–36.

Sieving analysis supplies quantitative values for the decrease in size of the limestone rubble. Thus the characteristics described on page 130 can be more exactly compared within the sediment, the cave and between various caves. Since stones are cleaned by such an analysis, their freshness or erosion, the sharp or rounded edges, and rolled and foreign materials can be more easily recognized. Washing analysis supplies quantitative values for earth and clay. Besides the help which it provides in the recognition of differences and similarities not visible to the naked eye, it also makes it possible to recognize when loess is a major component—in this way climatic readings can be made. Soil from fields can be recognized in a washing analysis by its characteristic grain-size distribution. Under a binocular microscope of 10–20 times magnification the components of the separate groups can be ascertained.

Simple chemical analyses to determine calcium carbonate, humus and phosphate contents make for an easy recognition of their origin and for their comparison with other caves. The values obtained from sieving and washing analyses and the determination of calcium carbonate content are values of weight which are best recalculated as percentages. Humus and phosphate contents are given in colour values. To provide a better impression than with rows of figures, all the values obtained should be drawn as *diagrams* and these are presented most clearly if the columns for the separate analyses are put side by side and the samples one on top of the other, in accordance with the profile. However the intervals can be small and regular because the size of the intervals in the profile does not imply time, but is merely dependent on the size of the rubble or the rapid change of unimportant more homogeneous sediments.

As every excavation means disturbance of the deposits, scaled drawings and photographs of important profiles should be made as well as possible. In addition there should be taken from at least one characteristic spot a lacquered strip so that the original full sequence of layers can be observed later. Where this is not possible one must be content with 'colour stripes', which at any rate preserve the colour impression of the separate layers in a small space. For these lacquered strips the method developed by Voigt has proved of value, but nowadays the so-called 'Capaplex' method of Herrnbrodt can be recommended which has the advantage that the profile need not be pre-dried. A simple method of producing colour stripes is described in detail by the author (*op. cit.*, pp. 37–39). The colour is indicated by Munsell Soil Colour Chart numbers. Ideally these colour values are determined on both the fresh section as well as on the dried samples, in order to include the colour change due to evaporation.

CAVE SEDIMENTS AND QUATERNARY GEOLOGY

The clearest time indicator for a chronological assessment of cave sediments is the last glaciation—the Würm Ice Age. Its effects were so penetrating and the deposits formed so recently that it is of advantage to deal first of all with the influence of this cold phase on sedimentation. From this point we can assess deposition in earlier and later phases.

The most striking glacial factors influencing sedimentation in caves are: an alteration of the snow line (the edge of the permanent snow field), the vegetation, tree and forest lines, the surface of ice streams, the boundaries of the ice caps, precipitation and the maximum penetration of perma-frost.

During the ice age, in all regions not covered by glaciers between the northern ice cap and the Alps, as well as far beyond, the water in ground and rock was locked up by *perma-frost* to great depths. Its effect on sedimentation in the interior part of a cave has already been discussed in the section on limestone rubble. We concluded there that the peak of a cold phase can be bordered by the coarse rubble of the advance phase of the glacier and the coarse rubble of the thaw, and itself leave no trace.

The *surfaces of the ice streams* allow us to recognize the mountains, peaks and the ranges which were free of ice and on which vegetation and animal life (within the zones of vegetation) were also possible side by side with glaciers. Caves which had been reached by glaciers were no longer visited by man or beast. Heavy precipitation, which is characteristic of the first part of a glacial advance and which possibly appears again later with the coming of a warmer oscillation, had both a direct and an indirect effect on sedimentation in caves. It provided the material necessary for glaciation and the descent of the snow line.

Figs. 26 and 27 provide information about the great significance of times of transition with their changes in the position of the snow, tree and forest lines. The columns in Fig. 26 signify the change in average height of the permanent snow line as well as the tree and forest boundaries in the central Alpine region from the Riss-Würm Interglacial through the Würm Glaciation to the present day. The names of the caves are put down in order of their heights above sea-level. The dotted and barred lines, which begin at the names of the caves and link up the columns, show their position in the landscape during the three periods of time. It must be stressed that maximum conditions are indicated. From this figure we can gauge the significance of the long transition times with their associated changes.

The case of the snow line is illustrated in Fig. 27. Every cave has its own column, which shows the extent by which the boundary of the permanent snow line must have descended, from its peak during the Riss-Würm Interglacial until it reached the cave. For the snow line to descend a thousand or more metres much precipitation and a long time were required. Much might have happened in the cave during this time. Man and beast could have visited it long after the start of the cold phase and also several changes could have left their marks. Thus one can see quite clearly that the duration of sedimentation and the point in time of its cessation under deep frost conditions could be different in every cave according to its situation. Caution must be advised when a chronological correlation is made between the fossil, cultural and archaeological layers of different caves. The beginning, duration and end of such layers must be specially examined in each cave. An uncritical correlation of the results from one cave can lead to erroneous deductions.

The examples illustrated in Figs. 26 and 27 come from the Alps and Jura. In other landscapes snow, tree and forest lines have different values, but they were always of consequence in some way or another. In the region of the great ice caps there were added

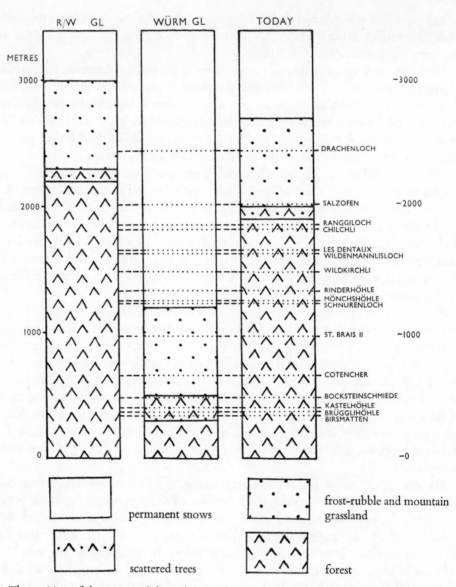

Fig. 26 The position of the snow and forest lines in the Riss-Würm Interglacial, the Würm Glaciation and today, in heights above sea-level, and the positions of caves within the region of the Alps and Jura.

the effects of these reserves of cold, and at sea coasts there was a possible amelioration of the climate and its extremes, in addition to glacial eustatic changes of sea-level.

As man and beast can also hunt and live above the forest line—at least in summer—their traces in caves are of little climatic significance. The cave is only uninhabitable in summer when the snow line reaches the cave and perma-frost penetrates the mountain. On the other hand caves below the snow line remained open the whole year round. But there the frost was also an effective deterrent, so that in wide regions of

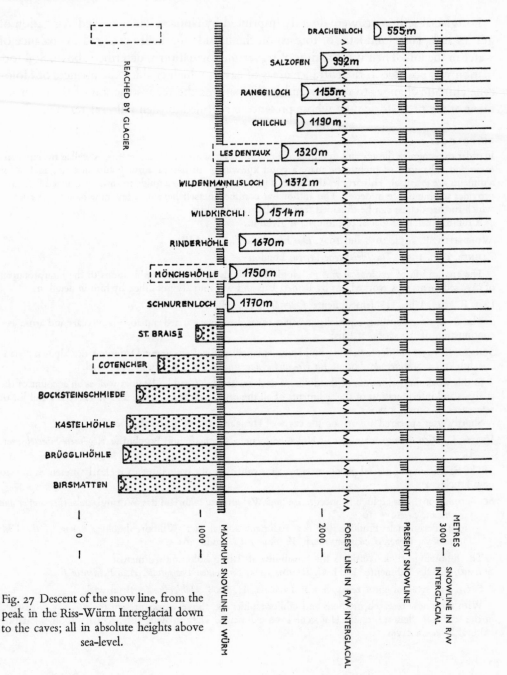

Fig. 27 Descent of the snow line, from the peak in the Riss-Würm Interglacial down to the caves; all in absolute heights above sea-level.

central Europe during the main cold phases man did not necessarily inhabit caves. But the increasing warmth at the end of the ice age again offered hunters caves to occupy in many places, which certainly made migrations and an expansion of population easier.

Postglacial sediments were directly imprinted by climate. The renewed vegetation of grasses and plants (and later of forests) on the hillside markedly changed the balance of water in the hill. Then was the time of travertine formation as described above. Soil formation was possible in the entrance areas of caves, which enabled the nuances of Holocene climatic changes to register and hence permits the reconstruction of the environment of the prehistoric men whose presence is revealed in their cultural remains.

REFERENCES

In order to recognize the age and duration of a culture layer within cave sediments, as well as the environment and behaviour of prehistoric man, a good knowledge of natural history and an exact analysis of sediments are essential. This article, therefore, is intended to provide a guide to this. Specialized literature provides an abundance of detail. The author has confined herself here to a few new basic works out of which further details can be obtained from bibliographical lists.

A full discussion of glacial phenomena is given in:

WOLDSTEDT, P. 1954, 1958 and 1965. *Das Eiszeitalter*, I, II and III

ZEUNER, F. E. 1959. *The Pleistocene Period*, London

The application of geological and pedological methods in various combinations to the interpretation of cave sediments was worked out by Robert Lais and was initially published by him in detail in:

LAIS, R. 1941. Über Höhlensedimente. *Quartär* 3, 1940, Berlin 1, 56–108

The work of the author, especially in Swiss caves, has been carried out for many years and arose as a continuation of the work of Lais:

SCHMID, E. 1958. Höhlenforschung und Sedimentanalyse. Ein Beitrag zur Datierung des alpinen Paläolithikums. *Schriften des Instituts für Ur- und Frühgeschichte der Schweiz*, no. 13, Basel.

In this work the techniques of the different analyses are described in detail as well as an account of the analyses and interpretation of the sediments of all the caves named in Figs. 2 and 3. There is a full list of references to similar caves.

Shortly after appeared a work on the caves of Hungary, also based on the work of Lais:

VERTÉS, L., 1959. Untersuchungen an Hölensedimenten. Methode und Ergebnisse. *Régészeté Füzetebs*, ser. II, 7

The significance of glacial phenomena for the evaluation of cave sediments is clearly presented in two new articles.

SCHMID, E. 1963. Zur alpinen Schneegrenze und Waldgrenze während des Würmglazials. *Eiszeitalter und Gegenwart*, 14, 107–110

—— 1964. Periglaziale Einflüsse bei der Sedimentation in der Wildkirchlihöhle. *Report of the VIth International Congress on Quaternary, Warsaw 1961.* Lodz, 165–9

The following article considers the possibility of dating holocene sediments:

SCHMID, E. Die Sedimente. In H.-G. BANDI, 1964. *Birsmatten-Basisgrotte. Acta Bernensia I*

For recent spelaeological research see: TRIMMEL, H. 1968. *Höhlenkunde.* Brunswick

With their new research methods and bibliographies the above works present the point now reached in the study of Pleistocene and Holocene cave sediments. They provide the necessary tools for dating cultural layers in caves.

PLANTS

14 *Pollen Analysis*

G. W. DIMBLEBY

SAMPLES TAKEN FOR POLLEN ANALYSIS may range from long series covering a span of thousands of years to the single sample for a spot determination of date. Basically the analysis consists of the identification and enumeration of the various types of pollen present in each sample; in other words, the preparation of a pollen spectrum for each sample. This in itself is not always a simple matter, especially in certain types of material, but the techniques are now well established and the inherent limitations of the method understood. As this aspect of the subject is fully covered in textbooks (e.g. Faegri and Iversen[5]) it is not proposed to deal with it here. What is of more concern is the interpretation of the pollen spectra so obtained.

Pollen analysis is often thought of as a technique for dating, but it only serves this purpose if the pollen spectra can be tied in to a time scale based on some direct dating method, such as radiocarbon dating. In recent years the greater accuracy of radiocarbon dating and the increasing resources available for it have reduced the importance of pollen analysis as a dating method. In fact, pollen sequences today are not infrequently augmented with radiocarbon determinations. Nevertheless, pollen analysis is itself increasing rather than decreasing in importance as its application to environmental studies is developed over a progressively widening field.

For many parts of the world a pattern of change has now been established in the pollen rain over a long period of the past, so that even isolated analyses may be fitted into their appropriate position in the sequence. Thus in Europe the Postglacial period has been divided up into zones, each having a characteristic tree pollen spectrum, reflecting the sequence of climatic changes which have taken place as the Postglacial developed. Knowing the present ecological tolerances of these tree species, it is possible within limits to assess the climatic features of each zone. However, each of these zones may cover two or three millennia, so their value for dating is restricted, though in some cases subdivision is possible, based on the behaviour of certain critical species. In Europe and elsewhere the zone and sub-zone boundaries have now been tied in with considerable accuracy to an absolute time scale, principally by C^{14} determinations on organic matter stratified immediately adjacent to these boundaries (Godwin, Walker and Willis[7]). Where such a system of absolute dating has not yet been worked out, pollen analysis is only capable of establishing relative chronology. For pollen analysis to be of value in dating it is not necessary to interpret the pollen spectra in terms of the plant communities on the ground; many correlations are based only on the percentages of the different pollen types, in particular the tree species, without any consideration of the ecological structure of the forests producing the pollen. In fact, as we shall see in the following pages, it may not always be possible to arrive at such ecological conclusions.

For the archaeologist, however, pollen analysis is potentially of much greater value than just as an indirect instrument for dating, important though this is. It can also give information on the ecological environment in which human remains and artifacts were situated, and a knowledge of the ecological environment may in turn point to the use— or misuse—of the land at that time.

Thus pollen analysis is of potential value in archaeology in three ways: (a) as a means of dating, (b) to provide evidence of the contemporary environment, and (c) as an indication of what man was doing to that environment. It is rare for these different facets to emerge equally from any one investigation and indeed sometimes one or more of them may be impossible of interpretation. Generally it may be said that a site which gives first-class material for dating tends to give only limited ecological information, and vice versa.

The Postglacial forest sequence in Europe has been worked out in detail from a large number of palynological investigations; the entry or disappearance of the different tree genera, together with the relative abundance of their pollen, characterizes the various pollen zones and sub-zones. For such information the ideal material is an unbroken sequence of stratified deposits in conditions which favour the preservation of pollen. Anaerobic peat deposits or lake sediments are therefore usual subjects for study. The information they provide, however, is not relevant to any particular piece of ground or plant community. It reflects the forest sequence of the district as a whole, which is what is required for dating purposes. Clearly, therefore, the ecological value of such information is limited. Nevertheless, the impact of man on the forest can be seen in such analyses, and, when seen, can be dated with some precision, but its expression will only be in general terms and will not be related to any given place. This is well illustrated by the work of Pearsall and Pennington[14] on the Windermere muds, in which they were able to show the increased grass pollen and the correspondingly decreased tree pollen percentages as the result of prehistoric occupation. The pollen analyses alone, however, could not tell them where in the district the main forest destruction had taken place, though by bringing other facts to bear, a definite conclusion was reached.

The ratio of non-tree pollen to tree pollen is a good guide to the density of the forest and the density is often dependent on man's activity. A marked increase in this ratio, due to an increase in the pollen of light-demanding herbs, is a usual indication of human influence. It is important to realize that in order to diminish the forest cover it is not necessary to cut trees down. Fire is a potent factor, damaging standing timber and destroying regeneration: at the same time it often has the incidental but cumulative effect of increasing the fire hazard. Grazing, too, can in the course of time destroy or mutilate a forest by constant attack on the next generation of trees. One need not hesitate, therefore, to attribute observed changes in the pollen spectra to human agency solely because that culture had not the mechanical means to clear forest. As far as we know fire was always available and it is significant that West[20] suggested that an episode of deforestation in the Hoxne interglacial deposits might be attributable to the influence of Palaeolithic man.

In every complete pollen sequence through the Postglacial period evidence will appear sooner or later of the effect of man in the environment. In Europe this usually starts in the Neolithic period, though, as we shall see later, Mesolithic man could cause local modification of his environment. But it was when some sort of husbandry, whether of stock or crops, became part of everyday life that the forest became an undesirable nuisance to man rather than just the setting in which he found himself and from which he won the necessities of life. Then the effects of deliberate clearance became sufficiently widespread to affect the pollen rain from a whole district and so show in the bog or lake analyses. Iversen[9] in Denmark has shown with great clarity the sequence

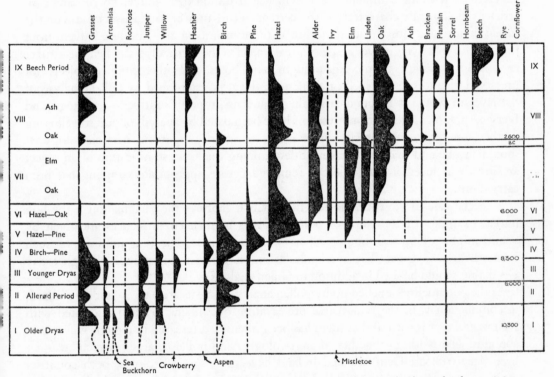

Fig. 28 Idealized diagram illustrating the Postglacial pollen sequence in Jutland. By kind permission of Dr Johs. Iversen.

of forest destruction (in which fire was the chief implement), cultivation and forest regrowth, which he calls *Landnam* (= land taking) and which is now widely recognized all over Europe. Fig. 28 is an idealized diagram of his showing the sequence for Jutland; the spread of heather, grasses and weeds of cultivation from the Neolithic onwards (zones VIII and IX of his classification) can clearly be seen. The non-tree pollen often gives some guide to the use being made of the land; the appearance of cereal pollen, distinguishable from that of other grasses, together with the pollen of weeds of cultivation such as plantain and goosefoot, is conclusive proof of the onset of cultivation. There will be differences in detail, of course, in regions of different plant geography, topography or soil.

Attention is now being devoted more and more to obtaining a detailed picture of how farming became established. By very close sampling through peat deposits it has been possible to show that the first forest clearances were often small and short-lived, the forest returning in full strength again and again (Turner[18]). Eventually extensive clearance occurred which in upland areas usually persisted right through to the present day.

Now, whilst all such changes in a peat bog sequence may be datable—within the precision of the pollen zonation—they cannot be related to particular sites or to particular cultures without complementary evidence from another source. For instance, an artifact typologically characteristic of a certain culture may be found associated with the *Landnam* horizon, thus equating culture with environment and land use. Adventitious finds of this sort may, however, be of great value to the archaeologist when the artifact itself is not datable by type; e.g. ploughs, skis, boats, and other wooden objects not preserved in land sites. In such cases the period can be established by pollen analysis of the layer in which it is found (assuming that it is properly stratified—*see* Faegri and Iversen,[5] p. 116). Objects from museums have been dated by analysis of peat still clinging to them—a reminder that cleanliness is not necessarily righteous in archaeology. It should also be said that the chances of determining the exact stratification of an object are greatly reduced if that object is removed before appropriate sampling has been carried out.

A special case of adventitious bog finds which captures the imagination is the bog burial; examples of the value of pollen analysis in such circumstances are given by Schütrumpf.[15] The anthropological as well as archaeological significance of such occurrences is so great that a reliable dating is of first importance, though today C^{14} dating would be used in addition to pollen analysis.

As the potentialities opened up by pollen analysis of peats are now so widely realized, in conjunction with the remarkable preservation of remains so often associated with such material, it is natural that there has been intensified research in regions where peat abounds. The working together of archaeologists and pollen analysts in such areas has been very fruitful; Denmark and Ireland have made great progress, both countries owing a great deal to the Danish palynologist, Knud Jessen. Moreover, the importance of peat investigations in many other aspects of Quaternary research has been recognized and the appropriate experts brought in. Such intensified work has led not only to more detailed knowledge of existing sites but the recognition of many new sites. Most important is the increasing number of actual occupation sites which has become known. Occupation sites of this sort—even though they may be the ephemeral settlements of nomadic people—make it possible more fully than before to correlate a culture with its environment and at the same time to give it a reliable dating. Again, for typologically important sites a C^{14} dating will probably be sought, but for many others reliance will still be placed on the pollen analysis alone. In some cases the date may be rendered more precise if the occupation can be related to one or more 'recurrence surfaces'—recognizable changes in the nature of the peat due to resurgence of bog growth as a result of the increased wetness of the bog surface. The ages of these surfaces may be known with reasonable accuracy, but it is often difficult to identify individual ones with certainty.

The Maglemosian site at Star Carr[1] is a fine example of how an actual occupation site well stratified in peat can be made to yield up a very comprehensive mass of evidence concerning the people, their environment and their way of life, to a degree that would not be possible either from isolated finds or from an archaeologically sterile bog profile. From a later period may be quoted Troels-Smith's investigation of the Neolithic Ertebølle culture in Denmark and his comparison of it with the Egolzwil lake-dwelling culture in Switzerland.[16] These are occupation sites preserved in stratified deposits, one in peat and the other in lake mud, but both providing material for pollen analysis (and for C[14] tests). In fact both proved to be of virtually the same date and both showed the clearing of the forest in preparation for agriculture; but whilst in Denmark it was the elm which suffered most by the clearance, in Switzerland it was the beech. Here then were similar and contemporary cultures producing similar effects in floristically different environments. The nature of the actual settlements was, of course, very different in the two cases, but this is not our concern here.

Not strictly occupation levels, and yet not adventitious finds either, are the trackways sometimes found embedded in peat bogs. Recently Godwin[6] has made a detailed study of the trackways of the Somerset Levels, using pollen analysis not only to confirm dating—mainly based on the C[14] date—but to demonstrate the ecological conditions of the Neolithic or of the Late Bronze Age when these tracks were constructed. He sees them as an attempt to keep communications open over land that was becoming increasingly swampy, an attempt which ultimately failed as peat growth relentlessly continued.

So far discussion has centred on sites associated with deposits formed under waterlogged conditions, but it must be recognized that in such places archaeological sites cannot give a complete picture of the total effect of man on his environment. Occupation sites embedded in peat were probably only occupied during the summer; during the winter the people must have moved away above the high water-table to influence another environment. In the case of the Swiss lake-dwellings, it is obvious that the occupation layer was not itself on the site of forest clearance. The pollen record of forest clearance refers to the dry land, to sites which cannot be precisely identified. In such cases, then, the ecological picture is either blurred or incomplete, and it must be recognized that this is an inherent limitation in the study of all sites liable to waterlogging (and hence to peat formation), particularly in the later prehistoric cultures. Contemporary with such occupations other people were living on the dry land and sometimes the wealth of information which can be obtained from peat sites blinds us to this fact. In a country such as Britain, in which the bulk of the land is well above the water-table at all times of the year, even in this damp Sub-atlantic climate, the conditions exemplified by the bog or water-side sites cannot be regarded as typical for the country as a whole. The fact is, of course, that normal terrestrial sites do not lend themselves to the same methods of study, though, as we shall see below, pollen analysis may still unexpectedly yield results even in such conditions.

Before turning to purely terrestrial sites, however, we must look at that very large group of sites which in their day were terrestrial but which are now buried beneath peat. This is most commonly the case where the onset of the wetter Sub-atlantic period, about 500 BC, resulted in the initiation of peat formation in many places where it had not taken place before. Thus in Ireland Jessen[11] found that the onset of Sub-atlantic peat formation generally followed the Late Bronze Age, and proof of the original normal terrestrial nature of some sites may still persist in the form of old field systems beneath several feet of peat. Sites in such a situation offer a very different problem from those we have discussed so far. As with all sites covered by peat, of course, the peat above the occupation is only relevant for the dating of the site in so far as the very lowest layer gives a latest possible date for the site, but there may be a long interval between the occupation of the site and the onset of peat formation.

To put this in its correct perspective it is necessary to introduce here a rather different principle, namely the analysis of the pollen in normal soils. It was pointed out at the beginning of this chapter that pollen analysis is ideally carried out in anaerobic stratified deposits. Under such conditions microbiological activity is excluded, though if a peat becomes drained intense microbiological activity may start up in the peat, destroying both the peat itself and the pollen in it. This is especially true of fen peats, which are of high base status. It might be expected, therefore, that pollen falling on the surface of a freely drained soil would be exposed to the same processes and rapidly be destroyed. On calcareous and circumneutral soils this is so, such pollen as they do contain being so corroded as to be largely unrecognizable. But with soils of greater acidity, especially those with a pH less than 5·5, pollen may be found in very large quantities. This pollen is not lying free in the soil, but is apparently stabilized in humic material; if soil is shaken up with water the pollen will not be extracted, but if the humus is broken down with caustic potash large quantities of pollen may be set free. For this reason, the pollen does not wash freely through the soil profile. It does move downwards, presumably in association with the movement of the humus, but the process is slow and, incidentally, independent of the size of the pollen grains. Thus a crude stratification is produced which reflects broadly the history of vegetation as long as the pollen has been accumulating.[2]

Acidity is not the only factor which favours pollen preservation. Any condition which reduces microbiological activity may have a similar effect; low temperature or aridity, for example. Indeed, the recent work of Martin[12] in Arizona has shown that even freely-drained calcareous materials can preserve pollen under those climatic conditions.

Now soils are not static but are maturing. Many of the soils of Europe, forming on material exposed during the Ice Age, were initially more or less calcareous, gradually becoming leached and more acid as time went on. This leaching process appears to have been more rapid in the higher rainfall areas, and, in soils of low base status particu-larly, to have accelerated following deforestation. Consequently, the pollen record seldom goes back as far as the primeval forest stage, but usually starts in the transition from forest to open country. This progressive acidification of soil has one other important effect, namely to bring about the elimination of those members of the soil fauna which are responsible for soil mixing: these animals, in particular certain earthworms, are intolerant of acidity. In cases where they do occur together with pollen they wreck any pollen stratification. Stratification may be as much a matter of actual quantities of pollen as of percentages. The usual pattern is that the highest concentration is at the surface and that it falls with depth until at 45 to 60 cm it peters out altogether. The high concentration at the surface is very important in recognizing buried surfaces (*infra*).

The interpretation of soil pollen analyses differs in one important manner from that of peat or lake deposits. The bulk of the pollen falling on a soil comes from the vegetation on the spot; the influence of more distant vegetation, particularly if the site is forested, is largely masked. In other words, a soil pollen spectrum is of much more use for the interpretation of the ecology of the site itself but is of correspondingly less use for dating purposes, because critical species (e.g. the calcicolous elm) may not occur in the local forest type. This drawback becomes most serious in deforested country when the representation of tree pollen, the essential basis for dating, may be so low that an adequate count cannot be obtained. On the other hand, if dating is not possible, at least there is a better chance of obtaining precise information about the environment and man's effect on it.

An effect of soil development which is of importance in the present context is the formation of a raw humus layer. Once such a layer has formed it tends to build up and it has been shown that for palynological purposes it may be treated like a peat. In other words, it collects the pollen, but does not transmit it to the underlying layers. Raw humus is susceptible to burning, however, and on heathlands, for example, it is repeatedly consumed by fire. Consequently, a marked 'unconformity' builds up between the pollen spectra of the contemporary raw humus and the underlying mineral soil, an 'unconformity' which can span a thousand or two years.

This point has considerable archaeological importance not only where raw humus exists today but also where it has existed in the past. The Mesolithic site of Cook's Study (near Holmfirth, Yorks.), excavated by Hallam,[8] is instructive in this connection. Here microliths were lying on slightly podzolized mineral soil beneath about 75 cm of peat of Sub-atlantic age. Above the flints and below the peat proper was a 5 cm band of darker organic matter, which, when dried out, showed much greater shrinkage than the over-lying peat (Plate Xa). The pollen analysis (Fig. 29) suggested that it was raw humus and not true peat; not only was the layer much richer in pollen than adjacent samples above or below, but the vegetation indicated by the pollen was grass-heath, a community which characteristically forms raw humus. The pollen diagram gives some indication of unconformity in relation to the more tree-rich spectrum beneath, so that there was a gap—of unknown duration—between the Mesolithic occupation and the raw humus overlying it. This is particularly important as there were indications of agriculture in the pollen from the raw humus layer.

Even in areas where peat has never formed pollen analysis can give valuable information about ancient man's environment and his influence on it. Wherever a soil surface

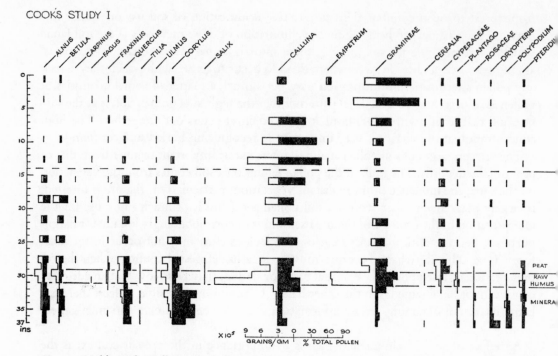

Fig. 29 Cook's Study. Pollen analysis through peat, raw humus and mineral soil of a Pennine Mesolithic site. Microliths occurred on the surface of the mineral soil.*

has been sealed it is possible that pollen will be preserved, particularly if the soil is acid. It is fortunate that from the Neolithic onwards the habit of constructing earthworks has brought about the preservation of many surfaces contemporary with the particular culture. In Holland Waterbolk[19] has drawn attention to the difference of environment in the Neolithic and Bronze Ages, with particular reference to the spread of heathland, basing his conclusions on the pollen content of surfaces buried beneath barrows. Similar work in this country[4] has shown the gradual retreat of the forest and the differing types of land use practised at high and low altitudes. Thus cultivation was widespread in the lowlands, but at higher altitudes final deforestation came about through forest pasture.[3]

It is not always easy to interpret the analyses of such buried surfaces. There is usually a mixture of pollen of trees and shrubs with that from grasses and herbs. Bearing in mind that under a tree cover many species, even if able to survive, flower much less profusely, it is clear that these grasses and herbs must have been growing in full light. Yet the woody species were sufficiently close at hand to contribute to the pollen rain. The only feasible interpretation is one of clearings within a generally forested area. Through comparative analyses the extension of such clearings can sometimes be traced until the condition is reached where the landscape is no longer forested.

* In Figs 29, 30 and 31 the histograms are double, the left-hand side representing the absolute pollen frequency in grains/gm and the right-hand side the percentages of total pollen plus fern spores.

It was said earlier that the surface of a soil contains the highest pollen content, and it is sometimes obvious that the soils buried underneath earthworks show a truncated pollen profile; that is, they have been stripped. This in itself is a point of interest, but it seriously restricts the value of such an earthwork for pollen analysis. However, it may happen that such a mound is made up of recognizable turves, and Waterbolk has used such turves for pollen analysis when the soil surface is disturbed. At the same time there is no proof that turves come from the immediate vicinity of the earthwork and in one case where a buried surface was also present I have found that they did not. Even where a mound is not obviously built of turves, a pollen profile through it can give interesting information about the structure. Thus it is sometimes found that barrows are constructed entirely of subsoil, since they contain little pollen except that which has demonstrably washed down from the new surface (Fig. 30). In other cases (Plate Xb; Fig. 31) the pollen content is high throughout, showing that they are built up of topsoil. Sometimes it can be shown that the mound is heterogeneous, and that some of the material did not come from the neighbourhood of the monument; likewise, it can also be shown that some, at any rate, of the material came from a surrounding ditch. Each case must be examined on its merits, but a complete profile through an earthwork, though laborious to analyse, can cast unexpected light on the mode of construction.

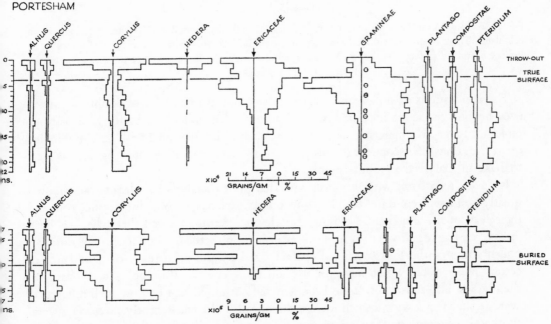

Fig. 30 Portesham. The upper set of curves shows the pollen distribution in and below the surface of a Bronze Age barrow. Pollen is only abundant near the surface, indicating that the mound itself was constructed of subsoil material. The lower set of curves shows the pollen spectra from the turf core down into the soil underlying the primary surface. The high proportion of ivy pollen is puzzling but may be due to the use of ivy for fodder. The barred circle indicates the presence of cereal pollen.

BICKLEY MOOR- BARROW
(COMPLETE SECTION)

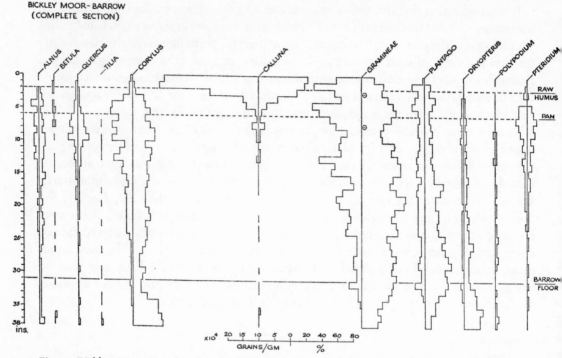

Fig. 31 Bickley Moor Barrow. A series of analyses through the mound of a Bronze Age barrow on heathland. There is abundant pollen throughout the mound, showing that it was built of topsoil. The present heathland surface contrasts with the agricultural condition in Bronze Age time, as indicated by the pollen analyses.

The applications of pollen analysis to archaeological material will doubtless extend even beyond the scope indicated here. We know that pollen can be found in various biologically inactive materials, and if these happen to be associated with human remains or artifacts they offer scope for investigation by this technique. It is often easier, however, to make an analysis than to interpret it.

It can be seen from what has been said that pollen analysis has already contributed greatly—and will continue to do so—to our knowledge of our distant ancestors and their way of life, but before closing this chapter it must be said that what has been discovered has recently led to some re-examination of the method itself. The different pollen zones of the Postglacial are characterized by the occurrence or abundance of certain pollen types which have been found to be critical; this applies particularly to the division into sub-zones. It has been generally assumed that because such differences were general over a wide area, they were climatically induced. Recently, however, several workers have questioned this, suggesting that man himself influenced some species more than others, and it so happens that the critical species are the ones most in question. Elm, for instance, was a tree particularly useful to primitive man, for cattle fodder and for making of bark bread. It is the species which best separates the Atlantic (zone VIIa) from the Sub-boreal (zone VIIb), being much less abundant in the latter. In Ireland,

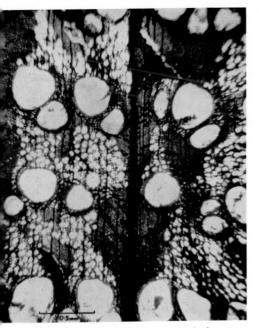

(a) Transverse section of oak (*Quercus* sp.), showing early and later vessels, and one broad and many narrow rays. Ring-porous.

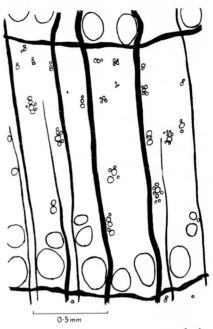

(b) Diagram of transverse section of ash (*Fraxinus excelsior*), showing 1–3 rows of large early vessels, later vessels in small clusters, and uniseriate and multiseriate rays. Ring-porous.

(c) Diagram of transverse section of willow (*Salix caprea*), showing scattered vessels, sometimes grouped, and uniseriate rays. Diffuse-porous.

(d) Diagram of transverse section of pine (*Pinus cembra*) showing tracheid, rays, and resin-canals.

(see page 178) PLATE XI

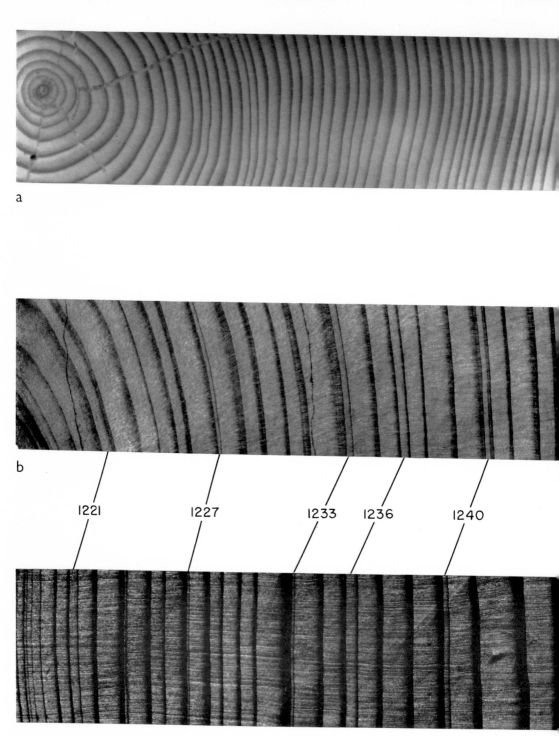

a

b

1221   1227   1233 1236   1240

c

Cross-dating and types of tree-ring series: (a) a complacent record lacking ring character; (b) and (c) sensitive tree-ring series which cross-date; (b) and (c) are from the thirteenth-century ruin Betatakin in northern Arizona.

PLATE XII (see page 191)

according to Mitchell,[13] elm declined at a later date than on the Continent or in the rest of the British Isles. Its disappearance therefore was not climatically determined. In the same way, Iversen[9] has shown that the decline of lime, another indicator species, was to be correlated with early agriculture rather than with time. Other important species similarly affected are ivy and mistletoe, which Troels-Smith[16] believes were used as fodder plants for stalled animals, especially in the winter, whilst birch, whose spread may indicate cooler conditions in the Sub-atlantic period, may also have been favoured by an increase in the practice of burning, after which it is a common colonizer.

It is impossible at present to say to what degree human influence has affected such species: no doubt it varied from place to place according to culture, climate and local ecology. We have seen that from earliest times man has had the power to influence his surroundings and it would be ecologically irrational to expect that his effects would not modify the floristic composition of the flora, particularly of the forest flora. Indeed, it is possible that his effects locally went beyond that; thus it is common to find from soil pollen profiles that mass movement of soil has taken place, which appears to be associated in many cases with early forest clearance. If such deforestation were general over a catchment area it is conceivable that flooding might increase, resulting in increased wetness of swampy land and so to increased peat growth in topogenous mires. Whether false recurrence surfaces have originated in this way I do not know, but we are only beginning to recognize how drastic were the effects early man had on his environment, in spite of the smallness of the populations. It is pollen analysis that is opening this field of knowledge to us, but we must not be surprised if some of our earlier beliefs and assumptions themselves come in for some re-examination.

REFERENCES

 1 CLARK, J. G. D. 1954. *Excavations at Star Carr*, Cambridge
 2 DIMBLEBY, G. W. 1961. *J. Soil Sci. 12*, 1–11
 3 —— 1961. *Antiquity 35*, 123–8
 4 —— 1962. *The Development of British Heathlands and their Soils*, Oxford
 5 FAEGRI, K. and IVERSEN, J. 1964. Textbook of Pollen Analysis (2nd edition), Oxford
 6 GODWIN, H. 1960. *Proc. Prehist. Soc. 26*, 1–36
 7 —— WALKER, D. and WILLIS, E. H. 1957. *Proc. Roy. Soc. Ser. B. 147*, 352–66
 8 HALLAM, J. S. 1960. *The Mesolithic of the Central Pennines*, (M.A. thesis, Liverpool University)
 9 IVERSEN, J. 1949. *Danm. Geol. Unders. 4 (3)*, No. 6
10 —— 1958. *Veröff. Geobot. Inst. Rübel Zürich 33*, 137–44
11 JESSEN, K. 1934. *Irish Nat. J. 5*, 130–4
12 MARTIN, P. S. 1963. *The Last 10,000 Years*, Tucson
13 MITCHELL, G. F. 1956. *Proc. Roy. Irish Acad. 57B*, 185–251
14 PEARSALL, W. H. and PENNINGTON, W. 1947. *J. Ecol. 34*, 137–48
15 SCHÜTRUMPF, R. 1958. *Praeh. Zeits. 36*, 156–66
16 TROELS-SMITH, J. 1956. *Science 124*, 876–9
17 —— 1960. *Danm. Geol. Unders. 4 (4)*, No. 4
18 TURNER, J. 1965. *Proc. Roy. Soc. Ser. B. 161*, 343–53
19 WATERBOLK, H. T. 1954. *De Praehistorische Mens en zijn Milieu*, Groningen
20 WEST, R. G. *Phil. Trans. Roy. Soc. Ser. B. 239*, 265–356

15 Wood and Charcoal in Archaeology

A. CECILIA WESTERN

PLANT REMAINS ARE VERY COMMONLY found on archaeological sites of all periods, and the most usual form in which they survive is as wood charcoal. On very dry or completely waterlogged sites parts of plants, twigs and branches, nuts and seeds, pollen, and even leaves or flowers, may survive in a recognizable condition, but in normal circumstances vegetable matter decays by the action of bacteria in the soil and can only survive when completely carbonized. Wood burned in an inadequate supply of oxygen forms charcoal, consisting of carbon which does not decay in the soil, and these fragments may be found by archaeologists upon ancient hearth sites. Wooden posts, beams or planks used in the construction of defensive structures, huts or other buildings may also be carbonized if destroyed by fire in too little air. In wells, lakes, rivers and bogs, where the soil is completely waterlogged and airless, wood and other organic matter survive for thousands of years. Examples of this are the Roman writing tablet from Chew Stoke, Somerset,[1] trackways of Neolithic and Bronze Age date from Somerset peat-bogs,[2] the Mesolithic brushwood flooring at Star Carr, Yorkshire,[3] dug-out canoes of oak and ash in the estuary of the Humber at North Ferriby[4] probably dating from 1500 to 1200 BC, boat-shaped coffins at Loose Howe, Yorkshire,[5] medieval wooden spoons, knife-handles and a casket from York,[6] and the various remains of wooden structures and objects from the Swiss lake-villages,[7] of which some hundreds from the Neolithic to Late Iron Age periods are known. In dry and desert countries wood can remain undecayed for thousands of years also, if the soil is completely dry, and numerous wooden objects, coffins, furniture, figurines, combs, and so on, dating from 3000 BC onwards have been found in Egypt.[8] Other examples of relatively dry preservation are the tomb chamber constructed of juniper or cedar logs inside a large Phrygian tumulus at Gordion, Anatolia,[9] dating from about the sixth century BC and containing remains of ornate wooden furniture, and the large numbers of wooden domestic articles and pieces of furniture found in the Middle Bronze Age tombs at Jericho.[10] In these cases preservation appears to be due, not to lack of moisture, although the objects seem to be dry when found, but to circumstances not yet completely understood preventing the survival of the bacteria causing decay. Wood carvings and other objects, dating from the fifth century BC, have also been found, well-preserved, together with other organic material, frozen into a solid block of ice at Pazyrik, in the Altai Mountains in Central Russia.[11]

It is of interest to the archaeologist to know what kinds of trees and shrubs have been used by ancient peoples for firewood, for building, and for the making of objects required in daily life or religious ritual. Such information may throw light on climatic differences at distant periods of time, on local vegetation and whether a district was forested, or merely supported grassland or scrub. It may also show whether local woods only were used or if timber was imported from elsewhere for special purposes, and to what extent craftsmen had discovered and appreciated the qualities of different timbers for specific purposes. Wood and charcoal remains also provide very suitable material for Carbon-14 dating. The problems of the chemical nature of charcoal and wood, particularly of the condition of wood such as that found in the Jericho tombs and the reason for its survival, are a detailed study more suited to a chemist or a specialist in timber utilization than to a wood-anatomist, and it is the identification of structure which will be dealt with here.

The standard work on the whole subject of the flora of the past in Britain is *History of the British Flora* by H. Godwin (1956). There is unfortunately nothing comparable to it at present for the Mediterranean and Middle East region, although much work is now being done on plant remains from these areas. For the anatomy of wood and its determination *The Structure of Timber* by F. W. Jane (1956) or *Textbook of Wood Technology* by A. J. Panshin and C. de Zeeuw (1964) should be consulted.

Most trees and shrubs can be distinguished by the structure of the wood. This statement does not generally apply to species, but on the whole it is true to say that one genus can be distinguished from another by wood anatomy. Apart from the tree ferns all the trees and shrubs of the world can be divided into two groups, the gymnosperms or softwoods, which are cone-bearing trees such as pine and cedar, and the angiosperms or hardwoods, such as oak and poplar. The latter group also includes the palms, but these have a different structure from either softwoods or hardwoods. Fig. 32 illustrates

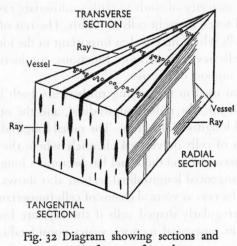

Fig. 32 Diagram showing sections and main features of wood

diagrammatically the basic structure of a piece of the trunk of a tree, and the three sections cut by the wood-anatomist to show three-dimensionally the structure of each kind of cell. The transverse section is the most important in identifying hardwoods and is cut straight across the trunk or branch. It shows the rays like the spokes of a wheel, and growth rings as concentric circles normally defined in hardwoods from a temperate climate by a band of denser tissue at the end of one growing season and by an increase in the size or number of the vessels of the new season's growth. Woods grown outside the temperate zone may not show distinct growth rings, due to lack of definite periods of growth and of rest, or may show more than one period of growth during the year and therefore it is better not to use the less accurate term, annual rings.

Most types of cells in wood are aligned longitudinally so they are cut through their shorter axis by a transverse section, and from an examination of this section temperate hardwoods may be divided into ring-porous and diffuse-porous woods. In a ring-porous wood (Plate XIa) the vessels formed early in the growing season are considerably larger than those formed later; there may be from one to four or even five rows of large early vessels, and normally the change from these to smaller late vessels is fairly sudden. The latter may be numerous or sparse, and solitary or in groups or strings variously arranged (Plate XIb), according to the genus or species of the wood. In a diffuse-porous wood (Plate XIc), on the other hand, there may or may not be a ring of vessels at the beginning of the season of growth, but there will be only a gradual reduction in the size of the vessels produced as the season advances. Here again the vessels may be numerous or sparse, solitary or in groups, clusters or strings, which may be arranged in a radial, obliquely radial or tangential direction. Ray cells are the only cells which have their longer axis at right angles to the direction of the trunk or branch, and grow in a radial or horizontal direction, so they appear in both ring-porous and diffuse-porous woods similar to the spokes of a wheel. They may be only one cell wide (uniseriate), two cells wide (biseriate), or any number up to about thirty or more cells wide (multiseriate), although in the majority of timbers with multiseriate rays they will be something between three and seven or eight cells in width. The rest of the wood consists of various other kinds of cells which may be less important in the identification, especially of charcoal. All wood cells have one or more functions, conduction or storage of food or water, or mechanical support of the tree.

The other two sections used in identifying timbers are both longitudinal cuts, one along the radius of the trunk, the radial longitudinal, and the other at right angles to the radius, the tangential longitudinal section. The radial longitudinal section shows the vessels as vertical chains of cells or vertical channels where the ends of the cells have broken down in the heartwood and the vessel has become a long tube, and the rays as horizontal bands. The tangential longitudinal section also shows the vessels as vertical chains or channels, and the rays as vertical chains of cells (uniseriate rays) or boat-shaped groups of rounded or irregularly shaped cells if the rays are biseriate or multiseriate. The shape of the rays in tangential sections varies considerably and ray width is a valuable diagnostic feature.

The two longitudinal sections also show three other minute features useful in identification, particularly vessel pitting, perforations, and spiral thickening. Each cell of which a vessel is composed, known as a vessel element, has secondary material laid down upon the inner sides of the walls, but this material is laid down unevenly, leaving thin areas called pits which usually coincide with pits of neighbouring vessel elements, and vary between genera in shape, size and arrangement. Details of pit shape are often invisible in charcoals, but the pits themselves are usually clearly in an 'opposite' arrangement where they are in vertical rows with one row of pits beside or opposite to those of the next row, or 'alternate' where the pits are fitted in alternately with those of the next row. The end walls of each element in heartwood may be broken down altogether, leaving merely a rim round the edge when the vessel becomes a tube, and this is known as simple perforation. Sometimes the end walls disappear in part, leaving a grid or ladder-like structure, scalariform perforation, or a network, reticulate perforation. Scalariform perforations may be further differentiated by whether there are few or many bars. The vessels of certain kinds of wood can also be distinguished by the presence of spiral thickening, an extra layer of material laid down spirally upon the cell wall.

Softwoods are examined in much the same way as hardwoods, except that in the transverse section almost all conifers are basically much alike, being composed of regularly arranged vertical tracheids which both provide support and conduct water (Plate XId). There are no vessels, and the most noticeable feature on this section is the much denser appearance of the late wood, where the tracheid walls are much thicker than in that formed earlier, and the dense late wood may in some timbers amount to as much as half of the total growth of one season. The change from thin to thick walls may be sudden or gradual, and this again is a generic or specific feature. The rays of a coniferous wood are uniseriate, except in rare instances when a small part of a ray may be biseriate. Resin canals, which appear as very large cells, are found in a few coniferous genera, but not in the majority. They are infrequently and irregularly spaced so that a very small section may not include any. In the tangential longitudinal section the same genera may have irregularly spaced resin canals included in the centre of some of the rays, which then appear boat-shaped and biseriate above and below the resin canals, although the other rays in the section will be uniseriate and straight-sided. The radial longitudinal section is very important in softwoods for a very minute feature known as crossfield pitting. These pits occur in the walls of the ray cells adjacent to vertical tracheids. Pits may be of various shapes, simple or with round, oval or slit-like openings, and borders of various widths, and these variations are constant in a genus. They are only visible for study at fairly high magnifications (about × 120).

The quantity of charcoals found on many archaeological sites makes it imperative that rapid methods of preparation for identification should be employed, since a fragment of charcoal of an indeterminate wood, perhaps distorted by heat, may require some hours for its identification. Ideally every fragment large enough should be examined, but in practice there is usually insufficient time to be so thorough, and a preliminary sorting can be quickly made with a × 10 hand lens, grouping the fragments into kinds that appear to be alike. This magnification may, with experience, suffice to determine the British ring-porous woods, but is usually inadequate for more than a rough grouping into types of wood for the diffuse-porous species, into those with numerous vessels evenly dispersed, those with fewer vessels arranged in strings or clusters, those with some very broad and conspicuous rays, and so on. Oak, a ring-porous timber, is normally fairly easy to distinguish, and much time could be saved if specimens of it were picked out from the rest by the archaeologist before submitting the whole group to the wood-anatomist. A quick check would then probably be enough to confirm the oak determinations. The first sorting out is done almost entirely on the transverse section, because a × 10 hand lens is of relatively little use on the longitudinal sections of charcoals, which are particularly hard to see. A detailed examination has then to be made using a microscope, and good detail can be observed at magnifications of about 40–50 and 100–120. Magnification above 120 is of limited use, except for special details, because a charcoal section is seldom flat, although this depends upon the preparation of the specimen.

Charcoals can be prepared in two main ways. The simplest and quickest way, which is obviously preferable if it gives adequate results, is to make fresh breaks in the charcoal in the three planes already described, to give a transverse section and radial and tangential longitudinal sections. Charcoal normally breaks quite cleanly, though not always exactly in the desired plane, but any unevenness leads to difficulties at higher magnification because the depth of focus decreases proportionately as the magnification increases. The charcoal fragment is broken into at least three small pieces, each presenting a clean, newly-broken face in the transverse, radial or tangential plane, and they are mounted on small lumps of plasticine on a glass slide for examination in turn under the microscope. If this method does not reveal enough, or accurate enough, detail the charcoal fragments, already broken to show the required sections, can be impregnated in a synthetic resin such as Lakeside 70C, ground down with grades of carborundum, and mounted on a microscope slide by the same technique as is used for making sections of rocks and soil samples. This is a slow and laborious process, requiring a certain amount of apparatus, and is impracticable where large numbers of specimens are involved, and moreover the heat needed for impregnation often causes cracking and warping. An alternative method is impregnation with Celloidin, followed by sectioning on a microtome,[12] but this is also very laborious where numbers of specimens are involved. It would be advantageous if an impregnating medium for cold application were available, to reduce the time involved and avoid any heating of the specimen.

A quicker and easier method of producing thin sections of charcoal would also be of assistance where microphotography is necessary. A fresh break on a piece of charcoal does not remain clean and bright indefinitely. It becomes dusty and smudged after a while, and though it may be kept as a piece of evidence, if it is to be re-examined in after-years it will probably have to be broken again. It is therefore valuable to be able to record the section permanently by means of a microphotograph, but it has already been noted that charcoals very seldom break perfectly flat, and it is therefore difficult, especially at magnifications of 100 or more, to get a photograph which is in focus all over the field. This difficulty should not be experienced when dealing with thin sections, either cut or ground, and so the practical detail of recording evidence is simplified where thin sections of charcoal can be used.

One of the difficulties in identifying charcoals is that of lighting the specimen. Charcoal is always dense and black, and often has smooth, highly reflecting surfaces. It is therefore important that the light should fall on the surface at a fairly high oblique angle, which can be achieved by having an internally lit microscope, so arranged that the light passes down the microscope tube as a hollow cylinder, which is then reflected on to the point upon which the objective is focused. Other forms of top lighting can also be used very well, but they become less efficient at very high magnifications when the objective is almost touching the specimen. The best angle of light varies between one specimen and another, and the disadvantage of the internal vertical illuminator is that the angle cannot be altered.

Dry wood from desert sites can vary considerably in condition, from very hard and solid to brittle and powdery, and is often heavily impregnated with crystals of gypsum and other minerals. It is frequently found in the form of an object which cannot be broken to provide a sample, but if it is merely the remains of beams or unidentifiable fragments of furniture or other objects it can often be treated as charcoal and examined on a fresh break, or impregnated, ground and mounted on a slide. Dry wood of this kind will only break to give a flat section if the wood is considerably decayed, but yet retains its form, otherwise it will break unevenly on the transverse section, leaving a torn end which shows nothing, and in this state it will have to be treated as a piece of modern wood, by sectioning on a microtome. But this leads to further difficulties, since it cannot be cut dry without tearing the cell walls, and boiling the specimen in water or caustic soda, as modern wood is prepared, may cause it to collapse. The wooden furniture and objects found in the tombs at Jericho appeared to be very dry when the tombs were first opened, but within minutes of the air being admitted were covered with drops of moisture. The wood mainly retained its shape, though it was calculated that it had shrunk as much as 25% in a radial and tangential direction, and somewhat less in length, but it was completely 'denatured', being apparently composed of tiny particles, probably of lignin, which retained their relative positions until they were disturbed, and the whole resembled cocoa powder gone into lumps. It is not known why this wood survived at all in this condition, and it has been found extremely difficult to deal with. It can, to a certain extent, be impregnated with synthetic resins, but not without causing considerable deformity, and so far the best way of identifying many of the specimens appears to be by examination of a fresh break. It is thus clear that ancient wood preserved in dry, or apparently dry, conditions presents a number of problems which are not yet solved, and further experiment is needed in the hope of finding an impregnating medium which would preserve objects without altering their external appearance and yet could be easily sectioned, as we already have for the treatment of waterlogged wood.

Wet wood may come from lakes, swamps, bogs, wells, river-banks or estuaries, ancient forests submerged by the sea or shipwrecks, when further problems may be presented because of the presence of salt or other minerals. Large branches of oak from between high- and low-water marks in the Lyonesse surface at Clacton, Essex, dating from the Mesolithic period, were impossible to section with a razor because all the large vessels were lined with a deposit of pyrite. This was hard and tore the surrounding tissue when compressed by the action of cutting, although specimens of diffuse-porous woods (maple, etc.) from the same conditions were easily sectioned by hand while still wet. It is most important that excavated wood should be kept in the same state of humidity that it was in before excavation. Wood from under the sea can therefore be kept immersed in changes of fresh water until examination, thus helping to reduce its salinity.

Impregnation of wet wood to prevent deformation and to preserve it in a condition fit for handling can be carried out by immersing it over a period in a water-miscible synthetic wax, polyethylene glycol. When thoroughly impregnated the specimens are removed from the wax bath, drained, when the wax hardens, and the surplus is removed by gentle wiping with a cloth damped in cold water. The wood then has the appearance of damp wood newly excavated, but the main advantage for the wood-anatomist is that it is soft enough for sections to be cut from it in the hand with a razor, and although these are apt to curl, as is frequently the trouble with tissues sectioned in wax, they uncurl rapidly in water, and can be floated off on to a slide for thorough examination. Unfortunately this method has, so far, been unsuccessful for dry wood, but wood excavated damp, but not thoroughly wet, can be kept damp and usually contains enough water to take up the wax without further wetting.[13]

The specimens or sections being set up, their structure can be studied three-dimensionally, and grouped and identified by means of suitable keys. These are either dichotomous, when one of two alternative features is selected which leads on to another pair of alternatives, gradually eliminating all but the correct genus, or a punched card or table key. The advantage of the latter keys is that for material in poor condition features can be picked out in any order and there is less risk of being unable to determine an identity because a feature in the middle of the series is invisible. Good examples of a lens key and microscope key of this kind are those produced by the Forest Products Research Laboratory at Princes Risborough,[14] although they deal with commercial timbers only. For charcoal identification a specially devised punch card key using both macroscopic and microscopic features will be found useful. Finally, the identity being reduced to a few possibles, the specimen is compared with wood and charcoal specimens of known woods, and also with normal sections. A good representative collection of named modern specimens, both wood and charcoal, is thus a vital tool. It is perhaps worth mentioning here that the roots of trees may be present in the ashes of fires, and these require a special comparative collection, and up to the present have tended to be overlooked.

In common with some other specialist studies of which archaeologists are making increasing use, the identification of timbers is mainly valuable as an aid to interpretation in conjunction with all the other evidence. This consists primarily of the archaeological and stratigraphical evidence of the site, the pottery and other artifacts, pollen, bones and shells, but wood and charcoal remains can often give valuable environmental information, besides the direct evidence of materials used for various purposes. Timber for structures, tools and weapons was probably selected for its purpose, to some extent at least, because of certain qualities, as well as for ease in felling and working with the tools available. Builders or craftsmen probably travelled some distance to find the timbers they required for their houses or their tools, and would certainly have taken trouble to make the hafts and shafts of their weapons of the best material available.

Firewood is more likely to have been supplied from near at hand, since in few areas of north-western Europe, at least, except in very cold areas or periods, can there have been a great shortage of fuel until a comparatively late date. Charcoal from hearths may therefore give some indication of the type of vegetation in the immediate locality, indicating close woodland, scrub, or open grassland with individual trees. In desert conditions, of course, it must have been necessary to fetch firewood from a distance, as Arab women do today, going as much as ten miles from their homes to collect huge bundles of scrub and thorn. In such areas fuel frequently consists of small shrubs and sub-shrubs, which increases the number of possible species considerably. For this reason it is advisable for the worker dealing with archaeological charcoal to limit his geographical field, since it is essential to know thoroughly the existing woody flora of the site. The fuel would also have been augmented by the waste material from timber collected for other purposes, and also probably by broken and discarded domestic objects.

Sometimes the wood from which an object is made is found to be an alien, that is, a species which either does not at present grow anywhere near the area concerned, or, it may be, never could possibly have grown anywhere near it because of what is already known of soil conditions, climate or altitude. In such case great caution is needed. It may be that the object as such was imported from elsewhere, either in course of trade or as a personal possession by a migrant or traveller, or it may indicate trade in timber in bulk, such as is known from literary evidence to have taken place from Syria to Egypt. But another factor to be taken into account is that ancient wood, and particularly charcoal, is often very difficult to identify with certainty and a determination of this kind may need to be supported by other evidence, perhaps of other macroscopic plant remains, of objects such as pottery, weapons or jewellery which can be paralleled with objects in the area where the suspected timber is known to grow or to have grown, or of written evidence of trade between the two places, as already stated. The horse chestnut, *Aesculus hippocastanum*, is a case in point. For various reasons this species is believed to be an introduction to this country, probably as late as the sixteenth century, and it is certainly native to the Balkans, but a number of identifications of this tree have been made, dating between the Neolithic and Romano-British periods, and it is interesting to note that they are nearly all of specimens of charcoal. These determinations have not upset the established belief, because *Aesculus* may easily be confused with *Populus* and *Salix*, unless the specimen is so good that it is possible to see very minute features, and this is frequently not the case. Thus the specimens may have been wrongly identified, or may possibly be intrusive. Points like these have to be borne in mind when endeavouring to interpret the meaning of a list of timbers represented among the wood and charcoal fragments from a site.

Present knowledge of the vegetation of Britain, Ireland and Scandinavia at different periods is fairly extensive, a large amount of work having been done on pollen and macroscopic plant remains from bogs, and therefore the identification of wood from sites in these areas contributes chiefly material to fill in a picture of which the main outlines and considerable details are already known. But it may be that evidence will be found for certain trees having returned to these islands, or having become widespread, earlier than is at present thought. The discovery of beech, *Fagus sylvatica*, in South Wales in the Iron Age proves an earlier and wider distribution for this tree than had been believed previously. The flora of the Mediterranean basin and the Middle East in the past is not so well known, although a good deal of work has been done on modern floras of the countries concerned, particularly since the Second World War. This problem is complicated by the facts of millennia of civilized life, constant movements of peoples and trade from early times, with consequent introductions of new plants and destruction of indigenous floras. Trees and plants valued for their timber, fruits or other products have probably been transported from one area to another by man, so that it is difficult in many cases to prove whether a plant is spontaneous or naturalized so long ago as to have escaped from cultivation and appear to be native. Some plants have certainly been greatly altered by selection and cultivation, and possibly grafting also, and it may conceivably be possible in the future, from investigation of grafted and natural samples, to discover when and where this practice began. These problems require much further study, including that from the linguistic angle, since some guidance can be obtained from the fact of an ancient language having names for certain plants.

Much more information of value might be discovered from the identification of timbers used for known purposes, for structures, for handles of tools and weapons, for domestic equipment, and so on, and this requires co-operation between excavator and wood-anatomist. The latter usually receives boxes or bags of samples marked with some such legend as 'PK 47/109' or 'Mer 15a NW Black Fill', which is meaningless to anyone not knowing the site or method of excavation, and this is where help can be given to the wood-anatomist by the excavator, to the advantage of both. If the specialist can be given some idea of what is expected, or hoped for, from the identification of the various samples submitted—'This may be a sleeper beam from a dwelling'; 'These were found associated with three axe-heads: could they be the remains of axe-handles?' —he is more likely to be able to make useful comments on his findings. It is his business to give any environmental and botanical information he can in his report, and to interpret his identifications in the light of such information. All this must then be interpreted and weighed by the archaeologist with all his other archaeological and environmental evidence, if specialist studies of various groups of material such as wood and charcoal are to play their full part in building up our knowledge of ancient times and peoples.

REFERENCES

1 TURNER, E. G. 1956. *J. Rom. Studies* 46, 115
2 GODWIN, H. 1960. *Proc. Prehist. Soc.* 26, 1
3 CLARK, J. G. D. 1950. *Ibid.* 16, 109–13
4 WRIGHT, E. V. and CHURCHILL, D. M. 1965. *Ibid.* 31, 1–24
5 WARD, H. and ELGEE, F. 1940. *Ibid.* 6, 90–95
6 WATERMAN, D. M. 1959. *Arch.* 97, 85–87
7 KELLER, F. 1866. *Lake Dwellings of Switzerland*, London
8 LUCAS, A. 1962, rev. ed. HARRIS, J. R. *Ancient Egyptian Materials and Industries*, London
9 YOUNG, R. 1958. *Am. J. Arch.* 62, 148–50

10 KENYON, K. M. 1960 and 1965. *Excavations at Jericho*, London, vols. 1 and 2
11 RUDENKO, S. I. 1960. *Culture of the Population of the Central Altai in the Scythian Period*, Moscow/Leningrad (in Russian)
12 Forest Products Research Laboratory. 1951. *The Preparation of Wood for microscopic examination*, D.S.I.R. Leaflet 40
13 ORGAN, R. M. 1959. *Studies in Conservation* 4, 96–105
14 Forest Products Research Laboratory. 1952 and 1961. *Identification of Hardwoods*, D.S.I.R. Bulletins 25 and 46

16 The Condition of 'Wood' from Archaeological Sites

WOOD CAN SURVIVE the centuries in a great variety of conditions and may be found hard or soft, brittle or tough, heavily impregnated with other materials or thoroughly leached. It often exhibits some facet of degrade by biological or chemical agencies with which is associated a very high moisture content. On the other hand, when incomplete combustion has occurred and the wood has been converted to charcoal, this charcoal will persist with little or no visible alteration unless it has been subject to very wet situations and distorted by pressure.

After the bombing of Rotterdam in 1940, the timber piles on which a large part of the city had been built attracted the attention of Varossieau[1] who made an anatomical investigation of the wood. His observations formed part of the evidence that certain fungi will decay wood by growing through the middle layer of the secondary cell wall and cause a degrade of wood termed 'soft rot'.[2-4]

There are many instances in which one suspects that biological or chemical degrade, or both, have taken place, yet no conclusive evidence has remained. The problem resolves itself into examining site conditions, observing the state of the wood before and after its removal from the place of burial, and studying the nature of the material in which it is buried. For example, under the Jewel Tower, Westminster, elm piles some six feet in length and pointed at one end formed the foundation for the fourteenth-century building. During repair work it was noted that some of the piling was in a decayed condition. The subsoil in one area consisted of a disturbed upper layer about a foot deep, fine green-grey clay some four feet thick, and a layer of sandy gravel beneath. Piles driven through the clay and projecting some six inches to a foot into the sandy gravel showed interesting differences in the process of decay. The tip in the sand was little more than a stain and had apparently been thoroughly decayed by wood-rotting fungi. The upper region in the disturbed topsoil layer and much of the heartwood lower down was also decayed. But the outer portion (about 1–2 in. in from the surface) of the middle section, in the anaerobic clay, was relatively sound and no traces of fungi could be detected. Thus there appear to be soil conditions under which the decaying organisms will not flourish whereas at quite close quarters decay is active.

In Dover,[5] oak piling from Roman harbour works was again found in two distinct sets. The timber as a whole had retained its shape, and presumably size, quite well and tool marks were still sharp. One set of piles had been considerably softened so that a finger could be pushed into the surface with little difficulty, and when cut up the wood broke cleanly across the grain, showing that the strength properties were greatly reduced. Other piles very closely associated with these were, however, found in a much tougher condition. The surface in some cases was softened, but the wood was extremely difficult to break across the grain and in part at least it retained a very considerable tensile strength. The chemical analysis[6] showed that the ash content in both sets was abnormally high; in addition the tougher wood in fact came from slow-grown timber which (in its natural state) one would have expected to be weaker. The reasons for such differences would be important to discover.

The most common feature of buried wood found in a well-preserved, recognizably 'woody' state is its so-called 'waterlogged' condition. This is distinct from the use of the term for wood that has become saturated with water and sunk. Softwood logs recently raised from Norwegian rivers after lying submerged for about a century show little change apart from an increased permeability, although the effect of the presumably low temperature in this case is difficult to assess. The outstanding characteristics of ancient 'waterlogged' wood, on the other hand, appear to be a very high moisture content (up to 700% on the oven-dry weight) allied to an extremely high shrinkage on drying, particularly in the tangential direction, and when dry the distorted timber is extremely hard and tough. Some botanical and chemical data are available,[7] and recent investigations[8,9] have been concerned with the mechanics of conserving woody material found in this condition. One is left with the thought that micro-organisms, including, perhaps, bacteria, may be responsible; or that continued subjection to the chemical effects of anaerobic waterlogged media might be sufficient—the results in both cases being similar: hydrolytic breakdown of the cell wall material.[10] Any attempt at isolating the micro-organisms present in such material is likely to be some centuries too late to find the original causal organisms still active. Nevertheless, accurate field observations could make an immediate contribution, especially where backed by anatomical and chemical laboratory work.

Accurate observations of the state of the wood and the conditions of burial could be important to fundamental research into the nature of the plant cell wall and the physiology of decay by micro-organisms. Analysis of a particular tree species on similar site conditions at progressive stages of degrade might well yield information as to the chemical and physical nature of the cell wall, which is not readily seen in the undegraded state. This in turn could yield information as to the mode of action of the micro-organism causing the degrade.

From the archaeological point of view, such studies might make it possible to identify not only the recognizable wood remains, but also the various 'fibrous residues' and stains in so-called post holes, sleeper trenches and coffins where little or no botanical evidence remains. Even if the identification went no further than 'wood', it could, in many cases, be of considerable importance to be sure of this fact. At the same time it might be possible to interpret conditions under which the degrade occurred and this might well have an important bearing on other archaeological evidence.

REFERENCES

1 VAROSSIEAU, W. W. 1949. *Houte in alle Tijden* 1 (5), 331–87
2 BAILEY, I. W. and VESTAL, M. R. 1937. *J. Arnold Arboretumn 18*, 193–205
3 BARGHOORN, E. S. and LINDER, D. H. 1944. *Farlowia 1*, 395–467

4 Savory, J. G. 1954. *Ann. appl. Biol.* 41, 336–47

5 Rahtz, P. A. 1958. *Archaeologia Cantiana* 72, 111–37

6 Farmer, R. H. 1955. Private communication from Forest Products Research Laboratory, D.S.I.R.

7 Barghoorn, E. S. 1949. *Papers of R. S. Peabody Found. for Archaeol.* 4, 49–83

8 Organ, R. M. 1954. *Studies in Conservation* 4, 96–105

9 Rosenquist, A. M. 1954. *Ibid.* 13–21 and 62–72

10 Barghoorn, E. S. 1949. *Harvard Bot. Mus. Leaflets* 14, 1–20

17 Dendrochronology

BRYANT BANNISTER

THE EMERGENCE OF DENDROCHRONOLOGY as a significant archaeological dating tool can be precisely determined in both time and space—June 22, 1929; Showlow, Arizona. To be sure, speculation on the nature of tree-rings can be traced back to the third-century BC writings of Theophrastus, and certainly the detailed observations of a long succession of botanists and naturalists have been instrumental in our understanding of growth rings and their implications.[85] But it remained for the astronomer A. E. Douglass, the recognized pioneer of the science of dendrochronology, to apply tree-ring phenomena in a systematic attack on the chronological problems of archaeology.

Douglass began his examination of tree-rings in 1901 while searching for a tool to be used in the study of sunspot cycles. He first became aware of the potential archaeological applications of his work some two decades later, at which time he commenced a ten-year investigation into the dating of the spectacular American Indian ruin Pueblo Bonito. This project stands out as a model of inter-disciplinary co-operation and culminated in the establishment of construction dates not only for Pueblo Bonito but for more than forty additional major ruins in the American South-West as well.[13,60] The dramatic conclusion to this historically important project took place on a summer night in the small town of Showlow where Douglass, after carefully studying the day's collection of tree-ring specimens excavated from a nearby ruin, realized that he had finally spanned the gap between a centuries-long floating chronology, made up from ancient construction beams, and a dated tree-ring record extending backwards from modern times.[14] The gap was bridged, scores of prehistoric ruins were immediately assigned absolute dates, and archaeological tree-ring dating became of age!

BASIC PRINCIPLES

The term dendrochronology refers both to the method of employing tree-rings as a measurement of time, wherein the principal application is to archaeology, and to the process of inferring past environmental conditions that existed when the rings were being formed, mainly applicable to climatology. While some would prefer to restrict the appellation to the former usage, it matters little to the archaeologist, for he stands to benefit from all aspects of tree-ring research.

The basic principles involved in dendrochronology are deceptively simple. Tree-rings, which are so obvious on the cross-sections of most trees, can be more accurately described as the transverse sections of successive layers of xylem growth—each layer having been formed by the tree in response to some environmental fluctuation, normally of an annual nature in seasonal climates. In conifers, the annual ring is composed of two parts: an inner band of large light-coloured cells that merges, sometimes very gradually, with an outer band of thicker-walled, dark-coloured cells which in turn usually terminates abruptly, leaving a sharply defined outer edge. A number of angiosperms and shrubs have annual rings of somewhat similar gross characteristics, but tree-rings of considerable complexity are also known to exist.[44]

In those regions where dendrochronology has successfully been applied to archaeological specimens there are basically two types of tree-ring series commonly found (Plate XII); or perhaps the two types should best be termed end points along a continuum of variation. In the first type, the rings are of relatively uniform thickness, as measured along a radius, and often exhibit a slow algebraic decrease in width as the tree approaches maturity. Such ring series lacking in distinctive character are termed complacent (Plate XIIa). In contrast, the second type of ring record is distinguished by variability of individual ring widths, even though there may be a gradual decrease in the relative size of rings as the tree grows older. These series (Plate XIIb, c) are called sensitive and are far more suitable for dendrochronological purposes.

Under certain conditions, contemporaneous ring records formed by sensitive trees will show remarkable similarity when compared with each other. The patterns of narrow and broad rings in one tree will closely match the patterns found in other trees (Plate XIIb, c). Cross-dating, which is based on this phenomenon, can be defined as the identification in different trees of the same ring patterns, each series of rings representing exactly the same period of years. It is cross-dating that stands as the fundamental principle underlying tree-ring dating, and it must be present before either absolute or relative dates can be derived.

The cross-dating principle gives rise to the two most important facets of tree-ring research. First, in regions that contain modern cross-datable trees which can serve as controls, proper application will permit the assignment of calendar years to each of the individual rings within a specimen. It is this feature, of course, which has been responsible for archaeological tree-ring dating in the absolute sense. Even where modern tree-ring controls are not available, relative dating is still possible. Second, the very fact that ring patterns which lead to cross-dating are present in trees at all implies the existence of some environmental factor, or complex of factors, which not only fluctuates itself on a year-to-year basis (when dealing with annual rings) but also has the capacity to induce similar and simultaneous growth responses on the part of trees over a given geographical area. The isolation and understanding of such controlling factors has been of interest to tree physiologists and dendrochronologists alike.

It should not be assumed that the conditions responsible for cross-dating are the same wherever the phenomenon occurs. For example, in the semi-arid regions of south-western United States, soil moisture is apparently the dominant controlling factor, whereas in Alaska and other northern latitudes temperature seems to be the chief determinant. Nor should it be assumed that cross-dating is universally present, for, in fact, only certain trees in an area cross-date with each other, only certain areas in the world contain cross-datable trees, and cross-dating between separated areas is usually non-existent.

A considerable body of literature pertaining to the basic principles of tree-growth and its dendrochronological implications has been produced. In the American South-West a few of the more important works are by Douglass;[11,12,15] Ferguson;[24] Glock;[41] Glock,

Studhalter, and Agerter;[44] and Schulman,[80] Bell,[3] Hawley,[47] Schulman,[77] and Willey[96] have treated the Mississippi drainage, while Weakly[91,92] and Will[94,95] have carried out investigations in the Great Plains of the United States. Lyon[57-59] has reported on New England tree-ring studies. The basic contribution to Alaskan dendrochronology is by Giddings,[28] although additional pertinent studies have been made by Giddings[30,31,33,35] and Oswalt.[68,69] Other treated regions in the Western Hemisphere include parts of Canada, western America, Mexico, and South America.[80]

Scandinavian scientists have produced a number of excellent studies. Some English-language summaries are Eklund[23] for Sweden, Høeg[48] for Norway, Holmsgaard[49] for Denmark, and Mikola[62] for Finland. Hustich[52,53] has dealt with trees throughout the northern latitudes. The works of Huber and Jazewitsch[50] of the Forestry-Botany Institutes of Tharandt and Munich are outstanding. Dobbs[9,10] and Schove[72,73] have been active in reporting tree-ring studies carried out both in the British Isles and in Scandinavia, and Messeri[61] has published on tree growth in Italy. To date little work has been done in Africa, although a few investigations have been made in Asia—Rudakov[70] in Russia, Gindel[37] in Israel, DeBoer[8] in Java, and Kohara[55] and Nishioka[63] in Japan. Bell and Bell[5] have provided a rather pessimistic view of the situation in New Zealand.

It should be emphasized that the above citations by no means constitute a complete list of tree-ring publications, although they are reasonably representative of the basic work being done in the designated regions. For the most part, these citations have been chosen because they deal with fundamentals and reflect the potentialities of tree-ring dating rather than merely recording archaeological results. Wherever possible, the more recent publications with bibliographies have been given so that the reader may investigate further if he wishes. A much more comprehensive review of tree-growth studies is presented by Glock,[42] with a highly critical assessment of dendrochronology in general.

REQUISITES OF ARCHAEOLOGICAL TREE-RING DATING

Before the tree-ring method can be applied to archaeological problems in any given region, there are several favouring circumstances that must exist and, unfortunately, these necessary conditions are by no means universal in nature. The first requirement is an ample supply of wood or charcoal tree-ring specimens in association with the archaeological environment to be dated. Not only must the prehistoric inhabitants of an area have used wood extensively, preferably for construction purposes, but the wood must be preserved so that both cellular and ring structure remain evident. Large areas of the world are immediately ruled out because either wood was not used extensively in ancient times or what was used has long since rotted away. On the other hand, certain regions are particularly favourable: the American South-West, northern Mexico, some arctic areas, Turkey, Egypt and various places in Europe and Asia where local conditions have ensured preservation. Charcoal, one of the most indestructible of materials as long as it remains uncrushed, is an excellent source of tree-ring records but its presence in quantity in archaeological sites is in part related to the cultural practices of the original inhabitants.[2]

The second major requirement for the establishment of tree-ring dating is that the specimens cross-date. As indicated previously, for cross-dating to occur the samples must contain clearly defined rings that show fluctuations of thickness throughout the series. The rings whether annual or multiple must be the result of a periodicity in growth factors which induces similar responses (measurable in variable ring widths) in trees within the region, and the specimens must contain enough rings to permit positive identification of like patterns in different pieces.

As long as tree-ring samples are available from a particular site and the specimens cross-date with each other, relative dates are possible. The establishment of absolute dates, however, is another matter. Even though contemporaneous relative dated specimens may be merged into a composite whole, forming a floating chronology, it is still necessary to build a known tree-ring chronology back far enough to overlap and cross-date with the unknown segment in order to achieve absolute dating. This is known as chronology building (Fig. 33) and although simple in concept usually requires considerable time and effort to accomplish. Starting with modern samples of known date, successively older and older specimens are cross-dated and incorporated into the matrix until a long-range tree-ring chronology is established. Depending on the materials available, this procedure may take many years to perform if, indeed, it is possible at all. Once a precisely dated master chronology is produced, however, the ring patterns contained in samples of unknown age may be cross-dated with the master chronology and assigned absolute dates.

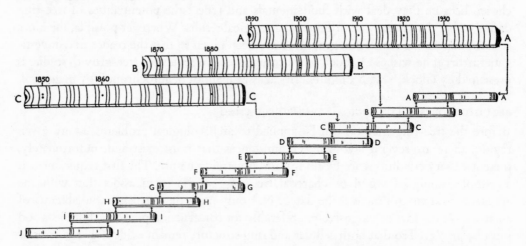

Fig. 33 Chronology building. A: radial sample from a living tree cut after the 1939 growing season; B–J: specimens taken from old houses and successively older ruins. The ring patterns match and overlap back into prehistoric times. After Stallings.[84]

COLLECTION AND ANALYSIS

The collection of tree-ring specimens is guided by the basic aim of preserving as complete a record of the ring series as possible. A full cross-section is preferable to a core or radial sample, although it often is not practical to obtain a complete transect when dealing with living trees or archaeological structures which are to be preserved. Various types of coring tools have been developed: among others, the Swedish increment borer which is designed for sampling living softwood trees, the brace-driven tubular borer with circular saw teeth which has proved effective on prehistoric beams,[12] and the power-driven long-core extractor developed by Bowers.[6] New type tools for sampling museum pieces and archaeological timbers are currently being tested.

Specialized techniques for collecting wood and charcoal from excavations are so closely related to particular field conditions that it is impracticable to describe them all. In general, however, special care must be exercised to prevent damage or loss of outside rings. Charcoal and certain types of wood usually need immediate application of some preservative. A solution of gasoline saturated with paraffin wax is both economical and effective but other preservatives may be equally useful. The standard archaeological procedures for handling any delicate and valuable artifact are called for, and detailed notes on provenience, physiology, and ecology of the collection area are vital.[41,2]

Before actual study can begin, specimens must be surfaced so that cellular structure is visible and the ring series may be examined with clarity. The importance of this step cannot be overemphasized since adequate surfaces are absolutely essential in the process of achieving precise dates. Charcoal and soft or rotten wood can readily be prepared with a razor blade, a technique that is rapid but fairly difficult to master. Excellent surfaces on small sections can be obtained with a sliding microtome, but for large cross-sections sanding is highly recommended. Although small hand-held belt sanders utilizing a series of graded sandpapers will do a presentable job, there now exist specially designed sanding devices which are capable of producing full transect surfaces that satisfy the most stringent requirements. One such device, the Bowers-Vossbrinck sanding machine, employs the 'abrasion along a line' principle and uses metal cutting belts 12 inches wide.

Noteworthy discussions of collection and sample preparation practices are to be found in Douglass,[16-20] Glock,[41] Hall,[45] Scantling,[71] and Smiley.[81]

In the analysis of tree-ring specimens for archaeological dating purposes the first objective is the establishment of cross-dating between samples. When absolute dating is involved, the process is carried one step further and cross-dated specimens are matched against a master chronology which itself is a product of previously cross-dated pieces. In its simplest form, therefore, the problem is reduced to recording individual ring series and comparing them with other series. Consequently, the initial requirement is the positive identification of each of the visible growth increments within the sample. Rings that are present on only a portion of their circumference, so-called 'false rings' or 'lines' which do not represent a full season's growth, microscopic rings—these and other anomalies must be recognized before cross-dating can be attempted. The subject of ring 'reading' is treated in detail by Douglass,[20] Glock,[41] and Schulman.[80] Additional problems such as completely absent rings (see references above) can only be solved through the process of cross-dating itself.

All of the different systems of tree-ring dating, and there are several currently being used throughout the world, are nothing more than alternate ways of representing growth patterns and establishing cross-dating. For the most part, the various techniques have been adopted because they are particularly suited to certain local conditions of tree growth and certain types of ring chronologies. Since the best known of these, the Douglass System, is basic to most subsequently developed methods, it alone will be discussed here. Further explanations of this system are to be found in Bannister and Smiley,[2] Douglass,[11,12,20] Glock,[40,41] Schulman,[80] and Stallings.[84]

The Douglass method, which has been most successfully applied in the American South-West, is primarily useful where highly sensitive trees constitute the main source of datable specimens and the amount of correlation between ring records is often of a very high degree. The technique emphasizes, first, those rings which deviate from the normal—noticeably narrow or broad rings—and, second, the internal relationship of these rings within the overall series. Comparison of one ring record with another is accomplished in three ways: the memory method, skeleton plots, and precisely measured ring widths. The memory method simply entails memorizing all of the ring patterns encountered. It is, of course, a very rapid and convenient way of comparing specimens but it does require a thorough knowledge of the local chronology. For the experienced investigator, however, the memory method supplemented by comparative wood samples is perhaps the most satisfactory way of verifying cross-dating.

When one is working with large quantities of materials or in unfamiliar areas, either temporally or geographically, the skeleton plot has proved to be an exceedingly useful tool.[41,84] Basically a specialized graph depicting the relative widths of diagnostic rings (Fig. 34), the skeleton plot has the advantage of being free of any age trend within the specimen since the size of each ring is judged in relation to neighbouring rings (compare Fig. 34A, B, with Fig. 35A, B). Thus skeleton plots of a standard scale can rapidly be compared with each other and, if cross-dating is found to exist, the plots may be merged to provide an easily understood representation of the site or local chronology (Fig. 34A). The skeleton plot method is considered only a preliminary step in the dating process, however, and it must be used with caution since it records only the most striking characteristics of a ring series rather than the totality of traits upon which dating must depend.

Various measuring devices designed to accurately record widths along a radius have been developed. The Craighead-Douglass measuring instrument,[19] the De Rouen Dendro-Chronograph, the Addo-X designed by the Swedish Forestry Research Institute,[22] and the German machine developed at the Forestry-Botany Institute in Munich[54] are but a few. After the measured values are translated into plotted graphs (Fig. 35) both visual and statistical comparisons can readily be made. Since absolute values are involved, however, standardization or correction for the effect of age is frequently necessary before the material can be used for the study of the relation between climate and growth. Age trend line introduction and standardization processes employed in the Douglass System are discussed by Schulman[79,80] and by Smiley, Stubbs and Bannister.[83] After standardization, the plotted curves express yearly values as percentage departures from average growth. Fritts (personal communication) is currently engaged in adapting standardizing processes to electronic computer techniques.

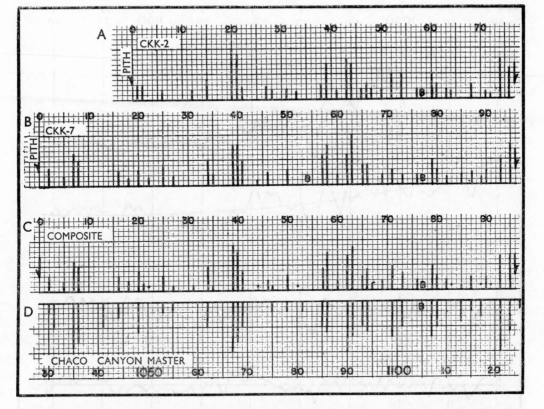

Fig. 34 Comparison of skeleton plots. A and B: skeleton plots of the ring series in two beams from the prehistoric ruin Kin Kletso, Chaco Canyon, New Mexico; C: composite plot of A and B; D: regional master chronology for Chaco Canyon. Matching of C with D establishes tentative dating of specimens (see text). The length of each vertical bar on the graph is inversely proportional to the relative width of the ring; average width rings are not recorded, and extra large rings are indicated by the letter B.

Another tree-ring dating method once used in south-western United States was developed by Gladwin.[38,39] This system depended upon a statistically constructed variation of the skeleton plot which recorded all rings. In Alaska, Turkey, Egypt, and New Zealand the Douglass System has been employed. In the wetter climates of Europe and in Scandinavia, the lack of highly sensitive trees with strong cross-dating tendencies precludes the use of the Douglass System. Various methods of statistical analysis involving coefficients of parallel and opposite variation, logarithmic plotting, special mechanical devices for automatically comparing series, and other innovations have been devised.

No matter what system of tree-ring dating is used, the validity of the results depends upon the preciseness with which cross-dating can be accomplished. Absolute identification can be secured by means of the forecast-and-verification method, wherein additional ring characteristics are sought and compared after test correlations have been made. When a sufficient number of positive verifications are found, the probability of chance correlations becomes increasingly remote and accurate cross-dating is assured.

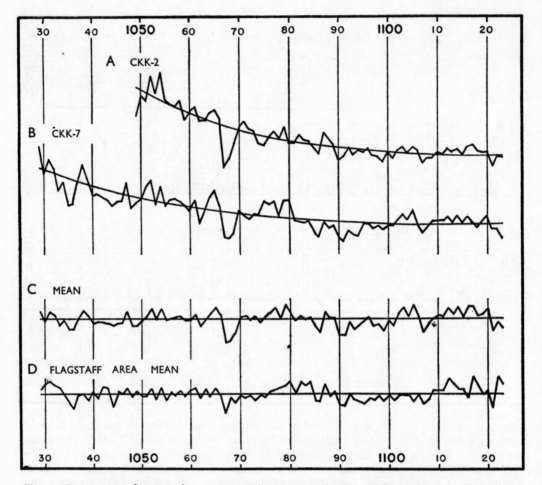

Fig. 35 Comparison of measured curves. A and B: measured ring widths (with standardizing lines superimposed) of the ring series in two beams from the prehistoric ruin Kin Kletso, Chaco Canyon, New Mexico; C: standardized mean of A and B with ring widths expressed as percentage departures from average growth; D: Flagstaff Area Mean in standardized form. Comparison of C with D leads to absolute dating of specimens (see text).

THE INTERPRETATION OF TREE-RING DATES

Once a tree-ring date has been established, its archaeological significance can vary greatly. After all, a tree-ring date can only be applied with authority to the specimen itself, and it may or may not be directly related to the archaeological context from which the specimen originated. There is a basic problem, consequently, of the time relationship that exists between the date of the specimen and the archaeological manifestation being dated.

Where the tree-ring dating method has been used extensively, as in Alaska and in the south-western United States, refined techniques of date interpretation have become increasingly necessary. The scheme that follows, therefore, is for the most part based on archaeological conditions as found in the American South-West, but because of their general nature the implied rules of interpretation should have relevancy wherever tree-ring dating is feasible.

The usual errors of interpretation that confront the archaeologist can be classified into four general categories:

Type 1. The association between the dated tree-ring specimen and the archaeological manifestation being dated is direct, but the specimen itself came from a tree that died or was cut prior to its use in the situation in question.

Type 2. The association between the dated tree-ring specimen and the archaeological manifestation being dated is not direct, the specimen having been used prior to the feature being dated.

Type 3. The association between the dated tree-ring specimen and the archaeological manifestation being dated is direct, but the specimen itself represents a later incorporation into an already existing feature.

Type 4. The association between the dated tree-ring specimen and the archaeological manifestation being dated is not direct, the specimen having been used later than the feature being dated.

If, for instance, a tree-ring date derived from a roofing timber were used to fix the time of construction of the roof, it would be an example of direct association; whereas, if the same date were used to determine the age of the contents of the roofed room, it would constitute an indirect application. It is quite possible, of course, to be confronted with a fifth type of general error, actually a variety of Types 2 and 4, which stems from the presence of intrusive specimens in unrelated archaeological environments. Since this problem is strictly an archaeological matter, however, it will not be discussed here.

The Type 1 error, wherein the association is direct but the dating is early, is usually caused by the presence of re-used beams. Judging from the situation in the American South-West, the re-use of construction timbers was an extremely common practice and hardly surprising when one considers that it was often far easier to salvage old logs from nearby abandoned structures than it was to fell growing trees with a stone axe. Obviously, the re-use of timbers in later structures can result in erroneous interpretation. Although the tree-ring date derived for the specimen may be perfectly correct, its application to the structure from which the specimen came would result in the assignment of too early a construction date. The aboriginal use of wind-fallen trees and driftwood logs, if not recognized as such, would introduce a similar tendency to overestimate the age of a feature incorporating this kind of wood. Even the stockpiling of beams before use would introduce a slight but consistent error of the same type.

In regions where wood was relatively scarce it is easy to envisage the problems caused by the re-use of old wood. Any wooden artifact might well tend to acquire heirloom status, and consequently any dates obtained would be subject to the Type 1 error. If a worked artifact were involved, even the process of shaping the wood could contribute to the magnitude of the error.

When the association is not direct but the dating is early, we are dealing with the Type 2 error. This usually comes about as a result of attempting to date artifacts within a room through the application of tree-ring dates derived from logs used in the construction of the room. The problem is basically archaeological in nature and resolves itself into the question of the temporal relationship between a room and its included contents. In short occupation sites the problem may be of only minor significance, whereas in sites of long occupation the problem can be critical. All too often there have been attempts to assign tree-ring dates to a particular item (pottery type for example) on the basis of dated beams in a room which might well have been constructed several centuries before the item in question was manufactured. Again, the tree-ring dates may be correct, their application to the construction of the room may be equally correct, but their assignment to the contents of the room could lead to highly fallacious interpretations. It is also theoretically possible to encounter Type 2 error when non-construction tree-ring dates derived from specimens in old trash are erroneously applied to later constructive features.

In the Type 3 error the association is direct but the dating is late. Over the course of years a prehistoric structure may well become weakened and in need of repair. If a particular roofing timber is replaced, perhaps centuries after the original roof was built, a tree-ring date derived from that timber would represent the time of repair and not the time of construction of the room. In some cases such dates, if recognized, are an advantage since they may give insight into the length of occupation of a particular structure. Dates from buildings that have been abandoned and then reoccupied and remodelled are subject to similar errors.

Finally, the Type 4 error occurs when the association is not direct but the dating is late. For the most part, this type of error is a result of applying dates from non-construction specimens to construction features. For example, firepit charcoal and wood or charcoal specimens found in room fill or trash mounds could conceivably give far more recent dates than the architectural features they are loosely associated with. On the other hand, non-construction dates used judiciously with construction dates from a single ruin may well indicate at least a minimum period of occupation.

Although the usual errors of interpretation can be identified with one or more of the four general types of error enumerated, it is not to be supposed that the specific error-producing situations mentioned are all that can be encountered. For one thing, these four types of chronological error can occur either independently or in combination with each other, and in the latter case the amount of error involved will either be increased or will tend to cancel out. Each dating problem, therefore, presents its own unique set of circumstances, and an understanding of both the dendrochronological and archaeological conditions involved is necessary for a satisfactory solution.

If it appears from the foregoing discussion that the chances of error associated with the time relationship problem are so high as to cast doubt on the interpretation of all tree-ring dates, it should be remembered that the extent of the danger involved is inversely proportional to the number of dated specimens from any given feature. If a single structure, for example, yields only one date, its interpretation is definitely subject to the types of error enumerated. If this same structure yielded 100 dated specimens the chances of fallacious interpretation would be greatly reduced. Errors of the Type 1 and

Type 3 varieties are particularly amenable to correction through the use of tree-ring date clusters. The fundamental premise is that if there are a number of tree-ring dates from a single structure or architectural feature which cluster about a single point in time, then dates that deviate from the cluster represent re-used or repair timbers, depending upon whether they are earlier or later than the majority. The same reasoning, with modification, would apply to groups of non-construction dates. In similar fashion, the clustering of archaeological traits or characteristics is useful when dealing with errors of the Type 2 and Type 4 varieties. Properly applied, the clustering techniques are powerful problem-solving tools, but they have limited use in those cases where there is an insufficiency of data.

A further complication in the interpretation of tree-ring dates is introduced when the condition of the outside of the dated specimen indicates that exterior rings have been lost through shaping, rot, burning, or some other eroding force. Again various techniques have been developed which tend to minimize this potential source of error. Both the time relationship problem and the problem of outside rings are discussed in detail by the author elsewhere.[1]

THE THREE MAJOR ARCHAEOLOGICAL APPLICATIONS OF TREE-RING DATA

A review of the archaeological applications of tree-ring data leads to a convenient threefold classification scheme. First, there are those applications wherein chronology, either relative or absolute, is the chief consideration. Second, there are those interpretations which depend upon the environmental histories recorded in the ring series themselves. And third, there is that class of fundamentally non-chronological information which stems from the juxtaposition of related dates and which gives rise to inferences of a cultural nature.

By far the most common use of archaeological tree-ring data has been in the field of chronology and the best example of this use is in the American South-West. Today in this area of heavy concentration of archaeological sites there exist a number of regional dendrochronologies which have relevance to fairly broad geographical areas, the longest extending back to the year 59 BC. In addition, more localized chronologies have been developed to aid in dating materials from specific locations.

The Laboratory of Tree-Ring Research at the University of Arizona in Tucson serves as a central repository for the major South-Western tree-ring collections and currently houses an estimated 125,000 individual archaeological specimens. These pieces come from about 2,000 prehistoric sites, some 800 of which have yielded at least one dated sample. Although precise numbers are difficult to determine, roughly 10,000 separate archaeological specimens from the South-West and adjacent regions have been dated.

A chronological history of the development of archaeological tree-ring dating in the South-West is given by Schulman,[80] and a more comprehensive view is to be found throughout the pages of the *Tree-Ring Bulletin* (1934 and following issues).[86] It would be impracticable to list all papers dealing with tree-ring dates in the region but recent summaries of dates have been published by Smiley;[82] Smiley, Stubbs, and Bannister;[83] and Bannister.[1]

As a result of the intensive tree-ring research carried out in the South-West, the pre-history of this area is better understood from the chronological point of view than it is in any other place in the world. Glock,[43] however, has questioned the accuracy of the South-West archaeological tree-ring calendars and has estimated that they may be 5% in error. Other workers, including the author, have confidence in the essential correct-ness of South-Western dendrochronologies, and this view is being continually confirmed by the cross-dating process and present-day research.

Outside the South-West there are numerous localities where the tree-ring dating method has been applied. Results range from the well-substantiated absolute dates of Alaska and Germany to the very preliminary analyses carried out on Turkish and Egyptian specimens. Not all of the studies here reported, however, have received un-qualified acceptance by other workers. Bell[3] has established dates for the Kincaid Site in Illinois; five log cabins in the Mississippi Drainage have been dated by Hawley;[47] Will[93-95] has derived dates from a number of sites in North and South Dakota; three dated sites in the Great Plains have been reported by Weakly;[89,90] and preserved wood in New England has been dated by Lyon.[56] Present efforts in the Missouri River Basin are summarized by Caldwell;[7] a summary for the Mississippi Valley is given by Bell[4] and for Nebraska by Weakly.[91] A current and as yet unreported project by the author on specimens from the Casas Grandes Site of Chihuahua, Mexico, has resulted in the establishment of a 500-year floating chronology.

The many dated sites in Alaska and the tracing of driftwood origins are largely the work of Giddings,[26-29, 32, 34, 36] Oswalt,[65-67] and VanStone.[87,88] Schulman[78] describes dating work carried out by Aandstad in Norway on six late structures whose approximate ages were already known. Ording[64] reports a floating chronology based on a hundred logs from Raknehaugen in south-eastern Norway, and Eidem[21] dated beams from eight houses in Flesberg. Høeg[48] has made a summary of Norwegian dating work.

Dendrochronological dating in Great Britain is documented by Schove[74,75] and Schove and Lowther,[76] while Zeuner[98] reports work on seventeenth-century wood from the City of London and on Beaker age stumps located near Clacton-on-Sea. Huber and his associates in Germany have succeeded in developing a relative chronology based on log palisades at the Bronze Age fort at Wasserburg or Bachau.[50, 51] Other floating chronologies have been derived for the Neolithic sites of Thaingen Weier and Egolzwil III in Switzerland and Ehrenstein near Ulm in south Germany and for the Bronze Age site of Zug-Sumph in Switzerland.[51] Absolute dating was accomplished on beams from the medieval town of Zeigenhain near Kassel, Germany.[50] Two recent summaries of European tree-ring work are Dobbs[10] and Zeuner.[98]

A prehistoric floating tree-ring chronology in Russia is reported by Zamotorin[97] while Kohara[55] documents an attempt to date a five-storied pagoda in Japan. The Middle East would appear to be potentially an excellent area for the development of at least relative chronologies. Although problems of importation and re-use of wood are associa-ted with Egypt, current research by the author on archaeological tree-ring specimens from Turkey and Egypt indicates that cross-dating exists in specific regions and that long relative chronologies are a definite possibility. Tree-ring dating in New Zealand is apparently not feasible because óf the lack of cross-dating.[5]

The relationship of tree growth to climate has been the subject of many dendrochronological studies, and certainly information of past environmental conditions as estimated from tree-rings constitutes a major contribution to archaeological knowledge. On the whole, however, the present state of tree-ring research indicates that caution should be exercised in making such interpretations. Tree growth itself is an immensely complex mechanism, and the various external and internal factors that influence growth and are responsible for the existence of cross-dating between trees are as yet imperfectly understood. Certain dominant controls such as temperature and soil moisture may be isolated, but quantitative evaluations of even these factors in ancient times are presently unobtainable. On a relative basis it may be possible to speak of droughts and other climatic fluctuations, but all too often the archaeologist has seized on such relative indications and has used them to explain away highly intricate archaeological situations and cultural behaviour. Great strides in understanding the significance of dendrochronologies have been made,[30] but still the newest mathematical techniques of analysis continue to demonstrate that the final answers have not yet been reached.[25]

A third application of tree-ring data is concerned with the internal relationships of associated dates rather than their placement in time. For example, Haury,[46] among others, demonstrated the exact developmental process of a multi-roomed pueblo in Arizona. If enough comparable data were available, it might be possible to identify culturally motivated construction practices among primitive peoples. Similarly, Huber found frequent building periods in the houses of Ehrenstein near Ulm and gained insight into the technology and economic conditions of the time. From a study of cutting dates derived for beams from a single roof, Bannister[1] was able to conclude that the prehistoric population of Chaco Canyon in north-western New Mexico practised stockpiling of their timbers before use. Also, by means of the clustering of dates derived from beams re-used in a later structure he[1] was able to infer the prior existence of a building which had not been discovered through usual archaeological techniques. These are but a few of the many cases of this type of application and by no means represent the range of possibilities along this line.

There is no doubt that the results of tree-ring research will continue to be important within the field of archaeology. The expansion of the method into as yet untested regions, the improvement of our knowledge of the meaning of rings as climatic indicators, and the application of tree-ring dates to problems of culture stability and change—these are the areas in which rapid future progress can be expected to occur.

REFERENCES

1 BANNISTER, B. 1959. *Tree-Ring Dating of Archaeological Sites in the Chaco Canyon Region, New Mexico*; MS, doctoral dissertation, Univ. of Arizona

2 —— and SMILEY, T. L. 1955. Dendrochronology, in SMILEY, T. L. (ed.) 'Geochronology, with Special Reference to Southwestern United States', *Univ. of Arizona Phys. Sci. Bull. 2*, 177–95

3 BELL, R. E. 1951. Dendrochronology at the Kincaid Site, in COLE, F. C., *Kincaid, A Prehistoric Illinois Metropolis*, Appendix I. Chicago

4 BELL, R. E. 1952. Dendrochronology in the Mississippi Valley, in GRIFFIN, J. B. (ed.) *Archaeology of Eastern United States*, Chicago, 345–51

5 BELL, V. and BELL, R. E. 1958. *Tree-Ring Bulletin 22*, nos. 1–4, 7–11

6 BOWERS, N. A. 1960. *Ibid. 23*, nos. 1–4, 10–13

7 CALDWELL, W. W. 1960. *Ibid. 23*, nos. 1–4, 14–17

8 DEBOER, H. J. 1951. *Proc. Koninkl. Nederl. Akademie Van Wetenshappen*, Ser. B, no. 54, 194–209

9 DOBBS, C. G. 1951. *Forestry 24*, no. 1, 22–35

10 —— 1960. *New Scientist, 182*, 1213

11 DOUGLASS, A. E. 1919. *Climatic Cycles and Tree-Growth*, vol. 1; *Carnegie Inst. of Washington Pub.* 289

12 —— 1928. *Ibid.* vol. 2

13 —— 1929. *Nat. Geog. Mag. 56*, 736–70

14 —— 1935. *Nat. Geog. Soc., Contributed Papers, Pueblo Bonito Series* no. 1

15 —— 1936. *Climatic Cycles and Tree-Growth*, vol. 3; *Carnegie Inst. of Washington Pub.* 289

16 —— 1940. *Tree-Ring Bulletin 7*, no. 1

17 —— 1941a. *Ibid. 7*, no. 4

18 —— 1941b. *Ibid. 8*, no. 2

19 —— 1943. *Ibid. 10*, no. 1

20 —— 1946. *Laboratory of Tree-Ring Research Bull.* no. 3, Univ. of Arizona

21 EIDEM, P. 1956. *Tidsskrift for Skogbruk 64*, no. 2, 96–116

22 EKLUND, B. 1949. *Meddelanden Statens Skogsforskningsinstitut 38*, no. 5, 1–77

23 —— 1956. *Tree-Ring Bulletin 21*, nos. 1–4, 21–24

24 FERGUSON, C. W. 1959. *Kiva 25*, no. 2, 24–30

25 FRITTS, H. C. 1960. *Forest Science 6*, no. 4, 334–49

26 GIDDINGS, J. L., Jr. 1938. *Tree-Ring Bulletin 5*, no. 2, 16

27 —— 1940. *Ibid. 7*, no. 2, 10–14

28 —— 1941. *Laboratory of Tree-Ring Research Bull.* no. 1, Univ. of Arizona

29 —— 1942. *Tree-Ring Bulletin 9*, no. 1, 2–8

30 —— 1943. *Ibid. 9*, no. 4, 26–32

31 —— 1947. *Ibid. 13*, no. 4, 26–29

32 —— 1948. *Ibid. 14*, no. 4, 26–32

33 —— 1951. *Ibid. 18*, no. 1, 2–6

34 —— 1952. *Proc. Am. Phil. Soc. 96*, no. 2, 129–42

35 —— 1953. *Tree-Ring Bulletin 20*, no. 1, 2–5

36 —— 1954. *Ibid. 20*, nos. 3–4, 23–25

37 GINDEL, J. 1944. *Ibid. 11*, no. 1, 6–8

38 GLADWIN, H. S. 1940a. Methods and Instruments for Use in Measuring Tree-Rings, *Medallion Papers*, no. 27

39 —— 1940b. Tree-Ring Analysis, Methods of Correlation, *Medallion Papers*, no. 28

40 GLOCK, W. S. 1933. *Pan-American Geologist 60*, 1–14

41 —— 1937. Principles and Methods of Tree-Ring Analysis. *Carnegie Inst. of Washington Pub.* 486

42 —— 1955. *Botanical Review 21*, nos. 1–3, 73–188

43 —— 1960. Dendrochronology, in *McGraw-Hill Encyclopedia of Science and Technology*, New York, 58

44 —— STUDHALTER, R. A. and AGERTER, S. R. 1960. Classification and Multiplicity of Growth Layers in the Branches of Trees at the Extreme Lower Forest Border. *Smithsonian Miscellaneous Collections 140*, no. 1

45 HALL, E. T., Jr. 1946. *Tree-Ring Bulletin 12*, no. 4, 26–27

46 HAURY, E. W. 1934. The Canyon Creek Ruin and the Cliff Dwellings of the Sierra Ancha, *Medallion Papers*, no. 14

47 HAWLEY, F. M. 1941. *Tree-Ring Analysis and Dating in the Mississippi Drainage*, Chicago

48 HØEG, O. A. 1956. *Tree-Ring Bulletin 21*, nos. 1–4, 2–15

49 HOLMSGAARD, E. 1956. *Ibid. 21*, nos. 1–4, 25–27

50 HUBER. B., and JAZEWITSCH, W. VON, 1956. *Ibid. 21*, nos. 1–4, 28–30

51 —— 1958. *Flora 146*, no. 3, 445–71

52 HUSTICH, I. 1948. *Acta Botanica Fennica 42*

53 —— 1956. *Acta Geographica 15*, no. 3

54 JAZEWITSCH, W. VON, BETTAG, G. and SIEBENLIST, H. 1957. *Holz als Roh- und Werkstoff 15*, 241–4

55 KOHARA, J. 1958. *Kobunkazai no Kagaku 15*, 12–17
56 LYON, C. J. 1939. *Science 90*, 419–20
57 —— 1946. *Tree-Ring Bulletin 13*, no. 1, 2–4
58 —— 1949. *Ecology 30*, no. 4, 549–52
59 —— 1953. *Tree-Ring Bulletin 20*, no. 2, 10–16
60 McGREGOR, J. C. 1938. *Museum of Northern Arizona Bulletin* no. 13
61 MESSERI, A. 1953. *Nuovo Giornale Botanico Italiano 60*, nos. 1–2, 251–86
62 MIKOLA, P. 1956. *Tree-Ring Bulletin 21*, nos. 1–4, 16–20
63 NISHIOKA, H. 1952. *Proceedings of the Seventh Pacific Science Congress 3*, 118–21
64 ORDING, A. 1941. *Meddelanden Norske Skogforsøksvesen 8*, no. 27, 91–130
65 OSWALT, W. H. 1949. *Tree-Ring Bulletin 16*, no. 1, 7–8
66 —— 1951. *Ibid. 18*, no. 1, 6–8
67 —— 1952. *Anthropological Papers of the University of Alaska 1*, no. 1, 47–91
68 —— 1958. *Tree-Ring Bulletin 22*, nos. 1–4, 16–22
69 —— 1960. *Ibid. 23*, nos. 1–4, 3–9
70 RUDAKOV, V. E. 1958. *Botanicheskiy Zhurnal 43*, no. 12, 1708–12
71 SCANTLING, F. H. 1946. *Tree-Ring Bulletin 12*, no. 4, 27–32
72 SCHOVE, D. J. 1950. *The Scottish Geographical Magazine 66*, no. 1, 37–42
73 —— 1954. *Geografiska Annaler 36*, nos. 1–2, 40–80
74 —— 1955. *Weather 10*, no. 11, 368–371, 395
75 —— 1959. *Medieval Archaeology 3*, 288–90
76 —— and LOWTHER, A. W. G. 1957. *Ibid. 1*, 78–95
77 SCHULMAN, E. 1942. *Ecology 23*, 309–18
78 —— 1944. *Tree-Ring Bulletin 11*, no. 1, 2–6
79 —— 1953. *Ibid. 19*, Nos. 3–4.
80 —— 1956. *Dendroclimatic Changes in Semiarid America*, Tucson
81 SMILEY, T. L. 1951a. *Archaeological Field Practices Regarding Tree-Ring Specimens*. Mimeographed paper, Laboratory of Tree-Ring Research, Univ. of Arizona
82 —— 1951b. *Laboratory of Tree-Ring Research Bull.* no. 5, Univ. of Arizona
83 —— STUBBS, S. A. and BANNISTER, B. 1953. *Laboratory of Tree-Ring Research Bull.* no. 6, Univ. of Arizona
84 STALLINGS, W. S., Jr. 1949. *Dating Prehistoric Ruins by Tree-Rings*. Laboratory of Tree-Ring Research, Univ. of Arizona, revised ed.
85 STUDHALTER, R. A. 1955. *Botanical Review 21*, nos. 1–3, 1–72
86 TREE-RING BULLETIN. 1934–. Published by the Tree-Ring Society with the co-operation of the Laboratory of Tree-Ring Research, Univ. of Arizona, Tucson
87 VANSTONE, J. W. 1953. *Tree-Ring Bulletin 20*, no. 1, 6–8
88 —— 1958. *Ibid. 22*, nos. 1–4, 12–15
89 WEAKLY, H. E. 1941. Letter to A. T. Hill, in (p. 205) HILL, A. T. and METCALF, G., *Nebraska History 22*, no. 2
90 —— 1946. A Preliminary Report on the Ash Hollow Charcoal, in CHAMPE, J. L., 'Ash Hollow Cave', *Univ. of Nebraska Studies N.S.* no. 1, appendix I
91 —— 1949. *Proc. Fifth Plains Conf. for Arch., Note Book* no. 1, 111–14
92 —— 1950. *Proc. Sixth Plains Arch. Conf., Anth. Papers* no. 11, 90–94
93 WILL, G. F. 1946. *North Dakota Agricultural College Bulletin* 338
94 —— 1949. *Proc. Fifth Plains Conf. for Arch., Note Book* no. 1, 114–16
95 —— 1950. *Proc. Sixth Plains Arch. Conf., Anth. Papers* no. 11, 95–97
96 WILLEY, G. R. 1937. *Tree-Ring Bulletin 4*, no. 2, 6–8
97 ZAMOTORIN, I. M. 1959. *Sovetskaya Arkheologiya 1959*, no. 1, 21–30
98 ZEUNER, F. E. 1960. Advances in Chronological Research, in HEIZER, R. F. and COOK, S. F. (eds.), 'The Application of Quantitative Methods in Archaeology', *Viking Fund Publications in Anthropology* no. 28, 325–43

18 Palaeo-Ethnobotany

HANS HELBAEK

IN THE NEOLITHIC several cereals were cultivated which are unknown to the modern farmer, for instance naked barley, Einkorn, and Emmer. This is common knowledge—but what are our sources? For grain is very perishable: it either sprouts or decays (it can keep for millennia only in deserts). What foundations have the statements and descriptions we read of plants which died many thousands of years ago and which were the indispensable basis for the existence of the ancient cultures? In many museums no evidence of a vegetable diet is exhibited and the visitor has little opportunity to form an opinion of the basis for statements on plants as food in prehistory. This chapter is concerned with demonstrating the nature of the archaeological plant material, and how this material is examined and interpreted in the laboratory. Discussion is confined to the Old World where wheat and barley were the established qualifications for human existence. It will appear that the evidence is abundant although some of it may seem remote and intangible.

Some kinds of material occur everywhere, others are limited to certain climatic regions. Thus mummy wheat is only found in Egypt, and the ritually murdered Iron Agers, whose stomach contents are such a valuable and rare source of information on prehistoric diets, have been found only in bogs within a restricted area in north-western Europe. Silica skeletons are commonest in the Arid Zone, while the two most important categories, carbonized grain and seeds, and the imprints of such, may be met with in any excavation all over the world except the Arctics.

The result of this particular study is a long story which has recently been touched upon in a series of brief surveys;[17,18,20,22] here it is proposed to give the reader an idea of the evidence itself and the technique by which results have been attained.

MUMMY WHEAT

The so-called mummified grain from Egyptian tombs is the nearest we can get to the original state of the food plants of antiquity. Because of the severe aridity, agriculture in Egypt is wholly dependent upon irrigation, either from small wells or, more important, by the distribution of the waters of the Nile through canals to the low-lying lands in the delta and to narrow strips along the banks further up the river. In the passages beneath the pyramids as well as in pits in the open desert, stores of grain may be found which have kept almost completely fresh for sometimes as long as five to six millennia. Indeed the husk may be a little darker than contemporary grain and it will oxidize like wood, but all the details, the tiny hairs on kernels, husks, internodes, etc., still remain and the cell structure is rather more easily observed than in fresh cereals.[10,13,28] Even the starch will still react to the iodine test and stain a deep violet. It might be expedient to point out that the very common belief is unfounded that mummy wheat is still viable. Even in its dormant state a seed is alive, so that assimilation and respiration must go on, and for this purpose moisture is necessary. Thus the complete desiccation which is the reason for the preservation of the grain is the very instrument by which it was killed—and indeed long ago. Although the microscope reveals the normal pattern of cells in the grain shell (seed case) numerous ruptures disturb the order in this vital protective organ. A few years after deposition the grain died from desiccation, and no superstition can revive it. (The belief that wheat found in ancient tombs can still be made to sprout and propagate is supported by the tales of the guides in the Egyptian Museum in Cairo, who repeat it daily to visitors from all over the world.) Incidentally, that particular species has not been grown in Egypt since the time of the Romans and nowhere can an authentic example of the live progeny of genuine mummy wheat be demonstrated.[29] However, before it became extinct in Egypt it was taken to Abyssinia where it has been grown ever since under the Ethiopian name of *Adaz*. Other races of the same species are grown in more remote mountainous districts in Europe and elsewhere, relics of local prehistoric strains. In Germanic languages it is called *Emmer*. Though wheat alone is reputed to be immortal, barley also was a very important cereal in ancient Egypt, used for bread and beer alike.[1] Many other plants were cultivated, particularly flax and a number of species of the pea family, but they still grow there and do not cause exaggerated speculation.

EVIDENCE PRESERVED IN BOGS

Generally speaking, a combination of moisture and oxygen is a prerequisite for the activity of putrefactive microbes. In Egypt there is little moisture; hence the plants may keep for ever. On the other hand, in peat bogs we find many categories of vegetable matter preserved because no fresh air is available and further because of the long-term action of humic acid. These circumstances afford us unlimited material for the study of the vegetational history of those regions where peat deposits are preserved, both in the form of wood, leaf, and fruit samples and in the form of pollen,[3] but as a source of the study of plant husbandry and past human diet the possibilities are somewhat limited. Starch is not preserved and even such plant parts as husks and grain shells are rarely reported from peat analyses. However, many seeds and fruits have such a tough shell that they will never disappear unless the bog dries up.

In the excavation of prehistoric marsh-dwelling sites in the foothills of the Alps large deposits of stones and seeds of berries may be encountered which have preserved their shape and sometimes even their characteristic colours. Most often they prove to come from juicy and more or less sugary fruits while carbonized plant remains seldom occur in such context. Such remains are the refuse from wine-making; already in the beginning of the second millennium BC—or maybe even earlier—people had discovered how to make attractive drinks of the berries which grew wild on the lower slopes of the Alps. They used mainly grapes of the wild forest vine which at that time grew in these areas, also blackberries, raspberries, elderberries, the fruits of the bittersweet nightshade, and cornelian cherry which is very common in the open forests in the southern foothills and which in certain tracts in northern Italy is still collected by the peasants and used for the same purpose. Some authors have suggested that these accumulations are human excrement, a suggestion which is contradicted by the massive occurrences of the stones of the cornelian cherry which are up to 1·5 cm long and certainly must be awkward eating on a large scale.

In northern Holland, north-west Germany, and in the Danish peninsula, human corpses of Iron Age date have sometimes been found in peat deposits. Peat is known to have been used for fuel in this region since the Neolithic, and the corpses seem to have been thrown into the small ponds left open by the peat cutters some two thousand years ago.[2,27] The corpses from Tollund and Grauballe have received particularly widespread publicity (Fig. 36).

The conditions for preservation of vegetable matter seem to differ if it has been enclosed in the intestinal canal; it is, at any rate, a fact that husks and seeds of grass removed from the stomachs of bog-found corpses may prove to be quite extraordinarily well preserved. Thus starch may be found which has kept its specific agglomerate structure and the ability to stain with iodine, while husks may have kept their otherwise easily perishable surface (epidermis). Many fragments of the inner integument (seed coat) of cereals may be encountered and even the protein cells which would not seem to be very resistant may cover the inner surface of the seed coat. These delicate pellicles are identified in part by their specific cell formations, in part by the microscopic hairs which may occur still attached to fragments of seed coat. The hairs from the grains of wheat, barley, rye, and oats are different and of good diagnostic value.

Sometimes many whole seeds and fruits are found in the remains of a meal, specially those that have a strong shell and have avoided grinding and chewing. Thus many fruits of willow weed and goosefoot made up considerable proportions of the meals and many were intact and macroscopically determinable. Apart from that, the stomach contents consist of a mud-like matter from which particles are selected by low magnification for examination by the high-power microscope. Very small fragments may suffice for an identification—in some cases half a square millimetre of tissue may be plenty. Under the microscope these mud particles present an inexhaustible variety of shape and colour, sometimes fragments consisting of a series of layers of different structure, at others bits of a single layer of tissue with its cells clearly exposed to observation and measuring, such as the corn spurrey seed coat shown in Plate XIIIc.

These 'Bog Men' subsisted on a highly mixed diet. For instance, Grauballe Man had in his intestinal duct the remains of 66 species of plants only seven of which were cultivated. Various plant diseases were established, such as ergot and smut, and the man himself must have suffered from more or less continuous stomach-ache caused by an intestinal worm (*Trichuris*), the eggs of which occurred literally by the million. All the non-cultivated plants were species the seeds of which were collected on the fallow field or in the meadow and forest, and they tend to show that life on the basis of agriculture was anything but carefree in those days, at least in that part of Denmark, which is mostly rather poor moorland. It should, however, be added that, as opposed to Tollund Man, he had had some meat also, judging by small splinters of animal bone among the plant remains.[7,16]

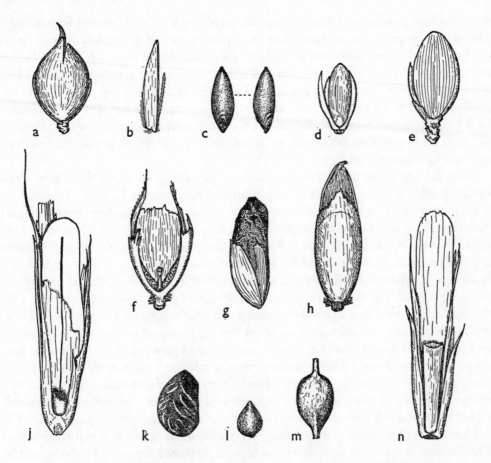

Fig. 36 Grasses, seed and fruits from the stomach of Grauballe Man (× 10): (a) Spikelet of *Echinochloa crus-galli*, dorsal view (the sterile floret is visible behind the fertile one); (b) floret of *Poa nemoralis*, lateral view; (c) grain of *Deschampsia caespitosa*, dorsal and lateral views; (d) palea and margins of lemma of *Setaria viridis*, distal view; (e) palea with remains of lemma of *Echinochloa crus-galli*, distal view; (f) palea with portion of lemma of *Sieglingia decumbens*, distal view; (g) floret of *Holcus* containing an *Ergot sclerotium*; (h) floret of *Sieglingia decumbens*, dorsal view; (j) floret with caryopsis of *Agropyron caninum*; (k) fruit of *Potentilla erecta*; (l) fruit of *Alchemilla*; (m) fruit of *Carex*; (n) floret of *Lolium perenne*, ventral view (this is an unusually long rachilla).

CARBONIZED MATERIAL

Charcoal is an extremely durable matter; if not exposed to high temperature or mechanical action it may keep and stay determinable indefinitely whether deposited under wet or dry conditions. The same applies to other forms of carbonized vegetable matter, and to the student of the dietary practice of the remote past this circumstance is of the greatest value.

Now and again one may meet in literature the expression 'spontaneous carbonization' in connection with deposits of prehistoric grain. The term serves to indicate that grain may turn into charcoal at ordinary temperatures if only kept underground long enough. This, in fact, is an invention; carbonization requires heat, and deposition of grain under conditions such as are met with in excavations would very soon result in putrefaction and complete destruction if the grain was not heated beyond roasting point.[4,9] There is too little cellulose and too much easily decaying starch in a cereal grain for the fermentation heat to turn it into charcoal. We may take it for granted that the carbonized food remains found in archaeological context have always been exposed to direct or indirect fire. It may have happened by an accidental house fire or it may be the consequence of miscarried parching.

From the earliest times it was customary to dry the grain artificially, the purpose varying with the circumstances. The primitive wheat species, Einkorn, Emmer, and Spelt, have a very tough and sturdy spikelet which does not release the grains in ordinary threshing; the spikes are beaten to pieces, but the grains are still enclosed in their individual husks. If the spikes are heated, however, the solid portion of the spikelet becomes dry and brittle and then it is possible to crush them. Therefore grain drying was used in all regions where these three species were grown. It was also employed in cool and rainy regions, such as the Hebrides, but here simply in order to store the harvest without risk of fungus attack and other damage, whichever species was involved. In hot and humid climate the drying aimed at preventing ill-timed sprouting. Of course the seed grain for the next season had to be put aside and preserved by other means since the germinating power is destroyed at a comparatively low temperature. This is expressly mentioned by Pliny in his *Historia Naturalis*. Our finds show clearly that no proper temperature control was possible in the primitive drying plants, even the comparatively sophisticated Roman kilns the ruins of which abound in southern England.

Thus it often happened that the grain was overdone, scorched or wholly carbonized. Then it was thrown on the midden—and was preserved for ever. In case of datable artifacts being found in the same strata the grain constitutes most valuable material for our study. And it is by no means always just small quantities we find; a pint is common, a gallon not unusual, and several finds of up to ten gallons are recorded in the annals of archaeology. Such large quantities mostly come from burnt houses; much useful information may be acquired for instance about the relative importance of the several cereals and legumes and about the weed flora of the fields, items that may reveal the economic status of a prehistoric community and of its contacts with the world abroad.[12,14,15,24]

The technique of identifying carbonized plant remains is based upon the same principles as in the case of other types of material, viz. comparison with fresh homologous plant parts. The examiner must, however, be intimately acquainted with the specific changes of shape, size, and proportions caused by heat in order to visualize the original appearance of the deformed and often mutilated carbonized matter and to put a name to it.

Complete carbonization turns the cereal grain into an amorphous mass almost devoid of traces of structure. It does, however, happen that some kernels are but imperfectly carbonized and then it may be possible to study the microscopic details of husks and grain shells. Even carrier tissue of starch bodies or the branching system of the fungi which attack grain left too long in wet condition (*Dematiaceae*) may occasionally be observed.

These exceptions come in handy to the study of crushed remains of carbonized foods such as bread and buns. It is sometimes possible to find evidence of the species from which the buns were made which occur in Bronze Age sites in central and southern Europe (and the Iron Age site of Meare in Somerset), and other similar material.[9] When plant matter carbonizes a lot of tar is formed, and this old and cindery tar is actually the main obstacle to identification as it is largely insoluble in agents which leave the cell tissues undamaged.

By and large carbonized grain is in a rather poor state as regards morphological detail, but now and again it happens that it passes through the process surprisingly unscathed. Thus for instance a collection of grains and spike parts got overheated in a pot in an Assyrian palace in northern Mesopotamia some 2,600 years ago; the remains are as good for determining the exact spike form as freshly harvested barley. The kernel may be precisely described: the wrinkling of the husks, the serration of the veins, the specific shape of the bases, the rachilla and the internodes with the remains of the lateral florets enable the classification of the race. One problem only eludes us: the colour of the grain. A great variety of grain colour is met with beyond Europe: the kernels and husks may be white, yellow, purple, violet, grey or black. Thus in the country where this old barley was grown, the modern product is yellow or purplish-black.

As a rule, carbonized plant remains from regions with little or no frost and a dry soil are much better preserved than those coming from northern latitudes. In frost and thaw the soil particles will move and eventually grind off the finer details of the fragile plant bodies. Even though most grain is fetched from some depth beneath the present surface, there will have been a time when it lay scattered among other debris on the ground before erosion, sand drift, and renewed human activity covered up the traces of the habitation site and kept the frost at arm's length; that is when the damage was done. One very attractive exception is shown in Plate XIIIb. It is part of a large heap of linseed, and the seeds of a weed which occurs in flax fields, Gold-of-Pleasure. The two plants were grown together in the Danish Iron Age and both kinds of seed were used for food because of their considerable oil content. On top of the seeds is seen the pear-shaped pod valve of Gold-of-Pleasure. These and many other food remains were found in Jutland in a house burnt down some time in the first century AD. Also in that house was a large vessel filled with malt (sprouted barley), the only example hitherto of prehistoric brewing encountered in Denmark.[5]

SILICA SKELETONS

In most excavations in arid zones, e.g. in Egypt and Mesopotamia, one comes across heaps or extensive strata of ash. It is of course desirable to find out what the fuel was since very often it has a bearing upon the common vegetable food of that time. Usually the ash will prove to consist of an amorphous powder mixed with small bits of structurally highly organized glass matter. These fragments are the silicious elements of the epidermis of the vegetative parts of grasses. During its growth the epidermis cell of grasses and some other families undergoes a 'mineralization'. The minute interstices of the fundamental cellulose framework of the cell wall will eventually be filled up with other organic substances as also quite prominently by silica. When the plant burns or decays this element of silica will remain, and if the plant part is protected against mechanical action, as for instance in the wall of a clay vessel, it will today represent a true copy of the cells exhibiting all their specific structural details.[21] The difference in dimensions and design in the epidermis of the various grasses may be very pronounced and thus it is possible to distinguish between the cultivated species by means of these glass-like objects when they are properly magnified. The attractive design of millet ash (husk) from an Assyrian palace is illustrated in Plate XIIId.

There would seem to be two reasons why silica skeletons figure less prominently in palaeo-ethnobotanical material from northern regions: the silica solidification in the epidermis is conspicuously heavier in hot and arid climates; and the formation of ice crystals in such delicate and unelastic structures is bound to prohibit their preservation.

GRAIN IMPRINTS

In areas in the Near East and elsewhere where no suitable building stone is available and where timber belongs to the imported luxuries, common houses are built of clay or mud mixed with straw, stubble or chaff. This was the technique ever since man became settled with the invention of agriculture. Such prehistoric houses are encountered in excavations, and in the chunks of wall and floor material there may be a multitude of imprints of plant parts yielding highly important information on the plants being cultivated when the house was occupied. Sometimes silica skeletons also are preserved even if no fire was involved.

The ceramic too, which was made at the fireplace in the house, very often contains imprints because the food was prepared at the same place and the grain and seeds spilled on the floor got stuck to the lumps of wet pottery material and were eventually kneaded into the clay. Grain imprints may occur in hand-made pottery from all agricultural regions of the world, and in Denmark they are particularly common. There are Bronze and Iron Age vessels of a moderate size which on their surface bear as many as 200 imprints of seeds and grains.[6,9,11,18,25]

If a dry seed is kneaded into the wet clay at the shaping of a vessel it will absorb moisture from its surroundings. Together with the water it will attract the finest particles of the clay which will form a fine-grain coat all over the surface of the seed. When the vessel is fired the seed will burn away, but the cavity left in the now hardened clay is lined with this fine-grain material in which minute morphological features of the plant body may be moulded. A cast of the cavity will show the seed in sufficient detail for an exact description and identification. Even small seeds may in this way leave determinable traces, for instance the seed of corn spurrey which is less than one millimeter in diameter.

As a rule, large particles of plants were picked off the clay by the potter, but in the large bricks from Mesopotamian monumental buildings one may come across more or less whole spikes. One of the best possible examples of this kind is illustrated in Plate XIIIa. In it is represented all necessary detail for a systematic classification of the type of two-row barley. Incidentally, these bricks which are upwards from 12 in. square may bear hundreds of determinable imprints of chaff and grains.

APPENDIX

Recently an attempt was made to throw light on the evolution of plant husbandry in Iraq.[26] This country, which consists of a mountainous region in the north (Kurdistan) and a southern alluvial plain (Mesopotamia), is within the general area where agriculture is believed to have originated. In the uplands the prototypes of the most important cultivated plants are still to be found, and the adjoining low-lying river plain would have been a natural area of development for the intensive irrigation agriculture which was the fundamental qualification for the rise of the vigorous Mesopotamian cultures of the fourth and subsequent millennia.

This project was carried out by a systematic tracking and determination of imprints in well-dated pottery and bricks from ancient habitation sites, palaces, and ziggurats, as also by examination of carbonized material and ash from the area in question. The investigator visited museums in Europe and Iraq; the ruins of numerous ancient cities in Mesopotamia, from Nimrud and Babylon in the north to Ur and Warka in the south, were examined from this particular point of view. The result was a quite coherent picture of plant husbandry stretching from the seventh millennium BC to the time of Harun-al-Rashid, c. AD 800.

In the beginning man had domesticated the wild Emmer and the wild two-row barley of the northern mountains and he also took up the cultivation of the wild flax. Presumably during the seventh millennium farmers migrated into the river plain in the south with its fertile alluvial soil, and there they eventually developed irrigation agriculture. This forcible change of environment led by mutation to the transformation of the two-row barley into the six-row form, and Emmer and flax attained a higher state of efficiency. General expansion in the seventh millennium brought agriculture from Anatolia to Europe and probably Egypt was colonized not long afterwards.[20,22,23]

The small-grain wild wheat, Einkorn, which was domesticated together with the wild Emmer attained a high state of development in Asia Minor and became the third member of the group of important cereals which were taken to Europe and, presumably via the Danube basin and the western Black Sea coastlands, spread all over that continent in the course of three millennia. Flax and some of the Oriental legumes, such as pea, lentil, and vetchling, accompanied the cereals as secondary cultivars. Millet turns up in Mesopotamia about 3000 BC, but the traces of that plant are not consistent in the Near East. Whereas during the third and second millennia it was widely grown in southern Europe, in Iraq we do not encounter it again until the middle of the first millennium, and in Egypt it does not seem ever to have been grown in antiquity. Certain interesting developments took place in Asia Minor at an early time, concerning naked barley and the free-threshing wheat (e.g. bread wheat), but the evidence is only just emerging and not yet published in detail.[30, 31]

This field of research is but one of numerous auxiliaries to modern archaeology. If we aim at the whole truth and nothing but the truth regarding the life and achievement of our remote ancestors, this study is as indispensable as the excavation and interpretation of the more conspicuous remains of ancient cultures, and it need not be emphasized that without correct dating of the plant remains all the endeavours of the palaeo-ethnobotanist are utterly futile. This applies to the corresponding fields within other natural sciences as well. The excavator must be informed and interested in these problems and he must give considerable attention to the recovery of the pertinent material. If he is alert, treasures of information may be acquired. The interpretation is comparatively simple; it requires only the prerequisites of all scientific research: special training, patience, and luck.

REFERENCES

 1 ABERG, E. 1950. In LAUER, J. P., LAURENT-TACKHOLM, V. and ABERG, E. Bull. Inst. d'Egypte 32, 153
 2 BECKER, C. J. 1948. Torvegraning i aeldre Jernalder. Nationalmuseets Arbejdsmark 1948, 92
 3 GODWIN, H. 1956. The History of the British Flora, Cambridge
 4 HARRIS, T. M. 1958. J. Ecol. 46, 447
 5 HELBAEK, H. 1938. Planteavl. Aarbøger 1938
 6 —— 1948. Les impreintes de céréals, in RIIS, P. J. Fouilles et Recherches de la Fondation Carlsberg 2, 3
 7 —— 1950. Aarbøger 1950, 311
 8 —— 1952a. Acta Archaeologica 23, 97
 9 —— 1952b. Proc. Prehist. Soc. 18, 194
10 —— 1953. Dan. Biol. Medd. 21, 8
11 —— 1954. Aarbøger 1954, 202
12 —— 1955a. The Botany of the Iron Age Vallhager Field, in STENBERGER, M. et al., Vallhagar, a Migration Period Site on Gotland, Sweden, Stockholm
13 —— 1955b. Proc. Prehist. Soc. 21, 93
14 —— 1956. In GJERSTAD, E. Acta Inst. Romani Sueciae, ser. 4, 27:2
15 —— 1957. In KLINDT-JENSEN, O. Nat. Mus. Skr. St. Ber. 2
16 —— 1958. Kuml 1958, 83
17 —— 1959a. Die Paläoethnobotanik des Nahen Ostens und Europas. Opusc. Ethnol. Mem. L. Biro Sacra. Akademiai Kiado, Budapest
18 —— 1959b. Science 130, 365
19 —— 1959c. Archaeology 12, 183
20 —— 1959d. Kuml 1959, 103
21 —— 1960a. Cereals and weeds in Phase A, in BRAIDWOOD, R. J. and BRAIDWOOD, L. Excavations in the Plain of Antioch, vol. 1, Chicago
22 —— 1960b. The Paleo-Ethnobotany of the Near East and Europe, in BRAIDWOOD, R. J. and HOWE, B. Prehistoric Investigations in Iraqi Kurdistan (Studies in Ancient Oriental Civilizations, no 31), Chicago ch. 8
23 —— 1960c. Iraq 22, 186
24 —— 1961. Anatolian Studies 11, 77
25 JESSEN, K. and HELBAEK, H. 1944. Dan. Biol. Skr. 3 (2)
26 JACOBSEN, T. and ADAMS, R. 1958. Science 128, 1251
27 JORGENSEN, S. 1956. Kuml 1956, 128
28 LAURENT-TACKHOLM, V. 1952. Faraos Blomster, Copenhagen
29 TACKHOLM, V., TACKHOLM, G. and DRAR, M. 1941. Flora of Egypt, Cairo
30 HELBAEK, H. 1966. Economic Botany 20, 4
31 —— 1969. Plant collecting, dry-farming and irrigation agriculture in prehistoric Deh Luran. In HOLE, F. et al., Prehistory and Human Ecology in the Deh Luran Plain, Ann Arbor

19 Palaeo-Ethnobotany in America

RICHARD A. YARNELL

THE ANALYSIS AND INTERPRETATION of archaeological plant remains provides information which has bearing on a variety of botanical and anthropological problems. Answers to questions about subsistence and ecology are coming more and more frequently to be derived with the assistance of botanists who in turn are often aided in their investigations of cultigen history and evolution by having access to plant remains recovered by careful excavators. While there is an appearance here of symbiosis, an inherent divergence of interest exists with regard to the kinds of information desired and the contexts of interpretation. Yet, overt conflict of interest continues as a rarity even though contact between botany and anthropology is steadily increasing. Perhaps this is largely due to a concurrent growth of appreciation for anthropological problems by the botanist and vice versa. In any case, the alliance is highly profitable and promises to be much more so in the future.

Analyses of plant remains from individual archaeological sites and groups of sites can be highly instructive of local patterns of technology and subsistence (and perhaps ultimately of economics and other aspects of the extinct socio-cultural systems under investigation). Given adequate material to work with they can provide relative quantitative data on plant food sources and other information such as local environmental conditions, importance of agriculture, preparation and utilization of various kinds of plant products, and, occasionally, indications of contact with other areas.

The importance of assistance from the botanist does not end here, however. The intricacies of interpretation are likely to be enough to tax the resources of the anthropologist and the botanist working together, let alone either by himself. For instance, it cannot be assumed that valid ecological inference can be made simply in terms of natural environmental conditions, especially if agriculture is present. Whenever man comes into contact with nature, he alters it, often drastically. The higher the level of technological development and the more extensive the archaeological remains, the more intensive is the disturbance likely to have been. It may not be meaningful to ask simply, 'What was the character of the natural vegetation?' Rather the question might be, 'What was the resultant character of the plant life as it responded to the changed conditions induced by man through his efforts to extract from his surroundings the goods necessary for his survival and for continued effectiveness in the functioning of his culture?' We need to know the habitat in order to understand the pattern of cultural adaptation, but also we must have knowledge of the impact of this adaptation on the plant life, animal life, etc., in order to achieve a realistic understanding of the nature of the habitat. We are dealing here with feedback systems which are somewhat more complex than the simple cause and effect models with which we are likely to feel more secure.

A few good starts are being made in this direction, but a more reassuring pheno-menon is the growing recognition that there is no simple dichotomy between cultigens and 'wild' plants. The trichotomy of cultigen, weed or weedy species, and climax species is not entirely adequate, as indicated by Harlan and Dewet,[39] but it is an im-provement. Furthermore, it provides a category for the remains of plants which may or may not have been intentionally cultivated, as an alternative to inclusion with those which presumably were not. The prominence and identity of material in this category can serve as a partial index of disturbance if the collection is adequate for statistical purposes. Unfortunately, weed seeds are usually smaller than the openings in screens ordinarily utilized during excavation for the recovery of small items; and there are still far too few workers to examine many sizeable collections or to interpret them adequately.

Thus, palaeo-ethnobotany can contribute to dynamic as well as static interpretations of the operation of cultural systems. It also has a place in culture historical studies, especially in so far as agriculture and the evolution of domestication are concerned, and it should prove to be useful in providing data for distributional studies and for indicating something about intercultural relationships. This could further develop through greater utilization of the data in synthetic approaches, from roughly synchronic to broadly diachronic.

Almost all of the current syntheses are being made by botanists and largely for their own purposes. Fortunately, their purposes tend to coincide with, or at least are comple-mentary to, the purposes of the anthropologist. As cultigens evolve, so does agriculture and culture in general; and the botanist is aware that his cultigens evolve only in habi-tats dominated by man, just as the anthropologist is aware that cultures evolve as parts of biotic systems.

Though an occasional writer comments upon the rarity of archaeological plant remains, the ninety-year period of 1876 through 1965 has produced at least 375 pub-lished reports of archaeological plant remains in America; and the total probably exceeds 500, not including unpublished recoveries. The geographical and chronological distribution of these reports is indicated in Table A. Undoubtedly this compilation is far from complete; however, it is probably representative for the most part. The overall distributions are 23% for Latin America, 39% for the United States west of the Great Plains, and 38% for the eastern United States and southern Ontario. The respective percentages for these regions are more nearly equal for the last fifteen years, largely because of the number of reports describing material recovered during recent excava-tions in Mexico.

Table B indicates the distribution of those reports prepared by botanists and ethno-botanists. The total of 165 is impressive, but there are still very few detailed reports available for specific localities at specific points in time. Thus the ecology potential of palaeo-ethnobotany in America has barely been tapped. Regional syntheses are rare; but syntheses of the archaeological reports of maize, beans, and the cucurbits are pro-gressing well, largely because of the number of botanists interested in the evolution of cultigens. Non-cultigens are not well represented by such studies, however. The

) One of the most perfect imprints of grain
~er encountered. Two-row barley from a
ick which was used about AD 800 in building
huge weir in the ancient Nahrwan Canal east
of Baghdad (×4).

(b) Portion of a carbonized heap of the olea-
ginous seeds of flax and Gold-of-Pleasure,
from a burnt Iron Age house in Denmark.
The pear-shaped object on top of the seeds is
the pod-valve of the Gold-of-Pleasure (×4).

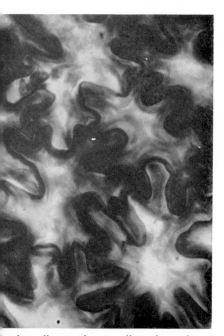

) The stellate epidermis cells in the seed coat
corn spurrey (*Spergula arvensis*) from the
omach of the Iron Age man from Grauballe,
Denmark (×400).

(d) Silica skeleton of millet husk found in an
Assyrian palace in Iraq which was sacked
shortly before 600 BC (×675).

(see page 206) PLATE XIII

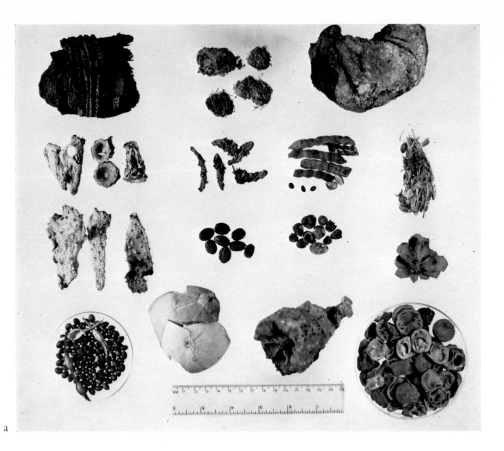

a

b

PLATE XIV (see page 215)

(a) Wild plant foods of the fourteenth century from Tonto National Monument Arizona (from upper left across): agave stem section, agave quids, prepared agave cake, prickly pear fruits, cholla buds, mesquite seeds and roasted pods, mesquite quid, young stem joints of prickly pear, jojoba nuts, acorns, pinyon cone, paloverde seeds and pods, buffalogourd, fruit of datil yucca, cracked walnuts. Bohrer 1962[7]. Southwestern Monuments Assn. Technical Series 2:96, Plate 12. (Courtesy of Vorsila L. Bohrer.) (b) Remains of cultivated sunflower (*Helianthus annuus*) from Newt Kash Hollow rock shelter, Menifee County, Kentucky, dating from *c.* 600 BC. (Specimens from the University of Kentucky.) 17:163, Figure 3. (Courtesy of Charles B. Heiser.)

Gourd-like warty squash shell (*Cucurbita pepo*) and torch canes *in situ* on the floor of Indian Avenue, lower Salts Cave, Mammoth Cave National Park, Kentucky, located approximately two miles from the cave entrance. Apparently these items were left by gypsum or mirabilite miners during the first millennium BC. Watson and Yarnell 1966[85]. Cave Research Foundation photo by Robert M. Keller.

(see page 215) PLATE XV

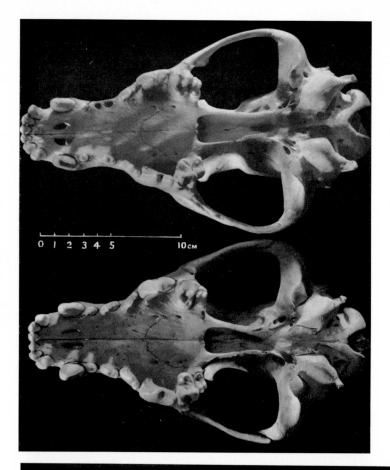

(a) Palatal views of the skulls of *Canis lupus lupus*, from the collection of the British Museum (Natural History). In the bottom skull the teeth are very large and they are abnormally compacted. There is no diastema between the first premolar and the canine, and the second premolar overlaps the third premolar (no. 1680; locality, Europe). In the top skull the teeth are evenly spaced and there is no overlap or displacement of the teeth. This skull represents the normal condition in wolves (no. 28.5.4.1; locality, north Sweden).

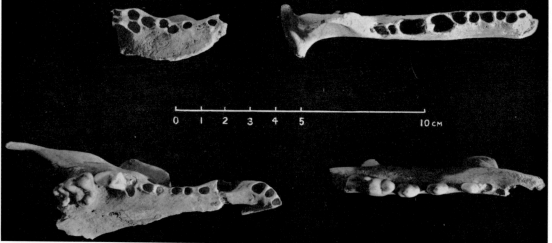

(b) Dog jaws from the Bronze Age site of Chios in Greece, to show the variability in tooth formation. Top left: fragment of maxilla with tooth sockets that are compacted and which held large teeth, crowded together; top right: mandibular ramus with the same type of tooth sockets as the maxilla at left. Bottom left: maxilla with the carnassial tooth and the two molars in position. These teeth are smaller and are not compacted in the jaw. Bottom right: fragment of mandibular ramus with the second, third and fourth premolars in position; small, widely-spaced teeth as in the previous specimen.

PLATE XVI (see page 303)

TABLE A

Distribution of reports of American archaeological plant remains by decade and region

| | South America | Middle America | United States and Canada | | | | | | Total |
			West	S.West	Plains	Mid-West	N.E.	S.E.	
1876–1885	3					2			5
1886–1895	1					1	1	1	4
1896–1905	1						1	1	3
1906–1915	1			5	1	2	2		11
1916–1925	4			11		2	3	5	25
1926–1935	2	3		22	3	8	2	3	43
1936–1945	2	6	1	36	4	10	6	5	70
1946–1955	12	11	5	28	6	4	8	5	79
1956–1965	10	30	1	39	9	23	7	16	135
Total	36	50	7	141	23	52	30	36	375

exceptions are almost exclusively weedy genera and species which may have been cultivated or semi-cultivated. But even here there are obvious gaps. For instance, *Chenopodium*, one of the most promising genera as indicated by the abundance of evidence, has attracted little attention in America among students qualified to synthesize the data, probably because it has not yet come to their attention to the extent necessary to stimulate investigation.

Analysis of archaeological plant remains in North America hardly exceeds three decades in age. It has been three times that long since Europeans began their early studies of Peruvian materials. In 1876 Saffray reported his study of plant remains in a Peruvian mummy bundle,[72] and Rochebrunne's *Recherches d'ethnographie botanique sur las flora des sepultures péruviennes d'Ancón*[70] appeared in 1879. During the following decade two studies by Wittmack were published,[92] including his *Die Nutzpflanzen der alten Peruaner*.[93] In 1910 Costantin and Bois reported plant remains from various

TABLE B

Reports of analyses and syntheses dealing with archaeological plant remains in America

| | United States | | | | |
	Latin America	South-west	East	General	Total
1876–1905	5				5
1906–1935	4	5	1	1	11
1936–1965	35	60	41	13	149
Total	44	65	42	14	165

Peruvian archaeological sites in *Sur les grains et tubercules des tombeaux péruviens de la Periode Incasique*,[15] but it was not until 1917 that a significant contribution by an American appeared. This is Safford's *Food-Plants and Textiles of Ancient America*[71] which deals with materials from North and South America. It was followed in 1922 by Harms' *Ubersicht der bischer in altperuanischen Gräbern gefundenen Pflanzenreste*[40] and in 1934–35 by *El mundo vegetal de los antiguos peruanos*,[94] a major report by Yacovleff and Herrera. Since that time the most significant contributions to Peruvian palaeo-ethno-botany have been the work of Margaret A. Towle at the Harvard University Botanical Museum during the past fifteen years. This was impressively climaxed in 1961 by her comprehensive monograph, *The Ethnobotany of Pre-Columbian Peru*,[84] in which there is a fuller description of the history and content of Peruvian palaeo-ethnobotanical studies.

Though scattered reports of plant remains from North American archaeological sites appeared during the final quarter of the nineteenth century and the first quarter of the twentieth, it was not until 1931 that the first significant analysis was published.[34] This is the study of plant remains recovered from rock shelters of the Ozark Plateau in Arkansas and Missouri in 1922–23. It was made by Melvin R. Gilmore, who was responsible for the founding of the Ethnobotanical Laboratory at the University of Michigan Museum of Anthropology in 1930. Gilmore identified the remains of 68 plant species from an abundance of material which was well preserved because of the perpetually dry condition of the shelter interiors. At least 30 species probably were utilized for food, and several were cultivated. So far there has been little additional interpretation of the significance of this material in the light of more recent knowledge of the archaeology of the eastern United States. This is largely a result of the difficulty of assigning the remains to particular cultural contexts because of the indistinct strati-graphy of the desiccated accumulations of debris and because the provenience of the specimens is not indicated. Nevertheless, Gilmore's Ozark Bluff-Dweller report is a major landmark of American palaeo-ethnobotany.

In 1937 Gilmore reported the general results of initial work at the Ethnobotanical Laboratory,[35] which had agreed to receive and examine archaeological plant remains and to furnish a report of the findings. This had the fortunate result of encouraging American archaeologists to become more aware of plant remains and their significance and the unfortunate result of establishing a tradition of furnishing palaeo-ethnobotanical data without receiving financial support, which has since worked to the detriment of this kind of investigation. By mid-1962 the Laboratory had received 418 consignments of plant remains which included 4802 lots.

In spite of the amount of work devoted to palaeo-ethnobotany by Gilmore, he published very little in this field. His reports to archaeologists have generally been quoted or abstracted in the texts of their publications. This has been the case also for his successor, Volney H. Jones, who nevertheless has compiled an impressive list of published reports, the majority of which have appeared as appendices to archaeological mono-graphs.

In 1936 Jones published two significant papers. One is a synthesis of what was then known of aboriginal cotton of the south-western United States and includes discussion of various archaeological specimens.[44] The other is his most widely cited contribution, the report of the plant remains recovered from Newt Kash Hollow rock shelter in eastern Kentucky.[45] Here, as in the case of the Ozark material, the specimens were abundant and well preserved because of desiccation. The remains of 40 plant species are reported, eight of which probably were cultivated or semi-cultivated. Nine or ten of the species represented probably were gathered for food, and nine or ten presumably were utilized for other purposes. One of the most interesting plants reported by Jones is tobacco which is not represented in other collections from prehistoric archaeological sites east of the Rocky Mountains.

The problem of context is present at Newt Kash Hollow, but apparently is not as serious as it is in the Ozark Plateau. Though the stratigraphy is indistinct, there appears to be a pre-maize agricultural level which has been radiocarbon dated at the seventh century before Christ, during the Early Woodland period. The similarity of the lower level Newt Kash material to the lower level Ozark rock shelter plant remains suggests that the latter also are Early Woodland in context, especially so now that very similar material from Salts Cave in west-central Kentucky has been radiocarbon dated at the first millennium BC.[85] This means that we know a great deal more about the palaeo-ethnobotany of the Early Woodland period than of any other prehistoric period of the eastern United States. The reason for this is that the later periods are represented almost exclusively by open sites in which the only plant remains are carbonized, are often difficult to recover intact or at all, and tend to be overlooked, though they are frequently abundant, even in regions with considerable rainfall.

The bulk of Jones' palaeo-ethnobotanical reports, published during the two decades between 1940 and 1960, deal with plant remains from archaeological sites in the south-western United States. The most notable of these are his reports on materials from a cave in Zion National Park, Utah,[46] and his report with Robert L. Fonner on plant remains from the Durango and La Plata areas of Colorado. However, the continued operation of the Ethnobotanical Laboratory as a centre for the receipt, analysis, and deposit of archaeological plant remains may eventually be recognized as among his most significant contributions to palaeo-ethnobotany.

Reports dealing with aboriginal American plant fibres are rare. The results of two studies by A. C. Whitford appeared in 1941 and 1943.[90,91] The earlier paper presents a large number of remarkable identifications of archaeological and ethnological fibres from the eastern United States. Whitford examined many specimens of fabric, cordage, etc., from ten museums and one private collection and was able to make identifications of 32 plant species. The other paper is a more general report on aboriginal North American fibre plants. The uniqueness of Whitford's contribution serves to emphasize one of American palaeo-ethnobotany's greatest present deficiencies, the acute shortage of available qualified personnel to identify archaeological plant fibres.

Approximately 30% of the American reports of palaeo-ethnobotanical analysis since 1940 have concentrated on the remains of Indian corn, and it has predominated in many others. Though G. N. Collins made earlier studies in the 1920's,[14] Edgar Anderson of

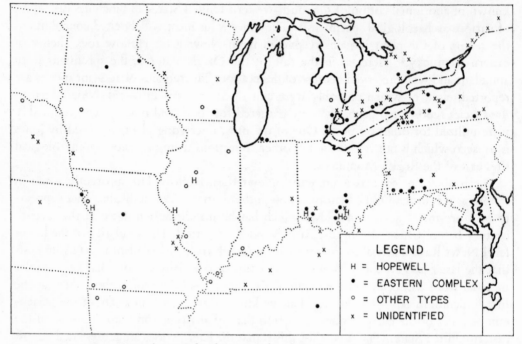

Fig. 37 Distribution of prehistoric archaeological corn in the Mid-West.

the Missouri Botanical Garden seems to have originated this trend when his analysis of maize from Cañon del Muerto, Arizona, was published in 1942.[1] During the next few years he reported several additional studies of archaeological maize from the southwestern United States. Then, in 1947, the climax of his palaeo-ethnobotanical work appeared.[9] This is a paper by W. L. Brown and Anderson on the Northern Flint corns which reports their analyses of archaeological and ethnological maize collections from many locations in the eastern United States. It is a notable contribution partly because it is the earliest systematic synthesis of data on the archaeological remains of a food plant, though it was preceded by Jones' survey of cotton.[44]

The 1939 monograph on the origin of maize by Paul C. Mangelsdorf and R. G. Reeves[62] undoubtedly did much to stimulate palaeo-ethnobotanical investigations of this plant. In fact, Mangelsdorf himself turned to archaeological maize analysis and reported the much-publicized Bat Cave corn of New Mexico in 1949 with C. E. Smith, Jr.[63] Prior to MacNeish's recent discoveries in Mexico, this was considered the oldest domesticated maize known. During the past 15 years, Mangelsdorf has made extremely important contributions to our understanding of the origin and development of Indian corn, largely as a result of his studies of archaeological remains from Mexico. [58,59,60] It has been fortunate indeed that the individual whom Hugh Cutler has singled out as 'the recognized authority on the origin of corn'[21] can be numbered among the most productive of American palaeo-ethnobotanists.

In 1945 there appeared what must be considered one of the most significant general studies extensively utilizing palaeo-ethnobotanical data. This is George F. Carter's

Plant Geography and Culture History in the American Southwest.[13] Although many of Carter's conclusions were immediately disputed, this work has often been cited; and some of its conclusions have since been supported by new data, though others have not. A major value of Carter's study is its indication of some of the kinds of problems to which the application of adequate palaeo-ethnobotanical data is essential.

In addition to Edgar Anderson, Liberty Hyde Bailey and W. W. Mackie, Carter acknowledges the technical assistance of Thomas W. Whitaker, who is probably the leading authority on the American Cucurbitaceae. Fortunately, Whitaker's examination of archaeological cucurbits has continued for the two past decades. His earlier work in palaeo-ethnobotany is probably best known from his 1948 paper on the bottle gourd,[86] and his report the next year on the 5000-year-old cucurbit remains from Huaca Prieta, Peru.[87] Since then, in co-operation with Hugh Cutler, he has analyzed and reported material from various archaeological sites and presented syntheses of the history and distribution of the American cucurbits. [24,88,89]

As well as working with Mangelsdorf on the Bat Cave corn, C. Earle Smith, Jr., has studied the other plant remains from this archaeological site.[76] More recently he has made extensive contributions in botany and palaeo-ethnobotany to the Tehuacan Archaeological-Botanical Project directed by R. S. MacNeish.[77,78,79] Soon to be published is his bibliography of American archaeological plant remains compiled with the aid of six other workers in this field and utilized extensively in the preparation of this review.[81] Smith's forthcoming survey paper on the origins of American crop plants is much needed and eagerly anticipated by this writer, at least.

The late Robert M. Goslin, formerly of the Ohio State Museum, was an excellent example of the kind of individual much needed in American palaeoethnobotany at the present time. His general knowledge of Ohio, as well as his knowledge of the archaeology and flora of that state, well suited him to make identifications of its plant remains and to synthesize the data, even though he was not professionally trained. His two publications on Ohio palaeo-ethnobotany are indications of the contributions to be made by the individual who is in a position to concentrate on the prehistoric utilization of plant products in a particular region.[36,37]

The most prolific contributor to North American palaeo-ethnobotany during the past decade has been Hugh C. Cutler of the Missouri Botanical Garden. Earlier he published on South American races of maize,[16] but the bulk of his recent reports deals primarily with his comparative analyses of archaeological maize from the eastern and south-western United States. Cutler's syntheses of the rapidly accumulating data are continually improving our view of the prehistory of Indian corn in the United States and northern Mexico. During the past three years alone (1963–65) at least 15 of Cutler's reports have been published, and others await publication. Fortunately, Cutler is an authority on the cucurbits and economic plants in general as well as maize. This places him in an almost unique position of value in the field of palaeo-ethnobotany. Some of his more notable contributions include his studies of the plant remains from Tularosa Cave and Higgins Flat Pueblo in south-western New Mexico,[17,18] maize from Heltagito rock shelter in Arizona,[19] plant remains from a cave in the Mexican state of

Durango,[8] maize and cucurbits from Mesa Verde, Colorado,[23] and American cucurbits in general.[24,88]

Two additional authorities on maize, Norton H. Nickerson and Leonard Blake, have contributed from the Missouri Botanical Garden; and another, Walton C. Galinat, has worked at the Harvard University Botanical Museum. Nickerson's studies date from the early 1950's and include his analyses of plant remains from the Oahe Dam area in South Dakota.[67] His most significant contribution to palaeo-ethnobotany is a study of maize cob morphology in which he deals extensively with ethnological as well as archaeological collections.[66] Blake's work is more recent and consist mostly of analyses of archaeological maize from the eastern United States, reported with Cutler (e.g. the Banks site in Arkansas).[22]

Galinat, who is currently at the University of Massachusetts at Waltham, has done important work on the influence of hybridization with teosinte on the evolution of maize, and his analyses of archaeological remains strongly reflects this emphasis.[31,32,33] He has worked with Mangelsdorf on the analysis of the extensive collections made by MacNeish from the caves of Tamaulipas and the Tehuacán Valley in Mexico,[59,60] Tehuacán maize is the oldest and most primitive yet found. In addition, Galinat has reported the plant remains from the important Lo Daiska site of eastern Colorado,[29] and he and J. H. Gunnerson have conducted an extensive study of eight-row maize in the south-western and eastern United States which has resulted in their interpretations of the historical relations between these two regions with respect to this plant.[30,31]

The leading authority on aboriginal beans in America is Lawrence Kaplan who, like Cutler, is also especially competent in general palaeo-ethnobotanical investigations. His work on plant remains from Mexico and the south-western United States has spanned the past decade. He has analysed MacNeish's beans from Tamaulipas and Tehuacán,[53,54] as well as those from various archaeological sites in the American south-west. His most extensive report so far is on his comprehensive study of cultivated beans of the pre-historic south-west.[51] Kaplan has analyzed all of the plant remains from Cordova Cave, New Mexico,[52] and has just completed analysis of what is probably the largest collection of carbonized plant material from a single site in America. It was recovered from an open Hopewellian site in Illinois by Stuart Struever, utilizing a flotation recovery technique which he developed.[82,83]

Human coprolites are rarely recovered from archaeological sites, because they are rarely preserved except under continually desiccated conditions. When they are subjected to careful analysis, they can furnish excellent evidence of subsistence activities. Jones reported faeces contents from Newt Kash Hollow shelter,[45] and R. L. Fonner analyzed the ones from Danger Cave and Juke Box Cave in Utah.[27] Coprolite analysis has been most highly developed by Eric O. Callen (see article in this volume) working with material from Huaca Prieta in Peru, Tamaulipas and Tehuacán.[11,12] In addition, he has examined several of the specimens from Salts Cave, Kentucky, at the request of P. J. Watson and R. A. Yarnell, which implemented their study of 100 human coprolites collected at points up to two miles from the cavern entrance (see Plate XV).[85] This Early Woodland material is strikingly similar to the Ozark and Newt Kash Hollow plant remains discussed earlier. The report indicates quantities of each plant food consumed and draws certain inferences about the ecology of the poeple.

Largely as a result of training and guidance from Volney Jones, Yarnell made a general study of the palaeo-ethnobotany of the mid-west region of North America.[96] Earlier he studied plants growing on Pueblo ruins in New Mexico, comparing the results to the palaeo-ethnobotanical record of the south-west generally.[98] He has studied plant remains from several sites in the eastern United States, receiving generous assistance from Hugh Cutler.

Another of Jones' trainees is Vorsila L. Bohrer who has produced one of the finest studies of archaeological plant remains yet to appear. It is a thorough analysis of 516 lots of well-preserved material from the cliff dwellings of Tonto National Monument in Arizona.[7] She presents the Tonto data in full descriptive and functional contexts and also includes comparative data from archaeological and ethnographic sources. This she is able to do because she previously compiled the ethnobotanical and palaeo-ethnobotanical data of the south-west and recorded them on punched cards which are on file at the University of Michigan Museum of Anthropology and constitutes a valuable resource for further studies.[6]

The Tonto cotton textiles were studied by Kate Pack Kent,[56] who had earlier prepared a comprehensive review of prehistoric south-western cotton cultivation and weaving.[55] More recently C. E. Smith, Jr., has reported on very old cotton from Tehuacán and presented a general study as well.[79]

Several plants, in addition to maize, cucurbits, beans, and cotton have received some attention, mostly in the context of regional surveys. South-western tobacco and *Croton* and eastern giant ragweed have been treated by Jones.[48,50,68] Yarnell has examined the evidence for prehistoric Pueblo utilization of *Datura*[95] and for cultivation of the annual marshelder, *Iva annua* var. *macrocarpa*, in the eastern United States,[97] though M. J. Black had previously presented the basic details of the marshelder problem.[5] Jonathan Sauer's monograph on the amaranths is a world wide survey but is hardly palaeo-ethnobotanical because of the near absence of archaeological remains.[73] This is probably due in part to small seed size resulting in non-recovery. The same could be said of tobacco and other plants, indicating that our present evidence strongly reflects the screen mesh sizes generally utilized during excavation.

Sunflowers in North America have largely been the domain of Charles B. Heiser, who has concluded that *Helianthus annuus* was domesticated in the central region of the United States. This is on the basis of phytogeographic and palaeo-ethnobotanical evidence.[41,42] Recently, he has turned his attention to plant domestication in Nuclear America and has reviewed the evidence on the origin and migration of the major American cultigens.[43] Heiser's conclusions here are somewhat indefinite, apparently because of insufficient palaeo-ethnobotanical evidence. As he states with reference to the problem of tracing origins, 'In the absence of archaeological remains or fossils, no absolutely reliable method exists to reach a definite answer for most of our crop plants.'

Robert L. Dressler made use of the palaeo-ethnobotanical evidence available at the time of his extensive survey of pre-Columbian cultivated plants of Mexico which he reported in 1953.[25] Since then Mangelsdorf, MacNeish, and Gordon Willey have usefully reviewed the early developments in Middle American agriculture, emphasizing the archaeological evidence of the major cultigens which MacNeish and others have greatly increased in recent years.[61]

So far neglected in this review is the work in pollen analysis which has strong significance for American palaeo-ethnobotany. Among the contributors are Elso S. Barghoorn, Paul S. Martin, Paul B. Sears, and James Schoenwetter. Sears' work includes studies of relevance to 'archaeological horizons in the basins of Mexico'[75] as does that of Barghoorn who earlier took part in the investigations of the Boylston Street Fishweir in Boston.[3,4] Martin has made extensive palynological studies in the American south-west where he has worked on very early cultural levels in Arizona and on pollen analysis of human coprolites from Glen Canyon.[65] Schoenwetter's work has been largely in the south-west also, and he has contributed to the American Bottoms archaeological project of Illinois.[74]

At least four general papers on the investigations of archaeological plant remains have been published in America. Gilmore's appeared in 1932 as part of his report of the activities of the Ethnobotanical Laboratory at the University of Michigan.[35] In 1947 Barghoorn presented a guide for 'collecting and preserving botanical materials of archaeological interest'.[2] The offerings of Jones and Cutler are especially instructive. Both appeared as portions of a general publication dealing with the disposition and analysis of non-artifactual archaeological materials.[20,47] This is the report of a conference sponsored by the National Academy of Science–National Research Council. Several other papers in this collection are worthy of note, especially those by Griffin and MacNeish.[38,57]

One of the most gratifying recent developments in American palaeo-ethnobotany is a symposium entitled 'Integrated Research in Economic Botany VI: Ethnobotany of some New World Cultures.' It took place December 30, 1964, in Montreal, Canada, at a meeting of the Society for Economic Botany. Five of the papers published subsequently in *Economic Botany*, Volume 19, Number 4, were presented by six of the currently most active workers in the field: Callen (coprolites from Mexico),[53] Galinat (maize in North America),[30] Kaplan (American *Phaseolus* beans),[53] Smith (American cultivated crops),[80] and Whitaker and Cutler (American domesticated cucurbits).[88] All of these papers deal primarily with the pre-Columbian archaeological record of plant remains. Table C indicates the results of some of the work of these individuals and others.

Many American archaeologists, in addition to those already mentioned, have displayed a cognizance of the significance of palaeo-ethnobotany. A few of them can be noted here for purposes of exemplification: Joseph R. Caldwell has emphasized plant remains in explicating his concept of 'primary forest efficiency.'[10] In a much-quoted but never published paper, Melvin L. Fowler has discussed the early development of agriculture in the eastern United States, utilizing the available palaeo-ethnobotanical evidence.[28] William A. Ritchie has shown a continuing interest in plant remains from

TABLE C

Antiquity of various American cultigen remains. Dates are in years before present and broadly approximate.

Sources: beans, Kaplan;[53] sunflower and cucurbits in east U.S., Watson and Yarnell;[85] others in southern Mexico, Smith;[79] others in northern Mexico and cotton in south-west U.S., Mangelsdorf, et al.;[61] maize in south-west U.S., Smith;[80] maize in east U.S., Yarnell.[96]

	Peru	Southern Mexico	Northern Mexico	South-west U.S.	East U.S.
Helianthus annuus sunflower			?	?	2,600
Lagenaria siceraria bottle gourd	5,000	7,500	9,000	2,300	2,600
Cucurbita pepo squash, pumpkin		3,000	9,000	2,300	2,300
C. moschata	4,000	5,000	3,000	1,000	?
C. mixta		7,000?	1,000	1,000	
C. ficifolia	4,000	?			
C. maxima	2,000				
Phaseolus vulgaris garden bean	2,500	7,000	6,000	2,300	600
P. lunatus lima bean	5,300	1,400	1,800	700	?
P. coccineus scarlet runner bean		2,200	9,000		
P. acutifolius var. latifolius tepary bean		5,000		1,200	
Zea mais maize	3,000	6,500	4,500	4,500	1,800
Nicotiniana rustica tobacco	?	?	1,600	?	?
Gossypium spp. cotton	4,000	?	3,700	3,000	
Amaranthus spp. amaranth		6,400	4,200	?	
Capsicum spp. chili pepper	4,000	8,000	9,000		
Manihot esculenta manioc	2,700	?	2,400		
Arachis hypogaea peanut	2,700	2,100			
Ipomoea batatas sweet potato	2,700	?			
Solanum sp. potato	2,700				

archaeological sites in the north-eastern United States,[60] and Charles Faulkner has systematically recorded the materials recovered in Tennessee.[26]

It is perhaps inevitable in a review of this sort that individuals and studies which might have been included are neglected. It should be stressed that this overview does not pretend to be complete or entirely comprehensive. I have, however, endeavoured to give some idea of the range of workers and research in this field, if not also some of the limitations of past studies.

REFERENCES

1 ANDERSON, E. 1942. *Am. J. Bot. 29,* 832–5
2 BARGHOORN, E. S. 1944. *Am. Antiq. 9,* 289–94
3 —— *et al.,* 1949. *Pap. Peabody Found. Archaeol. 4,* No. 1
4 ——, WOLFE, M. K. and CLISBY, K. H. 1954. *Harvard Univ. Bot. Mus. Leafl. 16,* 229–40
5 BLACK, M. J. 1963. *Pap. Mich. Acad. Sci. Arts and Let. 48,* 541–7
6 BOHRER, V. L. 1958, *Am. Anthrop. 56,* 99–104
7 —— 1962, *Southwest. Mon. Assn. Tech. Ser. 2,* 75–114
8 BROOKS, R. H. *et al.,* 1962. *Am. Antiq. 27,* 356–69
9 BROWN, W. L. and ANDERSON, E. 1947. *Am. Mo. Bot. Gard. 34,* 1–30
10 CALDWELL, J. R. 1958. *Trend and Tradition in the Prehistory of the Eastern United States.* Am. Anthrop. Assn. Mem. No. 88
11 CALLEN, E. O. 1965. *Econ. Bot. 19,* 335–43
12 —— and CAMERON, T. W. M. 1960. *New Scient. 8,* 35–40
13 CARTER, G. F. 1945. *Plant Geography and Culture History in the American Southwest.* Viking Fund Publ. Anthrop., no. 5
14 COLLINS, G. N. in GUERNSEY, S. J. and KIDDER, A. V. 1921. *Pap. Peabody Mus. 8,* 1–121
15 COSTANTIN, J. and BOIS, D. 1910. *Revue Gen. Bot. 22,* 242–65
16 CUTLER, H. C. 1946. *Harvard Univ. Bot. Mus. Leafl. 12,* 257–91
17 —— 1952. *Fieldiana: Anthrop. 40,* 461–79
18 —— 1956. *Ibid. 45,* 174–83
19 —— 1957a. *Plateau 30,* 1–16
20 —— 1957b. *Natl. Acad. Sci.-Natl. Res. Counc. Publ. 565,* 39–40
21 —— 1962. *Am. Antiq. 28,* 256–7
22 —— and BLAKE, L. 1965. *Southeast Archaeol. Conf. Bull. 3,* 75–7
23 —— and MEYER, W. 1965. *Soc. Amer. Archaeol. Mem. 31,* 136–52
24 —— and WHITAKER, T. W. 1961. *Am. Antiq. 26,* 469–85
25 DRESSLER, R. L. 1953. *Harvard Univ. Bot. Mus. Leafl. 16,* 115–73
26 FAULKNER, C. H. and GRAHAM, J. B. n.d. *Plant Food Remains on Tennessee Sites: A Preliminary Report.* MS (1965)
27 FONNER, R. L. 1957. *Soc. Amer. Archaeol. Mem. 14,* 303–4
28 FOWLER, M. L. n.d. *The Origin of Plant Cultivation in the Central Mississippi Valley: A Hypothesis.* MS (1957)
29 GALINAT, W. C. 1959. *Proc. Denver Mus. Nat. Hist. 8,* 104–16
30 —— 1965. *Econ. Bot. 19,* 350–7
31 —— and GUNNERSON, J. H. 1963. *Harvard Univ. Bot. Mus. Leafl. 20,* 117–60
32 —— MANGELSDORF, P. C. and PIERSON, L. 1956. *Ibid. 17,* 101–24
33 —— and RUPPÉ, R. J. 1961. *Ibid. 19,* 163–81
34 GILMORE, M. R. 1931. *Pap. Mich. Acad. Sci. Arts and Let. 14,* 83–102
35 —— 1932. *The Ethnobotanical Laboratory at the University of Michigan.* Univ. Mich. Mus. Anthrop. Occ. Contrib., no. 1
36 GOSLIN, R. M. 1952. *Ohio Archaeol. 2,* 9–29
37 —— 1957. Food of the Adena People, in WEBB, W. S. and BABY, R. S. *The Adena People,* no. 2, Columbus, Ohio
38 GRIFFIN, J. B. 1957. *Natl. Acad. Sci.-Natl. Res. Coun. Publ. 565,* 59–60

39 HARLAN, J. R. and DEWET, J. M. J. 1965. *Econ. Bot. 19*, 16–24
40 HARMS, H. VON. 1922. Ubersicht der bischer in alterperuanischen Gräbern gefundenen Pflanzenreste, in *Festschrift Edward Selar*, Stuttgart, 157–86
41 HEISER, C. B. 1951. *Proc. Am. Philos. Soc. 95*, 432–48
42 —— 1955. *Am. Biol. Teacher 17*, 161–7
43 —— 1965. *Amer. Anthrop. 67*, 930–49
44 JONES, V. H. 1936a. *Univ. New Mex. Bull. Anthrop. Ser. 5*, 51–64
45 —— 1936b. *Univ. K. Rpts. Archaeol. and Anthrop. 3*, 147–65
46 —— 1955. *Univ. Utah Anthrop. Pap. 22*, 183–203
47 —— 1957. *Natl. Acad. Sci.-Natl. Res. Coun. Publ. 565*, 35–8
48 —— 1965. *El Palacio 72*
49 —— and FONNER, R. L. 1954. *Carnegie Inst. Wash. Publ. 604*, 93–115
50 —— and MORRIS, E. A. 1960. *El Palacio 67*, 115–17
51 KAPLAN, L. 1956. *Am. Mo. Bot. Gard. 43*, 189–251
52 —— 1963. *Econ. Bot. 17*, 350–9
53 —— 1965. *Ibid., 19*, 358–68
54 —— and MACNEISH, R. S. 1960. *Harvard Univ. Bot. Mus. Leafl. 19*, 33–6
55 KENT., K. P. 1957. *Trans. Am. Philos. Soc. n.s. 47*, pt. 3
56 —— 1962. *Southwest Mon. Assn. Tech. Ser. 2*, 115–55
57 MACNEISH, R. S. 1957. *Natl. Acad. Sci.-Natl. Res. Counc. Publ. 565*, 28–9
58 MANGELSDORF, P. C. and LISTER, R. H. 1956. *Harvard Univ. Bot. Mus. Leafl. 17*, 151–78
59 —— MACNEISH, R. S. and GALINAT, W. C. 1956. *Ibid. 17*, 125–50
60 —— 1964. *Science, 143*, 538–45
61 ——, MACNEISH, R. S. and WILLEY, G. R. 1964. Origins of Agriculture in Middle America, in West, R. C. *Handbook of Middle American Indians*, Vol. 1, Austin, 427–45
62 —— and REEVES, R. G. 1939. The Origins of Indian Corn and its Relatives. *Texas Agric. Expt. Sta. Bull., no. 574*
63 —— and SMITH, C. E. JR. 1949. *Harvard Univ. Bot. Mus. Leafl. 13*, 213–47
64 MARTIN, P. S. 1963. *Am. Antiq. 29*, 67–73
65 —— and SHARROCK, F. W. 1964. *Ibid. 30*, 168–80
66 NICKERSON, N. H. 1953. *Am. Mo. Bot. Gard. 40*, 79–111
67 —— 1954. *Bür. Am. Ethnol. Bull. 158*, 163
68 PAYNE, W. D. and JONES, V. H. 1962. *Pap. Mich. Acad. Sci. Arts. and Let. 47*, 147–63
69 RITCHIE, W. A. 1965. *Early Man to Iroquois*. Garden City, N.Y.
70 ROCHEBRUNNE, A. T. DE. 1879. *Actes Soc. Linn. Bordeaux 3*, 343–58
71 SAFFORD, W. E. 1917. *Proc. 2nd Pan-Am. Sci. Congr. 1*, 146–59
72 SAFFRAY, DR. 1876. *La Nature 4*, 401–7. Paris
73 SAUER, J. D. 1950. *Ann. Mo. Bot. Gard. 37*, 561–632
74 SCHOENWETTER, J. 1964. *Am. Bottoms Archaeol. Ann. Rept. 3*, 29–31
75 SEARS, P. B. 1962. *Bull. Geol. Soc. Am. 63*, 241–54
76 SMITH, C. E. JR. 1950. *Harvard Univ. Bot. Mus. Leafl. 14*, 157–80
77 —— 1965a. *Fieldiana: Bot. 31*, 55–100
78 —— 1965b. *Ibid. 107–43*
79 —— 1965c. *Econ. Bot. 19*, 71–82
80 —— 1965d. *Ibid., 322–34*
81 —— *et al., In press. Ibid.*
82 STRUEVER, S. 1962. *Am. Antiq. 27*, 584–7
83 —— 1965. *Southeast Archaeol. Conf. Bull. 3*, 32–5
84 TOWLE, M. A. 1961. *The Ethnobotany of Pre-Columbian Peru*. Viking Fund Publ. Anthrop., no. 30
85 WATSON, P. J. and YARNELL, R. A. In press. *Am. Antiq.*
86 WHITAKER, T. W. 1948. *Southwest. J. Anthrop. 4*, 49–68
87 —— and BIRD, J. B. 1949. *Am. Mus. Nov. 1426*, 1–15
88 —— and CUTLER, H. C. 1965. *Econ. Bot. 19*, 344–9
89 ——, CUTLER, H. C. and MACNEISH, R. S. 1957. *Am. Antiq. 22*, 352–8
90 WHITFORD, A. C. 1941. *Am. Mus. Nat. Hist. Anthrop. Pap. 38*, 1–22
91 —— 1943. *J. N.Y. Bot. Gard. 44*, 25–34

92 WITTMACK, L. 1880–87. Plants and Fruits, in REISS, W. and STÜBEL, A. *Necropolis of Ancón in Peru*, Vol. 3, pt. 13, N.Y., London, and Berlin

93 —— 1888. *Congr. Internatl. Amer.* 7, 325–49, Berlin

94 YACOVLEFF, E. and HERRERA, F. L. 1934–35. *Revista del Museo Nacional 3*, 243–322: 4, 31–102. Lima

95. YARNELL, R. A. 1959. *El Palacio 66*, 176–8

96 —— 1964. *Aboriginal Relationships between Culture and Plant Life in the Upper Great Lakes Region*. Univ. Mich. Mus. Anthrop., Anthrop. Pap. no. 23

97 —— 1965a. *Florida Anthrop. 18*, 77–82

98 —— 1965b. *Am. Anthrop. 67*, 662–74

20 The Domestication of Yams: A Multi-disciplinary Approach

JOHN ALEXANDER

HOW AND WHEN YAMS WERE FIRST DOMESTICATED is still unknown in spite of their being a staple food of many millions of people in two continents and in spite of different domesticated species being found in three continents. Alone among the great cultivars they have, so far, failed to arouse the interest of more than a few botanists and historians and much work needs to be done before the problem of their domestication is solved. This summary of our present knowledge will serve to demonstrate how dubious general theories based upon work in one discipline or in one region are likely to be; a lesson which has relevance to the study of any kind of agri- or vegi-culture. Since yam remains have yet to be identified in an archaeological context and since the application of ethnographic and botanical evidence to tropical field archaeology has hardly begun, the direction which future research should take must be considered, for in the study of yams, perhaps, more than any other food crop success will come only through close interdisciplinary co-operation.

The problems are world-wide, for the natural family *Dioscoreaceae* is pan-tropical and this herbaceous vine is found wild in Africa, Asia and America. Many of the 600 species known store their nourishment in underground tubers which are, or can be made to be, good to eat and for this reason they are attractive to men. Two groups of problems can be distinguished; those of Regional Synthesis, in which the evidence from many different sources (ethnographic, botanical, etc.) must be assessed and fitted together to show the local pattern of use and development, and general ones of Field Archaeology, concerned with the finding of the settlements and cultivation areas of yam-growers.

Although little detailed work upon the chromosome history of the genus *Dioscorea*[1] has yet been done, there seems no doubt among botanists that wild yams have always formed part of the environment of men in the forested, tropical zones of the three continents already mentioned and Australia. It is also agreed that cultigens, man-made species, have been developed from local wild forms in the three first-mentioned continents.[2] It should therefore be apparent that before any general theories about the origins of yam domestication can be advanced, the evidence in each of the three continents will have to be studied and compared.

In South-East Asia the following botanical evidence is available: wild species are found from India to southern China and southward beyond Malaya into the Pacific Islands. Two important cultigens (*D. alata* L. and *D. esculenta* (*lour*)) are held to be of mainland origin and a third (*D. bulbifera* L.) originated either on the mainland or in the islands.[3] The ethnographic evidence shows that hunter-gatherers know, harvest and even replant wild yams in the area, and that tubers had every appearance of being a long-established part of their food supply.[4] The domesticated species, although widely grown on the mainland, are nowhere a major crop; many farming societies grow them as a subsidiary one and cultivation methods are skilful.[5] On literary evidence yams can be shown to have been known and presumably domesticated in south China by the third century AD and in India by the sixth century AD.[6] In the latter area it seems unlikely, on literary evidence, that they were present much earlier.[7] Direct archaeological evidence does not yet exist but it has been shown in recent years that men with equipment similar to that used by contemporary cultivators in Central China existed in the tropical forests of Assam, Thailand and Malaya as early as the second millennium BC.[8]

In the islands of the Pacific domesticated yams are still a major and sometimes even a staple crop. Botanically the species found are accepted as mainland ones, perhaps with some local cultigens.[9] Ethnography shows that they are expertly cultivated and that many groups are (within the historic present) using only stone tools.[10] Yams are widely used in the religious and social life of these groups. In the further islands, where wild yams are not found, the arrival of domestic species are recorded in oral tradition and can be dated to the first and second millennia AD.[11] Here, as on the mainland, no direct archaeological evidence for yam-growing exists. Groups with equipment similar to that possessed by farmers on the mainland have been found and dated, as on the mainland, to the second and first millennia BC.[12]

In the islands of the Indian Ocean, especially Madagascar and on parts of the East African Coastal Plain, yams of South-East Asian species, not related to local wild forms, are grown.[13] On physical anthropological and linguistic grounds the population of Madagascar is held to be of South-East Asian origin and a movement of peoples and plants across and round the Indian Ocean in the first millennium AD is generally accepted.[14]

A wide variety of evidence from Asia may therefore be summarized as pointing to an early domestication of yams on the South-East Asian mainland and a movement of plants and peoples both eastwards and westwards thence. There is no evidence to support a date earlier than the second millennium BC for this to have taken place.

In Africa a comparable body of evidence has been accumulated. Botanically it has been shown that indigenous wild yams exist from the Indian Ocean to the Atlantic and from the Sudan to Angola. It is generally agreed that two important cultigens (*D. cayenensis Lam.* and *D. rotundata Poir.*) as well as several minor forms have developed from indigenous species.[15] The existence of a number of peculiarly African yam pests, particularly four species of Dynastid beetle with very wide distributions, may be significant here.[16] The ethnographic evidence shows that the wild forms are harvested by hunter-gatherers and are also well-known as a famine food to farming societies throughout tropical Africa.[17] The domestic species are widely cultivated from the east to the west coasts as a subsidiary crop[18] and, in West Africa, are a staple in many areas.[19] Yams are expertly cultivated and within the historic present, stone as well as metal tools were used. Yams are as deeply entwined in the social and religious life of many communities as they are in the Pacific Islands. Literary evidence shows that yams were being cultivated in East and West Africa in the sixteenth century AD.[20] There is as yet no direct archaeological evidence of yam-growing but groups with equipment similar to that of farmers in the tropical savannahs[21] and to that of yam growers in the tropical forests have been found and can be dated to the second and first millennia BC.[22]

The evidence from Africa is therefore very similar in kind and date to that from South-East Asia and suggests a development of vegiculture in the tropical forests at a time in the second millennium BC when there is so far no archaeological evidence of connection between the two continents.

In South America wild yams are found through the forests of Brazil and Venezuela and at least one cultigen (D. trifida L.) is accepted by botanists as having been derived from local wild forms.[23] Ethnography shows that the wild forms are known and prized by hunter-gatherers and that the domestic forms are grown as a subsidiary crop from the Caribbean Islands to Brazil.[24] They are cultivated with stone or wooden tools but are nowhere a major crop. Literary evidence shows cultivated yams to have been present in the Caribbean Islands in the sixteenth and in Brazil in the seventeenth centuries AD.[25] The archaeological finds show groups with equipment similar to that of known but later cultivators to have been present in the area in the second millennium or possibly even the third millennium BC.[26]

The evidence from America is therefore broadly similar to that from the other two continents and suggests a development of vegiculture in the tropical forests at a time when there is no archaeological evidence for connection with other continents.

These facts do not square with the general theories so far advanced. They have been based on a mixture of mainly botanical and literary evidence, the ethnographic being neglected. The archaeological evidence from the tropical forests has only become available in recent years and has also been insufficiently considered.[27] Although the actual crops cultivated are not known, the mere presence of possible farmers in areas where yams are later important means that the problem must be considered as a prehistoric one, and that the literary and historical evidence which has been so much relied upon is really too late to be of use. Burkill and Sauer, the leading theorists, have both happened to concentrate on the evidence from Asia and have suggested a single source of yam-domestication there. A diffusion of plants it is held, then took them to the Pacific Islands, to Africa and later to America. If the answers to these problems really lie, in each continent, in or before the first millennium BC, then only Field Archaeology will find them. It will be necessary to excavate undoubted evidence of the presence of yams and/or of contact between the continents at this date.

To find this, a new approach to excavation in tropical forests will be necessary. The field problems are formidable for the Dioscoraea leave no seeds, nuts or pollen grains to be recognized and tropical conditions only rarely preserve leaves or woody fragments. Success may come from a study of many peripheral kinds of evidence and the co-operation of many specialists both before and after excavation will be necessary. It may come either from the gardens or the settlements of yam growers and some possible lines of research may be considered here.

YAM GARDENS AND CLEARANCES

Perhaps the most hopeful source of information will be the many surface sites already reported from the tropical forests in all three continents. Where scatters of stone tools have been found over areas of several acres[28] the areas should be re-examined, for those which have artifacts at some depth below the present surface will be of particular importance. They might well have been, and further field-work might locate others, on the lower slopes of hills or in valley-bottoms where earlier land surfaces have been covered by sheet erosion.[29] This erosion itself might well be the result of clearance for agri- or vegi-culture. The buried land surface might perhaps be identifiable from a scatter of charcoal (from forest clearance) or from a scatter of stone tools left after cultivation. Its status as a true soil could be checked by analysis and if it had been cultivated for yams, the mounding-up during growth, and the pits dug to harvest the crop, might well survive and be revealed by area excavation.[30] Really careful excavation might even be able to distinguish pits cut through the mounds.

If a surface on which events of this kind took place can be located, then widespread sampling will be necessary. The samples will, in most cases, need a preliminary examination on the spot, since the few which could be transported back to a laboratory might well be wrongly selected. The excavation team will have to include either a botanist or an excavation assistant trained, although not necessarily in any very detailed way, to recognize plant, insect and mollusc remains. At its simplest, this will make possible the retention of samples rich in evidence for later study, so that particularly interesting areas can be returned to and larger samples obtained. If suitably qualified help is available on the site, or when the selected samples are later submitted to specialists, more detailed work on the following lines must be undertaken.

First the character of existing yam cultivation in the area must be studied, probably with the help of Agricultural Research scientists in Government or University Departments of Agriculture.[31] The Botanical evidence not only of the appearance of cooked and uncooked tuber-fragments, the structure and silica skeletons of leaf and woody fragments of yams should be known, but also existing and deserted yam cultivation-plots should be visited and the vegetation pattern at different stages during crop-growth and forest regeneration be noted. In existing cultivations, the seeds, nuts and pollen of associated crops, as well as those of the characteristic local weeds, should be studied.[32] Entomologically, the insect, avid and molluscan tests found in local yam crops should be known, for the samples will have to be studied for durable fragments in the form of wing-covers, legs, eggs and shells, etc.[33] The study will need to be micro- as well as macroscopic.

SETTLEMENTS

By comparison with the cultivation plots, the location of the settlements of yam cultivators may be less easy. Whilst settlements in the forests have been, and will continue to be, located by scatters of pottery and other domestic debris, no progress will be made until the actual remains of yams are found. The search for organic matter must therefore be intensified and this will best be done in those areas (kitchens, stores and middens) where food fragments are likely to be found. The variety of botanical and entomological evidence may well be smaller than in the cultivation plots and this will only partially be compensated by ethnographic parallels for some of the objects found.

In kitchens local ethnographic evidence may show specialized equipment used in preparing yams; particular kinds of graters, mashers or pounders, earth or clay ovens, pots or griddles. These, in themselves, will not be conclusive, but if found will call for intensive study in the areas where they are concentrated. Burnt organic material will need particularly detailed study for yam fragments, but the baked clay from hearths, ovens, walls, as well as all sherds of pottery, should be examined for the matrices of burnt-out fragments of organic matter.[34]

Food stores and local methods of storing yams may be identifiable from the ethnographic evidence. Special huts identifiable from plans or sitings, clamps or storepits may be found.[35] If these can be identified, extensive sampling, for fragments of the yam pests likely to be concentrated here, will be necessary. As well as the insects, avids and molluscs mentioned above, microbe infections may also be identifiable.[36]

In middens, either pits or mounds, the individual strata of debris, recognized by careful excavation, will need examination for the kind of plant and insect evidence mentioned above. Once again preliminary examination of samples will need to be undertaken on the site and only the more rewarding ones retained for later work.

If both settlements and cultivation are found in the same area, the pottery and stone tool types may well link them, and particular societies may be identified. Dating must be expected to be by radio-active carbon (C-14) rather than by other methods.

Only when field work of this kind has been done in each continent will general theories have much validity. In the meantime, it should be evident that current theorizing, especially that which supports a single area of origin of yam domestication, is unsatisfactory.

This conclusion may perhaps be applied to the study of other early plant domestications, for archaeologists must realize that their best endeavours will always be insufficient if they confine themselves to the study of human artifacts. Only the excavation, under controlled conditions, of plant, insect and molluscan remains will satisfy a wider audience.

REFERENCES

1 SHARMA, A. and DE, D. 1965. *Genetica 28.1*, 112
2 WAITT, A. 1963. *Yams: Field Crop Abstracts*. Vol. 16.3 with bibliography, 145
  CHEVALIER, A. 1946. *Rev. int. Bot. appl.* no. 279–80, 26
  COURSEY, P. 1967. *Yams*, London
  BURKILL, I. 1953. *Proc. Linnean Soc. 164*
3 BURKILL, I. 1951. *Advanc. Sci. 28*, 443
  TING, Y. and CHI, C. 1948. *Journ. Agric. Assoc. 186*, 23 China
  ALEXANDER, J. and COURSEY, P. 1969. In DIMBLEBY, G. W. and UCKO, P. *The Domestication and Exploitation of Plants and Animals*, London
4 WAITT, A. 1963, *op. cit.*
  RADCLIFFE-BROWN, A. 1964. *The Andaman Islanders*, London, 220

5 BARRAU, J. 1956. *Journ. Agric. Trop. et de Bot. Appl.* 3.7–8, 285
  BASCORN, J. 1965. *Anthrop. Records 22*, 101
6 TING, Y. and CHI, C. 1948. *op. cit.* 23
  WRIGLEY, C. 1960. *Journ. African Hist.* I
7 OM PRAKASH. 1961. *Food and Drink in Ancient India*, Delhi
8 SHARMA, T. *Neolithic Cultures of Assam* (unpublished Ph.D. thesis London, 1966), summarizing the
  S.E. Asian evidence
  CLARK, J. D. G. 1961. *World Prehistory*, Cambridge, 204
9 BARRAU, J. 1965. *J. Soc. Océan 21*, 55
10 FORDE, D. 1964. *Habitat Economy and Society*, London, 187
11 SUGGS, R. 1960. *The Island Civilisations of Polynesia*, 154
12 E.g. BULMER, S. and R. 1964. *American Anthrop. 62.2, No. 4*
13 COURSEY, P. 1965. Yams, *World Crops 17(2)*, 75
14 FREEMAN-GRENVILLE, P. 1962. *Med. History of Tanganyika*, Oxford
15 IRVINE, F. 1954. *Textbook of West African Agriculture*, Oxford, 191
  CHEVALIER, A. 1946. *Op. cit.*
  COURSEY, P. 1967. *Yams*, London
16 GOLDING, F. 1928. *7th An. Bull. Dept. Ag. Nigeria*, 38
17 OKIY, G. 1960. *Journ. West Afric. Science Assn. 6.2*, 117
  CORKILL, N. 1948. *An. Trop. Med. and Parasit. 42.4*
18 *Ethnographic Survey of Africa, V.* 1965., 17. I.A.I.
  MACMASTER, D. *A Subsistence Crop Geography of Uganda* (unpublished Ph.D. Thesis, London, 1960)
19 COURSEY, D. 1965. *World Crops 17.2*, 75
20 PERIERA, D. 1936. *Esmeraldo de Situ Orbis.* Hakluyt Society
21 DAVIES, O. 1966. *Reports, 8th Congress Pre- and Proto-History*, Prague
22 —— 1960. *Trans. Hist. Soc. of Ghana 4.2*, 14
  FAGG, B. 1959. *Journ. Hist. Soc. Nigeria 4*
23 COURSEY, P. 1967. *Yams*, London
24 STEWARD, J. H. and FARON, L. C. 1959. *The Native Peoples of Southern America*, New York
25 CARTER, G. 1946. *American Anthrop. NS 48.1*
26 ROUSE, I. 1964. In *Prehistoric Man in the New World* (ed. JENNINGS, J. D. and NORBECK, E.), Chicago
27 BURKILL, I. 1953. *Op. cit.*; and 1960. *Journ. Linnean Soc. (Bot.) 56*, 319
  SAUER, C. 1952. *Am. Geog. Soc. Bowman Mem. Lecture*, series 2
  MORGAN, W. 1962. *Journ. Afric. Hist. III.2*, 235
28 DAVIES, O. 1962. *Proceedings of 4th Pan-African Congress of Pre- and Proto-History*
29 As at Nokk, Fagg (1959), *op. cit.*
30 This might be the explanation of the pits at Nteresso. DAVIES, 1966, *op. cit.*
31 E.g. *The Nigerian Federal Department of Agricultural Research*, Ibadan
32 An obvious related crop in more recent times has been Elaeius guinnensis for example. I am grateful to
  Dr T. Russell for information on this point.
33 TAYLOR, T. 1963. *Nig. Dept. of Ag. Research Mem. 50*, 15: and
  JERATH, M. 1965. *Nig. Dept. of Ag. Research Mem. 83*, for a discussion of insect pests.
  I am indebted to Drs Verdcourt and Eastcop for information on mollusca.
34 ALEXANDER, J. From discussion at the seminar on Yam Domestication (Duplicated paper, the Institute
  of Archaeology, London, 1966), yam fragments should be recognizable since cassava has been
  identified. SMITH, C. E. 1968. *Economic Botany 22, no. 3*, 259
35 E.g. IRVINE, F. 1954. *A textbook of West African Agriculture*, Oxford, 126
36 OKOFOR, N. 1966. *Expl. Agriculture 2*, 179

21 Diet as revealed by Coprolites

E. O. CALLEN

UNTIL COMPARATIVELY RECENTLY, the brittle nature of any desiccated coprolites (as distinct from fossil ones) only allowed seeds and bones to be identified. As far back as 1910, Young[35] found sunflower seeds, water-melon seeds and fragments of hickory shell in coprolites from Salts Cave, Kentucky. Among later workers, Volney Jones[19] was able to identify four different types of seeds and two types of nuts from Newt Kash Hollow Shelter, Kentucky, and Jennings[18] identified seeds and other plant remains, plus hair of deer or antelope, feathers and chips of bone from Danger Cave in Utah. In 1957 Webb and Baby[31] with R. M. Goslin reported seeds, bones, feathers, and grass-hopper and beetle fragments from coprolites recovered from caves in Ohio, and Mac-Neish[23] reported finding grasshopper and snail shell fragments in coprolites excavated from the Ocampo Caves, Tamaulipas, Mexico. Yarnell[34] examined coprolites from Salts Cave, Kentucky, and was able to identify fourteen different plants by their seeds, as well as fish scales, arthropod remains and bone. Meanwhile Martin and Sharrock[27] made a pollen analysis of coprolites from a selection of caves in Utah, and were able to identify ten or more genera of plants from each specimen tested. Further pollen analysis has been carried out by Benninghoff[4] using Salts Cave coprolites, but at the time of writing his results had not reached the stage of publication.

Except for the pollen analyses, most of these results have been obtained by a dry analysis of materials, hence only seeds, fibres, bones and other cutinized materials could be identified. However, Volney Jones[20] experimented with material soaked in alcohol and household detergent for forty-eight hours or longer, enabling him to put it through graduated screens, to give a coarse sorting by size, but no data have been published. Colyer and Osborne[12] working with coprolites of the Wetherill Mesa Project, soaked them in 2% lye for twenty-four hours or longer, and screened them to give a coarse sorting, but no results or data are given, other than photographs and identification of seed samples recovered.

The first successful identification of soft plant and animal tissues from coprolites, was made by Callen and Cameron[10] working on material from Peru. They soaked their material in a 0·5% aqueous solution of trisodium phosphate for seventy-two hours. In addition to softening the material, much of the bile pigment is extracted as well. Sub-sequent experience (Callen[7]) has shown that soaking for a week or more frequently allows the coprolite to fall apart naturally, and prevent further breaking of the plant fragments.

Using a modification of the trisodium phosphate method Ambro[1] and Cowan[13] reported at the annual meeting of the Society for American Archaeology on their analysis of coprolites from Lovelock Cave, Nevada. Here also graduated screens were used to get a rough estimate of different foods eaten. Their work forms the first of a series being initiated under R. F. Heizer[16] at the University of California, Berkeley. Also using the phosphate method, another series of analyses is being initiated under George Armelagos[3] at the University of Utah. Both of these should soon be producing valuable data. Using a different softening agent (sodium hydroxide and disodium EDTA), Samuels[30] examined coprolites from the Mesa Verde of the Wetherill Mesa Project, Colorado. He was searching for parasites, finding pinworm eggs only, plus soil nematodes and mites. Also searching for parasites is Andrew McClary[28] of Michigan State University, who is analyzing coprolites from the Shulz site in Michigan, using both the phosphate and hydroxide methods. According to Lorenzo[22] some work on parasites in coprolites is also being carried out in Mexico City.

Callen and Cameron[11] did not publish the full results of their first trisodium phosphate analysis until 1960. They had developed it on coprolites from the Huaca Prieta, Peru, obtained through the courtesy of Dr Junius Bird, of the American Museum of Natural History in New York. According to Bird,[5] who had excavated the site, the economy of the Huaca Prieta peoples was based on a primitive farming combined with fishing. There had been a definite pre-pottery and pre-maize culture, lasting from circa 2500–1250 BC, when pottery and maize were introduced more or less simultaneously. The huaca was finally abandoned as a habitation around 500 BC.

The plant remains sifted from the refuse showed that the diet had consisted mainly of squash, chilli peppers, beans of possibly four varieties, *Canna* lily rhizomes, and rhizomes of cattails, rushes and sedges. The presence of a few seeds seemed to indicate that fruits had been eaten in season.

Judging from the coprolites, the diet of these Huaca Prieta inhabitants appears to have consisted mainly of beans, cucurbits (squash, etc.), a starchy root, mussels and other sea organisms. Crab and sea urchin, as well as sundry fruits in season, were probably more in the nature of delicacies than staple foods. The absence of bones in the refuse led Bird to conclude that meat must have been rare in the diet. No bones were found in the coprolites.

The writer had a further opportunity to study coprolites intensively through the courtesy of Dr Richard S. MacNeish, formerly of the National Museum of Canada, Ottawa, now of the University of Calgary, Alberta, who had excavated them from two neighbouring caves near Ocampo, in south-western Tamaulipas, Mexico.[23] They were designated Tmc 247 and 248, and the material recovered from them covers the period from 7000 BC till the time of the Spanish Conquest, with a gap between 5500–4000 BC. It has therefore been possible to discover something about the changes in diet in that valley, over the centuries.

As before, the coprolites were soaked in trisodium phosphate, but benzene and salt (NaCl) flotation tests were introduced. In the benzene tests, chitinous (i.e. insect) material floats at the benzene/water interface, and in the salt tests parasite eggs rise to the top of the solution. However, as small seeds, including grass seeds and glumes, as well as fibrous debris tended to do so also, the use of salt tests was discontinued for lack of time.

The coprolites from caves Tmc 247 and 248 between them span eight cultural phases,

TABLE A

Huaca Prieta Coprolites: HP – 3 2500–1250 BC; HP – 5 800–500 BC

Pit: 500 BC — HP – 5 — — — HP – 3 — — 2500 BC

Layer	A2	A4	B1	B4	C3	Hse	D1	D3	E1	F	G	H1	I2	L3	M	O	P1	Pos Unk
bean	x	x	x	x	x	x		x	x	x	x	x	x		x	x		
Capsicum				x					x						x			
Cucurbita	x	x	x					x	x	x	x		x	x	x		x	x
fruit tissue								x	x	x			x	x				
other plant tissue	x		x	x	x	x		x	x	x		x				x		x
fresh food	x	x		x	x	x		x	x	x	x	x	x	x	x		x	x
roasted food				x			x		x		x		x		x			x
mussel			x	x			x	x		x		x		x	x	x		
crab							x	x	x						x			
sea urchin							x	x	x						x			
diatoms		x		x			x	x	x		x							
algae								x								x		
fish							x	x	x				x	x		x		
arthropod				x			x			x					x			

the oldest, Infiernillo, covering the period from 7000–5000 BC.[25] From the refuse of the cave floors, there were recovered: *Opuntia* (prickly pear),[23] *Lagenaria siceraria* (domestic gourd) and *Cucurbita pepo* (pumpkin),[33] and *Phaseolus coccineus* (runner bean).[21] From the coprolites, plentiful *Opuntia* and *Phaseolus* were recovered, but no *Lagenaria* or *Cucurbita*. However, plentiful *Capsicum* (chili peppers) as both seeds and fruit tissue, and *Agave* (maguey) leaf tissue were found in the coprolites.

In the following cultural phase, Ocampo, covering the period from 4000–2300 BC, the cave refuse contained the same plants as in the Infiernillo phase, with the addition of the French or green bean, *Phaseolus vulgaris*.[21] From the coprolites, *Opuntia*, *Capsicum*, *Phaseolus* and *Agave* were recovered as before, though it was impossible to identify the bean species, since the characters by which they are identified at present are destroyed when the bean is eaten. However, three additional plants were identified from the coprolites. *Cucurbita pepo*, represented by seeds, was found in coprolites of the lowest level, i.e. close to 4000 BC. A second plant was *Carthamnus*, the seeds of which were identified at Kew Botanic Gardens. This plant belongs to the sunflower family, and is known to have been a source of red dye in prehistoric times. Of greatest interest, however, was the presence of *Setaria* (foxtail millet), seeds of which were obtained from the lowest level of the Ocampo phase. This proved to be *Setaria geniculata*, identified by C. E. Hubbard,[17] of Kew Botanic Gardens. When eaten, these seeds were generally eaten in quantity, with many of them split or broken.[9] Their colour suggested that they had been roasted.

The next younger cultural phase is Flacco (2300–1800 BC), which developed directly from Ocampo,[21] and in the coprolites the new plants to appear were *Aloe*, and *Helianthus* the sunflower. This latter proved to be *Helianthus annuus* var. *lenticularis*, and was found in only two coprolites of the 68 examined from this phase. It has since been found in a number of Mesa de Guaje coprolites, as will be mentioned later. What is believed to be *Yucca* and *Amaranthus* were also found in coprolites of this phase.

According to MacNeish[21] there was a fundamental shift in diet with the advent of the Guerra cultural phase (1800–1400 BC). As can be seen in Table B, the amounts of *Agave*, *Opuntia*, *Capsicum* and bone in the coprolites dropped considerably, while the amounts of bean, squash, and *Setaria* increased. It was in this phase that maize (*Zea*) made its appearance, in the form of cobs in the refuse,[21] but none was found in the coprolites.

The fifth cultural phase, Mesa de Guaje, covers the period from 1400–400 BC, and the samples of coprolites available is large enough to be completely representative of the diet. Of the main plants identified, there was a drop in the amounts of the principal plants eaten, except *Opuntia*, and in the amount of bone recovered.[6] This work was

TABLE B

Ocampo Caves, Tamaulipas. Percentage Occurrence

		Agave	bean	*Capsicum*	*Cucurbita*	*Opuntia*	*Setaria*	bone
7000 – 5000 BC	Infiernillo	40	60	60	0	65	0	20
4000 – 2300 BC	Ocampo	49	20	41	7	84	32	24
2300 – 1800 BC	Flacco	62	12	54	23	82	40	19
1800 – 1400 BC	Guerra	50	17	36	33	64	42	7
1400 – 400 BC	Mesa de Guaje	60	30	46	34	41	37	37
200 – 900 AD	Palmillas	—	—	—	—	—	—	—
1000 – 1500 AD	San Lorenzo	80	47	67	33	87	47	40

carried out between 1958 and late 1961, and completed the first phase of the analysis of the Tamaulipas material. The second phase started in late 1965, and a further 43 Mesa de Guaje coprolites have been thoroughly studied by mid-1966, so that the figures for Mesa de Guaje had to be revised and are shown in Table B. At the same time the figures for *Capsicum* and *Opuntia* were revised, to combine the figures for seeds and tissues without duplication. The bone figures were also revised. Nevertheless, these Mesa de Guaje figures cannot be considered final until the pre-1962 material has been re-examined in the light of subsequently acquired knowledge. Out of these 43 additional coprolites studied, 34 contained the remains of meat, showing that the absence of bones does not necessarily mean that no meat was eaten.

In these 43 Mesa de Guaje coprolites, *Agave* was the most frequently eaten material identified. This was followed by *Phaseolus*, mesquite, various cactus fruits (but excluding *Opuntia*), *Capsicum*, *Setaria*, bone, *Cucurbita*, *Opuntia*, and *Helianthus*, in that order. The presence of mesquite (*Prosopis*) is noted for the first time, but re-examination of the earlier material will no doubt show that it was eaten in earlier cultural phases too. *Helianthus*, the sunflower, turned up in ten coprolites of the culture, as well as other composite seeds. *Amaranthus* was also present but less frequently, than *Helianthus*. Two further plants identified include *Tillandsia usneoides* and a fleshy bromeliad probably of the same genus. *T. usneoides*, 'Spanish Moss', has frequently been found adhering to the exterior of the coprolites, and thus probably not been eaten, but equally frequently it has turned up inside the coprolites, and consequently must have been swallowed. This plant is found in the tropical rain forest region. The other bromeliad, probably eaten for its fleshy leaf bases, was identified at Kew Botanic Gardens as belonging to the genus *Tillandsia*. It too is probably an epiphyte, but in the thornscrub/cactus vegetation amongst which the actual caves are situated.[23] The presence of *Lagenaria* seeds in two Mesa de Guaje coprolites should also be mentioned, as it constitutes the oldest record of these seeds being used as human food.[14]

The coprolites from the Mesa de Guaje cultural phase mostly came from a single excavation square, consequently they have been grouped according to their chief constituents. Out of the 43 coprolites, *Agave*/mesquite were the co-dominant plants in eight coprolites, though they had been eaten together 33 times. *Agave*/bean (probably *Phaseolus*) were co-dominant six times, though eaten together 33 times also. *Agave*/*Helianthus* were co-dominant thrice, though eaten together eight times, and *Agave*/*Capsicum* co-dominant twice along with meat, but eaten together 20 times, 16 of them with meat. *Agave* alone as dominant material occurred twice, bean twice, mesquite twice, *Cucurbita* twice, and *Capsicum*, cactus and meat once each. Other plants that were co-dominant in the coprolites included *Tillandsia usneoides*, the fleshy-leaved *Tillandsia* and *Aloe*. *Opuntia*, although it occurred frequently, was never a dominant or co-dominant material in a coprolite. *Zea* (maize) occurred only four times in these 43 coprolites, and *Cucurbita* thirteen times.

In 1960 MacNeish[21] stated that there was a fundamental shift in the diet of the Tamaulipas cave dwellers, with the advent of the Guerra phase (1800–1400 BC). With the arrival of maize in that valley, the bean, squash and maize diet made its appearance and became well established, according to observations of the refuse from the caves.[21] This would suggest that a definite agriculture must have been established in the Guerra phase, so that by the succeeding Mesa de Guaje (1400–400 BC) it would be well established. Later, however, MacNeish[25] wrote (p. 417) that the incipient agriculture stage of development in the Tamaulipas (Ocampo) Caves stretched to the end of the Mesa de Guaje phase, i.e. till 400 BC. While it might be agreed that the Guerra phase saw the end of the incipient agriculture stage, the evidence of the coprolites and refuse combined seem to suggest that a very definite agriculture had been established by the beginning of the Mesa de Guaje phase, whatever the other artifacts may have indicated.

Succeeding the Mesa de Guaje phase are La Florida and Palmillas, two phases from which no coprolites were recovered. Following them comes the San Lorenzo cultural phase (AD 1000–1500), which according to MacNeish[21] shows a definite degeneration in culture and agriculture. In the refuse of the Palmillas phase, *Manihot dulcis* (cassava) was found, and it became one of the dominant plants of the San Lorenzo diet. At the time of writing, seven coprolites of level 1 and eight from level 2 of San Lorenzo have been examined. *Manihot* was dominant in one and co-dominant in five others of level 1, and co-dominant in four coprolites of level 2, i.e. in a total of 10 out of 15 coprolites. Other co-dominant plants include *Agave* five times in fifteen, *Opuntia* three times, bone four times, *Cucurbita* twice and *Capsicum* twice. Interesting was the fact that when *Cucurbita* was dominant, the other plants eaten were mostly in the form of seeds.

From the final cultural phase of the Tamaulipas sequence, San Antonio (AD 1500–1740), only one coprolite was recovered. This proved to contain *Agave*, *Opuntia* and meat (with bones) as the co-dominant materials.

When the Tamaulipas coprolites were recovered, some were riddled with circular, pit-like holes, containing empty pupal cases or dead larvae and pupae of blow flies or flesh flies. The discarded larval skins of *Fannia scalaris*, the latrine fly, were frequent. Plentiful remains of *Musca domestica*, the house fly, and several adult fungus gnats were also present. Other dipterous insects recovered include *Drosophila* larvae of several species, as well as the larvae of *Hermetia illuscens*, the soldier fly.[29] Amongst beetle larvae those of *Thylodrias contractus*, the odd beetle,[26] were the most interesting. For this latter scavenger of dried animal material, including fur, there is definite fossil evidence of a Caucasian origin, so that it is reasonable to assume that the odd beetle was carried by man over the Bering Land Bridge as he migrated into the New World. Other beetle larvae frequently recovered were those of two different dermestid beetles, common pests of stored products.

Before the Tamaulipas material had been fully analysed, a further opportunity to apply the trisodium phosphate method was provided by Dr R. S. MacNeish in early 1962, with coprolites from the Tehuacán Archaeological-Botanical Project from southern Puebla, Mexico. Here too the caves were situated in a thornscrub-cactus vegetation, so that there was a likelihood that similar plants had been eaten. Table C shows the principal plants identified from these Tehuacán valley coprolites.

Ten cultural phases or complexes constitute the Tehuacán sequence,[24] but coprolites were recovered from only seven of them. The oldest of these is the El Riego phase, dated between 6500–5000 BC, though the coprolites were from the youngest layers, and probably dating from close to 5500 BC. The co-dominant materials of the diet were *Setaria* and *Ceiba*, along with some meat and such plant materials as cactus or *Agave* tissue. This appeared to be an already well-established diet, since *Setaria* and other seeds were found on the cave floors of the Ajuereado phase, dating from before 6500 BC, and looked upon by MacNeish[25] as belonging to the hunting and plant gathering stage of the sequence. Following the El Riego phase, comes the Coxcatlan phase, dating from about 5000–3400 BC. Here again there is a very obvious *Setaria/Ceiba* diet, probably a wet season diet. Several new plants appeared, particularly *Diospyros digyna* and *Lemaireocereus*. This latter appeared along with *Ceiba* in the coprolites, and from internal evidence, probably represents a dry season diet.

The succeeding Abejas culture (3400–2900 BC) is looked upon as the last phase of the incipient agriculture stage in the Tehuacán valley. The diet shows an almost complete absence of *Setaria* and *Ceiba*, and the materials that had been eaten, suggest dry season

TABLE C
Principal Plants from Tehuacán Coprolites

Plant	Common name	Part eaten	eaten in Tamualipas?
Setaria	foxtail millet	seeds	yes
Ceiba	silk-cotton tree *pochote*	starchy roots	no
Agave	*maguey*	leaf tissue	yes
Opuntia	prickly pear cactus	fleshy stems chiefly, fruits and seeds	yes
Lemaireocereus	organ cactus	fleshy stems chiefly, fruits and seeds	no
Cacti, other	*tuna*	fruits and seeds	yes
Diospyros	sapote	fleshy fruits	no
Cucurbita	squash	chiefly fruits, some seeds	yes
Prosopis	*mesquite*	pods and seeds	yes
Capsicum	chili	fruits and seeds	yes
Zea	maize	seeds	yes

meals. They were *Agave*/cactus meals with some meat, though one was exclusively squash and meat.

The main cave from which nearly all the coprolites were obtained, was apparently uninhabited during the next two cultural phases, but in a neighbouring cave two coprolites were recovered, both with *Agave*/*Lemaireocereus* as co-dominant materials, and containing no *Setaria* or *Ceiba*.

The next cultural phase constitutes the formative period of the Tehuacán sequence; Santa Maria is dated between 900–200 BC. Plentiful coprolites were obtained from the main cave, and showed that the *Setaria*/*Ceiba* diet was as popular as before. At the same time the *Agave*/*Lemaireocereus* diet, foreshadowed in the previous Ajalpan, and even back in the Coxcatlan phase, was common. New plants to appear in this Santa Maria phase were *Physalis*, the ground-cherry or cape-gooseberry, and *Manihot*, the cassava.

The classic period of the sequence is the Palo Blanco phase, dating between 200 BC–AD 700. The *Setaria*/*Ceiba* and *Agave*/*Lemaireocereus* diets were as popular as ever, and meat was eaten with practically every meal. However, in subsidiary caves of the valley there was an *Agave*/cactus diet, or a *Lemaireocereus* diet, along with meat in practically every case. It was always the local plants around the cave mouth that were being eaten. An interesting plant that turned up at this time was *Helianthus*, the sunflower, which will be referred to later.

In the post-classic period, Venta Salada, from AD 700–1540, there is a noticeable decline in the *Setaria*/*Ceiba* and *Agave*/*Lemaireocereus* diets.

This survey shows that in the Tehuacán valley caves, a diet of grass seeds (*Setaria*) and a starchy root (*Ceiba*) came into existence at the beginning of the incipient agriculture stage, or towards the end of the hunting and gathering stage. This diet continued through into the Christian era, almost to the time of the Spanish Conquest. It should be emphasized again, however, that this is a cave diet and not a city dweller's diet, for which there is evidence that it was almost certainly based on a maize, bean and squash agriculture.

In the Tamaulipas caves, 350 miles away in northern Mexico, many of the same plants were being eaten (Table C). The outstanding absentee from the diet is *Ceiba*. So far there has been no starchy root crop identified as being eaten there until the Palmillas phase (AD 200). Other absentees include *Lemaireocereus* and *Diospyros*, and all three of them are absent from the valley vegetation. *Tillandsia usneoides* as well as the fleshy *Tillandsia* sp. were recovered from both the Tamaulipas and the Tehuacán coprolites, though they were eaten more frequently in the former. *Helianthus*, known to have been eaten by Indians from Kentucky to Utah and Nevada by 2500 BC, first appeared in the Tamaulipas coprolites about 2000 BC (also about the time that maize was introduced into the valley), but did not appear in the Tehuacán caves till close to the Christian era, i.e. not before 200 BC.

The remarkable absence of maize from the cave diets can have several explanations. Grinding and cooking techniques may have reduced the grains to such fine particles that they were thoroughly digested, and not traceable in the coprolites. On the other hand, the cave users may have tended and harvested the crops for tribute or for their masters, and not for home consumption. Certainly the continued use of *Setaria* would suggest the latter.

Meat was eaten surprisingly frequently, but bones, by means of which it might be identified were generally absent. However, hairs were often swallowed and have provided a method of identifying this meat. Hairs soaked in trisodium phosphate show the medulla pattern clearly. Measurements of the width of the cortex and medulla, and studies of the medulla pattern have shown that different genera of animals can be distinguished from one another, i.e. deer from peccary from ring-tailed cat. Sometimes even different species of the genus can be differentiated, i.e. *Sylvilagus cunicularius* (Mexican cottontail) and *S. audubonii* (Audubon cottontail).[8] The cuticular or outside scale pattern of the hairs could not be distinguished very readily in the phosphate soaked hairs. It is the cuticular pattern that has been the means of identification used by several other workers, including most recently Appleyard and Wildman[2] and Douglas.[15] Hair identifications have been published as an integral part of the analysis of the Tehuacán human coprolites,[8] but a detailed study of the animal material from the same caves will have to await further work.

ACKNOWLEDGEMENTS

The writer is greatly indebted to: Dr Junius Bird and Dr Richard S. MacNeish for placing their materials and knowledge at his disposal; Dr C. E. Hubbard and Dr C. R. Metcalfe of the Royal Botanic Gardens, Kew; Dr F. M. McFadden of the United States Department of Agriculture in Oxford, North Carolina, and the various specialists in the Entomology Division of the Canada Department of Agriculture, Ottawa; the many biologists and archaeologists in North America, including colleagues at McGill University, who have contributed tidbits of information, but especially Emeritus Professor

T. W. M. Cameron, a never-failing source of help and encouragement during the initial stages of this work.

REFERENCES

1 AMBRO, R. D. 1966. *Soc. Amer. Archaeol.*, 31st ann. meeting, p. 3 (abstr.)
2 APPLEYARD, H. M. and WILDMAN, A. B. 1963. *Science in Archaeology*, chap. 52, 545–54
3 ARMELAGOS, G. J. 1966. Personal communication
4 BENNINGHOFF, W. S. 1966. Personal communication
5 BIRD, J. B. 1948. *Natural History 57*(7), 296–303, 334–5
6 CALLEN, E. O. 1963. *Science in Archaeology*, chap. 19, 186–94
7 —— 1965. *Economic Botany 19*(4), 335–43
8 —— 1967. *Amer. Antiq. 32*(4), 535–8
9 —— 1967. *The Prehistory of the Tehuacán Valley*, vol. 1, 261–89
10 —— and CAMERON, T. W. M. 1955. *Proc. Roy. Soc. Canada 51* (abstr.)
11 —— and CAMERON, T. W. M. 1960. *The New Scientist 8*(190), 35–40
12 COLYER, M. and OSBORNE, D. 1966. *Mem. 19, Soc. Amer. Archaeol.*, 186–92
13 COWAN, R. A. 1966. *Soc. Amer. Archaeol.* 31st ann. meeting, p. 3 (abstr.)
14 CUTLER, H. C. 1962. Personal communication
15 DOUGLAS, C. L. 1966. *Mem. 19, Soc. Amer. Archaeol.*, 193–201
16 HEIZER, R. F. 1965. Personal communication
17 HUBBARD, C. E. 1961. Personal communication
18 JENNINGS, J. D. 1953. *El Palacio 60*(5), 179–214
19 JONES, VOLNEY H. 1936. *Univ. of Kentucky Repts. Archaeol. and Anthrop. 3*(4), 147–65
20 —— 1965. Personal communication
21 KAPLAN, L. and MACNEISH, R. S. 1960. *Harvard Bot. Mus. Leafl. 9*(2), 33–56
22 LORENZO, J. L. 1966. Personal communication
23 MACNEISH, R. S. 1958. *Trans. Amer. Philos. Soc. N.S. 48*(6), 1–210
24 —— 1962. *Tehuacán Archaeological-Botanical Project Repts. 2*, 1–42
25 —— 1964. *Handbook of Middle American Indians*, vol. 1, chap. 12, 413–26
26 MARSH, D. C. and CALLEN, E. O. 1964. *Phytoprotection 45*(3), 134 (abstr.)
27 MARTIN, P. S. and SHARROCK, F. W. 1964. *Amer. Antiq. 20*(2), 168–80
28 McCLARY, A. 1966. Personal communication
29 McFADDEN, M. W. 1966. *Proc. Ent. Soc. Washington 68*(i), 56
30 SAMUELS, R. 1966. *Mem. 19, Soc. Amer. Archaeol.*, 175–97
31 WEBB, W. S. and BABY, R. S. 1957. *The Adena People, No. 2*. Ohio Hist. Soc.
32 WHITAKER, T. W. and BIRD, J. B. 1949. *Amer. Mus. Novitates No. 1426*, 1–15
33 ——, CUTLER, H. C. and MACNEISH, R. S. 1957. *Amer. Antiq. 22*(4), 352–58
34 YARNELL, R. A. 1966. Personal communication
35 YOUNG, B. H. 1910. *The Prehistoric Men of Kentucky*, Filson Club Publications No. 25

22 The Anthropology of Prehistoric Great Basin Human Coprolites

ROBERT F. HEIZER

THE POTENTIAL VALUE OF HUMAN COPROLITES dating from prehistoric times as a source of information on ancient diet and health conditions has been known for a long time,[1] but not until 1960, with the work of E. O. Callen and T. W. M. Cameron of McGill University, was a serious effort made to extract and publish significant cultural information from a large lot of dated human faecal remains recovered from a controlled archaeological investigation.[2] While coprolites in an excellent state of preservation are often found in cave or shelter sites with dry deposits, these items may also be preserved under moist conditions.[3] Once archaeologists become consciously aware of coprolites and begin to look for them in archaeological sites, it is possible that their occurrence, recognition, and recovery under special conditions may prove to be much wider than we now suspect.

The excavation in 1936 of Humboldt Cave in west central Nevada, which was filled with dry living refuse, produced numbers of human coprolites,[4] but efforts made in 1937 to secure identification of seeds which were clearly visible in them failed through lack of interest or response by experts. In 1950 a large collection of coprolites was made at nearby Lovelock Cave,[5] a big closed chamber filled with dry occupation trash, as well as at other nearby cave and shelter sites occupied in prehistoric times. This coprolite material, together with that excavated in the summer of 1951 from Hidden Cave on the southern border of Carson Lake, about forty miles to the south, was analysed by Norman L. Roust, then a graduate student at the University of California (Berkeley), and a summary of his findings has been published.[5a]

In the summer of 1965 Lovelock Cave was revisited by a University of California field party and a collection of about seven hundred coprolites was made from two locations in the cave. A total of fifty Lovelock Cave coprolites has been analysed at Berkeley during 1965–66. The present paper summarizes the information secured on kinds and quantities of materials preserved in identifiable form in the Nevada coprolites, and compares results of analysis of coprolites from the same site (Lovelock Cave) carried out independently in two separate investigations employing different techniques of examination.

TECHNIQUES OF ANALYSIS

N. L. Roust, working between 1951 and 1955, unaided and without the advantage of earlier work to build upon, devised a method of dry analysis of coprolites. Since the faecal pellet was crushed, its form was changed, but other than this, the dry analytical technique is non-destructive. The coprolite to be analysed is first weighed, measured, and described with reference to shape, colour, apparent texture, etc. It is then crushed to the point of pulverization, care being taken not to break visible items as they make their appearance during the reduction process. The volume of the powdered dry material is determined, and a grab sample—usually amounting to about 5 grams—is taken and its volume is determined and recorded. This aliquot is then picked over and all visible un-digested elements such as bone, hair, fibre, etc., are extracted with a forceps or dissecting needle. The residue, which Roust termed 'digested material', consists of a fine powder in which separate elements cannot be distinguished. Weight and volume determinations are made of each component of this aliquot, and a calculation is then made of the amount by weight and volume for the whole coprolite.

The wet analysis method which we used in 1965–66 is a modification of that devised by E. O. Callen. It is partially destructive. The hard, dry faecal pellet is first measured, weighed, and described. It is then cut in half and two samples, each weighing 2 to 3 grams, are extracted, placed in labelled containers (we use 35 mm metal film cartridge cans), and set aside to be utilized for pollen analysis and chemical analysis for some of the fifty or so constituents known to occur in human faecal material.[6] Pollen studies of coprolites have already produced important results[7] in illustrating the floristic nature of a locality and, in addition, may be expected to tell something about the season of the year the coprolite was voided. The specimen is then placed in a wide-mouth glass jar with a screw lid (important because this confines the disagreeable odour, which at times is incredibly strong), into which is poured a cup of 0·5% aqueous solution of trisodium phosphate. There it soaks for a week or more, and in the process becomes softened, and the seeds and other plant materials are reconstituted by rehydration. The jar is shaken occasionally to help break up the pellet.

When the jar is opened, the contents are poured into a conical screen with a 1 mm mesh which rests on the rim of an empty three-quart container. Water is poured through the screen while it is agitated, the effect of this washing being to carry off the finer residues smaller than 1 mm in diameter. These residues are allowed to settle for a day or so and then the brown liquid, charged with trisodium phosphate, is poured off. We have not saved this liquid, but perhaps this should be done by other workers. The chemicals in suspension in this liquid are the item referred to in Table A as 'weight loss'. The fine residues are then dried and passed through two more screens, one with a 0·495 mm mesh (32 meshes/inch) and the other with a ·147 mm mesh (100 meshes/inch). The very fine powdered material which passes through the smallest screen provides a third grade of fine residues.

The wetted coarsest components (i.e. those over 1 mm in diameter) are placed in six-inch petri dishes and scanned under a 5·5 diopter illuminated table magnifier, and each kind of constituent (bone, charcoal, feather, fibre, etc.) is picked out with tweezers or a dissecting needle. When this process is completed each element is dried and then weighed. The residues held by the 0·495 mm screen (i.e. those with diameters between 0·999 and 0·496 mm) are examined under 20× magnification and the percentages of the most abundant constituents are estimated, and the weight of each of these is calculated by estimation and recorded. The same is done with the residues held by the 0·147 mm screen (i.e. those between 0·494 and 0·148 mm in diameter). The finest residues (i.e. those less than 0·146 mm in diameter) contain little that is qualitatively or quantitatively identifiable and appear to consist of the indigestible portions of soft or well-chewed foods.

Comparing the two methods, it can be argued that each has its advantages and disadvantages. Dry analysis does away with the bother of the soaking, washing and drying processes, and in addition is non-destructive to the extent that nothing is thrown away. Wet analysis has the disadvantage of creating unpleasant odours, and is slower in that it requires time for soaking, washing, and drying. However, it has the great advantage of reconstituting the coprolite contents to their original size and form by rehydration and thus makes for easier and more positive identifications.

PREHISTORIC DIETARY ITEMS AND MENUS

There is not enough space to provide a detailed list of the items and quantities present in the 101 coprolites which have been analysed from Lovelock Cave,[7a] but the data in Table A summarizes this information for the two separate investigations.

Seeds, particularly those of *Scirpus* (bulrush) and *Typha* (cattail), occur in a majority of samples. *Siphateles*, the Lahontan chub which runs up to 4·5 inches in length, were a more or less regular item of diet. These were secured from the waters of Humboldt Lake, which lay about two miles north of the cave, with dipnets made of cordage extracted from *Apocynum*, such nets having been recovered from the cave deposits. Fish were apparently eaten whole and raw, or after being parched or toasted with glowing coals. Surprisingly large numbers of these small fish were occasionally eaten. One coprolite weighing 30·1 grams contained the bony remains of 29 *Siphateles* as well as those of two other lake species, and a second coprolite, also rich in fish remains, contained the bones of at least 51 *Siphateles*. By devising a relation of length of pharyngeal bones to total length of the live fish, Dr W. I. Follett has calculated that the fish bone in this coprolite was derived from live fish weighing 3·65 pounds.[7b]

The whole seeds found indicate which seeds were eaten, and it appears that the prehistoric peoples collected small amounts of a variety of seeds which they encountered casually.

There are rare occurrences of *Gammarus*, a freshwater amphipod, but since this animal is also eaten by birds, fishes, and large water insects, it cannot be proved that they were taken and eaten in quantity by man as a conscious dietary item. There are also rare occurrences of *Cybister*, the water tiger beetle, found minus the head, which was perhaps unpalatable and bitten off before the beetle was swallowed.

Bird eggs were apparently not much eaten, or if they were it may have been at periods of the year when the cave was not visited. Larger birds were eaten after their primary and secondary feathers were plucked out, but baby birds (nestlings) were apparently eaten whole and raw, as evidenced by their bones and down present in coprolites.

The absence of splinters of heavy mammal bone may indicate that large forms such as antelope, deer, and mountain sheep were not brought to the cave, but that their meat

TABLE A

Contents of Human Coprolites from Lovelock Cave, Nevada

	Wet Analysis Interior	(1965–66) Entrance	Dry Analysis (1951–55)
Total number analysed	30	20	51
Total weight (gr)	495·0	345·0	782·0
Average orig. dry weight (gr)	20·4	20·3	19·1
Maximum diameter (mm)	53·0	74·0	—
Per cent of coarse constituents (>0·147 mm) diam. to total weight	22·6	15·1	44·36
Per cent of fine constituents (>0·147 mm diam.) to total weight)	48·5	47·7	55·63
Per cent of weight loss (after rehydrating and drying) to total weight	28·9	37·2	—
Seed (per cent of total weight)	27·3	21·1	25·90
Fish bone (per cent of total weight)	8·8	10·1	5·32
Bird remains (per cent of total weight)	1·3	4·1	—
Fibre (per cent of total weight)	5·8	5·2	7·60
Coprolites with fish bone (no., %)	20 (66%)	15 (75%)	21 (41%)
Coprolites with *Typha* seed (no., %)	10 (33%)	14 (70%)	}35 (68%)
Coprolites with *Scirpus* seed (no., %)	24 (80%)	16 (80%)	
Coprolites with abundant bird remains	6 (20%)	10 (50%)	18 (35%)
Meal types:			
Seed and fish	15	8	
Seed	4	1	
Fish	2	–	
Seed and bird	6	5	
Fish, bird and seed	–	4	
Seed, fish, and fibre	2	–	
Fish, bird, and fibre	–	1	
Bird, seed, and fibre	–	1	
Fibre	1	–	

was stripped off where the animal was killed and the bones discarded. The problem of identifying evidence of large mammals in the coprolites is a difficult one. Aside from the presence of animal hairs which could have been ingested quite incidentally, we have not yet found any method of determining the presence of mammalian meat as an article of diet. Perhaps chemical analysis for amino acids will provide the answer.

AGE OF COPROLITES AND SEASON OF CAVE OCCUPATION

It seems probable that the coprolites from the interior of Lovelock Cave represent winter accumulations during a time when the cave occupants were eating mainly dried *Scirpus* seeds and dried fish. The entrance lot of coprolites probably reflect somewhat more pleasant temperature conditions which did not necessitate cave-living to keep warm, and the greater abundance of *Typha* seeds, fish, and ducklings implies that these coprolites were deposited in the autumn. Pollen determinations from the interior and entrance lots will probably throw definite light on the question of seasonality.

One coprolite from the cave interior lot has been radiocarbon dated at 1210 ± 60 years old (sample UCLA-1071 F), and one from the entrance lot at 145 ± 80 years old (sample UCLA-1071 E). We are indebted to Dr Willard F. Libby and Dr Rainer Berger for dating these specimens.

In view of the marked similarity of dietary elements present in the two lots, we may conclude that food-gathering practices in this area have not changed materially in the past millennium.

PARASITOLOGICAL EXAMINATION

While parasites have been noted in prehistoric desiccated coprolites from Israel,[8] Colorado,[9] and coastal Peru,[10] an examination of fifty interior and entrance samples from Lovelock Cave by F. L. Dunn, Hooper Foundation, University of California Medical Centre, failed to yield any evidence whatsoever of parasitic remains. Larval nematodes of the genus *Rhabditis*, which are present in some of the coprolites, demonstrate that helminths can survive in recognizable form in faecal pellets, so that the total absence of true parasitic types such as hookworms, whipworms, roundworms, etc., in the Lovelock Cave coprolites may be taken as indicating a parasite-free population. Dunn[11] has determined that in general, open-country, temperate latitude hunter-collector groups are either wholly or relatively free of parasitic infections.

One amorphous mass of faecal material contained Charcot-Leyden crystals which are commonly noted in modern diarrhoeal and dysenteric faecal specimens, particularly in association with intestinal amoebiasis resulting from infection of *Entamoeba hystolytica*. It is not possible to provide any estimate of how common such dysentery might have been, but approximately 4% of the collection of coprolites is in this category.

SOME ASPECTS OF DAILY LIFE AS INFERRED FROM COPROLITES

Some of the coprolites from Lovelock Cave are three inches in diameter, although this size is rare. Most of them are solidly packed with fibre and seeds and can have been voided only with considerable effort. They are usually well-formed, and in the opinion of authorities we have consulted, they are interpreted as evidencing fairly normal intestinal operation considering the coarseness of the diet.

Sanitary practices were apparently minimal. Not much is recorded in the ethnographic literature of the Great Basin Indians (or American Indians as a whole, for that matter) about disposal of body wastes, but the evidence from Lovelock Cave seems to indicate that the cave was used at the same time as a living area and latrine. Captain J. H. Simpson, in 1859, wrote the following about a visit to a Gosiute Indian camp in western Utah: 'The offal around [the house] and in a few feet of it was so offensive as to cause my stomach to retch, and cause a hasty retreat. Mr Bean told me the truth when he spoke of the immense piles of faeces voided by these Indians, about their habitations, caused no doubt by the vegetable unnutritious character of the food.'[12]

Recent investigations of the quantities of phosphorus, nitrogen, and calcium in the soils of archaeological sites in California have led to the conclusion that these elements are mainly, perhaps wholly, due in origin to human wastes.[13] It can be shown that one hundred persons can produce 1,852 pounds of nitrogen, 273 pounds of phosphorus, and 121 pounds of calcium per year. If most of the human body wastes are deposited in the immediate vicinity of houses (as, for example, in the case of the Gosiute cited above), a very substantial addition of these elements will occur in the course of time. The investigation of Eddy and Dregne[14] on the soil chemistry of archaeological camp and village soils in New Mexico provides data which are consistent with those of California.

The diet indicated, one of relative sameness over a long period of time, consisted of small seeds, fish, and aquatic birds, supplemented occasionally with small rodents, eggs and insects. The most notable implication of the diet is the dependence upon food items secured from the lake on which the main open settlement lay. The generalized picture of Great Basin Indians living in a water-deficient area, always hungry, wandering about on foraging trips to kill small rodents or collect seeds,[15] does not fit at all with the economic routine suggested by the coprolites which, rather, imply a relatively sedentary population exploiting limited food resources and securing from these an adequate subsistence.

POSTSCRIPT

A curious parallel to modern coprolite dissection, though only a partial one, existed on the aboriginal level. The simple hunter-gatherer peoples of the peninsula of Lower California had developed, long before the appearance of the Spaniards in the sixteenth century, a technique for extracting components of human coprolites. Johann Baegert, a Jesuit priest, in the middle of the eighteenth century described the native use of the *pitahaya* cactus (*Lemairocereus thurberi*) which bears a fleshy fruit in late summer and early autumn. In this water-deficient land where food was ever in short supply, the *pitahaya* harvest time was the one period when every one had enough to eat, although we may imagine that a steady diet of this fruit became tiresome. Baegert wrote: 'The pitahayas contain a great many small seeds, resembling grains of powder, which for reasons unknown to me are not consumed in the stomach, but are passed in an undigested state. In order to use these small grains, the Indians collect all excrement during the season of the pitahayas, pick out these seeds from it, roast, grind, and eat them with much joking. This procedure is called by the Spaniards the second harvest.'[16]

Aschmann[17] cites a number of accounts of the second harvest among the peninsula tribes, and these are all very much like Baegert's description, except for occasional bits of additional information such as the facts that the flour made from the salvaged seeds was stored to be eaten during the winter when other food was scarce, and that all the people defecated in a special place paved with flat stones or dry grass. This last observation is interesting because it suggests that in this situation a regular latrine was invented for the purpose of conserving the collective faeces whose undigested seeds, when extracted and stored, may have meant the difference between starvation and survival in the lean period of winter.

REFERENCES

1 Earlier investigations, usually in the form of incomplete analyses and inadequately reported on, are by JONES, V. H. 1936. *Univ. Kentucky Repts. in Archaeol. and Anthrop. 3*, 147–65; WAKEFIELD, E. G. and DELLINGER, S. C. 1936. *Annals of Intern. Med. 9*, 1412–18: WEBB, W. S. and BABY, R. S. 1957. *The Adena People*, Ohio State Univ. Press; YOUNG, B. H. 1910. *The Prehistoric Men of Kentucky*, Filson Club, Publ. No. 25

2 CALLEN, E. O. this volume: CALLEN, E. O. and CAMERON, T. W. M. 1960. *New Scientist 8*, 35–40; CALLEN, E. O. 1965. *Econ. Bot. 19*, 335–43

3 GRZYWINSKI, L. 1959–60. *Zoologica Poloniae 10*, 195–9; ibid., 1962. *Wiadomosci Parazytologiczne 8*, 548; TAYLOR, E. L. 1955. *Veterinary Records 67*, 216

4 HEIZER, R. F. and KRIEGER, A. D. 1956. *Univ. Calif. Publs. in Amer. Archaeol. and Ethnol. 47* (1)

5 LOUD, L. L. and HARRINGTON, M. R. 1929. *Univ. of Calif. Publs. in Amer. Archaeol. and Ethnol. 25* (1)

5a ROUST, N. L. 1967. *Univ. Calif. Archaeol. Survey, Rept. 70*

6 ALTMAN, P. L. and DITTMER, D. S. (eds.). 1964. *Biology Data Book.* Fed. Amer. Soc. Exper. Biol., Washington, D.C., Table 53; CONSOLAZIO, C. F. and JOHNSON, R. E. 1963. *Physiological Measurements of Metabolic Functions in Man*, McGraw Hill, Table 13–19, 451–2; WOLLAEGER, E. E. and COMFORT, M. N. 1947. *Gastroenterology 9*, 272–83

7 MARTIN, P. S. and SHARROCK, F. W. 1964. *Amer. Antiq. 30*, 168–80

7a For details of the 1965–66 analyses see HEIZER, R. F., AMBRO, R. D. and COWAN, R. A. 1967. In *Univ. Calif. Archaeol. Survey, Rept. 70*

7b For details see FOLLETT, W. I. 1967. *Univ. Calif. Archaeol. Survey, Rept. 70*

8 WITENBERG, G. 1961. *Bull. Israel Explor. Soc. 25*, 86

9 SAMUELS, R. 1965. *Soc. for Amer. Archaeol., Mem. 19*, 175–79

10 CALLEN, E. O. and CAMERON, T. W. M. 1960. *New Scientist 8*, 35–40

11 DUNN, F. L. 1968. In LEE, R. and DEVORE, I. (eds.). *Man the Hunter*, New York, 221–8

12 SIMPSON, J. H. 1876. *Report on Explorations Across the Great Basin of the Territory of Utah*, Engineer Dept. of U.S. Army, Washington, D.C., 56

13 COOK, S. F. and HEIZER, R. F. 1965. *Univ. Calif. Publs. in Anthrop. 1*; ibid. 1962. *Univ. Calif. Archaeol. Survey, Rept. 57* (1)

14 EDDY, F. W. and DREGNE, H. E. 1964. *El Palacio 71*, 5–21: ARRHENIUS, O. 1963. *Ethnos 1963* (2–4)

15 STEWARD, J. H. 1938. *Bur. Amer. Ethnol., Bull. 120*

16 BAEGERT, J. J. 1952. *Observations on Lower California.* Univ. Calif. Press, 68

17 ASCHMANN, H. 1959. *Ibero-Americana 42* (7), 80–81

ADDITIONAL NOTE (June, 1969). Since this article was written we have augmented the collection of human coprolites from Lovelock Cave and now hold over 5000 specimens. Examples from radiocarbon dated levels of ages ranging from 2,500 to 150 years old are available to interested persons for study.

ANIMALS

23 Pleistocene Mammals and the Origin of Species

BJÖRN KURTÉN

EVOLUTION BEGINS AT THE POPULATION LEVEL, but as it goes on its effects accumulate and, in time, bring about the origin of new species. The importance of this was recognized by the early evolutionists, who even tended to use the 'origin of species' as a synonym of evolution. And, in fact, the rise of a new species is the primary *irreversible* event in evolution.

A dog is a domesticated wolf; you can breed a dog with a wolf, and they will yield fertile offspring. If the human race became extinct, our surviving dogs would probably interbreed with the wolves, finally to merge with them in a single population. That is because the dog and the wolf still belong to one and the same species, and their differentiation is reversible.

On the other hand, horse and donkey have been bred with each other for many centuries, and yet they do not merge into one species. No matter how many times we try to penetrate the genetic wall separating these two animals, it will not succeed; they do not produce fertile offspring. The speciation of horse and donkey is irreversible.

However, since evolution is a gradual process, there are various intermediate cases, in which the interfertility between species is hardly impaired at all. In those instances there are other kinds of barriers between the species, making the separation irreversible in practice. The two species may inhabit separate areas, or the species hybrids may be less well adapted to their environment than the two mother species, or the members of different species may refuse to mate in nature, even though they can be induced to do so in captivity. The role of the animal species in evolution has recently been thoroughly discussed by Mayr.[1]

It is clear that the actual history of origin of a species is of great intrinsic interest to the student of evolution. At the same time, however, the appearance of new species, and the disappearance of old, when worked into a stratigraphic sequence, furnishes the Pleistocene archaeologist with a useful chronological tool. Both of these aspects—the evolutionary and the chronological—are of interest to the student of human origins and evolution; he will wish to relate the descent of Man to the evolution of the fauna in general, and in addition he may study the dynamics of species change in other forms of life, for which the fossil history may be better documented than that of Man.

IMMIGRATION OR EVOLUTION IN SITU?

The history of the Pleistocene in Europe appears to span more than three million years, judging from K-Ar dates for the basal Villafranchian (earliest Pleistocene) of Montagne de Perrier in France.[2] In the course of this great stretch of time, the mammalian fauna was almost continuously undergoing changes in its composition. New species were introduced by immigration or evolution; old species vanished by extinction or evolution. As far as the European scene is concerned, this sequence is comparatively well known, though of course many details remain to be filled out.[3] What is known about the appearance of new species in the Pleistocene of Europe?

Various mammal species appear in the fossil record quite suddenly, without any predecessor in earlier strata, from which they might be derived. Doubtless many of these instances simply result from the incompleteness of the fossil record, and future discoveries may show that the ancestral form after all did inhabit Europe and the species evolved in situ.

In some cases, however, it seems fairly clear that the species in question really evolved somewhere else and appeared on the European scene as an immigrant. These species are common as fossils and have a well-documented earlier history in other parts of the world. For instance, we know that North America was the centre of horse evolution in the Tertiary, and that one-toed horses (*Equus*) originally evolved in that continent, afterwards to migrate to the Old World. They evidently crossed the Bering Strait, first to populate Asia, then to push into Europe and Africa. In Europe they appear at an early stage in the Villafranchian, but not at its very beginning.

As another example, true elephants (the family Elephantidae) evolved outside Europe (authorities differ as to whether they originated in Africa or Asia) and entered Europe only about the middle of the Villafranchian, many thousand years later than the horses. Again, the aurochs (*Bos primigenius*) entered Europe in the Holstein interglacial, apparently as an immigrant from Asia, where ancestral forms are known in earlier strata.

On the other hand, there are numerous instances in which it seems evident that a species evolved in Europe, and that the actual transition from the ancestral to the descendant species is covered by the fossil documentation. Sometimes it may perhaps be maintained that the ancestral and descendant forms are so similar that they can really be retained in a single species. For instance, the living Barbary ape of Gibraltar has a fossil history in Europe extending back to the Villafranchian, but the material is perhaps not sufficient to prove beyond doubt that the Villafranchian species (*Macaca florentina*) is distinct from the living (*Macaca sylvana*). The same objection might be made against the lineage *Dama clactoniana*→*Dama dama*; the Holsteinian Clacton deer is evidently ancestral to the Late Pleistocene fallow deer, but are the two in fact different species?

There are also instances in which the two successive species are certainly distinct, but where there is a time gap in the record coinciding with the actual transition. It is, for instance, clear enough that the Villafranchian bear *Ursus etruscus* (last appearance at Tegelen, end of Villafranchian) was ancestral to the living brown bear, but the latter appears in Europe in the Holstein (in Asia it is known a little earlier, but not early enough to bridge the gap).

WELL-DOCUMENTED SPECIES TRANSITIONS

Still, there are many cases where the ancestral and descendant forms are so distinct morphologically that they definitely have to go into separate species, and yet are connected by a sequence showing a complete transition.

Probably the most famous instances are found among the elephants. The Villafranchian *Elephas meridionalis*, or southern elephant, gave rise to two distinct, evolving lineages. One of the lines continued to inhabit about the same type of environment as the ancestral form, and in this group the evolutionary change was quite moderate: it gave rise to the Middle and Late Pleistocene straight-tusked elephant (*Elephas antiquus*). The other line meanwhile evolved much more rapidly, passing through two distinct species-stages in the same time: the Middle Pleistocene steppe mammoth (*Elephas trogontherii*) and the Late Pleistocene woolly mammoth (*Elephas primigenius*). In this case the change in mode of life was more radical, for these animals adapted themselves to a Boreal and Arctic environment; consequently the rate of evolution was speeded up. All of the elephant transitions are documented by enormous amounts of fossils, but unfortunately no study encompassing all the available material has yet been made.

There are, however, other good instances of species evolution. The wolverine (*Gulo gulo*), which is now a sub-Arctic and Arctic form, evolved gradually from an ancestral species (*Gulo schlosseri*), which was much smaller and lived in a warm-temperate fauna in the earliest Middle Pleistocene. Transitional populations show gradual size increase and a shift into colder associations, until finally typical *Gulo gulo* are found in the Mindel glaciation.

The European dhole of the Pleistocene, *Cuon alpinus* (the species is still in existence in Asia), evolved gradually from more primitive types in the Middle and Early Pleistocene. The ancestral form, *Cuon majori*, is present in the Late Villafranchian of Val d'Arno.

The line of the brown and cave bears has a very good fossil record, apart from the gap mentioned above. Its history begins with a small form, *Ursus minimus*, in the late Pliocene and earliest Villafranchian. Gradual size increase and other changes led in the middle Villafranchian to the appearance of *Ursus etruscus*, which continued to evolve in the same direction. In the Middle Pleistocene it passed into *Ursus deningeri*, which finally (in the Holsteinian, e.g. Swanscombe) gave rise to the true cave bear, *Ursus spelaeus*. Meanwhile, the brown bear, *Ursus arctos*, had evolved elsewhere, probably in Asia. It appeared in Europe in the late Holsteinian and continued to exist here side by side with the cave bear for the rest of the Pleistocene. The two did not cross or merge and thus were good species at this time; their common ancestry is represented by the late Villafranchian *Ursus etruscus*. In this case the brown bear represents the conservative, slowly evolving line, and the cave bears the rapidly evolving, progressive line.

The history of the steppe lemming (*Lagurus lagurus*) in Europe goes back to the Villafranchian and early Middle Pleistocene, when the ancestral *Lagurus pannonicus* was very common in eastern Europe. Transitional forms occur in the Holsteinian; the modern species is present in the Late Pleistocene. The two species are distinguished by details in the dentition. The steppe lemming now inhabits southern Russia and western Siberia.

THE COMPOSITION OF THE FAUNA

As new species entered the European fauna, old species tended to disappear at about the same rate, so that the total number of species remained approximately constant. One phase of this species turnover is exemplified by Table A, representing the transition from the Cromer interglacial to the Holstein interglacial. Here are listed on one side the species that made their last appearance in the Cromer or the Mindel, and on the other those species that made their first apearance in the Mindel or the Holstein. (Note that this is not a complete list of the species then known to be in existence, but only the fraction of the fauna that took part in the change.) The total of the vanishing species is 36; the total of new appearances 44. The excess in the latter column almost certainly is

TABLE A

Replacement of Mammalian species in Europe, Cromer to Holstein

Last appearances in Cromer–Mindel	First appearances in Mindel–Holstein
Insectivora	
Sorex runtonensis	Sorex kennardi
Petenyia hungarica	Crocidura leucodon
Talpa fossilis	Crocidura suaveolens
Chiroptera	
Myotis baranensis	Rhinolophus hipposideros
	Myotis myotis
	Barbastella barbastella
	Pipistrellus pipistrellus
	Vespertilio serotinus
	Vespertilio nilssoni
	Nyctalus noctula
Primates	
Macaca florentina	Macaca sylvana
Homo erectus	Homo neanderthalensis
Carnivora	
Hyaena perrieri	Hyaena hyaena
Felis lunensis	Felis silvestris
Gulo schlosseri	Gulo gulo
Martes vetus	Martes martes
Pannonictis pliocaenica	Mustela erminea
Mustela palerminea	Mustela nivalis
Mustela praenivalis	Aonyx antiqua
Ursus deningeri	Vulpes corsac
	Ursus spelaeus
	Ursus arctos

Proboscidea

Elephas meridionalis	Elephas antiquus
	Elephas trogontherii

Perissodactyla

Dicerorhinus etruscus	Dicerorhinus kirchbergensis
Equus mosbachensis	Equus germanicus

Artiodactyla

Euctenoceros senezensis	Praemegaceros cazioti
Eucladoceros sedgwicki	Megaloceros giganteus
Cervus etuerarium	Dama clactoniana
Praemegaceros verticornis	Myotragus balearicus
Megaloceros savini	Bubalus murrensis
Dama nestii	Bos primigenius
Alces latifrons	
Praeovibos priscus	
Soergelia elisabethae	
Leptobos etruscus	

Rodentia

Muscardinus dacicus	Eliomys quercinus
Pliomys episcopalis	Dryomys nitedula
Mimomys reidi	Arvicola amphibius
Mimomys newtoni	Arvicola greeni
Mimomys pliocaenicus	Lagurus lagurus
Mimomys intermedius	Microtus agrestis
Lagurus pannonicus	Microtus gregalis
Allophaiomys pliocaenicus	Apodemus agrarius
	Micromys minutus
	Mus musculus

Lagomorpha

Hypolagus brachygnathus	Oryctolagus cuniculus

---

spurious; it does not represent an increase in the number of species but only an increase in our knowledge of the fauna that is closer to us in time and hence better documented. The main excess is indeed found among the bats (Chiroptera) which have the poorest fossil record.

The assumption that new species originate at a constant rate forms the basis of the so-called percentage dating, which was originally introduced by Lyell more than a century ago. Lyell characterized the successive divisions of the Tertiary period on the basis of the percentage of modern forms found in the molluscan faunas. In an analogous way the successive Pleistocene faunas might be characterized by the percentage of living species of mammals that they contain. For instance, the latest Pliocene faunas of Europe contain only a few modern species of mammals (some four to six in number). During the Villafranchian, the percentage of modern species gradually increased to about 10%;

in the Cromer it is between 40 and 50; in the Riss, more than three-quarters of the species are modern. In other continents the percentage of modern species probably built up in the same way, although not necessarily at the same rate. The extent to which these rates were synchronous in different continents is probably dependent on the amount of intermigration between them, and so it may be expected that the changes in Asia and Europe, for instance, were more closely correlated than, say, those in North America and Europe.

For instance, the Djetis fauna of Java, with an early form of *Pithecanthropus* (or *Homo erectus*), carries about 20% modern species. This is about the same as the European fauna of the Günz glaciation. In the somewhat younger Trinil fauna (with the classical *Pithecanthropus*) the percentage is about 50, or approximately the same as in the Cromer-Mindel in Europe.[4] This is quite consistent with the K-Ar date of 0·5 to 0·6 million years assigned to the Trinil.[5]

Naturally, we do not have to limit ourselves to the percentage of present-day species in the fossil fauna. We might, for instance, use the percentage of Eemian species, or of any other temporal assemblage suitable for the purpose. We might also use the gradually disappearing old species, for instance the percentage of Pliocene survivors in a given fauna. Various possibilities for the further development of percentage dating are thus available.[6] In this way the specific composition of a fauna may help to pinpoint its chronological position in a manner quite independent from that of the 'index fossils' that it may contain.

REFERENCES

1 MAYR, E. 1963. *Animal species and evolution*, Cambridge, Massachusetts
2 CURTISS, G. H. 1965. In DE VORE, P. L., *The Origin of Man*, p. 23, Chicago
3 KURTÉN, B. 1968. *Pleistocene mammals of Europe*, London
4 —— 1962. In KURTH, G. *Evolution und Hominisation*, 74–80. Stuttgart.
5 KOENIGSWALD, G. H. R. VON. 1962. In KURTH, G. *Evolution und Hominisation*, 112–19, Stuttgart
6 KURTÉN, B. 1960. *Comment. Biol. Soc. Sci. Fennica*, 21.5, 1–62
   —— 1960. *Ibid.*, 22:5, 1–14
   —— 1960. *Ibid.*, 23:8, 1–12

WOLF HERRE

THE WILD ORIGINS of domestic animals are of fundamental importance. The archaeological record reveals that at first man was only a food-gatherer who hunted wild animals for their meat, so that, in the settlements of the Palaeolithic and Mesolithic, remains of animals of the chase alone are found. It is only in Neolithic sites that the number of bones of the many species of game animals decreases: now only a few species occur frequently. Man had formed a new relationship with these animals—he had domesticated them. This event was of the highest significance for the development of human culture: man was freed of the vicissitudes of hunting by the adoption of an economy based on food production. When considering this general subject the discipline of zoology must be applied properly if sound conclusions regarding the history of civilization are to be reached.

Wild animals are adapted to different habitats and their geographical distribution differs according to their species, while their various qualities enable them to take part in the natural struggle for existence. Wild animals lack many characteristics which, today, constitute the value of their domestic counterparts. Thus the wild sheep and guanaco have a hairy coat like most mammals, but their wool is not of the type produced by the domestic sheep and alpaca, which can be spun. The aurochs and wild goat have only enough milk to rear their young; they cannot produce those quantities of milk which in their descendants, the domestic cow and domestic goat, are so important to man. Wild boars and wolves do not have the amount of fat or the growth of meat that make the domestic pig and domestic dog sources of food for many peoples. Similarly, the wild hen does not lay the large number of eggs that its domestic counterpart does. These are characteristics of domestication just as are peculiarities of colouring, morphological changes or modifications of behaviour, surveys of which have been compiled by Klatt,[22] Nachtsheim[27] and Herre.[10,11]

It can be seen, therefore, that wild animals have undergone considerable changes during the course of domestication; man has developed different specialities in them which often render them unfit for the struggle for existence in the wild and which characterize them as domesticated. One is thus led to consider the zoological causes of these peculiarities, and the cultural problems concerning the general causes of the adoption of domestication and the development of domestic animals in different cultures in particular.

THE CONCEPT OF SPECIES

Many discussions on the domestication of animals are based on the fact that domestic animals occur in more varied forms than wild species. It often seems incredible that such a variety should have evolved from so few wild species. For this reason some people were of the opinion that domestic forms had sprung from a crossing of different wild species. Let us therefore elucidate the term 'species'.

In order that zoology might progress it was necessary to arrange animal forms in some sort of order. At first current scientific thought used the term 'species' in a static sense so that the important characteristics were those which made a simple diagnosis possible. Hence an individual would be described as a type-specimen of the species; its characteristics served as a guide for classifying other individuals as belonging to that species. Linnaeus, the founder of zoological systematics, realized however that it was the group that determined the characteristics and not the characteristics that determined the group. He knew that characteristics varied, but later the fact that variation existed led to the conclusion that only the individual constituted a real unit and that supra-individual units were merely man-made abstractions, and hence 'artificial' rather than 'natural'.[25] In the last decades the opinion that the individual belongs to a supra-individual unit, especially and clearly in the case of the higher animals, has once more gained ground. This supra-individual unit is the breeding community, and populations which, given free choice in selecting a mate, represent breeding communities, are defined as 'species'. Thus the species is a biological reality.[15,16]

This thesis of modern zoological systematics, for the perfection of which the work of Kleinschmidt,[23] Rensch,[35] Huxley[19] and Mayr[24] has been especially valuable, has important consequences affecting research into domestic animals. The populations of domestic horses, asses, cattle, sheep, pigs, dogs, etc., form, among themselves and with only that wild species from which they originate, a natural breeding community, given free choice of mate. Each of these communities therefore constitutes a species. It has not been possible, as yet, to break down the barrier between *natural* breeding communities in domestication. Man has, for instance, crossed domestic horses and donkeys for at least 4,000 years to produce mules.[17] He has not, however, succeeded in producing a new natural breeding community, a species.[15,16] Research into domestic animals is, therefore, faced with the task of showing clearly the origin of the various domestic animals from their wild species, and it is wrong to speak of phylogeny as applying to domestic animals. The changes that have come about during domestication must be regarded as morphological development within the species (a significant fact in the formation of biological theories).[16a,b]

THE NATURE OF DOMESTICATION

In order to study the causes of the special changes of wild animals under domestication it is necessary to examine the nature of domestication in the biological sense. Very different opinions have been expressed on this subject; Röhrs[41] has produced the most recent critical summary of this question.

Domestication is a relationship between man and some species of animals, but while domestic animals are of use to him, the fact that man makes use of these animals does not constitute parasitism, since with domestication man took on responsibilities as well. The unrestrained life of the hunter was replaced by an existence which gave freedom for the development of his mental faculties. At first domesticated animals received little tending; the primitive domestic animal found its own food and was not kept in stalls. But man formed a sexual barrier against the wild individuals of the species, made a selection of the more tractable animals and, instead of the small groups formed by animals in the wild state, he made his animals live in large flocks and herds from which he was able to take animals for slaughter, when needed. Man was king over his herd, but there are limits to any form of husbandry that merely exploits its resources; in intensive husbandry, a higher quality animal is eventually achieved. The more man aims at this higher quality in his domestic animals, the greater the attention they must receive, so that man becomes the servant of his animals. A remarkable psychological readjustment was necessary to bring this about, entailing a readjustment of social structure.

There are indications that animals seem to appreciate the advantages offered by man—they seek association with him of their own accord. A relationship between two animal species for their mutual benefit is called, in zoological parlance, symbiosis. Thus domestication has been described as symbiosis between man and the domestic animals. Other species of animals are thought to have a relationship comparable to domestication: ants, for example, are supposed to keep domestic animals.[20,46]

The decisive factor in domestication by man is, however, the sexual isolation of parts of the wild species and the keeping of large herds under his control and for his own use. This new social structure requires suitable forms of behaviour, and steps are therefore taken to eliminate animals that hinder the formation of large herds.[10] Thus, even in the early stages of domestication, man begins using a method of selection which is different from natural selection. The formation of large herds offering greater protection for the individual than the smaller natural group[39] also brings about a change in the working of selection. Consequently other and fewer individuals fall victim to selection than would do so in the natural struggle for survival. The conditions of domestication widen and alter the *Lebensraum* of the wild species so that more variations within the species survive. In addition to this, man isolates only small sections of the wild species. The result of this, as Sewall Wright[45] has shown, is that, in isolation, combinations of genes become different from those resulting from free mating; thus characteristics become frequent which are uncommon in the wild species. This is another reason why the breadth of variation of characteristics must become greater in domestication. Man is able to derive benefit from such circumstances and he starts selecting characteristics which are of particular value to him. If he sets up new sexual barriers among the domestic animals, the formation of selected breeds is brought about, a step which must be regarded as a new cultural achievement demonstrating an ability to direct consciously processes which are conditioned by domestication.

Such brief observations alone show that domestication is more than mere symbiosis in the zoological sense. Domestication is an expression of the constructive abilities which man owes to the evolution of his brain. Röhrs[41] is therefore right when he says that only man possesses genuinely domesticated animals. The domestication of animals represents an achievement peculiar to man; he actively influences the relationship between himself and the animals.

If this interpretation is valid, it leads one to the conclusion that the greater variety of domestic animals compared with their original species is not a result of particular physiological conditions in the domesticated state, for example being kept in stables, the kind of food, etc., but that it comes about through special selection. In order to examine this statement further, one must look for domestic animals which have always been kept in relatively free and primitive conditions which, on the whole, differ from those of the original species only in the conditions of selection and not in their immediate environment. Such animals are the domesticated reindeer of northern Europe and Asia, and the llama and alpaca of South America.[7,9,10,12,13]

The domesticated reindeer enables groups of human beings to settle in desolate areas because it is capable of finding its food even under a thick cover of snow. To do this it ranges over great distances. Man follows the herds as a nomad and has thus adapted his way of life to that of the domestic animal. Domestic reindeer are never kept in stables and no fodder for them is provided by man; but he creates large herds to satisfy his demand for food. This has only become possible through the elimination of rutting-fights by the castration of all fully grown stags, leaving the business of reproduction to the younger males. This intervention may seem unimportant but its result is that the reindeer has all the characteristics of domestication which are known from other domesticated animals.

The llama and alpaca are the domesticated forms of the guanaco, the llama serving as beast of burden, the alpaca as a supplier of wool. These herds of domestic animals live in parts of the Andes that can only be described as unsuitable for habitation by man. They are never kept in stalls either, and they find their own food; but they live in large herds. And they, too, show the general characters of domestic animals. The variability in the herds of domestic reindeer as well as of llama and alpaca is very much greater than in the original species. This variability offers material for many directions of selection. Both through the forces of environment and the mental abilities of man certain directions of selection are brought into effect. The camel should also be mentioned in this group. It enables man to colonize semi-desert and desert areas. The unfavourable nature of this environment, however, can lead to such a marked deterioration in the condition of the domestic camel that whole sections of the population are endangered. Because of this, effective social agreements are made between different groups of camel nomads.[44a]

WHAT CHARACTERIZES A DOMESTIC ANIMAL?

The archaeologist who wants to find out the origin of domestication will want to know whether there are characteristics which distinguish the remains of wild animals from those of domestic ones. The numerical ratio of the species of animals found on prehistoric sites gives the first clues to any domestication. In the case of hunters the number of species present is usually larger and the distribution of age and sex is generally more even than in the case of a herding community. In domestication some species of animals predominate and the distribution of, for instance, age groups indicates habits of utilization.[16d]

More important still is the analysis of changes within the breed after the transition to domestication. An accurate knowledge of the variability of the wild species is necessary and any examination of the history of domestic animals must be based on systematic zoological studies. Wild species are not static units, but change in space and time. Thus some original species have died out after the beginning of domestication, e.g. the aurochs; others have changed their areas of distribution, e.g. wild sheep and wild horses, while others have a different geographical distribution of their sub-species today from that of the time of domestication. Such factors make the study of the history of domestic animals more difficult.

Today, the value of domestic animals is determined above all by their physical qualities; the study of material from prehistoric settlements tells us nothing about these. Skeletal remains play a special part in research into the history of domestication. If the bones of the wild species of the old domestic animals, for example, sheep, cattle, pigs, horses and dogs, are compared with those of the domestic animals, at first an extension of the range of variations and eventually a selection in favour of smaller size and variation of form become apparent. In the domestic state therefore a greater variability also occurs in the skeletal parts. The transition between the wild form and the domestic animal at the beginning of domestication, however, is fluid, and it is difficult to determine with single bones, whether they are of wild or domestic forms. Particular characteristics in the domestic state can even lose their specific value and without them an individual may be assigned to a different group. It is therefore necessary to study a large quantity of material in order to determine the variability of the whole population.[161]

It has frequently been concluded from the decrease in physical size in the earliest stages of domestication, that the animals degenerated compared with the wild species. This overlooks important biological facts. In the initial stages of domestication man did not yet make adequate provision for the animals' fodder and he prevented the animals from roaming around freely. Thus when food was scarce domestic animals suffered more than wild ones and small individuals with smaller food requirements had a better chance of survival than large, so that the proportion of small animals increased. In addition to this, it is probable that primitive man preferred small animals as he could control them better. Reduction in size is not however a necessary result of domestication; fundamentally, the state of domestication produces variation extending in all directions: in domestication there also appear individuals which are larger than in the wild species. If man knows how to preserve these variations he is also able to increase the physical size of an animal beyond the range realized in the wild species. The domestic horse, the rabbit and the domestic fowl are examples of this.

A change in size generally brings about changes in morphology and individual characteristics. Peculiarities can be more striking between large and small domestic animals, or between domestic animals and their original species, than differences between wild species. If, therefore, only peculiarities of morphology are taken into account and the differences of proportion, which are correlated to size, are not explained, the wrong conclusions may be reached on the origins of domestication, as Klatt[21] showed in 1913;

more recently Röhrs[40] has applied the allometric formula to these problems, a decisive contribution to research on this subject.

Studies into the influence of physical size on the form of the body and its parts show that there are governing factors that change single characteristics. Such factors are, among others, sex, growth pattern, age and nutrition. Female animals are generally smaller than males, but there may be considerable sexual dimorphism in other characteristics also. This fact used to be overlooked and differences that were due to sex were regarded as a peculiarity of the domestic animal or as a characteristic of a breed. In the case of cattle, it was especially Siewing[44] who pointed out the significance of such influences; in the case of sheep, Reitsma[34] showed that discussions concerning special centres of domestication lose their basis if the sexual dimorphism of sheep is taken into consideration. In general, sexual differences decrease in domestication.

Klatt has drawn attention to another important phenomenon. In every population there are lightly and heavily built individuals. In domestication, the range of even these characteristics widens. Klatt, therefore, distinguished growth patterns because skull, skeleton and organs often differ in the same sense. Growth patterns occur in all sizes; and because of variations in size and growth pattern many peculiarities of morphology can be understood. Meunier[26] has done particularly valuable work on their theoretical elucidation and recording. Hammond[5] has studied the influence of feeding on physical proportions.

From research into the origin of domestic animals, we have shown that in the gradual transition from wild animals to domestic animals the range of variation of all characteristics reached in the wild species is extended and eventually moved outside this range. However, the greater variation between domestic animals calls for a very careful consideration of correlative ties and modifying changes if conclusions on the origin of domestication are to be sound. One has to examine again and again the way in which the characteristics of domestic animals are to be classified within the ranges of variation; there are no characteristics which are absolutely valid for distinguishing a state of domestication.

The living conditions of wild species bring about severe selection which keeps the range of variation narrow. As a result of this, inferences can, with a high degree of probability, be drawn from single characteristics to apply to the whole body. This is no longer the case with domestic animals. Here single characteristics do not always vary correspondingly with each other,[8,4,29] and must thus be first considered within the range of variation in order to exclude merely coincidental individual variations before significant conclusions are drawn from them.

WHAT IS A BREED?

This question leads one to the problem of making subdivisions among the domestic animals. The increase in the breadth of variation under domestication often leads to extreme individuals of very different physiques; these are often subdivided into breeds, but individuals whose characteristics result from special gene combinations or hereditary changes do not yet constitute a breed so long as they are merely extremes of a uniform variation. They are only potential preliminary stages towards breeds. One may only speak of breeds when groups of individual domestic animals (populations) show certain accumulations of characteristics which can be statistically recorded within the overall range of variation. The environments of domestic animals and man bring about the selection of such combinations of characteristics.

A population with accumulations of characteristics brought about by its environment is called a geographical breed;[15-16] it will exhibit broad variability. Of greater relevance to the history of civilization are the selected breeds, created by man through the selection of animals according to definite breeding objectives and through sexual isolation, which show a narrow range of variation. Such selected breeds are a sign of a highly developed culture; nor are they static units immune to change. Often, it is true, the name remains the same but qualities change and with them morphology. Selected breeds are 'improved' towards higher performance when man's abilities increase, or they disappear when sexual isolation discontinues. If breeds of domestic animals which, isolated in space as geographical breeds or isolated sexually as selected breeds, have been developing in their own way for some length of time are then intermingled, new and remarkable variations will occur which will often range beyond that of the two original breeds. Thus the way is opened for new selection. Modern animal breeding and its selective breeding are characterized by such processes.

THE PROCESS OF DOMESTICATION

The number of animal species hunted by man is large, but the number of species that became important to him as domestic animals is small. He must have made a choice.

It can be seen that nearly all domestic animals originated from social wild species, i.e. in the individuals of the wild species there was already an inclination towards sociability which facilitated an association with man. But a choice was made even from social species. Species with dangerous offensive equipment and with fierce rutting-fights (such as fallow, roe and red deer) became domesticated animals only when, through some special biological factor, they made habitable by man areas which otherwise would have been uninhabitable. This happened, for instance, in the case of the reindeer.[10,11]

Domestic animals did not all originate in the same part of the world; this can be seen from the fact that the original species live in different geographical areas. Any given wild species can, however, only have become domesticated in its natural area of distribution. Reed[33] has recently emphasized this point. At the time of its domestication the wild horse had its home exclusively north of the Caucasus, the wild ass in northeastern Africa; consequently they could not have been domesticated in the same area. The wild form of the domestic llama and alpaca, the guanaco, which lives only in South America, may be cited as a further example. It may be assumed on this basis that the domestication of wild animals is carried out when a certain level of civilization is reached, as Zeuner[46] and Reed[33] also suggest. There is also the conception of the prehistorian Schwantes to be considered, that ideas travel faster than goods; with this in mind one might think that only the idea of domestication was passed on and put into practice with different species at different places.

Cattle are of interest in this connection. Of them several wild species with differing ecological peculiarities have been domesticated. *Bos primigenius*, the aurochs, was an animal of the open deciduous forests and of parkland; from it came the domestic cow. The sub-tropical areas are the home of the buffalo, *Bubalus arnée*, used in hot and moist areas instead of the descendants of the aurochs. The Gayal, which goes back to the Gaur as wild cattle, is also adapted to tropical swampy areas. The domestic yaks, on the other hand, are the cattle of the cold high mountains of Tibet. Similar observations apply to geese. In Europe and North Africa *Anser anser*, the grey goose, was domesticated, in East Asia *Anser cygnoides*. It can therefore be assumed that there are cases of the new domestication of animal species after the pattern of older ones.[1a]

However, a comparison of the areas in which domesticated animals originated shows that a certain level in the cultural development of the peoples was a prerequisite for domestication. The numbers of domestic animals whose homes are in Europe and Asia are large, while in Africa, where wild species abound, only the domestic ass and the domestic guinea-fowl came into being. In Australia and North America no domestication took place, disregarding the turkey, which probably originated in Mexico. In South America, it was only in parts of the Andes where a high standard of civilization developed that guanaco and guinea-pig were domesticated. Zoological-geography can therefore give reference points in relation to questions concerning the centre of domestication. Only in the region of the Titicaca basin do the distribution areas of *Lama guanaco* and *Cavia aperea* overlap, and only in the region of Mexico do those of the turkey and Muscovy duck. Populations capable of domestication must have lived in these areas.[16d]

If one seeks reasons for such domestication, the following is of importance. All wild cattle have found a similar use in the economy of man; the donkey takes the place of the horse as transport; the camel and llama fulfil a similar task, and the equivalent of the sheep is found in the alpaca. It is possible, therefore, that similar universal requirements have led to the domestication of animals, that experience of the possibilities of the uses that they could be put to spread more rapidly than the animals themselves, so that the same demands were met by different animals.

It is beyond doubt however that domestic animals were brought to areas in which the original species were unknown. This is certainly true of the horse which came to occupy an important position among the domestic animals south of the Caucasus; that is, in areas which were the home of other wild equids. Goats and sheep also became important domestic animals quite early in areas where the wild species had long since died out or had never existed.

From such examples of the influence of man on their distribution domestic animals have come to be considered as originating in essentially the same area and from there starting a march of conquest. Zoological data do not support this view even if one species alone is considered. Pigs may be used as an example. The subspecies of the wild boar show peculiarities between western Europe and eastern Asia. Such differences also occur between the domesticated pigs of these areas, evidence of different instances of domestication of the same wild species.

Archaeological finds support this; in several places gradual transitions from wild populations to domestic animals can be demonstrated; Pira[30] was the first to draw attention to this fact with his study of pigs in the Baltic area. In more recent times Reed[33] has recorded the same phenomenon in pigs from prehistoric settlements in Iraq.

Such findings apply also to cattle; Röhrs and Herre[42] have described a population in transition from the aurochs to the domestic cattle on the southern shore of the Bosphorus, and Nobis[29] one in Schleswig-Holstein. Another aspect of this question may be mentioned to support the assumption that the same species was domesticated several times. It is now certain that the first settlements in the Near East, in which the first domestic animals occurred, are earlier than those of northern Central Europe. Had the domestic animals been imported one would expect those in the earlier settlements of the north to show a clear difference from the wild species. However some direction transitions from the wild populations of Central Europe have been found, suggesting an indigenous domestication.

THE BEGINNING OF DOMESTICATION

After these predominantly zoological considerations it is necessary to consult the evidence relating to the history of civilization in order to discover the point of time at which the domestication of the various species occurred. In the older literature quite a number of erroneous views are expressed because archaeological research did not progress at an equal rate in all fields. Apart from this, errors occurred because the fauna from areas where domestication had happened was rarely so well known that the gradual changes during domestication could be recorded with accuracy; also the shifting of the ranges of variation in local populations was ascertained in such a way as to make statements on the actual beginning of domestication hardly possible. So far, the best preparatory work for such an analysis has been done on the Cimbric peninsula.[3,38]

For a long time it was generally thought that the chronological order in which domestic animals followed one another was the same in all parts of the world, and, for a long time, the Near East was considered to be the original home of domestic animals— *ex oriente lux!* The dog was considered to be man's oldest domestic animal; but results from recent excavations must lead one to a different conclusion.

Reed[33] made a critical examination of the new data according to which sheep are shown to be the oldest domestic animals. In Zawi Chemi, Shanidar (Iraq), groups of humans kept sheep as domestic animals as early as 9000 BC. A little later the goat was domesticated; even in the oldest levels of Jarmo and Jericho the goat is recognizable as a domesticated animal, therefore the practice of domestication must have been carried on for some time before the deposition of the strata. The domestic pig has also a long history. It is true that in the pre-pottery levels of Jarmo only remains of large wild boar were found, but with the occurrence of pottery the presence of domestic pigs is also clear. The distinct differences that can immediately be recognized here between wild boar and domesticated pigs force the conclusion that the pig was not domesticated in Jarmo but earlier, in another place. It may be assumed that this happened around 6500 BC.

According to the archaeological evidence available so far, domestic cattle are of a more recent origin. Their first identifiable occurrence as such is at the Halafian site of Banahilk, which places the date for domestication in the period 5000–4000 BC. For this reason the reports of Röhrs and Herre on the animal remains from the oldest Neolithic permanent settlement of Fikirtepe on the southern shore of the Bosphorus are of interest. Bittel dates the settlement in the early fourth millennium BC. Röhrs and Herre found undoubted remains of domestic sheep, domestic goats and domestic pigs; the cattle, however, formed a population of transition from aurochs to domestic cattle. Independently of Reed's conclusions, the same picture emerges from this evidence of the order in which the domestication of these species took place in the Near East.

In the same way, the new ideas on the appearance of the domestic dog in the Near East gain in importance because of the independent nature of their evidence. It was previously thought that the dog was the oldest domestic animal in the Near East because Bate[1] had reported a domestic dog from the Natufian, that is, 8000 BC. Röhrs and Herre were puzzled that no evidence of domestic dogs could be found in the varied material from Fikirtepe; they only found the humerus of a wolf. Bate's statements were then checked and found to be without foundation. Other early prehistoric settlements in the Near East yielded no evidence of dogs either, and Röhrs and Herre called for an accurate analysis of wild canids from that area before conclusions were made on the domestication of the dog. Such a study has meanwhile been presented by Clutton-Brock.[2] It showed that the remains of a canid which Bate had regarded as a domestic dog were of a small subspecies of wolf. Reed examined the remains of canids from Jarmo; he too was forced to allocate these few bones to wolves. Thus it was not possible to find any evidence to establish the domestic dog among the first domestic animals. Whether Zeuner's view[47] concerning a domestic dog from Jericho can be maintained remains to be seen. The domestic dog is certainly not the oldest domestic animal in the Near East.

In Central Europe, especially to the north, on the other hand, the dog is certainly the oldest domestic animal.[4] It is probable that dogs originated from the wolves of Central Europe and were domesticated at a stage of cultural development as early as the Mesolithic. This is, therefore, a case of autochthonous domestication and not one of the importation of a domestic animal. There is evidence also of the domestication of aurochs and wild boar in Central Europe,[30,29] which seems to be more recent than that in the Near East (this must, however, be clarified by further dating), while the order in which species were domesticated is different. This is more evidence to indicate that the idea of domesticating wild animals spread faster than the domestic animals themselves. This is of great significance especially in evaluating the sequence of domestication from a zoological point of view.

The mounting archaeological evidence, taken as a whole, shows that the beginning of domestication is not to be regarded as a uniform process but as a varied one. Present ideas may be extended and modified by further new archaeological findings. In this connection, fresh information provided by Ducos, as well as by Samson and Radulesco,[31] is important as it indicates that the domestication of sheep may also have occurred at several different places, such as Asia Minor, south and south-east Europe.

THE REASONS FOR DOMESTICATION

Both the zoological facts and recent archaeological finds again pose the question of why men domesticated animals, thereby not only creating advantages for themselves but also taking on the responsibility of looking after the animals. As an answer the psychological explanation was advanced that among primitive peoples the social instinct of man had extended to young wild animals and that thus a more intimate relationship developed between individuals and social animal species in particular, which resulted in domestication. However, Reed has said, quite rightly, that the rearing and fondling of young animals is practised a good deal to this day without any further consequences. The above explanation overlooks the fundamental fact that it is the sexual isolation of parts of wild populations which constitutes the decisive step towards domestication. The work of Meggitt ([23a], 1965) also supports this.

The view that hunting peoples invented domestication became more important, and the idea of the dog as the first domestic animal fits into this line of thought. This theory has been varied in many ways, especially in Europe. It was thought that wolves realized the advantages of hunting together with man, joined him voluntarily and thus brought the domestic dog into being. Sauer[43] has already said sharply that such ideas arose from romantic minds and were without foundation. Modern hunting peoples do not know the use of the dog as a helper in hunting and it is certain that the dog only became a hunting companion in fairly recent times. Furthermore, Degerbøl[4] discovered that wherever the dog appeared as the oldest domestic animal it had been used as food. Even today the dog is eaten in wide areas of the world, in Asia and among the aborigines of South America. It must also be remembered that as a beast of prey the wolf has its special food requirements and that it is unlikely that the food refuse of small groups of prehistoric men was sufficient to make the domestication of this animal possible. Nor does archaeological evidence now support the thesis of the dog as the oldest domestic animal.

Another major theoretical standpoint recently demolished is that religious factors were of primary significance in the origins of domestication, particularly of the ox. The latest archaeological evidence shows that the ox was not present at the first stage, although it became one of the most important and versatile domestic animals at a very early date. One must therefore examine whether the religious ideas of prehistoric men were already so deep-rooted as to provide the impetus for such a culturally significant act as domestication. What has been discovered so far hardly supports such a thesis.

So far it has become certain that the first domestic animals were easily fed herbivorous animals whose main importance lay in their meat-producing qualities, as the wild animals did not form wool or produce large quantities of milk. The first domestic dogs, too, served as producers of meat. The provision of meat seems, therefore, to have been an important reason for domestication, a view supported by the fact that the same animal species, or other wild species that were similar to the domesticated form, were domesticated at different times, but at presumably similar cultural stages. As Reed, too, points out, it is becoming increasingly clear that domestication begins when a growing human population changes over to a more settled and culturally higher form of life. So the view suggests itself that the keeping of domestic animals arises from the necessity of ensuring a regular food supply for larger groups of people. Therefore domestication is probably dependent on a certain cultural stage and at the same time a prerequisite for the further development of culture. However, this is another matter about which archaeology will have to provide further information.

THE MAIN HISTORICAL FEATURES OF THE DOMESTICATION OF HORSES AND CATTLE

It is not intended to give here a general survey of the historical development of all domestic animals. Some data on the horse and ox may serve as examples of the most important domestic animals.

The home of wild horses lies to the north of the big mountain chains which run through Europe and Asia from east to west. Once their numbers were large; the wild horse was an important animal of the chase for Palaeolithic men. In the course of the early Holocene the area of distribution and the numbers of animals decreased greatly, and today it is only in east Asia that there are small populations of the wild horse. If the up-to-date palaeontological evidence and the results of modern zoological systematics are considered, *Equus przewalskii* is the only species from which the domestic horse can have originated.[15,16] It is difficult to give a complete and accurate picture of the beginnings and the place of the domestication. Hančar[6] mentions the early Tripolje culture in the South-East European wooded steppe and the Afanasje culture of the Siberian wooded steppe, and the end of the third millennium BC as places and times at which wild horses were domesticated. Huppertz[18] adds the view that horses were domesticated in central Asia and came, domesticated, from there to China as early as 4000–3000 BC.

According to what is known today, the horse had little importance at first as a domestic animal because it was only a supplier of meat, but after it had crossed the Caucasus probably in the middle of the third millennium BC., following the example of the use of the ox, it was harnessed to the cart. In the ancient East, in the mountain country of Syria, Asia Minor, the Caucasus, the cart developed into the horse-drawn chariot which helped to overthrow and form empires. The use of the horse in war gained it a special position as an important element of political power. The riding of the horse is more recent than the chariot, at least in the orient. According to Hančar, the development of the horse into a riding animal took place in the Altai-Sajan area around 1500 BC, with the mounted warrior replacing the chariot from 1000 BC. Huppertz thinks that the development of the horse into a riding animal began in central Asia, and it is certain that it was from Asia that mounted warriors and their horses came into world history. The horse, however, gained importance also as a helper to the animal breeder, at first probably in Caucasian and South Siberian areas. In Central Europe, its chief use for a long time was as a beast of burden, a draught animal before the plough and a source of meat. Thus the 'social position' differs very much from one area to another. In Europe it is predominantly a working animal, in the region of Asia Minor and in parts of Asia it is the companion of the socially privileged classes. It needs further ethnological study to determine how far this statement is true.

When it comes to the question of the biological change undergone by the horse in domestication, modern research permits quite accurate statements, particularly for Europe. On average the Przewalski horses stand 140 cm high at the withers. At the beginning of domestication, this height is known to have been decreased without the formation of a breed becoming immediately evident. Horses of the La Tène period grew to a height of 130 cm. Horses of the pre-Roman Iron Age in Britain are said to have reached a height of only 120–125 cm at the shoulder. It is certain that in the ancient Mediterranean civilizations thoroughbreds were already being developed, though evidence from osteological remains is not yet conclusive. In Central Europe, differences between geographical breeds of horses become distinguishable only as late as 300 BC: in the region immediately to the north of the Alps, horses were of lighter build than on the North Sea coast. According to studies made by Nobis[28] a rapid development took place in the Migration period: the original heavy cart-horse was developed from smaller geographical breeds of horses of broad build, and big horses became frequent. This process continued into the Middle Ages when, through selection, bigger and bigger domesticated horses were developed, reaching a height of up to 160 cm at the withers. These were the knights' chargers and side by side with them survived the small country horses of the farmers. The first horses to reach Iceland during the time of the Vikings were of heavy build but developed into ponies in the course of adaptation to the unfavourable environment.

All this shows that wild animals extended their range of variation when domesticated. From this wide variation selections were made which led to widely different forms in domestic horses. In modern times crossing and subsequent selection became important as a method of breeding.

Domestic horses became so important to mankind because they did not remain mere meat animals, but lightened human toil and were eventually decisive in warfare. The ox, on the other hand, has remained in a more modest position as a domestic animal, though more important in the development of early mankind than the horse.

It is true to say that all domestic cattle descend from the aurochs, *Bos primigenius*. Adametz named a further species of origin, *Bos brachyceros*; this turned out to be a misinterpretation, a domestic ox having been incorrectly dated. The same applies to Reed's assumption[32] that, side by side with the aurochs, another smaller species of wild cattle had lived in the Near East.[33]

India is generally believed to be the area where the aurochs originated, spreading thence to much of Eurasia and Africa. From Africa it was not, however, able to populate south Europe, as from the Pleistocene there was no longer a land bridge with Europe. The Pleistocene aurochs was of massive build, and was divided up into subspecies; *Bos primigenius trochoceros* lived in Europe, *Bos primigenius hahni* in Egypt, and *Bos primigenius namadicus* in India. The aurochs of the Holocene was smaller; it is called *Bos primigenius primigenius*. This subspecies was widely distributed, became rarer in the Middle Ages and died out in the seventeenth century. There are, however, many records available concerning the appearance of the aurochs.[36,37]

In the several different regions where the aurochs was domesticated a notable and uniform variation appeared at a very early stage. Domestic oxen became generally smaller than the wild species. In the larger animals, the skull still showed a predominance of the characteristics of the wild animal; hence the term 'primigenius cattle'. In the smaller animals, changes dependent on size led to stronger morphological differences;[21] such animals are called 'brachyceros cattle'. As the development towards the domestic ox progresses, brachyceros cattle become predominant; it is however not justifiable to regard these individuals as a separate breed, as the variability in their stock is very large. Only when the breadth of variation narrows down and special characteristics become frequent that are not connected with sexual differences or with castration can breeds be designated, as indicating the breeders' intention and ability. Such phenomena can be identified in highly developed cultures, such as those of Egypt and Rome. In Central Europe, influence through breeding remained slight for a long time. The number of small animals, which could survive times of food scarcity, increased up to the Middle Ages. Neolithic cattle stood from 115 to 138 cm high at the withers, that is, they resembled modern medium-sized breeds. From the Middle Ages, a minimum size of 95 cm is known.

Concerning the history of breeding, it is noteworthy that large cattle, different from the smaller country cattle, lived in the area of the Roman castella north of the Alps. These large animals have been called 'pseudoprimigenius cattle'; they did not, however, attain any great importance in breeding. By the ninth and tenth centuries, no effects of such animals can be traced in the area of the Rhine. Crossing as a method of breeding does not seem to have been practised in the Middle Ages, it has assumed importance only in modern times. Selection from the geographical breeds offered sufficient possibilities for the realization of breeding aims.

What had first been a meat animal was soon used to draw the plough; the cart was invented for it and it also became important as a milking animal. Cattle have to be considered as the most important domestic animals of peaceful men. Sheep, goats and pigs are also distributed widely as domestic animals. According to the evidence so far known concerning the history of sheep and goat, it seems probable that they were widely distributed as domestic animals even in early times, while the pig was domesticated in Europe as well as in Asia Minor and East Africa.

Altogether the domestic animals illustrate that a high degree of adaptability is inherent in wild animals. Man therefore found it possible to change radically the shape and qualities of an animal according to his needs, and it cannot be predicted how far such endeavours will lead. Man has the ability to change domestic animals today as much as ever.

REFERENCES

1 BATE, D. M. A. 1937. In GARROD, D. The Stone Age of Mount Carmel, Oxford, vol. 1
1a BOHLKEN, H. 1964. Vergleichende Untersuchungen an den Schädeln wilder und domestizierter Rinder. Z. wiss. Zool. 170, 323–418
2 CLUTTON-BROCK, J. 1962. Z. Tierzüchtung u. Züchtungsbiologie 76, 326–33
3 DEGERBØL, M. 1933. Danmarks Pattedyr i Fortiden, Copenhagen, vol. 1

4 —— 1962. *Z. Tierzüchtung u. Züchtungsbiologie 76*, 334–41
5 HAMMOND, J. 1960. *Farm Animals*, London, 3rd ed.
6 HANČAR, F. 1956. *Das Pferd in frühistorischer und früher historischer Zeit*, Vienna and Munich
7 HERRE, W. 1943. *Zool. Anz. 141*, 196–214
8 —— 1951. *Anat. Anz. 98*, 49–65
9 —— 1952. *Zool. Garten N-F. 19*, 70–98
10 —— 1955a. *Das Ren als Haustier*, Leipzig
11 —— 1955b. Domestikation und Stammesgeschichte, in HEBERER. *Die Evolution der Organismen*, Stuttgart, 2nd ed., 801–56
12 —— 1958a. Abstammung und Domestikation der Haustiere, *Handbuch der Tierzüchtung*, Hamburg, Bd. I
13 —— 1958b. *Z. Tierzüchtung u. Züchtungsbiologie 71*, 252–72
14 —— 1959. *Naturwissenschaftl. Rundschau* 87–94
15 —— 1961a. Der Art- und Rassebegriff, *Handbuch der Tierzüchtung*, Hamburg, Bd. III, 1, 1–24
16a —— 1961. *Schriften des Geographischen Instituts des Universität Kiel, XX*
16b —— 1962. *Zool. Anz. 169*, 1/2
16c —— 1964. *Zool. Anz. 172*, 403–25
16d —— 1966. *Festschrift Jankuhn*, in the press
16e —— 1966. Zoologische Betrachtungen zu Aussagen über den Domestikationsbeginn. *Palaeohistoria 12*, 283–5
16f —— 1967. Gedanken zur Erhaltung des Wildpferdes Equus przewalskii Poljakow 1881. *Equus (Berlin) 1*, 304–25
17 RÖHRS, M. 1958. *71. Wiss. Veröffentl' d. deutschen Orient-Gesellschaft*, 60–79
18 HUPPERTZ, J. 1962. *Z. Tierzüchtung u. Züchtungsbiologie 76*, 190–208
19 HUXLEY, J. 1948. *The New Systematics*, London
20 KELLER, G. 1905. *Naturgeschichte der Haustiere*, Berlin
21 KLATT, B. 1913. *Arch. Entw. Mech. 36*, 387–471
22 —— 1927. Entstehung der Haustiere, *Handb. d. Vererbungswissenschaft*, Berlin, Bd. III, 1–107
23 KLEINSCHMIDT, O. 1902. Der Formenkreis Falco-Hierofalco, *Aquila 9*, 1–49
23a MEGGITT, M. J. 1965. The Association between Australian Aborigines and Dingoes, in *Man, Culture, and Animals*, Washington, D.C.
24 MAYR, E. 1957. *The Species problem*, Washington
25 —— LINSLEY, E. G. and USINGER, R. L. 1953. *Methods and principles of systematic zoology*, New York
26 MEUNIER, K. 1959. *Z. wissenschaftl. Zoologie 162*, 328–55
27 NACHTSHEIM, H. 1949. *Vom Wildtier zum Haustier*, Berlin, 2nd ed.
28 NOBIS, G. 1955. *Z. Tierzüchtung u Züchtungsbiologie 64*, 201–46
29 —— 1962. *Ibid. 77*, 16–31
30 PIRA. 1909. *Zoolog. Jahrb.*, Suppl. Bd. X, H.2
31 RADULESCO, C. and P. SAMSON. 1961. *Z. Tierzüchtung u. Züchtungsbiologie 75*, 282–321
32 REED, C. A. 1960. A review of the archaeological evidence on animal domestication in the prehistoric Near East, in BRAIDWOOD, R. J. and HOWE, B. *Prehistoric investigations in Iraqi Kurdistan*, Chicago
33 —— 1961. *Z. Tierzüchtung u. Züchtungsbiologie 76*, 34
34 REITSMA, G. C. 1932. *Het Schapp*, Wageningen
35 RENSCH, B. 1929. *Das Prinzip geographischer Rassenkreise und das Problem der Artbildung*, Berlin
36 REQUATE, H. 1957. *Bonner Zoologische Beiträge 8*, 207–29
37 —— 1957. *Z. Tierzüchtung u. Züchtungsbiologie 71*, 297–328
38 —— 1962. *Ibid. 77*
39 RÖHRS, M. 1958. Ökologische Beobachtungen an wildlebenden Tylopoden Südamerikas, *Verhandl. Dtsch. Zoologen 1957 in Graz*, 538–54
40 —— 1959. *Z. wissenschaftl. Zoologie 162*, 1–95
41 —— 1961. *Z. Tierzüchtung u. Züchtungsbiologie 76*, 7–22
42 —— and HERRE, W. 1961. *Ibid. 75*, 110–27
43 SAUER, O. 1952. *Agricultural Origins and Dispersals*, New York
44 SIEWING, G. 1960. Das Hausrind, in HERRE, W. *Die Haustiere von Haithabu*, Neumünster, 19–71

44a SWEET, L. E. 1965. Camel Pastoralism in North Arabia and the Minimal Camping Unit, in *Man, Culture, and Animals*, Washington, D.C.

45 WRIGHT, S. 1940. The statistical consequences of Mendelian Heredity in relation to speciation, in HUXLEY, J., 161–83

46 ZEUNER, F. E. 1954. Domestication of animals, in SINGER, C., HOLMYARD, E. J. and HALL, H. R. *A History of Technology*, Oxford

47 —— 1958. *Palestine Exploration Quarterly 19*, 52–55

48 —— 1963. *A History of Domesticated Animals*, London

25 Social Organization as a Population Regulator

V. C. WYNNE-EDWARDS

POPULATIONS OF ANIMALS living in a natural state normally remain in stable equilibrium with the world around them: this has long been recognized. The explosive increase of one species or the dwindling to extinction of another, though they both occur, are exceptions rather than the rule, and many of the conspicuous upsets in Nature's balance that have come to notice in the last hundred years or so have been tipped off not spontaneously but by human interference.

BALANCED POPULATIONS

The factors that produce a population equilibrium have interested zoologists a great deal, especially in the last fifty years, though much longer ago Darwin attempted to analyse them in Chapter 3 of *The Origin of Species* (1859).[4] The ecological norm can be regarded as tending towards a steady state, in the sense that, though animal populations commonly suffer transient setbacks and losses, their numbers generally return more or less rapidly towards the status quo, and do not increase beyond an upper limit or ceiling. This is in sharp contrast to human populations, with their continuous upward trend, which appears to have been going on in some of the old-established peoples of Europe and Asia for two millennia at least, and gives cause for present alarm. Interest in the subject has been increasing lately because of the growing threats to man's biotic environment, and the realization that we need to understand the principles of population ecology in order to conserve the world we live in.

Like so many biological processes the balancing of populations is a complex phenomenon, and one cannot on the basis of everyday experience and common sense explain with any certainty what brings it about. Darwin was fully conscious of this in putting forward his own tentative views, which he based on the previous ideas of Malthus. He took it for granted that all living organisms must continuously be striving to the utmost to increase in numbers, although they cannot succeed in doing so indefinitely because they are opposed by a variety of extraneous forces. These 'checks to increase' appear to arise (i) from the fact that all food supplies are finite, and (ii) that many species serve as food themselves for predators; (iii) from the 'climate' or physical environment which can often be seen to exact a toll, and (iv) from the mortality caused by parasites and disease. Later generations of biologists have almost invariably accepted these deductions as if they were the last word on the subject, although evidence has been accumulating for many years which reveals that the argument is based on a misconception and is fundamentally wrong.

ENDOGENOUS CONTROL OR HOMEOSTASIS

Evidence has come from the innumerable experiments that have been done since Darwin's day with populations of laboratory animals of many kinds. These show that the animals employed, whatever they are, possess adaptations which give them a large measure of endogenous control over income and loss in their own populations. For example, the size to which small goldfish in a bowl will grow, assuming they are ideally fed and cared for, depends on how many fish there are in relation to the volume of water; and if the fish, after remaining several years at a constant size, are transferred to a larger tank, they will at once begin to grow again. Experience with guppies, which breed freely in aquaria, reveals further that they control their actual numbers in a corresponding fashion, and once the ceiling is reached they will keep the 'biomass' of their population constant in relation to the water volume for an indefinite period, which may cover many generations of fish. Duplicate experimental tanks maintain the same ceiling biomass and come to have nearly identical population structures.[6]

Darwin's checks are not involved here at all: the guppies are given plenty of food and an equable climate; they have no predators and no diseases. Yet they cannot be induced to exceed a biomass of roughly 2 grams per litre. If part of the stock is removed, the remainder by breeding will build up the numbers to the same ceiling as before. If extra fish are added, cannibalism brings the stock down to the standard level. Essentially the same kind of result has been found in animals as diverse as fruit-flies (Drosophila), flour beetles (Tribolium), water-fleas (Daphnia), fish, amphibia and mammals (such as laboratory rats and mice, and voles). Darwin's basic assumption that organisms are always striving to increase in numbers turns out in fact to be far too sweeping.

More and more self-regulatory phenomena are also being discovered nowadays among wild populations of animals, and there is no room any longer to doubt that they are of general occurrence in all but the most primitive invertebrate groups. Darwin's hostile forces are of course perfectly real, and there are numerous cases where, most of the time, a given population is being held down below its acceptable ceiling by the pressure of one or more of them. But should their pressure ever ease for long enough, the regulatory mechanism latent in the population itself will take over and impose a ceiling, as soon as a sufficient density is reached. Unknowingly, and regrettably, man apparently shook off his own regulatory machinery in the course of becoming civilized, and now lacks either experience or even memory of its existence. It is probably this more than anything else that has prevented us, from Malthus almost to the present, from recognizing all around us the built-in homeostatic mechanisms of other species.

THE GENERAL THEORY

If animals are adapted to regulate their own numbers the question arises, what determines the optimum ceiling level? I began to study this question about fifteen years ago and have since developed a general hypothesis to resolve it, based on the proposition that, for the majority of animals, limitation of their own population density is the only reliable way of saving the food supply from over-exploitation. My main conclusion, as will appear shortly, is that self-regulation always, necessarily and fundamentally depends on social behaviour.

What follows in this chapter has been written from an essentially zoological point of view, with animal populations primarily in mind; but it is abundantly clear that human beings inherit social institutions from their ancestors, and that this process has been going on since pre-human times. A comparative study of animal sociology suggests that the functional evolution of society has proceeded continuously from a remote geological era, and that its primitive origins were common at least to whole classes and phyla of animals. Whether sociality is polyphyletic, and arose in parallel more than once, for instance in the vertebrates and arthropods separately, we do not know and need not consider here. What must be clearly understood is that sociality has nothing primarily to do with gregariousness: it is perfectly possible for 'solitary' animals like cats or bears to have an elaborate social organization. Sociality can in fact be readily demonstrated as a general attribute of animals, though like many another biological system it tends to be better developed and more readily evident in the higher forms.

One of the many resemblances between human and other animal species is that they are all typically broken up into partially isolated local inter-breeding groups, which continue to perpetuate themselves indefinitely on the same ground. There is usually no more than a small trickle of infiltration from outside, which brings in new genes from time to time and, among human populations at least, new skills. The integrity of the local group is of great ecological and cultural importance, and this is in no way better illustrated than by the amazing navigational powers that have been evolved in parallel by all the regular two-way migrants, whether they are insects, fish, amphibia, turtles, birds, bats, seals or Cetacea. They have become free to travel far away only because they have the ability to return and resume citizenship, whenever the time comes round, in their own parochial self-regulating group.

Over-population in relation to food typically arises in the short term because current stores have been used up before any succeeding ones are ready for use; and in the longer term because such heavy inroads are being made upon the food resources that they cannot recover before the next season comes round: yields consequently diminish and the food productivity of the habitat is lowered. Persistent overgrazing, as is well known, leads for this reason to the downgrading of pastures, and overfishing to the chronic depletion of fish stocks. The optimal exploitation rate is the one that spins each crop out until other foods in turn become available, and at the same time allows the highest sustainable harvest to be utilized year by year. It generally entails that the demand be curbed while the food is still plentiful, and before its capacity to renew itself completely the following season has been impaired. In terms of available biomass, different food organisms can be expected to vary enormously in the degree of exploitation to which they may be subjected with impunity. With perennial grasses, all that need be left to regenerate the pasture is a small fraction of the amount that can safely be consumed, by a herd of ruminants for example, in the course of the grazing season; but when these same ruminants are preyed upon by carnivores, such as lions, the bulk of the standing stock must at all times be left on the hoof, and only a small fraction removed for food each year. Similarly beavers, which cut down whole poplar trees in order to eat the bark and foliage, must always leave the majority of available trees as a standing reserve because the rate of tree regeneration is so slow.

It is readily apparent that, although food is generally the commodity that ultimately limits the carrying capacity of the habitat, the population dependent on it must not be allowed simply to increase until further growth in numbers is chronically held in check by general starvation. Famine is a catastrophe especially likely to damage the food resource and lead to its permanent depletion. What is required instead is a regulating mechanism that can (i) resist the build-up of population beyond the point where sufficient food remains to go round without overtaxing the resource, and (ii) off-load to a safe distance any excess of population that may notwithstanding arise in the habitat.

Acute food-shortage leads to competition between members of the population in which the stronger sex may be expected to outlive the weaker. Although numbers can be progressively reduced by starvation in this way, the relief of pressure comes too late because the food resource has in typical cases already been damaged before any mortality results. To forestall the damage entirely, therefore, some other comparable type of competition requires to be substituted, that will lead at a much earlier stage to checking population growth or discharging the surplus as the case may be, and thus imposing an asymptote on density before the danger level is approached.

COMPETING FOR RIGHTS INSTEAD OF FOR FOOD

The existence of competition for such substitute goals or rewards is in fact almost everywhere conspicuous in the higher animals, such as vertebrates and arthropods. In the simplest systems competition takes place for space instead of food, and single individuals, family groups or larger aggregates hold territories to the exclusion of their competitors. Provided their behaviour mechanisms make them insist on at least an adequate minimum size for their territory, consistent with an ample self-contained supply of food, population density can be held at or below any ceiling that is fixed by a natural selection as advantageous. The territory simply becomes a conventional substitute, as far as competition is concerned, for the food it contains. Contest for ownership can be intense and can be seen to lead to the expulsion of supernumerary competitors in the process of achieving density limitation, exactly as postulated above. Territories of this kind occur fairly frequently among birds, as well as in all the other classes of vertebrates and in some insects and crustaceans. In man we can see their counterpart in the land-tenure patterns of farming communities.

In more involved systems the conventionality of the substituted goals of competition becomes increasingly exaggerated, and their connection with the food sources they ultimately represent gets more abstract and less direct. Solitary mammals like foxes, for example, evidently have to achieve acceptance by the community in the use of one or more holes or earths, which form part of a network of traditional dens extending over the country. Here there are no actual defended feeding-territories, although each individual has a customary 'home range' which freely overlaps that of other mutually tolerated individuals. Nevertheless the end result is exactly the same, holding down the population density of foxes below the level at which they would deplete the stocks of their prey. Competition is for 'rights' in the use of living quarters and hunting grounds; but once these rights have been secured the possessors do not quarrel about the actual food. Abstract rights of this kind often appear to be the automatic prerogative of the possessor of some tangible token prize, such as a recognized nest-site or hiding place. In a crowded sea-bird colony, for instance, there is frequently a well-defined perimeter to the nesting area, within which the successful competitors manage to secure their token holdings; birds that are unable to stake a claim inside the perimeter are inhibited from nesting outside, so that here it is the number of breeders that is limited by an established convention. Nest-site holders automatically acquire rights as established residents to seek food in the surrounding waters, and to breed as well.

It has been shown in a number of instances, including the red grouse (*Lagopus scoticus*)[5] and Australian magpie (*Gymnorhina tibicen*),[2] that not all members of a population have equal rights. Some habitual residents may enjoy access to the food resources and yet be inhibited when it comes to breeding. This stems from an aspect of conventional competition which is directed less towards tangible possessions than towards achieving acceptance or personal rank in a communal group. In actual practice, competition for real property and for abstract status are often inextricably mixed; but both forms of competition are in fact discharging the same basic function, which is to limit population density by a process of excluding any surplus that exceeds the acceptable level. Feeding rights are almost invariably involved in status competition; control of breeding rights, sometimes involved also, is of course similarly connected with the process of securing density limitation. Some form of status hierarchy is recognizable, at least in a few species, in every group of animals where property-competition occurs; the two are parallel and closely related phenomena.

A BIOLOGICAL DEFINITION OF SOCIETY

Conventional competition usually involves not only conventional rewards, whether real or abstract, but conventional methods of competing. The rewards themselves assume all the vital importance of the primary resources they replace. Failure to secure conventional rights normally precludes reproduction, and often culminates in expulsion from the habitat, starvation, and premature death. Vital as success is, therefore, to every contestant, conventional competition nevertheless characteristically stops short of deadly combat. In its place are substituted threat, bluff, and other more sophisticated displays of superiority. Generally these are quite sufficient to settle the contest, so that resort to brute force, and ultimately killing, is seldom required.

According to the writer's hypothesis, the rise of this edifice of conventional competition can be identified causally with the evolution of social behaviour; the two are alternative facets of one great adaptational complex. In many cases it is of course quite clear that competition for conventional rewards by conventional methods is a social process, particularly if it entails an *ad hoc* assembly of individuals at a customary place and time. Such an example would be the dawn assemblies of black grouse (*Lyrurus tetrix*) or sage-hens (*Centrocercus urophasianus*) on their traditional strutting grounds in spring, where the individual status and condition of the males is decided by sustained ritual tournaments. But the conventionalized rivalry of male dogs meeting by chance in the street is in fact hardly less typical of what we regard as a social phenomenon. The hypothesis recognizes conventional competition, in short, as the true essence of social behaviour, and defines a society as 'an organization of individuals capable of providing conventional competition among its members' ([8]p. 132.).

This is viewing the phenomenon of sociality from a novel direction, and it reveals an aspect that at first seems to depart considerably, and perhaps unacceptably, from the preconceptions commonly held on the subject. It must be remembered, however, that, although Allee[1] and his predecessors in the field have emphasized the universality of social behaviour among animals and the superficiality of the notion that some species are social while others are not, there has never been any accepted criterion by which true sociality could be identified. 'Social' and 'society' as biological terms are almost as vague as their everyday dictionary definitions, which pick out the qualities of gregariousness, companionship, interdependence, co-operation, and the like. Allee stressed the fundamental importance of mutual aid, for the benefit of the group; Tinbergen[7] recognized the importance of the reaction of the participants on one another, and the corollary that there is an underlying biological function; but no single characteristic function emerges to nail the phenomenon down.

It is not unreasonable to postulate, therefore, that the everyday definition may apply only to part of the wider biological phenomenon of sociality, emphasizing the element of cohesion and brotherhood, but overlooking, or perhaps unconsciously expurgating because in human contexts it is often disturbing, the accompanying element of rivalry. The most cursory survey of the phenomena of social behaviour suggests that this is by no means an improbable supposition. Within the coherent bird-flock or school of fish, an 'individual distance' between the members is often jealously observed, denoting the latent rivalry present even among equals. The members of societies are often not equal, in which case their rank has in most cases been competitively determined. And if this evolves a permanent submissiveness in the subordinates and an unresisting assumption of a lower status, as with the worker castes in social Hymenoptera and termites, it is not difficult to see that the primitive competitive machinery has merely been suppressed, and that social rank in these special cases has become predetermined by nutrition in early life. In the primitively social *Polistes* wasps, the removal of the queen at once frees the workers from her inhibitory dominance and within twenty-four hours some of them may begin to lay eggs.

At the other extreme the antagonistic element in social behaviour predominates so greatly that we lose sight of the fact that the phenomena in question are social at all. Song-birds aggressively defending their exclusive feeding territories appear to be the antithesis of a social community; yet it is well known that territories often tend to be coherently grouped together. When the males join in a synchronized chorus of song at dawn or dusk, each emulating his audible neighbours, the elements of sociality are unmistakable: it is just that the 'individual distance' is misleadingly large.

Contemporary human societies sometimes exist for the declared purpose of conventional competition, as happens in many forms of sport. At other times the competitive element is fugitive or more or less completely allayed, resulting only in the emergence of the necessary superiors or officials who conveniently 'dominate' the group. A vast array of human social institutions lies somewhere in between these situations. Even in so advanced a social species as our own the brotherhood of society is typically capable of arousing the competitive element whenever conditions of stress arise.

If this is a correct interpretation, the test of sociality is whether or not it is potentially capable of providing the conventional machinery by which surplus individuals can be excluded from the group or eliminated from the habitat, or recruitment regulated, or reproductive output adjusted, and population density thereby ultimately controlled. 'Potentially' is a necessary qualification in the case of man, as far as reproductive output is concerned, since this vital element in the machinery, although it survived into historic times among tribes living by hunting or temporary agriculture, or as nomad herdsmen, appears to have atrophied with the rise of permanent agricultural and urban communities.

POPULATION HOMEOSTASIS

In most animals the machinery of population regulation is partly behavioural, partly physiological. Behaviour is always involved in the spacing-out mechanisms which disperse the population over the ground, either as individuals or pairs or flocks, and, when the habitat is full up to its acceptable capacity, force whatever surplus of population there may be to get out and go elsewhere. Antagonistic behaviour subjects individuals to stress, and this leads to more or less acute physiological consequences. In the vertebrates it is a normal function of the endocrine system, and in particular of the adrenal cortex, to respond to social pressure and in turn to influence 'target' organs elsewhere in the body. The status of the individual, determined by social competition, is very commonly reflected in the state of its reproductive organs and is sometimes manifested externally by the development of scent-glands or skin and plumage colours. Lack of success in gaining a recognized position in the social milieu generally inhibits sexual maturation; and in some species an incipient threat of malnutrition can condition the fertility level of the population as a whole. Under stress, submissive individuals die simply of inanition, or fail to escape as they normally would from predators, or succumb to the burden of the parasites they already carry. Behaviourally, they may be lacking in ardour and fail to mate, or they may neglect their offspring.

In most of the mammals, physiological responses to population pressure are well developed: the maturation of the gonads, the frequency of ovulation and size of the litter are all commonly subject to density-dependent influences. In primitive man on the contrary, physiological mechanisms for regulating numbers had already become almost vestigial. Fertility in man is little affected by social stress, and there is not nearly enough stress-induced mortality to make this in any way effective as a population regulator. Control of density therefore depended almost completely on behavioural devices, for example on tribal land-tenure systems, and the expulsion or execution of individuals, on warfare, and especially on family limitation. The latter appears to have been imposed largely by traditional precepts, enjoining deferment of marriage, or the prolonged lactation of infants coupled with a concurrent ban on sexual intercourse, or the practice of contraception, abortion or infanticide. Obedience to the dictates of authority and fear of punishment are generally compelling forces among simple people; they appear to be part of an innate, socially valuable adaptation that, as usual, allows rights to be conferred on some and restraints on others in the interests of the continued safety and survival of the society as a whole.

The endogenous regulation of population density, depending on processes that are automatic and self-contained within the population concerned, is a typical form of homeostasis. Its operation is not necessarily perfect, and, especially among species living where the habitat is violently or repeatedly disturbed, as happens under most regimes of human land-use, animal numbers tend to get out of hand and pest conditions are gener-ated. To achieve the appropriate response from the population in order to adjust or restore the balance between population density and consumable resources, the members first require to be suitably conditioned; and it appears that there is a large category of social phenomena in animals the function of which is to provide an index of the density of population existing at the time. As pointed out at length elsewhere,[8] such 'epideictic' phenomena are especially conspicuous in anticipation of seasonal and other changes in density levels, and above all among adults immediately before they reproduce. The dawn chorus of birds, already referred to, is a typical epideictic display, indicating by its intensity and volume the standing density of territory-holders as well as their com-petitive ardour. In the case of the black grouse, one and the same tournament can per-haps condition the participants to the population pressure currently existing in the area served by the 'lek', rank the assembled individuals in a hierarchy, and eliminate from participation as breeders an appropriate quota of the subordinates. Possibly some of the tribal gatherings and initiation ceremonies so widespread in primitive human popula-tions fulfilled similar functions.

In general, the intensity of any form of conventional competition or display tends to be proportional to the number of contestants; that is to say, to be density-depend-ent; and this feature alone may often be sufficient to make it an effective epideictic index.

SOCIAL AND ANTISOCIAL

It would be a mistake to convey the impression that all conventional behaviour contains a latent element of competition, or that it is necessarily social at all. Courtship activities for instance are usually highly conventionalized; young birds and mammals communi-cate by conventional signals with their parents and vice versa. These are activities on the fringe of sociality, as understood here, and social only to the extent that the whole population is affected by whether the courtship succeeds or not, and whether the parents give sufficient food and care and are thus more or less successful in rearing their young. It is a significant and essential feature of social behaviour that it has a survival value for the society itself as a continuing unit, and is concerned with individuals only as com-ponents of the social group. A good illustration of this is the hierarchy, a typical social phenomenon, which exists only within a coherent group and vanishes completely if the individuals part company with one another.

Social organizations appear to have evolved as entities in their own right, each with its characteristic structures, codes and adaptations. They have been improved and perfected by natural selection, discriminating in favour of efficient systems which preserve the balance between population and environment without detriment to resources or prejudice to what the future brings. Less efficient systems are eliminated because they lead either to overpopulation and cumulative damage, or to the attenuation and extinction of the group. The process is one of intergroup selection.[9]

Antisocial behaviour among individual members, although it may advance their own interests, is by definition potentially detrimental to the survival of the group. It appears to have been firmly and almost universally suppressed by natural selection, acting at this overriding level. Total compliance with the social code, even when this entails the restriction or inhibition of fertility, exclusion from food and shelter, expulsion from the habitat, or summary death to the individual concerned, is consequently the normal routine of social life. The element of personal independence and individuality with which man intersperses his own customary social conformity, and the option open to him to conform or not, appear to have at most a rudimentary counterpart in other species. At one end of the scale the consequences of this 'free will' are anti-social, and these the conventional code attempts to curb by punishment; but they have presumably been more than outweighed in the past on the other side by the freedom it offers the talented individual to exercise his originality and inventive powers, and so contribute materially to the survival and rapid advancement of the society to which he belongs.

CARR-SAUNDERS' THEORY OF THE OPTIMUM NUMBER

In the context of archaeology it is especially interesting to find that this hypothesis of population regulation via the social system, in so far as it may be applied to man, had been largely anticipated forty years earlier by Carr-Saunders.[3] By making an exhaustive and masterly survey of the literature he was able to establish, first that those still-surviving primitive peoples about whom sufficient was known appeared all to have lived originally on traditional tribal areas, within recognized territorial boundaries. Second, that they normally remained in balance with the food resources of their own domains and thus maintained adequate and permanent nutritional standards, and physical well-being. Third, that most if not all practised one or more of the restrictive customs already mentioned, which resulted in family limitation.

In explanation he offered a biological hypothesis, based on the economic conception that in every natural and cultural environment there is a certain optimum number of inhabitants, such that it secures the highest return of goods per head for their labours. It must be a very great advantage to any population to approximate to that desirable density; but it will not be achieved simply by allowing starvation to limit numbers, because famine is attended by social instability and nullifies all the accumulated skills of the community in hunting, or cultivating the ground, by which their economic welfare is ordinarily sustained. Limitation must come from within, and this at once suggests an intelligible explanation for the widespread restrictions on effective fertility that have been recorded.

The economic principle of the optimum number would in Carr-Saunders' view apply only when social organization had developed to the point where men were able to reap the benefits of co-operation. This was the condition that seemed to him to provide the indispensable link between sociality and the regulation of numbers; whereas in my own view, as we have seen, society is regarded very differently, as providing the medium of conventional competition, which results when required in imposing the actual population ceiling. On my hypothesis, successful husbandry of resources depends primarily on controlling consumer demand, and only rarely and secondarily on mutual aid as a means of augmenting the output of 'goods'. Carr-Saunders' argument could be applied only to societies in which mutual aid conferred an important advantage, and this restricted his perspective to human societies, going back he surmised at most to Lower Palaeolithic times; it precluded any wider application of the theory to animals in general.

There are therefore two important and closely connected points of difference between our two theories, first as to the biological function of society, and second as to the nature of the economic benefits that accrue from it. Otherwise they are strikingly similar. Both realize that social codes enable the interests of the individual to be subordinated to those of the community, and that the evolution of this extremely advantageous type of adaptation must imply that selection has acted between social groups, as evolutionary units in their own right, giving preferment to those 'practising the most advantageous customs'; for no amount of selection at the level of the individual can evoke or modify social systems which enforce restrictions on individual liberties (e.g. the freedom to take food or property, or to reproduce), as a means of protecting the future and survival of the group as a whole, or its human counterpart the state.

ACKNOWLEDGEMENT

Part of this chapter has already appeared in print elsewhere,[10] and I am most grateful to the Zoological Society of London for permission to incorporate an amended version of it here.

REFERENCES

1 ALLEE, W. C. 1931. Animal aggregations, a study in general sociology, Chicago
2 CARRICK, R. 1963. Ecological significance of territory in the Australian magpie (Gymnorhina tibicen). Proc. XIII Intern. Ornith. Congr., Ithaca, 740–53
3 CARR-SAUNDERS, A. M. 1922. The population problem, a study in human evolution, Oxford
4 DARWIN, C. 1859. The origin of species, London. (Cited from '6th Edition with additions and corrections', 1891)
5 JENKINS, D. WATSON, A. and MILLER, G. R. Population studies on red grouse Lagopus lagopus scoticus (Lath.) in north-east Scotland. J. Anim. Ecol. 32, 317–76
6 SILLIMAN, R. P. and GUTSELL, J. S. 1958. Experimental exploitation of fish populations. U.S. Fish and Wildl. Serv., Fishery Bull. 58 (No. 133), 214–52
7 TINBERGEN, N. 1953. Social behaviour in animals, London and New York
8 WYNNE-EDWARDS, V. C. 1962. Animal dispersion in relation to social behaviour, Edinburgh and London 132
9 —— 1963. Intergroup selection in the evolution of social systems. Nature 200, 623–26
10 —— 1965. Social organization as a population regulator. Symp. zool. Soc. London, 14, 173–78

26 The Ageing of Domestic Animals

I. A. SILVER

THE METHODS for determining the age at death of domestic animals by examination of their hard parts differ little from those used in ageing any other animals. However, owing to the close association of domestic animals with man much more detailed information is available in relation to age changes in the skeleton and dentition than in the case for any animals other than man himself. The science of ageing an animal by the appearance of its teeth in life (or death) is probably as old as animal husbandry.

Really accurate estimates of the age of an animal can be made only when the following conditions are fulfilled—(a) that it belongs to a species or breed of which the age characteristics are well documented, (b) that its plane of nutrition is known, (c) that most of the teeth and a representative selection of bones are available and (d) that it is not yet fully adult. Archaeological material cannot satisfy all these criteria, since, first, age characteristics are well known only for modern domestic animals, most of which are considerably selected and inbred. Tooth eruption dates and epiphysial fusion dates differ very significantly between individual breeds within a single species. It is a reasonable assumption that bony remains from sites dated before intensive selective breeding began will show age characteristics similar to the more primitive of modern domestic animals rather than to those more highly specialized, provided that the archaeological material is definitely the same species as its modern counterpart. Second, the plane of nutrition of the animal can only be guessed at, usually from the bones whose age is to be determined, which leads to a danger of circular argument. Third, it is only under rather favourable circumstances that several bones can be identified positively as belonging to one animal. Fourth, it is fortunate that where food animals are concerned many are slaughtered before reaching adulthood and this slightly simplifies the task of ageing many bones.

METHODS—BONES

Assessment of age. This relies on a number of factors which are linked with the embryological, foetal and post-natal method of bone development and growth. With the exception of the clavicle and some parts of the skull, bones are first preformed in cartilage which then ossifies and becomes rearranged structurally. The process of ossification is constant for each bone. Long bones usually show a primary centre of ossification in the middle of the shaft and at least one epiphysial centre at each end (Fig. 38a). Complex bones such as vertebrae have more centres (Table A). Cartilaginous zones, the epiphysial plates, persist between the primary and secondary centres, allowing growth, until a relatively constant age for each particular epiphysis when the cartilage becomes ossified and the primary and secondary centres fuse. There are, however, some regions of cartilage which do not ossify, even in old age, although calcium salts may be deposited within cartilage, giving it a superficial appearance of bone. The costal cartilages and the proximal parts of the suprascapular cartilages of large animals may be affected in this way.

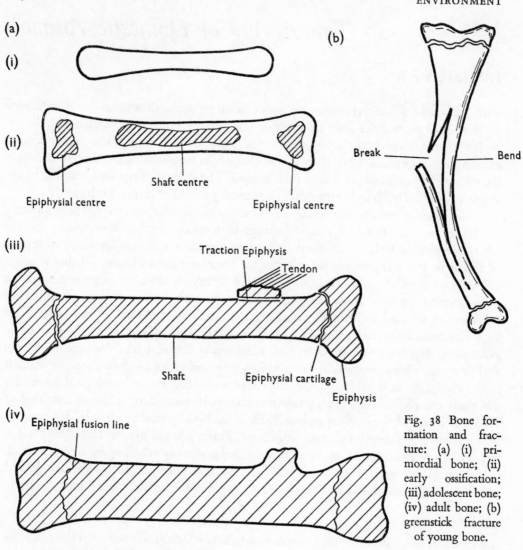

(a)

(i)

(ii)

Epiphysial centre

Shaft centre

Epiphysial centre

(iii)

Traction Epiphysis

Tendon

Shaft

Epiphysial cartilage

Epiphysis

(iv) Epiphysial fusion line

(b)

Break

Bend

Fig. 38 Bone formation and fracture: (a) (i) primordial bone; (ii) early ossification; (iii) adolescent bone; (iv) adult bone; (b) greenstick fracture of young bone.

Once a skeleton has started to ossify, the age of an animal may be determined fairly accurately by noting the regions where epiphysial fusion has occurred. From the point of view of the skeleton, full adulthood is reached when all epiphyses are fused and from this time onwards the indications of advancing age are very much less precise. The following changes in bones take place during the adult period, and serve as a rough guide (if evidence of tooth wear is lacking) as to whether the animal is a young, middle-aged or elderly adult. At first the shafts of the limb bones are relatively long and slender and the extremities are large. There are few surface marks on the bone and prominences for tendon and muscle attachments are small. In the mid-adult phase the bones become more rugged in appearance and the extremities are relatively narrower.

TABLE A

Ossification centres and ages of fusion in post-cranial skeleton of domestic animals.

Bone	Ossification Centres	Fusion
Vertebrae	Body 1 Arch 2 + Spine 1 Epiphyses 2	Horse, ox—body and arch fuse at or just after birth; bodies fuse with epiphyses at 5 years. Pig, sheep, dog—body and arch fuse at 3–6 months.
Atlas	4	Horse and ox—wings not fused till 6 months.
Axis*	7	Epiphysis between body and odontoid in horse open till 3–4 years.
Sacrum†		Body epiphyses may never fuse. Unite with each other before uniting with body.
Costal cartilages‡ Sternum	Manubrium 1 Sternebrae, 2 each	Sternebral centres fuse early except in last sternebra of ruminants which remain in 2 parts till old age.

* Anterior notch of axis becomes a foramen in old horses.
† Bases of spines fuse in old horses. Spines fuse in young adult cattle and sheep.
‡ Ossify or calcify commonly in old age.

Bone	Ossification Centres	Fusion				
		Horse Ass	Ox	Sheep	Pig	Dog
Scapula	Bicipital tuberosity	1 yr 8 mo.	7–10 mo.	6–8 mo.	1 yr.	6–7 mo.
	Tuber spinae	3 yrs				
Humerus	Proximal epiphysis	3–3½ yrs.	3½–4 yrs	3–3½ yrs.	3½ yrs	15 mo.
	Distal epiphysis	15–18 mo.	12–18 mo.	10 mo.	1 yr.	8–9 mo.
Radius	Proximal epiphysis	15–18 mo.	12–18 mo.	10 mo.	1 yr.	11–12 mo.
	Distal epiphysis	3½ yrs	3½–4 yrs	3 yrs	3½ yrs	11–12 mo.
Ulna	Olecranon*†	3½ yrs	All at 3½–4 yrs	All at 2½ yrs	All at 3–3½ yrs	9–10 mo.
	Distal end	Before 2 birth mo.				11–12 mo.
Metacarpus	Proximal epiphysis‡§	Before birth	Before birth	Before birth	Before birth	Before birth
	Distal epiphysis	15–18 mo.	2–2½ yrs	18–24 mo.	2 yrs	8 mo.
1st Phalanx	Proximal epiphysis	13–15 mo.	Before birth	Before birth	2 yrs	7 mo.
	Distal epiphysis	Before birth	1½ yrs	13–16 mo.	Before birth	Before birth

TABLE A continued:

Bone	Ossification Centres	Horse Ass	Ox	Sheep	Pig	Dog
2nd Phalanx	Proximal epiphysis	9–12 mo.	Before birth	Before birth	1 yr	7 mo.
	Distal epiphysis	Before birth	1½ yrs	13–16 mo.	Before birth	Before birth
3rd Phalanx	No true epiphysis¶	Partly ossified at birth				
Pelvis (os innominata = os coxae)	Fusion of main bones	1½–2 yrs	7–10 mo.	6–10 mo.	1 yr.	6 mo.
	Ilium—Tubercoxae Ischium—sciatic tuberosity Pubis—Acetabular bone	All fused at 4½–5 yrs	All fused by 4½ yrs	All fused by 3½ yrs	All fused by 6–7 yrs	Sciatic tuberosity at 2 yrs
Femur	Proximal end (2 epiphyses)‖	3–3½ yrs	3½ yrs	2½–3 yrs	3½ yrs	1½ yrs
	Distal end (1 epiphysis)	3–3½ yrs	3½–4 yrs	3–3½ yrs	3½ yrs	1½ yrs
Tibia	Proximal epiphysis	3–3½ yrs	3½–4 yrs	3–3½ yrs	3½ yrs	1½ yrs
	Distal epiphysis★★	20–24 mo.	2–2½ yrs	1½–2 yrs	2 yrs	13–16 mo.
Fibula	Proximal epiphysis	Doubtful 2–3 yrs	Fused with tibia 2–3 yrs		3½ yrs	15–18 mo.
	Distal epiphysis	Fuses with tibia 1–3 mo.	Separate bone	Separate bone	2½ yrs	15 mo.
Fibular Tarsal (Calcaneum)	Tuber calcis	3 yrs	3–3½ yrs	2½–3 yrs	2–2½ yrs	13–16 mo.
Metatarsal	Proximal epiphysis	Before birth	Before birth	Before birth	Before birth	Before birth
	Distal epiphysis	16–20 mo.	2¼–3 yrs	20–28 mo.	2¼ yrs.	10 mo.

★ Interosseus radio-olecranon ligament ossifies in horse at 3–4 yrs.
† Radio-ulnar ligament ossifies in dog at 2 yrs.
‡ Metacarpals 3 and 4 of ruminants are joined by cartilage at birth.
§ Ossification occurs at 3–8 mo. (old figures give 12–15 mo.).
¶ In old horses the lateral cartilages may ossify to form 'side bones'.
‖ A traction epiphysis at 3rd trochanter in horse ossifies variously from 2 to 4 yrs.
★★ Lateral malleolus separate at birth to 3 mo. in foal.

Marks caused by blood vessels become obvious and tendon attachments may ossify to give 'traction epiphyses'. Smaller prominences associated with muscle attachment appear, and depressions at muscle origins are deep. The cortex of the bone is thick and the bone is heavy. In senility, calcium resorbtion takes place resulting in a bone with a thin cortex and large medullary cavity. Rarefaction is common. Similar changes may occur in pregnancy.

Certain pathological features may be present which can also be a guide to the probable age. For instance, so-called 'greenstick' fractures occur only in young bones (Fig. 38b); malignant bone tumours usually appear in the adolescent or young adult but arthritic changes and signs of healed inflammatory changes, especially on the legs of large animals, are commonest in middle to late life. Changes in the alveoli of the jaws where teeth have been lost in life may be useful as guides to age. The alveolar cavity is slowly filled with bone after loss of a tooth, and if no cavity at all is present, particularly at the site of a deep-rooted tooth, it is an indication that the jaw is probably not from a young adult. The size of the maxillary sinuses in horse, ox, sheep and goat gives a fairly close correlation with age even when teeth or other parts of skull are missing. The lower the floor of this sinus, the older the animal. In extreme old age, high-crowned teeth may grow right out of the jaw leaving the floor of the maxillary sinus below the level of the palate. In the foal, the maxillary sinus is almost full of developing teeth, at $5\frac{1}{2}$ years it is full of embedded parts of permanent teeth and in old age it is largely filled with air.

In the horned domestic animals the cavity of the frontal sinus extends into the bony horn-core. A horn-core from a young animal normally has a rather narrow cortex and a large sinus cavity. With advancing age the cavity is reduced and the cortex thickens. Horn-cores showing signs of repaired damage are more likely to come from mature animals. If the horn itself survives it will be found to show annual growth rings, the first of which appears at two years of age in cattle.

RADIOGRAPHIC EVIDENCE OF EPIPHYSIAL FUSION

Smith[34] has studied the epiphysial fusion age of the limb bones of 12 sheep in the Clun Forest breed, by radiography. The ages for epiphyseal closure are summarized in the following table and are mostly earlier than those quoted in the general table. However, the following factors must be considered: (1) Clun Forest is a very early maturing breed of sheep. (2) The sheep were kept under good nutritional circumstances. (3) Only females were used over 10 months. (4) Radiographic evidence of epiphysial closure does not necessarily imply that the fusion is complete or sufficiently strong to withstand the stresses likely to be imposed on archaeological material. Nevertheless, Tschirwinsky[35,36] who boiled his material for 8 hours to determine whether epiphysial fusion had occurred, quotes figures which are closely comparable with those of Smith.

Epiphysial Fusion in Clun Forest Sheep

Bone	Scapula	Humerus					Radius		Ulna	
Epiphysis	Tubercle	Prox.	Distal	Tuber-osity	Epicondyles Lat.	Med.	Prox.	Dist.	Prox.	Dist.
Fusion age (months):										
Smith	5	17	4	28	4	6	4	21	21	26
Tschirwinsky		16–21	3				3	16–21		

Bone	Meta-carpus	1st Phalanx	2nd Phalanx	Femur				Tibia		
Epiphysis	Distal	Prox.	Prox.	Prox.	Dist.	Trochanter Maj.	Min.	Prox.	Dist.	Tu-bercle
Fusion age (months): Smith	16	10	8	17–18	18–20	17–19	13	25	15	30
Tschirwinsky	15–16			16	16–21	16	10	16–21	10	

Bone	Calcaneum	Metatarsus	1st Phalanx (hind)	2nd Phalanx (hind)
Epiphysis	Tuber Calcis	Distal	Prox.	Prox.
Fusion age (months): Smith	15	15	9	6
Tschirwinsky		15–16		

Detailed assessment of age. The tables above indicate the ages at which the epiphyses of the major bones fuse with the shaft in the common domestic mammals. There is unfortunately no complete agreement on exact fusion ages and the figures given in the tables are means and as far as possible these data refer to 'scrub' crossbred animals. High planes of nutrition and sheltered conditions tend to accelerate epiphysial fusion.

Certain features may be amplified as these are not obvious in tables. The proportions of the skull change strikingly with age. In young mammals the brain case is large relative to the face, but during the growing period the face usually increases in size faster than the cranium. Taking the horse as an example (Table B), in a young foal the bones of the forehead are convex, but as growth occurs the frontals and nasals flatten and may become concave in old age. The maxillary region of the face is also primarily convex but it becomes concave as the cheek teeth grow out of the skull. The relationship of the rostral end of the facial crest to the cheek tooth immediately below it, is as follows: in the new-born, the posterior part of the third premolar, in the three-year-old the posterior part of the fourth premolar, and in the mature adult the first molar. The pre-maxilla in young horses has a downward curve which is gradually lost with age. The caudal border of the vertical ramus of the mandible becomes narrow and sharp in very old horses. The long axis of the bony orbit in the young adult is on a line passing through the necks of the incisor teeth and the external auditory opening but in old age it is lower and on a line joining the occipital tubercle and the rostral end of the zygomatic crest.

The cranium behind the post-orbital bars is wider in a young than in an adult animal: the various prominences, especially the lachrymal tubercle and nuchal and sagittal crests, increase with age, and the infra-orbital foramen, which in early life is present as a slit, becomes large and almost round in old age.

METHODS—TEETH

General. The teeth are the most durable and in many ways the most informative hard

TABLE B

The skull of the horse—centres of ossification and fusion ages.

Bone	Centres of ossification	Fusion ages	Notes
Occipital	Supraoccipital 2 × exoccipital Basioccipital	Supra with exocc. at 18 mo. Basi with exocc. at 3–4 mo.	4 bones at birth but only 1 bone in adult
Sphenoid	One in each of 4 wings One in body = 5	With occip. at 5 yrs	
Ethmoid	2 in each lateral mass 1 in perpendicular plate = 5		At birth perpendicular and cribriform plates are cartilaginous Often paired in young animals
Interparietal	2 main centres	With parietals at 3–4 yrs With supraoccipital at about 5 yrs	Fusion v. variable Central part more convex in foal than adult
Parietal	Each has one centre	Parietals fuse across midline about 4 yrs Parieto-occipital fusion 5 yrs Parieto-squamous fusion 12–15 yrs	No external parietal crest in foal
Frontal	Each has one centre	With each other or parietals only in old age	
Squamosal (Squamous temporal)	Each has a single centre	With parietal at 12–15 yrs	
Periotic (Petrosal or Petrous temporal)	At least 2	At or soon after birth	Rarely fuses with adjoining bones
Pterygoid Maxilla Lachrymal Palatine Zygomatic	1 each (Some may have small secondary centres)		Normally remain separate. May unite with adjoining bones in old age
Premaxilla	1	The two bones fuse across mid line at about 4 yrs	
Nasal	1	Mid line suture is unfused even in old age	
Mandible	2 in each branch	The 2 centres fuse before birth. The 2 halves fuse at 2–4 mo.	

structures of the body. It may be possible to infer, from a single tooth, not only the species or feeding habits of an animal, but also its age and approximate size. However, for accurate determination of age from teeth it is necessary to have at least a selection of them from an animal, preferably still embedded in the jaw. The teeth which give the best indication of age in the adult are those of the 'high-crowned' or hypsodont type which grow out of the jaw at an approximately constant rate as they are worn away, and whose character changes not only in regard to length but also in respect of the crown pattern of the interfolded layers of cement, enamel and primary and secondary dentine. It is unfortunate that maximum accuracy in ageing of teeth can be accomplished only in the infantile and adolescent animal, the same periods in which bones give their most reliable indication of age. There are, however, as in the case of bone, certain signs to be found in the teeth of adults which will indicate whether they are from young, middle-aged or senile animals. Although changes in horse teeth are dealt with in detail in the tables it is worth noting that the first molar is rather commonly attacked by caries in the young to middle-aged adult, whereas caries in other cheek teeth is much less common and is usually an indication of advanced age. In cattle, the incisor teeth are always movable in the jaw in life, so that there is a relatively large amount of soft tissue in the incisor alveoli. Thus it is common to find in normal cattle that the roots of the incisors are much smaller than the alveolar cavity. On the other hand, especially in carnivores, if the teeth show roots which are markedly smaller than the alveoli, and the alveolar walls are rough, then it is probable that the specimen suffered from paradontal disease and was old. A common sequel to this condition is readily detectable in archaeological material due to the resorbtion and destruction of bone at the original abscess site. The tooth most often affected by abscesses of the root is the carnassial tooth of the upper jaw (premolar 4) in old dogs. Frequently the maxillary bone over the roots of this tooth is eroded so that a sinus develops between alveolus and the surface.

Very heavily worn teeth, or jaws showing alveoli from which teeth have been lost in life, naturally indicate an old animal, but considerable caution must be exercised in coming to such a conclusion unless there is confirmatory evidence from other (skeletal) sources. Young dogs which eat large quantities of bones or play with and chew hard materials such as wood or stones, may present a pattern of tooth wear suggestive of extreme senility, whereas old animals which have eaten mainly meat and have not had to scavenge may have almost unworn teeth. In this latter case, however, there is nearly always some wear on the canines and carnassials and the tips of the incisors. Among herbivores the type of soil and herbage plays a major part in tooth wear. Animals on sandy soil and short grass show the highest rate of wear, whereas animals feeding largely on foliage or on lush grass from soft soils with a low silica content show only slow tooth abrasion. Certain areas are well known at the present time to produce rapid tooth wear. For instance, ponies living on Dartmoor often seem, on the evidence of their teeth, to be as much as two years older than they are in fact.

Details of ageing by teeth in individual species. (1) *Horse.* Table C gives tooth eruption dates in live horses, that is the age at which the tooth cuts the gum and not the age at which it first appears out of the bone. In archaeological material teeth which are unworn and project only slightly above the jaw line are best regarded as being at a stage represented by the earliest dates given here. If a tooth shows the slightest evidence of wear then it must have been erupted, and in all probability will have been erupted for at least 2–3 months. Teeth usually take about six months from eruption to come into full wear.

TABLE C

Tooth eruption ages in the horse.

Tooth		Deciduous teeth	Permanent teeth
Incisors★			
Central	I/I	Present at birth	2½–3 yrs
Lateral	I/I	3–4 wks	3½–4 yrs
Corner	I/I	5–9 mo.	4½–5 yrs
Canine	I/I	Rarely emerges from jaw	4–5 yrs
Premolars			
1	I/I Wolf tooth	Inconstant, 6 mo.	Inconstant, 2½ yrs
2	I/I	⎫	2½ yrs
3	I/I	⎬ Present at birth	2½ yrs
4	I/I	⎭	3½ yrs
Molars			
1	I/I	⎫	Wide variation. 7–14 mo. Usually present by 1 yr
2	I/I	⎬ Absent	2–2½ yrs
3	I/I	⎭	3½–4½ yrs

★ It is usual for the upper milk incisor teeth to be replaced by permanent teeth slightly earlier than those of the lower jaw.

It is of great importance to distinguish permanent from deciduous incisor teeth and the following characteristics may be used. The milk teeth have a definite 'neck'; they are grooved on the lingual and smooth on the labial surfaces; they are small and the enamel is white; they often show signs of resorbtion of the root due to the presence of following teeth; when present in the jaw they are arranged in a semi-circle. The permanent incisors appear as follows (Fig. 39a): they are long and curved and diminish gradually from crown to root without a neck, the curve being restricted to the crown region, the root being straight; they are grooved on the labial aspect; the enamel is a dirty white and the infundibulum is much deeper than in milk teeth; there is a

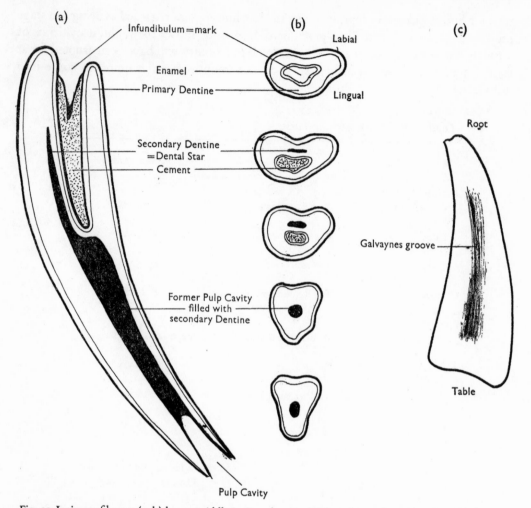

Fig. 39 Incisors of horse: (a, b) lower middle incisor: longitudinal section and cross-sections viewed from above (note the outer layer of cement has been omitted to avoid confusion); (c) upper lateral incisor, showing Galvayne's groove.

considerable change in cross-section from the crown to root, the crown being twice as wide laterally as it is antero-posteriorly whereas in the root region the antero-posterior diameter is twice the lateral (Fig. 39b).

When all the teeth have erupted and are in wear, it is necessary to resort to other characters for determining age. The incisor teeth of horses show valuable clues to age provided that tooth wear has remained within normal limits. The first is the infundibulum or mark, and the second is the star, which is formed by the filling of the pulp cavity with secondary dentine of a colour different from that of the primary dentine. (Fig. 39a, b). The third is that the shape of the table (the biting surface) varies with age in a constant manner. Lastly, the labial groove (of Galvayne) of the upper corner incisor is confined to the middle third of the tooth so that it remains within the jaw until approximately the tenth year (Fig. 39c), it is half-way down the erupted front of the tooth at 15, the full length at 21 and only the distal half shows a groove at 30 years. The following list shows the expected appearance of teeth at differing ages.

Birth	Milk central incisors and premolars
1–5 months	Milk central plus lateral incisors and premolars
6–12 months	Milk central plus lateral plus corner incisors and premolars plus first molar
1 year	Infundibulum worn out of central incisors. Corner incisors in wear but thin walled. Incisor teeth close together
18 months	Infundibulum lost from lateral incisors. First molar in wear
2 years	Incisor teeth wide apart. Infundibulum lost from corner incisor. Second molar appears
2½ years	Permanent central incisor and first and second permanent premolar cut. Second molar in wear
3 years	Permanent central incisor and first and second permanent premolar in wear
3½ years	Permanent lateral incisor and third permanent premolar cut plus lower canines
4 years	Permanent lateral incisor in wear. Upper canine may appear (males). Third molar appears
4½ years	Permanent corner incisor appears. Upper canine usually present as a sharp knife edge—but only in males. Third molar in wear
5 years	Permanent corner incisor in wear, but inner wall still level with jaw and the upper tooth is much longer laterally than antero-posteriorly. Canine in wear. Star on central incisor
6 years	Upper corner incisors, diameters almost equal laterally and a.p. and inner walls in wear. Infundibulum very shallow on central. Star on lateral incisor
7 years	Upper corner square, often with a posterior 'hook'. Lower corner in wear on inner as well as outer walls, all of which are thick. Infundibulum lost from central incisor. Canines blunt
8 years	Infundibulum lost from lateral incisors and very shallow on lower corners
9 years	All infundibular marks absent on incisors. No labial groove on upper corner beyond alveolar cavity. Central incisor table is triangular
10 years	Appearance of Galvayne's groove on labial aspect of upper corner incisor. Lateral incisor table triangular
11 years	Corner incisor table becoming triangular
12 years	All incisor table markedly triangular
13 years	Often a posterior hook on corner incisor
15 years	Galvayne's groove ½ down erupted part of upper corner incisor
18 years	Central incisor table width = thickness a.p.

21 years	Galvayne's groove reaches full length of erupted part of tooth.
	Narrowing of lower jaw and separation of roots of incisors marked
26 years	Width of central incisors = $\frac{1}{2}$ a.p. diameter
30 years	Galvayne's groove half-way off upper corner incisor

The rate of wear of horse teeth is not constant, e.g. between 5 years and 7 years the incisors are worn away at about $\frac{1}{4}$ inch per year while later in life the rate is much reduced so that over 20 years of age the incisors are ground off at about $\frac{1}{4}$ inch per 5 years. The lower cheek teeth tend to wear faster than the upper as they have a smaller surface area; also the central cheek teeth wear faster than those at each end of the row. In old horses this often leads to an undulation of the surface of cheek teeth. Very smooth molars and premolars are also characteristic of old age.

Lastly, the arrangement of the incisor teeth in the jaw is referable to the age of the animal. In youth the upper and lower teeth meet to form a vertical line with their labial surfaces (Fig. 40). As the animal ages the angle at which the teeth meet becomes progressively less than 180° until in old age, the incisors, especially of the lower jaw, protrude almost horizontally from the jaws (Fig. 40).

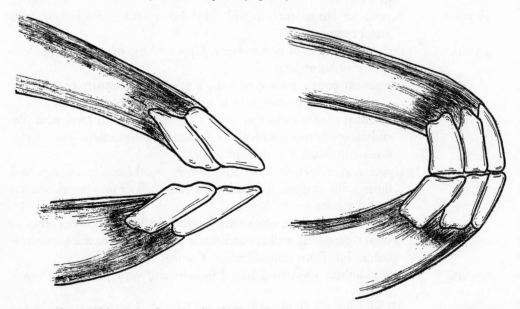

Fig. 40 Change of the angle of profile of teeth; this is due to the curvature of the crown and straight roots.

No doubt horse dealing is almost as old as domestication of horses and dealers are distinguished by the ingenuity they show in attempting to improve on the natural appearance of horses' teeth, to the confusion of their clients. The common forms of deception consist of the production of an 'artificial infundibulum' in old incisor teeth by burning a hole and the filing away of the front of the incisors to reduce the acuteness of the angle at which they meet. Both of these practices help to produce a 'young' old horse. Both are easily detected if the normal arrangement of dentine and enamel is

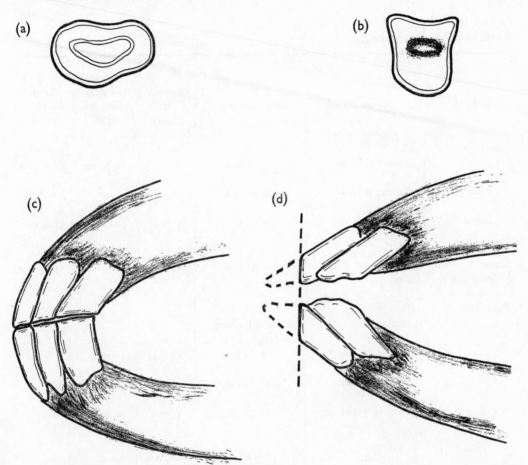

Fig. 41 'Bishoping'; (a) natural mark; enamel surround is present; tooth is wider than long; (b) false mark; no enamel surround; tooth is longer than wide; (c) young teeth, meeting at 180°; (d) old teeth, filed to give 180° front surface.

understood (Fig. 41). In the first case no enamel surrounds the false 'mark' and in the second the enamel will be missing from the front of the filed incisors (Fig. 41). This type of 'faking' used to be very common and is known as 'Bishoping', which suggests a rather disreputable connection with the church. Another trick which has a long history is that of removing the milk incisors in order to 'force' the permanents and give a very young horse a more mature appearance. This is easily detected by reference to the molars and premolars.

(2) *Ox*. The teeth of cattle show great variation in eruption dates depending on breed, management and nutrition. The better the housing and feeding and the more highly bred, the earlier the eruption of teeth. It is noticeable in the early works on domestic animals that the ages given for tooth eruption may be as much as twice that given by modern authors for improved breeds—see Table D. It seems reasonable to take the older figures as more applicable to archaeological material unless there is independent

TABLE D
Tooth eruption ages in the ox.

Tooth		Deciduous teeth	Permanent teeth	Chauveau 19th century	Commercial Crossbred stock 1950. MR*	Ranch cattle MR*
Incisors						
1 central	o/1 ⎫	Present at birth	14–25 mo.	18 mo.	20–24 mo.	22–24 mo.
2 middle	o/1 ⎬	Present at birth	17–36 mo.	30 mo.	30 mo.	30–36 mo.
3 lateral	o/1 ⎭	Present at birth or in first 2 wks	22–40 mo.	42 mo.	36 mo.	42 mo.
Canine (=incisiform corner)	o/1	At birth or in first 2 wks	32–48 mo.	54 mo.	42–48 mo.	54–60 mo.
Premolars						
1		Occasional	Occasional, always lost before 3 yrs			
2	1/1	Birth to 3 wks	24–30 mo.	18 mo.	30 mo.	
3	1/1	Birth to 3 wks	18–30 mo.	30 mo.	30 mo.	
4	1/1	Birth to 3 wks	28–36 mo.	42 mo.	36 mo.	
Molars						
1	1/1		5–6 mo.	6–9 mo.	6 mo.	
2	1/1	Absent	15–18 mo.	30 mo.	15–18 mo.	
3	1/1		24–30 mo.	4–5 yr	24 mo.	

* MR: Miller and Robertson.[18]

evidence that the system under which the animals were kept afforded good protection against weather and periodic starvation. Some features not obvious from the table are given below:

Birth to 3 months	Incisor crowns overlap
6 months	Incisors are side by side
1 year	Spaces between incisors, heavily worn
2 years	Central permanent incisors show some wear
2½–3 years	2 pairs permanent incisors in wear
3–4 years	3 pairs permanent incisors in wear
4–5 years	4 pairs permanent incisors in wear with some overlapping of teeth

5–10 years	Progressive wearing of incisors and reduction of overlap with eventual almost complete loss of crown leaving root stumps with 'tips' of enamel only
12–14 years	Widely separated stumps of incisors
14–16 years	Gradual closing up of stumps of incisors

Separate incisor teeth can be placed as young if the labial surfaces bear longitudinal wavy lines, or aged if these are absent. The incisors are at first convex in outline and are levelled by wear. This wear removes the enamel to expose a line of yellow dentine. Within this a darker streak appears later (the secondary dentition) which changes in shape with age; from being long (transversely) it shortens, then widens into a square and finally becomes round in the root.

It is worth noting that the last milk premolar of the lower jaw is very large in ruminants and has 3 cusps. It may be easily mistaken for a permanent tooth.

TABLE E

Tooth eruption ages in the sheep.

Tooth		Deciduous teeth	Permanent teeth	
			Modern figures (improved breeds)	Semi-wild, hill sheep, old figures (1790)
Incisors				
Central	0/1	Birth to 1 wk	12–18 mo.	18 mo.
Middle	0/1	Birth to 1 wk	18–24 mo.	30 mo.
Lateral	0/1	Birth to 2 wks	27–36 mo.	42 mo.
Canine (corner incisor)	0/1	Birth to 3 wks	33–48 mo.	50 mo.
Premolars				
1		Usually absent	Usually absent	
2	1/1	Birth to 6 wks	21–24 mo.	30 mo.
3	1/1	Birth to 6 wks	21–24 mo.	30 mo.
4	1/1	Birth to 6 wks	21–24 mo.	40 mo.
Molars				
1	1/1		5 mo. (upper) 3 mo. (lower)	6 mo.
2	1/1	Absent	9–12 mo.	18 mo.
3	1/1		18–24 mo.	3–4 yrs

(3) *Sheep*. Sheep vary widely in the age at which they reach maturity, the so-called improved breeds maturing much earlier than hill breeds. Figures published by authors in the late eighteenth and early nineteenth centuries suggest that at that time sheep were regarded as having similar tooth eruption dates to cattle, but modern authorities, referring to modern breeds of sheep, give eruption dates which are considerably younger. The incisors of sheep are long and narrow so do not show the same changes as those of the ox. They are normally held rigidly in the jaw. Sheep teeth come into wear 3–5 months after they are erupted.

(4) *Goat* (Table F: improved breeds early dates, rough goats late dates).

(5) *Pig*. Like sheep, pigs have been selected into a great many breeds whose maturation varies considerably. Only very general reliance can be placed on eruption dates as indication of age. The pig is peculiar in that the first premolar is not deciduous and is

TABLE F
Tooth eruption ages in the goat.

Tooth		Deciduous teeth	Permanent teeth*
Incisors†			
Central	0/1	Birth	15 mo.
Middle	0/1	Birth	21 mo.—27 mo.
Lateral	0/1	Birth	27 mo.—36 mo.
Canine (corner incisor)	0/1	1–3 weeks	36 mo.—40 mo.
Premolars			
1		Usually absent	Usually absent
2	1/1	3 mo.	17–20 mo.—30 mo.
3	1/1	3 mo.	17–20 mo.—30 mo.
4	1/1	3 mo.	17–20 mo.—30 mo.
Molars			
1	1/1		5–6 mo.
2	1/1	Absent	8–10 mo.—12 mo.
3	1/1		18–24 mo.—30 mo.

* Early dates: improved breeds; later dates: rough goats.
† Incisors are frequently broken in old goats due to eating twigs.

TABLE G
Tooth eruption ages in the p

Tooth		Deciduous
Incisors		
Central	1/1	1–3 wks 4–14 days
Lateral	1/1	10–14 wks 6–12 wks
Corner	1/1	Birth
Canine		Birth
Premolars		
1	1/1	
2	1/1	7–10 wks
3	1/1	1–3 wks 1–5 wks
4	1/1	1–4 wks 2–7 wks
Molars		
1	1/1	
2	1/1	
3	1/1	

* As usual, data from late 18th-

variable in appearance, also alone of the domestic animals it possesses a tooth, the canine, which grows throughout life. Very long lower canines (more than 8 inches) indicate an old animal.

The lower incisors become heavily worn from digging and in old pigs the molar and premolar crowns may be worn flat or even concave.

(6) *Dog and Cat*. The domestic carnivores are relatively long-lived yet their teeth provide little evidence of age after the first eight months of life.

At one year all dog incisors are in wear but still have the *fleur-de-lys* shape which is completely lost by two years. Cats frequently lose the incisor teeth in middle age.

(7) *Camel*. Although the ageing of camels by their teeth has been practised in Arabia since before the tenth century, information on the subject is still rather vague.

TABLE H
Tooth eruption ages in the dog.

…manent teeth	Old Data* Permanent	Tooth	Deciduous teeth	Permanent teeth
2–17 mo.	2½–3 yrs	**Incisors** Central I/I		3–5 mo.
		Lateral I/I	4–6 wks	
7–20 mo.	2½–3 yrs	Corner I/I		
–12 mo.	6–12 mo.	Canine I/I	3–5 wks	5–7 mo.
–12 mo.	12 mo.	**Premolars** I I/I	Absent	4–5 mo.
½–6½ mo. constant		2 I/I		
2–16 mo.	2 yrs	3 I/I	5–8 wks	5–6 mo.
2–16 mo.	2 yrs	4 I/I		
2–16 mo.	2 yrs			
		Molars I I/I		4–5 mo.
–6 mo.	1 yr	2 I/I		5–6 mo.
–13 mo.	1½–2 yrs	3 I/I		6–7 mo.
7–22 mo.	3 yrs			
…thors give late eruption dates.		Similar ages are given by 18th-century authors.		

TABLE I

Tooth eruption ages in the cat.

Tooth		Deciduous teeth	Permanent teeth
Incisors			
Central	1/1	⎫	
Lateral	1/1	⎬ 3–4 wks	3½–5½ mo.
Corner	1/1	⎭	
Canine	1/1	3–4 wks	5½–6½ mo.
Premolars			
1		Absent	Absent
2	1/0	⎫	
3	1/1	⎬ 5–6 wks	4–5 mo.
4	1/1	⎭	
Molars			
1	1/1	Absent	5–6 mo.

Domestic Fowl. Owing to the very short period during which growth takes place it is not practicable to age skeletal remains except into 'young' and 'old'. Long bones in birds do not have epiphysial centres of ossification, the whole epiphysis being cartilaginous in youth. The epiphyses of long bones all ossify early (under six months). The 'keel' of the sternum is largely cartilaginous in young birds, and gradually ossifies. This process is completed between 5 and 8 months according to breed. Spurs develop on the metatarsals of males and their length is some indication of age. Old females may also develop spurs.

CONCLUSIONS

The ageing of animals from skeletal remains of any antiquity cannot be an exact science, and calls for the exercise of considerable judgement. Despite selective breeding the horse and dog seem to have retained a more constant skeletal development with age than have other domestic species. In particular, sheep and pigs are very difficult to age on the evidence of teeth alone owing to their responsiveness to feeding and management changes. It is unfortunate that the translations from Arabic of works of the thirteenth century are not always clear in respect of nomenclature of teeth and that earlier writers such as Aristotle and Varro are far from objective in their methods of ageing. Nevertheless medieval authors from Asia and Europe provide useful information on unimproved

TABLE J

Tooth eruption ages in the camel.

Tooth		Deciduous teeth	Permanent teeth
Incisors			
Central	0 or 1/1	4–6 wks	0/1 4 yrs
Middle	1/1	3–4 mo.	0/1 5 yrs
Lateral	1/1	8–9 mo.	1/1 6 yrs
Corner (Canine)	1/1	10–12 mo.	1/1 6½ yrs
Premolars			
1 (canine type)	0/0		1/1
2	1/0	⎫	0/0 ⎫ 4–5 yrs
3	1/1	⎬ 4–6 mo.	1/(1) ⎬ Lower P.M.3 if erupted is usually shed by 6–7 yrs
4	1/1	⎭	1/1 ⎭
Molars			
1	1/1		1 year
2	1/1		3 yrs
3	1/1		5 yrs

For further details *see* Cornevin and Lesbre,[7] Monod,[19] and Lesbre.[16]

animals in many instances. Where it can be established that one breed of animal only is present in an excavation site, and if a reasonably complete set of bones and teeth for one or two individuals can be assembled, then relationship of tooth wear to epiphysial fusion dates may be determined and applied to the rest of the more fragmentary material from the same site.

There is little difficulty in classifying animals as young, aged or senile, but to decide ages to the nearest six months or year clearly requires very close study and considerable luck in obtaining appropriate bones or teeth.

REFERENCES

1 ARISTOTLE. *Natural History of Animals*, bks 2 and 4; first detailed record of observations but with many errors
2 ABU-BEKR. *c.* 1400. *Le Naceri*, bk 2, p. 54; transl. PERRON, M., Paris, 1859; difficult translation but earliest good details on horse, camel, sheep and goat; also, first details of tooth forgery in Arabia
3 BROWN, G. T. 1860. *Dentition as indicative of the age of the animals of the farm*, London

4 CHAUVEAU, A. 1888. *Traité d'anatomie comparée des animaux domestiques*, Paris, 4th ed.

5 —— 1891. *Comparative anatomy of the domesticated animals*, transl. FLEMING, G., London; useful for summary of nineteenth-century views on ageing by bones and teeth

6 COLUMELLA. *De Re Rustica*, bk 4; early observations on horse teeth

7 CORNEVIN, C. and LESBRE, X. 1894. *Traité de l'âge des animaux domestiques*; the most comprehensive book available on ageing of sheep, goats, camels, horses, dogs, cats, rabbits and guinea-pigs by examination of teeth; well illustrated

8 CRESCENZI, P. DE. *c.* 1260. *Opus ruralium commodorum*, bk 12; ageing in medieval Europe

9 DAUBENTON. *Instruction pour les Bergers*, Pamphlet *c.* 1800; ageing sheep up to 5 years

10 DUPONT, M. M. 1893. *L'âge du cheval et des principaux animaux domestiques*, Paris

11 FRANCINI, HORACE DE. 1607. *Hippiatrique*, bk 1, ch. 7

12 GIRARD FILS. 1824. Receuil de médecine veterinaire, *Mémoire sur les moyens de reconnaître l'âge du cheval*; good practical account of horse teeth

13 GIRARD, J. 1834. *Traité de l'âge du cheval augmenté de l'âge du bœuf, du mouton, du chien et du cochon*

14 HAYES, M. H. 1915. *Veterinary notes for horse owners*, London, 8th ed.; excellent photographs of horse teeth at various ages

15 HUIDEKOPER, R. S. 1891. *Age of the domestic animals*, Philadelphia

16 LESBRE, F. X. 1893. *Bulletin de la société centrale vétérinaire*, p. 147 ; dentition des camélides

17 MAYHEW, E. 1849. *The horse's mouth, showing the age by the teeth*, London; illustrations

18 MILLER, W. C. and ROBERTSON, E. D. S. 1947. *Practical animal husbandry*, Edinburgh, 5th ed.; good diagrams on horse and cow. Useful for modern horse, cattle, sheep, pig and dog

19 MONOD, O. O. 1892. Receuil de mémoires et observations sur l'hygiène et la médecine vétérinaire militaire, *De l'âge du Chameau*, Paris

20 NEHRING, 1888. *Landwirtschaftliche Jahrbücher*; comparison of teeth in wild and domestic pigs

21 NICKEL, R., SCHUMMER, A. and SEIFERLE, E. 1960. *Lehrbuch der Anatomie der Haustiere*, Berlin; the most recent information on bones and teeth

22 PESSINA. 1830. *Sul modo di conoscere dai denti l'età dei cavalli*; extremely detailed ageing of horse teeth

23 PLINY. *Natural History*, bk VIII; repetition of Aristotle

24 RUINI, CARLO. 1626. *Anatomia de Cavallo, infermità e suoi remedii*, Venice, bk 1, ch. 41; the most detailed information on horse up to that time

25 SAUNIER, GASPARD DE. 1734. *La parfaite connaissance des chevaux*, La Haye

26 SIMONDS, J. B. 1854. The age of ox, sheep and pig, *Roy. Agricultural Soc.*, London; good detail; distinguishes well-bred and common stock

27 SISSON, S. 1953. *Anatomy of the domestic animals*, ed. CROSSMAN, J. S., Philadelphia, 4th ed.; the best information in English on epiphysial fusion dates except for sheep and goat

28 SOLLEYSEL, DE. 1664. *Le parfait maréchal*, Paris; details of horse teeth up to 8 years and of faking practices in Europe

29 TAQUET, J. 1607. *Phillipica ou haras de chevaux*, Paris, Anvers ed.

30 VARRO. *De Re Rustica*, bk 2

31 VEGETIUS, PUBLIUS. *c.* 450. *Artis veterinariae sive mulo medicinae*, bk 4

32 VIBORG. 1823. *Mémoires sur l'éducation, les maladies, l'engrais et l'emploi du porc*, Paris; the first useful information on pig teeth

33 XENOPHON. *On Equitation*, bk 1, ch. III; first reference to ageing by teeth

34 SMITH, R. N. 1956. *Vet. Rec.* 68, 257

35 TSCHIRWINSKY, N. 1889. *Landw. Jb.* 18, 463

36 —— 1910. *Arch. mikr. Anat.* 75, 522

27 The Origins of the Dog

JULIET CLUTTON-BROCK

IN 1787 John Hunter[16] submitted a paper to the Royal Society on 'Evidence to show that the dog, wolf, and jackal are all of the same species'. He postulated that because the dog will interbreed with both wolf and jackal to produce fertile progeny, the three groups should be considered as a single species. This discussion was one of the first essays written on a subject that has become increasingly popular with anatomists and archaeologists. That is, whether the dog is descended from the wolf, from the jackal or from a wild dog that is now extinct.

There are two main problems that confront the osteologist working in this field, firstly, the detection of very early domestic dogs and the features that distinguish their remains from those of wild canid species, and secondly from what wild ancestors the dog has actually evolved.

Because the skulls and particularly the teeth are the most commonly found remains of canids on archaeological sites, osteologists have concentrated on their distinctive features rather than on those of the appendicular skeleton. The skulls of modern breeds of dog can be distinguished from those of wild wolves and jackals and it is usually possible to identify dog skulls from archaeological sites in Europe and Asia when these sites are Neolithic or later. It is, however, extremely difficult to distinguish dog remains from Mesolithic sites.

Dog remains were identified from the Natufian levels of Mount Carmel by Bate[13] in 1937 but a re-examination of this material by Clutton-Brock,[1] and later by Kurtén,[18] and Reed[20] has convinced these authors that the skull in question cannot be distinguished from that of the small Arabian wolf[15] that is found in the Near East at the present day.

Canid remains have, in recent years, been identified from Mesolithic and Pre-Pottery Neolithic sites in many parts of the world and it is still a question of debate whether these were wild, tamed, or domesticated animals. (In this context, a *domesticated* animal is one that has been bred in captivity and can be considered as being economically useful to the community.)

Degerbøl[10, 11] has identified dog remains from the Mesolithic site of Star Carr in Yorkshire, England and from Maglemosian sites in Denmark.

Lawrence[19] has also identified very early dog remains, indeed these may be the earliest yet to be described, and surprisingly they come from North America, from Cave sites in Idaho that have been dated at 9500–8400 BC. She has also described finds of dog from a very early site in Turkey at Cayönü dated at 7000 BC.

Zeuner[23] identified dog remains from the Pre-Pottery Neolithic levels of Jericho but a reassessment by measurement of this material shows that again these jaws cannot be said to be dog rather than wolf (Clutton-Brock[3]). Other early sites in Western Asia that have produced large canid remains are Jarmo in Iraq,[20] Belt Cave[7] on the shores of the

Caspian Sea and several sites in South Western Iran.[16] In Gujarat, India, large canid remains have been found at the microlithic site of Langhnaj.[2]

The canid remains from Early Neolithic Jericho and several other Asiatic sites consist of a relatively few bones and jaws of *Canis* Spp. and great numbers of fox remains. All these were intermingled with the remains of food animals such as goats, pigs, and cattle. It has therefore been concluded that both foxes and wolves were eaten by the Pre-Pottery Neolithic people along with any other meat that could be caught.

The difficulty about the identification of all these canid remains (except for the fox which is always recognizable) lies in the fact that wolf and primitive dog are so anatomically similar. It can however be said that there is no evidence to suggest that the jackal played any part in the ancestry of these Mesolithic 'dogs'.

A great deal of literature has been written on the distinctions between the skulls of dogs, wolves and jackals. As long ago as 1892 Goudry and Boule[14] listed the characters, that were known to them to be distinctive and amongst these they stated that in the wolf the length of the upper carnassial tooth is greater than that of the two molars, measured together, whereas in the dog and jackal the length of the carnassial is less than, or at the most equal to, the length of the two molars. The authors stated that the Indian wolf, *Canis lupus pallipes* Sykes, 1831, was an exception to this rule and that it had short carnassial teeth like the dog. This exception has in the past been lost sight of and the character has been frequently used as a supposedly distinctive feature to identify canid remains from archaeological sites. It is a potentially useful diagnostic feature because the part of the maxillary bone that holds these teeth is a most commonly found fragment. It was thought necessary therefore to reassess the results of Goudry and Boule. The appropriate measurements were made on all the skulls of European and Indian wolves, jackals and dogs that are in the collection of the British Museum (Natural History). These measurements are presented in the form of a graph (Fig. 42) where the central axis represents a carnassial index of unity. Those skulls in which the carnassial length exceeds the combined lengths of the two molars fall to the left of the central axis, whilst those in which the carnassial length is shorter than the length of the two molars fall to its right.

It can be seen from the graph that as far as modern dogs are concerned, the results of Goudry and Boule are strikingly confirmed, for only a single specimen had a carnassial index greater than unity. The European wolves, however, although significantly different from dogs, do in a number of individuals show a carnassial index less than unity. The Indian and Arabian wolves as stated by Goudry and Boule overlap the dogs in carnassial index. The Natufian canid remains fall well within the range of the Arabian wolf, so they cannot be identified as dog on the basis of this measurement, nor can it be stated that they were derived from the Egyptian jackal, *Canis aureus lupaster* Hemprich and Ehrenberg, 1833, as Bate[13] contended.

Reduction in size of the carnassial teeth is typical of highly domesticated dogs and it becomes exaggerated in those of very large body size. This is well illustrated in the graph, where the carnassial teeth of the largest specimens of domestic dog, these being Great Danes and bloodhounds, are, for the size of dog, very short and considerably shorter than the length of the two molars. The upper carnassials of these specimens are

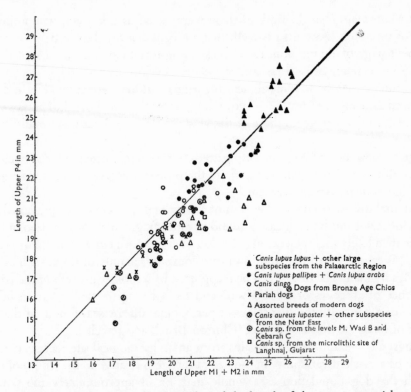

Fig. 42 Graph to show the relationship of the length of the upper carnassial
tooth to the combined lengths of the upper first and second molars in dogs,
wolves and jackals and in the canid specimens from Natufian levels in Palestine.
The diagonal line represents a carnassial index of unity.

very much smaller than those of the large European wolves, although the dogs have the
greater body size. The tooth measurements of this group of dogs are shown on the
extreme right of the range for dogs on the graph.

The changes that occur in the size and shape of canid skulls as the result of domestication or even of taming alone, are well authenticated. Not only are these changes shown
by the remains of primitive domestic dogs from archaeological sites but they are also
to be seen in captive wolves.[10, 11] The first alteration to the animal as a result of taming
or domestication is an overall reduction in size. In the skull this reduction in size is seen
as a shortening of the jaw bones without a corresponding reduction in the width so that
the characteristic wide muzzle of the dog is produced. As a result of this shortening of
the muzzle, the teeth become compacted in the jaw and they may be much displaced.
It is especially common for the third upper premolar and the fourth lower premolar to
overlap the carnassial teeth that lie behind them. It is not known, however, how frequently the teeth of wild European wolves are displaced in this way and the condition
may be more common than is generally supposed, so that this feature alone should not
be taken as proof of taming or domestication. Plate XVIa shows the palatal views of two

skulls of *Canis lupus lupus* L. Both of these were, as far as is known, wild animals and yet one of the skulls (bottom) has teeth that are considerably displaced.

The next stage of alteration in the domestic dog is reduction in the size of the teeth, especially the canines and carnassials. With the development of long-faced breeds of dogs the muzzle may be secondarily lengthened so that the teeth are widely and irregularly spaced and lose the feature of crowding, as in the greyhound. The jaws can be distinguished, however, from those of the wild wolf by the relatively small size of the teeth.

In highly domesticated dogs the cusp pattern of the teeth is often reduced in complexity, especially that of the premolars, where the posterior accessory cusps may be much reduced in size if not entirely absent.

Periodontal disease occurs in the teeth of a very high percentage of present-day dogs and if evidence of this bone disease is found in canid fragments from archaeological sites it is more than likely that they belong to a dog or at least to a tamed canid. For periodontal disease is caused by an unnatural soft diet consisting mainly of slops, such as is often fed to dogs by man. The disease can be recognized by a spongy growth of the jaw bone, by evidence of abscesses or by the bone and teeth having 'rotted' away in life.[6] The mandible of a dog with the first stages of periodontal disease was found on the Bronze Age site of Snail Down in Wiltshire (Clutton-Brock and Jewell[5]).

Amongst a collection of dog remains from an archaeological site there is commonly found to be a marked variability in the size of the teeth relative to the length of the jaw, although the dog population as a whole may be of approximately the same sized animals. An example of this was found on the Bronze Age site of Emporio on the island of Chios, Greece.[4] On this site the dogs were rather small animals that were slightly larger than an English fox terrier. There were 22 mandibles and 11 maxillae found throughout all levels of the Bronze Age trenches. Some of these had large teeth that were compacted in the jaw and others had small widely spaced teeth. Presumably breeding was at random amongst such a dog population and the size and degree of crowding of the teeth must be a natural variation that is probably augmented by the effects of domestication. Measurements of two extreme variants from Chios are given in Table A.

If the added lengths of the teeth, premolar 2 to molar 3, are expressed as a percentage of the directly measured length of the tooth row from the anterior edge of the second premolar to the posterior edge of the third molar, then this index can be used to show the degree of crowding of the teeth. In the mandible of type I (Plate XVIb, top right) whose tooth measurements are given in the table, where the tooth row is short and the teeth large the index is 102·8%, whereas in the second type (bottom right), where the tooth row is absolutely longer and the teeth smaller, the index is 72·6%.

In the material from Chios the second type of jaw, that is with small widely spaced teeth, is more common than the first type, only two mandibles from a total of nine having large compacted teeth. (The remaining thirteen mandibles were too fragmentary to allow any assessment to be made of their tooth development.) This material may be compared with a collection of dog remains from the Bronze Age barrow site of Snail Down in Wiltshire. In these specimens the teeth are very large and are compacted in

TABLE A

Measurements of two extreme variants of Bronze Age dogs from Emporio, Chios in Greece.

	Type I	Type II
	mm	mm
Length of tooth row from the anterior edge of premolar 2 to the posterior edge of molar 3	58·5	62·0
Depth of mandible below premolar 4	c. 18·0	c. 19·7
Length of premolar 2	7·8	6·6
Length of premolar 3	10·0	8·2
Length of premolar 4	10·5	9·8
Length of molar 1	21·0	18·6
Length of molar 2	8·4	7·7
Length of molar 3	3·0	4·0

four out of five of the mandibles. The dogs from Snail Down were considerably larger animals than those from Chios and they represent a different type of dog, with large heavy jaws and powerful teeth, showing the influence of the great wolf of northern Europe.

The question remains of what was the ancestry of the domestic dog. Trouessart[11] believed that all domestic dogs of Europe and Asia and the dingo were derived from the Indian wolf, *Canis lupus pallipes*, with the exception of the Ancient Egyptian dogs which he believed were derived from the Egyptian jackal, *Canis aureus lupaster*. Since his time there was for many years a general neglect of the Indian wolf as the supposed ancestor of the dog, despite its very close resemblance to primitive domestic dogs. The Indian wolf is extraordinarily similar in size and skull shape to the dingo and also the Indian pariah dog with which it freely interbreeds. There can be no doubt, at least, that these two forms of the dog have evolved from the Indian wolf. The dogs identified from Prehistoric sites in Western Asia must also have been descended from this subspecies of wolf. On the other hand the much larger dogs from Star Carr in Yorkshire, England and the Danish sites could have evolved from tamed European wolves. There is no palaeontological evidence for the existence of a species of wild dog other than those that are known at the present day which could have given rise to the domestic dog. The classification of dogs from archaeological sites and the history of some of the more ancient breeds has been further discussed by Zeuner.[24]

It has been demonstrated by Crisler[8] and by Fentress[12] how easy it is to tame the Canadian timber wolf and how dog-like their behaviour becomes. Whilst Schenkel[21] and others have shown how very closely similar the social behaviour of the dog is to that of the wolf. So that on behavioural grounds as well as anatomical it is assumed that the wolf is the ancestor of the dog.

The interbreeding of dogs with wolves is well authenticated and has occurred, since ancient times, both naturally and with the intervention of man. Pliny wrote of how the Gauls tied up their female dogs in the woods so that they might mate with wolves and thereby strengthen the breed. Eskimos in North America are known to cross their husky dogs with wolves for the same purpose. In general, however, the separate identity of dogs that have been bred from the northern wolves and of those that have been bred from the smaller Asiatic wolf cannot have survived because of the trading and inter-breeding that has occurred between all types of dog since Mesolithic times. The dingo is probably one of the only breeds of present day dog that can be considered as derived purely from the Indian wolf. This hypothesis of the mixed origin of the dog was be-lieved in and expounded by Darwin[5] and it is in fact surprising how little knowledge has been gained on the much discussed subject of the ancestry of the dog since he wrote his book, *The Variation of Animals and Plants under Domestication*, first published in 1868.

ACKNOWLEDGEMENTS

I am greatly indebted to Dr F. C. Fraser, lately Keeper of Zoology at the British Museum (Natural History), and to Miss J. E. King of the Osteology Department for the facilities they have offered to me during the course of this work.

Miss Ann Grosvenor Ellis took the photographs of the canid skulls. I wish to acknow-ledge permission granted to me by the trustees of the British Museum (Natural History) to reproduce photographs of the two wolf skulls.

REFERENCES

1 CLUTTON-BROCK, J. 1962. Near Eastern canids and the affinities of the Natufian dogs. *Tierzüchtg. Züchtungsbiol. 76*, 326–33
2 —— 1965. *Excavations at Langhnaj. Part II: the fauna.* Deccan College, Poona, 43 pp.
3 —— 1969. Carnivore remains from the excavations of the Jericho Tell. In: *The Domestication and Exploitation of Plants and Animals.* Ed. DIMBLEBY, G. W. and UCKO, P. J. London. In the press
4 —— Animal Remains from Emporio. In: HOOD, M. S. F. *Excavations of the Bronze Age Site of Emporio, Chios, Greece,* London. In the press
5 CLUTTON-BROCK, J. and JEWELL, P. A. Wild and domestic fauna from the Bronze Age Barrow cemetery of Snail Down, Wiltshire. In: THOMAS, N. *Excavations at Snail Down.* London. In the press
6 COLYER, F. 1936. *Variations and Diseases of the Teeth of Animals,* London
7 COON, C. S. 1951. *Cave Explorations in Iran 1949.* Museum Monograph. Univ. Pennsylvania, Phila-delphia, 1–124
8 CRISLER, L. 1959. *Arctic Wild,* London
9 DARWIN, C. 1868. *The Variation of Animals and Plants under Domestication,* London
10 DEGERBØL, M. 1943. *Saertryk of Dyr Natur Og Ms. København 1942–43,* 11–36
11 —— 1961. On a find of a preboreal domestic dog (*Canis familiaris* L.) from Star Carr, Yorkshire, with remarks on other domestic dogs. *Proc. Prehist. Soc. 27,* 35–55
12 FENTRESS, J. C. 1967. Observations on the behavioural development of a hand-reared male timber wolf. *J. American Zoologist, 7,* No. 2, 339–51
13 GARROD, D. A. E. and BATE, D. M. A. 1937. *The Stone Age of Mount Carmel,* Oxford, vol. I, 157–253
14 GOUDRY, A. and BOULE, M. 1892. *Matériaux pour l'Histoire des Temps Quaternaires,* Paris, vol. IV, 123–9
15 HARRISON, D. L. 1968. *The Mammals of Arabia II.* Carnivora, Artiodactyla, Hyracoidea. London. 195–206

16 HOLE, F. and FLANNERY, K. V. 1967. The prehistory of Southwestern Iran: a preliminary report. *Proc. Prehist. Soc. XXXIII*, 147–206

17 HUNTER, J. 1787. Observations tending to show that the wolf, jackal and dog are all of the same species. *Phil. Trans. Roy. Soc. Lond.*, 1787

18 KURTÉN, B. 1965. The carnivora of the Palestine caves. *Acta zool. fenn.* Jan. 1965. 74 pp.

19 LAWRENCE, B. 1967. Early domestic dogs. *Sonderdruck aus Z.f. Säugetierkunde, 32*, H.1, 44–59

20 REED, C. A. 1961. Osteological evidence for prehistoric domestication in southwestern Asia. *Tierzüchtg. Züchtungsbiol, 76*, 31–8

21 SCHENKEL, R. 1967. Submission: its features and function in the wolf and dog. *J. American Zoologist, 7*, No. 2, 319–29

22 TROUESSART, E. L. 1911. *C.R. Acad. Sci. Paris 152*, 909–13

23 ZEUNER, F. E. 1958. Dog and cat in the Neolithic of Jericho. *Palestine Exploration Quarterly 19*, 52–55

24 ZEUNER, F. E. 1963. *A History of Domesticated Animals.* London. 79–111

28 The Palaeopathology of Pleistocene and more Recent Mammals

DON BROTHWELL

DISEASE is the result of biological variability, trauma, or malfunction, and as such one expects to find traces of it throughout time, both in invertebrate and vertebrate remains. The study of anomalous fossil remains can supply valuable information regarding the exact extent to which animal groups were prone to a particular disorder. As evolution is likely to have taken place in pathogenic organisms no less than other animal varieties, it is also evident that such remains are likely to provide evidence of the antiquity of a particular variety of disease. Owing to the nature of the remains, only abnormalities affecting bone can usually be identified.

Pathological studies on ancient animal remains are as yet few, but with the increasing interest and study in the field of such osteological material, it seems only a matter of time before far more data are assembled. The information to be revealed is threefold:

(1) It helps to establish the range and antiquity of various diseases found in animals other than man.

(2) In some instances it may directly reflect upon the environment of the animal and of man.

(3) In the case of certain infectious diseases, it might eventually be possible to identify the precursor, that is the carrier, of a specific type of disease before man emerged or contracted it.

The present essay is meant to be a very brief review of what has been discovered about one particular group of animals, the mammals, during the period of man's existence, and what may still be revealed by further work.

One of the earliest references to the pathology of fossil animal bones was made by E. J. C. Esper (1742–1810),[3] on the femur of a cave bear (*Ursus spelaeus*). Admittedly, his diagnosis would appear to be quite wrong, for he suggested an osteosarcoma, whereas the deformity seems likely to have been the result of a fracture and callus formation, with some necrosis.[5] Later, in 1820, Cuvier[2] described the skull of a hyena from Gaylenreuth displaying a severe injury to its occipital crest, which had healed before death. Interest in the pathology of animal bones was also developing in England about that time and William Clift,[1] in a paper on cave fauna, notes inflammatory changes in the metacarpal and metatarsal bones of bovines present. A wolf mandible also displayed chronic abscessing and periodontal disease of the alveolar bone.

Other papers noting pathological upsets in Pleistocene animals followed, and in particular the cave bear has been well described (for further references see Moodie;[6] Pales[7]).

VARIETIES OF DISORDER

In Table A, a synopsis of the palaeopathology of Pleistocene and more recent mammals is given. In particular, fractures, periostitis, osteomyelitis, and arthritic disorders are well

TABLE A

A synopsis of the pathological conditions recognized in Pleistocene and more recent mammals. *

Order *Carnivora*
    Family *Canidae*
        Canis familiaris: fracture, 'osteophytic growth', periostitis
        Canis lupus: tumour (? myositis), abscesses, periodontal disease
        Aenocyon dirus (giant wolf): fracture, osteo-arthritis, osteomyelitis
    Family *Hyaenidae*
        Hyena: fracturing, osteo-arthritis
    Family *Ursidae*
        Ursus spelaeus: osteomyelitis, fractures, osteo-arthritis, 'necrosis', 'amputa-
            tion', kyphosis, vertebral collapse, caries, chronic abscesses, periodontal
            disease
    Family *Felidae*
        Panthera pardus: fracture
        Smilodon californicus (sabre-tooth cat): spondylitis, periostitis, exostosis,
            fractures
Order *Perissodactyla*
    Family *Equidae*
        Equus sp. Pleistocene: hyperostoses (? the result of an osteogenic sarcoma)
Order *Primates*
    Family *Cercopithecidae*
        Papio hamadryas (baboon): Paget's disease (?), rickets, spondylitis (?)
Order *Edentata*
    Superfamily *Megalonychoidea*
        Mylodon robustus (ground sloth): fracture, 'necrosis'
Order *Proboscidae*
    Family *Mammutidae*
        Mammut americanus: fracture, necrosis, caries, abscess
Order *Artiodactyla*
    Infra-order *Palaeodonta*
        Platygonus (peccary): periostitis
    Sub-order *Tylopoda*
        Camel, Texas Pleistocene: pathological phalanx
    Family *Cervidae*
        Rangifer tarandus: ankylosed phalanges, fracture, osteitis
    Family *Bovidae*
        Symbos cavifrons (musk ox): fracturing, chronic suppurating sinusitis
        Bos primigenius: osteo-arthritis, chronic abscess, periodontal disease,
            dental tumour (?)
        Ovis: osteo-arthritis
        Bos longifrons: osteo-arthritis

---

* The list is not meant to be an exhaustive compilation.

represented. As accidental injury and blood-stream infection produced fracturing and inflammatory changes in the dinosaurs, millions of years before the mammalian radiation, it is not surprising to see such anomalies in fauna of the last million or so years. An added factor is however the appearance of man, and a number of cases of animal injury may have resulted from his quest for food or as a result of defending himself. Pales,[7] for example, describes an inflammatory reaction to be seen on the lower jaw of a cave bear from Ariège which he considers may have resulted from a wound by a human artifact. Another type of deduction is sometimes possible, as demonstrated by Saint-Périer.[8] He describes a fractured, osteomyelitic, and partly healed reindeer metacarpal. He concludes that as the beast lived many months in this incapacitated condition without being killed by man, there was probably a surplus of game in that area at that time.

Arthritic disorders are also clearly in evidence in giant Jurassic/Cretaceous reptiles, and are therefore not surprising in the mammals. Much evidence is at present rather obscured by lack of agreement as regards terminology, and as Zorab[10] has recently pointed out, various earlier authors would appear to have used the term 'ankylosing spondylitis' (an arthritic disorder which may result in ossifications at the vertebrae uniting them into a single block) rather than 'osteo-arthritis', which seems a much more common condition—producing 'lipping' and deformity at some articular surfaces. Union of some lumbar vertebrae by extensive bony bridging in *Smilodon californicus* may be an example of the former, whereas the latter disorder seems to be fairly common in the European cave bear. In man, osteo-arthritic deformity may be broadly correlated with age, and it would be interesting to know whether similar information could be obtained from its occurrence in other mammals. In a study of osteo-arthritis in a Romano-British dog, Harcourt[11] has been able to argue that the degree of disability in this animal supported the view that it was a house dog (survival being less likely in any other situation).

Disorders of the mouth do not appear to be so common, relatively speaking, although this difference may result as much from a lack of interest—and thus of recording—as of actual infrequency. *Ursus spelaeus* has provided examples of caries cavities, chronic abscessing and alveolar bone destruction through periodontal infection. A recently discovered skull of *Bos primigenius* from Cambridgeshire[9] is of interest in that restricted alveolar destruction and possibly chronic abscessing are associated in this case with lack of dental alignment on the left side, presumably resulting initially in food impaction and gum irritation.

There seems little doubt that the considerable variety of tumours affecting modern men were not all present even a few thousand years ago. Their infrequency in earlier mammals is even more marked. A pelvic fragment of *Canis lupus* (Pleistocene) displays a bony projection of a spongy appearance, which might be the result of a tumour. The molar of a Pleistocene bovid from Charente has an extremely swollen root which Pales thinks could be a tumour, but could on the other hand be hypercementosis. Another very debatable case is to be seen on a posterior cannon bone of a Pleistocene horse from

Gironde, France. Pales[7] describes a 'diaphysial hyperostosis' which could perhaps be the result of an osteogenic sarcoma.

Few other anomalies have so far been noted, and some of these are questionable.

DISCUSSION

As I have already said, the palaeopathology of earlier animal forms, as of man, is a multi-purpose study. It is to be hoped that with the increasing detailed examination of excavated animal remains, some attempt at establishing the more common diseases, such as arthritis, will be made. Even where diagnosis is uncertain, the publication of accurate reference illustrations is worth considering, as in the recent study of *Myotragus baledricus*.[12] Radiographic examination, at least of the more complete bones, might be revealing, especially as regards 'lines of arrested growth'. As in the study of ancient human pathology, there is also a need for very precise description and careful diagnosis, especially in the case of the rarer anomaly, where a single example may be of extreme importance. So far it has not been possible to link up the origin of some human diseases with the pathology of earlier or contemporary mammals. It seems reasonable to suppose, however, that some human parasites were originally carried by other mammalian forms. The transmission of the plague bacillus from rats to men immediately comes to mind as an example of the adaptability of a parasitic organism to another host, but there is in fact a variety of parasitic groups affecting both man and other animals (either the same species or similar ones). As Hare[4] points out, the *Salmonella* which produce typhoid and paratyphoid fever have cousin-species in oxen and pigs, which closely resemble the human varieties. *Corynebacterium diphtheriae*, causing diptheria, resembles to some extent *C. ovis* of horses, *C. pyogenes* of cattle, pigs and sheep, and *C. murium* a pathogen of mice. Some human viruses also have relatives producing disease in animals. For example, the main habitat of the yellow-fever virus is certain species of monkeys, and it is transmitted from these to man by *Haemagogus* mosquitoes.

By Neolithic times, contact between some forms of animal and man had become closer than ever before, and it is possible that this period in particular is a critical one from the point of view of the transmission of certain forms of disease to man. The continued study of animal palaeopathology may help to substantiate this.

Finally, it must be remembered that disease may be as much a killer in other vertebrate populations as in man, and in the case of food animals, epidemics have obvious repercussions for the particular human society concerned.

REFERENCES

1 CLIFT, W. 1823. *Phil. Trans. Roy. Soc. Lond. 113*, 81 (quoted by Moodie)
2 CUVIER, G. 1812. *Recherches sur les Ossemens fossiles*, Paris (quoted by Moodie)
3 ESPER, E. J. C. 1774. *Ausführliche Nachrichten Von neuentdeckten Zoolithen unbekannter vierfüssiger Thiere*, Nuremberg
4 HARE, R. 1954. *Pomp and Pestilence. Infectious Disease, Its Origins and Conquest*, London
5 MAYER, DR. 1854. *Nova Acta Leopoldina*, 673–89
6 MOODIE, R. L. 1923. *Palaeopathology. An introduction to the study of ancient evidences of disease*, Chicago
7 PALES, L. 1930. *Paléopathologie et Pathologie comparative*, Paris
8 SAINT-PÉRIER, R. DE 1936. *Arch. Inst. Paléont. hum. 17*

9 SHAWCROSS, F. W. and HIGGS, E. S. 1961. *Proc. Camb. Antiq. Soc. 54*, 3–16

10 ZORAB, P. A. 1961. *Proc. Roy. Soc. Med. 54*, 415–20

11 HARCOURT, R. A. 1967. *J. small Anim. Pract. 8*, 521–2.

12 WALDREN, W. H. and KOPPER, J. S. 1968. *The Myotragus Baledrious. Paleopathology and the Palynological Analysis of the Soil of the Deposit.* Deya Archaeological Museum, Mallorca.

29 An Assessment of a Prehistoric Technique of Bovine Husbandry

CHARLES HIGHAM and MICHAEL MESSAGE

'Ascertainable truth is piecemeal, partial, uncertain and difficult.'
Bertrand Russell

THE PURPOSE OF THIS PAPER is to show that it is possible to assess the pattern of bovine husbandry practised at any given prehistoric site. Hitherto all attempts at assessing the economic significance of the faunal spectra derived from prehistoric settlement sites have been severely handicapped by a lack of adequate comparative material from modern cattle of known breeds. This is not the case here since we have at our disposal large samples of material from three modern breeds of cattle (*vide infra*); a study of which is to be published shortly.

The present paper represents a preliminary report of an attempt to reconstruct the bovine economy practised at Troldebjerg, a settlement of the Danish Funnel Necked Beaker Culture situated on Langeland and dated to the end of the third millennium BC.[1]

A definitive study of the entire faunal spectrum from Troldebjerg is in preparation. However, all the indications are that the final reconstruction of the pattern of bovine husbandry at Troldebjerg will not depart significantly from that to be presented here.

The primary prehistoric bovine material to be considered is currently housed in the Zoological Museum of the University of Copenhagen. In addition, reference is made to certain data derived from the collection of Danish *Bos primigenius* bones housed in the same institution. Both collections were made available through the kindness of Professor M. Degerbøl, the Director of the Sub-Department of Quaternary Zoology.

The three modern comparative domestic bovine samples are from adult animals of three different breeds. The first comprises selected bones from the fore and hind limbs of 40 three-year-old Aberdeen Angus steers and 40 cows of the same age and breed. The second includes the equivalent bones from 26 Red Danish cows, with ages ranging from $2\frac{1}{2}$ to 10 years, collected from the slaughterhouse of the Kødfoderfabriken Sjaelland at Ortved, supplemented by the same bones from 6 cows and 2 bulls of the same breed, but with ages of from $1\frac{1}{2}$ to 5 years, and collected from the Veterinary High School of the University of Copenhagen. The final modern sample is derived from the data published by Zalkin[26] in his study of the Kalmyk bovine. For comparative purposes, reference is also made to some of the material published by Lehmann[16] and Stampfli[21] in their studies of *Bison bonasus*.

As far as the bones to be considered are concerned, the preliminary nature of this article necessitates that most attention will be paid to three bones only: the metacarpal, the radius and the mandible including the dentition. The choice of the first two bones was dictated by the fact that in modern bovines, they display marked sexual dimorphism

(Howard[11] and Zalkin[26]). The choice of the mandible and dentition resulted from this bone's unique potentiality for the reconstruction of a detailed picture of the variation in the frequency of mortality with age (Kurtén[15]).

MATERIAL: BASIC METRICAL ATTRIBUTES

Table A contains, for both the modern and ancient material, the basic statistical attri-

TABLE A

The Metrical Attributes of Modern and Prehistoric Bovine Metacarpals, Radii, and Lower Third Molars (dimensions in mm.)

Sample	Dimension	N	O.R.	X̄
Kalmyk ♀	Metacarpal: Max. distal width	59	52·0–65·0	59·7±0·38
Kalmyk ♂	,, ,, ,,	13	64·0–79·0	70·5±0·86
Kalmyk ♂	,, ,, ,,	10	65·0–82·0	72·6±1·44
Red Danish ♀	,, ,, ,,	32	60·0–70·3	65·0±0·37
Red Danish, Adult ♂	,, ,, ,,	1	—	72·3
Red Danish, Young ♂	,, ,, ,,	1	—	69·8
Aberdeen Angus ♀	,, ,, ,,	40	54·5–65·2	60·1±0·32
Aberdeen Angus ♂	,, ,, ,,	40	64·0–74·0	67·7±0·35
Troldebjerg, Pooled	,, ,, ,,	39	53·0–73·0	62·1±0·90
Troldebjerg, Group 'A'	,, ,, ,,	19	53·0–63·5	57·2±0·47
Troldebjerg, Group 'B'	,, ,, ,,	20	64·0–73·0	67·3±0·66
Kalmyk ♀	Metacarpal: Maximum length	59	189·0–224·0	207·1±1·11
Kalmyk ♂	,, ,, ,,	13	206·0–240·0	221·7±2·86
Kalmyk ♂	,, ,, ,,	10	193·0–228·0	208·0±3·04
Red Danish ♀	,, ,, ,,	32	197·2–228·3	215·7±1·13
Red Danish, Adult ♂	,, ,, ,,	1	—	206·6
Troldebjerg, Group 'A'	,, ,, ,,	7	192·0–203·0	197·6±1·22
Troldebjerg, Group 'B'	,, ,, ,,	8	207·5–214·0	210·0±0·76
Red Danish ♀	Radius: Max. distal width	32	79·0–92·1	84·8±0·62
Red Danish, Adult ♂	,, ,, ,,	1	93·6	
Red Danish, Young ♂	,, ,, ,,	1	91·5	
Troldebjerg, Pooled	,, ,, ,,	40	65·5–88·0	77·3±1·40
Troldebjerg, Group 'A'	,, ,, ,,	26	65·5–74·0	70·1±0·58
Troldebjerg, Group 'B'	,, ,, ,,	14	80·0–88·0	83·6±0·71
Danish *Bos primigenius*	Maximum length of Lower third molar	36	45·0–54·0	48·7±0·36
Troldebjerg	,, ,, ,,	99	32·3–45·0	39·2±0·25
Kalmyk ♀	Ratio of distal	59	24·1–31·5	28·9±0·16
Kalmyk ♂	width to	13	30·0–34·0	31·9±0·35
Kalmyk ♂	length ×100	10	32·5–40·0	34·9±0·57
Kalmyk ♂	for the metacarpal	13	30·0–34·0	31·9±0·35

* Significant (p<0·05)

butes of the metacarpal and radial dimensions, and the metacarpal ratios, which have been used in the present study. From that Table, it can be seen that the extent of variation in the metacarpal length about the mean is statistically identical for Kalmyk cows, steers and bulls, whereas although the mean values of that dimension are statistically identical for the cows and bulls, it is significantly greater (p<0·01) for the steers. In the case of the maximum distal metacarpal width, again the extent of the variation about the mean is identical for cows, bulls and steers, but now the mean itself is statistically identical for the steers and bulls, and for both, significantly (p<0·01) greater than the mean for cows. Consequently, the shape of the sexed Kalmyk bovine metacarpals, as

s	V	C.D.	'Student's' t	F-ratio on comparison with
				Pooled Troldebjerg:
2·99±0·27	5·00	} 1·77	} 11·70**	3·66**
3·10±0·61	4·38			Pooled Troldebjerg: 3·30**
4·55±1·02	6·27	—	} 1·24	Pooled Troldebjerg: 1·53
1·97±0·26	3·03			Pooled Troldebjerg: 8·19**
—	—			
—	—			
2·05±0·23	4·10	} 1·78	} 15·68**	Pooled Troldebjerg: 7·57**
2·22±0·25	3·28			Pooled Troldebjerg: 6·45**
5·64±0·63	9·08			
2·06±0·33	3·60	} 1·98	} 12·12**	Troldebjerg, Group B, 2·38
3·02±0·48	4·37			
8·52±0·79	4·11		} 5·39**	Kalmyk ♂, 1·26
10·12±1·99	4·55			Kalmyk ♀, 1·07
9·60±2·15	4·61			Kalmyk ♂ 1·11
6·39±0·79	2·96			
3·25±0·86	1·64	} 2·29	} 8·82**	Troldebjerg, Group B, 2·27
2·15±0·53	1·02			
3·54±0·43	4·17			
6·58±0·76	8·90			
2·96±0·41	4·23	} 2·40	14·26**	
2·65±0·50	3·19			
2·16±0·25	4·23	} 2·04	} 20·67**	Troldebjerg, 1·32
2·48±0·18	6·31			
1·23±0·11	4·25	} 1·19	} 2·47*	
1·30±0·25	4·08		} 4·63**	
1·80±0·40	5·16	} 1·94	} 13·25**	
1·30±0·25	4·08			

** Significant (p<0·01)

expressed in the ratio of the distal width to length, reveals sexual polymorphism, the bones of cows, steers and bulls showing significant and progressive increases in robustisity.

Whereas we have at our disposal, metacarpals and radii from a large number of mature Red Danish cows, and from one mature and one immature bull of the same breed, we have none from mature steers. The reason for this is that steers of this breed are almost all slaughtered before the distal epiphyses of the bones in question have fused. On the basis of the material to hand, however, the length of the adult bull's metacarpal falls well within the range for the corresponding dimension in cows, while the distal width of the same bone exceeds that for any of the female specimens. Furthermore, the distal width of the metacarpal from an 18-month-old bull is already at the extreme upper end of the female range, and with continuing growth, would probably have exceeded in size all the available bones from females. Exactly the same situation holds for the distal width of the radius.

It would seem, therefore, that the metrical attributes of the Red Danish bovine metacarpals reveal similar characteristics as were observed for the Kalmyk breed, while the distal width of the radius, like that of the metacarpal, reveals sexual dimorphism.

With the Aberdeen Angus material, the situation is different. There is a large number of cows' and steers' limb bones, but no equivalent bones from bulls. Furthermore, as a result of the way in which the material was prepared, it was not possible to obtain measurements of overall metacarpal length, nor maximum distal width of the radius. Nevertheless, as was the case for the Kalmyk material, the extent of the variation around the mean maximum distal width for steers' and cows' metacarpals is statistically identical, while the mean itself is significantly ($p < 0.01$) the greater in steers.

It is concluded, therefore, that in modern bovines, the metacarpal reveals sexual polymorphism in which the bones of cows, bulls and steers may be differentiated on the basis of their shape. With fragmentary metacarpals in which it is possible to measure only the maximum distal width, however, the bones of steers and bulls cannot at present be separated.

The Troldebjerg faunal sample includes approximately 5,000 bovine bone fragments. Of the adult metacarpals, 15 are complete and 24, while fragmentary, possess their distal articulating ends. The estimate of the variability for the pooled (i.e. complete and fragmentary) specimens on the basis of the distal width has been compared with the corresponding estimates for modern sexually homogeneous samples (Table A), nearly all the resultant values of the F Ratio being significant ($p < 0.01$). Such a high estimate of sample variance suggests strongly that the Troldebjerg metacarpal sample is heterogeneous in one or more respects.

In Fig. 43, which is a plot for the Troldebjerg metacarpals of the distal width against distal transverse diaphysial width, the data, on visual grounds, appears to fall into two groups with a division at 62 mm on the distal width axis. It will, however, be noted that three specimens with distal ends of 62, 62 and 63·5 mm could reasonably be assigned, again on visual grounds alone, to either of the two presumptive groups. The 95% equal probability ellipses have been calculated from the sample mean vectors and covari-

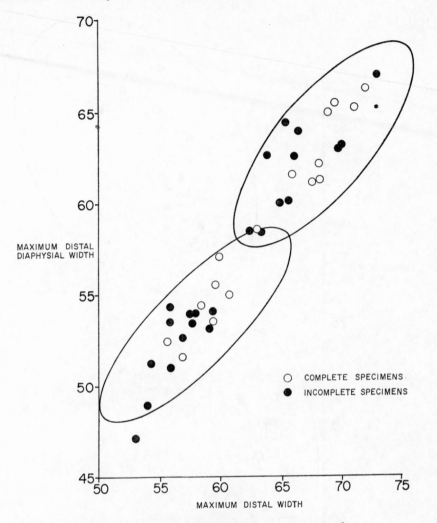

Fig. 43 Scatter diagram of Troldebjerg bovine metacarpals.

ances after Jackson's[14] method, with the three doubtful specimens included in the calculation for each presumptive group. As may be seen in Fig. 43, two of the three specimens do indeed fall within the region of overlap between the two ellipses, and they have therefore been assigned at random to either group. It would appear, therefore, that the high estimate of sample variance of the Troldebjerg metacarpals results from the presence of two types of adult bone.

The variability of the distal width of the pooled Troldebjerg radii is significantly greater ($p < 0.01$) than that for modern Red Danish female specimens, the value of the F Ratio in this case being 6.33. In the scatter diagram of the maximum distal width against the width of the articulating surface corresponding to the cuneiform, the material again falls into two groups. Calculation of the 95% equal probability ellipses

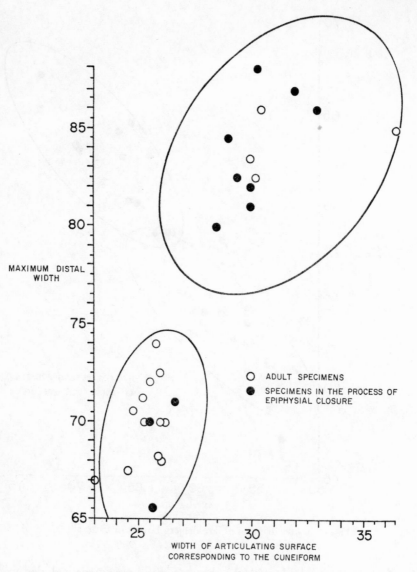

Fig. 44 Scatter diagram of Troldebjerg bovine radii.

from the mean vectors and covariances of the two presumptive groups reveals that there is no region of overlap. Again, therefore, the high sample variance reflects the presence of two distinct types of adult bones. Henceforth, the smaller sized group will be called Group A, and the larger sized group, Group B.

The establishment of two groups of mature bovine metacarpals and radii from Troldebjerg poses the question of the relationship between these groupings. This question is meaningful in the present context, since it is not possible to match individual radii and metacarpals. In theory, at least, those groupings could represent two, three or four types of bovines: the possible associations are shown in Table B.

TABLE B

Theoretical Pairings of Grouped Troldebjerg Bovine Metacarpals and Radii

I	Radius	A	B	A	B		A	B				A	B			A	B
2	Metacarpal	A	B		A	B			A	B	A	B		A	B	
$\frac{2}{1} \times 100$		81·4	80·5	–	68·4	–	–	–	–	–	–	96·0	–	–	–	–	–

In modern Red Danish cows in which such matching has been possible, it is found that the maximum distal metacarpal width and the distal width of the radius in the same animal are highly correlated ($r=0·51$; $p<0·01$), while the ratio ($\times 100$) of the mean of the former dimension to that of the latter is 76·6. Where in Table B it was possible to calculate the same ratio, the values varied widely. It is clear, however, that the ratios obtained when it is assumed that groups A and B of metacarpals correspond, respectively, with groups A and B of radii, are very close to the figure obtained for the modern sample. It is held, therefore, that group A radii and metacarpals come from animals of the same type; similarly for group B radii and metacarpals.

DISCUSSION

It must be emphasized from the outset that the nature of the available material itself necessitates that no explanation which may be advanced to account for the grouping displayed by the mature bovine bones from Troldebjerg can ever be regarded as certainly being the correct one. Nevertheless, in the light of the characteristics of the comparative material, both ancient and modern, some interpretations can be shown to be considerably more probable than others.

The five most obvious explanations which might be advanced, either singly or in combination, to account for the grouping shown by the mature bovine bones from Troldebjerg are the admixture of:

(i) domestic bovine remains with those from *Bison bonasus*;
(ii) domestic bovine remains with those from *Bos primigenius*;
(iii) the remains of domestic bovines raised on differing planes of nutrition;
(iv) the remains of males and females from the same breed of domestic bovines;
(v) the remains of distinct breeds of domestic bovines.

In their study of Danish bison remains, Degerbøl and Iversen[7] attributed the six late- and post-glacial finds at their disposal to a new sub-species: *Bison bonasus arbustotundrarum*. Since the settlement at Troldebjerg was not established until some 5,000 years after the date of the chronologically most recent finds of Danish bison, it would seem to be highly improbable that the bovine material from Troldebjerg contains any bison remains.

The probability that that contention is correct is increased by two other lines of evidence. Thus both Stampfli[21] and Lehmann[16] have drawn attention to a number of specific points of morphological dissimilarity between a given bone in cattle and in bison. When the bovine material from Troldebjerg was examined in the light of those points of difference, the morphology of each bone from Troldebjerg was clearly incompatible with its having been derived from a bison.

Lehmann[16] also considered the value of the ratio of breadth to height of the trochlea of the humerus in both modern *Bos* and in modern *Bison*; in the former genus the ratio varied from 66 to 75, while in the latter the range was 58 to 65. The same ratio for the modern bovine humeri from Troldebjerg was found to be distributed as follows:

Magnitude of ratio:	67	68	69	70	71	72	73	74
No. of specimens:	1	6	18	29	27	20	4	1

Thus for the Troldebjerg bovine humeri, not only is there no overlap in the value of the ratio with its value in modern bison, but also the range of values from Troldebjerg falls completely *within* the modern range.

In view, therefore, of the consensus of the preceding lines of evidence, it is held that the observed grouping of the bovine material from Troldebjerg is not the result of the admixture of the remains from domestic cattle and *Bison bonasus*.

The second explanation which might be advanced to account for the grouping of Troldebjerg bovine bones is admixture of domestic cattle remains with those of *Bos primigenius*. Now, numerous finds (e.g. at Svaedborg and Holmegaard) of bones from Danish Maglemosan Culture settlements indicate the presence of a race of large bovines in Jutland during the boreal pollen zone by *c.* 7300–5500 BC: these bones have been ascribed to the species *Bos primigenius*.[5]

The archaeological evidence indicates that these bovines were hunted, and it has been suggested that their hunting, allied with the increased forest density characteristic of the Atlantic pollen zone (*c.* 5500–3000 BC) led to the virtual disappearance of this animal from the Danish Islands. Any surviving herds of *Bos primigenius* would have been increasingly restricted to the less densely forested portions of Jutland. Consequently, although no bog finds of *Bos primigenius* from the Danish Islands have been dated to the Sub-Boreal pollen zone (*c.* 3000–500 BC), it is possible that some herds of *Bos primigenius* did survive on Langeland during the occupation phase of Troldebjerg.

On that basis, therefore, the possibility that the grouping of the Troldebjerg bovine material does result from an admixture of the remains of domestic cattle and *Bos primigenius* requires further consideration. Now from Table A it can be seen that although the extent of the variation in the length of the lower third molar about the mean is statistically identical for both the Danish *Bos primigenius* and the Troldebjerg bovines, the means themselves are significantly different ($p < 0.01$) and, furthermore, the degree of overlap, reflected in the value of the coefficient of difference, is less than 1%. On the evidence provided by that dimension it would seem to be most unlikely that there is any admixture with *Bos primigenius* in the Troldebjerg bovine sample.

It might be argued, however, that the size of *Bos primigenius* was declining up to the Sub-Boreal period, and that the available sample of Danish *Bos primigenius* lower third molars is biased in favour of specimens derived from chronologically earlier, and therefore larger, individuals of the species. Thus the Pindstrup cow[5] has been dated to pollen zone 7.

To date, that specimen is not only the smallest but also, chronologically, the latest example of Danish *Bos primigenius* yet discovered. Moreover, the data from the skeleton of that animal indicates quite clearly that whereas certain dimensions, such as the length

TABLE C

The Dimensions of Bovine Metacarpals from Troldebjerg (Nos. 1–15) *and Danish* Bos primigenius (Nos. 16–33) *in mm*

	Maximum Length	Proximal Width	Minimum Diaphysial Width	Distal Width
1	192·0	58·6	29·0	57·0
2	196·0	59·8	31·6	60·6
3	196·2	60·3	31·6	58·5
4	197·0	59·0	33·2	60·0
5	199·2	59·2	31·1	59·8
6	200·1	59·6	30·1	59·5
7	203·0	54·7	32·0	55·7
8	207·5	65·1	40·0	68·1
9	207·5	59·6	34·3	66·0
10	209·0	64·4	35·0	68·0
11	210·0	67·0	40·2	67·5
12	210·0	65·0	39·0	69·0
13	211·0	67·2	38·7	72·0
14	211·5	68·8	38·0	71·0
15	214·0	69·0	39·5	69·5
16	229·0	63·0	39·5	67·0
17	232·0	70·2	39·5	67·0
18	233·5	66·1	37·0	65·0
19	243·5	83·0	48·6	83·1
20	244·0	69·6	39·0	67·5
21	244·1	70·0	38·1	70·2
22	247·0	77·0	49·6	74·2
23	247·6	77·5	50·0	80·2
24	247·7	81·2	44·3	80·0
25	248·5	86·0	51·4	83·2
26	249·0	74·3	41·0	77·0
27	249·0	70·2	39·2	67·5
28	250·0	90·2	50·6	84·0
29	252·0	78·0	49·1	82·0
30	252·0	89·5	52·0	86·3
31	255·0	85·5	52·5	81·0
32	261·2	83·0	51·6	86·5
33	263·5	83·0	50·0	83·5

of the lower third molar, do not overlap with the ranges of the same dimensions in the Troldebjerg material, other dimensions, such as the maximum distal width of the metacarpal, certainly do.

From Table C, however, it is clear that while there is overlap between the most broad distal widths of the Troldebjerg bovine metacarpals with the most narrow distal widths of the metacarpals from *Bos primigenius*, the lengths of the Troldebjerg metacarpals never overlap with those of the metacarpals from *Bos primigenius*. This disparity in metacarpal length, together with the distinction in size of the lower third molars between the Troldebjerg bovines and Danish *Bos primigenius* is held to indicate that the bovine sample from Troldebjerg contains no bones from *Bos primigenius*.

The site of Troldebjerg lies some two miles inland from the eastern shore of the island of Langeland. The island itself is some 25 miles long and 10 miles broad, and, during the occupation period of that site, most probably possessed two distinct microenvironments: inland forest and shoreland meadow.[13] If selected bovines were raised on the shoreland meadows while the remainder were raised in forest clearings, then it might be argued that the observed groupings of the Troldebjerg bovine metacarpals and radii resulted merely from the effects of differential planes of nutrition. Indeed it is now well established[3] that differential planes of nutrition for individuals of the same breed of cattle exert a marked effect upon their body weights and certain of their dimensions.

It is possible therefore, that the observed groupings do result from the effects of the cattle at Troldebjerg being raised on two different planes of nutrition: one high and one low. However, the eastern shore of Langeland, i.e. the coast lying to the seaward side of Troldebjerg, comprises a low cliff with a narrow rocky zone extending from its base to the sea. It is possible, therefore, that there was an absence of shore meadows, with their superior grazing potential, on the coast nearest to Troldebjerg. Certainly, however, during the summer months, the inhabitants of Troldebjerg may have taken some selected part of their herd to the low-lying western shore of the island, where such meadows did exist. Moreover, the necessary period of winter feeding would not have erased the differential effects of such a manoeuvre upon the sizes of the animals comprising the herd as a whole. At this juncture, therefore, it might seem that the observed groupings of the metacarpals and the radii do result from the effects of raising cattle on two different planes of nutrition.

The data of Black, Knapp and Clark[2] indicate that in cattle, the height at the withers is virtually unaffected by food supply. Zalkin[26] has shown that the length of the bovine metacarpal is highly correlated with the height at withers. It is most improbable, therefore, that the finding that the lengths of the metacarpals in group B are significantly greater than those in group A reflects *per se* that the parent animals were raised on differing planes of nutrition. It is concluded, therefore, that the primary reason for the bovine metacarpals from Troldebjerg falling into two groups must be sought among the two remaining possibilities.

This is the most appropriate point in the present discussion at which to consider the question of sexual dimorphism. It has been demonstrated by our work which has not yet been published, that the size and shape of the metacarpal and the size of the distal end of the radius display sexual dimorphism, while Howard[11] has claimed similar characteristics for the metacarpals of *Bos primigenius*.

Were it postulated that the bones comprising group A of the mature metacarpals from Troldebjerg come from females, and those comprising group B from males, then the statistical relationships between the dimensions under consideration should, in the light of modern data, be predictable. Thus, the variance of the maximum distal metacarpal width about the mean should be statistically identical for the two groups, although the means themselves should be significantly ($p<0.01$) different. Furthermore, the extent of overlap for that dimension between the two groups, as reflected in the coefficient of difference, should be of the same order as it is in modern cattle. From Table A, it can be seen that all predictions hold. By analogy, therefore, with the situation in modern cattle, group A comprises metacarpals from female, and group B from male cattle.

In the herd of Troldebjerg of course, the male animals may have been either all bulls, or a mixture of bulls and steers. In modern Kalmyk cattle, while the extent of variation in metacarpal length about the mean is statistically identical for cows, steers and bulls, the mean itself is significantly ($p<0.01$) greater in steers than it is in cows and bulls; indeed, the mean lengths of Kalmyk cows' and bulls' metacarpals are statistically identical.

If the lengths of the *complete* metacarpals in groups A and B are compared, it is found that the variances are statistically identical, while the mean lengths are significantly different ($p<0.01$). On this basis, again by analogy with the situation in modern cattle, it would seem that the complete metacarpals from group B are predominantly, if not entirely, derived from steers. The point here is, of course, that since there is an overlap in this dimension for Kalmyk bulls and steers, it is possible that one or more of the shorter metacarpals in group B in fact come from bulls. A consideration, however, of the shape of the complete metacarpals themselves, in terms of their distal width to length ratios, suggests very strongly that most, if not all, are from steers.

At this stage in the argument, therefore, it would seem possible to conclude that the two groups of mature metacarpals from Troldebjerg represent females (group A) and males (group B); the majority of the latter having been castrated.

Now it might be objected that the conclusion that the observed groupings of bovine metacarpals and radii results from their sexual polymorphism assumes that only one breed of domestic bovines was represented at Troldebjerg. In the light of this, therefore, it might be postulated that those groups arose because, in fact, there were two breeds of domestic bovines at Troldebjerg, but of different size, and in which the bones displayed no sexual dimorphism. Alternatively, there might have been more than one breed of the same size, but in which the bones did display sexual differences.

Strictly, of course, neither of those views can be either confirmed or denied on the basis of the evidence to hand. Nevertheless, the former is considered to be unlikely in the light of the undoubted sexual polymorphism of the metacarpal in the modern bovine, and the almost certain occurrence of sexual dimorphism in *Bos primigenius*, from which early breeds of domestic cattle are assumed to have developed (Howard, 1962).[11]

It is considerably more difficult to arrive at any clear-cut conclusion concerning the second genetic proposal outlined above. A detailed consideration of its implications, however, strongly suggests that the domestic bovines at Troldebjerg could be viewed as belonging to one breed. Furthermore, in terms of the present assessment of the economic significance of the age distribution of mandibles and sexed limb bones, resolution of that problem is, *per se*, irrelevant.

Table D shows the result of ageing the bovine teeth and mandibles from Troldebjerg after the dynamic method adopted by Kurtén.[15] It is clear that the mortality among

TABLE D

The Mortality Frequencies of the Troldebjerg Bovine Mandibles and Dentition

Age stage of Dentition Development (after Higham, 1967)	Approximate age in months (after Silver, 1963)	Percentage of Total sample
1	Foetal	0·0
2	Birth–3 weeks	0·0
3	1–4	0·0
4	5–6	0·6
5	6–7	1·2
6	7–9	2·2
7	8–13	0·0
8	15–16	2·8
9	16–17	6·8
10	17–18	6·8
11	18–24	0·0
12	24	4·1
13	24–30	5·1
14	30	5·1
15	30–31	7·2
16	31–32	2·4
17	32–33	2·4
18	36	4·8
19	38	2·8
20	40	14·5
21	40–50	12·8
22	50	13·3
23	Over 50	5·1

N = 98

animals less than one year old was very low (4%), that it rose to a maximum for animals between 40 and 50 months of age, and that some 18% of the animals survived beyond the latter age. That the deaths were not equally distributed between age groups was confirmed (p<0·01) with the aid of the Kolmogorov-Smirnov test. However, since bovine mandibles and teeth do not display sexual dimorphism,[6] it is not possible to use them to consider differential mortality between the sexes over a given period of post-natal life: nevertheless, such an objective may be achieved.

Thus in a given herd the numbers of male and female calves born over a period of time will be effectively equal. It should be possible, therefore, by taking advantage of the facts that the epiphyses of all anatomical bones do *not* fuse at the same age, and that certain bones display marked sexual dimorphism, to see whether or not there is differential mortality between the sexes over a given period of post-natal life.

In modern, and presumably also in prehistoric, bovines the distal metacarpal epiphysis fuses at from 2 to $2\frac{1}{2}$ years of age. From Troldebjerg there are 20 mature presumably male, and 19 mature presumably female metacarpals giving a sex ratio (male:female) of $1\cdot0:0\cdot95$, which is not significantly different from one of 1:1. On this basis, therefore, there was no overall selective mortality of either sex for animals less than 2 to $2\frac{1}{2}$ years of age.

In modern, and again presumably in prehistoric bovines, the distal radial epiphysis fuses at from $3\frac{1}{2}$ to 4 years of age. The Troldebjerg material yielded four mature, presumably male, and 18 mature, presumably female, radii, giving a sex ratio (male : female) of $1\cdot0:4\cdot5$, which is significantly ($p<0\cdot01$) different from one of 1:1.

In attempting to interpret the preceding osteometric findings in terms of animal husbandry it is necessary that due attention be given to the former vegetation around, and the local geography of Troldebjerg. The site itself is situated on the eastern edge of a low drumlin flanking a small lake which lies some two miles inland from the sea. Immediately before the arrival there of the Neolithic settlers this region possessed a mixed oak forest which gave way, around the lake margins, to reeds and willow. The settlers, however, proceeded with the aid of fire and axe to establish cereal fields in place of the forest.[13]

Now there is no evidence that ploughs were used at Troldebjerg; instead the agricultural regime practised was very similar to that of *Brandwirtschaft* employed in the colonization of Central Finland, particularly during the sixteenth and seventeenth centuries.[20] Under this regime the technique is to grow cereals, exploiting the natural fertility of the soil in one area and, when this has been exhausted, to clear new plots. A feature common to recent manifestations of *Brandwirtschaft* is periodic movement to exploit virgin areas as a result of the rapid impoverishment of the land within the vicinity of a given settlement.[17]

The inhabitants of Troldebjerg belonged, therefore, to the group of cultures which practised 'shifting agriculture';[4] by analogy with the then contemporary cultures in Switzerland which also practised a form of *Brandwirtschaft*,[24] the period of occupation would probably not have exceeded 50 years.[12]

The present study of the bovine remains from Troldebjerg has revealed what we believe to be the major characteristics of the pattern of cattle husbandry practised there. The first is that the inhabitants of Troldebjerg were proficient at overwintering young cattle. Thus 96% of the bovine mandibles and teeth from this site come from animals which survived their first winter. This is a startling finding since natural mortality in wild bovines is highest over their first winter.[19] Furthermore, approximately 80% of the cattle at Troldebjerg survived their second, and approximately 60% their third, winter.

Now, young calves are susceptible to food shortage and 2- and 3-year-old animals require more fodder with increasing age. The fact that such large proportions of both types of animal survived the winter suggests that the inhabitants of Troldebjerg were not only skilled at overwintering calves without difficulty, but also that adequate winter fodder was available. Certainly it is known that during the Swiss Neolithic, considerable care was given to the collection of winter fodder for cattle: indeed, at Thayngen Weier a hut was devoted to the storage of leaves and twigs.[9] Such activity remains *de rigeur* in Finland today,[17] and Frödin[8] has emphasized the current role of swamps and mires as sources of cattle fodder in Central Sweden. The view that collection, for winter fodder, of leaves, twigs and 'wasteland hay' was undertaken at Troldebjerg receives support from the finding at Danish Funnel Necked Beaker Culture settlements of flint knives specialized for use in the collection of leafy fronds.[22] Furthermore, with an agricultural regime primarily concerned with cereal cultivation, the bovines themselves might have been able to glean stubble fields during the autumn.

The special feature of the bovine husbandry practised at Troldebjerg was the maintenance of a large proportion of the castrated bovines to an age of three to four years. Such animals may be maintained for either one, or possibly both, of two reasons: for meat or for tractive power. However, whereas the fattening of animals for the former purpose may be undertaken from birth, their training for the latter purpose is not usually commenced until they are $2\frac{1}{2}$ to 3 years of age.[23] At Troldebjerg it is quite clear that male cattle died preferentially between $2\frac{1}{2}$ and 4 years of age. Since the inhabitants were so proficient at overwintering, it would seem most probable that this pattern of male mortality was due to selective killing, and not to natural causes. In turn, this suggests that the primary objective of raising castrated bovines to such an age was for the provision of meat, rather than tractive power. The validity of this assertion is supported by the collateral artifactual and agricultural evidence: ploughs were not used and indeed were not needed for the pursuit of *Brandwirtschaft*. Moreover one of the most profitable ages at which to kill cattle for meat is between $3\frac{1}{2}$ and 4 years of age, when under modern conditions, the animals will have attained some 90% of their maximum possible weight. Subsequent increases in weight with age are very gradual, animals attaining 99% of the maximum at 7 years of age (Brody[3] reviews this question). Under prehistoric conditions, at $3\frac{1}{2}$–4 years of age almost certainly the animals would have achieved something less than 90% of their potential maximum weight, but already would have reached the point where the subsequent growth would not justify further provision of winter fodder.

The evidence of the metacarpals shows that by age $2\frac{1}{2}$ years, the proportion of male and female bovines which died at Troldebjerg was equal. Consequently irrespective of the nature of the factors which determined those deaths, whether or not they operated singly or in some combination, and whether or not their relative importance remained constant with age, they had a net effect which displayed no sexual bias. Essentially the factors concerned may be divided into two groups: sex independent and sex dependent. Under the former heading would be included accidental death from natural causes (e.g. predators and disease), together with the selective culling of animals which failed to thrive, displayed physical deformity, or possessed traits (e.g. colour) which were undesirable in the eyes of the stock rearer. Under the latter heading would be included such factors as the planned killing of young steers for meat and of young females which were held to be surplus to future breeding requirements.

It is unlikely that any significant proportion of the deaths of animals less than $2\frac{1}{2}$ years of age is due to natural causes. The fact that 40% of the specimens in the available metacarpal sample are immature strongly suggests that the deliberate killing of such young animals occurred. At present, however, we cannot evaluate the relative importance of each of the suggested reasons for such an appreciable killing of animals less than $2\frac{1}{2}$ years of age, and giving rise thereby, whether deliberately or not, to equal mortality between the sexes.

A further effect of the pattern of bovine mortality at this site is that, of the animals older than $3\frac{1}{2}$–4 years at death, some 80% were female. This situation ensured not only the replenishment of the herd, but also the provision of milk and its derivatives in appreciable quantities. *A priori* the surviving males could be a mixture of oxen and bulls, or bulls alone. Since there is no archaeological evidence for the use of the plough at Troldebjerg, it might be argued that the remaining males were indeed bulls. Clearly at least one, and preferably two, bulls must have been maintained at any one time for breeding purposes. To maintain more bulls, however, would have been difficult, economically disadvantageous, and biologically unnecessary. It is not impossible that certain oxen were maintained for general draught purposes. The nature of the available evidence, however, does not, at present, permit any estimate to be made of the ratio of adult bulls to adult oxen.

The pattern of sexed bovine mortality which has emerged from the present study indicates that the primary aim of the bovine husbandry practised at Troldebjerg was that of meat production. To that end, steers were raised to an age (3–4 years) at which they would have been approaching maximum body size. There is no evidence that plough oxen were maintained, a situation that reflects the inhabitants' practice of *Brandwirtschaft*. At the same time, care was taken to provide an adequate supply of mature cows for the purposes of not only herd replenishment but also the provision of meat and dairy produce.

The available osteological material also suggests that the number of bulls maintained at any one time was small, a situation indicating a sophisticated attitude to one of the problems of bovine husbandry. Furthermore, it is clear that the inhabitants of Troldebjerg were adept at overwintering their young stock and were critical of the potentialities of individual animals. The latter contention derives from the relatively high, but sexually non-differentiated, mortality among immature cattle.

The research described in this paper was undertaken to see if it is possible to assess the pattern and economic significance of bovine husbandry practised at a given prehistoric settlement site, in the light of palynological, archaeological and modern comparative osteological material. The fact that that aim has been fulfilled for Troldebjerg implies that further studies of this nature will provide for the prehistorian, the type of information hitherto available only to the student of Economic History or Historical Geography.

REFERENCES

1 BECKER, C. 1954. *Acta. Arch.*, 49–150
2 BLACK, W., KNAPP, B. and CLARK, A. 1938. *J. Agr. Res. 56*, 465–72
3 BRODY, G. 1945. *Bioenergetics and Growth*, London
4 CLARK, J. G. D. 1952. *Prehistoric Europe: The Economic Basis*, 1952, London
5 DEGERBØL, M. 1962. *Zeit. f. Tierz. u. Zücht. 76*, Pt. 2/3, 243–51
6 —— 1963. *Occ. Paper No. 18 of the Royal Anthropological Institute*, 69–79, London
7 —— and IVERSEN, J. 1945. *Danm. Geol. Under. II Raekke, No. 73*
8 FRÖDIN, J. 1952. *Inst. f. Samm. Kult.*
9 GUYAN, W. 1954. *Mon. z. Ur-u. Fruh. d. Schweiz., XI*, 221–72
10 HIGHAM, C. 1967. *Proc. Prehist. Soc. XXXIII*, 84–107
11 HOWARD, M. 1962. *Zeitf. Tierz. u. Zücht. 76*, pt. 2/3, 252–64
12 HUBER, B. and JAZEWITSCH, W. 1958. *Flora 146*, 445–71
13 IVERSEN, J. 1941. *Danm. Geol. Under., II Raekke, No. 66*, 1–68
14 JACKSON, J. 1956. *Industrial Quality Control XII, No. 7*, 4–8
15 KURTÉN, B. 1953. *Acta Zoologica Fennica 76*
16 LEHMANN, U. 1949. *Neues Jahrb. f. Min., Geol., u. Palaeont. 90*, 163–266
17 MEAD, W. 1953. *Farming in Finland*, London
18 SILVER, I. 1963. In HIGGS, E. and BROTHWELL, D. *Science in Archaeology*, 250–68, London
19 SKINNER, M. and KAISON, O. 1947. *Bull. Amer. M. of N.H. 89*, 123–256
20 SOININEN, A. 1959. *Scand. E.H.R. 7*, 150–66
21 STAMPFLI, H. 1963. In BOESSNECK, J., JEQUIER, J.-P. and STAMPFLI, H., Seeberg Burgäschisee-Sud; Die Tierreste, *Acta Bernensia, II, 3*
22 STEENSBERG, A. 1943. *Nat. Skr.*
23 THIRSK, J. (*ed.*) 1966. *The Agrarian History of England and Wales, Vol. IV*, London
24 WELTEN, M. 1954. *Mon. z. Ur-u. Fruh. d. Schweiz. XI*, 61–81
25 WINTHER, J. 1935. *Troldebjerg*, Rudkøbing
26 ZALKIN, V. 1960. *Journal of the Moscow Society of Experiments of Nature, Biology Dept., No. 1.* Moscow
27 —— 1962. *Академия Наук СССР Материалы и Исследования по Археологии СССР No. 107*

30 Osteological Differences between Sheep (Ovis aries Linné) and Goat (Capra hircus Linné)

J. BOESSNECK

IT IS WELL KNOWN that to distinguish between the bones of sheep and goat presents great difficulties. After the useful groundwork done notably by Cornevin and Lesbre,[4] as well as by Gromova,[5] Boessneck, Müller and Teichert[2] recently re-examined this problem and attempted its solution by the study of a comprehensive collection of material. Their investigations were concerned only with the domesticated forms of *Ovis* and *Capra*, i.e. *Ovis aries Linné* and *Capra hircus Linné*. This limitation to domestic forms on the one hand narrows down the problems of differentiation to just one (typical) species or 'super-species' from either genus, on the other it makes the task more difficult because of the greater variations between individuals among domesticated animals. The investigation aimed at making possible the identification of bones and bone fragments originating from deposits on archaeological sites. Generic differences, if any, in the relationship between different parts of the skeleton were not considered.

The following is an extract from the considerably more extensive publication by Boessneck, Müller and Teichert.[2] It is confined to the most important features of the bones most frequently discovered in the excavation of settlement sites. Only the chief characteristics of the skull are dealt with and, in order to save space, most of the illustrations have been omitted; in any case, the larger parts of the skull seldom present difficulties. If necessary, the numerous illustrations in the original work, mentioned above, should be consulted. Horn cores, and their effect on the skull structure, are not dealt with here. Differentiation of the lower jaw and of the teeth is especially difficult and is, therefore, not considered here. With regard to the spine, I confine myself to dealing with the first two cervical vertebrae, but quite often other cervical vertebrae, and the lumbar and sacral vertebrae may be distinguished. In the case of the sacrum, in particular, I would draw attention to the work recently published by Boessneck and Meyer-Lemppenau,[1] which considers the differences of genus and sex in *Ovis aries*, *Capra hircus*, *Capra ibex ibex*, *Rupicapra rupicapra rupicapra* and *Capreolus capreolus capreolus*. Of the bones of the extremities, this extract does not include the carpal bones, although distinction is often possible, nor the patella, os malleolare, or the smaller tarsal bones. For work on the pelvis, I refer the reader to the dissertation by Lemppenau[8] on differences of sex and genus in Central European ruminants, which goes far beyond the scope of this study.

The analysis of the material, the numerous calculations of indices, and a larger list of references can be found in the original work. As in that work, the abbreviations O for Ovis aries and C for Capra hircus are used in the following.

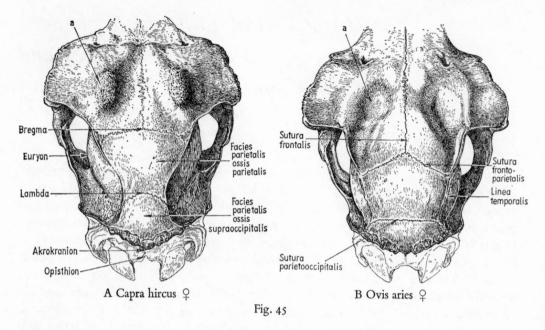

A Capra hircus ♀   B Ovis aries ♀

Fig. 45

THE SKULL

The characteristic differences in the skull are found in the pre-orbital region, the nasal bone, the region of the pyramidal eminence, and in the roof of the cranium.

For O, the external lacrimal fossa is considered the best generic characteristic. It lies in the aboral and basal part of the pars facialis of the lacrimal bone and extends to the dorsal part of the pars facialis of the zygomatic bone. It develops postnatally; it is always absent in C. In C there is usually a noticeable permanent fontanelle between the nasal and lacrimal bones, the fontanella naso-lacrimalis, which, in most cases, is closed orally. In O, this fontanelle closes but a gap may remain between the nasal and lacrimal bones and maxilla which continues as the so-called incisura nasomaxillaris. The frontolacrimal suture is more strongly serrated and indented in C, while in O it may run almost straight for some distance. Intermediate forms occur, particularly in strong-horned rams.

A notable difference between C and O is that in C the sinus frontales extend into the aboral part of the nasalia but the differences in the form and size of the nasal bones depend more on race and growth development.

As further differences in the facial bones only the deeper choanae and the mostly large foramen sphenopalatinum in O, in contrast to C, should be mentioned.

In the cranium there are marked differences in the bones of the pyramidal eminence. All three of its component parts, mastoid, tympanicum and petrosum, are larger in C; the mastoid is very prominent in the nuchal plane (Fig. 46A) as well as laterally, while the mastoid process of O is wedged-in as a narrow bone between the squamous temporal bone and the occipital bones (Fig. 46B). This characteristic again represents one of the best distinguishing features between the skulls of the two genera. The tympanicum in C is also less wedged-in and protrudes farther basally. The processus muscularis at the tympanicum is usually short and flat in C, while it is usually long and pointed in O. When viewed from the inside of the skull the petrosum in O is inserted between the parietal and occipital bones like a wedge with a narrow base directed orobasally. In C it is wider and normally forms an irregular quadrangle or pentagon. Another characteristic feature in C is an eminence on the oral border of the inner side of the petrosum, while in O there is only a hint of this.

Turning now to the cranium we find, first of all, that in C the coronal suture runs right across its roof and forms two right angles with the frontal suture (the so-called T-shape, see Fig. 45A). In O, the fronto-parietal suture usually forms an angle which is open towards the occiput (the so-called Y-shape, see Fig. 45B). Two angles of more than 90° are formed with the frontal suture. Apart from intermediate forms, the most important exception found in O is a slightly bent arch instead of the open angle towards the occiput. The lambdoid suture behaves similarly but vice versa. Apart from some exceptions, it forms an open angle or an arc towards the occiput in C, and in O, apart from its lateral part, it runs almost straight across the cranial surface (Fig. 45). Further, in C the fossae temporales are closer together than in O (Fig. 45). These marked differences produce marked dissimilarities in the form of the facies parietalis of the parietal and of the facies parietalis of the supra-occipital bone, as can be seen from Figs. 45A and 45B. The proportional differences of cranial length and breadth can be expressed as indices which, as they do not overlap in the genera, can be utilized for the identification of finds. For the parietal index the basic measurement is the distance akrokranion-bregma (Fig. 45A), for the lambdoid index, the distance akrokranion-lambda (Fig. 45A). In both cases the least width between the temporal lines is referred to. For C, the parietal index in the narrower sense, with the width as a percentage of the length, was 27–60%, for O it was 63–100+%; in the lambdoid index the results were 70–145% for C, and 155–300% for O.

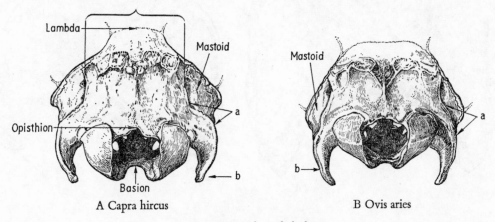

A Capra hircus   B Ovis aries

Fig. 46 Occipital, nuchal plane.

However, the supra-occipitale of C is higher than of O not only in the area which belongs to the cranium but also in the neck area (Fig. 46). One can usually determine parts from this region by measuring the smallest breadth of the supraoccipitale (i.e. the smallest breadth of the occiput—Fig. 46A), and expressing it as a percentage of the total height of the supraoccipitale (opisthion-lambda; Fig. 46A); there were only a few cases of the results overlapping. In C, the results varied from 80–110%; in O, from 100–145%. Study of the exoccipital bones showed that, on the whole, the jugular processes project farther in C than in O, they are also shorter and often thicker (Fig. 46B).

Skulls of hornless sheep usually have a slight dent where the horn-cores normally are or, more rarely, they have a small conical bump. Hornless goats have large protrusions instead of horn cores (Fig. 45Aa). Further, in C there is sexual dimorphism: in ♂♂ the frontal bulges forward to a high bump which in ♀♀ is less pronounced if it is there at all.

Apart from this, sexual dimorphism shows itself in both horned and hornless races of both genera, the skulls of ♀♀ being built on smaller, more delicate and slimmer lines than those of the corresponding ♂♂. In addition, there are in horned individuals differences in the size and shape of the horns: these will not be discussed here.

ATLAS AND EPISTROPHEUS

In order to facilitate the determination of genus when dealing with the cervical vertebrae it is useful to try first to ascertain the sex. The vertebrae of the ♂♂ are thicker, more massive and, within a race, usually larger. These features may make identification easier. Concerning the atlas, it is also useful to note the thickness of the ventral arch: in the stronger ♂♂ the ventral arch is thicker at the median vertebral entry, in the dorsoventral direction, than the height diameter of the overlying spinal canal. This observation is valid for strong hornless ♂♂ as well as for horned ones.

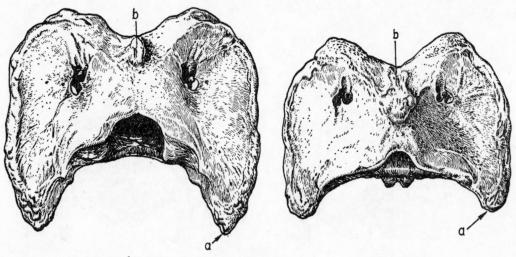

A Capra hircus ♂   B Ovis aries ♂

Fig. 47 Atlas, dorsal aspect.

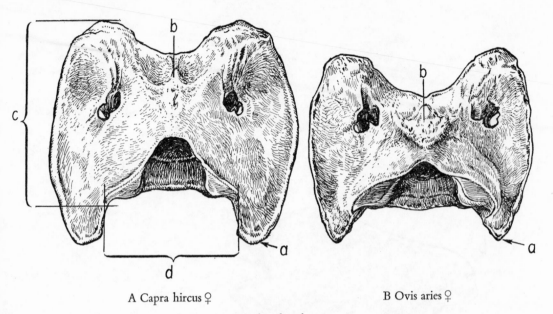

A Capra hircus ♀   B Ovis aries ♀

Fig. 48 Atlas, dorsal aspect.

The atlas is usually a little longer in C than in O and in C ♀♀ altogether longer than in the ♂♂; for the purpose of distinguishing genera, however, this feature is useful to a limited extent only. In C, the transverse processes overtop the caudal articulation considerably; in ♂♂ they often end in a point (Fig. 47Aa); in ♀♀ they are mostly flattened (Fig. 48Aa). In typical examples of O they project less, having a more pointed ending in the ♀♀ (Fig. 48Ba) and a blunt, uneven ending in the ♂♂. These differences are, however, nothing more than a rule which is not free from overlapping examples. An important feature is found in the dorsal tubercle. In C it is situated cranially and slopes down steeply in front with a sharper crest (Figs. 47 and 48Ab). In O the dorsal tubercle, which in typical cases is of a bumpy nature, reaches farther caudally and slopes less steeply cranially (Figs. 47 and 48Bb). The original work by Boessneck, Müller and Teichert[2] mentions deviations from this rule (p. 41). In some cases, on the ventral side two depressions can be observed next to the ventral tuberosity. If these are deep the atlas probably belongs to C, for deeper depressions in O are exceptional; if, on the other hand, they are only shallow, badly defined dents then identification by this criterion is not possible. In O these depressions may be almost entirely absent. The ventral tuberosity itself is, in O, heavier, ending caudally in a big bump. In C, it is narrower, more ridge-like, including the tuberosity in which it ends. This distinguishing mark is, however, also rather uncertain.

In the epistropheus, the genera are distinguished from one another by the height of the spinous process. This is higher in C than in O, and in ♂♂ higher than in ♀♀. This feature, however, depends of course on the horn development, which in turn depends

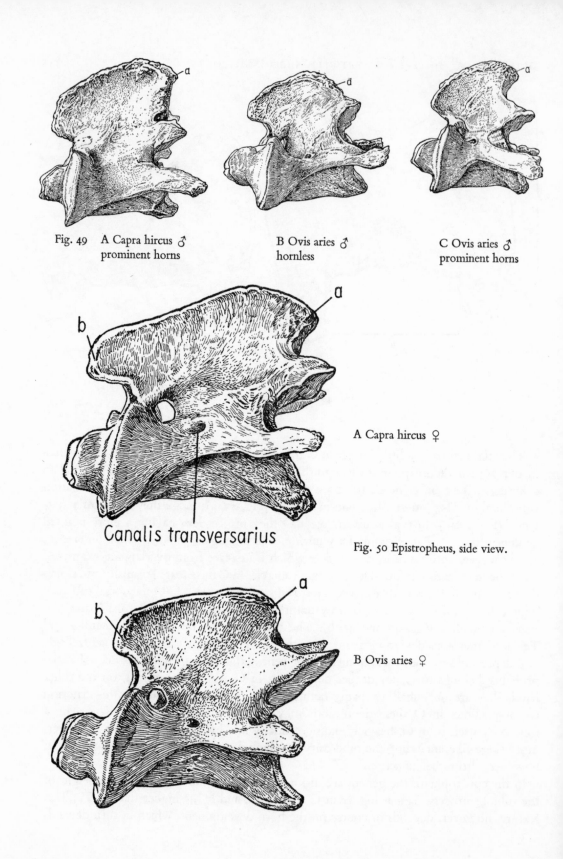

Fig. 49   A Capra hircus ♂
prominent horns

B Ovis aries ♂
hornless

C Ovis aries ♂
prominent horns

A Capra hircus ♀

Canalis transversarius

Fig. 50 Epistropheus, side view.

B Ovis aries ♀

on the age of the individual (Figs. 49 and 50). The caudal and cranial ends of the spinous process offer uncertain distinguishing features. In C, the caudal end is frequently drawn-out caudodorsally in the form of an acute angle (Figs. 49 and 50Aa) while in O it normally slopes in the form of an arch (Fig. 49Ba). It is obvious that there are intermediate forms, but things can be altogether different as is shown in Fig. 49Ca. Cranially, too, in C, the spinous process generally projects farther than in O (Fig. 50b) and ends in a larger arch. In O the extremity is more pointed generally, though not in the case of our example, Fig. 50b. The spinous process in O is broader on the whole, or its crest broadens more at its conclusion. In typical cases of C it is narrow and angular. In common with a number of other writers we found that the transverse canal is often absent on one or both sides in C; this is very exceptional in O. Only Hildebrand's findings ([7], p. 345), using 8 sheep and 9 goats. run contrary to this. He states 'The transverse canal was absent in half of my sheep skeletons, a third of the goat bones . . .'. Finally, for determination of sex by means of the epistropheus it may be useful to decide on the state of development of the ventral crest. In older ♂♂, without clear distinction between horned and hornless individuals, the ventral crest broadens caudally, in O becoming a blunter, in C a more angular, dome.

Consideration of all the criteria makes it possible, in many cases, to determine sex and genus from finds of the atlas and the epistropheus. The problem is, however, complicated by the possibility that the animals may have been castrated, especially in the case of sheep.

THE SCAPULA

Frequently only the head and neck parts of the scapula are found and so the differences in this region are of very great importance. In the region of its neck, the shoulder blade is, in C, slimmer and more elongated (Figs. 51 and 52), than in O, and the distance between the distal end of the spine and the glenoid cavity is greater. The relation of this distance to the shortest length at the neck of the scapula can be used for distinguishing purposes although there is a zone of overlapping, particularly in young animals (see Boessneck, Müller and Teichert,[2] diagram I). On the scapula of O, because of its more compact build, which feature is, however, of little use for distinguishing purposes, the margo cervicalis is more strongly arched inwards than in C (Fig. 52). Usually in O a pecten rises on the side opposite the collum (Fig. 52Ba) which is absent or only hinted at in C. It develops only gradually as a ridge for muscle roots and is, therefore, absent in the scapulae of young sheep. In addition, there are two ill-defined differences: the supraglenoid tubercle is, on the whole, more strongly developed in O, reaches farther down beyond the glenoid cavity and, when viewed laterally, it appears to be more rounded-off than in C (Fig. 51). In C the form of the glenoid cavity tends to be circular, in O elliptical. However, the scapulae of juvenile goats in particular often have an elliptically shaped fovea articularis.

The subscapular fossa is broader in O and is predominantly flat cranio-dorsally (Fig. 52B) while in C it usually is limited to a distinct eminence which flattens out towards the vertebral border (Fig. 52Ab). If the spine of the scapula is extant it also makes

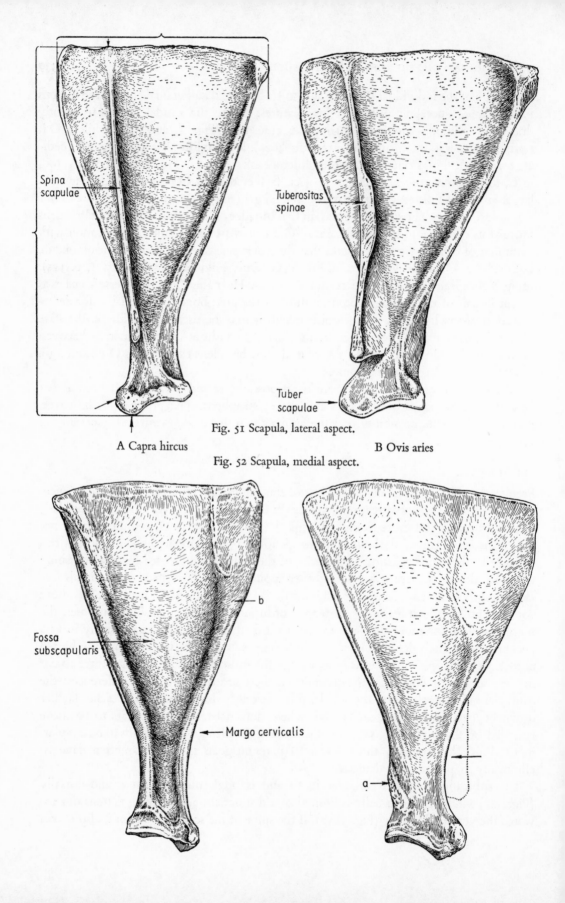

Spina
scapulae

Tuberositas
spinae

Tuber
scapulae

A Capra hircus

B Ovis aries

Fig. 51 Scapula, lateral aspect.

Fig. 52 Scapula, medial aspect.

Fossa
subscapularis

b

Margo cervicalis

a

identification possible. In O it has in the middle a pad-like thickening, the spinal tuberosity, which is turned over caudally; on the other hand, it projects cranially near its termination in the acromion. In C it is sharper, does not form a tuberosity and runs in a straight or almost straight line often projecting cranially to some extent. In young sheep and animals of smaller primitive races, however, the spinal tuberosity may be merely indicated. In old goats, on the other hand, slight traces may be found in exceptional cases.

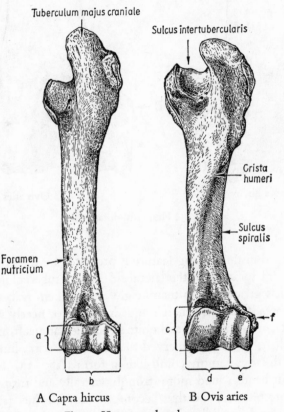

A Capra hircus   B Ovis aries

Fig. 53 Humerus, dorsal aspect.

THE HUMERUS

It is true that the humerus of C is built on altogether more elongated lines than that of O (Fig. 53), but this difference can only be used in a limited fashion for the purpose of differentiation. Proximally, the best distinguishing feature is the tuberculum majus craniale. It is high and narrow in C and overtops the articular head and the tuberculum majus caudale considerably and is inclined steeply (Fig. 53A). Even if occasionally it inclines more strongly over the intertubercular sulcus the total impression remains the same. Compared with this, the tuberculum majus craniale in O is broad and projects less far (Fig. 53B). It usually projects only half as much from the upper rim of the tuberculum majus caudale as in C. Even with a more pronounced medial bend of the end of the tubercle the broader intertubercular sulcus is not arched over so much (Fig. 53B).

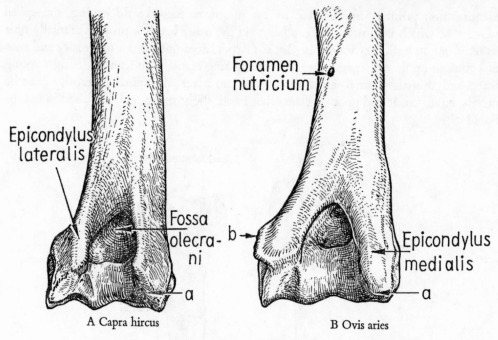

Fig. 54 Humerus, distal end.

A further less-marked distinguishing feature is presented by the area for the insertion of the tendon of infra-spinatus on the lateral side of the tuberculum majus. As a rule, in O, this surface has greater width than height and is often oval, whereas in C it has more height than breadth and is generally quadrangular or nearly square. However, it is not rare to find transitional forms and quite strong deviations from this norm.

Passing to the shaft, it will be observed that in O the crista humeri, adjoining the deltoid tuberosity distally, is more comb-like in form (Fig. 53B). In the region of the deltoid tuberosity it bends round more strongly laterally and turns over farther. In C it is straighter, more blunted, and thus becomes quite indistinct (Fig. 53A). In O, the foramen nutricium in the middle of the shaft lies on the posterior side of the bone, a little distal to the median line and usually closer to the lateral border (Fig. 54B). In C it may be situated in the same region but more in the area of transition between the posterior and lateral sides or even as far as the lateral side. If this is so, determination by this feature alone is often uncertain. In C, the foramen may, however, also lie a little farther distally, in the area of transition between the anterior and medial sides (Fig. 53A). Then determination is easy. In the humeri of goats there is quite a foramen nutricium in both places.

In the examination of archaeological bones the differences at the distal end are most important as this part of the humerus is mostly recovered. In O, the trochlea humeri is stouter, its medial part is higher and tapers more strongly from medial to lateral than in C (Fig. 53). In younger animals it is, however, relatively slim in build in both genera. In O the trochlear surface often shows a granular thickening at the end of the lateral border (Fig. 55BC). In C this is either absent or only slightly indicated. It must be stated that on humeri of prehistoric or early historic sheep there is quite often only a slight trace of the thickening, or it is completely absent. In contrast to C, the pit of the lateral epicondyle in O is surrounded by a more strongly developed epicondylar surface which originates proximally and shows a tendency to develop into a crest-like process (Figs. 54 and 55Bb). In O, the distal part of the medial epicondyle ends in an angle between a right- and obtuse-angle (Figs. 54 and 55Ba). In C, on the other hand, the angle seems to have been cut off obliquely (Figs 54 and 55Aa). In C, the transition from the shaft to the lateral epicondyle frequently takes place in the form of a narrow high ridge which continues to the end of the epicondyle (Fig. 54A). In O, this part is broad and only slightly arched (Fig. 54B).

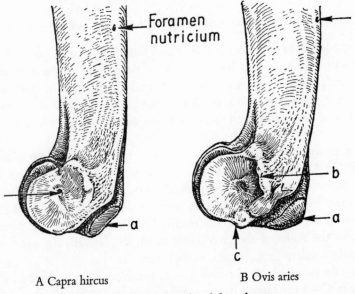

A Capra hircus   B Ovis aries

Fig. 55 Humerus, distal end, lateral aspect.

THE BONES OF THE LOWER ARM

In the bones of the lower arm the best difference between the genera is found in the region where the ulna adjoins the proximal end of the radius. In C the lateral coronoid process of the ulna grows together with the lateral facet of the radius and together with it, in most cases, forms a laterally projecting edge (Fig. 56Aa). In O, the lateral coronoid process of the ulna does not project so far nor does it unite with the radius (Fig. 56B). Moreover, in C, the two shafts grow together proximally to the radio-ulnar interosseous space. Only the articulus radio-ulnaris proximalis and its immediate neighbourhood is by-passed. Finds of the proximal ends of radii with fragments of attached ulnae are likely, therefore, to be from C, for, in O, the proximal ends of the bones

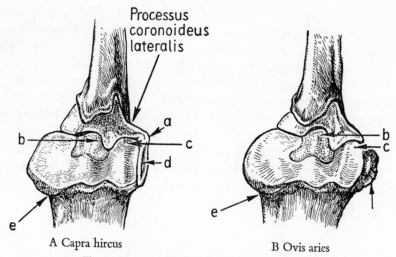

Processus
coronoideus
lateralis

A Capra hircus   B Ovis aries

Fig. 56 Ossa antebrachii, dorsal proximal end.

grow together over short distances only in exceptional cases of old animals. In the radii of young goats in whom the ulna has not yet become attached in the proximal region, a quite large, bumpy surface, often with angular borders, can be recognized which stretches farther distally than in O. In O the contiguous surfaces at the proximal ends of radius and ulna are small, and only in some older animals are they angular and bumpy.

It is evident from the preceding paragraph that the proximal interosseous space lies further distally in C than in O. In C, it originates in a curve as a result of the inter-crescence of the proximal parts of radius and ulna, while in O it comes between the contact surfaces of the two bones, ending as a cleft. From the distal end of the above-mentioned interosseous space towards the distal interosseous space, the surface formed by the union of the shafts of the two bones is, on the lateral side, often accompanied by a well-marked sulcus in C, which is absent in O.

Considering the radius alone, the best feature for distinction is offered by the stronger development in O of the lateral bicipital tuberosity at the proximal end (Fig. 56B). In the majority of cases the weakly developed ledge in C is marked by a sulcus directed dorsovolarly (Fig. 56Ad) which, in O, was found more or less clearly marked in only a few cases.

In the shaft of the radius there are differences of degree near its distal end. The distal part of the diaphysis may look as if it had been pressed together with two fingers in a mediolateral direction and had, as a result, given way with its axial part in a dorsal direction. Extreme cases of this type were found in some ♀♀ of C. To a lesser degree the 'compression' occurred in radii of both genera. It is absent, however, in many radii of O and of many young animals of both genera. In these, the end of the shaft is curved to an approximate semicircle. With the stronger 'compression' the medial border is also marked more strongly and bent back further as if it had given way to the pressure in a volar direction. The area between the medial border and the dorso-medial longi-

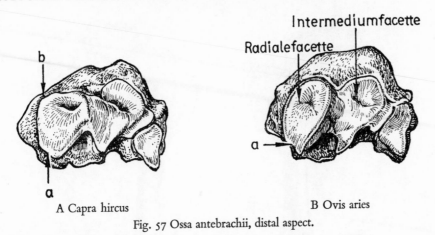

A Capra hircus   B Ovis aries

Fig. 57 Ossa antebrachii, distal aspect.

tudinal border then becomes larger. This feature is, again, characteristic of C and occurs only exceptionally in O, without reaching the extreme limits.

In the distal epiphysis there are two useful distinctions. In C, the facet for the articulation with the os carpi intermedium (Fig. 57B) is more deeply indented in the area where it broadens dorsally than in O, and the dorsal edge of the articulation reaches lower down in C. In O, the facet for the os carpi radiale is longer, narrower and almost drop-shaped (Fig. 57B); in C it may be broader and more angular, especially in the dorsal part (Fig. 57Ab).

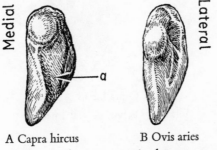

A Capra hircus   B Ovis aries

Fig. 58 Olecranon, proximal aspect.

In the ulna, the olecranon of C is longer than in O. The tuber olecrani is, as a rule, thicker in C than in O, the outer side in C being more strongly curved while the inner edge, viewed from above, is usually almost straight or even slightly bent (Fig. 58A). In O, the inner side is usually slightly curved at this place (Fig. 58B). On the tuber olecrani of C a laterally sloping, smoother face or groove can be seen whose partial lateral termination is formed by a more or less distinct border which runs dorsovolarly (Fig. 58Aa). Dorsolaterally the face slopes down without limits to the lateral side of the olecranon. The smooth face and terminating border are absent in O (Fig. 58B), but even in C they may be developed only indistinctly. When the surface of contact with the radius has been preserved it is more uneven and longer in C and the lateral coronoid process is drawn out farther (see p. 341).

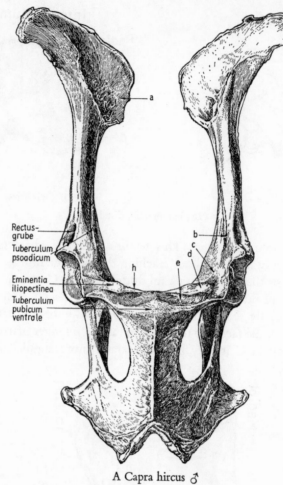

Rectus-
grube

Tuberculum
psoadicum

Eminentia
iliopectinea

Tuberculum
pubicum
ventrale

A Capra hircus ♂
Fig. 59 Pelvis, ventral aspect.

THE PELVIS

Firstly, the most important differences of sex will be briefly described. The pelves of
the ♂♂ can be often recognized in the various races by their size and sturdy build alone.
The pelves of the ♀♀ are more spacious and wider in proportion to their length than
those of the ♂♂ (Fig. 59 compared with Fig. 60). The widening of the pelvic space of
♀♀ as a birth channel takes place without any corresponding increase in the outer contours of the bone. Because of this the ♀ pelvis is built more lightly.

The body of the ilium is slenderer and longer in ♀♀ and the ala is smaller than in ♂♂
(Figs. 59 and 60). In the pelvis of ♂♂ the ala of the ilium is drawn out as a flat surface,
caudally of the sacral tuberosity (Fig. 59a). The sacral tuberosity of the ♀ pelvis ends in
a high point (Fig. 60Ba) or is also drawn out a little caudally; it occurs in this way in
many cases of C (Fig. 60Aa) though not to the same extent as in ♂♂.

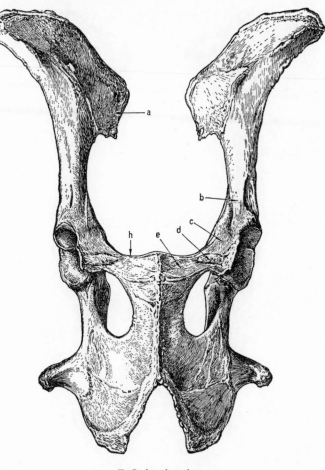

B Ovis aries ♂
Fig. 59 Pelvis, ventral aspect.

The body of the ilium of the ♂ pelvis becomes strengthened and rounded in its transition to the acetabulum and the pubis at their ventromedial side, which results in several subtle differences in the sexes: the pit for the origin of the rectus femoris (Fig. 59A Rectusgrube) is terminated by a narrow pad (Fig. 60b) in the ♀ pelvis which, in this region, has a steep or indented medial wall. In the ♂ pelvis the area medial to this muscle pit is flatter and wider. The distances from the medial edge of the muscle pits to both edges are approximately equal (Fig. 59b). The ventro-medial border of the acetabulum in pelves of ♂♂ is generally around twice or more than two times the width of that in corresponding or equally large ♀♀ pelves (Figs. 59c and 60c). The ilio-pectineal eminence is pad-shaped in ♂♂ and often sharp-edged in ♀♀ (Figs. 59d and 60d). In ♀♀ it usually forms the cranial termination of the pelvic floor, but this is not so in ♂♂. The pecten ossis pubis (Fig. 60B) justifies its name only in the case of ♀♀, for only

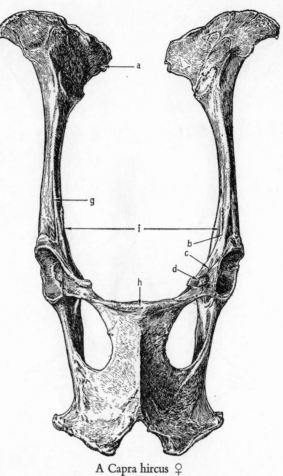

A Capra hircus ♀

Fig. 60 Pelvis, ventral aspect.

in them does it protrude as a more or less sharp process. In the pelves of ♂♂ the strong pubic branches develop a dorsal or craniodorsal border and a ventral or caudoventral edge which enclose a wide groove (Fig. 59e). The anterior part of the pubis especially in ♂♂, becomes thicker near the symphysis. Often the ♂ pelvis develops a ventral pubic tubercle as a large tuberosity (Fig. 59A); frequently it develops a dorsal pubic tubercle either in addition to or instead of that mentioned above. In ♀ pelves the tubercles are developed weakly, if at all. It must be pointed out that, in general, the ♀ pelvis is subject to greater changes which make it more typical, as it were, according to the frequency of delivering young. Pelves of animals that have not yet given birth to young are more difficult to tell apart from the pelves of ♂♂.

The tabula ischiadica stands more steeply in the ♂, less sloping in the ♀, making the cavity narrower or wider. The ischial arch forms a narrower V in the ♂ and one that is farther open in the ♀; this difference is, however, subject to extensive overlapping. The pelvic floor is shorter and wider in the ♀, longer and narrower in the ♂ animal.

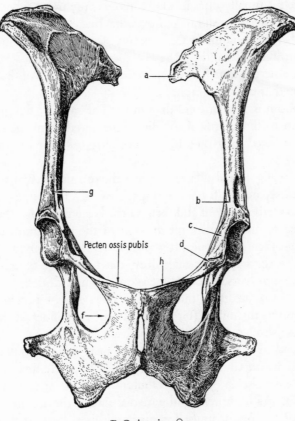

B Ovis aries ♀
Fig. 60 Pelvis, ventral aspect.

The determination of sex—not considering castrates and hermaphrodites which occur quite frequently in C—is thus not difficult with the complete pelves and even possibly with many of the fragments (compare also Lemppenau[8]).

Passing to the distinction of genus, it must be noted first that the pelvis of C is, on the whole—though with quite a lot of overlapping—longer and narrower than that of O (Figs. 59 and 60). On the slenderer body of the ilium of ♀♀ goats the ventral side forms a high vault (Fig. 60Ag), while it is arched only a little in the body of the ilium of ♀♀ sheep which is altogether shorter (Fig. 60Bg), As a result, in O ♀♀, the muscle ridge which runs near the ventral edge of the body of the ilium (linea glutaea ventralis), mostly lies very near the ventral edge from a lateral aspect; in C ♀♀, it is more strongly arched over ventrally. Furthermore, in C ♀♀, the medial termination of the muscle pit for the musculus rectus femoris protrudes considerably like a pad (Fig. 60Ag). Thus, in C ♀♀, the tubercle for the musculus psoas minor (tuberculum psoadicum) usually lies completely on the medial side of the body of the ilium and does not reach as far as its ventral edge, which it usually does in O. Moreover, the psoas tubercle has a tendency in O to draw out farther caudally, often even beyond the pit for the musculus rectus femoris close to the acetabulum. In C, it usually does not reach the caudal end of the pit for the musculus rectus femoris, or barely does so. This latter difference is valid also for the ♂ sex, while there is usually only an indication in the ♂♂ of the other distinguishing features discussed in this paragraph.

The ala of the ilium is smaller in C than in O. The ratio of the greatest diameter of the ala of the ilium to the length of the ilium, measured from the cranial edge of the labium acetabuli, showed 0·47–0·66 for C, and 0·63–0·89 for O, with approximately 5% overlapping.

Because of the strong sexual differences (see above), the cranial region of the pubis has to be discussed separately for ♀♀ and ♂♂. In C ♀♀ the pubic floor mostly slopes down gradually towards the front and forms a thicker pubic ridge (Fig. 60Ah); in O ♀♀ it slopes down steeply and forms a pit in front of the pubic rami proper. Young ♀♀ have a thicker pubis than older ones. It was observed in the pelves of the ♂♂ of C that the eminentia iliopectinea in most cases drew out to a ridge which forms the cranial termination of the transverse groove mentioned when discussing the sexual differences (Fig. 59Ah). O often has a more or less independent pecten ossis pubis as the anterior termination of this sulcus (Fig. 59Bh). In the remainder of the material investigated features were similar to those described for C.

At the cranial end of the foramen obturatum near the acetabulum a small, usually semicircular part is 'ligatured' in C. This completely or partly tied-off area forms a dent or groove on the medial side of the acetabulum. In contrast to this, O has a uniform foramen obturatum and no notch on the medial side of the acetabulum. In most cases, this feature presents an opportunity for distinguishing the two genera. In the ♂♂ of both genera as well as in the ♀♀ of C, the foramina obturata form a narrower oval; in the ♀♀ of O they mostly widen in their caudal part (Fig. 60Bf).

The pelvic symphysis is longer in C than in O. This difference catches the eye in most ♀♀ (Fig. 60) while it is indistinct in many ♂♂. The posterior border of the arcus ischiadicus stands at a steeper angle to the symphysis in C, and the pelvic exit is altogether narrower than in O.

One of the best and most familiar distinguishing features is presented by the lateral process at the tuber ischiadicum. It is longer in O than in C. While in O it usually projects far to the side of the extreme point of the acetabulum and rarely protrudes only on the same level, it does not reach this point in C or, as we were able to observe a few times in ♂♂, does so only just (Figs. 59 and 60).

THE FEMUR

The os femoris projects farther proximally and distally in O than in C (for details see Boessneck, Müller and Teichert,[2] p. 95).

The head of the femur is more ball-shaped in C, better defined against the slenderer collum; in O it is more roller-like, elongated in a lateromedial direction (Fig. 61). In C, the head quite often forms a shelf towards the saddle (Fig. 61Aa). In O, the transition

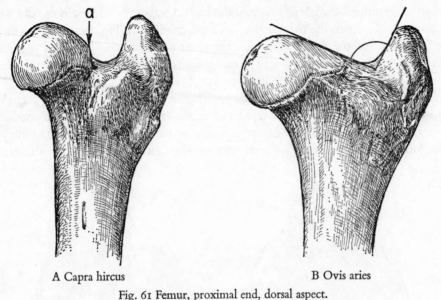

A Capra hircus   B Ovis aries

Fig. 61 Femur, proximal end, dorsal aspect.

takes place mostly gradually without or with only an insignificant change of the contour (Fig. 61B). The trochanter major stands nearer the head in C and is less curved outward than in O (Fig. 61). The surface which is situated craniolaterally at the trochanter and is covered by a synovial bursa, is usually curved forward like a bump in C; this is either not present in O or is only slightly so (Fig. 62a). However, in O there is a tendency to draw forward farther the corner proximal to this surface (Fig. 62Bb).

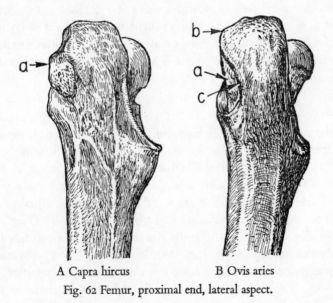

A Capra hircus   B Ovis aries

Fig. 62 Femur, proximal end, lateral aspect.

Thereby the terminating edge of the area, the linea trochanterica lateralis usually swings to the anterior border in the proximal part of the trochanter (Fig. 62BC), not so in C.

The distal half of the facies aspera on the shaft of the femur broadens more in C than in O. In C it takes up more, and often far more, than half of the width of bone at this spot, in O less than half or a little more than half.

A synovial pit on the trochlea patellaris presents an important, frequently mentioned indication of the genus. It is characteristic of C while it is absent in O. It notches the trochlea from the distal end or it lies completely or partially isolated in the pulley-like groove. However, there are individuals even among C in whom the pit is absent.

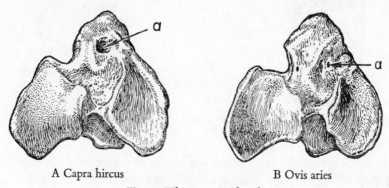

A Capra hircus   B Ovis aries

Fig. 63 Tibia, proximal end.

THE TIBIA

Of all the medullated bones, the tibia is the most difficult to distinguish. It was only at the proximal end that we found an almost consistent difference in the form of a circular pit of a diameter of several millimetres with nutritient foramina at its bottom which was characteristic of C (Fig. 63Aa). O has one or several foramina nutricia in its place (Fig. 63Ba). Errors were possible in only a few cases which were due to unconformity in some individuals.

THE TALUS AND THE CALCANEUS

In some examples of the talus of C which, on the whole, is built on slenderer lines, the trochlea or its lateral articular ridge is inclined slightly medially with reference to the head, while in O and in other tali of C which are indistinguishable by this feature the two parts stand on top of each other without an angle. The projection at the proximo-plantar angle of the medial articular ridge of the trochlea is usually more strongly developed in O than in C, and more strongly in ♂♂ than in ♀♀ (Figs. 67 and 68). In ♀♀ of C, a projection may be completely absent or may accompany the plantar end of the ridge only as a narrow ledge (Fig. 68A). In strong ♂♂ of O—in exceptional cases also in C—the projection on the other hand juts out considerably plantarly and medially as a lobe (Fig. 67B). The ♀♀ of O as well as the ♂♂ of C lie between these extremes

Fig. 64 Talus, dorsal aspect.

Fig. 65 Talus, medial aspect.

Fig. 66 Talus, plantar aspect.

Fig. 67 Talus, proximal aspect ♂

Fig. 68 Talus, proximal aspect ♀

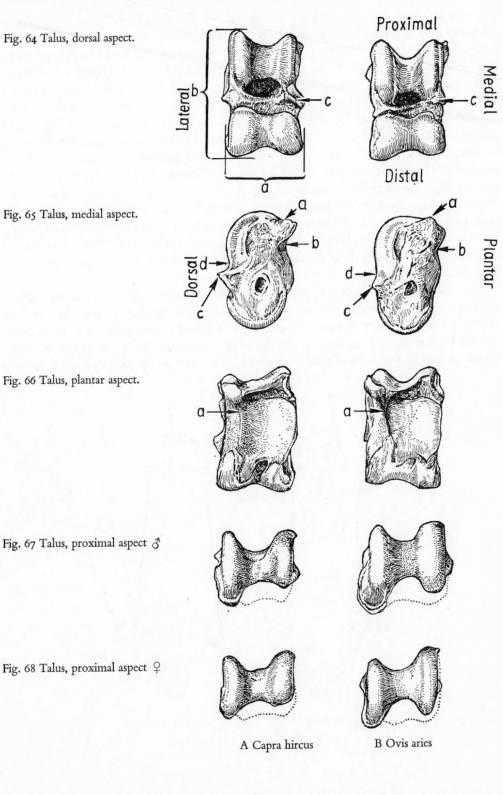

A Capra hircus   B Ovis aries

(Fig. 68B and 67A), and also the less extremely developed tali of ♂♂ O and ♀♀ C. There are many overlappings. From a medial aspect the projecting lobe usually reaches higher in O than in C and is heavier (Fig. 65a). In a distal direction it is less defined in O (Fig. 65b), and altogether the medial region of the trochlea in O, compared with the head of the talus, appears heavier than in C (Fig. 65). A rather good feature appears to exist at the distal end of the medial articular ridge: in C, a sharp ridge usually standing obliquely, protrudes dorsally and medially between trochlea and head (Figs. 64AC and 65AC). It is developed more weakly in O, placed more obtusely and usually more horizontally (Figs. 64BC and 65BC). However, transitions from both sides occur also in this feature. In O, the articular surface for the calcaneus on the plantar side of the bone goes up higher proximally-medially (in Fig. 66 at a) in a plantar direction. The medial edge of the articular surface usually projects noticeably over the lateral edge in O; in C, both project roughly equally in a plantar direction. In O, a pad or thickish connecting piece runs from the medial edge of the articular surface to the plantar lobe of the medial articular ridge (Fig. 66Ba); in C, there is nothing like this or only an indication of it (Fig. 66Aa).

The calcaneus of C is longer and slimmer than that of O, and also usually slightly curved plantarly, however, only rarely as markedly as in the case of our Fig. 69A. The depth of the body—dorsoplantar direction—as a rule increases more in a distal direction in O than in C, especially on the dorsal side medially above the articular surface to the talus (Fig. 69). The plantar part of the tuber calcanei projects beyond the dorsal

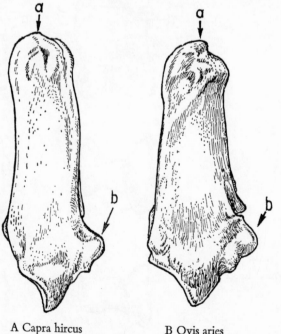

A Capra hircus   B Ovis aries

Fig. 69 Calcaneus, lateral aspect.

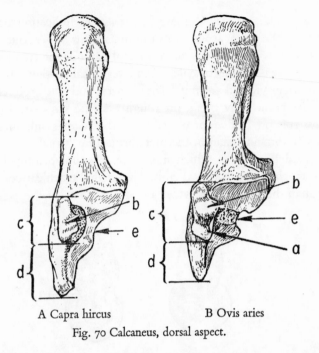

A Capra hircus   B Ovis aries

Fig. 70 Calcaneus, dorsal aspect.

part farther in O than in C (Fig. 69a). The condyle in the centre of the articular facet for the os malleolare usually stands out proximally and distally more clearly in O than in C (Figs 69b and 70b). The distal, indented part of the articular facet is drawn out longer in O than in C (Fig. 70Ba). As a result of this, the articulation part at the lateral process is longer than the articulation-free part of this process or roughly of the same length; on C, on the other hand, it is shorter or, at the most, equally long (Fig. 70c to d). The articular facet for the os malleolare is usually also relatively narrower in O than in C. The greatest width of this facet expressed as a percentage of its greatest length was 50–66% in C, 37–52% and in isolated cases up to 55% in O. Less than one-fifth of the values was above 50% in O and under 52% in C. The two articular surfaces for the talus—the narrow one on the medial side of the lateral process for the lateral side of the ankle-bone and the large one on the sustentaculum tali for the plantar face of the talus—often join together as one in C, rarely so in O (Fig. 70e).

THE METAPODIA

To begin with, it can be difficult in distal parts to decide whether the remnant of bone in question is of a metacarpus or a metatarsus. On the distal part of the diaphysis, the dorsal side in the region of the coalescence suture between the IIIrd and IVth metapodic radius is suitable for distinction. In the metacarpus, this suture is as if engraved with a knife and terminates near the distal end of the diaphysis. The dorsal face of the distal end of the diaphysis is convex or at least flat. In the metatarsus a wider, more or less distinct sulcus runs through on the dorsal side of the distal end of the diaphysis right to the end. Thus the dorsal side of the distal end of the diaphysis is indented, which is usually quite clear in C, and in O there is at least an indication of it. The greatest difficulties in telling the metacarpus from the metatarsus are encountered at the distal epiphysis. Distinction is possible on the peripheral parts of the two trochlear condyles. In metacarpi those parts of the trochlear condyles distal to the axis of the foot form roughly a semi-circle, viewed from a lateral aspect, and with reference to the longitudinal axis of the bone, they break off roughly at the same level (Fig. 71A). In the metatarsus, they run on farther proximally on the plantar side and merge into the diaphysis with less notching than in the metacarpus (Fig. 71Ba).

It is possible to determine to which side a metapodium belongs by comparing the sizes of the two trochleae at the distal ends. The medial trochlear condyle is developed more strongly than the lateral. It is wider and deeper.

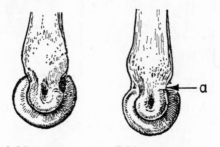

A Metacarpus   B Metatarsus

Fig. 71 Metapodia distal epiphysis, Capra hircus.

The metapodia of C are shorter and wider than those of O. However, as the diagrams II–VI in our original work show, the possibility of errors is increased when distinguishing by use of the proportions of width and length alone. Some strong rams have such massive metapodia that their width-length index falls right in the middle of the variation range of C. On the other hand, the metapodia of lightly built C ♀♀ may reach beyond the limit into the upper or middle range of variation of small sheep. Nevertheless, appreciation of the length-width index does help one to come to the correct conclusion as to the genus of animal from which the bone originated. Concerning sex dimorphism in whole metapodia of O see Calkin[3] and Haak.[6]

For the purpose of distinction at the proximal end the main feature to be considered, particularly for the metatarsus, is the perforation of the articular surface by formations of synovial pits. Such perforations are rare in metacarpi; but when they do occur the metacarpus can be recognized as belonging to C. They often occur in the metatarsus of C. One to three sometimes strikingly large holes, varying from circular to triangular, are observed. In O, it is rare to find a perforation which is then roughly circular and has a diameter of at most 2–3 mm.

At the distal end, the proportion of the size of the trochlear condyles distant of the axis of the foot, to the size of the verticilli forms a marked distinguishing feature for the metacarpus; in the metatarsus the difference is not so clear. In C the peripheral parts of the trochlear condyles are relatively smaller than in O (Fig. 72). Often they are also more sharply defined against the axial part of the trochlear condyle and are more deeply notched-in immediately adjoining the verticillus (Fig. 72). One measures the dorsovolar or dorsoplantar diameter of the peripheral trochlear section immediately adjoining the verticillus, i.e. where it is smallest, at least in C, and puts it in proportion to the parallel diameter of the verticillus (Fig. 72Aa to b). In the metacarpus the index calculated for the medial trochlea was always over 63 in O; in C it was in one instance exactly 63, but for the rest it was always below that. In the metatarsus, there was an overlapping area between 59, the smallest figure for O, and 62·5, the largest for C.

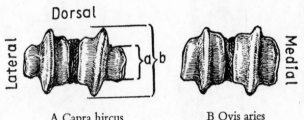

A Capra hircus   B Ovis aries

Fig. 72 Metacarpus distal aspect.

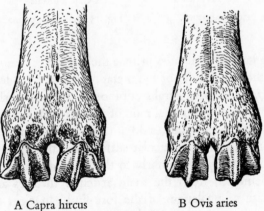

A Capra hircus   B Ovis aries

Fig. 73 Metacarpus distal aspect, dorsal view.

In cases of doubt, additional features can be used. The verticilli on the trochlea are more sharply edged and steeper in C than in O, particularly when viewed from the volar or plantar aspect, and from the distal aspect (Fig. 72). In C, the axial halves of the trochlear condyles with the verticilli diverge more strongly in a proximal direction than in O (Fig. 73). The fossulae which join on to the distal trochlear condyles proximally—two each dorsally and volarly or plantarly over each trochlea—are, as a rule, more strongly developed in C than in O (Fig. 73).

THE PHALANGES

In general, it can be said that the phalanges of the fore-limbs are more massive than those of the hind-limb, being thicker and usually also longer. The inner phalanges are, as a whole, again bigger than the outer. Individual phalanges, however, can seldom be classified either in the one or in the other respect with any degree of certainty.

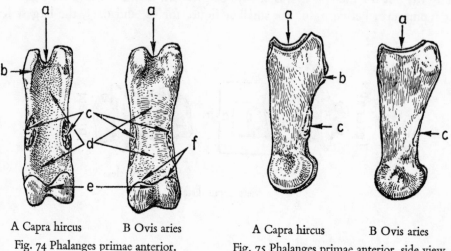

A Capra hircus   B Ovis aries   A Capra hircus   B Ovis aries
Fig. 74 Phalanges primae anterior.   Fig. 75 Phalanges primae anterior, side view.

At the proximal end of the phalanges primae the differences are reflected which were observed for the trochlear condyles of the metapodia. For C, a deeper leading groove is characteristic (Fig. 74a), the peripheral section of the articular surface rises higher over the axial (Fig. 75a), and the longitudinal radii of the articular sections are more strongly bent than in O (Fig. 75a). These features do not, however, remain without some overlapping or uncertainty. The small articular surfaces for the ossa sesamoidea phalangis primae, which join on volarly or plantarly to the proximal articular surfaces, are, as a rule, more clearly delimited from the main articular surfaces and are larger in C, particularly in the case of phalanges of the fore-limb. In clear cases among C, the dorsovolar or dorsoplantar diameter of the articular surface for the os sesamoideum distant of the axis of the foot is a quarter or more of the length of the corresponding articular section for the metapodium. The axial ligament tubercle on the posterior side of the proximal end shows a stronger tendency in C than in O of being drawn out distally to a high ridge (Figs. 74Ab and 75Ab). The originating points for ligaments on the lateral borders of the volar or the plantar face at the commencement of the distal half (Figs. 74c and 75c) usually stand out more clearly in C than in O. The posterior side of the body is frequently concave in C (Fig. 74Ad), more rarely flat; but in O it is mostly flat (Fig. 74Bd) or convex. The best distinguishing feature on the fetlock is found at the distal end. In C, the posterior edge of the distal articular surface as a rule forms a right angle or more acute angle with its vertex at the articular groove (Fig. 74Ae). In

O, the angle is obtuse and wide open (Fig. 74Be); sometimes there is hardly an indication of it. The articular sections stand out more clearly in C than in O.

The phalanges secundae of the fore-limb are distinguished not only by their greater thickness (see above), but also by having a larger distal articular region which reaches farther proximally and whose medial sector is directed more steeply distally than in the phalanges secundae of the hind-limb. In the cases that are easiest to distinguish the distal articular surface of phalanges secundae of the fore-limb, on the dorsal side, goes as far as half along the length of bone, whereas in the phalanges secundae of the hind-limb it reaches only about one-third of the length. However, overlapping in these features is considerable. The front phalanges secundae show a difference at the proximal end in the proportion of length to width. The dorsovolar diameter is here smaller in C than the lateromedial diameter, or is of equal size; in O, the proximal end is of greater length than width or as wide as it is long. This feature can be used in O to determine the genus if it has otherwise been possible to establish that the bone belongs to the fore-limb; but for C it can be used quite generally, because in phalanges secundae of the hind-limb the proximal end is of greater length than width in both genera. As in the phalanx prima, though with considerable overlappings, the posterior edge of the trochlear condyle is more strongly indented in C than in O (Fig. 76a) and has a tendency in C to be drawn up far proximally in the peripheral half (Fig. 76Ab). This 'drawn-up' portion of the articular surface may finally continue in a ridge (Fig. 76Ac). In O, the peripheral halves of the articulation are drawn up only a little farther than the axial halves (Fig. 76Bb). In C, the axial part of the distal trochlear condyle projects more steeply and farther distally (Fig. 76d) and is smaller compared with the peripheral part than in O (Fig. 77). However, these differences are blurred when phalanges secundae from front and hind limbs have not been separated out beforehand, because there are similar differences between the front and the hind phalanges.

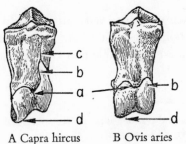

A Capra hircus B Ovis aries

Fig. 76 Phalanges secundae anterior.

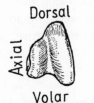

Dorsal

Axial

Volar

A Capra hircus

Peripher

B Ovis aries

Fig. 77 Phalanges secundae anterior, distal aspect.

The differentiation of the phalanges tertiae is easier than that of many other bones. The phalanges tertiae of C are narrow, as if they had been pressed flat between two fingers in the anterior half, the mass escaping dorsally and distally. Thus a sharp dorsal edge is formed the course of which is extremely variable. In O, the phalanges tertiae

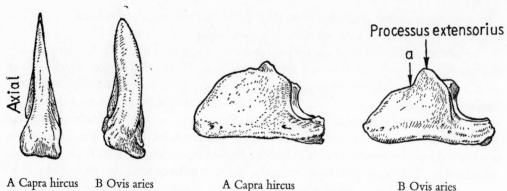

A Capra hircus   B Ovis aries   A Capra hircus   B Ovis aries
Fig. 78 Phalanges tertiae, distal aspect.   Fig. 79 Phalanges tertiae.

are wider and smaller (Fig. 79), the dorsal edge is usually blunter. The processus exten-
sorius is relatively small in C, relatively large in O (Fig. 79). In O there is often a saddle
in front of it (Fig. 79Ba) which may, however, occur similarly in C. The narrow sole
surface of the phalanges tertiae of C forms an isosceles triangle with a very short base
(Fig. 78A). The sides of this triangle, as they merge into the side surfaces, form two angles
of approximately 90°, at least in the anterior half of the phalanx. In O, the side edges of
the sole surface are more curved, the outside edge convex, the inner edge in its anterior
third also convex, but in its middle part concave (Fig. 78B). Apart from this, the inner
edge of the sole surface loses its sharp angle with the inner surface of the phalanx,
long before it reaches the middle; the sole surface is rounded-off and merges gradually
into the axial side. In C, the sole surface stands almost vertically to the sagittal plane of
the bone; in O it is inclined more strongly to this plane from proximoaxial to disto-
peripheral.

CONCLUSION

Distinguishing between sheep and goat bones is often not easy even with the help of
the features mentioned above, especially when the bones in question are fragmentary
food remains. With some practice, however, at least a considerable part can be determined.

REFERENCES

1 BOESSNECK, J. and MEYER-LEMPPENAU, U. 1966. Geschlechts- und Gattungsunterschiede am Kreuzbein
    der kleineren mitteleuropäischen Wiederkäuer. *Säugetierkundliche Mitteilungen 14*, 28–36
2 —— MÜLLER, H.-H. and TEICHERT, M. 1964. *Kühn-Archiv 78*, 1–129
3 CALKIN, V. I. 1961. *Bjull. Moskovsk. Obšč. isp. prirody, otd. biol. 66*, 115–32
4 CORNEVIN, CH. and LESBRE, F. 1891. *Bull. Soc. d'Anthropol. Lyon lo*, 47–72
5 GROMOVA, V. I. 1953. *Trudy komissii po izuč. četvertičn. perioda, t. lo, vyp. 1*
6 HAAK, D. 1965. *Metrische Untersuchungen an Röhrenknochen bei Deutschen Merinolandschafen und Heid-
    schnucken*, Diss. Munich
7 HILDEBRAND, M. 1955. *California fish and game 41*, 327–46
8 LEMPPENAU, U. 1964. *Geschlechts- und Gattungsunterschiede am Becken mitteleuropäischen Wiederkäuer*.
    Diss. Munich

31 Bird Remains in Archaeology

ELLIOT W. DAWSON

REMARKABLY little appreciation has been shown of the value of bird remains in archaeological sites in Europe despite the stimulus provided by Clark's [37],[38] major reviews of the fowling activities of prehistoric man, and the knowledge of domestic associations of many kinds of birds in historic times.[86]

The reasons for this lack of study are, firstly, that large mammal bones, often the predominant faunal remains from such sites, have provided what seemed to be an adequate picture of the food supply and hunting of the ancient peoples, and the extra information from the relatively few bones of birds was not considered worth their detailed examination. Secondly, it has often been supposed that identification of small bird bones is difficult. This is quite true, the difficulties being comparable with those for many of the smaller mammals, which have been equally neglected. Had a book such as Cornwall's[47] guide been available for even the larger or commoner birds much more could have been attempted by the informed archaeologist who had only Lambrecht's[109] treatment for reference. The lack of comparative skeletons in museums has meant that the identification of bird remains has become essentially specialist work limited to those few zoologists who have managed, largely through their own enthusiasm, to build up adequate collections of bones of living birds, so that the third reason for the neglect of bird remains in archaeology is the lack of adequate collections and interested specialists.

In other parts of the world the situation has varied from this extreme, through North America where bird remains have been studied from a considerable number of sites and where correlations and discoveries of some interest have emerged, to the other in New Zealand where a whole phase of Maori culture, the *Moa*-hunter (or 'Archaic') Period, was largely based on the hunting of these giant ratite birds, the Dinornithiformes. The relative abundance and importance of various animals in the supply of food or clothing materials for prehistoric peoples has determined the proportions of bird, fish, shell-fish, and mammal remains found in their occupation sites. In Europe, large mammals were a chief source of these materials; in North America both birds and mammals were used for particular purposes, while in New Zealand, with its lack of native land mammals, *Moas*, small birds, seals and whales, fish, and shell-fish were used in varying proportions from the *Moa*-hunter Period to European times, and the tracing of these variations, as the *Moa* became rarer, has been beautifully demonstrated by Lockerbie.[117] Hence, in New Zealand, the study of bird remains has become of very great importance both in view of the current intensive archaeological research, and in relation to the many natural deposits, in caves, swamps, and sand-dunes, of extinct birds, some of which were known to the earliest Maoris.[48],[49],[51],[52],[56],[59],[60]

Lately, increased interest has been shown in bird remains in Europe and the work of Bramwell and some others in Great Britain is providing results of some significance.

It was in Europe that the pioneer work was done on birds in archaeological sites, and this makes it surprising that their significance has been overlooked to a great extent. The work of Japetus Steenstrup in 1848 on the Danish shellmounds of Jutland showed that from the identification of the bones of birds and mammals found in these places one could derive quite an amount of information about the climatic conditions and the vegetation at the time when the middens were being formed in addition to purely cultural information about the hunting range of the former inhabitants. Winge[193] carried on such studies and the tradition has been maintained by Troels-Smith[173] and others in assessing the value of bird remains found at early Neolithic sites in west Zealand.

What can one derive from a study of bird remains? What has already been achieved in this way from various sites throughout the world? How can these bird remains be identified, and what are the problems involved? Some answers to these questions, with examples and references for further reading, follow and may provide suitable encouragement for archaeologists likely to encounter such material.

THE USE OF BIRD REMAINS IN ARCHAEOLOGY

The 'remains' of birds found in archaeological sites include bones, feathers, mummies, eggshell, guano, and, perhaps, the painting and carving of replicas of the contemporary avifauna on caves, trees, stones or artifacts. Each of these kinds of relic has its value in interpreting the everyday life and background of the dwellers in these sites. From identification of the bones a list of species can be compiled and comparisons can be made with the present-day avifauna of the region. From what is known of the present habits of movement or migration of these birds, evidence may be found of seasonal occupation of the sites or of a particular hunting or trading range of the peoples formerly inhabiting them.

Although there have been several later studies (e.g. an analysis of animal remains in preceramic sites of 5,000 to 3,500 years old in Florida by Neill, Gut, and Brodkorb[138]) the classic example is Howard's[93] interpretation of the bird remains from the Emeryville shellmound, a large prehistoric Indian site on the shore of San Francisco Bay, California. The bones found there were predominantly of water birds, indicating a hunting range restricted to the vicinity of the shore. Most of the birds were ducks, mainly winter visitors, and geese, at present entirely winter visitors from October 1st to the end of April. Bones of the Merganser were correlated with the present-day occurrence from January 1st to April 11th. Howard concluded: 'On this evidence, then, we can say with certainty that the shellmound was occupied during the winter months.' From the abundant bones of cormorants (Phalacrocoracidae), of which nearly half were of young nestling birds, it was concluded, based on the knowledge of the habits and nesting times of the present-day species in the area, that the 'optimum time' of taking young cormorants of the age found in the mound is from the middle of June to the end of July; and, therefore, the Emeryville mound must have been inhabited by the Indians during the summer months also. The avifauna of the mound indicated a continued occupation by the Indians throughout the year even though there are no bones of birds limited to the intervening spring and autumn months.

While such correlations are justifiable, some caution must be observed when accounting for the presence or absence of bones of certain birds in occupation sites (cf. Gilmore[79]). A comparison has been made between birds from Indian middens in Oregon and those in Puget Sound, Washington, by Professor Loye Miller.[134] At the latter site many groups of birds, well represented in Oregon, were rare or completely absent, notably condors and eagles. Some correlation seemed likely between their absence and the ritual usage of condors, eagles, and ravens by Indians of various tribes.[133] Owls and crows were also, according to him, 'shielded by Indian psychology' in North America (cf. Friedmann[74]), and, in Roman Britain, ravens had peculiar semi-domestic associations which accounted for their abundant remains near dwelling sites.[86] Trade with distant tribes may account for the presence of some otherwise inexplicable bones,[55] and intermingling with earlier deposits may provide a complex situation.[48,49,55]

Broken bones or artifacts made from bird bones are of very great interest also. In most New Zealand sites bone awls, needles, or bird spear-points occur. Discussing those from the *Moa*-hunter camp at the Wairau Bar, Duff[60] provided an example: 'The chief value of these awls to archaeology is that they were selected from the stoutest and soundest portions of the skeleton . . . and being preserved in large numbers provide a ready indication of the presence of extinct creatures, whose bones have not otherwise survived. Thus at Wairau the only indication of the extinct eagle (*Harpagornis*) is, apart from a practically indestructible claw, three awls worked from the distal tibia and ulna.'

Eggs and eggshell may provide useful information, as in New Zealand, where *Moa* eggs were found with *Moa*-hunter burials at Wairau presumably used as water-bottles, replacing the *Lagenaria* gourds of the tropical homeland, and suggesting, because of their increasing rarity, 'some superiority of rank of the deceased'.[60] Engraved or painted eggs also occur in some sites (cf. Breuil and Clergau[26]). Ceremonial bird burials, a feature of some Indian cultures, have been discussed[175, 90] (cf. also Blanc and Blanc [16]), and the use of captive macaws and other parrots in providing feathers for 'religious paraphernalia' accounts for isolated skeletons in certain Pueblo sites.[103] A later report on the Pueblo del Arroyo provides an amusing archaeological sidelight interpreted by bird bones: 'Another interesting find . . . the incomplete skeleton of a macaw, one of those gorgeous red-blue-and-yellow parrots (*Ara macaw*) from tropical Mexico and south. The skeleton is especially interesting to me because the sternal apparatus had been fractured by a blow and subsequently healed. Presumably the bird had bitten a careless finger somewhere on the trail to Chaco Canyon, or after arrival there, and had been felled by a stick in angry hands.' This find 'provided evidence of an apparent clash of tempers. We may imagine a sudden painful bite from an irritated beak and a sharp, angry blow in retaliation. Landing full on the bird's breast, the blow resulted in a permanent injury', which was described in full anatomical detail.[104] Mummies of birds, as made in ancient Egypt, are also of interest.[127,161]

Some indication of the former presence of various birds, which may confirm the identification of bones found in the sites or may indicate a wider knowledge of the natural world by the peoples concerned, can be derived from pictographs,[86,25] petroglyphs,[134] dendroglyphs,[100] and artifacts (e.g. Webb and Baby[176]). Again on the New

Zealand scene some of the large birds of rock paintings of South Canterbury are possibly contemporary work of the *Moa*-hunters.[60] Guano, also, has its role in aiding the archaeologist, and an example is Kubler's[107] attempt at a chronology based on guano deposition.

EXAMINATION AND IDENTIFICATION OF BIRD BONES

With a little experience bird bones can be easily separated from those of the smaller mammals, such as the rabbit, and, provided a few bones of birds now common in the area can be studied, most archaeologists, aided by a good memory, should be able to attain a working knowledge of at least the major families of birds encountered. This is about as far as the non-zoologist can go with safety, and for many archaeological purposes this is sufficient. The archaeologist rarely wants detailed identification but rather help in interpreting what material information he has.

For the ornithologist concerned with the more detailed identification of the bones, there are a number of problems and pitfalls, some of which may be mentioned here. There is the problem of the palaeontologist, the fitting of what is essentially a fossil, a 'thing dug up', devoid of feathers and the other external characters used by the present-day ornithologist, into the framework of the zoologist dealing with living animals, a problem comparable with that of the palaeobotanist who must name fossil pollens which are identical with those of Recent plants but may have had different leaves. Many zoologists are sceptical of how far such correlation can be carried, and as a concession to those who insist that an identical *part* (bone, or pollen) may not be correlated with an identical *whole* (bird with feathers, or plant with leaves) one has to make the identification, *Corvus* aff. *corax*, for example, meaning a species closely comparable with *corax*, the present-day Raven, if not identical. This naming problem arises with all fossils, even those characterized by morphological features common to both fossil and living specimens, but, since palaeontology, and indeed any science, can only advance by making or assuming provisional correlations, one may be justified in making specific identifications. This is just how Owen[149] deduced the former existence in New Zealand of 'a struthious bird nearly, if not quite, equal in size to the ostrich, belonging to a heavier and more sluggish species', from an unprepossessing fragmentary limb bone. Lydekker[120] and Miller[128] have also demonstrated that, within reason, such a correlation is the most practical procedure; but it is important that those concerned should be familiar with this problem. However, a number of workers insist on identifying down to subspecies on a basis of the present-day distribution, particularly where geographical subspecies, not necessarily separable osteologically, inhabit different regions or different islands (cf. Wetmore[187]). For example, a New Zealand crow bone found in a North Island deposit would be *Callaeas cinerea wilsoni*, the Blue-wattled Crow (or North Island *Kokako*), despite the absence amongst the bones of the coloured wattles distinguishing it from the Orange-wattled (South Island) Crow, *C. cinerea cinerea*. Provided that this assumption is stated no great harm may be done but to the archaeologist, not 'in the know', a confusing picture of events may result. An undifferentiated *Kokako* population may have been widespread in New Zealand at the time of the deposits since it is evident that many profound changes in the New Zealand avifauna have occurred within Recent times and not all of these are solely attributable to the advent of Polynesian Man.[50] One must not assume that the present range or habitat of a bird is identical with its distribution in former times when the archaeological deposit was forming. In New Zealand a large rail, the Takahe (Notornis), now restricted to small colonies in the mountainous, snow-grass country of the south-west of the South Island, was formerly widespread[87,192] and the virtually extinct flightless ground parrot or Kakapo (Strigops habroptilus) occurred within living memory in many parts of the country.[191] The specialized habitat of Notornis might imply differences in tolerance of the bird towards its environment in earlier times or the wider distribution of its present habitat and climate.

Similarly, Blanc[15] used the presence of the remains of the Great Auk (Alca impennis) in the Grotta Romanelli in southern Italy as an indicator of a cold climate,[28] but Bate[8] has said of the Great Auk remains from Gibraltar: 'The occurrence of the Great Auk in Mediterranean region in Palaeolithic times does not necessarily imply a very different climate to that obtaining at the present day. That this bird was commonly known only from more northerly latitudes within historic times may be responsible for its being usually considered an entirely northern, though not an arctic species.'

A fine example of the danger of assumption of present-day distributions is provided by the pelican remains in the Iron Age peat of East Anglia (cf. K. A. Joysey, first edition of this volume). Records of living stray pelicans in Britain during the last few hundred years have been of Pelecanus onocrotalus, the White Pelican. It was reasonable to assume, therefore, that the peat bones (Pollen Zone VII–VIII, 500 BC) would be those of the same species. K. A. Joysey's thorough critical examination of the peat birds has established them as Pelecanus crispus, the Dalmatian Pelican, also recorded as presumably breeding birds at the Iron Age settlement of Glastonbury[1,2] up to the Roman occupation.[68]

In some areas, notably sand-dunes where the wind may scour out deposits intermingling the remains from different strata, another problem arises, one that the field archaeologist can do much to eliminate. In New Zealand, bones of Moas which had died probably in pre-human times became mixed with overlying midden debris, which might or might not have contained Moa bones once used for food.[48] This situation resulted in earlier workers identifying the site as a Moa-hunter camp or, if indeed there were Moa bones in the later midden, in providing a longer species list of Moas used for food than warranted and, hence, of projecting the existence of certain genera into human times. Only careful field work in collecting and the distinguishing of such primary and secondary associations can save the zoologist this embarrassment.

Similarly, care must be used in analysing and interpreting the size ranges of the essentially selected animals found in midden debris; their robustness, perhaps, is not necessarily indicative of the normal size range in the region.[32] Again, it is not often realized, even by ornithologists, how much variation in size there is in living birds and this must be considered when making comparisons with earlier faunas.[132] Gilmore's[80] guide to the organization and significance of the identification of mammal remains can be read with profit by every archaeologist desirous of the services of the specialist zoologist, and by every such zoologist invited to undertake such identifications. A number of references should also be consulted by those seeking ecological information from midden debris.[198,79,81,116,189,190,43,44,45,201,170,124,125,126] Correlations between climatic conditions and the presence of various bird remains are feasible by ornithologists conversant with the living bird, and reference should be made to A. H. Miller's[130,131] work in California and to Gentilli's[77] treatment of the Australian scene. The preparation of illustrated guides or keys to the bones likely to be encountered may be useful, modelled on those produced for mammals.[20,47]

GEOGRAPHICAL SUMMARY

A selected listing of the main work involving collections, identifications, and interpretations of bird bones from archaeological sites includes the following references, although many published reports on late Pleistocene and Recent bird faunas not directly associated with human activities are also relevant.

Europe

Scandinavia: Investigations of the Danish 'kitchen middens' of Jutland provided the first evidence of the archaeological significance of bird bones.[167] Winge published a number of lists of identifications from later excavations,[193-197] and birds have been reported from other sites[75] including rock shelters in Norway[29] and in other Danish sites,[171,146,136] although little interpretation of their significance has been made. An imaginative picture has been provided by Troels-Smith[173] from an early Neolithic site in Denmark, e.g.: 'A large number of birds lived at the lake—swans, mallards, pintails, and shovellers had their nests in the swamp, and in the twilight the teal passed over the peat islet with whirring wings.' Here the bird remains were interpreted in relation to the possible seasonal occupation of the site: 'Bones from barely fledged birds indicate a habitation in June and July, and finds of bittern and other migratory birds point to the summer half year. Characteristic winter visitors among the migratory birds have not been found.' And it was concluded—'Hence we can be sure that the dwelling place was inhabited in the months, June, July, August, and September, while there is nothing to indicate that it was inhabited during the rest of the year.'

Brønsted,[30] recounting the excavation of the Gokstad Viking ship (AD 870), related the 'exotic and unexpected discovery' of bones and feathers of a peacock lying beside the steering oar. In Sweden, within recent years, interesting work has been carried out in medieval and prehistoric sites by Lepiksaar,[113,115] notably at the Iron Age Vallhagar in Gotland (AD 200-550) and in Lund (AD 1020-1040).[13] Investigations have also been made on the sea birds of early middens including an unknown species of petrel.[112,114] In another Swedish publication, Rausing[153] has discussed the application of natural sciences to archaeology, and the work of Sirelius[165] should be noted for Finland.

Germany: A number of Neolithic sites, especially Magdalenian and Azilian caves in southern Germany,[160] have produced notable bird faunas (see also Soergel[166]). Particular interest is attached to the Late-Glacial site of the 'Reindeer Hunters of Meiendorf' near Hamburg[157] where the birds found were largely species found in tundra environment, confirming the findings from the age of the reindeer calves that it was only a summer camp (cf. also Rust[158]).

Switzerland: The lake dwellings have provided bird bones and some discussion has been made.[156,105,139,154] Neolithic sites near Berne have been investigated more recently.[101]

France: Excavation reports, mentioning identifications or offering interpretations of the bird fauna in France, are relatively numerous, and the classic work is Milne Edwards's contribution[135] in Larter and Christie's *Reliquiae*, dealing with the fauna of caves and sites in the south-west of France. Other Magdalenian and Azilian sites in the Dordogne and in the Pyrenees have been discussed by Astre,[5, 6] and there are notes of interest on other caves and shelters.[121, 110, 10]

The Monaco grottoes have been investigated by Boule[18] and the figures of the bones may be helpful as a guide.[19]

Great Britain: During the earlier part of this century, E. T. Newton, already noted for his researches into the extinct bird fauna of the Mascarene Islands, published numerous lists of birds identified from Pleistocene and later occupation caves; however little ecological interpretation was attempted.[141–145] Alfred Newton, also, was interested in bird remains, especially those of the Great Auk, from middens,[140] and Auk bones are still an interesting feature of some sites elsewhere.[85,119,172,37,28] Gurney[86] presented an historical review of prehistoric birds in general terms with some interesting information on the ancient domestication of geese, fowls and pigeons, particularly in Romano-British times; cf. also the prehistoric origin of the fowl[169] and the domestic goose.[155] Gurney's records of the keeping of birds in medieval England, taken from various 'Household Books', are of particular interest in urban archaeology following reconstruction in Britain. Lowe[118] has discussed the introduction of the pheasant and fowl based on distinguishing osteological features. Fowl bones have also been reported on from beneath a Romano-British floor (AD 130) at Cirencester [41] and a reviewer noted: 'Well-attested remains of *Gallus* from early Roman sites in this country are not yet sufficiently common to pass unnoticed.' (*Ibis 92*, 335). Bird remains were common at Glastonbury and have been reported on by Andrews;[1, 2] they include evidence of the breeding of pelicans in England shortly before Roman times (cf. also Forbes *et al.*[68]).

Many of the British (and Middle East) bird remains were identified by Miss D. M. A. Bate, formerly of the British Museum (Natural History), e.g. Hawkes and Hull.[9] The death of Miss Bate in 1951 prevented many important findings being published, and much material still awaits identification. Arkell's[4] tribute to her still challenges future workers to follow her lead. For this reason the current work of Bramwell in caves in Somerset and Derbyshire is very welcome.[21–23] Bell[11,12] had earlier given a detailed summary of sites containing bird remains, with lists of the species found, but no ecological correlations were discussed. Bramwell's[24] excellent treatment of Late-Glacial and Postglacial distribution of British birds, with a useful map showing locations of sites, must be commended. Lydekker's[120] earlier account of the difficulties of identifying bird remains in Britain should also be considered.

At other occupation sites, bird bones may appear of less importance, as at Star Carr;[39],[40] here, 'Fowling played' what Clark called 'a definite, though very sub-ordinate part in the quest for food. . . . The good representation of water birds . . . is only what might be expected from the location of the site, but the rarity of land birds . . . can only mean that no serious attempt was made to secure the avifauna of the forested hinterland.'[39]

Ireland: Many caves throughout the Irish Republic and Northern Ireland have produced bird remains in sufficient quantity to make them of considerable interest.[168] Coleman[42] has produced an important paper which lists caves, the birds found, and gives many references to the original sources.

Gibraltar: A rich bird fauna was found in the Devil's Tower rock-shelter and 33 species, including the Great Auk, were identified by Miss Bate,[8] indicative of a mild climate with cool summers. This conclusion was verified by the finding of both the Alpine Chough (*Pyrrhocorax pyrrhocorax*) and the Red-billed Chough (*P. graculus*), the former being now restricted to high mountains. Both species have been found also in the Monaco caves.[19]

Italy: A. C. and G. A. Blanc[14],[15],[16] have published various lists of bird remains from late and post-Monastirian deposits in southern Italy, many species of which are now restricted to more northerly regions (but cf. Bate[8]). They have recently given an intriguing account of the identification of bones of a black or a griffon vulture sacrificed in the sixth or seventh century BC in the area of the Comitium in the Roman Forum. An interesting correlation was suggested between this find of a bird 'sacred to Mars and preferred to any other bird for taking omens' and the story of the founding of Rome when Romulus saw his flight of twelve vultures.

General: Clark has presented several accounts of early man's activities in Europe associated with the bird fauna. Correlations were made of the birds and climatic con-ditions and, from the literature, he has summarized lists of the fauna of Mesolithic sites throughout Europe covering the range 8300 to 500 BC. References to the original sources can be found in his bibliography.[35], [36] Later, he correlated the movements of the Magdalenians of the Dordogne with the movements of the reindeer to their summer grazing grounds and he provided a brief summary of the European scene.[38]

Clark's [37] review of fowling activities, read in conjunction with accounts of more modern fowling,[123] is especially valuable, and, with Moreau's[137] account of 'vicissitudes of the European avifauna since the Pliocene', is the basic reference for Europe.

North Africa, the Middle East and India

Bird remains feature in some of the North African cultures investigated by McBurney, but little has yet been published except from the earlier sites on which McBurney and Hey[122] have remarked: '. . . in contrast with later North African cultures no use seems to have been made of marine shell-fish, snails, or birds.' From the Sahara, Breuil and Clergeau[26] have reported on a Palaeolithic decorated ostrich egg.

Hilzheimer[92] calculated that 2·5% of his animal bones in his Mesopotamian site were birds but he could not identify them for lack of comparative material. Reports on other

Middle East sites have been given by Vaufrey[174] and by Josien.[102] Bird bones were collected in quantity from the Mount Carmel excavations[76] but, owing to Miss Bate's death, the identifications have not been completed and much material still awaits examination. Coon[46] gave a more detailed account of the fauna of Belt Cave, Iran, and, although the species of birds had not been identified, he was able to analyse the material quantitatively and correlate the percentages of birds found with the hunting and gathering activities of the inhabitants of the various caves, providing an illustration of what the archaeologist can do even if no zoologist can be induced to identify his material.

In India and Pakistan, a few reports have been made, notably Rang Mahal,[115] Mohenjo-Daro,[163] and in West Pakistan.[61] Basham[7] has given some account of the capture and domestication of birds in pre-Muslim India.

North America

Several lists of identifications of bird remains from archaeological sites in this region have appeared and those of Howard,[93] Brodkorb (in Neill et al.[138]) and Miller[133] may be cited as containing ecological or archaeological interpretations of interest. A further selection of reports on bird remains from Indian occupation sites follows:

Alaska: Friedmann[69-74] on Eskimo sites ranging from 50 to 1,500 years old.

British Columbia.[64]

Washington State.[134,33]

California.[93,98,57,58] Attention is also drawn to Howard's[96] survey of trends in avian evolution in Pleistocene to Recent times and her treatment of direct ancestral forms of birds in a continuously forming site in relation to 'temporal' subspecies,[97] and, hence, to subspecific identification of bird bones.

Nevada: Heizer and Kreiger[91] recorded 19 species of birds from the Humboldt Cave.

Oregon.[182,133]

Utah and Arizona.[129,89,27,134]

Ohio.[82-84,184]

Illinois.[150-152]

Florida: Close co-operation between zoologists and archaeologists has produced some reports of note, especially relating to earlier cold phases in the climate of Florida.[28,138,177,178,88,34,162,164]

New Mexico:[94,95,183,184] The use and distribution of turkeys, particularly among the Pueblo people, has also been of interest here, in other parts of America,[27,111,108,104,161] and in Europe.[17]

Central and Southern America and the West Indies

The Yucatan caves have been reported on by H. I. Fisher,[65] and pre-Columbian mounds in the Argentine by Kraglievich and Rusconi[106]. Middens and caves in the West Indies have been extensively investigated by Wetmore;[179-181,185,186,188] see also Chabanaud[34] and R. R. Howard.[99]

Australia

Although subfossil birds have been recorded in considerable number, little mention has been made of birds in midden debris. Gill[78] has recorded birds from one aboriginal midden, and Gentilli's[77] geographical summary provides the necessary background information for future studies.

New Zealand

With the earlier phase of Maori culture based on the hunting of *Moas*, these birds, together with their contemporary small birds, form an important feature of midden debris in early archaeological sites and persist into later sites in the form of worked bone artifacts often made from subfossil remains. Extensive accounts of the *Moa* have been given by Archey[3] and by Oliver,[147] while Duff[60] has dealt, in great detail, with the cultural aspect of *Moa* remains. Oliver[148] and Falla[63] have provided the background information on the New Zealand avifauna as a whole. Falla[62] has reported also on the small birds of the *Moa*-hunter middens at Wairau. Since Duff's work, the use of radiocarbon dating has enabled Lockerbie[117] to demonstrate a gradual change in the diet of the early inhabitants of southern New Zealand from *Moa*-hunter (or 'Archaic') to 'Classic' Maori culture up to European times, based on his own skilful excavations. At Pounawea, Lockerbie found a *Moa*-hunter layer (AD 1145) with plentiful *Moa*, whale and seal bones with a few shellfish. Above this was an occupation layer (AD 1455) where the *Moa* was less abundant and fish had become common. In the uppermost part of the site (AD 1665), *Moa* bones were very scarce and shellfish must have provided most of the menu. Later sites closer to European times (False Island, 1636, 1762; Murdering Beach, 1817) contain nothing typical of the *Moa*-hunter Period.

Many New Zealand sites are in shifting sand-dunes where secondary or false associations may be formed by the mingling of midden debris with earlier deposits,[48] giving a longer list of birds from a site than should be the case (cf. Dawson[49]). Despite Lockerbie's[117] demonstration that many species of *Moa* can occur in the one site, great care in collecting and identifying *Moa* remains still has to be observed in all localities. Stratification in most New Zealand sites is undeniable and excavations in the earlier natural deposits can reveal much of the history of the site (Dawson and Yaldwyn[56] and unpubl.). Study of the many species of small birds which disappeared in a geologically short space of time on the arrival of Polynesian Man, as well as others already on the way to extinction due to climatic effects, is a necessary adjunct to the examination of archaeological bird remains and many points of interest are becoming evident.[50-54,66,67] *Moa* remains from known occupation sites are being examined more critically and lists of purely archaeological *Moa* bones are appearing.[159,199,200]

The zoologist is as busy with his own researches as the archaeologist is with his and to many zoologists making such identifications would be the 'drudgery' that Gilmore[80] mentioned. The archaeologist would do well to enlist the sympathy and enthusiasm of his consulting zoologist in explaining the particular interest attached to the remains submitted for identification and he should avoid unnecessary duplication of material.

Cultural inferences must be left to the archaeologist but the zoologist should provide all the biological evidence that can be deduced from the material and he should ensure that publication of results of biological significance is made in purely biological journals as opposed to the zoologist's report added as an appendix in an archaeological journal far removed from the eye of fellow zoologists.

REFERENCES

1 ANDREWS, C. W. 1899. *Ibis* (7) 5 (19), 351–8.
2 —— 1917. In BULLEID, A. and GRAY, H. ST G., *The Glastonbury Lake Village*, II, 631.
3 ARCHEY, G. 1941. *Auckland Inst. and Mus. Bull.* no. 1.
4 ARKELL, A. J. 1951. *Arch. News Letter 3* (11), 169–70.
5 ASTRE, G. 1949. *Bull. Soc. Hist. nat. Toulouse 84*, 233–6.
6 —— 1951. *Ibid. 85*, 151–71.
7 BASHAM, A. L. 1954. *The Wonder that was India*, London.
8 BATE, D. M. A. 1928. *J. Roy. Anth. Inst. 58*, 92–113.
9 —— 1947. In HAWKES, C. F. C. and HULL, M. R. *Rep. Res. Comm. Soc. Antiq. London 14*, 354–5.
10 BAYOL, J. and PAULUS, M. 1947. *Bull. Soc. Etud. Sci. nat. Nimes 48*, 79–99.
11 BELL, A. 1915. *Zoologist* (4) 19 (893), 401–12
12 —— 1922. *Ibid.* 251–3
13 BERGQUIST, H. and LEPIKSAAR, J. 1957. Medieval animal bones found in Lund, in *Archaeology of Lund. Studies in the Lund Excavation Material*, I, 11–84
14 BLANC, G. A. 1921. *Arch. Antrop. Etnol.* (Firenze) *50*, 1–39, 7 pls.
15 —— 1928. *Ibid. 58*, 3–24
16 —— and BLANC, A. C. 1958. *Nature 181* (4627), 66
17 BÖKÖNYI, S. and JÁNOSSY, D. 1959. *Aquila 65*, 265–9
18 BOULE, M. *et al.* 1919. *Les Grottes de Grimaldi (Baouse-Rousse)*, Monaco
19 —— and VILLENEUVE, L. DE. 1927. *Arch. Inst. Paléont. hum. 1*
20 BRAINERD, G. W. 1939. *Ohio Sta. Archaeol. & Hist. Qtly. 48*, 324–8
21 BRAMWELL, D. 1957. *Proc. Univ. Bristol Speleol. Soc. 8* (1), 39
22 —— 1960a. Some research into bird distribution in Britain during the late glacial and postglacial periods, *Bird Report, 1959–60, of the Merseyside Naturalists' Assoc.*, pp. 51–8
23 —— 1960b. *Proc. Somerset Archaeol. and Nat. Hist. Soc. 104*, 87–90.
24 —— 1960c. The Excavation of Dowel Cave, Earl Sterndale, *Peakland Archaeol. Soc.* (Newsletters 14–17, 1957–60, reprinted, and *J. Derbyshire Archaeol. and nat. Hist. Soc. 1959, 79*)
25 BREUIL, H. 1938. *C.R. 13th Congr. préhist. France*, 478–88, 559–64, 673–84
26 —— and CLERGEAU, A. 1931. *Anthropologie 41*, 53–64
27 BREW, J. O. 1946. Archeology of Alkali Ridge, Southeast Utah, *Papers of the Peabody Museum, Harvard 21*, 121
28 BRODKORB, P. 1960. *Auk 77* (3), 342–3
29 BRØGGER, A. W. 1908. *Vistefundet. En aldre stenalders Kjøkkenmødding fra Jaederen*, Stavanger, 332–47
30 BRØNSTED, J. 1940. *Danmarks Oldtid*, Copenhagen
31 BULLEN, R. P. and SLEIGHT, F. W. 1959. Archaeological investigations of the Castle Windy midden, Florida, *William L. Bryant Found. Amer. Studies, Report* no. 1
32 BYERS, D. S. 1951. *Am. Antiq. 16* (3), 262–3
33 CARLSON, R. L. 1960. *Ibid. 25* (4), 562–86
34 CHABANAUD, P. 1946. *Mém. Mus. Hist. nat. Paris 22*, 121
35 CLARK, J. G. D. 1936. *The Mesolithic Settlement of Northern Europe*, Cambridge
36 —— 1944. Man and nature in Prehistory with special reference to Neolithic settlement in Northern Europe, *Occ. Pap. Univ. London Inst. Archaeol.*, no. 6
37 —— 1948. *Antiquity 22*, 113–30
38 —— 1952. *Prehistoric Europe*, London
39 —— 1954. *Excavations at Star Carr*, Cambridge

40 CLARK, J. G. D. 1956. Star Carr, a Mesolithic site in Yorkshire, in BRUCE-MITFORD, R. L. S. (ed.), *Recent Archaeological Excavations in Britain*, London, 1–20

41 CLIFFORD, E. H. 1948. *Trans. Brist. & Glos. Archaeol. Soc.* 67, 381–95

42 COLEMAN, J. C. 1947. *J. Roy. Soc. Antiq. Ireland* 77 (1), 63–80

43 COOK, S. F. and HEIZER, R. F. 1947. *Am. J. Phys. Anth. N.S.* 5, 201–20

44 —— and TREGANZA, A. E. 1947. *Am. Antiq.* 23 (2), 135–41

45 —— —— 1950. *Univ. Calif. Publ. Amer. Archaeol. Ethnol.* 40 (5), 223–62

46 COON, C. S. 1951. *Mus. Monogr. Univ. Mus. Pennsylvania* 1, 156–7

47 CORNWALL, I. W. 1956. *Bones for the Archaeologist*, London and New York

48 DAWSON, E. W. 1949a. *N.Z. Bird Notes* 3 (5), 132–3

49 —— 1949b. *J. Polynes. Soc.* 58 (2), 58–63

50 —— 1952. *Emu* 52 (4), 259–72

51 —— 1958. *Ibis* 100 (2), 232–7

52 —— 1959a. *Proc. XVth Int. Congr. Zool.* 1958, 450–2

53 —— 1959b. *Notornis* 8 (4), 106, 111–5

54 —— 1961. *Ibid.* 9 (5), 171–2

55 —— 1962. A possible association of Maori and Kakapo (*Strigops habroptilus*; Aves, Psittacidae) in the Wellington district, N.Z. *Rec. Dominion Mus.* 3 (6)

56 ——and YALDWYN, J. C. 1952. *J. Polynes. Soc.* 61 (3–4), 283–91

57 DeMAY, I. S. 1941. *Condor* 43 (6), 295–6

58 —— 1942. *Ibid.* 44 (5), 228–30

59 DUFF, ROGER. 1949. *Pyramid Valley. The Story of New Zealand's Greatest Moa Swamp*, Christchurch

60 —— 1956. *The Moa-hunter Period of Maori Culture*. Canterbury Mus. Bull. 1, Wellington

61 FAIRSERVIS, W. A. 1956. *Anth. Pap. Amer. Mus. nat. Hist.* 45 (2), 169–402

62 FALLA, R. A. 1942. Bird remains from *Moa*-hunter camps, *Rec. Canterbury (N.Z.) Mus.* 5 (7), 43–9

63 —— 1955. New Zealand bird life past and present, *Cawthron Lecture Series* no. 29 (Cawthr. Inst. Sci. Res., N.Z.)

64 FISHER, E. M. 1943. *Bull. Bur. Am. Ethnol.* 133, 133–42

65 FISHER, H. I. 1953. In HATT, R. T., FISHER, H. I., and LANGEBARTEL, D. A., Faunal and archaeologica researches in Yucatan caves, *Cranbrook Inst. Sci. Bull.* 33

66 FLEMING, C. A. 1952. *Rep. 7th Sci. Congr. Roy. Soc. N.Z.*, 1951, 114–23

67 —— 1957. *J. Polynes. Soc.* 66 (3), 271–90

68 FORBES, C. L., JOYSEY, K. A. and WEST, R. G. 1958. *Geol. Mag.* 95 (2), 153–60

69 FRIEDMANN, H. 1933. *Condor* 35 (1), 30–1

70 —— 1934a. *J. Wash. Acad. Sci.* 24 (5), 83–96

71 —— 1934b. *Ibid.* 24 (5), 230–7

72 —— 1935. *Ibid.* 25 (1), 44–51

73 —— 1937. *Ibid.* 27 (10), 431–8

74 —— 1941. *Ibid.* 31 (9), 404–9

75 FRÖDIN, O. 1906. En svensk kjökkenmödding. *Ymer* 1906, 17–35

76 GARROD, D. A. E. and BATE, D. M. A. 1937. *The Stone Age of Mount Carmel*, Oxford, vol. I

77 GENTILLI, J. 1949. *Emu* 49 (2), 85–129

78 GILL, E. D. 1954. *Mankind* 4 (6), 249–54

79 GILMORE, R. M. 1946. *Am. Antiq.* 12 (1), 49–50

80 —— 1949. *J. Mammal.* 30 (2), 163–9

81 GOGGIN, J. M. 1948. *J. Wash. Acad. Sci.* 38 (7), 225–33

82 GOSLIN, R. M. 1945. *Wils. Bull.* 57 (2), 131

83 —— 1955. *Ohio J. Sci.* 55 (6), 358–62

84 —— 1957. Food of the Adena people, WEBB and BABY, *The Adena People* (q.v.)

85 GRIEVE, S. 1885. *The Great Auk, or Garefowl (Alca impennis, Linn.)—its History, Archaeology, and Remains*, London

86 GURNEY, J. H. 1921. *Early Annals of Ornithology*, London

87 GURR, L. 1952. *Trans. Roy. Soc. N.Z.* 80 (1), 19–21

88 HAMON, J. H. 1959. *Auk* 76 (4), 533–4

89 HARGRAVE, L. L. 1939. *Condor* 41 (5), 206–10

90 HEIZER, R. F. and HEWES, G. W. 1940. *Am. Antiq.* 42 (4), 587–603

91 HEIZER, R. F. and KREIGER, A. D. 1956. *Univ. Calif. Publ. Amer. Arch. & Eth.* 47 (1), 1–190

92 HILZHEIMER, M. 1941. *Stud. Ancient Orient Civiliz.* no. 20

93 HOWARD, H. 1929. *Univ. Calif. Publ. Zool.* 32 (2), 301–94

94 —— 1931a. *Condor* 33 (5), 206–9

95 —— 1931b. *Ibid.* 216

96 —— 1947a. *Auk* 64 (2), 287–91

97 —— 1947b. *Condor* 49 (1), 10–13

98 —— and MILLER, A. H. 1939. *Publ. Carnegie Inst. Wash.* 514, 39–48

99 HOWARD, R. R. 1956. *Am. Antiq.* 22 (1), 47–59

100 JEFFERSON, C. 1955. *J. Polynes. Soc.* 64 (4), 367–441

101 JOSIEN, T. 1952. *Arch. Suisses d'Anth. gén.* 21 (1), 28–62

102 —— 1955. *Israel Explor. J.* 5 (4), 246–55

103 JUDD, N. M. 1954. *Smithson Misc. Coll.* 124

104 —— 1959. *Ibid.* 138 (1), 1–222

105 KELLER, F. 1866. *The Lake Dwellings of Switzerland and Other Parts of Europe*, London

106 KRAGLIEVICH, L. and RUSCONI, C. 1931. *Physis* 10, 229–41

107 KUBLER, G. 1948. Towards absolute Time: Guano Archaeology, in *A Reappraisal of Peruvian Archaeology, Soc. Amer. Archaeol. Mem.* 4, 29–50

108 LANGE, C. H. 1950. *El Palacio* 57 (7), 204–9

109 LAMBRECHT, K. 1933. *Handbuch der Palaeornithologie*, Berlin

110 LANTIER, R. 1945. *Proc. Prehist. Soc.* 11, 49

111 LEOPOLD, A. S. 1948. The wild turkeys of Mexico, *Trans. 13th N. Amer. Wildlife Conf.* 1948, 393–400

112 LEPIKSAAR, J. 1950. *Göteb. Mus. Årstr.* 1949–50, 143–6

113 —— 1955. The bird remains from Vallhagar, in STENBERGER, M. (ed.), *Vallhagar, a Migration Period Settlement on Gotland Sweden*, Copenhagen, vol. II, 814–31

114 —— 1958a. *Zoologisk Revy* 4, 77–85

115 —— 1958b. Bone fragments from Rang Mahal, in HANNA RYDH (ed.), 'Rang Mahal. The Swedish Archaeological Expedition to India 1952–1954', *Acta Arch. Lund* 3, 196–200

116 LEROI-GOURHAN, A. 1952. Étude des vestiges zoologiques, in LAMING, A. (ed.), *La Découverte du Passé*, Paris

117 LOCKERBIE, L. 1959. From *Moa*-hunter to Classic Maori in Southern New Zealand, in FREEMAN, J. D. and GEDDES, W. R. (eds.), *Anthropology in the South Seas. Essays presented to H. D. Skinner*, New Plymouth

118 LOWE, P. R. 1933. *Ibis* (13) 3 (2), 332–43

119 LUCAS, F. A. 1890. *Rep. U.S. Nat. Mus.* 1887–88, 493–529

120 LYDEKKER, R. 1891. *Ibis* (6) 3 (11), 381–410

121 MAYET, L. and PISSOT, J. 1915. *Lyon Ann. Univ.* 39, 74–7

122 McBURNEY, C. B. M. and HEY, R. W. 1955. *Prehistory and Pleistocene Geology in Cyrenaican Libya*, Cambridge

123 MACPHERSON, H. A. 1897. *A History of Fowling*, Edinburgh

124 MEIGHAN, C. W. 1958a. *Am. Antiq.* 24 (1), 1–23

125 —— 1958b. *Ibid.* 131–50

126 —— 1958c. *Ibid.* 383–405

127 MEINERTZHAGEN, R. 1930. In NICOLL, *Birds of Egypt*, London

128 MILLER, A. H. 1929. *Univ. Calif. Publ. Bull. Dept. Geol. Sci.* 19 (1), 1–22

129 —— 1932. *Condor* 34 (3), 138–9

130 —— 1937. *Ibid.* 39, 248–52

131 —— 1939. *Proc. Sixth Pacific Sci. Congr.*, pp. 807–10

132 MILLER, L. 1944. Ornithology of the looking glass, in *Science in the University*, Berkeley, Calif., 267–78

133 —— 1957. *Condor* 59 (1), 59–63

134 —— 1960. *Wils. Bull.* 72 (4), 392–7

135 MILNE EDWARDS, A. 1876. Observations on the birds whose bones have been found in the caves of the South-West of France, in LARTER, E. and CRISTY, H., *Reliquiae Aquitanicae*, London, 226–47

136 Møhl, U. 1957. Contribution on animal bones, in Klindt-Jensen, O., *Bornholm i Folkevandringstiden*. Nationalmus. Skr., Større Beretninger II, 1–323

137 Moreau, R. E. 1954. *Ibis 96* (3), 411–31

138 Neill, W. T., Gut, H. J. and Brodkorb, P. 1956. *Am. Antiq. 21* (4), 383–95

139 Neuwiler, E. 1924. *Mitt. Antiq. Ges. Zürich 29* (4), 109–20

140 Newton, A. 1870. *Ibis* (2) 6 (22), 256–61

141 Newton, E. 1922. *Proc. Univ. Bristol Speleol. Soc. 1* (2), 64, 73

142 —— 1923a. *Naturalist* Aug. 1923, 264–5

143 —— 1923b. *Proc. Univ. Bristol Speleol. Soc. 1* (3), 119–21

144 —— 1924. *Ibid.* 2 (2), 121

145 —— 1925. *Ibid.* 2 (2), 159–61

146 Nordmann, V. 1936. *Danm. Geol. Unders.* (3) 27, 128

147 Oliver, W. R. B. 1949. *Dominion Mus. Bull.* no. 15

148 —— 1956. *New Zealand Birds*, Wellington

149 Owen, R. 1840. *Proc. Zool. Soc. London* 7, 169–71

150 Parmalee, P. W. 1956. Faunal analysis, in Fowler, M. L. and Winters, H., Modoc Rock Shelter, preliminary report, *Illinois Sta. Mus. Rep. Investig.*, 4 (and see *Am. Antiq. 24*, 257–70)

151 —— 1957. *Trans. Ill. Sta. Acad. Sci. 50*, 235–42

152 —— 1958. *Auk 75*, 169–76

153 Rausing, G. 1958. *Lund Hist. Mus., Från Forn. och Medell.* no. 3

154 Reinerth, H. 1926. *Die jüngere Steinzeit der Schweiz*, Augsburg

155 Riddell, W. H. 1943. *Antiquity 17*, 148–55

156 Rütimeyer, L. 1862. *Neue denks. allg. Schweiz Ges. Naturwiss. 19*, 113–15

157 Rust, A. 1937. *Das altsteinzeitliche Rentierjägerlager Meiendorf*, Neumünster

158 —— 1943. *Die alt und mittelsteinzeitlichen Funde von Stellmoor*, Neumünster

159 Scarlett, R. J. 1952. *Rep. 7th Sci. Congr. Roy. Soc. N.Z.* 1951, 198–9

160 Schmidt, R. R. 1912. *Die diluviale Vorzeit deutschlands*, Stuttgart

161 Schorger, A. W. 1961. *Auk 78* (2), 138–44

162 Sellards, E. H. 1916. *Eighth Ann. Rep. Florida Sta. Geol. Surv.*, 121–60

163 Sewell, R. B. S. and Guha, B. S. 1931. Zoological remains, in Marshall, J. (ed.), *Mohenjo-Daro and the Indus Civilization*, London, vol. II, 649–73

164 Shufeldt, R. W. 1917. *Ninth Ann. Rep. Florida Sta. Geol. Surv.*, 35–42

165 Sirelius, U. T. 1934. *Die Volkskultur Finnlands. I. Jagd und Fischerei*, Berlin and Leipzig

166 Soergel, E. 1955. *Jh. ver. vaterl. Natur. Würtemb. 110*, 121–4

167 Steenstrup, J. 1857. Et bidrag til Gerrfuglens, *Alca impennis* Lin., naturhistorie, og saerligt til kundskaben om dens tidligere Udbredningskreds, *Vid. Medd. nat. For. Kjøbenhavn. 1855* (3–7), 33–116

168 Stellfox, A. W. 1938. *Irish Nat. Journal 7* (2), 37–43

169 Stubbs, F. J. and Rowe, A. J. 1912. *Zoologist* (4) 16 (347), 1–14

170 Taylor, W. W. (ed.). 1957. The identification of non-artifactual archaeological materials, *Nat. Acad. Sci. Publ. 565*, Nat. Res. Council, Washington

171 Thomsen, T. and Jessen, A. 1907. *Mém. Soc. Roy. Antiq. Nord*, 1902–7, 161–232

172 Ticehurst, N. F. 1908. *Brit. Birds 1* (10), 309–11

173 Troels-Smith, J. 1960. *Ann. Rep. Smithson. Inst. 1959*, 577–601 (transl. from *Natur Verd.*, July 1957)

174 Vaufrey, R. 1931. *Anthropologie 41*, 262

175 Wallace, W. J. and Lathrap, D. W. 1959. *Am. Antiq. 25* (2), 262–4

176 Webb, W. S. and Baby, R. S. 1957. *The Adena People No. 2*, Ohio State Univ. Press

177 Weigel, P. H. 1958. *Auk 75* (2), 215–16

178 Weigel, R. D. 1959. *Florida Anth. 12* (3), 73–4

179 Wetmore, A. 1918. *Proc. U.S. Nat. Mus. 54*, 513–22

180 —— 1922a. *Bull. Amer. Mus. Nat. Hist. 46*, 297–333

181 —— 1922b. *Smithson. Misc. Coll. 74* (4), 1–4

182 —— 1928. *Condor 30* (3), 191

183 —— 1931. *Ibid. 33* (2), 76–7

184 —— 1932. *Ibid. 34* (3), 141–2

185 —— 1937. *J. Agric. Univ. Puerto Rico 21* (1), 5–16

186 —— 1938. *Auk* 55 (1), 51–5
187 —— 1956. *Smithson. Misc. Coll. 131* (5), 1–105
188 —— 1959. *Ibid. 138* (4), 1–24
189 WHITE, T. E. 1953. *Am. Antiq. 18* (4), 396–8
190 —— 1956. *Ibid.* 21 (4), 401–4
191 WILLIAMS, G. R. 1956. *Notornis* 7 (2), 29–56
192 —— 1960. *Trans. Roy. Soc. N.Z. 88* (2), 235–58
193 WINGE, H. 1900. Report on bird remains, in MADSEN, A. P. et al., *Affaldsdynger fra Stenalderen Danmark*, Copenhagen and Paris, 179–82
194 —— 1903a. *Vid. Medd. fra naturhist. For. Kjøbenhavn., 1903,* 61–110
195 —— 1903b. Knoglerne (pp. 194–5), in SARAUW, G. F. L., En Stenalders Boplads i Maglemose ved Mullerup, Sammenholdt med Beslaegtede Fund. Bidrag til Belysning af Nystenalderns Begyndelse i Norden, *Aarbog. Nord. Oldkynd. Hist.* (2) 18, 194–5
196 —— 1920. *Mém. Soc. Roy. Antiq. Nord. 1918–19,* 241–359
197 —— 1931. *Ibid. 1926–27,* 1–128
198 WINTEMBERG, W. J. 1919. *Canad. Field Nat. 33,* 63–72
199 YALDWYN, J. C. 1959a. *N.Z. Arch. Assoc. Newsletter* 2 (4), 20–5
200 —— 1959b. *Ibid.* 25
201 ZEUNER, F. E. 1959. *The Pleistocene Period,* London

SUPPLEMENTARY REFERENCES

AMADON, D. 1963. Comparison of fossil and recent species: some difficulties. *Condor* 65, 407–9
ARMSTRONG, E. A. 1958. *The Folklore of Birds,* London
BARTON, P. L. 1968. Bibliography of New Zealand archaeology and related subjects, 1961–65. *N.Z. Archaeol. Assn. Newsletter 11(1),* 57–64
BLAKE-PALMER, G. 1956. An Otago coastal occupation site with *Dinornis* remains. *J. Polynes. Soc.* 65(2), 161–3, pls. A–C
BRODKORB, P. 1963. Catalogue of fossil birds, Part I (Archaeopterygiformes through Ardeiformes). *Bull. Fla. State Mus. (Biol. Sci.)* 7(4), 179–293
—— 1964. Catalogue of fossil birds. Part 2. (Anseriformes through Galliformes). *Bull. Fla. State Mus. (Biol. Sci.)* 8(3), 195–335
BRODKORB, P. and DAWSON, E. W. 1962. Nomenclature of Quaternary coots from oceanic islands. *Auk* 79(2), 267–9
BUIST, A. G. and YALDWYN, J. C. 1960. An 'articulated' moa leg from an oven excavated at Waingongoro, South Taranaki. *J. Polynes. Soc. 69* (2), 76–88, pls. 1–5
BURCHAK-ABRAMOVICH, N. I. 1962. (Study of the birds of the ancient epoch of the Bospor Kingdom). *Ornitologia* 5, 438–43 (in Russian)
COLEMAN, J. C. 1965. *The Caves of Ireland,* Tralee
CUMBERLAND, K. B. 1962. Moas and men: New Zealand about A.D. 1250. *Geographical Rev.* 52(2). 151–73
DAWSON, E. W. 1962. A first record of the extinct New Zealand coot from the North Island. *Notornis* 10(2), 85
—— 1968. Bird bones for archaeologists: aids to identification and interpretation. *N.Z. Archaeol. Assn. Newsletter 11* (in the press)
DUFF, R. 1960. An 'articulated' moa leg from South Taranaki. *J. Polynes. Soc. 69(4),* 411–12
DUFF, R. S. 1964. *The problem of Moa extinction.* Cawthron Memorial Lecture No. 38
FALLA, R. A. 1962. The Moa, zoological and archaeological. *N.Z. Archaeol. Assn. Newsletter 5(3),* 189–91
FLANDERS, R. E. and CLELAND, C. E. 1964. The use of animal remains in Hopewell burial mounds, Kent County, Michigan. *Jack-pine Warbler* 42, 302–9
FLEMING, C. A. 1962. History of the New Zealand land bird fauna. *Notornis 9(8),* 270–4, 2 figs
—— 1962. The extinction of Moas and other animals during the Holocene period. *Notornis 10(3),* 113–17, 2 figs
—— 1962. New Zealand biogeography. A palaeontologist's approach. *Tuatara 10(2),* 53–108, 15 figs

GOLSON, J. and GATHERCOLE, P. W. 1962. The last decade in New Zealand archaeology. Part I. *Antiquity* *36(143)*, 168–74, 1 map (reprinted in *N.Z. Archaeol. Assn. Newsletter 9(1)*, 4–10, 1965). Part II. *Antiquity* *36(144)*, 271–8, 8 figs. (reprinted in *N.Z. Archaeol. Assn. Newsletter 9(1)*, 11–18)

GRUHN, R. 1961. The archaeology of Wilson Butte Cave, South Central Idaho. *Occ. Pap. Idaho State Coll. Mus. 6*, 1–202

HAMON, J. H. 1961. Bird remains from a Sioux Indian midden. *ASB Bull. 8*, 26

HATTING, T. 1963. On subfossil finds of Dalmatian Pelican (*Pelecanus crispus* Bruch.) from Denmark. *Vidensk. Medd. dansk. naturh Foren. Kbh 125*, 337–51, 10 figs., 3 tables

HARTREE, W. H. 1960. A brief note on the stratigraphy of bird and human material in Hawkes Bay. *N.Z. Archaeol. Assn. Newsletter 3(4)*, 28

HOLMAN, J. A. 1964. Osteology of gallinaceous birds. *Quart. J. Fla. Acad. Sci. 27*, 230–52

HOOIJER, D. A. 1961. The fossil vertebrates of Ksâr'akil, a palaeolithic rock shelter in the Lebanon. *Zool. Verh. 49*, 1–68, 2 pls

HOWARD, H. 1964. Fossil anseriformes, pp. 233–326. In DELACOUR, J. *The Waterfowl of the World*, vol. 4, London

KRETZOI, M. 1962. Prähistorischer Grosstrappen-Fund und die Geschichte der Trappen. *Aquila 67/68*, 189–90

KROSCHE, Ö. 1963. *Die Moa-strausse*, Wittenberg Lutherstadt: Ziemsen

KRUTCH, J. W. and ERIKSSON, P. S. (eds.) 1962. *A Treasury of Bird Lore*, New York

MILLER, L. 1961. Bird remains from Indian middens in the Dakota area. *Bull. S. Calif. Acad. Sci. 60 (3)*, 122–6

—— 1963. Birds and Indians in the West. *Bull. S. Calif. Acad. Sci. 62(4)*, 178–91. table I

MOHL, U. 1957. Knoglematerialet fra Dalshøj og Sortemuld. In JENSEN, KLINT, and BORNHOLM, O. in Folkevandringstiden. *Skr. Nat. Mus. Kbh. Større Beretninger 2*

MOREAU, R. E. 1963. Vicissitudes of the African biomes in the late Pleistocene. *Proc. Zool. Soc. Lond. 141(2)*, 395–421, 4 figs

OLSEN, S. J. 1959. The archaeologist's problem of getting non-archaeological artifactual materials interpreted. *Curator 2(4)*, 335–8

—— 1967. Osteology of the Macaw and Thick-billed Parrot. *Kiva 32*, 57–72

PARMALEE, P. W. 1967. Additional noteworthy records of birds from archaeological sites. *Wilson Bull. 79*, 155–62

PRICE, T. R. 1963. Moa remains at Poukawa, Hawkes Bay, *N.Z. Archaeol. Assn. Newsletter 6(4)*, 169–74

—— 1965. Excavations at Poukawa, Hawkes Bay, New Zealand. *N.Z. Archaeol. Assn. Newsletter 8(1)*, 8–11

PRYNNE, M. 1963. *Egg-shells*, London

SCARLETT, R. J. 1962. Subfossil records of the Little Grey Kiwi in the North Island. *Notornis 10(2)*, 84–5

—— 1962. Interim list of Moa species from North Island archaeological sites. *N.Z. Archaeol. Assn. Newsletter 5(4)*, 245–6

—— 1966. A pelican in New Zealand. *Notornis 13(4)*, 204–17, figs. 1–11

SCHÜZ, E. 1966. Über Stelzvögel (Ciconiiformes und Gruidae) im Alten Ägypten. *Vogelwarte 23*, 263–83

STEINBACHER, J. 1960. Die Moas. Zur Neuaufstellung ihrer Skelette im Senckenberg-Museum. *Natur u. Volk 90*, 142–52, figs

STRESEMANN, E. 1960. Über 'Vorkolumbische Truthähne' in Ungarn und überdas Perlhuhn in der Kulturgeschichte. *Zool. Jahrb. Syst. Ök. Geogr. 88*, 31–56

TCHERNOV, E. 1962. Palaeolithic avifauna in Palestine. *Bull. Res. Council Israel* (B) *Zool. 11(3)*, 95–131

THOMSON, A. L. 1964. *A New Dictionary of Birds*, London

TROTTER, M. 1965. Excavations at Ototara Glen, North Otago. *N.Z Archaeol. Assn. Newsletter 8(3)*, 109–14

—— 1965. Avian remains from North Otago archaeological sites. *Notornis 12(3)*, 176–8

TYLER, C. 1958. Some chemical, physical and structural properties of Moa egg shell. *J. Polynes. Soc. 66*, 110–30, 2 pls

—— 1964. Einige chemische, physikalische und strukturelle Eigenschaften der Eischalen. Ein Rückblick. *J. f. Orn. 104*, 57–63

—— and SIMKISS, K. 1959. A study of the egg shells of ratite birds. *Proc. Zool. Soc. London. 133(2)*, 201–43, 12 text-figs., 3 pls

WILKES, O. R. and SCARLETT, R. J. 1964. Further Heaphy River excavations. *N.Z. Archaeol. Assn. Newsletter 7(3)*, 128

—— —— and BORAMAN, G. 1963. Two Moa-hunter sites in North-west Nelson. *N.Z. Archaeol. Assn. Newsletter 6(2)*, 88

WILLIAMS, G. R. 1962. Extinction and the land and freshwater-inhabiting birds of New Zealand. *Notornis 10(1)*, 15–32

—— 1962. Extinction and the Anatidae of New Zealand. *Wildfowl Trust Ann. Rep. 15*, 140–6

WOOLFENDEN, G. E. 1965. Bird remains from a Kentucky Indian midden. *Quart. J. Fla. Acad. Sci. 28*, 115–16

YALDWYN, J. C. 1962. Faunal material-bone. Pp. 256–63, table 3, in SMART, C. D. and GREEN, R. C. A stratified dune site at Tairua, Coromandel. *Dominion Mus. Rec. Ethnol. 1(7)*

32 Remains of Fishes and other Aquatic Animals

M. L. RYDER

THIS ACCOUNT concentrates on vertebrate fishes, but all aquatic animals of archaeological interest are mentioned because there is little distinction archaeologically between the group of animals known zoologically as fishes, and the other aquatic animals that are gathered, caught, or hunted in water. Table A classifies the aquatic animals that are likely to be found on an archaeological site; most of these have been mentioned in this account, and there are no doubt others that have been omitted.

TABLE A
Aquatic animals of archaeological importance.

Invertebrates (skeleton, if any, mainly external)	Phylum *Coelenterata*	corals
	Phylum *Arthropoda*	crayfish, crabs, lobsters, barnacles (*Crustacea*)
	Phylum *Mollusca*	shell-fish, cuttlefish, octopus
	Phylum *Echinodermata*	sea urchin
Vertebrates (internal skeleton)	Phylum *Chordata*	fishes
		Amphibia—frogs, newts
		Reptiles—turtles
		Mammals—Rodents: beaver
		Carnivores: otters, seals, sea-lions, walruses
		Cetacea: whales, dolphins
		Sirenia: dugong (sea-cows)

FISHES

Fishes breathe by gills. They have a body that is divided into a trunk and a muscular tail. There is a tail fin with dorsal and ventral lobes, and there are paired pectoral and pelvic fins representing limbs. On the back and belly are median unpaired dorsal and ventral fins. In the lowest fishes (including the sharks and rays, Fig. 80a) the skeleton is cartilaginous; in the more advanced fishes, the teleosts (Fig. 80b), the skeleton is bony, and the gill slits are covered by a bony flap, the operculum. Most fishes have an external skeleton of small scales which are formed in the skin.

There seems to be no agreed way of classifying fishes; different sources often give a different name and status to even the major groups. The classification of Goodrich[1]

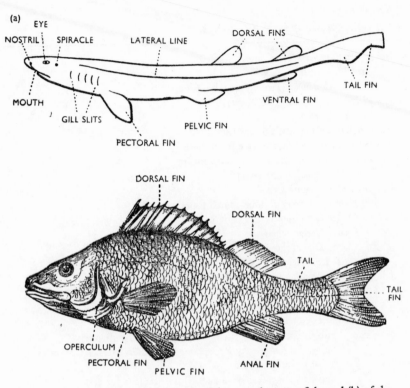

Fig. 80 External features (a) of the dogfish, a cartilaginous fish, and (b) of the perch, a bony fish.

is authoritative and detailed, and another is given by Norman[2] for British fishes, which Wells[3] apparently follows. The classification given in Table B is simplified from Romer[4] with additions from Young.[5] The most recent is by P. H. Greenwood et al.[55]

Evolution of the fish skeleton and survey of fish types. A brief consideration of its evolution will give a better understanding of the fish skeleton. The eel-like lampreys, lacking jaws and rayed fins, are the most primitive living vertebrates, and as adults they live parasitically on other fishes. Their skeleton is cartilaginous and includes a simple cranium, gill-bars, and a poorly developed backbone. The evolutionary advance to bony fishes is accompanied by the development of jaws with teeth, and paired fins. Jaws are thought to have arisen from the first pair of skeletal bars that lay between the gill openings in the ancestors of the lampreys. The possible way in which this took place is illustrated by Zeuner.[6] Teeth have their origin in the shark group. The skin of sharks contains pointed scales (denticles) that give it a rough texture (shagreen). The teeth of sharks are similar to denticles, and it seems likely that teeth arose from the denticles along the edge of the mouth, becoming enlarged in the process. The first function of teeth was to prevent prey escaping from the mouth, and for this reason the teeth of fish usually point backwards into the mouth.

Sharks (the *elasmobranchs*) range in size from the small dogfish, common around

TABLE B
Brief classification of main fish groups.

Class *Agnatha* (jawless vertebrates)
    Three fossil orders
    Order *Cyclostomata* (*Petromyzon*—lampreys)
Class *Placodermi* (archaic jawed fishes)
    Two fossil orders
Class *Chondrichthyes* (cartilaginous fishes)
    Order *Cladoselachii* (primitive fossil sharks)
    Order *Elasmobranchii* (sharks, skates and rays)
    Order *Holocephali* (chimaeras)
Class *Osteichthyes* (bony fishes)
    Sub-class *Crossopterygii* (lobe-finned fishes)
        Order *Osteolepidoti*
        Order *Coelocanthini*
        Order *Dipnoi* (lung-fishes)
    Sub-class *Actinopterygii* (ray-finned fishes)
        Order *Palaeoniscoidei* (*Polypterus*—bichir)
        Order *Chondrostei* (*Acipenser*—sturgeon)
        Order *Holostei* (*Amia*-bowfin, *Lepidosteus*—gar-pike)
        Order *Teleostei*
            Sub-order *Isospondyli*: *Clupea* (herring), *Salmo* (trout)
            Sub-order *Ostariophysi*: *Cyprinus* (carp), *Tinca* (tench), *Silurus* (cat-fish), *Rutilus* (roach)
            Sub-order *Apodes*: *Anguilla* (eel), *Conger* (conger eel)
            Sub-order *Mesichthyes*: *Esox* (pike), *Belone* (gar-fish), *Exocoetus* (flying-fish), *Hippocampus* (sea-horse), *Gasterosteus* (stickleback), *Syngnathus* (pipe-fish)
            Sub-order *Acanthopterygii*: *Zeus* (john dory), *Perca* (perch), *Labrus* (wrasse), *Uranoscopus* (star gazer), *Blennius* (blenny), *Gadus* (whiting), *Pleuronectes* (plaice), *Solea* (sole), *Lophius* (angler-fish)

Britain, to the large whale sharks of the tropics, but form only a small proportion of living fishes. The rays and skates mainly eat shell-fish, and their teeth have been modified into flattened crushing plates. In addition, their body has become flattened for living on the sea-bed; their pectoral fins have become enlarged, and their tail has been reduced. Some of the denticles in the tail have enlarged to form spines.

A much more important group are the *Osteichthyes*. In these the cartilaginous skeleton has become replaced by bone, and additional bones, known as dermal or membrane bones, have arisen. These have no cartilaginous precursor in the embryo. At the beginning of their evolution the *Osteichthyes* divided into two groups: the *Crossopterygii* (lobe-finned fishes) and the *Actinopterygii* (ray-finned fishes). The *Crossopterygii* were not successful as fishes, but were important in giving rise to the land vertebrates. The first order (Table B) is extinct and the second order (*Coelocanthini*) was thought to be extinct until the first of several specimens was caught off South Africa in 1939. The third order (*Dipnoi*, or lung-fishes) has only three types, one in each of Australia, South America and Africa. These have short jaws and fan-shaped crushing teeth. The skeleton of the paired fins consist of pre- and post-axial jointed radials articulating with a median jointed axis, a structure that gave rise to the limb of land vertebrates.

In the *Actinopterygii*, except in rare instances, the paired fins are composed only of a web of skin supported by slender rays. The oldest ray-fins (*Palaeoniscoidei*), a living representative of which is the Nile bichir, have thick, shiny, rhomboid scales. The bichir has a dorsal fin that is divided into a series of parts, and the pectoral fins have a fleshy lobe. The sturgeon (*Chondrostei*), like the bichir, is a survivor of an ancient group. The tail fin is shark-like, the jaws lack teeth, the skeleton is almost entirely cartilaginous, and the scales comprise many small denticles, and five rows of large bony scutes. The *Holostei* are represented today by the fresh-water gar-pikes (Central and North America) and bowfin (North America).

The *Teleostei* include all fishes familiar to us, except those already mentioned, and number about 20,000 species. The scales have become thin and flexible, and overlap, and the hind ends of the jaw bones are not fixed to the skull, allowing a wide gap. Most of the group live in the sea, and are more abundant in shallow coastal waters where food is plentiful. The smaller numbers that inhabit the high seas are unlikely to be encountered by archaeologists. Many teleosts live in fresh water and there are 34 species of fresh-water fishes in Great Britain,[7] to which have recently been added 10 aliens, e.g. rainbow trout, bass and carp; Fitter[7] thinks that the carp might have been introduced in the Middle Ages. Wells[3] describes 164 British sea fishes (of all types). The majority of teleosts lay numerous eggs that float near the surface, but some lay eggs that develop on the bottom. The salmon lives in salt water, but ascends fresh-water streams to breed; that is, it is anadromous. The eel on the other hand is caradromous, it lives in streams, and migrates to the ocean, crossing the Atlantic, to spawn; the young elvers spend three years on the return journey.

There are great variations in size and body shape among the teleosts from the 'standard' streamlined bodies (Fig. 80b) of fast-swimming fishes such as the trout, to the elongated eel shape, as well as many bizarre shapes, e.g. the sea-horse. The teleosts are on the whole flattened laterally, so that the flat-fishes (plaice and sole) have become adapted to bottom living by turning over on to their side, the dorso-ventral flattening found in the rays being impossible in fish that were already thin laterally. The head appears incongruous, having two eyes on one side, because the eye of the underside migrates around to the upper surface in the young flat-fish. Despite these different shapes, the teleosts are a difficult group to classify, and it is a disadvantage to those students interested in the skeleton that their identification is often based on external features.

The classification into sub-orders followed here (Table B) is that of Young.[5] The *Isospondyli* (salmon, trout and herring) show primitive features in the large maxillae (upper jaw bones), and the posterior position of the pelvic fins. In the *Ostariophysi* (carp, roach and catfish) the anterior vertebrae are modified to form a separate chain of bones, the Weberian ossicles, joining the swim-bladder to the ear. The *Apodes* (eels) have many primitive features. The *Mesichthyes* (pike, flying-fish, sea-horse) link the more primitive types with the more highly developed *Acanthopterygians* (perches, flat-fishes and gadids—cod, haddock, ling). These have stiff spines at the front of their dorsal and anal fins, the body is short, as is the maxilla bone, and the pelvic fins lie far forward (Fig. 80b).

The skeleton of fishes in detail. What are fish bones like when encountered in archaeological excavations? The only parts that are likely to be preserved from cartilaginous fishes are teeth and denticles—particularly any that have become enlarged to form spines (Fig. 81a). The bones of bony fish are irregular in shape, and have a rough texture.[8] They often have sharp points, and are often brown in colour as opposed to the yellow-white bones of higher vertebrates. Some fish bones appear very like horn. One has done well if one can state that fish bones have been found, because to go further and identify species is very difficult even when comparative material is available. Skull bones on the whole have specific differences, but in my experience the most common fish bones are vertebrae, and although these can be reported as say 'of cod size', the difficulty is that large vertebrae from a small species might be similar in size to the small ones of another, but larger, species. As with the identification of any animal material, the only way is to build up a reference collection of known skeletons from the area in question. However, it is advisable to measure the diameter of each vertebra found, and to report the frequency with which each diameter occurs. Then, later, someone with a greater knowledge of fish bones may be able to use these statistics to identify the species to which they belong.

The cartilaginous elasmobranchs are described by Daniel.[9] The denticles (placoid scales), like teeth, are made of a core of dentine (ivory), the base of which is surrounded by cement (bone), and the point of which is covered with a cap of enamel. The point of a spine is bent acutely upon the base, which is bean-shaped, and much larger than the spine itself (Fig. 81a). The cartilaginous skeleton is impregnated with calcium salts and may well be preserved

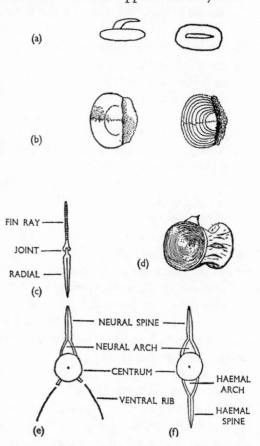

Fig. 81 (a) Spine of a ray (enlarged placoid scale), side view (left), top view (right); only the spine projects above the skin surface: the oval base-plate lies within the skin; (b) cycloid scales of herring: one annual growth ring (left), eight growth rings (right); (c) dorsal fin of bony fish showing supporting radial; (d) archaeological specimen of a centrum from bony fish—note broken arch; (e) trunk vertebra and (f) tail vertebra from bony fish. (b) After Kyle,[11] (d) from Ryder.[8]

in certain conditions. The brain-case or cranium has a nasal capsule at the front, a large orbit at each side, and an auditory capsule at the back. Attached to the back of the skull is the vertebral column. The upper jaw is not fused to the cranium, but is suspended by a cartilage and some ligaments. Both upper and lower jaws bear teeth. Behind the jaws are the skeletal arches of the gill slits. The cartilaginous vertebrae consist of a basal centrum or body, with concave ends, on top of which lies the neural arch. In the tail there is also a ventral haemal arch. In some elasmobranchs (e.g. the rays) the vertebrae of the trunk region are fused into a continuous rod. The median and paired fins are supported by jointed cartilaginous rods known as radials. The edge of the fin is strengthened by horny dermal fin rays known as ceratotrichia. The radials of the paired fins form a series starting with larger rods at the base. These basal rods articulate with the girdles lying transversely across the body. The pectoral (shoulder) girdle is an incomplete hoop, whereas the pelvic girdle is merely a transverse rod.

The typical bony teleostian fishes have a relatively shorter body than the elasmobranchs, and in some of them the pelvic fins are in front of the pectoral fins. The thin bony scales may be circular or oval in shape; some have smooth edges (cycloid scales), others have serrated edges (ctenoid scales), and are rough to the touch.[10] This distinction can sometimes help to distinguish species, e.g. the dab has ctenoid scales, whereas the plaice has cycloid scales.[11] The eels do not have visible scales, and the silurids never have them. The scales show rings of growth which indicate the age of the fish. In spring and summer when growth is rapid many rings are laid down, but as the growth slows and almost ceases in winter the rings become fewer in number, and closer together. These winter rings form a band which marks off a year's growth, though some may be due to unequal growth in summer[11] (Fig. 81b).

Age can also be determined from similar rings on the otoliths or ear-stones. These are elongated and often angular, porcelain-like aggregations of calcium carbonate found free in each ear cavity. They have a flattened appearance, and show growth rings on their broad face (Plate XVII). As otoliths are sure to be as old as the fish, they probably give a more accurate indication of age than scales, which can begin to grow during life. Otoliths are also useful in indicating fish when all other remains have decayed. Gregory[12] states that certain species have characteristic otoliths that allow identification, and Mr J. M. Moreland of the Dominion Museum, Wellington, New Zealand, has found otoliths useful in the identification of archaeological material.[13] Certain bones, too, exhibit growth rings; Kyle[11] illustrates them in an opercula bone, and Wells[3] states that the fin rays (of cod) when sectioned transversely, show microscopic growth rings. Such a microscopic approach, similar to that described in other chapters by Sandison and myself, is likely to be used increasingly in the future.[14, 15] The horny plugs in the ears of whales show six-monthly growth rings that indicate age.

The skull can be divided into brain case, additional dermal bones (bones lacking a cartilaginous precursor in the embryo) and splanchno-cranium (jaws and gill arches). It is a complicated structure of often flattish irregular-shaped bones (Fig. 82). Gregory[12] illustrates the skulls of many teleosts, but the bones readily separate from one another, as can be seen if the head of a fish is boiled, so the skull is unlikely to be found intact.

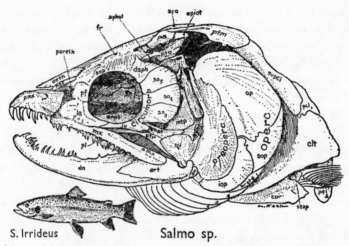

Fig. 82 Skull of bony fish (*Salmo irrideus*—a Pacific Salmon). Key from Gregory[12] (some bones not mentioned in the present text are omitted): dn—dentary, art—articular, qu—quadrate, pmx—premaxilla, pl—palatine, mx—maxilla, pareth—parethmoid, fr—frontal, sphot—sphenotic, soc—supra-occipital, epiot—epiotic, ptm—post-temporal, supcl—supra-cleithrum, clt—cleithrum, pcl—post-cleithrum, cor—coracoid, scap—scapula, brste—branchiostegal rays. From Gregory.[12]

Apart from the jaws, other bones in the roof of the mouth bear teeth. The gill cover or operculum is supported by four flat bones, and the branchiostegal membrane below the operculum is supported by branchiostegal rays. These are often found as archaeological remains, and consist of stoutish, curved bones, not unlike the ribs of a mammal, ending in a blunt point. There are five gill arches; the inner surface of these often bears teeth, and the posterior border often has small spine-like processes known as gill rakers. The teeth of teleosts are like those of the cartilaginous fishes. The vertebral column is composed of distinct bony vertebrae. The body of each vertebra has concave ends, and is constricted in the middle into the shape of an hourglass (Fig. 81d). Dorsally there is a pair of processes that unite to form the neural arch. In the trunk region each vertebra bears a pair of ventro-lateral processes to which ventral ribs are attached (Fig. 81e). In the tail region these processes are bent downwards and united to form the haemal arch. The haemal arches are extended to form the haemal spines (Fig. 81f). In the region of the ventral fins (Fig. 83) there are radials below the haemal spines, and the radials articulate with the fin rays. In some fishes the radials of the tail fin are flattened to form plates lying in the median plane of the body.

The neural arches are prolonged to form neural spines. These are surmounted by radials (Fig. 81c) in the regions of the dorsal fins, and the radials articulate with the dermal rays that support the fins. The fin rays of bony fishes (lepidotrichia) are bony, jointed, and often branched, unlike the horny unjointed ceratotrichia of cartilaginous fishes. In the more highly evolved bony fishes the joint between the fin rays and the radials enables the fin to be raised and lowered.

The bones of the pectoral (shoulder) girdle (Figs. 82 and 83) corresponding to those of the cartilaginous fishes comprise the dorsal scapula, the ventral coracoid, and the meso-

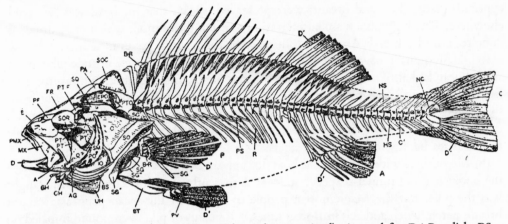

Fig. 83 Skeleton of perch. Key from Young[5] (some bones omitted): A—anal fin, B+R radials, BS—branchiostegal rays, BT—basipterygium, C—caudal (tail) fin, C′—centrum, D′—dermal fin rays, HS—haemal spine, NS—neural spine, O—operculum, P—pectoral fin, PS—rib processes, PV—pelvic fin, R—ribs, SG—shoulder girdle. After Dean.

coracoid. There are also some dermal bones, the cleithrum, post-cleithrum and supra-cleithrum. The supra-cleithrum articulates with the post-temporal of the skull, attaching the pectoral girdle to the back of the skull. The pectoral fin articulates with the girdle by means of several short radials, and the web of the fin is supported by rays that articulate with the radials. The first (anterior) ray is larger than the rest, and often articulates directly with the scapula. In some fishes, e.g. the silurids (catfish), this articulates independently from the rest of the fin and is armed with spikes on each side. These rays are very characteristic, and some were found in the recent Seelands dig in Australia (see below). The pelvic skeleton consists of only a single, flat triangular bone, the basipterygium, on each side, and the radials of the pelvic fin are much reduced.

ARCHAEOLOGICAL SURVEY

1. *Fish remains in Europe and the Near East.* Perhaps the earliest aquatic animals used for food were shell-fish. The Neanderthal men of Devil's Tower, Gibraltar, derived much of their food from limpets and mussels, and shell-fish appear to have contributed to European subsistence ever since.[17] However, a diet in which shell-fish are the mainstay is normally associated with a low level of attainment and shell-fish occupied only a subsidiary place in communities which hunted and fished with vigour. On the other hand, a hominid older than *Zinjanthropus* found recently in Tanganyika[18] had apparently eaten catfish.

(a) Upper Palaeolithic hunter-fishers. Although remains of fishing gear are rare, abundant fish bones, and representations in Magdalenian cave art, show that fishing was already carried out in Upper Palaeolithic times.[16, 17] The Magdalenians of the Dordogne caves (France) caught pike, trout, dace, chub, bream and white bream, as well as salmon. It is likely that the salmon were caught at some distance away when they came upstream in summer. The lack of salmon skull bones in the caves, whereas skull bones of the frailer cyprinids (dace, chub and bream) were preserved, shows that the head was removed elsewhere. This suggests a seasonal migration to catch the salmon, which were dried, as done recently by North American Indians to be eaten in the caves in winter.

Representations in cave art in northern Spain and southern France include pike, trout and salmon, and also, near the coast, flat-fish and tunny. But the latter do not prove sea-fishing. Well-preserved fish bones are rare on coastal sites, and these are mainly from species like wrasses that could be taken close inshore. The inhabitants of the Grimaldi caves on the Mediterranean shore ate many shell-fish. Perhaps these people were unable to fish at sea because of the lack of boats.

(b) Mesolithic hunter-fishers. The boat first appeared in Mesolithic times together with the hook, net and funnel-shaped trap.[16, 17] Apparently the most common fish caught was the pike, but the Maglemosian people of the north European plain also caught bream, perch, tench and eels in Boreal times.[16] Remains of pike were found impaled on spear-points in lake deposits at Kunda, Esthonia, and in southern Sweden. On one lake site in north Zealand 80 upper and 64 left lower jaw bones of pike were found. The preponderance of skull bones at Svaerdborg may indicate that the pike were dried to be eaten elsewhere. The suggestion quoted by Clark[16] that the head bones were more likely to survive is not borne out by my experience, which is that the most common fish bones to survive are vertebrae. Surprisingly, no osteological evidence of fishing was found at Star Carr,[19] the early Mesolithic lake-side site at Seamer near Scarborough, Yorkshire.

Towards the end of Mesolithic times there is evidence for the beginning of sea-fishing from boats.[16, 17] The Tardenoisian middens of Téviec and Hoëdic on the south coast of Brittany yielded bones of sea-fish. Although fishing was more important than hunting, shell-fish still predominated and wrasse and other labrid remains indicated inshore fishing only.

Cod bones were found in an Early Atlantic level at Cushendun in Northern Ireland, and early sites on Oronsay have yielded remains of black sea-bream, probably caught from the rocks, as well as conger, haddock, common sea-bream, ballan wrasse, thorn-back ray, skate, a number of sharks, and claws of crabs, which suggest fishing from boats.

Several Mesolithic III sites on the Littorina shores of Denmark had middens containing marine shell-fish, yet the vertebrate fish were mainly fresh-water types.[16] At Ertebölle most of the fish remains were from eel, roach and pike, yet bones from cod, flounder and gar-fish indicate sea-fishing. The occurrence of remains of large haddock and coalfish, which live at depths of from 40 to 100 metres, shows that the Ertebölle people of Denmark must have caught fish by line from boats at a good distance from the shore. Clark[17] considers that this off-shore fishing was more effective after the advent of farming: there were numerous haddock and cod bones in the Sölanger midden, most of which is Neolithic.

(c) The Neolithic period to the Iron Age. The advent of farming, and its continued development, increased the population, and this increased the demand for fish. Improved tackle (barbed hooks, metal fish-spears, net sinkers, and the development of weirs) increased the efficiency of fishing. But the full possibilities were not realized until historical times, the development of herring fishing, for example, being associated with the rise of an urban economy.

From Neolithic times then the fisherman was usually a farmer, fishing being a seasonal occupation that led to seasonal settlements. At Jarmo in Iraq, a few fish and fresh-water crabs added to protein variety.[20] The 'lake dwellings' of Europe have yielded many fish scales and fish bones. The most common species from the Swiss sites were pike, and Clark[16] considers that many of the roach, dace, chub and perch caught may have been used as live-bait for pike. Other fish caught by the inhabitants were carp, burbot, and a salmon.

Although most lakes and rivers were fished to satisfy day-to-day needs, certain fisheries were developed around the anadromous salmon and sturgeon, and the cara-dromous eel. Clark[16] gives evidence of salmon fishing at certain points on Irish rivers (cf. the North American Indians); the lack of fish remains at such sites supports the sug-gestion that the fish were cured and taken away. It is likely that the sturgeon was fished seasonally in the Danube, remains having been found on two sites.[16] Although eel remains have been recovered from Stone Age sites in Jutland and Gotland, there is little evidence that eels were fished extensively. Young may have been taken in the run up-stream, but remains of these are unlikely to survive.

There is evidence for a line fishery off the northern and western shores of Britain based on cod, but including coalfish, dogfish, skate, other rays, conger, gurnet, grey mullet, wrasse, haddock, tope, angel-fish, bream, rudd and accompanied by crab catching.[16] Petrie in 1866 found 'apparently sillock or coalfish' bones in the midden at Skara Brae on Orkney, as well as cod bones and a building mortar to which ground fish bones had been added.

Off-shore fisheries were carried on in the Skagerrak by people occupying the northern parts of the west coast of Sweden at the close of the Stone Age.[16, 17] The contents of three middens yielded mainly cod, ling and haddock with smaller numbers of ballan wrasse, whiting and pollack, all of which are bottom feeders. One of the eight haddock from Rotekärrslid, and two of the ninety-seven from Rörvik were larger than the maxi-mum size caught there today, and many of the ling were large. This apparent reduction in size might appear to be associated with recent over-fishing, but it must be noted that only two of the forty-eight cod from Rörvik were as much as 0·97 m. long as compared with the present maximum of 1·5 m. and there is evidence that fishing, by reducing competition among the fish, stimulates growth.[5]

A midden at Anneröd yielded cod and numerous haddock, as well as whiting, pollack, tunny and flounder. That this fishery was by line is suggested by a Bronze Age rock-engraving in south Sweden showing men fishing from a boat with a hook and line.[17] A Neolithic settlement at Hemmor, Gotland, yielded 5,343 cod bones, and numerous fish-hooks, indicating line-fishing. Sea-fishing in Denmark, continued to be concentrated on the southern shores of the Kattegat. The Sölanger midden has already been men-tioned; cod was also found at the Bronze Age site of Fyen, and at the Iron Age site of Borrebjerg on Sejerö.

Clark[17] considers that the biggest sea fisheries in prehistoric Europe were those of

Norway; the deep fjords bring bottom-feeding fish close in to shore. The earliest traces were found at Viste, near Stavanger, which was occupied by hunter-fishers probably before farming spread to Norway. Here cod was the most common fish; other remains came from haddock, ling, pollack, torsk, conger, ballan wrasse and striped wrasse.[16] Later, fishing accompanied farming and became seasonal in character, which must have resulted in the drying of fish (see medieval period below). Two engravings of skin-covered boats show halibut caught on a line.

Herring remains are almost absent from prehistoric sites in Europe, although herring fishing was well established by Domesday. Clark[17] considers that herring fishing was not developed because the needs of small communities of farmer-fishers did not justify the labour involved in making the nets.

(d) The ancient Mediterranean civilizations. The classical archaeologists of Mesopotamia, Egypt, Greece and Rome tended to concentrate on art treasures, and it is not often that animal remains appear in publications about these periods. Hilzheimer,[21] in what he states is the first study of bones from a Mesopotamian site, lists fish among the remains from Tell Asmar, the period of which is given as from Early Dynastic III to Gutian. These formed 3·4% of the total remains from both domestic and wild animals; no species are given. Bird bones formed only 2·5% of the remains. Braidwood and Reed[20] state that the irrigation canals of Sumer were a source of fish.

Engravings and other representations of fish become more common in this period. One species that is abundantly represented in ancient art is the Nile fish *Tilapia nilotica*. Thompson[22] illustrates an engraving of one of these from a Vth Dynasty tomb. He also shows an engraving of two men carrying a giant Nile perch (*Perca nilotica*) from Medum (*c.* 2780 BC). According to Childe[23] the ancient Egyptians imported dried fish from the Arabian Sea, and Thompson[22] states that salted fish are well preserved on Egyptian sites. Along with many other animals fishes were mummified.[24] With the advent of these civilizations literary sources are added to representations and remains, and with the ancient Greeks the first interest in biology arose; Aristotle knew a great deal about fishes. Thompson[22] lists ancient Greek names for fishes, and gives many illustrations, e.g. his frontispiece illustrates a well-known vase of the fourth century BC showing a tunny-merchant cutting up fish. The ancient Macedonians are said to have been the first to fish with artificial flies.

The Romans held fishing contests, cultivated oysters, and had fish-ponds in their markets to ensure that fish would be fresh, although they imported sea-fish from Germany.[25] In Rome there was a sacrificial custom in which small fishes were caught in the Tiber and burnt alive in honour of the god Vulcan.[26] One oyster shell comprised the only remains from fish that I found among some animal bones from the Roman cemetery in Trentholme Drive, York, excavated by Mr L. P. Wenham in 1957–58. There had been other shells in previous years among these bones which came from food buried with the dead for their journey into the next world.

(e) The Medieval period. The only fish bone reported from an Early Christian Crannog in Northern Ireland was a branchiostegal ray that was probably from cod.[27] The inhabitants of a tenth-century settlement at Mawgan Porth, Cornwall, ate mussels, but the only evidence of fishing came from a few perforated stones that may have been used as net or line sinkers.[28]

The animal remains of thirteenth-century date found at Clough Castle, Co. Down,[29] included the following marine mollusca: edible cockle (*Cardium edule*), great scallop (*Pecten maximus*), common periwinkle (*Littorina littorea*), edible mussel (*Mytilus edulis*) and oyster (*Ostrea edulis*). In addition there were remains from cod (including vertebrae) and probably wrasse, haddock and perch (scales). Some of the cod bones showed a diseased condition known as hyperostosis (extra growth of bone). The cause of this is unknown; it is found today and may be associated with age.

The excavations carried out during the last ten years at Kirkstall Abbey (1152–1540) yielded numerous oyster and mussel shells, as well as a few cockles and whelks (*Buccinum undatum*).[30] These are thought to have been eaten more before the monks were allowed to eat meat, because fewer were found in a midden associated with the meat kitchen built about 1450. These shell-fish must have come from the coast and some fifteenth-century records of Fountains Abbey[31] refer to oysters being bought at York, Hull and Scarborough (respectively 25, 50 and 70 miles from Leeds). I know of no records of the way in which these were transported; they may have been carried in barrels of salt water, but it is now known that if oysters are kept cool and moist they become dormant and remain alive for months.* It is of interest that the same records mention 'seal fish' which were apparently regarded as being fish rather than 'flesh'. The oyster shells at Kirkstall were only about half the size of modern adult oysters, and had only one or two (annual) growth rings, indicating that they were young.[32]

The midden yielded only a small proportion of fish bones among the thousands of animal bones found.[33] There were about as many fish bones as bird bones, and most were apparently too large to have come from fresh-water fish. In 1956 eight large vertebrae, probably from cod, were found, and there were branchiostegal rays of normal cod size. In 1957 forty fish bones were found; one vertebra had a diameter of 7 mm being comparable in size to a modern salmon vertebra. There were eleven other vertebrae, and the frequencies of the diameters (in mm) of those found in 1956 and 1957 are: 12 mm (1), 13 (1), 16 (4), 17 (3), 18 (2), 19 (3), 20 (1), 22 (2), 23 (2). There were also branchiostegal rays, fin rays, ribs, and skull bones that could not be identified. One skull bone was from a fish larger than cod. In addition, there was a dermal spine from a large ray (Fig. 82). In 1958 the fish bones were of cod size; there were two skull bones, two branchiostegal rays, and three vertebrae with diameters of 13, 16 and 17 mm. Some of the unidentified bones may have been from haddock, ling or the fresh-water pike. Fitter[7] says that this was transported to likely ponds in the Middle Ages, and Kirkstall along with other monasteries had its own fish-ponds. The records of Fountains[31] mention salmon, cured sprats (*Clupea sprattus*), and that 'stock-fish' (dried or salted fish, probably cod and ling) were bought at the above three ports. Speed (1631) said that dried fish were imported from Norway and Iceland.

Excavations carried out at Pontefract Priory (1090–1540) from 1957 to 1959 yielded

* The Inca runners could carry fish and shell-fish from the Pacific 170 miles over the mountains and deliver it fresh to Cuzco.

about 300 animal bones of which thirteen were from fishes, and only six of these were stratified.[34] One bone was definitely from cod, and most of the others were of cod size; three vertebrae had diameters of 12, 13 and 23 mm. There was one mussel shell, and thirty-five oysters, which were larger than those from Kirkstall.

About 400 animal bones, of which five were from fishes, were found in excavations in Petergate, York, in 1957 and 1958, through levels dating from the fourteenth century back to the eleventh century.[35] These comprise two parts of the pectoral girdle, of which one had a knife cut, and was identified as cod, a skull bone, and two vertebrae 14 and 16 mm in diameter. The second of these was from the extreme anterior end (disk-shaped) and was therefore the largest in the body. There were 147 oyster shells, 49 cockles, one scallop and one whelk. It is known that the Archbishop of York had 'salmon garths' on the river Ouse, and a record of 1465 mentions the large number of pike that were eaten at one of his feasts.

Of about 3,000 bones found during the first ten years' excavation at the village of Wharram Percy, deserted about 1500, perhaps 50 were from fishes.[36] Cod bones were identified amongst these, and many were of cod size, but there were a few smaller ones, possibly from fresh-water fish. The diameters (in mm) and dates of the vertebrae (frequency in brackets) were as follows: thirteenth century, 14, 22; fourteenth century, 5 (2), 6, 8, 9, 11, 16, 17, 18, 20 (first of column), 20 (2), 24; fifteenth century, 5, 12, 13. There was one oyster shell, and a fragment that was possibly from a whelk shell. It is most interesting that sea-fish, including shell-fish, reached this isolated village on the Yorkshire Wolds.

2. *Whales and Seals in Europe*. Whales[37] and seals[38] were hunted off European shores as early as the Stone Age, but space forbids a consideration of the details, which are discussed by Clarke.[17]

3. *Findings outside Europe*.

(a) *Africa*. Goodwin[39] describes prehistoric coastal fishing methods in South Africa. He describes tidal fish-traps (*vywers*) made of 'dry' stone walls. These occur for at least 1,000 miles roughly from Cape Town to Zululand. Many are still in use, often with ground-bait; they are covered at high tide, and as the tide ebbs, water is lost through the stones leaving any fish stranded. At Oakhurst shelter near George, some distance from and 300 feet above the sea, there is a series of local Later Stone Age strata. In the pre-Wilton levels few fish bones or otoliths occur, whereas above that level they increase in number and variety and include scales. As otoliths would not have disappeared, the appearance of fish remains is comparatively recent, and is associated with the discovery of a means of catching fish in quantity. The lack of other implements indicates these traps which are accordingly Wilton and post-Wilton in date.

Species identified include bishop (*Pagrus*), elft (*Pomatomus*) and eagle ray (*Myliobatis*). At Klip Kop cave, Hermanus, fishes of the generea *Pagrus*, *Dentex*, *Sparus*, and *Diplodus*, all in the modern fauna, were identified. This local Wilton culture is characterized by the replacement of microliths with shell implements. The shells used were *Mytilus* (common mussel) and *Donax*. The same sequence occurs in many middens along the coast: the earliest levels have neither fish nor pottery; the next have fish but no pottery, and the most recent levels contain fish and pottery. Some middens associated with some *vywers*, possibly used a century ago, comprised conical heaps of shells 3–4 ft high, and 9–10 ft in diameter, and each heap contains only one type of shell, possibly reflecting the way in which available supplies were used.

(b) *Asia*. Mongait[40] does not mention sea-fishing in his general survey, *Archaeology in the USSR*. But in the third or Serov phase (third millennium BC) of the Siberian Neolithic he says that fresh-water fishing played as great a role as hunting. Fish were caught with nets, harpoons, and arrows, the fish-hook being invented later in the same phase. Stone images of fish are common, and even though schematic, they are good representations of salmon, whitefish, ling, sturgeon and others. Two of these are illustrated;[40] one 28 cm long is an exact representation with mouth, eyes, fins and scales, whereas the other has only the shape of a fish, with a mouth. It was thought that these images were used in a ritual to ensure fishing success. Now it is considered that they were used as decoys, and each has several holes from which the stone could have been suspended. A pile settlement in the Charozero District of the second millennium BC had heaps of fish scales and bones between the dwellings, as well as remains of woven fish-traps and bone harpoons. In the early Chinese Neolithic between 3500 and 2000 BC there were at least two riverine cultures in which farming activities were supplemented by well-developed fishing and mollusc-collecting activities. The later Neolithic in south China had a maritime orientation.[41]

(c) *Oceania*. Gifford[42] excavated a coastal site in Fiji and another not far inland. These have since been dated as belonging to the first century BC. The artifacts resemble those of Melanesia to the west, rather than Polynesia to the east. He found two main cultural levels: lower layers without shell, upper layers with shell, and either the earlier people did not eat shell-fish, or they dumped the shells elsewhere. Bones of vertebrate fish, domestic pig, and evidence of cannibalism were found in each level. The weight of the fish bones found was 3,113 g. compared with 4,950 g. of bones from other animals. Although most of the fish bones could not be identified, e.g. vertebrae, some identifications were made from jaws, and evidence of 20 species as well as several genera was obtained. Five of the species had not been reported from Fiji before. The weight of bones found at the different levels, and the depths at which the different species were found, are indicated in tables. The only other aquatic vertebrate found was the green turtle (*Chelonia mydas*). This is the shore turtle of tropical seas that is commonly eaten by man.

There was so much shell material that only sufficient shells were collected to indicate species; the many species identified (shown in tables) are all found in Fijian waters today, and some are still eaten. The large white cowry (*Ovulum ovum*) which is used today as an external house decoration was not found in the excavations; on the other hand, a smaller cowry (*Cypraea eburnea*), used as a personal ornament, was found. When spider shells (*Pterocera lambis*) are collected today, the sharp projections are immediately broken off. The animal is often obtained by shattering the shell, and the fragmentary specimens indicate that this was done in the past. Shell had been used to make knives, fish-hooks and ornaments. A few small crustacean fragments were found, and these were mainly concentrated in the shell layer. Four species of crab were identified, and only one of these was among the two species eaten today. Two echinoderms—a sand dollar and a heart urchin—were identified, as well as specimens of coral.

Gifford and Shutler[43] excavated eleven sites in New Caledonia, a large island about 1,000 miles off the coast of Queensland, which has cultural relationships with other parts of Melanesia. There were fewer fish bones than in Fiji, although nine of the eleven sites were on the coast; whereas in Fiji 1·08 g. of fish bone per cubic foot was found, here the weight was only 0·75 g. Whether this represents a true difference in the use of fish, or whether the smaller yield in New Caledonia is due to the reported practice of burning fish bones is not clear. Nevertheless, a total of 5,652 g. of bones from fishes was found, compared with 4,316 g. from other animals, including mammals introduced by Europeans. But the uneven distribution of fish bones, the absence of bones from domestic animals, and the scanty evidence of cannibalism, suggested that molluscs, and possibly also descapods (crustaceans), had been the principal sources of protein. Many of the fish bones could not be identified, but of the fourteen species recorded, nine had not been reported from New Caledonia before. Bones of the green turtle and also the loggerhead turtle (*Caretta caretta*) were found.

Mollusc shells were the most abundant animal remains; these were more plentiful in the coastal sites, and whereas in Fiji it was clear that the shells had been carried to the sites by man, here this is certain only in the inland sites. The 255 species identified were mostly marine types and comprised both bivalves and univalves, with which *Nautilus* was included, but two, *Arca scapha* and *Gafrarium tumidum*, were found in large quantities indicating frequent use for food. The author, however, admits that in some instances he has taken the liberty of omitting the doubt in the identification expressed by the malacologist, and instead listed the species as a definite identification. As there is no indication of where this has been done, the value of all the identifications is in my opinion reduced. The heaviest concentration of shells at one site was in the 24- and 30-in. levels, which later radiocarbon dating has shown to be of the sixth century BC. One level of another site was dated as first century AD. The change of species at different levels in one site suggested an environmental change; an increase in *Arca scapha* and decrease of *Potamides semitrisulcatus* suggested more sand and less mud in earlier times. Shell artifacts were next in abundance to potsherds; these comprised net sinkers, fish-hooks, money and personal ornaments. Octopus lures were also found.

Decapod shell fragments, chiefly from crab, with occasional lobster, were abundant at one site. Of the total of 6,550 g. of decapod shell from various sites, 6,369 g. came from this site. The abundance here may be explained by its proximity to shallow water, and the scarcity of shell on other sites suggested that crabs did not form a prominent part in the diet. Sea-urchin shell fragments, mostly spines, came from three sites and there were stone-like coral remains; these may merely represent beach debris, but a possible use of coral additional to the hair bleach suggested at Fiji is as a file in the manufacture of shell artifacts.

Gifford[44] excavated five sites at Yap, 'the island of stone money' which lies at the western edge of Micronesia. It is in the longitude of Tokyo, about 750 miles east of the Philippines, and is culturally associated with the Marianas Islands to the north. Radiocarbon dates show the sites to range from the second to the nineteenth century AD. Fish bones (4,053 g.) were the most abundant vertebrate remains, and the density of 2 g. per cubic foot shows that fish were used more than in Fiji and New Caledonia. In general the upper levels yielded more than the lower levels and the distribution is indicated in tables. Six species were determined, but eight genera and three families had representatives that could not be specifically determined. The frequency of each identification was indicated, and these are of interest because few fishes have ever been recorded from Yap. Again the only other aquatic vertebrate found was the turtle.

Except for coral, molluscs were the most abundant organic remains; 167 species were identified of which 52 were bivalves and 115 univalves (including *Nautilus*). The distribution by site and depth was shown in tables. The stratigraphic distribution of species indicated a constancy of food habits.

Fleming[45] discussed the use of the stratigraphical succession in a marine fauna to establish a chronology in New Zealand. He said that differences in species of mollusca in successive midden groups that had suggested changes in the distribution of the tohemanga = toheroa (*Amphidesma ventricosum*) could have been due to different food habits of the successive peoples, but the status of the toheroa is still changing on modern beaches. Decrease in the size of molluscs in more recent middens suggested the silting of estuaries, but no indication had been found of local changes in molluscan faunae comparable with those of the Yoldia and Littorina seas of the Baltic. Seal remains, however, suggested a more extensive prehistoric distribution than at present.

The first period of New Zealand prehistory is known as the Archaic Phase of New Zealand Eastern Polynesian culture.[46] This period was originally known as the *Moa*-hunter culture; *Moa*-hunter sites have been shown by radiocarbon dating to range from the eleventh to the fifteenth century. These sites commonly have shell middens and artifacts include bait-hooks, stone and bone lure-hooks and barracouta harpoon points. Ornaments found include shells and teeth from the sperm whale, porpoise and shark (*Carcharodon*). An excavation of a *Moa*-hunter site at Sarah's Gully on the Coromandel Peninsula in the North Island of New Zealand yielded abundant seal remains.[47] At the coastal site of Pounawea, which according to radiocarbon dating was first occupied before AD 1140, the diet at first consisted principally of *Moa*, with some other birds, and fish, seal and whale, but few shell-fish.[48] By AD the *Moa* had become less plentiful, and more fish and shell-fish were being eaten. Finally by AD 1660 the *Moa* had become very scarce (as a result of continued killing by the Maoris) and the diet consisted principally of shell-fish, fish, seal and small birds. The scarcity of the *Moa* caused many sites to be abandoned, new settlements being established near the new source of food on the coast. Some coastal sites, e.g. on False Island, were almost wholly connected with fishing. A large midden dated AD 1480±50 contained great quantities of fish bones, as well as mussel, paua and large cockle shells.

When European contact was established in the eighteenth century the Classic Maori phase of New Zealand Eastern Polynesian culture was dominant.[48] Sites of this period have yielded whalebone weapons, metal fish-hooks with and without barbs, more highly developed barracouta points, and lures with hooks, often in the shape of small fish. Again there were whale and shark-tooth ornaments; and there were trumpets made from a *Charonia* shell. Fortified *pa* sites are common in this period but it is not certain whether or not these extend back into the archaic period. Green[49] in a survey of *Moa*-hunter sites on the Coromandel coast said that they had mussel, limpet, periwinkle and paua shells in that order, along with bones of seal, whale and a variety of birds in addition to the *Moa*. The middens of *pa* sites on the other hand contain primarily pipi and cockle shells.

Australia, to prehistorians, is the least-known continent. At most, this vast area has been covered by five excavations of chronological or cultural significance.[50] In the excavation of a rock shelter at Fromm's Landing on the Lower Murray river, South Australia, eleven distinct levels were encountered.[51] The tenth of these has been dated by the C^{14} method as being 4850 ± 100 years old. Fish bones were found in most levels, but in only two instances was it possible to distinguish species. These were *Oligorus macquariensis* (Murray cod) which was found in several levels, and the broken spine of *Bathytoshea* (Sting ray). Four bone muduks, thought to have been used as fish gorges, were found in levels five to seven. Mollusc shells were found at all levels, and there was no significant change of species with depth. The following aquatic molluscs were identified: univalves, *Notopala hanleyi*, *Lenameria tenuistriata* (*waterhousei* and *confluens*), and *Plotiopsis tetrica*, bivalves, *Corbiculina angasi*, *Velusinio ambiguus* and *Alathyria jacksoni*, the last two of these being fresh-water mussels common in the Murray today.

Finally, in 1960, the excavation of a rock shelter was commenced at Seelands on the banks of the Clarence river in northern New South Wales. Five levels down to a depth of four feet six inches were encountered and a radiocarbon date[52] of level II gave the result AD 1040 ± 80. The fish bones, vertebrae (diameter relatively small, e.g. about 3–8 mm and often compressed laterally or dorso-ventrally), ribs, branchiostegal rays, and a few jaws were submitted by the present author to Mr G. P. Whitley of the Australian Museum in Sydney. He reported that owing to their fragmentary nature and the lack of a representative collection it was on the whole impossible to identify species. There was, however, a movable fin-ray from a catfish, and three other bones were probably from catfish. There are two species of catfish in NSW today. The shells were submitted to Dr D. F. McMichael at the same museum. He reported that there were five species of aquatic molluscs, all bivalves. There were two fresh-water mussels (*Cucumerunio novae-hollandiae* and *Velesunio ambiguus*) both found in the Clarence today. The others were marine types, although the sea is at least thirty miles away, including the common pipi (*Plebidonax deltoides*), well known to have been eaten by the aborigines; a ship worm probably belonging to the genus *Nausitora*; and finally a member of the family *Gariidae*.

CONCLUSIONS

1. There has been a tendency for all animal remains to be neglected, and 'fish' remains have probably received the least attention. This is probably due to the difficulty of

identifying species: even experienced people require a full collection of comparative specimens which takes a long time to acquire, especially in a new area such as Australia, in which there are many species.

2. Diet helps to indicate the cultural attainment of a people. Fishes, and other aquatic animals, have apparently been important as food from earliest times. In some collecting communities with a riverine or maritime orientation fish formed the main source of food. Shell-fish were probably the first aquatic animals to be collected, and remains of shell-fish on their own probably indicate a primitive people with a low level of attainment.

3. Shells provide a useful raw material, and the artifacts of some cultures are based almost entirely on shell.

4. The identity of fish species can indicate: (a) the extent to which different fishing methods were developed; (b) zoological distribution; and (c) changes in climatic as well as geological environment.

5. The identity of different bones of the body can indicate practices such as fish-drying, in which the head is removed.

6. The study of fish remains in future is likely to depend more and more on specialized knowledge possibly involving microscopical and chemical techniques.*

ACKNOWLEDGEMENT

I wish to thank my colleagues in the History and Zoology departments of the University of New England, Australia, for their helpful advice during the preparation of this article.

REFERENCES

 1 GOODRICH, E. S. 1909. *Cyclostomes and Fishes*, Part IX of LANKESTER, SIR RAY (ed.), Treatise on Zoology, London
 2 Norman, J. R. 1953. *Fishes* in List of British Vertebrates, British Museum (Natural History)
 3 WELLS, A. L. 1958. *The Observers Book of Sea Fishes*, London
 4 ROMER, A. S. 1941. *Man and the Vertebrates*, 3rd ed., Chicago
 5 YOUNG, J. Z. 1954. *The Life of Vertebrates*, Oxford
 6 ZEUNER, F. E. 1958. *Dating the Past*, 4th ed., London
 7 FITTER, R. S. R. 1959. *The Ark in our Midst*, London
 8 RYDER, M. L. 1969. *Animal Bones in Archaeology*, Oxford
 9 DANIEL, J. F. 1934. *The Elasmobranch Fishes*, Berkeley, Calif.
10 GOODRICH, E. S. 1908. *Proc. Zool. Soc.*, 751
11 KYLE, H. M. 1926. *The Biology of Fishes*, London

* A method has recently been evolved in South Africa to obtain a relative dating of shell middens.[54] Shells of *Mytilus perna* from stratified coastal middens were dissolved in dilute acetic acid, and the ratio of conchyolin (horn-like substance) to calcium carbonate in the shell was estimated. This ratio was found to decrease with the increasing age of the shells, and could therefore be used to indicate the relative age of the middens. The method was applied to Later Stone and Iron Age deposits on the Natal coast, and the results obtained were consistent with the relative dating deduced from stratification. The method is apparently capable of distinguishing between middens of different age providing the soil environments are identical. This is important because clearly an acid soil will remove calcium carbonate, and the conchyolin may decay more rapidly in some conditions than others.

12 GREGORY, W. K. 1959. *Fish Skulls*, Laurel, Florida (originally published 1933 in *Trans. Am. Phil. Soc. 33*)
13 Personal communication
14 ANDERSON, H. and JORGENSEN, J. B. 1960. *Stain. Technol. 35*, 91–95
15 MOSS, M. L. and POSNER, A. S. 1960. *Nature, 188*, 1037
16 CLARK, J. G. D. 1948. *Ant. J. 28*, 45–81
17 —— 1952. *Prehistoric Europe: The Economic Basis*, London
18 LEAKEY, L. S. B. 1961. *Nature 189*, 649f.
19 CLARK, J. G. D. 1954. *Star Carr*, Cambridge
20 BRAIDWOOD, R. J. and REED, C. A. 1957. The achievement and early consequence of food production, *Cold Spr. Harb. Symp. Quant. Biol. 22*, 19–31
21 HILZHEIMER, M. 1941. Animal remains from Tell Asmar, *Studies in Ancient Oriental Civilization*, no. 20
22 THOMPSON, D'ARCY W. 1947. *A Glossary of Greek Fishes*, Oxford
23 CHILDE, V. G. 1936. *Man Makes Himself*, London
24 LORTET, L. C. and GAILLARD, C. 1907. *Arch. Mus. Lyon 9*, Mém. 2
25 BROGAN, O. 1936. *J. Rom. Stud. 26*, 195–222
26 ROSE, H. J. 1933. *Ibid. 23*, 46–63
27 JOPE, M. 1955. *Ulster J. Arch.* 3rd ser., *18*, 77–81
28 BRUCE-MITFORD, R. L. S. (ed.) 1956. *Recent Archaeological Excavations in Britain*, London
29 JOPE, M., 1954. *Ulster J. Arch.* 3rd ser., *17*, 103–63
30 RYDER, M. L. 1959. *Agric. Hist. Rev. 7*, 1–5
31 FOWLER, J. T. (ed.). 1918. Memorials of Fountains, III, *Surtees Soc. 130*
32 YOUNG, C. M. 1960. *Oysters*, London
33 RYDER, M. L. 1961. In OWEN, D. E., Kirkstall Abbey Excavations, 1955–59. *Pub. Thoresby Society, Leeds, 48*, 107
34 —— 1965. In BELLAMY, C. V., Excavations at Pontefract Priory, *Pub. Thoresby Society, Leeds, 49*, 110
35 —— 1969. In WENHAM, L. P., Excavations in Petergate, York (forthcoming)
36 —— 1969. In HURST, J. G., Excavations at Wharram Percy (in the press)
37 CLARK, J. G. D. 1947. *Antiquity, 21*, 84–104
38 —— 1946. *Proc. Prehist. Soc. 12*, 12–48
39 GOODWIN, A. J. H. 1946. *Antiquity 20*, 134–41
40 MONGAIT, A. 1959. *Archaeology in the USSR*, Moscow; 1961. Harmondsworth
41 FAIRSERVIS, W. A. 1959. *The Origins of Oriental Civilization*, New York
42 GIFFORD, E. W. 1951. Archaeological Excavations in Fiji, *Anth. Recs. 13*, 3, Berkeley, Calif.
43 —— and SHUTLER, D., JR. 1956. Archaeological Excavations in New Caledonia, *Anth. Recs. 18*, 1
44 GIFFORD, W. S. and GIFFORD, D. S. 1959. Archaeological Excavations at Yap, *Ibid.* 2
45 FLEMING, C. A. 1953. Materials for a Recent Geochronology of New Zealand, *Report of 7th Sci. Congress, Roy. Soc. N.Z.*
46 GOLSON, J. 1959. Culture Change in Prehistoric New Zealand, in FREEMAN, J. D. and GEDDES, W. R. (eds.), *Anthropology of the South Seas*, New Plymouth
47 —— 1959. Excavations on the Coromandel Peninsula New Zealand, *N.Z. Arch. Assoc. News Letter 2* (2), 13–18
48 LOCKERBIE, L. 1959. From Moa-Hunter to Classic Maori in Southern New Zealand, in FREEMAN, J. D. and GEDDES, W. R. (eds.), *op. cit.*[46]
49 GREEN, R. 1959. A Survey of Sites on the Coromandel Coast, *N.Z. Arch. Assoc. News Letter 2* (2), 23
50 MULVANEY, D. J. 1959. *Nature 184*, 918
51 —— 1960. *Proc. Roy. Soc. Victoria 72* (2), 53–85
52 McBRYDE, I. 1961. *Antiquity 35*, 312–313
53 McMICHAEL, D. F. 1961. *J. Malac. Soc. Austral.* no. 5, 51
54 SCHOUTE-VANNECK, C. A. 1960. *S. Afr. J. Sci. 56*, 67–70
55 GREENWOOD, P. H. *et al.* 1966. *Bull. Amer. Mus. Nat. Hist. 131*, 339–456

33 Non-Marine Mollusca and Archaeology

B. W. SPARKS

THE STUDY OF THE PAST DISTRIBUTIONS, occurrences and associations of non-marine Mollusca in the Quaternary period has two main aims: first, to find out as much as possible about such Mollusca for their own sake, and second, to use the Mollusca to determine the age of the beds in which they were found and the natural conditions prevailing during their deposition. The very fact that the first aim exists indicates that knowledge is incomplete and that, therefore, the second aim cannot be fully realized. In addition, the incompleteness of knowledge about modern Mollusca limits the inferences that may be drawn from the accumulations of dead Mollusca found in deposits. Further work on modern Mollusca, in the identification of species in the juvenile state and on their ecology in particular, might be expected to illuminate the past, while studies on past Mollusca are necessary to understand some aspects of present distributions. The position is exactly similar when one considers studies of non-marine Mollusca made in conjunction with other studies, for example, Quaternary botany, archaeology, or geomorphology, because it is not only a question of interpreting, for example, the archaeology in the light of the Mollusca, but of gleaning information from the archaeology concerning the distribution and occurrence of Mollusca at different periods.

Mollusca are useful because of their wide distribution, their preservation in a variety of deposits, their large numbers and their comparative freedom from human influences, at least when compared with such vulnerable larger animals as the vertebrates. They prefer habitats with a sufficiency of lime for building their shells and, although different species have different degrees of tolerance of non-calcareous habitats, only one species, *Zonitoides excavatus*, is at present a calcifuge, though it does not seem to have been one always in the past.[5] Thus, the richer the base-status of the locality, whether it be land or freshwater, the richer the fauna generally is. In non-calcareous localities not only is the number of species restricted, but the shells produced are thinner and hence less adapted to preservation. Furthermore, the shells are more readily weathered and destroyed by the acid deposits formed in such localities. Provided, then, that the district is not one of acid rocks, soil and vegetation, Mollusca may be expected in a wide variety of river, lake, marsh, woodland and open-land deposits.

Preservation varies enormously. Although the shells will be preserved in well-aerated oxidized deposits, they are affected by leaching. Most of them are very thin and hence even though the shell itself may not be destroyed, the fine detail of ornamentation, often a diagnostic feature, may suffer severely. Percolating water may precipitate calcium carbonate and, even though this may not cement the shells into the deposit, it may encrust and obscure features of the shell. The differences between the degrees of preservation are so great that Quaternary faunas as old as that from the organic parts of the Cromer Forest Bed are sometimes far better preserved than Postglacial specimens from superficial deposits on Chalk downland.

If the shell survives at all, its shape is likely to be preserved accurately simply because of the rigid form of the shell. In certain sediments crushing does occur, especially of bivalve shells and particularly the large ones such as the species of *Unio* and *Anodonta*. Small closely coiled gastropods, such as *Vertigo* and *Vallonia* spp. (Fig. 84), are probably the least susceptible to crushing. But even though crushing may remove a whorl or two it often leaves the first two or three whorls intact and the species may very often be identified from that part of the shell. Again the large numbers of Mollusca preserved usually mean that not all the specimens will be broken and, even though broken and juvenile specimens are unidentifiable, there will be a residue of unbroken identifiable specimens.

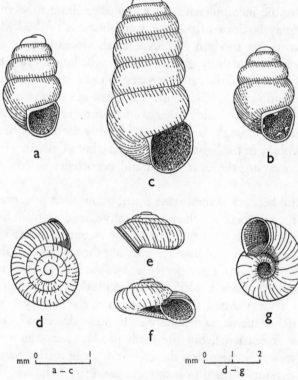

Fig. 84 Cold Quaternary Mollusca: (a)–(b) *Vertigo parcedentata* (Al. Braun). Barrington, Cambs. (c) *Columella columella* (Benz). Laceby, Lincs. (d)–(g) *Vallonia tenuilabris* (Al. Braun). Little Chesterford, Essex. (d)–(g) From Sparks (*Proc. Malac. Soc. Lond.* 30 (1953), 112).

It is not completely true to say that Mollusca, being small and lowly creatures, are not subject to human interference, because the Postglacial spread of widespread alteration and cultivation of the earth's surface by man seems to have wrought greater changes in

Mollusca faunas than occur from one interglacial to another, largely because the micro-climate near the surface has generally become drier. Yet it is probably safe to assume that, on the one hand, Mollusca have occupied most of their climatic and ecological range and, on the other, that these ranges have not been so reduced by human persecution as to be unrepresentative and, therefore, useless in reconstructing conditions from past distributions of Mollusca.

With these introductory remarks made, it seems possible to discuss the use of non-marine Mollusca in archaeology under the three headings of their value as indicators of age, climate and local conditions.

MOLLUSCA AS INDICATORS OF THE AGE OF A DEPOSIT

The idea that certain species of Mollusca might be usable to date deposits of Quaternary age was probably inherited from the use of zone fossils in geology. The ideal zone fossil is one either with a very wide distribution, such as a floating marine creature, or one widely dispersed after death, often by flotation, such as an ammonite. Rapidly evolving species are also required so that the length of time it is possible for an animal to represent is limited. None of these three conditions is met by Quaternary non-marine Mollusca. They are far from widely dispersed, being, on the contrary, controlled in their distribution by local conditions. Further, it seems practically impossible to detect evolutionary changes in non-marine Mollusca in the Quaternary period—at least that is my own experience mainly with British species.

Certain species are or appear to be limited to one particular horizon. For example, *Viviparus diluvianus* seems to be confined in England to the Hoxne Interglacial, *Viviparus glacialis* to the Cromer Interglacial and earlier beds, and *Nematurella runtoniana* (Fig. 85e, f) to the Cromer Interglacial. But each species is known from very few localities, two of them from only two localities, so that whether they are really as confined in their distribution as they seem to be awaits further discoveries of older Quaternary deposits. Such deposits need to be dated independently for obvious reasons. Some idea of the possibilities may be gathered from the fact that in the Netherlands *Viviparus diluvianus* also occurs in the much earlier Tiglian horizon, so that, in view of the proximity of the two countries, it may well turn up at this level in England when more deposits are known.

An extension of the idea of zone fossils is to be found in the linking of particular types of fauna with certain phases of the Pleistocene. The clearest example of this is in the attribution of the 'loess' fauna to the cold period associated with the Last Glaciation. The main features of this type of fauna are a very high frequency of *Pupilla muscorum* associated with *Columella columella* (Fig. 84c) and *Vertigo parcedentata* (Fig. 84a, b). These occur with marsh species, such as *Succinea arenaria* or *oblonga*, species characteristic of small bodies of water, for example *Planorbis leucostoma* and sometimes with *Pisidium obtusale lapponicum* and *Pisidium vincentianum*. On the Continent *Vallonia tenuilabris* (Fig. 84d–g) is also commonly found. Of course, all the species may not occur in a single deposit, as the fauna will vary somewhat with the local conditions. Probably the first five or six examples of this fauna to be found in Britain proved to be Last Glaciation in age, but

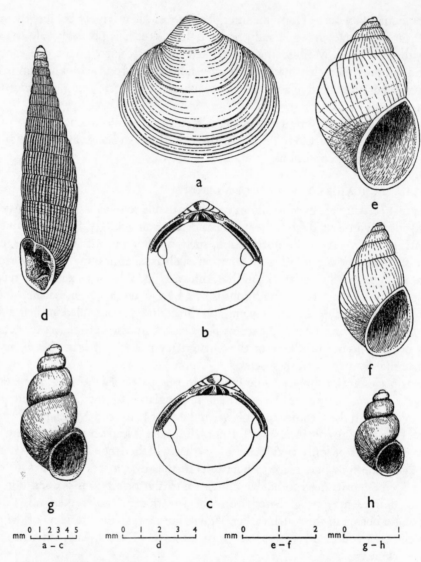

Fig. 85 Interglacial Mollusca: (a)–(c) *Corbicula fluminalis* (Müller). Swanscombe, Kent. (d) *Clausilia pumila*, C. Pfeiffer. Barnwell, Cambs. (e) *Nematurella runtoniana*, Sandberger. Little Oakley, Essex. (f) *Ditto*, ditto. West Runton, Norfolk. (g)–(h) *Belgrandia marginata* (Michaud). Bobbitshole, Ipswich, Suffolk.

examples were later found at Little Chesterford in Essex and Thriplow in Cambridge-shire, which are unlikely to be as recent and more likely to represent a period of cold climate associated with the previous Gipping glaciation. The same has proved true on the Continent: faunas of this type, but earlier in date than the Last Glaciation, have been found in the Netherlands, Germany and Czechoslovakia. It is clear that the fauna is an indication of distinctive local conditions, which were repeated in the Pleistocene, the apparent relation with the Last Glaciation being due to the fact that so many more deposits of this age are preserved. It is still true, however, that when such a fauna is found the odds are that the deposit is Last Glaciation in age, but the inference can no longer be fully relied on.

Another example of a facies fauna, possibly of a more complex type, has recently been discussed by Sparks and West.[15] It is a freshwater fauna dominated by *Planorbis laevis* and *P. crista* in the early parts of interglacials. It has been reported from the beginning of the Hoxnian, Ipswichian and Postglacial periods and is thus comparable with the 'loess' fauna discussed in the last paragraph. More examples of this type might be expected to occur as work proceeds.

It is generally unsafe to attempt to correlate deposits by the nature of their assemblages of Mollusca, except perhaps within short distances within one river basin. For example, four or five fossiliferous sites are known in the highest terrace at Cambridge within a distance of about four miles. Certain features of the faunas recur from site to site and within the same area it ought to be possible to link in any future discoveries of the same type of Last Interglacial fauna. But to correlate on the basis of Mollusca faunas from one river basin to another is an extremely uncertain operation. An extremely interesting and important application of the numerical study of Mollusca to the interpretation of the subaerial deposits of the North Downs in Kent, especially the Late Glacial deposits, has been made by M. P. Kerney, of Imperial College, London, who has shown that it is possible to recognize definite periods of the Postglacial in that area by the Mollusca contained in the beds.

Another possibility, the use of percentage of extinct species present as a guide to the age of a deposit, fails because of the comparatively small differences in such percentages and because the variations between deposits of a single age are so great. Of the species of Mollusca known from the Cromer Interglacial approximately 21% are now extinct: for the Hoxne Interglacial the figure is about 17%, for the Ipswich Interglacial it is about 15% and for the early part of the Postglacial it is about 5%. These figures are obtained by lumping faunas. When individual faunas are compared it is found, for example, that the Hoxne deposit itself has no extinct species, while some rich Postglacial deposits may contain 4 or 5% of extinct species.

Perhaps the clearest examples of snails being introduced at certain definite periods are to be found in the Postglacial period. It has long been known[3] that many of our most common snails are late in their introduction into the British fauna and their presence or absence may point to a Postglacial age and sometimes to a particular part of the Post-glacial period. *Pomatias elegans*, a species characteristic of dry, friable calcareous soils, occurs in large numbers in many Postglacial deposits, but is only known by isolated fragments from two or three interglacial deposits. In abundance, then, it is fairly safe to conclude that it indicates a warm part of Postglacial time. The two largest British land snails, *Helix pomatia* and *Helix aspersa*, are nearly everywhere indicative of a date no earlier than Roman except that the latter is reputed to occur earlier in the south-western peninsula. *Helicella virgata*, *Helicella caperata* and *Helicella gigaxii* are all late. The first is reputed to occur early in the Postglacial in the south-west but elsewhere to be absent from Roman deposits: it is known from a few interglacial deposits but these could probably be differentiated by other features of the mollusc faunas. The second, *Helicella caperata*, only occurs late in Postglacial time as a rule, though it has been found in deposits which are probably Bronze Age or earlier in dry valleys near Hitchin, while it is known fossil in south-west England. The third, *Helicella gigaxii*, is known fossil in south-west England but is only common in post-Roman times. *Monacha cantiana*, which is very common on cultivated land at the present time, is probably even later and Kennard[3] suggested a Norman age for its introduction. Many of these species, which are largely or entirely confined to the Postglacial, are xerophilous and have been found mainly in subaerial deposits at the foot of chalk slopes, in dry valleys and on the Chalk itself, often in association with archaeological remains. Deposits of this type of interglacial age are virtually unknown, largely because either glacial or preglacial denudation has removed them or because they have had any Mollusca weathered out of them. This may explain the very rare occurrence of some species in interglacials and their Postglacial abundance, but it does not explain a complete absence in interglacials because other xerophiles have become incorporated in river deposits in small numbers, e.g. *Pupilia muscorum* and *Helicella itala*. There are other species in the Postglacial period which do not everywhere survive the early part of that period and, where they persist later, do so in greatly reduced numbers. In eastern England *Lauria anglica*, *Acanthinula lamellata*, *Acicula fusca*, *Vertigo substriata*, *Vertigo parcedentata* (or *genesii*), *Vertigo angustior*, *Vertigo moulinsiana*, *Vertigo alpestris* and *Ena montana* all fall into this class and indicate an early Postglacial date.

Non-marine Mollusca, then, may sometimes be used for giving approximate ideas of dating, though rarely is the indication precise and often it is non-existent. The more that these creatures are studied carefully, especially in conjunction with the archaeology of the Postglacial period, the greater will become our knowledge of the spread across England or disappearance locally of certain species and hence the more exact the indication of dates to be gleaned from the snails in other deposits.

MOLLUSCA AS INDICATORS OF CLIMATE

Most non-marine Mollusca have a wide distribution. For example *Vallonia pulchella* is known from the Ahaggar region of the central Sahara, from most of Europe up to and within the Arctic Circle in Scandinavia, from much of northern Asia and also from North America. Such a distribution is probably an extreme one, but commonly one reads that the species occurs from Sicily to the North Cape and over most of Europe and western Asia. On the face of it animals of this sort offer little hope of drawing useful climatic deductions, but the position is not as hopeless as it seems to be. The problem can be approached in two ways: either by considering the presence or absence of certain key species or by considering the overall composition of the fauna.

Certain species occur only in cold deposits. These have mainly been mentioned in considering the loess type of fauna earlier in this chapter. They are *Columella columella*, *Vertigo parcedentata* (Fig. 84), *Pisidium vincentianum* and *Pisidium obtusale lapponicum*. On the other hand there are species which are confined to the interglacials and to the warmer parts of the Postglacial. Most famous of these is the bivalve *Corbicula fluminalis*

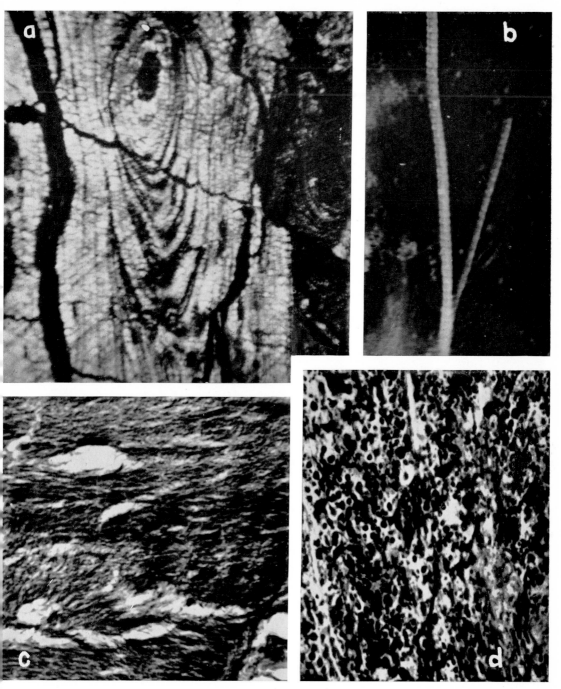

(a) Sample of mandible Circeo IIa: section of decalcified bone seen through a polarizing microscope; signs of tissue's deterioration are present. (b) Unidentified bone fragment found in close proximity to mandible Circeo IIIb. Electron micrograph of decalcified bone. Two collagen fibrils with the 640 Å overperiod. (c) Sample of mandible Circeo IIa. Section of decalcified bone, stained according to the Mallory method. A space previously occupied by an osteocyte is evident. (d) Unidentified bone fragment found in close proximity to mandible Circeo IIIb. Microradiogram of a section of decalcified bone. The tissue appears to be drilled by several 'Bohrkanäle'.

(see page 526) PLATE XXIII

(a) Wool off a piece of skin from a frozen burial mound in the Altai Mountains; fourth or fifth century BC. (b) Fine-wool fibre in parchment from the Dead Sea Scrolls. (c) Medium-wool fibre in parchment from the Dead Sea Scrolls.

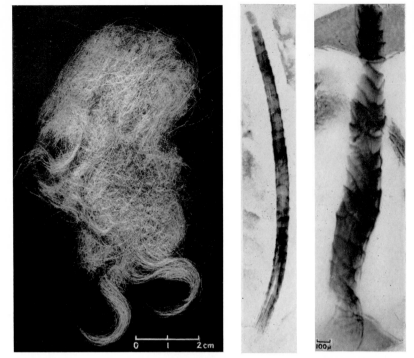

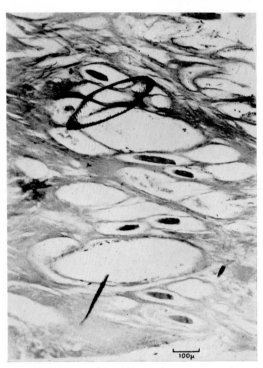

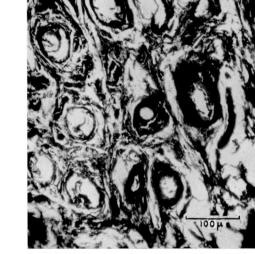

(d) Follicle group from a hairy sheep in a parchment from Hatfield, Yorkshire, dated AD 1403. Note the coarse fibre with a latticed medulla displaced from the primary follicle, and fine fibres in secondary follicles. From Ryder.[22]

(e) Follicle remains characteristic of cattle skin in a specimen of medieval shoe leather from excavations in York; three of the follicles contain hairs.

PLATE XXIV (see page 539)

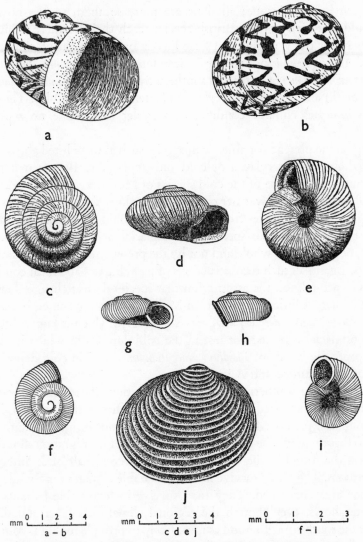

Fig. 86 Interglacial Mollusca: (a)–(b) *Theodoxus serratiliniformis*, Geyer. Swanscombe, Kent. (c)–(e) *Helicella crayfordensis*, Jackson. Grantchester, Cambs. (f)–(i) *Vallonia enniensis*, Gredler. West Runton, Norfolk. (j) *Pisidium clessini*, Neumayr. Swanscombe, Kent. (f)–(i) From Sparks (*op. cit.*).

(Fig. 85a–c), which at present occurs in the Nile and thence eastwards to Kashmir, but there are other useful species as well. *Pisidium clessini* (= *astartoides*, Fig. 86j), *Theodoxus serratiliniformis* (= *cantianus*, Fig. 86a, b) and *Helicella crayfordensis* (Fig. 86c–e) are not known living but may be presumed southern from their occurrence only in association with true interglacial faunas. *Belgrandia marginata* (Fig. 85g, h) now known only from a few localities in the south of France; *Helicella striata* and *Clausilia pumila* (Fig. 85d), south-east European species, which spread north-westwards in interglacial periods; *Vallonia enniensis* (Fig. 86f–i), another species known from interglacials and now found mainly in the southern half of Europe; all these are more southern species now extinct in Britain. In addition many of the British species reach their northern limits in Britain and in Denmark or the very south of Scandinavia on the continent. Among these are *Acicula fusca*, *Azeca goodalli* (not found in Scandinavia), *Helicodonta obvoluta* (northern limit in Holstein), *Ena montana* (reaches southern Sweden), *Vertigo moulinsiana* (northern limit in Denmark) and *Truncatellina cylindrica* (extends as far as Oslo). The presence of these species indicates climatic conditions no cooler than those now prevailing in Britain.

Depending on the presence or absence of species such as these listed above, the climate can be classed as truly interglacial or cold and steppe-like. But even here there are certain difficulties. In the case of the cold species of Mollusca very little is known about their survival into periods of warmer climate. By analogy with plants one might expect them to linger in certain places from which they would eventually be ousted by the spread of more thermophilous species in interglacial or Postglacial time. The fauna should, then, be judged as a whole and not by the presence or absence of small numbers of key species. Again, all such reconstructions of past climates and local conditions from biological evidence rely on the assumption that species do not change their ecological requirements. There is little evidence from Mollusca of such changes, but an exception must be made of *Discus ruderatus*, a Boreo-Alpine form which is known in interglacial and warm Postglacial deposits, but not in the cold deposits in which it might be expected. The opposite is true of *Pisidium vincentianum*, found in cold deposits, but now living in south-east Europe and Asia.

The presence of the southern species is an indication of reasonably warm climatic conditions, but again care needs to be exercised. In the first half of an interglacial period or in the Postglacial period, Mollusca presumably will not immigrate until the climate suits them, so that there will be a lag reflecting the rate of immigration. Southern species may, however, be found in the deposits from the second half of an interglacial for a number of reasons. They may survive in less favourable climates for a while before they die out in the area concerned. They may survive in favourable habitats, where the micro-climate allows, even though the regional climate has deteriorated. Limestone slopes facing the south come to mind as most likely to provide highly favourable micro-climates. Mollusc faunas, after all, really reflect small-scale variations of environment, although one tends to interpret them in more regional terms. Finally it is very difficult to distinguish in deposits between contemporary and derived shells. The shells are too fragile to stand much battering, but such limited derivation as the washing out of a bed of river alluvium after a few millennia with the redeposition of the included Mollusca is sufficient to confuse the climatic interpretation. This is known to have happened with pollen and the possibility of it happening with Mollusca cannot be eliminated.

More may be learned about the nature of the climate from a careful study of the Mollusca. For this purpose the frequency of different species must be known and this requires the extraction of Mollusca from a bulk sample of the material concerned rather than their selection by eye from the material in the field. Owing to variations in size and colour-contrast between the shells and the matrix containing them, selection by eye gives a very distorted picture of the fauna. Hence washing followed by sorting of the sample under a low-power microscope is required both for the deduction of the climate and the local conditions indicated by the fauna.[7]

As a rule it is not possible to consider the variations of a single species through a freshwater deposit as an indication of climate, because the local conditions prevailing during deposition rarely remained sufficiently stable for the species of Mollusca to reflect solely climatic change. This is probably less true of land faunas as Kerney's[10,11] work has shown. As a result, it is necessary to form the Mollusca into distributional groups to offset local ecological changes.[6-9] About four such groupings suffice and they are based upon present distributions in Scandinavia:

(a) Species reaching to or almost to the Arctic Circle
(b) Species reaching approximately 63°N
(c) Species reaching 60°-61°N, i.e. approximately the limit of the oak
(d) Species only reaching the very south of Scandinavia or being confined to the Continental mainland

A model distribution of these groups through an interglacial period would show their successive appearance and disappearance in reverse order, the peaks of the warmer groups probably occurring a little after the middle of the interglacial. The distribution of the Mollusca is somewhat asymmetrical with respect to the climatic optimum, partly because appearance depends on the rate of immigration, while disappearance depends on ability to withstand deteriorating conditions. It is clear, however, that the periods of colder climate at the beginning and end of interglacials are characterized by highly tolerant faunas, while the middles have still a majority of species of such type, although less tolerant species are present in varying, usually small, amounts.

In practice, acquaintance with such distributions, allied with a consideration of such factors as the number of species, and the dominance or otherwise of the fauna by one or two species, and the relative proportions of land and freshwater species, would enable an experienced fossil malacologist to make a shrewd estimate of the climate. The position is, however, too complex to allow a hard and fast rule whereby simple proportions of the fauna can be used to infer the climate directly.

MOLLUSCA AS INDICATORS OF LOCAL CONDITIONS

Just as the distribution of Mollusca is exceedingly broad, so often is the range of habitat in which a given mollusc is found. It is true that certain of them are restricted, for example *Ancylus fluviatilis* is only characteristic of streams with a stony bottom and an absence of mud, while *Pomatias elegans* is more or less confined to friable soils in calcareous districts, but many have a wide range of either land or freshwater habitats. This leads to a considerable degree of uncertainty at times in inferring the local conditions represented by a fauna. If Mollusca with very restricted distributions are present they probably define the local conditions fairly precisely, but with fossil assemblages the possibility of mixed faunas is always present. That this happens is easy to see for example in the case of river deposits containing a small proportion of dry-land Mollusca.

It is easy to infer the washing in and transporting of the latter by the stream. When one finds, on the other hand, a predominantly marsh fauna, together with *Pomatias elegans*, *Vallonia costata*, and *Carychium tridentatum*, the inference of local conditions becomes more difficult. Unless the ecology of species has changed—and if one makes that assumption too easily the basis of fossil work disappears—such mixtures must imply two environments in close juxtaposition. But is it to be assumed that the juxtaposition is spatial or that it is temporal? Mollusca vary so much with small differences of vegetation and elevation that a mixed marsh and dry-land fauna of the type suggested above might be interpreted as meaning dry calcareous hummocks projecting through a marsh. A consideration of the minor relief might suggest whether such an idea is plausible or not. Alternatively, there may have been a marsh, in which calcareous muds were deposited and which dried out sufficiently for its invasion by dry-loving species. There would then be a mixture of faunas more or less at one level. It might be possible to tell whether this happened by taking samples above and below the mixed horizon—assuming, of course, a fair thickness of deposits, which is by no means always present.

A good example of the mixed type of faunas representing spatial variations in the detail of environment is provided once more by many of the cold loess faunas. These usually contain a very high percentage of the xerophilous species, *Pupilla muscorum*, in association with smaller numbers of species characteristic of marshes and poor bodies of water, such as *Succinea* spp., and *Planorbis leucostoma*. Such a mixture is probably best interpreted as representing a set of hummocks of, at least partly, wind-blown silt separated by marshy slacks.

But there are many deposits the faunas of which are less readily interpretable because of the range of possible conditions. However, although many species have a range of habitat,[1,2] it commonly appears that if one were searching for living specimens one particular sort of habitat would be more likely to yield specimens than others. If it is assumed that this habitat is indicated by the species concerned, it becomes possible to start to interpret local conditions by forming ecological groups of species, comparable with the distributional groups outlined above, and studying their percentage variations.[7-9] As with the latter groups, if some such assumptions are not made, it is hardly possible to start serious work on the interpretation of fossil groupings of Mollusca. One hopes that a predominance of Mollusca of a particular group, made up of different species, is cumulative evidence of a particular form of environment. It may not be, but the chances are that it is.

The groups of freshwater Mollusca used have been:

(a) Slum species, i.e. those which will stand exceedingly poor water conditions, such as poor aeration, periodic drying, large temperature changes consequent upon the small size of the body of water. Only certain species can stand such conditions, although such species may be found elsewhere.

(b) Catholic species, i.e. those which are found in practically every type of freshwater environments except the worst 'slums'.

(c) Ditch species: a term designed to cover those species which prefer plant-rich slow streams.

(d) Moving water species, i.e. those more commonly found in larger bodies of water, streams, or ponds, where movement is assured either by currents or by winds. The bodies of water are 'larger' and 'moving' by mollusc standards.

With land Mollusca it may be possible to separate such groups as marsh and associated species, xerophiles, open-habitat species and 'woodland' species, the last being a vague term designed to cover rather retiring Mollusca and those commonly found in damp scrubland.

Such groupings have been used and checked in several ways:

(a) By the consistency of the results. For example, high percentages of 'slum' freshwater Mollusca are usually associated with a predominance of marsh and associated species among the land Mollusca. Also, one begins to see recurring groupings of the species of large genera, for example with the small bivalve *Pisidium*, the combination of *casertanum* with *personatum* seems to point to slums, the combination of *subtruncatum*, *milium* and *nitidum* is a typical catholic one, while *amnicum* (possibly with *clessini*) and *henslowanum* and *moitessierianum* is more characteristic of moving water.

(b) By inferring local conditions from the form of the deposit and checking that the Mollusca agree. This is most easy to do in Postglacial deposits, for example alluvial valley fills, where marginal samples differ from central samples in the land/freshwater ratios and in the percentages of the subdivisions of each group.

(c) Most important, by comparison with the conclusions drawn from the study of macroscopic plant remains taken from the same samples. Very close agreement has been reached mainly from the study of Pleistocene freshwater and marsh deposits for it is in these that plant remains are well preserved. Many archaeologically important deposits are not of this type but were formed on dry land. Nevertheless, the fact that the conclusions drawn from Mollusca have been cross-checked by several methods gives more confidence in the interpretation of the Mollusca of those deposits where no such checks are available.

CONCLUSION

Mollusca may therefore be used in deriving conclusions about climatic and local conditions and less certainly about the age of deposits. Their abundance and comparative freedom from human interference make them very useful for percentage variation studies. The interpretations are probably most accurate when a deposit is thick enough to show variation through time, but even single samples yield something of value. It must be remembered, however, that human beings usually take a wider view of environment than snails, so that the conclusions drawn from the latter are valid only for small sections of the human environment.

REFERENCES
1 BOYCOTT, A. E. 1934. *J. Ecol.* 22, 1–38
2 —— 1936. *J. Anim. Ecol.* 5, 116–86
3 KENNARD, A. S. 1923. *Proc. Malac. Soc., Lond.* 15, 241–59

4 ELLIS, A. E. 1926. *British Snails*, Oxford
5 KERNEY, M. P. 1959. *Proc. Geol. Assoc. 70*, 322–37
6 SPARKS, B. W. 1957. *Phil. Trans. Roy. Soc. Lond., B, 241*, 33–44
7 —— 1961. *Proc. Linn. Soc. Lond. 172*, 71–80
8 —— and LAMBERT, C. A. 1961. *Proc. Malac. Soc. Lond. 34*, 302–15
9 —— and WEST, R. G. 1959. *Eiszeitalter und Gegenwart 10*, 123–43
10 KERNEY, M. P. 1963. *Phil. Trans. Roy. Soc. Lond., B, 246*, 203–54
11 —— BROWN, E. H. and CHANDLER, T. J. 1964. *Phil. Trans. Roy. Soc. Lond., B, 248*, 135–204
12 LOŽEK, V. 1965. *Geol. Soc. America, Special Paper 84*, 201–18
13 SPARKS, B. W. 1964. *J. Anim. Ecol., 33* (Supplement), 87–98
14 ANT, H. 1963. *Abh. Landesmuseum f. Naturkunde zu Münster in Westfalen, 25*, 125
15 SPARKS, B. W. and WEST, R. G. 1968. *Geol. Mag. 105*, 471–81

34 Marine Mollusca in Archaeology

N. J. SHACKLETON

AT MANY ARCHAEOLOGICAL SITES, especially those near the sea, abundant sea shells are found. These molluscan remains have generally received scant attention in the past, and much of their potential has been wasted. The object of this paper is to outline some aspects of their usefulness to the archaeologist.

The variety of information which may be derived from molluscan remains is surprisingly large. It is here classified under three headings, each quite separate and self-contained. First to be considered is the economic and cultural information which can be derived from an on-site examination of the mollusca, the uses to which the shells have been put as well as the contribution of shellfish to the diet of the inhabitants. In the second section the mollusca are discussed as a key to the past climate at the site. The somewhat technical nature of this section is justified by the fact that at present the only known method of determining numerical temperature values for the geologic past is through oxygen isotope studies. The third section deals with the contribution to the absolute dating of the site which may be made by the mollusca. Though the technique of radiocarbon dating is familiar to the archaeologist, the particular advantages which shells offer may not be so well known, nor are the hazards of basing radiocarbon dates on shells as widely appreciated as they should be.

Among the many people whose stimulus has encouraged the author to make this essay into some of the science within archaeology Dr Colin Renfrew deserves special mention. If the text which follows holds any interest for the archaeologist this is largely due to his enthusiasm.

MOLLUSCA AND THE STUDY OF THE ECONOMY

Many of the coastlines of the world are lined by huge mounds of shells, the legacy of peoples whose livelihood was drawn almost entirely from the sea. Along the coasts of South Africa people pursuing this way of life, known as strandloopers, were found by the earliest European visitors. Very large shell midden deposits have been described along the coasts of Denmark, Florida, Peru, Australia, Eastern Russia and many other places. Frequently the shells are so numerous that they are entirely ignored by archaeologists except inasmuch as they may conceal artifacts.

At the other extreme Tsountas[1] during his excavations of Bronze Age tombs in the Cyclades found very few shells, which, he says, are there by chance and do not constitute evidence on diet. Even in this case it might reasonably be deduced that the odd limpet was part of the undertaker's snack rather than there through some natural agency. To this day a fisherman on a remote Cycladic Island will take a handful of limpets for sustenance when he goes off in search of rabbits.

At some sites it seems certain that the vast majority of the shells represents food refuse. An evaluation of the species eaten, and any variations during the period of occupation of the site, adds to our knowledge of living patterns. Detailed examination may reveal a great deal more. For example, a small isolated heap of shells might be discovered in excavation. This may enable an estimate to be made of how many people sat down to a meal together. A palaeotemperature analysis of the outer edge of a selection of the shells could indicate at what time of year the meal was eaten.

If the site is one at which shellfish are fairly uniformly abundant in the food refuse, it might be shown that it had all been collected at the same season, demonstrating a seasonal occupation of the site. If there were also remains of other foodstuffs then it might be that shellfish were eaten at a particular period of the year when other food was scarce.

It is considerably easier to estimate how much meat is represented by a heap of shells than by a few bones. For most species the internal volume of the shell, determined by filling it with water and weighing or measuring the volume of the water, is a very good estimate of the meat volume. Some shells such as cockles do not fill the whole volume all the year round but the error introduced by this uncertainty would never be very large. Shumway[2] was able to make speculative estimates as to how great a population the site which he described might have supported, on the basis of the number of shells found. Though this is less easy on a site where shellfish do not form the principal constituent of the diet, it still might be feasible if one could demonstrate that shellfish were the principal constituent during a particular season.

The habitat which a particular molluscan species occupies today is generally quite well known to the marine biologist. This comprises the range of water depth the species inhabits, its temperature tolerance and the type of substrate it prefers. Thus an examination of the assemblage of species represented at a site gives us information as to the climate and type of coastline when the site was inhabited. It cannot be taken for granted that the coastline was as today, since changes of sea level may profoundly alter the character of the coastline. Shumway[3] shows that at the present time there is not sufficient rocky coastline to supply the large number of mussels (*Mytilus californianus*) which were evidently available when the site he describes was occupied. However, the conditions implied by the assemblage are consistent with the rather rapidly rising sea level which is postulated during the period of retreat of the Wisconsin ice sheets.

Sometimes the size range of a particular species may give us some insight into the economy of the site. At the Neolithic site of Saliagos in the Aegean the size range of limpets (*Patella* spp.) was determined and one particular accumulation[4] consisted of shells significantly smaller than were found elsewhere. It was found that limpets smaller than about 25 cm were not normally collected, so that a collection averaging about 20 cm (this implies only half the meat content) may well indicate a period of scarcity. At present little work has been done to pursue this line of study.

At certain sites there are abundant mollusc remains but with an indication that they are not primarily food refuse. An early example is the Upper Palaeolithic rock shelter at Ksâr 'Akil in the Lebanon.[5] Here out of the 1,500 marine mollusca examined over 1,000 belong to one or other of the species, *Nassarius gibbulosus* (Linné) and *Collumbella rustica* (Linné), both of which are too small to have been collected for food. Moreover, considerably over half of these small shells have been modified by grinding a hole in the last whorl, or in some cases by grinding away so much that only a ring of shell remains. It is interesting that all the five specimens of *Nassarius gibbulosus* described from Jericho[6] have also been modified. One is forced to the conclusion that even at a Palaeolithic site molluscan remains may be present for a variety of reasons, some of which are beyond our present understanding. In view of this, a very careful examination of the state of each shell should be made.

In the first instance, each shell should be examined to ascertain whether it was collected alive or washed up on the beach. This can most easily be done with the aid of a collection of living and beach-worn specimens. Very often shells collected on the beach have holes worn in them, but on careful examination it is generally easy to distinguish a man-made hole from a natural one. Sometimes the former are made by grinding the convex part of a shell on a flat stone. The two examples of *Cypraea lurida* Linné illustrated from Jericho (Biggs[6], figure 2b and c, inadvertently described in the figure caption as *Cypraea livida*) appear to have been treated this way. In other cases (for example, certain specimens from the Late Neolithic site at Saliagos) the sharp edge of a stone, or maybe a worked obsidian edge, has been used to file a groove through the shell, or a point has been used as a drill.

The small holes drilled by boring molluscs should not be confused with man-made holes, though they do of course still have significance since they may well have been collected on account of the holes already present. Similarly one should beware of attributing to prehistoric man holes which have come about during burial or excavation. For example, the crystalline structure of the limpet shell makes it rather liable to break across parallel to the base of the cone, producing a smaller cone and a ring. Confusion does not arise so long as these possibilities are borne in mind while the shells are being examined.

It is sometimes the case that molluscs are collected as food but the shells are subsequently put to some other use. Limpets (*Patella* spp.) are sometimes used as scrapers, leaving a section of the edge much worn away. Alternatively the edge may be smoothed carefully all round to make a good spoon or scoop. The same species can be made into a pendant. All these usages were described from the Saliagos site.[7] It is not always possible to tell whether a limpet has been used as a scraper since the edge is often damaged in removing the animal from the rock.

This section in particular cannot hope to provide an exhaustive study of the material under discussion. The cultural and economic information which can be elicited from a study of molluscan remains will always depend on the nature of the site and equally on the imagination of the excavator or his consultants. It is to be hoped that the few ideas outlined here will soon be greatly expanded by other workers.

PALAEOTEMPERATURE ANALYSIS OF MOLLUSCA

The temperature of the sea in which a mollusc lived can, in certain circumstances, be estimated by an analysis of the relative abundance of the oxygen isotopes in the calcium carbonate shell. It will be necessary to discuss briefly the principles involved in order to consider the applicability of the technique to archaeological problems. A rather more detailed review is given by Epstein.[8]

Three stable isotopes of oxygen exist in nature; they have mass numbers 16, 17 and 18 and in the earth's atmosphere they are present in the ratio $99 \cdot 759 : 0 \cdot 0374 : 0 \cdot 2039$.[9] It is the variations in the relative abundance of the isotopes in the many components of the earth's crust which are of interest to geologists. The molecular ratio $^{18}O^{16}O/^{16}O_2$ is most valuable and easily determined; it is measured using a mass spectrometer. The ratio is usually expressed in geological work as a δ-value,

$$\delta = 1000 \frac{^{18}O^{16}O/^{16}O_2 \text{ (sample)} - {}^{18}O^{16}O/^{16}O_2 \text{ (standard)}}{^{18}O^{16}O/^{16}O_2 \text{ (standard)}}$$

where the standard is generally the 'PDB' standard, named after a fossil belemnite from the Pee Dee formation, in Southern Carolina, on which it is based.

In the ocean the δ-value of the oxygen in combination as water varies a little from place to place. When calcium carbonate is deposited from the water either inorganically or, for instance, by a mollusc, it has a δ-value which depends both on the δ-value of the water and on the water temperature. It is this minute temperature dependence which opens the way to a determination of fossilized temperatures. The temperature T may be derived from a determination of the δ-value of the oxygen in the carbonate, δ_s and the δ-value of the oxygen in the water, δ_w by means of the expression:

$$T = 16 \cdot 5 - 4 \cdot 3(\delta_s - \delta_w) + 0 \cdot 14(\delta_s - \delta_w)^2$$

The amount of material needed for a single measurement may be as little as $0 \cdot 5$ mgm calcium carbonate.[10] It is possible to analyse seasonal layers in a single shell and this technique was used in the analysis of some of the molluscs from the Haua Fteah cave (Cyrenaica) and the Arene Candide cave (Italian Riviera).[11] The analytical errors are generally less than $1°C$; results are not necessarily valid at this level of precision however, for two good reasons. One is that the isotopic composition of the water remains a problem (see below). The other is that ocean temperature fluctuates appreciably over quite short periods, so that long-term means must be based on large numbers of determinations.

In most of the layers from which molluscs were analysed at Haua Fteah the range of temperatures recorded by single shells is about $10°C$. This is about equal to the observed seasonal variation in monthly mean temperature at Apollonia on the Cyrenaican coast ($15 \cdot 5°C$ to $26 \cdot 5°C$).[12] In both this cave and the Italian one, the rise in temperature following the last glaciation, as well as the rather marked temperature maximum between about 6500 and 4500 years B.P. and a minor temperature minimum at about 4000 years B.P. are fairly convincingly shown.[13]

On the other side of the globe at San Diego, California, a site occupied by the La Jolla people between 7500 and 5500 years ago contains a large quantity of shellfish food refuse. A few palaeotemperature measurements there suggested a higher temperature than the present, though the occupation was not long enough to give the detailed information that was obtained from the Mediterranean sites, nor were enough measurements made for a comparable weight to be attached to them. However, additional evidence of a warmer climate was provided by a study of the species represented in the molluscan assemblage.[14] Of interest to archaeologists is the fact that at present air temperatures closely follow ocean temperatures, as is shown by the plots of annual means of sea and air temperature from 1916 to 1946 reproduced by Hubbs.[15]

As mentioned above, this method of determining palaeotemperatures depends on a knowledge of the isotopic composition of the water in which the mollusc lived (for which reason it has no usefulness for freshwater molluscs). The bulk of the oceans is so great that it might be thought that their isotopic composition would remain constant. However, this has proved not to be the case, as suggested by Olausson[16] and recently demonstrated experimentally by Shackleton.[24] The reason is that the extensive ice sheets which built up during the glacial phases of the Pleistocene were composed of isotopically light snow, as is the Antarctic Ice Sheet today; this in turn is due to the fact that water molecules containing ^{16}O evaporate more readily than those containing ^{18}O. This effect yields an apparent palaeotemperature for a glacial phase which is lower than the real one, if no allowance is made for it, so that actual temperature changes tend to become exaggerated in the isotope record. It may be useful to regard the curves published by Emiliani primarily as a portrayal of the waxing and waning of the ice sheets, rather than as a representation of temperature changes.[25]

The implication of this brief discussion is that, at present, the actual temperature values obtained by isotopic analysis should be treated as subject to correction. There is no reason to suppose that adequate understanding of them will be long in coming. Even uncorrected, isotopic temperatures provide a climatic parameter of some value.

Mollusca from archaeological sites may be especially valuable for palaeotemperature work because in addition to being datable they are frequently associated with a particular sea level stand. A knowledge of the sea level enables the amount of ice on the earth's surface to be estimated, and this information may then be used to make a correction to the isotopic temperature. In the case of the San Diego site mentioned above, where the evidence for a climatic optimum provided by oxygen isotope studies is corroborated by an analysis of the species present, limits may be put on the possible change in ocean isotopic composition since that time. The higher isotopic palaeotemperature cannot be entirely due to isotopic changes in the ocean but must be partly due to the independently demonstrated temperature maximum.

Even where the interpretation of long-period temperature variations detected by the oxygen isotope method is open to doubt at present, the detailed information available is interesting. The fact that seasonal variations in temperature are clearly shown means that the season of death of a mollusc is preserved in the isotopic record. An examination of the results from Haua Fteah[18] reveals that shellfish were eaten all the year round since there is no systematic tendency for the outermost readings to be characteristic of a particular season. In the same work it is evident, though not explicitly stated, that even during the cold period during which the Mesolithic layers were deposited the summer-winter temperature variation was as great as it is now. The fascination in this rather complicated technique lies in the abundance of specific information on past earth temperature which it is able to provide.

RADIOCARBON DATING OF MARINE MOLLUSCA

The shells of mollusca consist mainly of calcium carbonate in the form of either calcite or aragonite, with a small amount of organic protein. This organic matter, conchiolin, is present to the extent of one or two per cent in modern shells.[19] Both the organic and inorganic fractions contain carbon and can therefore be dated by radiocarbon estimation. Most of the radiocarbon dates based on shell material which have been published have utilized carbon from the shell carbonate. This is readily released as carbon dioxide by the action of acid.

Unfortunately, the carbonate of old shells is rather liable to contamination, generally with modern carbon. This is rather difficult to detect since the mechanism is a partial recrystallization of the carbonate with replacement of the carbon from the carbonate ion in the groundwater around the shell. However, the contamination is easily demonstrated by separating the inner and outer fractions of the shell and dating them separately; several laboratories have performed this experiment. For example, Dyck et al.,[20] publish (Table 3, page 27) measurements on the inner and outer fractions of four shells. For each of their samples the inner sample appears older, the difference being equivalent to about 5% contamination by modern carbon in the outer fraction. This affects the apparent age of the most recent shells by a few hundred years, and the oldest by about three thousand years. It is clear that where possible the outer 30% to 50% of shells should be leached away before dating, and that thick and solid shells are to be preferred.

If there is no shortage of material, which may often be the case when abundant shellfish food refuse is available at an archaeological site, a far more reliable date may be obtained using only the organic fraction of the shell. This organic matrix is chemically rather stable and is far less liable to contamination than is the carbonate. The procedure for dating this fraction has been described by Berger et al.[19] These authors list three methods; in the first, and simplest, the carbonate is dissolved away in dilute hydrochloric acid, leaving the organic residue. This is then combusted for radiocarbon analysis just as normal organic samples are.

The weight of shell which is required to supply sufficient organic matter for a radiocarbon estimation will vary according to the age of the shells since the organic matter gradually decomposes. In general several kilograms of shell will be needed.

There is also a more fundamental problem encountered in connection with the radiocarbon dating of shells. This concerns the initial activity of the incorporated carbon. The initial activity of the plant material which is usually dated depends upon the state of balance between the production of ^{14}C in the upper atmosphere by cosmic activity on the one hand and its disappearance both by radioactive decay and by transfer to the oceans and the biosphere on the other. Analogously the initial activity of the carbon present as bicarbonate ions and other compounds in the ocean depends on the balance between the assimilation of ^{14}C from the atmosphere and its deposition in the bottom sediments.

To facilitate discussion of the variations in initial activity which we find in nature Broeker and Olson[21] have defined a quantity Δ, given by the expression:

$$\Delta = \delta\,^{14}C - (2\delta\,^{13}C + 50)\left(1 + \frac{\delta^{14}C}{1000}\right)$$

The quantity Δ thus represents the difference in parts per thousand (usually referred to as 'per mil') between the ^{14}C activity of the sample under consideration and the ^{14}C activity of the international ^{14}C standard (95% N.B.S. Oxalic Acid), corrected for isotopic fractionation through the term in δ^{13}C.

If a modern sample has a negative Δ-value this means that it appears to have a finite age instead of appearing contemporary. On the other hand many samples collected today have a strongly positive Δ-value because they contain ^{14}C generated by nuclear weapons as well as that ^{14}C produced by cosmic activity.

Marine molluscs utilise the bicarbonate ions in sea water in depositing the carbonate of their shells. Thus the initial ^{14}C activity of the shell depends on the Δ-value of the bicarbonate ions in the water. This may be measured in sea waters from different parts of the world; a technique for doing this is described by Broeker et al.,[22] and about 300 such measurements are listed by Broeker and Olson.[21]

Values of Δ around -50 per mil are typical, although there is a wide range and in some of the ocean deeps a figure of -100 per mil is quite usual. A mollusc which lived in water in which the ^{14}C Δ-value was -50 per mil would have an apparent ^{14}C age about 400 years greater than its actual age, if no correction were made for this effect.

The effect of isotopic fractionation causes further confusion. It happens that if ^{13}C/^{12}C ratios are not determined in order to make a correction for isotopic fractionation then shell material appears about 400 years younger than plant material. It is apparent that quite fortuitously these two effects tend to cancel each other out. For this reason Broeker and Olson[23] recommend that for shell samples taken from open coasts between 40°N and 40°S latitude, the raw date, not corrected for either of the above effects, should be taken as sufficiently accurate for most purposes.

For the present this certainly seems reasonable advice, but it is of the utmost importance that all laboratories and users of radiocarbon dates make it quite clear just what corrections have or have not been made. So long as this is done, as our understanding of the exchange between ^{14}C in the atmosphere and the ocean is improved we shall be in a position to re-assess the meaning of earlier age determinations.

It is here that workers in the ^{14}C field could usefully enlist the help of archaeologists. Shell samples are needed from sites where the age can be assessed by other means, and at least for the last 10,000 years sites of former human habitation provide the best opportunities. Here is a tool for investigating ^{14}C in the oceans in the past as well as the present. It should be added that there is also a need for shell material collected at any known time, prior to the use of nuclear weapons, in the more recent past. This is important because samples collected today only have bearing on the distribution of atom-bomb radiocarbon, and though this can help in the understanding of the natural distribution, it becomes increasingly difficult to discover the natural distribution which we seek to understand and utilize.

REFERENCES

1 TSOUNTAS, C. 1898. Kykladika 1. *Eph. Arch.* 105
2 SHUMWAY, G., HUBBS, C. L. and MORIARTY, J. R. 1961. *Ann. New York Ac. Sci. 93(3)*, 37–132
3 *Ibid.,* 112
4 SHACKLETON, N. J. 1968. In *Excavations at Saliagos near Antiparos* by J. D. Evans and C. Renfrew
5 ALTENA, C. O. VAN REGTEREN. 1962. *Zoologische Mededelingen (Rijksmuseum van Nat. Hist. Leiden) XXXVIII, no. 5,* 87–99
6 BIGGS, H. E. J. 1963. *Man LXIII,* 125–8
7 SHACKLETON, *op. cit.*[4]
8 EPSTEIN, S. 1962. In *Researches in Geochemistry. Ed.* P. H. Abelson, 217–40, New York
9 NIER, A. O. 1950. *Phys. Rev. 77,* 789–93
10 SHACKLETON, N. J. 1965. *Jour. Sci. Instr. 42,* 689–92
11 EMILIANI, C., *et al.* 1964. In *Isotopic and Cosmic Chemistry,* ed. H. Craig, S. L. Miller and G. J. Wasserburg, 133–56, Amsterdam
12 *Ibid.,* 146
13 *Ibid.,* 148
14 SHUMWAY, *et al., op. cit.,*[2] 109–12
15 HUBBS, C. L. 1948. *Sears Foundation; Journal of Marine Research VII,* 459–82
16 OLAUSON, E. 1965. *Progress in Oceanography 3,* 221–52
17 EMILIANI, C. 1955. *Journal of Geology 63,* 538–78
18 EMILIANI, *et al., op. cit.*[11] Figures 8 to 25
19 BERGER, R., HORNEY, A. G. and LIBBY, W. F. 1964. *Science 144,* 999–1001
20 DYCK, W., FYLES, J. G. and BLAKE, W. JR. 1965. *Radiocarbon 7,* 24–64
21 BROEKER, W. S. and OLSON, E. A. 1961. *Radiocarbon 3,* 176–204
22 ——, TUCEK, C. S. and OLSON, E. A. 1959. *Int. Jour. Appl. Radiation and Isotopes 7,* 1–18
23 BROEKER and OLSON, *op. cit.*[21], 179, para. 1
24 SHACKLETON, N. J. 1967. *Nature 215,* 15–17
25 —— and TURNER, C. 1967. *Nature 216,* 1079–82

35 Molluscs as Food Remains in Archaeological Sites

CLEMENT W. MEIGHAN

CONTEMPORARY CIVILIZATIONS use molluscs only as incidental or luxury food and not as a base for subsistence. However, students of culture history cannot ignore the past existence, over most of the world, of a type of culture primarily dependent on shellfish as the staple food. For archaeological sites of this culture type, molluscan remains are primary indicators of the people's adaptations to their environment, serving for the archaeologist as the same sort of evidence represented by animal bones in the sites of hunters or crop remains in the sites of farmers. Techniques for identification and interpretation of shell remains are therefore important in understanding a wide range of prehistoric sites.

The extent of cultures based, to a greater or lesser degree, on the gathering of shell-fish is little appreciated. Sites of such cultures are generally small with unelaborate remains, lacking even the drama associated with sites of successful hunters. The mention of shell middens or 'kitchen middens' brings immediately to mind the Mesolithic sites of the Baltic (Ancylus Sea), which indeed are the very source of the name 'kitchen midden'. Yet sites representing cultures of this general kind are found all along the oceans of the world, from Arctic to tropics, and also hundreds of miles inland on major rivers where freshwater molluscs could be obtained in quantity. Shell middens are therefore among the most abundant of archaeological sites, being available for study almost everywhere in the world.

The definition of a shell–midden site has never been standardized and there is some confusion in the use of this term by different authors. So far as the physical nature of the site is concerned, 'shell midden' has been applied to any archaeological deposit containing a visible quantity of molluscs. Hence the name has been used for archaeological deposits containing 1% or less of molluscan remains (by weight) as well as deposits composed almost entirely of shell. A midden containing more than about 30% shell (by weight) appears visually to be almost pure shell since the other main components (rock and soil) have a greater density and occupy a smaller volume. Also, the shells are usually white in colour and more apparent visually than other materials.

These distinctions in proportion of shell present have an immediate functional correlate in being rough indicators of the intensity of mollusc gathering and in theory the degree of reliance placed on this food resource. Unfortunately, this simple determination of shell proportion is not the whole story and may in fact be quite misleading. It is necessary to recognize three broad categories of sites quite different in cultural meaning, yet all of them describable in terms of their physical components as shell middens.

These are:

1 Shell middens which are hunter-gatherer sites in which the mollusc remains represent a food staple in the economy of the people. This does not mean that the total diet, nor necessarily even the major portion of it, consisted of molluscs, but that molluscs were a staple food, contributing significantly to the survival of the people. This is not merely a question of quantity, but, as has been pointed out by numerous writers, the use of molluscs introduces an important element of stability into a hunter-gatherer economy. The characteristic feast-or-famine situation resulting from seasonal availability of most plants and animals does not apply to shellfish which can be collected all year round. Hence, the use of molluscs by hunter-gatherers provides a food resource to tide the people over during periods of scarcity in other foods. It permits a more stable population, both in numbers (less starvation) and in degree of nomadism since people are less frequently forced to move in search of food. The work of Kroeber[9] shows that hunter-gatherer peoples in North America maintained roughly twice the density of population along the coasts as they did inland. A major reason for this was the relatively secure food supply available in the form of molluscs.

2 Shell middens representing mixed economy in which agriculture provided the staple food for the people but shellfish were used as a significant protein supplement. In general, these are shellmounds containing sherds since pottery is seldom associated in quantity with hunters and gatherers. Numerous shellmounds in Mexico, Panama and the Andean area appear to fit this category.

3 Shell middens representing market-towns or semi-commercial collecting of shellfish for export to the interior as well as local use. These are the product of highly organized agricultural civilizations and are still being produced today in many parts of the world. Aboriginally, sites in this class have been studied by the writer in such locations as Barra de Navidad, Mexico, where a shell midden represents a thriving commerce in salt and shellfish dating back a thousand years, and near Arica, Chile. The latter sites include fishing communities of the Inca empire that apparently exported both fish and shellfish in return for agricultural products.

These distinctions are somewhat arbitrary when applied to any individual shell midden, but they are very important in using existing methods of midden analysis and interpretation. Such methods have been developed from studies of hunter-gatherer middens of 'Mesolithic' type and can provide useful information for this kind of community. While middens of hunter-gatherer peoples represent the commonest form of shell midden, there are enough of the other varieties to necessitate some caution in applying midden analysis techniques. By and large, one shellmound looks pretty much like another, and it is important to know that apparent physical similarity may mask major differences in the kinds of communities leaving the remains.

Existing midden analysis methods which seek ecological and population data are all based on the assumption that the molluscs in a site were consumed locally. If the amount of export was at all large, it is impossible to interpret the site by conventional methods. Conventional midden analysis can also yield good data on other animal resources (fish, birds, mammals) but ordinarily the importance of plant foods can only be crudely guessed at from the kinds of artifacts present, plant remains seldom surviving. If the site was one of mixed economy including agriculture, the relative importance of plant foods cannot be quantified except from historical sources.

An unanswered question of interest is the age of the shell-midden way of life. Because of differences in the definition of 'shell midden' it is not possible to say where the oldest site of this kind has been found. The meaningful question is not 'Where is the oldest site containing molluscs?' but rather 'Where is the oldest site showing use of molluscs as a significant food resource?' Molluscs have been used for ornament long before they were used for food. Their use as food may well have been forced by scarcity of other food such as game animals. The average molluscan flesh is certainly not very appealing in appearance and the earliest humans apparently existed for uncounted millennia before that anonymous hero ate the first oyster. In any event, shell middens of real antiquity are rare or absent in world archaeology. The shell middens of northern Europe, associated with the Mesolithic, are well known. However, early Mesolithic sites do not appear to be shell middens and many Mesolithic sites such as Star Carr (Clark[4]) are completely lacking in orientation toward molluscan foods. A full-blown shell-midden subsistence is hard to demonstrate prior to about 7,000 to 8,000 years ago in northern Europe (Clark[3]). In North America, the oldest dated shell middens are also in this time range. In Peru, pre-ceramic shell middens in the 6,000 to 7,000 year range are known. In Japan, it appears that older true shellmounds exist, perhaps to 9,000 or more years ago. Even allowing for our fragmentary knowledge these dates are suggestive of a correlation with the end of the ice age and the beginning of the Holocene, not only in northern Europe but over most of the world.

The general shift from a kind of Palaeolithic big-game hunting to the more general-ized hunting and gathering, characteristic of shell-midden dwellers, has been linked to the extinction of the large animals of the Pleistocene and the consequent necessity for using lesser food resources. Chronologically, the connection between the onset of the Holocene and the inception of shell middens seems probable. The functional explanation of the shift in resources (i.e. the larder was bare of reindeer and mammoth) seems less probable.

It may be that by the end of the Pleistocene, human population had increased to the point where more systematic exploitation of the environment was inevitable. In other words, it was not so much a decline in the number of game animals as an increase in the number of mouths to feed that triggered an active development of new food resources. Such development involved greater use of land resources (plants and small game) but also turned to the previously little used foods of the rivers and the sea. At first, the change could simply extend man's land activities to marine resources—hunting seals on the beach as if they were land animals, and collecting molluscs as if they were fruits to be picked from a plant. Considerably later comes the use of boats and systematic fishing activities.

MIDDEN ANALYSIS

The purpose of midden analysis is to determine the constituents of an archaeological deposit as exactly as possible. The data can then be applied to interpretations of ecology, chronology, population and various changes through time. Midden analysis characteristically seeks a wide range of data concerning all components of a site which may be informative: not only molluscs but artifacts and raw materials; bird, mammal, and fish bones; soil samples; and pollen samples are part of midden analysis. Hence a broad range of quantitative methods employed under the general term of midden analysis related to the use of molluscs are discussed. The citations given in the references are examples only and not intended as a thorough listing of works dealing with midden analysis. For a further bibliography on the subject, it is suggested that one consults R. F. Heizer and S. F. Cook.[8]

The steps in data collection and analysis include:

1. Selection of samples to be analysed. Fortunately for the archaeologist, it is not necessary to screen and sort a mountain of midden to determine the components present with a fair degree of accuracy. A series of small samples can suffice. The analysis of shell components by use of small samples probably yields more reliable results than for other kinds of midden components such as bone. This is because shell comes closest to the ideal material for sampling—molluscs are very abundant in the average shell midden, are finely divided, and more or less evenly distributed within the site deposit. The very important paper of Treganza and Cook[13] investigates the number of samples necessary and the reliability of various sample sizes in yielding a true picture of midden components. They conclude that a series of 15 to 25 small samples (4 or 5 pounds of midden each), will yield a reasonably correct indication of site constituents. Ordinarily the samples are taken from the side walls of open excavations—this permits the investigator to select 'average' midden and avoid obvious lenses and concentrations which would skew the results. When this procedure is not feasible, cores can be taken with a soil auger.

2. The samples are passed through a screen. What passes through the screen (mainly soil) is classed as 'residue' and not further analysed. The material caught by the screen becomes the sample to be analysed. Obviously the size of the screen mesh is important here and various workers have used screens varying in mesh from half an inch to as fine as one-sixteenth of an inch. Several workers including the writer, have experimented by passing the same sample through screens of varying fineness to see what effect the particle size had on the results. It is clear that the results differ by a few percentage points when finer mesh screens are used and there is no doubt that a more precise knowledge of the sample is obtained with a finer sorting (Greenwood[7]). On the other hand, the gain in accuracy has to be balanced against practical considerations of labour time. The sorting of one complex sample to a quarter-inch size usually takes a few hours but can take much longer. Sorting to one-sixteenth of an inch will increase the time by at least 500%. The question is whether the gain in information is significant enough to justify the expense of the finer sorting. Each worker has to set his own standards here;

the experience of the writer has been that a quarter of an inch sorting is the smallest practicable size for most site analysis.

3. The material retained by the screen is washed, sorted, and identified. Even when the great bulk of the material consists of shell fragments the other components are of great importance. Indeed, the fundamental fact to be determined is the importance of molluscan resources relative to other means of subsistence. This cannot be determined without detailed midden analysis.

Ordinarily samples from an open midden will contain, besides residue, stone, bone, charcoal and molluscan fragments. Taxonomic identification of these materials is difficult and sometimes impossible because of the small size of the fragments. Considering only the molluscs, the situation is not quite so difficult. Even with quarter-inch fragments of shell, differences in lustre, colour, texture and surface marking permit sorting of the fragments into piles representing individual species (or genera) of shells (see Meighan[11] for photographs of sorted shell fragments). If one takes a quarter-inch fragment of shell to a conchologist and asks for a taxonomic identification, he will of course be told that this is impossible because the piece does not show the characteristics needed for identification. However, with samples from archaeological sites, genus and species identifications can often be given with some assurance. The archaeologist will have some whole shells from the site to indicate the range of species present, and generally the great bulk of the shell sample will consist of only two or three species which were favoured food resources. The site of Zuma Beach, in Southern California, is an extreme example (Peck[12], Ascher[1]). Although more than thirty species of molluscs have been collected from the site, analysis of the midden samples shows that the molluscan food resource was over 99% mussels—all other species were picked up casually. Many of the species were primarily used for ornaments or implements, or were simply stray shells picked up on the beach. The identification of the fragments in midden samples can ordinarily be rapidly reduced to a very small number of possibilities and recognition of only three or four species commonly will take care of almost all the molluscs in the midden samples.

In passing, the example of the Zuma Beach site shows the problem of interpretation arising from the all-too-common practice, in archaeological reports, of presenting a list of molluscan species present without any data on the relative frequency of each species. A list of thirty species from the Zuma Beach site is by itself misleading about the molluscan food resources present since it implies that the aboriginal population was systematically exploiting a wide range of molluscan foods whereas in fact only one species was of significance in the diet.

The identification of molluscs is easier for the archaeologist to attempt on his own than is the identification of such remains as bird or animal bones. Published keys of shells are available for many regions of the world; these can ordinarily be used by the archaeologist for preliminary sorting and identification. Before publication it is most desirable to have the identifications and terminology checked by a conchologist to avoid mis-identifications, use of obsolete species names, and similar errors.

4. Once identified, a tabulation of the components in the sample shows the relative

importance of different molluscs. Further it permits estimation of the actual food resources represented by the total site deposit. It is only at this point that a true picture of molluscan use can be gained. The shells, representing the discarded refuse of food sources, are an indirect indicator of how much mollusc flesh was used. However, there is considerable variability in the ratio of shell to meat in different mollusc species.

Cook and Treganza[6] have calculated the relationship between types of edible food and bone and shell remains, including:

	Weight of edible flesh	Weight of remains preserved in site
Mammal and bird bone	20	1
Mussels	1	2·35
Clams (San Francisco Bay)	1	3·5
Clams (Southern California)	1	5
Haliotis (Bonnot[2])	1	3·8

These figures show that there is considerable variation in the amount of edible flesh evidenced by molluscan remains, depending on the species of mollusc and the region where they are found. More important is the ratio of flesh to bone weight for mammal and bird bone. These figures indicate that one gram of bird bone in a midden represents as much edible flesh as 100 grams of clam shells. The shells so apparent in a shell midden do not have to indicate primary dependence on molluscs for food, since small quantities of less visible components may indicate food resources of even greater importance to the inhabitants of the site. For example, the Little Harbor site on Catalina Island off Southern California yielded midden samples with about as high a proportion of shell as has been recorded (up to 58% of the sample's weight being shell). Yet complete analysis of the other components in the midden shows that molluscs could not have been more than about half of the flesh foods utilized, the other half being fish, birds, and sea mammals (Meighan[10]).

One difficulty in carrying midden analysis to the final step of calculating food resources is that accurate shell to flesh ratios are not available for many species. Not only is there considerable regional variation, even for related forms, but many of the molluscs important in aboriginal economies are forms of no importance today and hence no figures for shell to meat weight are available. The smaller barnacles, for example, appear completely insignificant as a food resource. Yet they form significant amounts of midden shell in some places and could have been used in soups to yield a food resource. More important yet would be the determination of flesh to bone ratios for fishes. It appears likely that very small weights of fish bone may represent a considerable quantity of fish used for food, particularly in sites where the preservation of fish bone is poor.

Even after all these analytical steps, there is an area of subsistence that cannot ordinarily be interpreted from midden analysis, namely the use of plant foods. In the average midden site, no plant remains are preserved and indications of plant usage are restricted to the tools of plant preparation (milling stones and the like) plus rare carbonized seeds

or other plant parts. No matter how precisely the midden samples are sorted and tabulated, there remains the unknown factor of plant foods—this factor at present cannot
be quantified for most sites. It would be of value to have careful midden analyses for
the shell middens in very dry areas of the world, such as coastal Peru, to see what
evidence of plant foods would appear in the samples. Even in these cases, however,
quantification of results would be most tenuous since ordinarily only the edible parts
of the plant are harvested and brought to the kitchen, not the whole plant. Hence, while
every clam or mussel has a physical residue likely to be in the village dump, not every
bushel of corn or pot of beans has an equivalent 'garbage' factor. The plant refuse is
likely to be left in the fields, fed to animals, used for fuel, or otherwise disposed of.
Therefore, even a village site in which all refuse has been preserved can seldom provide
quantitative data on the use of plant foods.

GENERAL CONSIDERATIONS

Despite the shortcomings of molluscan analyses, they do contribute data of importance
concerning a broad range of archaeological sites. Imperfect techniques are not worthless
techniques, and use of existing methods can greatly amplify our knowledge of shell-
midden dwellers. Only a small handful of the uncounted thousands of shell middens in
the world has been studied for molluscan content. It is therefore impossible to draw
general conclusions about the cultural stages in which molluscs play a central part in
the subsistence. This is unfortunate not only because shell-midden economies were important to so many peoples in the past, but also because it is in precisely this level of
cultural development that the genesis of later civilizations must have developed. The
careful study of molluscan remains from individual sites may not only amplify knowledge of the site but also contribute to comparative data of importance. The sorts of
data available from molluscan remains include:

1 Species lists, providing possibilities for conclusions about:
   a Selection of resources—what molluscs were used from those available in the
   environment. Some molluscs are favoured food resources, others ignored or used
   only incidentally.
   b Inferred technology—while little in the way of tools is needed for most mollusc
   collections, some types must be dug from the sand and some types require tools to
   detach them from the rocks.
   c Environment of the site zone—many molluscs are very sensitive to changes in
   salinity and water treatment and all have a natural habitat of clearly defined nature
   (rocky shore, mud flats, etc.). Molluscs present in a site therefore reflect the past environmental conditions.
2 Quantitative analysis, providing possibilities for conclusions about:
   a Proportions of shell species to each other, reflecting the relative importance of
   different molluscs in the diet.
   b Proportions of molluscan foods to other foods in the diet—the degree to which
   the culture depended upon molluscs.

c Changes through time. These include primarily shifts to other food resources, or shifts from one mollusc to another. Such trends are explainable in terms of environmental changes (silting in of lagoons, ocean temperature change, etc.) or cultural effects, principally the over-exploitation of favoured foods.

For the future, not only the quantity of information in these areas must be increased, but also the reliability through improved sampling and analysis methods. Finally, it is to be hoped that some standardization, or at least convertibility, of sampling methods will be developed. Existing reports describe molluscan sample in terms of whole shells per unit volume, weight per unit volume, or percentage of total weight in a sample. Some reports give relative percentages for components but not the total weight or volume of the sample. These differing approaches are indicative of an era of experimentation in which archaeologists are seeking new means for drawing conclusions from their data, and the next few years will no doubt see marked improvement in both the quantity and quality of molluscan analysis.

REFERENCES

1 ASCHER, R. 1959. *Southwestern Journal of Anthropology 15*, No. 2, 168–78
2 BONNOT, P. 1948. *California Fish and Game 34*, No. 4
3 CLARK, J. G. D. 1952. *Prehistoric Europe: the Economic Basis*, London
4 —— 1954. *Excavations at Star Carr*, Cambridge
5 COOK, S. F. 1946. *Amer. Antiq. 12*, 50–3
6 —— and TREGANZA, A. E. 1950. *Univ. of California Public. in American Arch. and Ethnol, 40*, No. 5, 223–62, Berkeley
7 GREENWOOD, R. S. 1961. *Archaeological Survey Annual Report, 1960–61*, 409–22, Los Angeles
8 HEIZER, R. F. and COOK, S. F. (eds.) 1960. *The Application of Quantitative Methods in Archaeology*. Viking Fund Publications No. 28, New York
9 KROEBER, A. L. 1939. *Cultural and Natural Areas in Native North America. Univ. of California Public. in American Arch. and Ethnol. 38*, Berkeley
10 MEIGHAN, C. W. 1959. *Amer. Antiq. 24*, 383–405
11 —— et al. 1958. *Amer. Antiq. 23*, 1–23
12 PECK, S. L. 1955. *An Archaeological Report on the Excavation of a Prehistoric Site at Zuma Creek: Los Angeles County, California. Arch. Survey Assoc. of Southern California, No. 2*, Los Angeles
13 TREGANZA, A. E. and COOK, S. F. 1948. *Amer. Antiq. 14*, 287–97
14 WISSLER, M. 1959. *Archaeological Survey Annual Report, 1958–59*, 147–50, Los Angeles

36 Molluscs from Human Habitation Sites, and the Problem of Ethnological Interpretation[*]

H. E. J. BIGGS

IN PREVIOUS CHAPTERS ON MOLLUSCS, this important invertebrate group of animals has been considered generally in terms of marine and non-marine forms, and also from the point of view of their food value to earlier communities. My own contribution is intended to emphasize other ways in which information on past societies can be derived from the identification and consideration of molluscs. As in recent primitive communities, animals were not simply used as food in earlier cultures, but provided raw materials needed in art, dress, magico-religious ceremonials and in trade. This type of information, highly relevant to the proper reconstruction of the anthropology of earlier peoples, is in fact the most difficult to derive with any certainty from excavated material—if it is preserved at all. With proper co-operation between archaeologist and biologist, and with due caution in interpretation, some conclusions can however be reached. Although this subject could to some extent be exemplified by reference to vertebrate remains, I plan to illustrate the field by reference to my own research group, the mollusca.

A major difficulty in some work on excavated molluscs, at least in my experience, is that sometimes there is a lack of associated precise field data. At times this may be critical to proper interpretation. In excavations at Jericho, Kathleen Kenyon did in fact keep shells from a close proximity carefully together in envelopes. Because of this, it is now possible not only to identify the specimens as all *Glycymeris* and *Cardium*, but to conclude that these holed shells probably formed a single necklace (Biggs,[2] Fig. 1). Except in food midden or natural deposits, every effort should certainly be made to save and catalogue shells associated with habitations. Incidentally, they should also be cleaned with care; and for instance, in washing out large numbers of *Melanopsis praemorsa* (Linné) I was able to carefully collect a number of minute and delicate extra species not previously known from prehistoric deposits. Saving merely representative specimens is unsatisfactory. Where only one or two shells are found, these should not be considered as valueless. On the other hand, it is important not to make too much of them, and as Oakley[12] has recently said in his study of fossil collecting and early folk-lore, there is a temptation to place too much symbolic meaning on such finds. Of course, it is to be expected that some specimens will pose questions which are unanswerable for the present. What, for instance, is the reason for the modifications to several specimens of

---

[*] This short paper may be considered by some readers as very marginal to scientific work in archaeology. It depends on one's classification of ethnology. We include it in order to emphasize that the scientific specialist can assist, indeed can provide the primary information, from which socio-cultural interpretation can be derived.—Eds.

Nassarius gibbosula (Linné) from Jericho?[2] Each was worn down on either side until little less than the thickness of a pearl button, and showing the spiral coil of the septum.

SHELLS AND ECONOMICS

It is well known from ethnographic observations on recent primitive peoples that shells may be utilized in various ways, at family, community and inter-tribal levels. Within the family unit, in some cultures, shell has been used for general domestic and agricultural needs. To give New World examples, well-shaped vessels were made by the Hopewell people of Illinois and Missouri[5,11] from conch shell (*Busycon perversum*), a trait also found in Middle Woodland times.[13] Mussel shell spoons have similarly been found at prehistoric Illinois sites. Larger and more robust mussel shells were also made into hoes, and at the Hopewellian Steuben site, they were fairly numerous (though not all intact).[11]

Much has been written on the subject of shells as money, although archaeological evidence is as yet poor. One possibility is mentioned by Fischer.[6] Referring to the hoards of *Nassarius neritea* (Linné) in the Grimaldi cave, he says '. . . on est plutôt tenté d'y voir un trésor "en espèces"; rappelons à cet égard les amas de "Koroni" (*Marginella amygdala*) de Tombouctou qui, d'après les traditions locales, auraient précédé comme monnaie les "Cauris" (*Cypraea*) et auraient été enfouies par ordre du chef de la ville lors de l'introduction des Cauries' (p. 91).

The use of purple dye from some species of the genus *Murex* has long been known, and especially from the Mediterranean area. The shell form is not difficult to identify, and in almost all collections from eastern Mediterranean sites will be found a few examples of one or other of the larger species. At Tell Rifa'at in Syria and positioned well inland, M. V. Seton-Williams discovered a mass of *Murex* fragments—clear evidence I think of this industry. Even in the small sample sent to me for examination were at least twenty specimens, estimated by counting the number of apices present. Not all inland finds need be indicative of dye extraction, however, and the few examples of *Murex truncatus* at Jericho may perhaps have been collected for other reasons. In the case of one large species, *Murex brandaris* L., frequently excavated in the Mediterranean area, the shell is sufficiently impressive (Plate XVIIIb) to have been perhaps of decorative or ritual value. Identification of this genus is thus not sufficient in itself to be meaningful culturally, and much work remains to be done on this group—as represented at archaeological sites. To my knowledge, no attempt would appear to have been made to relate early occurrences of the crushed purple-bearing *Murex* shells to the development of textiles and dyeing.

By the careful identification of genera or species foreign to the site of discovery, even from very small fragments, there is of course the hope of building up evidence of trading. Tower,[14] for instance, has worked on shells excavated at various sites in the American southwest and claims that they confirm the existence of certain suggested trade routes in prehistoric times. He concludes that 'It now seems possible that when the final picture of trade in marine mollusca in the prehistoric southwest is outlined, the archaeologist will possess a valuable tool for the determination of economic and cultural relations between the sites and between the pre-Columbian peoples of the American southwest' (p. 46).

Similar conclusions might perhaps be derived from the presence of Red Sea shells at Jericho.[2] Here, it could be that the trade route in Neolithic times passed either along the coastal plain and down into Egypt, or, more directly, along the Arabah to Aqaba. I suspect it was the latter, but until more shell samples are available and have been examined, this must remain uncertain. It seems important to emphasize that careful and correct shell identification is vital to the correct construction of trade routes by these specimens. Henderson[8] stated this point clearly with regard to the study of *Haliotis fulgens* and *Haliotis rufescens* from sites in Washington state. In a similar way, Leechman[9] warned of the confusion which could follow the mis-identification of similar species, for example, as in various types of abalone.

CEREMONIAL AND RITUAL USES

Great care and much caution is needed here. Conclusions should not go far beyond facts. This type of problem, and the alternatives which must be considered in attempting its solution, can be illustrated by reference to a discovery of a Triton shell, *Charonia variegata*. A fine specimen was excavated by Seton-Williams at Tell Rifa'at, sixty-three miles from the nearest seaport. It seems most unlikely that it was transported this distance with the meaty interior intact, and it was not holed at the apex for blowing (as this and related species usually are). On present evidence, therefore, one must tentatively conclude that this may have been for ceremonial reasons, indeed, as it was a Greek site, one even wonders whether it had been used for some form of Neptunian ritual! (Plate XVIIIe.)

The use of shells as ceremonial trumpets is known from various recent ethnographic evidence, but archaeological examples are as yet few. Boekelman[3] has studied the evidence for them in the United States and records that *Strombus galeatus*, *Melongena patula* and *Murex nigritus* were all used as trumpets by early Amerindians of the west coast. Somewhat pointedly he reflects that: 'If all sea shells found, even though apparently unworked would be saved with the same care that worked artifacts are preserved, it is quite possible that shell trumpets may be reported in some of the Mississippi Valley mounds. Time and again we have heard of field workers of excavations where unworked shells, and especially broken specimens, were not even removed from the sites' (p. 30).

Much has been written on fertility cults and charms, but little being of real value. I am therefore hesitant to offer more hypotheses, though some mention nevertheless deserves to be made, if only in relation to a few sites and specimens. Castiglioni and Groid[4] have suggested that the semilunar laminae found on various sites of Late Palaeolithic date in Italy and several other localities in the western Mediterranean have significance as fertility charms. The objects are made from fragments of *Cardium* and *Glycymeris* (both marine bivalves). Some support might be given to this idea by recent discoveries of further examples. Amongst the mollusca collected by C. B. M. McBurney in a Late Palaeolithic cave in Mazanderan, North Persia, and entrusted to me for examination,

I have found similar semilunar laminae (Plate XVIIId). In this instance, they were fabricated from *Didacna crassa*, a species of the same family living in the Caspian Sea as the *Cardium* of the Mediterranean.

A similar question arises in relation to the mollusca recovered from Çatal Hüyük by J. Mellaart, and examined by me. Amongst them was a single valve of what appears to be *Arca antiquata*, or at least a variety which does not appear to be a Mediterranean species. I have seen a similar shell from a Greek site rubbed down at the umbo and holed, probably for wearing, but this example has no hole. It has been suggested that one view of the shell (Plate XVIIIa) is similar to the female external genitals, and in view of the use of such structures in primitive art, this is not entirely out of the question. Without more definite ethnological evidence associated with such specimens, it is not possible of course to arrive at a more certain answer to the occurrence of such shells.

DRESS AND DECORATION

Finally, this brief note on the relationship between malacology and ethnological reconstruction, should consider more mundane aspects. Shells which have formed part of a necklace or similar decorative object, have in all cases perforations. If only a fragment of shell is threaded, there may be difficulty of identification. Care must also be exercised in attributing all cases to deliberate perforation, for in almost all random collections of valves of *Glycymeris* and *Cardium* from the Mediterranean coast a percentage will be found to be holed at the umbo, simply by wave action and beach wear. Occasionally, intentional working is very clear, and on one valve of an *Arca* shell I have examined from a Greek site, scratches are plainly visible and clearly result from deliberate wear. Details of technique may sometimes be obtained, and the use of sections cut from Indian Chank shell to make bangles has been discussed by Wilkins[15] in his report on the mollusca from Rang Mahal, Bikaner. He also illustrates the angle at which the shell was cut to obtain the largest number of bangles from one shell. Pendants could also be made of shell, those from the Crable Site,[10] Illinois, showing the range in size and design which could occur at one site. Whole whelk shells were used as pendants by the early Missouri Indians,[5] who bartered for these shells from the Gulf of Mexico. Returning to the Old World, there is even the possibility that some form of 'buckle' was produced from the cowry, an early specimen from a Syrian site (Plate XVIIId) being a possible example (broken and presumably discarded structures of this type occurring at Jericho).

I hope it is clear from what I have said that the interpretation of data on molluscan remains—beyond that related to dietary and chronological fields—is difficult. Good co-operation between archaeologist and malacologist is the only way to ensure the extraction of the fullest possible information on the ethnology of earlier populations from shells.

REFERENCES
1 BIGGS, H. E. J. 1960. *J. Conch.* 24, 379–87
2 —— 1963. *Man* 153, 125–8

3 BOEKELMAN, H. J. 1936. *Am. Antiq.* 2, 27–31
4 CASTIGLIONI, O. C. and GROID, A. 1965. *Natura 56*, 101–20
5 CHAPMAN, C. H. and CHAPMAN, E. F. 1964. *Indians and Archaeology of Missouri*, Columbia
6 FISCHER, P.-H. 1949. *J. Conchyl. 89*, 82–93
7 HEIZER, R. F. and FENANGA, F. 1939. *Am. Anthrop. 41*, 378–99
8 HENDERSON, J. 1930. *Nautilus 43*, 109–110
9 LEECHMAN, D. 1942. *Am. Anthrop. 44*, 159–162
10 MORSE, D. F. 1960. *Central States Archaeo. J. 7*, 124–34
11 —— 1963. *Anthrop. Papers Mus. Anthrop. Univ. Michigan*, No. 21, Ann Arbor
12 OAKLEY, K. P. 1965. *Antiquity 36*, 1–16, 117–25
13 PERKINS, R. W. 1965. *Bull. Illinois Archaeo. Survey*, No. 5, 68–92. Univ. Illinois, Urbana
14 TOWER, D. B. 1945. The use of marine Mollusca and their value in reconstructing prehistoric trade routes in the American Southwest. *Papers, Excavators Club, II*, No. 3
15 WILKINS, G. L. 1959. *Acta Archaeo. Lund. 3*, 189–95

SECTION III   MAN

37 Sex Determination in Earlier Man

SANTIAGO GENOVÉS

OFTEN A MAJOR STUDY of skeletal remains is made with practically no more than a cursory investigation of sexual differences, and much laborious and useful work is undertaken, particularly on small samples or on 'unique' specimens, which would lose almost all its usefulness if the sex assignment proved to be incorrect. Consequently, it seems a good idea to lay stress on certain points before giving a general account of the methods followed in order to reach a reasonably accurate sex diagnosis.

In his celebrated memoir *L'Homme fossile de La-Chapelle-aux-Saints* Marcellin Boule[1] wrote (p. 5): 'la méthode des mensurations, employée comme méthode directrice a le très grave inconvénient de donner l'illusion d'une précision mathématique dont la Nature, essentiellement mobile et changeante, ne saurait s'accomoder'. Quite often the measuring of bones instead of being a tool has become practically the master of the physical anthropologist; and, as Leakey[2] pointed out, the fact that two things, whether skulls or teeth or pieces of bone, have the same length, breadth, and height does not necessarily mean that they have the same shape or that both are, morphologically speaking, identical. I agree with Leakey that it is important to stress at all times that no single measurable character of any bone will serve by itself to distinguish two different individuals racially or sexually as the case may be, but that only after critical examination of the combination of all the characters can we arrive at results which will be of value. Furthermore, characters which by their own nature might have escaped measurement or expression in an equivalent way may have to be called in to help supply the correct answer.

In spite of the great advances in genetics and the views of authorities like W. C. Boyd,[3] who have strongly criticized the traditional methods of physical anthropology, advocating that practically the only approach to the subject is the genetical one, the fact remains that in practice the anthropologist is often confronted with the problem of assigning sex to a bone, and the only practical way in which this can be accomplished is by combining measurements and morphological observations in a fashion as logically valid as possible. It must be admitted that from a strictly genetical point of view the worker may be observing or measuring 'characters' which are of different orders and fall under the influence of different factors. On the other hand, if the measurements and observations are generally in keeping with the normal patterns of growth, morphology, and function of the bone, they may prove to be of value in sex discrimination in spite of the fact that a phenotype is being considered which perhaps in the future might be subdivided into smaller factors. This may be so no matter how obscure or inexplicable the different genetic or other forces concerned in the adult appearance of the complete character may be. We are still far from understanding to what extent genetic, environmental, hormonal, or other factors are responsible for the final shape a bone assumes.

To return to the anthropological problem, it may at first sight appear that metrical and morphological methods are too crude to determine sex differences in bones which have been affected by these various factors. However, the fact is that if the analysis does not rely on the infallibility of just one character, it may be possible to discriminate unless, as it sometimes happens, a picture of what can be called intersexuality appears. Thus it is not advisable to trust to a single metrical or morphological character, no matter how seemingly infallible, when undertaking sex-determinations.

THE SEX-RATIO

In earlier populations as in modern ones we have examples of varying sex-ratios. Among the Pecos Indians, Hooton[4] reported an excess of males (of more than 10 years of age) in all the periods extending into the last phase of occupation, the sex-ratio being 176·5 males to 100 females.

Angel[5] finds in ancient Greece that in most cemeteries the males preserved for study outnumber the females two to one. On the other hand, Neel[6] shows with data from a recent census that in the United States 50% of the women give birth to 88% of the boys born in each generation, and Ferembach[7,8] shows that in prehistoric groups the sex-ratio, as also the differential fertility and mortality, can greatly modify the outward appearance of a population.

We have considered the above explanation pertinent in order to show:

(1) That contrary to what is usually believed in earlier populations it is not uncommon to find unequal proportions between the sexes.

(2) That factors are constantly changing the sex-ratio, so that this changes from one age to another amongst the individuals of a population and from one generation to the next.

Therefore, what is found in one archaeological stratum *need not* serve as a pattern for postulations about remains found in adjacent strata, whether above or below.

SEXUAL DIMORPHISM IN PREHISTORIC REMAINS

The question of whether the sexual dimorphism in prehistoric populations is greater or less than in recent ones is a fruitless one unless we specify the prehistoric remains to which we are referring. The various modern human groups do not have the same degree of sexual dimorphism. For example, it is known that the sexual dimorphism in Bantu pelves is much less marked than those of Bushmen and Europeans[10] and that some characters (e.g. the pre-auricular sulcus) are of practically no value in a Bantu population.

If we depend on indirect data from other primates, there are several facts which suggest that a pronounced sexual difference *in size* is a primitive condition. Prehistoric races of orang-utan[11] as well as of the Celebes macaque[12] possess a more marked sexual difference in canine size than the corresponding living forms.[13]

In what ways do ancient human remains display sexual dimorphism? Morant[14] and von Bonin[15] find that Upper Palaeolithic European populations are, in many respects, similar to their more recent descendants, whence Brothwell[16] infers a similar type and degree of sexual dimorphism. Keith[17] believed that sexual dimorphism was less pronounced in Neanderthal 'races' than is the rule among modern ones,[18] and Hooton[4] contends that sex differences are less pronounced in primitive peoples than among Europeans.

In the remains of Tabun I, there were found in the superior ramus of the pubis (McCown and Keith[19]) characteristics which, whilst separating them from the rest of the known Neanderthals—including the specimens from Skhul—could not be duplicated in modern man. It was thought that they might possibly be attributed to the sex factors. Later, however, Stewart[20] showed that in Shanidar I and III (both Neanderthals and apparently male) the same situation is produced in the superior pubic ramus as found in Tabun I, which proves that *these pelvic features are not sex-induced changes.*

What is reasonable in the question of sexual dimorphism of prehistoric remains is that we can make more or less legitimate suggestions from these remains, from comparisons with other primates, or with more recent populations. However, such suggestions will frequently be erroneous, attributing to sexual dimorphism what might be in fact a simple intra or extra group variation, or a stage in evolutionary development.

Elsewhere,[21] the present author reached the following conclusions with reference to prehistoric skeletal remains:

'Since the relation between skulls and post-cranial bones from different sites of more or less contemporary deposits is still very far from being elucidated, sexing one specimen on the evidence afforded by corresponding bones of another should be attempted only with great caution.

'Sexing palaeanthropic material on the basis of bones that do not correspond is very inadvisable, even with specimens from contemporary deposits.'

That extreme caution in this respect should be observed when dealing with prehistoric bones of great age is exemplified by the great numbers of them which have opposed diagnoses from specialists (Table A).

One could, of course, make a larger table with other remains for in the above table are figured only those which have Neanderthal affinities. One can also quote cases from America. Thus Minnesota *Man* seems in fact to be a *Girl*[22-24] and Tepexpan Man is very probably Tepexpan Woman.[25,26] It is clear that in these and in other cases, the original error was due largely to natural ignorance of the progress which has been made in sex diagnosis in recent years.

Apart from a series of standards and techniques to which we shall briefly refer later, it must be stressed that one cannot judge prehistoric remains by the same criterion as modern ones. Frequently the diagnosis was based on traces of muscular insertions, forgetting that in early remains, and in the majority of our so-called 'primitive contemporaries', the cultural environment and different division of work, amongst other factors, can put a good part of the female population to fulfilling tasks which require considerable muscular exertion. This would certainly affect bone size and form.

TABLE A
Sexes assigned to Neanderthal remains by different anthropologists.

Anthropologists	Spy I	Spy II	Skhul IX	Galilee	Gibraltar I	La Quina H₅	Ehringsdorf III
Fraipont & Lohest (1886)	♀	♂	—	—	—	—	—
Virchow (1887)	♂	♂	—	—	—	—	—
Schaaffhausen (1887)	♂	♂	—	—	—	—	—
Sollas (1907)	♂	♂	—	—	♂	—	—
Keith (1911)	♂	♂	—	—	♂	—	—
Henri Martin (1913)	—	—	—	—	—	♀	—
—— (1923)	—	—	—	—	—	♂?	—
Keith (*ante* 1925)	—	—	—	♂	—	—	—
—— (1925)	—	—	—	—	Probably ♀	Probably ♀	—
—— (1927)	—	—	—	♀	—	♀	—
Morant (1927)	♂?	♀?	—	♀?	♀?	♀?	—
Weidenreich (1927)	—	—	—	—	—	—	♀
Hrdlička (1930)	'Weak' ♂, or ♀	♂	—	♂	♀	♂	♂
Keith (1931)	—	—	—	o?	♀	♀	♂
Vallois (1937)	♂	♂	—	o?	—	Probably ♀	♀
McCowan & Keith (1939)	—	—	♂	♂	♀	♂	—
Howells (1946)	—	—	—	—	—	—	'Seemingly' ♀
Trevor (*post* 1949)	♂	♂	—	—	—	—	—
Clark Howell (1951)	♂	♀	♂	♂	♀	♀	♂
Boule & Vallois (1952)	—	—	—	—	—	♀	♂

Thus Wood Jones,[27] working on Egyptians, found foetuses in pelves with characteristics which were to him distinctly masculine, and Faulhaber[28] says, referring to the prehispanic remains of Tlatilco (Mexico): 'As for the sexual characteristics, the number of cases in which the female skeletons have an extremely robust appearance, similar in this character to the males, is surprising, although according to the pelvic characters they are unquestionably women.'

METHODS OF SEX DETERMINATION

In agreement with many authorities[29-35] and contrary to the opinion of Hanna and Washburn,[36] I believe it impossible to base sex determination on one character alone —either metric or morphological. Masculine characteristics in one bone may be accompanied by feminine traits in another, or in another segment of the same one. This is equally true of both modern and prehistoric remains.

Up to now, I have outlined the various difficulties which exist. I believe, however, that with care and by using diverse methods, one can, both in populations and even in individuals, arrive at a wholly satisfactory sex diagnosis. Obviously, the further away we are in time from the present, the more difficult it will be, especially if we are dealing with specimens whose phylogenetic affinities are still somewhat incomprehensible. In anatomy books, in anthropometric works, or in works on identification from skeletal remains,[37-48] there is a résumé of the traits, mostly anatomical, to observe and evaluate for sex diagnosis. Although they are not all in agreement with each other (and neither is the author with the evaluation of some of the criteria given), I believe nevertheless that it is easy and within the reach of all archaeologists to familiarize themselves with these, and also to undertake sex diagnosis. As various authors have reviewed the traits of value in sexing, I will not enter into great detail here.

Practically all the bones in the human body have at some time been an object of study with a view to determining the degree of sexual dimorphism. To a certain degree, all make a contribution towards arriving at a diagnosis. However, we can say that there are three areas to be considered in the first instance, and these afford the best results. They are the pelvis, as a whole and for its particular traits; the skull and face, as a whole and for their particular traits; and the articular surfaces of the bones, chiefly long bones.

PELVIS

The prepuberal pelvis. According to some authors, several of the pelvic characters enabling a determination, or a good assessment, of sex are established early in development, in some instances even before birth.[49-51] However, others[52-56] maintain that features of the pelvis strongly indicative of sex only become apparent at puberty when the bones of the female pelvis, and in particular the pubic bones, respond by active growth changes to the hormonal stimuli produced by the sex hormones. Nevertheless, Boucher[57] finds significant statistical differences in the greater sciatic notch, using British foetal material, and also in the sub-pubic angle[58] in prenatal remains of American Whites and Negroes. With her method $\frac{\text{Breadth} \times 100}{\text{Depth}}$ of the greater sciatic notch, she managed to distinguish without error the 34 foetal pelvic specimens which she had at her disposal. Although her results are very promising, they need confirmation.

The adult pelvis as a unit. For obvious reasons, the number of works on the female pelvis far surpasses those on the male pelvis; the former has been studied above all in relation to childbirth, and to the various stages of pregnancy, giving rise to the frequent confusion between the characteristically female pelvis and that of the childbearing woman. That is to say, in normal circumstances, female pelves are not so wide, brachypellic or platypellic, as the case may be, as it has been supposed and described.

Innominate bone. Whilst it is rare to be able to reckon upon a complete pelvis, one very frequently has at one's disposal nothing more than some fragments. Generally speaking, certain parts of the innominate bone can be of more value to us than fragments of other bones in the matter of sexing.[32, 47]

Genovés[59,60] after the analysis of forty-four absolute measurements, nine indices and thirteen morphoscopic characteristics on this bone concludes that one index, three absolute measurements, and four morphoscopic characteristics are valuable for sex diagnosis.

It has been made evident[61,62] that the main sexual difference in the *sciatic notch* is not its width or depth or the index between both measurements, but the fact that the perpendicular from the maximum-width line to the deepest point of the notch divides the width into roughly two equal chords in females, whereas in males the upper chord is the smaller. Thus the features of the innominate bone to be considered in sexing are as follows:

1. The sciatic notch index: composed of the distance in projection between the perpendicular at the point of greatest depth, starting from the line determining the width of the greater sciatic notch, and the highest point of this width, times 100, divided by the width of the greater sciatic notch.

2. Middle width of pubis. This is the distance from the mid-point of the anterior border of the pubic symphysis to the nearest point on the inner border of the obturator foramen.

3. Minimum lower width of the ilium, which is the shortest distance between the supra-acetabular point and the anterior border of the greater sciatic notch.

4. Maximum vertical diameter of the acetabulum, following the direction of the general axis of the body of the ischium.

5. Pre-auricular sulcus. In the postero-inferior border of the ilium.

6. Composite arch of the anterior border of the auricular facet and the anterior border of the greater sciatic notch.

7. Shape of the greater sciatic notch.

8. Relative massiveness of the upper area of the medial portion of the pubis or pubic crest.

By using either a series of metrical characters, standardized morphoscopic characters or a combination of both composed in the manner described above, an accuracy of 95% can be expected.

Using a general discriminant function, Howells[35] reaches 96·53% of correct classifications determined with at least a 95% of probability of exactitude. Six *os coxae* measurements are used.

Although it was in favour for some years, and has a certain amount of utility,[35,63] I shall not deal with the ischio-pubic index of Hanna and Washburn[31] for it presents many technical deficiencies.[30,31–33,59,63]

SKULL AND FACE AS A WHOLE

The skull has traditionally been the anatomical unit most used in sex diagnosis. In general terms the male skull has a higher cranial capacity than the female. Moreover, a female skull capacity rarely reaches 1,500 cc. To Hrdlička a capacity of above 1,450 cc suggests a male whereas a capacity of 1,300 cc or less suggests a female.

The male skull, besides being generally bigger than the female skull, looks more solid, and usually has a more receding frontal.[64] The malars and the mandible are stronger and more solid, and the facial skeleton in general is relatively bigger and longer.

The supra-orbital ridges are more prominent in male remains. They have more marked mastoid processes and also external occipital protuberances. Keen[29] arrives at an 85% accuracy in sex determination by using (a) the supra-orbital ridges, (b) the occipital crest and nuchal lines and (c) the ridge at the upper rim of the auditory meatus (posterior root of the zygomatic process of the temporal). In the experience of Keen,[29] Machado de Sousa,[65] Giles and Elliot[66] and of the author, this last characteristic is of considerable value, for it is well marked in the majority of male skulls and generally weak in females. Starting with multivariate techniques[66] which lead to more refined ones, and using nine measurements (glabello-occipital length; maximum skull width; basion-bregma height; basion-nasion; maximum bi-zygomatic diameter; basion-prosthion; prosthion-basion height; palate external breadth; and the mastoid height), Giles and Elliot[67] obtain an accuracy of 82–89% by discriminant function analysis.

In the mandible, the gonial angle is more open in females, whilst the ascending ramus, the condyle and the symphysis are higher amongst men.[68] The ascending ramus is also wider in males, and the chin more square, quite frequently showing lateral protuberances.[69] After a metrical and morphoscopical examination, Morant says, 'It will be safe to conclude that sexual differences are more marked for the mandible than for the cranium.' Anatomically, following Morant's methods,[68] Cleaver[70] managed to sex accurately 85% of his samples. Using the bigonial diameter, the mandibular symphysis height, the mandibular ramus height and the mandibular ramus minimum breadth, Hanihara[71] obtains an 85% correct classification in the mandible by means of discriminant function analysis. Giles[72] obtains the same percentage of certitude by similar methods but using nine mandibular measurements.

Although there is no question that discriminant function analysis represents theoretically the highest degree of discriminatory power to our respect, it can be seen that with less elegant and sophisticated means, but with valid osteometric knowledge and judgement,[68,70] thirty years ago the same results had been obtained.

ARTICULAR SURFACES OF THE BONES—ESPECIALLY THE LONG-BONES

Just as the vertical diameter of the acetabulum is found amongst the four characteristics of greatest value in the innominate bone for sex discrimination, the femur and humerus heads, as also their distal articular surfaces and those of the other long-bones, are very valuable for sex determination. Generally, in male and female long-bones of the same general size, the articular surface of the second will be appreciably less than that of the first. Obviously, this is better appreciated in femur and humerus heads, although others (e.g. the sigmoid notch of the ulna or the upper articular surface of the astragalus) can be very useful.[26,47]

Although long-bone criteria are not commonly used, there is an extensive literature dealing directly with sex differences in these bones.[73–76] Dwight,[77] in a fairly ample series, found that the diameter of the femur head has a mean of 49·7 mm and 43·8 mm for men and women respectively, with only one male specimen having a value lower than the female one, and only two females above the male mean. Thieme and Schull[78] in a study of North American Negroes calculated means of 57·17 mm and 41·52 mm for the diameter of the femoral head in men and women respectively. They conclude that it is 'the best single measurement for discriminating the sexes in this series' of the eight characters studied. By using for preference the femur head, the epicondylar width of the humerus and other characteristics of the long-bones and pelvis they were able to reach an accuracy of 98·5% in known material and one of 97% when the material was unknown.

WITH ALL THE SKELETON

It is evident that when the whole skeleton is at our disposal sex assignation becomes a rather cursory matter. This is, however, a most unusual happening in anthropological practice. Treating by means of discriminant function analysis six measurements (basion-bregma height; maximum length of femur; length of *cavitas glenoidalis* of the scapula; the ischium-pubis index—with Genovés'[60] modified technique—and the total breadth of the atlas, a misclassification of only 1·01% is obtained.[63]

SOME OTHER CHARACTERISTICS

Apart from what appears below about the scapula by Bainbridge and Genovés[79] and apart from the various data provided by Vallois,[80] Olivier and Pineau[81] give the following data: (1) A scapula is female if the breadth of the glenoid fossa is less than 2·61 mm; (2) the height of the bone less than 144·4 mm; (3) the length of the spine less than 127·9 mm; and (4) the weight less than 38·58 g; the bone is male if these dimensions are more than 26·8 mm, 15·75 mm, 141·4 mm, and 61·78 g respectively.

From the articles by Olivier et al.[82] on the clavicle the useful data in Table B has been taken.

Although it has traditionally been desirable to use the sacrum for sex determination, Piganiol and Olivier[83] reach the conclusion that the only element of any value in this respect is the weight. This is of little use in fragmentary material.

TABLE B

Dimensions of clavicle used in determination of sex.

	Female if less than	Male if more than
Maximum length	138 mm	150 mm
Maximum breadth	20·5 mm	25·5 mm
Perimeter at the middle of the diaphysis	32 mm	36 mm
Weight	8 g	20 g

Various authors have attempted to use the sternum in sex discrimination, but I believe that its use is too open to error, and in any case, it is very rare to find a complete sternum of prehistoric date (*see* Serra[84] and especially Ashley[85] in this respect).

Some authors[74,75] have revived in recent years the method of using the weight of the bones as characteristics of sex discrimination, but its value seems to be very low and almost never applicable to early remains.

Gejvall[88] has suggested standards for verifying sex (and age) of cremated remains. This method seems promising, but certainly needs further elaboration.

CONCLUSIONS

Although some important aspects of sex determination have been neglected in the past, new statistical procedures are gaining greater attention, not only for their application to articular surface measurements, but also in that these methods are being applied to other parts of the skeleton such as the skull, sternum, pelvis and scapula.

Pons[77] achieves 95%, 94% and 89% correct estimates using four femoral, six pelvic, and five sternal measurements respectively. Bainbridge and Genovés[79] applied their method to various metrical characteristics of the scapula from a population of known identity, comprising twenty-six males and twenty females, with the following results:

At the 99–87% limits 21 individuals were 'sexed'.
At the 87–80% limits 2 more individuals were 'sexed'.
At the 84–20% limits 10 more individuals were 'sexed'.

Several authors such as Pons,[89] Bainbridge and Genovés,[79] McKern and Munro,[90] Brothwell,[91] Hanihara,[63] Giles and Elliot,[67,92] Steel,[93] and later Giles,[72] Hanihara,[63] and Howells,[35] have applied Fisher's method of discriminant functions or the concept of 'size and shape' introduced by Penrose[82] for racial diagnosis. Perhaps, by following these methods, we shall in the future possess true limits of accuracy for the sex determination of various parts of the skeleton, and for a range of human populations both prehistoric and recent. This is a desirable goal which is not so far distant.

This requires deep knowledge of mathematical procedures and of statistical techniques. For archaeologists, in practical cases consultation with pp. 51–56 of Brothwell,[48] of pp. 79–118 of Genovés,[47] or of pp. 112–52 of Krogman[45] is suggested.

REFERENCES AND NOTES

1 BOULE, M. 1911–13. Ann. Paléont. 6, 106–72; 7, 21–192; 8, 1–70
2 LEAKEY, L. S. B. 1953. Adam's Ancestors, London, 4th ed.
3 BOYD, W. C. 1950. Genetics and the Races of Man, Boston
4 HOOTON, E. A. 1930. The Indians of Pecos Pueblo; a Study of their Skeletal Remains, New Haven
5 ANGEL, J. L. 1954. Human Biology, Health and History in Greece from First Settlement until Now. Yearbook Am. Phil. Soc., 168–74.
6 NEEL, J. V. 1958. Hum. Biol. 30, 43–72
7 FEREMBACH, D. 1960. Boletim da Soc. Portug. de Ciencias Naturais sér. 2a, 8, 1–6
8 —— 1960. Trabalhos de Anthropologia e Etnologia 18, 5–23
9 ORFORD, M. 1934. S. Afr. J. Sci. 31, 586–610
10 HEYNS, O. S. 1945. A Critical Analysis of the Bantu Pelvis with Special Reference to the Female; D.Sc. thesis, Univ. of the Witwatersrand, Johannesburg
11 HOOIJER, D. A. 1948. Zoo. Med. Museum Leiden 29, 175–301
12 —— 1950. Verh. Ken. Ned. Akad. v. Wetenschappen Amsterdam, Afd. Natuurk II, 46, 1–164
13 —— 1952. Proc. Ken. Ned. Akad. v. Wetenschappen Amsterdam, ser. C, 55, 375–81
14 MORANT, G. M. 1930. Ann. Eugen. Lond. 4, 214

15 BONIN, G. VON. 1935. *Hum. Biol.* 7, 196–221
16 BROTHWELL, D. R. 1961. *Man.* 61, 113–16
17 KEITH, SIR ARTHUR. 1931. *New Discoveries Relating to the Antiquity of Man*, London
18 Though he expressed this opinion cautiously and stated that it was subject to modification in the light of further discoveries
19 McCOWN, T. D. and KEITH, SIR ARTHUR. 1939. *The Stone Age of Mount Carmel*, Oxford, vol. II
20 STEWART, T. D. 1960. *Science* 131, 1437–8
21 GENOVÉS, S. T. 1954. *J. Roy. Anth. Inst.* 84, 131–44
22 JENKS, A. E. 1936. *Pleistocene Man in Minnesota: a fossil Homo Sapiens*, Minneapolis
23 HRDLIČKA, A. 1937. *Am. J. Phys. Anth.* 22, 175–99
24 JENKS, A. E. 1938. *Am. Anth.* 40, 328–36
25 DE TERRA, H. J. ROMERO and STEWART, T. D. 1949. Tepexpan Man. *Viking Fund Publications in Anthropology*, no. 11
26 GENOVÉS, S. T. 1960. *Am. J. Phys. Anth.* 18, 205–18
27 WOOD JONES, F. 1907–8. *The Archaeological Survey of Nubia, II: Report on the Human Remains*, Cairo
28 FAULHABER, H. in GENOVÉS S. (ed.). *Homenaje a Juan Comas*, Vol. II, 83–122, Mexico City D.F.
29 KEEN, J. A. 1950. *Am. J. Phys. Anth.* 8, 65–78
30 STEWART, T. D. 1954. *Ibid.* 12, 385–92
31 GAILLARD, J. 1960. *Bull. et Mem. de la Soc. d'Anthrop. de Paris*, IIe s., t. 1, 255–67
32 —— 1961. *Ibid.*, IIe s. t. 2, 92–108
33 FEDELI, M. 1962. *Riv. di Antropologia XLIX*, 201–12
34 LARNACH, S. L. and FREEDMAN, L. 1964. *Records of the Australian Museum* 26, 259–308
35 HOWELLS, W. W. 1965. *Bull. et Mem. de la Soc. d'Anthrop. de Paris.* IIe s., t. 7, 95–105
36 HANNA, R. E. and WASHBURN, S. L. 1953. *Hum. Biol.* 2, 21–27
37 TESTUT, L. 1928. *Traité d'Anatomie humaine* (ed. LATARJET, L., Paris)
38 KROGMAN, W. 1939. *FBI Law Enforcement Bull.* 8, no. 8
39 STEWART, T. D. 1948. *Am. J. Phys. Anth.* 6, 315–28
40 BRASH, J. C. (ed.) 1951. *Cunningham's Text Book of Anatomy*, London, 9th ed.
41 HRDLIČKA, A. 1952. *Practical Anthropometry* (ed. STEWART, T. D.), Philadelphia, 4th ed.
42 BOYD, J. D. and TREVOR, J. C. 1953. Problems in Reconstruction; I: Race, Sex, Age and Stature from Skeletal Material, in SIMPSON, C. K. (ed.) *Modern Trends in Forensic Medicine*, London, 133–52
43 CORNWALL, I. W. 1956. *Bones for the Archaeologist*, London
44 OLIVIER, G. 1960. *Pratique anthropologique*, Paris
45 MONTAGU, M. F. A. 1960. *A Handbook of Anthropometry*, New York
46 KROGMAN, W. M. 1961. *The Human Skeleton in Forensic Medicine*, Springfield
47 GENOVÉS, S. 1962. *Introducción al Diagnóstico de la Edad y del Sexo en Restos Oseos Prehistóricos*, Mexico City D.F.
48 BROTHWELL, D. R. 1963. *Digging up Bones*, London
49 FEHLING, H. 1876. *Arch. Gynaek.* 10, 1–80
50 THOMSON, A. 1899. *J. Anat. Lond.* 33, 359–80
51 VILLEMIN, F. 1957. *Strasbourg Méd. J.* 33
52 KONIKOW, M. 1894. *Arch. Gynaek.* 45, 19–42
53 LE DAMANY, 1904. *J. Anat. Paris*, 40, 387–413
54 KAPPERS, J. ARIENS. 1938. *Biemetrische Bijdrage tet de Kennis van de ontogenestische entwikkeling van het menschelijk Pekken*, Assen
55 YAMAMURA, H. 1939. *Jap. J. Obstet. Gynaec.* 22, 268–341
56 HEYNS, O. S. 1947. *S. Afr. J. Med. Sci.* 12, 17–20
57 BOUCHER, B. J. 1955. *J. Forensic Med.* 1, 51–54
58. —— 1957. *Am. J. Phys. Anth.* 15, 587–600
59 GENOVÉS, S. T. 1959a. *Diferencias sexuales en el hueso coxal*, México
60 GENOVÉS, S. T. 1959b. *Bull. et Mém. de la Soc. d'Anth. de Paris* 10ème sér., 10, 3–95
61 LAZORTHES, G. and LHEZ, A. 1939. *Arch. Anat. Strasbourg* 27, 143–70
62 LETTERMAN, G. S. 1941. *Am. J. Phys. Anth.* 28, 99–116
63 HANIHARA, K. K., KIMURA, and MINAMIDATE, T. 1964. *Japanese J. Forensic Med.* 18, 107–14
64 WOO, J. K. 1949. *Am. J. Phys. Anth.* 7, 215–26
65 MACHADO DE SOUSA, O. 1954. *Revista de Antrop.* 2, 11–18

66 GILES, E. and BLEIBTREU, H. K. 1961. *Amer. Anthrop. 63*, 48–61
67 —— and ELLIOT, O. 1963. *Am. J. Phys. Anthrop. 21*, 53–68
68 MORANT, G. M. 1936. *Biometrika 28*, 84–122
69 ALBUQUERQUE, R. M. 1952. *Contribuções para o Estudo da Antrop. Portug. 5*, 65–196
70 CLEAVER, F. H. 1937–8. *Biometrika 29*, 80–112
71 HANIHARA, K. K. 1959. *J. Anthrop. Soc. Nippon, 67*, 191–7
72 GILES, E. 1964. *Am. J. Phys. Anthrop. 22*, 129–36
73 DWIGHT, T. 1894. *Boston Med. and Surg. J. 22*, 1–12
74 —— 1904. *Am. J. Anat. 4*, 18–31
75 PARSONS, F. G. 1914. *J. Anat. Lond. 48*, 238–67
76 PEARSON, K. 1915. *Biometrika 10*, 479–87
77 DWIGHT, T. 1900. *J. Anat. Lond. 24*, 61–68
78 THIEME, F. P. and SCHULL W. J. 1957, *Hum. Biol. 29*, 242–73
79 BAINBRIDGE D. and GENOVÉS, S. T. 1956. *J. Roy. Anth. Inst. 86*, 109–29
80 VALLOIS, H. V. 1928–46. *Bull. et Mém. de la Soc. d'Anth. de Paris* 7ème. sér., *9* (1928), 129–68; 7ème sér., *1* (1929), 110–91: 8ème sér., *2* (1932), 3–153: 9ème. sér., *7* (1946), 16–110
81 OLIVIER, G. and PINEAU, H. 1957. *Arch. d'Anat. 5*, 67–88
82 —— 1951–6. *Bull. et Mém. de la Soc. d'Anth. de Paris* 10ème. sér., *2* (1951), 67–99 and 121–57; 10ème. sér., *3* (1952), 269–79: 10ème. sér., *4* (1953), 553–61: 10ème. sér., *5* (1954), 35–56 (with CHALBEUF, M. and LALUQUE, P.) and 144–53; 10èmé. ser., *6* (1955), 282–302: 10èmé. ser., *7* (1956), 225–61 (with CAPLIEZ, S.) and 404–47
83 PIGANIOL, G. and OLIVIER, G. 1958. *C.R. de l'Assn. des Anatomistes (54e. réunion)* no. *100*, 589–94
84 SERRA, J. A. 1941. *Contribuições para o Estudo da Antrop. Portug. 4*, 33–159
85 ASHLEY, G. T. 1956. *J. Forensic Med. 3*, 27–43
86 VALLOIS, H. V. 1957. *L'Anth. 61*, 45–69
87 OLIVIER, G. and PINEAU, H. 1958. *Bull. et Mém. de la Soc. d'Anth. de Paris* 10ème. sér., *9*, 328–39
88 GEJVALL, N.-G. 1959. Vanligaste Ben: Nagot om Bearbetning Av Branda Ben Och Deras Vetenskapliga Värde. *Särtryck ur Fvnd*. Göteborg
89 PONS, J. 1955. *Trabajos del Instituto Bernardino de Sahagún 14*, 137–59
90 McKERN, T. W. and MUNRO, E. H. 1959. *Am. Antiq. 24*, 375–82
91 BROTHWELL, D. R. 1959. *Deutschen Ges. f. Anth. 6*, 103–9
92 GILES, E. and ELLIOT, O. 1962. *VIe. Cong. Int. Scis. Anthrop. et Ethnol. 1*, 179–84
93 STEEL, F. L. D. 1962. *J. Roy. Anthrop. Inst. 92*, 212–22
94 PENROSE, L. S. 1954. *Ann. Eugen. London 18*, 337–43

38 Estimation of Age and Mortality

SANTIAGO GENOVÉS

THERE ARE TWO SIDES to the problem of determining the age of prehistoric remains: first, what we can ascertain about the age distribution and life expectation of earlier populations, either by analysing their skeletal remains, or by examining the vital statistics of present-day human groups whose state of cultural development is comparable with the peoples being studied by the prehistorian; second, starting with the data provided by well-identified remains, and by legitimate morphological methods of deduction obtaining formulae for the estimation of age in skeletal remains. During the last few years the criteria for the second point have changed considerably. Nevertheless, the data regarding this aspect are far more abundant than for the first.

Precision in the diagnosis of age in a skeleton has been a subject for study chiefly owing to the interest displayed in it by physical anthropologists, and to its application in the field of forensic medicine. Only recently have we taken account of the value it holds in the study of earlier populations. It must, however, be said at the outset that recent studies have shown once more that, although we can arrive at a fair degree of exactness in age estimates, the variability *within* and *between* the races is considerable. Indeed, there remains much to be discovered in this field of study, which means that the estimation of age in either individuals or populations is still subject to a variable margin of error.

Before continuing, a few explanations are necessary. In the first place we cannot depend on having skeletal series representing prehistoric populations which are statistically large enough in number and which are perfectly identified as regards the characteristics of age. We base our deductions chiefly on data taken from more recent and better known groups, and from those which we have reason to believe possess—because of their racial affinities, geographic location, and cultural similarities—characteristics homologous to the peoples we are trying to analyse. Moreover, we shall be concerned here solely with prehistoric man belonging to the species *Homo sapiens*, for if we venture into previous morphological stages, the problem becomes greater and more complex.[1]

Apart from the cultural elements often associated with skeletal remains—which can indirectly shed some light on the subject of age estimation and the numbers and demographic characteristics of a population—we rely in the first instance on the number and state of development of the bones, and on certain characteristics in them which have been successfully related to definite ages.

It may be noted here that although we are at present considering age, it has in fact quite a close relationship with sex. It is well known that in general the developmental stage of bone growth in relation to chronological age is more advanced in females than in males. Thus it is estimated, for example,[2] that in girls the ischio-pubic ramus is joined at approximately $4\frac{1}{2}$ years whilst in boys this occurs at about 7 years; also that fusion of the three primary elements of the pelvis takes place at about 10 years and 14 years respectively.

DEMOGRAPHY AND MORTALITY

Until very recently the essential criteria for age estimation in adults consisted of observing the degree of obliteration of the cranial sutures. It is because of this that excessive age estimates were misguidedly made in the past on prehistoric man.

Expectation of life in prehistoric groups. At the very beginning of this century[3] investigations began to be made into the life expectation of earlier man, finding that chances of long life were very small. Lately, a fair number of authors have concerned themselves with this problem.[4-12] Vallois,[5] for example, has considered in detail life expectation in Upper Palaeolithic and Mesolithic man (Table A). It will be seen that an age of over 50 years was very seldom attained, and although he considered suture criteria in this work, the evidence of the post-cranial remains does not fundamentally contradict these findings. Further data on age variability in earlier groups is given in Tables B and C. From other considerations there is no doubt that there exists a close relationship between the cultural level and the expectation of life in earlier times.

TABLE A

Expectation of life of Upper Palaeolithic and Mesolithic man.

	No.	Age				
		12–20	21–30	31–40	41–50	51–60
Upper Palaeolithic and Ibero-Maurusian men	86	15 (17·4 %)	31 (36 %)	27 (31·4 %)	11 (12·8 %)	2 (2·3 %)
Mesolithic men	50	6 (12 %)	35 (70 %)	6 (12 %)	1 (2 %)	2 (4 %)

From Vallois.[5]

Mortality of sub-adults. Until recently, little attention has been given to this subject. The small quantity of sub-adult remains, their lack of inclusion in normal population statistics, and their frequent state of severe fragmentation, have contributed to their being overlooked for quite a long time. A further complicating factor is the possible practice of burying stillbirths or young infants in places away from the main cemeteries, which thus are usually missed. Nevertheless, after considering such problems, Howells[8] deduces that the percentage of mortality among sub-adults was between 55 and 60%.

Sex differences in mortality. Many authors are in agreement that in prehistoric times and early historic periods mortality among females was considerably more frequent before the age of 40 years than for males.[4-7,9,11,13-15] This greater female mortality during the earlier age periods (contrary to what happens today) is usually attributed to causes related to pregnancy, although other reasons have also been suggested.

TABLE B

Mortality by age in populations of different epochs.

Origin	Period	n	Distribution by ages					Authors
			0–12 %	13–20 %	21–40 %	41–60 %	61–x %	
Several	Lower Palaeolithic (*H. neanderthalensis*)	20	40·0	15·0	40·0	5·0	0·0	Vallois (1937)**
—	Upper Palaeolithic	102	24·5	9·8	53·9	11·8	0·0	**
—	Mesolithic	65	30·8	6·2	58·5	3·0	1·5	**
Spanish Levant	Neo-eneolithic	101	24·7	14·8	41·6	17·8	1·0	Fusté (1952)
Anatolia	Chalcolithic and Copper Age	104	31·7	12·5	34·6	17·3	3·8	Several (Senyürek, 1951)
—	Chalcolithic to 13th cent. BC	122	20·4	13·1	40·9	19·6	5·7	Senyürek (1947)†
Aulnay-aux-Planches	Neolithic	28	0·0	7·1	64·3	25·0	3·6	Riquet (1943) and Fusté (1952)*
Austria	Bronze	273	6·9	17·2	39·9	28·6	7·3	Franz and Winkler (1936)**
Ancient Greeks	—	2,022	18·7	23·4	33·8	13·6	10·1	Several (Richardson, 1933)†
Egyptians	Roman era	141	19·8	14·1	39·7	16·3	9·9	Pearson (1901–1902)†
Ancient Romans	—	8,065	38·1	19·9	30·0	7·1	4·6	MacDonell (1913)†
Spain and Lusitania	Roman era	1,996	9·4	16·4	38·8	19·9	15·2	
Africa	Roman era	10,697	9·9	9·4	28·4	19·6	32·4	
Lower Austria	1829	—	50·7	3·3	12·2	12·8	21·0	Franz and Winkler (1936)**
—	1900	—	44·3	2·0	12·1	15·7	25·9	
—	1927	—	15·4	2·7	11·9	22·6	47·4	
France	1896–1905	—	25·3	2·6	11·5	17·3	43·3	Vallois (1937)**
		n	0–14	15–19	20–39	40–59	61–x	
Spain	1948	299,178	21·8	2·3	11·8	16·3	47·7	Statistical Year Book, 1950
—	1949	315,512	20·7	2·0	10·8	16·2	50·3	1951
—	1950	300,112	19·7	1·9	10·1	15·9	52·4	1952
—	1951	321,083	17·6	1·5	8·7	15·7	56·6	1953

From Fusté,[6] p. 328.

* Compilation of the Aulnay-aux-Planches series (Riquet 1943) and of the Dolmen des Bretons (Fusté 1952), of the same locality.

** The limit between the first two categories of ages is at 14 years.

† According to Senyürek, 1951.

TABLE C
Percentage of male and female deaths in relation to age at death.

Age Group	Bronze Age of Lower Austria		Egyptians of Roman times	
	%M.	%F.	%M.	%F.
Adolescents (14–20 yrs)	10	25·9	6·5	18·1
Adults (21–40 yrs)	37·5	52·8	44·2	65·9
Mature Adults (41–60 yrs)	45	13	29·5	11·3
Senile (> 60 yrs)	7·5	8·3	19·6	4·5

From Vallois,[4] p. 530.

METHODS OF DETERMINING SKELETAL AGE[16]

Up to the age of about 30 years, the estimation of age for fairly complete specimens can be made with reasonable accuracy by considering methodically three groups of processes. These are dental eruption, synostosis of the bones, and epiphysial union of the bones—especially the long-bones. For later age periods, transformations on the articular surface of the pubic symphysis and certain structural changes within the bones themselves are employed.

DENTAL ERUPTION AND OTHER CHANGES

Milk dentition. Although sex differences in dental maturation are slight, there is good evidence that eruption can be influenced by outside factors.[17] In Table D data for Korean, North American and Japanese boys are compared to show the degree of variability.

TABLE D
Eruption of primary teeth (in months): comparison of Korean, American and Japanese infants.

	Maxillary			Mandibular		
	Korean	American	Japanese	Korean	American	Japanese
Central incisors	9–11	6–9	7–9	7–9	5–7	7–9
Lateral incisors	11–14	7–11	8–11	11–14	6–8	8–11
Canines	15–19	16–20	17–20	15–19	14–18	16–19
First milk molars	13–19	10–18	15–20	13–19	8–16	15–20
Second milk molars	19–29	20–28	23–36	19–29	16–24	22–26

From Duk Jin Yun. 1957. *Am. J. Phys. Anth. 15,* 261–8.

Permanent dentition. Hurme,[18] in what is probably the largest sample of actual populations, provides the data presented in Table E. In regard to this he writes:'A glance at the table shows that the minima and maxima at the 95% level are quite apart, ranging from a little over 3 years to more than 6½ years, not counting the third molars. Thus

TABLE E
Normal variability in emergence of human permanent teeth.

Sequence	Tooth Max.	Tooth Mand.	95 % range (yrs) Males	95 % range (yrs) Females	Sex diff. (yr)
1	—	M₁	4·64 – 7·78	4·37 – 7·51	·27
2	M¹	—	4·83 – 7·97	4·65 – 7·79	·18
3	—	I₁	5·01 – 8·07	4·73 – 7·79	·28
4	I¹	—	5·88 – 9·06	5·61 – 8·79	·27
5	—	I₂	5·98 – 9·42	5·62 – 9·06	·36
6	I²	—	6·75 – 10·59	6·28 – 10·12	·47
7M 8F+	P¹	—	7·52 – 13·28	7·15 – 12·91	·37
8M 7F+	—	C	8·30 – 13·28	7·37 – 12·35	·93
9	—	P₂	7·94 – 13·70	7·30 – 13·06	·64
10	P²	—	8·10 – 14·26	7·80 – 13·96	·30
11	—	P₂	8·18 – 14·76	7·60 – 14·18	·58
12	C	—	9·00 – 14·38	8·29 – 13·67	·71
13	—	M₂	9·45 – 14·79	8·99 – 14·33	·46
14	M²	—	9·99 – 15·37	9·58 – 14·96	·41
15	—	M₃	16·5(?) – 27·0(?)	16·5(?) – 27·0(?)	small
16	M³	—	16·5(?) – 27·0(?)	16·5(?) – 27·0(?)	small

From Hurme,[18] p. 379.

the chances of error are considerable in using teeth for purposes of estimation of age, and the desirability of supplementing this estimate with evidence of some other kind becomes easy to understand.'

With this in mind, and only then, should we apply tooth emergence data (Table F) to earlier material. As regards the third molars, we can say that for Europeans (and those of European origin) the main eruptional period is 17–22 years, although sometimes they are much later. Account should of course be taken of the fact that congenital absence of one or more thirds is not uncommon, the frequency of absence for modern populations ranging from a few per cent to over 30%.

Dental attrition. The degree of wear on the teeth can be used in populations where we *already know* the cultural circumstances, in order not to fall into considerable error, and in the total absence of other data. To rely on attrition in populations of whom we know little can lead to serious errors.

Other dental procedures. Approaching the problem from another angle, Zander and Hurzeler[19] have clearly shown that cementum thickness is directly related to age for single-rooted teeth with healthy supporting tissues. Likewise, Nalbandian and Sognnaes[20] have initiated studies in which they correlate chronological age with criteria such as secondary dentine, periodontal attachment, cementum apposition and root sclerosis. Employing the multifactorial approach introduced by Gustafson[21] to various modifications amongst which are figured those mentioned above, it is possible that valid results will be obtained in the future.

TABLE F *Estimates of age of tooth emergence, means of means (in years). † The sexual dimorphism in Negro, American, and Caucasoid American and English populations.*

Group	Source	Method	Range of Size of n	Maxillary Teeth						
				I^1	I^2	C^1	P^1	P^2	M^1	M^2
Male										
American Negro	Steggerda & Hill	L, m	From 9 to 50	7·77 / ·66	8·45 / ·81	11·74 / ·97	10·82 / 1·09	11·92 / 1·03	6·79 / ·79	12·64 / ·92
Zulu	Suk	C, med.	492	5·98 / 1·07	6·98 / 1·40	10·17 / 1·55	10·11 / 1·35	10·66 / 1·19	5·26 / ·69	11·36 / 1·21
Maya	Steggerda & Hill	L, m	25 to 67	8·35 / ·67	9·30 / ·88	11·79 / 1·13	10·29 / 1·01	11·63 / 1·03	6·88 / ·55	12·49 / ·99
Pima	Dahlberg	C, med.	470	7·83 / ·71	8·74 / ·75	11·66 / 1·41	10·08 / 1·28	11·33 / 1·36	5·98 / ·77	11·67 / 1·21
American	Cattell	C, med.	3,863	7·33 / ·74	8·42 / ·79	11·50 / 1·20	10·33 / 1·59	11·08 / 1·31	6·33 / ·79	12·16 / 1·13
English	Ainsworth	C, med.	2,000	7·42 / ·69	8·81 / ·94	11·73 / 1·12	9·96 / 1·42	10·89 / 1·50	6·34 / ·68	12·33 / 1·06
New Zealand	Leslie	C, med.	1,427	7·26 / ·80	8·32 / ·90	11·40 / 1·12	11·01 / 1·37	11·74 / 1·29	6·47 / ·78	12·47 / 1·33
Female										
American Negro	Steggerda & Hill	L, m	8 to 50	7·13 / ·60	8·31 / ·88	10·39 / ·85	10·07 / ·79	10·97 / ·81	6·90 / ·45	11·85 / ·75
Zulu	Suk	C, med.	516	6·18 / ·93	7·14 / 1·25	9·72 / 1·44	9·76 / 1·27	10·06 / 1·23	5·77 / ·57	10·92 / 1·38
Maya	Steggerda & Hill	L, m	13 to 55	8·27 / ·85	8·63 / ·76	10·89 / 1·00	9·96 / ·94	10·92 / ·94	6·69 / ·70	12·09 / 1·01
Pima	Dahlberg	C, med.	487	7·47 / ·69	8·34 / ·98	10·94 / 1·59	9·63 / 1·23	10·73 / 1·34	5·80 / ·79	11·38 / 1·29
American	Cattell	C, med.	3,826	7·08 / ·68	8·00 / ·79	11·08 / 1·07	9·92 / 1·31	10·92 / 1·42	6·16 / ·57	12·08 / 1·13
English	Ainsworth	C, med.	2,000	7·20 / ·63	8·37 / ·94	11·20 / 1·12	9·77 / 1·13	10·72 / 1·33	6·12 / ·68	12·07 / 1·03
New Zealand	Leslie	C, med.	1,335	6·83 / ·69	7·86 / ·61	10·82 / 1·02	10·52 / ·99	11·24 / 1·20	6·38 / ·78	12·20 / 1·28

(continued overleaf)

TABLE F (continued)

Group	Source	Method	Range of Size of n	$_1I_1$	$_2I_2$	$_1C_1$	$_1P_1$	$_2P_2$	$_1M_1$	$_2Mt_2$
Male										
American Negro	Steggerda & Hill	L, m	From 9 to 50	6·95	7·94	10·99	10·86	11·48	6·97	12·33
				·59	·76	·94	·87	·90	·70	1·02
Zulu	Suk	C, med.	492	5·47	5·96	9·63	10·11	10·75	5·23	11·04
				·73	1·04	1·31	1·38	1·28	·71	1·17
Maya	Steggerda & Hill	L, m	25 to 67	7·41	8·40	11·16	11·14	11·99	6·76	11·86
				·67	·53	·90	1·00	1·08	·62	1·07
Pima	Dahlberg	C, med.	470	6·26	7·65	10·78	10·43	11·39	5·89	11·29
				·89	1·21	1·28	1·29	1·45	·67	1·25
American	Cattell	C, med.	3,863	6·25	7·58	10·66	10·58	11·33	6·16	11·66
				·68	·79	1·02	1·36	1·54	·79	·86
English	Ainsworth	C, med.	2,000	6·49	7·72	10·80	10·86	11·80	6·24	11·86
				·69	·71	1·09	1·33	1·50	·69	1·09
New Zealand	Leslie	C, med.	1,427	6·38	7·42	10·78	11·34	12·18	6·46	11·89
				·59	·83	·93	1·42	1·44	·76	1·13
Female										
American Negro	Steggerda & Hill	L, m	8 to 50	6·28	7·19	9·73	10·23	10·77	6·33	11·43
				·79	·70	·92	·87	·90	·62	·99
Zulu	Suk	C, med.	516	5·85	6·23	9·12	9·76	10·24	5·49	10·61
				·73	1·03	1·07	1·12	1·32	·75	1·49
Maya	Steggerda & Hill	L, m	13 to 55	7·15	8·09	10·32	10·24	11·16	6·68	11·49
				·78	·81	·81	·87	·90	·76	1·10
Pima	Dahlberg	C, med.	487	6·15	7·32	9·66	9·87	10·73	5·43	10·80
				·75	1·02	1·25	1·30	1·46	·99	1·05
American	Cattell	C, med.	3,826	6·08	7·25	9·66	10·08	11·08	6·00	11·42
				·52	·68	·91	1·13	1·42	·45	1·07
English	Ainsworth	C, med.	2,000	6·23	7·50	9·90	10·36	11·21	5·95	11·52
				·65	·72	·95	1·22	1·46	·68	1·03
New Zealand	Leslie	C, med.	1,335	6·19	7·16	9·74	10·54	11·73	6·30	11·36
				·60	·62	·94	1·18	1·35	·59	1·47

Mandibular Teeth

From Dahlberg A. and Menegaz-Bock, R. 1958. *J. Dent. Res.* 37, 1123–40, Table VIII.

SYNOSTOSIS OF BONES

The pelvis. Although a certain degree of variability exists, the union of the ischium and pubis in the ischio-pubic ramus and the union of the three elements composing the acetabulum, are of use in the case of pre-adolescents (Table G).

TABLE G
The pelvis: union of the conjoined rami and of the acetabulum.

Year of Union of Conjoined Rami	Author	Year of Union Acetabulum
—	Stevenson (1924)[22]	at 15–16
7th year	Wood Jones in *Buchanan's Anatomy* (1949)[23]	14–16
4–4½ in females 7 in males	Francis (1952)[24]	females at 10 males at 14
8 in females later in males	Smout (1943)[25]	—
9th year	Grant (1952)[26]	—
—	McKern and Stewart (1957)[27]	at 17 (final age)

The sacrum. Allowing for bone variations, union of the bodies of the sacral vertebrae begins at about 16 years and proceeds from the lower segments upwards. At about 23 years, ossification is complete, although in a number of cases the union between the upper segments S_1 and S_2 is not completed until about 30 years.

The skull. Contrary to the criteria traditionally accepted until recent times, the process of suture obliteration in *Homo sapiens* does not follow a well-defined pattern.[27,28] Various authors have thrown grave doubts on the idea that the sutures are directly related to the growth of the skull, and as a result, to the age of the individual.[29-37] Thus the only union of bones in the skull which we are now able to employ is at the basi-sphenoid synchondrosis. This gap between the basi-sphenoid and basi-occipital is obliterated about adulthood, as various authors have found (Table H).

TABLE H
Closure of the basi-sphenoidal synchondrosis.

Author	Begins–Ends
	yrs
Cunningham (1951)[34]	18–25
Prinsloo (1953)[35]	23
Hrdlička (1952)[36]	18–19
McKern and Stewart (1957)[27]	18–21
Genovés and Messmacher (1959)[37]	18–20
Vallois (1960)[5]	17–23
Singer—Comments to Vallois, 1960	17–25

EPIPHYSIAL UNION OF THE BONES, ESPECIALLY THE LONG-BONES

The distal epiphysis of the humerus and proximal epiphyses of the ulna and radius. These show the first signs of union, which is generally complete by 18 years.

The epiphyses of the femur, tibia and fibula. According to the majority of authors, the process of epiphysial fusion of these bones has already been completed by the age of 19 years, making it possible to estimate 17–18 years for a specimen with partial ossification and less than 17 years if the process has not yet begun.

The ischial tuberosity. The epiphysial portion of the ischial tuberosity unites with the rest of the ascending ramus of the ischium at about 19 years, and towards 20 years completes its process of ossification.

Iliac crest and vertebral epiphysial plates. If the plates and crest are separate the person is under 19 years. If there is partial obliteration, the age is probably between 19 and 20 years. Over the age of 20 years union is usually complete.

Proximal epiphysis of the humerus and distal epiphyses of the ulna and radius. The ossification process of the epiphyses is relatively slower, for it begins at about 18 years and does not end until about 21–22 years of age. Although these three epiphyses have been grouped together, there is evidence that the humerus head undergoes a slight retardation in its ossification relative to the other two.

Medial extremity of the clavicle. This presents certain difficulties on account of the polymorphism of the articular surfaces. Nevertheless we can say that although the process of fusion generally begins at about 18 years, it is quite often retarded and may begin as late as 25 years. Normally the fusion ends between 27 and 30 years, with the last site of union being located in the form of a fissure along the inferior border.

The relation between minimal diameter of the medullary canal and the minimal diaphysis diameter at the same level seems to provide a useful criterion in long bones to determine the age of the specimen.[38]

CHANGES AT THE ARTICULAR SURFACE OF THE PUBIC SYMPHYSIS

Todd[39] described ten phases through which the symphysial surface of the pubis passes in its metamorphosis from adolescence up to 50 years or more. With slight variations other authors have since corroborated the usefulness of this method.

Whilst the non-specialist can, with sound criteria and within certain limits, use the guides which have so far been indicated for the estimation of age, it is far more difficult for him to succeed in using the criteria of the pubic symphysis in the same form. Nevertheless it seems worth giving here, at least very concisely, the ten phases of Todd, with slight corrections proposed by Brooks[28] (McKern and Stewart[27] have reproduced these basic changes in plastic casts which can be obtained):

(1) 17·5–19·5 years: surface crossed by horizontal crests separated by a distinct groove; margins not defined. (2) 19·5–21·5 years: the grooves begin to fill up, starting from the posterior margin which begins to be noticeable. (3) 21·5–24·0 years: the grooves become progressively obliterated and the posterior margin shows up more clearly; the anterior margin is slightly bevelled. (4) 24·0–26·0 years: posterior margin clearly delimited by the 'dorsal plateau'. The bevelled anterior margin acquires a

considerable extension, with the lower border beginning to appear. (5) 26·0–27·0 years: sporadic beginnings of the formation of a 'ventral rampart'; the posterior and inferior borders become more and more defined and the upper border begins to appear. (6) 27·0–33·5 years: upper and lower borders are better defined; ventral rampart reaching its final stage of evolution. (7) 33·5–38·0 years: the granular surface of the symphysial area grows smaller and exotoses appear on it. (8) 38·0–42·0 years: the surface becomes smooth, having for the first time a complete border on the articular area. (9) 42·0–50·5 years: the posterior border becomes more visible and more prominent than the rest. (10) 50·5 or more years: the surface acquires an eroded appearance and a look of disordered ossification; the border begins to disintegrate.

It must be emphasized that after the age of 30 the symphysial surfaces of the pubic bone are often quite altered and distorted in bone remains belonging to females who have borne children, and therefore the symphysis appears in age to be much beyond those normally representing the actual ages.[40,41]

These, nevertheless, are certainly the best criteria for age estimates after 18 years. Indeed, because of the very favourable results, too much attention is being paid to them, forgetting other criteria which are still of value as supporting evidence.

MORPHOSCOPIC ALTERATIONS IN BONES

From birth until death the bones experience a series of primary changes. To these we have just referred. There are others, however, which we can call secondary, being of a morphoscopic or sometimes metrical nature. These are more subtle and less well defined but, when used with discretion, can be of some little value. For example, from 35 years onwards, the sciatic portion of the major sacro-sciatic ligament begins to ossify, thus forming a characteristic bony lip. Because we have no other guide than the pubic symphysis between the ages 30 and 50 years, the ossification of this ligament can be very useful. Another feature of interest is that of vertebral 'lipping' (osteo-arthritis), which develops fairly regularly and especially after the age of about 40 years.[42] Hence the feature can be used to separate the older age groups.

It must be noted that McKern[43] establishes, first, that in complete remains, instead of the usual practice of emphasizing complete skeletal coverage, dependable age estimations can be obtained from the combined maturational activity of a small number of critical areas. Second, that the use of other criteria than the pubic symphysis is only justified when this region is missing or damaged. Although this seems correct from the statistical point of view, it does not agree with the criteria of Brooks[28] nor with my own. In the first place it is a very rare thing to have for examination complete skeletons, and in the second, it is preferable to base one's opinion on different processes, especially when, as in the case of the pubic symphysis, the margin of error can be great for the non-specialist. Nevertheless, it seems worth reproducing here the graph from McKern,[43] demonstrating the relationship between certain known and predicted skeletal ages (Fig. 87).

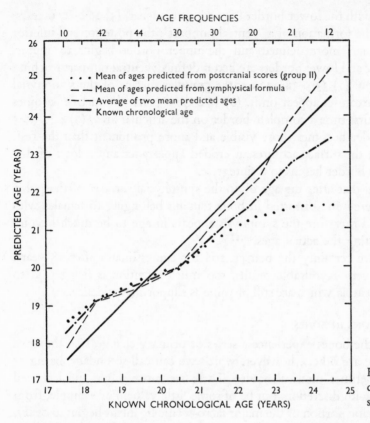

AGE FREQUENCIES

Fig. 87 Relationship between certain known and predicted skeletal ages. From McKern[43]

OTHER METHODS

Continuing along the lines of Wachholz[44] in the past century, Schranz,[45] Berndt,[46] and Hansen[47] distinguish a number of phases in the spongy structure of the femoral and humeral heads. Although the margins of error are very great, and thus it cannot be

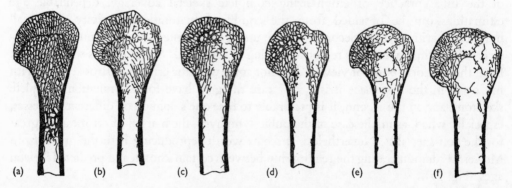

Fig. 88 Morphological changes in the upper epiphysis of the humerus from younger (a) to older (b–f) ages. From Nemeskéri et al.[48]

used by itself, there is no doubt that great benefit can be gained from it. Nemeskéri and others[48] have tried with similar results to subdivide the types of structural change. Considering this evidence, six phases of structural modification can be identified as shown in Fig. 88.

A microscopic determination of age arrives at ± 5 years of the actual one in 86·3% of the cases using selected cortical bone in a sample of 51 specimens from birth to 82 years old.[49]

For a general appraisal of the application of biochemical methods to biological reconstruction see Lengyel and Nemeskéri,[50] For general consultation, Brothwell,[51] pp. 57–67, Genovés,[52], pp. 15–47, and Krogman,[53] pp. 18–111.

REFERENCES AND NOTES

1 Weidenreich, for example, estimated the ages of the 'Sinanthropus' individuals and those from Ngandong—but they are likely to be far from the truth:
   WEIDENREICH, F. 1943. *Palaeontologica Sinica 10*
   —— 1951. *Am. Mus. Nat. Hist., Anth. Papers* no. 43, 205–90
2 FRANCIS, C. C. 1952. *The Human Pelvis*, London
3 PEARSON, K. 1901–2. *Biometrika 1*, 261–4
4 VALLOIS, H. V. 1937. *Anthropologie 47*, 499–532
5 —— 1960. Vital Statistics in Prehistoric Populations as Determined from Archaeological Data, in HEIZER, R. F. and COOK, S. F. (eds.) 'The Application of Quantitative Methods in Archaeology', *Viking Fund Publications in Anthropology* no. 28, 181–222
6 FUSTÉ, M. 1955. La duración de la vida en las poblaciones humanas del levante español durante el período neo-eneolítico. *Homenaje Póstumo al Dr D. Francisco Pardillo Vaquer*, Barcelona, 325–33
7 —— 1954. *Trabajos del Inst. 'Bernardino de Sahagún' Antrop. Etnol. 14*, 81–104
8 HOWELLS, W. W. 1960. Estimating population numbers through archaeological and skeletal remains, in HEIZER, R. F. and COOK, S. F. (eds.) *op. cit.*[5]
9 GOLDSTEIN, M. S. 1953. *Hum. Biol. 25*, 3–12
10 NEMESKÉRI, J. 1956. *V. Int. Congr. Anth. Eth. Sci.* (From Howells[8])
11 MACDONELL, W. R. 1913. *Biometrika 9*, 366–80
12 WILLCOX, W. F. 1938. *Congr. int. de la Population*, Paris, no. 2, 14–22
13 FRANZ, L. and WINKLER, W. 1936. *Z. f. Rass. 4*, 157–63
14 SENYÜREK, M. S. 1947. *Am. J. Phys. Anth. 5*, 55–66
15 —— 1951. *Belleten 15*, 447–68
16 Without doubt the most complete work on the subject of ageing is that of McKern and Stewart (a). Together with those of Vandervael (b) and Cabot Briggs (c) it has been used widely here, for these improve on and add to earlier works such as Stevenson (d), Todd and Lyon (e and f) and Augier (g).
   (a) McKERN, T. W. and STEWART, T. D. 1957. *Skeletal Age Changes in Young American Males, Analyzed from the Standpoint of Age Identification*. Quartermaster Research and Development Center, Massachusetts.
   (b) VANDERVAEL, F. 1952. *S.A.S.* no. 25–26
   (c) CABOT BRIGGS, L. 1958. *Initiation à l'Anthropologie du Squelette*, Algiers
   (d) STEVENSON, P. H. 1924. *Am. J. Phys. Anth. 7*, 53–93
   (e) TODD, T. W. and LYON, D. W. JR. 1924. *Ibid.*, 7, 325–84
   (f) —— —— 1925. *Ibid. 8*, 23–71
   (g) AUGIER, M. 1932. *Anthropologie 42*, 315–22
17 HURME, V. O. 1954. *Child Development 19*, 213
18 —— 1957. *J. Forensic Sci. 2*, 377–88
19 ZANDER, H. A. and HURZELER, B. 1958. *J. Dental Res. 37*, 1035
20 NALBANDIAN, J. and SOGNNAES, R. F. 1960. *Am. Ass. Adv. Sci.*, Pub. no. 65, 367–82
21 GUSTAFSON, G. 1950. *J. Am. Dental Ass. 41*, 45–54
22 STEVENSON, P. H. 1924. *Op. cit.*[16(d)]

23 Wood Jones, F. (ed.) 1949. *Buchanan's Manual of Anatomy*, London, 8th ed.

24 Francis, C. C. 1952. *Op. cit.*[2]

25 Smout, C. F. V. and Jacoby, F. 1943. *Gynaecological and Obstetrical Anatomy of the Female Pelvis*, London; 2nd ed., 1948; 3rd ed., 1953

26 Grant, J. C. B. 1952. *A Method of Anatomy*, Baltimore, 5th ed.

27 McKern, T. W. and Stewart, T. D. 1957. *Op. cit.*[16(a)]

28 Brooks, S. T. 1955. *Am. J. Phys. Anth.* *13*, 567–97

29 Moss, M. L. 1954a. *Ibid.* *12*, 373–84

30 —— 1954b. *Am. J. Anat.* *94*, 333–61

31 Mednick, L. W. and Washburn, S. L. 1956. *Am. J. Phys. Anth.* *14*, 175–91

32 Lachman, E. 1958. *Am. J. Roentgenol.* *79*, 721–5

33 Christensen, J. B., Lachman, E. and Brues, A. M. 1960. *Ibid.* *83*, 615–27

34 Brash, J. C. (ed.) 1951. *Cunningham's Text Book of Anatomy*, London, 9th ed.

35 Prinsloo, I. 1953. *J. Forensic Med.* *1*, 11–17

36 Hrdlička, A. 1952. *Practical Anthropometry* (ed. Stewart, T. D.), Philadelphia, 4th ed.

37 Genovés, S. T. and Messmacher, M. 1959. *Cuadernos del Inst. de Historia (Mexico)*, Ser. Antrop. no. 7

38 Eliakis, E. and Iordanidis, P. 1963. *Annales de Medicine Légale 43*, 12–18

39 Todd, T. W. 1920. *Am. J. Phys. Anth.* *3*, 285–334

40 Johnston, F. E. and Snow, Ch. E. 1961. *Amer. J. Phys. Anthrop.* *19*, 237–44

41 Stewart, T. D. 1962. *Amer. J. Phys. Anthrop.* *20*, 143–48

42 Stewart, T. D. 1958. *The Leech 28*, 144–51

43 McKern, T. W. 1957. *Am. J. Phys. Anth.* *15*, 399–408

44 Wachholz, L. 1894. *Friedreichs Beitr. ger. Med.* *45*, 210–19

45 Schranz, D. 1933. *Dt. Z. ges ger. Med.* *22*, 332–61

46 Berndt, H. 1947. *Z. ges. Inn. Med.* *2*, 122–48

47 Hansen, G. 1953–4. *Wiss. Z. Humboldt-Univ. Berlin 3*, 1–73

48 Nemeskéri, J. I., Harsányi, L. and Ascádi, G. 1960. *Anth. Anz.* *24*, 70–95

49 Kerley, R. E. 1963. (Summary) *Amer. J. Phys. Anthrop.* *21*, 404

50 Lengyel, I. and Nemeskéri, J. 1963. *Z. Morph. Anthrop.*, *54*, 1–56

51 Brothwell, D. R. 1963. *Digging up Bones*, London

52 Genovés, S. T. 1962. *Introducción al Diagnóstico de la Edad y del Sexo en Restos Oseos Prehistóricos*, Mexico City D.F.

53 Krogman, W. M. 1961. *The Human Skeleton in Forensic Medicine*, Springfield, Ill.

39 Stature in Earlier Races of Mankind

L. H. WELLS

STATURE IS ONE OF THE CHARACTERISTICS on which we chiefly rely in identifying individual human beings and also, in some measure, human population types or 'races'. Accordingly, in building up a living mental image of men of earlier periods, stature is among the characteristics which we most wish to be able to assess.

As late as the eighteenth century opinions on the stature of early man belonged to the realm of folk-lore rather than science. With the expansion of the horizons of human prehistory in the nineteenth century, inquiry into the stature of early man acquired a new significance; Broca's discussion of the stature of the Cro-Magnon fossil skeletons may be taken as marking the beginning of serious study of this problem.

THE VARIATION OF STATURE IN LIVING MAN

Anthropologists have attempted to attach absolute values to the otherwise elastic concepts of 'tall' and 'short' stature. From accumulated evidence, the mean stature of the male half of the world's living population appears to be approximately 165·0 cm (5 ft 5 in); Morant[16] gives the actual mean value from nearly four hundred samples recorded up to 1926 and representing populations from all parts of the world as 164·6 cm. Taking this mean value as a starting point, it has been found consistent with experience to label statures below 160·0 cm as 'short', and those of 170·0 cm and upwards as 'tall'. By a further extension, statures below 150·0 cm may be termed 'very short', and those of 180·0 cm and upwards 'very tall'. Both individual statures and the mean statures of population groups can be placed in these categories. The terms 'dwarf' and 'giant' are applied respectively to individuals below 130·0 cm and above 199·9 cm, limits which appear effectively outside the range of normal human variation. The term 'pygmy' is applied not to individuals but to populations whose mean stature is less than 150·0 cm, so that at least half of their members are likely to belong to the 'very short' category. There is no corresponding term for 'very tall' populations, which in fact hardly exist; Morant[16] observes that a mean stature of 180·4 cm appears to be the largest on record, whereas at the other extreme a mean as low as 143·0 cm is to be found.

The mean stature of females is approximately 10·0 cm less than that of males, the difference being about 6% of the male stature; this proportion holds with increasing and decreasing stature, and the limits of the stature categories for the female are adjusted accordingly.

Morant[16] points out that it is only in very extreme cases that the variations in stature of human populations do not overlap considerably. For some purposes it is useful to know the actual range of a series of measurements, that is the highest and lowest individual measurements encountered. Statistically, however, the variation around a mean is measured by the average amount by which individual measurements exceed or fall short of the mean; this figure is known as the standard deviation. By expressing the difference between an individual measurement and the mean of a series as a proportion of the standard deviation of the mean, the probability that the individual could have belonged to this particular series can be evaluated. In the case of stature the standard deviation varies for different population samples between 5·0 and 8·0 cm. A statistical argument against including an individual in a certain group on the ground of stature requires a difference between the individual stature and the group mean at least 2·5 times the standard deviation of the mean, e.g. the chances that an individual with a stature of 138·2 cm could have belonged to a population whose mean stature is 162·4 cm with a standard deviation of 6·5 cm are only about 1 in 10,000, the difference being 3·7 times the standard deviation.

Normal stature is known to be controlled genetically by the interaction of a large number of inherited factors. At the same time environmental influences, in particular nutrition, operating during the growth period may affect stature very considerably, preventing the genetic potentialities of the individual from being realized. Thus an appreciable fluctuation of stature from generation to generation could be caused by external circumstances in a genetically stable population.

STATURE AND THE SKELETON

Stature is divisible into two moieties, axial (head + trunk) length and lower limb length. Within a single population the proportion between these moieties varies appreciably from individual to individual, some being long-trunked and short-legged, others short-trunked and long-legged. The mean ratio between these moieties may differ from one population to another; thus leg length forms a greater proportion of stature in American Negroes than in White Americans.[26] Leg length in turn has two main components, femoral length and crural (tibio-fibular) length; the relation of femoral to crural length varies from individual to individual, and the mean femoro-crural ratio may differ from one population to another.

Upper limb length, though not a direct component of stature, in the normal individual is broadly proportionate to leg length and so indirectly to stature. However, in addition to individual and group variations in the proportion of arm length to stature and of upper-arm to forearm length, the length of the upper limb bones is affected by differential use of the two arms (handedness). Unfortunately it cannot be simply assumed that the preferred limb has been overdeveloped, nor alternatively that the neglected limb is underdeveloped; under different conditions both effects may be found in varying degrees.

In the most advantageous circumstances it would be difficult, and usually completely impossible, to assemble the trunk skeleton accurately enough for an estimate of axial length, although a method for estimating stature from the length of the vertebral column was developed by Dwight (Telkkä[24]). Stature estimates from the skeleton are therefore practically always founded on the lengths of the long bones of the limbs. From what has been said, it would be inferred that the stature could best be assessed from the combined femoro-crural length, less accurately from either the femoral or the crural length, and still less accurately from the lengths of the upper limb bones. This has in fact proved to be the case (e.g. Trotter and Gleser[26]). At the same time it follows that all these estimates, even the femoro-crural, are subject to a measure of inescapable uncertainty. Even in one population group, individuals of identical stature may have appreciably different limb-bone lengths, and conversely bones of identical length may have belonged to individuals differing appreciably in stature; these variations will be even more accentuated if individuals belonging to distinct population groups of differing limb proportions are compared.

DEVELOPMENT OF TECHNIQUES FOR STATURE ESTIMATION

The credit for the first scientific contribution to this subject may perhaps be claimed for the English surgeon-anatomist William Cheselden (1668–1752), who in 1712 communicated a paper to the Royal Society on 'The dimensions of some bones of extraordinary size which were dug up near St Albans.'[6] Of these bones (possibly Romano-British), Cheselden concluded that 'if all the parts bore a due proportion this man must have been eight foot high'. From the measurements given by Cheselden, it appears probable that his specimen was a pituitary giant, so that his estimate may well have been of the correct order; it is however his qualifying clause, 'if all the parts bore a due proportion', which deserves notice.

The history of successive attempts to devise formulae for estimating stature from limb-bone lengths has been reviewed by Telkkä[24] and by Trotter and Gleser.[25] The widely followed methods of Manouvrier and of Pearson are founded upon Rollet's study on the limb-bone lengths of 50 male and 50 female southern French individuals, published in 1888; Telkkä rightly comments on the small size of the foundation on which a great edifice has been erected.

Manouvrier's and Pearson's methods held the field for several decades, the former, as Telkkä notes, being more frequently used by continental European, and the latter by British and American workers. Some workers have questioned the validity of these methods even as applied to all European populations; in particular, Pearson's method has been considered to underestimate the stature of tall individuals. To remedy the supposed defects of the Manouvrier and Pearson techniques, Breitinger[3] attempted to develop a method using limb-bone lengths measured by indirect methods in living European subjects of known stature. This procedure allowed data from a much greater number of subjects to be used, but in the opinion of some other workers it merely substituted one set of uncertainties for another.

Both Manouvrier and Pearson regarded their methods as applicable to human material of all physical types, regarding differences in average proportions between types as less considerable than individual variability in proportion within a single type. Pearson[18] deals with the inescapable error due to individual variability in a surprisingly off-handed way, so that his reference to the matter may easily pass unnoticed, and his estimates are presented with a spurious impression of precision.

Alternative formulae have been presented by Stevenson[22] for Chinese material, by Telkkä[24] for Finns, and by Dupertuis and Hadden[8] for American Whites and Negroes. The work of the last-named authors is however superseded by that of Trotter and

Gleser,[25],[26] which is revolutionary in being based on directly measured limb-bone lengths of individuals whose stature was recorded during life. Their first study was based on comparatively small American White and American Negro series, their second on much larger series of both these groups and on a smaller Mongoloid series. These series are of males only; in their earlier study Trotter and Gleser correlated their living-stature series with cadaver-length series for both male groups, and on the basis of this comparison developed estimation formulae from cadaver-length series of American White and American Negro females to replace those of Dupertuis and Hadden.

In both their studies Trotter and Gleser lay great stress on the inescapable range of error in estimation. They maintain that the limits of 95% certainty in estimation are between 7·0 and 8·0 cm on either side of the estimate for the lower limb bones, and 8·0 to 9·0 cm for the upper limb bones. However distressing these wide limits may be, Trotter and Gleser insist that they cannot be reduced by statistical juggling, as some authors have suggested. These errors of estimate apply strictly only to populations substantially identical with those upon which the formulae were founded; for other populations they may well be considerably too small.

Most earlier investigators have taken as the best estimate of stature the average of the estimates obtained from all available bones and combinations of bones. Trotter and Gleser regard this procedure as statistically fallacious, and argue forcibly that the best single estimate available, i.e. that with the lowest error of estimate, should be adopted. They also reject the pooling of results obtained from different populations to derive 'general' or inter-racial formulae, such as that constructed by Dupertuis and Hadden,[8] who combined Pearson's data with their own data for American Whites and American Negroes.

Telkkä[24] has compared some estimates obtained by his own method and those of Manouvrier, Pearson, and Breitinger; estimates by Manouvrier's methods tend to be lower than those by Pearson's method for short statures, and higher for tall statures, while estimates by Breitinger's and Telkkä's methods are consistently somewhat higher than those by Pearson's method. Almost all the discrepancies are very much less than the error of estimate by any of the formulae. The author[31] has similarly compared estimates by Pearson's formulae, the 'general' formulae of Dupertuis and Hadden, and the original and revised Trotter-Gleser formulae for American Whites and Negroes. Dupertuis and Hadden's general formulae and the revised Trotter-Gleser White American formulae give closely similar results; those obtained by Pearson's method are lower, the difference being usually small at the lower end of the range but rising considerably with increasing bone length. The revised Trotter-Gleser American Negro formulae give estimates surprisingly close to those obtained by Pearson's formulae, so that the latter would appear, contrary to expectation, to predict the stature of present-day American Negroes better than that of White Americans.

Applied to modern Sicilian measurements published by Graziosi,[11] Pearson's formulae for the lower limb bones give estimates agreeing much better with records of living Sicilian stature than do those obtained by the American formulae. It is also to be noted that Trotter and Gleser's American White formula for tibial length overestimates the mean stature of Allbrook's[1] present-day British series by about 2·5 cm (1 in), although the mean statures of the British and American White groups differ very little, whereas Pearson's formula founded on a French series of shorter stature comes very close to the true value. It is by no means certain, therefore, that the American White formulae are to be preferred for estimating the stature of earlier European populations.

Allbrook, [1] in estimating East African Negro statures by a modification of Breitinger's technique, has found that different estimation formulae are needed for 'Nilo-Hamite' and 'Bantu' groups; the Trotter-Gleser Negro formulae give reasonable estimates for the former of these groups, but are very unsatisfactory for the latter.

'NEAR-GIANT' AND 'NEAR-DWARF' STATURES

Pearson found that his formulae failed conspicuously to predict the stature of true giants (above 200 cm) and true dwarfs (below 130 cm). He concluded that the formulae gave an approximation to the middle part of a complex curve representing the varying relationship between limb-bone lengths and stature, and that they broke down for statures below 150·0 cm and above 179·9 cm, that is for 'very short' and 'very tall' individuals: 'In the region of what may be termed sub-giants and super-dwarfs, namely, from about 180–200 cm and 150–130 cm, a very small change in the long bone length makes a remarkable change in stature.' He therefore suggested that outside of the limits of 150 cm and 180 cm his formulae should not be used, but that stature should be estimated from curves plotted for the different long bones. Further he suggested that the points of inflection of the curves might have 'a biological as well as a mathematical significance', that is presumably that at these levels the genetic mechanism controlling stature changed significantly. Pearson seems to have regarded these critical levels as absolutely fixed; it would seem more natural to suppose that they are fluctuating, and that there is a zone of overlap between 'normal' tall or short individuals and true sub-giants or super-dwarfs.

More recent investigators have largely passed over this question of limits. Telkkä has tabulated his results for the range 155–185 cm, and does not discuss the validity of his formulae outside this range. Trotter and Gleser[25] did not extrapolate below 152·0 cm (5 ft), which was the lower limit of stature for acceptance into the US forces; they regard their formula as valid up to 198·0 cm stature, i.e. over the whole of Pearson's 'sub-giant' range. The question of limits is in fact very pertinent since it affects the estimation of stature in individuals belonging to very tall and very short or pygmoid races of living men, especially in Africa, and also of some of the most notable examples of early man.

STATURE ESTIMATES IN EARLIER HISTORIC AND PREHISTORIC PERIODS

Broca[5] prefaced his discussion of the stature of the Cro-Magnon skeletons with the comment: 'It is impossible to determine correctly the stature of any imperfect and disarticulated skeleton; it is not even safe to apply to this determination the relationship between the length of the femur and the height of the body that medical jurisprudence has adopted; for these relations have been determined for men of our own race, and we know that the proportions of the body notably vary among existing races; and there is more reason why they may have varied in races which have died out in the course of ages.'

Trotter and Gleser[25] have expressed even stronger reservations: 'It is perhaps impossible to determine which equations are best for application to skeletal remains of older races for which there are no records of actual stature. In fact, Kurth has suggested on the basis of his recent experience in estimating stature of middle Europeans of the 8th to 10th century that measurement, when possible, of the overall length of the skeletal remains *in situ* is preferable to stature estimated from the long bones according to equations based on more recent populations.' This defeatist conclusion would limit the possibility of stature estimation to undisturbed burials in the extended position. Against this it may be urged that available formulae, provided we do not press the result too hard, can in fact give a reasonable indication of the probable stature of earlier groups. In dealing with individual specimens, the full range of inescapable variation attending any estimate has to be borne in mind, but estimates based on the means of population samples of reasonable size are more likely to be near the truth.

There are now available as alternatives, for material of European origin, the formulae of Manouvrier, Pearson, Breitinger, Telkkä, Trotter and Gleser, and Allbrook; for Mongoloid material, those of Stevenson and of Trotter and Gleser; and for Negroid material, the American formulae of Trotter and Gleser and at least two sets of formulae devised by Allbrook, one founded on 'Nilo-Hamite' and the other on East African 'Bantu' data. For remains which can be assigned with confidence to one of these groups, the choice can be reduced to a few alternative methods. The problem of choice is much more difficult when dealing with remains which cannot confidently be assigned to one of these groups, and which may not even belong to the species *Homo sapiens*.

No attempt at a complete review of all the data available concerning stature in past times will be made in this paper; consideration will be given only to certain classes of evidence: (1) the mean stature of a number of populations, mainly west European, belonging to historic and later prehistoric periods; (2) estimates of individual stature of some pre-Neolithic European specimens, (3) estimates of individual stature of some prehistoric African specimens, and (4) estimates related to individuals possibly or probably not of the species *Homo sapiens*. To further simplify the problem consideration will be limited almost wholly to male specimens.

Historic and late prehistoric European populations. The data considered have been divided into two groups, one consisting of mean femoral lengths of British population samples ranging from medieval to Neolithic, and the other of femoro-tibial lengths mostly of west European populations over the same range. Where other evidence was not available, series quoted by Pearson[18] have been included; these have previously been reconsidered by Dupertuis and Hadden.[8] When both femoral and femoro-tibial length estimates for British series are available, the difference between the two estimates is well below the error of estimate by either formula.

The fluctuation of British mean femoral stature estimates from the Neolithic to the medieval period (Table A) covers a range of about 7 cm (3 in) by the Pearson formula and 9 cm (3½ in) by Trotter and Gleser's American White formula. If the Pearson estimates were considered better for shorter, and the American for taller statures, this range might be increased to as much as 12 cm (5 in). The lowest value is found for the

TABLE A

Mean femoral stature estimates for some British male series.

	No.	Femur Length	Pearson	Trotter-Gleser (1958)
		cm	cm	cm
Medieval (Rothwell) (Parsons[11])	76	45·6	167·0	171·3
Anglo-Saxon (Munter[17])	161	46·4	168·5	173·2
Iron Age (Maiden Castle) (Goodman and Morant[10])	26	44·1	164·2	167·8
Round Barrow (Beddoe, in Pearson[18])	27	47·8	171·2	176·4
Neolithic (Beddoe, in Pearson[18])	25	45·8	167·4	171·8

Iron Age population of Maiden Castle, the highest for Beddoe's Round-Barrow series, who appreciably exceed Munter's Anglo-Saxons (this larger series gives a lower femoral length than Beddoe's for the same period). Over this whole period it may be said that British mean stature has fluctuated between medium and tall.

It is valuable to have some idea of the variation around these means. In this instance a consideration of the greatest and least femoral lengths (Table B) may serve as a measure of this variation. The least femoral lengths of the medieval, Anglo-Saxon, and Iron Age series differ but little, corresponding to stature estimates in the upper part of the 'short' range on both Pearson's and the American formulae. The greatest lengths differ more widely; the medieval series has one exceptionally high measurement, the next being much lower. Disregarding this, the fluctuation of the upper end of the range appears to follow that of the mean. Preferring the American formula to that of Pearson may raise the estimates for the tallest statures by as much as three inches. On the other hand, recourse to Pearson's curves would increase the estimates for the tallest statures in both the medieval and the Anglo-Saxon series very considerably; the stature of the

TABLE B

Extreme femoral stature estimates for some British male series.

		Femur Length	Pearson	Trotter-Gleser (1958)
		cm	cm	cm
Medieval (Rothwell):	least	40·9	158·2	160·4
	greatest	49·0	173·4	179·2
		(54·3)	(183·4)	(191·5)
Anglo-Saxon:	least	40·4	157·3	159·3
	greatest	52·7	180·4	187·8
Iron Age:	least	40·0	156·5	158·3
	greatest	47·7	171·0	176·2

exceptionally tall medieval specimen would be raised into the 'giant' category. A single exceptional specimen of this type may well be that of an abnormal individual, but in the Anglo-Saxon series the number of long femora is so considerable that it seems highly doubtful whether they can be claimed as abnormal 'sub-giants' in Pearson's sense.

The femoro-tibial stature estimates for west European series (Table C) show a similar range in mean values, between 164 cm and 171 cm by Pearson's formula, and between 167 cm and 175 cm by the American formula; thus Pearson's formula makes most of these populations to be of medium average stature, whereas the American formula makes most of them tall. The Reihengraber, Anglo-Saxon and Frankish series, compared with the Gallo-Roman and British Iron Age series, suggest that the Teutonic migrations produced a shift towards taller stature in western Europe. The Franco-Belgian 'Neolithic' series should probably be taken, in more modern usage, to cover also the Chalcolithic and Early Bronze Age periods. For comparison it may be noted that an Early Bronze Age series from Austria[9] gives a mean stature estimate of 164·7 cm by Pearson's formulae, and 168·2 cm by those of Breitinger. The predynastic Egyptian population of Nagada[29] had a mean stature just below or just above 170 cm, depending on whether the Pearson or the American formulae are used.

TABLE C
Mean femoro-tibial stature estimates for some European series.

	Femoro-tibial Length	Pearson	Trotter-Gleser (1958)
	cm	cm	cm
French (10th–11th century)	82·6	167·0	171·2
Franks (500–800 AD)	82·0	166·3	170·4
Anglo-Saxon	83·5	168·1	172·3
S. German Reihengraber	85·5	170·4	174·8
Gallo-Roman	81·4	165·6	169·7
British Iron Age (Maiden Castle)	80·5	164·6	168·5
French and Belgian 'Neolithic'	79·9	163·9	167·8
Predynastic Egyptian (Nagada)	83·9	168·5	172·8
Mesolithic (Teviec, Brittany)	76·5	159·9	163·5

At the end of last century considerable play was made with the idea that during the Neolithic period, at least in central Europe, a 'pygmy' type existed alongside of the normal medium-statured population. The original evidence for this view, according to Pearson,[18] consisted of three adult skeletons only, one probably male and two female. The lower limb-bone lengths of these three are at the extreme lower end of the range of variation of British Neolithic, Iron Age, and Dark Age series. In themselves, these specimens afford no more evidence of a distinct pygmy population than individuals of similar proportions in a Dark Age Scottish series[32] do of the 'dwarf Picts' of tradition.

Pre-Neolithic Europeans. Since prior to the Neolithic period stature has to be deduced from individual skeletons rather than from the means of series, the estimates must be presumed liable to an even greater margin of uncertainty. A comparison of Upper Palaeolithic and Mesolithic male stature estimates by the methods of Manouvrier, Pearson, and Breitinger has been made by Pittard and Sauter;[19] in the present survey this has been supplemented by a comparison of femoral, and where possible also of tibio-femoral, stature estimates by Pearson's method and that of Trotter and Gleser. Some observations on Upper Palaeolithic female stature estimates have been assembled by von Bonin.[27]

Short male series of the Mesolithic period have been recorded from Teviec, Brittany (Table C) and from Mugem, Portugal.[12,19] Both groups give mean stature estimates around the boundary between 'low' and 'medium' stature, with a range from 'low' or even 'very low' to the boundary of 'tall' stature. The single skeleton of this period from Cuzoul de Gramat (Table D) has limb bones considerably longer than the average for both these groups though within the upper limit of both; stature estimates for this skeleton place it within the upper half of the 'medium' stature range. The evidence that the Mesolithic population of western Europe was appreciably shorter in stature than its successors from the Neolithic period onwards is thus by no means conclusive. There are however some grounds for considering that the varieties of the European physical type became differentiated during the Mesolithic period; this may have included differentiation in mean stature.

Of male skeletons belonging to the latter part of the Upper Palaeolithic (Magdalenian and contemporary phases), that from Chancelade is notable for its low femoral length, slightly below the mean of the Teviec Mesolithic group and approximating to the least measurements in historic British series. The estimated stature of this man is on or slightly below the boundary between 'short' and 'medium'; this has been advanced along with other arguments for dissociating the Chancelade specimen from other Late Palaeolithic remains and looking for its affinities among short-statured types of man. Other Late Palaeolithic male skeletons from western Europe, such as those of Veyrier, Haute-Savoie, Obercassel near Bonn, and Gough's Cave, Cheddar, Somerset, are unquestionably of modern European type. These all have considerably longer femora than the Chancelade man, their estimated statures approximating to the means of Neolithic and later west European populations. It is perfectly possible, and indeed probable, that the Chancelade individual belongs to the same group as the others, and that the average stature of the inhabitants of western Europe at that period was very much the same as in later periods.

In point of stature, two skeletons from San Teodoro Cave, Sicily,[11] might well be grouped with these, but some craniological arguments as well as their geographical separation may make it preferable to keep them apart.

Broca,[5] in spite of his reservations already quoted, considered that the taller of the two males from Cro-Magnon (the 'old man') must have exceeded 180·0 cm in stature. It must be pointed out that the limb-bone lengths for this skeleton cited by Pearson and later workers are estimations; the only intact lower limb bone is the tibia of the second

TABLE D

Pre-Neolithic European male statures.

	Length	Pearson	Trotter-Gleser (1958)
	cm	cm	cm
Cuzoul de Gramat			
Femoral	44·7	165·3	169·2
Femoro-tibial	81·5	165·7	169·8
Chancelade			
Femoral	40·8	158·0	160·2
Obercassel			
Femoral	44·7	165·3	169·2
Veyrier			
Femoral	46·1	168·0	172·5
Gough's Cave			
Femoral	44·0	164·0	167·6
San Teodoro 1			
Femoral	44·2	164·2	168·1
Femoro-tibial	81·6	165·8	169·9
San Teodoro 4			
Femoral	42·5	161·2	164·1
Gr. des Enfants			
Femoral	52·2	179·4	186·6
Femoro-tibial	97·2	183·9	189·6
Barma Grande I			
Femoral	53·2	181·3	189·0
Femoro-tibial	96·8	183·5	189·1
Barma Grande II			
Femoral	49·1	173·6	179·4
Femoro-tibial	89·3	174·8	179·6
Gr. de Cavillon			
Femoral	47·0	169·7	174·6
Femoro-tibial	87·4	172·6	177·2
Paviland			
Femoral	47·6	170·8	176·0
Combe-Capelle			
Femoral	42·5	161·2	164·1

male, which measures 37·5 cm, corresponding to statures of 167·8 cm by Pearson's formula, 172·7 cm by the Trotter-Gleser formula for White Americans, and 170·0 cm by Allbrook's modern British formula.

Four skeletons from the Grimaldi (Mentone) group of caves provide more satisfactory evidence. A skeleton from the Grotte des Enfants and the taller of two from Barma Grande (B.G. I) appear to have had longer limb bones than the taller Cro-Magnon individual, who was more closely matched by the shorter Barma Grande skeleton (B.G. II). The skeleton from the Grotte de Cavillon agrees with the second Cro-Magnon skeleton; that from Paviland Cave, Glamorgan, comes close to these two (Sollas[21]). From Table D it will be seen that stature estimates for these skeletons by the Pearson and Trotter-Gleser formulae differ by more than 5 cm and sometimes as much as 8 cm (2 to 3 inches), but by both methods the two tallest individuals (Grotte des Enfants and B.G. I) both fall into the 'very tall' class and the other three into the 'tall' class. It must be noted that if Pearson's curve of stature variation is used instead of his formula, the stature estimates for the two tallest skeletons would be increased almost to the lower limit of 'giant' stature. Verneau, using Manouvrier's methods, ascribed to this group of skeletons a mean stature of 187 cm; Sollas, using Pearson's method, reduced this to 179 cm. The estimates assembled by Pittard and Sauter give averages of 175 cm for Pearson's method, and 180 cm for both Manouvrier's and Breitinger's.

While the Grimaldi group of skeletons could be regarded as those of a local isolated group of special genetic character, the Cro-Magnon, and still more the Paviland examples suggest that tall stature was a widely dispersed character in western Europe at this period. The evidence of the Predmost III skeleton[19] shows that it occurred also in eastern Europe. However, the Combe-Capelle skeleton, which is regarded as probably the earliest Upper Palaeolithic specimen from western Europe, has a much shorter femoral length, placing its estimated stature in the lower half of the 'medium' range. These divergent pieces of evidence can be regarded as indicating either two population groups of quite different stature, and so presumably having a distinct history, existing simultaneously in the earlier Upper Palaeolithic, or a very thinly scattered population derived from a single origin, within which local foci of distinctive character, possibly of a purely transitory nature, might appear as a consequence of temporary isolation and inbreeding. How far the strikingly tall men of the earlier Upper Palaeolithic were ancestral to their shorter successors at the end of this period is not, even now, completely clear.

TABLE E

Prehistoric African femoral lengths (male).

	Length	Pearson	Trotter-Gleser Negro (1958)	Trotter-Gleser White (1958)
	cm	cm	cm	cm
Asselar	45·0	165·9	166·7	169·9
Nakuru IX	50·2	175·7	177·6	182·0
Makalia I	48·4	172·3	173·9	177·8
Willey's Kopje I	49·2	173·8	175·5	179·7
II	51·6	178·3	180·6	185·2
III	52·2	179·4	181·8	186·6
Elmenteita 1	51·5	178·1	180·4	185·0
3	45·5	166·9	167·8	171·1
Naivasha	41·5	159·3	159·4	161·8
Gamble's Cave 4	51·0	177·2	179·3	183·9
5	52·0	179·1	181·4	186·2
Fish Hoek	43·5	163·1	163·6	166·5
Tuinplaats (Springbok Flats)	50·0	175·3	177·2	180·5

In this connection it must be remembered that the duration of the Upper Palaeolithic may well have been comparable with the whole span of post-Palaeolithic time.

Prehistoric Africans. Table E presents femoral stature estimates for a number of noteworthy prehistoric specimens from Africa south of the Sahara.

The rather insecurely dated Asselar skeleton from the southern fringe of the Sahara[2] is important as probably the earliest specimen to show a predominance of Negroid characters. On this ground the stature estimate by Trotter and Gleser's Negro formula might claim preference; however, it differs hardly at all from that obtained by Pearson's formula. All the estimates indicate a medium stature comparable with the means for living central and southern African Negro groups.

The long series of East African specimens recorded by Leakey[13,14] are divisible into three chronological groups, Neolithic (Nakuru, Makalia, Willey's Kopje), Mesolithic (Elmenteita), and Upper Palaeolithic (Naivasha, Gamble's Cave). All appear to be predominantly 'Europoid' rather than Negroid, and may perhaps be included under the term 'Palaeo-Mediterranean' proposed by Briggs.[4] A noteworthy feature of the whole series is the great femoral length and inferentially tall stature of most of its members. The Elmenteita specimens however show a considerable range of variation, and equal variability might be expected also in the earlier and later groups. Nevertheless the short femoral length of the Naivasha specimen[14] contrasts so strongly with the others as to bring the correctness of its sexing under consideration; if it is truly male, it raises the possibility of a second, much shorter statured element in this population.

The two South African specimens considered both have substantial claims to more than merely relative antiquity.[33] The Fish Hoek skeleton, despite its strongly paedomorphic cranial characters, is clearly not pygmoid in stature; the femoral stature estimates place it closer to the mean stature of modern Hottentots than of modern Bushmen.[35] It is to be noted that no pygmoid remains of unquestionable geological antiquity have yet come to light in Southern Africa. The great length of the Tuinplaats femur sets it far apart from all later South African human types, and suggests some affinity with the East African series, but in its craniology this individual displays Bushmanoid traits not observed in any of the East African specimens; it is not completely impossible that this anomalous combination of characters might find a counterpart in the Naivasha skeleton.

Earlier humans. The myth of the 'gorilloid' build and stance of the 'classic' Neanderthal type must now be considered completely exploded;[23] nevertheless the massive lower limb bones of this type present almost as distinctive a character as does its skull. It is to be noted that in these respects the Neanderthal type specimen is not as extreme as are the Spy skeletons which have done most to foster our conception of the type. These bones, it must be urged, are not especially short. The results in Table F, for what they are worth, indicate that the Neanderthal and Spy individuals could both have fallen into the medium range of modern human statures. The lower limb bones of the La Chapelle aux Saintes skeleton appear to have been of the same order of length; those of the La Ferrassie skeleton may however have been appreciably shorter. It has been argued that in this type the actual stature was reduced by a slouching stance; directly

TABLE F

Femoral and femoro-tibial stature estimates for earlier human types.

	Length	Pearson	Trotter-Gleser (1958)		
			White	Negro	Mongoloid
	cm	cm	cm	cm	cm
Neanderthal					
Femoral	44·1	164·2	167·8	164·8	167·4
Spy					
Femoral	42·8	161·8	164·8	162·1	164·6
Femoro-tibial	75·9	159·2	162·7	159·0	163·0
Skhūl IV					
Femoral	49·0	173·4	179·2	175·1	177·9
Femoro-tibial	92·4	178·4	183·5	178·0	183·0
Trinil					
Femoral	45·5	166·9	171·2	167·8	170·4

contrary to this is the suggestion that the lower limb was short relative to the trunk so that the stature would be underestimated from it.

McCown and Keith[15] demonstrated that the limb bones from the Skhūl Cave at Mount Carmel were entirely different from those of the classic Neanderthal type both in length and morphology, being much more closely paralleled by those of the tall group of European Upper Palaeolithic skeletons. This is clearly demonstrated by the lower limb bones of Skhūl IV (Table F); the limb bones of other specimens in the Skhūl group appear to be even longer but are not so well preserved. The interpretation of these findings has been much debated; recent evidence, however, tends very forcibly to dissociate the Skhūl group from other Near Eastern 'Neanderthaloids' including those from the neighbouring Tabūn Cave, and there are good arguments for regarding this group as 'proto-*sapiens*' and genetically ancestral to the tall Upper Palaeolithic stock of Europe. In contrast, the limb bones of the female skeleton from the Tabūn Cave appear to indicate that this individual was of medium stature like the European Neanderthal group.

Among the skeletal fragments plausibly associated with the Broken Hill skull from Zambia is a complete tibia, the length of which is 409 mm;[20] the entirely normal character of this bone has sometimes but quite baselessly been considered an obstacle to associating it with the 'Neanderthaloid' skull. A very wide range of stature estimates can be obtained from this bone: Pearson 175·8 cm, Breitinger 177·0 cm, Trotter-Gleser 'White' 180·9 cm, Trotter-Gleser 'Negro' 174·9 cm, Allbrook 'British' 177·9 cm, Allbrook 'Nilo-Hamite' 173·0 cm, Allbrook 'Bantu' 167·3 cm. All except the last point to a tall stature comparable with those of the Skhūl remains; this resemblance can be interpreted in more than one way.[30]

The more complete of two tibiae from Ngandong, Java, has a length of 365 mm.[37] Assuming this to be male, the methods of estimation listed in the preceding paragraph give results varying from 170·3 cm (Trotter-Gleser 'White') to 156·3 cm (Allbrook

'Bantu'), all the intervening values falling into the 'medium' range; if considered female, however, this specimen would indicate a moderately tall stature.

The only measurable limb bone which may possibly be attributable to the Java-Pekin group of fossil men (*Homo erectus*) is the femur belonging to the original Trinil group of finds. The essentially 'modern' character of this bone was again at first an obstacle to its acceptance; latterly it has been seen as consistent with the probable sequence of man's structural evolution as interpreted, e.g., by Washburn.[28] Whatever estimation formulae are applied to this bone, the inferred stature comes out to be close to, though somewhat above, the average of modern humanity (Table F). Other limb-bone fragments from the Java and Pekin deposits are consistent with the conclusion that *Homo erectus* tended to a stature round about the average of *Homo sapiens*.

No complete long bones of the South African australopithecines are at present available for stature estimation; nevertheless it is evident that *Australopithecus africanus* must have been of pygmoid proportions, whereas *Paranthropus robustus* was probably considerably taller as well as more robustly built. An incomplete tibia from the 'Zin-janthropus' living floor at site FLK I, Olduvai Gorge, Tanzania, has an estimated length of approximately 277 mm.[36] The array of stature estimates to be obtained from this measurement by methods applicable to modern human beings in the normal stature range extends from 152·0 cm to 134·0 cm; in terms of the variation in existing man, all are thus 'short' or 'very short', the lowest approaching the 'dwarf' category. Estimates by a number of procedures suggested by Pearson[18] for pygmy and dwarf skeletons are consistently lower, from 134·0 cm down to 125·0 cm. clustering around the upper limit of the dwarf range. It appears likely that this tibia does not belong to the robust australopithecine *Zinjanthropus boisei* but either to a smaller australopithecine or to a very primitive hominine (*Homo habilis*). At the present time the evidence for considering the earliest hominines to have been of pygmy stature is only tenuous, and positive evidence for any early hominine or even hominid having been of giant stature is non-existent. It remains possible, therefore, that the extreme variations in stature encountered in modern *Homo sapiens* may have been developed within this species only in comparatively recent times.

REFERENCES

1 ALLBROOK, D. 1961. *J. Forensic Med. 8*, 15–28
2 BOULE, M. and VALLOIS, H. V. 1932. *Arch. Inst. Paléont. Hum. 9*
3 BREITINGER, E. 1937. *Anth. Anz. 14*, 249–74
4 BRIGGS, L. C. 1955. The Stone Age races of Northwest Africa. *American School of Prehistoric Research, Peabody Museum, Harvard University.* Bulletin no. 18
5 BROCA, P. 1865–75. On the human skulls and bones found in the cave of Cro-Magnon, near Les Eyzies. In LARTET, E. and CHRISTIE, H. *Reliquiae Aquitanicae*, London, 97–122
6 CHESELDEN, W. 1712. *Phil. Trans. Roy. Soc. London* (abridged) 5 (1703–12), 671–2
7 DRENNAN, M. R. 1936. *Am. J. Phys. Anth. 21*, 205–216
8 DUPERTUIS, C. W. and HADDEN, J. A. 1951. *Am. J. Phys. Anth. N.S. 9*, 15–53
9 EHGARTNER, W. 1959. *Mitt. Anth. Ges. Wien 88–89*, 8–90
10 GOODMAN, C. N. and MORANT, G. M. 1939. *Biometrika 31*, 295–312
11 GRAZIOSI, P. 1947. *Riv. Sci. Prehist. 2*, 123–223

12 LACAM, R., NIEDERLANDER, A. and VALLOIS, H. V. 1944. *Arch. Inst. Paléont. Hum. 21*

13 LEAKEY, L. S. B. 1935. *The Stone Age Races of Kenya*, London

14 —— 1942. *J. E. Afr. Nat. Hist. Soc. 16*, 169–77

15 McCOWN, T. D. and KEITH, A. 1939. *The Stone Age of Mount Carmel. Vol. II. The fossil human remains from the Levalloiso-Mousterian*, Oxford

16 MORANT, G. M. 1939. *Biometrika 31*, 72–98

17 MUNTER, H. 1936. *Ibid. 28*, 258–94

18 PEARSON, K. 1899. *Phil. Trans. Roy. Soc. London* (A) *192*, 169–244

19 PITTARD, E. and SAUTER, M. R. 1946. *Archives Suisses d'Anthrop. Generale 11*, 149–200

20 PYCRAFT, W. P. 1929. Description of the skull and other human remains from Broken Hill. *Rhodesian Man and Associated Remains*, London, 1–51

21 SOLLAS, W. J. 1913. *J. Roy. Anth. Inst. 44*, 325–74

22 STEVENSON, P. H. 1929. *Biometrika 21*, 303–21

23 STRAUS, W. L. and CAVE, A. J. E. 1957. *Quart. Rev. Biol. 32*, 348–63

24 TELKKÄ, A. 1950. *Acta. Anat. 9*, 103–17

25 TROTTER, M. and GLESER, G. C. 1952. *Am. J. Phys. Anth.*, N.S. *10*, 463–514

26 —— 1958. *Ibid. 16*, 79–123

27 VON BONIN, G. 1935. The Magdalenian skeleton from Cap-Blanc in the Field Museum of Natural History. *Univ. Illinois Bull. 32*, no. 24

28 WASHBURN, S. L. 1951. *Trans. N.Y. Acad. Sci.*, Series II, *13*, 298–304

29 WARREN, E. 1897. *Phil. Trans. Roy. Soc. London* (B) *189*, 135–227

30 WELLS, L. H. 1957. The place of the Broken Hill skull among human types. *Proc. 3rd Pan-African. Congr. Prehist. Livingstone, N. Rhodesia, 1955*, London, 172–4

31 —— 1959a. *J. Forensic Med. 6*, 171–7

32 —— 1959b. *Proc. Soc. ant. Scot. 90*, 180–91

33 —— 1959c. *Man 59*, 158–60

34 PARSONS, F. G. 1914. *J. Anat. 48*, 238–67

35 WELLS, L. H. 1960. *S. Afr. Journ. Sci. 56*, 277–81

36 DAVIS, P. R. 1964. *Nature 102*, 967–68

37 DAY, M. 1965. *Guide to Fossil Man. A Handbook of Human Palaeontology*, London

40 Cremations

NILS-GUSTAF GEJVALL

THE INTEREST IN PREHISTORIC cremated bones displayed by archaeologists has increased to a very remarkable extent during the last ten years. From being considered either valueless or at any rate not worth the trouble, either of recovery in the field or of the great care demanded for their proper storage, samples of cremated bone have suddenly become most important, and a large number of excavation reports, in Sweden at least, are nowadays accompanied by an analytical study of cremated remains. It is only the shortage of qualified bone specialists that seriously restricts the progressive expansion of such studies.

Just over thirty years ago the celebrated Swedish anthropologist and anatomist, Professor C. M. Fürst, made the following declaration in reply to an inquiry from the then Chief Inspector of Antiquities in Stockholm: 'I would straight away place on record my considered opinion, based on experience, that cremated remains of human bones in burial urns are almost always devoid of any anthropological interest, especially in cases of such in a mass cemetery. From an anthropological point of view, therefore, these bones are of no scientific value, and I consider that nothing is lost if they are neither submitted to nor preserved in the Museum.'[1] Archaeologists, however, continued to recover such material, and in the discussions that followed the above-mentioned declaration on the principles to be adopted at the National Museum of Antiquities in Stockholm, it was resolved nevertheless that all cremated bones should be collected, in the expectation that methods would be devised in the future which would make it possible to use them for scientific purposes.

Opinions on such osteological remains have, however, varied very considerably; some scholars have sought to find indications of anthropological characteristics in them,[2] and this in itself is neither an impossibility nor an exaggeration for those who have in fact come to recognize how much can, under favourable conditions, survive in the way of identifiable fragments, even after cremation. Others, doubtless on the *a priori* assumption that it is too fantastic even to venture on making a morphological examination of shattered and distorted skeletal fragments, and insufficiently acquainted with material from prehistoric cremation burials, have adopted a pessimistic attitude towards all attempts to make a categorical estimate of the age or sex of a dead person on the basis of surviving cremated remains.[3]

In England, too, there has been a markedly increased interest in prehistoric cremations in latter years. A series of meticulous studies have been published by F. P. Lizowski,[4-6] and Calvin Wells' recent paper on the cremated bones from a fifth- to seventh-century urn-field at Illington, Norfolk,[7] is a further indication that this subject is becoming much more widely recognized.

On the Continent, a series of investigations were carried out during the Second World War on the bone material recovered from a number of urn cemeteries, but these papers (like so many anthropological studies and not least those of the author) have appeared in a large number of local periodicals that are difficult to come by or as appendices attached to archaeological excavation reports, so that it would not be easy to give an exhaustive catalogue of them all. Two authors may be mentioned here, Ursula Thieme in Germany[8] and Aemilian Kloiber in Austria.[9] Unfortunately, neither of these gives any information about the procedures employed, and this was one of the reasons why the author, in a short and fully illustrated summary,[10] has tried to draw the attention of archaeologists to the fact that it really is profitable to make such investigations as a matter of course.

A later paper, dealing with the cremated bones from 200 graves of the late Celtic period in a cemetery in south-west Sweden,[11] includes a description of the methods that have been consistently followed since then at our Osteological Laboratory in Stockholm. At the time of writing, the contents of no less than over 5,000 cremation burials have already been examined, using the same procedure throughout.

Before proceeding to a closer study of the material, we will add a reminder that the first stages in the investigation of cremations are the same as in all studies of skeletal material, namely to establish the *number of interred individuals*, their approximate *age at death* and their *sex*.

PHYSICAL CHARACTERISTICS OF THE MATERIAL

These must, of course, depend directly on the firing temperature, any treatment that may have taken place before deposition (e.g. crushing to reduce the fragments to a standard size), also the nature of the encasement of the bones, under which we must include the various kinds of container (urn with or without lid or covering stone, comparatively perishable tree-bark boxes caulked with resin, etc.), and finally the amount of pyre debris, charcoal and ash, and the soil type and precipitation conditions in the burial area.

As a result of a series of comparisons with present-day cremations from the Northern and Southern Crematoria in Stockholm, the former an old and the latter a modern establishment, and of a number of experiments with the re-burning of pulverized bone samples from prehistoric (including late Celtic) cremations, the author has become convinced that cremating techniques in prehistoric times must have attained a very high level of efficiency. This in turn presupposes a tradition extending far back in time. Thus it very frequently happens, even after modern cremation, that a proportion of blue or blue-grey areas of bone are found, especially in the cross-section of compact bony parts, e.g. in the diaphyses of long bones, showing that organic matter still survives there. When such samples are re-heated under blast, after they have been pulverized, the blue colouration disappears, and it can be demonstrated that a slight diminution in weight has occurred.

In prehistoric times, of course, burning took place in the open, on a pyre that was exposed to wind and weather. There was no restriction on the duration of a cremation other than (perhaps) nightfall; there was no great risk of deficient oxygenation, while the remains were accessible throughout the whole process and could be pushed back into the flames with sticks or other implements to ensure effective combustion. Only heavy rain or snow would be needed to minimize or delay the completion of cremation.

Nowadays, because cremation is carried out in an enclosed chamber, oxygen has to be forced by various means through air vents into the incinerator (the cremation oven), and indeed the effectiveness of the combustion cannot be assessed until the whole process has been completed and the 'ashes' collected in a receptacle. The time taken for a modern cremation is normally in the order of $1\frac{1}{2}$ to 2 hours, and the oxygen deficiency usually occurs while the 'ashes' are cooling in the receptacle, in which they lie in a fairly compact mass.

Size. In prehistoric samples this varies from microscopically small parts and fragmentary bones up to pieces a couple of decimetres in length. The latter are rare, however, and in fact occur only in large, intact urns. Otherwise, the fragments in any given sample can usually be characterized without further ado as being of a certain average size (e.g. 1·5–2·5 cm), and this, together with the general appearance of the individual pieces of bone, is a fairly reliable indication that some mechanical breaking-up must have taken place. The bone remains were perhaps simply crushed with a stone after they had cooled, in order either to get them into the burial container or to make them easier to handle. Precisely the same is done with the remains after the cremation process at the present day; special apparatus is used, consisting of a powerful fan to blow away the ash (the true ash), a magnet to extract all the coffin nails and the large numbers of various metal fittings which the undertaker insists on using to make the coffins more expensive, and finally a crusher to reduce the bone remains (nowadays mistakenly called the 'ashes') to suitable dimensions, normally 1–2 cm.

In the Second World War, as in the First, it became expedient to make urns from paper pulp. Several of these have subsequently been disinterred and their contents transferred to metal containers. On inspection of such re-interments one can immediately see that, even during the short time that the cremated bones have lain in the earth, they have completely assimilated the soil colouring from it, and it is impossible to distinguish them from prehistoric samples—this is worth remembering for the field archaeologist. It is also worth noting that even in urns from the Bronze Age the characteristic smell of burning can still hang over the cremated bones.

As regards changes suffered by the sample after interment, it is obviously to be expected that in areas with a high water content in regions where winters are cold, further fragmentation will take place as a result of repeated frosts, that soils with a high acidity can erode the bone, and again that depositions lying at shallow depth may sometimes have served as a substratum for the roots of plants and thus have suffered secondary erosion. Uncalcined or incompletely combusted parts may in some instances be affected by processes of decay, but as a general rule the bones from cremation burials have undergone little alteration. Only the remains of aborted foetuses and new-born babies, and poorly combusted cremated bones may, on occasion, crumble into a morphologically unrecognizable state.

Colour. Cremated bones can vary from chalk-white, through grey, grey-brown and brown, or grey-blue and blue, to coal-black. Blue-green and bright verdigris green shades also occur, but these are usually a result of lying close to metal objects among the grave goods. The general rule is that large bone amounts of lightish colour shades, comprising a high proportion of big fragments (high mean size) and with unaltered, sharp fracture edges, derive in the main from well-protected interments (urns with lids or covering stones in dry soils), whereas strongly humus-stained or charcoal-mixed fragments bespeak simpler cremation pits. Cremated burials of the pre-Roman Iron Age embrace the remains of individuals of all age groups, from foetuses to the elderly, both males and females, from well-preserved urns with covering stones and containing the whole of the bones recovered from the pyre, to simple cremation pits with a very few scraps of charcoal and a mere token deposition of a tiny fraction of the burnt bones. All this, like the factors mentioned above, must to a considerable extent determine the chances of developing a method by which the material can be made scientifically productive, and the fundamental principle must be to recover every single scrap of information that the fragments can be made to yield. The results achieved by an investigation are thus a measure of the length of time that can be spent on repeated re-examinations of the material. The important factors are primarily the following: quantity and weight of the bones and the ratio between the two; size of the fragments; identifiable fragments and morphological observations on them (Plate XIX); and certain metrical series of wall thicknesses and the statistical use of these (discussed in DETERMINATION OF SEX, below).

IDENTIFICATION OF THE FRAGMENTS

During the process of cremation of the human (or animal) cadaver on the funeral pyre, the soft parts are the first to disappear, followed by the distortion and shattering of the bones that makes it so difficult to identify individual fragments among the burnt remains. An intensively trained and experienced eye, research at a crematorium and comparative studies between modern cremated bones before crushing and prehistoric bone samples, are the essential prerequisites for learning to recognize more and more fragments (Plate XIXa shows a typical sample of cremated bones). One important difference that may be pointed out is between the ways in which compact bone tissue, e.g. the shaft bones, and spongy bone, e.g. the epiphyses, are altered during cremation. The compact bone normally cracks and breaks into pieces, as do the crowns of all teeth that had erupted at the time of burning, whereas teeth that were not yet ready but lie in various stages of growth in the jaw, and the roots of the erupted teeth can normally be recovered whole or reassembled. The spongy bone tissue, which of course has this texture specifically in order to withstand pressures from different directions, shrinks slightly during burning but in general retains its shape. The articular heads of thigh bones and upper arm bones, complete vertebrae and various bones of the middle hand and middle foot are among the normal finds.

The way in which the compact bone shatters is not completely haphazard. Some degree of regularity can be observed, and one factor that is often overlooked is the common tendency for the lines of the cracks to follow trajectories of the bone, i.e. features indicating 'the interdependence of structure and function' . . . 'one of the fundamental laws of biology.'[12] By studying this fracture formation on the different bones of the body caused by cremation (Plate XIXb, c, e, and f show examples from the thigh bone and radius) and at the same time memorizing the shape of the different cross-sections of these bones at different points along their lengths, it is possible to train oneself to pick out a given part of a given bone of each individual from a sample of bones from cremation burials. The various morphological details can be learnt either from a text-book or on an uncremated skeleton.[13]

ENUMERATION OF INDIVIDUALS

One may expect, especially when examining all the interments from a large cemetery, to come across graves that contain remains of more than one individual. It is also important for the archaeologist to know the total of individuals, since it may otherwise be impossible to reach a correct interpretation of particular associations of finds. There is, moreover, the accidental chance that at some time in the history of a given population there befell some misfortune, some passage of arms, an epidemic or some other event that resulted in the simultaneous deaths of a number of individuals, who were thereupon buried together. Religious beliefs and customs may also on occasion lie behind multiple interments.

The prerequisites necessary for a reliable estimate of the total of individuals in a grave are: that a sufficient quantity of the remains from the pyre were deposited to provide a reasonable chance of success; that some *singly-occurring* or *paired* bones of every individual are present; and, of course, that they have not been broken up beyond recognition. In practice, the author normally looks for such skeletal parts as the odontoid process of the second cervical vertebra (a *dens axis* is shown in Plate XIXd), the petrous part of the inner ear (*petrosum . . mastoid*) (Plate XIXj, k, l), the supraorbital region (Plate XIXg, i), the glabella (the protuberance above the nasal root) (Plate XIXh, i), jaw parts and their articulating processes (*processus articulares mandibulae*), the articulating heads of the upper arm and thigh bone (*capita humeri et femoris*), the pilaster region of the thigh bone and all teeth and tooth fragments (cf. Plate XIXo), including root parts, etc. The above are then used throughout the whole investigation and should be placed separately in a box or bag for control on any future occasion. In addition, certain other pieces from the middle regions of the shaft bones are extracted for sex determination, of which more will be said below (DETERMINATION OF SEX). By grouping together those skeletal parts that occur singly or in pairs in each individual, it is possible to calculate the number of persons represented (or at least the minimum number), but of course the smaller the volume of bones deposited, the less certain will be the results. If there are only few fragments, it will be impossible to estimate the total of individuals at all. Nevertheless, there are individual similarities in form between paired bones, e.g. that part of the petrous region that faces the brain cavity and contains the outlet for the auditory nerve (*meatus auditorius externus*), that make it possible, if one left and one right section of this region are both represented, to distinguish between different individuals (cf. Plate XIXk, l). Similarly, if there is a wide divergence in age between two individuals in the same grave, this can be demonstrated from a large variety of different skeletal parts (DETERMINATION OF AGE, below). If different individuals were cremated on separate occasions, or interments deposited at different times, this too will be detectable, in which cases this fact is usually reflected in different shades of colouration and peculiarities in the stratigraphy, which it is the duty of the archaeologist to observe and record meticulously.

As an example of a burial rite where the cremated bones of one individual after another (probably of the same family) were scattered horizontally, ultimately forming what almost amounted to a small burial mound, we may cite the Middle Grave Field of late Celtic date at Vallhagar on Gotland. This type of grave, before the osteological analysis showed it to represent a concentration of several individuals, had surprised archaeologists by the occurrence of several specimens of the same class of iron objects, e.g. shield-bosses and swords, in each structure.[14]

DETERMINATION OF AGE

The determination of the individual ages at death is based mainly on the same principles as for uncremated skeletal material, but the same limitations apply as in the calculation of the total number of individuals. As far as adults over the age of thirty are concerned, any anthropological age determination must necessarily be both relative and subjective, not least because we have no means of knowing how those characteristics on which such estimations are based were manifested when the individual was alive; still less do we know of the genetical background of the population from which the individual came. All these points were underlined by the author in his dissertation on 364 medieval skeletons from North Sweden.[15]

Cremated remains of foetuses, new-born babies, children of various ages, adolescents and young adults up to the age of 25–30 years can be aged no less precisely than un-cremated skeletons, with the aid of the surviving teeth and tooth fragments and the degree of synostosis of the various articulating processes (epiphyses and certain other bones in the body become firmly fused with their respective diaphyses according to a known time-scale to be found in text-books on anatomy).[13] The various sutures of the skull also change with increasing age, and it is always worthwhile extracting from the sample all the vault fragments (cf. Plate XIXn) and examining their cross-section by eye. A combination of the shape of the tooth roots, the width of the root canals, the root apices, the cross-section of the vault, the degree of sutural obliteration and the ratio of the weight of the sample to its volume, will give a good indication of the relative gradation of the age groupings above twenty years into *adult*, *mature* and *senile*. Further than this it is dangerous to venture, even in cases where the complete inventory of bones is available.

A number of comprehensive series of age determinations carried out by these methods formed the basis of the mortality curves published by the author in various papers and collated in his doctorate thesis.[16]

DETERMINATION OF SEX

Anyone who has been engaged in skeletal studies knows how difficult it can sometimes be to sex uncremated bones. Surely, then, it must be quite impossible to grapple with the problems of cremated ones? The answer is No; and in the following paragraphs the author will proceed to try to explain the way in which he has attempted to deal with the question.

The difference between the sexes is most often sought on skeletal material in the so-called secondary sexual characters; in males a more robust cranium with more powerful and coarser supraorbital parts, a more prominent region above the nasal root (or glabella) (cf. Plate XIXg, h), larger *processus mastoides*, more powerful and larger *capita humeri et femoris* and, in general, more pronounced muscle relief. All these characters are *normally* less strongly manifested in the females (cf. Plate XIXi). Every population, however, exhibits a certain number of intersexes or intermediates between the definitely male and the definitely female individuals from an osteological point of view. We may expect at least 20% of the adult individuals in a collection of cremated material to be morphologically indeterminable, partly comprising these intermediate types, partly pathological cases and partly because sex-determinative fragments will probably have failed to survive in some of the samples under investigation.

There will always still remain, therefore, after the sexing of the individuals with

TABLE A

Statistical treatment of the comparative material.

	Maximal measured wall thickness in measurement area Ia.	Wall thickness at Ib.	Wall thickness of femur in measurement area 2.	Vertical diameter of caput humeri	Transversal diameter of caput humeri	Wall thickness of caput humeri in measurement area 3c.	Wall thickness of radius in measurement area 4
Males							
Mean value ($\bar{x}$)	6·5	13·0	6·7	44·4	38·9	4·1	2·7
Standard deviation (σ)	1·3	3·3	1·6	2·3	2·7	0·8	0·5
Mean error ($\Sigma\bar{x}$)	±0·2	±0·8	±0·2	±0·3	±0·4	±0·1	±0·1
Total (n)	46	17	47	56	44	30	32
Coefficient of variation	20·0	25·4	23·9	5·2	6·9	19·5	18·5
Range	10·0–4·5	23·0–8·5	11·5–4·0	52·5–40·0	47·5–37·0	6·6–2·6	3·6–1·8
Females							
Mean value ($\bar{x}$)	5·9	11·5	5·3	41·8	35·5	2·7	2·0
Standard deviation (σ)	1·3	2·3	1·1	2·4	2·4	0·8	0·4
Mean error ($\Sigma\bar{x}$)	±0·2	±0·5	±0·2	±0·3	±0·4	±0·1	±0·1
Total (n)	45	22	41	47	39	32	26
Coefficient of variation	22·0	20·0	20·8	5·7	6·8	29·6	20·0
Range	9·2–4·0	17·0–8·0	8·5–2·2	45·0–34·5	40·5–32·0	5·0–1·7	2·9–1·2
t for the difference	2·14	1·59	4·95	6·12	6·01	9·90	4·95
Probability value (P)	0·02	0·1	<0·001	<0·001	<0·001	<0·001	<0·001

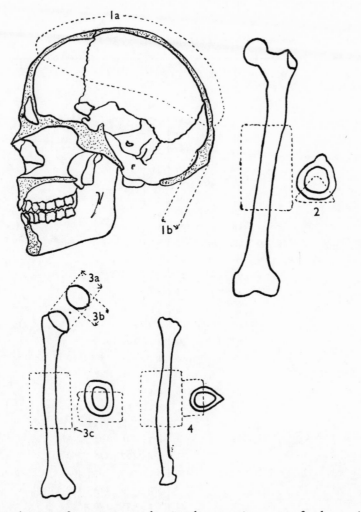

Fig. 89 Schematic diagram of measurements, showing the approximate areas for the metrical series and the position of the measurements within each area. The figures correspond to the headings of the relevant columns in Tables A–D as follows: 1a: maximal measured wall thickness of the vault in measurement area 1a; 1b: wall thickness of the cranium between *protuberantia occipitalis externa* and *eminentia cruciata* (these are easily recognizable fragments); 2: wall thickness of the thigh bone within an area near the middle of the diaphysis and directly opposite the pilaster; 3a, 3b, and 3c: vertical and transversal diameters of the articular head of the upper arm, and wall thickness at the middle of the diaphysis; 4: wall thickness of the radius within an area near the middle of the diaphysis. From Weinmann and Sicher.[12]

typically male or female supraorbital regions, *capita humeri et femoris*, etc., a number of individuals that cannot be sexed by direct means.

For such cases the author has attempted to evolve a procedure based on the established fact that, out of any two individuals of equal size, the walls of the bones of the female will on average be $\frac{1}{3}$–$\frac{1}{4}$ thinner than those of the male. In 1948 the author was able to demonstrate statistical proof of this hypothesis when an opportunity arose of taking

TABLE B

Sex determination of cremations by various methods.

Females	mm	Males
	69 2·5	
	95 2·6	
Females	209 2·7	Males
	107 2·8	
	2·9	
	114 3·0	
51 49	53 3·1	
	204 3·2	
166 73	207 3·3	
164 97	175 3·4	
133 199 160 68 67 31 174 59 222 196	71 3·5	
224 | 198 96 92 80	47 3·6	
61 13	173 3·7	
159 44 | 128	55 3·8	116
110	39 3·9	12 77 | 130 33 90
158 11	211 4·0	137 153 | 84 144 219 120 134
180 170	100 4·1	105 | 146
125 119 | 124	214 4·2	138 139 | 30 45 184 205
	4·3	21 27 | 87 88 115 118 | 197
	216 4·4	14 149 188 | 127 65
	63 4·5	117 121 | 123 155 189 | 17 104 206
	4·6	58 113 |
	4·7	101 194
	4·8	167 | 215 | 182
	210 4·9	190 62 162
	5·0	29 143 157 102 |
	41 5·1	171 | 176
	5·2	74 140
	5·3	91 60
	5·4	20 | 32 | 25
	5·5	
	5·6	148 |
	5·7	
	5·8	
	5·9	141 |
	6·0	23

In the framed column in the middle, the mean thickness of the vault wall in mm; on the left side the female burials, on the right the males. On either side of the central frame, enclosed with solid lines, the determinations based on morphological features (supraorbital regions, shoulder joint heads, etc.); between the solid and the dotted lines, the determinations on biometric grounds, arranged in descending order of certainty from the middle outwards. From Gejvall.[11]

TABLE C

Example of a points system for interpolation of a prehistoric cremated individual into the metrical series for modern cremations.

Grave 59, containing 1½ litres of bones, i.e. low in the range of bone volumes.

	Column							
	VI.	1a	1b	2	3a	3b	3c	4
Grave 59	3·5	5·0	6·6+	5·0	—	—	2·6	1·6
Mean value for ♀ in the modern sample (*cf.* Tab. A)	—	5·9	11·5	5·3	41·8	35·5	2·7	2·0
Points	—	♀	♀	♀	—	—	♀	♀

The result is 5 ♀ points in 5 columns (considering the similarity of the measurements), implying that the individual should be placed on the female side of Table B. This position is further supported by the value of 3·5 for the mean thickness of the vault wall shown in col. VI.

This procedure makes it possible to build onto Table B; outside the solid line delimiting the morphologically sexed individuals are interpolated the determinations arrived at by statistical means, arranged in descending order of certainty from the middle outwards.

From Gejvall.[11]

measurements, following the same procedure throughout, on 50 male and 49 female modern cremations selected at random and placed at his disposal in Stockholm. There was no question here of any difficulty in finding the skeletal parts required for measuring. The relevant metrical series are shown in Table A and Fig. 89, and the statistical treatment of the values derived from these measurements shows that a proven sexual difference exists in the majority of the experimental metrical series.

At the same time, all the morphological sexual characters listed above in connection with prehistoric cremations were recorded for this material, and age determinations were also carried out, which the author was able to check directly against the records of the crematorium offices several days later. The age determinations proved to a great extent to fall within the correct limits, and only two of the sex determinations were wrong. A multitude of information of forensic and criminological value was recovered from these studies, but they lie outside the scope of the present discussion.

When applying the results thus achieved to the prehistoric material, it is most convenient to start with morphologically sexed individuals (i.e. on the basis of supraorbital regions, etc.) and then, for the remainder, to employ statistically the average wall-thicknesses given by the male and female individuals thus determined. In practice this can be done either by straight comparisons or by using a simple points system such as that described by the author in his 1948 paper on cremations (an example of which is given in Tables B and C).

It would be wrong to leave the subject of prehistoric cremations without some mention of the animal bones that occur in them together with the human bones. First, a curiosity. A prehistoric cremation can sometimes be assigned even to a specific season of the year, as in the case of a number of early Roman Iron Age graves, if jaw fragments of

TABLE D

The mean values of the biometric series and the division of the comparative material into different age groups.

Age Group	1a ♂	1a ♀	1b ♂	1b ♀	2 ♂	2 ♀	3a ♂	3a ♀	3b ♂	3b ♀	3c ♂	3c ♀	4 ♂	4 ♀
I. Over 70 yrs	7·1	6·2	12·1	11·9	6·8	5·1	44·1	39·5	41·1	35·6	3·9	2·5	2·9	1·7
n	14	26	9	13	16	23	15	22	15	21	9	16	10	11
II. 50–70 yrs	6·3	5·5	13·9	11·4	6·7	5·3	44·8	37·5	42·4	34·6	4·1	2·8	2·6	1·9
n	24	12	6	8	22	10	26	12	21	11	14	9	15	9
III. under 50 yrs	6·0	5·7	14·8	9·7	6·7	5·7	44·2	39·5	41·8	36·4	4·3	3·0	2 6	2·4
n	8	8	2	2	9	9	15	10	12	8	7	8	7	7

From Gejvall.[11]

lamb (the remains of a burial feast?) are included. Lambs are born in March–April, and their age can be determined from the associated tooth fragments. The occurrence of various animal species in prehistoric cremation graves (bear, in the form of the first claw phalange, from the skin in which the corpse was wrapped (cf. Plate XIXm), dog, horse, ox, sheep and/or goat, pig, elk, deer, various kinds of bird, fish, etc.) and the distribution of these species over the various periods and regions, open up a completely new field of research which the author has discussed in a recently published paper,[17] and which sheds fresh light on burial rites, economy and hunting activities, and on the incidence of want and plenty at different periods in earlier times.

REFERENCES AND NOTES

1 Letter dated 22nd August 1930 in the Stockholm Archaeological and Topographical Archives, D. no. 1394 1930
2 KRUMBEIN, C. N. 1934–5. *Anthropologische Untersuchungen an urgeschichtlichen Leichenbränden, Forschungen und Fortschritte 10–11*, 411
3 HUIZINGA, J. 1952. In Dubiis Abstine. In *Proc. State Service for Archaeological Investigations in the Netherlands*
4 LIZOWSKI, F. P. 1955–6. *Proc. Soc. Antiq. Scot. 89*, 83
5 —— 1956. The Cremations from Barclodiad y Gawres, in POWELL, T. G. E. and DANIEL, G. E., *Barclodiad y Gawres*, Liverpool
6 —— 1959. *J. Roy. Soc. Antiq. Ireland 89*, 26
7 WELLS, C. 1960. *Antiquity 34*, 29
8 THIEME, U. 1940. Untersuchungsergebnis des Leichenbrandes aus 7 Gräbern von Bornitz, Kr. Zetz. Nachrichtenblatt für deutsche Vorzeit, Leipzig, 16 Jahrg. Heft 10–11
9 KLOIBER, AE. 1943. *Mitt. Anth. Ges. Wien.* 72
10 GEJVALL, N.-G. 1947. *Bestämning av brända ben från forntida gravar, Fornvännen*, Stockholm, H 1 (English summary)
11 —— and SAHLSTRÖM, K. E. 1948. Gravfältet på Kyrkbacken i Horns socken, Västergötland in *Kungl. Vitterhets Historie och Antikvitets Akademiens Handlingar*, Stockholm, Del. 60:2 (German summary)

12 WEINMANN, J. and SICHER, H. 1955. *Bone and Bones. Fundamentals of Bone Biology*, St Louis, 127. The author is fully aware that measurement area No. 4 (middle area of diaphysis of radius) could be mixed up with the opposite area of the ulna. In practice, and for this rough method, this should, however, imply but minor sources of error.

13 BRASH, J. C. 1937. *Cunningham's Text-book of Anatomy*, Oxford, 7th ed. or: u.p. RAUBER-KOPSCH, *Lehrbuch und Atlas der Anatomie der Menschen* I, Leipzig, 1947, 17 Aufl.; in the present edition (19th) the valuable tabular summaries of obliteration and epiphysis-fusion have unfortunately been omitted—interest in osteology is apparently not in the ascendant in medical schools!

14 GEJVALL, N.-G. 1955. The Cremations at Vallhagar, in STENBERGER, M. (ed.), *Vallhagar, A Migration Period Settlement on Gotland Sweden*, Stockholm, II, 705

15 —— 1960. *Westerhus, Medieval Population and Church in the Light of Skeletal Remains*, Kungl. Vitterhets Historie och Antikvitets Akademien, Stockholm, 42 (Monograph Series)

16 —— *Ibid.*, plate 5

17 —— 1961. *Acta Archaeologica Lundensia*, ser. in 4°, 5, 157–173

41 *The Palaeopathology of Human Skeletal Remains*

MARCUS S. GOLDSTEIN*

PALAEOPATHOLOGY, a term apparently first used by Sir Marc Armand Ruffer,[39] is concerned with the diseases which can be demonstrated in earlier human and animal remains. Thus the materials of study in human palaeopathology have been the skeletal and soft tissue remains of 'ancient' peoples, occasionally also the art objects left by these people which depict the human figure in ways suggestive of morbid conditions.

Obviously the physical anthropologist and physician who usually undertake the studies in human palaeopathology are dependent on the archaeologist for their material. In turn, the role of pathology in prehistory, so far as it can be ascertained, should be of relevant interest to archaeology. For disease, disability, and death are integral aspects of the biology of a population and its culture. Angel,[3] for example, has pointed to the close relationship between health and the course of civilization in ancient Greece. Studies in palaeopathology in recent years, as noted by Sigerist,[43] Ackerknecht,[4] Brothwell,[9] and others, have tended to include, in addition to a description of diseased conditions of bones, an 'epidemiology' of the skeletal population recovered by the archaeologist. That is, there has been a consideration of health status of the group in terms of prevalence of disease, age and sex distributions, estimates of age at death and average life span of the group, and relationships with culture changes observed in different strata or periods of time. An early example of such a 'reconstruction of the growth and decline' of an early population is the classic work on the Pecos Indian Pueblo by Hooton[23] in 1930. Such studies, regrettably enough, tend to be limited in number and scope because a large 'population' of skeletal material is not often uncovered, especially of early man. Even when a large burial site is found, the remains may be too fragmentary or in too poor a state of preservation for study.

SCOPE OF THE PRESENT CHAPTER

This essay is meant only as a brief general survey, and will thus note only the major literature on the subject, especially since about 1945, and indicate briefly the type of information which palaeopathology has revealed.

Several previous publications have reviewed in detail the field of palaeopathology. Moodie[28] in 1923 published a comprehensive work on animal and human palaeopathology which includes an extensive bibliography. A volume by Pales[35] in 1930, *Paléopathologie et Pathologie comparative*, gives the most complete pre-war bibliography (660 titles) and exhaustive treatment of the subject to that time. Sigerist[43] in his illumina-

* The views here expressed are the author's and do not necessarily represent those of the Department of Health, Education and Welfare of Washington, D.C.

ting book *Primitive and Archaic Medicine* published in 1951, reviews the field and lists the literature published between about 1930 and 1944. Shorter but nevertheless excellent general reviews of the subject have also been published in recent years by Vallois,[52, 53] Krogman,[26] Angel,[3] and Ackerknecht.[4] More recently, multi-authored studies have appeared, edited by Jarcho[56] and Brothwell and Sandison.[54] Together with the earlier works, these provide a good basic series of references on this subject.

THE FINDINGS OF HUMAN PALAEOPATHOLOGY

Disturbances in development. The older literature[35, 43] cites congenital club-foot in ancient Egypt and deformity attributed to hydrocephalus in an Egyptian of the Roman period, and instances of open sacrum and possible Paget's disease from Neolithic France. More recently Angel[1] reported a case of congenital hip dislocation in a series of 132 skeletons (31 well preserved) of Greeks dating from Neolithic to Byzantine times. The skeletal remains of 9 prehistoric Huron Indians from Ontario, Canada,[25] showed a 'strong, active male, at least 50 years of age' with two congenital anomalies: an asymmetrical distortion of the skull involving all the bones of the face which, according to the author, probably caused 'a severe tilting of the head on the neck' (torticollis?); and a lesion of the lumbar region of the vertebral column that probably caused low-back pain and sciatica. Brothwell[9] reports on a Neolithic skeleton from Britain in which the long bones of the left arm are much shorter than those of the right, and of scoliosis of an apparently congenital origin found in five early British skeletons, one dating back to the Bronze Age. Instances of hip dislocation have been found in skeletons from Neolithic France[35] (Fig. 57e), Bronze Age Britain,[9] Early Iron Age Greece,[1] and pre-Columbian America.[21, 25]

Mention may also be made of a possible case of mongolism in an Anglo-Saxon population. According to Brothwell,[8] the skull of a child of about nine years of age manifested symptoms generally associated with mongolism, such as marked microcephaly, hyperbrachycephaly, small sphenoid body and high angle of basi-occipital, thinness of cranial bones, small maxilla but fairly normal mandible size, and minor anomalies of the dentition. Finally, the subject of congenital variation as seen in early skeletal material is reviewed in a general way by Brothwell and Powers.[55]

Inflammation of bone. Sigerist[43] has remarked that inflammation in the skeleton is a normal defence reaction to a pathological agent or injury, occurring in the periosteum (periostitis) or in the marrow (osteomyelitis), and that the great majority of all pathological changes found in early human bones are the results of inflammatory processes. Chronic inflammatory diseases that affect the joints (arthritis deformans), or spondylitis deformans when it is in the spinal column, are included under this category.

According to Straus and Cave,[51] the 'old man' of La Chapelle-aux-Saints, a member of the Neanderthal group, was afflicted with spinal osteoarthritis that caused him 'to stand and walk with something of a pathological kyphosis'; these authors also point to a flattening and deformation of the right mandibular condyle in the La Chapelle man, 'attributable to an osteoarthritis of the temporo-mandibular joint', and note a like but more severe condition in two other Neanderthal mandibles, those of La Quina and La Ferrassie.

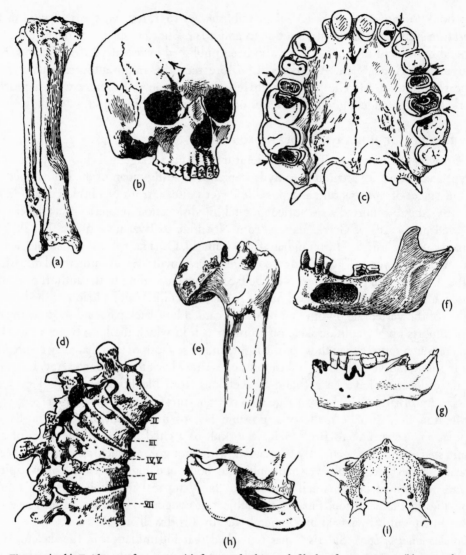

Fig. 90 (a, b) Evidence of trauma: (a) fractured tibia and fibula of a Peruvian; (b) an early Egyptian skull. (c) The palate of Rhodesian Man; arrows point to the caries cavities. (d) Part of the vertebral column of a Neolithic skeleton from Germany, with vertebral collapse and fusion strongly suggestive of tuberculosis. After Moodie.[28] (e) Deformed femur head of the French Neolithic period; the anomaly probably indicates a congenital dislocation of the hip. After Pales.[35] (f–i) Examples of early Egyptian oral pathology: (f) a large cystic cavity; (g) chronic abscessing at the root of a lower first molar; (h, i) lateral and palatal views of edentulous skulls. After Ruffer.[39a]

Stewart[49] has reported osteoarthritis in Shanidar I from Iraq: this Neanderthaloid skeleton, judged to be about 45,000 years old, shows osteophytes or 'lipping' in his cervical and lumbar vertebrae, as well as a pathological flattening of the mandibular condyle similar to that of La Chapelle man noted above.

Several reports have pointed to the prevalence of inflammatory lesions (arthritis, periostitis, and osteomyelitis) in the skeletons of prehistoric American Indians,[10, 21, 25, 38, 46] Neolithic France,[29] Greece,[1] and Britain,[9] and the late Copper Age in Hungary.[18] Such inflammatory conditions are not indicative of specific diseases, since they could have been caused by different agents.[43]

Tuberculosis of bone. Perhaps the first definite European evidence of human skeletal tuberculosis, according to Morse,[30] is from a Neolithic cemetery in Germany (Fig. 90d). Sigerist[43] notes that Elliot Smith and Ruffer, in 1910, found an Egyptian mummy of the XXIst Dynasty (*c.* 1000 BC) with inflammation and destruction of bone indicative of Pott's disease. Possible manifestations of Pott's disease have also been reported in pre-Columbian American Indian remains.[36, 38, 46] American Indian clay figurines and effigy water-bottles of pre-Columbian times are cited by Ritchie[35] as '. . . faithful representations of persons afflicted with Pott's disease . . .' although this view has been questioned sharply by Morse.[30] The latter, after detailed consideration of the evidence for skeletal tuberculosis in the pre-Columbian American Indian, found it all negative and concludes that tuberculosis did not exist in the prehistoric American Indian.

Syphilis and Yaws. Whether syphilis originated in the New World or Old has been an uncertain and moot issue for many years.[45] Possible syphilitic lesions have been noted in pre-Columbian remains in Oklahoma,[10] Texas,[21] and California,[38] although in each instance the diagnosis was far from being definitive and the number of cases was very small. Other cases are discussed by Goff.[54]

Of interest in this connection is the citation quoted by Brothwell[9] of '. . . an edict of Edward III to the Mayor and Sheriffs of London in 1346, which describe a disease of a syphilitic nature communicated by "carnal intercourse with women in stews and other secret places".'

It seems fair to say that the evidence as to where syphilis originated is still too meagre and uncertain to warrant any firm conclusions.

Yaws, a treponemal disease largely limited to tropical regions and at times mistakenly diagnosed as syphilis, has been discovered by Stewart and Spoehr[50] in the skeleton of an individual from a prehistoric site (*c.* AD 854±145) in the Mariana Island group in the Western Pacific (Fig. 91c). They note that the specimen '. . . gives evidence not only of the presence, but of the character of yaws in the Western Pacific before the introduction of syphilis.'

A provocative suggestion has recently been made by one authority,[15] that the various species of treponemal infections have been 'mere variants of one basic organism', and that 'Interspecific competition may partially determine whether a population contracts yaws or syphilis.'

Leprosy. According to Møller-Christensen,[27, 54] the earliest case of leprosy found in the skeleton is that of a Copt (mummy) from the sixth century.

Møller-Christensen, it may be mentioned, on examining the skeletons representing about 200 persons who had been inmates of a Danish medieval leper hospital, discovered a diagnostic characteristic of the disease in the skeleton, namely, '. . . changes in the distal part of the *aperture piriformes* . . . roentgenologically characterized by atrophy of

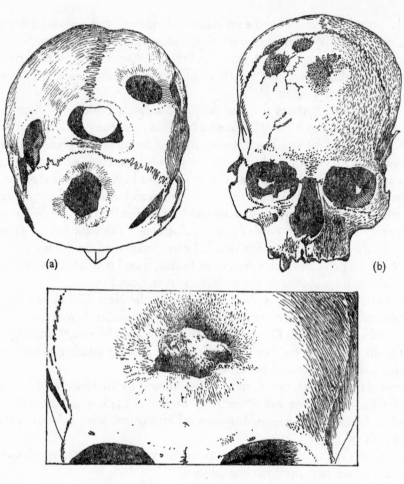

(a)   (b)

(c)

Fig. 91 (a) Upper aspect of a pre-Columbian skull from Cusco, Peru, with seven trephine openings. After Oakley *et al.*[33] (b) Facial aspect of a Bronze Age skull from Jericho. After Oakley *et al.*[33] (c) Part of the frontal region of a skull from the Western Pacific, dated to the ninth century AD; a crater-like lesion is suggestive of yaws. After Stewart and Spoehr.[50]

the anterior nasal spine and the maxillary alveolar process', or *facies leprosa*. Some 76 per cent of the examined crania manifested this diagnostic criterion. Typical bone changes in leprosy are shown in Fig. 92.

Traumatic injury. Cranial injuries (e.g. Fig. 90b) as a possible cause of death, or traumatic lesions in the form of fractures healed by the formation of calluses (e.g. Fig. 90a), have occurred at all times before and since the advent of man, as evinced in skeletal remains from all parts of the world.[1, 9, 10, 17, 21, 29, 38, 43]

Tumours. Except for benign osteomata, tumours in prehistoric man are apparently rare.[43] According to Brothwell,[54] however, there are more examples in early skeletal series than previously suggested in the literature. To give examples of neoplastic conditions, Nemeskéri and Harsányi[31] cite a case of 'Tumour multiplex (Myeloma)' in a

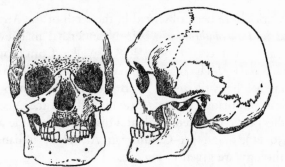

(a)

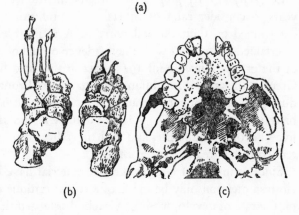

Fig. 92 Bone changes in leprosy, after Møller–Christensen.[27] (a) Facial and lateral aspects of Case 2, showing bone changes in the upper alveolar region. (b) Both feet of Case 1, displaying considerable deformity and loss of bone. (c) Palatal aspect of Case 4, showing a large perforation.

(b)   (c)

skeleton from a medieval site in Hungary (ninth to twelfth centuries AD; 1 case in 1055 skeletons). The oldest example of a tumour in man appears to be a sarcomatous overgrowth (Fig. 93b) on the chin of the Kanam mandible from Kenya, East Africa, which has been dated as possibly Middle Pleistocene.[34] A honeycomb type of hyperostosis over the vertex of a skull from the Egyptian XXth Dynasty (c. 1200 BC), according to Rogers,[37] 'suggests the reaction to an angioblastic or sarcomatous meningioma'. Other examples of tumours are shown in Fig. 93.

Trephination. Trepanning should perhaps be mentioned in a review of palaeopathology since it is evidence of possible surgical therapy for the alleviation of pathological conditions. Thus Brothwell[9] remarks on a Beaker period skeleton in Britain with signs of congenital scoliosis associated with a trephined hole in the head, and suggests the latter may have been an attempt to cope with the scoliosis. Evidence indicative of at least a possibility that early peoples performed trephination to alleviate mastoid inflammation has been noted,[33] as well as to relieve pressure on the brain due to injury.[26] Trepanning was practised in Europe during Neolithic times,[29, 40] in Africa in the Bronze Age,[33] and in ancient Peru.[47] Stewart[48] and Lisowski[54] have recently reviewed the skull surgery performed by Stone Age man in different parts of the world. Examples of trepanning from the New World and Old World are shown in Fig. 91.

Dental pathology. A large literature is extant on dental palaeopathology. Only some representative examples of recent papers on the subject are here mentioned.

Caries have been observed in the teeth of the Australopithecine apes of South Africa and in *Pithecanthropus*.[6, 13, 14] Neanderthal man evidently suffered from periodontal disease and abscessed roots,[43, 52] as well as from tooth fracture and faulty dental microstructure.[24, 44] The relationship of nutrition to dental pathology in early human populations has been discussed by Brothwell,[6] who also reports on caries and periodontal disease in British remains extending from the Neolithic to the seventeenth century.[9] Others have reported on dental disease among the ancient Minoans in Crete (*c.* 1750–1550 BC),[11] and pre-Columbian American Indians.[19, 38] A few cases of early oral pathology are given in Fig. 90.

Longevity of early peoples. As already mentioned, an effort has been made in recent years to consider rates of mortality in prehistoric groups, based on age at death as determined on their skeletal remains. A rough idea of average life span can thus be ascertained and related with the incidence of pathology and general biology and culture of the group. Since about 1945, data in this field have been published on the ancient Greeks,[2] the ancient inhabitants of Anatolia,[42] Bronze Age British,[7] groups in Hungary during the late Copper Age and ninth to twelfth centuries,[18, 31] and several pre-Columbian Indian groups,[10, 12, 16, 20, 38] virtually all indicating that relatively few individuals lived beyond middle life, and that mortality among females in the earlier years of life tended to be greater than in males.

Since estimates of age on skeletal material have often been based on cranial suture closure, mention may be made of a recent critique of this method,[5] as well as a report on the rate of development of vertebral osteoarthritis as a means of identifying skeletal age.[49] This subject is discussed in greater detail by Genovés, elsewhere in this volume.

COMMENTS AND CONCLUSIONS

Plainly, human palaeopathology reveals that our prehistoric ancestors were also subject to disease and disabilities even as we; that mortality in infancy and the early years of life was very high, with individual survival generally limited to very young adulthood.★ No doubt acute infectious diseases eliminated whole families and even larger groups in prehistoric times, as they have done throughout history until very recently even in west European countries.[22]

Archaeology, both as an essential contributor of the source material to, and a potential beneficiary of the findings from, the field of palaeopathology, has a legitimate and considerable interest in the progress of the latter. It may be appropriate therefore to mention several ways in which, in the author's opinion, the skeletal material provided by the archaeologist might be better utilized in studies of palaeopathology.

First, there are still large lacunae in the diagnoses of lesions on the dry bone. Hooton[23] long ago suggested that the clinical pathologist and anatomist co-operate in the preservation of skeletal material of known clinical history for the purpose of acquiring satisfactory criteria in the study of palaeopathology. In any event, there is surely a need for

★ According to the basic studies of Schultz,[41] diseases and developmental defects are common even in monkeys and apes in their natural environment, although many so affected nevertheless survive and successfully compete in their natural habitat.

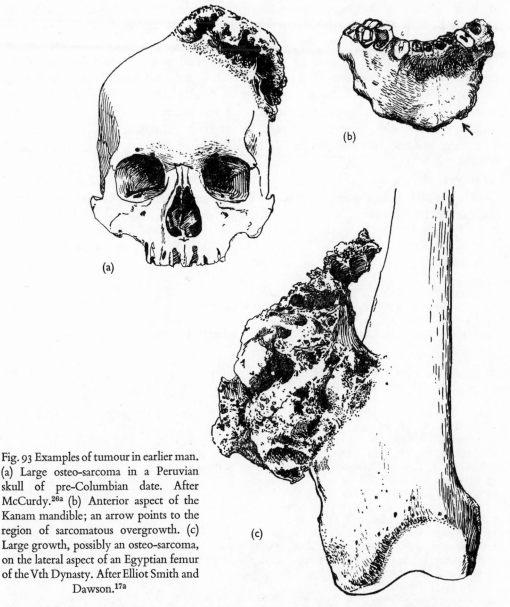

Fig. 93 Examples of tumour in earlier man. (a) Large osteo-sarcoma in a Peruvian skull of pre-Columbian date. After McCurdy.[26a] (b) Anterior aspect of the Kanam mandible; an arrow points to the region of sarcomatous overgrowth. (c) Large growth, possibly an osteo-sarcoma, on the lateral aspect of an Egyptian femur of the Vth Dynasty. After Elliot Smith and Dawson.[17a]

closer collaboration between the physical anthropologist and the pathologist in the detection and diagnosis of diseases in the skeleton, thereby making the results of palaeo-pathology more meaningful for the archaeologist as well as for others. Second, there is a definite need for compiling the bits of information on palaeopathology that are often 'buried' in archaeological reports and the like. In many instances the skeletal remains uncovered in an archaeological excavation are few in number, and hence a report on them, including observations on pathology, appears as a brief addendum to the archaeo-logical monographs. Such fragmentary data on skeletal remains and palaeopathology may or may not be significant in any single instance; when multiplied a hundredfold they might well reveal much of interest to a large circle of workers. It is suggested therefore that 'clearing-houses' be established at places willing to assume the responsibility, to which could be sent all publications containing data on palaeopathology. And third, deriving from the second suggestion, it is proposed that broad surveys of the palaeopathology of a whole country or region be developed, especially with knowledgeable respect to archaeological relationships, as was recently done by Brothwell[9] for Britain. Such surveys, appearing at periodic intervals, should be of pertinent interest to the medical historian and physical anthropologists as well as to the archaeologist.

ACKNOWLEDGEMENT

I wish to thank Miss Rosemary Powers of the British Museum (Natural History) for the excellent illustrations.

REFERENCES

(a) General

1 ANGEL, J. L. 1946. Am. J. Phys. Anth. 4, 69–97
2 —— 1947. J. Gerontol. 2, 18–24
3 —— The Interne (Jan.–Feb. 1948), 15–17, 45–48
4 ACKERKNECHT, E. H. 1953. Palaeopathology, in KROEBER, A. L. (ed.) Anthropology Today, New York, 120–126
5 BROOKS, S. T. 1955. Am. J. Phys. Anth. 13, 567–597
6 BROTHWELL, D. R. 1959. Proc. Nutrit. Soc. (Great Brit.) 18, 59–65
7 —— 1960. Advancement of Science 64, 311–322
8 —— 1960. Ann. Human Genetics (London) 24, 141–150
9 —— 1961. The paleopathology of early British Man: An essay on the problems of diagnosis and analysis. J. Roy. Anth. Inst. 91, 318–344
10 BRUES, A. M. 1959. Bull. Oklahoma Anth. Soc. 7, 63–70
11 CARR, H. G. 1960. Man 157, 1–4
12 CHURCHER, C. S. and KENYON, W. A. 1960. Hum. Biol. 32, 249–273
13 CLEMENT, A. J. 1956. Brit. Dental J. 101, 4–7
14 —— 1958. Ibid. 104, 115–123
15 COCKBURN, T. A. 1961. Science 133, 1050–1058
16 COOK, S. F. 1947. Hum. Biol. 19, 83–89
17 COURVILLE, CYRIL B. 1950. Bull. Los Angeles Neurol. Soc. 15, 1–21
17a ELLIOT SMITH, G. and DAWSON, W. R. 1924. Egyptian Mummies, London
18 GÁSPARDY, G. and NEMESKÉRI, J. 1960. Acta Morphologica (Budapest) 9, 203–218
19 GOLDSTEIN, M. S. 1948. Am. J. Phys. Anth. 6, 63–84
20 —— 1953. Hum. Biol. 25, 1–12
21 —— 1957. Am. J. Phys. Anth. 15, 299–312
22 HARE, R. 1954. Pomp and Pestilence. Infectious Disease, Its Origins and Conquest, London
23 HOOTON, E. A. 1930. The Indians of Pecos Pueblo. A Study of Their Skeletal Remains, New Haven
24 KALLAY, JURAY. 1951. Am. J. Phys. Anth. 9, 369–371
25 KIDD, E. 1954. Am. J. Phys. Anth. 12, 610–615
26 KROGMAN, W. M. 1949. Scientific American 180, 52–56
26a McCURDY, G. G. 1923. Am. J. Phys. Anth. 6, 217–329
27 MØLLER-CHRISTENSEN, V. Ten Lepers from Naestved in Denmark. A Study of Skeletons from a Medieval Danish Leper Hospital, Copenhagen
28 MOODIE, R. L. 1923. Palaeopathology. An Introduction to the Study of Ancient Evidences of Disease, Urbana, Illinois

29 MOREL, C., JR. 1957. *La Médecine et la Chirurgie Osseuse aux Temps Préhistoriques dan la région des Grands Causses*, Paris

30 MORSE, D. 1961. *Am. Rev. Respir. Dis. 83*, 489–504

31 NEMESKÉRI, J. and HARSÁNYI, L. 1959. *Homo 10*, 203–226

32 NETTLESHIP, A. 1954. *Bull. Hist. Med. 28*, 259–269

33 OAKLEY, K. P., BROOKE, W. M. A., AKESTER, A. R. and BROTHWELL, D. R. 1959. *Man 59*, 1–4

34 —— and TOBIAS, P. V. 1960. *Nature 185*, 945–947

35 PALES, L. 1930 *Paléopathologie et Pathologie comparative*, Paris

36 RITCHIE, W. A. 1952. *Am. J. Phys. Anth. 10*, 305–317

37 ROGERS, L. 1949. *Brit. J. Surg. 36*, 423–424

38 RONEY, J. G., JR. 1959. *Bull. Hist. Med. 33*, 97–109

39 RUFFER, M. A. 1921. *Studies in the Paleopathology of Egypt*, Chicago

39a —— 1920. *Am. J. Phys. Anth. 3*, 335–382

40 SCHRODER, G. 1957. *Fortschr. auf dem Gebiete der Roentgenstrahlen und der Nuklearmedizin 87*, 538–543

41 SCHULTZ, A. H. 1956. The Occurrence and Frequency of Pathological and Teratological Conditions and of Twinning Among Non-Human Primates, in HOFER, H., SCHULTZ, A. H. and STARCK, D. *Handbook of the Primates*, New York, I, 965–1014

42 SENYUREK, M. S. 1947. *Am. J. Phys. Anth. 5*, 55–66

43 SIGERIST, H. E. 1951. *A History of Medicine*; vol. 1, Primitive and Archaic Medicine, New York

44 SOGNNAES, R. F. 1956. *Am. J. Path. 32*, 547–577

45 STEWART, T. D. 1940. Some historical implications of physical anthropology in North America. In Essays in Historical Anthropology of North America, *Smithson. Miscell. Coll. 100*, Washington, D.C.

46 —— 1950. Pathological changes in South American Indian skeletal remains, in STEWARD, J. H. (ed.), *Handbook of South American Indians 6, Bur. Am. Ethnol. 143*, 49–52

47 —— 1956. *Bull. Hist. Med. 30*, 293–320

48 —— 1958. Stone Age skull surgery: A general review with emphasis on the New World, *Smithson. Report for 1957*, publ. 4333, 469–491, Washington

49 —— 1958. *The Leech 28*, 144–151

50 STEWART, T. D. and SPOEHR, H. 1952. *Bull. Hist. Med. 29*, 538–553

51 STRAUS, W. L. JR., and CAVE, A. J. E. 1957. *Quart. Rev. Biol. 32*, 348–363

52 VALLOIS, H. V. 1948. *La Clinique 43*, 7–13

53 —— 1949. Paléopathologie et paléontologie humaine. In *Homenaje a Don Luis de Hoyos Sainz*, Madrid, 333–341

(b) *Recent major surveys*

54 BROTHWELL, D. R. and SANDISON, A. T. (eds.) 1967. *Diseases in Antiquity*, Springfield. Especially chapters by Morse, Goff, Møller-Christensen, Hackett, Lisowski, Brothwell, Bourke and Wells.

55 BROTHWELL, D. R. (ed.) 1968. *The Skeletal Biology of Earlier Human Populations*, Oxford. Studies by Sandison, Marshall, Brothwell and Powers, are particularly relevant.

56 JARCHO, S. (ed.) 1966. *Human Palaeopathology*, New Haven. Especially relevant to this review are the papers by Stewart, Putschar, Osborne and Miles, Roney, Moseley, and Frost.

42 The Study of Mummified and Dried Human Tissues

A. T. SANDISON

TECHNIQUES FOR PRESERVATION of the human body in Ancient Egypt attained an elaboration perhaps only approached by contemporary mortuary practice in the United States of America.[1a,1b] The methods used are, however, entirely different; modern embalming techniques utilize formaldehyde for tissue *fixation* while mummification implies virtual *desiccation* of tissues. Strictly speaking the term 'mummy' should be restricted to the product of Ancient Egyptian embalming; nevertheless preservation of the human body has been obtained by chance circumstance or deliberate intent in cultures widely separated in space and time. Such preservation, usually the result of simple dehydration, has been reported by anthropologists from the five continents. Places of interest to the anthropologist in this respect include the Canary Islands,[1c,2] Peru, the Torres Straits Islands, Australia, Oceania, Central and West Africa and North America.[2,3] Anthropologists in the past[3,4] saw these phenomena as evidence of cultural diffusions but this view is no longer tenable. Other dried bodies have been reported, e.g. from the crypt of the Capucin convent in Palermo and St Michan's Church, Dublin.[1b] True Egyptian mummies, sun-dried bodies, naturally desiccated bodies from the above locations as well as Moorleichen (bodies preserved in the peat-bogs of Schleswig-Holstein, Holland and Denmark),[45,57,63] all provide or could provide material of palaeohistological interest.

Mummification in Egypt had a sophisticated Osirian religious background but in the beginning was probably introduced as a substitute for the wonderful preservation of the body noted to result from simple desiccation in predynastic sand-burials.[5] As funerary practice became elaborate, entombment removed the body from close proximity to hot dry sand and some mode of preservation became imperative. Mummification, at first the prerogative of the pharaoh, then of royalty and nobility, became almost universal by the close of the New Kingdom. Despite this democratization it is certain that the techniques varied in complexity and cost.[6]

During the Old Kingdom the results of embalming were poor; the majority of Middle Kingdom specimens are friable and ill-preserved although notable exceptions are recorded. The New Kingdom has yielded many well-embalmed bodies especially from the XXIst Dynasty but continued deterioration set in after the XXVIth so that by Roman times preservation was usually mediocre and largely achieved by covering the body with hot resinous substances often described as bitumen. Excellent salted specimens have come from the Coptic period. Ironically perhaps the best preserved bodies are predynastic, preserved by simple desiccation by the hot sand.

The Ancient Egyptians were themselves the first Egyptologists and in later periods were keenly interested in their own history and archaic practices.[7] Nevertheless there is an unfortunate lack of information concerning embalming techniques in the ancient records; details are given only of liturgy and ritual. The most valuable account is given by Herodotus (c. 450 BC)[8] but this, although it is probably a reasonable account of later practice, may not have great relevance to the techniques of say the XXIst Dynasty. Diodorus Siculus (c. 60 BC)[9] also writes on embalming but adds little of scientific value. Briefly we learn that in the most expensive embalming the brain was removed via the nostrils by an iron hook, that the trunk viscera (except heart and kidneys) were removed and that the body was treated with natron. Debate continues as to whether natron was used in solution or solid form;[10a] some experiments made by the writer tend to support the argument that dry natron was used.[10b] Occasional comments on mummification by early Christian writers and medieval Arab scholars add little to our knowledge. In medieval Europe interest in mummies was largely confined to their therapeutic use. Bellonius[11] and Paré[12] in the sixteenth century and Greenhill,[13] Rouelle,[14] Hadley[15] and John Hunter in the eighteenth century made some observations. Napoleon's expedition to Egypt led in the nineteenth century to more important studies, e.g. those of Denon,[16] Baron Larrey[17] and in Britain those of Granville,[18] Osburn[19] and Thomas Pettigrew[1c] whose fine book, published in 1834, was long the standard work. In the present century, the studies of Ruffer,[20-35] Lucas,[10a] Elliot Smith,[6,36,37] Wood-Jones,[37] Derry,[37] and Warren R. Dawson[2,6,38] have consolidated our knowledge of the techniques and results of ancient embalming methods.

HISTOLOGICAL STUDIES

It did not occur to Pettigrew[1c] to submit tissues from his mummies to microscopic examination although already mummy bandages had been thus studied. Mummy tissue is at first sight unpromising material so that it is in some ways surprising that as early as 1852 Johan Czermak[39] the distinguished Viennese laryngologist made accurate drawings of tissues from two mummies, which he had teased out in caustic soda. He depicted hair, tendon, cartilage, nerve, muscle and adipose tissue and used the micrometer to measure the structures. In 1904 Wilder[40] described the restoration of dried human tissues using 1–3% caustic potash for rehydration, checking the process at the desired stage with 3% formalin. Wilder studied Peruvian mummies and sun-dried bodies of Cliff-dweller and Basket-maker Indians of south Utah and demonstrated blood vessels, sarcolemma, neurilemma, adipose tissue, Meibomian glands of eyelid, medullary kidney tubules and portal tracts of liver. In 1909 Shattock[41] made frozen sections of the aorta of Pharaoh Merneptah and demonstrated calcification. Ruffer[21,26] at this time embarked on his important studies in Cairo and in a fine series of papers described naked-eye and histological appearances in normal and pathological mummy tissues. He used fluids containing alcohol and sodium carbonate to soften the brittle tissues, passed them through graded alcohol and chloroform to paraffin wax for section. He described many tissues, e.g. skin, muscle, nerve, blood vessels, heart, lung, liver, kidney, stomach, intestines, testis and breast. His death at sea in 1917 was a grievous loss to palaeopathology.

American palaeohistology was firmly consolidated in 1927 when Wilson[42] described tissues from Basket-Maker and Cliff-Dweller Indians using a softening fluid similar to

Ruffer's; he studied skin, muscle, lung, etc. In the same year Williams[43] reported studies of two Peruvian mummies, following his discovery that soft tissues could be dissected after soaking for a few hours in weak formalin. Histological preparations were made after submersion of tissues in 1% formalin then passing them through alcohols to paraffin or collodion. Later Williams[44] reported further work on bone sections from preserved bodies from Utah, Arizona and New Mexico including an Arizona Basket-Maker baby.

Turning now to Eurasia, Aichel[45] reviewed the histological appearances of German Moorleichen or peat-bog bodies; studies had been made of connective tissues, bone, nerves, alimentary tract, breast, etc.

Simandl[46] described the appearances of skin and muscle from a XIXth or XXth Dynasty female mummy after treatment in 30% alcohol followed by progressive alcohol dehydration to paraffin wax. He utilized many staining methods and also made frozen sections but failed to show convincing sudanophilia of adipose tissue. In 1938 Shaw[47] applied modern staining methods to canopic jar material from an XVIIIth Dynasty tomb; these tissues were soft and cut readily without special treatment; the results were of considerable interest.

Busse-Grawitz[48] reported a study of Egyptian mummy and American tissues; he found no cells nor nuclei but on culture observed cellular structures. On the basis of these findings he suggested altering Virchow's famous dictum 'Omnis cellula e cellula' to 'Omnis cellula e substantia viva'—a conclusion which will not be generally acceptable; probably the structures seen by Busse-Grawitz were of fungal nature. Following his studies Gürtler and Langegger[49] studied Theban mummy tissue before and after various treatments and found no evidence to support Busse-Grawitz. They noted that connective tissues were well preserved but saw neither cells nor nuclei. At this time Jonckheere[50] attempted to make sections of tissues from the Royal Scribe Boutehamon of the XXIst Dynasty at Thebes but was not successful. Graf[51] described histological studies of Egyptian tissues and of ancient Swedish skeletons; he used 1·2% saline to soften the tissues followed by 4% formalin.

Later Sandison[52] reported an elaboration of Ruffer's technique for mummified tissues which has also been used by Rowling[53] on human mummy material from different periods and by Ryder[54] on mummified Theban cat skin and parchments. This method involves softening by rehydration followed by conventional dehydration then double-embedding in celloidin and paraffin for section with any microtome.

Routine staining methods are readily applicable. A further modification by Sandison[55] introduced the use of an automatic Histokinette processing machine to accelerate the progress of tissues and obviate hand transference. Large specimens, e.g. entire temporal bone with external ear of a mummy, were cut in vertical section with ease. The method proved useful for such large bone-sections after decalcification utilizing an ion-exchange resin. This method has yielded excellent sections of bone from Bronze Age, Iron Age, Romano-British, Anglo-Saxon and medieval periods; the latter included a portion of the femur of King William the Lion of Scotland recovered when his tomb was cleared at Arbroath in 1816.[96c] Sandison[52] had previously found the neutral decalcifying fluid of White useful for small bone fragments. Graf[51] used 5% nitric acid or 1–3% trichloracetic acid respectively for ancient Swedish and Egyptian bones. Andersen and Jørgensen[56] used 2% citric acid and 20% sodium citrate at pH6 for decalcification of archaeological bones prior to histochemical examination.

Schlabow et al.[57] describe in a most elegant paper the detailed examination of a fourteen-year-old female bog body from Windeby, including a comprehensive histological, histochemical and chemical examination of the well-preserved brain. Sandison[58] reported successful demonstration of sudanophilic lipid by frozen section of rehydrated mummy tissue and the application of some simple histochemical tests and polarimetry.

Leeson[59a] cut ultra-thin sections of skin from an American Indian burial of uncertain date after embedding in methacrylate, submitted these to electron microscopy and demonstrated cell membranes, nuclear membranes and chromatin, although organelles, not surprisingly, were absent. Further electron microscopic studies on palaeohistological material have been made.[59b]

With regard to more recent preserved human tissues Born[60] describes the histological investigation of a naturally desiccated eighteenth-century European body using oil of cloves and double-embedding in celloidin and paraffin. Hunt[61a] reported histological studies of naturally mummifying bodies from the notorious Christie murder case. He noted that tissues from these bodies (stored in an airy cupboard for about 50, 70 and 100 days), which had been firm, became soft and offensive in 4% formalin. An attempt to cut frozen sections failed but the tissues could be hardened in alcohol for twenty-four hours and then processed. Other specimens fixed in Heidenhain's Susa did not require hardening. Evans examined tissues from thirty-three adipocerous bodies inhumed in triple coffins in a dry environment for periods between 103 to 127 years.[61b]

It should be mentioned here that mummified and dried tissues from all periods develop a brown turbidity in alcoholic solutions.

RESULTS

The conventional variants of the haematoxylin and eosin stains of the routine histologist give a poor histological picture, as a rule, with diffuse imprecise tinctorial renderings. This should not discourage investigators since very considerable detail may emerge with carefully chosen stains. In general cell outlines and nuclei are lacking although in the epidermis, for example, investigators[26,44,52] have noted persistence of cell membranes and nuclei, and cell and nuclear membranes have been seen on electron microscopy.[59a,b]

All workers in the various fields of palaeohistology are agreed that connective tissues survive mummification and desiccation better than epithelia. Organs largely composed of epithelium, i.e. glandular organs, may only be identifiable by virtue of their connective tissue and vascular framework; nevertheless they are usually readily recognizable even in the absence of their delineated epithelial cells. For this reason stains such as van Gieson, Mallory, Masson, phosphotungstic acid haematoxylin, Heidenhain's iron haematoxylin, orcein, Verhoeff's and Weigert's elastica stains are often valuable. Sandison[52] has utilized these stains to distinguish connective tissues and to demonstrate muscle striations in appropriate instances (Plate XXa). Nerves are well outlined also by such methods

(Plate XXb); if elastica and connective tissue stains are combined the structure of blood vessels in normal and pathological states may be studied with relative ease (Plate XXc). Adipose tissues, tendon, cartilage and bone are also readily visualized in well-preserved tissues. It is of interest to note the striking contrast in the staining of adjacent articular cartilage and bone in mummy sections stained by the periodic-acid Schiff method[52] (Plate XXd). Andersen and Jørgensen[56] have studied metachromasia of cartilage and bone in archaeological material.

It is possible to obtain excellent staining of the skin by phosphotungstic acid haematoxylin if the epidermis remains. Hair follicles, sweat glands and sebaceous glands may often be noted in the cutis while well-delineated squamous cells with nuclei may remain in the epidermis (Plate XXIa). Sandison[62] has demonstrated stainable and bleachable melanin in the coats of the mummy eye (Plate XXIb). It is sometimes possible to obtain a positive Perl's reaction in mummy tissues but it is not certain if such a reaction is reliable. Exogenous pigment, e.g. carbon, has been demonstrated in the lungs of Basket-Maker Indians,[40] in Egyptian mummy lungs[21] and in XVIIIth Dynasty canopic lung.[47]

Simandl[46] and Shaw[47] attempted staining for lipid in frozen sections but were unsuccessful: Sandison[58] demonstrated that frozen sections may indeed reveal sudanophilic lipid capable of study by polarimetry and special staining methods.

It may be stated confidently that many sections of mummy and dried tissues show bacterial bodies which have been present in the tissues since the onset of putrefactive changes which are checked by embalming. Moulds may also be present; further, if mummy tissue is allowed to become damp modern moulds may be detected on the surface of tissues.[62] Some moulds may readily be mistaken for red blood cells; Wilder,[40] Williams[43] and Busse-Grawitz[48] claimed to have recognized red blood cells but were probably mistaken. Sandison[52] noted erythrocyte-like structures in mummy thyroid gland; these had the tinctorial properties of red blood cells when stained by van Gieson, Heidenhain's iron haematoxylin, Lieb's phosphotungstic acid haematoxylin, Mallory's trichrome and Lendrum's eosin-phloxine tartrazine methods. They measured $3 \cdot 25$ μ in diameter while red blood cells from fresh human tissue similarly processed measured $4 \cdot 0$ μ. Born[60] has discussed the probable fungal origin of red blood cell-like structures. It seems probable that 'white blood cells' described by some workers are also fungal. Occasional intrusive larvae may be noted in sections, almost certainly derived from eggs laid between the time of death and wrapping of the body and which may continue to develop for some time after wrapping. Sandison[62] noted the larva of a Piophila species in a section of mummy eye.

There are few studies of brain; Rowling[53] had disappointing results except in one instance where the provenance of the material is uncertain and is probably modern. Schlabow et al.[57] demonstrated remains of nerve fibres but no neurones in the wonderfully preserved brain of a fourteen-year-old female Moorleiche dating from about the beginning of the Christian era.

Turning again to more recent material Born[60] showed that, in a naturally mummified body dating from the early eighteenth century, collagen and elastic tissues were demonstrable but that the epidermis was lost and no nuclei could be demonstrated. This is of interest when compared with Ruffer's[26] study of naturally desiccated predynastic Egyptian bodies in which preservation was so good that epidermal nuclei and muscle striations were easily seen and in which even the intestinal contents were shown to contain vegetable cells, partially digested muscle fibres and starch granules. This latter information is of interest from the dietary point of view; a few similar studies have been made, e.g. by Glob[63] on Moorleichen and Wilder[40] on American dried bodies.

Mant[64] described natural mummification of parietes and internal organs (which were still recognizable) of a well-nourished man exhumed after four years in a sandy grave. He further described the excellent preservation of the body of a woman buried for 26 months in a mass grave in a concentration camp; histological examination of the neck tissues showed collagen, fatty tissue and the ghosts of muscle cells. Hunt[61a] has shown that while skin structure was relatively normal 20 days after death, in a second body naturally mummified for 50 days much of the epidermis was lost, nuclei were scanty but muscle striation preserved. A third body dead for 70 days in similar conditions showed very scanty nuclei but still evident muscle striation; the latter was still evident in a fourth body dead for 100 days. In all these bodies there was extensive surface growth of moulds but these, being aerobic, did not penetrate deeply. The same author in a study of a body exhumed after three years' burial in a coffin states that no skin nuclei were then apparent but that fibrous tissue and adipose cell outlines were still evident when stained with haematoxylin laked by a wetting agent. Evans found good histological preservation of myocardium, lung, liver, gall bladder, kidney, breast, uterus with fibroids, testis, eye, blood vessels with medial calcification, skin, nerves and striated muscle in bodies inhumed for over 100 years in triple coffins.[61b] It is hoped that further forensic medical investigations of this sort will also be reported: they may both throw light on natural mummification and aid our understanding of embalming.

Finally attention may be drawn to other laboratory studies of mummified tissues. Blood group serology has now been widely applied to archaeological tissue including bone. Graf[65] demonstrated a spasminogenic substance, presumably histamine, in mummy tissues while Sehrt[66] claimed to show glycolytic activity in mummy tissues put up with pancreatic extract and dextrose. Schmidt,[67,68] Mair[69] and Lipworth and Royle[70] investigated the lipids of ancient Egyptian brains while Aberhalden and co-workers[71,72] reported investigations on amino-acids. Trotter[73] studied hairs of Peruvian dried bodies from Paracas.

Unfortunately many of the earlier palaeohistological studies such as those of Ruffer are illustrated not by photographs but by drawings which are difficult to evaluate. Opinions on histological matters are frequently subjective to some extent so that if any of the material examined by earlier palaeohistologists is available in paraffin block form it would be of great interest to have further sections cut, stained by modern methods and published as photomicrographs.

Suggested procedures. The histologist or pathologist confronted with a wrapped mummy for study should consider radiological examination before unrolling the specimen. Apart from visualization of such artefacts as jewellery or amulets [74] much information can be obtained on the presence of bone and joint disease and of possible calcification of arteries.[75-79] If there is evidence of much disorganization of the skeleton or of multiple fractures without evidence of reaction the mummy is likely to be in poor condition (this state of affairs in a XXVIth Dynasty mummy examined radiologically by the writer was confirmed on unrolling). If the body is attractively bandaged it may be better to conserve it as a specimen for exhibition.

Many mummies show considerable carbonization of bandages and much dust may be released during unwrapping. This may irritate the eyes, nose and throat; a mask to cover the nose and mouth may be helpful. One is reminded of Belzoni's words:[80] '. . . though, fortunately, I am destitute of the sense of smelling, I could taste that mummies were unpleasant to swallow . . .' There may be difficulty in removing the last layers of bandages because of resinous materials and instruments may be necessary. This should be avoided if possible since epidermis, when present, may be lost. On the skin surface, and about the head especially, attention should be directed towards the presence of larvae or pupae; these may be of interest to the entomologist.[1,81,27,62] After unwrapping, further radiographs of areas of interest may be taken and better definition may thus be obtained. If it is desired to dissect large portions of the body these may be photographed and then placed in rehydrating fluid.[52] Much brown turbidity will develop in the fluid which may be changed as required. The specimen imbibes fluid and at this stage any adherent bandage may be removed. This process must be watched carefully to prevent maceration of the specimen; the process may be checked by transferring the specimen to 10% formal-saline in which it can safely be left. It may be of interest to rephotograph the specimen at this stage. A head treated as above will approach more closely to its original contours, especially eyelids, nose, mouth and ears.[40,62] (It might be worthwhile trying this technique on some of the Royal Mummies in the Cairo Museum in order to obtain a more accurate idea of their appearance in life; it would however require great courage to commit such priceless specimens to the rehydrating bath.) After rehydration dissection may be undertaken, e.g. in a limb the neurovascular bundles can readily be traced and removed.

At this stage selected specimens may be processed by the double-embedding method[52] or, if an automatic processing machine is available, by that of Sandison.[55] In the hand-transfer method the specimens are carried over in perforated glass tubes from one fluid to the next. In the automatic method the portions, which may be quite large, are processed in stainless steel cassettes. If the portion contains bone preliminary decalcification is essential; the method of Sandison[55] using ion-exchange resin may be recommended and has proved successful with large specimens. Andersen and Jørgensen[56] recommend 2% citric acid and 20% sodium citrate for decalcification; this also seems satisfactory.

After paraffin embedding the blocks may be cut on any conventional microtome, e.g. the Cambridge Rocking Model. As explained above, routine haematoxylin and eosin stains rarely give good results and resort should be made to methods which differentiate between collagen and epithelia. The writer has found phosphotungstic acid haematoxylin of particular value for bringing up latent detail. Heidenhain's iron haematoxylin, orcein, Verhoeff's and Weigert's elastica stains have proved valuable in the study of blood vessels. The histologist should not be shy of attempting more special methods such as the periodic-acid Schiff technique, Fontana silver stain, and others where appropriate. Andersen and Jørgensen[56] have employed carbolfuchsin-picro ponceau, toluidine blue and azure-A in studies of archaeological bone. In studies of lipids using frozen sections the tissues must, of course, not be exposed to fat solvents. The use of the cryostat should not be forgotten in planning such investigations.

PALAEOPATHOLOGICAL AND PALAEOHISTOPATHOLOGICAL STUDIES

'Palaeopathology' was coined by Ruffer in 1913 to indicate 'the science of disease which can be demonstrated in human and animal remains of ancient times' and it seems reasonable to extend the term as indicated above to imply the recognition of disease in ancient tissues by histological studies. Of course it is not only by examination of actual remains that we derive information about human disease in ancient tissues. For the historical period information is available from the great Egyptian medical papyri, from Greek and Roman writers etc. although there are sometimes conflicts in interpretation; art forms may also give information of value, e.g. Egyptian statues and statuettes, tomb painting,[25] Greek votive offerings, etc. Unexpected light is thrown by Mochica Peruvian pottery (c. 300 BC–AD 500) on the probable existence of *Uta* (a form of cutaneous leishmaniasis) at this period as well as information about amputation, circumcision and many variant sexual practices of which we would otherwise be ignorant.[82,83]

There is now a modern comprehensive work on palaeopathology[84a] and an excellent synopsis is given by Sigerist[84b] in his monograph on primitive and archaic medicine. Valuable older books include Ruffer's collected papers[85] and those of Moodie[86] and Pales;[87] Williams' paper[44] is also useful. None of these is now in print.

Much palaeopathological study concerns bones, considered elsewhere in this book by Dr Marcus Goldstein. Nevertheless, soft tissues have also provided considerable evidence of disease.

Mitchell[93] interpreted the appearances of an Old Kingdom mummy from Deshasheh as evidence of poliomyelitis. Gout in an early Christian of Philae was described by Smith and Dawson[6] and the presence of uric acid in tophae was confirmed by W. A. Schmidt. Smith and Dawson[6] also illustrate a case of leprosy of the hands and feet in an early Christian period Nubian specimen. Both of these cases were re-examined by Rowling,[53] who agrees with the diagnoses. The writer has obtained, by courtesy of Professor V. Møller-Christensen and Dr J. B. Walter, skin and peripheral nerve from the Christian leper but has not so far found it possible to demonstrate the bacillus of leprosy by Ziehl-Neelson staining although bacilli have been seen in methenamine silver stained sections. There is no doubt that Pott's disease (tuberculous spinal osteitis) occurred in Egypt: Smith and Ruffer[23] described a classical case with a large psoas abscess in the mummy of a priest of Ammon of the XXIst Dynasty but failed to demonstrate acid-fast bacilli. Other cases are described by Derry.[37]

With regard to tumours there is a marked paucity of evidence possibly because the expectation of life in earlier times was short. Moreover, most examples are to be found in the skeleton, with a few exceptions. Smith and Dawson,[6] for example, suggested carcinoma of the ethmoid and of the rectum as being causal in the production of erosion of the skull base and sacrum in two Byzantine bodies; this is slender evidence but may be correct. Møller and Møller-Christensen[96a] diagnose secondary carcinomatosis of the cranium in a medieval Danish skull. These and other cases are discussed by Brothwell[96b] and Sandison[96c]. Possibly the most convincing evidence of neoplasm of soft tissues came from Granville[18] who diagnosed (without histological confirmation) cystadenoma of the ovary, possibly malignant, in a mummy now known to be Ptolemaic. The writer has noticed a small squamous papilloma of the skin in a mummy.[84a]

Ruffer and Ferguson[22] described a variola-like eruption of the skin in an XVIIIth Dynasty middle-aged male mummy from Deir-el-Bahari; histological section was consistent with smallpox. Elliot Smith[36] described a similar eruption on the skin of Ramesses V and Ruffer[29] further discussed these two cases and other cutaneous lesions in the Royal Mummies. Ruffer tentatively diagnosed malaria in some Coptic bodies with splenomegaly[31] and conclusively proved the existence of bilharziasis in Ancient Egypt by demonstrating calcified ova of *Bilharzia haematobia* in the straight kidney tubules of two XXth Dynasty mummies.[20,21]

Other kidney lesions noted by Ruffer[21] included unilateral hypoplasia of kidney; in another XVIII–XXth Dynasty mummy the kidney showed multiple abscesses with gram-negative bacilli resembling coliforms. Long[97] described arteriosclerosis in the kidneys of the Lady Teye of the XXIst Dynasty. Shattock[98] described and analysed renal calculi from a IInd Dynasty tomb; oxalates and conidia were noted. A vesical calculus found in the nostril of a XXIst Dynasty priest of Amen contained uric acid covered by phosphates.[6] Ruffer[21] described three mixed phosphate uric-acid calculi from a predynastic skeleton. A bladder stone in a Basket-Maker Indian body is reported by Williams.[99]

Smith and Dawson[6] also refer to the finding of multiple stones in the thin-walled gallbladder of a XXIst Dynasty priestess. Two faceted gallstones were discovered between ribs and iliac crest of an arthritic male skeleton in Grave Circle B at Mycenae of date about 1600 BC.[100] Shaw[47] noted in the canopic-preserved gallbladder of an XVIIIth Dynasty singer that spaces resembling Aschoff-Rokitansky sinuses were present: this suggests chronic cholecystitis. Ruffer[26] mentions fibrosis of the liver in a mummy and equates this with cirrhosis but insufficient evidence is given to evaluate this. Little has been written about alimentary disease in mummies. Smith and Dawson[6] report appendicular adhesions in a Byzantine period Nubian body: these are almost certainly the result of appendicitis. Ruffer[26] describes what may well be megacolon in a child of the Roman period and prolapse of rectum in Coptic bodies.[31] Elliot Smith[36] mentions two probable cases of scrotal hernia—Ramesses V shows a bulky scrotum now empty after evisceration, while the scrotum of Merneptah was excised after death by the embalmers, possibly because of the bulk of a hernia.

Some interesting studies of lung have been published. Anthracosis in Egyptian mummy lungs was described by Ruffer[21] and by Long.[97] Wilder noted similar changes in Basket People bodies of Utah.[40] Shaw[47] reported anthracosis in the lungs of Har-mosĕ of the XVIIIth Dynasty but he had also suffered from emphysema and lower lobe bronchopneumonia. The writer has noted anthracosis of the lungs and hilar lymph nodes in a Guanche body studied by Brothwell, Gray and Sandison. Ruffer[21] reported pleural adhesions and diagnosed pneumonia in two mummies, one XXth Dynasty and the other Ptolemaic; the latter may have been pneumonic plague although the evidence is far from complete. Long[97] reported caseous-like areas in the lung of a XXIst Dynasty lady and Wilder recognized possibly bronchopneumonia in a Basket-Maker Indian baby. In the writer's opinion these diagnoses must be accepted with some reserve in view of the possible confusion of moulds as leucocytes. With regard to anthracosis this seems to enhance lung preservation; in the lungs of a much decomposed coalminer exhumed 2 years after burial in a wet cemetery the writer noted that dust disease was still easily diagnosed and bronchial cartilages and vessels were relatively well preserved.

Elliot Smith[36] described lactating breasts in the recently delivered Queen Makere and Wilder[40] noted parous breasts and os cervix in a Basket People Indian woman. Williams[44] reported an observation by Derry that Princess Hehenhit of the XIth Dynasty had a narrow pelvis and died not long after delivery with vesicovaginal fistula. Smith and Dawson[6] described violent death in an unembalmed sixteen-year-old pregnant Ancient Egyptian girl and postulated illegitimate conception. The Archaeological Survey of Nubia revealed a deformed Coptic negress who died in childbirth as a result of absent sacro-iliac joint contracting the pelvis.[37] Male Egyptian mummies show circumcision throughout the dynasties until abandoned in the Christian period. Cameron[90] described a eunuchoid Middle Kingdom mummy with a curious penile appearance reminiscent of incisional operation.

With regard to vascular disease, we are here on firm ground and have direct evidence. Blood vessels are often well preserved in Egyptian mummies and dried bodies. Czermak[39] described aortic calcification and Shattock[41] made sections of the calcified aorta of Pharaoh Merneptah. Elliot Smith[36] noted this change in his macroscopic description of the royal body and also described calcification of the temporal arteries in Ramesses II. Ruffer[21,24,26] described histological changes in Egyptian mummy vessels from the New Kingdom to the Coptic period. Long[97] examining the mummy of the Lady Teye of the XXIst Dynasty described degenerative disease of the aorta and coronary arteries with arteriosclerosis of the kidney and myocardial fibrosis. Moodie[76] described radiological evidence of calcification of superficial vessels of a predynastic body. Williams[44] reported arteriosclerosis with calcification and calcified thrombus in a Peruvian mummy of AD 700. Buchheim[101] gives a good review of arterial disease in Ancient Egypt. It is often difficult to assess the older descriptions which are unaccompanied by photographs; Sandison[102, 84d] examined and photographed mummy arteries using modern histological methods (Plate XXIc, d). Arteries were tape-like in mummy tissues but could readily be dissected. Arteriosclerosis, atheroma with lipid depositions, reduplications of the internal elastic lamina and medial calcification could readily be seen. (A word of warning may be given here that atheromatous lesions in mummy arteries tend to form sectoral clefts: this should not be interpreted as dissecting aneurysm.)

Miscellaneous conditions noted in mummies include pediculosis, baldness in men and women and comedones of face (Ruffer[27]). The writer has also noted and confirmed histologically comedones in an elderly male mummy head.[84d] Wilder[40] described infantile eczema in a Utah Indian baby and an infective dermatosis in a Peruvian mummy. Wood Jones[103] described judicial hanging and decapitation in Roman Egyptian skeletons and Elliot Smith[36] reconstructs the death by violence of Pharaoh Seknenre. Glob[63] illustrates sacrificial hanging and throat-cutting in Moorleichen. Examinations of more recent remains include those of Don Francisco Pizarro[104] where the autopsy, 350 years after his murder in Lima, confirmed the historical account of his death. Porter[105] gives an account of the autopsy on John Paul Jones 113 years after his death; the body had been preserved in alcohol. The findings of pulmonary scarring and of interstitial nephritis fit well with his known medical history.

In conclusion it may be said that future palaeohistopathological studies might give further information on vascular disease, the presence of lesions inducing fibrosis, both inflammatory and neoplastic, and the presence of parasites such as helminth ova and others. It is to be hoped that such studies as well as gross examinations of bones and joints will continue to be made since information of value to the archaeologist, anthropologist, and pathologist, as well as to the general and medical historian, might be forthcoming.

ACKNOWLEDGEMENTS

I am grateful to Messrs J. G. Scott, J. D. Boyd and Cyril Aldred for assistance in obtaining material for my studies; to Cyril Aldred for continued advice on Egyptological matters; and to Messrs W. Penny, N. L. Russell, D. McSeveney and W. Mason (all Fellows of the Institute of Medical Laboratory Technology) for technical assistance.

REFERENCES

1a MITFORD, J. 1963. *The American Way of Death*. London
1b GALE, F. C. 1961. *Mortuary Science*, Springfield, Ill.
1c PETTIGREW, T. J. 1834. *A History of Egyptian Mummies*, London
2 DAWSON, W. R. 1928. *J. Roy. Anth. Inst. 58*, 115
3 ELLIOT SMITH, G. 1929. *The Migrations of Early Culture*, Manchester
4 PERRY, W. J. 1937. *The Growth of Civilization*, Harmondsworth, 2nd ed.
5 BREASTED, J. H. 1912. *Development of Religion and Thought in Ancient Egypt*, London
6 ELLIOT SMITH, G. and DAWSON, W. R. 1924. *Egyptian Mummies*, London
7 ALDRED, C. 1960. *The Egyptians*, London
8 HERODOTUS 1921. Text and trans. by A. D. Godley, London, vol. I
9 DIODORUS SICULUS 1933. Text and trans. by C. M. Oldfather, London, vol. I
10a LUCAS, A. 1948. *Ancient Egyptian Materials and Industries*, London, 3rd ed.
10b SANDISON, A. T. 1963. *J. Near East Studies 22*, 259
11 BELLONIUS 1553. *De Admirable Opera Antiquorum*, Paris
12 PARÉ, A. 1575. *Les Oeuvres*, Paris
13 GREENHILL, T. 1705. NEKPOKHΔEIA *or the Art of Embalming*, London
14 ROUELLE, M. 1754. *Mém. de l'Acad. Royale des Sciences*, Paris
15 HADLEY, J. 1764. *Phil. Trans. Roy. Soc. 54*, 1
16 DENON, V. 1803. *Travels in Upper and Lower Egypt*, London, vol. 1
17 LARREY, D. J. 1812. *Memoires de Chirurgie Militaire*, Paris
18 GRANVILLE, A. B. 1825. *Phil. Trans. Roy. Soc. 1*, 269
19 OSBURN, W. 1828. *An account of an Egyptian Mummy*, Leeds
20 RUFFER, M. A. 1910. *Br. Med. J. 1*, 16

21 —— 1910. *Cairo Sci. J.* 4, 1
22 —— and FERGUSON, A. R. 1910. *J. Path. Bact.* 15, 1
23 ELLIOT SMITH, G. and RUFFER, M. A. 1910 *Zur Historischen Biologie der Kranksheitserreger*, 3 Heft
24 RUFFER, M. A. 1911a. *J. Path. Bact.* 15, 453
25 —— 1911b. *Bull. Soc. arch. Alex.* 13, 1
26 —— 1911c. *Mém. Inst. Égypte*, 6 (3)
27 —— and RIETTI, A. 1912. *J. Path. Bact.* 16, 439
28 —— —— 1912. *Bull. Soc. archéol. Alex.* 14, 1
29 —— 1914. *Mitt. Gesch. Med. Naturw.* 13, 239
30 —— 1914. *Ibid.* 13, 453
31 —— 1913. *J. Path. Bact.* 18, 149
32 —— and WILLMORE, J. G. 1914. *Ibid.* 18, 480
33 —— 1917. *Cairo sci. J.* 9, 34
34 —— 1918. *J. Path. Bact.* 22, 152
35 —— 1920. *Am. J. Phys. Anth.* 3, 335
36 ELLIOT SMITH, G. 1912. *The Royal Mummies*, Cairo
37 —— WOOD-JONES, F. and DERRY, D. E. 1908–10. *Archaeol. Survey of Nubia, Bulls. & Report on Human Remains*
38 DAWSON, W. R. 1929. *Mém. Inst. Égypte* 13
39 CZERMAK, J. N. 1852. *S. B. Akad. Wiss., Wien* 9, 427
40 WILDER, H. M. 1904. *Am. Anth.* 6, 1
41 SHATTOCK, S. G. 1909. *Proc. Roy. Soc. Med.* 2, 122
42 WILSON, G. E. 1927. *Am. Nat.* 61, 555
43 WILLIAMS, H. U. 1927. *Arch. Path.* (Chicago) 4, 26
44 —— 1929. *Ibid.* 7, 890
45 AICHEL, O. 1927. *Anth. Anz.* 4, 53
46 SIMANDL, I. 1928. *Anthropologie* (Prague) 6, 56
47 SHAW, A. B. 1938. *J. Path. Bact.* 47, 115
48 BUSSE-GRAWITZ. 1942. *Arch. exp. Zellforsch.* 24, 320
49 GÜRTLER, J. and LANGEGGER, P. A. 1942. *Anat. Anz.* 93, 185
50 JONCKHEERE, F. 1942. *Autour de l'autopsie d'une Momie*, Brussels
51 GRAF, W. 1949. *Acta. Anat.* (Basel), 8, 236
52 SANDISON, A. T. 1955. *Stain Technol.* 30, 277
53 ROWLING, J. T. 1961. *Disease in Ancient Egypt: evidence from Pathological Lesions found in mummies.* M. D. Thesis. Univ. of Cambridge
54 RYDER, M. L. 1958. *Nature* 182, 781
55 SANDISON, A. T. 1957. *Nature* 179, 1309
56 ANDERSEN, H. and JØRGENSEN, J. B. 1960. *Stain Technol.* 35, 91
57 SCHLABOW, K., HAAGE, W., SPATZ, H., KLENK, E., DIEZEL, P. B., SCHÜTRUMPF, R., SCHÄFER, U. and JANKUHN, H. 1958. *Prähist. Z.* 36, 118
58 SANDISON, A. T. 1959. *Nature* 183, 196
59a LEESON, T. S. 1959. *Stain Technol.* 34, 317
59b MACADAM, R. F. and SANDISON, A. T. 1969 *Medical History* 13, 81
60 BORN, E. 1959. *Zbl. allg. Path. path. Anat.* 99, 490
61a HUNT, A. C. 1953. In CAMPS, F. E., *Medical and Scientific Investigations in the Christie Case*, London, Appendix 6
61b EVANS, W. E. 1962. *Med. Sci. and Law* 2, 155
62 SANDISON, A. T. 1957. *Medical History* 1, 336
63 GLOB, P. V. 1959. *Jernaldermanden fra Grauballe*, Aarhuus
64 MANT, K. 1953. Recent Work on Changes after Death, in Simpson, K. (ed.), *Modern Trends in Forensic Medicine*, London
65 GRAF, W. 1949. *Nature* 164, 701
66 SEHRT, E. 1904. *Berlin, klin. Woch.* 41, 497
67 SCHMIDT, W. A. 1907. *Z. allg. Physiol.* 7, 369
68 —— 1908. *Chemikerztg.* 32, 769
69 MAIR, W. 1913. *J. Path. Bact.* 18, 127

70 LIPWORTH, A. and ROYLE, F. A. 1915. *Ibid. 19*, 474
71 ABERHALDEN and BRAHM. 1909. *Z. physiol. Chem. 61*, 419
72 ABERHALDEN and WEIL. 1911. *Ibid. 72*, 15
73 TROTTER, M. 1943. *Am. J. Phys. Anth. 1*, 69
74 WINLOCK, H. E. 1936. *Bull. Met. Mus. Art 31*, 274
75 BERTOLOTTI, M. 1913. *Nouv. Icongr. Salpêt 26*, 63
76 MOODIE, R. L. 1931. Roentgenologic Studies of Egyptian and Peruvian Mummies. *Field Mus. Nat. Hist.* III
77 DANFORTH, M. S. 1939. *Bull. Mus. Art. Rhode Isl. Sch. of Des. 27*, 36
78 JONCKHEERE, F. 1942. *Autour de l'Autopsie d'une Momie*, Brussels
79 ZORAB, P. A. 1961. *Proc. Roy. Soc. Med. 54*, 415
80 DISHER, M. W. 1957. *Pharaoh's Fool*, London
81 MURRAY, M. A. 1910. *The Tomb of Two Brothers*, Manchester
82 MASON, J. A. 1957. *The Ancient Civilizations of Peru*, London
83 POSNANSKY, A. 1925. In *Festschrift. zur Feier des. 25-jährigen Bestehens der Frankfurter Gesellschaft für Anthropologie and Urgeschichte*
84a BROTHWELL, D. and SANDISON, A. T. (eds.). 1967. *Diseases in Antiquity*, Springfield, Illinois
84b SIGERIST, H. E. 1951. *A History of Medicine*, New York, vol. I
85 RUFFER, M. A. 1921. *Studies in the Palaeopathology of Egypt*, Chicago (This volume includes references 20–35 and some other papers of interest)
86 MOODIE, R. L. 1923. *Paleopathology, an Introduction to the Study of Ancient Evidences of Disease*, Urbana
87 PALES, L. 1930. *Paléopathologie et Pathologie comparative*, Paris
88 HRDLIČKA, A. 1914. In *Smithsonian Miscellaneous Collections, 61*
89 SALIB, P. 1961. *J. Bone Jt. Surg. 43A*, 303
90 CAMERON, J. 1910. In Murray, M. A. *Tomb of Two Brothers*, Manchester
91 BUDGE, E. A. W. 1924. *A Guide to the 1st, 2nd and 3rd Egyptian Rooms*, British Museum, London
92 STEWART, T. D. 1943. *Am. J. Phys. Anth. 1*, 47
93 MITCHELL, J. K. 1900. *Trans. Ass. Am. Phys. 15*, 134
94 MacCURDY, G. G. 1914. *Am. J. Phys. Anth. 6*, 217
95 ROGERS, C. L. 1949. *Br. J. Surg. 36*, 423
96a MØLLER, P. and MØLLER-CHRISTENSEN, V. 1952. *Acta. path. microbiol. scand. 30*, 336
96b BROTHWELL, D. 1967. In *Diseases in Antiquity*, Springfield, Illinois
96c SANDISON, A. T. 1968. In *The Biology of Earlier Human Populations*, Oxford
97 LONG, A. R. 1931. *Arch. Path* (Chicago) *12*, 92
98 SHATTOCK, S. G. 1905. *Trans. path. Soc. Lond. 56*, 275
99 WILLIAMS, G. D. 1926. *J. Amer. med. Ass. 87*, 941
100 MYLONAS, G. E. 1957. *Ancient Mycenae, The Capital City of Agamemnon*, London
101 BUCHHEIM, LISELOTTE. 1956. *Therap. Berichte 28*, 108
102 SANDISON, A. T. 1962. *Medical History 6*, 77
103 WOOD-JONES, F. 1908. *Brit. med. J. 1*, 736
104 McGEE, W. J. 1894 *Am. Anth. 7*, 1
105 PORTER, H. 1905. *Century Magazine 70*, 927

43 Buried Bone: The Experimental Approach in the Study of Nitrogen Content and Blood Group Activity

J. D. GARLICK

BURIED ORGANIC MATERIALS decompose in a variety of ways and at a variety of rates. Sometimes this variation may be of little account in the interpretation of analytical results useful to archaeology. In radiocarbon dating, for example, whatever the quantity and chemical combination of carbon remaining from the original organic material of a partially fossilized specimen (provided direct and indirect effects of contamination can be excluded), the ratio of C^{12} to C^{14} will give within reasonable limits an estimate of the age of the specimen.

In other cases, however, the quantities and composition of surviving organic materials in a buried specimen may be crucial to the investigation, and can only be interpreted in the light of the environment since burial. This paper outlines the experimental approach in the study of two such characteristics of bone—its nitrogen content as an aid to dating; and its blood group activity.

In both studies most of the progress has so far been made by laboratory work in many parts of the world, but the Experimental Earthworks sponsored by the British Association for the Advancement of Science now offer an opportunity for field studies too.[17,19,26] The first earthwork was constructed on Overton Down, Wiltshire, in 1960, and the second near Wareham, Dorset, in 1963. They are allowing both empirical and experimental study of the changes occurring over time in batches of materials buried within them and successively removed at intervals of 2^n years. The results given in this paper are from uncooked and boiled animal bone and uncooked human bone recovered from the Overton Down earthwork. Some batches of material were buried high in the chalk bank (pH about 8); others near ground level in the turf core (pH about 6·3).

BONE NITROGEN

Fresh, dry, defatted compact bone from large mammals contains on average between 4 and 5% organic nitrogen by weight. More than nine tenths of bone nitrogen is contained in its structural protein—collagen. Other organic substances, including a small proportion of gelatin-like soluble collagen and the protein from the network of vessels in bone, contribute the remaining fraction.[12] Tests for nitrogen in fossil bone are thus essentially tests for surviving collagen and its breakdown products. Much of the non-collagen nitrogen is contained in soluble and relatively unstable substances which are not likely to persist for long periods in buried bone. Only when total nitrogen falls to a very low level would residues of substances other than collagen be likely to contribute significantly.

Immature bones contain more nitrogen, especially near growth zones, and bones from aged animals may contain less.[33] Some workers have reported that nitrogen values decrease from outside to inside of ox femur shaft,[29] but others do not find this to be so.[33] The bones of small mammals such as the rabbit and rat seem to be more variable but tend to show lower values.[29,44]

Collagen[15]

Collagen is a fibrous water-insoluble protein which accounts for up to a quarter of the weight of fresh bone. It forms a rather lower proportion of the dentine of teeth,[31] and is also an important component of many other tissues, including skin and tendon. The basic collagen molecule, which contains about 18% N, is composed of three coiled polypeptide chains with an amino-acid composition notable for its high glycine and hydroxyproline content. The three chains are held close together by hydrogen bonds between the glycine residues on adjacent chains, and other types of linkage may form as collagen matures.[44] Bundles of individual collagen molecules (which are about 1/10,000 mm in diameter) are arranged in fibrils of up to 1/00 mm diameter, in which the overlapping of successive molecules produces the characteristic 640 Å banding seen under the electron microscope (Plates Ia and XXIIIb). Oriented alongside the collagen molecules in bone are crystals of inorganic hydroxyapatite, which can be removed by mild acid or other decalcifying treatment. There are also small quantities of other organic substances such as sugars in preparations of collagen.[12]

In some respects collagen is not a stable protein, for even in hot water the individual polypeptide chains separate and form the less organized gelatin, a substance readily broken down by proteolytic enzymes. In other respects, however, it is a remarkably stable substance, for in its unaltered state it is very resistant to proteolytic enzymes such as trypsin, particularly when associated with hydroxyapatite, and it can survive in an environment of micro-organisms which rapidly break down other proteins.[14, 22] The collagen-mineral complex can be completely broken down *in vivo*, as during wound repair, but the precise mechanism remains unclear.[15,41] Otherwise collagenase—an enzyme which degrades collagen—is produced by only a few micro-organisms, mainly species of *Clostridium*, and especially *Cl. histolyticum*, the agent responsible for gas gangrene.[22,28] In laboratory studies collagenase activity disappears in strongly acid conditions (pH below 4 or 5), is greatest in a neutral or slightly alkaline medium (pH 7 to 8), and may persist, depending on the particular system, in strongly alkaline conditions (pH 9).[22] Various agents, including ferrous iron and heavy metals, are known to inhibit collagenase, which can also be destroyed by enzymes produced by other organisms.[22,24] Denatured collagen can easily be broken down to short peptides and their constituent amino-acids. Most of these are more or less soluble substances which would sooner or later leach out of buried bone.

The rate of disappearance of nitrogen from buried bone is thus likely to depend in the short term on the presence and suitability of the environment for micro-organisms which produce collagenase. Over longer periods of time it is probable that collagen decomposes in other ways. Collagenase activity produces a thinning and tapering of collagen fibrils without changing their characteristic 640 Å banding.[22] The characteristics of Pleistocene and earlier altered collagen (see p. 37) suggest some less specific breakdown process. Environmental factors which have been suggested as influencing the rate at which collagen degrades and its nitrogen is removed include the composition, pH and hydrology of the matrix; oxygenation; temperature; and changes brought about by the soil flora.[5,9]

LABORATORY METHODS

Preparation of Specimens

After selection or treatment to eliminate recent contamination, specimens may be prepared by pounding, cutting or gentle drilling. High-speed drilling or grinding produces enough heat to convert collagen to gelatin.[31] Drying above 100°C may also have this effect, although previous desiccation at a lower temperature reduces or eliminates it.[31,33] Preparations for testing will normally include water-soluble and insoluble fractions. The first contains any soluble organic substances, including peptides or free amino-acids from collagen breakdown; the insoluble residue any unaltered collagen. Alternatively the collagen can be isolated by one of the standard procedures for bone and dentine decalcification.

Nitrogen Determination

Of the many quantitative tests available for organic nitrogen the *Kjeldahl Method* is the one used by most workers in this field.[47] Samples are digested for twelve hours or more with hot sulphuric acid in the presence of suitable catalysts. This converts the nitrogen of organic substances to ammonium sulphate, which is measured as ammonia freed from the digest by strong alkali. The method is both accurate and sensitive with most fresh biological materials, but is unreliable when the nitrogen is in oxidized form, as in nitro compounds. In such cases the oxidized nitrogen must be reduced before digestion. Many procedures are available, but probably the simplest is to add glucose to the digestion mixture. This is effective with most resistant compounds of this type.[47] Collagen, whether isolated or in whole bone or dentine, is readily converted by the direct Kjeldahl method, although somewhat longer digestion may be necessary with the tissues of older individuals.[44]

   The original test for organic nitrogen was by the *Dumas Method*, in which the material under test is burnt in an atmosphere of carbon dioxide, and any oxidized nitrogen then reduced. This converts nitrogen to gaseous form, which is collected and measured directly. The method requires careful procedures and may be unreliable with very small quantities of nitrogen, but very few types of organic nitrogenous compound are difficult to convert, and the method is generally more powerful than Kjeldahl's.

Amino-acids

The proportion of hydroxyproline in collagen is so high that the amount of collagen or its breakdown products can be estimated from hydrolysates of fossil bone by standard quantitative tests for this amino-acid (hydroxyproline is found in only small proportions in other animal and plant tissues). Chromatographic techniques allow the complete amino-acid pattern to be analysed, and this may distinguish contaminants from the residues of non-collagen bone protein (see Plate Ib).

Contamination

Work on radiocarbon dating of fossil bone and antler has shown that considerable contamination by younger organic material may occur.[3,4,6,23] Much of the contaminating material may be deposited from percolating water, but debris from micro-organisms could presumably account for a significant proportion of intrusive nitrogen. Fertile soil contains, of course, a considerable amount of nitrogen,[8,10] and a specimen of matrix from one of the Overton bones buried in the turf layer contained about 1% N by a direct Kjeldahl test. Even the chalk fragments surrounding the specimens buried high in the bank contains about 0·3% nitrogen in non-resistant form.

Various treatments have been suggested for clearing specimens of contaminants for radiocarbon tests. Apparently the most satisfactory method is to decalcify the bone or dentine with acid and treat the residual collagen with alkali to remove insoluble contaminants.[6] By this procedure only residual collagen can be isolated, of course, and its breakdown products will be lost.

Collagen and its breakdown products can also be distinguished from contaminants by amino-acid analysis, provided particular amino-acids have not been preferentially eliminated by microbial or other agencies. This becomes increasingly likely with older specimens owing to the varying long-term stability of particular amino-acids.[1,16] and possibly to the differing solubilities of amino-acids or peptides with particular amino-acid compositions.

Indirect effects of contamination may also be important, particularly as they will usually be difficult or impossible to identify and measure. For example micro-organisms or substances absorbed from ground-water could interfere with the breakdown of surviving collagen, perhaps by inhibiting collagenase activity, and so preserve a higher nitrogen content than would be expected from the general conditions of burial.

BONE NITROGEN AND ARCHAEOLOGY

In Section 1 of this volume Oakley (pp. 37 to 43) shows that where a body of consistent data is available for a particular type of site an intrusive burial such as the Galley Hill skeleton can be clearly distinguished by its nitrogen content; this is confirmed by fluorine tests, which give parallel results. Only in special conditions, as in Siberian permafrost or the La Brea tar pits of Los Angeles, do bone specimens retain most of their nitrogen over long periods, and in most excavated bone the nitrogen content is considerably reduced. Without consistent data from the same or comparable sites, however, nitrogen values may give little clue to the age of the material. Mean values of around 1% N, for example, may be found in Saxon, Neolithic or earlier European material from diverse sites.

NITROGEN IN HISTORICAL BONE

A recently reported series of Kjeldahl tests on human bone ranging from 2 to 700 years old or more[20] showed no significant drop in nitrogen content up to 50 years, followed by a steady fall to about 2% N at 700 years, with values of 1·1% and 1·3% N for two specimens between 200 and 800 years old. This series shows a much more delayed initial fall in nitrogen content than the Overton bones, but fits well with Saxon compact bone from the U.K. tested by the author, which contained between 0·9 and 1·4% N in different parts of a single long bone, with less than 5% of this soluble and none resistant.

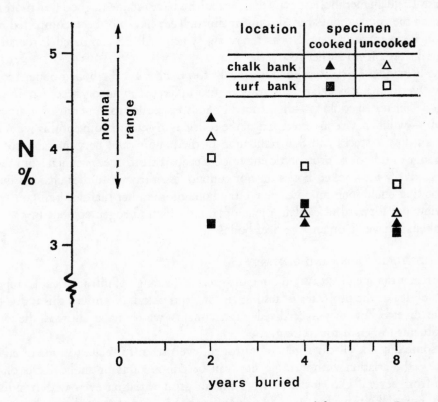

Fig. 94 Kjeldahl nitrogen content of animal bones recovered from Overton Down artificial earthwork.

The results for the Overton material are shown in Figure 94. The animal specimens were long bones and scapulae from sheep; some were immature, and at burial would be expected to fall in the upper end of the normal range. Samples of compact bone were prepared by slow hand-drilling into the cleaned specimens. It will be seen that after two years' burial the nitrogen content was generally still within although towards the lower end of the normal range for fresh bone, but after four years there was a considerable mean fall to between 3 and 3½% N. After eight years' burial the values have dropped hardly if at all from the four year level (the variation within and between bones exceeds the mean difference between the four and eight year recoveries). The addition of glucose to the digestion mixture did not increase the nitrogen value for any of the animal bones. Despite the presumably greater leaching in the chalk bank the upper burials on the whole contain as much nitrogen as the lower, and an identical proportion (about 5%) in soluble form. However it is tempting if premature to note that in both four and eight year recoveries the chalk bank uncooked bone had less nitrogen than the uncooked turf core specimens.

The three human bones recovered after four years all contain just over 4% N by glucose-Kjeldahl method, and why these specimens have retained a good deal more nitrogen than the animal bones remains unexplained. Tests have not been completed on the human bone from the eight year recovery, which will be compared in detail with material stored from earlier recoveries.

The behaviour of cooked bone is difficult to predict, and the boiled bone recovered from Overton has not so far shown any regular difference in nitrogen content from uncooked. The initial cooking—the cleaned bones were boiled for an hour or more before burial[18]—would have converted part of the collagen to gelatin. Some of this would have been lost in the stock, and that remaining in the bone would be vulnerable to attack by a range of microbial proteolytic enzymes. Yet apart from one specimen from the two year recovery the cooked bones do not contain less nitrogen. Other changes induced by cooking could, one supposes, make the bone more rather than less resistant. This is the view put forward to explain the anomalously high nitrogen content (2·5% N) of a cooked, believed Roman Age beef bone.[20]

POST-PLEISTOCENE BONE AND DENTINE

The greater the age of excavated bone the greater the range of nitrogen values reported, and the greater the problems of testing and interpretation. No doubt this is due partly to the diverse but very specialized environments which have allowed the organic constituents to persist for so long.

In some but not all cases general nitrogen levels seem to relate to type of environment.[5,7,25] Variation within single sites can be considerable or slight. Tests on large series from several U.S. localities have shown great variation even within individual bones, especially in wetter sites.[7] On the other hand most of the collagen has persisted in a large series from a 4000 year old cemetery in a sandy soil in Hungary,[21] and there is apparently little variation between skeletons.

The results of tests on an apparently uncontaminated specimen of Predynastic Egyptian ivory from a well-documented tomb at Naqada illustrate the difficulties in interpreting some older material (Table A). The higher Kjeldahl values after reduction must mean that some of the nitrogen is in oxidized form not susceptible to direct digestion. The Dumas method apparently converts yet further nitrogenous material resistant to Kjeldahl digestion even after reduction. Several other early Egyptian ivories tested also gave generally but not invariably higher values by the Dumas method. Some showed a similar pattern of resistant nitrogen concentrated in the soluble fraction,

TABLE A

| Method of Testing | Percentage of specimen weight | |
	Total N	Water-soluble N
Kjeldahl, standard digestion	0·24	trace
„ with added glucose	0·75	0·43
„ prior reduction by HI and P	0·63	not tested
Dumas Laboratory 1	1·1	„
„ Laboratory 2	1·2	„

while others showed it in both soluble and insoluble fractions. The total direct Kjeldahl N varied from rather more than 0·1% to above 1% N, with a lower variance in the insoluble fraction.[35] Fresh human dentine contains ±3·5% N, and collagen accounts for a greater proportion of this than in bone.[32] The nitrogen content in bone and ivory would generally be expected to follow a similar pattern during fossilization, but this might not be so at low nitrogen levels, for the insoluble non-collagen nitrogen in elephant ivory is apparently considerably raised.[34]

It has not so far been possible to identify the composition and probable origin of the various nitrogenous fractions in this material; in particular it is not known if the resistant nitrogen is collagen-derived, and therefore properly included in the total nitrogen for dating purposes. Adequate amino-acid analysis is impossible on small samples from valuable museum objects, and it is hoped that the problems will be solved by detailed study of expendable specimens which show the same indigestive behaviour.

PLEISTOCENE BONE AND DENTINE

Nitrogen values reported from Pleistocene fossils range from over 3% N in some of the Late Pleistocene Rancho La Brea tar pit bones to less than one hundredth of this value in Early and Middle Pleistocene specimens.[11] Material with many of the microscopic and chemical features of collagen may persist in bone and dentine for millions of years, but subtle changes can occur in surviving collagen fibrils which reduce the banding frequency from 640 Å to 600 Å or even less in earlier fossils.[43] Collagen accounts for a variable but nearly always reduced proportion of the total nitrogen,[11,16] and the relatively unstable hydroxyproline falls sharply as a proportion of total amino-acids present.[2,16] A technical difficulty is that the protein or peptides of fossil and even of more recent desert-dried bone may require prolonged treatment to convert them to amino-acids, and incomplete hydrolysis would underestimate hydroxyproline, which is among the more resistant.[42]

Whether the change in banding and loss of hydroxyproline are part of a single breakdown process is not known. Nor is it clear what environmental conditions or time-span are necessary for these changes to come about.[30] They are already present in 14,000 year old Nubian skeletons from a sandy matrix,[27] which contain only a trace of residual Kjeldahl nitrogen, but apparently not in much earlier Eurasian specimens.[25,46] The La Brea Late Pleistocene bones show the amino-acid change but preserve the 640 Å banding.[16,50]

Although surviving collagen has been identified by electron diffraction in a Miocene fossil,[45] the organic nitrogen in pre-Pleistocene fossils seems generally to be in peptide or free amino-acid form.[1] The proportions of the various amino-acids differ greatly from those in collagen, apparently as a result of their varying long-term stability, and the amino-acid content of the matrix may be higher than that of the fossil itself.[2] The traces of organic nitrogen in pre-Pleistocene fossils are so variable, and their origin so uncertain, that gross nitrogen values are of little or no foreseeable value for dating such early material.

BLOOD GROUP ACTIVITY IN BURIED BONE

Glemser's article in the first edition of this work (pp. 437–446) gave a full account of the methods, difficulties and achievements of fossil blood group studies. In the right conditions blood group activity can persist in human remains for many thousands of years, but, as with collagen, blood group substances do not disappear in a constant fashion. Indeed it is possible that the apparent blood group of a buried bone will change rather than disappear over the course of time. What is known of the biochemistry of blood group differences makes this not improbable.

At least in the ABO and related systems the differences between the major blood groups lie in the particular type and arrangement of a relatively few sugar residues in part of a large mucopolysaccharide molecule.[37,38] If particular sugars are removed the blood group specificity will change. Micro-organisms are a likely source of change or error.[48] Not only do many strains possess blood group specificity related to the human ABO groups, but enzymes produced by microorganisms, including some species of *Clostridium* are able to remove sugars from blood group substances and so produce new specificities.[36,39,49,50]

Only the ABO antigens can generally be identified in old bone, and conditions must be ideal for antigens of other systems, such as Rh or MN, to be preserved. Only a few series of tests for antigens of other systems have been reported, and their interpretation can be problematical.[21]

Details of the many practical difficulties in identifying fossil blood groups and attempts to resolve them are described in Glemser's article.[13] The most frequent finding is that blood group activity is so reduced that standard techniques fail to identify any group. Contamination presents difficult problems, for there is no simple means of differentiating genuine blood group reactions from those produced by soil or other microorganisms. There are, however, slight differences between human and microbial ABO-like specificities, and with appropriate reagents it should be possible to distinguish intrusive blood groups, provided the human antigens have not themselves changed after burial.

The Wareham and Overton earthworks will again allow an empirical study of the fate of blood group activity in bone buried in diverse environments.[17] Bones of known

ABO groups are buried at both sites, and the MN and Rh groups were also tested for the Wareham material. Three of the seven specimens recovered from Overton after four years' burial could be correctly grouped, although their activity was considerably reduced. In a fourth bone A activity had nearly disappeared. Of the two further bones A activity was not detected in an AB specimen from the chalk environment, nor B activity in a B specimen from the turf layer. There was no sign of new (false) blood group specificities.

More delicate tests, including fluorescent antibody techniques,[21] should allow much more detailed testing of later recoveries. Through the study of micro-organisms present in the bones and their matrix it may also be possible to identify the agents responsible for loss or change of blood group specificity.

CONCLUSIONS

In some conditions of preservation both nitrogen content and blood group activity of buried bone can already yield much useful information for the archaeologist and anthropologist. The aim must be to specify more closely the conditions of burial and the techniques of testing which will allow reliable information to be extracted from a wider range of excavated material. Much progress will stem from laboratory research in the many fields of study concerned, including biochemistry, microbiology and immunology. Equally important will be field experiments such as the Experimental Earthworks in which to follow through time and in different environments the inter-action of the many variables involved.

REFERENCES

1 ABELSON, P. H. 1955. *Yrbk. Carnegie Inst.Washington, 54,* 107–9
2 ARMSTRONG, W. G. and TARLO, L. B. H. 1966. *Nature 210,* 481–82
3 BARKER, H. 1967. *Nature 213,* 415
4 BARKER, H. and MACKEY, J. 1961. *Radiocarbon 3,* 39–45
5 BERGER, R., HORNEY, A. G. and LIBBY, W. F. 1964. *Science 144,* 999–1001
6 BERGER, R. and LIBBY, W. F. 1966 *Radiocarbon 8,* 467–97
7 COOK, S. F. and HEIZER, R. F. 1959. *Am. J. Phys. Anth. 17,* 109–15
8 —— 1965. *Studies on the Chemical analysis of Archaeological Sites,* Berkeley and Los Angeles
9 CORNWALL, I. W. 1956. *Bones for the Archaeologist,* London
10 —— 1958. *Soils for the Archaeologist,* London
11 DOBERENZ, A. R. and P. MATTER III, 1965. *Comp. Biochem. Physiol. 16,* 253–58
12 EASTOE, J. E. and EASTOE, B. 1954. *Biochem. J. 57,* 453–59
13 GLEMSER, M. S. 1963. *Science in Archaeology,* 1st ed. pp. 437–46
14 GROSS, J. and LAPIERE, C. M. 1962. *Proc. Nat. Acad. Sci. 48,* 1014–22
15 HARKNESS, R. D. 1961. *Biol. Rev. 36,* 399–463
16 HO, TONG-YUN, 1965. *Proc. Nat. Acad. Sci. 54,* 26–31
17 JEWELL, P. A. (ed.) 1963. *The Experimental Earthwork on Overton Down, Wiltshire, 1960,* London
18 JEWELL, P. A. 1968. Personal communication
19 JEWELL, P. A. and DIMBLEBY, G. W. (eds.) 1966. *Proc. Preh. Soc. 32,* 313–42
20 KNIGHT, B. and LAUDER, I. 1967. *Med. Sci. Law. 7,* 205–208
21 LENGYEL, I. and NEMESKÉRI, J. 1963. *Z.Morph. Anth. 54,* 1–56
22 MANDL, I. 1961, *Adv. Enzymol. 23,* 164–264
23 MÜNNICH, K. O. 1957. *Science, 126,* 194–99
24 NEUMANN, R. E. and TYTELL, A. A. 1950. *Proc. Soc. Exp. Biol. N.Y. 73,* 409ff.

25 OAKLEY, K. P. 1963. In *The Scientist and Archaeology* (ed. E. Pyddoke), pp. 111–19. *See also* pp. 37 to 43 of this volume.

26 PROUDFOOT, V. B. 1965. *Adv. Sci. 22*, 125–33

27 RACE, G. J., *et al.* 1968. *Am. J. Phys. Anth. 28*, 157–62

28 ROBB-SMITH, A. H. T. 1953. In *Nature and Structure of Collagen* (ed. J. T. Randall) London

29 ROGERS, H. J., WEIDMANN, S. M. and PARKINSON, A. 1952. *Biochem. J. 50*, 537

30 SHACKLEFORD, J. M. 1966. *Am. J. Phys. Anth. 25*, 291–98

31 STACK, M. V. 1951. *Brit. Dent. J. 90*, 173–81

32 —— 1953 in *Nature and Structure of Collagen* (edit. J. T. Randall) London

33 STROBINO, L. J., and FARR, L. E. 1949. *J. Biol. Chem. 178*, 599

34 TOMES,   . 1895–6. *J. Physiol. 19*, 217

35 UCKO, P. J. 1965. *J. Roy. Anthrop. I. 95*, 214–39

36 WATKINS, W. M. 1962. *Immunol. 5*, 245–66

37 —— 1966. *Science 152*, 172–81

38 WATKINS, W. M. and MORGAN, W. T. J. 1959. *Vox Sang. 4*, 97–119

39 WATKINS, W. M., ZARNITZ, M. L. and KABAT, E. A. 1962. *Nature 195*, 1204–6

40 WEIDMANN, S. M. and ROGERS, H. J. 1950. *Biochem. J. 47*, 493

41 WOODS, J. F. and NICHOLS, G. Jr. 1963. *Science 142*, 386ff.

42 WYCKOFF, R. W. G., DOBERENZ, A. R. and McCAUGHEY, W. F. 1965. *Biochim. Biophys. Acta 107*, 389–90

43 WYCKOFF, R. W. G., WAGNER, E., P. MATTER III and DOBERENZ, A. R. 1963. *Proc. Nat. Acad. Sci. 50*, 215–18

44 GROSS, J., LAPIERE, C. M. and TANZER, M. L. 1963. In *Cyvodifferentian and Macromolecular Synthesis* (ed. M. LOCKE) New York and London, pp. 175–202

45 ISAACS, W. A., *et al.* 1963. *Nature 197*, 192

46 ASCENZI, A. 1969 this volume, pp. 526–38

47 BRADSTREET, R. B. 1965. *The Kjeldahl Method for Organic Nitrogen*, New York and London

48 THIEME, F. P. and OTTEN, C. M., 1957. *Clm. J. Phys. Anth. 15*, 387–97

49 KABAT, E. A., 1956. *Blood Group Substances*, New York, pp. 88–91

50 WYCKOFF, R. W. G. and DOBERENZ, A. R., 1965. *Proc. Nat. Acad. Sci. 53*, 230–33

SECTION IV MICROSCOPY AND RADIOGRAPHY

44 *The Application of X-rays to the Study of Archaeological Materials*

DON BROTHWELL, THEYA MOLLESON,
PETER GRAY AND RALPH HARCOURT

WITH THE DISCOVERY of X-rays in 1895 by Wilhelm Röntgen, a powerful new technique was made available for the study of ancient materials. In physics, the impact of the discovery was immediate, and within the first year over a thousand articles, large and small, were published on this subject. Seventy years after the discovery, there is still a remarkably limited application of X-ray techniques to the study of archaeological specimens. This may be partly explained by time limitations and the unavailability of equipment or laboratory help, but it seems equally to be the result of a failure on the part of the archaeologist in general to realize the potentialities or ask in what way their own particular materials or studies might be assisted by one or other form of X-ray analysis. The various X-ray techniques now known were, of course, not all available from the beginning, the well-known medical radiography being well established before the advent of X-ray diffraction analysis, this in turn being a 'mature' procedure by the coming of X-ray microscopy only a few years ago.

It is not our task here to enter into a detailed description of the principles involved or structure of the various equipment used in X-ray studies. It is more important to emphasize that although equipment is expensive—and thus out of easy reach of archaeological research institutions—the wide use of X-ray methods in industrial, general scientific, and medical work means that prospects of technical advice and help should be within the range of many archaeologists. In the case of the radiography of bone, wood or metal objects, the major cost may be only that of the film, X-ray and dark-room equipment being in very common use in many countries (facilities being extendable to archaeological research where 'tactful' approaches are made).

Elsewhere in this volume, attention is given to certain aspects of the application of X-rays to archaeological material, and these topics need only brief mention here. Leo Biek (page 568) points to the importance of radiographs in showing morphological detail on objects whose surfaces are encrusted with either oxidized or 'foreign' deposits. Ironwork, in particular, can be valuably explored by this means. Frederick Matson, discusses the non-destructive technique of X-ray fluorescent spectrometry (page 592). The equipment is becoming increasingly more available in certain laboratories, and so far has perhaps been especially helpful in studying ceramics. The surface area needed for examination purposes need not be more than 10 mm. across, and thus small fragments of pottery are sufficient for analytical purposes. In contrast to this technique, which leaves the specimen intact, X-ray diffraction analysis may be more destructive, although only very small quantities need to be powdered for analysis. Useful general references to these two analytical techniques are Aitken[1] and Barker.[2]

From the studies which have now been made, it would seem possible to predict that future X-ray work is likely to fall mainly into two broad categories: first, that concerning the chemical composition of excavated objects; second, pertaining to the biology of earlier humans, animals and plants. What follows is a brief and general review of some research avenues, to show the diversity of information which has been, or promises to be, forthcoming.

X-RAY DIFFRACTION ANALYSIS

This technique offers a relatively quick and accurate way of determining the major components of an excavated object, where analysis is desirable. Unlike the radiocarbon laboratories, those undertaking X-ray diffraction work who are sympathetic to the needs of the archaeologists are not well known, and the facilities vary from country to country. In Britain, two laboratories which have wide experience of archaeological materials for study by this method are the British Museum Research Laboratory[2] and the Department of Mineralogy at the British Museum (Natural History). Few if any laboratories are likely to be unselective in the samples they accept for analysis, and requests for analyses without a clear statement as to the archaeological relevance of resultant data are likely to meet with resistance.

When X-rays are passed through a small powdered fraction of the sample sent for analysis, a characteristic powder diffraction pattern is obtained and recorded. From this pattern the composition of the sample may often be identified.

This method is already very well established and widely used as a means of identification. The pioneering work of Hanawalt, Rinn, and Frevel has led to the eventual publication of a reference file of such patterns by the American Society for Testing Materials, known as the A.S.T.M. Index, which is brought up to date yearly. Not only is new information added each time, but existing data are often revised and even replaced by more up-to-date and accurate data.

The advantage of the X-ray powder method in museum work is that it is non-destructive and requires only very little material, usually not more than a few tenths of a milligram. This makes it possible for the same sample to be used for other determinations as well. The X-ray diffraction method can often be used where other methods fail but it too has its limitations and is best used in conjunction with chemical and/or other methods to effect an identification. Differences in texture also show up and may often help in interpreting a mixture of two or more constituents.

It should, however, be noted that minor or even, in an unfavourable case, major constituents of a sample may not be detected at all, whereas minute amounts of another constituent may give an identifiable powder pattern. Substances amorphous to X-rays will never produce a diffraction pattern. Thus, the bright red staining on a recent human bone sample sent to one of us [D.R.B.] could not be identified by X-ray diffraction. It was later found to be a colloid, also amorphous to X-rays. Nevertheless the X-ray powder method has been usefully and successfully employed in a number of widely different problems, both in archaeology and other fields of science. The most readily remembered of these is perhaps the Piltdown skull problem, where the identification of gypsum, $CaSO_4 2H_2O$ in addition to apatite, $Ca_5(PO_4)_3(F_1OH)$ led to the discovery that the bones had been treated chemically to make them look older. Other problems encountered by the Department of Mineralogy, B.M. (N.H.) include the composition of some human and animal urinary calculi; bezoar stones, medieval jewellery, gemstones found in graves at archaeological sites; medieval 'niellos'; devitrification products of ancient and other glass; different types of pottery and glazes; pigments used by Renaissance masters; various 'jade' objets d'art and jade axe-heads from all over the world.

X-RAY MICROSCOPY

It was not until 1948 that the first true X-ray microscope was devised. Unlike contact microradiography, which depends upon the normal X-raying of thin specimens in contact with photographic emulsion (and the enlargement of the resulting image), projection microscopy permits the photography of sharp enlarged images. Equipment is very expensive at present, a major supplier in Europe being High Voltage Engineering (Europa) N.V., Amersfoort, Holland. This type of microscopy has been applied successfully to the study of such divergent materials as blood cells, metals, plant tissues, ceramics and formaminifera. The microscope projects a magnified image of the specimen on to a film or fluorescent screen with an ultrafine focus X-ray tube. Initial magnification for the camera attachment ranges from $\times 10$ to $\times 150$.

Although still in its infancy, the technique holds much promise, perhaps especially for certain bio-archaeological investigations. In the case of bone changes and histology, it already promises to provide a valuable new dimension in the study of osseous tissue. So far, however, little skeletal material has been considered in this way. Possibly it holds the most promise for the palaeobotanist, although it is early to say, and some workers seem to regard the technique with caution or scepticism (Dimbleby, personal communication). Nevertheless, as fragments of plant tissue, wood or otherwise, may be extremely minute and fragmentary (and may cause considerable problems in conservation), any additional techniques to explore and record tissue morphology are clearly worth considering.

Because of the considerable penetrating power of X-rays, and the great depth of field which can be achieved, it seems possible that prior to the rehydration of selected coprolites (if the sample is large), they might usefully be scanned by means of microradiography. Where not all the faeces are to be broken down for analysis, X-ray scanning of this type could clearly help in selecting parts which looked most promising from the point of view of enclosed food debris. Also, before rehydration separated the parts of the coprolite, it would reveal any likely relationships between the harder tissue—especially bone-fragments.

THE USE OF X-RAYS IN THE STUDY OF ANIMAL BONES

In many respects the radiographical aspects of the study of both human and animal bones are very similar, as indeed are the types of disease in each which leave their mark on bone. These, briefly, are fractures, inflammations, tumours and various proliferative or degenerative conditions.

The massive size of the bones of the larger animals introduces some technical difficulties but these are not insuperable.

The range of pathology so far claimed in prehistoric mammals has been briefly surveyed in the first edition of this book.[3] It is sufficient here simply to exemplify ways in which X-rays can be used in the proper diagnosis and study of abnormality. Plate XXIIc shows an Iron Age dog femur which one of us [R.H.] suspected of fracture. However, the degree of alignment of the broken parts and the resorption of the callus, was such that radiography was necessary for confirmation.

It is frequently assumed, possibly incorrectly, that in prehistoric times domestic farm animals necessarily went very hungry, if not nearly starved, during the winter. Work carried out in a series of experiments on Scottish hill sheep may help to confirm or correct this belief. It was shown that clearly recognizable resorption with thinning of the cortex and rarefaction of cancellous bone occurred in animals which had a reduced calcium and phosphorus intake and that the bones of animals fed a diet deficient in protein and calories showed definite radiographic differences from those which had been adequately fed. Such resorption was consistently more marked in some bones than others; the mandible, cervical vertebrae and skull being the most sensitive indicators.[4,5,6,7]

Other workers have demonstrated transverse trabeculae and osteoporosis in the bones of pigs fed a diet which contained inadequate protein and total calories.[8]

Lines of retardation can be seen in animals although they are harder to recognize than in humans. In both ruminants and pigs these are, in some cases, retained for a considerable period.[9] Plate XXIIa, b shows these 'trabeculae of malnutrition' in sheep. If the number of such lines in the bones of a faunal group could be reliably and consistently correlated with the age, estimated by other means, and found to be similar then it seems reasonable to infer that a seasonal dietary deficiency occurred. If this could be established it would be a contribution towards explaining the reason for the reduction in size that so consistently seems to accompany domestication. Conversely, if it were shown that the winters did not impose undue hardship then, equally valuable, the diminution in size would suggest that prehistoric stockowners practised deliberate selective breeding. At present there is little evidence that they did.

As far as is known to us very little work of this sort has been done with excavated, as opposed to modern material. This, of course, is consistent with the general neglect to which all aspects of the study of excavated animal bones have been subjected, at any rate, in Great Britain.

As in the case of studies of Man, variation in the thickness of cortical tissue in long bones is to be found in other mammals. Little work seems to have been done relating differences to breeds or to nutritional and other environmental factors. Such work might eventually be very profitable on early stocks, although the broken nature of many animal bones may make direct observation rather than radiographic examination, easier.

Also, as in the study of Man, any consideration of dental development and eruption sequences in other mammals would be dependent upon the use of X-rays. To our knowledge, this field has still to be explored as regards earlier and wild domestic stocks. Similarly, any investigation of variation in internal tooth morphology (pulp size and shape, thickness and shape of dental tissues) would need the assistance of radiographs— but this also is a neglected aspect (though Kursén (on page 671) demonstrates the type of external dental variation present in prehistoric mammals).

TABLE A

Date of Publication	Material (site)	Specimen	Author and other details
1895	X-rays discovered by Röntgen.		
1902	Šipka, Předmost, Krapina	jaws	Walkhoff,[55] internal structure.
1903	La Naulette, Spy, Goyet	jaws	Walkhoff,[55] tooth development.
1904	Krapina, Spy	femora	Walkhoff,[55] structure.
1908	Heidelberg	jaw	Schoetensack.[41]
1909	Le Moustier	jaw	Klaatsch.[28]
1913	Piltdown	parietal and teeth	Underwood,[49] stereoscopic
1914	La Rochette	teeth	Elsner,[20] taurodontism.
1919	Obercassel, Neanderthal	femora	Bonnet,[12] structure.
1920	Eringsdorf	jaw	Virchow[51]
(1924)	Rhodesian	skull	Bertram—not published.
1926	La Quina	jaw	Martin.[31]
1927	Pithecanthropus	femur	Dubois,[19] structure.
1928	Gibraltar	jaw	Buxton,[14] stereoscopic.
1933	Sinanthropus	teeth	Black et al.,[11] pulp-cavity size.
1936	Engis	skulls	Fraipont.[21]
1937	Wadjak, Choukoutien	skulls	Weidenreich.[57]
1938	London	skull	Young,[61] mineralization.
	Swanscombe	skull	Le Gros Clark,[15] mineralization.
1948	Saccopastore	teeth	Sergi.[42]
1949	Teshik Tash	skeleton	Rohklin.[38]
1951	Solo	skull	Weidenreich,[58] post-jugular fossa.
1953	Dolni Vestonice	skull	Jelínek.[26]
1956	Les Cottes	skull	Patte,[34] palaeopathology.
1957	Fossil man tooth eruption		Garn et al.[22]
1958	Rhodesian, Florisbad, Saldanha	skulls	Singer.[45]
1960	Fossil man radiographic survey		Weiner—Wenner Gren.
1961	Fond-de Foret	femur	Twiesselman.[48]
1962	Neanderthal	femur	Nemeskéri,[33] age.
	Kanam	jaw	Tobias.[46]
1964	Lantien	jaw	Ju-Kang.
1966	Kedung Brubus	jaw	Tobias.[47]
1967	Neanderthal frontal sinuses		Vlček[52]
1968	Šala	frontal sinus	Vlček.[53]

RADIOGRAPHIC STUDIES OF FOSSIL MAN

Because the problems of studying fossil man are generally the same as those in working on other early mammals, and the subject has a long history, it would seem worth consideration in some detail.

The first important radiographic studies of fossil hominid material were probably made by Otto Walkhoff at the beginning of the century. Only five or six years after the discovery of Röntgen rays he was fully aware of the importance and possibilities of the new technique. Inspired by Darwin's work on variation Walkhoff seems to have X-rayed as many fossil human remains as he could get hold of and incorporated his findings in fully comprehensive monographs on the structure and function of the primate skeleton. He associated with Selenka[54] and Gorjanovič-Kramberger[23] in this work.

Thus by 1903 the Krapina, Prédmost, Šipka, Spy, La Naulette and Goyet mandibles had all been radiographed and examined for internal trabecular structure, chin development, and tooth morphology.[55] By 1904 similar studies had been made on the femur including an age assessment of the Krapina femora from the state of the internal trabecular structure, and a comparison of the Spy femur with other fossil and modern human femora as regards mechanical functioning.[56,23]

Attention was paid to such details as orientation; and the quality of the radiographs is good even by today's standards. Unfortunately this very high standard was not maintained. During the next fifty years, although some radiographs were taken of fossil hominid material, especially of jaws and teeth as taurodonty came to be associated diagnostically with primitiveness and the Neanderthalers, comprehensive survey studies of the range of variation in normal material do not seem to have been made. A resumé of the history of radiography as applied to fossil man is seen in Table A.

Techniques and Problems

Fossil material by its fragmentary and often mineralized nature can raise special radiographic problems.

Heavily mineralized bones require greatly increased dosages if the X-rays are to penetrate the radio-opaque impregnating minerals. Young[61] commented on this feature after X-raying the London skull and pointed to the degree of mineralization as an indication of the fossil nature of the bone. Le Gros Clark[15] compared the Swanscombe skull with that of a seventeenth-century Londoner in the same way. (This could never be more than a relative method of dating bone.) It has been particularly difficult to get good radiographs of the Rhodesian skull. Bertram tried unsuccessfully in 1924 before the general availability of powerful industrial equipment. Eventually good radiographs were obtained in 1953 by Solus Schall Ltd., using 109 kV and a two-minute exposure time. A modern skull would take about 70 kV for 0·6 seconds. Sometimes the matrix filling the bone cavity will make adequate radiographic detail almost impossible, as was the case with the Upper Pleistocene Singa skull. To examine mineralized bone, especially jaws, fully it may be necessary to make different exposures for thick areas with tooth roots and for thin areas with tooth crowns, since the heavy dosage necessary to penetrate the body of the jaw would obliterate the crowns of the teeth and any other thin areas.

The question of standardization needs consideration. Singer[45] asks that the X-ray head—specimen distance should be constant for a given bone so that radiographs are comparable. Attention needs to be paid to the orientation of material. Particularly when it is fragmentary the temptation is to let the bone 'rest naturally on the film' which obviously rules out any possibility of standardization. However exposures should also be made from a number of directions if the radiographs are to be correctly interpreted. Limitations of orientation as well as indifferent quality of the radiographs aided the misidentification of the Piltdown jaw.[27,30,49] This was only rectified in 1955 when new radiographs were made.[16] New and better radiographs were also instrumental in the reassessment of the taxonomic position of the Kanam jaw fragment.[46]

Insufficient use has been made of stereoscopic radiography in this field although stereo-pairs were taken of the Piltdown parietal as early as 1913 and Buxton[14] did use stereoscopic radiographs for his identification of the teeth of the Gibraltar child's mandible. There is also scope for the wider use of microradiography particularly of pathological material (Moseley *in* Jarcho[25]) and for other specialized techniques such as image intensification for comparison of bone structures.

Cranial Studies

In the past there has been sporadic use of X-rays when it should have been routine to the study of any fossil material. Today, however, the work of Rohklin[38], Jelínek[26], Corrain[17], Vlček[53] and others indicates that there has been considerable improvement in this direction. Radiographic examination of the frontal sinuses should form an integral part of any primary description of new fossil frontals.

Radiographs showing the degree of development of the frontal sinuses have been used to assess the individual's age, e.g. Ca verde,[17] Peche de L'Azé,[35] Tzeyang,[36] Fontéchevade I,[50] Šala.[53] It is surprising how often an assessment of the frontal sinus has been attempted without using radiographs, even when the jaws and teeth of the same skull have been X-rayed.

Vlček's[52] recent work on the variation of the frontal sinuses of Neanderthal man marks a turn to a more general outlook. Sergi is interested in the form of the Neanderthal maxilla but has only come to use X-rays latterly in his studies, e.g. Monte Circeo[44] although he has frequently used them for examination of jaws and teeth.[42,43]

Many other studies on the skull of fossil man could be made. Singer[45] used lateral view radiographs to compare the form of the frontal bone in the Florisbad, Rhodesian and Saldanha skulls. Weidenreich[58] described what he called a post-jugularis fossa from the radiographs of the base of Solo VI and XI skulls. Variations in cortical thickness,[26] prognathism, and the hypophysial fossa for example, could be studied radiographically, as well as entirely new studies on say comparative bone densities.

Dental Radiography

Dental radiography has been important in the study of fossil man and the fossil primates

since tooth form and development so often has a taxonomic significance and more particularly is a means of assessing the age of the individual.

In the past there has been a lot of confusion over the order of tooth eruption in man.
Recent work on modern and ancient populations has done much to clarify the picture.
The eruption sequence in modern man is a variable phenomenon and cannot be used as a
taxonomic criterion within known hominids. Existing variation in modern man must
be considered when attempts are made to compare extinct hominids with modern man
and far more information is needed on dental development in the various populations of
modern man.[22, 29]

Equally there has been a certain amount of confusion as to the significance of the size
of the pulp-cavity of the teeth of the primates in general and fossil man in particular.
Thus most jaws of fossil man, including the Australopithecines,[37] *Sinanthropus*,[11, 57] as
well as the classic Neanderthalers[23] have been X-rayed.

Post-cranial Studies

Bonnet[12] was one of the few early workers to examine the internal structure of the long-
bones of the Neanderthalers as a group. The Obercassel femora were compared radiographically with other femora from Spy, Krapina and Neanderthal. Dubois[19] X-rayed
the femur from Trinil and from the form of the trabeculae deduced that the femur of
Pithecanthropus, if not entirely constructed for the same locomotion as that of man, was
adapted for an erect gait—hence *Homo erectus*. Gorjanovič-Kramberger[23] was evidently
aware of changes to the internal trabecular pattern with age when he compared the
Krapina femur of an adult and a much younger individual.

A sufficient number of published radiographs is now available for such studies on the
internal structure and ageing as those of Nemeskéri[32, 33] on femora and Atkinson[10] on
vertebrae, using more recent archaeological material, to be made on a wider range of
fossils. Similarly, studies of the mechanical structuring of bones of the sort carried out
by Roth-Lutra[39] might be applied to fossil men.

Anomalies

Rather surprisingly, little radiographic work on fossil man has been done in this field
though many workers have stressed that it is essential to any study of the pathological
remains of fossil man. [40, 59]

Dubois[19] X-rayed the *Pithecanthropus* femur from Trinil but does not comment on
the radiological aspects of the gross exostosis present. Patte[34] used radiographs in his
examination of the skull from Les Cottes and diagnosed a traumatic abscess or a very
persistent osteomyelitis. The bone thickness had been reduced by erosion of the external
table. New radiographs of the Kanam jaw revealed that two of the teeth had ante-
mortem fractures running up the roots, reaching the root-canals and pulp-cavities,
which have the effect of artificially widening the canals and bulging the neck region of
each tooth.[46]

The peculiarities of weathering, soil erosion and uneven mineralization can cause
certain pseudo-pathological changes in fossils. Wells[59] outlines a number of ways in

which radiographs can simulate abnormal conditions. Decker and Bohrod[18] warn that medullary artifacts in prehistoric bones can be due to the irregular deposition of silicon compounds.

Further, the same X-ray pattern may be produced by different processes (Blumberg and Kerby in Jarcho[25]) or the process producing the pattern may not be fully or correctly understood (Marshall in Jarcho[25]). Thus great caution is called for, and consequently the extended use of all available analytical techniques including radiography, before attempting to diagnose an anomalous condition.

RECENT WORK ON THE RADIOGRAPHIC STUDY OF EGYPTIAN MUMMIES

Investigation of a wrapped mummy of an ancient Egyptian by an anatomist, pathologist or an archaeologist entails the laborious task of unrolling the specimen, and ends frequently in its destruction. Furthermore, even if the unwrapped mummy is not disturbed, it is known that this procedure will eventually have a deleterious effect upon the exposed body. A far simpler and harmless investigation can be undertaken by merely X-raying the mummy either in its wrapping or coffin (wooden or cartonnage). The films, which will form a permanent record, can readily be copied and sent to other establishments for study and comparison.

The late Professor Sir Grafton Elliot Smith fully realized the importance of radiography, and in his Preface to *The Royal Mummies* he states, 'In the case of many of the mummies, especially those in the best state of preservation, there was singularly little that an anatomist could do, provided of course that he refrained from damaging the body. In such mummies as those of Ramesses III, for instance, the anatomist can add little to what any one can see for himself by looking at the body encased in its resinous carapace. Examination with the aid of X-rays would, no doubt, have provided much additional information.' At the time Elliot Smith was examining the Royal mummies, there were no adequate X-ray facilities. In 1931 Roy L. Moodie, having X-rayed the Egyptian and Peruvian mummies in the Chicago Field Museum of Natural History, remarks 'Roentgenology supplements all other methods of learning of physical troubles in early times.'

During recent years, a systematic radiographic skeletal survey of the mummies of ancient Egyptians in the museums in this country and on the Continent has been undertaken with the following objects in view:

1 *Determination of the presence or absence of human bones within the coffin or wrappings*
Many museums in this country and on the Continent possess mummies acquired by travellers of the last century as a souvenir. In many cases these worthies were exploited by the native dealers. We learn from C. R. Scott in 1837, 'for the eagerness with which every sort of trash is purchased by travellers makes the trade a very profitable concern, and opens a wide door for fraud, by the encouragement it gives to the *manufacture* of mummies'. A good example of a fake mummy is illustrated in the Kodak Publication, *Medical Radiography and Photography (Fig. 11).*[63] The late Warren R. Dawson also informed the writer that he and Elliot Smith once opened an apparently intact fine

cartonnage coffin, and found it packed, not with a wrapped mummy, but a conglomeration of modern rubbish.

2 Determination of sex and age

A coffin can usually be dated by its style and orthography, but it cannot always be assumed that it contains the original inhabitant. Thus, a coffin bearing the name and titles of a man may contain the mummy of a female, and vice versa. It is likely that native dealers filled an empty coffin with a mummy to make the 'lot' more attractive, and, no doubt, more expensive. Again, a mummy showing a late period style of embalming may be found in a coffin of a much earlier date. Examples of such substitutions are mummies nos 45, 52 and 64 in the British Museum. Ageing the mummy is fairly simple before the fusion of the epiphyses, and it is noteworthy that Professor R. H. Harrison[62] appears to have solved the problem of the contents of the coffin found in Tomb 55, Valley of the Kings, by the use of X-rays. After fusion of the epiphyses the matter is not so straightforward, but a general estimation may be given by the condition and state of the bones and teeth. The appearance of an unwrapped mummy of a female in one museum caused the curator to estimate the age at death to be about 75. Radiographs showed the bones to be those of a girl aged about 17.

3 Correlation of radiographic findings with known embalming techniques

This has proved a success in numerous cases, and vague labels such as 'Mummy of an ancient Egyptian, thought to be at least 3000 years old' can be replaced by ones of a more definite character.

4 Demonstration of amulets within the bandages

Amulets, made either of faience or metal, were frequently incorporated within the mummy wrappings. These, being radio-opaque, can readily be detected and removed under radiographic control if thought necessary. Numerous, well executed amulets are within the bandages of the British Museum mummy No. 22939, and are illustrated in Gray.[63, 65]

5 Demonstration or absence of palaeopathological features

There appears to be a popular misconception that a mummy is associated with both direful diseases and misfortune. With regard to the former, one of us [P. G.] once had an assistant who blankly refused to approach an unwrapped mummy for fear of contracting both consumption and venereal disease!

The mummy, lying in an extended position, presents the palaeopathologist with the least of his problems. The bandages and sycamorewood or cartonnage coffins are radiolucent, and, thereby, cause no significant obstruction to the radiographs. In the case of a genuine mummy, the skeleton is intact and the bones are free from soil contamination. However, it must be admitted that when the use of packing material was in vogue fine bone detail is obscured, and some of the embalming agents can cause pseudo-pathological features.[64] It is further admitted that the causation of death can rarely be stated, but this is not surprising when one considers how many fatal diseases leave no tell-tale X-ray evidence in the skeleton. The commonest complaint encountered is spinal arthritis, but other bone lesions have been noted. The soft tissues, contrasting well with the bandages and the bony structures, have, on occasions, shown evidence of arterial disease.

X-RAYS AND NORMAL HUMAN VARIATION

We have discussed so far the value of radiography in relation to man by reference to recent work on Egyptian mummies and the slowly growing studies on fossil man. Wells[66] has previously considered other aspects. It would seem of value to mention, by way of final comment here, the possibilities of more extensive work on normal variation in earlier populations—especially those of Neolithic and more recent times. This field has recently been reviewed at some length by Brothwell, Molleson and Metreweli,[13] who indicated a variety of differences which had been, or might be successfully explored by, radiography. Except in the confirmation or study of abnormality, few workers have given consideration to this in the past, other than for the internal architecture of certain long bones and its relation to developmental age (see Genovés, page 440).

In the case of the skull, at least seven separate aspects can be listed as worthy of radiographic consideration.

1 The shape of the pituitary fossa. Burrows and colleagues[67] have shown by reference to a post-medieval English and a Negro series that there are both intra and inter-group differences, but their work has still to be extended to earlier groups.

2 Cranial thickness. Although Getz[68] has demonstrated possible inter-group differences in recent series, no extension back in time appears to have been made yet.

3 Sinus complexity of the temporal bone. As yet, only early Amerindians have been studied for differences in mastoid pneumatization.[69]

4 Endocranial size and shape.

5 Middle meningeal artery patterns. On the internal aspect of the parietals, grooves show the branching of the meningeal vessels. This pattern is known to be very variable, in fossil as well as recent Man. Detailed studies, using X-rays, should be possible.

6 Cranial base morphology. The architecture of this part of the skull is complex, radiographs providing useful additional information.

7 Frontal sinus variation. This is a very variable part of recent and earlier skull series, and in early British groups differences have already been demonstrated.[13]

Some of these categories mentioned will clearly be biologically more meaningful than others, and in particular, the frontal sinus system and cranial thickness deserves far more consideration in earlier peoples.

In the case of the post-cranial skeleton, thickness of the cortical tissue of the long bones should receive more attention than it has previously, especially as there is a growing body of data on this aspect in living populations.

REFERENCES

1 AITKEN, M. J. 1961. *Physics and Archaeology*, New York
2 BARKER, H. 1967. In *The Application of Science in Examination of Works of Art*, Museum of Fine Arts, Boston, 218

3 BROTHWELL, D. R. 1963. In *Science in Archaeology*, London, 275–8
4 BENZIE, D., *et al.* 1955. *J. Agric. Sci. 46*, 425
5 —— 1956. *Ibid.*, *48*, 175
6 —— 1959. *Ibid.*, *52*, 1
7 —— 1960. *Ibid.*, *54*, 202
8 PLATT, B. S. and STEWART, R. J. C. 1962. *Brit. J. Nutr. 16*, 483
9 NODDLE, B. 1968. Personal communication
10 ATKINSON, P. J. 1967. *Calc. Tiss. Res.* 1, 24–32
11 BLACK, D. *et al.* 1933. *Geol. Mem. Ser. A, No. 11*
12 BONNET, R. 1919. In VERWORN, M. *et al. Der diluviale Menschenfund von Obercassel bei Bonn*, Wiesbaden
13 BROTHWELL, D. R., MOLLESON, T. and METREWELI, C. 1968. In BROTHWELL, D. R. (ed.) *The Skeletal Biology of Earlier Human Populations*, London
14 BUXTON, L. H. DUDLEY. 1928. In GARROD, D. R. *et al. J. Roy. Anthrop. Inst. 58*, 57–85
15 CLARK, W. E. LE GROS, 1938. *J. Roy. Anthrop. Inst. 68*, 58–60
16 —— 1955. In WEINER, J. S. *et al. Bull. Br. Mus. (Nat. Hist.) Geol. 2*, No. 6, 225–87
17 CORRAIN, C. 1963. *Mem. Mus. Civ. Storia Nat. 11*, 11–16
18 DECKER, F. H. and BOHROD, M. G. 1939. *Am. J. Roentgen. 42*, 374
19 DUBOIS, E. 1927. *Konink. Akad. Weten. Amsterdam, 29*, 1275–7
20 ELSNER, F. W. 1914. *Arch. Anthrop. 13*, 127–9
21 FRAIPONT, C. 1936. *Arch. Inst. Paléont. num. mém. 16*
22 GARN, S. M., KOSKI, K. and LEWIS, A. B. 1957. *Am. J. phys. Anthrop. 15*, 313–31
23 GORJANOVIĆ-KRAMBERGER, K. 1906. *Der Diluviale Mensch von Krapina in Kroatien*, Wiesbaden
24 —— 1907. *Anat. Anz. 31*, 97–134
25 JARCHO, S. 1966. *Human Palaeopathology*, Yale Univ. Press
26 JELÍNEK, J. 1953. *Anthropozoikum. 3*, 37–92
27 KEITH, A. 1924. *The Antiquity of Man*, London
28 KLAATSCH, H. 1909. *Zeit. Ethnol. 41*, 537
29 KOSKI, K. and GARN, S. M. 1957. *Am. J. phys. Anthrop. 15*, 469–88
30 LYNE, C. W. 1916. *Proc. Roy. Soc. Med. 9*, 33–62
31 MARTIN, HENRI. 1926. In *Recherches sur l'évolution du Moustérien dans le gisement de la Quina (Charente). 4*, 128–9. Angoulème
32 NEMESKÉRI, J., HARSÁNYI, L. and ACSÁDI, G. 1960. *Anthrop. Anz. 24*, 70–95
33 —— and HARSÁNYI, L. 1962. *Anthrop. Anz. 25*, 292–7
34 PATTE, E. 1955. *Anthropologie, Paris. 59*, 39–61
35 ——1957. *L'enfant néandertalien de Peche de l'Azé*, Paris
36 PEI, W. C. and WOO, J. K. 1957. *Acad. Sinica. mem 1*
37 ROBINSON, J. T. 1956. *Transvaal Mus. Mem. 9*, 21–2
38 ROHKLIN, D. G. 1949. In GREMIATSKI, M. A. (ed.) *Teshik-Tash: Palaeolithic Man*, Moscow
39 ROTH-LUTRA, K. H. 1965. *Anthrop. Anz. 27*, 278–88
40 SANDISON, A. T. 1968. In BROTHWELL, D. R. (ed.) *The Skeletal Biology of Earlier Human Populations*, London, 205–43
41 SCHOETENSACK, O. 1908. *Der Unterkiefer des Homo heidelbergiensis*, Leipzig
42 SERGI, S. 1948. *Riv. Antrop. 36*, 95
43 —— 1954. *Riv. Antrop. 41*, 306–44
44 —— 1960. *Acc. Naz. Lincei. 28*, 594–9
45 SINGER, R. 1958. In KOENIGSWALD, G. H. R. VON (ed.) *Hundert Jahre Neanderthaler*, Utrecht
46 TOBIAS, P. V. 1962. *Actes 4th Congr. Pan Af. Prehist. etude Quat.*
47 —— 1966. *Zool. Med. 41*, 307–20
48 TWIESSELMANN, F. 1961. *Inst. roy. Sci. nat. Belgique. 148*, 164
49 UNDERWOOD, A. S. 1913. *Br. Dent. J. 56*, 650–52
50 VALLOIS, H. V. 1958. *Arch. Inst. Paléont. hum. 29*, 262
51 VIRCHOW, H. 1920. *Die menschlichen Skeletreste aus dem Kämpfeschen Bruch im Travertin von Ehringsdorf bei Weimar*, Jena
52 VLČEK, E. 1967. *Anthrop. Anz. 30*, 166–89
53 —— 1968. *Anthropozoikum 5*, 105–24
54 WALKHOFF, O. 1902. In SELENKA, E. (ed.) *Studien uber Entwickelungsgeschichte der Tiere*, Wiesbaden

55 ——1903, in ibid.
56 —— 1904. Das Femur des Menschen und der Anthropomorphen in seiner functionellen Gestaltung, Wiesbaden
57 WEIDENREICH, F. 1937. Palaeont. sinica 101
58 —— 1951. Anthrop. Pap. Am. Mus. Nat. Hist. 43, 205–90
59 WELLS, C. 1967. In BROTHWELL, D. R. and SANDISON, A. T. (eds.) Diseases in Antiquity, Springfield, 5–19
60 WOO, JU-KANG. 1964. Vert. PalAsiatica, 8, 12–27
61 YOUNG, M. 1938. Biometrika, 29, 277–321
62 HARRISON, R. G. 1966. J. Egypt. Arch. 52, 95–119
63 GRAY, P. H. K. 1967. Med. Radiog. Photog. 43, 2
64 —— 1967. In BROTHWELL, D. R. and SANDISON, A. T. (eds.), Diseases in Antiquity, Springfield, Illinois
65 DAWSON, W. R. and GRAY, P. H. K. 1968. Catalogue of the Egyptian Antiquities in the British Museum. Vol. I. Mummies and Human Remains, London
66 WELLS, C. 1963. In Science in Archaeology, London, 401
67 BURROWS, H., CAVE, A. J. E. and PARBURY, K. 1943. Brit. J. Radiol. 16, 87
68 GETZ, B. 1959. Acta Morph. Neerl-Scand. 3, 221
69 GREGG, J. B., STEELE, J. P. and HOLZHUETER, A. 1965. Am. J. Phys. Anthrop. 23, 51

45 Microscopy and Prehistoric Bone

ANTONIO ASCENZI

THE MICROSCOPE has been profitably used in the study of prehistoric bone for more than a hundred years. Many problems had to be dealt with, but they can be arranged, as Jaekel pointed out some 70 years ago, under three main headings. Under the first heading comes the vast number of studies directed towards the microscopic investigation of the process of fossilization and the chronological data which can be obtained therefrom. The second heading covers the comparative histology of prehistoric vertebrate skeletons yielding information essential to palaeontological research. Under the third heading are grouped all those studies which concern the microscopic investigation of skeletal pathology. These three groups will be dealt with separately; however only the first group will receive extensive treatment, as the other two have been amply discussed in other chapters.

MICROSCOPIC CHARACTERISTICS AND THE STATE OF PRESERVATION

Prehistoric bone and *fossilized bone* are certainly not synonymous terms. There are famous instances where animal remains have become embedded in frozen mud and preserved almost unaltered throughout many thousands of years, not only in their bone but also in their soft parts. As regards the bones, such material is particularly valuable, because it furnishes a large amount of organic substance (ossein) which can be microscopically compared with fresh bone as has recently been done by Ezra and Cook.[34] Similarly Randall and his colleagues [78] were able to obtain a quantity of collagen sufficient for electron microscopic study from a tusk of *Elephas primigenius*, aged between 10,000 and 15,000 years, found in the frozen mud of Siberia. They were able to show that the periodic structure of the fibrils had remained unchanged. Moreover, complementary studies with wide-angle X-ray diffraction showed that even the minutest periodic structures had been preserved. These results confirmed the previous observations of Bear [19] who examined the collagen of a tusk of *Elephas primigenius* by low-angle X-ray diffraction and found that the overperiod of the fibrils averaged 640 Å.

The fortunate circumstance of finding animal and human remains preserved in frozen terrain is unhappily not the rule. Usually bones buried in the earth are subject to far-reaching changes which finally lead to fossilization.

The first students who applied microscopy to fossil bones [77] were forcibly struck by the fact that in general their specimens showed no substantial changes of structure, making it possible to compare them histologically with the bones of present-day animals. This led to the investigation by microscopic, chemical and physical methods of the process of fossilization in the hope of finding laws which could be used to make chronological deductions. The fruitfulness of this microscopic research which was already considerable in the past has recently become greatly enhanced by technical refinement and the introduction of new apparatus.

In order to appreciate the results hitherto achieved, it may be as well to recapitulate briefly some fundamental concepts on the structure of bone tissue. Bone contains cells, the osteocytes, furnished with fine branching processes. Between these cells lies a metaplasmic ground-substance, consisting of an organic component (ossein) and an inorganic component. Ossein consists of collagen fibres running in bundles which are cemented together by osteomucoid. Depending on the orientation of collagen fibres, coarse fibred bone and parallel finely fibred bone can be distinguished. The inorganic component has a micro-crystalline structure corresponding to an apatite, the nature of which is still uncertain.[26] The crystallites are orientated in the direction of the collagen fibres.[35,57,12,37] Finally the bone contains vascular cavities, known as Haversian canals, and marrow cavities.

In the process of fossilization the bone's components are modified as follows: (a) gradual disappearance of all organic structures, i.e. the osteocytes and the ossein; (b) their replacement by material carried in the water of the ground; (c) substitution of the chemical elements constituting the crystalline lattice of the apatite. These various transformations can be followed microscopically.

The disappearance of the marrow cells and of the osteocytes is the first phenomenon to occur after death and is due to autolysis following the activation and the setting free of intracellular enzymes. This is the main reason why it is impossible to establish the blood group in fossil bones, group specific elements being present only in the marrow. Though the osteocytes are no longer directly visible, their external profile can still be seen, because the surrounding calcified metaplasm faithfully follows the original outlines. Moreover, the cavity which was previously occupied by the osteocyte and its processes often stands out clearly, owing to the deposits of brown or blackish foreign material which it contains. This also applies to teeth in which this material collects in the canaliculi of the dentine, replacing the fine processes of the odontoblasts that filled them in the living tissue. This was already noted by those authors who were the first to apply the microscope to the study of fossilized bones [77] and to fossilized teeth.[2,71] In fact, Quekett was of the opinion that the essential factor in the process of fossilization was exactly the substitution of the osteocytes and the contents of the major cavities of the bone by material coming from the earth. This view was opposed by Aeby[1] who systematically investigated bones of various geological ages and found that the filling of the cavities previously occupied by the osteocytes is not a constant phenomenon synchronized with the process of fossilization. Actually it can happen that in highly fossilized bone these cavities are completely empty. Aeby, therefore, concluded that fossilization is not due simply to foreign material being deposited in cavities previously occupied by cells, but rather to a chemical metamorphosis of the inorganic components of the metaplasm or apatite. In this he saw the explanation for the excellent state of the histological structure.

That was definitely the end of Quekett's belief in the possibility of dating fossil bone by the filling of the osteocyte cavities.

What has been said about the filling of the osteocyte cavities applies equally to the filling of the larger vascular and marrow cavities. The material in these larger cavities being more abundant, it can be studied by means of the polarizing microscope along mineralogical lines as was done by Rogers [80] on a wide scale.

A further step in our understanding of the process of fossilization by means of the microscope is to the credit of Schaffer.[87] It was known that the metaplasm of fresh bone is optically anisotropic. This applies both to the apatite and the collagen fibres of the ossein. Before Schaffer this had been established by Valentin[96] and by von Ebner.[31,32] The latter author had also noted that whenever bone is artificially deprived of ossein, it retains its birefringence, but that this is susceptible to variations of intensity and sign, depending on the refractive index of the fluids in which the sections are embedded. Thus the birefringence which is monoaxially positive with reference to the orientation of the collagen fibres in fresh bone, might in the presence of fluids with a suitable refractive index become negative (Fig. 95). Taking these discoveries as his starting point, Schaffer examined vertebrate bones of various geological ages ranging from the Lias to the 'Diluvium' under the polarizing microscope. He found that only the bones from 'Diluvial' beds behaved as regards optical anisotropy in the same manner as fresh bones, while animal bones of greater age showed a behaviour of the birefringence which with increasing age of the specimen became more and more similar to that of tissue artificially deprived of ossein. The author concluded that in the course of fossilization bone slowly but progressively loses its collagen fibres.

Schaffer[88] subsequently extended his investigations to fossil teeth and obtained exactly analogous results.

The physical bases of von Ebner's experimental findings which led to Schaffer's discoveries were established much later by Wiener[98] who worked out the theory of optical anisotropy of composite bodies. The merit of having recognized how this theory could also be applied to bone belongs to Schmidt.[90] Today quantitative studies on the optical anisotropy of bone tissue based on Wiener's theory are a fruitful field of research on the question of solving some of the basic problems of ultrastructure.[8,10,13]

The correctness of Schaffer's conclusions was recently confirmed by Baud and Morgenthaler[16], Ascenzi[11] and Oakley.[70] By using the optical as well as the electron microscope, these authors demonstrated the persistence of ossein in skeletal fragments which were thousands and even tens of thousands of years old. Baud and Morgenthaler's material was obtained from 7 human skeletons ranging in age from a minimum of 450 years (the beginning of the sixteenth century) to a maximum of 10,000–12,000 years (Magdalenian epoch). After decalcification, the yield of ossein from these fragments decreased in proportion to the duration of their preservation. Whether they were examined by optical, polarizing or electron microscope, the results were in full agreement. The normally birefringent ossein was markedly stainable with fuchsin by van Gieson's method, owing to its high content of collagen. The electron microscope showed the fibrils to be well preserved and their overperiod measured on the average 640 Å.

Even more significant were the studies of Ascenzi,[11] because they were conducted on bone of an even earlier geological age. He used a small fragment of the Neanderthal mandible Circeo IIa and some fragments of the fauna accompanying the Neanderthal mandible Circeo IIIb. Considering that it was possible to establish the exact age of the

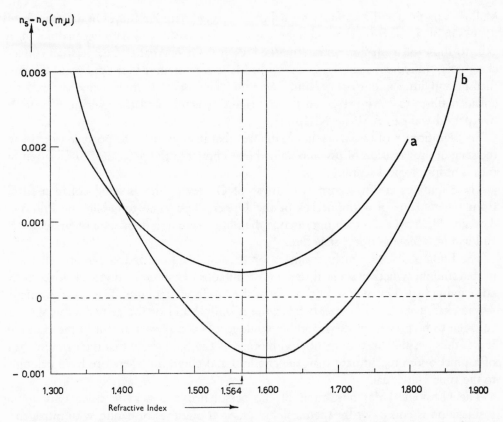

Fig. 95 Curves of form birefringence pertaining to highly calcified normal bone (a) and to bone deprived of ossein (b), according to Ascenzi and Bonucci. For embedding fluids with range of refractive index between 1·480 and 1·720, the birefringence of the bone deprived of ossein is negative.

deposits in which these bones were found, the importance of these studies is evident. The mandible Circeo IIa was discovered in 1939 by A. C. Blanc together with the Neanderthal cranium Circeo I in the Grotta Guattari, Monte Circeo. The mandible Circeo IIIb was found in 1950 by Ascenzi and Lacchei[92] in the ossiferous wall outside the entrance of the above-mentioned cave. According to Blanc these remains belong to the Epiwürm II. From the fragment of the Circeo IIa mandible as also from those of other bones a relatively large amount of organic material was obtained. As the mandibular fragment was small, it was only examined under the optical microscope, while the rest of the material was also investigated by the electron microscope.

The ossein of the Circeo IIa mandible appeared surprisingly well preserved. Its structure was that of a lamellar bone which in some areas showed some osteonic units (Plate XXIIIa). Between the lamellae the small elongated lacunes formerly occupied by the osteocytes were clearly visible. The tissue showed a feeble affinity for haematoxylin, a transitory metachromasia with toluidin-blue, a fair staining with methyl-blue by

* Cf. *Man 51*, January 1951, Art. 7.

Mallory's method and no affinity for Schiff's reagent (Plate XXIIIc). On the other hand the ossein obtained from the fragments of animal bones showed staining qualities more akin to those of fresh bone, i.e. a marked affinity for haematoxylin, persistent meta-chromasia, intensive staining both with Mallory's methyl-blue and van Gieson's fuchsin and little affinity for Schiff's reagent. The electron microscope showed the collagen fibres to have preserved their periodic structure and the average size of the overperiod was 640 Å (Plate XXIIIb).

The significance of this work lies in the fact that it shows it to be possible to estimate the state of preservation of ossein obtained from bones in the process of fossilization by means of histological staining.

These findings are in accord with those of Oakley[70] who isolated collagen fibrils from the remains of a rhinoceros of the Upper Pleistocene found in the Piltdown deposits. Under the electron microscope the fibres were in a poor state of preservation and had no visible periodic structure.

The finding of collagen in fossilized or presumably fossilized bones proved useful in determining whether skeletal remains of dubious origin do or do not belong to the same individual. This was so in the case of the Piltdown cranium. The electron micro-scopic examination of fragments from the mandible and of the cranial vault showed collagen to be present in the mandible while it was completely absent in the cranium. It was thus possible, in conjunction with other methods, to show that the mandible was of a much more recent date than the cranium and could not therefore have belonged to the same individual.[69]

The histological demonstration of the persistence of ossein in bone undergoing fossilization is borne out by chemical and physical methods of dating with nitrogen [50] and with C^{14}.[93] In fact both elements used in these techniques are derived from the collagen.

When in advanced fossilization the ossein has disappeared, the fine canaliculi which are left when the bundles of collagen fibres have gone, are filled with extraneous material which, usually being dark in colour, gives to the tissue a finely striated appearance.[87,21]

Various methods have been employed in the microscopic study of the transformations undergone by the bone's apatite in the course of fossilization. In the past, measurement of the refractive index by means of Becke's line was used. Actually the refractive index of fossil bone cannot be regarded as an exponent of only the chemical changes in the apatite's crystalline lattice, but rather as an exponent of the whole complex process of substitution of the organic structures by penetrating mineral material. Normally the refractive index of ossein alone is 1·530,[14] while that of apatite alone is 1·600.[7,8,10,14] Obviously the whole bone has an intermediate refractive index which in adult animals in whom the depositing of calcium salts has been completed is 1·564.[14] As regards fossilized bone, the systematic measurements conducted by Rogers[80] on a large series of animals of various geological ages, ranging from the Ordovician to the Pleistocene, established two important facts: first, that there is no constant relationship between geological age and the refractive index; second, that the refractive index often greatly exceeds that of the apatite alone, suggesting that in the bone as a whole and in the

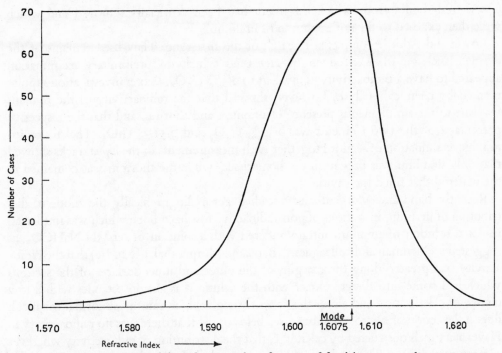

Fig. 96 Frequency diagram of the refractive index of a series of fossil bones, according to Rogers. The mode of the measured refractive indices (n=1·6075) is higher than the refractive index of fresh bone deprived of ossein (n=1·6)

apatite in particular dip changes have taken place through the influx of extraneous material (Fig. 96).

Autoradiography is a highly selective microscopic technique for the study of the changes taking place in the apatite's lattice during fossilization.[60,22] However, this can only be used when radioactive elements are present. Strutt[95] was the first to report the presence of radioactive elements of the uranium series in fossilized bones, but it was only in the last ten years that specific research was undertaken.[52,54,28,24,3] It could be shown that though the radioactivity varied considerably from one specimen to another, it was always greater than that of the surrounding earth. Smith and Bradley[94] reported that in the dinosaur bones which they examined the uranium content varied from 0·04 to 0·135%, while the adjoining rock contained only 0·001 to 0·005%. Oakley[69,70] was able to establish that as a general rule the uranium concentration in cenozoic human and animal bones increases proportionately with the passage of time. Moreover, a strict correlation between uranium and fluorine was noted.[3]

These findings led to the conclusion that the uranium is localized in the apatite where, as elsewhere in phosphates, it finds suitable chemical and structural conditions. The demonstration of the elective depositing and the mechanism by which it takes place was largely the result of studying autoradiograms microscopically. These investigations were made (a) on fossilized bones containing uranium, (b) on fossilized bone which did not contain uranium, but was exposed to the action of a dilute solution of uranium,

(c) on fresh bones from which the ossein had been artificially removed and which were then exposed to the same solution of uranium.

Bowie and Atkin[23] conducted research of the first type. They used remains of the dermato-skeleton of a specimen of *Homostius* which on preliminary examination appeared to have a radioactivity equivalent to $0 \cdot 5\%$ U_3O_8. Closer investigation supplemented by chemical analysis, however, showed that the radioactivity of the remains was due to the simultaneous presence of uranium and thorium and that the respective percentage of the two elements was $0 \cdot 32\%$ U_3O_8 and $0 \cdot 51\%$ ThO_2. The autoradiographic examination of sections together with measurements of the *alpha* tracks showed that only uranium was present in the bone tissue, while the thorium was contained in the material that filled the cavities.

Recently Baud and Morgenthaler[18] studied autoradiographically the mode of distribution of uranium in sections of non-radioactive fossilized bone which was immersed in a 1% solution of uranium nitrate buffered with a solution of $0 \cdot 025N$ $NaHCO_3$, as suggested by Neuman and colleagues.[65] Baud and Morgenthaler found (a) that the radioactivity was greater along the margins of the outer and inner surfaces of the sections which had come into direct contact with the solution, as also in osteones with a low degree of calcification and along the zones through which ran the abnormal canaliculi due to the action of micro-organisms (see below); (b) that there was no radioactivity in Haversian canals obstructed by calcite; (c) that the distribution of radioactivity wherever present was diffuse. The authors, therefore, concluded that the amount of uranium present in a fossil bone depends, apart from extrinsic, also on intrinsic factors. These are the porosity and the permeability of the tissue which in turn depend on its submicroscopic structure as also on the physical and chemical composition of the inorganic component. It is the inorganic component which conditions the processes of adsorption and exchange. This is generally in accordance with the results obtained by Amprino[4] who conducted similar investigations, using fresh, instead of fossil bone, which he artificially deprived of ossein.

The way in which uranium attaches itself to phosphates in general and bone apatite in particular is still controversial. If in the case of the bone it can be excluded that this constitutes a separate phase[18] in the form of UO_2 or UF_4 or $Ca (UO_2)_2(PO_4)_2.8H_2O$ (autunite), there remain the following possibilities to be considered: either the uranium is chemically adsorbed on the surfaces or internal discontinuities of the crystalline lattice in the form of U^{+4} ions or as isolated $(UO_2)^{+2}$ radicals;[51] or else the uranium (U^{+4}) substitutes the calcium present in the apatite lattice;[58,28,38] or the $(UO_2)^{+2}$ radical substitutes two Ca^{+2} ions.[66,67]

The fact that fluorine and uranium behave analogously in fossil bone makes it possible to use measurements of the radioactivity of the latter element for relative chronological calculations and this has led to the establishment of important data.[70]

Only few electron microscopic studies of the apatite of fossilized bone have been made and it would be worth while to take them up again with more suitable methods. Ascenzi[9] found that fragments of *Elephas antiquus* from Saccopastore (Rome) contained no collagen and showed a mineral structure which was not unlike that of fresh bone artificially deprived of ossein. In the following year (1950) Barbour[15] reported similar findings. Moreover she pointed out variations in the size of the mesh of the mineral structure due to the process of fossilization. She did not express an opinion on the significance of this finding, but it is probable [9,16] that this is caused either by an increase in crystalline material or by a reduction of that which was originally present. The latter alternative, that is, a rarefaction of the mineral framework, might find a confirmation in the work of Baud and Morgenthaler,[18] who in fossil bone found microradiographically visible zones of far-reaching demineralization.

It remains to be mentioned that as far back as 1864 Wedl described, in both recently deposited and fossil bones, canaliculi which had no similarity with those present in normal tissue (Plate XXIIId) and which contained fine brownish filaments. He was of the opinion that these findings were caused by a fungus. They were also observed by Roux[86] in fossil bones and fully confirmed by Schaffer,[87, 89] who designated them 'Bohrkanäle', that is, drilled canals. They have been recently studied by Morgenthaler and Baud.[64] The appearance of this type of canal leads to the progressive elimination of any structure.

In those cases in which greater or lesser parts of the bone tissue become destroyed they are replaced by material which is brought in from the ground.[21]

From what has been said it follows that the microscopic changes which take place in bone undergoing fossilization not only depend on the passage of time, but above all on the environmental conditions of the deposits in which they are found. Therefore, in the present state of our knowledge, they do not furnish criteria for absolute dating.

THE HISTOLOGICAL STRUCTURE OF THE SKELETON IN THE PREHISTORIC VERTEBRATES

The fact that fossil bone retains its microscopic structure makes comparative histological research possible. This has been done systematically in fishes and reptiles.

It was Owen,[71] Williamson[99] and Pander[73-76] who undertook the first histological studies of the skeletons of fishes. After the death of Pander, these studies lay dormant for over 40 years, except for a few isolated contributions[27] and Rohon's publications.[81-85] However the latter author's microscopic interpretations are often inexact (cf. Gross[46]). In 1907 Gebhardt's work was published, as also that of Goodrich. After the first World War there arose a renewed interest in the palaeontology of palaeozoic fishes and this led to a revival of histological studies in the field by Stensiö, Obrutschew, Heintz, Hoppe, Bryant, Stetson, Brotzen (cf. Gross[46,47]). But the most valuable body of research, both in scope and thoroughness, is that published by Gross between the years 1930 and 1959. Leaving aside the many problems which concern the structure of the exoskeleton, it can be briefly said of the histology of the endoskeleton that the bone is structurally primitive. It is primary or coarse fibred bone of variable feature containing primary osteones. These last are particularly abundant in the Arthrodires and the Crossopterygians. Secondary osteones on the other hand are rare. However, it is probable that if specimens of the same species, but of different size, were examined, they would show that the differentiation of bone in fossil fishes, as judged by the number of secondary osteones, is largely a function of the bodily mass and thus a mechanical and mineral metabolic exigency. That this does in fact apply to the vertebrae of *Thynnus thynnus* L. has recently been shown by Amprino and Godina.[6]

Valuable studies on the skeletons of fossil reptiles have been made by Kiprijanoff,[56] Seitz[91] and Gross.[45] Minor contributions limited to specific problems are those of Broili[25] and Moodie[63] on the ossified vertebral tendons of *Trachodon* and those of Nopcsa[68] concerning the development of the ribs also of *Trachodon*.

These various studies go to confirm that reptilian skeletal development follows the same laws in the geologically oldest and in surviving forms. Nevertheless the gigantic dimensions reached by the Dinosaurs of the Cretaceous induced a structural complexity similar to that of the largest surviving mammals. On that particularly touches the structure of the diaphyses of the limbs which has been the object of major attention; this does not differ, even in its most simple expression, from that of the amphibians. Thus the diaphysial shaft consists of primary periosteal bone of homogeneous structure with a trace of stratification which can be more or less pronounced. It is traversed by vascular canals which have primary osteones. More rarely one comes across that particular type of periosteal bone which Gross calls 'laminar Periostknochen' owing to its peculiar structure. In it laminae are orientated concentrically with reference to the axis of the bone and are separated from each other by an ample vascular network which is also arranged concentrically. This has been seen in *Theromorpha* (*Kannemeyeria*), *Thecodontia* (*Erythrosuchus*), *Dinosauria* (*Plateosaurus*). Secondary osteones, though usually rare, reach their maximum development in *Brachiosaurus*, *Diplodocus*, *Bronthosaurus* and *Iguanodon*.

The ossified intervertebral tendons of *Trachodon* also have a complex structure and are rich in longitudinally orientated secondary osteones.[25] It may be assumed that this is due to their particular mechanical function of making the vertebral column rigid. Contrary to Dollo,[30] Broili expressed the opinion that the abundance of Haversian canals and hence of blood vessels could be the result of the direct ossification of muscles, a view which hardly seems acceptable.

The histological structure of skeletons of other classes of fossil vertebrates has received less attention (Moodie[62]). From what is known it may be concluded that generally speaking the bone structure of extinct forms is no different from that of surviving ones (cf. also Ezra and Cook[34]). This also applies to fossil man in whom microradiography has shown that the statistical distribution of the osteones in relation to the degree of calcification is identical with that of modern man.[17]

A problem of great palaeontological as well as of forensic interest is the possibility of determining microscopically the species to which a bone fragment belongs when this cannot be ascertained macroscopically. Demeter and Mátyás[29] claimed to be able to distinguish about 40 mammalian species by the histological characteristics of their bones. This was doubted by Eggeling[33] and recently by Amprino and Godina.[5] The latter showed that within the Order, the Genus and the Species the type of bone structure varies, depending upon which bone is examined, the size of the species, the age of the individual and differences in the speed of growth, as also in relation to other less easily recognizable factors. Undoubtedly the problem requires further study.

THE HISTOLOGICAL PATHOLOGY OF PREHISTORIC BONE

Bone is the only tissue which can bear evidence of the diseases which have afflicted the vertebrates in the most distant past. Histological contributions on the pathology of the skeleton are not numerous and are scattered in the vast literature pertaining to medicine, palaeontology and anthropology. Particularly valuable, therefore, was the work of Moodie who, as long ago as 1923, produced the first collection and treatment not only of the macroscopic, but also of the microscopic lesions found in prehistoric vertebrates. A similar collection of all known data was made by Pales[72] and, recently, by Ákos Palla.[103]

The earliest indications of skeletal pathology reach back to reptiles of the Permian and it may be said that in this as well as in subsequent periods traumatic lesions, i.e. fractures, dominated the scene. In these fractures the histological appearance of the callus showed no features that were essentially different from those of ordinary present-day pathology. Moodie's observation that in fossil reptiles the structural complexity of the callus is greater than that of the normal bone, it having a particularly large number of secondary osteones, certainly needs checking. In calluses which complicating osteomyelitis had rendered septic, histological examination showed only indirect signs of inflammation, such as more or less conspicuous structural irregularities consisting of communicating cavities with fistular pathways. But those formations which Renault[79] interpreted as fossilized microbes cannot be regarded as direct evidence of a causal agent, because they are often seen in perfectly healthy bone and are probably due to post-mortem putrefaction. The same can be said for inflammations not resulting from fractures, for instance maxillary alveolitis and osteomyelitis of dental origin.

Chronic arthritis which was already present among the large Secondary dinosaurs and became increasingly common in later epochs, as in *Machairodus* and above all in *Ursus spelaeus*, showed nothing of histological significance as compared with the findings of modern pathology.

The microscope has furnished certain indications for the recognition of some tumours of the bone which produce rather characteristic features, as do the angiomas.

In a comprehensive study of pachyostosis Kaiser[55] has recently confirmed that, subject to the structural differences among species, skeletal pathology is remarkably uniform.

Finally, Michaëlis[59] pointed out in fossilized human bones microscopic signs which would prove the pre-Columbian origin of syphilis.

Before concluding this brief section, it might be as well to mention that, taken singly, the various contributions on the pathological histology of fossil bones often reveal, especially in the older papers, a lack of terminological precision which creates some uncertainty in the value of their findings. It is to be hoped that in future research there will be a stricter adherence to generally accepted pathological concepts.

PROSPECTS FOR FURTHER STUDY

What has been said regarding the contribution to the study of prehistoric bone which microscopy has made, should give some idea of the length of the road that has been travelled, but it should also provide an orientation for future research.

As for our knowledge of the way in which the process of fossilization takes place, there can be no doubt that the greatest use will be made of systematic studies on the progressive disappearance of the ossein and the ultrastructural modifications which take place in the apatite of the bone. As far as the ossein is concerned, this will have to be further investigated by histochemical methods, by the use of the electron microscope and by employing the polarizing microscope for quantitative estimations. The electron and polarizing microscope will also be of the greatest use in the analysis of ultrastructural modifications of the apatite. Wherever possible it will be necessary to associate these studies with (a) the chemical analysis of ossein; (b) chemical and X-ray spectrographic analysis of the apatite; (c) absolute chronological measurements by the C^{14} technique, using specimens of ossein; (d) studies on the manner in which liquids from the ground circulate in skeletal parts; (e) geological and geochemical investigations to clarify the conditions in the environment in which fossilization takes place. In this way it would become possible to arrive at precise conclusions concerning the microscopic aspects of the process of fossilization in bone making reference to the nature of the deposits and to absolute time.[100, 101, 102]

Autoradiographic studies, on the way in which various radioactive elements are exchanged for elements making up the bone's apatite, would increase our knowledge of the transformations which the inorganic fraction of bone tissue undergoes.

As regards palaeontology, histological studies on the skeletal structure of those groups of vertebrates which have hitherto received little attention would be welcome. It might also be worth while to study systematically the characteristics of bone collagen of extinct species wherever this has been preserved. It might also be profitable to go further into the question of histologically ascertaining the species to which a bone belongs.

It seems superfluous to stress the already considerable interest in the histological investigation of palaeopathological problems.

REFERENCES

 1 AEBY, CHR. 1878. Arch. f. mikrosk. Anat. 15, 371–82
 2 AGASSIZ, L. 1833–43. Recherches sur les poissons fossiles, Neuchâtel
 3 ALTSCHULER, Z. S., CLARKE, R. S. and YOUNG, E. J. 1958. Geological Survey, Professional Paper 314-D, pp. 45–90
 4 AMPRINO, R. 1953. Experientia 9, 291–3
 5 —— and GODINA, G. 1947. Commentationes Acad. Pontificia Scientiarum 11, 329–464
 6 —— 1956. Pubbl. Staz. Zool. Napoli 28, 62–71
 7 ASCENZI, A. 1948. Rend. Accad. Naz. Lincei (Cl. Sc. Fis. Mat. e Nat.) (VIII) 4, 777–83
 8 —— 1949a. Nature 163, 604
 9 —— 1949b. Riv. di Antrop. 37, 143–8
10 —— 1950. Science 112, 84–86
11 —— 1955. Am. J. Phys. Anth. 13, 557–66
12 —— and BENEDETTI, E. L. 1959. Acta anat. 37, 370–85
13 —— and BONUCCI, E. 1961. Ibid. 44, 236–62
14 —— and FABRY, C. 1959. J. Biophys. and Biochem. Cytol. 6, 139–42
15 BARBOUR, E. P. 1950. Am. J. Phys. Anth. 8, 315–30
16 BAUD, C.-A. and MORGENTHALER, P. W. 1952. Arch. Suisses d'Anth. Gén. 17, 52–65

17 —— 1956. *Ibid. 21,* 79–86
18 —— 1959. *Ibid. 24,* 45–52
19 BEAR R. S. 1944. *J. Am. Chem. Soc. 66,* 1297–305
20 BLANC, A. C. 1939. *Rend. Accad. Naz. Lincei* (Cl. Sc. Fis. Mat. e Nat.) (VI) *29,* 205–10
21 BLEICHER. 1893. *Bibliographie anatomique 1,* 93–96, 123–8
22 BOWIE, S. H. U. 1951. *Bull. Geol. Survey G.B. 3,* 58–71
23 —— and ATKIN, D. 1956. *Nature 177,* 487–8
24 —— and DAVIDSON, C. F. 1955. *Brit. Mus. Nat. History Bull. Geology 2,* 276–82
25 BROILI, F. 1922. *Anat. Anz. 55,* 464–75
26 CARLSTRÖM, D. and ENGSTRÖM, A. 1956. Ultrastructure and distribution of mineral salts in bone tissue, in BOURNE, G. H., *The Biochemistry and Physiology of Bone,* New York
27 CLAYPOLE, E. W. 1894. *Proc. Amer. Micros. Soc. 15,* 189–91
28 DAVIDSON, C. F. and ATKIN, D. 1953. *C. R. XIX Congr. géol. internat. Alger* Sec. 11, 13–31
29 DEMETER, G. and MÁTYÁS, J. 1928. *Z. Anat. u. Entwg. 87,* 45–99
30 DOLLO, L. 1887. *Arch. de Biol. 7,* 249–64
31 EBNER, V. VON. 1874. *Sitzgsber. Akad. Wiss. Wien., Math-.naturwiss. Kl.* (III) *70,* 105–43
32 —— 1875. *Ibid. 72,* 49–138
33 EGGELING, H. VON. 1938. Allgemeines über den Aufbau knoecherner Skeletteil, in BOLK, L. VON, GÖPPERT, E., KALLIUS, E. and LUBOSCH, W. *Handb. d. vergl. Anat. d. Wirbelt. 5,* 275–304
34 EZRA, H. C. and COOK, S. F. 1959. *Science 129,* 465–6
35 FERNANDEZ-MORÁN, H. and ENGSTRÖM, A. 1957. *Biochim. et biophys. acta 23,* 260–4
36 GEBHARDT, F. A. M. W. 1907. *Verhandl. anat. Ges., 21 Vers. Würzburg,* 72–90
37 GLIMCHER, M. J. 1959. *Revs. modern Phys. 31,* 359–93
38 GOLDSCHMIDT, V. M. 1954. *Geochemistry,* Oxford
39 GOODRICH, E. S. 1907. *Proc. Zool. Soc. London,* 751–74
40 GROSS, W. 1930. *Geol. Paläont. abh. 18,* 121–56
41 —— 1931. *Paläontographica 75,* 1–62
42 —— 1933a. *Abh. Preuss. Geol. Landesanst.* H. 145, 41–77
43 —— 1933b. *Paläontographica 79* (A) 1–74
44 —— 1933c. *Abh. Preuss. Geol. Landesanst.* H. 154, 4–83
45 —— 1934. *Z. Anat. u. Entwg. 103,* 731–64
46 —— 1936. *Paläontographica 83* (A) 1–60
47 —— 1947. *Ibid. 96* (A) 91–158
48 —— 1957. *Ibid. 109* (A) 1–40
49 —— 1959. *Ibid. 113* (A) 1–35
50 HEIZER, R. F. and COOK, S. F. 1952. *Am. J. Phys. Anth. 10,* 289–303
51 HENDRICKS, S. B. and HILL, W. L. 1950. *Proc. Nat. Acad. Sci. Washington 36,* 731–7
52 HILL, W. S. 1950. *Ciencia e Investigación 6,* 43–44
53 JAEKEL, O. 1891. *Neues Jahrbuch f. Mineral., Geol. u. Paläon.,* I, 178–98
54 JAFFE, E. B. and SHERWOOD, A. M. 1951. *U.S. Geol. Survey, Trace Elements Memorandum,* Rep. no. 149, 1–19
55 KAISER, H. E. 1960. *Paläontographica 114* (A) 113–96
56 KIPRIJANOFF, V. 1881–3. *Mem. Acad. Sci. St. Petersburg 28,* 1–103; *30,* 1–55; *31,* 1–57
57 KNESE, K.-H. and KNOOP, A.-M. 1958. *Z. Zellforsch. 48,* 455–78
58 McKELVEY, V. E. and NELSON, J. M. 1950. *Econ. Geology 45,* 35–53
59 MICHAËLIS, L. 1930. *Veröffentl. Kriegs- und Konstitutionspathol. 6,* 1–92
60 MILLER, B. L. and HOECKER, F. E. 1950. *Nucleonics 8,* 44–52
61 MOODIE, R. L. 1923. *Paleopathology,* Urbana, Illinois
62 —— 1926. *Biologia generalis 2,* 63–95
63 —— 1928. *Am. Museum Novitates,* No. 311, New York
64 MORGENTHALER, P. W. and BAUD, A.-C. 1956–7. *Bull. Soc. Suisse Anthrop. et Ethnol. 33,* 9–10
65 NEUMAN, W. F., NEUMAN, M. W., MAIN, E. R. and MULRYAN, B. J. 1949a. *J. Biol. Chem. 179,* 325–33
66 —— 1949b. *Ibid. 179,* 335–40
67 —— 1949c. *Ibid. 179,* 341–8
68 NOPCSA, F. B. 1933. *Proc. Zool. Soc. London,* 221–6

69 OAKLEY, K. P. 1955a. Analytical methods of dating bones, *Advancement of Science 11*, 3–8
70 —— 1955b. *British Mus. Nat. History Bull. Geology 2*, 254–65
71 OWEN, R. 1840–5. *Odontography*, London
72 PALES, L. 1930. *Paléopathologie et pathologie comparative*, Paris
73 PANDER, CH. H. 1856. Monographie der fossilen Fische des silurischen Systems der russisch-baltischen Gouvernements, *Buchdruck. d. keis. Akad. d. Wiss.*, St. Petersburg
74 —— 1857. Ueber die Placodermen des devonischen Systems, *ibid.*
75 —— 1858. Ueber die Ctenodipterinen des devonischen Systems, *ibid.*
76 —— 1860. Ueber die Saurodipterinen, Dendrodonten, etc des devonischen Systems, *ibid.*
77 QUEKETT, J. 1849. *Trans. Micros. Soc., London 2*, 40–42
78 RANDALL, J. T., FRASER, R. D. B., JACKSON, S., MARTIN, A. V. W. and NORTH, A. C. T. 1952. *Nature 169*, 1029–33
79 RENAULT, B. 1896. *Ann. des Sci. nat. bot.* (VIII) 2, 275–349
80 ROGERS, A. F. 1924. *Bull. Geol. Soc. Am. 35*, 535–56
81 ROHON, J. V. 1889. *Mém. Acad. Imp. Sci. St. Petersburg* (VII) *36*, no. 14
82 —— 1892. *Ibid.* (VII) *38*, no. 13,
83 —— 1893. *Ibid.* (VII) *41*, no. 5,
84 —— 1899. *Sitzgsber. Böhm. Ges. Wiss., Math.-naturwiss. Kl.*, no. 8, 1–77
85 —— 1901. *Ibid.*, no. 16, 1–31
86 ROUX, W. 1887. *Ztschr. f. wissen. Zool. 45*, 227–54
87 SCHAFFER, J. 1889. *Sitzgsber. Akad. Wiss. Wien., Math.-naturwiss. Kl.* (III) *98*, 319–82
88 —— 1890. *Ibid.* (III) *99*, 146–52
89 —— 1894. *Anat. Anz. 10*, 459
90 SCHMIDT, W. J. 1933. *Ber. Oberhess. Ges. Natur- u. Heilk., Naturw. Abt., Giessen 15*, 219–47
91 SEITZ, A. L. L. 1907. *Nova Acta Abh. keiserl. Leop.-Carol. deutsch. Akad. Naturf. 87*, 231–370
92 SERGI, S. and ASCENZI, A. 1955. *Riv. di Antrop. 42*, 337–403
93 SINEX, F. M. and FARIS, B. 1959. *Science 129*, 969
94 SMITH, K. G. and BRADLEY, D. A. 1951. *Papers Michigan Acad. Science, Arts and Letters 37*, 257–63
95 STRUTT, R. J. 1908. *Proc. Roy. Soc. London* (A) *81*, 272–7
96 VALENTIN, G. 1861. *Die Untersuchung der Pflanzen- und Tiergewebe in polarisiertem Lichte*, ENGELMANN, W., Leipzig
97 WEDL, C. 1864. *Sitzgsber. Akad. Wiss. Wien. Math.-naturwiss. Kl.* (I) *50*, 171–93
98 WIENER, O. 1912. *Abh. sächs. Ges. Wiss., math. phys. Kl. 32*, 509–604
99 WILLIAMSON, W. 1849. *Phil. Trans. Roy. Soc. London 140*, 435–75
100 WYCKOFF, R. W. G., McCAUGHEY, W. F. and DOBERENZ, A. R. 1964. *Biochem. Biophys. Acta 93*, 374–7
101 SHACKLEFORD, J. M. and WYCKOFF, R. W. G. 1964. *J. Ultrasrtucture Res. 11*, 173–80
102 WYCKOFF, R. W. G. and DOBERENZ, R. 1965. *Proc. Nat. Acad. Sci. N.Y. 53*, 230–3
103 PALLA, A. 1962. *Paläopathologie*, Jena

46 Remains Derived from Skin

M. L. RYDER

THIS CHAPTER discusses the microscopic examination of skin, leather and parchment, and the light it throws on the history of domestic animals. Among animal remains on archaeological sites, skin and hair are preserved less often than bone. They, and textiles derived from them (see chapter by Appleyard and Wildman), decay rapidly in the damp climate of northern Europe, and are destroyed by alkaline soil, but are well preserved in acid waterlogged conditions such as peat bogs. Skin is preserved well in the dry climate of the Near East, good examples being ancient Egyptian leather, and the parchment from the Dead Sea Scrolls. Another classic example of preservation is that of skin in the frozen wastes of central Asia. The frozen burial mounds of the local Early Iron Age (about the fifth to the first centuries BC) that have been excavated in the Altai Mountains have yielded skins of sheep and goats, and the hair of yaks, in addition to leather, carpets, and fur, wool and silk clothing.[1]

The animal from which skin remains have come has mainly been identified from any hairs remaining above the surface. Leather has been identified from the characteristic pattern on the skin surface, known as the grain pattern, which varies with species.[2] According to Plenderleith[3] it is almost impossible from the appearance of a parchment to identify the animal from which it has been derived. The method described here, which depends on the microscopic examination of hair remaining in the skin, provides a useful new approach to the study of ancient specimens.

This method was derived from one of the lines I followed in wool research at the Wool Industries Research Association, Leeds, which is to make a microscopic study of the size, numbers and grouping of wool fibres in specimens of skin from different breeds of sheep. In this way differences in the skin that cause differences in the fleece can be determined. In order to examine tissues under the microscope, they have to be cut into sections (thin slices) with a microtome (an instrument rather like a bacon slicer). In order to study the number and grouping of wool fibres in the skin, the sections are cut horizontally, i.e. parallel to the skin surface. The sections are then mounted on glass slides and stained to make the different parts visible before being examined under the microscope.

The skin is first treated with a fixative which precipitates the proteins of the living cells. Then, as the fixative is usually dissolved in water, and as the tissue is supported during the cutting by being embedded in wax, it has to be dehydrated before it can be put into the wax. This is done by passing the tissue gradually through alcoholic solutions of increasing strength, until absolute alcohol is reached. Then the tissue is passed through a solvent such as xylol which will mix with both alcohol and wax.

This histological method has been detailed so that the reader will appreciate the preparation that is necessary before a fresh specimen can be examined. The essential first stage, in order to obtain good microscopic detail, is considered to be the fixation, and this must be carried out soon after death. I was therefore surprised to find that dried skin gave almost as good preparations of the microscopic structure of the follicles in which hairs and wool fibres grow, as fresh skin that had been fixed. This came about when my interests widened to include wild sheep and the history of domestic sheep,[4],[5] and it happened that the only source of skin from some of the wild sheep was from dried skins in museum collections. The good preparations obtained from dried skin in turn suggested that, if archaeological material was available, the method might be used to study the evolution of domestic animals towards the different breeds in existence today. Ancient specimens of skin, that might show what the coats of primitive domestic animals were like, were therefore sought.

Skin from the sheep that the ancient Egyptians mummified would have been ideal for this, but according to the British Museum no mummified sheep are available in Britain. In addition, with sheep, the body was apparently not mummified whole; the different bones of the body are found jumbled together in a basket of papyrus, to one corner of which is attached the head, so that the whole resembles the shape of a sheep.[6] It would seem unlikely therefore that much, if any, skin would be preserved with this method. Dr A. T. Sandison kindly sent me a leg from an Egyptian mummified cat and good preparations were obtained from the brittle skin on this (see below). This mummy was from Bubastes and is of the Ptolemaic period (323–30 BC).

A few specimens of ancient leather have been examined and most of these had evidence of having been made from cattle skin; they either contained cow hairs, or follicle remains characteristic of cattle. The idea of using parchment came to me when I was studying local history in Yorkshire by examining old parchment documents, and discovered that many had a well-defined hair pattern which I later found was well known to archivists. It was fortunate that the first specimens that came available were fragments of the Dead Sea Scrolls,[4] which were provided by Professor D. Burton and Dr R. Reed of Leeds University. The results obtained from these stimulated the provision of other material for study. Only a short strip of parchment 0·5 cm wide is required and this can often be taken from the junction of a membrane without spoiling the appearance of a document. A sample can sometimes be taken from the end of a sealing tag, and bookbindings can be sampled from the part folded inside the cover.

THE STRUCTURE OF SKIN

The skin of mammals consists of two main layers: a thin, outer, epidermis, and a thicker, inner layer known as the dermis or corium (Fig. 97). This is composed mainly of fibres of the protein collagen, which is quite distinct from the protein keratin which is the substance of hairs, nails and horns. The hairs grow from pits in the skin called follicles, and these, and their associated glands, are derived as downgrowths from the epidermis. The layer of the dermis in which the follicles are enclosed is known as the papillary layer. This is the layer that gives leather its characteristic grain. Beneath the papillary layer the collagen fibres of the dermis are coarser, forming a more open network, and this layer is known as the reticular layer. At the base of the dermis, many animals, e.g. cattle,

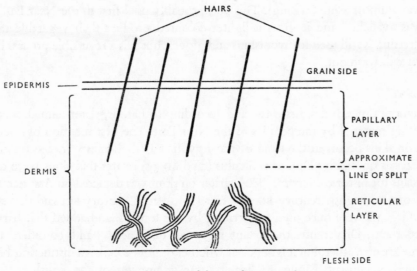

Fig. 97 Vertical section of skin to show main layers.

have a fatty layer. During the preparation of leather and parchment the hairs and the epidermis are removed, and today, in order to obtain a thinner product, the skin is often split in a region roughly corresponding to the boundary between the papillary and reticular layers.

METHODS OF PRESERVING AND TANNING SKIN

Skin may be left untreated, as with rawhide and parchment, or it may be tanned to produce leather. Tanning is a chemical process that preserves the skin, tending to make it impervious to water, but retaining the natural pliability. The main tanning methods involve (a) oils, (b) vegetable extracts, and (c) minerals.[2] Oil tannage is probably the oldest method and may go back to Palaeolithic times; the Eskimos have probably used fish oil since prehistoric times. Milk, butter and egg yolk were used by Asiatic peoples, and they, and the Indians of North America, used brains to emulsify the oil. Oil-tanned skin can be readily washed, and was used for cheap clothing in the past, which was sometimes made from old parchments.[7] Oil is still used in the preparation of chamois leather, which is made from the flesh side of a split sheepskin. The tanning action of smoke, which depends on substances such as aldehydes, was used by primitive peoples, and persisted until recently in Siberia and China.

Further west, vegetable tanning was probably used by Neolithic times. In ancient Egypt, acacia pods provided the tanning material, whereas in northern Europe tanning was done with an infusion of oak bark. The process became more elaborate, and involved dehairing and defatting the skin. Alkali is necessary to remove the hair, and lime has probably been used for at least 2,000 years, but the first materials were probably urine, and later, ashes. The chemical effect of combination with the skin proteins in vegetable tanning is different from that of oil, but is similar to that of the chromium salts used in the modern mineral tanning process. The only mineral process of ancient times was alum dressing (tawing). This was probably used first in the Near East where alum was available, and it gives a lighter-coloured product than vegetable tanning. Alum dressing is still used for woolskins and gloves, but it is a reversible process because the alum will wash out.

PARCHMENT

From remote times, hides, first raw, and according to Latour,[8] later tanned, were used as a writing material by the peoples of the Near East. The first mention of documents written on skins occurs in the time of the Egyptian IVth Dynasty (c. 2600–2500 BC).[9] Next, Ctesias quoted by Diodorus Siculus (died AD 34) relates that skins were used by the Persians for historical records. The 'writer on skin' was depicted on Assyrian monuments from the eighth century BC and Herodotus (fifth century BC) said that skins of sheep and goats were once used for writing by the Ionians, and added that barbarians still used them. Driver lists the extant Egyptian documents, and considers that at least some are on leather, but it is not clear whether or not he makes a distinction between leather and parchment. Mongait,[1] listing some documents of the eighth century AD found in a Sogdian castle in Tajikistan, mentions paper and leather but not parchment. True parchment did not appear until the second century BC. The word parchment Latin: *pergamena*) is in fact derived from Pergamum, the name of the city in Asia Minor in which parchment was developed. The development of parchment was probably the result of a gradual improvement in methods of preparing skin for writing. But the high cost of papyrus may have acted as a stimulus; it is said that parchment was invented by Eumenes II (197–159 BC) of Pergamum as a substitute because the Egyptian pharaoh had forbidden the export of papyrus to Eumenes' country in the hope of preventing the growth of the famous library at Pergamum.

The manufacture of parchment has changed little through the ages. The skin is limed in order to loosen the hair or wool which is then scraped away with a curved knife. Any remaining flesh or fat is scraped from the under-surface (flesh side); the skin is then stretched on a frame, and the scraping continued. Parchment was originally made from the entire skin, but in more recent times it was (and still is) made from the flesh side of a split skin, the grain side (containing the hair roots) being used for bookbinding. Apart from the liming, which is often repeated to remove the grease, and which according to Plenderleith[3] leaves the parchment in an alkaline condition, the skin receives no further chemical treatment, i.e. it is not tanned. The manufacture of this very durable material therefore involves little more than drying under tension, during which it is rubbed with pumice in order to obtain a smooth surface. But despite this, the flesh side can usually be distinguished from the grain side by its rougher texture, and in books, the pages are usually mounted grain to grain and flesh to flesh in order to give a uniform appearance.

According to Plenderleith[3] the most common source of parchment is sheepskin, and my studies confirm this. Saxl,[7] on the other hand, claims that among medieval parchments, whereas those from sheep predominated in England, those from goats predominated on the Continent. I have not yet had the opportunity to examine continental parchments, so have no evidence about the source of parchments there. Calf parchment, for which the term vellum should strictly be reserved, is usually thicker and harder than sheep or goat parchment, and is used for bookbinding rather than writing.[34]

DATING

In the Leeds University Department of Leather Industries a method has been evolved which gives a rough indication of the date at which leather or parchment was made.[10] This depends on the shrinkage temperature of collagen fibres from the material. Samples are rehydrated in distilled water for an hour, fibres are teased from them, and mounted between cover-slips on the heating stage of a microscope. Heat is applied and the temperature at which the fibres begin to shrink (ranging from about 25° to 60°C) is noted. In general, older specimens have a lower shrinkage temperature. Fragments from the Dead Sea Scrolls were found to have shrinkage temperatures comparable with other ancient specimens of known age, and so a date was indicated which was in agreement with that obtained by palaeographic and radiocarbon methods.

HISTOLOGICAL METHOD

The first specimens of dried skin were merely softened in carbolic xylol (25 g. phenol in 75 ml. xylol) before being embedded in wax prior to sectioning. Then Sandison's softening fluid was found to give better results.[4] This consists of 90% alcohol—30 vols; 1% formaldehyde—50 vols; 5% aqueous sodium carbonate—20 vols.[11] The effect is for the dilute alkali (sodium carbonate) to attack the skin slightly and swell it, while the alcohol and formaldehyde act as fixatives. The more delicate material such as ancient parchments was left in this fluid for only 20 mins., whereas the harder material (leather and recent parchments) was softened for 24 hours. Specimens were dehydrated in the usual way, left in carbolic xylol overnight, and wax embedded *in vacuo* for 30 mins.

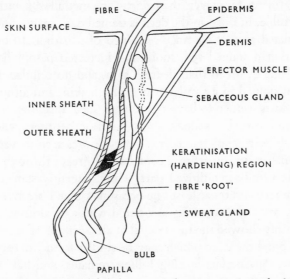

Fig. 98 Primary wool follicle in vertical section. From Ryder.[6,4]

Sections were stained with the Sacpic method. In this the cell nuclei are stained purple-black with haematoxlylin, and there are two other dyes, red basic fuchsin, and green, acid picro-indigo-carmine, which is in fact a mixture of yellow picric acid and blue indigo-carmine. This staining method shows the different structural features of the skin and follicles; for example, hairs and wool fibres in the skin show three successive zones representing stages of growth (Fig. 98). The soft root part of the fibre is acidophil and stains green with picro-indigo-carmine; then there is a keratinization (hardening) zone which is basiphil, and stains red with basic fuchsin; and finally the fully formed part of the fibre, composed of keratin, stains yellow with picric acid. Part of the inner sheath stains red and other parts of the follicle and skin stain varying shades of green.

STAINING REACTIONS AND STRUCTURAL DETAILS

Modern dried wool-skins from museum collections gave the same staining reactions as fixed, fresh skin. The taxidermist in preparing such skins may preserve them with salt, alum or oil, or not at all. At least one specimen known to have been preserved with alum gave the same staining reactions as fresh skin. Cells and their nuclei were visible, but the detail was naturally not as good as in fixed, fresh skin. The collagen of the dermis in sections of modern chamois leather (oil tanned) stained blue-green, as in fresh skin, and there were no follicle remains because this leather is made from the flesh side of the skin.

According to Sandison[12] hair and follicles in the skin of human mummies are often well preserved, and he found[13] (see chapter by Sandison) that the eyelids, including hair follicles and eyelashes, were remarkably well preserved.* Early in the series of sections of skin from the mummified cat that Dr Sandison sent me, the sections showed hairs cut above the skin surface. These had stained blue or mauve instead of the usual yellow, and they were somewhat degenerate and swollen, which may have come about during the softening treatment. However, the ladder-type medulla[14] (central core) of the fibre was frequently visible. In the skin the dermis stained dark green, but had the appearance of having coagulated so that no trace remained of its original fibrous nature. Within the skin the hairs had stained red, indicating increased basophilia. The follicle walls stained a paler shade of green than in fresh skin, and no cellular detail remained.

Old parchment stained in a similar way to fresh skin, and although the collagen of the dermis sometimes seemed to have coagulated, most specimens retained their fibrous nature. The dermis usually stained green, and sometimes yellow, but occasional patches, usually thicker areas, stained red. Wool fibres seen in vertical section usually showed the normal transition from a root stained green, through a red keratinization region, to a yellow fully-keratinized part. This frequently stained orange, instead of yellow, and often red, and on at least one occasion a blue fibre was seen. Cellular detail was very variable and not necessarily associated with age, although eighteenth-century parchments probably showed the most detail of all. Sections of parchment often showed maroon debris around the edge which may be similar to the maroon staining of leather mentioned below. Parchments lacking follicle remains, and having an open mesh of

* Natron (sodium sesquicarbonate) was used in the embalming process.

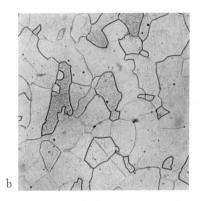

a

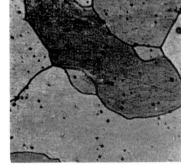

c

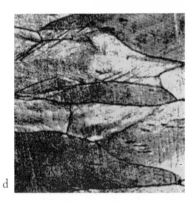

b

(a) Spontaneous cracking in ancient silver ($\times$ 100). Unetched.
(b) Pure iron ($\times$ 100). Etched.

(c) Cast and fully annealed copper ($\times$ 100). Etched.
(d) Cold-worked copper ($\times$ 100). Etched.

d

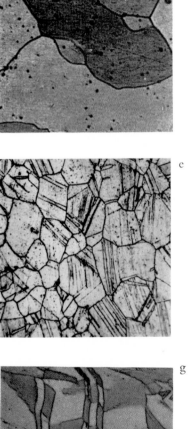

e

(e) Slip-bands due to cold-working ($\times$ 100). Etched.
(f) Twinned structure of copper or low-tin bronze after being worked and fully annealed ($\times$ 80). Etched.

f

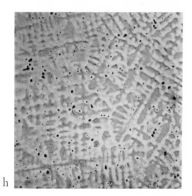

g

(g) Copper after working, full annealing and then again being cold-worked ($\times$ 150). Etched.
(h) Cast low-tin bronze ($\times$ 100). Etched.

h

(see page 555) PLATE XXV

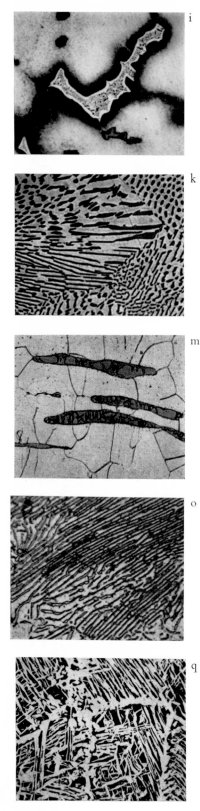

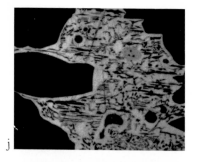

(i) 'Burnt' structure in bronze formed from solid solutions ($\times$ 100). Etched.
(j) Duplex structure in bronze. Typical of eutectic or the eutectic-like structure ($\times$ 100). Etched.

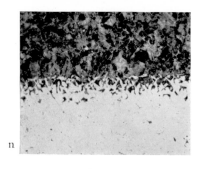

(k) Eutectic in silver-copper alloy ($\times$ 100). Etched.
(l) Widmannstätten pattern in meteorite ($\times$ 10). Etched.

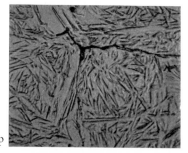

(m) Wrought iron ($\times$ 200). Crystals of iron and streaks of slag. Etched.
(n) Superficially carburized iron ($\times$ 100). Pearlite dark, ferrite light. Etched.

(o) Eutectoid structure of pearlite in slowly cooled steel ($\times$ 100). Etched.
(p) Martensite in steel quenched from very high temperature ($\times$ 250). Etched.

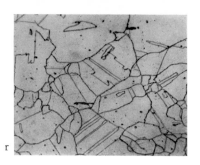

(q) 'Meteoric' structure in man-made steel heated to a yellow-heat and cooled in air ($\times$ 100). Etched.
(r) Neumann bands (thin twins) in man-made iron ($\times$ 100). Etched.

PLATE XXVI (see page 555)

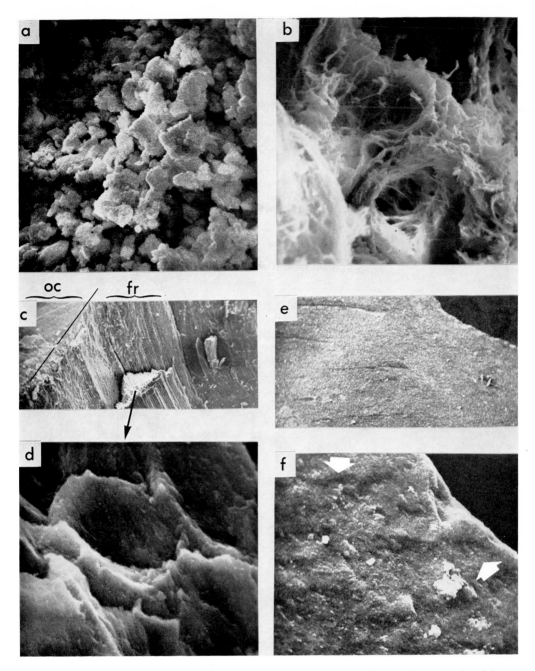

Archaeological material as seen by scanning electron microscopy. (a) Surface detail on a Medieval femur from Winchester, which had macroscopic evidence of mild osteitis. B.M. (N.H.) sample. × 30,000. Plate No. P1/472. (b) Cellular detail of plant debris from a rehydrated coprolite from Salts Cave, Kentucky. Sample kindly provided by Dr R. Yarnell. × 1,500. Plate No. E.M.1/437. (c) Fractured fossil enamel of *Australopithecus*. Occlusal (oc) and broken (fr) regions are seen. × 130. Plate No. P1/433. (d) Detail of part of the fracture surface seen in c. Fracture surface cuts across enamel prisms, and shows crystalline texture. × 6,400. Plate No. P1/437. B.M. (N.H.) sample. (e) Low power view of part of a Natufian half-moon flint. B.M. (N.H.) specimen E 4594. Apparent abrasive marks are seen. × 55. Plate No. P4/562. (f) Close-up of region near the cutting edge of specimen in e. Surface irregularity clearly seen. × 2,100. Plate No. P4/564.

(see page 564) PLATE XXVII

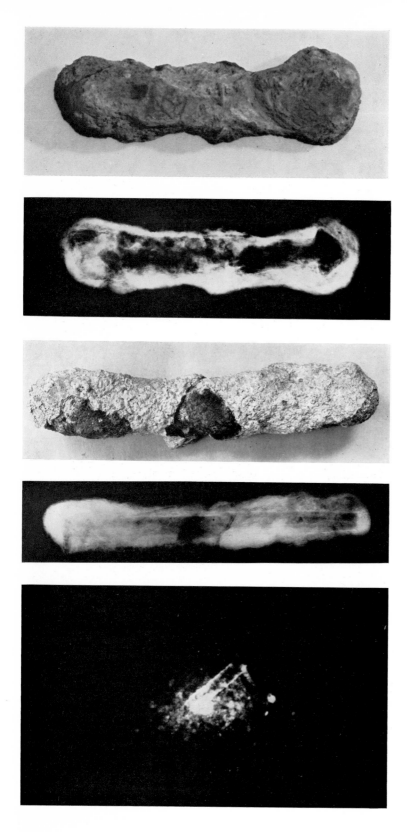

Voids (dark) in shapes of iron objects totally 'exhausted' by corrosion, revealed by X-radiography: *Above*, socketed ?ballista bolt head in clay from collapsed walls. *C.* 1900 years old. Pen Llystyn, Caerns.; p. 569.[27] Approx. 1/1. *Below*, Ship's nail from wreck in sand at 20 m. depth on bed of Mediterranean off Marseilles; p. 569.[28] Approx. ×2/5.

X-radiograph showing (?iron oxide) lining of tunnel in fired clay, originally occupied by ?souring chopped grass temper. *C.* 1400 years old. Buckden, Hunts.; p. 569 (report forthcoming in *Proc. Camb. Ant. Soc.*). Approx. ×5. (Cf. Pl. XXIX *lower*).

PLATE XXVIII (see page 567)

Horn-shaped tuberculous growth of iron corrosion products from ?cramp (still) holding wood and completely 'exhausted' by corrosion. X-radiograph shows transfer of nearly all iron from cramp to growth, as a result of burial in aerated waterlogged well filling in chalk. *C.* 1600 years old. Rudston, Yorks.; p. 569.[25] Approx. × 1/4.

Potsherd with (internal) oriented texture ('sweep'), formed by potter's throw, seen in X-radiograph as aligned streaks (dark) due to grass temper. In the upper part, streaks run at an angle to final, horizontal smoothing and grooving of surface. They would register as 'voids' whether the grass were green (in raw clay), charred (reduced fired) or ashed (oxidised fired). *C.* 800 years old. Approx. 1/1.

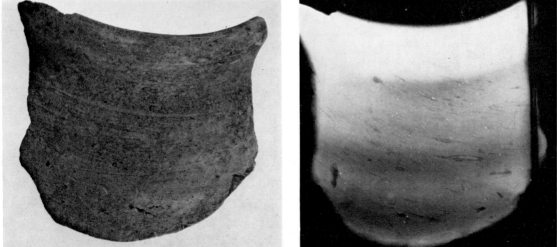

PLATE XXIX (see page 567)

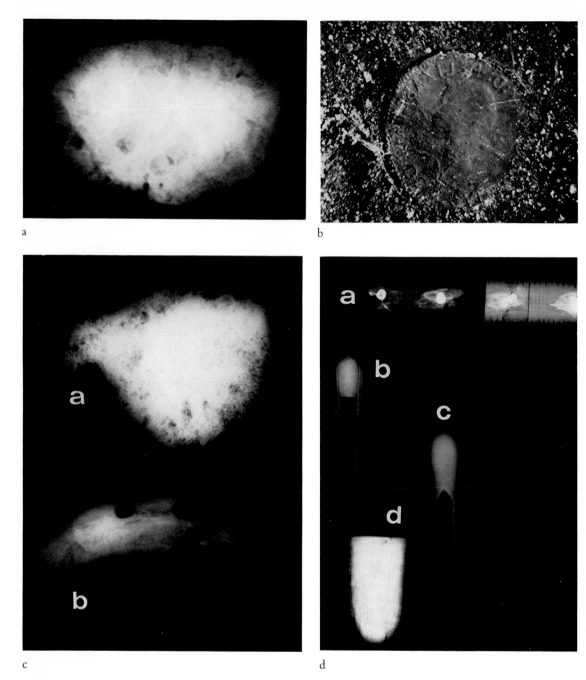

(a) X-radiograph of lump of clay showing identifiable snail shells unbroken inside it (dark helical shapes with white outlines). *C.* 700 years old. Norwich; p. 569 (*Norf. Archaeol. XXXIII, Part II,* 1963, 139: this find not specified). (b) Impression of a halfpenny on specimen of 'raw' fleece, buried flesh side up in sand with the coin over one corner, after recovery five years later. Many of the fibres remain but all the skin has gone except where covered by the coin. Wareham, Dorset; p. 120.[31] (c) X-radiograph clearly showing characteristic difference between porous iron 'slag,' a, and straightgrained wrought iron, b, where obscured by corrosion products on surface. *C.* 1900 years old. St Eval, Cornwall; p. 569 (report forthcoming in *Proc. Prehist. Soc.*). Approx. ×4/5. (d) X-radiograph of objects of bone (a, b: straightgrained, clear) and 'ivory' (c, d: convolute, fuzzy). P. 569: a, part of comb; b, c, parts of ?pigment tubes, b with stopper; d, chessman. Approx. ×4/5.

PLATE XXX (see page 567)

Close examination of micro-environment of an artifact for associated, altered material. *C.* 1400 years old. Sewerby, Yorks.: p. 567,[35] also see p. 120: *Above:* Back of copper alloy brooch with iron pin showing textile and other organic residues. Approx. ×5/4. *Below left:* Detail of above, area approximately in middle of lower half of square head, shows two fibre bundles spun into a thread encased in iron corrosion products; short lengths of unravelled fibre ultimates preserved by copper corrosion products (top left); and some fly pupa cases as partial casts in iron corrosion products (bottom right). Approx. ×40. *Below right:* Detail of thread on left, showing fibre ultimates to be hollow. Approx. ×150.

PLATE XXXI (see page 567)

(a) Thin section of an axe-hammer from Pembridge, Herefordshire (×25).

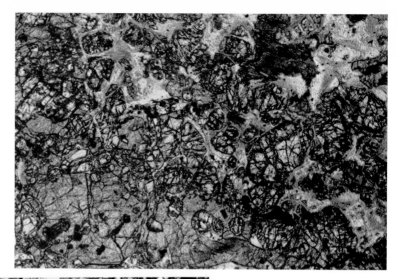

(b) Thin section of pictrite from an outcrop in Hyssington Parish, Montgomeryshire, for comparison with (a). In both these slides, the semi-rounded, greatly cracked grains are olivine; greyish material with cleavage, forming a large patch to the bottom and left, is augite; white is felspar, with the cloudy patches therein, apple-green chlorite and the black patches are iron ore.

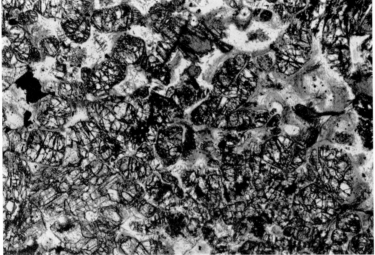

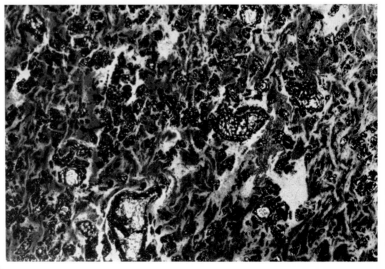

(c) Thin section of the very distinctive metamorphosed laterite from Tievebulliagh, Co. Antrim (×25).

PLATE XXXII (see page 571)

coarse collagen fibres suggesting the flesh side of a split skin, were found as early as the thirteenth century, but they only became common from the sixteenth century onwards. It would be interesting to find an historical record of the period at which the splitting of skins began. Apparently the earliest method of making a skin thinner was to shave away the flesh side.[15, 34]

Archaeological specimens of presumably vegetable-tanned *leather* usually appeared brown or black before sectioning, and often stained maroon throughout. This maroon stain seemed to be a convenient method of distinguishing leather from untanned skin or parchment, supplementing chemical tests for tanning. But as most specimens examined were from excavations, and had therefore been in contact with soil, some modern (strop) leather was examined to see whether the maroon stain was due to tanning or to decay. In fact the collagen fibres at the flesh side of the skin stained a dirty blue-green, with parts yellow, red and maroon. The grain side was darker, the collagen fibres being mainly grey-blue and the follicle remains maroon. The darker blue-green staining was confirmed in some modern Egyptian sheep or goat leather and in some modern 'Morocco' bookbinding made from the grain side of sheep skin. Thus, whereas untanned skin tends to retain the bright blue-green stain of fresh skin, leather stains darker and has a tendency to stain maroon.

Next it was decided to determine which component of the stain gave the maroon result, and this was carried out with a medieval specimen, by staining different sections separately with each of the different stains. The sections were a pale brown colour before staining, and this colour was apparently unchanged by haematoxylin. Picro-indigo-carmine on the other hand stained the collagen fibres olive green (cf. the flesh side of the strop leather) while the follicles remained brown. Basic fuchsin stained the whole skin bright maroon; the maroon colour therefore derives from this stain, and indicates an increased basophilia in leather, particularly after degradation. The hairs, too, in leather often stained maroon, but surprisingly they were sometimes colourless, i.e. completely unstained, and sometimes stained bright blue.

IDENTIFICATION OF ANCIENT SPECIMENS

Until about the middle of the last century it was thought that hairs had no particular arrangement in the skin. Then it was found that they were arranged in characteristic groups, and towards the end of the century it was found that many mammals had two kinds of hair follicle within the group. But it was not until about the nineteen-twenties that the full significance of this difference as it affects the fleeces of sheep was realized: one type of follicle tends to grow finer wool fibres than the other. The two kinds of follicles are now known as primary follicles and secondary follicles. The primaries, formed first in the foetus, are usually the largest, and are arranged in rows in the skin often of three primaries each. The secondaries are more numerous and lie to one side of the primaries. The primary trio with its associated secondary follicles constitutes the follicle group which is the unit of the fleece (Fig. 99). The fundamental difference that distinguishes them in the skin is that the primaries have a sweat gland and erector muscle, whereas the secondaries have neither of these. Both types do, however, have

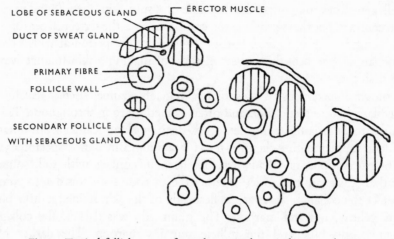

Fig. 99 Typical follicle group from domestic sheep in horizontal section.

sebaceous glands, the glands that produce wool grease. The secondaries being usually the smallest follicles tend to grow finer fibres than the primaries, and therefore the more secondary follicles a sheep has in its skin, the finer on the whole will be the fleece. The relative number of secondary follicles is expressed as the secondary-primary follicle ratio, or S/P ratio; in general the higher the S/P ratio the finer is the fleece.

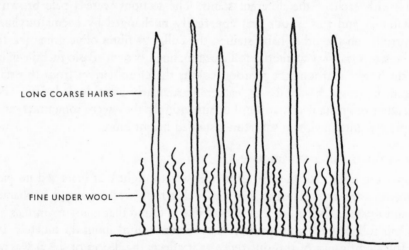

Fig. 100 The double coat of a wild sheep. From Ryder (*New Scientist*, 27th October 1960).

Wild sheep from which the domestic sheep arose have a double coat consisting of an outer-coat of very coarse, hairy fibres known as kemps, and a short, under-coat of very fine woolly fibres[6] (Fig. 100). And as the outer-coat kemps grow from the primary follicles, and the under-coat wool grows from the secondaries, examination of the skin shows considerable difference in size between the primary and secondary follicles. There is an apparent fundamental difference in the arrangement of the follicles in the skin between wild sheep and domestic sheep. In wild sheep (Fig. 101b) the secondary

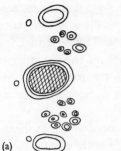

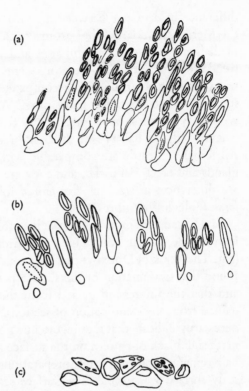
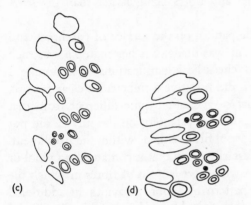

(a)

(b)

(a)

(b)

(c)

(d)

(c)

Fig. 101 Follicle groups from (a) domestic goat;
(b) wild (mouflon) sheep; (c) Shetland sheep;
(d) Soay sheep. (a, c, d) From Ryder.[4]

Fig. 102 Follicle groups from the Dead Sea Scrolls;
(a) fine-wooled sheep; (b) medium-wooled
sheep or hairy sheep (see text); (c) hairy sheep.
From Ryder.[4]

follicles frequently lie between the primaries, whereas in most domestic sheep, as already mentioned (Fig. 99), the secondaries are usually grouped to one side of the primaries.[4]

The hairy primitive sheep such as those belonging to the African and Asiatic breeds, which are among the most primitive in existence today, have a somewhat intermediate grouping with the secondaries beginning to move from between the primaries (Fig. 102c). These are still much larger than the secondaries, and produce the hairiest fibres of the fleece. This arrangement is similar to that in the goat (Fig. 101a), but the goat has fewer secondaries. Woolly primitive domestic sheep, such as the Soay and Shetland, have appreciable difference in diameter between the primaries and secondaries, and the secondaries are grouped in a wedge, only the points of which are between the primaries (Fig. 101c and d). Such an arrangement is often found in the coarser-fleeced British breeds such as the Scottish Blackface, the long hairy fibres of which make them somewhat similar to the sheep of the hairy primitive group (cf. Plate XXIVd). In the more highly evolved domestic sheep the secondaries have spread out beyond the wedge and in general become grouped at one side of the primaries. Modern medium-wooled sheep, e.g. the longwools and down breeds, have less difference in diameter between the primaries and secondaries. Fine-wooled sheep, e.g. the Merino, have large fibre groups with many secondaries, and hardly any difference in diameter between the primaries and secondaries (cf. Fig. 101a). The evolutionary trend after domestication therefore seems to have been a movement of the secondaries from between the primaries, accompanied by a tendency for the primaries to become smaller, and to grow less hairy fibres. As more secondaries have developed in finer-wooled types, these have spread away from the primaries.

Knowledge of hair type in different breeds of cattle is not as advanced as it is in sheep. All follicles in cattle are comparable with the primaries in sheep, i.e. they have sweat glands and erector muscles, and they are distributed at random in the skin. But there are differences in size, the *first-formed* follicles and fibres being larger than the *later-formed* follicles and fibres.[16]

Saxl [7] made attempts to use the hair follicle pattern on the surface of parchments to identify the animal from which the parchment was made, but her material was such (e.g. The Book of Durrow) that she could not check her identifications by sectioning. I found that examination of the surface pattern did not give a sufficiently clear picture, and that the impression gained from the surface was often quite different from that gained from the examination of sections. In addition, a pattern on the surface did not necessarily indicate that there would be good wool fibre remains within the parchment, neither did lack of pattern on the surface necessarily mean that it contained no wool or hair remains. Sometimes my preparations showed short lengths of fibres in which the scaly surface was visible. The surface scale pattern of a fibre provides an additional feature to help identification.[14] It will be noted that the 'danger' claimed by Appleyard and Wildman on p. 628 is not as great as they imply because identifications in parchment are made mostly on the grouping of fibres, and less on the appearance of individual fibres.

One of the oldest specimens examined[4] was from some Aramaic documents originating in Egypt in the fifth century BC.[9] The specimen stained bright green, so it could be parchment or could have been preserved with oil or alum, but it had apparently not been vegetable tanned. There were traces of large follicles, as well as fine fibres, suggesting a hairy sheep or goat. Remains of follicle bulbs showed cell nuclei, and the fine fibres were apparently not pigmented and had scales visible. Two of these had a diameter of 12 microns, and two more had diameters of 24 and 18 microns respectively.*

All available evidence suggests that the sheep was domesticated in south-west Asia, possibly as early as 10,000 BC.[17] It is not known what the fleeces of the earliest domestic sheep were like, but it has always been assumed that they were hairy and pigmented brown or black like wild sheep. The next specimen to be described was therefore of even greater interest than the last. This was a piece of sheepskin from Scythian excavations in the Altai Mountains.[18] It came from frozen burial mound No. 5 at Pazyryk, and was kindly supplied by N. J. Merpert, Scientific Secretary of the Institute of Archaeology in Moscow. The sample was taken from the shoulder region of the skin, and was dated as being of the fourth or fifth century BC. The wool was intact (Plate XXIVa) and

* Diameter measurements were made with a Lanameter projection microscope.

had a slight yellow-brown discoloration; the microscopic preparations confirmed that it was not pigmented.[19] This therefore compares with the whiteness of Iron Age wool in the west. Cloth from the Roman period apparently had fewer pigmented fibres than wool from the Bronze Age oak-coffin burials of Denmark.[20]

The fleece was double coated with hairs extending in a shallow curl 4 cm beyond the under-wool to a length of 12 cm. This was the maximum staple length (in fact comparable with the maximum in wild sheep)[6] because the hairs in the skin had brush ends that are formed preparatory to moulting. These were the coarsest fibres; a goat is likely to have had coarser fibres: there were no kemps. The under-coat wool was dense and mixed with the hair, and had no staple crimp (cf. wild sheep).[6] A whole mount of the coat fibres showed hairs that were typical of those found in sheep, i.e. the central medulla or core of the fibre occupied no more than about half the width of the fibre, and they were roughly 75–90 microns in diameter. The surface scale edges were prominent, and the scale pattern was apparently an irregular mosaic. The fine, non-medullated fibres were typical fine wool fibres, having smooth, near, scale margins, and a few were as fine as 12 microns, but most of them had a diameter between 20 and 26 microns. This is comparable with the under-wool of modern hairy sheep; the under-coat of the goat tends to be finer, as in the last specimen. There were also a few non-medullated fibres of medium diameter, i.e. about 40 microns. These had an irregular waved mosaic, being like wool from a down breed, and some of them had the more diagonal scale edges that have a tendency to occur in lustre longwools (fibres of down breeds and longwools are illustrated in Appleyard,[21] p. 113).

Sections of the skin stained bright green and the wool fibres stained bright yellow. These were well preserved, having a clear scale pattern. Some of the sebaceous glands remained as a grey mass near a wool fibre. Despite particles of earth in the wool attached to the skin there was no maroon staining; the skin may have been preserved with butter. Vertical sections of the skin showed that the follicles had an acute slope, which is a primitive feature, and that there was a well-developed fat layer, which in my experience is uncommon in sheep. The follicle grouping seen in horizontal sections was that of a hairy, primitive animal. The secondaries formed a wedge between the primaries, and their relatively large number and their lack of extreme fineness are in accordance with the specimen being from a sheep rather than a goat. The secondary fibres occasionally showed the bilateral staining characteristic of crimped fibres.[14] The primaries were narrower within the skin than above it, and had lost their medulla, because they had formed brush ends preparatory to moulting.

The overall picture obtained from this specimen was of a hairy primitive sheep with some generalized characters. The moulting and short staple length are primitive features; e.g. the staple length was comparable with some modern Asiatic, hairy breeds, but was only about one-third as long as the fleece of the modern Scottish Blackface. However, the specimen was comparable in fineness with the less hairy grades of Scottish Blackface wool, the hairs in particular being much finer than the coarse kemps of the coarse Scottish Blackface fleeces, and of the wild sheep. This fineness, lack of pigment, and the wider range of fibre types than in the wild sheep, are interesting in a sheep that is apparently primitive. There is a tendency today for the different fibre types to be associated with different breed types, but most of the range of fibre types are still found in breeds such as the Scottish Blackface.

Sections of a sample of Egyptian leather dated 300 BC stained blue-green with maroon patches, suggesting vegetable tanning, and the fibrous nature of the skin had mainly been lost. There were fine fibres (one had a diameter of 8 microns) and larger, pigmented follicle remains. Occasionally these had medium fibres (about 50 microns in diameter) and some of them had a narrow medulla. This specimen seemed to be from calf.

Some twenty fragments of parchment from the Dead Sea Scrolls were examined,[4] and five from the nearby site of Muraba'ât, which are grouped here with the Dead Sea Scrolls for convenience, although, whereas the Dead Sea Scrolls are generally agreed to date roughly from the time of Christ, the Muraba'ât parchment came from caves used during the Jewish revolt of AD 132–135; these are situated to the south of those in which the Dead Sea Scrolls were found.

Only four parchments had clear groups; one of these was a calf and this and another calf specimen were the only ones with pigmented fibres. The others are shown in Fig. 102, a fine-wooled sheep (a), a medium-wooled sheep (b), and a hairy animal (c) that could have been a sheep or a goat, although the relatively large number of secondaries suggested that it was from a sheep. Three other samples had both fine and coarse fibres, and were therefore hairy animals. One of these had two fine fibres 12 microns in diameter, and a larger non-medullated fibre 42 microns in diameter. Another had fine fibres, 6, 8 and 12 microns in diameter, and a fibre with a diameter of 16 microns in which there was a medulla 12 microns wide. Medullae occupying such a large proportion of the fibre usually only occur in coarser fibres, and a similar unidentified fine animal fibre in a Bronze Age textile specimen from Amesbury was found to have a wide medulla by Appleyard.[22]

The medium-wooled type had appreciable difference between the diameter of the primary and secondary fibres, and a Soay-type grouping in which there was a wedge of secondaries pointing between the primaries (Fig. 102b). Short lengths of fibres had a scale pattern with diagonal scale edges (not found in the Soay) suggesting a longwool type (Plate XXIVc). Six other samples had fibres of medium-wool size (primaries ranging in diameter from 32 to 42 microns and secondaries around 20 microns in diameter) and three of these had diagonal scale edges. The intact wool of the Altai sample has enabled a reassessment to be made of these findings published in 1958.[4] First, the group (Fig. 102b) was similar to that of the Altai specimens and the primary fibres had brush ends. Therefore instead of being medium wool these fibres may be hairs that had narrowed preparatory to moulting. Second, the significance of the apparent long-wool type fibres may lie more in these fibres being present in a hairy type, as in the Altai specimen, than their indication of a primitive long-wool type. It is only as more specimens become available that answers to these problems will be found.*

* Leather and wool supplied by Prof. Y. Yadin from the Cave of the Letters, in Judea (AD 135) confirm the existence of a medium-wooled sheep, with a high proportion of fine fibres, which was the predominant type in that time and place.[5]

The fine-wooled type is even more interesting. This had large groups of fine fibres that are found today, in even larger groups, in Merino sheep. Two other samples had fibres as fine as this one (12–16 microns in diameter) and these had a scale pattern that was suggestive of the Merino (Plate XXIVb). It is known that modern Merinos came from Spain about 200 years ago, but little is known of their history before that.[6] These findings support hints that the Merino originated in the Near East. One fragment from the Dead Sea Scrolls, although apparently parchment, was found to consist of plant tissue when sectioned, and so was presumably papyrus.

The only specimen linking the ancient with the medieval specimens was some Egyptian leather of the Coptic period (seventh to twelfth century AD) from the British Museum. This had a well-defined grain pattern on the surface, and was clearly leather which the museum authorities thought was pigskin. In fact when sectioned it was found to be from a hairy sheep or a goat. The collagen stained a dirty green, but there was hardly any maroon staining, the original brown colour of the unstained sections remained in the follicle walls. The follicles had pigmented cells and the fibres were moderately pigmented, so the skin was from a brown animal or a brown patch on an animal. Some of the coarser fibres had a latticed medulla and of three fibres that could be measured one had a diameter of 94 microns with a medulla 64 microns wide; the figures for another fibre were 58 and 34 microns respectively, and a third, non-medullated fibre had a diameter of 34 microns. These measurements are more comparable with those of a hairy sheep than a goat.

MEDIEVAL AND RECENT SPECIMENS

Parchment. The study of the Dead Sea Scrolls stimulated provision of further material for investigation, and about 150 British parchments ranging in date from 1193 to 1871 have been examined.[23] The source of most of these was known, and there were three collections: from Hereford, Yorkshire and Scotland. The assumption has been made that parchment was made in the region of the place in which the document was written. However, certainly as early as the seventeen-nineties, it was clear that the parchment had not necessarily been made locally: a parchment of that date from Hereford bore the name of a London stationer. Also, there is evidence of livestock movement as early as the Middle Ages. One of the medieval sources of parchment was the Royal Manor of Hatfield, Yorkshire, and there is a record of AD 1323 of sheep being taken from East Anglia to re-stock Royal Manors in the north.[24]

Only one of these British parchments showed a clear follicle grouping, so the identifications were made mainly from individual fibres. Even those with many well-preserved follicles or fibres did not show the follicle arrangement. The remains in the medieval parchments were on the whole no better preserved than those in the Dead Sea Scrolls, possibly owing to the wetter British climate, although many of the medieval parchments were of excellent quality. The seventeenth- and eighteenth-century ones were on the whole of the worst quality, being the thickest, but showed most histological detail, e.g. cell nuclei in the follicle bulbs and surface scale patterns on the wool fibres. The nineteenth-century ones were the thinnest, and contained the fewest remains. This is possibly owing to increased efficiency in the removal of wool fibres from the skin before manufacture, or to the practice of using only the flesh side of the skin to make parchment.

The criterion of fibre diameter used for identification led to descriptions: fine (7–18 microns), fine to medium (about 18 microns to about 35 microns) and medium (about 35–60 microns). These descriptions give no indication of breed, which is the main interest in this period when the different breed types must have been evolving. Sometimes, however, further information could be gained from indications of follicle grouping and fibre scale pattern so that suggestions of type, e.g. down breed (in the fine to medium group) and longwool (in the medium group), could be added. But too few specimens have yet been examined to indicate the distribution of these types. However, the Scottish parchments, which were from the fifteenth to seventeenth centuries, had pigmented follicle remains suggesting the primitive domestic Soay sheep. This is of interest because it tends to confirm the scanty evidence that this breed remained in Scotland until as late as the eighteenth century. Three of the medieval English parchments had pigmented fibres closely resembling those of the Soay.

Hairy types were easily distinguished because of the presence of both coarse and fine fibres, and hairy sheep could usually be distinguished from goats, e.g. modern goat primary fibres are about 160 microns in diameter compared with about 80 to 100 microns in the Herdwick sheep, and the secondary fibres of the goat are as fine as 10 to 15 microns, whereas those of the Herdwick are around 20 microns in diameter, e.g. a parchment from Hatfield dated 1403 had a primary fibre 108 microns in diameter with a medulla 100 microns wide, and three secondaries 18, 20 and 22 microns in diameter (Plate XXIVd). A parchment from Startforth, Yorkshire, dated 1727 was identified as goat from the scale pattern of the fibres actually protruding for about half an inch above the parchment surface. One of the two Dead Sea Scroll samples identified as calf had a patch of hairs above the surface. The only British parchments that was certainly from calf was from the cover of a book from Fountains Abbey dated 1450. This had pigmented hairs, and although the cover appeared like parchment, there were areas of maroon staining in the skin suggesting a form of preservation.

Hairy sheep were apparently kept in all periods. Whereas most of the fine wools came from the medieval period, the medium wools became more common in the sixteenth century and predominated after that date, those of the eighteenth century being the coarsest, e.g. 50 to 60 microns in diameter. The findings so far therefore support the doubtful historical records of the extreme fineness of medieval wool. And as many of the medium wools are likely to have been longwools, historical evidence[25] for an increased supply of long wool during the sixteenth and seventeenth centuries is also supported. There was evidence, however, of the existence of medium and fine to medium-wooled sheep in the Middle Ages that could have been the ancestors of the longwool, the origin of which has recently been much discussed.[24–27]

Leather. The earliest medieval samples of leather came from a tenth-century shoe found in excavations at the South Corner Tower of the Roman Fortress at York.[28] The leather was examined by Miss Betty M. Haines of the British Leather Manufacturers Research Association who, using vertical sections, identified it as being made from cattle hide, and said that the leather had a break in the middle which had arisen from incomplete penetration of tan. My own (horizontal) preparations from a black, brittle fragment showed follicle remains which confirmed that the leather was from cattle, but only a few degraded hairs remained.

Another sample from York came from excavations carried out in Petergate by Mr L. P. Wenham in 1957 and 1958. The finds dated from the eleventh to the fourteenth century, and among many animal bones (see my chapter on fish remains) were found a number of shoes which were described by Mr J. H. Thornton of Northampton College of Technology. The fragment of leather examined[29] was black and moderately brittle, but sections showed many follicle remains with a few well-preserved cattle hairs (Plate XXIVe). The hairs had little pigment, and so could have come from a white (or grey) animal (or patch on an animal). Some hairs stained the usual yellow colour, others stained green or blue and some were colourless. Some pieces of stitching from the shoes were clearly leather, but some could possibly have been bits of yarn made from flax fibres. However, when these were mounted on a microscope slide the fibres could not be separated easily as they can be in a yarn, and when a piece was sectioned and stained, a microscopic examination confirmed that the fibres were collagen fibres (stained maroon) from leather, and not flax fibres.

Another piece of medieval leather examined was found during excavations at Pontefract Priory in 1959.[30] This was attached to a buckle of thirteenth to fourteenth century date, and microscopic examination showed follicles characteristic of cattle skin, but no hairs. Two specimens of shoe leather supplied by Dr A. E. Werner of the British Museum research laboratory were examined. One came from the boat found at Kentmere in the Lake District, dated by C-14 to AD 1320±130,[33] and the other came from a fifteenth-century grave at Lincoln Cathedral. Both were made from cattle skin; the Kentmere leather showed clear traces of follicles, whereas the Lincoln leather had less well-defined follicles, but had a few degraded hairs.

Finally, I was recently sent a specimen by Mr D. M. D. Thacker of Llantilio Crossenny, Monmouthshire. This came from under the hinge of a door leading to the Chapel of the Pyx at Westminster Abbey. The door had once been covered with skin which was reputed to be that of Richard de Podlicote, a monk who in 1303 robbed the king's treasury and was flayed when caught. The specimen appeared like parchment, but was thicker than sheep or goat parchments and more comparable with a calf parchment. The hairs lacked pigment completely, which is unusual for human hair, and they had a moderately dense arrangement even for the scalp. Comparison with both human and cattle skin led this to be identified as calf.

More recent evidence has enabled an hypothesis on fleece evolution in domestic sheep to be put forward,[5, 35] and the Çatal Hüyük textiles have been shown to be flax and not wool.[31] Evidence of Auroch skin and changes in the coat of the ox have been described.[32]

A microscopic examination of skin and wool remains can therefore often reveal details that give a surprising amount of information that is of interest to biologists, as well as to archaeologists and agricultural historians.

REFERENCES

1 MONGAIT, A. 1959. *Archaeology in the USSR*, Moscow. 1961. Harmondsworth
2 GANSSER, A. 1950. *Ciba Review* (81) 2938–2964
3 PLENDERLEITH, H. J. 1956. *The Conservation of Antiquities and Works of Art*, Oxford
4 RYDER, M. L. 1958. *Nature 182*, 781–783
5 —— 1964. *Nature 204*, 555–9
6 —— and STEPHENSON, S. K. 1968. *Wool Growth*, London and New York
7 SAXL, H. 1954. *An investigation of the Qualities, the Methods of Manufacture and the Preservation of Historic Parchment and Vellum with a View to Identifying the Species of Animal used*; M.Sc. Thesis, Leeds University
8 LATOUR, A. 1949. *Ciba Review* (72) 2630
9 DRIVER, G. R. 1957. *Aramaic Documents of the Fifth Century BC*, Oxford
10 BURTON, D., POOLE, J. B. and REED, R. 1959. *Nature 184*, 533–534
11 SANDISON, A. T. 1955. *Stain Technol. 30*, 277–283
12 —— Personal communication
13 —— 1957. *Medical History 1*, 336–339
14 RYDER, M. L. 1963. A Survey of the Gross Structure of Protein Fibres; in HEARLE, J. W. S. and PETERS, R. H. (ed.), *Fibre Structure*, London
15 WATERER, J. W. 1956. Leather; in SINGER, C. *et al.* (ed.), *A History of Technology*, Oxford, vol. II
16 LYNE, A. G. and HEIDEMAN, MARGARET, G. 1959. *Austral. J. Biol. Sci. 12*, 72–95
17 READ, C. A. 1962. *Z. Tierzücht Zücht Biol. 76*, 31–8
18 RUDENKO, S. I. 1953. *Kul'tura Nasileniia Gornogo Altaia v. Skitskoe Vremia*, Moscow
19 RYDER, M. L. 1961. *Austral. J. Sci. 24*, 246–248
20 CLARK, J. G. D. 1936. *The Mesolithic Settlement of Northern Europe*, Cambridge, 117
21 APPLEYARD, H. M. 1960. *Guide to the Identification of Animal Fibres*, Leeds
22 —— Personal communication
23 RYDER, M. L. 1960. *Nature 187*, 130–132
24 TROW-SMITH, R. 1957. *A History of British Livestock Husbandry to 1700*, London
25 BOWDEN, P. J. 1956. *Econ. Hist. Rev. 9*, 44–58
26 RYDER, M. L. 1959. *Agric. History Rev. 7*, 1–5
27 —— 1964b. *Agric. Hist. Rev. 12(1)*, 1–12; (2), 65–82
28 STEAD, I. M. 1958. *Yorks Arch. J. 39*, 515–537
29 RYDER, M. L. 1969. Animal remains from York (forthcoming)
30 BELLAMY, C. V. 1965. Excavations at Pontefract Priory. *Ibid.*, forthcoming *Publications of the Thoresby Soc. 49*, 110
31 RYDER, M. L. 1965. *Anatolian Studies 15*, 175–6
32 —— 1964. *Proc. Prehist. Soc. 30*, 193–7; *Proc. Soc. Ant. Scot. 97*, 166–79
33 Personal communication from D. M. Wilson.
34 RYDER, M. L. 1964. *J. Soc. Archivists 11*, 391–9
35 —— 1969. Changes in the coat of sheep and cattle following domestication. In DIMBLEBY, G. W. and UCKO, P. J. (eds.) *Domestication and Exploitation of Plants and Animals*, London

47 *Microscopic Studies of Ancient Metals*

F. C. THOMPSON

EVEN TODAY IT IS IMPOSSIBLE to produce any metal in a state of absolute purity, in other words all our metals are in reality alloys. So long, however, as the impurity content does not exceed that which is characteristic of the extraction technique used, they may, for all normal purposes, be regarded as commercially pure materials. Thus a copper of the later third millennium BC[1] which contained only 97·4% of copper with 0·87% of tin, over 0·5% of lead and more than 1% of other impurities would to the metallurgist be merely an impure copper despite the tin which is present. When the impurities exceed the amount inevitably present in view of the works practice of the age, the presumption is that deliberate additions had been made and the term alloy then becomes justifiable.

With the exception of the metals which are found native, mainly iron, copper and gold, all the metallic articles *except* those of iron or steel had, until very recently, started life in the liquid state. In that condition most metals are miscible in each other in all proportions—lead being the main exception—but on solidification one of three things may happen. In the first place the metals in solution in each other in the molten state may remain in solution in the solid, yielding an alloy of the 'solid solution' type. Secondly, they may separate out more or less completely, giving what is termed a 'eutectic' in which both metals have frozen out simultaneously to produce a constituent which is a mechanical mixture of the two. Finally, the metals may combine to form compounds which are just as definite chemical compounds as is common salt. On which of these types of alloy has been formed depend both the microstructure and the properties.

As far as the properties are concerned, the solid solutions are by far the most important since they are harder than the metals of which they consist but yet have sufficient ductility to enable them to be worked both hot and cold. Further, when cold-worked the hardness is still further increased. The eutectics, being merely mixtures of the component metals, have broadly the properties of a metal, i.e. are relatively soft as compared with the solid solution. They have, however, relatively low melting points and are the essential constituents of the lower melting point solders. The intermetallic compounds are all characterized by high hardness and extreme brittleness, are unworkable and have rarely found any real field of application. When present in an alloy consisting mainly of a solid solution, however, they may exert a useful influence by providing a hard scaffold and thus increasing the strength appreciably. This is effected, however, at the expense of some loss of ductility, i.e. workability. As typical of these three classes of alloy structure may be mentioned the brasses with less than thirty-five

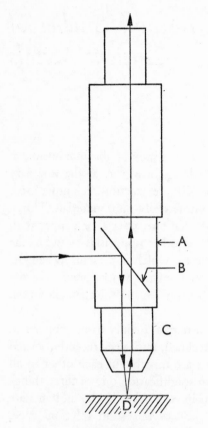

Fig. 103 Microscope with vertical illuminator.

per cent or so of zinc (solid solutions), soft solders (eutectics) and high-tin bronzes of the speculum metal type which may consist almost entirely of the copper-tin compound Cu_{31} Sn_8.

Although special microscopic equipment is produced for metallurgical work, the basic necessities are neither complicated nor expensive. Since for all practical purposes it is impossible to produce metallic sections so thin as to be transparent, such structures must be viewed by reflected light and the main, indeed almost the only essential piece of apparatus additional to the microscope itself is a 'vertical illuminator' by means of which the surface to be examined may be conveniently illuminated. Light from a reasonably intense source enters through a hole in the side of the illuminator A, Fig. 103, strikes a reflecting surface B and is concentrated by the objective, C, on to the specimen D. After reflection it again passes through the objective and travels up the microscope tube to the eye-piece. In some ways this arrangement is even simpler than that employed for transparent slides since the objective forms its own condenser. Two forms of reflector are in common use, one a plain glass cover slip which reflects a proportion of the incident light and later transmits a part up the tube. It will be apparent that this involves a considerable loss of illuminating power but it has the advantage that, since the whole aperture of the lens is available for the formation of the image, a high degree of resolution is obtained. In the other type the reflection is effected by means of a prism which covers half the field of the objective with a corresponding loss of resolution in one direction but with the formation of a much brighter image. Except where high resolution at high magnifications is required, and this rarely happens in the sort of work with which we are concerned here, there is not much to choose between the two methods.

To obtain a surface suitable for examination, an area of the metal must first be given a mirror polish. This area need not in general be large and for many purposes a $\frac{1}{8}$ in. circle is sufficient, though there are cases where a more extensive examination may be desirable. Where hand-polishing is used, a flat is ground or filed on the article and the marks gradually eliminated by rubbing on specially prepared emery papers of finer and finer grade. On changing from one paper to the next the direction in which the rubbing is done is changed through 90° so that the scratches due to the coarser papers are removed each time. The Blue Back papers I.G. to 4/O, available from the English

Abrasives Corporation Ltd., provide a suitable series for most purposes. One word of warning may be given. The surface of the specimen can become quite hot if too much pressure is used in the rubbing down and, especially in the case of a quenched steel, the temperature may rise to an extent which will bring about quite appreciable changes in the structure of the metal.

Having obtained a surface which is flat and covered only by the finest scratches, these in their turn must be removed by polishing. This may be done by rubbing the specimen, after having most carefully washed off every trace of grit, on damp selvyt cloth stretched on plate glass and dressed with Silvo or Brasso for non-ferrous metals or specially prepared alumina for iron or steel. Diamond powder is even more effective but is more expensive. Among the brands of alumina powder on sale the 5/20 grade supplied by Griffin and George may be recommended. Since the clarity of the final structure depends entirely on the care and skill used in carrying out these processes, it will be apparent that there is much virtue in the old saying 'More haste, less speed'.

At this stage a pure metal if examined under the microscope would appear a structure-less blank and to develop the structure etching with some appropriate reagent which will dissolve away the polished surface is required. Before doing this, however, it is in the highest degree desirable to examine the sample in this unetched state. Flaws of all kinds such as the cracks in age-embrittled silver, Plate XXVa, inclusions of slag, the presence of insoluble particles of lead, etc. are far more clearly revealed at this stage than is the case when the etching treatment has developed other structural features.

The final part of the preparation, the etching itself, is done with a reagent chosen according to the nature of the material under examination, and very many reagents are used by the specialist. For perhaps 99% of normal investigations two will however be found adequate: for non-ferrous metals and alloys a solution of 10% ferric chloride acidified with 2% hydrochloric acid, and for iron and steel a 2% solution of nitric acid in alcohol are commonly used. (Pour the nitric acid slowly into the alcohol in an open dish.) It is worth bearing in mind that it is always possible to re-etch a specimen if the structure is not sufficiently clearly developed but that if over-etched it will mean going right back to the emery papers and starting all over again. After etching the specimen, it must be thoroughly washed in running water and then equally thoroughly dried in absolute alcohol or some similar dehydrating medium. All this may sound somewhat complicated, but with a little practice and patience there is nothing beyond the resources of anyone prepared to take the necessary trouble.

NON-FERROUS METALS

The structure of a pure metal in the as-cast state is shown in Plate XXVb and consists of irregularly shaped grains separated by boundaries which show up dark after the etching. These grains are the individual crystals of varying orientations. Some etching reagents colour the crystals differentially according to their orientations (c), but this must not be taken to imply any difference of composition. The best safeguard here is to note that all sorts of degrees of colouration are to be observed. When cold-worked, e.g. by hammering the edge of a blade, these grains become elongated (d), and in addition are crossed by numerous straight lines called 'slip-bands' (e). On reheating such a worked metal the structure remains unaffected until a certain 'temperature of recrystallization' has been reached when new crystals make their appearance which are no longer elongated and in which slip-lines no longer occur. Such cold-worked and annealed material is, however, characterized by the broad bands shown in Plate XXVf which are due to twinning of the crystals and which, with an appropriate etching technique, may separate light and dark areas within a single crystal. If the metal with such a twinned structure is again cold-worked, the grains are once more distorted and slip-bands formed anew. The evidence of the earlier twinning is not, however, eliminated but the originally straight twin boundaries are now bent and irregular (g). From this appearance under the microscope then it would be possible to say quite dogmatically that the sample in question was a non-ferrous metal which had been cold-worked and then annealed above the temperature of spontaneous recrystallization and, following this, had again been worked. It is not possible, however, to say how often the cold-work—annealing—cold-work cycle had been repeated; it might have been done twenty times and still yield exactly the same microstructure. However, should the working be done 'hot' at a temperature above that of recrystallization—this amounts structurally to simultaneous working and annealing—a twinned structure identical to that of Plate XXVf will be obtained. This recrystallization temperature not only differs from metal to metal, but is also markedly influenced by the impurities present in solid solution, the temperature rising as the material becomes less and less pure. Some *very* pure metals, among them gold, copper and silver, will recrystallize spontaneously after cold-work even at ordinary temperatures in the course of time. Thus gold nuggets have been found to show a structure indistinguishable from that of Plate XXVf due to grain-gold being autogenously welded into bigger and bigger masses under the hammering of the gravel in river beds and the spontaneous recrystallization in the course of millennia of the deformed grains. Further, the more severe the cold-work the more readily does the metal recrystallize. Once recrystallization is complete the initially small grains commence to grow, becoming larger and larger as both the temperature of annealing and the time at that temperature are increased. It is rarely possible, therefore, to do more than say in broad, general terms that the metal with the larger grain size has probably been heated to the higher temperature or, alternatively, that it has been kept there for a longer time.

NON-FERROUS ALLOYS

Passing on now to the non-ferrous alloys which form a single solid solution much of what has just been said also applies. Plate XXVf for instance might equally well be either a pure metal or a solid solution in the cold-worked and annealed state. There are, however, two cases in which the structures are not the same. A solid solution in the as-cast state shows the structure of (h) whilst the pure metal is shown in (b). The 'dendritic' structure of (h) results from changes in composition of the solid solution which occur during the solidification process together with the curious manner in which it passes from the liquid to the solid state. Unlike a material such as common salt which forms a minute cubic crystal which grows as a cube, metals start from a crystal nucleus and grow by throwing out solid arms usually in three directions at right angles to each other. From these other branches grow until the whole mass is solid. In the alloy the primary arms are of the purest composition, the impurities increasing as solidification goes on. On annealing at a sufficiently high temperature and for a sufficiently long time, the variations of composition are wiped out by diffusion and finally the structure of the cast and fully annealed alloy differs in no way from that of (b). This diffusion is a process requiring time, and alloys are frequently found in which the dendritic pattern is still incompletely removed even when the material has been worked and then fully recrystallized by annealing.

It will be apparent from the identities of most of the structures of similarly treated pure metals and solid solutions that the microscope is not a substitute for chemical analysis although in some cases an approximation to the composition can be given. Its real function is to enable the treatment, thermal and mechanical, to which the alloy has been subjected to be determined, and, with certain exceptions, this can often be done with certainty.

Another feature of the structure of a solid solution, not found with pure metals, is that which results from heating it to a temperature at which partial fusion has taken place, i.e. the material has been 'burnt'. Just as the alloy freezes over a range of temperature, so does it melt progressively as the temperature rises. In (i) is shown a typical structure obtained when fusion has just commenced, the duplex constituent, a eutectic, forming initially at the grain boundaries where the impurities tend to concentrate.

Although, as has already been mentioned, some metals do dissolve in each other in all proportions even in the solid state, in most cases there is only a limited range of solid solubility after which another constituent, or 'phase', is formed. In the brasses for instance the solid copper can dissolve not more than 39% of zinc, above which a second phase makes its appearance. For our purposes, however, the more interesting case is provided by the alloys of copper and tin, the bronzes. With low tin contents that element remains in solution, yielding in the case of a casting the structure of (h). As the amount of tin increases another, eutectic-like, constituent makes its appearance (j). These structures in the bronzes are greatly influenced by the rate of cooling from high temperatures and it is, therefore, dangerous to attempt to predict the composition from an isolated microscopic structure.

Another interesting example of a eutectic structure is found in the silver-copper system. The maximum amount of copper which solid silver can dissolve is about 9% and usually it is less. When the silver becomes saturated with copper any increase in the copper content results in the appearance of the silver-copper eutectic whose structure is shown in (k). The higher the copper content the more of the eutectic is present until at about 30% the whole alloy is composed of this constituent. Since the eutectic has the lowest melting point of any alloy of these metals, it forms the essential constituent of the silver solders and has in fact been recognized as such in a plated coin of Neapolis[2] of about 300 BC.

Since with the exception of 'speculum metal' the intermetallic compounds found little or no application in ancient metallurgy, this brief account of the structures of the non-ferrous metals and alloys fairly covers the period from man's first use of native copper down to around the Middle Bronze Age. An exception occurs, however, in connection with the very curious alloys containing appreciable amounts of arsenic, lead, antimony or iron which seem to usher in the true bronzes—in the metallurgical sense—in which a fairly constant tin content of some 10–12% was used. These rather remarkable alloys, which suggest deliberate research [3] on the part of the craftsmen of the time, weld together the earlier use of varying and relatively low additions of tin and the later, more sophisticated alloys, and often have more complicated structures which cannot be discussed here.

IRON AND STEEL

That the earliest iron known to and used by man was of meteoric origin there can be no doubt, and the belief that such iron is too brittle to be worked into usable forms was effectively disposed of by Zimmer[4] when he showed that of the metallic meteorites known in 1916 no less than 99% possessed sufficient ductility to permit them to be forged down either hot or cold. It is well known that meteoric iron may be distinguished from the early man-made iron by invariably containing nickel from about 3% to around 35%, often together with not inappreciable amounts of cobalt. Terrestrial iron itself is, however, often made from ores which contain small amounts of nickel much of which will find its way into the metal. The presence, therefore, in such iron of some 1% or so of nickel must *not* be taken as any indication of a meteoric origin. There is, however, one problem which still awaits a complete solution. When meteoric iron corrodes away entirely what happens to the nickel originally present? Does it remain in the rust and so still provide evidence of its origin or does it pass away as soluble salts in the water responsible for the corrosion? An answer to these questions might at times be of immense value.

The characteristic structure (Plate XXVI 1) of certain types of meteorite is well known. It must not be overlooked, however, that this structure is *not* typical of all, or perhaps even of the majority, of metallic meteorites. Further, when a meteorite with this structure is reheated to a good red heat transformations occur as a result of which it is permanently eradicated, the structure then becoming quite indistinguishable from that of a man-made metal of the same composition.

Since the whole of the man-made iron, and later steel, manufactured in antiquity had a totally different origin from that of the copper and bronzes, it is not surprising that corresponding differences are to be found in the microstructures. None of this iron or steel was ever molten, the product of the furnaces being merely a crumbly, coke-like lump of semi-solid particles of iron.

When the 'ball' of spongy iron is withdrawn from the furnace the metal is admixed with molten slag, bits of charcoal, etc. which are in part, but in part only, expelled during the subsequent heatings and hammerings. It follows that the bars produced still contain some slag which has been drawn out into threads by the working, the whole structure under low magnifications almost resembling a whirlpool. At higher magnification (m) the structure consists of light grains of iron, called 'ferrite' by the metallographer, and slag. Such iron is soft and is incapable of being hardened by quenching, though some degree of hardening can be induced by cold-work. It is to such iron that Polybius refers in his description[5] of the Roman defeat of the Celts at the battle of Addua where, discussing the long Celtic swords, he says that these were 'easily bent, and would only give one downward cut with any effect, but that after this the edges got so turned and the blades so bent, that, unless they had time to straighten them with the foot against the ground, they could not deliver a second blow'.

An enormous step forward was taken when it was realized that when this iron was heated in glowing charcoal something happened as a result of which the metal became much stronger and far more capable of retaining a sharp cutting edge. The explanation is provided by Plate XXVIn in which it will be seen that in addition to the soft, white ferrite there is now a second, dark-etching constituent 'pearlite' which, at a sufficiently high magnification, shows a duplex structure of iron and iron carbide, Fe_3C, very much like that of a eutectic (o). It is in fact a 'eutectoid', i.e. a eutectic but formed from a solid, as distinct from a liquid solution. The carbon which has been absorbed during the heating in very hot charcoal is found entirely in these pearlitic areas which, therefore, increase in amount as the time and temperature of the carburization have increased. With this increase in the proportion of pearlite to ferrite goes a corresponding increase in the hardness. By controlling the treatment it was, as (n) shows, possible to carburize a cutting edge but still leave a soft but tough backing, or alternatively to convert the whole article into steel.

In addition to this increase of hardness, such steely iron (steel is only iron into which varying amounts of carbon have been introduced) possesses a further, and even more important, property, namely that of being hardened much more intensely if it be heated to a temperature above about 750°C, a red heat, in a reducing atmosphere and then quenched in cold water. The explanation of such quench-hardening is evident from (p). The duplex, pearlitic structure of the unhardened steel has disappeared and in its place a new phase 'martensite' with a needle-like structure has been induced. Lightly etched in the alcoholic nitric acid solution—a few seconds are normally adequate—martensite appears as a light brown constituent and it is to the formation of this intensely hard material that the hardening is attributable. The early smiths must have discovered very soon that just as the carburization was possible only in the atmosphere within the mass of glowing charcoal, so any reheating of the steel in an oxidizing atmosphere would, by burning out the carbon, undo all the good which had been obtained by the previous treatment, by leaving a soft and unhardenable skin of practically pure iron.

When the degree of carburization had been substantial, and when the quenching was drastic, as in cold water, a blade although very hard would be distinctly brittle and liable to break. To reduce this brittleness the quenched steel may either be reheated to a low temperature—even boiling water will have some effect—or alternatively the quenching may be made slightly less severe. There can be no doubt that the latter technique was that adopted by the earliest workers and from this fact were derived the remarkable quenching fluids which were used. The symbolism of the belief in the efficiency of the urine of a red-headed boy is fairly obvious, and such nostrums persisted until well after the Middle Ages. Indeed, when the writer was a student, he was informed that there was an old-established Sheffield firm that still imported barrels of camels' urine from Egypt for this purpose. As the tempering treatment is carried out at progressively higher temperatures the rate of etching of the martensite becomes faster and faster until instead of the light, straw-coloured martensite a black-etching, microscopically structureless constituent is produced.

The technical details which must be satisfied if the best results are to be obtained are of the utmost importance. Learning by experience was quite evidently slow and it is to the unusual skill of certain smiths that blades to which magical properties were ascribed were due. The well-known letter of the Hittite king Hattusilis III (1275–1250 BC) probably to the king of Assyria[6] must refer to a quenched steel worked with all the skill and art available anywhere at that time: 'They will produce good iron, but as yet they will not have finished. When they have finished I shall send it to you. Today now I am dispatching an iron dagger-blade to you.' A single blade of sufficient value to be an appropriate present from one important king to another was most certainly not 'iron', and almost as certainly was a carburized and quenched steel with a microstructure not dissimilar from that of (p).

In conclusion two other typical structures may be discussed. Although all ancient steels in the unhardened state contain pearlite usually with more or less ferrite, the distribution of these constituents is by no means constant even when the amount of carbon present is the same. When the steel has been cooled down from a relatively low temperature, say a dullish red heat, the pearlite areas are small and arranged in a purely higgledy-piggledy manner. As the temperature to which the steel was heated gets higher and higher the size of the pearlite regions increases and a triangular pattern analogous to the Widmanstätten structure in meteorites is gradually formed (q). By itself, however, this pattern is no evidence of a meteoric origin and can be induced in any steel by appropriate very high-temperature treatment; it merely shows that the last time the specimen cooled down it was from a very high temperature—a yellow heat in the case of (q)—a rate of cooling that was reasonably slow and without any mechanical treatment such as hammering.

The final structure to be considered (r) shows crystals of ferrite crossed by relatively straight bands all parallel with one another within a given grain but changing direction from one crystal to the next. These Neumann bands are found only in the ferrite and afford evidence of some slight distortion of the material, usually by sudden stresses such as might occur on the edge of an axe. First found in meteorites, they are sometimes believed, erroneously, to provide proof that the material is in fact meteoric in origin. This is not the case since such Neumann bands are by no means uncommon in more or less pure, man-made iron especially if the metal is somewhat brittle due, for instance, to a rather high content of phosphorus.

The treatment given here has necessarily been sketchy and only the simplest examples have been discussed. It is hoped however that it may have provided sufficient evidence of the sort of assistance, often obtainable in no other way, which the microscope can give in the examination of ancient metals, and at the same time of showing how desirable it is when more complicated structures do occur of calling on the aid, usually gladly given, of someone more experienced in the interpretation of metallographic evidence.

ACKNOWLEDGEMENTS

The thanks of the writer are due to the President and Council of the Royal Numismatic Society for permission to use several of the illustrations from his paper published in the *Numismatic Chronicle*, Sixth Series, Vol. XVI, p. 329, 1956, and to Dr E. S. Hedges whilst Director of the Tin Research Institute for Plate XXVh and Plate XXVIi and j.

REFERENCES

1 BURTON-BROWN, T. 1951. *Excavations in Azarbaijan, 1948*, London, 193
2 THOMPSON, F. C. and CHATTERJEE, A. K. 1951. *Nature 168*, 158
3 —— 1958. *Man 58*, 1
4 ZIMMER, G. F. 1916. *J. Iron and Steel Inst. 94*, 306
5 NEWTON FRIEND, J. 1923. Iron in Antiquity; *J. Iron and Steel Inst. Carnegie Schol. Mem. 12*, 219
6 GURNEY, O. R. 1952. *The Hittites*, Harmondsworth, 83

48 The Study of Archaeological Materials by Means of the Scanning Electron Microscope; an Important New Field

DON BROTHWELL

THE 'STEREOSCAN' or scanning electron microscope is a recent product of the Cambridge Instrument Company, based on principles developed by Professor C. W. Oatley of the Cambridge University Engineering Laboratories. The instrument uses a fine probe of electrons to directly examine the microtopography of solid bulk specimens, a fact of special import in that archaeological materials are not usually suitable for other forms of electron miscroscopy. It permits the examination of surfaces whose roughness or other characteristics would render extremely difficult, or impossible, their observation at high magnification in the conventional transmission electron microscope. Also, the specimen detail can be resolved to 200–500 Å with a depth of focus that is at least 300 times greater than that of a light microscope. The direct reading magnification system provides a range of magnification claimed to be × 50 to over × 50,000, but in my own experience it is likely to have most archaeological value within the range × 1,000 to × 30,000.

The machine is attracting considerable interest in various biological fields, including anatomy and palaeontology, and in numerous branches of the physical sciences. With practice, scanning can be fairly rapid, and as the specimen stage allows for objects of up to about 15 mm in diameter and several millimetres thick, a considerable surface area of a specimen (or specimens) can be covered. For high resolution work, the specimen must be covered with a thin layer of silver or gold evaporated *in vacuo*. 'Wet' specimens need careful freeze-drying before plating. There are in fact different views on coating procedure, and some believe that there should be a first layer of carbon.

It would be out of place to discuss the controls of this machine in detail here. The important fact is that the specimen can be viewed on a screen, with quick increase or decrease of magnification. A second screen, synchronized to the viewing screen, is fitted with camera attachment, so that photographic record can be made of any view considered important. Although stereo-photography may prove of little value in the case of archaeological material, it might be mentioned that by means of stereo-pair photographs and using a stereometer,[2] one can produce accurate contour drawings from such illustrations.

It is inevitable that any attempt to discuss a potentially valuable, though as yet unexplored, research field will consist of optimistic talk and little fact. Nevertheless, there would still seem to be a good case for discussing, albeit briefly, the important new dimension of high magnification scanning microscopy. Even in disciplines where the machine has been in use over the past two years or so, little more than ground work has been achieved, and there are as yet no reference atlases of scanning microscopy ot the type now available for the conventional electron microscope. It is thus of primary importance, if the technique is soon to have any value for archaeology, to assess the variety of materials that may advantageously be studied by this machine. To my knowledge, few specimens have been considered, and the Stereoscan microscope at the British Museum (Natural History) is perhaps the first to be used to study the human past. In our case, the specimens are mainly of bio-archaeological interest, but there is no doubt that its applications in the study of earlier cultures are far wider than this.

BONE

Although both human and animal bones from archaeological sites have been mainly considered in terms of their macroscopic appearance, there has been some recent attention to the microscopy of ancient human bone.[4] By scanning microscopy, we can hope to get closer to the processes of calcification (or osteolysis), as shown for instance in the granular nature (Plate XXVIIa) of the external surface of a medieval femur from Winchester ($\times$ 30,000). We might hope to see structures not previously seen or expected, and for example in our preliminary work on palaeopathological bone, we have been able to record spicular structures in an Amerindian specimen not previously seen.

Confirmation of bone tissue where the fragments are very small can also be attempted. In the case of suspected bone from Sutton Hoo, high magnification pictures of the cancellar tissue were possible by this method (K. P. Oakley, personal communication).

DENTAL TISSUES

Because teeth are often found in a well-preserved condition on sites, they are potentially important structures for study by the Stereoscan, and recent work by Alan Boyde[1] has shown the wealth of information on dental tissues which can be obtained by this means. Our own work at the B.M. (N.H.) has been concerned so far with determining how much detail remains in earlier human teeth and in the fossil primates (including the hominids). In Plate XXVIIc is shown a piece of fractured enamel of *Australopithecus*, displaying part of the occlusal surface (oc) and the fractured region (fr) with the columnar enamel prisms. Plate XXVIId gives detail at one broken surface (parallel to the occlusal surface) and shows that the cellular detail remains, so that comparative studies of prism pattern should be possible in earlier hominids and primates.

HAIR

The textile industry has been quick to realize the value of this new instrument,[3] and there is no reason to think that the identification and analysis of ancient fibres will not also benefit in a similar way. Fibres from Sutton Hoo have been studied in this way, and I have scanned hair from a protohistoric site in Africa and from the Niah Cave, Borneo. The major problem is cleaning the fragile material without damaging it, and even then post-mortem changes may considerably obscure details of cuticular morphology.

COPROLITES

The analysis of coprolites is shown to be of importance by its full representation in this volume. As in other biological fields, especially in botany, scanning microscopy may aid identification and comparison. Plate XXVIIb shows plant debris from a Salts Cave coprolite, Kentucky, in which detail is excellent at × 1,500. Obviously some tissues more than others, especially of plants, will be more meaningfully considered by this means.

ARTIFACTS

Some years ago when I became interested in replica methods of recording and analysing attritional marks on ancient teeth, I suggested to colleagues that this was equally applicable to a consideration of certain stone artifacts. Having recently noted possible abrasive marks on fossil teeth in Stereoscan photographs, it seems similarly possible to urge a consideration of tool scratch patterns by this means. The only artifact time has permitted me to view in this way (a Natufian half-moon flint) appears not to have the cereal 'polishing' it was suspected of having (Plate XXVIIe, f). Instead, the grooves appear under high magnification (× 2,100) to be more probably a reflection of the flint microstructure at the fracture surface.

As I have said, it is not easy to review the potentialities of a new field when there is as yet hardly any data available. Even from this short comment, however, it should be clear that the instrument opens up a new world of high magnification micro-topography to the archaeologist.

ACKNOWLEDGEMENTS

I should like to acknowledge the co-operation of my colleague Miss Theya Molleson. Special thanks are due to Dr Alan Boyde, of University College, London, who gave encouragement in the early stages of our work, as well as good advice. The staff of the B.M.(N.H.) Electron Miscrocope Unit, and especially Mr Brian Martin, gave invaluable assistance (and continue to do so). Dr Richard Yarnell kindly supplied the Salts Cave coprolite sample.

REFERENCES
 1 BOYDE, A. 1964. Ph.D. Thesis, University of London
 2 BOYDE, A. 1967. *J. Roy. Microscop. Soc. 86*, 359–70
 3 SIKORSKI, J. 1967. *J. Bradford Textile Soc.* 98–9
 4 JARCHO, S. (*ed.*) 1966. *Human Palaeopathology*, New Haven

SECTION V ARTIFACTS

49 *Artifacts*

L. BIEK

STRICTLY, EVERY PIECE of evidence of early human activity should be categorized an artifact. In precise scientific terms this word denotes an accidental anomaly in a rigidly controlled experiment or observation, but in the present context the concept must be seen against a general background of human purpose impressed on inanimate material. While in this section of the book no special study deals with the modification of natural scenery, methods of construction or even craftsmanship, the implicit connection is clear enough and also extends into other sections of the book.

Thus prehistoric stone axes are linked with forest clearance,[1] certain baked clay objects with Roman reclamation works[2]—all are artifacts, whose effects have a direct bearing on pollen analysis and soil profile development. So have earthworks which in turn by their manner of construction determine the fate of smaller artifacts buried in them.[3] Perhaps the connection between the various aspects of a particular activity is shown most clearly in relation to something like the spectrographic analysis of bronzes. This cannot properly be considered in isolation from the nature of all the raw materials involved—ores, clay, wood or charcoal—or from the furnace characteristics, efficiency of crucibles and moulds, and forging skill.[4,5] In fact a piece of slag may in this sense be more significant than a dagger!

The recognition of a true artifact may be the most important task of all, especially for very early periods. Distinction between a natural and a man-made fire may be crucial,[6,7] and can be difficult; the same applies generally to problems of recognition by the ancients,[8] as for instance over the use of an iron ore as a building stone.[9] And the most obvious example is the establishment of true man himself as defined by his ability to make artifacts at all.[10]

Even when considered in this special sense, as small finds, the material must still be related first of all to its environment during burial. Any 'exposure' of this kind produces in time an equilibrium between artifact and ambient medium which is disturbed on excavation,[18] and which reflects a general tendency to return to raw materials or basic structure. The further a 'mineral' material has been taken from its state of rest, the greater the forces working for its return.[30] Materials of organic origin normally suffer total microbiological disorganization (p. 539). Whatever the equilibrium, it often constitutes evidence that may be easily and rapidly lost. The fragility of the principal object quite apart, if the object is simply considered for itself, certain details of structure which 'do not belong', or even altered features, may be overlooked and destroyed. Often an astonishing amount of associated fine detail is recoverable (Plate XXXI). [22,23,31]

Wood and other organic material from waterlogged deposits, as well as significant features contained in the attached soil, quickly suffer physical and chemical changes that alter their shape and nature unless they are protected from the atmosphere. As an overwhelming proportion of this material comes from such deposits, at least in temperate climates, these considerations are of great importance, especially as they also involve clear evidence of the fate of the material during and even before burial.[11,12] In another sense, an appreciation of the ambient soil may be crucial in attempts to date, for example, a glass linen smoother from its extremely fragile weathering skin,[34] or a pottery sherd from its inherent thermoluminescence (see p. 106 above).

Seen in isolation, artifacts present a variety of problems for scientific investigation. Where the material remains essentially unaltered by working—as do stone, wood and bone—its identification is best considered along with the natural environment and by the same specialists. But usually some modification of the raw material occurs and the preparation, in the widest sense, of the substance from which the artifact is made introduces further stages of appraisal. As the complexity of processing increases so separate specialties are multiplied; at the same time, the separate studies of methods by which any one material was prepared, and worked, need all the more to be considered together, in relation to one another.

Even in the simplest cases, such as the selection or crude extraction of fibres and their fabrication into textiles, it is not difficult to consider the two aspects separately. The use of parchment little affects the issue, but leatherworking is clearly distinct from manufacture.[13] In the case of pottery—although still involving a relatively simple transformation by heat of a material that remains basically itself—there are a number of different aspects ranging from the geological through the technicalities of the wheel to the chemical effects of firing. Similarly the manufacture, application and setting properties of plasters and mortars require separate but integrated consideration.[14]

The production of totally new and 'unnatural' materials provides the climax in this development. From the selection of raw materials to the final anneal, the making of a glass vessel involves several highly specialized activities which all have to be taken into account when devising a programme for investigation. This applies even more in the case of metals where the extraction processes involve additional complexities, and fabrication virtually provides another degree of freedom.

Certain features emerge from a consideration of the problem as a whole. Most specialist examinations have various tools and approaches in common. Thus the microscope is universal, and indeed symbolic, as a first step. It suggests the number of materials involved and defines the limits of the problem. This is clearly essential from the start. Any one item, even when not a composite assembly, may require several specialists, and there will be an optimum order in which they should see it. This order will depend on whether the specific value of the artifact is intrinsic or relative, largely typological or scientific, or lies in its use as dating evidence. But many of these factors will remain obscure until after microscopic examination.

This may be followed by one or more of the many non-destructive tests now available,[15] before proper specialist investigation begins. Among these X-radiography has proved to have a wide range of usefulness,[16] showing up details of internal structures in a variety of materials (Plates XXVIII–XXX), but particularly marked in the case of 'iron objects' of uncertain shape and doubtful stability.[16,17] There is here a vital distinction between *revelation* of significant evidence and its (attempted) *exposure* by some form of 'cleaning'. It is theoretically impossible to return to the original surface by any cleaning method. Radiography and similar techniques can almost always provide the required information, and more simply and quickly, without removing any evidence which might come to be regarded as valuable in the future. Any cleaning must always be to some extent both destructive and subjective. This clearly indicates how intimately examination is related to conservation in almost all cases. While the latter introduces fresh aspects[18] it is entirely dependent on the former. On the other hand, conservation in the widest sense must be a primary factor in decisions from the start wherever there is any risk of losing evidence by exposure.

Ultimately the material of such objects may be completely altered (p. 118). Conservation by exposure then becomes impossible if there has been extensive interpenetration of artifact and environment. Corrosion products can grow right out of an iron object to mineralize, and even encase,[26] associated wood—leaving only a frail, exhausted shadow at the core of the original artifact whose final surface may be completely distorted.[24,25] Sometimes plausible, but totally misleading, outlines or shapes are produced by corrosion[26] or pseudo-stalactitic growths.[25] (Plate XXIXa, b).

In the limit, a featureless lump with a regular outline may contain a void, in the shape of an object which has completely corroded out, its altered material forming the surrounding shell. On the inside surface of this shell there is a faithful negative fossil impression of the original surface of the object. Revelation of shape by X-rays is very good for iron (Plate XXVIII), [27,28] but information about lumps of altered silver[27] can only be recovered by some such mechanical 'shelling' and casting as has been used for iron.[29]

Results of specialist investigations on artifacts are most useful in separate reports, by the specialists, rather than as extracts quoted in the main text. Even when it must be restricted to a short note, the specialist contribution should be clearly recognizable and unedited, otherwise its value may be considerably reduced, to the detriment of future work. When no scientific examination is possible, at least a brief specialist description should be sought. Specialist reports on artifacts have been systematically abstracted since 1934.[19-21]

At the same time, all scientific evidence from artifacts, and indeed from all other aspects, of any one site greatly benefits by co-ordination at a scientific level. It is now widely accepted that, to ensure its full recognition, all material should be submitted to specialist examination. But the significance of any one artifact may not be clear even to the specialist until he knows about all the others. Precise distinctions—as for instance between various 'slags', over-fired pottery and certain forms of lava, which bear a family resemblance to each other—may become vital and require further work. However, the principal advantage of such co-ordination lies in its provision of an over-all scientific picture which to everyone concerned is of far greater value than the algebraic sum of the individual features.

REFERENCES

1 IVERSEN, J. 1954. *Arch. Newsletter*, May, 8; *Ill. Lond. News*, 1st May, 722; and see p. 169 above
2 RIEHM, K. 1961. *Antiquity 35*, 181–91
3 JEWELL, P. A. 1958. *Adv. Sci. 14*, 165–72. See also [31] p. 123 above
4 COGHLAN, H. H. 1956. *Notes on the Prehistoric Metallurgy of Copper and Bronze in the Old World*, Oxford; TYLECOTE, R. F. 1962. *Metallurgy in Archaeology*, London
5 —— 1960. *Sibrium 5*, 145–52
6 OAKLEY, K. P. 1955a. *Proc. Third Pan-African Congr. on Prehistory*, London, 385–6
7 —— 1955b. *Proc. Prehist. Soc. 21*, 36–48
8 CHILDE, V. G. 1956. *Piecing Together the Past*, London, 162–3
9 FOX, LADY (A.) 1957. *Trans. Devon Assn. Adv. Sci. Lit. Art, 89*, 33 and 73–5
10 OAKLEY, K. P. 1949. *Man the Toolmaker*, London
11 BIEK, L. 1959. In RICHARDSON, K. M. *Arch. J. 116*, 107–9
12 —— 196-. In RAHTZ, P. A. *Chew Valley Lake*, London (forthcoming)
13 WATERER, J. W. 1956. In SINGER, C. (ed.), *History of Technology*, London, II, 147–90
14 DAVEY, N. 1961. *A History of Building Materials*, London
15 HALL, E. T. 1959. *Archaeometry 2*, 43–52; SCHALL, W. E. 1968. *Non-Destructive Testing*, Brighton; Moss, A. A. 1954. *Museum Techniques: The Application of X-Rays, Gamma-Rays, U. V. and I. R. Rays to the Study of Antiquities*, London: STANFORD, E. G. et al. 1968. *Progress in Applied Materials Research*, 8, London. See especially 205–37: MULLINS, L. *The Evolution of Non-destructive Testing*. Also previous volumes (*1–3* appeared as *Progress in Non-destructive Testing*); BRITISH NATIONAL COMMITTEE FOR NON-DESTRUCTIVE TESTING, 1967, Ottawa. *Proc. Fifth Internat. Confce, on Non-destructive Testing*. Also previous Conference Reports; BARTON, J. P. 1965. Radiology Using Neutrons, *Studies in Conservation 10*, 135–41; THOMSON, G. (ed.) 1963. *Recent Advances in Conservation*, London
16 BIEK, L. 1963. *Archaeology and the Microscope*, London, 128ff
17 LOOSE, L.; KOZLOWSKI, R. 1960. *Studs. Conserv. 5*, 85–8; 89–101
18 PLENDERLEITH, H. J. 1956. *The Conservation of Antiquities and Works of Art*, Oxford
19 STOUT, L. and GETTENS, R. J. (ed.) 1932–42. *Technical Studies in the Field of the Fine Arts*, Harvard
20 GETTENS, R. J. and USILTON, B. M. (ed.) 1955. *Abstracts of Technical Studies in Art and Archaeology, 1943–1952*, Washington
21 International Institute for Conservation of Historic and Artistic Works. From 1955. *Abstracts of the Technical Literature on Archaeology and the Fine Arts*. From 1966, b; *Art and Archaeology Technical Abstracts*. Also *Ausgrabungen und Funde 11*, 1966, also previous issues
22 RYDER, M. L. et al. 1964. *Proc. Prehist. Soc. 30*, 193–8; also see 1966, *Proc. Soc. Antiq., Scot. 97*, 175–6
23 CROWFOOT, E. et al. 1961. In HURST, J. G. *Med. Arch. V*, 292–3
24 BIEK, L. 1965. In ADDYMAN, P. V. and BIDDLE, M. *Proc. Camb. Ant. Soc. LVIII*, 126. N.B. *erratum*: Para. 4, penultimate line, first word—for 'wood' read 'iron'
25 —— 196-. In STEAD, I. M. *Excavation of a Roman Well at Rudston, Yorks., 1967* (forthcoming)
26 —— 196-. In SAUNDERS, A. D. and ADDYMAN, P. V. *Lydford* (forthcoming)
27 —— 1963. In FROST, H. *'Barbarossa' Wreck* (forthcoming); also see *Under the Mediterranean*, 263 and Pl. 2
28 —— 1969. In HOGG, A. H. A. *Arch. J. CXXV*, 184
29 KATZEV, M. L. and VAN DOORNINCK, F. H. JR. 1966. *Studies in Conservation 11*, 133–41
30 E.g. VERNON, W. H. J. 1949. *J. Roy. Soc. Arts 97*, 578–610
31 SAUTER, F. and ROSSMANITH, K. 1965. *Archaeologia Austriaca, XXXVII*, 1–6
32 HOPF, M. 1965. *Jahrb. Röm.-Germ. Zentralmus, Mainz. 10* (1963), 68–75
33 EGGINS, H. O. W. (ed.) 1969. *International Biodeterioration Bulletin 5*; and previous issues
34 NEWTON, R. G. 1963. In HOLDEN, E. W. *Sussex Archaeol. Coll., CI*, 164; ibid., 1966. *Glass Techn. 7*, 22–5; ibid., 1969. *Glass Techn. 10*, 40–2
35 BIEK, L. 196-. In RAHTZ, P. A. *Excavation at Sewerby Park, Yorks.*, 1959 (forthcoming)

50 Petrological Examination

F. W. SHOTTON

ON PAGE 778 OF WILLIAM DUGDALE's *Antiquities of Warwickshire*, published in 1656, there is an excellent engraving of a small stone axe, shaped by chipping except for ground surfaces meeting at the cutting edge. It is stated to be in the possession of Sir Elias Ashmole, though it is apparently not now in the Ashmolean Museum. The illustration accompanies a reference to an earthwork at Oldbury, near Nuneaton, and Dugdale writes: 'On the North part of this Fort, have been found, by plowing, divers Flint stones, about four inches and a half in length, curiously wrought by grinding, or some such way, into the form here exprest: the one end shaped much like the edge of a Pole-Axe, which makes me conjecture that, considering there is no flint in all this part of the Countrie, nor within more than xl. miles from hence, they being at first so made by the native Britans, and put into a hole, boared through the side of a staff, were made use of for weapons, inasmuch as they had not then attained to the knowledge of working iron or brass to such uses.'

We have here, I think, not only the earliest recognition in Britain of a prehistoric stone implement but also the first use of petrology for deducing that the object had been imported from some considerable distance. From the sapient way Dugdale writes, one feels that he was able to recognize flint and that he knew it occurred in the Chalk of eastern England. Geological knowledge was so embryonic in his time that we cannot object that his 'more than forty miles' is actually not less than seventy-five.

Nevertheless we have to wait until this century before we find the petrological examination of stone objects becoming an important aid to archaeological deduction. One of the more famous pioneering examples was the demonstration by Dr H. H. Thomas that the circle of small stones (the 'blue stones') at Stonehenge came from Carn Meini in the Prescelly Mountains of Carmarthenshire.[10] Archaeologists since then have exercised their minds on the dual problems of what particular significance this stone had (we know it was also used for axe-making) and how the boulders were transported a distance which is 140 miles as the crow flies but certainly far longer as Early-Bronze Age man went.

It is only within the last twenty years that the petrological examination of small objects has been systematically pursued, prompted particularly by the Council for British Archaeology's investigation of stone axes. Under this scheme, a comprehensive account has been given for the counties of Cornwall, Devon, Somerset, Gloucester, Wiltshire, Dorset and Hampshire,[4,8,9] and interim accounts for Hereford, Shropshire, Worcester, Warwick and South Staffordshire [6,7] but there is also a steadily-accumulating store of knowledge about the rest of Britain which is not yet published. Slowly the detail is being filled in to the complex picture of axe-making factories and the dissemination of their products by trade during the Neolithic and Bronze Age. In the tools of earlier times, exact recognition of the nature of the rock is less rewarding, for in general

Palaeolithic man used local materials—flint where he could get it, though often from river or glacial gravels, but in default of this, chert from the Carboniferous Limestone or quartzite pebbles from the Bunter or glacial gravels.

It should not be thought that petrological examination is important only in the case of axes. It is useful for all tools, particularly for such objects as hones which were often made from highly-prized stone carried long distances. Querns, millstones, building stone and roofing slate are examples of other objects where understanding is enhanced if an exact knowledge of the rock is obtained. (See particularly[13].)

The preparation of a microscope slide of a rock—a 'thin section'—follows practice which is standard in all departments of geology. Initially a thin slice is removed from the object by two parallel cuts of a diamond wheel. Inevitably this leaves a gap in the specimen which may be 4 mm wide and 15-20 mm deep, but this is a price which has to be paid if a thin section is to be made. The injury can be filled with plaster and if painted skilfully it may be difficult to detect that anything has been removed. Indeed, the writer has on more than one occasion received from museum curators axes for sectioning which had already been so treated.

The cut-out rock fragment is smoothed on one side which is then attached to a glass slide by a transparent cement such as Canada Balsam or 'Lakeside'. The rock is now rubbed away with suitable abrasives until it is only 0·03 mm thick, when a cover glass is cemented upon it. Thus a thin section is prepared but the reader will appreciate that this bald account conceals a considerable amount of technical skill and experience on the part of the preparator. At this thickness the majority of the minerals found in rocks are transparent, some colourless, some with typical colours, and only a few still remain opaque. Moreover, as the section can be looked at in ordinary, plane-polarized and cross-polarized light and the investigator can use various accessories of the petrological microscope, mineral identification can nearly always be made with precision. Not only, then, can a rock be placed into its fundamental class of igneous, sedimentary, meta-morphic or pyroclastic (and often this is impossible on simple examination by eye), but the further identification of the minerals present, their shape and size, relative proportions and textural relations to each other, gives to a rock a uniqueness which can be described and recognized when it is met with again in another specimen. Reference to the illustration of a thin section (Plate XXXII) will show how many distinctive features it has, even when the reproduction takes no account of colour.

THE PETROLOGICAL EXAMINATION OF STONE AXES

The nation-wide survey of stone axes has not, so far, attempted to differentiate those made of flint. A thin section of this rock is quite distinctive, but we do not need such a section to tell us that the material is flint. On the other hand, no one has yet found micro-characteristics which will enable us to separate the flints of Yorkshire from those of Lincolnshire, Suffolk, Kent, Sussex or Antrim, still less to be more precise in localization, so that thin section work in this direction is unrewarding.

The case of the non-flint axes and hammers (often loosely spoken of as 'stone' axes) is quite different. Up to the present, about 21 petrological categories or 'Groups' have been defined, with some further subdivided. Not all these groups are of equal significance, for a few have been based on only two or three similar specimens in a restricted region and such a group may not be recognized further afield as work extends over the country. Most of the groups, however, include many examples and their number steadily increases as the area of investigation widens.

THE PRODUCTS OF KNOWN AXE-FACTORIES

Before the idea of petrological examination had really started, Hazzledine Warren had discovered the litter of flakes and rough-out cores at Graig Lwyd and recognized that it marked a Neolithic factory site. Since then other working sites have been located elsewhere. To the rocks used at these factories, group numbers have been allocated, as follows:

VI. Great Langdale, Westmorland.
VII. Graig Lwyd, near Penmaenmawr, Caernarvonshire.
IX. Tievebulliagh and Rathlin Island, Antrim.
XXI. Mynydd Rhiw, Lleyn, Caernarvonshire.

There are now also known to be a number of working sites around Scafell in various Ordovician ashes not unlike but still not the same as Group VI.

The *Langdale* rock is a fine-banded, epidotized andesitic ash—the result of a shower of volcanic dust into the Ordovician sea. In the writer's opinion it produces the finest of all axes and it was widely disseminated by trade throughout the land. So highly prized was the rock that numerous working places were set up on the screes below the outcrop of the stratum, itself nearly two thousand feet above sea level.[1]

The *Graig Lwyd* factory is also now known to be a series of working sites. The rock in this case is igneous—to give it its technical name, an epidotized micro-granodiorite—which congealed within the neck of an old volcano.

Mynydd Rhiw has only recently been discovered[2] and appears not to have been as extensive as the two mentioned previously. Like Group VI, the rock is a compact Ordovician volcanic ash but its details are very different from Langdale and there is no possibility of confusion.

The factory sites in Antrim perhaps illustrate better than any others how carefully prehistoric man chose the material for his tools. The rock at *Tievebulliagh* is a dark grey, fine-textured, very hard stone of unmistakable appearance in thin section (Plate XXXIIc), breaking rather like flint and restricted to a small outcrop—as well it might be in view of the special way in which it arose. Everyone knows the Tertiary basalt flows of Northern Ireland, typified by the Giant's Causeway, but fewer are aware that the lavas flowed out when the region enjoyed a moist tropical climate, so that the tops of individual flows are often weathered into bright red laterite soil. These red surfaces of varying thickness can be seen separating the flows. Now at Tievebulliagh a volcanic neck pierces a succession of these lava flows, the neck being also filled with a plug of basalt. The heat of this, when molten, could do nothing to the unweathered lava flows, but it baked the red soils, in particular one thicker than the rest, and for a short distance around itself the neck produced this black flint-like rock which was so attractive to prehistoric man for the purpose of axe-making. In more recent years another factory has been discovered at *Rathlin Island* and its products are indistinguishable from Tievebulliagh because exactly the same geological situation has been chosen and the end-product is therefore similar. Axes from these factories abound in Ireland but are also found, though in much reduced numbers, across the Irish Sea.[3]

PETROLOGICAL GROUPS OF UNDISCOVERED FACTORIES

There are bound to be numbers of implements made from the same rock and to which, therefore, a Petrological Group number can be given, even though no factory site is known. It is obvious also that, working from geological advice, it might be possible to pin-point the place from which the rock came and then to discover the working site. So far it has to be admitted that no success of this kind has yet been achieved but there is no doubt that it ultimately will be.

Group I is a most distinctive rock which in the past would have been simply called 'greenstone', but now 'uralitized gabbro'. It is the type of rock which we would expect in Cornwall and although examples of this axe have been found almost all over England, there is such an overwhelming preponderance of finds near Penzance that there can be no doubt of the approximate source. Because an exact match to the rock could not be found at any known outcrop, Keiller, Piggot and Wallis[4] suggested that the factory site was low-lying and had been drowned by the post-Neolithic rise of sea level. In these days of exploration of the sea-floor by skin divers, there is still a prospect of the site being found.

Group VIII is a fine rhyolitic ash much used for axes, particularly for many found in South Wales, but there is a strong suspicion that several closely similar rocks have been included in this group and the products of more than one factory, perhaps widely separated, may have been confused.

Group XII is the best example of a most distinctive rock—picrite—which has been matched exactly with a source.[7] It occurs in Hyssington parish in Montgomeryshire. How distinctive the rock is in its minerals and texture and how exactly it matches the parent source is apparent in Plate XXXIIa, b. We now know that there are two small outcrops of picrite separated by about a mile and indistinguishable from each other. At either or both the rock could have been worked by Bronze Age man, but from it he made only perforated axe-hammers by a process of pecking and grinding and to find the factory waste will be far more difficult than in such cases as Langdale or Graig Lwyd where thousands of flakes litter the site. It is significant that two implements with their perforations not yet finished have been found in the same parish as the alleged parent source.

Group XIII is 'preselite'—the well-known spotted dolerite from the Prescelly Hills which was used in the Stonehenge ring of smaller stones and also for a modest number of axes and axe-hammers. Although the parent outcrop is quite restricted, the site of the factory is still unknown.

Group XIV is a small one—only about fourteen axe-hammers have yet been put into this group—but the rock is so distinctive that we can be certain that a small factory worked a sill of camptonite in the Cambrian rocks of Griff, near Nuneaton.[6]

Group XV is a form of sandstone used extensively, mainly for axe-hammers and perforated adzes, and this is a good example of a rock which, though distinctive, occurs over such a large outcrop that we can do no more than suggest a source, or sources, in the southern part of the Lake District.[6]

Group XVIII is widespread, a distinctive quartz-dolerite which can be matched with some dykes in Scotland and north England but even more obviously with the Great Whin Sill which outcrops along more than a hundred miles of massive crags in Northumberland and Westmorland, in Teesdale and the Farne Islands. These great scars must have been a constant invitation to tool-making man but he had so much to choose from that his factory sites will be difficult to find.

Group XX is a coarse epidotized volcanic ash which is being recognized in increasing numbers now that work is being done in the north Midlands. Charnwood Forest is the probable parent source.[6]

OTHER USES FOR MICROSCOPICAL PETROLOGY

Hones have been in common use for sharpening steel since Roman times. June E. Morey and K. C. Dunham[5] have shown that amongst a collection of medieval whetstones in Yorkshire half are made from one type of rock, a fine-grained quartz-mica granulite, which they suggest came from Aberdeenshire. This indicates how carefully raw material was selected and the extent to which it was traded.

Querns and *millstones* need rocks of special characteristics—they must be made of hard minerals and yet they must have a limited proportion of softer grains or crystals which wear away to maintain a rough pitted surface on the stone. The grits of the Carboniferous formation appropriately enough known as the Millstone Grit, which occurs dominantly in Yorkshire, Lancashire, north Staffordshire and Derbyshire, is pre-eminently suitable in this country. The Romans certainly knew this, for petrologists constantly recognize this rock at sites far removed from the outcrops.

It is very obvious that the advice of the geologist will often be sought about the materials used in construction—*building stone, slates* and *natural tiles, tesserae, road metals* and so on. At times it is worthwhile making a thin section to look for special features of diagnostic significance, but in many cases it is the larger-scale features of bedding, grain size, colour and identification of contained fossils which are of more use.

Petrological examination need not be restricted to natural raw materials. Although comparatively little work has been done on *ceramics*, thin sections of pottery, bricks or tiles will reveal the size and nature of the gritty component of the clay and may enable conclusions to be drawn about the origin of this,[14] whilst the mineralogy may give an indication of the temperature of kilning. The petrology of *slags*, too, is a highly specialized study, but exact identification of the crystalline part of these can indicate what product was being produced and perhaps what type of ore was being smelted.

Again, it is the trained mineralogist who will identify the minerals used in jewellery and suggest from where they might have come. Here he may well encounter extra-

British imports. Particularly is this the case with amber which, in quantity, will always suggest physical links with the Baltic countries.

There are, of course, other cases of importation across the sea, particularly in and after the Roman occupation. The Romans brought in their most-prized ornamental stones, such as the imperial purple porphyry from Egypt, and they rather strangely had a predilection for slabs of basalt from the region of Niedermendig in the Eifel. In pre-Roman times, examples of sea commerce are less numerous, though the occurrence of northern Irish (Group IX) axes in England and Scotland has been noted. A considerable number of jadeite axes (more than 70) have been recorded from England, Scotland and Ireland[11,12] and although no certain source of this rock has been located, it is almost certainly extra-British and European. The most unexpected case concerns a few axes rich in corundum (emery) which have been matched in Crete. Perhaps we are more prepared for such a conclusion after the evidence of the carved daggers at Stonehenge showing Minoan influence.

Finally it must be emphasized that the petrologist is engaged in a fascinating sort of detective work which can be used equally well to detect fraud (or perhaps one should say, to prevent misrepresentation, since archaeological fraud is seldom deliberate). Amongst the axes which are sent in from all sorts of collections or circumstances of finding, a small proportion look 'wrong'—their typology is non-British, or they are of exotic-looking stone. Petrological examination can sometimes indicate that the rock comes from a known distant source, and very often it can at least suggest that the raw material is most unlikely to be British. Amongst such dubious examples are specimens from museums where curating has been poor and labels which have become detached have been wrongly stuck on again, or private collections where the owner relies on his memory. When such specimens are dug up, it is reassuring to find how often they are in the garden of a house once occupied by the local doctor or parson who was an enthusiastic collector, but whose surviving relatives had little respect for his 'old junk'.

Nevertheless, the writer has met a few cases where the circumstances of discovery have been given in great detail, though usually at second-hand and certainly quite erroneously. One of these concerned a beautiful flint dagger or spear-head. The sister of the finder recalled the exact spot on the farm in Warwickshire where it had been ploughed up, yet it was made of an unusual finely-banded coloured flint which exactly matched the artifacts of the Ohio Indians and nothing else. One can cite also a block of sandstone carrying a Roman inscription, originally in a Birmingham garden, where the possibility of its being of local origin had to be balanced against the chance of its being an imported collector's piece. Petrological examination came down clearly on the side of the second possibility, for the thin section revealed fossil foraminifera which were identified as probably Miocene in age. The sandstone could not have been British, but it could easily have been Mediterranean. Last of all may be mentioned part of a 'stone' statue, typically Roman and found near to a known Roman site—but it showed the unmistakable texture and mineralogy of concrete and was undoubtedly a Victorian copy.

REFERENCES

1 BUNCH, B. AND FELL, C. 1949. *Proc. Prehist. Soc. 15*, 1
2 HOULDER, C. H. 1960. *Trans. Caern. Hist. Soc. 21*, 1-5
3 JOPE, E. M. 1953. *Ulster J. Arch. 15*, 31
4 KEILLER, A., PIGGOT, S. and WALLIS, F. S. 1941. *Proc. Prehist. Soc. 7*, 50
5 MOREY, J. E. and DUNHAM, K. C. 1953. *Proc. Yorks. Geo. Soc. 29*, 141
6 SHOTTON, F. W. 1959. *Proc. Prehist. Soc. 25*, 135
7 —— CHITTY, L. F. and SEABY, W. A. 1951. *Ibid. 17*, 159
8 STONE, J. F. S. and WALLIS, F. S. 1947. *Ibid. 13*, 47
9 —— —— 1951. *Ibid. 17*, 99
10 THOMAS, H. H. 1923. *Ant. J. 3*, 239
11 SMITH, W. C. 1963. *Proc. Prehist. Soc. 29*, 133
12 —— 1965. *Ibid. 31*, 25
13 SHOTTON, F. W. 1968. *Proc. Geol. Assoc. 79*, 477
14 PEACOCK, D. P. S. 1968. *Proc. Prehist. Soc. 34*, 414

51 Obsidian Analysis and the Obsidian Trade

J. R. CANN, J. E. DIXON and COLIN RENFREW

OBSIDIAN IS A VOLCANIC GLASS whose mechanical properties, which resemble those of flint, make it suitable for the manufacture of tools. There are relatively few sources of the material. The purpose of obsidian analysis is to establish characteristics of each source which will serve to distinguish it from other sources. Artifacts found in archaeological sites can then be examined with the same criteria, and the source of the material identified. This procedure, which furnishes valuable information for early prehistoric trade, is that of characterization. The method of trace element analysis has provided the most promising approach to the problems of obsidian.

CHARACTERIZATION

'Dr Halley was at Stonehenge in the year 1720 and brought a piece of it to the Royal Society. I examined it with a microscope. 'Tis a composition of crystals of red, green and white colours, cemented together by nature's art, with opake granules of flint of stoney matter. The Doctor observed from the general wear of the stones that the work must be of an extraordinary antiquity, and for ought he knew, 2 or 3,000 years old.' This passage by Stukeley,[1] written in 1740, which goes on to discuss the source of the Stonehenge stones on the basis of Halley's microscopic examination, records the first scientific characterization study brought to the aid of archaeology. It foreshadows notably the work of Thomas[2] which established the identity of the spotted dolerite of the Stonehenge blue stones with that found in the Prescelly Mountains of South Wales. Naturally Halley did not have the geological evidence at his disposal to make such an attribution, but his attempt is an instructive one, as equally his adventurous guess towards the Antiquity of Man.

Petrographic methods were not adopted again in archaeological investigations until the end of the nineteenth century, when Lepsius[3] attempted to identify Greek marbles in thin section, and Fouqué and Washington[4] rather ingeniously examined thin sections of pottery from the island of Santorin in order to confirm its local origin. By the same means Ordoñez was studying obsidian in Mexico as early as 1892.[5] The method has been widely and successfully used since then, notably for the study of the British Neolithic axe trade. Of recent years other analytical methods have been used for characterization, notably optical spectroscopy and neutron activation.

The basic problem in all these cases is one of identifying the source of material found in excavations by comparing its properties with those of material known to come from a particular place. The procedure of distinguishing the sources from one another may be termed characterization. At least three factors bear on the solution of this problem: the degree to which the sources may be uniquely characterized by measurements of one or more parameters, the number of sources in a given region, and the area over which practicable identification of material with source is to be attempted, and the extent to which material may have come from sources other than the nearest.

The first factor is in many ways the most important. On the one hand a totally successful world-wide characterization of all sources, would eliminate the significance of the other factors. At the other extreme, in the case of flint, the determinable parameters may either be so constant over the whole of the source region (as is the case with composition and refractive index), that no individual sources may be distinguished, or vary so rapidly and randomly (as with colour and translucency) that the density of distinguishable sources rise to perhaps several per square foot. In such a case the third factor becomes all-important, and the area of practicable identification will clearly be useless for archaeological purposes.

Similar difficulties bedevil the tracing of the pure white marbles used abundantly in ancient Greece. Most of the measurable variations between widely separated samples may be exhibited in the material from one single quarry.

In cases where a useful but limited distinction between the source is practicable, the second and third factors become very important. If the sources are closely spaced and difficult to characterize, the area over which useful results may be obtained will be severely limited. Clearly at places distant from the source region the attribution to a specific source may then prove impossibly difficult. But within the region itself some information of value may be gained. Washington's work on Santorin, for example, confirmed that much of the pottery found there incorporated a filler of volcanic origin, which conveniently limited the number of possible sources for it within the region in question. It was reasonably concluded that the pottery was made on Santorin itself. If, on the other hand, the problem had concerned the possibility of imports from the Aegean into a more distant area, such as Libya perhaps, the observation would have been of little value.

The third factor is an important one also, and its judicious consideration can often enhance the value of the enquiry. In modern times the trade in manufactured goods reaches world-wide proportions, but to the prehistoric archaeologist, some limitations will be acceptable. For example, in most cases an archaeologist working in the Old World will be content to rule out New World imports, and since prehistoric man was surely too shrewd to bring 'coals to Newcastle', or amber to the Baltic, imports from a very distant source can often be disregarded in cases where adequate sources were available much nearer at hand.

It has become evident in the study of the distribution of obsidian artifacts in the Mediterranean region that, from the very earliest times, factors other than simple linear distance have indeed affected the utilization of sources. Not only natural barriers but aesthetic considerations, and the adherence to established patterns of trade seem to have played a role. Indeed at sites where a long record of habitation can be established, the complex and changing picture of source utilization that may be built up for a particular material can provide a great amount of valuable indirect evidence for social conditions in the region as a whole. In the case of so evidently mobile a material as obsidian, therefore, the third factor listed must be considered with great caution.

The distribution of sources and the relative ease with which they may be character-ized are in fact, particularly favourable in the case of obsidian. The first two factors thus work in its favour, and make obsidian well suited to the kind of characterization study described in the following sections.

OBSIDIAN

Obsidian is a natural glass formed by the cooling of certain types of lava which have a content of silica greater than 65%. Such lavas are very viscous, and crystallization is normally inhibited, but several factors combine to make the formation of obsidian suitable for tool-making an unusual occurrence. First these lavas also contain a high content of water and other volatiles and usually erupt explosively to form fragments of pumice. In order to produce a massive glass the cooling must be slow enough to allow the escape of the volatiles; but if the lava cools too slowly it may crystallize partly or completely and thus lose its glassy nature. Crystallization may also begin if the lava is held for some time in magma chambers beneath the volcano, with the formation of numerous large crystals of quartz and felspar, which are found set in a glassy base after the lava has been erupted. These cause the resultant rock to fracture irregularly. Finally the action of ground water, and particularly the hot water associated with eruptive centres hydrates the obsidian. While this process provides the basis for obsidian dating,[6] the conchoidal fracture is in consequence lost and eventually the obsidian crystallizes completely. Thus good obsidian is only found near geologically recent volcanoes.

Geologists, however, include in the term obsidian rocks which contain large quan-tities of phenocrysts or many vesicles (gas holes), or when they have been so affected by hydration that they splinter rather than fracture conchoidally. Geological reports of obsidian associated with a particular volcano must therefore be treated with caution by the archaeologist until it can be established that the obsidian fulfils the archaeological requirements enumerated.

Properties

Obsidian can be distinguished from other materials by its glassy lustre (although this is not always present) and by its fine conchoidal fracture. Some varieties of chert or flint may be confused with obsidian, but their surfaces are normally duller, their refrac-tive indices lower (1·40 to 1·45 as opposed to 1·49 to 1·52 for obsidian) and, in the final result, they burn badly in the spectrograph because of their high water content, and have a low trace element content.

Geologists have long divided obsidians into three broad types: alkaline, calc-alkaline and peralkaline. These types can be recognized by their chemistry and by the petro-graphy of the rocks associated with them in the same volcanic region.

The variation in the physical properties of obsidian reflects this broad division in a general way.

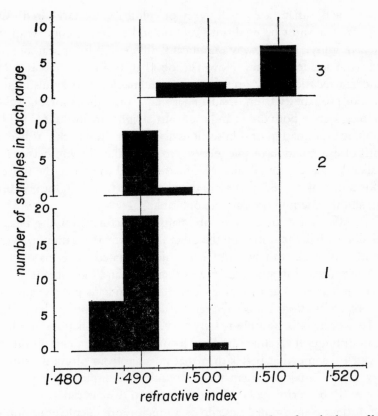

Fig. 104 Histogram showing the range of refractive index of 52 obsidians of known trace element content and geological affinity. 1 and 2 Alkaline and calc-alkaline obsidians. 2 13 specimens from Lipari. 3 Peralkaline obsidians.

Figure 104 is a histogram of the refractive indices of the first fifty-two obsidians on which we have made trace element determinations. In 1 and 2 are plotted alkaline and calc-alkaline obsidians together, as determined by trace element content and geological setting, 2 representing the thirteen specimens of Lipari obsidian that were measured. The obsidians represented in 3 are peralkaline.

It can be seen from this that obsidians with refractive index lower than 1·495 are probably alkaline or calc-alkaline (Groups 1, 2, 3, 4a of our final classification) while those with refractive indices greater than 1·505 are very probably peralkaline (Groups 4b, 4c, 4d, 5, 6). Those with intermediate refractive indices are indeterminate. Density is less reliable a guide as the presence of even a small quantity of vesicles can change the overall density appreciably, but in general peralkaline obsidians have a higher density than alkaline and calc-alkaline ones.

The appearance of obsidian is, in fact, a more reliable guide than either density or refractive index in making this division. It transpires that almost all peralkaline obsidians are green, greenish or sometimes brown in transmitted light whereas alkaline

and calc-alkaline obsidians are usually grey or colourless (or rarely red). Other indications of appearance must be used with caution and in conjunction with the results of
more detailed study. In this way significant differences in appearance may be distinguished from accidental ones. However, obsidian from the sources in Melos proves
to have a characteristic pearly grey lustre which enables it to be distinguished with a
high degree of probability from obsidian deriving from other sources.[7] Obsidians from
several sources, seen in both direct and transmitted light, are illustrated in Plate XXXIII.

Petrographic examination of thin sections also has its drawbacks. While it is possible,
on the basis of examination of phenocrysts, to make the division between the alkaline
and calc-alkaline and the peralkaline obsidians referred to above, the more suitable the
obsidian for tool-making, the fewer are the phenocrysts, until in the best obsidians they
are absent, and the method becomes inapplicable.

It is thus difficult to characterize obsidians satisfactorily on the basis of physical
properties alone: their chemistry, on the other hand, provides a more powerful method.
The chemistry of rocks can be most conveniently stated in terms of the content of
major elements (present in amounts greater than 1%) and the content of trace elements
(less than 1%). The content of major elements in obsidians covers only a small range
because of the restriction, stated above, on the composition of lavas that can form
obsidian. However, it is possible readily to recognize peralkaline obsidians, and, less
certainly, to distinguish alkaline obsidians from calc-alkaline ones, on this basis. Thus a
division which is somewhat better than that possible from physical properties may be
made. Nevertheless, major element analysis requires a considerable expenditure of time,
and cannot easily be performed on less than 2 grams of material.

The use of trace element analyses allows a much more detailed division to be made.
In addition the analyses may be performed on only 60 milligrams of sample. The
obsidians of a single volcano or of a group of volcanoes close together have trace
element contents that are closely convergent: indeed they appear to lie within the limits
of error of the analytical method. This is a phenomenon which has often been noticed
for other volcanic rocks, and which has been demonstrated by us for obsidians from
Lipari[8] and from Melos.[7] In the case of obsidians of the same broad compositional
type, but from volcanoes in different places, the trace elements may show differences by
up to a factor of 10, although this is not invariable. The variation in trace element
content between obsidians of different types may be as much as 1,000 times, or more.
Thus it is possible by trace elements easily to divide the three broad compositional
types from one another, while within types subdivisions may be made which allow, in
favourable cases, the obsidian of a single volcano to be completely characterized.

Sources
The chief known sources of obsidian suitable for tool-making are shown in Fig. 105.
Some of the sources, for example, in Iceland and Ascension Island, are not in areas
occupied in prehistoric times. The rest may be divided into six main areas:

(a) the Mediterranean region and (b), the American cordillera, where all three types
of obsidian are present, (c) Central Africa (dominantly peralkaline), (d) the East Indies

(dominantly calc-alkaline), (e) New Zealand (peralkaline and calc-alkaline), and (f) Japan. Obsidians from most of these regions are illustrated in Plate XXXIV. All of these regions are suitable for characterization studies, but particularly so are the Mediterranean region and the American cordillera, where sources of different types are spread out over a large area well inhabited in prehistoric times.

Of the several sources in the Mediterranean, those of Lipari[9] and Melos[10] are the best known and the most extensively used. Those of Central Europe[11] were in fact already used in the Mesolithic period. The abundant sources of South Anatolia and Armenia, as well as providing the material for the numerous surface scatters of Neolithic date in the area[12,13] were already known in Palaeolithic times.[14] Obsidian was traded from them widely throughout the Near East. In Africa obsidian has long been in use. The Kenya sources were used in Palaeolithic times (Plate XXXIVg) and the Abyssinian sources were well known to Pliny.[15] Obsidian was used too in the Canary Islands.

In the Far East there are fewer sources: none, in fact, is known in Central Asia. However, in Japan obsidian tools are common.[16] Tools were made at the Easter Island source (Plate XXXIVf) and the sources in New Zealand were also exploited.[17]

In America the magnificent mirrors and carving of the Aztecs and their predecessors (Plate XXXIVe) are rivalled only by the obsidian statuettes made by the Egyptians.[20, 21] The Central American sources have been listed by Heizer and his colleagues.[18] In northwest America there are several sources: arrowheads from California and Oregon (Plate XXXIVc and d) are illustrated for comparison with an example from the Aegean (Plate XXXIVb).

CHARACTERIZATION METHODS

Obsidian was first considered as an object of trade in the early years of this century.[10,19] Most of the early work on characterization attempted to make use of physical properties such as refractive index and appearance.[22,23] These approaches can be deceptive if complete characterization is attempted in as complex a region as the Mediterranean. This is well illustrated in Crete by the case of the white-spotted obsidian, occasionally found in Minoan contexts (Plate XXXIVd), which was originally assigned on the basis of appearance to an origin in Lipari[24] but which in fact comes from the Island of Giali.[7]

However, in more simple areas, or where the problem is a more straightforward one, such as the tracing of obsidian from a particular source with well-defined characteristics, physical properties can give useful information. Mention has already been made of the pearly-lustred Melian obsidian, which may be traced, using this property, throughout the Aegean. In New Zealand, a similar problem, that of the spread of obsidian from Mayor Island (off the east coast of North Island) has been successfully solved by Green and his collaborator.[25,17] This variety is peralkaline, and shows the characteristic green colour and high refractive index (1·497–1·507) while the other obsidians of North Island, which are calc-alkaline, lack this green colour and have refractive indices between 1·487 and 1·494. The obsidian from Mayor Island can therefore readily be distinguished from other obsidians when it is encountered in

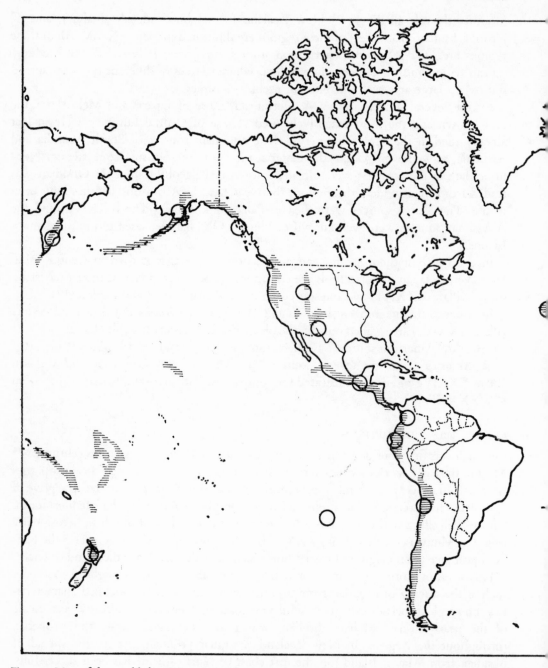

Fig. 105 Map of the world showing regions of recent volcanic activity (shaded). The principal known
obsidian sources are indicated by circles.

excavations. We have also used this green colour to distinguish peralkaline obsidian
from Pantelleria from alkaline obsidian from Lipari at the site of Skorba in Malta,[8]

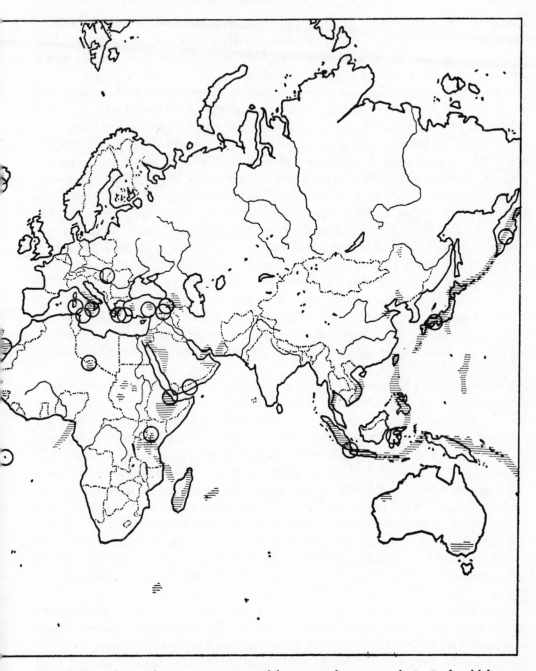

though here the evidence was supported by trace element analysis. It should be emphasized that such methods are only suitable in simple areas or where the investigation has limited aims.

Major element analysis has once been used, despite the difficulties mentioned above, for archaeological purposes. Georgiades[26] analysed six obsidian samples from the calc-alkaline source of Melos and the alkaline source of Antiparos, and was able to make a distinction between them. However, the time and the quantity of material required are great enough to make it difficult to apply such methods to large numbers of samples, while the distinctions are not always very certain.

Trace element analysis has proved the most certain and general way of characterizing obsidian, and can be applied to large numbers of samples, for the method is quick and (in the case of optical spectroscopy) requires little material. By 1966 we had made some 380 analyses of obsidian from sources and archaeological sites using optical spectroscopy[7],[8],[41] and achieved a satisfactory division into groups, which it has proved possible to subdivide in several cases. Optical spectroscopy has recently been used in New Zealand also for the study of obsidians.[27] Weaver and Stross[28] report a preliminary analysis of specimens from Central America, using X-ray fluorescence as their analytical technique.[29] Although their results are not quoted in parts per million, it may be seen that they agree well with our results for the Old World, particularly in the high content of zirconium present in certain (significantly green) obsidians from Teotihuacan and La Venta in Mexico which must be of peralkaline type. Here too should be mentioned the work of Cornaggia, Fussi and D'Agnolo,[30] for while they used physical properties and chemistry in combination, their most striking results were obtained by optical spectroscopy. They carried out a preliminary survey of obsidian in the West Mediterranean, but the validity of their conclusions is reduced by the small number of samples analysed.

The method of optical spectroscopy is widely known in archaeological circles, since it has been used for the analysis of metals,[31] faience[32] and other materials. Although it does not give a high accuracy ($\pm 25\%$), in contrast with X-ray fluorescence, for example, it has the advantage of necessitating the destruction of only 60 milligrams of specimen, as compared with 2 grams for X-ray fluorescence. A general account of the method may be found in Aitken[33] and more detailed accounts of the method used by us in Nockolds and Allen[34] and in our original paper.[8] By measuring the intensities of particular lines in the spectrum of the light produced when the specimen is burned in a carbon arc, the concentrations of 20 or more trace elements may be found.

A further analytical method which has been used to determine trace elements, as well as major elements, is neutron activation.[35] The analyses are accurate, and have already given an insight into the obsidian trade in the northern United States.[36] The method is now being applied to Old World obsidian also.[37]

In the interpretation of the analyses, by whatever means these may be obtained, the aim is to produce a division into groups on the basis of trace element content. Ideally such groups would contain all the specimens analysed from a single source and only those specimens (including, of course, artifacts analysed whose material derived from the source). It has proved most convenient to make a preliminary division on the basis of the amount of barium and zirconium present, as these were the two elements showing the greatest variation (Fig. 106). The plot illustrated divides the specimens so that the first requirement of grouping is satisfactory: *all the specimens from a given source fall within a single group.* At this stage each group contains obsidian from several sources,

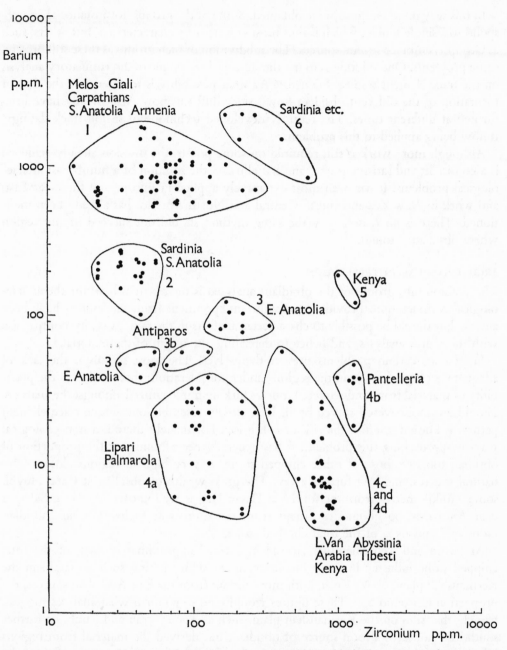

Fig. 106 The content of barium and zirconium of certain Old World obsidians, measured in parts per million. Each dot represents a single specimen, and the division into groups (which is supported by other trace-elements) is indicated.

but the groups may be further subdivided by plotting other pairs of elements (such as strontium and iron for Group 2).

In this way up to ten groups are obtained. Some of the groups, for instance 2b, correspond to a single source, which is thus most satisfactorily characterized, but others, such as Group 1, embrace several sources. The subdivision of such groups as these still present some problems. One solution is to use the statistical technique of discriminatory analysis on the trace element results obtained.[38] Another possibility is to determine the date of formation of the different obsidian flows, since different flows will usually have been formed at different times. The recently developed technique of fission track dating[39] is now being applied to this problem.

Although more work is still required on some points, the division already achieved is a consistent and satisfying one, and has allowed the solution of a number of archaeological problems. It has been most extensively applied in Europe and the Near East, and work in New Zealand and in Central and North America has already been mentioned. There is no reason why the same method should not succeed in any region where obsidian is found.

ARCHAEOLOGICAL INTERPRETATION

The division into groups of the obsidians analysed is the essential basis for the archaeological consideration. Provided that sufficient specimens from the sources have been analysed, it should be possible to characterize artifacts in the same way, by comparison with the source analyses, and hence to determine the origin of the material.

In practice certain problems present themselves. The most serious is the lack of adequate geological cover in the regions under consideration: there is always the possibility of material from undiscovered sources lurking unrecognized amongst the analyses. Should an undiscovered source by ill luck closely resemble one whose trace element pattern is known, there is the risk of confusion. Fortunately there is a non-geological way of approaching this problem. It has generally been found that the proportion of obsidian tools to those of other chipped stones is very high in regions close to the natural sources, and low further away. The great wealth of obsidian at Çatal Hüyük some 130 kilometres from the source at Hasan Dağ is well known. Again at Saliagos near Antiparos, 60 kilometres distant from the sources at Melos, the rich obsidian industry forms 95% of the total chipped stone.

At Jarmo and Tell Shemshara, obsidian formed approximately 40% of the total chipped stone industry in Early Neolithic times, while at sites such as Sarab, in the Kermanshah plain, or Ali Kosh, both more distant from the East Anatolian sources, the proportion is around 2%. These figures would tend to confirm what analyses suggest, namely that sites on the Kermanshah plain, such as Tepe Guran and Sarab, or further south, did not have a local source of obsidian, but derived the material from regions where it was in more abundant supply, and ultimately from the sources of the Lake Van region of Eastern Anatolia.

Sometimes analyses of artifacts form a group for which no source has yet been identified. This need cause no surprise in view of our limited geological knowledge of the Near East. Here the distribution of findspots of the particular group of material is relevant. For example at Jericho, where obsidian is present although rare in Pre-pottery

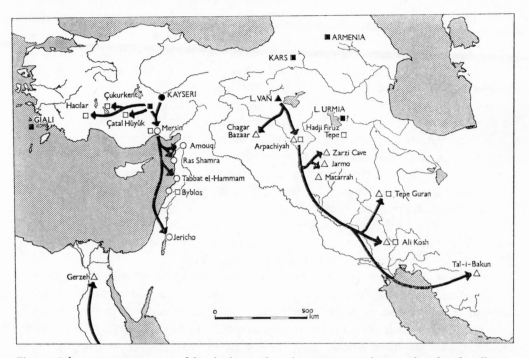

Fig. 107 Schematic representation of the obsidian trade in the Near East in the seventh and sixth millennia BC. Obsidian in the Levant came chiefly from sources in Central Anatolia; that found to the east of the Syrian desert from sources near Lake Van in Eastern Anatolia.

Neolithic times, all the specimens analysed fall in Group 2b. Other Group 2b artifacts are known from early sites along the Levantine coast, and from surface finds in the Kayseri region of South Anatolia. Up until 1963 the exact location of the source in question was not known. The concentration of Group 2b finds in the Kayseri region suggested that the source should be somewhere in that vicinity, and subsequent field-work succeeded in locating it near the village of Ciftlik, some 100 km south-west of Kayseri.[41] And from this source obsidian was exported to Jericho already in the seventh millennium BC.

This very early and widespread trade is indeed the most striking outcome of the analyses that have been conducted in the Old World. A schematic indication, for the Near-Eastern region, such as it appeared on the basis of analyses up to December 1965 is given in Figure 107.[40] More recent analyses have considerably extended this picture,[41] but they have not changed it in essentials. It is clear that in the seventh and sixth millennia, obsidian was exported from Group 1 sources such as that of Acigöl, west of Kayseri, westwards to Çatal Hüyük and Çukurkent, and south to Mersin and Byblos. The Group 2b source material was exported chiefly in a southern direction to Mersin, Ras Shamra, Byblos and Jericho.

At the same time the Group 4 source at Nemrut Dağ, near Lake Van, with another similar source near Bingöl, was supplying obsidian in large quantities to aceramic sites in Iraqi Kurdistan such as Jarmo and Tell Shemshara. This and other sources in Eastern Armenia, yet to be precisely located, supplied more distant settlements such as Tepe Guran, Sarab, Ali Kosh and even Persepolis (Tal-i-Bakun) in the sixth millennium. There is evidence, too, that the trade was already under way in the Mesolithic (food gathering and incipient cultivation and domestication) stage of Karim Shahir.

Looking westwards a similar picture is found. A comprehensive project of research in the Aegean has shown that Melos was supplying sites in Thessaly, Macedonia and Crete with obsidian as early as the sixth millennium BC.[7] In the West Mediterranean too the trade was early and widespread.[8]

Although obsidian was prized for the manufacture of tools principally in the Neolithic period, its use for the production of vases and statues persisted in the Old World until Classical times, and until much more recently in the Americas. The obsidian of Giali, for example, was used by the Minoans of Crete exclusively for the manufacture of stone vases. And Phidias himself used Melian obsidian to embellish his statue of Zeus at Olympia, one of the Seven Wonders of the Ancient World.

By the methods described, very precise information may be obtained about patterns of prehistoric trade. While it would always be unwise to base important deductions upon the results of a single analysis, the agreement of several analyses gives very strong evidence indeed. Such patterns, based on categorical and material evidence are more reliable than conclusions drawn from stylistic parallels of pottery or chipped stone. They give evidence of cultural contact, and suggest surprisingly efficient communications at an early date, heralding those of more extensive Chalcolithic trade. Obsidian would appear indeed to be the earliest object of trade which can be recognized and characterized with accuracy today.

REFERENCES

 1 STUKELEY, W. 1740. Stonehenge, a Temple Restored to the Druids, 5
 2 THOMAS, H. H. 1923. Ant. Jour. III, 239
 3 LEPSIUS, G. R. 1890. Griechische Marmorstudien
 4 DUMONT, A. and CHAPLAIN, J. 1888. Les Ceramiques de la Grèce Propre I
   WASHINGTON, H. S. 1895. Am. Jour. Arch. IX
 5 ORDOÑEZ, E. 1892. Memorias de la Sociedad Cientifica 'Antonio Alzate' VI, 33
 6 FRIEDMANN, I. and SMITH, R. L. 1960. American Anthropologist 25, no. 4, 476
 7 RENFREW, C., CANN, J. R. and DIXON, J. E. 1965. Ann. Brit. Sch. Arch. Athens 60, 225
 8 CANN, J. R. and RENFREW, C. 1964. Proc. Prehist. Soc. XXX, 99
 9 DAVID, N. C. 1959. Bull. Paletnologia Italiana 67–8, 205
10 BOSANQUET, R. C. 1904. 'The obsidian trade', in ATKINSON, T. D., et al., Excavations at Phylakopi in Melos
11 JANŠAK, S. 1935. Praveké Sídliska s Obsidiánovou Industriou na Východnom Slovensku
12 MELLAART, J. 1958. Istanbuler Mitteilungen 8, 82
13 TODD, I. A. and PASQUARÉ, G. 1965. Anatolian Studies XV, 95
14 KÖKTEN, I. K. 1952. Ankara Üniversitesi Dil ve Tarih-Čografya Fakültesi Dergisi X, 167
15 PLINY, Nat. Hist. xxxvi, 169
16 MUNRO, H. G. 1911. Prehistoric Japan
17 GREEN, R. C. 1964. Newsletter New Zealand Arch. Ass. 7, no. 3, 134
18 HEIZER, R. F., WILLIAMS, H. and GRAHAM, J. A. 1965. Contributions Univ. California Arch. Res. Fac. I, 94
19 PEET, T. E. 1909. The Stone and Bronze Ages in Italy, 150

20 LUCAS, A. 1948. *Ancient Egyptian Materials* (3rd ed.), 473
21 WAINWRIGHT, G. A. 1927. *Ancient Egypt, III*
22 FRANKFORT, H. 1927. Studies in Early Pottery in the Near East, Part II, *Roy. Anth. Inst. Occ. Paper No. 8*, 190
23 By Dr Phillips, using thin sections, *see* GARSTANG, J. 1953. *Prehistoric Mersin*, 26
24 EVANS, A. J. 1921. *The Palace of Minos at Knossos I*, 87 and 412
25 GREEN, R. C. 1962. *Newsletter New Zealand Arch. Ass. 5, No. 1*, 8
26 GEORGIADES, A. N. 1956. *Praktika tis Akademias Athinon 31*, 150
27 GREEN, R. C., BROOKS, R. R. and REEVES, R. D. 1967. *N.Z. Journal of Science 10, no. 3*
28 WEAVER, J. R. and STROSS, F. H. 1965. *Contributions Univ. Calif. Arch. Res. Fac. 1*, 89
29 *cf.* HALL, E. T. 1960. *Archaeometry 3*, 29. An application of similar methods to Californian obsidian is reported by PARKS, G. A. and TIEH, T. T. 1966. *Nature 211*, 289
30 CORNAGGIA CASTIGLIONI, O. FUSSI, F. and D'AGNOLO, M. 1962 and 1963. *Atti della Società Italiana di Scienze Naturali e del Museo Civico di Milano, CI, CII*
31 BRITTON, D. and RICHARDS, E. E. 1963. In BROTHWELL, D. and HIGGS, E. S. (*eds.*) *Science in Archaeology*, 499
32 STONE, J. F. S. and THOMAS, L. C. 1956. *Proc. Prehist. Soc. XXII*, 37
33 AITKEN, M. J. 1961. *Physics and Archaeology*, 60
34 NOCKOLDS, S. R. and ALLEN, R. 1953. *Geochimica et Cosmochimica Acta IV*, 105
35 AITKEN, M. J. 1961. *Physics in Archaeology*, 166
36 GRIFFIN, J. B. and GORDUS, A. A. 1966. A preliminary study of Hopewellian obsidian in the United States, Paper read to the *VIIth Congress of Prehistoric and Protohistoric Sciences, Prague*, August 1966
37 Research by Mr Gary Wright, in collaboration with Professors Griffin and Gordus is under way at the University of Michigan, Ann Arbor
38 RENFREW, C., CANN, J. R. and DIXON, J. E. 1965. *Ann. Brit. Sch. Arch. Athens 60*, 236, fig. 5
39 BRILL, R. H. 1965. *Archaeometry 7*, 51: FLEISCHER, R. L., PRICE, P. B., WALKER, R. M. and LEAKEY, L. S. B. 1965. *Nature 205*, 1138
40 We wish to thank Miss Carolyn Hull for drawing this map
41 RENFREW, C. DIXON, J. E., CANN, J. R. 1966. *Proc. Prehist. Soc. XXXII*, 30

52 Some Aspects of Ceramic Technology

FREDERICK R. MATSON

THE POTTERY FOUND IN MOST archaeological sites that were occupied by man after he began to farm and to settle on the land has changed very little in its appearance since it was fired and used. Although most excavated vessels are broken or exist only as remnants in the form of one or more potsherds, they serve as important evidences of the people who made and used them. Sherds are little affected by burial in the earth—they endure while metals corrode and disintegrate, and objects made of bark, wood or skin decay. Pottery preserves in its shape, decoration and physical properties a permanent though very fragmentary record of some of man's activities. Therefore, it must be studied intensively if the archaeologist is to reclaim from it all that is possible of the record remaining in such objects, and of their associations with other materials, in his excavations of ancient villages and towns.

If the mineralogical, physical and chemical properties of pottery are selectively determined in the light of the archaeological problem being studied, information can be obtained about the raw materials selected and used by the potter, their treatment before being formed into pots, the manner of fashioning the vessels and of firing them, and perhaps the uses to which they were put. The role of the potter as the active and controlling agent in these procedures must be kept in mind, and the function of his products in his community cannot be overlooked. We are concerned with the analytical data of products made by man, data which will help us better to understand this man's culture. Each study increases our historical knowledge of technological developments in areas of the world where ceramic products have been manufactured through long periods of time.

It is not necessary to have available expensive equipment in well-arranged laboratories in order to undertake the basic technological examination of pottery and other ceramic objects. Careful observations by one understanding the ceramic processes of pottery forming and firing can produce valuable information of direct use in the archaeological study of the wares. In this paper simple procedures requiring little laboratory equipment will be discussed first, followed by examples of the spectacular results obtained with special analytical equipment. Although technological pottery studies are the subject of this discussion, it should be recognized that similar approaches can be used in the examination of other important ceramic materials used by man such as brick, glass, glaze, enamel, faience, pigments, cement and plaster.

A close examination of the interior and exterior surfaces of sherds and of freshly fractured cross-sections through body walls can tell much about the ware and its production if one has some understanding of the properties of clays and the changes that occur as the surface of a semi-dried vessel is worked to its final condition by the

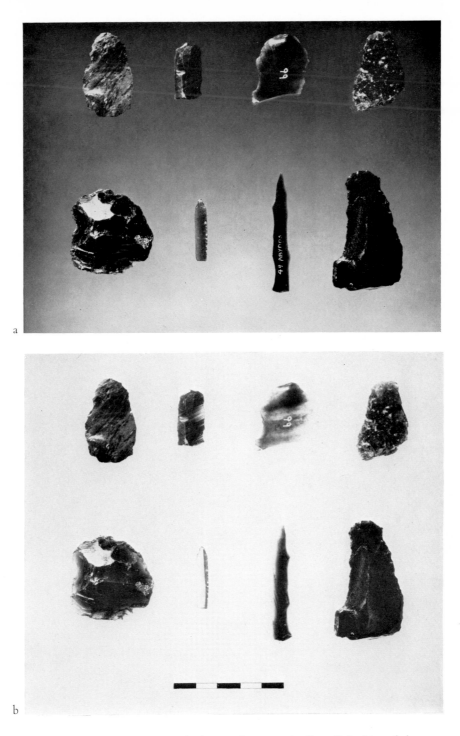

Variation in the appearance of obsidian artifacts, seen in direct light (a), and the same objects in transmitted light (b). 1: (top left): Sardinia, mottled red; 2: Çatal Hüyük, Anatolia, striated; 3: Hungary, cloudy; 4: Knossos, Crete, obtained from Giali, white-spotted; 5: (second row, left): Liparia; 6: Çatal Hüyük, transparent; 7: Egypt, obtained from Abyssinia, green; 8: Kenya, entirely opaque.

(see page 578) PLATE XXXIII

The world-wide use of obsidian. (a) Near East: amulet from Chalcolithic Chagar Bazaar; (b) Europe: arrowhead from Saliagos, Greece, Neolithic; (c) North America, arrowhead from California, Karuk indians; (d) North America, arrowhead from Oregon; (e) Central America, mask from Mexico, Teotihuacan culture; (f) Pacific Islands, Easter Island; (g) Africa, hand-axe from Kenya, Palaeolithic. All *c.* three-quarters natural size. Objects a, c–g illustrated courtesy of the Curator, Museum of Archaeology and Ethnology, Cambridge.

PLATE XXXIV (see page 578)

potter, and as the well-dried ware is fired. A hand lens or a low-power binocular microscope helps one see the details sought, especially if oblique lighting can be arranged so that shadows are cast which emphasize the surface striations and textural variations. It is desirable to examine all of the sherds excavated at a site in this manner, if possible, after they have been washed, catalogued and assembled as parts of restorable vessels. When the latter is not possible, they should be sorted as to wares and then grouped according to the vessel area from which they came—rims, bases, shoulders, handles, body pieces, etc. By examining the entire ceramic production in groupings one can most effectively evaluate the materials and select characteristic as well as unique items for more intensive study. It is misleading to choose a sample for further analysis unless the selection is made with a background knowledge of the variations within the site's ceramic spectrum. In this connexion an appreciation of elementary statistical procedures and methods of sampling are useful.

One further step is desirable for the ceramic examiner. He should have a practical knowledge of the local clays available to the potters, and in his off hours of relaxation at the dig he should have sought such clays, tempered them with water, considered their textural variations, and attempted to make simple pots from them. I have done this with some success in Iraq, Iran and the eastern United States, and have found that this experience helped me to understand the ancient potter at work as I studied his sherds.

In the first sortings it is helpful to check the broken edges for fracture patterns transverse and parallel to the body walls that might indicate how the vessels were formed. In a large collection of sherds it is usually possible to find a few whose fractures show evidence of the junction of the body walls and the base, the joining of coils of clay while building the walls, or the addition of a rim to the formed vessels. The absence of such breaks in the fabric does not necessarily show more than that the potter was skilful, yet it could, with small pots, indicate that each was formed from one lump of clay.

If a paddle and anvil technique was used in the final shaping of the vessel to compact its walls, round out its base and prevent serious cracks from forming as the pot dried, its use can sometimes be recognized by the slight depressions on the interior surface that were caused by the rounded anvil, and by paddle marks on the exterior. When a wooden paddle has a carved design on its surface or a piece of coarse textile has been wrapped around it as in some parts of North America and the Far East, to mention but two areas of the world, it is easy to recognize this technique. If a smooth paddle is used, however, the surface must be carefully examined. I have seen the walls of olive jars in the Lebanon thinned and the bases of water jugs in Afghanistan rounded by the use of the paddle and anvil, and have been impressed by the force of the blows given as well as by the tough resiliency of the clay. This technique has probably been used far more frequently in the past than has been recognized.

Ridgings and striations on the exterior and interior surfaces of body sherds and the finishing marks on both faces of basal sherds can indicate whether or not the vessel was formed on a potter's wheel. This is not a simple matter to determine when examining sherds from the time period when the wheel was first being used as in the Uruk period in the ancient Near East—very roughly about 3,300 BC. It is possible to fashion a pot by hand and then add a wheel-turned rim as has been done in Upper Egypt in recent times. It is also possible to rework the surface of a partly dried vessel on a simple wheel or lathe, scraping off the surface irregularities. This treatment leaves parallel striations on the smoothed surface, scratch marks caused by the dragging of mineral inclusions along under the scraping tool as it moves across the slightly moist clay surface. Usually the interior of narrow-mouthed vessels is not as well finished as the exterior, and the basic techniques of forming the piece can often be seen there.

A slip is sometimes applied to the surface of jars and to one or both surfaces of bowls. If this is a red slip on a clay body that fires to a brown or yellow colour there is no trouble in recognizing it. Such slips appear on pottery in the Near East from the very earliest ceramic strata of simple agricultural villages that were occupied well before 4,000 BC. They were also common on pottery made in Europe and the Americas in later times. The red burning clay was available in the Near East on the mountain slopes, but it may have been enriched with abraded powder from soft ferruginous rocks, for well-worn fragments of such rocks are found in some of the excavations. Often, however, a yellow, tan or red surfacing is termed a slip when in reality its colour is due to a concentration of salts on the surface of the vessel or is caused by the wet hand of the potter as she smooths the surface of the piece she is fashioning. Wet smoothing concentrates the finest clay particles in a thin layer at the surface where they may develop a more intense colour when fired because the diluting effect of the coarser ingredients is masked by this fine-textured layer. Such a film, termed by Childe a 'self-slip', may be described by a hasty observer as an intentionally applied slip. If it cannot be determined whether or not a slip is present from the careful examination of a significant series of sherds and this information would be useful, then a thin section of a characteristic sherd, should be prepared. When it is examined under a petrographic microscope it will usually show whether or not there is a layer of foreign material on the surface.

Freshly fractured edges of sherds uncontaminated by adhering clay or lime deposits will show clearly the textural variations in the ware and the degree to which it has been fired. When sherds are sorted under a binocular microscope with respect to texture, one quickly learns to recognize major variations in the quantity and size of the mineral grains present and is able to classify the sherds into one or more fabrics. If the core of the sherds is black or grey in colour, care is necessary so that one is not misled by the colour contrast between the mineral grains in the dark core and those in the tan to red oxidized clay zones near the surfaces. Whether the mineral inclusions were intentionally added as tempering material or occur naturally in the clay is a question of some interest that can be answered when one is familiar with the local clays and the possible variations from gravel admixtures through sandy to very fine that occur in them. The local deposits of sandy clays used for pottery in glaciated regions can often be traced to river banks of flood plains. Some such clays must be washed to remove the coarsest inclusions before they can be used successfully. If shell has been added to the clay as was done by some North American Indians, or straw was included as in many agricultural areas of the world, there is no difficulty in recognizing the intentional admixture.

A correlation between the size and shape of the vessels and the purity of the clay from which they were formed may at times be of interest. Fine-textured clay, naturally river-washed or intentionally levigated, may have been used for the smaller and finer wares while large storage jars and the coarser, thicker domestic wares may tend to contain more mineral grains, for they give structural strength to the plastic vessel as it is shaped, and help prevent excessive cracking during drying. Detailed identification of the mineral inclusions and the study of sherds whose texture and appearance suggest that they are foreign to the site can best be done under a petrographic microscope by a mineralogist.

Estimates of the weight percentage of the tempering inclusions in the clay may be desirable if the textural variations seem significant in the study of the kinds of pottery made. If so, it is a simple matter to prepare briquettes as comparison standards. The series shown in Plate XXXVa have been useful when studying shell-tempered pottery. Crushed shell that had passed through a 14-mesh sieve but was retained on one of 20 mesh was mixed with a fine clay in the weight percentages shown, and the tempered clay was formed into small briquettes. After firing, the test pieces were broken in half. Those shown in the left-hand column were then ground to a smooth flat surface while those in the right-hand column were retained in their fractured form similar to that of the edges of sherds. This scale greatly aided in the classification and analysis of shell-tempered pottery. The thickness of the briquettes approximated that of the pottery being studied. The ground surfaces in the first column suggest that a similar treatment of some sherds might be of use, through the study of the orientation of the shell platelets, in determining how the pottery was fashioned. Similar series tempered with sand, straw, asbestos or other materials used by the potters can be prepared when needed. They give a degree of precision to the work and are particularly useful when one tries to replicate and understand the potter's procedures. However, too fine steps in the scale must be avoided as they can cause confusion and may lead to a degree of precision that is false, since the early potters were not necessarily consistent in their product as made in many households over long periods of time. Compositional limits for tempering within which the potters worked can be determined, because they were controlled by the desirable working properties of the tempered clay and also by the successful production of fired pots.

The dark core that appears in many sherds can be used as a means of studying the manner and degree of low-temperature firing of pottery. Dark-cored wares occur in all parts of the world and do not necessarily indicate a primitive stage of ceramic development. All they really show is that the pottery had been fired insufficiently with respect to both temperature and duration of the firing to eliminate this dark zone. Usually this will mean that a kiln was not used. With many clays a low firing temperature will not impair the usefulness of the vessels, and it certainly requires less fuel. Since all clays contain some organic matter derived from decomposing plant materials, they will turn black in the initial stages of firing but will then become lighter and lighter greys as the carbonized organic material is removed through oxidation. The natural colour developments of this carbon-freed clay, now no longer under strong internal reducing conditions, can then be seen. The surface regions will quickly brighten in colour, but it may take quite a while to eliminate the black or grey zone in the core, as its oxidation is dependent upon the porosity of the clay body—a sandy clay being much more open in structure than a very fine-textured untempered one. Then too, some clay minerals hold more strongly than do others the adsorbed organic matter. The total amount of organic material present is of course an important consideration, for in addition to the naturally occurring carbonaceous ingredients, some peoples have added dung to their potting clay to make it more plastic. In such cases it will take a longer time at a given temperature to oxidize all of the carbon if the ware is not very porous.

The series of test briquettes shown in Plate XXXVb illustrate the phenomena just described. Prepared pieces of a sandy Tigris River clay from south of Baghdad were fired at 500°C in an oxidizing atmosphere, one trial piece being drawn from the kiln every five minutes for half an hour. When cool, the briquettes were cut in half and the core faces were ground smooth so that their colour zones could be compared. As can be seen in the left-hand column, the clay first darkened and then became progressively lighter in colour as the firing progressed, yet a grey core remained after half an hour. Some of the Tigris clay was then levigated to remove much of the sand that it contained, and a series of fine-textured briquettes was prepared. Both sandy and fine clay test pieces were then fired at 600°C in the same manner as in the preceding series. A faint trace of a grey core remained in the sandy clay after 25 minutes, but had completely disappeared after half an hour. The black core of the fine clay remained massively present, however. Similar test firings at 700° and 800°C did not entirely remove the black core from the fine clay.

This experiment emphasizes the effect of texture and porosity on the rate at which a clay can be oxidized. Since time and temperature are interrelated variables in all ceramic firings, it can be seen that with longer firing periods at the test temperature the core can be oxidized, but not always to the same colour as the surfaces. When one has the data at hand that such experiments provide, one can make some reasonable estimates concerning the firing processes used by the potter. When doing so, the core colour of the rim, body and basal sherds must be carefully considered for they may differ greatly in one vessel as well as from jar to jar. It is sometimes possible to determine the probable manner of firing the pots—upside-down, right-side-up, several in one firing, etc. Such studies provide good training for student archaeologists.

Similar experiments showing the colour developments at higher temperatures can be carried out under both oxidizing and reducing conditions for a local or an imported clay, and a firing temperature scale can thus be developed that is useful when studying kiln-fired wares. I have discussed the results of such higher temperature studies else-where.[5]

In the preceding pages it has been shown that one can learn much about the techno-logical aspects of ancient pottery by comparatively simple means and thus gain an insight into the problems the potters faced and solved in selecting their materials and in shaping and firing their wares. More refined and detailed analytical methods are available, and can be used when the questions they may help answer have been co-operatively proposed by the archaeologist and the technologist, and the sherds to be so tested have been carefully selected. Examples will illustrate some analytical approaches, many of which are still in their exploratory stages of development.

The petrographic microscope is one of the most useful tools of the ceramic technologist. Carefully prepared paper-thin slices of sherds, about 0·03 mm in thickness, can be studied at high magnifications. These thin sections can be used to identify and compare the mineral inclusions in the sherds with those of local clays. If the two differ significantly in their mineral fabric the sherds may represent imported wares which can then be described in mineralogical terms. It is then possible to prepare and analyse thin sections of sherds of the areas from which the importation is suspected in the light of one's knowledge of ancient trade and of the geological nature of the regions. This technique is useful only if there are readily recognizable differences in the mineral inclusions in the clays from the regions in question. Thin sections can also be checked for the orientation of the particles with respect to the surfaces of the sherd; this may yield information about the manufacture of the pottery, while the grain-size distribution, knowing that of the local clays, can suggest whether or not the clay had been levigated before use. The addition of tempering materials can often be recognized, and changes in the degree of oxidation of some minerals may help show the extent to which the pottery had been fired. Experience with the mineralogy of sedimentary materials is a most useful preparation for one who wishes to study petrographic thin sections.

An example of the identification of an imported ware at the long-occupied pueblo of Pecos, New Mexico, and the location of its place of origin will illustrate one application of petrographic methods, in this case to a ware tempered with crushed potsherds. Miss Shepard, who has conducted many successful petrographic analyses, summarizes the results of one aspect of her Pecos studies as follows in her useful volume, *Ceramics for the Archaeologist* (pp. 383–384):[11]

'A black-on-white type at Pecos has the same finish and style as the black-on-white pottery of the Galisteo Basin, some 30 miles away. Was the Pecos pottery imported or made locally? The potsherd temper seemed at first to offer little hope of answering the question, but thin sections showed that many of the temper particles were from culinary ware (blackened and coarse textured), tempered with rock—andesite or diorite. Galisteo culinary ware is tempered with this kind of rock, that of Pecos is sand-tempered. The sherd temper is, therefore, from Galisteo, for Pecos people obviously would not go 30 miles for sherds when there was an abundance of them on their own trash heaps, and this type of sherd-tempered pottery must have been brought into Pecos.' This information was then used by Miss Shepard and A. V. Kidder in the study of the trade relationship in its many aspects between Pecos and the Galisteo Basin.

Spectrographic analyses have long been used to determine the relative proportions of the elements present in trace amounts or in small quantities in ancient metals and glasses. They are now being used with success in studies of the regional distribution of some kinds of pottery. The small powdered sample of a body that is to be analysed is ignited in an electrode arc and the elements that are present in relatively small amounts can be identified by the characteristic spectra of light that they emit. In coarse-textured pottery it is difficult or impossible to obtain a representative sample for such analysis because of the variation in the quantity and size of the mineral grains of several types that will be present in each sample chosen. Two sherds from the same pot could differ markedly in their overall composition and in the relative amounts of the less frequent elements that are present, depending on the chance distribution of the coarser mineral grains in each sample analysed. This difficulty does not apply to all wares, so within limits, emission spectroscopy can be useful in pottery studies. Quantitative spectrographic analyses can at times be made if one can prepare a set of samples of known chemical composition as standards that approximate the compositions of the specimens being tested.

Sayre[9] (pp. 156–157) has made quantitative spectrographic analyses of powdered samples of the clays from fifteen wine jars of unknown provenance that were excavated in the Agora, the ancient market place of Athens. Many wine amphorae have a tax stamp impressed on one of their handles while the clay is still plastic which shows the place of manufacture and presumably the source of the wine. Sayre also analysed clays from stamped jars of known origin, and found that of the fifteen just mentioned, eleven had a composition like that of jars made on the island of Knidos, while the remaining four agreed in composition with jars from Rhodes. His work can aid materially in tracing the ramifications of the Aegean wine trade in classical times.

Mrs E. E. Richards[7] has been making a series of spectrographic analyses of Romano-British mortaria, searching for ranges of concentration for certain elements that may be characteristic for samples known to come from specific kiln sites. Her preliminary work has already met with success.

Physicists are now working with archaeologists in several countries in trying to apply some of the newer analytical techniques to the solution of archaeological problems. The Research Laboratory for Archaeology and the History of Art at Oxford which has excellent research physicists interested in instrument design and application on its staff is a good example of this effective interaction between members of the two disciplines. Each type of instrumental analysis presents certain advantages within certain ranges of application, and these limits are still being determined and in some cases modified by further refinements in instrument design. A few examples of recent work will illustrate the imaginative application of some of the newer techniques.

Nuclear bombardment and activation of archaeological materials has produced interesting results. At the invitation of Dr Robert Oppenheimer, a small discussion group composed of archaeologists and physicists met at the Institute for Advanced Study at Princeton, New Jersey, in 1956 to consider the possibility of applying nuclear analytical techniques to the solution of archaeological problems. As a result of this meeting, E. V. Sayre and his associates at the Brookhaven National Laboratories studied carefully selected sherd groups whose places of origin were questioned on archaeological grounds. One problem selected was that of the Fine Orange Ware, a distinctive type in Mesoamerica that occurs at several Mayan sites. A small quantity of this ware was found among the sherds in the excavations at Piedras Negras, but it was an important ceramic item at Kixpec, a site some distance away. Was the pottery of this type found at Piedras

Negras imported from the region of Kixpec? Bowl fragments of Fine Orange Ware from both sites as well as the normal Piedras Negras pottery were exposed to neutron irradiation in the Brookhaven nuclear reactor in order to produce neutron activation in the test pieces. The artificially induced neutron activity of materials that have been exposed in an atomic pile under the same conditions will decrease at a rate determined by the relative amounts of the activated chemical elements present in the sample. Therefore, the decay rate is a means of characterizing the chemical composition of a sample. The gamma rays emitted are suitable for such measurements. The rates of decrease in the gamma ray activity of these artificially activated Mayan sherds showed that the Fine Orange Ware from both sites had the same relative concentration of chemical elements, while the typical Piedras Negras pottery was quite different in its decay rate. These results confirmed the archaeologists' assumption that the Kixpec region was the centre of manufacture for the Fine Orange Ware.

Another problem investigated by Sayre was that of one type of Roman *terra sigillata*, the Arretine ware, which often was stamped when formed so as to show its place of manufacture. Stamped Arretine sherds known to have come from bowls made at Arretium received nuclear bombardment with similar ware of uncertain origin that was found in other regions. Some of the pieces from foreign regions had the same decay rate as those from Arretium, while others that Howard Comfort, who defined the problem and supplied the materials, suspected because of differences in texture as having been ancient forgeries—though they bore the stamp ARRET so that they would have greater market value—were found to differ from the true Arretine pieces. It is likely that this analytical technique will be used to help trace the place of origin of many of the Roman wares widely dispersed throughout Europe and the Mediterranean countries, and can probably be applied with success to the study of Greek trade in its widespread ramifications. Preliminary studies of Gaulish Samian pottery at the Research Laboratory for Archaeology, Oxford, by Miss Emeleus and Miss Simpson [2,12] have made it possible to group the samples 'in a manner that is understandable both geographically and archaeologically'.

A great advantage of this technique of nuclear bombardment is that it is non-destructive. Museum pieces from which chips cannot be removed for other forms of analysis can be exposed in a nuclear reactor, and after the necessary decay rate measurements have been made they can be stored in a protected place until their radioactivity has disappeared or is negligible. They can then again be safely exhibited or handled in study collections.

Another non-destructive technique is that of X-ray fluorescent spectrometry which has been successfully used at the Boston Museum of Fine Arts and at Oxford. The equipment is now available in many university and industrial laboratories so it should be fairly accessible to archaeologists. The test specimen is bombarded with X-rays and the characteristic fluorescence that is then emitted by chemical elements receiving this induced activation can be measured spectrometrically and the elements can be identified.

Young and Whitmore [13] have used this instrument at Boston to characterize the composition of certain types of Japanese and Chinese wares through the use of sherds that have been excavated at known kiln sites. Such work will help in the specific identification of some of the Far Eastern wares from regions where little controlled archaeological excavation has yet been done although beautiful objects from these areas have long appeared on the markets and in private collections and now grace museums throughout the world. Hall[3] discusses the advantages and limitations of X-ray fluorescent spectrometry, and points out that the analysis is largely of elements occurring very close to the test surface, so weathered or corroded surfaces can seriously affect the usefulness of the measurements.

A new tool that is still being refined and rebuilt on both sides of the Atlantic in order to attain greater effectiveness and smaller areas of analysis is the electron probe which can identify the elements present in a spot as small as five microns in diameter. Its use in archaeological studies is largely potential although Roberts[8] describes his 'electron gun', an X-ray microanalyser.

There are other new techniques being tried in archaeological studies which are of direct application in the broad field of ceramic technology, particularly when glasses and glazes are considered. Many of these techniques are discussed in the papers in the volume on the Boston Seminar that was edited by Young.[9] Current work in progress is effectively reported in the small annual bulletin, *Archaeometry*, published by the Research Laboratory for Archaeology and the History of Art, Oxford.

Ceramic technological studies have been conducted on a limited scale for a long while. In 1883 Anatole Bamps [1] presented a paper at the Fifth International Congress of Americanists in which he pointed out the usefulness of microscopic studies with particular reference to Peruvian pottery. He summarized the microscopic studies of Wilhelm Prinz which showed that some black and red pottery were made from the same paste and that the colour bands seen in cross sections of sherds did not indicate the building up of successive layers of different clays but showed the degree of firing. Bamps also recognized the value of microscopic work in tracing the origin of widely distributed wares and pointed out the danger of drawing conclusions from the chemical analyses of pottery when the mineralogical composition of the pastes was not considered. These points are still valid today and must repeatedly be emphasized.

Over the past eighty years many technological studies have appeared in widely scattered publications, often as little known appendices or footnotes in archaeological reports. Lucas's valuable volume, *Ancient Egyptian Materials and Industries*[4] summarizes his long years of distinguished work in Egypt. Miss Shepard's *Ceramics for the Archaeologist*[11] provides a detailed introduction to the nature of ceramic materials and processes as well as to many aspects of ceramic analyses. Its examples are drawn chiefly from the south-western United States and Central America, the two regions in which she has worked with great distinction. Her bibliography and those in Matson's papers of 1955 and 1960 will suggest a basic set of references for those interested in further reading.

In this paper it has not been possible to consider all aspects of the technological study of pottery. The surface decoration of wares in terms of pigments, vitrified slips and glazes has not been discussed. There have been several excellent studies of the nature and replication of the so-called Greek 'glaze' found on the red figured and black figured wares. A citation of the recent literature in this field is available (Matson,[6] p. 50). The higher fired wares leading to the development of stoneware and porcelain form another subject of immediate interest to students of Far Eastern and post-medieval European ceramics.

Technological studies can be carried out most effectively when the field archaeologist is aware of the potentialities of such work and systematically collects samples of the possible raw materials that were used and saves for study more of the miscellaneous items that occur in excavations. Lumps of tempered unfired potter's clay, for example, have been found in American Indian sites, crucible fragments and refuse slag appear in the Near East, and kiln-site wasters abound in the Far East. Ceramic technological studies based on carefully collected field samples and the identification of well-defined problems can significantly advance our knowledge of man's development and his ways of life.

REFERENCES

1 BAMPS, A. 1883. C. R. Congres. int. des Americanistes, 5ᵉ Sess, Copenhagen, 274 ff.
2 EMELEUS, V. M. 1960. Archaeometry 3, 16–19
3 HALL, E. T. 1960. Ibid. 3, 29–35
4 LUCAS, A. 1948. Ancient Egyptian Materials and Industries, London, 3rd ed.
5 MATSON, F. R. 1955. The American Ceramic Society Bulletin 34, 33–44
6 —— 1960. The Quantitative Study of Ceramic Materials; in HEIZER, R. F. and COOK, S. F. (ed.) 'The Application of Quantitative Methods in Archaeology', Viking Fund Publications in Anthropology 28, 34–59
7 RICHARDS, E. E. 1959. Archaeometry 2, 23–31
8 ROBERTS, G. 1960. Ibid. 3, 36–37
9 SAYRE, E. V. 1959. Studies in Ancient Ceramic Objects by Means of Neutron Bombardment and Emission Spectroscopy; Application of Science in the Examination of Works of Art, 153–180; proc. of seminar (Sept. 15–18, 1958) Research Laboratory, Mus. of Fine Arts, Boston
10 —— MURRENHOFF, A. and WEICK, C. F. 1958. The Nondestructive Analysis of Ancient Potsherds through Neutron Activation; Brookhaven Nat. Lab. Rep. no. 508
11 SHEPARD, A. O. 1956. Ceramics for the Archaeologist. Carnegie Inst. of Washington, Publ. 609
12 SIMPSON, G. 1960. Archaeometry 3, 20–24
13 YOUNG, W. J. and WHITMORE, F. E. 1957. Far Eastern Ceramic Bulletin 9, 1–27

SUPPLEMENT

This brief note will serve as a bibliographic guide to several useful publications of the past five years. New editions of two of the classical works have appeared. Lucas' Ancient Egyptian Materials and Industries has been revised and enlarged by J. R. Harris.[6] Miss Shepard has prepared a Foreword to the fifth printing of Ceramics for the Archaeologist in which she reviews ceramic studies that have appeared in the period 1954–64.[9] Successive volumes of Archaeometry (Volume 10, 1967 being the most recent) continue to include articles of technological ceramic interest. In the I.I.C. Abstracts published by the International Institute for Conservation of Historic and Artistic Works (now in volume 7, 1968) over 5,000 annotated abstracts have been listed that pertain to the technical literature on archaeology and the fine arts. This is a good source to check for reports on ceramics. Extensive spectrographic studies of Greek potsherds from twenty-one sites in the eastern Mediterranean region have led Catling to the provisional conclusion, subject to revision by the results of data currently being analysed, that the sherds studied represent thirteen production centres, and that ware from six of these was exported to other areas.[2] A detailed petrographic study of an imported decorated vessel excavated at Cahokia in south-western Illinois suggests to Bareis and Porter the region in which it was manufactured.[1] Compositional tests have been made by Hofmann and Theisen with an electron probe of the black vitrified slip of Attic pottery and of the red surfacing of Terra Sigillata.[5] Laser-beam probes will doubtless be used soon for ceramic analyses. Noble's well-illustrated and annotated book advances our understanding of the ceramic problems and techniques of classical Greece.[8]

Non-laboratory aspects of ceramic studies continue to augment our store of technological data. Hampe and Winter, a classicist and a professional potter, travelled together and visited potters at work in many present-day Greek and Italian villages.[3,4] Their detailed commentary, clear photographs, and sketches of kiln construction, provide a most useful record of contemporary craft processes that are rapidly disappearing. The Wenner-Gren Foundation for Anthropological Research sponsored a ten-day conference on *Ceramics and Man* at Burg Wartenstein, south of Vienna, at which the seventeen participants discussed the archaeological, ethnological, ecological and technological aspects of pottery made in the Americas, Europe, North Africa, the Near East, and South-east Asia. These papers have now been published.[7]

It is encouraging to note those directing specialized ceramic studies are increasingly concerned with the problem of the better use of their data to understand man the potter in his cultural milieu.

REFERENCES

1 BAREIS, C. J. and PORTER, J. W. 1965. *American Antiquity 31*, 95–101
2 CATLING, H. W., RICHARDS, E. E. and BLIN STOYLE, A. E. 1963. *The Annual of the British School of Archaeology at Athens 58*, 94–115
3 HAMPE, R. and WINTER, A. 1962. *Bei Töpfern und Töpferinnen in Kreta, Messenien und Zypern*, Mainz
4 —— 1965. *Bei Töpfern und Zieglern in Süditalien, Sizilien und Griechenland*, Mainz
5 HOFMANN, U. and THEISEN, R. 1965. *Zeitschrift für anorganische und allgemeine Chemie 341*, 207–16
6 LUCAS, A. and HARRIS, J. R. 1962. *Ancient Egyptian Materials and Industries*, London, 4th ed.
7 MATSON, F. R. (*ed.*) 1965. *Ceramics and Man*. Viking Fund Publications in Anthropology, 41
8 NOBLE, J. V. 1965. *The Techniques of Attic Painted Pottery*, New York
9 SHEPARD, A. O. 1965. *Ceramics for the Archaeologist*. Carnegie Inst. of Washington, Publ. 609

53 Optical Emission Spectroscopy and the Study of Metallurgy in the European Bronze Age

DENNIS BRITTON and EVA E. RICHARDS

THE FRAMEWORK OF THE LATER PREHISTORY of Europe has long been standardized in the sequence: Neolithic, Bronze Age and Iron Age. But within it our interpretations are constantly shifting. More and more, for example, are we appreciating that in many regions the first use of metal comes already among cultures generally styled 'Neolithic'.[1] This metal is not bronze but copper, as spectroscopic analyses have proved, and so a sort of 'Copper Age' forms a prelude to the Bronze Age itself. For the next thousand years, roughly from 1600 BC to 600 BC, bronze was the metal chiefly used for tools, weapons and ornaments through most of Europe.

But spectroscopic analyses do more than modify our view of the traditional 'Three Ages' system. The technology of copper and its alloys holds a crucial position in the early industrial history of Europe, and the extensive trade that a Bronze Age of necessity implies formed a major step in our economic development. If we are to appreciate this story in all its aspects every means of study must be applied, and one of these is analysis by optical emission spectroscopy. Yet this is no magic key to open all doors. On the contrary, an uncritical use of its results would soon lead us astray. Our best hope of a right understanding lies in using the various methods together, wherever possible checking their conclusions against each other. So in focusing our attention on one approach, we shall nevertheless refer to others, some based purely on archaeology and some of a technological kind. First the technique itself is described, then the problems of interpretation discussed, and finally a short review is given of some notable applications.

THE PRINCIPLES AND TECHNIQUE OF OPTICAL EMISSION SPECTROSCOPY

Of the methods which may be used to analyse a material for the chemical elements contained in it, spectroscopy offers a combination of advantages which make it specially suitable for the study of archaeological specimens. Sometimes from a single experiment on no more than 10 milligrams of a substance, the elements present may be identified and their relative amounts measured. Few other analytical procedures have the ability simultaneously to identify as many as a score of constituents and to estimate their concentrations over a range as wide as four orders of magnitude (i.e. from 0·001% to 10%). An outline of the principles underlying the method and some of the practical aspects will be described here.

The transmission of energy by radiation is familiar to everyone: the heat from the sun reaches us as light; the wireless programmes reach us by radio-frequency radiation; X-rays are well known to be a very penetrating form of radiation. All these forms of radiation are fundamentally the same phenomenon, in that they can be regarded as wave motion. They differ from one another only in their wavelength. Furthermore, the radiation which we perceive visually we call visible radiation or light. The different colours of the rainbow, into which white light is split when it passes through the water droplets acting as minute prisms, are again different in wavelength. The corresponding experiment in a laboratory, the resolution of light into colours by means of a prism, was achieved by Newton three hundred years ago.

In 1817 Frauenhofer set up the first spectroscope, consisting of a slit, prism and theodolite which enabled him to observe separately light of different colours. With this instrument he observed spectral lines in the light of the sun. Before the middle of the nineteenth century Fox Talbot, the inventor of photography, applied this invention to the recording of spectra. He was also the first to observe that the light emitted by certain elements when introduced into an electric arc consisted of characteristically coloured rays. By 1861, the basis of the spectroscopic method of analysis was firmly established by Kirchoff and Bunsen. They showed that the spectrum of an element consists of a number of lines (rays of light of different wavelengths) which are characteristic of that element and at the same time independent of its state of chemical combination.[2]

The lines of a spectrum have different intrinsic intensities, more light is emitted at certain wavelengths than at others under a given set of circumstances. The most important factor which determines the intensity of the spectrum as a whole is the concentration of the element producing it. Qualitative spectrographic analysis consists of the comparison of the wavelength of the lines in the spectrum of the sample with the spectra of the pure elements. Quantitative analysis depends on the measurement of the intensity of a chosen line for each of the elements whose concentration in the sample is required. The intensities of the same lines in the spectra of synthetic or chemically analysed samples are used for comparison. It is important that the reference material, whose composition is known, should be similar in kind to the samples of unknown composition.

The general layout of a spectrograph is shown in Fig. 108. The light emitted by the source (A) is gathered into a narrower beam by a lens (L) outside the spectrometer. It then passes through a narrow slit (S) (0·01–0·02 mm), is then reflected through a right angle and falls on the collimating lens (C). This is so placed that the beam reaching the prism (P) or grating consists of parallel rays. The light is refracted by the prism or diffracted by the grating. In either case the light which returns to the photographic plate (E) is spread out: different wavelengths are focused at different points along the photographic plate.

The source of light is an electric discharge between two electrodes maintained either at a high, alternating (spark) or low, direct (arc) voltage with respect to one another. It is the collision of the atoms, present in the gaseous state, with the electrons of the discharge which leads to the emission of light characteristic of these atoms. There are a number of ways of introducing the sample to be analysed into the discharge. The electrodes are usually made of graphite. The bronze may be converted into a mixture of

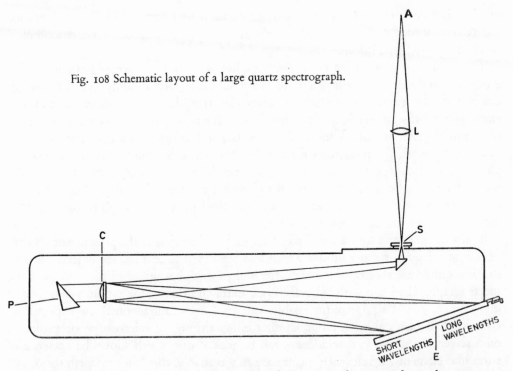

Fig. 108 Schematic layout of a large quartz spectrograph.

the oxides of its constituents; this is mixed with pure graphite powder in known proportion and packed into the cup hollowed out of the lower electrode. This method is also suitable for the analysis of ore and mineral samples. At the high temperatures generated in an electric arc, the mixture volatilizes. The dimensions of this cup are critical, and a new one has to be used for each exposure. Alternatively, the metallic sample is cast into a small globule and it is this which is placed into the electrode cup. In yet another method a solution of the bronze (0·2 ml of a 2·5% weight/volume solution) is placed into a thin-bottomed cup, which constitutes the upper electrode. The solution seeps through the porous graphite and the minute droplets volatilize into the park discharge.

In all methods the electrical characteristics of the discharge, the shape and distance from one another of the electrodes are critical and must be strictly controlled in order to obtain reproducible results. The quantitative determination of as many as twenty elements in one, or possibly two experiments, requiring between 2 and 10 mg of bronze, is quite feasible as a routine operation, by suitable initial choice of experimental conditions.

It is for this reason that spectrochemical analysis is the most widely used method in industry for the determination and control of the composition of alloys of all kinds. It is also widely used in the routine analysis of minerals, rocks and ores. Several hundred papers are published each year describing the optimum conditions for the spectrochemical analysis of particular materials. It is impossible to summarize here the various methods recommended for copper alloys, but critical reports are published by the British Non-Ferrous Metals Research Association, and by the American Society for the Testing of Materials. Most of the methods which have been used for archaeological work are quoted by Pittioni.[3]

If the spectrum is recorded on a photographic plate, only a narrow horizontal strip is exposed to the light, so that spectra of many (in some spectrographs up to 30) samples can be recorded on the same plate. Since the elements likely to be present in a bronze emit light mostly in the near ultra-violet and blue region of the spectrum, ordinary, unsensitized plates are satisfactory. These are fast and simple to process, but again, for quantitative work the conditions for development must be standardized. An enlarged photograph of the spectrum of a bronze is reproduced in Plate XXXVI. Some of the lines which have been found suitable for quantitative estimation of the main elements present are marked. The wavelengths are measured in Ångstrom units, one hundred million of which are equal to one centimetre.

If only qualitative information is required, such as for instance the presence or absence of lead in scrapings from a mould which had been used to cast bronze objects, then all that is required are spectra of the elements looked for, photographed through the same spectrograph. The plate with the reference spectra and that of the unknown are placed in a comparator. This apparatus enables one to view simultaneously two spectra on two different plates alongside one another either through a microscope or projected on a screen. Either way, coincidences can be picked out which show the presence of particular elements. If reference spectra are not available, then the wavelengths of un-identified lines can be computed from their position on the plate with respect to known lines. Compilations of all known lines of all the elements are available and can be used for identification in these cases.

The complete spectrum of an element is unique, although occasionally one or more of its lines may have a wavelength so nearly the same as that of some other elements that they will not be resolved in an ordinary spectrograph. For this reason it is customary in identification work not to rely on a single coincidence between the reference and unknown sample. The most sensitive lines of the elements, which are not necessarily the strongest ones, will persist down to concentrations as low as 1 part per million (0·0001%) for the consumption of as little as 1 mg of the specimen. This means that many elements can be detected when there was no more than one millionth of a gram present in the discharge. Quantitative work at these concentration levels is possible but difficult.

Although in the most modern equipment for routine spectrochemical analysis the photographic plate has been replaced by direct reading facilities, most of the analyses of archaeological interest have been done with the more conventional type of spectro-graph. Since the amount of illumination at a particular wavelength depends on the amount of the element emitting at that wavelength, the amount of blackening produced by a particular spectral line has to be measured. Visual estimates of the blackening are used for semiquantitative work, but as the variation in intensity is usually continuous it is difficult to decide where the boundary between such terms as medium and strong etc. will lie. The numerical evaluation of the blackening is carried out by means of a photoelectric device called a microphotometer. As the blackening produced is not strictly proportional to the amount of illumination, due to the peculiarities of the photographic process, fairly elaborate calibrations have to be carried out when the method is first set up. By means of these calibrations the blackening of the lines is converted into percentages of the appropriate elements.

It adds greatly to the value of these analytical results if the overall experimental error, as observed by replicating experiments, is assessed by a standard statistical method.

Most of the conclusions reached about archaeological material on the basis of composition relies on *differences* in the concentrations of particular constituents arising from differences in origin, date, method of manufacture and purpose. It is most important that no finer distinctions should be drawn than are warranted by the accuracy of the analysis. If for instance it is found that the standard deviation (this is the statistical definition of error due to random causes) of the determination of lead by a particular procedure is 10% and supposing that 5·0% of lead is found in a bronze, then the actual value has an even chance of being within 0·3 of this figure, while the odds against the real value being less than 4·2 or more than 5·8 are 9 to 1, and it has only one chance in a hundred of lying outside the range 3·7–6·3. These probabilities should be considered when the bronze is to be distinguished from another on the basis of its lead content.

When developing the analytical method it is important to ensure that the experimental error is less than the intrinsic variations in composition within the archaeological groups which are to be compared. On the other hand, extreme accuracy involves considerable expenditure of time. In archaeological work it is usually necessary to accumulate analytical data about a large number of samples. A compromise between sufficient accuracy and reasonable speed has therefore to be reached. This compromise will vary from problem to problem.

PROBLEMS OF INTERPRETATION

The information provided by optical spectroscopy is essentially descriptive. It tells us things we could never know merely by looking, but it leaves in our hands the problem of using this extra knowledge as a source for prehistory. In practice, interpretation involves two steps, the first in terms of technology, the second by way of archaeological reconstruction.

From the analysis we try to follow back the sequence of processes which led to the finished product. Our first question is: did the smith use copper by itself or did he aim at the deliberate production of an alloy? Some objects are of very pure copper and the traces of other metals in them may be regarded as impurities derived from the ore. But during the full Bronze Age alloys were in general use, the extra components being arsenic, tin, or tin and lead. Whenever the proportion of these rises much above 1% the possibility of intentional alloying must be considered.[4] To define the exact processes by which these alloys were made is often difficult and may be in part impossible. In any case, other evidence besides the analyses themselves must be taken into account, in particular the experience of geologists and metallurgists. For example, could the alloy be derived from selected kinds of copper ore, perhaps with skilful control of the smelting processes? The arsenical coppers of the later Neolithic and the Early Bronze Age may have originated in that way.[5] Or should we rather suppose that the other components were smelted from their own ores? This is certainly the usual explanation for the alloys of copper with tin and with tin and lead.[6]

When the main components shown by the analysis have been considered, others remain which presumably came in as impurities from the ore or ores. If the material is unalloyed copper, clearly all these are derived from the copper ore. Even in the alloys of copper with tin and lead, the ores of copper are again the likely source for many of the impurities. With the arsenical alloys, as already mentioned, the arsenic itself may be an impurity of this kind. It seems that the ores of copper are the sources for the bulk of the impurities, and from this arises a fascinating possibility. The combination of impurities in the smelted copper will broadly reflect that of the parent ore. Further, both objects and ores can be grouped according to their impurities, again taken not individually but in their recurrent combinations. Can knowledge of this kind enable us unambiguously to match finished objects with specific ore deposits? If it can, then we might learn a great deal about the economic organization of these early industries. The regions where copper was extracted could be compared with the overall dispersion of the products, and the importance of the various deposits at different periods could be assessed. Besides we should greatly increase our chances of discovering the sites of early mining and smelting, about which so little of a definite kind is known outside Austria.

But the obstacles are indeed formidable. First there are theoretical difficulties. The correlation between ores and the copper smelted from them is in terms of the combination of certain elements in both. But a direct quantitative comparison is hazardous and perhaps without meaning, since the several elements will pass over from the ore to the smelted metal in differing proportions, and these ratios might in fact have varied with the process used: how uniform were the extractive techniques and how standardized a product was achieved? Then it is known that the composition of the ore body itself varies from place to place through its depth, and into the bronze-smith's melt might even go ingot metal or scrap from more than one source. The practical difficulties lie in the assembly of all the information needed. Even if we suppose that the objects in question each contain copper from only one ore deposit, it is obvious that the comparisons of single analyses are of no value. What is needed is a soundly based assessment of the range of variation likely in the copper from all the probable ore sites, some of which may have been worked out long ago. The objects too must be grouped in terms of ranges of variation in their composition. It is doubtful if valid results can be achieved except by great numbers of analyses, and these may require statistical evaluation before they are used as evidence. If such problems are to be tackled effectively, it is certain that patient and long-term study on a considerable scale is necessary. At least outside Austria, which we shall mention again below, it is questionable whether or not these exacting conditions have been fulfilled so far.

In terms of technology two kinds of information are yielded by the study of spectroscopic analyses. The first is the definition of the metals used, and within the limits of

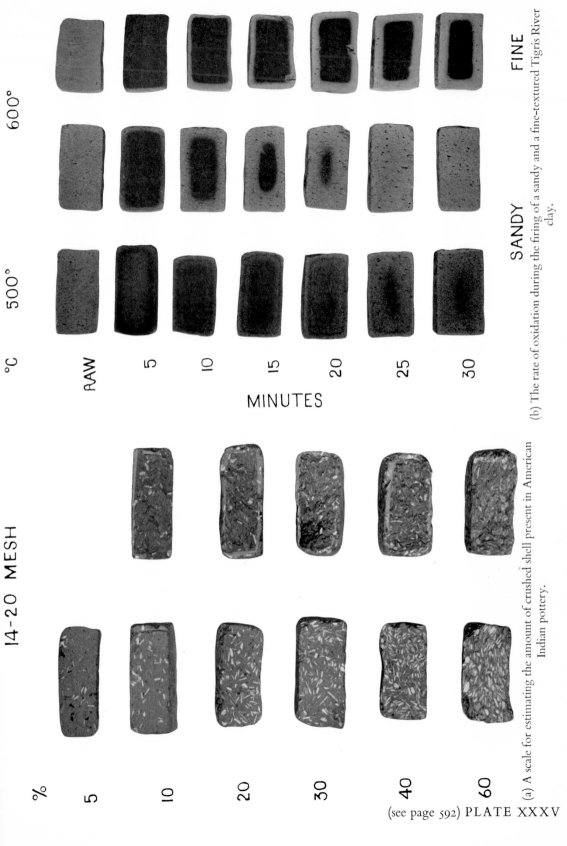

600°   FINE

SANDY

500°

°C

RAW

5

10

15

20

25

30

MINUTES

(b) The rate of oxidation during the firing of a sandy and a fine-textured Tigris River clay.

14-20 MESH

%

5

10

20

30

40

60

(a) A scale for estimating the amount of crushed shell present in American Indian pottery.

(see page 592) PLATE XXXV

(a) Axes of copper and bronze from Britain and Ireland (×1:2). Left to right: flat axe of copper (Ireland, later Neolithic); flanged axe of tin bronze (Corkstown, Co. Tyrone, Early Bronze Age); palstave of tin bronze (Andover, Hants, Middle Bronze Age); socketed axe of leaded tin bronze (Hammersmith, London, Late Bronze Age). (Pitt Rivers Museum, Oxford.)

Sb 2598·1

Au 2676·0

Fe 2739·5

Cu 2768·9

As 2780·2

Pb 2833·1
Sn 2840·0

Ni 3050·9

Bi 3067·7

Zn 3345·9

Ag 3382·9

(b) Spectrum of a bronze in the near ultra-violet region.

PLATE XXXVI (see page 603)

the method, the results are direct and unequivocal. The second concerns the sources of copper, and here the difficulties involved mean, at present, conclusions of a rather tentative sort for most regions of Europe. When historical reconstructions are attempted, we should keep in mind the very different character of these kinds of evidence, and to start with at least consider them separately. It is also valuable to form our ideas of what happened first of all from the archaeological standpoint alone. Then the new data from the side of technology, with an independent source, can be compared. But if all the evidence is thrown together at the beginning, we lose helpful possibilities of cross-checking our interpretations, and indeed may easily succumb to arguments that are essentially circular.

SOME EXAMPLES OF APPLICATION

Single analyses are of little value and may easily mislead: conclusions with real meaning must be based on large series of results. Awareness of this fact has been rather slow in taking root generally, although systematic research has been done on several aspects of the European Bronze Age.[7] Here some of the main examples are mentioned, with a few details to illustrate the different kinds of approach.

The pioneers of this method were W. Witter and H. Otto, whose researches in connection with the Landesmuseum of Halle/Saale had started already in 1931.[8] They were concerned with the beginnings of metallurgy in central Europe and by 1952 had completed about 1,500 analyses. Both the sequence of metals used and possible sources of copper were studied, and they realized the need for a knowledge of the likely ore deposits. Their conclusions are of great interest but call for checking by further work. The correlations between objects and ores require more detailed information about copper deposits—they did not themselves study samples of ores, and their broader historical suggestions should be viewed against comparative evidence from other regions. This applies particularly to the possibility of an independent growth of bronze metallurgy in central Europe.

It is in Austria that the systematic study of both objects and ore deposits has been pursued intensively and with notable success. This work began slightly later than that of Witter and Otto, about 1935, and it is particularly due to H. Pesta and R. Pittioni.[9] The other aspects of the story have also been given special attention, particularly the problems connected with early mining, and the treatment and smelting of the ore. Research has been concentrated on the regions of early exploitation in Salzburg and the Tyrol, where all the major deposits of copper ore have now been examined. Care has been taken to analyse samples from different depths in the deposit so as to define correctly the range of impurities characteristic of the ore-body as a whole. By 1959, Pittioni had available no less than 1,925 analyses of ores and material from ancient smelting places.

On this very substantial basis, study can now, it is claimed, be directed with confidence to the problem of correlating the ore deposits with likely products. Several aspects of the Copper Age, Bronze Age and the Urnfield Period have been studied in detail and these analyses are yielding results of great interest for the early economic history of central Europe. Two instances must suffice. Hoards of ingots are well known in the Early Bronze Age of the *Voralpenland*, and on the basis of 452 analyses the ores of Slovakia are suggested as the likely origin for much of this metal. On the other hand an intensive study of material from the Urnfields of the North Tyrol (581 samples) points to a major source in the copper deposits of the Bertagrube near Schwaz. In his review of 1959, Pittioni was able to report a grand total of 3,391 analyses, and added reassuringly that the possibilities of research were by no means exhausted!

It is a familiar paradox that the splendour of Bronze Age metal-working in Scandinavia rested entirely on imported materials. Here there is no challenge to locate ores exploited in remote antiquity but great opportunities for the study of technological development. The magisterial work of A. Oldeberg on this theme[10] covers the later periods as well: we are concerned only with the Bronze Age sections. Oldeberg deals with each metal in turn as it occurred in the North. Frequent illustrations are drawn from the long series of analyses incorporated in the book—747 from all periods. For the earliest use of copper and its alloys he relies much on the work of Witter and pursues for Scandinavia his suggestions about the sequence of metals and sources of copper. But Oldeberg's interests carry him right through the Bronze Age, and for the later phases too he has much to say on possible sources of metals. Particularly valuable is his study of the development of metallurgical techniques through successive periods of Scandinavian antiquity. In both these fields, he has used perceptively the results of spectroscopic analysis as a basic source for prehistory.

Since 1949 a very extensive survey has been undertaken at Stuttgart through the collaboration of S. Junghans, E. Sangmeister, E. Scheufele, H. Klein, and M. Schröder.[11] The programme now embraces the same chronological span as that of Otto and Witter but is expanded to consider the original spread of metallurgy in copper and bronze from the first centres in the Near East throughout Europe. From this wider view it is hoped that historical conclusions can be drawn that are of real validity. The results of the first six years' work, based on 2,302 analyses, were published in 1960 and deal with central and western Europe.[12] Other regions will be the subject of future publications. By 1960, 2,700 new analyses could be claimed, with samples collected for a further 3,000.

Great care has been taken to set out separately the general picture of cultural development for each region as derived from the usual methods of archaeology. Only then are the results of the analyses considered. One major theme is the origin and spread of true tin bronze metallurgy. Almost everywhere in central and western Europe a distinct phase is revealed in which copper alone was used, and then the new and superior alloy spreads throughout Europe—to all appearances, quite suddenly. Its earliest use in the regions so far considered is said to be in the *Schlaner Gruppe* of the Únětice Culture in Bohemia, probably about 1700 BC. Only future work will show whether an independent invention is involved or diffusion from the south-east.

The other main field of inquiry concerns the groups of copper as defined by their impurities. The work of Otto and Witter is greatly refined, with statistical evaluations to fix precisely the boundaries of the groups. Thirteen groups emerge and account for almost all the results. The occurrence of these groups is then plotted geographically and the main concentrations of each determined. Also their utilization by the different archaeological cultures is studied, in both space and time. Only when all parts of Europe have been thus examined will the problem of locating the sources be taken up in detail.

From all this comes the basis for a broad historical sketch in which the original account derived purely from archaeological techniques is combined with the new knowledge. What emerges is a general sequence in three stages. In the first, well before 2000 BC, knowledge of metal-working is confined to the south-east and south-west of Europe. From these two regions metallurgy spreads in the early second millennium to many parts of central and western Europe, and a number of new copper groups appear, suggesting the exploitation of fresh sources. The initial schools of metal-working were masters of quite complex methods of casting, but these skills were lost in the spread of the craft, and many of the earliest products in temperate Europe were made simply in open moulds, often with much subsequent forging (*Blechstil*). Only in the third phase, and significantly just with the diffusion of bronze metallurgy, was the older competence transcended and closed mould casting—for which the new metal was so well suited—became very general. About this time too, in the seventeenth century BC and later, the exploitation of new ore deposits is indicated, and these have been identified with sources in the Bavarian and Austrian Alps. By the end of the Early Bronze Age this 'alpine copper' had in many regions come to dominate the market.

Our final example brings us at last to Britain and shows the way in which we may apply to familiar material information about the kind of metal used. The evidence for Middle Bronze Age metalwork, especially in southern Britain, has been studied in detail by the usual archaeological methods of typology and association.[13] These showed its place in the prehistory of the region and related it to the independent sequences of the Continent. The material so defined was contrasted archaeologicaly with another group, which is broadly its successor and used to delimit our Late Bronze Age. Large numbers of specimens from both these assemblages, a total of 471, were analysed.[14,15] In each group tin had been added in rather variable amounts to the copper, but the Late Bronze Age material alone had as well an addition of lead, also variable but hardly ever absent (Fig. 109).

This interesting information is in some ways rather puzzling. For certain purposes the leaded alloy has technical advantages: the melting point is lower, and the molten metal would flow more easily into long or complex moulds. These properties might suit very well many of the typical forms of the Late Bronze Age and also its aspect of mass-production. But compared with plain tin bronze the castings would frequently be poorer in mechanical qualities. Perhaps economic factors were involved too, and we should recall that over much of southern Britain all the constituents would have to be imported. Besides an intriguing technological point, the analyses have proved for the first time an ancillary industry of some importance and uncovered a fresh aspect of Bronze Age trade. But they do not strictly provide a new method of dating—of deciding what is Middle and what Late Bronze Age. Those terms properly refer to assemblages defined by archaeological criteria. The reality of these groupings is buttressed by the analyses, though the sequence of alloys does not by itself furnish a yardstick for chronology.

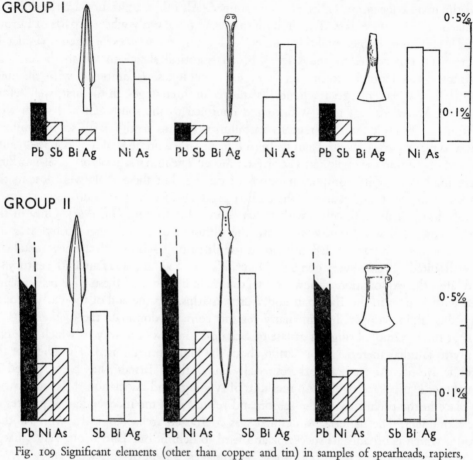

Fig. 109 Significant elements (other than copper and tin) in samples of spearheads, rapiers, swords, and axes from Britain. GROUP I: Middle Bronze Age; GROUP II: Late Bronze Age. From Brown and Blin-Stoyle.[14]

This picture for the Middle and Late Bronze Age of southern Britain is being complemented by studies of the earlier phases. The initial contribution was the notable work by H. H. Coghlan and H. J. Case on the first metallurgy in the British Isles.[16] For southern Britain the material between this programme and the Middle Bronze Age has also been sampled.[17] It is in the later Neolithic, perhaps from about 2000 BC on, that the first metal objects are known, such as the tanged flat daggers from Beaker graves. The metal here seems always to be copper, though sometimes so arsenical as to suggest deliberate choice of ores and perhaps control of the smelting. The broad butt flat axes that probably belong to the same period are of similar material. The clearest light on the start of a real Bronze Age is shed by the sequence of graves in the Wessex culture.[18] The earliest burials include six-rivet daggers, flat or with a midrib. Some of these are of copper—again this may be arsenical, but others are truly of bronze, containing a deliberate addition of tin, which rises once above 12%. In later graves, marked by two- or three-rivet daggers, bronze seems universal, and in 14 out of 22 daggers of this kind so far analysed the tin content is above 12%. The same alloy, with abundant tin, is found consistently in the hoards with flanged axes which belong to this second phase, and perhaps date from about 1550 BC onwards.

These results document very clearly the growth of knowledge in the alloying of copper (Plate XXXVIa). They show as well an interesting relation between the kind of metal and the methods of casting like that already observed for the Continent. Here too the first forms are of copper and cast flat in open moulds, with subsequent hammering and grinding. Next the first closed mould forms appear, cast in low tin bronze or the arsenical copper which has many of its advantages. Then bronze with rather higher tin content becomes standard and remains so throughout the Middle Bronze Age, until it was supplanted in its turn, sometime after 1000 BC, by the leaded alloy of the Late Bronze Age.

REFERENCES AND NOTES

1 JUNGHANS, S., SANGMEISTER, E. and SCHRÖDER, M. 1960. *Metallanalysen kupferzeitlicher und frühbronzezeitlicher Bodenfunde aus Europa*. Berlin, 8–34, and Beilage 1

2 TWYMAN, F. 1951. *Metal Spectroscopy*, London

3 PITTIONI, R. 1959. *Archaeologia Austriaca 26*, 67–95

4 JUNGHANS, S. *et al.*, *op. cit.*, 57ff.

5 COGHLAN, H. H. and CASE, H. 1957. *Proc. Prehist. Soc. 23*, 96

6 —— 1956. *Notes on the prehistoric metallurgy of copper and bronze in the Old World*, Oxford, 16–18, 23–25. The analysis of ingot metal might be instructive and show at what stage the lead became part of the mixture.

7 PITTIONI, R. *op. cit.*
HAWKES, C. F. C. 1962. *Atti del VI Congresso Internazionale delle Scienze Preistoriche e Protistoriche I*, 33–54

8 OTTO, H. and WITTER, W. 1952. *Handbuch der ältesten vorgeschichtlichen Metallurgie in Mitteleuropa*, Leipzig

9 PITTIONI, R. *op. cit.* 69ff., 93ff.

10 OLDEBERG, A. 1942–3. *Metallteknik under förhistorisk Tid*, Lund

11 *Bericht der Röm.-German. Komm. 35* (1954) 77 ff.; *Germania 35* (1957) 11 ff.

12 JUNGHANS, S. *et. al.*, *op. cit.*
BUTLER, J. J. and VAN DER WAALS, J. D. 1964. *Helinium 4*, 1–39

13 SMITH, M. A. 1959. *Proc. Prehist. Soc. 25*, 144–187

14 BROWN, M. A. and BLIN-STOYLE, A. E. 1959. *Ibid.* 188–208

15 *Archaeometry 2*, 1959, supplement

16 *Proc. Prehist. Soc. 23* (1957) 91–123

17 BRITTON, D. and RICHARDS, E. E. 1962. *Archaeometry 4*

18 APSIMON, A. 1954. *10th Ann. Rep. London University Inst. of Archaeology*, 37–62

54 The Analytical Study of Glass in Archaeology

RAY W. SMITH

GLASS HAS TRADITIONALLY been neglected by archaeologists, and its historical development has been only imperfectly understood. Thus, only in rare cases has the archaeologist been able to date graves by glass found in them. Usually it is the association of glass with other materials, such as ceramics and coins, that permits its dating. Now, with the technical study of ancient glass receiving more attention than ever before, there is a good prospect that the situation will be rectified.

Technological research on ancient glass presents several particularly difficult problems. One of these, due to the special nature of the substance, is the determination of the raw materials used. In view of the amorphous character of glass, one might say that its components have lost their individual identity, and crystallographic observations, for example, give no clue to the types of materials that were placed in the glassmaker's crucible.

It has been observed, moreover, that glassmaking formulae were virtually identical through centuries on end and across vast areas. As a result, the most piercing and accurate analyses attainable are essential to the full determination of regional and chronological differentiations. Fortunately, methods are becoming available which will surely elevate technological research on ancient glass to a new level of effectiveness.

It should be pointed out forthwith that an 'analysis' of a specimen does not necessarily justify the effort put into it. It has been long known that nearly all ancient glass is of the soda-lime variety. If an analysis is so sketchy that it reveals no more than this fact it obviously contributes nothing to our knowledge. To carry significance, a chemical analysis of ancient glass must reveal in what respects the specimen conforms to or departs from the characteristics of the various recognizable groups of glass in antiquity.

Unless and until there is a comprehensive and well-organized backdrop of analytical data against which analyses can be compared and thus interpreted, they are of only limited usefulness. But this is a prodigious commitment. There are well over one hundred 'area-periods' in ancient glass, so that several thousand reliable and accurate analyses in great depth, of well-authenticated specimens of known origin in time and place, will have to be available before any single analysis can justify a narrow definitive attribution.

It is clear that the first phase[7] of a research programme should be the organized accumulation of data. Investigation of highly specialized problems could well be deferred in some cases to a later date.

A good beginning has been made at the Brookhaven National Laboratory in the United States, where Dr Edward V. Sayre has studied several hundred specimens of ancient glass.[4] This work has revealed (see Fig. 110, Table A) that ancient glass in the

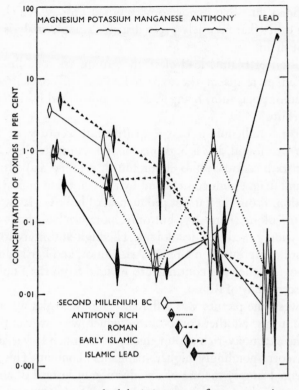

Fig. 110 Standard deviation ranges for concentration
of various metal oxides in the five main categories of
western ancient glass.

TABLE A

Mean concentration of the oxides that best characterize ancient glass.

Glass group	No. of Specimens	Mean percent concentrations and standard deviation ranges				
		Magnesium MgO	Potassium K$_2$O	Manganese* MnO	Antimony Sb$_2$O$_5$	Lead PbO
Second millennium BC	15	3·6 (4·6–2·9)	1·13 (1·89–0·69)	0·032 (0·046–0·021)	0·058 (0·32–0·011)	0·0068 (0·048–0·0010)
Antimony rich	34	0·86 (1·24–0·60)	0·29 (0·47–0·17)	0·022 (0·035–0·014)	1·01 (1·93–0·53)	0·019 (0·077–0·0047)
Roman	73	1·04 (1·47–0·73)	0·38 (0·63–0·22)	0·41 (1·60–0·10)	0·040 (0·089–0·018)	0·014 (0·057–0·0033)
Early Islamic	66	4·9 (6·5–3·6)	1·45 (2·2–0·94)	0·47 (1·07–0·21)	0·021 (0·035–0·012)	0·0088 (0·047–0·0016)
Islamic lead	6	0·33 (0·47–0·24)	0·026 (0·051–0·013)	0·022 (0·031–0·016)	0·081 (0·19–0·035)	36 (40–33)

* Some glasses with a characteristic dark blue or violet colour contain considerably more manganese than colourless glasses of the same type. It has been assumed that manganese was added deliberately to such glasses as a colorant, and they have been excluded in calculating the average manganese values.

Occident was divided into five major compositional groups, which were sufficiently distinct from each other that in nearly every instance a single analysis can clearly assign an object to one of them.

With the exception of Islamic lead-glass, the groups are soda-lime glass. The categories are described in terms of the expected ranges of concentrations of the five elements, magnesium, potassium, manganese, antimony, and lead, which most clearly differentiate the groups.

Glass of the second millennium BC group (fifteenth century BC to about seventh century BC), wherever found, has a high magnesium content. Glass of the antimony-rich group (about sixth century BC to about fourth century AD) is characterized by a lower potassium and magnesium content and by the consistent appearance of antimony in high concentration. From the earliest production of hollow glassware antimony was used deliberately in colour chemistry, but only sporadically. About the sixth century BC it began to be widely used as a decolorant. The high-antimony formula apparently became the standard composition in Greece, Asia Minor, and Persia during the fifth and fourth centuries BC, and the type continued to be used from the Euphrates valley eastward during the ascendancy of Rome.

Farther to the west, the picture was different. The great glassmaking centres of the Syrian coast began to use another composition, which we now call the Roman group. It differed from the antimony-rich group chiefly in its much lower antimony content, and usually in its correspondingly higher manganese content. This suggests that the distinction represented simply the use of one decolorant instead of another.

The Roman group is also found in the production of glass centres in Egypt, Byzantium, Italy, and the Western Provinces, remaining with little change through the Byzantine, Frankish, and Saxon periods. Whereas there is as yet no case known of the antimony-rich formula being used in southern Syria and on the Syrian coast, it does occur, and sometimes frequently, in areas farther to the west.

The emergent story of antimony and manganese in Italy and the Western Provinces is as follows. Manganese seems to have been the only decolorant used until towards the end of the first century AD, when antimony was introduced. During the remaining Roman centuries both decolorants were used, sometimes together, sometimes singly, and occasionally glass was made without a deliberate decolorant.

By the fourth century antimony was on its way out, and with the fifth century it apparently ceased to be used, both in the West and very likely elsewhere.

During its use as a decolorant, antimony must have been preferred to manganese, as it is an incomparably better decolorant. Presumably manganese was used through considerations of economy and availability. In any case, antimony must have been considered by the ancient glassmaker as a magic and mysterious substance, for here was a product which could impart both deep and luxurious colour to his product, as well as eliminate all signs of unwanted tints, producing a sparkling, limpid, crystal glass.

The early-Islamic group (introduced eighth–tenth century AD, or earlier) is marked by a return to the higher magnesium and potassium concentrations of the second millennium BC group, but, in general, without showing the low manganese content of the early glass. This glass is sufficiently similar to that of the second millennium BC group that the assumption has been voiced of an uninterrupted continuation of the same glassmaking tradition. The present analyses, however, would suggest that a lapse of many centuries occurred between the production of these two categories of glass. Certainly, glasses of both the antimony-rich and Roman groups were produced in some of the areas destined to become Islamic. The possibility, however, that the early formula was used without interruption in certain regions (Mesopotamia, Parthia, or Central Asia?) merits investigation.

The identification of the Islamic lead-glass group (introduced eighth–tenth century AD?) is based upon only six analyses, but the six glasses came from a variety of sources and yet possess remarkably similar compositions. Islamic lead-glass contains considerably more lead and less alkali and lime than most of the occasional New Kingdom high-lead glass. It is distinctly different from the lead-barium Chinese glass reported by Seligman and Beck,[5] and also from the two main types of eleventh–thirteenth century AD Russian lead-glasses described by Bezborodov.[1]

Two extensions of the foregoing findings are urgently needed. The initial and terminal dates of each group must be closely established, and it will be important to determine where each major change in glass composition first appeared, as well as to uncover the reasons for the changes. We do not yet understand, for example, the considerable decrease in potassium and magnesium around the middle of the first millennium BC and the increase in these elements again after the middle of the first millennium AD. The minor differentiations, moreover, which must surely exist within a group, either on a regional or a chronological basis, need to be exhaustively explored.

A few regional differentiations have already emerged. The antimony-rich Achaemenian glass from Persepolis, for example, shows systematically somewhat less titanium, zirconium and lead than early high-antimony glass from Greece (Phidias workshop) and Asia Minor. Early Islamic glass from north-eastern Iran seems to differ from material found in other parts of Iran, and clearly there is significantly less manganese in glass of the same group from sites in Mesopotamia and north-western Iran than in finds from other Islamic areas.

The most useful single technique in this work has been arc spectrography. While there is nothing novel in the use of this method in glass analysis, it produced for years simply qualitative results. Sayre,[4] however, had developed his methodology to the point where results are reproducible with standard deviations within twenty per cent of reported values. Arc spectrography offers the advantage that it is rapid, recording the concentrations of a large number of elements with one or two exposures. A disadvantage is that the operation consumes the specimen. Certain elements, also, do not show up satisfactorily in arc spectrography, for example phosphorus.

X-ray fluorescence has also proved its usefulness for our purposes. It is non-destructive, and either powdered samples or complete specimens of considerable size can be examined. In the latter case, a coloured spot may be caused by the exposure, but it is easily eliminated by moderate heating. The data produced by X-ray fluorescence is valid only for that portion of a specimen which lies close to the surface, a fact that must be considered if there is any surface contamination, decay, or lack of homogeneity. It has been determined that X-ray fluorescence is able to handle somewhat smaller samples than those required by arc spectrography, and that it can satisfactorily measure the concentrations of the five elements of Table A.

An important refinement of X-ray fluorescence, called the electron microbeam probe, is now available. This apparatus focuses its beam on an area only one micron in diameter, and can thus be used on extremely small specimens. Although the method has already been applied to archaeological problems, very little, if any, use of it has been made with ancient glass.

Several applications of the electron microbeam probe in respect to archaeological glass suggest themselves readily. One of them might well reveal the identity of a component material in glass of the fifth century AD. At that time glassmaking competence was in retrogression almost everywhere. Through carelessness or inability the impure matrix of a vessel frequently showed red streaks. The phenomenon was particularly frequent in the Rhineland. It is assumed that the glassmakers did not melt their batches at a sufficiently high temperature to achieve complete homogeneity, and that the red streaks represent movement of one of the imperfectly fused materials during the inflation of the paraison on the master's blowpipe.

If the microscopic beam of the electron probe were passed across the surface of such a vessel, there would be a sudden increase in the recording of concentrations for some elements and decreases for others at the moment the scanning cuts across one of the hairlines of these red streaks. This evidence might establish the approximate composition of one of the substances going into the batch, and lead to its identification with some type of natural deposit available to the ancients.

Another valuable use for the electron microbeam probe would be in determining the colour chemistry of fused mosaic plaques.[6] These precious tiny slices sometimes carry six or more colours of glass, both opaque and transparent, in closely spaced, minute areas. A scanning with the microbeam probe would quickly reveal the oxides by which each colour effect was set up. If one or two colours showed a divergence in its basic composition from the others, the possibility would have to be considered that the glass factory, unable to produce certain colours, had to go afield for these special shades.

Supplementing arc spectrography and the X-ray fluorescence equipment, flame photometry and colorimetry have been used with success for special purposes. Older methods of wet chemistry are still used effectively in the examination of archaeological glass specimens, and will continue to be applied, particularly to specialized problems involving small numbers of specimens. As the newer techniques are further refined and become more rapid, sensitive, accurate and economical, they are likely to be increasingly used. This will certainly be the case in larger programmes where extensive series of specimens are to be examined.

There can be little doubt that future research on ancient glass will turn to still unused, advanced methods of analysis. Sayre, for example, has already used the atomic reactor at Brookhaven with success on Greek pottery, and his preliminary investigations of ancient glass with the same neutron activation method show that certain patterns in the rare earths are present and can be uncovered in this way. Neutron activation can work with concentrations below the limits of spectrographic sensitivity, in fact can detect and measure some elements down to concentrations of a few parts per million million. The method is thus advantageous in the study of 'trace-trace' elements. As it is arduous and time-consuming, however, its use is likely to be confined for the present to problems beyond the reach of other methods.

Before examining further the probable future course of technological research on ancient glass, it is advisable to consider the proper objectives of this research. As the available basic analytical data expand, which is rapidly occurring, the archaeologist will expect the technologist to submit his findings in a form susceptible of far-reaching interpretation.

We have seen that a specimen of ancient glass can now be assigned to a compositional group on the basis of its analysis. This is analytical dating of a sort, but is only useful to the extent that the range in time of a group is not inordinately long. It is not enough to be able to determine, shall we say, that a given specimen belongs to the antimony-rich group and was made somewhere between the sixth century BC and fourth century AD. The span of a thousand years must be reduced to a century or less. The archaeologist, moreover, will insist on knowing where the specimen was produced.

Actually, there is a widespread misconception about the importance of 'dating techniques'. As valuable as it frequently is for the technologist to tell the archaeologist how ancient an object is, it would be obviously absurd to conclude that the usefulness of a method begins and ends with its ability to 'date'. The period of production of much ancient glass is already known from such circumstances as style, inscriptions, and association with other dated objects.

What we are after is much more basic and comprehensive. The objective is no less than that of archaeology itself—the advancement of human knowledge through the study of ancient cultures. We believe that man's understanding of himself, his future and his relationship to the order of things will immensely benefit from an expanded comprehension of his origins and his past. To be sure, the improved ability to date our objects will be an important result of the current technological advances. But this is only a small segment, albeit a significant one, of the range of benefits that technology is busily preparing.

We must at long last determine which substances were used as raw materials in each period. Little progress has been made in this direction. It is still moot, for example, whether plant ashes or soda deposits were used as the necessary alkalis. The resolution of these questions will open the way for an attack on a problem of far-reaching significance—the identification of individual deposits. If this can be accomplished, the door will open for significant new light to be shed on trade routes in antiquity.

A hint of these possibilities is contained in the recent observation that the basic composition of glass did not change in the Western Provinces with the break-up of Roman power in the fourth century AD. The analysis of a piece of Frankish glass from the Rhineland, for example, of the seventh century AD, is very little divergent from that of a beaker found at Pompeii from the first century. As it is commonly believed that no local source of soda alkali was available to the glassmakers in the West, it would appear that commercial traffic on the Mediterranean continued to be active, despite the political dislocations attendant on the events of the fourth century.

Ancient glass and its manufacturing background will not be adequately understood until more is known of furnace design and shop techniques. At each juncture of development there was a maximum level of accomplishment, determined in some measure by the highest attainable furnace temperature. This was dependent in turn on the type of fuel used as well as on furnace design. It is likely that changes in these practical conditions will have coincided at times with new departures in glass composition and with marked changes, up or down, in the quality of the product.

Firing circumstances in ancient glass furnaces, that is, the existence or absence of reducing conditions, will have profoundly affected the level of glass competence. And finally, chemistry of decolorization and the achievement of an extensive glass palette are matters that should be fully explored.

Research on the shop traditions of ancient glassmakers necessitates an ambitious pilot plant programme. We can learn with certainty how the ancients made their products in no other way than by doing it ourselves. When the raw materials used in antiquity are positively identified by careful analytical research, they should be melted down in the proportions used for the known ancient groups, and each type of glass fashioned under conditions duplicating as closely as possible the confirmed or presumed circumstances that obtained in these early shops.

This means constructing crucibles and furnaces and the use exclusively of tools and shop equipment which, in the absence of direct knowledge, may be assumed to have been available in the early periods of the art. The results of this exercise will surely be astonishing in given instances. Before drawing any conclusions as to how a type of glass was fashioned, every possible bit of evidence must be derived from the objects themselves. Visual examination can reveal tool and mould marks. The study of ancient glass surfaces, using the microscope if necessary, frequently produces clear evidence of an object's manipulative background.

No inquisitive observation of ancient glass should proceed without close attention to its bubble pattern. These virtually always-present flaws speak volumes. The size, shape, orientation and distribution of bubbles illuminate the handling of an object from the time an incandescent blob of fused raw materials is withdrawn from the crucible until hardening of the matrix on the blowpipe or pontil, or within a mould, precludes any further fashioning except by the cold technique of abrasion. The behaviour of bubbles in viscous glass is still only imperfectly understood. Full interpretation of bubble evidence cannot be achieved until all contributing factors have been precisely determined at the laboratory level.

One of the end products of forthcoming research on ancient glass will be some understanding of the structure of the vast industry that created it. We need to know whether it was competitive or monopolistic, whether it controlled its sources of raw materials or had to bid against other consumers for its basic substances. And where was the fountainhead at each period, whence came the epochal advances of early glass history.

It will be valuable to determine, for example, whether there were several 'sides' to the industry at any given period. Did the expansion of the industry in the first century AD occur from a Syrian and an Egyptian base separately? Or was there indeed any distinction, organizationally or technically, between the glassmaking of Sidon and Alexandria? How revealing it would be to determine that two distinct types of glass, compositionally speaking, were being made concurrently in the Rhineland at the end of the second century AD, and that one of them was identical with Syrian, the other with Egyptian production of the same time.

How, then, are these matters to be settled? Probably not by sole reliance on analytical methods presently in use. Many of the differentiations, albeit systematic ones, that will be the keys to important problems, will be found only in the extremely low concentrations of 'trace-trace' elements, or in subtle differences in the amounts of larger constituents. Thus an even greater degree of sensitivity and accuracy will be required in analytical methods. Neutron activation, for example, is likely to be increasingly used.

A purely hypothetical case will illustrate the possibilities of 'trace-trace' analysis. When analysed by normal methods, glass found at Pompeii from the first century AD is indistinguishable in composition from that made at Sidon. It may well be that both were made from the same materials with a common source. A systematic distinction might still be present if the crucibles were made from local clays in each instance. In Pompeii, shall we say, the corrosive action of the hot furnaces drew a minute concentration of an element from the crucibles into the batch, whereas this element, not being present in the clay used for Sidonian crucibles, cannot be found in glass from Sidon. The point is that such a minor systematic distinction would be impossible to detect except by 'trace-trace' methods.

There is good reason to believe that isotopic studies will have to be applied to the analysis of archaeological specimens. It is known that systematic isotopic ratio differences for some elements are to be found in nature, according to the geologic history of a substance or other circumstances, and that in some cases one or more isotopic ratios will accordingly vary from deposit to deposit. In any case, the availablity of the mass spectrometer suggests that isotopic research in various directions could benefit research on ancient glass.

The perfection of an ingenious new direct dating technique for glass will be watched with keen interest. Brill and Hood[2] have announced that decay in buried glass specimens proceeds under the influence of annual temperature or humidity cycles in such a manner that visible discontinuities in the cross-section of a layer of decay can be counted under the microscope as one would count the rings on a sawed tree trunk. Four specimens of ancient glass have thus far been examined in this way. They were found at ancient sites in Nishapur (Iran) and Sardis (Turkey). In all cases the number of layers counted corresponded approximately to the presumed age of the specimens on the basis of other evidence. The technique will be useful on glass which acquires a tight layer of decay, permitting cross-sections to be prepared.

The Brill-Hood method will be particularly valuable in special cases. For example, there are periods where the date of glass is seldom known. This is true of glass made between the seventh and eleventh centuries AD in the Middle East. Such specimens are not found in graves, and usually come from refuse heaps or other places which are disturbed or otherwise unsuitable for normal stratification dating. Due to these difficulties it has not been possible thus far to determine when and where the early Islamic composition was introduced. We know that it was not used in Egypt on glass weights and vessel stamps until the tenth century. It is further demonstrable that it was in use in Mesopotamia and Persia by the tenth century and probably in the ninth. But it occurs in certain objects from these areas which may well be earlier, their dates being still uncertain.

If the Brill-Hood technique can be perfected, it could be used to date with certainty a series of glass objects embracing a cross-section of glass accomplishment in various Islamic areas during these difficult centuries. This should provide the answer to the riddle of when and where the older 'Roman' composition was first abandoned in favour of a newer and doubtless more advanced glassmaking formula.

Meanwhile, excellent progress has been made with some of the specialized problems of glass research. Turner, for example, has been particularly active in exploring the methods used by the ancients to produce opacity and a range of desirable colours and in investigating other aspects of ancient glassmaking. Bezborodov[1] has analysed large numbers of specimens found in southern Russia, of which only a part qualify as ancient under the arbitrary definition of Sayre and Smith.[4]

As early as 1938 Seligman and Beck[5] examined numerous ancient Chinese glass objects, revealing that many such objects are rich in lead and others in barium, the latter not occurring in occidental glass except in traces. Caley[3] has now published a comprehensive résumé of analytical work on ancient glass.

The developing surge of research on ancient glass can proceed, as we have seen, on the basis of extensive preliminary published work. Perhaps there is danger that it will move forward too impetuously in some respects. Certainly there is need for much basic research before many of the ultimate projects are undertaken. Some of these necessary preparatory investigations have been mentioned. Others are:

(a) A searching study of the phenomenon of ageing, including the process of surface decay of buried and submerged glass. Some good work has been done in this direction, but little progress has been made in determining the precise relationships through which physical and chemical situations within the glass produce different types of decay at various rates when in contact with given soil conditions.

(b) Investigation of the selective absorption by plants of elements in the soils in which they grow.

(c) A survey of the raw materials which might have served the glass industries of antiquity in all areas accessible to presumed glass-manufacturing centres. This must include not only conventional chemical analysis, but the determination of 'trace-trace' concentrations and the investigation of isotopic ratios of possible usefulness in glass research.

(d) The detection and measurement of the maximum number of chemical elements which can be found in ancient glass, using a limited and carefully selected series of specimens typical of all periods and areas. In this work the most sensitive methods known should be used, irrespective of cost. This broad investigation should precede any extensive 'trace-trace' analyses in specific projects. Certainly many more elements than have been reported can be detected in ancient glass, and until the basic work has been performed it will be impossible to estimate where the most promising 'trace-trace' research can be undertaken.

The basic work alone that lies ahead is an immense commitment. It cannot all be done soon, and some of it will have to wait until the results accrue incidentally from programmes unrelated to glass research.

The stage is thus being set for large-scale research on ancient glass, work that will illuminate the field to a degree still visualized by few. It is doubtful, indeed it is perhaps not desirable, that such a programme will be authoritatively directed from any central point. Certainly the magnitude of the task will require the participation of numerous laboratories. It is to be hoped, in any case, that ample cross-contacts will be maintained between those undertaking glass research so that each contributes the most significant and effective work possible within the limitations of his facilities and resources, and that the programme as a whole advances purposefully towards its worthwhile goals.

REFERENCES
1 BEZBORODOV, M. A. 1956. Glass manufacturing in ancient Russia (in Russian), *Izdatel, Akad. Nauk Belarus S.S.R.*, no. 4758, Minsk
2 BRILL, R. H. and HOOD, H. P. 1961. *Nature 189*, 12–14
3 CALEY, E. R. 1961. Analyses of Ancient Glasses, 1790–1957; *Corning Mus. of Glass, Publ. Mon.*, Vol. 1
4 SAYRE, E. V. and SMITH, R. W. 1962. *Science 133*, 1824–26
5 SELIGMAN, C. G. and BECK, H. C. 1938. *Mus. Far East. Antiq., Bull.* no. 10, Stockholm
6 SMITH, R. W. 1957. Glass from the Ancient World. *Corning Mus. of Glass Publ.* nos. 98–121
7 —— 1958. *Archaeology 11*, 111–116

55 Fibres of Archaeological Interest: Their Examination and Identification

H. M. APPLEYARD and A. B. WILDMAN

THIS CHAPTER IS CONCERNED WITH the fibres which are found at archaeological sites, whether they are from fabrics or skins and with particular emphasis on any diagnostic features of their microstructure. Garments and the construction of fabric remains have already been adequately described elsewhere.[2,5] We have not taken part in any of the field work connected with these discoveries but have examined samples of fabrics, yarns or loose fibres for those who have been directly connected with the excavations or who are responsible for the preservation of the finds.

For the dating of the samples reliance has been placed upon the information supplied with them. The date of these samples must be determined by other relics found on the same site. Unaccompanied textile remains are very difficult to date.

All animal fibres of archaeological interest examined by us have had one common feature, they were all stained various shades of brown ranging from a light yellowish-brown to a very dark brown; this also applied to most of the vegetable fibres. Difficulty has therefore been experienced in commenting on the colour of many of these fibres, that is whether or not they have been dyed or whether the colour is due to natural processes in the course of the years in storage.

Some fabrics may have been bleached originally but it is not possible now to say if they had any treatments comparable to present-day finishing processes. It is known that bleaching and scouring processes did exist in ancient times; there are references to bleaching and scouring of cloth dating back to Roman and early Egyptian times.[7] One of the early works on bleaching is a review by Dr Francis Home of the methods used in Britain and Holland.[8]

THE PREPARATION OF FIBRES FOR EXAMINATION

In this chapter the names given to different types of cuticular-scale pattern and other structural features of mammalian fibres are from Wildman's classification.[12] The manner in which the sample of fibres is manipulated depends upon several factors but particularly upon its size and state of preservation. The historical value of excavated garments, coverings and skins or fragments of these means that in almost all instances samples which are available for fibre examination and identification are necessarily small; usually, therefore, extremely little material is available for any chemical tests, cross-sectioning and other manipulations. The whole sample is generally used for these examinations and the process of preparing representative sub-samples of archaeological material, so necessary for samples of modern textiles, is not usually carried out: when, for example, a small sample of cloth is in a very poor state of preservation it will easily disintegrate and cannot be handled to the extent of sub-sampling; special measures have in fact to be taken to protect the sample from the effects of even the minimum necessary manipulation. Frequently samples consist of a few scraps of degraded warp and weft thread or even just a tiny collection of fibre fragments. In addition to the samples already mentioned fragments of skin and hair are occasionally received from archaeological sites.

First of all, if the sample is fabric with a recognizable weave, the type of weave is noted in the manner set forth in the detailed descriptions of some samples given later in this paper. When the fabric piece is extremely fragile it is treated prior to laboratory manipulation with polyvinyl acetate solution to hold it together and prevent it breaking into small fragments.

A small amount of any sample suspected of consisting wholly or partly of fibres of vegetable origin is submitted to staining and solubility tests designed to reveal their presence. Reference is made later in the paper to the preparation for examination of fibres of vegetable origin.

Small samples of fabric are examined dry through stereoscopic binoculars using objectives with magnifications of from × 1·25 to × 10, to observe the weave and general cloth construction.

The preparation of fibre whole mounts. Whole mounts of fibres are often made and their preparation is a routine operation with each sample submitted; indeed where the sample is very fragile it may be the only kind of mount possible for examination microscopically. Washing or cleaning the fibres in ether or benzene is not usually possible with archaeological samples and the fibres are therefore mounted straight away in the mounting medium.

The best medium for this purpose is liquid paraffin, its refractive index (1·470) being sufficiently different from that of the keratin of animal fibres (1·548) to allow cuticular-scale margins to be visible but not so far different to produce undesirable optical effects; the relatively high viscosity of paraffin is also an advantage in helping to hold fragile fibres, preventing them from disintegrating on the microscope slide.

Whole mounts reveal the relative thickness of fibres, the presence of pigment, its type and distribution and sometimes also the medulla and the pattern formed by the external margins of the cuticular scales.

Cross-sections of fibres. Sometimes information provided by whole-mount examination is not sufficient to identify fibres: transverse sections of fibres show more precisely the type and distribution of natural pigment, the relative thickness of the cuticle and the structure of the medulla. These characteristics constitute very useful evidence for fibre identification: furthermore it is usually possible to obtain cross-sections of even the most fragile fibres (Plate XXXVIIIc). Good cross-sections of fibres at thicknesses of approximately 20–25 μm may be cut using a Hardy type hand microtome which is described elsewhere.[12] The fibres, again without cleaning in any way, are inserted with celloidin in the slot of the microtome and cut in the ordinary way; if the fibres available are very few in number they may be surrounded in the slot by wool or other available fibres which then form a packing material.

Preparation of fibres to show their cuticular-scale patterns. The patterns formed by the external margins of the cuticular scales are among the most important aids to the identification of mammalian fibres; this is particularly so where the fibres are of sufficient length to facilitate the observation of pattern sequences along their lengths: fibres in archaeological samples are often rather short and broken and therefore less precise identifications are possible than with fibres of more recent origin which are not so degraded. Nevertheless, and this will be demonstrated later in the chapter, the cuticular scale pattern of even short lengths of fibres can be a valuable clue to their identity, and fortunately it is possible to obtain casts of the scale patterns of some of these fibres. Methods of making such casts are described elsewhere in detail:[12] perhaps the best method for these fibres is the one in which the fibres are placed between two slides one of which is coated with a thin film of polyvinyl acetate (PVA): the whole preparation receives slight pressure in a light press, which incorporates a warm plate, whilst being warmed to the melting point of the PVA. The preparation is then cooled, the slides separated and the fibres peeled out leaving a cast of the surface of the fibres in the PVA (Plate XXXIXd). When the fibres are too fragile even for this treatment, the semi-embedding technique is employed; in this method the fibre remains on a microscope slide, and a medium with a refractive index near that of keratin, e.g. celluloid solution or glycerine jelly, is allowed to drain along both sides of the fibre. The upper surface is not covered and only the under half of the fibre is in contact with the medium. Sometimes PVA is used for this purpose. Where possible the scale-cast method is employed, because this eliminates from the preparation pigment and other fibre details which otherwise may obscure the scale margins.

THE IDENTIFICATION OF FIBRES FROM ARCHAEOLOGICAL SITES

Mammalian fibres can only be identified by methods of microscopy: keratin is common to all of them and therefore chemical and staining methods are of no use. Fibres from different families and orders or groups of mammals can be distinguished microscopically but those from different animals of the same species naturally resemble each other in many features: however, as elaborated below, it is sometimes possible to distinguish fibres as originating from, for example, a variety of sheep such as Down, mountain or lustre type when it is not possible to specify the precise breed of origin. From whole mounts alone one may in some instances determine the origin of a fibre; some animal fibres, such as, for example, mohair, camel hair and cashmere, are very uniform in fibre thickness along their lengths as opposed to wool fibres which are very variable along their lengths. If, for example, in addition to a very uniform fibre thickness, the scale pattern can be seen in the whole mount to be an irregular waved mosaic (Fig. 112a), with the characteristic steeply-sloping margins of fine camel hair, then the fibre may be identified immediately. However, the scale margins cannot always be seen in whole mounts of archaeological specimens and usually it is best where possible to cut cross-sections and also prepare casts of the cuticular surface. Evidence such as the distribution of pigment, relative thickness of cuticle, type of medulla and pattern of scale margins can be built up from these different preparations and a more accurate diagnosis made.

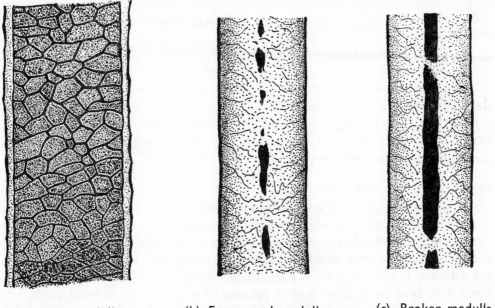

| (a) Lattice medulla | (b) Fragmental medulla | (c) Broken medulla |

Fig. 111 Types of medulla.

An example of the diagnostic value, with some fibres, of cross-sections is provided by Plate XXXVIIIc. These fibres were identified as human hair because of the dense concentration of pigment granules towards the cuticle and the characteristic shape of the narrow medulla.

We have stated that where the scale margins of fibres can be seen their pattern even on short lengths of fibre, together with evidence from whole mounts and perhaps cross-sections, enables a statement of their possible origins to be made with some confidence. Fibres may be identified as originating for example from certain groups of sheep: the cuticular-scale pattern of coarse outer-coat fibres from mountain sheep, e.g. Scottish Blackface, is of the type known as irregular mosaic (Fig. 112b) and this together with the presence of a coarse lattice type medulla (Fig. 111a) is characteristic. Again, the scale margins of medium to coarse lustre wool fibres form an irregular mosaic pattern of a rather different kind,[12] the fibres being either non-medullated or with a narrow interrupted or fragmental medulla (Fig. 111b). Fine wool fibres, for example from Down sheep which are quite common in medieval remains in Britain, are non-medullated with a cuticular-scale pattern of the irregular mosaic type with smooth margins and often of the waved variety (Fig. 112a).

Skin fragments. Fragments of skin which have been used for a variety of purposes, such as clothing, burial wrapping, sheaths for weapons and as parchment, can usually be readily identified by an experienced investigator. Pieces of material thought to be skin may be softened and relaxed in softening fluids and they may be sectioned on a microtome. The sections when stained by any of several nuclear and cytoplasmic stains show portions of epidermis connective tissue and root sheaths of follicles; they may even show follicle bulbs at the base of several follicles. The presence of fibre follicles may even be detected in softened fragments without any necessity for staining. Plate XXXVIIIb is a photograph of a section of parchment from the Dead Sea Scrolls in which fibres in their follicles may be seen. These sections were prepared by Dr M. L. Ryder.

There is an element of danger in attempting to identify fibre remains in parchment: these fibres are usually very short and each consists of the basal portion only of the original fibre: only one type of scale pattern therefore is shown. Several types of fibres have a similar scale pattern in this basal region, the pattern changing to a more distinctive and characteristic one further up the fibre.

DESCRIPTIONS OF SAMPLES EXAMINED

Fibres of vegetable origin. Fibres of vegetable origin often decay faster than animal fibres. This is particularly noticeable on sites where the soil is acidic. Examples of fabrics have been unearthed which contained fragments of vegetable fibres in the weft direction. Such examples are usually from cloths made chiefly from animal fibres and decorated with a weft yarn made from vegetable fibres. In some of these fabrics the animal fibres have been comparatively well preserved but gaps have occurred in the weft direction where the vegetable fibres had been. Vegetable fibres from some sites where the conditions have been favourable for preservation have been unearthed.

The earliest examples of vegetable fibres have been from Jutish and Saxon sites in Britain and from a sixth-century site in Turkey. The example from the Jutish site consisted of a few strands of fibres attached to the back of a brooch. These fibres were very fragile and could only be examined in whole mount; the fibres were not strong enough for other preparations, and were too discoloured for staining tests to be of any use. All that could be said of these fibres was that they were of vegetable origin.

Fibres from the Saxon site were quite well preserved. These were from very small fragments of woven cloth, but unfortunately they were very dark in colour so that

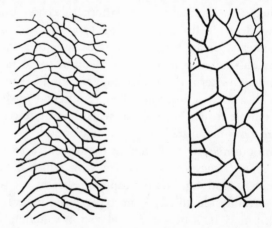

Fig. 112 Some cuticular-scale patterns. (a) Irregular mosaic: waved (b) Irregular mosaic

staining tests were of no value; their microscopical appearance showed that they were bast fibres and were very similar to flax.

A stronger and better-preserved sample of vegetable fibres from a plain-weave cloth was found among unstratified material at an Anglo-Saxon cemetery at Fonaby.[4] This sample was dark in colour and was strong enough to withstand sectioning. The cross-sectional shape of these fibres and the shape and size of the lumen suggested that they were flax; microscopical evidence only could be obtained from this sample (Plate XXXIa).

By far the best examples of vegetable fibres so far examined came from sixth-century Turkish tombs. These were from samples of cloth in plain weave which had been decorated with coloured silks. Several samples were examined and all were very well preserved; the weft from one was very clearly cotton. All the other samples had a similar appearance when viewed in whole mount; only one, however, was unstained and staining tests listed by the Textile Institute were used.[11] From these tests, appearance in whole mount and cross-section it was reasonably certain that this particular yarn consisted of flax fibres. The other yarns were certainly made from bast fibres and from microscopical preparations they were similar to flax (Plate XXXIXa).

Fibres of animal origin. Animal fibres, especially wool fibres, are particularly interesting because they provide evidence of the different types of fibres used by peoples in early periods of history. In view of the very wide range of types and qualities of wool used in the textile trade today it is most interesting to discover what types of wool have been produced in former days. Britain today produces many types of wool from the fine Southdown to the coarse mattress type of wool grown by the Scottish Blackface sheep. Leggett states that there were both wild and semi-domesticated sheep in Britain at the time of the Roman invasion, and suggested that the Romans introduced improved methods of breeding.[10]

The production of wool became of great importance to the economy of England and, according to Carus-Wilson,[1] in the thirteenth century English wool was in demand by the Continental weavers because of its good quality, especially wool from the Lindsay region of Lincolnshire which was required for fine-quality cloth in Flanders. Historians suggest that the sheep in England in these early periods were of the fine-wooled varieties, and evidence to support this has been found in some of the samples we have examined.

There is also evidence to support the idea that there were at least two types of sheep in Britain, even as early as the date of the Roman invasion. Roman historians reporting on conditions in Britain at the beginning of their occupation claimed that two kinds of cloth were woven by the natives in the eastern part of England, one a thick, harsh cloth, the other a fine-spun wool cloth woven in a check design in different colours.

Only a few samples from the Bronze Age have been examined and these were not very rewarding; one sample, preserved in PVA, was so badly damaged that it was not possible even to say whether the fibres were of animal or vegetable origin. Another sample, also preserved in PVA, was recognized as being of animal fibres, but there was not enough evidence to say what type of animal fibre. The only interesting feature in these fibres was that they were medullated, the medulla being very wide in comparison with the diameter of the fibres which was 12–15 μm. A third sample from the Bronze Age was most tantalizing; they were animal fibres; cross-sections were made and one very short length of scale pattern was found, but did not provide sufficient evidence for identification purposes. The thickness ranged from approximately 10–30 μ, the finer fibres were not medullated but some of the coarse fibres had a fine lattice type medulla, all were pigmented and in some fibres the pigment granules were arranged bi-laterally. By contrast it was most interesting to examine an extremely well-preserved sample of fibres sent to us by Dr M. L. Ryder. This sample was from a whole skin found in a frozen burial mound in Siberia; it was dated 500 BC. The skin was thought to be from sheep or goat. The fibres were in a remarkably good state of preservation; the scale structure was exceedingly clear, as clear as on newly grown wool fibres. The features of the fibres showed quite clearly that they were wool. The sample included fine non-medullated fibres of approximately 15 μ diameter, fibres of medium thickness, non-medullated and approximately 40 μ in diameter, and some coarse medullated fibres of approximately 85 μ diameter. An interesting feature of these coarse fibres was the width of the medulla; it was much narrower than one would expect in wool fibres of this thickness. These coarse fibres were dissimilar from those of known primitive breeds which have a wide lattice type medulla.

Roman site. Work on a Roman site at Ghirza in Tripolitania revealed two samples of pigmented animal fibres, one, a repp cloth consisting of fibres of medium thickness with interrupted medulla in some fibres. In whole mount the fibres were seen to be too regular in thickness along their length for wool fibres. Scale casts were made of fibres where the scale pattern still remained, the scale margins were crenate and the patterns were very similar in appearance to those seen on fibres from the common goat. The second sample from this site was of unspun hair, and this example serves to show the value of observing the pigment distribution. In cross-section the distribution of pigment granules and the size and shape of the medulla were clearly visible. When these sections were compared with sections of known human hair the chief difference was in the thickness of the layer of cuticular scales. Human hair has a thick layer of cuticle whereas the fibres in the sample had a thinner layer than one would expect to find on human hair; this could have been the result of degradation of the outer surface. Other factors, that is, distribution of pigment and the size and shape of medulla, matched those seen in human hair. Pigment in human hair is often densest near the cuticle, becoming less dense near the medulla. Where the scale pattern could be seen on these fibres it was of the same type as that seen along the length of human hair, i.e. waved, crenate with near to close margins. There was, therefore, enough evidence to be as definite as one can be on these samples to identify these fibres as being of human origin (Plate XXXVIIIc).

Samples from the caves at Muraba'ât. Several samples from the caves at Muraba'ât in Jordan were examined some time ago. The fabrics from which these samples were taken were described by Crowfoot,[2] some were plain weave, some fine tapestry and some regular tapestry. The probable date of these is given as AD 132 and onwards. Some of these fibres were very badly degraded and were beyond recognition, others were comparatively well preserved and there was sufficient evidence to indicate their origin. Of the samples examined two could not be identified, four were identified as wool and another probably wool, two were almost certainly camel hair and one was goat hair; the last three samples provided the greatest interest.

Some of the fibres were coarse and had a continuous medulla and streaky pigment distribution characteristics of camel hair, others were fine and had scale patterns similar to those seen on fine fibres from the camel. A difficulty arose with one of these samples of coarse fibres. It had been suggested that this sample could possibly be goat hairs now some coarse fibres from the common goat have features which are similar to those of coarse fibres from other animals. One feature which makes the identification of goat hair certain is a scale pattern on some coarse fibres which is transitional between smooth and rippled-crenate margins. To find this pattern it is necessary to make casts of as long a piece of fibre as possible; the small size of the available piece of yarn and the condition of the surface of the fibres made it difficult to find this particular pattern.

Cross-sections of these fibres were cut and several were found which had contours similar to some goat fibres. The distribution of pigment in these fibres was significant; in a number of goat fibres the pigment is in large aggregates arranged in a radial pattern, and this distribution was found in some fibres in this particular sample. It was this evidence which led to the conclusion that the original suggestion that the sample was made from goat hair was correct.

Saxon period. A short piece of yarn from a Saxon cemetery was one of the few samples which was made from coarse wool fibres. The scale margins were easily seen and the scale patterns were similar to those seen on coarse fibres from present-day British mountain breeds and on the coarse fibres from some of the primitive breeds of sheep such as the Mouflon and Urial.

The form of the fabrics found at Sutton Hoo and Broomfield Barrow were in good condition and were described by Crowfoot[3] as diamond twill, twill in two colours and tablet weave. Unfortunately the fibres were not in such good condition. The weaves were also described as being similar to those of Scandinavian origin, particularly from Denmark. In only one of these samples could the fibres be identified as being wool; the scale pattern was clear on some fibres, and a few were medullated. Fibres in the other samples were too badly degraded for a full identification; they could be described only as being of animal origin.

Anglo-Saxon period. Two samples from Taplow Barrow consisted of both coarse and fine fibres. One fragment of cloth was a 2/2 twill and thought to have been part of a cloak, the other was a plain weave. Unfortunately fibres from these samples were badly degraded and very little detail could be found on the surface of the fibres. The coarse fibres had the wide lattice-type of medulla found in the coarse fibres from British mountain wools and coarse fibres from primitive breeds.

This example and the previous one from the Saxon period suggest that at these periods in British agriculture double-coated breeds of sheep were extant, that is sheep with long coarse outer-coat fibres and short fine under-coat fibres.

The sample thought to be from a cloak also contained a number of pigmented fibres, some very densely pigmented and others only sparsely. This was also a feature of both primitive breeds and some of our present-day British mountain breeds.

Several samples from a site at Fonaby in Lincolnshire were examined; some could only be identified as being of animal origin. One of these samples from unstratified material, labelled US95b by Hawkes,[4] was of particular interest. This was a tuft of hair found lying on but not attached to a sample of cloth in plain weave (US95a).[4] Some of these fibres were pigmented and parts of the fibre follicles were still attached to the root ends. No scale patterns could be found on these fibres but they were strong enough for sections to be cut. It was seen from these cross-sections that the fibres had contours and shape and size of medullae similar to those of body hair from cattle. The shape of cattle body hair is elliptical in cross-section; the medulla is also elliptical and concentric with the outer edge of the fibre.

The root ends of these fibres were similar to those on fibres which are removed from pieces of skin. There is a trade practice in use at the present time of obtaining wool from small pieces of skin by leaving a pile of skin pieces to stand in a moist condition until the skin has rotted away leaving the wool fibres intact for use in textiles. The presence of this type of root end on the tuft of fibres (US95b) suggests that they could have come from a hide used as a covering.

Sixteenth-century sample from Northern Ireland. An example of wool fibres being preserved in a bog was found at Flanders Farm, Dungiven. The sample, part of a fabric, was well preserved. The fibres were degraded but it was possible to make quite good casts which showed wool-type scale patterns. In whole mount most of the fibres were seen to be fine, others were of medium diameter and had broken medullae, some of the fibres were densely pigmented.

Archaeological field experiment. An archaeological field experiment has been organized by the British Association at Overton Down, near Marlborough. Textile fabrics were buried in an earthwork on a chalk site and samples of fabrics will be recovered at intervals. Samples of wool cloth have been supplied by the Wool Industries Research Association and the recovered samples will be examined and compared with control samples in the Association's laboratories. It is hoped that this experiment will provide some of the answers to problems relating to the preservation of textiles, including degradation and discoloration of fibres. Archaeologists of the future will be able to reap the benefits of this experiment. A report after the first few years of the experiment has now been published.[9]

ACKNOWLEDGEMENTS

The authors wish to thank Miss E. Crowfoot and Miss A. S. Henshall for supplying the material for examination, Mrs S. E. Hawkes for permission to refer to the samples from Fonaby and to Mr R. L. S. Bruce-Mitford of the British Museum, for permission to refer to the samples from Sutton Hoo and Taplow Barrow. We are indebted to Professor Burton, formerly of the Leather Department of the University of Leeds, and his colleagues for samples of parchment from the Dead Sea Scrolls. We thank also Dr D. J. Smith and Lady Brogan, Department of Classics and Ancient History, King's

(a) Part of the pneumatic tube system installed at the north face of the Brookhaven reactor. Here a small container, bearing sample material, is being inserted into one of the tubes. The container is then sped into the reactor under pneumatic pressure, for bombardment by neutrons. The sample, now radioactive, is quickly returned for use in some experiment. The system is useful in making radioactive isotopes of short half-life, which lose their radioactivity in seconds, or minutes. Delivery can be made either into this face of the reactor, or directly into one of several adjoining laboratories. Photo courtesy Brookhaven National Laboratory.

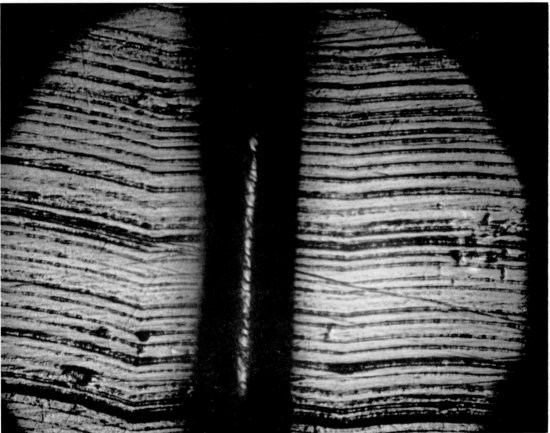

(b) Photomicrograph showing the laminar structure of a small piece of weathering crust on glass. The dark central band is a human hair placed across the layers to show the relative scale of sizes. Photo courtesy Corning Museum of Glass.

(see page 614) PLATE XXXVII

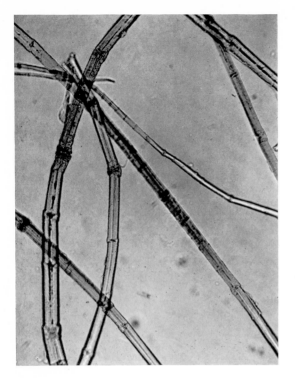

(a) Whole mount of fibres from sixth-century Turkish tombs (× 200).

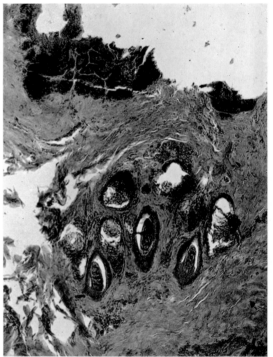

(b) Section of parchment from the Dead Sea Scrolls (× 88).

(c) Cross-section of unspun fibres from Ghirza (× 200).

PLATE XXXVIII (see page 624)

(a) Cross-section of fibres from Fonaby: packing of wool fibres (×190).

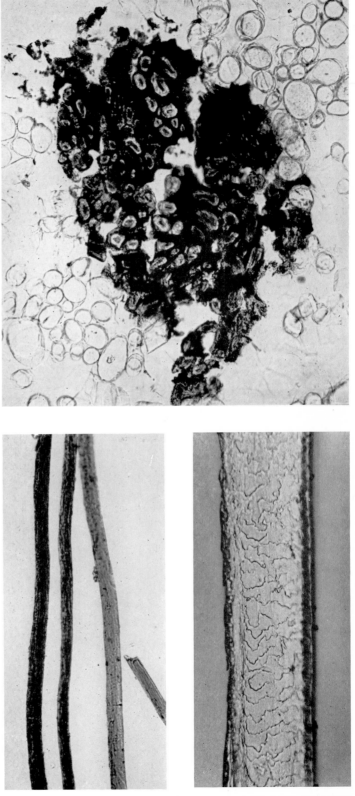

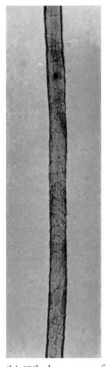

(b) Whole mount of fibres from Muraba'-ât (×200).

(c) Whole mount of pigmented fibres from Taplow Barrow (×210).
(d) Scale cast of fibre from Muraba'-ât. (×400)

(see page 624) PLATE XXXIX

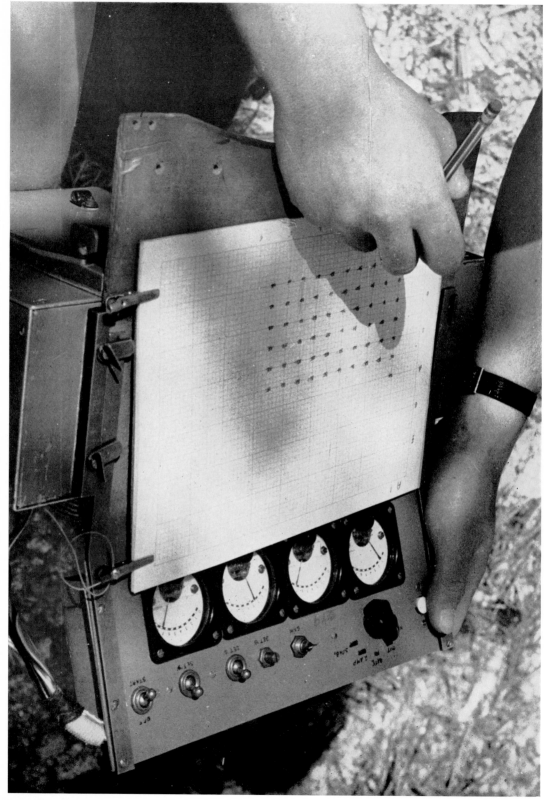

Taking readings with the proton magnetometer. Photo Thomas Thompson.

PLATE XL (see page 681)

College, Newcastle upon Tyne, for permission to refer to the samples from Ghirza. The technical assistance given by various members of the staff of the Biology Department of the Wool Industries Research Association is highly appreciated.

REFERENCES

1 CARUS-WILSON, E. 1952. The Woollen Industry; in POSTAN, M. and RICH, E. E. (ed.) *Cambridge Economic History of Europe*, Cambridge
2 CROWFOOT, E. 1961. Les Grottes de Murabaat, *Discoveries in the Judaean Desert*, Oxford, II
3 CROWFOOT, G. M. Personal communication
4 HAWKES, S. E. Forthcoming publication
5 HENSHALL, A. S. 1951–52. Early Textiles Found in Scotland. *Proc. Soc. Ant. Scot.*
6 —— Forthcoming publication
7 HIGGINS, S. E. 1924. *A History of Bleaching*, London
8 HOME, F. 1771. *Experiments on Bleaching*, Dublin
9 JEWELL, P. A. and DIMBLEBY, G. W. 1966. The Experimental Earthwork on Overton Down, Wiltshire, England. The First Four Years. *Proc. Prehist. Soc. 32*, 313–41
10 LEGGETT, W. F. 1947. *The Story of Wool*, New York
11 TEXTILE INSTITUTE. 1965. *Identification of Textile Materials*
12 WILDMAN, A. B. 1954. The Microscopy of Animal Textile Fibres, *Wool Ind. Res. Ass.*

SECTION VI STATISTICS

56 *Archaeology and Statistics*

DONALD J. TUGBY

LIKE ANY OTHER SCIENCE, archaeology describes the variables and relations with which it deals in a language of its own. The translation of this language into statistical language should be easy because statistical terms are abstract, while archaeological terms are concrete. The variables of statistical language, like x, y and z, have no specific content, but those of archaeological language, like 'site', 'horizon' and 'artifact', are circumscribed by the empirical reality to which they point.

When an archaeological problem is translated into statistical language, the statistical variables are given content, but are not made subject to the rules of archaeological language—they have to obey only the rules about relations among variables in a statistical model. This model is based on the idea that a set of observed events could occur by chance only with a certain probability. The model makes assumptions about the mathematical properties of the data fed into it. To use the model we must check that the assumptions are met, translate the archaeological terms into statistical terms, carry out the statistical operations and translate the result back into archaeological terms. This archaeological solution will be accompanied by a statement that the set of archaeological events could have occurred by chance only with a certain degree of probability, say, once in a hundred times.

This statement, known as the level of significance, distinguishes a result arrived at by statistical means from a result arrived at by any other means. In short, the statistical procedure and the manner in which the result is stated, reflect our belief that culture and environment affect the form of artifacts in a non-random fashion. This has long been a conventional belief in archaeology, being enshrined in the notion of configuration and, since Taylor,[1] in that of conjunction. Statistics enables the belief to be objectively tested.

PROBLEMS AND VARIABLES

Let us suppose that we are in some archaeological heaven. In an area, two hundred untouched surface sites await attention. What problems do they pose? In the first place we shall want to identify the traits in the sites and classify them; then we shall want to distribute the sites in a space-time framework; and finally we shall want to account for the processes by which the differences among the sites have arisen. We shall hope that traits, our elementary units of analysis, are regularly associated to give types and types occur regularly together as assemblages. Other archaeological units,

TABLE A

Archaeological objectives and archaeological units (A.U.). The arrows show the progressive association of units to form units of a higher order

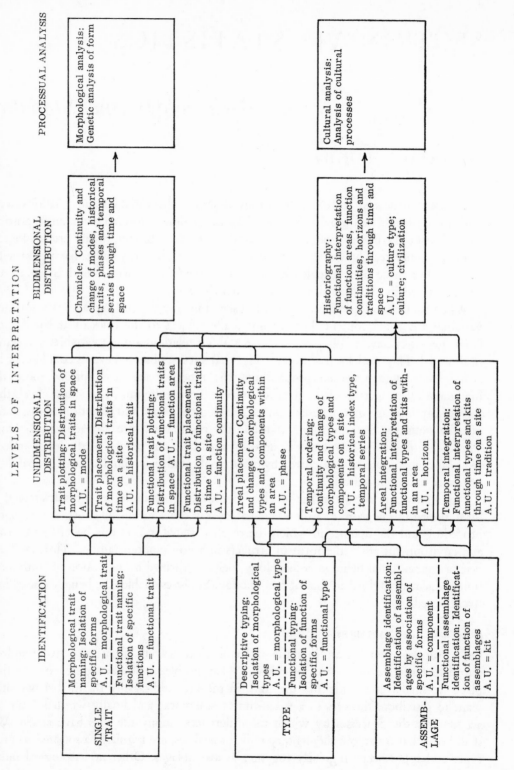

LEVELS OF INTERPRETATION

	IDENTIFICATION	UNIDIMENSIONAL DISTRIBUTION	BIDIMENSIONAL DISTRIBUTION	PROCESSUAL ANALYSIS
SINGLE TRAIT	Morphological trait naming: Isolation of specific forms A.U. = morphological trait Functional trait naming: Isolation of specific functions A.U. = functional trait	Trait plotting: Distribution of morphological traits in space A.U. = mode Trait placement: Distribution of morphological traits in time on a site A.U. = historical trait Functional trait plotting: Distribution of functional traits in space A.U. = function area Functional trait placement: Distribution of functional traits in time on a site A.U. = function continuity	Chronicle: Continuity and change of modes, historical traits, phases and temporal series through time and space	Morphological analysis: Genetic analysis of form
TYPE	Descriptive typing: Isolation of morphological types A.U. = morphological type Functional typing: Isolation of function of specific forms A.U. = functional type	Areal placement: Continuity and change of morphological types and components within an area A.U. = phase Temporal ordering: Continuity and change of morphological types and components on a site A.U. = historical index type, temporal series		
ASSEMB-LAGE	Assemblage identification: Identification of assemblages by association of specific forms A.U. = component Functional assemblage identification: Identification of function of assemblages A.U. = kit	Areal integration: Functional interpretation of functional types and kits within an area A.U. = horizon Temporal integration: Functional interpretation of functional types and kits through time on a site A.U. = tradition	Historiography: Functional interpretation of function areas, function continuities, horizons and traditions through time and space A.U. = culture type; culture; civilization	Cultural analysis: Analysis of cultural processes

like horizons and traditions, we shall form by relating traits, types and assemblages to space and time.

From archaeological experience we can expect that our types will intergrade with one another[2] and that when we attempt to classify our sites there will always be transitional forms, like the 'hybrid industries' of Paterson,[3] which cannot be allotted to a class. We shall have to break up the continuum of features in time and space by arbitrarily choosing cutting points determined by the variables, like type of site, shape of lip, ecological situation and so forth, to which we pay attention.

For scientific economy we shall try to choose a set of variables that constitute a meaningful problem and at the same time keep the number of variables small. By attending to only a part of the area at once, by using variables that consist of clusters of lower order units, or by dealing with only form or function, a contrast stressed by Thompson,[4] this difficulty will be resolved. Assuming that our choices are related to form and function, degrees of association and distribution in space and time, the commonly recognized dimensions of archaeology,[5] each combination of choices we make will be related to one of the archaeological objectives shown in Table A. The arrows in the table signpost the path of research along which units of a lower order are progressively associated to form units of a higher order.

We shall need to transpose theoretical dimensions like time and space into three sets of variables that can be defined in the field for practical work: A series of situations, a series of archaeological units and a series of criteria for judging the differences between units, such as presence and absence of a feature, measurements of a feature and counts of the relative frequency of features. Situations, units and criteria will be our operational variables.

We shall reach higher levels of interpretation (shown across the top of Table A) as we proceed. First, we shall identify units, then discover the association of units in space and/or time and finally discover processes, or the association of units of the highest level of abstraction.[6]

ANALYTICAL POSSIBILITIES

So far we have used archaeological language. Let us now translate it into statistical language. Cultural change takes place by transformations in units from situation to situation. The matrix in Figure 113 is a model of this process. Adjacent rows (classes of situations) in the matrix contain similar but not identical sets of units. The rows and columns cannot be re-ordered without destroying the progression in the matrix, a property that reflects the sequence of culture change. The units can be classified in three classes characterized by their occurrence in situations 1, 2 and 3, 4 and 5, and 6, 7 and 8 respectively. For a different archaeological objective the classes of situations can be classified in three super-classes characterized by combinations of units B and C, D and E and F and G respectively.

Another simple way of handling the same data is to note the number of times each combination of two units occurs, enter the counts in a matrix, and to sort the matrix so that the highest counts are near the diagonal and the lowest farthest away as in Fig.

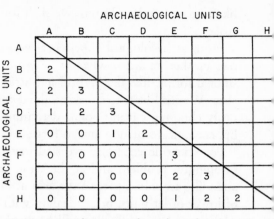

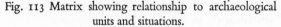

Fig. 113 Matrix showing relationship to archaeological units and situations.

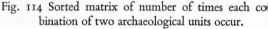

Fig. 114 Sorted matrix of number of times each combination of two archaeological units occur.

114. Note that the order of units is the same as in Fig. 113. If the entries in the original matrix are based not simply on presence or absence but on some kind of measure or count then the 'Xs' in Fig. 113 will be replaced by some kind of measure of association between a class of situation on the one hand and a class of archaeological unit on the other. Such a matrix we shall call an association matrix. It may or may not be possible to order the association matrix in a manner analogous to the serial order in the matrix of Fig. 114, namely with the highest associations near the diagonal and the lowest near the margins.

For illustrative purposes we have been using a matrix in which is shown the association of situations and archaeological units. We can equally well construct matrices showing the association of criteria and situations or the association of criteria and archaeological units. We can look at any of these matrices in terms of the similarity between the columns or the similarity between the rows, just as, when we considered the matrix of Fig. 113, we could classify the situations in terms of units or the units in terms of situations. Each of these ways of looking at the matrix is known as the transpose of the other. The complete model of analytical possibilities is presented in Fig. 115 by setting up criteria, situations and archaeological units as axes in three-dimensions and representing the association matrices as planes at right-angles to one another. With three planes, each of which can be viewed in two ways, we have six techniques labelled O, P, Q, R, S, and T after the analogous techniques of factor analysis as described by Cattell.[7]

IDENTIFICATION

The archaeological objectives of Table A other than trait naming can now be transposed into operations in terms of O . . . T techniques. Trait naming is a fundamental operation depending solely on archaeological judgement.

Descriptive typing: Isolation of morphological types.
Functional typing: Isolation of the function of specific forms.

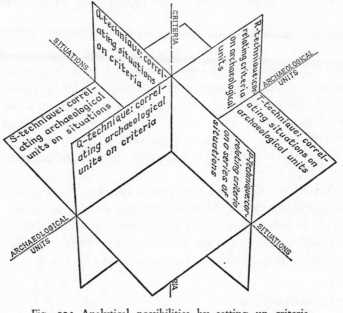

Fig. 115 Analytical possibilities by setting up criteria, situations and archeological units as axes in three dimensions.

In descriptive and functional typing we begin with a sample of specimens and a series of traits and end with a set of morphological and functional types. We want to know which traits go with which. We can adopt a Q-type approach or an R-type approach. An R-type solution can be achieved by simply counting the number of times each combination of two traits occurs, assembling these figures in a matrix and sorting them so that the highest figures are close to the diagonal as in sorting the matrix of Fig. 114. We should then be able to establish a typology by looking for breaking points or areas of low overlap in the series. Tugby[8] used this method for classifying axes and choppers from south-east Australia and Clarke[9] used the method for establishing a typology of British Beaker pottery. We could use a specimen by specimen matrix but this would be less economical because there would be a far larger number of cells in the matrix which would be more difficult to sort.

> Assemblage identification: Identification of assemblages by association of specific forms.
> Archaeological unit = component.
> Functional assemblage identification: Identification of function of assemblages.
> Archaeological unit = kit.

In assemblage identification we begin with established morphological and functional types, examine their associations and end with components and kits. This is a Q- or

R-type problem of the same structure as the typing problem and calls for the same techniques.

Another possible approach to the problem of the classification of types and assemblages is cluster analysis[10] which will yield a classification in terms of classes and subclasses. In cluster analysis an R-type sort is followed by a Q-type sort: First, in the cluster analysis of variables, the criteria are correlated in order to reduce the number of criteria while still accounting for the variation among the objects to be classified; and second, in the cluster analysis of objects, the objects whose profile of scores on the reduced criteria are similar are classed together. Clements[11] used a type of cluster analysis with ethnographic data from north-west California and achieved a classification very similar to that of Kroeber.

Sneath and Sokal[12] use a method similar to a specimen by specimen (Q-type) sort to set up a biological taxonomy. They suggest that taxonomic distance can be determined objectively in terms of degree of association, and a diagnostic key can be constructed by examining the original specimen by criteria matrix, just as we suggested a classification of archaeological units by examination of Fig. 113.

UNIDIMENSIONAL DISTRIBUTION

Trait plotting: Distribution of morphological traits in space. Archaeological unit = mode.

Functional trait plotting: Distribution of functional traits in space. Archaeological unit = function area.

In trait plotting we begin with morphological traits, demonstrate their distribution in space and end with a new unit, the mode. Analogous operations with functional traits yield function areas.

Trait placement: Distribution of morphological traits in time on a site. Archaeological unit = historical trait.

We begin with morphological trait and end with a morphological tradition or historical trait. Historical traits are traits of short duration in time which can be used as markers in the archaeological sequence.

Functional trait placement: Distribution of functional traits in time in a site. Archaeological unit = functional continuity.

We begin with a functional trait and end with a functional continuity (previously called functional tradition by Tugby).[13]

Areal placement: Study of the continuity and change of morphological types and components within an area. Archaeological unit = phase.[14]

Areal integration: Functional interpretation of functional types and kits within an area. Archaeological unit = horizon.[15]

Temporal ordering: Continuity and change of morphological types and components in a site. Archaeological unit = historical index type; temporal series.

Temporal ordering is the objective of a site description.

Temporal integration: Functional interpretation of functional types and kits through time in a site. Archaeological unit = tradition.[16]

Temporal integration is the ultimate objective of the analysis of a site as such. If the analysis is carried further a new objective at a different level of interpretation must be defined. For example, if the site is compared with neighbouring sites then the objective becomes one of bidimensional distribution rather than unidimensional distribution.

All objectives of unidimensional distribution have their limiting case: For distribution in space, the study of a single site; and for distribution in time, the study of a single phase or horizon. In these trivial cases the problem is reduced to one of typological analysis and can be appropriately handled by the techniques already mentioned. In all other unidimensional objectives the common concern is with the comparison of sets of archaeological units distributed in time or space and their ordering in a series. We can make use of a matrix of the kind shown in Fig. 113, in which the sequence of the archaeological units along the margin of the matrix cannot be altered without destroying the order within the matrix. If the raw data is entered in a matrix which is then sorted so as to achieve a serial order like the order of the matrix in Fig. 113 then this seriation can be interpreted as due to change in time or space as the case may be. The correct interpretation can be made if the order of the data in one of these dimensions is already known. This information might be obtained by inspection, for example by making a trait plot and showing that the distribution is not orderly.[17] The early end of a chronological series cannot be determined from the matrix itself but only from independent evidence, e.g. stratigraphy.

In the Robinson-Brainerd method the members of a set of assemblages are compared with one another with respect to their percentage content of different archaeological units, their scores on a coefficient of likeness are entered in a matrix, and the matrix is sorted by the same method as that used to sort the matrix of Fig. 113. The process is the analogue of the Q-technique. Belous[18] sorted the non-ceramic Central Californian material using the Robinson-Brainerd method and his results are in fair agreement with the sequence postulated by Heizer, and Flanders[19] has used the method in a re-examination of Mill Creek ceramics. A computer programme for the Robinson-Brainerd method has been devised by Ascher and Ascher.[20]

The Central Californian data has been re-examined by Dempsey and Baumhoff[21] using a method they call contextual analysis, in which the index of likeness between sites depends on the presence or absence of types rather than on the relative frequency of types. The indices are sorted in a Q-type matrix in the same way as in the Robinson-Brainerd method. Dempsey and Baumhoff's results show a high level of agreement with Heizer's sequence. Contextual analysis reduces sampling errors and provides a scale for placing new sites chronologically, but, as pointed out by Lipe[22] presence or absence is not a valid criterion for constructing an index of likeness when the inter-grading of deposits or change in a metrical character over time take place.

A rapid field method for solving a Q-type seriation problem by plotting three selected traits on graph paper has been invented by Meighan.[23] A mathematical rationale for the method and an internal check on the validity of the results have been provided by Ascher.[24] The usefulness of the cumulative percentage frequency graph for com-paring components whose temporal order is known has been pointed out by Jelinek.[25]

The Q-type analysis is reduced to its simplest form when two very similar assem-blages whose spatial distributions overlap are compared[26] or when two archaeological units are compared using only one criterion at a time, for example a single trait or a small combination of traits. In other words the analysis is reduced to only a small part of the Q–R matrix. For such simple comparisons the choice of an appropriate statistic depends on the assumptions that can be made about the parent population from which the samples to be compared are drawn, the independence of the samples and the type of scale formed by the data. In a nominal scale the classes of units or situations can be identified by numbers; in an ordinal scale the classes can be ranked; in an interval scale the intervals between any two classes are of known size and in a ratio scale there is, in addition, a true zero, and the ratio between any two points on the scale is independent of the unit of measurement. Parametric statistics such as the comparison of means test, the t test and the F test can be used with data drawn from a population which is nor-mally distributed or almost so. Non-parametric statistics such as the chi-square test, are well described by Siegel.[27] The use of the chi-square test in archaeology is demon-strated by Spaulding.[28] The median test, a variety of chi-square, has been used by Anderson[29] for a comparison of pueblo pottery types.

The steps in making comparisons using statistics are as follows: First, make assump-tions about the method of sampling and the relationship between the units; second, on the basis of the assumptions choose an appropriate statistic and determine by the theory of probability the range of possible values the statistics can have (the values are set out in tables); thirdly, decide at what level of probability the second assumption about the relationship between the units will be rejected; fourthly, calculate the statistic; and, fifthly, make a decision to reject or not to reject the second assumption. The latter is usually posed in the form of a null hypothesis, for example, that there is no difference between the units.[30] In making the decision two types of error can occur: Reject the null hypothesis when in fact it is true (Type I error); and accept the null hypothesis when in fact it is false (Type II error). Type I error can be reduced by using a high level of probability for rejecting the null hypothesis, but Type II error rises at the same time. The only way of reducing the risk of Type I error without raising the risk of Type II error is to increase the sample size.

It is not very useful to compare two unlike archaeological units when the difference between the units is obvious from inspection except for purposes of formal proof. On the other hand, it may be impossible to detect the difference between the units except by increasing the risk of a Type I error. A cautious analyst who is not prepared to take this risk will be inclined to make a Type II error. For archaeological purposes it is advantageous to compare a large number of samples by a method that uses the small differences between samples, which may not be significant in themselves, to order the samples in a series.

BIDIMENSIONAL DISTRIBUTION

Chronicle: Continuity and change of modes, historical traits, phases and temporal series through space and time.

Historiography: Functional interpretation of function areas, function continuities, horizons and traditions through time and space. Archaeological unit = civilization; cultural type.[31]

The fundamental problem in both chronicle and historiography is the confounding of differences that occur in time and space. Matrix analysis yields only one seriation. Before this method can be used a bidimensional problem must be reduced to a problem in unidimensional distribution, so that, after analysis, the seriation if any can be assigned to the uncontrolled dimension.

PROCESSUAL ANALYSIS

Morphological analysis: Genetic analysis of form—study of the processes of change in form through time and space considered without reference to function.

Cultural analysis: Study of processes accounting for changes in culture through time and space.

Morphological analysis and cultural analysis are used in different admixtures in non-statistical analyses. Paterson's[32] account of the Lower Palaeolithic industries of Europe uses form almost exclusively and Meighan's[33] analysis of Californian cultures is based on technology with some inferences about social and religious features, but Binford's[34] analysis of the changing utilization of native copper in eastern North America shows that in processual analysis morphological data are related to cultural and environmental data of all kinds.

Statistical models are indifferent to the type of data fed into them. Any model appropriate for the problem in hand can be used for morphological or cultural analysis. Stated in conventional terms the basic problem of cultural analysis is to separate the effects of processes like diffusion and migration from processes like innovation and evolution. The ideal analytical method is one which enables the effect of one set of variables to be accounted for while the effect of another set is examined. This can be achieved by simplifying the problem, for example, by confining the analysis to an area within which rapid diffusion is assumed to have taken place, a strategy adopted by Rouse in a classical study of the Fort Liberté region.[35] The statistics of time series might be useful and have been used by Belous.[36]

The problem can also be simplified by ignoring the difference between cultural processes in space and in time. The Mid-West Taxonomic System, for example, attempted to analyse total variability in culture without separating out change in time. The additional assumption can be made that cultural evolution has taken place through fixed stages. The Guttman method of scale analysis has been used by Carneiro[37] for the study of cultural evolution under this assumption. The rationale of the Guttman method has been set out by Goodenough[38] and the relations of the method to matrix analysis commented on by Tugby.[39] In the simple Guttman method used by Carneiro a seriation is achieved by ranking units according to the appearance of new traits; it is assumed that old traits are retained. The method might therefore be validly used for limited problems like the analysis of the progressive overlay of one culture upon another, for example, the spread of conquest through an area.

The classical method of experimental science for handling many variables at the same time is to control the effects of some variables while examining the effects of others. Among the methods by which this can be done, such as analysis of variance, multiple correlation, partial correlation and analysis of co-variance, the choice of the method depends on the form of the data. There are both parametric and non-parametric versions of some of these methods.

Multiple correlation is used to indicate how much of the total variance in a variable can be accounted for by all the other variables taken together; partial correlation refers to the correlation between any two variables when the effects of the other variables are controlled. The latter might have a useful role in processual analysis. The computation that these methods require can be carried out by computer. Regression analysis, which predicts the value of one variable from that of another, and multiple correlation with processing of the data by computer have been used in a Q-type problem to show the difference in function of rooms at Carter Ranch Pueblo.[40] In the full report on this project Freeman and Brown[41] differentiate sampling error and real differences due to function or temporal change and demonstrate the use of regression analysis to test hypotheses.

Sometimes a problem can be simplified by trying to account for the effects of a large number of variables in terms of a smaller number of underlying variables. This is the aim of factor analysis which attempts to abstract a set of factors from a matrix of association like the Q–R matrix by using different techniques in turn, each technique being intended to clarify the factors found in the previous technique. A difficulty in using this method in archaeology, as in any other field, is to conceptualize the factors once they have been found. Factor analysis can also be used for contructing classifications or indices, those variables that correlate most highly with a given factor being given the most weight. Driver and Schuessler[42] have factor analysed the north-west Californian data used by Clements and achieved a classification that agrees highly with that of Kroeber.

OTHER POSSIBILITIES FOR ANALYSIS

The objectives of Table A are derived from different combinations of the conventional dimensions of archaeology. The model of analytical possibilities in Fig. 115, however, suggests other unconventional problems that might be tackled using the methods already described that derive from an association matrix. P-technique, which consists of correlating criteria used to examine a single archaeological unit in a variety of situations, might be used to show the adaptation of a type to changes in ecology occurring either through time or space.

O-technique, which is the transpose of P-technique, consists of correlating situations with respect to a set of criteria used for examining one cultural unit; it might be used to reveal the common elements in a series of situations in which a certain phase occurs, or to reveal cyclical changes of climate associated with differences in the expression of a tradition. In S-technique cultural units are correlated with respect to one criterion on a series of occasions. For example a set of traditions might be compared with respect to their response to a series of situations like periods of increasing aridity. In T-technique, which is the transpose of S-technique, situations are correlated on one criterion on a series of cultural units. The technique is analogous to the test-retest method used in psychological testing to find out how reliable a test is. It could be used in archaeology to group together situations which have a similar effect on archaeological units, for example situations in which microliths are produced.

The six techniques are related to one another in Fig. 115 by transposability but can be classified in other ways, for example, in terms of the variable they hold constant or the correlation they share. R- and P-techniques share the correlation of criteria and should be the principal methods for examining the structure and cohesion of archaeological units because they correspond respectively to diffusion and evolution. Once a researcher has related his problem to the framework of analytical possibilities in Fig. 115 he will perceive, given always that the assumptions of the statistics are met, that any of the methods derived by manipulation of a matrix of association or the methods for comparison of archaeological units can be applied to the problems posed by the planes of the framework.

VALIDITY OF THE RESULTS

Any archaeological analyst must ask himself the following questions: Are my variables correctly chosen, properly sampled and accurately measured and are my results correctly interpreted? Traits must be named and variables chosen relevant to the problem before analysis can begin. The analyst must then decide which of all possible relations among the variables he will examine. The decisions are archaeological decisions made on the basis of archaeological insight and experience, and are independent of the subsequent statistical analysis, although they may preclude the use of statistics if there is no statistical model corresponding to the structure of the chosen problem.

Ideally, most statistics require the use of random samples, but adjustments can be made in the calculation of the statistic for non-random samples if the degree of non-randomness is known. Simple random sampling is not always the best method of sampling from the point of view of economy of effort and cost. For some problems, like the comparison of classes of unequal size, stratified sampling, i.e. sampling within each class or strata of the total population, may be more appropriate. Rootenberg[43] has detailed the steps in a stratified sampling design. Disproportional stratified sampling in which rare classes of specimens are over-represented in the sample, has been proposed for large collections by Cowgill.[44]

Sometimes the labour of data gathering can be reduced by cluster sampling, i.e. dividing the whole population into heterogeneous groups or clusters and sampling randomly among the cluster. The number of statistics that can be used with cluster sampling is usually restricted and correction factors must be used. A method of cluster sampling for archaeology has been described by Vescelius[45] and systematic cluster sampling with a random start has been used by Ascher and Ascher.[46] Archaeologists who want to use statistical analyses may have to adapt their field methods to meet the sampling assumptions. A start in this direction was made by Treganza and Cook[47] who demonstrated the validity of sampling a habitation mound by a method that was later used for a comparative study of Californian Indian mounds.[48] The role of sampling in a research design has been dealt with by Binford.[49] The method of sampling to be used in any study depends upon the intended technique of analysis, but whatever method is adopted the effect of the sampling procedure on the validity of the results must be assessed.

Errors of measurement are a common source of invalidity caused by lack of standard procedures and differences among workers in their use of measuring tools. Measurements of the length of the same Australopithecus tooth by different workers ranged from 9·60 mm to 11·0 mm for example.[50] Errors of measurement can be assessed by re-measuring a portion of the sample, but systematic errors, i.e. errors which are always in the same direction and which are important in biasing the results, may be missed nevertheless. Some errors of measurement might be controlled by using automated tools.[51]

The interpretation of the results often takes the form of an attempt to establish causation. If two variables are shown to be associated it is still not possible to say that one causes the other. In analysis the designation of variables as dependent and independent is often a matter of convenience. In archaeology, however, the sequence of events in time, if known, provides an in-built guideline for analysis which can be supplemented by common sense. It is obvious, for example, that a change in firing technique does not cause an increase in rainfall, but the reverse causal sequence is at least possible. The gross dimensions of archaeology like time and space conceal effective variables like soil type and temperature. An analysis may prove inconclusive because the effective variables have not been identified. In archaeology there is no practical criterion of validity, i.e. an interpretation cannot be checked by referring to subsequent events in nature. It is possible, however, although rarely done, to formulate an archaeological hypothesis which can be tested by subsequently gathering data; it was this approach which led Dubois to the discovery of Pithecanthropus. Excavation can be planned to fit the problem and eliminate some of the variables. Archaeological experiments using statistics, like those of Ascher and Ascher,[52] and Sonnenfeld,[53] perform a similar role in archaeological research—they enable the interpretations about events in the real world derived from axiomatically based theory to be checked against experimentally based observation.

ACKNOWLEDGEMENTS

The author is indebted to Professor J. A. Keats, University of Newcastle, N.S.W., for some perceptive comments on a draft of this article, and to Mr R. B. J. Wilson, University of Queensland, who tried to persuade the author to write clearly. The author is responsible for the errors and ambiguities that remain.

1 TAYLOR, W. W. 1948. *Memoirs of the American Anthropological Association 69*

2 A point well made in FORD, J. A. 1954. *Am. Anth. 56* (1), 42–54

3 PATERSON, T. T. 1945. *Proc. Prehist. Soc. 11*(1), 1–19

4 THOMPSON, R. H. 1956. *Southwest. J. Anth. 12*(3), 327–32

5 SPAULDING, A. C. 1960. In DOLE, G. E. and CARNEIRO, R. L. (*eds.*) *Essays in the Science of Culture,* 437–56, New York

6 The descriptive, distributional and genetic ways of correlating phases are distinguished in ROUSE, I. 1955. *Am. Anth. 57*(4), 713–21; three levels of organization in scientific analysis: Observation, description (of distribution) and explanation are recognized in WILLEY, G. R. and PHILLIPS, P. 1962. *Method and Theory in American Archaeology,* Chicago, 4

7 CATTELL, R. B. 1952. *Factor Analysis,* New York

8 TUGBY, D. J. 1958. *Am. Antiq. 24*(1), 24–33

9 CLARKE, D. L. 1962. *Proc. Prehist. Soc. 28*(15), 371–82

10 TRYON, R. C. 1955. *Univ. Calif. Pub. Psychol. 8*(1), 1–100

11 CLEMENTS, F. E. 1954. *Am. Anth. 56*(1), 180–99

12 SNEATH, P. H. A. and SOKAL, R. R. 1962. *Nature 193* (4818), 855–60; SOKAL, R. R. and SNEATH, P. H. A. 1963. *Principles of Numerical Taxonomy,* San Francisco

13 TUGBY, D. J. 1964. *Am. Antiq. 31*(1), 1–16

14 WILLEY, G. R. and PHILLIPS, P. 1962. *Method and Theory in American Archaeology,* Chicago, 62

15 *Ibid.,* 33

16 *Ibid.,* 34–7

17 For an example see TUGBY, D. J. 1958, *op. cit.* 8

18 BELOUS, R. E. 1953. *Am. Antiq. 18*(4), 341–53

19 FLANDERS, R. E. 1960. *J. Iowa Archaeol. Soc. 10,* 1–35

20 ASCHER, M. and R. 1963. *Am. Anthrop. 65*(5), 1045–52

21 DEMPSEY, P. and BAUMHOFF, M. 1963. *Am. Antiq. 28*(4), 496–509

22 LIPE, W. D. 1964. *Am. Antiq. 30*(1), 103–4

23 MEIGHAN, C. W. 1959. *Am. Antiq. 25*(2), 203–11

24 ASCHER, M. 1959. *Am. Antiq. 25*(2), 212–14

25 JELINEK, A. J. 1962. *Am. Antiq. 28*(2), 241–3

26 For example, the Adena and Hopewell trait lists are compared using a correlation coefficient in WITHERSPOON, Y. T. 1961. *Am. Antiq. 26*(B), 433–6

27 SIEGEL, S. 1956. *Non-parametric Statistics,* New York

28 SPAULDING, A. C. 1960. In HEIZER, R. F. and COOK, S. F. (*eds.*). *The Application of Quantitative Methods in Archaeology, Viking Fund Pubs. in Anth. 28*

29 ANDERSON, K. M. 1956. *Am. Antiq. 22*(2), 303–7

30 A good example of the use of the null hypothesis in curve-fitting is in FITTING, J. E. *Am. Antiq. 30*(4), 484–91

31 *Op cit.*

32 PATERSON, T. T. *op. cit.*

33 MEIGHAN, C. W. 1959. *Am. Antiq. 24*(3), 289–305

34 BINFORD, L. R. 1962. *Am. Antiq. 28*(2), 217–25

35 '. . . time distributions have been traced within the Fort Liberté region as a whole because it seems evident that the region was culturally homogeneous', ROUSE, I. 1939. *Prehistory in Haiti. Yale Univ. Pubs. in Anthrop. 21,* 13

36 BELOUS, R. E. *op. cit.*[18]

37 CARNEIRO, R. L. 1962. *Southwest. J. Anth. 18*(2), 149–69

38 Goodenough, W. H. 1963. *Southwest. J. Anth. 19(3)*, 235–50
39 Tugby, D. J. 1964. *Man 64(181)*, 144–6
40 Longacre, W. A. 1964. *Science 144 (3625)*, 1454–5
41 Freeman, L. G. jr. and Brown, J. A. 1964. *Fieldiana: Anthropology 55*, 126–54
42 Driver, H. E. and Schuessler, K. F. 1957. *Am. Anth. 59(4)*, 655–63
43 Rootenberg, S. 1964. *Am. Antiq. 30(2)*, 181–8
44 Cowgill, G. L. 1964. *Am. Antiq. 29(4)*, 467–73
45 Vescelius, G. S. 1960. In Dole, G. E. and Carneiro, R. L. (eds.). *Essays in the Science of Culture in Honor of Leslie A. White*, New York
46 Ascher, R. and M. 1965. *Science 147 (3655)*, 243–50
47 Reported in Heizer, R. F. and Cook, S. F. *Southwest. J. Anth. 12(3)*, 229–47
48 Cook, S. F. and Treganza, E. E. *Univ. of Calif. Pubs. in Am. Arch. and Ethnol. 40*, 223–62
49 Binford, L. R. 1964. *Am. Antiq. 29(4)*, 425–41
50 Robinson, J. T. 1965. *Curr. Anth. 6(4)*, 404–5
51 Sorenson, J. L. 1964. *Am. Antiq. 30(2)*, 205–6
52 Ascher, R. and M. *op. cit.*[46]
53 Sonnenfeld, J. 1962. *Am. Antiq. 28(1)*, 56–65

57 Classification by Computer

F. R. HODSON

THE HIGH-SPEED COMPUTER is being brought more and more into archaeological research since it makes practicable a wide range of techniques for analysing descriptive numerical data of the sort often assembled by archaeologists (cf. Chenhall[3]). In those branches of archaeology where the practice is to describe material numerically, in palaeolithic studies, for example, the computer may be brought into service directly. However, some available computer techniques for analysis seem so powerful, that it may prove worthwhile converting seemingly non-numerical archaeological data into a numerical form.

The purpose of this chapter is not to give a general review of the scope of the computer in archaeology, but to describe briefly the results of analysing two specific and contrasting groups of archaeological material by some available computing programmes. It is hoped that this summary will give some idea of the difficulties and the potentialities of this range of analytical techniques.

The general problem to be solved may be illustrated by the artifacts shown on Fig. 116 Here a group of objects (Iron Age brooches) are seen to be functionally related, but to vary through a wide range of minor features. How are the relationships between the objects to be judged and then represented in a meaningful classification? In many archaeological situations, some objects of such a group may be better documented (by association, for example) than others, and the problem is to extend this information, where justified, to the less-well documented material. Or, all of the group may be equally badly documented, and the problem is to extract as much legitimate information as possible from the interrelationships between the members of the group; to see in fact whether any underlying structure or trends are implied by their morphology. In both cases, the archaeologist has to use his judgement to relate individuals to each other. The more complicated and numerous the individuals are, the more difficult this task becomes. The individuals may, as here, be single objects, or they may be whole assemblages: the basic problem remains the same.

To investigate the consistency that may be expected from judgements of this kind, a few professional archaeologists and an anatomist were asked to classify from photographs the twenty-eight brooches from Münsingen, Switzerland, illustrated on Fig. 116, together with two alien brooches, one from Hallstatt in Austria and one from the British Isles.[8] They were asked to place similar brooches together and to represent their classifications as two-dimensional diagrams. These are shown as Figs. 117 and 118.

For the purpose of this experiment, the analysts were to assume that no external evidence was available to assist their classification. In fact, the brooches from Münsingen are well documented chronologically by the horizontal stratification of the cemetery in which they were found.[7] This evidence of relative date provides an inde-

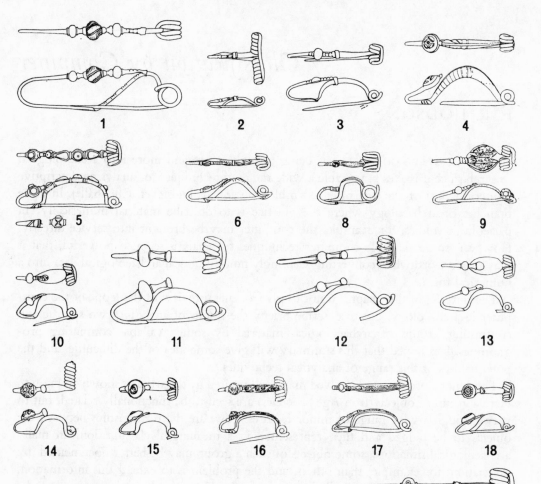

1 **2** **3** **4**

5 **6** **8** **9**

10 **11** **12** **13**

14 **15** **16** **17** **18**

19 **20** **21**

22 **23** **24** **25**

26 **27** **28** **30**

pendent way of checking the performance of the different analysts, since it is probable that chronological differences were a major factor behind morphological variation of the brooches. For this reason, symbols indicating the position of each brooch in the cemetery have been added to the diagrams. The symbols are graded from light to dark in five stages to correspond with five arbitrary zones in the cemetery running from north to south, i.e. approximately from early to late. By studying the position of the different symbols on the diagrams, it should be clear whether suggested configurations have any chronological, and hence, it may be assumed, any morphological significance.

The analysts' diagrams, Figs. 117 and 118, may be discussed first in general terms. Archaeologist 4 classified the brooches basically into a series of interrelated clusters. Archaeologist 3 and the Anatomist into a more or less linear development without discrete clusters, Archaeologists 1 and 2 into clusters that are themselves related in a linear fashion ('Phases' I, II and III). Thus there are considerable differences in the general interpretation of the structure within the set. Specific interpretations of individual brooches cannot be discussed in detail, but it may be noticed that some brooches are consistently allotted the same neighbours by most analysts (cf. brooch 10), while others are not consistently grouped at all (cf. brooch 5).

Judged between themselves, then, it may be said that despite a tendency to agree for some brooches, there is a surprising difference of opinion on others and on the general interpretation of the structure behind the group.

When judged by the independent criterion of 'likely date' i.e. by the grouping of the graded symbols, it may be seen that for two diagrams, those of Archaeologist 2 and the Anatomist, there is a clear trend of symbols from light to dark (from left to right) which corresponds with the likely date, and which implies that there is a correlation between the shape of the brooches and relative chronology. However, no overall, clear trend of symbols is visible on the other diagrams, although clustering of similar symbols is apparent on the diagram of Archaeologist 3.

This experiment is extremely limited, but is sufficient to illustrate the differences in classification that are likely to occur where even a small number of relatively complex units are concerned. With more units, the difficulties of classification will increase and a satisfactory mechanical method of ordering the material would be an advantage. I have attempted to try out some available methods of classification by computer on this specific group of material and on a small series of complex assemblages.

Ideally, any such procedure should be able to indicate, as appropriate, clustering or linear ordering or both. However, this is asking a great deal, especially where large numbers of units are involved, and there are some situations where clustering or linear ordering alone may reasonably be demanded.

Some numerical methods for the linear ordering of archaeological material have already been developed in the United States, most notably by Brainerd[2] and Robinson[12] but also by Dempsey and Baumhoff[5] and by Ascher.[1] The successful application of

Fig. 116 Bronze fibulae from the Iron Age La Tène cemetery at Münsingen, Switzerland. Scale just under half life size. (After Hodson, Sneath and Doran[8].)

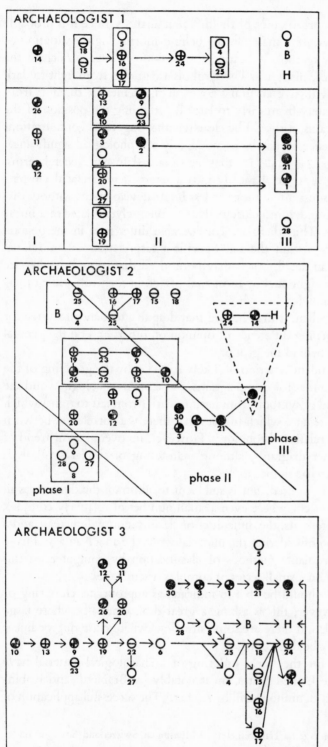

Fig. 117 Intuitive classifications of thirty fibulae (see Fig. 117). Symbols represent five approximate phases of deposition from early (light) to late (dark). (After Hodson, Sneath and Doran[8].)

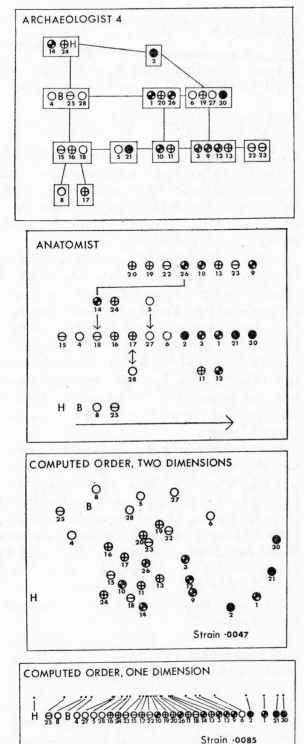

Fig. 118 Intuitive and computed classifications of thirty fibulae. Symbols as for Fig. 117. (After Hodson, Sneath and Doran[8].)

these techniques is limited to situations where it is safe to infer direct linear development within the material, and the performance is limited because the various units
(generally assemblages represented by the relative proportions of pottery types) are
arranged in order, but are not spaced out in any way. That is to say that a series of units
A–G that could most adequately be represented in one dimension as

A   BC   D   EF   G

would necessarily be recovered by these ordering methods as A B C D E F G.

Kendall[9] has provided a mathematical formulation for some ordering procedures
particularly relevant to the 'sequence dating' of large numbers of assemblages like the
Egyptian tombs studied by Petrie. A satisfactory method for the linear ordering and
spacing of small numbers of units is provided incidentally by the *Analysis of Proximities*
procedure to be described later.

Numerical methods for the *clustering* of archaeological material have been proposed
by Tugby[15] for stone axes and choppers, and for Beakers by Clarke.[4] Both authors
attempt to recognize significant clusters of *attributes* by reordering a matrix that records
the number of times attributes are found associated with each other. These preliminary
studies seem to involve difficulties that have still to be resolved (Matthews[11]). However,
a wide range of clustering techniques have been developed recently for biological
classification, especially by Sneath,[14] and with Sneath's co-operation a series of brooches
from Münsingen have been analysed by two *Numerical Taxonomy* programmes. Here
again, the known 'likely date' of the brooches is available to check the performance
of the procedures: it would be hoped to find a marked chronological cohesion within
computed clusters.

As with many other methods of multivariate analysis, the procedure to be described
starts from a matrix of *similarity coefficients* calculated between each pair of the units to be
analysed (cf. Robinson's *indexes of agreement*).[12] However, before any coefficients can
be calculated for objects like these brooches, they must first be described numerically,
i.e. by the presence, absence or inapplicability (+, –, or /) of a range of characters.
With this kind of artifact, the description has to cover not only directly measurable
features such as dimensions, number of coils to the spring and so forth, but also decorative features that are not measurable but that have somehow to be converted into a
form where the +, –, / code is applicable.

These considerations give rise to three methods of treatment that may be called
here A, B and C.

(A) Some features may be scored by their simple presence or absence (e.g. internal
cord to the spring).

(B) For a graded series (number of coils to the spring, ratios, etc.), the grading may
be preserved by breaking up the total variation range into arbitrary divisions and scoring
as follows, with one less 'character' column required than the number of grades defined:

	A	B	C
Brooch 1 (1st Ratio)	+	+	+
Brooch 2 (2nd Ratio)	+	+	−
Brooch 3 (3rd Ratio)	+	−	−
Brooch 4 (4th Ratio)	−	−	−

In this way, Brooch 1 would show $\frac{2}{3}$ agreement with Brooch 2, $\frac{1}{3}$ with Brooch 3, and $\frac{0}{3}$ with Brooch 4.

(c) For complex qualitative differences (types of decoration, etc.) coding is less straightforward and a rational solution has to be found for each contingency as it arises. Decorative motifs have to be split up into as many single elements as seem necessary, which may then be scored by their simple presence or absence (A). However, if this procedure seems likely to distort the pattern of scoring (similarity between undecorated brooches, for example, would be exaggerated through the common absence of a long series of motifs), it is possible to set conditions (C). For example, one series of characters would be listed as follows:

(1) Bow decorated +, or undecorated −   (A)
(2) If − : score /,   ⎫   dotted decoration   (C)
(3)   if + :   ⎬   zig-zag decoration   (C)
(4) continue for   ⎭   curvilinear decoration   (C)

To describe the brooches, 146 character columns were used: 81 columns, scored by method (B), dealt with dimension ratios (bow height, width and thickness, catch-plate length, total foot length, diameter of foot decoration, length and width of foot finial, and diameter of coils, all relative to the total length), angles (at the front and back of the bow) and the number of coils to the spring. The other characters were required to describe (by methods A and C) features of the coils and the decoration on the bow and foot.

The coefficient used was the *Simple Matching Coefficient* (S_{SM}) described by Sokal and Sneath.[14] (133) It is calculated as the proportion of character agreements, both negative and positive, out of the number of possible agreements. For example, two brooches 1 and 2 might be described against ten characters a–j, as follows:

	a	b	c	d	e	f	g	h	i	j
Brooch 1	+	+	−	+	/	−	−	+	+	−
Brooch 2	+	−	−	/	+	−	+	−	+	−

In this example there would be five agreements (features a, c, f, i, j) out of 8 possible agreements (features a, b, c, f, g, h, i, j). The symbol / implies that no comparison could be made, and so features d and e are ignored in the score which is, in this instance, $\frac{5}{8}$ or 62·5%.

Similar coefficients for 109 brooches in all were compared on a Mercury Computer of London University by an available Numerical Taxonomy programme. The coefficients were analysed by two contrasting procedures: *single*, and *average link* cluster analysis (Sokal and Sneath[14] (180)).

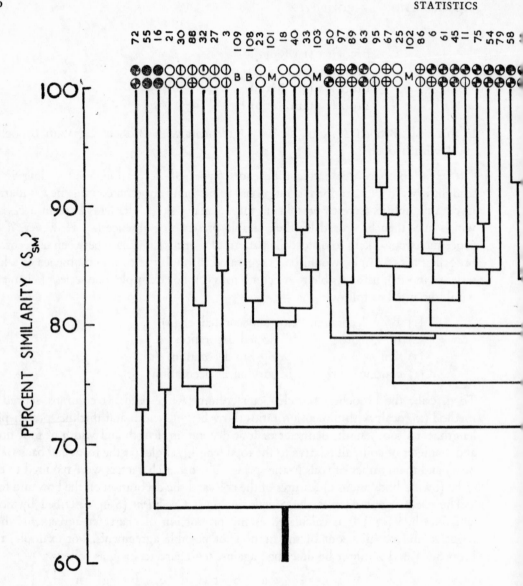

Single-link Cluster Analysis, where an aspirant is allowed to join an existing cluster if its similarity with any member of that group reaches the stipulated standard, was found to be of doubtful value, since chains of 'transitional' forms were liable to be produced and hence the clusters lacked the required cohesion.[8]

An *Average Link Cluster Analysis* of 72 brooches, however, produced a very satisfactory classification (Fig. 119). For this procedure, where an aspirant is allowed to join an existing cluster only when its average similarity with *all* members of the group reaches the required standard, a special computer programme was kindly written by J. A. and A. J. Hirsh. The dendrogram (Fig. 119) drawn out from the results of the com-

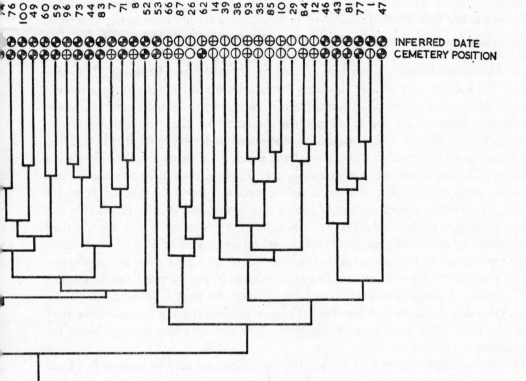

INFERRED DATE
CEMETERY POSITION

Fig. 119 Average-link Cluster Analysis of seventy La Tène brooches from Münsingen, except two from the Thames ('B') and three from the Marne ('M'). Date symbols represent a best archaeological estimate ('inferred date') and horizontally stratified zones of discovery ('cemetery position'). (After Hodson, Sneath and Doran[8].)

putation shows how groups are gradually enlarged as the criterion of similarity falls, until all the brooches are included in one group at about 65%. It will be seen that the chronological cohesion within groups (judged by the symbols for 'likely date'), remains high as far down as the 80% level of group formation. As far down as this level, only one cluster is chronologically unsatisfactory. This is made up of brooches 63, 95, 67 and 25, which turn out to be a series of rather simple 'roof-bow' brooches that seem to have changed little with time. The chronological cohesion of groups shown on this diagram suggests not only that the type of analysis (the Average-Link method) is producing satisfactory morphological groups, but that the preliminary methods of describing brooches numerically and of calculating similarity coefficients are basically sound.

A contrasting technique of analysis that should indicate linear ordering as well as clusters has been tried out on the small group of brooches illustrated on Fig. 116. The relevant programme was developed for archaeological purposes by J. E. Doran from a multidimensional scaling procedure devised by Shepard[13] and Kruskal.[10] This procedure also starts from a table of similarity coefficients, but it converts the information into a configuration or 'map' of points (representing in this case the brooches), where the distance between the points reflects their similarity, i.e. the greater the similarity between objects the closer they would be represented and vice versa. It is hoped that any latent clusters or trends within the material would be clear from the configuration retrieved. This configuration or map may be set up in one, two, three or more dimensions: the greater the number of dimensions, the more accurately the data will be represented, but clearly, a representation in one or two dimensions is most practicable. An important feature of the method is that a measure of goodness of fit (the 'strain' value) is calculated for each configuration, so that an indication is given of how well the data is being represented. In Doran's version of the method, as used here, a random configuration of points is set up first in any number of dimensions (typically three) and the starting configuration is progressively improved by moving the points iteratively until the strain value fails to improve. A number of different random starting configurations may be tried, and the best of all final configurations (i.e. that with least strain) selected for interpretation.

The final configuration in a higher number of dimensions may be collapsed to form the starting order in fewer dimensions. A one-dimensional representation is equivalent in some respects to seriation, but with spacing as well as ordering indicated, and with an expression given of how well the data are being represented.

The lower two diagrams of Fig. 118 show configurations computed by Doran's programme for the brooches of Fig. 116. If the procedure is working as desired, similar brooches should be close together, and any major trend should be reflected in the major dimension of the diagram. As for the configurations produced by the human analysts, it should be possible to judge how well these tasks are performed by studying the graded symbols of 'likely date'. It is at once apparent with the two-dimensional diagram that a trend of symbols from top left to bottom right has in fact been retrieved, and adjacent symbols are broadly similar. Judged by these criteria, the computed configuration in two dimensions compares remarkably well with human analyses. The computed diagram suggests no very discrete clusters within the group although the Hallstatt brooch (H) is well separated from the remainder. Good outside evidence suggests that this brooch is in fact earlier than all the La Tène brooches from Münsingen, as the two- and one-dimensional configurations (although not all the human analysts) suggest.

It must be emphasized that the purpose of this experiment is to see how well a mechanical procedure may estimate and represent the relationships between complex units. The chronological aspect is introduced primarily as a check on results since in this specific instance chronology may be expected to be a principal factor behind the morphological differences that are being analysed.

By its performance in this experiment, Doran's programme for the *Analysis of Proximities* appears to be suitable for situations where a relatively small number (up to fifty or thereabouts) of very complex units are to be analysed. An obvious archaeological situation of this sort occurs with series of palaeolithic flint assemblages which, following Bordes' methods, are currently described numerically by the relative proportions of a large range of categories of flints. It may be doubted whether any really satisfactory procedure for analysing such data has yet been demonstrated.

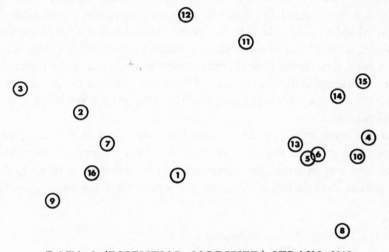

DATA A (ESSENTIAL, MODIFIED) STRAIN ·0018

Fig. 120 'Best' two-dimensional configuration of sixteen Mousterian assemblages. (After Doran and Hodson[6].)

A very restricted analysis of this kind of material has been attempted using Doran's programme.[6] The basic problem here, as with the brooches, is to establish the relationship between the different assemblages judged in this case by their inventory of flint artifacts: to see in fact whether any natural clusters or trends within the data may be retrieved.

For this preliminary analysis, data from sixteen Mousterian assemblages published by Bordes and his followers were selected, and a similarity coefficient was calculated between each pair of assemblages. The matrix of these coefficients was then analysed and typical low-strain configurations in two and one dimensions are illustrated on Figs. 120 and 121. The two-dimensional configuration differs from that recovered for the fibulae in suggesting a more obvious structure of clusters, with main groups at the

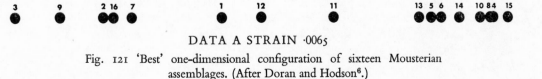

DATA A STRAIN ·0065

Fig. 121 'Best' one-dimensional configuration of sixteen Mousterian assemblages. (After Doran and Hodson[6].)

two ends of the longest axis, and with a separate pair of assemblages (11 and 12) between and to one side of them. Assemblage 1 perhaps hints at a link between the two main groups.

In interpreting the configurations of brooches it could be seen that the long axis of the two-dimensional configuration and the general order in one dimension showed a definite, if generalized correlation with time. There is no need to assume that a similar chronological interpretation should be put on the two Mousterian configurations. In fact, such a result would be to a certain extent surprising, since Bordes, whose method of data description was behind the analysis, suggests that major typological differences between the Mousterian are likely to be due to cultural rather than chronological factors. However, the evidence of some stratified assemblages included in the analysis does suggest that here, too, chronological development may represent the major discernible trend, since stratigraphically earlier assemblages are consistently placed to the right of later ones (1 − 2 − 3; 4 − 6/5 − 7; 8 − 9; 11 − 12). This order is retrieved in one dimension as well as in two.

Whether the same trend would be found if more than these sixteen Mousterian assemblages were analysed together remains to be seen. However, this analysis does demonstrate one way in which the computer may be called on to present complicated numerical data in a simple but objective way as a basis for discussion and interpretation.

REFERENCES

1 ASCHER, M. and R. 1963. *American Anthropologist* 65, 1045
2 BRAINERD, G. W. 1951. *American Antiquity* 16, No. 4, 301
3 CHENHALL, R. G. 1965 (*ed.*). *Newsletter for Computer Archaeologists*, Arizona State University
4 CLARKE, D. L. 1962. *Proc. Prehist. Soc.* 28, 371
5 DEMPSEY, P. and BAUMHOFF, M. 1963. *American Antiquity* 28, No. 4, 496
6 DORAN, J. E. and HODSON, F. R. 1966. *Nature*, 210, No. 5037, 688
7 HODSON, F. R. 1964. *Bulletin Inst. Arch. Univ. London* 4, 123
8 ——, SNEATH, P. H. A. and DORAN, J. E. 1966. *Biometrika* (in press)
9 KENDALL, D. G. 1963. *Bull. I.S.I. Ottawa* 34, 657
10 KRUSKAL, J. B. 1964. *Psychometrika* 29, 1
11 MATTHEWS, J. 1963. *Nature* 198, No. 4884, 930
12 ROBINSON, W. S. 1951. *American Antiquity* 16, No. 4, 293
13 SHEPARD, R. N. 1962. *Psychometrika* 27, 125, 219
14 SOKAL R. R. and SNEATH, P. H. A. 1963. *Principles of Numerical Taxonomy*, San Francisco and London
15 TUGBY, D. J. 1958. *American Antiquity* 24, No. 1, 24

58 Evolution at the Population Level: a Statistical Approach

BJÖRN KURTÉN

STUDENTS OF EVOLUTION frequently write about two 'kinds' of evolution, micro-evolution and macro-evolution. The meaning of these terms tends, however, to change with the viewpoint of the student. The geneticist may refer to a delicate shift in the gene balance within a few generations as micro-evolution, while macro-evolution to him may be the rise of a new subspecies. To a palaeolontologist micro-evolution may be the origin of new species and macro-evolution that of new families or orders.

In a study of Quaternary mammals it is probably best to draw the dividing line at the species level; the evolutionary role of the species is unique.[1] The present chapter will be devoted to the infra-specific changes—evolution on the population level—the earlier one (Chapter 23) being on the trans-specific evolution. The distinction is a real one in the sense that species-formation is an irreversible step, even though macro-evolution is generally regarded as simply a continuation, or accumulation, of micro-evolution.

Any two wolves belong to the same species, *Canis lupus*, yet they will always differ a little from each other, just like two human beings; and a local wolf population is made up by a number of such individual beings, each of which is unique. Again, two wolf populations in different areas consist of different individuals, and so will differ a little from each other in their averages and ranges of variation. An intensive study of many variables in the two populations may finally make it possible to assign even single individuals or a small group of unknown provenance to one or the other of the local populations.

As with the wolf, so with other species; and as with the differentiation in space, so with the differentiation in time. An excellent example has been provided by Giles,[2] who made a multivariate study of Pleistocene and Recent coyote in western North America. Even the often fragmentary palaeontological material may provide a basis for classification by means of discriminant functions that may be used as a quite sensitive dating tool. Fortunately, infra-specific changes were comparatively rapid in the Pleistocene, as a result of the environmental instability of this climatically turbulent epoch. Populations were changing all the time, even within relatively short time intervals.

For instance, the dentition of the cave hyena, *Crocuta crocuta* (Fig. 122) shows a series of marked changes from the Eemian Interglacial to the Würm Glaciation. The results of a study of British cave hyena material from the Eemian (Tornewton Cave, Kirkdale Cave, Joint Mitnor Cave, Barrington gravels) and the Würmian (Kent's Cavern) Uphill Cave, King Arthur's Cave, Coygan Cave, Ffynnon Beuno, Creswell) indicate that the changes seen in the following tables occurred.

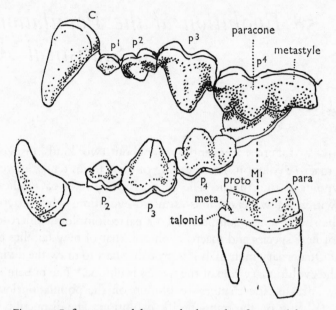

Fig. 122 Left upper and lower cheek teeth of spotted hyena (*Crocuta crocuta*) in partial occlusion, external view. C: canines; P: premolars, with serial numbers (P⁴: upper carnassial); M₁: lower carnassial, also shown separately in internal view (reversed, front end to the right) to exhibit dental elements: paroconid, protoconid, vestigial metaconid, and vestigial talonid.

(1) The jawbone became somewhat larger and heavier (Table A);

TABLE A

Width of the jawbone under the third premolar.

Age and locality	No. of specimens	Mean width	Standard Deviation	Coefficient of Variation
		mm	mm	
Eemian Interglacial				
1 Tornewton Cave	15	21·47±0·35	1·34	6·3
2 Barrington Gravels	12	21·25±0·29	1·01	4·8
Würm Glaciation				
3 Kent's Cavern	69	23·09±0·40	1·92	8·2
4 Four Würm Caves★	6	23·67±0·56	1·37	5·8

★ The four Würm Caves are: Creswell, Uphill, Ffynnon Beuno, and Coygan.

(2) The lower carnassial became distinctly broader (Table B);

TABLE B
Greatest width of the lower carnassial.

Age and locality	No. of specimens	Mean width	Standard Deviation	Coefficient of Variation
		mm	mm	
Eemian Interglacial				
1 Tornewton Cave	93	13·38±0·06	0·60	4·5
2 Kirkdale Cave	15	13·55±0·18	0·68	5·1
3 Joint Mitnor Cave	27	13·55±0·13	0·70	5·1
4 Barrington Gravels	7	13·57±0·27	0·72	5·3
5 2–4 combined	49	13·55±0·10	0·69	5·1
Würm Glaciation				
6 Kent's Cavern	177	13·95±0·05	0·65	4·7
7 Uphill Cave	10	13·86±0·18	0·56	4·0
8 King Arthur's Cave	7	14·21±0·30	0·79	5·6
9 Coygan Cave	5	14·15±0·32	0·72	5·1
10 Ffynnon Beuno	5	14·30±0·22	0·50	3·5
11 7–10 combined	27	14·15±0·14	0·72	5·1

(3) The incidence of the vestigial metaconid cusp in the lower carnassial (see Fig. 122) increased from about 11% to 44 % (Table C);

TABLE C
Incidence of the metaconid in M_1 (the lower carnassial).

Age and locality	Number of specimens — Total	Metaconid present	%
Eemian Interglacial			
Tornewton Cave (Hyena Stratum)	103	10	10
Kirkdale Cave	16	2	12
Joint Mitnor Cave	33	6	18
Barrington Gravels	8	—	0
Würm Glaciation			
Kent's Cavern	199	85	43
Brixham Caves	4	3	(75)
Uphill Cave	10	3	(30)
King Arthur's Cave	6	2	(33)
Coygan Cave	2	—	(0)
Ffynnon Beuno	5	3	(60)
Long Hole	2	2	(100)
Creswell	2	2	(100)
Total, Eemian	160	18	11
Total, Würm	230	100	44

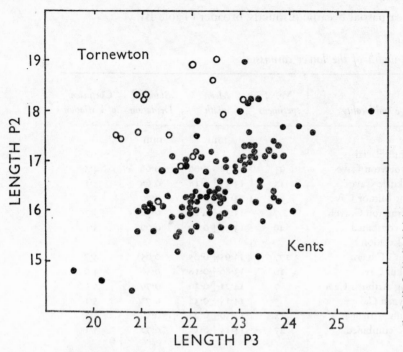

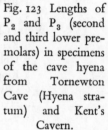

Fig. 123 Lengths of P_2 and P_3 (second and third lower premolars) in specimens of the cave hyena from Tornewton Cave (Hyena stratum) and Kent's Cavern.

TABLE D

Lengths of second and third premolars.

Age and locality	No. of specimens	Mean length	Standard Deviation	Coefficient of Variation
		mm	mm	
P_3, Eemian Interglacial				
1 Tornewton Cave	52	21·52±0·10	0·74	3·4
2 Barrington Gravels	16	21·75±0·22	0·88	4·0
3 Joint Mitnor Cave	26	21·67±0·08	0·42	2·0
P_3, Würm Glaciation				
4 Kent's Cavern	210	22·56±0·07	0·96	4·3
5 Coygan Cave	8	22·94±0·26	0·73	3·2
6 Five Würm Caves★	21	22·43±0·20	0·93	4·1
P_2, Eemian Interglacial				
1 Tornewton Cave	27	17·44±0·17	0·87	5·0
2 Barrington Gravels	11	17·50±0·33	1·09	6·2
3 Joint Mitnor Cave	10	17·22±0·25	0·79	4·6
P_2, Würm Glaciation				
4 Kent's Cavern	156	16·53±0·06	0·80	4·8
5 Coygan Cave	5	16·42±0·10	0·22	(1·3)
6 Five Würm Caves★	22	16·72±0·20	0·95	5·7

★ The five Würm caves are: Creswell, Uphill, Brixham, Ffynnon Beuno and King Arthur's Cave.

(4) The second lower premolar became shorter and the third lower premolar longer, on an average, causing a marked displacement of the scatter of the points in a diagram of the lengths of these teeth (Fig. 123, Table D);

(5) The third upper premolar became markedly longer in relation to its width (Fig. 124, Table E);

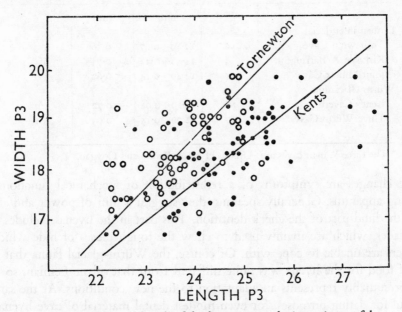

Fig. 124 Width and length of third upper premolar in specimens of the cave hyena from Tornewton Cave (Hyena stratum) and Kent's Cavern, with trend lines for the two samples.

TABLE E
Dimensions of third upper premolar.

Locality	No. of specimens	Mean	Standard Deviation	Coefficient of Variation
		mm	mm	
Width of P³				
Tornewton Cave	59	18·32±0·11	0·82	4·5
Kent's Cavern	54	18·33±0·11	0·82	4·5
Length of P³				
Tornewton Cave	61	23·70±0·10	0·82	3·5
Kent's Cavern	68	24·72±0·13	1·09	4·4

(6) The upper carnassial blade became distinctly stouter (Table F).

TABLE F
Blade width of the upper carnassial.

Age and locality	No. of specimens	Mean width	Standard Deviation	Coefficient of Variation
		mm	mm	
Eemian Interglacial				
Tornewton Cave	58	11·89±0·07	0·56	4·7
Kirkdale & Barrington	5	11·58±0·33	0·73	6·3
Joint Mitnor Cave	21	12·40±0·14	0·62	5·0
Würm Glaciation				
Kent's Cavern	86	12·19±0·08	0·72	5·9
Three Würm Caves★	17	12·29±0·15	0·63	5·1

★ The three Würm caves are: Uphill, Ffynnon Beuno and Coygan.

All these changes are symptoms of a redistribution of mechanical functions in the masticating apparatus. Generally speaking they suggest a shift of power and efficiency towards the hind part of the cheek dentition. This part in the hyenas includes the carnassial blades, which are mainly used to chew the tough pieces of hide which other meat-eaters are unable to cope with. Of course, the Würm-glacial fauna that was the source of food for the hyena was quite different from that of the Eemian, so that the change presumably represents an adaptation to the new conditions. At the same time it is useful for dating purposes, for even modest dental material of cave hyena can be readily dated.

Similar considerations apply to other species. Unfortunately this sort of analysis has so far been carried out only in very few instances. Its potential usefulness in dating is great, but the results are also of interest as such, for the study of rates and modes of evolution. Here are some instances of infra-specific changes which may be of use in connection with dating problems.

The Dirk-toothed cat, *Megantereon megantereon*, increased in size gradually during the Villafranchian and Middle Pleistocene; maximum size is reached at Choukoutien.

The Issoire lynx, *Felis issiodorensis*, has a bicuspid lower carnassial in the earliest Villafranchian; later on, a small third cusp (metaconid) became increasingly frequent.

The cave lion, *Felis leo*, became gradually smaller from a maximum in the Cromerian interglacial.

The wolf, *Canis lupus*, became gradually larger in the sequence from the Cromerian to the Würm.

The cave bear, *Ursus spelaeus*. A very large fossil material of this species is known from Eemian and Würmian Continental deposits. There is a clear progression from somewhat smaller and more primitive Eemian forms to very large Würmian ones;[3] the change continued during the Würm.[4]

Horses tend to become smaller in Europe from the Villafranchian to the Middle and Late Pleistocene, perhaps partly due to infra-specific change but also in part to repeated immigration or evolution of new, smaller species. As in many other instances, analysis of Pleistocene horses is still in a preliminary stage.

In Middle Pleistocene red deer, *Cervus elaphus*, on the Continent there is a repeated fluctuation between the Asiatic 'acoronate' form (in which the antlers terminate with a simple fork) and the European type of stag (with a cup formed by three or four tines). This is in rapport with climatic changes, the 'acoronate' form appearing in colder and more continental phases than the 'coronate', and is evidently due to an oscillation of the geographic ranges of these subspecies.

The Irish elk, *Megaloceros giganteus*, of the Holsteinian interglacial, differs from its Late Pleistocene descendant in the size and shape of the antlers.

The size of the fallow deer, *Dama dama*, was gradually reduced during the Late Pleistocene and Postglacial.

The aurochs, *Bos primigenius*, also decreased in size from a maximum in the Holsteinian; at the same time its horns became more curved and more nearly circular in cross section.

The list might be greatly extended; more details may be found in Kurtén.[5] For most forms the details and the short-term changes remain to be worked out.

The evolutionary changes in fossil species may help to date the archaeologist's finds, but they may also cast unexpected light on the environment of early man and the interaction between man and beast. In this respect the study of size changes at the end of the Pleistocene may be illuminating. A few mammals have increased in size in the Postglacial, many have remained unchanged, but a great number have showed a remarkable dwarfing.[6]

The causes of such changes have not yet been definitely established. In many instances we know that mammal species react on secular temperature changes by increase or decrease in size, for instance lowered temperature may be associated with size increase, and vice-versa (Bergmann's rule). But there are also instances in which this explanation becomes highly improbable.

Some cases of dwarfing may represent a reaction of the population to a deterioration of the environment or some component in it, such as the amount of food available. Then the smaller size makes it possible to keep the population at or near its optimal density in spite of the reduction of food or space or whatever the deficiency may be; small size will thus be adaptive, and favoured by natural selection. I think this is a probable explanation in some instances, as exemplified by the carnivores of Palestine at the transition from the Palaeolithic to the Neolithic.[7]

Three species that had been almost stable in size during the Würm show a sudden, dramatic dwarfing in the Mesolithic; they are wolf, wild cat, and spotted hyena. The hyena indeed, after an almost incredible process of shrinking, eventually became extinct; this would suggest that the dwarfing was in fact due to adverse conditions setting in.

In contrast the red fox reached maximum size in the Mesolithic, suggesting that this species thrived in the conditions that killed the hyena and dwarfed the wolf and cat. Perhaps all this is due to climatic changes, but it is difficult to disregard the possible effect of Mesolithic man; perhaps the red fox may have profited from some scavenging role in conjunction with the human population.

However that may be, the situation was changed completely with the beginning of the Neolithic; rapid dwarfing was now the lot of the fox. We can only dimly sense the complex constellations of factors that bring about these changes, but whatever they are they have a direct bearing on the evolution of human cultures and society during this period. Perhaps the study of other, analogous sequences may help to bring out their significance.

REFERENCES

1 MAYR, E. 1963. *Animal species and evolution*, Cambridge, Mass.
2 GILES, E. 1960. *Univ. California Publ. Geol. 36*, 369–90
3 DONNER, J. J. and KURTÉN, B. 1958. *Eiszeitalter u. Gegenwart 9. Mottl, M. 1964. Mitteil. Mus. Bergbau etc., Graz, 26*
4 MUSIL, R. 1965. *Anthropos*
5 KURTÉN, B. 1968. *Pleistocene mammals of Europe*, London
6 DEGERBØL, M. 1933. *Vidensk. Meddel. Dansk Nat. hist. For.*, 96
  KURTÉN, B. 1960. *Cold Spring Harbor Symp.*, 24, 205–15
7 KURTÉN, B. 1965. *Acta Zool. Fennica*, 107

59 Stones, Pots and People: a Plea for Statistical Caution

DON BROTHWELL

IN THE PREVIOUS CONTRIBUTIONS to this section on statistics, some of the possibilities of applying statistical methods to excavated remains have been considered. Although some warnings have already been made, it is my sole and specific job to expand further on some of the difficulties of considering archaeological data statistically. Certainly this is a period of archaeo-statistical optimism, and it is at periods such as this that an 'outsider' like myself can see the research problems in a different and perhaps more critical light than those who are actually immersed in the machinery of analysis.

It is not usual for techniques to be explored and applied at the same time, and to the same degree, by various disciplines, and generally speaking, archaeology has been very late in making full use of the battery of statistical methods available. There is, however, perhaps some value in this, for the archaeologist can learn something from the past mistakes of others, not only in the type and limits of analysis, but also in the varied problems of sampling.

Because I am by research interest a human biologist, what follows will be tempered by experience in another field—one with a far longer history and more mature background of precise data analysis.

HISTORY

It seems, actually, to be quite incorrect to think that all archaeological material has only come under statistical attention in the past decade or two. If we take the broad view (not a very popular one) that anything pertaining to earlier human populations and revealed by excavation has archaeological interest, then archaeo-metrics are more than a century old. Beginnings were specialized and limited, of course, the earliest work being perhaps the measurement and analysis of early human skeletal remains. By the end of the last century and the beginning of this, the biometric school of Pearson, in London, had set a particularly high standard, although their conclusions on stature, cranial morphology and so forth, are now dated.

Animal remains also received metrical attention during the nineteenth century, as evidenced by the careful report on the skeletal material resulting from the extensive excavations of General Pitt-Rivers.[23]

In the field of ceramics and stone artifacts, progress was much slower. Excepting the early (and then continuous) simple tool classifications, pottery first received more precise attention, although the results had little impact. Relevant here is Kluckhohn's[18] assessment of Leslie Spier's work, he writes: 'In a notable (and incredibly neglected) paper, Spier in 1919 applied the theory of random sampling to establish potsherd sequences by seriation, with results which were not only important from the point of view of the specific archaeological problem, but which would seem to have the most significant implications for stratigraphic method generally.' (p. 377.)

This appears to be not the only neglected early paper. McBurney[20] says of the early analysis of tools: 'The first serious use of statistics I can call to mind is in an unjustly neglected paper by the geologist J. D. Solomon on the Lower Palaeolithic of East Anglia published over thirty years ago. It is a relatively simple analysis of absolute measures and ratios of hand-axes from different sites and horizons.'

Following Spier, William Strong[27] applied fairly elaborate statistics in 1925 to the analysis of some 40 pottery traits to be found on ceramics from Ancon, Peru. By the early 1930's, in the New World at least, such analyses of material culture objects were being looked on with general favour. The statistical approach, Kroeber[19] wrote (p. 11): 'clarifies concepts, sharpens definition of problems, and reveals new problems which call for more exact factual investigation'. Statistical applications are now well beyond the bounds of simple electrical calculators, as the recent symposium on *The Use of Computers in Anthropology*[17] so clearly shows.

Scientific research can have its crazes, and perhaps the more elaborate the research tool or computer programme, the greater the temptation or attention. Investigations on human skeletal remains have an interesting history in this respect. Beginning with simple calculations of indices and means, it graduated through Pearson's Coefficient of Racial Likeness, to the more elaborate D^2 of Mahalanobis, and other multifactorial 'distance' statistics. Because the raw data is often crude and samples small (perhaps not even representative), an alternative and more simple biometric approach has recently been suggested by Penrose.[22]

The present period in human biology might be viewed (at least by some of us) as a time of particular caution in interpreting osteometric results. Thus an important law, equally applicable to archaeo-metric investigations, is that impeccable statistics are not a guarantee of impeccable results. So much depends upon what is offered to the computer (and it is so easy to *under*-estimate the limitations of the raw data).

NOMENCLATURAL AND TEMPORAL DIFFICULTIES

Just as in biological taxonomy, it seems important in archaeo-metric investigations to have, at least as far as is possible, a clear and properly balanced idea of the classificatory merits of the data being considered. A computer can indicate distances of cultural assemblages of clusters of traits from one another, and can indicate numerical *but not cultural* significance. It can also provide any number of correlations, the value of which will initially depend upon perceptive selection of data on the part of the investigator. Finally, however, the most difficult job of interpreting the results as indicators of cultural change (and all this simple phrase means, in terms of trait mutation, drift, trait intrusion and so on) must remain for the archaeologist. Regrettably, the nomenclature constructed by the social anthropologist, to refer to division of living populations can not be extended back through time. Rouse and Cruxent[25] state the present situation well when they say: 'The method of tribal identification has proved to be unsatisfactory for several reasons. The sources are frequently so imprecise that they permit contradictory identifications. . . . In its stead, the archaeologists of Europe and America are now accustomed to establish, purely archaeologically, units of culture, distinct from the tribes mentioned in historic sources. . . . The problem is to extract from the refuse criteria that may be used to group the communities into units which will serve as substitutes for the tribes of ethnology. . . . The culture which is shared by a group of communities is known variously as a "complex", "focus", "phase", "style" or "industry".'

This state of affairs can make life very difficult, especially for studies 'marginal' to the material culture aspects of archaeology. For instance, the origins of domestication of a particular plant or animal might be related to a particular tribal group which could conceivably not be distinguishable by an assemblage of artifact traits. Similarly, simple reference to a certain 'Beaker People' might rather obscure the fact that the group

TABLE A
Possible alternatives in tradition segmentation (from Haury et al.[11]).

```
                                                                    ↑
Direct               A B C
Tradition            A B C
                     A B C                                          Time
                     A B C
                     A B C
─────────────────────────────────────────────────────────────────────
                         A B C D                                    ↑
                         A B C D
Converging             A B      C D
Tradition              A B        C D                               Time
                       A B          C D
                       A B            C D
─────────────────────────────────────────────────────────────────────
                 A B D                                              ↑
                   A B D                      C D
Diverging            A B D                    C D
Tradition              A B D                C D                     Time
                         A B D            C D
                         A B          C D
─────────────────────────────────────────────────────────────────────
                         A B C D E F G                              ↑
                         A B C D E F
Elaborating            A B C D E
Tradition              A B C D                                      Time
                       A B C
                       A B
─────────────────────────────────────────────────────────────────────
                         A B                                        ↑
                         A B C
Reducing               A B C D
Tradition              A B C D E                                    Time
                       A B C D E F
                       A B C D E F G
```

really consisted of a number of separate relatively inbreeding communities, perhaps separated by linguistic or religious barriers not evident in the available culture traits.

Perhaps we should take the problem of population versus culture traits or traditions just a little further, in order to emphasize that in temporal studies one must be continually aware of the complex of alternative explanations for trait changes. In a recent American archaeological memoir on the study of cultural stability, various alternatives (Table A) which might explain varying tradition segmentations through time, were discussed. Although in diagrammatic representation, the alternatives are easy enough to understand, when presented to the archaeologist as a mosaic of statistical data whose pattern can change markedly through time, they are by no means so easy to decipher. Similarly, if we consider the evolution and progress of just *one* trait in, say, six hypothetical populations over a period of time (Table B), it is clearly most important to understand the theory of such differences, although this does not make statistical analysis for such variation any easier.

TABLE B

Various alternative possibilities of culture trait discovery and spread in six hypothetical populations where o = culture trait, and 1, 2 . . . 6 = populations.

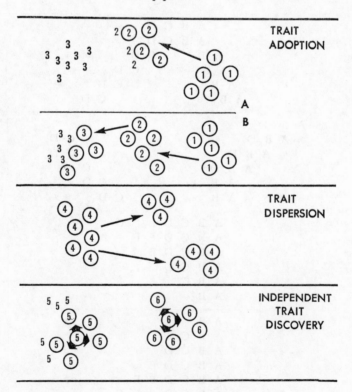

ENVIRONMENT (ARTIFACTS AND ARCHAEO-METRICS)

In a recent broadcast talk, Eric Higgs[15] emphasized that the study of *areas* rather than *sites* was a growing archaeological field; also, that the study of recent populations temporally and spatially—and in terms which can be meaningful to the prehistorian—was essential to the future healthy development of archaeological interpretation. Such remarks also emphasize the need on the part of the archaeologist to think in terms of early peoples contending with changing environments and a large spectrum of economies; of population increases and movements. Early communities are not simply a series of pots or stone tools (even though some studies go a long way to suggesting this). This broad dynamic outlook is well illustrated in recent studies by Desmond Clark[5,6] in Africa. In terms of a single tool variety, an example of a more progressive thinking is given by Posnansky[24], who rightly points out that the evolution of the handaxe is *not* just a matter of form change; the significant point is that it becomes a more efficient cutting tool.

The variability of stone tool varieties depends initially on two factors: (a) the raw materials available, and (b) the 'versatility' of the group given the need for a particular artifact. The first factor I suspect has been vastly underrated in various ways. Even over small areas, size of flint or suitable rock nodules could vary considerably, and, as a result of this, tool size (the industry seen at Vertesszöllös in Hungary shows how small 'heavy' tool types can become without losing all value). But not only size can be affected, for if only for manipulative reasons, shape may also be modified. Shape differences are of course very obvious between flint and quartzite (or igneous) rocks. Thus, a slightly different artifact shape and size—though how much different seems to need clarification with reference to recent stone-using populations—does not necessarily mean that we have a different population or culture. Significant differences in certain tool measurements between two or a limited series of tools must, therefore, be regarded with caution. Similarly, significant differences between tool types in 'highland' and 'lowland' sites in close proximity (assuming approximate contemporaneity) may also not necessarily indicate a cultural difference, but rather evidence of summer and winter residence by the same population. In such an instance, one could conceivably have differences resulting from variations in raw materials at hand, as well as the influence of varying economic pursuits throughout the year.

Assessment of the versatility or inventiveness of a group through time is also no easy problem when remnants of their material culture is all that is at hand. Moreover, it is important to appreciate early in the analysis of artifact assemblages that rate of change (whether by gradual 'indigenous' modification, or by the adoption of intrusive techniques) must never have been uniform—even supposing equal opportunities for change on the part of a number of communities. Just as in biology micro-evolutionary change is the sum of various factors (including mutation, gene intrusion, and founder effect), so in archaeology it is essential to think similarly in terms of a complex mosaic which is ever changing both spatially and temporally. In the same way, archaeo-statistics, like biometry attempts to provide more precise information about major evolutionary steps as well as minor changes, which may only be marginal or even irrelevant to a consideration of major trends. Both aspects have their part in the proper consideration of earlier cultures, but must be correctly recognized if the significance of results is to be properly used by the archaeologist.

MISFITS AND MISINTERPRETATIONS

In his readable introductory work on statistics, *Facts from Figures*, M. J. Moroney points out that 'the number of wireless licences purchased over the last twenty years or so correlates extremely highly with the numbers of people certified insane in the same years'. This mathematical association can be seen to be dubious without much further thought, but regrettably misfits and pseudo-associations of this sort are usually far from easy to evaluate.

In an endeavour to look a little further into the question of misinterpretations, but at the same time have some 'control' over the data presented, I have undertaken a brief study of British gravestone morphology in a number of nineteenth- and twentieth-century cemeteries. To make it easily digestible, the data is presented as histograms in Fig. 125. In order to finally set the stage for unbiased interpretation of these results it is suggested that the reader forget their date and their association with recent undertaker

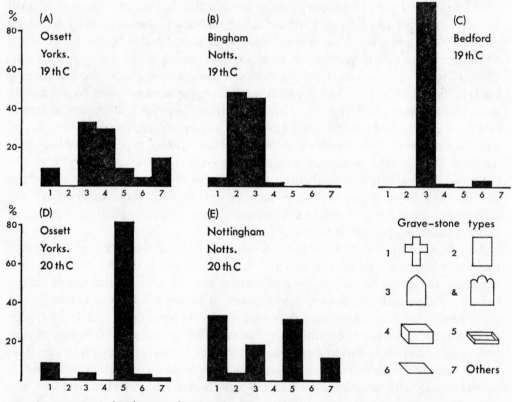

Fig. 125 Frequency distribution of various grave-stone types in a nineteenth- and twentieth-century English cemetery series.

'cults'. Two samples are from the same town in Yorkshire (A and D), two are from Nottinghamshire (B and E), and the other is the southernmost, from Bedfordshire (C). Three are nineteenth-century (A, B and C) and two are of recent date (D and E).

Now, supposing such material culture objects were from protohistoric or pre-historic levels, what conclusions could one draw? Without doubt, some of the frequency differences are *statistically* highly significant. Some of the deductions, alternative and complementary, which could be made about these variations might be listed briefly as follows:

(1) All show very different traditions in their form of stone working.

(2) Series A and B are markedly 'heterogeneous', whereas E is distinctive for the 'homogeneity' of type.

(3) As well as spatial differences, there are marked temporal ones. Thus, in series A and C, frequencies 3 and 4 decrease markedly whereas 5 increases significantly in the more recent of the two groups. In B and D groups, varieties 2 and 3 predominate in the early group, being replaced later by frequency peaks at 1 and 5.

(4) In terms of cultural development versus culture contact and intrusion, the data would seem to demand the following considerations. In the earlier period, there is increasing variation as one progresses northwards, a fact which might suggest that the northern community was showing a greater rate of tradition segmentation, or that it was a multi-hybrid culture—a melting pot for various intrusive elements. On the other hand, in the two more recent series, it is the more southern group which shows the greatest heterogeneity, the Yorkshire population having become more 'stable'.

Now, returning to the nature of the material and its date, the differences are clearly insignificant in terms of major cultural change, though statistically very significant. The differences may be a factor of the stonemason's preferences, type of stone available, cost variations, and perhaps even cultural 'drift' (haphazard movements of community preference from one form to another over a period of time). Of course this is an absurd example, but the problems outlined are very real ones for the archaeologist nevertheless.

Perhaps the recent controversy over the astronomical significance of Stonehenge would be a more apt—certainly a more applicable—example of doubtful conclusions following elaborate statistics (the raw data, in this case, also being open to question). Ever since 1740, when William Stukeley first observed that certain stone alignments pointed approximately to the sunrise at the summer solstice, there has been debate about possible astronomical implications. The detailed consideration by Hawkin and White[12] of this question might be regarded as the final crystallization of views and analyses in support of Stonehenge astronomers. Hawkins confidently states that 'I have demon-strated beyond reasonable doubt that the monument was deliberately, accurately, skil-fully oriented to the Sun and the Moon.' In Atkinson's[1] reasoned criticism of this new interpretation, which he pointedly entitles 'Moonshine on Stonehenge', he casts doubt upon some of the archaeological statements pertinent to the study, the suitability of the plans referred to for computational data, and the correctness of the tests of significance.

Thus, we see that what is a very worthwhile subject for study and testing—astronomy in prehistoric cultures—may so easily be 'fogged-up' by over-enthusiasm and some dubious calculating.

FROM MATERIAL CULTURE TO POPULATION

Perhaps one of the most important, and yet generally neglected, parts of archaeo-statistics is concerned with the 'translation 'of data on the material culture of a group into terms of family and population size. This may be concerned with such variables as numbers or size of pottery, spatial distribution of sites or finds, or the analysis of habitation numbers and sizes. Surprisingly, although New World archaeologists have shown themselves aware of the demographic potentialities of such data, Europe seems rather to lag behind. To an 'outsider' such as myself, this would seem to be partly the result of an extreme concentration on typology. If this seems an unfair statement, I can only say in my defence that in a recent attempt to review palaeodemography, I found only a

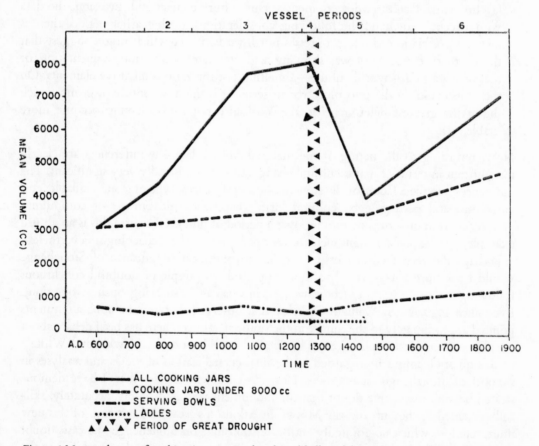

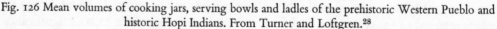

Fig. 126 Mean volumes of cooking jars, serving bowls and ladles of the prehistoric Western Pueblo and historic Hopi Indians. From Turner and Loftgren.[28]

handful of European archaeologists who had ever considered the question of population. However, my concern here is to demonstrate the type of population evidence one might tentatively derive from cultural evidence, and for the sake of brevity, only pottery and habitation data will be considered.

In searching for pertinent data on pottery I was in fact interested to note that in the case of British prehistoric or more recent pottery, no one seemed to have considered volumetric analysis. Also, there would seem to be no proper culinary consideration of such containers as beakers, food vessels, and 'funerary' urns,* and it would seem important to consider their possible use in terms of family units. The Bronze Age beaker, for instance, would seem to be a little too large as a domestic article for one individual, and thus what number of persons should it be equated with? In a recent visit to Patamona Indian villages in Guyana, I was pleased (socially but not medically) to be offered a 'communal' drinking bowl at various dwellings. The thick cassava or maize drinks were in vessels of comparable volume to the beaker, and seemed to be ideal for small family groups (fairly low fertility was usual among these Amerindians). Clearly there are various problems of this sort which are worthy of metric investigation, modern ethnographic findings being useful if considered with care.

The type of family information which can be derived from excavated vessels is well exemplified by the work of Turner and Lofgren[28] on prehistoric western Pueblo Indians. Changes in cooking jar volumes would appear to have had special significance, and showed the most fluctuation (Fig. 126). These changes would seem to be correlated with increasing population numbers from AD 600 to AD 1200 (showing a thirty-fold increase), than by decimation and gradual regrowth.

Moving to another form of analysis, Cook and Heizer[8] have recently reviewed, by means of fairly diverse examples, the general problem of the quantitative expression of relationships between population and settlement size. The formulations devised, and their discussion, rightly rest on careful numerical data. To summarize the precepts they work on, they state (p. 8): 'If there is to be a truly quantitative analysis of space-population or other similar relationship, all pertinent variables must be cast in absolute numbers. The reasonable and appropriate variables must be designated as independent. The data must be graphed and studied with respect to the governing type of function. The semi-log formulation may be employed when *rates* are involved, and the log-log formulation for static attributes unless otherwise clearly indicated. Strength of association may be tested by the use of the correlation coefficient and the standard error of estimate. If any particular situation requires exhaustive analysis, then more sophisticated mathematical and statistical methods should be considered.'

The types of relationship they were exploring are seen in Fig. 127, which shows the regression of log total floor space (ordinate) against log mean number of persons per village (abscissa). This log-log relationship is clearly highly significant in this case, but it is important to note that they show in other data, that correlations can sometimes be

---

* Although some continental types were clearly made for the purpose, the majority in Britain surely had a primary use as cooking or storage vessels.

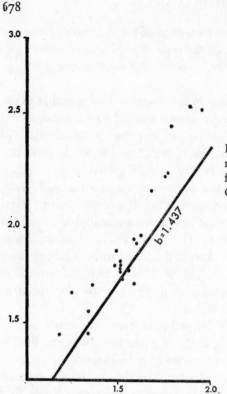

Fig. 127 Log total floor space (ordinate) against log mean number of persons per village (abscissa). Dots are single family units (for selected Amerindian groups). Data from Cook and Heizer.[8]

noticeably disturbed by additional factors. Nevertheless, such methods are clearly worth further extension and careful application.

STATISTICS AND ARCHAEOLOGY OF THE FUTURE

There is, of course, no doubt at all that statistical methods and the use of the computer for data storage, is as inevitable in archaeology as in any other sciences. Judging from such research in other fields, the archaeologist still has a variety of statistical teething troubles to come, even in primary matters such as the value of different distance statistics relative to the types of data.[16]

Complex multifactorial analyses have now been attempted on mammal skeletons,[10,13] and perhaps soon, the simple measurements of palaeobotany (as for instance seen in Helbaek[14]), will be followed by methods which will allow more data to be considered at the same time. Even non-metrical variation is yielding to more precise scoring and analysis in the biological field (Berry[2]). 'Matrix analysis'[4] has been applied to pottery[7] and 'factor analysis' to Mousterian tools.[3] The computer will digest and compare artifact density at varying levels, spatial complexes of post-holes, grave orientations, and indeed whatever the archaeologist wisely or unwisely wants it to do. It is only a matter of time before other methods, such as trend-surface analysis,[21,26] seduce the archaeologist.

The prospects are clearly exciting, if at the same time somewhat alarming to the majority who must undertake archaeological data analysis. Perhaps a little consolation might be found in a recent remark of J. D. Doran;[9] 'In the foreseeable future, the "computer-archaeologist" should obtain much more flexible and informal computing facilities, while the conventional archaeologist, who only occasionally has a use for a computer, will find more people to guide him, and may even find that he can use the machine himself while *it guides him.*'

ACKNOWLEDGEMENTS

I should like to thank Christy Turner and the editor of the Southwestern Journal of Anthropology, for permission to reproduce Fig. 2. Some aspects of the text benefited from discussion with David Clarke, Eric Higgs, Isobel Smith and Paul Ashbee.

REFERENCES

1 ATKINSON, R. J. C. 1966. *Antiquity 40*, 212–16
2 BERRY, R. J. 1968. The biology of non-metrical variations in mice and men. In BROTHWELL, D. R. (ed.), *The Skeletal Biology of Earlier Human Populations*, Oxford
3 BINFORD, L. R. and BINFORD, S. R. 1966. *Amer. Anthrop. 68*, 238–95
4 BRAINERT, G. W. 1951. *Amer. Antiq.. 16*, 301–13
5 CLARK, J. D. 1964. *S. Afr. Archaeo. Bull. 19*, 93–101
6 CLARK, J. D. 1966. *Amer. Anthrop. 68*, 202–29
7 CLARKE, D. L. 1962. *Proc. Prehist. Soc. 28*, 371–82
8 COOK, S. F. and HEIZER, R. F. 1965. *The Quantitative Approach to the Relation between Population and Settlement Size*, Rep. Univ. Cal., Berkeley, No. 64
9 DORAN, J. D. 1967. Electronic computers and archaeology: a computer scientist's viewpoint. Unpublished MS *Research Seminar on Archaeology*, Institute of Archaeology, London
10 GILES, E. 1960. *Univ. Cal. Pub. Geol. Sci. 36*, 369–90
11 HAURY, E. W. *et al.*, 1956. *Amer. Antiq. 22*, 31–57 (Mem. Soc. Amer. Arch. No. 11)
12 HAWKINS, G. W. and WHITE, J. B. 1965. *Stonehenge Decoded*, London
13 HEALY, M. J. R. 1965. Descriptive uses of discriminant functions, in *Mathematics and Computer Science in Biology and Medicine*, London
14 HELBAEK, H. 1961. *Anatolian Studies, 11*, 77–9
15 HIGGS, E. S. 1967. *The Listener, 77*, 425–7
16 HUIZINGA, J. 1965. *Proc. Kon. Ned. Akad, v. Wetensch.* c.68, 69–80
17 HYMES, D. (ed.) 1965. *The Use of Computers in Anthropology*, London
18 KLUCKHOHN, C. 1939. *Amer. Anthrop. 41*, 345–77
19 KROEBER, A. L. 1935. Preface: in KLIMEK, S. Culture Element Distributions: I, The Structure of Californian Indian Culture. *Univ. Cal. Pub. Amer. Archaeo. and Ethnol. 37*, 1–70
20 McBURNEY, C. B. M. 1964. Uses and abuses of statistics in Archaeology. Unpublished MS *Research Seminar on Archaeology*. Institute of Archaeology, London
21 MERRIAM, D. R. and SNEATH, P. H. A. 1966. *J. Geophys. Res. 71*, 1105–15
22 PENROSE, L. S. 1954. *Ann. Eugen. Lond. 18*, 337–93
23 PITT-RIVERS, A. 1898. *Excavations in Cranborne Chase*. Privately printed
24 POSNANSKY, M. 1959. *Man 59*, 42–4
25 ROUSE, I. and CRUXENT, J. M. 1963. *Venezuelan Archaeology*, New Haven
26 SNEATH, P. H. A. 1967. *J. Zool. Lond. 151*, 65–122
27 STRONG, W. D. 1925. *Univ. Cal. Bub. Amer, Archaeo. and Ethnol. 21*, 135–90
28 TURNER, C. G. and LOFGREN, L. 1966. *Southw. J. Anthrop. 22*, 117–32

SECTION VII   PROSPECTING

60 Magnetic Location

MARTIN AITKEN

MAN HAS BEEN GUIDED by the earth's magnetism for many centuries, certainly since the tenth century AD when the laws of Gottland prescribed penalties for Baltic sailors who tampered with the compass.* Ancient mariners knew too that compass directions were liable to be erratic near to certain coasts and that this was due to deposits of lodestone—fragments of which formed the active element of early compasses. A particular form of iron oxide (*magnetite*, Fe_3O_4) is responsible for the strong magnetic properties of lodestone and towards the end of the nineteenth century mineral prospectors in Sweden began to use *anomalous* compass readings—checked by reference to the sun or to the pole-star—as a method of locating rich iron-ore deposits.

Magnetic surveying is now an important and highly developed aspect of geological prospecting and very sensitive measuring techniques are used. One of these is the *proton magnetometer*, developed from the magnetic property of the nucleus termed 'free precession', which was first observed experimentally only in 1954.[9] By adapting the proton magnetometer for archaeological use it is possible to detect the following categories of buried remains:

(1) iron objects;
(2) fired structures such as kilns, furnaces, ovens and hearths;
(3) pits and ditches filled with top-soil or rubbish; and, in some circumstances:
(4) walls, foundations, roads and tombs.

The detection of iron objects hardly needs explanation; no one who has tried to take a compass bearing close to an iron fence will doubt the reality of the magnetic disturbance (or anomaly) from it. The disturbances from the other categories listed are very much weaker and arise because of subtle magnetic effects produced by fire and high humus-content. This means that the greater the involvement of a site with the basic human activities of smelting, cultivation, pottery-making, cooking, excretion, etc., the greater is the ability of the proton magnetometer to locate its various features.

The particular advantages of the proton magnetometer compared to more conventional magnetic field instruments, and compared too to resistivity surveying, are the ease and rapidity with which measurements can be made. An acre can be covered in upwards of four hours, depending on how many features are found. Plate XL shows

* Breathing over the compass after eating onions is one of the practices specifically condemned.

the instrument developed by the Oxford Archaeological Research Laboratory. Each measurement is initiated by pressing the white push-button and the digits subsequently indicated by the four meter-dials are recorded directly in plan form by the operator. A second operator moves the detector over the area being surveyed; this is temporarily marked out, 50 ft by 50 ft at a time, by a string net of 10 ft mesh. The chart of readings obtained from an area containing two pottery kilns and a ditch is shown in Fig. 128.

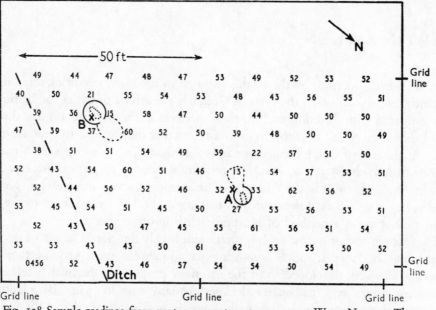

Fig. 128 Sample readings from proton magnetometer survey at Water Newton. The readings shown cover two unit squares each 50 ft by 50 ft. The detector-bottle was at 3 ft above ground level. Fig. 131 shows detailed measurements on traverses through 'A' and 'B'; Romano-British pottery kilns were found beneath these points. From Aitken.[3]

The simplicity of operation of the proton magnetometer is only achieved at the cost of complex electronics, and the instrument is expensive—upwards of £600. Another instrument based on the nuclear free-precession phenomenon is the proton *gradiometer*. This is a little cheaper to construct, and in its simplest form—the 'Bleeper', which is adequate for most types of archaeological site—the cost should be only £150. The *fluxgate* magnetometer is another alternative to the proton magnetometer or gradio-meter. It has important advantages but is not at present available in a form suitable for archaeological surveys. Its cost seems likely to be comparable to that of the proton magnetometer.

PRINCIPLES

Thermo-remanent magnetism. A lump of crude clay heated to a dull red heat (about 700°C) acquires a weak *permanent* magnetism on cooling—the phenomenon is termed *thermo-remanent* magnetism. It is the basis of magnetic dating (see pp. 76–87), and was first investigated towards the end of the nineteenth century.[5] The same effect occurs with soil and stones, as long as a small percentage of iron oxide is present—which is nearly always the case (among rocks, chalk is an obvious exception). The effect can be very simply demonstrated by holding an ordinary builder's brick close to a compass: the thermo-remanent magnetism is sufficient to cause a deflection of half a degree or more. On a larger scale, the thermo-remanent magnetism acquired by volcanic lava as it cools from the molten state gives rise to an appreciable magnetic anomaly in the region of a volcano. Thermo-remanent magnetism is carried by all types of igneous rocks, being strongest in recently-formed basalts and weakest in granites.

The thermo-remanent magnetism of baked clay has been exhaustively studied experimentally by Thellier[10] and a theoretical interpretation given by Néel.[8] The effect results from the *ferrimagnetism* of *magnetite* (Fe_3O_4) and *haematite* (α-Fe_2O_3). The average iron oxide content of the earth's crust is 6·8 per cent, and most soil, clay and rock can be expected to contain significant quantities of magnetite and/or haematite, uniformly dispersed in fine grains. Each grain of haematite forms a magnetic *domain*; within a domain the magnetization is uniform. In unbaked clay (soil, or rock) the domains point in random directions (Fig. 129), and because of mutual annulment, their net magnetic effect is very small. At a high temperature however, the intrinsic magnetization of each domain weakens and thermal agitation permits some of the domains to be lined up along the lines of force of the earth's magnetic field (Fig. 129b). On cooling, the domains remain 'frozen' in this lined-up situation. At the same time the intrinsic domain magnetization returns to its normal value and the net magnetic effect is now appreciable—simply because the magnetic fields from the domains now add together instead of cancelling out.

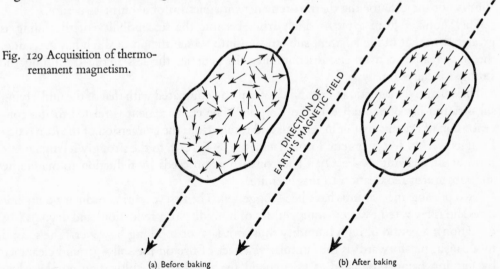

Fig. 129 Acquisition of thermo-
remanent magnetism.

DIRECTION OF
EARTH'S MAGNETIC FIELD

(a) Before baking   (b) After baking

As long as the temperature has reached 675°C (a dull red heat) there is no further increase in the subsequent thermo-remanent magnetism. The duration of heating is unimportant. The effect produced by heating to a lower temperature than 675°C depends on the clay; for a typical clay the effect would be 10% of maximum after cooling from 200°C, 30% after 400°C, 50% after 500°C and 90% after 600°C.

In the case of magnetite the grains are larger than can be occupied by a single domain and explanation is more complex. However, the experimental behaviour is similar to that of haematite except that the degree of magnetization acquired is very much stronger, although the stability of the 'frozen-in' domains is not so hard. The latter factor only matters in magnetic dating, but the former gives rise to a wide variation in the strengths of the anomaly to be expected from fired structures. The specific remanent magnetization of clay cooled from dull red heat can vary between 0·0001 and 0·1 e.m.u. per gram of clay (for refined clays, such as china clay, relatively free from iron, the figures are very much lower). The lower limit applies to red, highly oxidized clay in which conversion of iron oxide to haematite is nearly complete, and the upper limit to grey reduced clay in which magnetite is predominant.

Enhancement of soil susceptibility. The anomalies from pits and ditches arise from a different effect from thermo-remanent magnetism. It is not quite true to say that at ordinary temperatures the magnetic domains are unaffected by the external magnetic field. Some degree of alignment does occur, and a small magnetization results.

Magnetic *susceptibility* expresses the magnetization *induced* in 1 gram of the sample when it is placed in a magnetic field of 1 oersted, *without any heat treatment*. (The specific magnetization is obtained by multiplying the susceptibility by the earth's field strength— about 0·47 oersted in Britain). Induced magnetization is essentially temporary; in whatever direction a sample is turned, the magnetization always lies along the direction of the lines of force of the earth's magnetic field. Consequently disarrangement of the filling of a pit or ditch does not greatly* affect the strength of the anomaly from it. This is not the case for the thermo-remanent magnetism of a burnt structure.

The anomaly from a pit or ditch arises because the susceptibility of the filling is greater than that of the adjacent sub-stratum into which the pit or ditch has been dug, thereby creating a magnetic discontinuity. In general, the less sterile the filling the stronger is the anomaly.

The enhanced magnetic susceptibility of top-soil compared with that of the underlying sub-stratum has been studied by Le Borgne.[7] The enhancement is related to the concentration of organic matter in the soils and results from the conversion of the iron oxide from its weakly ferrimagnetic form, haematite (α-Fe_2O_3), to the strongly ferrimagnetic form of maghaemite (γ-Fe_2O_3). The conversion proceeds by reduction to magnetite and subsequent reoxidation to maghaemite.

Two possible mechanisms have been suggested. The first[6] occurs at ordinary temperatures and is favoured by alternating periods of humidity (for reduction) and dryness (for oxidation): a period of high humidity must not last for too long however. The second mechanism put forward[7] is the cumulative effect of fire on the soil—ground clearance by burning being postulated as inherent in the methods of cultivation employed in ancient times. Although high temperatures have intervened in this case, the anomaly is due to enhancement of instantaneous susceptibility rather than thermo-remanent

---

* There is some growth of anomaly with time if the filling is left undisturbed. This effect is due to viscous magnetism. With soils, the viscous component is not usually as great as the instantaneously induced component, although it may be of a comparable magnitude.

magnetization since the latter is subsequently destroyed by disarrangement as cultivation of the ground proceeds. Le Borgne has shown that burning can produce a rapid enhancement of susceptibility and to a higher degree than can be achieved with the first mechanism.

The susceptibility of artificially produced magnetite (dispersed in kaolin) and maghaemite (dispersed in sand) is of the order of 0·001 e.m.u. per gram for concentrations of 1%.[7] However, the susceptibilities found in natural soil samples will differ widely for the same concentrations due to variations in the grain size of the magnetic particles. On most archaeological sites visited by the author the susceptibility of the top-soil has been between 0·00005 and 0·0002 e.m.u. per gram. Sites with top-soils below and above these limits are described as 'weak' and 'strong' respectively.

In general the susceptibilities of samples taken from the filling of an archaeological feature are greater than that of the top-soil. This is presumably due either to the higher humus concentration in the pit (particularly in the case of a rubbish pit, latrine and food-storage pit that has gone foul) or to the greater degree of burning that the filling has suffered as a result of its close association with occupation.

The creation of an anomaly depends not only on the actual value of the susceptibility but also on the magnetic *contrast* between the feature and the material that surrounds it. Fig. 130 gives the susceptibility of specific magnetization, as appropriate, for some common materials. The question of contrast is important in respect of

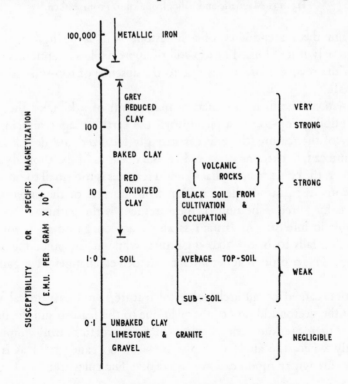

Fig. 130 Magnetism of some archaeological materials.

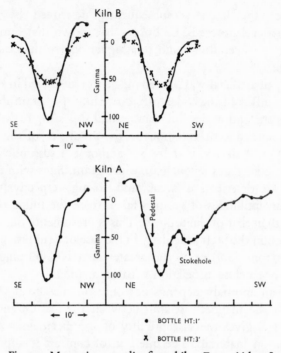

Fig. 131 Magnetic anomalies from kilns. From Aitken.[3]

walls. Although the susceptibility of a limestone wall is negligible, it can create a detectable anomaly if it is buried in top-soil of appreciable susceptibility: however the anomaly is in the reverse sense and is due to the absence of top-soil rather than to the presence of wall.

Anomaly detection. The thermo-remanent magnetism of a kiln, or the greater depth of high-susceptibility top-soil in a pit, distorts the earth's magnetic field from normal in the vicinity of the feature (the effect is strongly localized and doubling the distance from the feature can, in extreme cases, reduce the strength of the anomaly by a factor of eight). However, the effect from archaeological features is too small to cause a detectable error in the compass; instead, the deviation from normal of the *magnetic intensity* (or *field strength*) is measured. The unit of measurement is the gamma,* and the normal value of magnetic intensity in Britain is about 47,000 gamma. In some equatorial regions the value falls to below 30,000 gamma, while at the poles the value reaches 70,000 gamma. The proton magnetometer can detect changes of 1 gamma without difficulty.

The distortion caused by an archaeological feature is not easy to calculate because it results from the vector addition of the field due to the feature and the normal earth's field. However there are four general rules which are worth bearing in mind. These are applicable only where the angle of dip is between 60° and 70°N as is the case for N.W. Europe. Elsewhere modification is needed.[13] The rules are:

* 100,000 gamma = 1 oersted (CGS e.m.u.) = 79·6 ampere turn-metre^{-1} (MKS).

(a) The maximum of the anomaly lies to the *south* of the feature. The displacement is not greater than one-third of the depth of the centre of the feature.

(b) The separation between the two points, in a straight-line traverse, at which the anomaly has half its maximum value, is not less than the depth of the feature.

(c) A *reverse* anomaly may occur to the *north* of the feature at a distance equal to the depth. The reverse anomaly does not exceed 10 per cent of the maximum anomaly strength, except where the cause is modern iron.

(d) The anomaly is very small (less than 2%) at distances greater than three times the depth of the feature.

Actual traverses above two Romano-British kilns are shown in Fig. 131. The anomaly is shown as a dip rather than a peak as this corresponds to the sense of the proton magnetometer indication (*infra*); the anomaly does in fact represent an *increase* above the normal magnetic intensity.

The above rules apply primarily to isolated features such as kilns and pits. For linear features such as ditches, the anomaly depends upon the orientation. The anomaly for a ditch running north–south is nearly twice as great as that for an identical ditch running east–west. For an east–west ditch the reverse anomaly (lying to the north) may amount to 60% of the anomaly maximum, and should not be mistaken for a wall or rampart.

The sensitivity of magnetic surveying to iron is inconveniently high, and although, by detailed measurements, it is possible to distinguish between anomalies from iron lying in the surface and those due to genuine features, such measurements impede progress. Surface iron is most readily identified by measuring the width of the anomaly (rule (b)); if this width is not much greater than the height of the detector above the ground then clearly the cause lies close to the surface. Widespread iron (such as chicken netting) produces an irregular anomaly and is easy to recognize. The magnetic gradients produced by iron are often too strong for the proton magnetometer to operate satisfactorily and a 'killed signal' is another sympton of iron.

INSTRUMENTS

The proton magnetometer. The detector consists of a half-pint bottle of water or alcohol around which a 1,000-turn electrical coil is wound. The magnetic intensity is deduced from the behaviour of the protons which form the nuclei of hydrogen atoms in the water or alcohol. An essential preliminary to measurement is the three-second *polarizing period*. During this, a current of an amp is passed through the coil thereby producing a magnetic field of several hundred oersteds along the axis. This aligns a majority of the protons in that direction. When the polarizing current is cut off the protons try to align themselves along the lines of force of the earth's field. However, because they can be regarded as miniature gyroscopes, they perform gyrations about that direction instead. The frequency of gyration is exactly proportional to the magnetic intensity of the earth's field.

The proton gyrations are detectable because when gyrating in phase they produce an alternating voltage of about a microvolt in the coil around the bottle. This is fed, via a flexible cable which can be several hundred feet long, to the low-noise, highly-selective amplifier in the instrument itself. The use of special transistor techniques enables the frequency to be measured to an accuracy of 1 part in 50,000 within half a second; this corresponds to a sensitivity of 1 gamma. Greater sensitivity, say, down to 0·2 gamma, can be obtained without difficulty, though for archaeological application this is rarely required. The polarizing period is timed automatically within the instrument. At its conclusion frequency measurement takes place; the answer shown on the indicating meters is proportional to the reciprocal of the magnetic intensity. The greater the magnetic intensity, the lower the number indicated.

The polarization period is necessary before each measurement because internal magnetic inhomogeneities within the liquid cause the proton signal to die away after three or four seconds. This normal duration of signal may be reduced by an external magnetic gradient such as exists close to a piece of iron. Observation of the duration of the proton signal can be a useful check of whether an anomaly is due to iron. In some cases the signal decays too quickly for the frequency measurement to be performed—hence the term 'killed signal'.

Detailed circuits for the proton magnetometer have been described by Waters and Francis[11] and Scollar.[4] An instrument suitable for archaeological work is manufactured by the Littlemore Scientific Engineering Co., Oxford. Field instruments are also manufactured by Barringer Research Ltd., Toronto, and by Wardle and Davenport, Leek, Staffordshire, England. A much more sensitive form of nuclear magnetometer—the alkali vapour magnetometer manufactured by Varian Associates, California—has recently been tried[12] out on the plain of Sybaris, South Italy, by the applied Science Center, University of Pennsylvania Museum, Philadelphia.

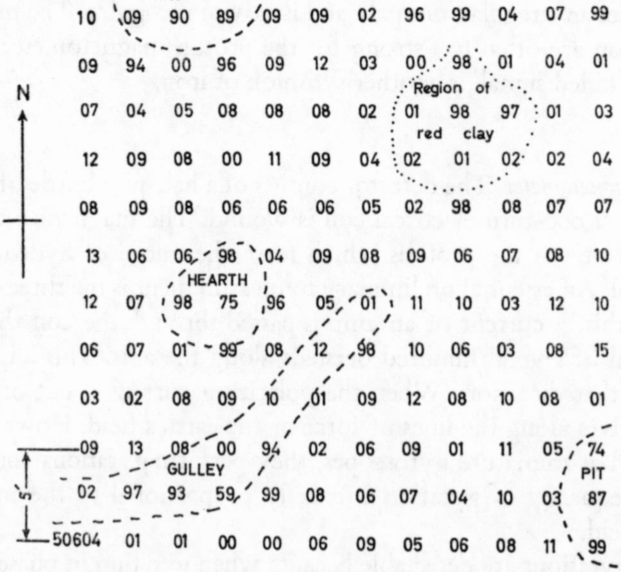

Fig. 132 Proton magnetometer readings.

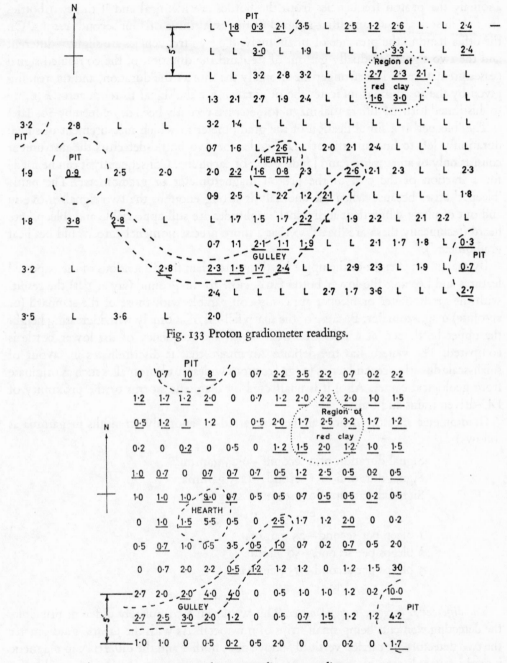

Fig. 133 Proton gradiometer readings.

Fig. 134 Fluxgate gradiometer readings.

The proton gradiometer. This instrument uses the same basic nuclear phenomenon of proton free-precession. Two bottles are used in this case, carried at either end of a vertically-held staff which is five feet or more long. In the absence of a magnetic anomaly the proton frequencies from the bottles are identical and if the two bottles are fed, in series, to an amplifier a signal of the usual three or four seconds results. On the other hand in the presence of an anomaly, the two frequencies are slightly different and the two signals gradually get out of step and the duration of the combined signal ceases prematurely. The stronger the anomaly the shorter the duration, and the reading given by the instrument indicates the time taken for the signal to reach zero. A more sophisticated form of differential magnetometer has recently been developed by Scollar.[4]

The 'bleeper' is a simplification of the gradiometer in which measurement of signal duration is left to human estimation.[3] Besides the two bottle-detectors the instrument consists only of an amplifier and loudspeaker or earphone. Consequently it can be made for a fraction of the cost of the proton magnetometer or gradiometer. The name 'bleeper' arises because when the anomaly is strong enough, the two signals move in and out of phase while their individual amplitudes are still appreciable and 'bleeps' are heard (technically these are 'beats' so that a more precise nomenclature would be 'beat gradiometer').

By making the height of the upper bottle greater than the dimensions of the expected features and keeping the lower bottle fairly close to the ground (say at 1 ft) the results with the gradiometer or bleeper are easily comparable with those of the standard (or absolute) magnetometer. Because of the sharp fall-off of anomaly with increasing height the upper bottle acts as a reference with which the frequency of the lower bottle is compared. The system has the definite advantage that it discriminates in favour of small-scale disturbances and tends to ignore more widespread anomalies such as originate from geological causes. Also, it is unaffected by magnetic storms or the proximity of DC-driven trains and trams.

Gradiometer measurements can be converted to anomaly strengths in gamma as follows:

> Signal duration of 2 seconds—6·25 gamma
> Signal duration of 1 second—12·5 gamma
> Signal duration of 0·5 second—25 gamma
>   etc., etc.
>
> 1 bleep per second—25 gamma
> 2 bleeps per second—50 gamma
> 3 bleeps per second—75 gamma
>   etc. etc.

The differential fluxgate magnetometer. This works on a completely different principle, the detecting elements being small strips of mu-metal. As with the proton gradiometer the two detectors are carried vertically above one another and the difference in magnetic intensities is indicated on a meter. An instrument of this type developed suitable for archaeological use has been described by Alldred[6] and some comparative trials of this and the two preceding instruments are shown in Figs. 132–34.

The fluxgate has two immediate advantages over the proton-type instruments. Firstly the reading is continuous. Secondly the fluxgate magnetometer, because of the small size of its detecting elements, can be used in strong magnetic gradients which preclude use of the proton magnetometer. Like the proton gradiometer it ignores widespread anomalies, magnetic storms and DC trains and trams.

Against these advantages must be balanced a greater complication in initial setting-up and in operation, and the fact that it has not yet been developed in a lightweight form suitable for archaeological use.

SURVEY LOGISTICS

Magnetic surveying is only a means to an end and to be worthwhile, the time and effort expended must be negligible compared to that required to trial-trench the same area. Consequently competent organization is vital. It is also important that the survey is carried out scientifically; measurements made solely to test out a preconceived archaeological idea can all too easily produce false support for that idea.

The standard procedure employed by the author is as follows. The area is first marked out with stout pegs (which must of course be free from nails!) so as to form a grid of 50 ft squares. Each square is covered in turn by a net stretched between the four corner pegs; the mesh size of the net is 10 ft and the middle of each 10 ft length is marked with a coloured tag. These enable the bottle to be moved over the square on a 5 ft mesh; this involves 100 measurements per square, approximately 1,800 per acre. In order to avoid shrinkage in wet weather it is essential that the string used for constructing the net is plastic-covered.*

Each square takes approximately 10 minutes to complete. Any abnormal readings are then investigated by more closely spaced measurements, firstly in order to determine the maximum strength of the anomaly, secondly to find its spatial extent, and thirdly to pin-point its centre on the ground.

A significant proportion of sites present serious handicaps to surveying. Trees, undergrowth, long grass, clover, nettles and thistles, etc. may impede movement of the cable and net so seriously as to rule out a survey. The proximity of AC electrical power cables and of radio transmitting stations is liable to cause interference with operation of the instrument. Iron litter on the surface, water pipes and gas mains, wire fences (to within 30 ft) produce their own disturbances which may mask, or simulate, archaeological features. Differentiation can be made with careful detailed measurements but this impedes progress. Another, more fundamental, difficulty occurs with sites on igneous geological formations. As mentioned earlier, igneous rocks have acquired an appreciable thermo-remanent magnetism as they cooled from the molten state. From recent basalts (of the Tertiary) the magnetic disturbance is far too strong to permit detection of archaeological features. In older basalts (100 million years or greater), and in granites, the effect is much weaker and archaeological surveying is possible.

The presence of DC power lines (such as are associated with DC trains and trams) creates difficulty only with the proton magnetometer. With the gradiometer and with the fluxgate the magnetic field associated with DC current affects both detectors equally

* Obtainable from James Lever, Box 6, Everlastic Rope Works, Bolton, Lancs.

and so cancels out. The same is true of transient variations of the magnetic intensity due to ionization currents in the upper atmosphere. On 'magnetic storm days' changes of upwards of 10 gamma may occur within 10 minutes even though the detector is kept at the same point. To survey with the proton magnetometer under such conditions it is necessary to have a second reference detector-bottle at a fixed position on the site and make check measurements with it at frequent intervals. In such circumstances a differential magnetometer of the type described by Scollar[4] is highly advantageous and the reader is referred to that source for a fuller discussion of surveying procedures.

RESULTS

Several hundred archaeological sites have now been surveyed with the proton magnetometer, Most of these have been highly successful though it must be emphasized that the degree of success is highly dependent on the suitability of the site for this technique. The magnetic effects from various types of feature are summarized in the following sections. Unless stated to the contrary anomaly strengths refer to measurements with the detector-bottle 1 ft above ground level.

Kilns. No difficulty has ever been experienced in finding kilns. Pottery kilns have been detected magnetically and confirmed by excavation, on the following sites: Brill, Downpatrick, Hartshill, Rossington Bridge, Savernake, Wappenbury, Water Newton. Of these the most outstanding was Hartshill where two dozen Romano-British kilns were located in advance of quarrying operations.

The anomaly strength from a kiln is usually 100 gamma or more, depending on the depth. In the sites covered, the depth of the old ground surface below the present-day surface has not been greater than 4 ft. At Hartshill the kilns were so close to the surface that the magnetic gradients were strong enough to give a 'killed signal'. This suggested surface iron but as soon as the turf was removed in order to confirm this on the first anomaly, the distinctive red upper rim of a pottery kiln was evident. On the other hand at Water Newton, where the old ground surface was about 2 ft down, the anomalies from kilns were not decisively different from that from a highly humus-laden pit (cf. Figs. 131 and 135).

Hearths. There is much less baked clay in a hearth so that the anomaly is smaller and hearths can escape detection. At High Rocks hill-fort an anomaly strength of 40 gamma was obtained from a hearth about eighteen inches below the surface whereas at Gwithian a hearth 1 ft down produced only 20 gamma. At Rainsborough hill-fort a hearth 9 in down produced an anomaly of 35 gamma (see Fig. 132).

Pits. Magnetic surveying was originated as a method of finding kilns, but it is also efficacious in locating pits and there is no known case of a pit going undetected. The strength of the anomaly is variable, depending on the susceptibility of the filling. This in turn depends on the degree of burning and humifaction—the 'dirtiness' of the filling —as well as on the basic iron content of the soil. Of the sites visited six stand out as examples of the immense value that magnetic surveying has in exploring the visually blank interiors of forts and camps: Barley, Burrough, Danes Camp, Madmarston, Rainsborough, Waddon Hill. Except for the first and last, these sites are on limestone

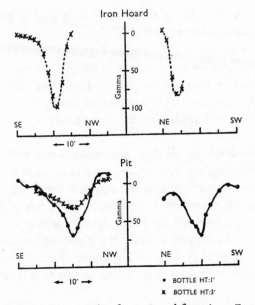

Fig. 135 Magnetic anomalies from pit and from iron. From Aitken.[3]

and conditions are evidently suitable for formation of high-susceptibility top-soil apart from any added enhancement due to archaeological occupation. Soil susceptibilities in the range 0·0001 to 0·001 e.m.u. per gram were encountered, and pit anomalies as high as 100 gamma. At Barley, on chalk, the average soil susceptibility was lower and consequently the anomalies were smaller—not greater than 30 gamma from a pit 5 ft across, 3 ft deep beneath eighteen inches of overlay. A difficulty with sites on chalk is the presence of irregularities in the surface of the chalk, which because of the consequent greater depth of top-soil give rise to anomalies. Such anomalies can usually be distinguished from genuine pit anomalies because of the better-defined shape of the latter, found when investigated with a detailed traverse.

Ditches. In general ditch-fillings are more sterile than pit-fillings. In some cases the filling is entirely rampart fall-in with little silting of top-soil. The anomaly may then be too small for detection. A compensating factor with ditches is their geometrical form. Anomalies, which considered in isolation would be indistinguishable from random fluctuations due for example to natural variations in the condition and depth of the top-soil, may acquire significance when seen in plan form. This is similar to recognition or geometrical features in aerial photography.

The classic example of magnetic ditch location is at Verulamium,[1,2] where an inner fosse, sectioned near to Bluehouse Hill, was followed for over half a mile. Closely-spaced traverses were necessary (traverses 10 ft apart, readings 2 ft apart along each traverse) in order to keep track of the ditch when it passed through other magnetic features. The anomaly varied between 5 and 20 gamma, presumably depending on the condition of the fill. The magnetic indications were confirmed by sectioning near either end; the ditch was about 15 ft across and deep. The ditch was followed along three sides of an approximate rectangle; one of the corners happened to lie exactly between the wickets of the corporation cricket-pitch—clearly out-of-bounds to digging!

Comparative surveys using different instruments. Figs. 132, 133 and 134 show the readings obtained over the same area by using a proton magnetometer, a proton gradiometer, and a fluxgate gradiometer respectively. Subsequently the area was stripped and the archaeological features examined. This was carried out in the course of the excavation of the Iron-Age hill-fort at Rainsborough by the Oxford University Archaeological Society in 1961.

The area covered in detail by all three instruments was 25 ft by 25 ft. Part of the standard-spaced survey using 100 readings per square of 50 ft by 50 ft is also shown in Fig. 133. For the proton magnetometer the detector-bottle was at 1 ft above ground level, for the proton gradiometer the lower bottle was at 1 ft and the upper bottle at 7 ft, and for the fluxgate gradiometer the lower detector was at 1 ft and the upper at 3 ft. In all cases the reading as obtained directly from the instrument is recorded. For the proton magnetometer (Fig. 132) only the digits from the two most sensitive meters are recorded; a change from 00 to 99 is only a change of 1 unit, that is an *intensification* of the magnetic intensity by 1 gamma.

For the proton gradiometer (Fig. 133) the readings represent the time (in seconds) for the proton signal to reach zero (see sub-section on the proton gradiometer). Where this exceeds 3·5 seconds, 'L' is recorded. Readings indicative of an anomaly of normal polarity (i.e. an increase in intensity) are underlined. Clearly a more immediate picture of the anomalies is obtained with the gradiometer and this compensates for its more tedious operation. This is also the case for the fluxgate gradiometer (Fig. 134), where the readings indicate the vertical magnetic gradient in gamma per foot, underlining having the same significance as before.

REFERENCES

1 AITKEN, M. J. 1960. The magnetic survey; Appendix to FRERE, S. S. *Excavations at Verulamium 1959, 5th Interim Report Antiq. 40,* 21–24
2 —— 1961a. The magnetic survey. Appendix to FRERE, S. S. *Excavations at Verulamium 1959, 6th Interim Report 41,* in press
3 —— 1961b. *Physics and Archaeology,* London and New York
4 SCOLLAR, I. 1965. *Archaeo-Physika (Beihefte der Bonner Jahrbücher) 15,* 21–92
5 FOLGHERAITER, G. 1899. *Arch. Sci. phys. nat. 8,* 5–16
6 ALLDRED, J. C. 1964. *Archaeometry 7,* 14–19
7 LE BORGNE, E. 1965. *Archaeo-Physika (Beihefte der Bonner Jahrbücher) 15,* 1–20
8 NÉEL, L. 1955. *Advances in Physics 4,* 191–243
9 PACKARD, M. and VARIAN, R. 1954. *Phys. Rev. 93,* 941
10 THELLIER, E. and THELLIER, O. 1959. *Ann. Géophys. 15,* 285–376
11 WATERS, G. S. and FRANCIS, P. D. 1958. *J. sci. Instrum. 35,* 88–93
12 BREINER, S. 1965. *Science 150,* 185–93
13 TITE, M. S. 1966. *Archaeometry 9,* 24–31

ANTHONY CLARK

THE DETECTION of buried archaeological remains by measurement of the electrical resistivity of the soil is a well-established technique that has been in use for fifteen years. Instrument design and the theory of resistivity measurement have recently been concisely summarized by Aitken,[1] but the last general description of field technique in English appeared in 1953,[2] since when experience has been gained in this subtle aspect of the subject, and some novel ideas have been advanced in scattered papers; also instruments are now more freely available to the amateur. The bias of this review will therefore be towards problems of survey and interpretation.

Soil resistivity measurement has been used as a geological and civil engineering aid since the second decade of this century, but it occurred to no one to apply it in archaeology until 1946, when Atkinson first used the method in his excavation of a group of Neolithic henge monuments at Dorchester, Oxfordshire. The technique was tried because of the need to locate as quickly as possible filled-in ditches and pits visible only as crop marks from the air, and not closely related to reference points on the ground. The success of the method was remarkable, and led to its enthusiastic application on other sites, but results were sometimes disappointing and development was slow for the next ten years.

Clearly Atkinson's first surveys had chanced to be made in almost ideal conditions, and refinements of interpretation and technique would be necessary before some other types of site could be tackled. Also the first instruments tried for archaeology were naturally those already available for commercial earth testing and geophysics. These are generally designed for work on a larger scale and are commensurately substantial and expensive, and not adapted for the archaeological requirement of rapid traversing along a straight line. Resistivity survey therefore tended to remain in the hands of a few specialists.

In 1956 the writer had the opportunity to use a simple two-terminal transistorized resistance meter designed by the Distillers Company Instrumentation Laboratory. This was tried prior to the first excavation of the Romano-British township of Mildenhall-Cunetio, Wiltshire, and readily detected the foundation of the town wall.[3] The extreme compactness, relative cheapness and low current consumption of a transistorized circuit seemed eminently desirable archaeologically, and such an instrument, using the conventional four-terminal system, was designed by John Martin and the writer. The successive excavations at Cunetio served as testing ground and control, and the instrument became commercially available in 1960.

The advent of magnetic detection in 1958 provided the archaeological armoury with a powerful new weapon. Whereas resistivity surveys are most conveniently made in straight lines, an area can be quickly examined with a magnetometer, which is also unaffected by the dampness of the soil. Magnetic measurement is superior in its ability to locate isolated, and often small, objects with magnetic fields, such as refuse pits, iron objects and baked-clay structures such as kilns. Resistivity, however, is particularly at home with linear features such as ditches and is more reliable for the detection of buildings and stone structures generally; and the apparatus is usually much cheaper at present. Resistivity can also be used in towns and close to power lines, where stray fields interfere with magnetic measurement. Clearly magnetic and resistance detection will remain supplementary to each other, although it should be remembered that most things that can be detected with a magnetometer can also be detected with a resistivity meter, if sometimes more tediously.

What of the future of resistivity measurement technique? Since the first edition of this book appeared, the trend has been to replace separate probes by integrated systems needing little or no ground penetration. In the most advanced, instrument, probes and a semi-automatic recorder form one compact unit (see p. 706).

PRINCIPLES OF SOIL RESISTIVITY MEASUREMENT

The ability of a mass of soil or rock to conduct electricity is due to water in the interstices which contains salts dissolved from the material and humic acids of biological origin. If an electrical potential (voltage) is applied between two electrodes connected to different points on the mass, the solution will separate into positive and negative ions by the process of electrolysis, and these will flow respectively to the negative and positive electrodes thereby setting up an electric current. The ratio of the applied voltage to the magnitude of the current is known as the resistance between the electrodes, and varies with the compactness and dampness of the mass and on the solubility and quantity of the salts and acid.

A crude soil resistivity meter can be made by inserting two metal probes a few inches into the ground, say a foot or more apart, connecting a battery across them, and measuring the ratio of the voltage to the current that flows between the probes. Not being constrained as in a wire, the current does not pass straight from probe to probe, but spreads out into many curving paths through the earth, some of it going considerably deeper than the horizontal separation of the probes. Herein lies the great power of resistivity measurement: the deep current penetration obtainable with only a short length of probe insertion. However, the readings of such a simple instrument are adversely affected by (i) probe polarization, the accumulation of oppositely charged ions close to each electrode, causing a continuous rise in resistance reading; (ii) probe contact resistance, which is usually much greater than the resistance value for the bulk of the soil between the probes and can vary considerably from one insertion to another; and (iii) natural earth currents and voltages of chemical origin where the probes make contact with the ground. Replacement of the battery by an alternating current power source obviates all these troubles except (ii), but this is overcome by using a four-probe system[5] as shown in Fig. 136. In this an AC current flows between the two outer probes, and the resultant voltage difference between the two inner detector probes is measured by a system which draws no current from them. The instrument is arranged to divide

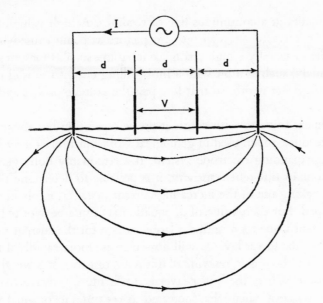

Fig. 136 The Wenner four-probe arrangement, showing
spread of current paths through homogeneous soil.

the voltage, V, by the current, I. This gives a resistance value, R, which, by the
formula

$$\rho = 2\pi dR \quad \ldots \ldots \ldots \ldots \ldots \ldots \quad (1)$$

where d is the spacing between the probes, gives an average specific resistivity, ρ, which
is assumed to apply at the centre point of the electrode system to a depth of about $1 \cdot 5d$,
providing the soil is fairly homogeneous. ρ is in ohm-centimetres, ohm-feet, etc.,
depending on the unit used to measure d. In most archaeological work, d is kept constant and the whole of the multiplying factor $2\pi d$ becomes a constant and ρ is proportional to R, so that there is no need to work out this expression for comparative readings
taken with equal spacing along a line. The presence of media more or less resistive than
the normal soil causes distortion of the regular current pattern shown in Fig. 137, and

R high   R low

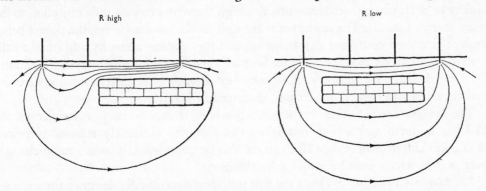

Fig. 137 Approximate indication of the distortion of current paths as the probe assembly passes over a
high resistance feature, showing how a low reading can be obtained over the centre of the feature.

consequent anomalies in a continuous line of readings. A high value of R is due to a high value of V relative to I which one can picture as being caused by current lines crowded near the surface by a high resistance intrusion such as masonry; conversely, a conductive anomaly, such as a pit with a moist filling cut into subsoil rock, draws the current lines to a greater depth, so that few pass the voltage probes and a low reading is registered.

The normal linear traverse with constant probe separation has already been alluded to. Another procedure, much used in geological work but more rarely in archaeology, is known as the expanding electrode system. If a reasonably homogeneous top layer is underlain by one of different resistivity, it is possible to determine the depth of the lower layer by making use of the increasing current penetration obtained as the probe spacing is increased. For each value of d, equation (1) must be worked out. This will give a fairly constant value for ρ until d is large enough for the current pattern to reach and be distorted by the lower layer. ρ will now increase more rapidly if the lower layer is more resistive than the upper, or will fall if it is less resistive. It is worthwhile to plot a graph of ρ against d. Where the lower layer is much more resistive than the upper, d approximates to its depth when ρ has increased to $1 \cdot 5$ times its original value.

INSTRUMENTS

The Megger Earth Tester.[5] This instrument was used by Atkinson for the first archaeological resistivity trials in 1946. It has the advantage over others that the reading is obtained by direct observation of a dial, although the operator must generate the working voltage by turning a handle. The Megger is a substantial wooden instrument mounted on a tripod. One disadvantage is that its accuracy is more readily affected by dry conditions than is the case with null balance instruments such as those described below. Atkinson devised for the Megger a switching system which operates in conjunction with five probes to enable consecutive four-probe readings to be taken along a line with the minimum of probe movement and time loss.[6]

The Tellohm.[7] This instrument is available in two forms, one designed for general use, the other a larger and more sensitive version for geophysical work. The latter seems usually to be chosen by archaeologists, although the writer can see little objection to the more compact model. The instruments are well finished and accurate, the power being derived from self-contained dry batteries, and the reading taken by adjusting a calibrated dial to give a zero (or null) reading on a meter. Using a Geophysical Tellohm, the United Kingdom Ministry of Works Test Branch have developed a system for making rapid area surveys which will be described below.

The Gossen Geohm.[8] This instrument, much used in Germany, is similar to the Tellohm in form and action, but more compact and extremely reasonably priced in Europe. Unfortunately, like all the meters so far considered, it lacks a rapid changeover switch, which must be supplied by the user.

The Martin-Clark Meter.[9] This is the first instrument specifically designed for archaeological work. Unlike the other instruments, which use rotary choppers or vibrating systems, the AC voltage is derived from a transistor oscillator which applies only a small voltage to the earth, but this is compensated for by the use of a very sensitive amplifier so that only light leads need be used and the battery is very long-lasting. The instrument is of the null-balance type. The compactness of the M-C meter enables the operator to hold it in one hand: he can thus follow the probes as they are moved so that the leads need only be of minimal length. Perhaps the most useful feature of the instrument is the changeover switch invented by Martin. This consists of four fixed spring contacts within the instrument and a rotating turret with five contacts and leads outside. At any setting of the switch, the four lower leads (1, 2, 3 and 4 in Fig. 138) are in use in the order in which they are seen from above, the top being spare. When the

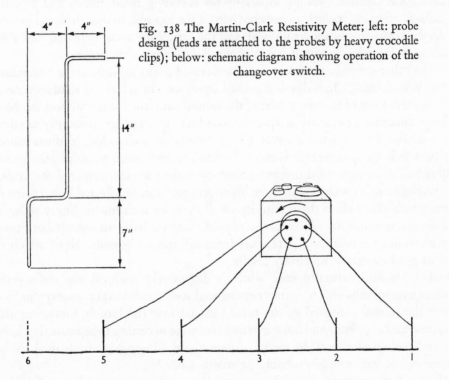

Fig. 138 The Martin-Clark Resistivity Meter; left: probe design (leads are attached to the probes by heavy crocodile clips); below: schematic diagram showing operation of the changeover switch.

turret is rotated one-fifth of a turn in the direction of movement, the former spare lead (5) becomes the leading one of the next group of four and, while the second reading is being taken, the new spare lead (1) is moved by the probe handler to position (6) ready for the third reading. Thus both instrument operator and probe handler work simultaneously without time-wasting intervals. This method of working is exactly the same as that devised by Atkinson, but the switch is much simpler than his and, being rotated in the direction of movement, counteracts the twisting of the leads that is inherent in this method of moving the probes. Probes and leads are colour coded and, as the instrument operator works close to the probes, no instructions have to be exchanged with the probe handler.[10]

The probes, of $\frac{3}{8}$ in mild steel, are also designed for compactness combined with easy removal and easy and accurate insertion, and the design, suitably insulated, is recommended for use with any instrument (Fig. 138). The upper crank is used as a handle, and for insertion the foot is placed on the lower crank which also acts as a depth stop.

SUITABILITY OF CONDITIONS

As already stated, the ability of a soil mass to conduct electricity depends on the presence of salts and acids in water solution. The best agricultural land is usually a rich loam upon a well-drained subsoil, such as Chalk or gravel, and such conditions can be expected to give good resistivity results, especially for revealing filled ditches and pits. In clay, the subsoil often differs little in resistivity from the top soil, so that the latter are difficult to detect, but masonry shows up well, and the writer has accurately detected a Roman building at a depth of about 2 ft in a clay soil awash with rainwater.

At the other extreme are sandy soils. In elevated positions such as the Greensand hills of the Weald, these often develop podsol conditions in which all soluble material has been dissolved out of the upper part of the subsoil, and top soil is scant indeed. Not only is the ground then practically incapable of conducting electricity, especially in a drought, but a similar fate sometimes overtakes the silting of archaeological disturbances and prevents their being detected. Such land often becomes more tractable after prolonged cultivation. Although most modern resistivity meters are compensated for probe contact resistance to a remarkable degree, their accuracy can be affected in very dry conditions, which also reduce the sensitivity of all types of instrument. Stony soils, besides making the insertion of probes physically difficult, are liable to exhibit both poor and variable contact conditions, quite apart from soil inhomogeneity, all of which factors tend to produce erratic resistivity results.

Difficulties also naturally arise where a deceptively uniform top soil overlies an inhomogeneous subsoil. The writer experienced such conditions on a survey in Norfolk, where the subsoil consisted of the mixed glacial material loosely known as Boulder Clay, and extra readings and interpretative care were necessary to separate the geological and archaeological effects. In such a situation, the filtering methods used by Scollar (see below, p. 707) would probably be worth while.[11]

The resistivity surveyor must also pay attention to the surface condition of the ground. Soil fairly freshly ploughed is usually well aerated and loose in texture. This tends to give high and erratic probe contact resistance because such well-ventilated soils tend to be dry, and included air pockets, being of infinite resistance, have the same effect as stones. It is therefore important to try to push the probes well down to furrow level, or to compact the soil around them with the foot. In a grass field on a Chalk subsoil, the writer found that a little-used track smoothed by wheeled vehicles and by people walking gave resistivity values on an average only two-thirds as great as the field generally. This can be accounted for by the small surface area of the compressed soil, resulting in a low water evaporation rate, and by moisture absorbed and transpired by the more luxuriant growth of grass in the rest of the field. Scollar found that a field of beet gave lower values than a rye field because of the protection against evaporation afforded by the broad leaves of the beet. Fertilizers probably also have an effect. To sum up: an absolute change of top-soil resistivity can be expected from one field to another, or from one part to another of a single field. This may be due to a change of soil depth, or of surface condition, or crops growing or recently harvested, but such effects should not inhibit the indication of buried remains.

A little rain before a survey is often useful in improving contact conditions, and the short circuiting effect of even heavy rain is often less than might be expected, as the instance cited above of the survey on clay demonstrated; and the onset of heavy rain halfway through a survey has also had no immediate effect. This is probably because freshly fallen rain first passes through the uppermost layer of the soil from which most electrolytes have already been dissolved, and the process of solution must also take some time, so that the water is at first hardly more conductive than distilled water; the first rain after a drought probably has more effect. Even prolonged rain for several days has not affected the ease with which the foundation of the Roman wall of Cunetio (soil: loam on Clay-with-flints on Chalk) can be detected, although the magnitude of the indication is not as great as in drier weather; on the other hand, similar conditions have almost completely masked the much more subtle indications of small Neolithic ditches in the light loam on Chalk soil of Salisbury Plain. The converse conditions of general drying out of the soil will also suppress any resistivity contrast. Scollar has observed that the indications of a Roman town wall, which normally have the expected high values with respect to the surrounding soil, can become completely reversed to give lower values after much rain, presumably because water collects on top of the relatively impermeable masonry.[12]

Generally masonry and brick will give relatively high, and silted ditches and pits low, resistivity readings, but there are exceptions. For instance, apart from the rather abnormal case above, a wall may be represented by a robber trench filled with low resistivity material, and a ditch may be wholly or partly filled with loose stones, especially when the filling has been deliberate.

CHOICE OF PROBE SEPARATION

This is a problem which the resistivity surveyor must consider very carefully on each site if he is to obtain the maximum information. The accepted rough rule is that a measurement, using the equidistant Wenner probe spacing, will detect remains down to a depth about equal to the horizontal probe spacing, d. Thus, if the probes are too close together, deeper features may be missed; on the other hand wider spacing, although giving deeper penetration, reduces the precision of location and, as the current spreads through a larger volume of soil, may fail to detect the smaller features and tends to suppress the effect of large ones. There is, of course, no definite limit to the penetration, the current falling off gradually with increasing depth.

Some workers recommend preliminary tests by the expanding electrode procedure (see above) at points away from the remains and, if their position is known at all, over part of the remains themselves, so as to ascertain the spacing likely to give the greatest contrast between remains and soil, and any variations of subsoil depth over the area of the site. If one is searching for filled ditches or pits expected to show as interruptions in the subsoil, a spacing must be chosen which is greater than that at which the subsoil begins to affect the preliminary readings appreciably; on the other hand, masonry often rises well above subsoil level, perhaps to the lowest ploughing depth, and in such cases can be detected with a much narrower spacing which is also valuable for the definition of individual small walls.

In practice, however, the top soil is often too shallow for this procedure to have much value; and there is usually regrettably little time for such preliminary work, and the surveyor must choose his spacing more rapidly and arbitrarily. This is often quite easy. For instance, remains which have been discovered by aerial photography, or ground observation, of crop marks or soil marks, are rarely much below plough depth (say 1–2 ft), especially if the crop mark has given a well-defined picture; and conditions that give a good crop mark can usually be relied upon to produce good resistivity results. Other sites are found by chance or intent during excavation. If such indications are supplemented by some preliminary work with the humble but neglected auger, or even by simple probing, a suitable spacing can be reliably chosen. An auger of some type is a most valuable addition to the resistivity surveyor's equipment.[13]

To prevent a survey from being too time consuming, it may be necessary to make preliminary traverses with a greater probe spacing than the ideal, but once the broad position of remains has been defined, traverses with smaller spacing can be made at selected places. However little preliminary work is done, a spacing of 1 metre, or 3–4 ft, can almost always be relied upon to produce results on the average site. Such spacings give fairly precise horizontal location of remains, with a limit of detection in the region of 4–5 ft and sites with a greater overburden than this are rare.

SURVEY PROCEDURE

The simplest type of survey is the straight line traverse using the five-probe system described above. This is particularly useful when tracing a linear feature such as a wall or ditch. A plastic or metallized linen measuring tape (not a metal tape or chain because of their conductivity) is laid along the ground as nearly as possible at right angles to the feature, and to start the five probes are placed in line along it from the zero point. If a 100 ft tape is used, with a 4 ft probe spacing, this will mean that the first reading occurs at 6 ft along the tape, and the last at 94 ft. In order to allow for this, and to obtain a representative idea of the resistivity level of the undisturbed ground, the tape should be amply extended on either side of the buried feature: this will help greatly in deciding whether a resistance anomaly is due to the feature sought or to variable ground resistivity. The results should be written down and plotted as a graph with resistance as abscissa and distance as ordinate. If an area survey is contemplated, individual traverses of this type give a useful preliminary indication of whether remains are clearly enough defined. When a fairly wide spacing has to be used, intermediate readings can be obtained by repeating a traverse with the zero point advanced by a distance equal to half the probe spacing $(d/2)$. This halves the reading interval and gives a more complete resistivity picture. If even closer coverage is required, the whole probe assembly (without the fifth probe) can be moved a very short distance between readings, but there is rarely much advantage in this.

Although our two-dimensional diagrams do not show it, the current spreads sideways as well as downwards; therefore some effect can be expected from features not actually crossed by the line of survey, and care should be taken to keep traverses at least a distance of $1 \cdot 5d$ from any modern anomaly such as an excavation trench.

An area survey is a more elaborate approach with which the approximate plan of remains can be defined in good conditions. The readings are obtained by making a series of parallel simple traverses, usually separated by a distance equal to the probe spacing. This will give a square grid of resistance values which should be plotted to scale in plan form. Staggering alternate traverses by a distance equal to half the probe spacing (see Fig. 139e) gives a slightly more even coverage of the ground, but the extra trouble in laying out hardly seems justified. 'Contours' or 'isographs' of equal resistance are then sketched in sparingly and should give an approximate outline of the remains. The choice of contour interval can usually be made by inspection, those passing through regions of steeper resistance gradient being generally the most useful. Contours drawn where resistance changes are small tend to wander aimlessly about the plan and are distracting and best omitted. Theory indicates that the minimum significant contour interval is about half the standard deviation of the readings. This is tedious to calculate, and Atkinson suggests the use of an approximation obtained by taking ten random series of ten consecutive readings and subtracting the lowest reading from the highest in each group. Add these differences together and divide the sum by ten to give the mean range of readings. Divide this by six and round it off to the nearest convenient unit or fraction of a unit to give the smallest significant contour interval.

As a quicker alternative to contouring, readings can be shown as shaded marks in which the density of shading is related to the resistivity at the point. In a published plan Schwarz[14] places a small circle at each point: a clear circle indicates a resistivity range of 75–95 ohm-metres, a circle with one quadrant blackened, 96–120, two quadrants, 121–160, three quadrants, 161–220, and completely blackened, 221–300 ohm-metres. This method gives a useful broad indication of the anomalies present.

An interesting alternative method of area surveying is used by the United Kingdom Ministry of Works Test Branch. To quote Aitken's description: the system 'employs a dozen or so probes each connected to a terminal on a multi-bank switch on the instrument; this successively energizes consecutive sets of four probes down the line. When a probe has served its purpose on one traverse it is moved to the corresponding position on the parallel traverse adjacent.' A drawback is that there is a considerable mass of equipment and the system is not convenient for long linear surveys.

In the case of a building, such as a Roman villa, once a survey of either of the above types has located the broad position of remains, the potential excavator will probably require the indication of individual walls which may be ill defined if a fairly large probe spacing has been used for the original survey. If the building lies just below the tilth, a probe spacing of 1 ft should be suitable for this, and if it is required to locate the centre of the wall with great precision, the electrode assembly should be advanced as a whole by steps of 6 in or less, instead of in the usual way, so that the fifth probe becomes super-fluous. Note, however, that if such a high resistance anomaly, embedded in a generally less resistive medium, is smaller in width than about $6d$, the readings may not rise to a simple maximum at the centre of the wall, but will have two peaks symmetrically disposed about the centre, giving an 'M' pattern. This is probably because, as indicated in Fig. 137, some of the current passes beneath the feature when the current electrodes are close to its edges, so that the voltage drop measured by the inner probes is too small. If this effect does not occur, one may assume that the wall is set in a dry subsoil or flooring. An inversion of this phenomenon, a 'W' effect, occurs with narrow features of relatively low resistivity, but these are less frequently encountered. To avoid these effects, and to obtain the sharpest possible indication of a narrow feature, the 'broadside on' approach advocated by Palmer can be used.[13] In this, the group of four electrodes is set out at right angles to the line of travel, and remains parallel to the linear feature as it is moved across it.

With small probe spacings, accuracy is essential. Aitken has calculated that, to keep the total error in the measured resistance within 14%, 1 ft spacing must be accurate to within $\frac{1}{2}$ in. The permissible error increases proportionally to d. Deviations from the straight line and variations of a few inches in depth of insertion have negligible effect, but it is worth keeping the latter as constant as possible to avoid excessive variations in contact resistance.[16]

Examples of rapid survey methods. In tracing the exact positions of circular ditches revealed by air photography, Atkinson has used the following method: linear traverses are made across the approximate position of the feature, and when one of these produces a double ditch type anomaly, it is assumed to be a chord of the circle. Halfway between the anomalies, another traverse is laid out at right angles: this should be a diameter of the circle, which is confirmed if two anomalies at suitable spacing are again recorded. The halfway distance between the two new anomalies is assumed to be the centre of the circle, and a second diametrical traverse is laid out at 45° to the first to check this. At Cunetio (Fig. 139), Annable and the writer have traced the external bastions of the town wall as follows. The line of the wall was established with two long traverses (a and b) at right angles to its line. Using information derived from a trench cut else-where, the exact width of the wall was superimposed upon the graphs of these traverses, and the front face line of the wall thus established marked on the ground with pegs 8 ft away from these pegs, a new traverse (c) was laid out at right angles to the first two, in other words 8 ft outside the wall and parallel with it. Measurements along this immed-iately revealed the positions of two bastions, and a trench was laid out over half of the one giving the strongest indication after its distance of projection from the wall had been determined with a fourth traverse. The survey took two men about one hour including the plotting of the results, and the trench gave precisely the information required without any adjustment.[17]

ALTERNATIVE ELECTRODE ARRANGEMENTS

One of the difficulties in resistivity measurement in low resistance conditions such as

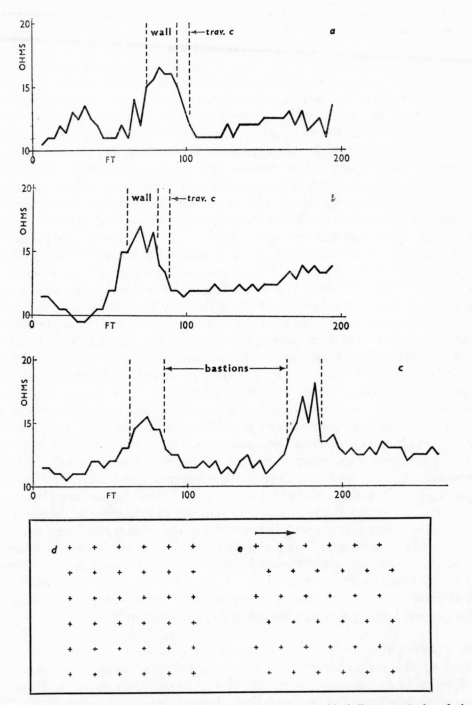

Fig. 139 a, b, c: The three traverses used to locate two wall bastions at Mildenhall (Cunetio); $d=4$ ft; d, e: two ways of arranging measuring points in an area survey; e, in which the arrow indicates the direction of traversing, gives a slightly more even ground coverage.

clay or boggy soil is that readings are often very low (in the region of 1 ohm) and the variations caused by buried remains proportionately small. Some instruments have poor discrimination in this region, and Palmer has proposed that the normal Wenner probe configuration be modified so that the inner voltage probes are closer to the current probes. This increases the voltage measured and gives higher values of R more suitable for the instrument and easier to read. Aitken considers that such a configuration increases errors due to the voltage probe penetration, and probe location certainly becomes more critical, although Palmer has solved this by linking the adjacent probes with insulators. An objection to this approach is that it reduces the power of the method to provide accurate positional information. Workers at the University of Birmingham favour the opposite approach of closing up the inner probe spacing (the Schlumberger configuration).[18] Although this gives lower readings, Rees considers that the results are superior in definition to the Wenner arrangement. With special switches, the rapid traversing method used with this can be adapted to the Schlumberger and Palmer configurations. However, Dunk, working on the shallow remains of a Roman villa with current probes 8 ft 6 in apart and detector probe separation of 6 in, mounted the electrodes on a hinged board, thus simplifying probe movement and eliminating the need for measurement of spacings.[19] More recently, the writer has obtained good results with a square array in the form of a table, opposite pairs of legs acting as current and detector probes. In the prototype, the legs are of the lightest Dexion slotted steel angle, the ends of which are squeezed flat and sharpened to form blade-shaped electrodes 2 ft 6 in apart. The top is a 1 ft 6 in square of 12 mm plywood on which are fixed a Martin-Clark meter and a clip-board for plotting. Struts of wood with aluminium brackets keep the system rigid and also form handles. The total weight is only 16 lb. This assembly can be rapidly operated by one person; the blade electrodes, easily inserted and giving a large contact area, and the extreme contact resistance independence of the latest instruments, ensure adequate contact in most conditions with the lightest pressure. Further improvements under development are a semi-automatic plotter which graphs the results as they are obtained and an adjustable table giving variable electrode spacing. The compact electrode geometry promises to give fewer anomalous results than do linear probe systems with little sacrifice of detection depth: theory shows that the 2 ft 6 in square system has a penetration equivalent to a Wenner array over 6 ft long. Other non-linear arrays are also being studied.[20] To prevent short-circuiting in wet conditions, it is important in all linked electrode systems to ensure that the insulated frameworks are well clear of the ground and treated with paint or silicones so that rain will form separate droplets rather than a continuous layer.

IMPROVEMENT OF RESULTS

However good the instrument, and however carefully the measurements are made, all soil resistivity measurements are subject to a greater or lesser degree to fluctuations superimposed upon the archaeological indications and complicating the picture. These variations may be due to variations in the dampness, nature or depth of the soil containing the remains. Even a modest inhomogeneity in the top soil can affect the passage of current past the voltage probes, and on this current depends the measured value of R.

Scollar has paid special attention to the problem of separating archaeological effects from those of subsoil variation. One of his methods is to literally filter archaeological variations from the broader soil variations by plotting the difference between each reading and an average of surrounding values, and is used to produce 'background free' plots of area surveys. This and other procedures are effective, but sometimes involve making assumptions about the size of the remains beneath the ground and need to be used with caution. Analytical procedures involve a lot of arithmetic, for which there is often little time or justification—in the end one must simply dig.

REFERENCES

1 AITKEN, M. J. 1961. *Physics and Archaeology*, London and New York, 60
2 ATKINSON, R. J. C. 1953. *Field Archaeology*, London, 2nd ed., 32, and in PYDDOKE, E. 1963. *The Scientist and Archaeology*, London
3 CLARK, A. *Illustrated London News*, 1 June 1957, 900
4 Known as the Wenner configuration. Originally derived by WENNER, F. 1916. *Bulletin of the U.S. Bureau of Standards 12*, 469
5 Evershed and Vignoles Ltd., Acton Lane Works, Chiswick, London, W.4.
6 A circuit for this is given by Atkinson in *The Scientist and Archaeology*
7 Nash and Thompson Ltd., Oakcroft Road, Chessington, Surrey.
8 P. Gossen and Co., Erlangen, Bayern, West Germany
9 Martin-Clark Instruments, 19 The Crossways, Onslow Village, Guildford, Surrey
10 An advantage of Atkinson's original switch is that it can be made up from standard wafer switch components
11 SCOLLAR, I. 1959. *Bonner Jahrbücher 159*, 284
12 From a study of the relation between rainfall and size of ditch anomalies on a sandstone site in England, it was concluded that best results can normally be expected between May and September: AL CHALABI, A. A. and REES, A. I. 1962. *Bonner Jahrbücher 162*, 266. French workers have found that there can be a considerable diurnal variation in readings caused by temperature changes: HESSE, A. 1962. *Archaeometry 5*, 123
13 A useful auger for quick results, consisting of a slotted steel probe, is made by And. Mattson, Mora, Sweden; available from J. H. Steward Ltd., 406 Strand, London, W.C. 2
14 SCHWARZ, G. T. 1958. *Jahrbüch der Schweizerischen Gesellschaft für Urgeschichte 47*, 59
15 PALMER, L. S. 1960. *Proc. Prehist. Soc. 26*, 64
16 Aitken examines the effect of such errors in some detail
17 ANNABLE, F. K. 1958. *Wiltshire Archaeological Magazine 207*, 233
18 REES, A. I. 1962. *Antiquity 36*, 131
19 DUNK, A. J. 1962. *Bonner Jahrbücher 162*, 272
20 The fundamental theoretical paper for these studies is UHLIR, A. 1955. *Bell System Technical Journal 34*, 103

Index of Sites

Algeria, 138, 143
Ali Kosh, 588, 590
Ambrona, 146–8
Amesbury, 550
Amri, 146
Ancaster, 29
Anneröd, 385
Arene Candide Cave, 410
Asselar, 463, 464
Athens (Agora), 598

Babylon, 213
Baluchistan, 139
Banahilk, 266
Barley, 692–3
Bat Cave, 220, 221
Belt Cave, 303, 367
Bickley Moor Barrow, 176
Bingöl, 590
Blossom, 69, 71
Bodega Bay, 69, 70
Borrebjerg, 385
Breedon-on-the-Hill, 29
Broken Hill, 465
Broomfield Barrow, 631

Caesar's Camp, Keston, 131
Cannington, 29
Cañon de Muerto, 220
Casas Grandes, 202
Cassington, 129
Çatal Hüyük, 426, 553, 588–9
Cave of Letters, 550
Cayönü, 303
Chaco Canyon, 138, 141, 197, 198, 203
Charozero, 389
Chew Stoke, 178
Chios, 306–7

Chorrera, 69, 71–2, 73
Clacton, 126, 183, 202
Circeo, 529
Cirencester, 365
Clarion Line, 126
Clough Castle, 387
Coal Valley, 97
Coldrum, 38
Combe-Capelle, 462–3
Cook's Study, 173–4
Copilco, 127
Cordova Cave, 222
Coygan Cave, 661
Crable Site, 426
Creswell, 42–3, 661
Cunetio, 695, 704–5
Cushendun, 384
Cyrenaica, 138, 145

Danger Cave, 222, 235
Dead Sea Rift, 136
Deir-el-Bahari, 498
Deshasheh, 497
Devil's Tower, Gibraltar, 366, 383
Dighton's Cliff Extension, 96
Doveholes, 43
Dover, 188

Ecuador, 65, 74
Egolzwil, 171, 202
Ehrenstein, 202, 203
Eifel, 97, 98
Elmenteita, 464
Emeryville, 360
Ensay, 29
Epirus, 143, 145
Ertebølle, 171, 384
Etruria, 139

Ffynon Beuno, 661
Fikirtepe, 266
Fiji, 389
Fish Hoek, 464
Flanders Farm, 632
Flesberg, 202
Florisbad, 36, 519
Fonaby, 629, 632
Fontéchevade, 116
Fountains Abbey, 387
Fromm's Landing, 392
Fyen, 385

Gafsa, 138, 146
Galley Hill, 37, 38–9, 506
Gamble's Cave, 463–4
Gebel Akhdar, 136
Ghirza, 630
Giali, 590
Gibraltar, 37
Glastonbury, 363
Glen Canyon, 224
Goddard, 69, 70
Gokstad, 364
Gordion, 178
Gotland, 364, 385, 473
Gough's Cave, 461
Goyet, 518
Graig Lwyd, 573
Grauballe, 208–9
Grimaldi Cave, 424, 463
Grotta Guattari, 529
Grotta Romanelli, 363
Grotte de Cavillon, 462
Grotte des Enfants, 462–3
Grotte du Trilobite, 43
Gwithian, 692

Hadhramaut, 143

Hallstatt, 649
Hartshill, 692
Haua Fteah, 410–11
Heltagito Rock Shelter, 221
Hemmor, 385
Hidden Cave, 244
Higgins Flat Pueblo, 221
High Rocks Hill Fort, 692
Hoëdic, 384
Hokkaido, 74
Hotchkiss, 69, 70
Huaca Prieta, 222, 236, 237
Humboldt Cave, 244, 367

Illington, 468

Jarmo, 265, 266, 303, 385, 588, 590
Jericho, 178, 179, 183, 265, 266, 303, 304, 409, 421, 423–5, 589
Jewel Tower, Westminster, 188
Joint Mitnor Cave, 661
Juke Box Cave, 222
Jutland, 385

Kastro Orovon, 139
Kentmere, 553
Kent's Cavern, 43, 661
Kincaid, 202
King Arthur's Cave, 661
Kingsley Cave, 69, 70
Kirkdale Cave, 661
Kirkstall Abbey, 387
Klip Kop Cave, 388
Krapina, 518, 520
Ksâr 'Akil, 408
Kunda, 384

La Brea, 506, 509
La Castella, 111
La Chapelle-aux-Saints, 481
La Ferrassie, 481
La Naulette, 518
La Quina, 481
Langdale, 573
Langhnaj, 304
Lepcis Magna, 139
Lipari, 582–4
Little Chesterford, 398
Little Harbor, 420
Liucheng, 45

Lloyd's Site, 37, 40
Lo Daiska, 222
London, 79, 202
Loose Howe, 178
Lovelock Cave, 235, 244, 247–8
Lund, 364

Maiden Castle, 459
Makalia, 464
Marib Dam, 140
Markkleeberg, 146
Mascarene Islands, 365
Mawgan Porth, 386–7
Mazanderan, 425
McClure, 69, 70
Meare, 211
Medum, 386
Meiendorf, 364
Melos, 582–3, 588, 590
Mesa Verde, 222, 236
Mildenhall, 695
Mississippi Drainage, 202
Mohenjo-Daro, 367
Mount Carmel, 303, 367, 465
Mugem, 461
Münsingen, 649
Muraba'ât, 550, 630
Mynydd Rhiw, 573–4

Naivasha, 464
Nakuru, 464
Naqada, 508
Neanderthal, 520
Negev, 139, 140, 141
Nemrut Dağ, 590
Newark Bay, 29
Newt Kash Hollow, 219, 222, 235
Ngangdong, 465
Niah Cave, 565
Niedermendig, 132
Nimrud, 139, 213
Nonsuch Palace, 29
Normanton Down, 130
North Ferriby, 178
Nutbane, 129–30

Oahe Dam, 222
Oakhurst, 388
Obercassel, 461, 520
Ocampo, 236–7

Ohio, 37
Olduvai, 61, 96, 97, 126
Olorgesailie, 96, 126
Olympia, 139
Oronsay, 384
Ostia, 140
Ouarizane Valley, 138
Overton Down, 133, 503, 507–8, 632
Ozark Plateau, 218, 219

Paracas, 495
Paviland, 462–3
Pazyrik, 178, 548
Pecos, 597
Petersgate, York, 388
Peterson, 69, 70
Piedras Negras, 598–9
Piltdown, 36, 39–42, 515, 519
Pompeii, 621
Pontefract Priory, 387–8, 553
Portesham, 175
Powder River, 148
Prědmost, 518
Prescelly, 574, 578
Pueblo Bonito, 191
Pueblo del Arroyo, 361

Rabat, 139
Rainsborough Hill Fort, 692, 694
Raknehaugen, 202
Rang Mahal, 367, 426
Richborough, 140
Rigler Buttes Site, 74
Robin Hood's Cave, 42, 43
Rome, 79, 532
Rörvick, 385
Rotekärrslid, 385

Saliagos, 408, 588
Salts Cave, 219, 222, 235, 566
Salzgitter-Lebenstedt, 146
San Teodoro, 461
Santorin, 578–9
Sarab, 588, 590
Sarah's Gully, 391
Sarmay Hegau, 97
Seamer, 384
Sedgeford, 29
Shanidar, 69, 72, 265, 431, 482
Shanidar Cave, 69, 72

Shulz site, 236
Sidon, 621
Sierra Nevada, 98
Šipka, 518
Skagerrak, 385
Skara Brae, 385
Skhul, 431, 465
Skorba, 584
Snail Down, 306
Solänger, 384, 385
Spy, 520
Star Carr, 171, 178, 303, 307, 366, 384, 417
Stonehenge, 129, 571, 578
Sutton Hoo, 565, 631
Svaedborg, 384
Swanscombe, 35, 36, 38, 126, 148, 253, 518

Tabun, 431, 465
Tamaulipas, 222, 235, 236, 238, 239–42
Taplow Barrow, 631
Tean, 29
Tehuacan, 222, 223, 240–2
Tell Asmar, 386
Tell Rifa'at, 424–5

Tell Shemshara, 588, 590
Tepe Guran, 588, 590
Tepexpan, 127, 431
Tesuque, 148
Téviec, 384, 461
Thaingen Weier, 202
Thatcham, 127–8
Thetford, 132
Thornborough Middle Rings, 129
Thriplow, 398
Tievebulliagh, 573
Tlatilco, 432
Tollund, 208
Tonto National Monument, 223
Tornewton Cave, 661
Torralba, 146–8
Trentholme Drive, York, 386
Trinil, 520
Tripolitania, 141
Troldebjerg, 315–30
Tuinplaats, 464
Tularosa Cave, 221

Uphill Cave, 661
Ur, 213
Utica, 140

Val d'Arno, 253
Verulamium, 131, 693
Veyrier, 461
Viste, 386

Wadi Derna, 146
Wadi Hasa, 139
Wadi Lebda, 143
Wadi Kofrein, 146
Wairau Bar, 361
Wareham, 503
Warka, 213
Wasserburg, 202
Wayland's Smithy, 128
Wharram Percy, 29, 388
Willey's Kopje, 464
Winchester, 29
Windeby, 493

Yap, 391
Yayahuala, 66
York, 178, 388, 552–3

Zeigenhaim, 202
Zion National Park, 219
Zuma Beach, 419

General Index

ABO blood groups, 510, 511

abscessing, 310, 312, 482, 486

absolute dating, 35 n., 45, 72, 93, 114, 167, 195

Adaz, 207

aerial photography, 121, 702

Agave, 238, 239–40, 241

age estimation: domestic animals, 283–302; man, 440–51, 486

age groupings, 26

Agropion canoninum, 209

Ailuropoda, 44

Alchemilla, 209

aleppo pine (*Pinus halepensis*), 146

alluvial succession, 135–7

Aloe, 238, 239

alpaca, 257, 260, 263

Amaranthus, 225, 239

amino acids, 37, 505–6, 509–10

Amphidesma ventricosum, 391

amputation, 497

aneurysm, 499

angel-fish, 385

animals, 251–427; domestic, 257–72; characteristics of, 260–2; species concept, 257–8; X-ray of bones, 516

anthracosis, 498–9

aortic calcification, 499

Apocynum, 246

appendicitis, 498

^{40}Ar/^{39}Ar method *see* potassium-argon dating

Ara macaw, 361

arc spectrography, 617

Arca scapha, 390

archaeomagnetism, 24, 76–87, 106; anomalies, 78–9; archaeological applications, 84–7; Curie points, 76–7, 80; direction of field, 79–80, 82–4; measurement of intensity, 84–7; metrical treatment and sample collecting, 80–1; stability of remanent magnetism, 77–9; *see also* magnetic location

Archiskodon africanavus, 42

arsenic, 560, 607, 608

arteriosclerosis, 499

arthritis, 312, 481, 482, 483, 523, 535

artifacts, 27–8, 30, 567–70; from bird bones, 361; electron microscopy, 566; flint, 129, 571, 572, 576; pollen analysis, 170; obsidian, 62–75, 579, 582–3; shell, 390, 393, 423–6; stone, 571–7; and statistics, 673–4

ass, 263

atheroma, 499

aurochs *see Bos primigenius*

Australopithecus, 466, 486, 520

autoradiography, 531–2, 536

axes, jadeite, 576; *see also* bronze, stone

barley, 206, 207, 208, 211, 213

bass, 379

bats (*Chiroptera*), 152, 255; guano, 159

beans, 216, 222, 225, 236–7, 238, 239; *see also Phaseolus*

bears, 43, 151–2, 159–60, 252, 253, 666; *Ursus arctos*, 253; *U. deningeri*, 253; *U. etruscus*, 252, 253; *U. minimus*, 253; *U. spelaeus*, 253, 311, 312, 535, 666

beech (*Fagus sylvatica*), 186

beetles, 240, 246; flour-beetles (*Tribolium*), 274

bilharziasis, 498

biology of ancient populations, 26–7

birch, 177

bird remains, 359–75, 387, 392, 420; archaeological use, 360–2; in coprolites, 246–7; examination and identification, 362–4; geographical summary, 364–9

bishop (*Pagrus*), 388

'Bishoping', 295

bison, 315; *B. bonasus*, 315, 321, 322

blood groups in bone, 510–11

boar, wild, 257, 264, 265, 266

bogs *see* peat deposits, Moorleichen

bones: ageing, 283–9, 473; blood grouping, 510–511; in coprolites, 236, 238, 242, 246–7; in caves, 151–2; dating, 35–45; electron microscopy, 565; fossil, 518–21, 526–33; histological structure, 533–5; inflammation of, 481–3; microscopy, 526–38; nitrogen content, 503–10; survival in altered form, 120, 121; X-rays in bone study, 516–21

Bos brachyceros, 269

Bos primigenius, 252, 257, 264, 265, 266, 312, 315, 321, 322, 323, 324, 325, 667; *B.p. hahni*, 269; *B.p. namadicus*, 269; *B.p. primigenius*, 269; *B.p. trochoceros*, 269

brain, 494

Brandwirtschaft, 327, 329

brasses, 554, 559

bream, 383, 384, 385

breed: defined, 262–3

breeding, animals, 257–72: cattle, 315; history of, 270; interbreeding, 258, 308; pelicans, 365; plants, 186

Brill-Hood, glass dating method, 621, 622

bronze, 608, 610–13; axes, 612; microscopy, 559, 560

buffalo (*Bubalus arnee*), 264

burbot, 385

C¹⁴ dating *see* radio-carbon dating

cacti, 238, 240, 241; pitahaya cactus, 249

calculi, renal and vesical, 498

calfskin, 543, 550, 552, 553

Callaeas cinerea wilsoni, 362

callus formation, 535

camel, 260; ageing, 299, 301; hair, 626, 631

Canis sp.: *C. aureus lupaster*, 304, 307; *C. lupus lupus*, 306; *C. lupus pallipes Sykes*, 304, 307

Capsicum (chili pepper), 225, 236–7, 238, 239, 240, 241

carbon reservoir, 47, 48, 50

carbonized remains, 121, 132, 188, 206, 207, 209–211, 420; *see also* charcoal

carburization, 561–2

carcinoma, 497–8

carex, 209

caries, 312, 482, 486

carnassial index, 304–6

carp, 379, 385

Carthamnus, 237

cashmere, 626

cassava *see Manihot*

castration: animals, 328; man, 499

cat: ageing, 299, 300; dirk-toothed (*Megantereon megantereon*), 666; ringtail, 242; sabre-tooth, 42, 44; wild, 667

catfish, 381, 383, 392

cattle, 261, 264, 313; ageing, 296–7; domestication, 261, 265, 266, 269–70; hair, 540, 632; husbandry, 315–30; skin, 540, 543, 548, 553

caves: cave rock, 156; fauna, 151–2; fillings, 125; mode of layer formation, 157; origins and forms: endogene, 152–3, exogene, 153; position, 154–6; research methods, 161–2; sediments, 151–61

Ceiba, 240–2

ceramic technology, 592–602; analytical techniques, 597–600; firing, 575, 595–6; shaping, 593–4; slips, 594, 602; texture analysis, 575, 594–5; X-ray, 513, 599

cereals, 120, 132, 206, 214; pollen, 169, 175

charcoal, 157, 178–87, 181–2, 193, 195, 209–11, 232

Chenopodium, 217

Chinese drugstore fossils, 44

cholecystitis, 498

chronometric dating, 35, 45, 74

chub, 383, 384, 385; Lahontan (*Siphateles*), 246

circumcision, 497, 499

clams, 420

climate, 124–5, 135, 178; cave deposits, 150, 158, 159–60, 166; deep sea cores, 110–14; dendrochronology, 203; fish, 393; molluscs, 397, 398, 399, 400–403, 408–12; pollen analysis, 129–30, 166, 176–7; soil magnetism, 684; timbers, 178

cloth, 624–5, 628–9, 630–2; *see also* fibres, textiles

club-foot, 481

coalfish, 384, 385

cobalt, 560

cockle (*Cardium edule*), 387, 388, 391, 392, 408

cod, 380, 384, 385, 386, 387, 388

coffins, 118, 119, 120, 178, 189, 521–2

collagen: in bone, 36–7, 503, 504–5, 506, 509–10, 528, 530, 532; in skin, 540, 544, 545; in ivory, 526

colorimetry, 618

computers, 649–60

congenital dislocation of the hip, 481, 482

conger, 384, 385, 386

copper, 555, 559, 603, 605, 607, 608, 611, 612

coprolites, 222, 235, 250; benzene tests, 236; diet; from, 235–43, 246–9; electron microscopy, 566; Great Basin, 244–50; methods of examination and analysis, 235–6, 242, 244–7; pollen analysis, 224; salt tests, 236

coral, 390, 391

corn spurrey, 212

Corynebacterium diphtheriae, 313; *C. murium*, 313; *C. ovis*, 313; *C. pyogenes*, 313

cotton, 220, 223, 225

cowry (*Ovulum ovum*; *Cypraea eburnea*), 389

crabs, 236–7, 384, 385, 390

cremations, 27, 120, 468–79; age determination, 473; animal remains, 477–8; enumeration of individuals, 472–3; identification, 471–2; physical characteristics, 469–71; sex determination, 473–8

Croton, 223

cucurbits, 216, 224–5, 236, 238, 239, 240

Cuon alpinus, 253; *C. majori*, 253

Curie Points, 76–7, 80

Cybister, 246

cyst, 482

dace, 383, 385

Daphnia (water fleas), 274

dating, 24–5, 35–108, 137–9; bones, 35–45, 503–510; *see also* absolute dating, archaeomagnetism, chronometric dating, dendrochronology, fission track, fluorine, nitrogen, radio-carbon, relative dating, stratigraphical dating

Datura, 233

Dead Sea scrolls, 539, 540, 547, 550, 551

deep-sea cores, 109–17; dating, 115–16; Globigerina ooze, 109–12; oxygen isotype analysis, 114; sampling, 110–11; temperature fluctuations, 110–14

deer, 235, 242, 260, 266; *Dama clactoniana*, 252; fallow (*D. dama*), 252, 263, 667; red (*Cervus elaphus*), 263, 667; roe, 263

deltas, 140

demography, 441–3

dendrochronology, 24, 64, 72, 191–203; archaeological applications, 201–3; interpretation, 198–201; methods, 194–8; principles, 191–3; requisites for, 193–4; techniques, 194–8

dermatosis, infective, 500

Deschampsia caespitosa, 209

desiccated remains, 132, 539; animal, 539; coprolites, 222, 235–50; man, 490–502; wheat, 206–207; wood, 178, 183; *see also* mummies

developmental disturbances, 481

discontinuous traits, in the human skull, 27

disease, 310–13, 480–9, 497–500; *see also* palaeopathology, plant diseases

ditches, 129, 130, 681, 684, 687, 693–4, 696; *see also* pits

dog, 251, 257, 261, 265, 266, 267; origins, 303–9, 312; ageing, 299

dogfish, 377, 385

domestication, 25–6; animals, 257–72; beginnings, 265–6; cattle, 315–30; nature of, 258–60; plants, 169, 206–50; reasons for, 267–8; sheep, 548

Donax, 389

donkey, 251, 258

Drosophila, 240, 274

duck, 360; Muscovy, 264

duckling, 248

dysentery, 248

earthworks, 125, 566; duration of construction, 131; experimental, 120, 133, 503, 507–8, 510–511, 632; over ancient soils, 128–30; and pollen analysis, 175

earthworms, 128, 173

Echinochloa crus-galli, 209

echinoderms, 390

ecology *see* environment

eczema, 500

eel, 379, 381, 384, 385

eggs, 360, 361, 366

Einkorn, 206, 210, 213

elasmobranchs, 377, 380

electron microscope, 526, 528, 530; scanning, 28, 564–6

electron probe microanalyser, 600, 602, 618

Elephantidae, 252; *Elephas antiquus*, 253, 532; *E. meridionalis*, 253; *E. planifrons*, 41, 42; *E. primigenius*, 253, 526; *E. trogontherii*, 253

elft (*Pomatomus*), 388

elk (*Megaloceros giganteus*), 667

elm, 173, 175–7, 188

Emmer, 206, 207, 210, 213

emphysema, 498

Entamoeba hystolytica, 248

environment and archaeology, 25–6, 33–4, 125, 139, 150, 179, 215, 251; and disease, 310; from mollusc remains, 390; from pollen analysis, 168–9, 170–1, 173, 174; from timbers, 184–5

Epimachairodus, 42, 43, 44

Equus, 252; *E. przewalskii*, 268, 269; *E. sanamensis*, 44; *see also* horse

Ergot sclerotinum, 209
estuaries, 140
evolution, 251–6; population level, statistical approach, 661–8

fabrics *see* cloth, fibres
Fannia scalaris, 240
Fergusonite, 88
ferri-magnetism *see* archaeomagnetism, magnetic location
ferrite, 560, 562
fibres, 624–33; animal, 120, 539–53, 568, 624, 626, 629–32; in coprolites, 247; descriptions, 628–32; identification, 626–8; preparation, 624–6; survival in altered form, 120, 121; vegetable, 624, 628–9
fibrosis of the liver, 498
fish, 236–7, 246–8; ageing, 381; archaeological survey, 383–94; evolution, 377–83; and homeostasis, 274; remains, 376–94
fishing, 383–6, 388–92, 417
fission track dating, 24, 58–61
flame photometry, 90, 618
flat-fish, 379, 380, 384
flax, 207, 211, 213, 629
flounder, 384, 385
fluorescence *see* X-rays, microscopy
fluorine analysis, 24, 36, 37–43, 44, 532
fluvial geology, 135–50
forest clearance, 128, 168–9, 171, 174, 177, 232, 327
forest lines, 163–6
forgery, detection of, 576, 799; *see also* 'Bishoping'
fossil fuel effect, 50
fossilization of bones and teeth, 518–21, 526–33
fowl, domestic, 257, 261, 365; ageing, 300
fowling, 366; *see also* bird remains
fox (*Vulpes*), 304, 667, 668
fracture, 310, 312, 482, 484, 535
frost action, 157–8, 163–4, 211–12
frozen remains, 178, 526, 539, 548
fruits, 207, 236, 237

Gafrarium tumidum, 390
Galley Hill skeleton, 37, 38, 39, 506
gallstones, 496
Gallus see fowl, domestic
Gammarus, 246
gar-fish, 379, 384
Gariidae, 392
Gaur, 264

Gayal, 264
geochemical reconnaissance, 121
Gigantopithecus, 44–5
glacial deposits, 125, 162–4
glass, 132, 568; analytical techniques, 614–23; arc spectrography, 617, 618; dating, 619, 621–3, 568; in fission track dating, 59–61; isotopic studies, 621; X-ray fluorescence, 617–18
Globigerina-ooze, 109–12
Globigerinoides sacculifera, 111
Globorotalia menardii, 113; *G. m. flexuosa*, 113; *G. tumida*, 112
goat, 264; ageing, 287, 298; domestication, 257, 264, 265, 266, 270; hair, 631; osteological differences from sheep, 331–56; skins, 539, 542–543, 548, 550, 551; *see also* hair, skin
gold, 555, 558
Gold-of-Pleasure, 211
goose (*Anser anser*; *A. cygnoides*), 264, 365
Gossen Geohm, 698
gourd *see* cucurbits, *Lagenaria*
gout, 497
grain *see* cereals, palaeoethnobotany
grasses, 120, 208; pollen, 168, 169; *see also* cereals, palaeoethnobotany, pollen analysis
grasshopper, 235
Great Auk (*Alca impennis*), 365, 366
guanaco, 257, 260, 263, 264
gurnet, 385
guinea-fowl, 264
guinea-pig (*Cavia aperea*), 264

haddock, 380, 384, 385, 386, 387
Haemogogus mosquitoes, 313
haematite, 76, 77, 683
hair: animal, 120, 539–53; in coprolites, 242, 247; electron microscopy, 565; human, 630; meat identification, 242; *see also* fibres, skin, wool
halibut, 386
Harpagornis, 361
Haversian canals, 527, 532, 534
hearths, 80, 84, 681, 692
helium, 88
Hermetia illuscens (soldier fly), 240
hernia, scrotal, 498
herring, 379, 386
hickory shell, 235
hide *see* skin
Hipparion, 44
hippopotamus, 39, 40, 41
Holcus, 209

holly (*Ilex aquifolia*), 132
Holostei, 379
homeostasis, 274, 279–80
Homo habilis, 60, 466
Homo neanderthalensis see Neanderthal man
Homo sapiens sapiens, 116, 466
hones, 575
horse, 251, 258, 261, 263, 667; ageing, 287, 289, 290–5; domestication, 268–9, 313; *see also Equus*
horse chestnut (*Aesculus hippocastanum*), 185
hunting, 257, 260, 267, 359; *see also* fowling
Hyaenidae *see* hyena
hyena (*Crocuta crocuta*), 151, 310; statistical analysis of evolution, 661–6, 667

Indian corn *see* maize
inflammatory changes in bone, 481–3, 535
ionium dating, 93
iron: magnetic location, 687, 688, 696; microscopy, 560–2; survival of, 119; X-ray, 513
isotopic fractionation, 47, 49, 621
ivy, 175, 177

jackal, 303–8
Java man *see Pithecanthropus*

K⁴⁰/Ar⁴⁰ dating *see* potassium argon
kidney disease, 498
kilns and fired structures, 575, 595, 602; dating, 78, 79, 80, 82, 83, 84, 106; locating, 681, 682, 686, 687, 692, 696; plant remains, 210
'kitchen middens', 360, 364, 384, 385, 387, 391, 407–9, 415–21; problems of analysis, 418–21

Lagenaria (domestic gourd), 237, 239, 361; *L. siceraria*, 225
lake deposits, 125, 127–8, 145–6; lake dwellings, 207, 385; pollen analysis, 168–9, 171; *see also* Swiss 'lake dwellings'
Landnam, 169–70
laurel (*Laurus canariensis*), 146
lead, 555, 560, 607, 608
leather, 539, 541, 545, 550, 551, 568; dating, 543; survival, 120, 121; staining reactions, 543, 550; tanning, 541–2, 545
Lemaireocerus, 240–1, 242; *L. thurberi*, 249
lemming (*Lagurus lagurus*), 253; *L. pannonicus*, 253
lentil, 213
leprosy, 483–4, 485, 497
lime, 177
limpet (*patella* sp.), 383, 392, 408, 409

'lines of arrested growth', 313, 516
ling, 380, 385, 387, 389
linseed *see* flax
lion, cave (*Felis leo*), 666
llama, 260, 263, 264
lobster, 390
Lolium perenne, 209
lynx, Issoire (*Felis issiodorensis*), 666

Macaca sp., 252; *M. florentina*, 252; *M. sylvana*, 252
'*Machairodus*', 42, 535
McLeod manometer, 90
magnetic location, 681–94, 695–6; ferrimagnetism, 683; instruments, 687–91; magnetic susceptibility, 684; principles, 682–6; survey logistics, 691–2; thermoremanent magnetism, 682–4, 686
magnetic fields, 76, 78, 79–80, 81, 82–3, 84
magnetic susceptibility, 68, 684
magnetite, 76, 77, 681, 683
magnetometers, 80–2, 695; astatic, 81, 86; differential fluxgate, 690–1, 694; proton, 681–2, 687–688, 694; rotating, 81, 85
maize, 216, 219–22, 225, 239
malaria, 498
malt, 211
mammals: palaeopathology, 310–13, 516; Pleistocene, 251–6; species in Europe, 254–5
mammoth, 40, 43, 127
man, 430–512
Manihot esculenta, 225, 239–41
manioc *see Manihot*
marshelder (*Iva annua v. macrocarpa*), 223
Martin Clark Resistivity Meter, 698–700
Mastodon, 41, 44
Megger Earth Tester, 698
mesquite (*prosopis*), 238, 239, 241
metallurgy, 609–13; Bronze Age, 610–13; Iron Age, 560–2
metals: alloys, non-ferrous, 558–60, 607–8; iron and steel, 560–2; microscopy, 555–63; non-ferrous, 557–63; preparation, 555–7; spectroscopy, 603–13
meteorites, 560, 562
Micro-Kjeldahl test, 37
microphotometer, 607
micropodzol, 119, 120
microscopy: ancient metal, 555–63; ceramic technology, 594; and charcoal, 182–3; hair, 539; petrology, 572, 575; in prehistoric bone, 526–537, 564–6; skin, 539, 549, 553

microtome, 539, 625, 627

millet, 212, 213

millstones, 575

Minnesota skeleton, 431

mistletoe, 177

MN blood groups, 510, 511

Moas, 359, 361, 368, 391, 392

mohair, 626

molluscs: as food, 415–22; ethnological interpretation, 423–7

molluscs, marine *see* shellfish

molluscs, non-marine, 395–406; as age indicators, 397–400; as climatic indicators, 397, 398, 400–3; and local conditions, 403–5

Moorleichen, 170, 490, 500; diet, 206, 208

mortality, human, 27, 440–52, 473, 486; *see also* age estimation

mouse, 313

mullet, 385

mummies, 63, 490–501; bird, 360, 361; blood groups, 495; cat, 540, 544; embalming techniques, 490–1; fish, 386; hair, 494, 544; histology, 491–3; pathology, 497–500; sheep, 540; X-ray, 521–3; *see also* palaeopathology

mummy wheat, 206–7

Murray cod (*Oligorus macquariensis*), 392

Musca domestica, 240

mussel (*Mytilus edulis*), 236–7, 383, 386, 387, 388, 391, 392, 408, 420

myocardial fibrosis, 499

Myotragus baledricus, 313

Nautilus, 390, 391

Neanderthal man: diet, 383; microscopy of bones, 528–30; pathology, 481–2, 486; sex, 431, 442; stature, 465; X-ray, 518, 520

necrosis, 310

neutron activation analysis, 90

'New Archaeology', 30–4

nickel, 560

nitrogen analysis, 24, 36–43, 44; of bone, 503–10, 530

nuclear bombardment, 598–9

oak, 179, 181, 183, 188–9

oats, 208

obsidian, 60, 578–91; green, 66, 586; grey, 66; rhyolitic, 64, 65; sources, 582–5; trachytic, 64, 65; trade, 583, 588–90

obsidian dating, 24, 62–75; advances in technique, 73–4; cultural factors, 67–72; hydration rate estimation; 63, 72, 74; measurement technique, 62–3; mechanical and chemical changes, 67

omegatron, 91, 102–3, 104

optical emission spectroscopy, 586, 598, 603–13; application, 609–13, interpretation, 607–9; principles and techniques, 603–7

origin of species, 251–6

ossein, 527–30, 532–3, 536

osteo-cytes, 527

osteomyelitis, 311, 312, 481, 535

osteones, 534, 535

osteo-sarcoma, 310, 487

ostrich, 366

ovarian cystadenoma, 498

ox, 267, 269, 270, 313; ageing, 287, 295–7

oxalic acid, 50–1

oxygen isotope studies, 114, 407, 409–12, 621

oyster (*Ostrea edulis*), 386, 387, 388

Paget's disease (*osteitis deformans*), 481

palaeoethnobotany, 206–28; American, 215–28; bog evidence, 207–8; carbonized material, 132–206, 207, 209–11; cereals, 206–14; grain imprints, 206, 212–13; mummy wheat, 206–7

palaeogeography, 140–4

palaeohydrology, 144–6

palaeomagnetism, 76, 98

palaeopathology: human bones, 480–9; mammals, 310–14, 516; microscopy, 535; soft tissues, 491–500, 522–3; *see also* disease

paper chromatography, 37

paradontal disease *see* peridontal

Paranthropus, 466

parasites, 313; in coprolites, 236, 248; in mummies, 500; *see also* worms, intestinal

parchment, 539, 540, 541, 542, 552, 568, 627, 628; dating, 543; Dead Sea Scrolls, 539, 540, 547, 550, 551; medieval, 551–4

pathology *see* disease, palaeopathology

paua, 391, 392

pea, 207, 213

peanut (*Arachis hypogaea*), 225

pearlite, 561, 562

peat deposits: pollen and stratigraphy, 127, 168, 170–2, 174, 177, 185, 322; preservative powers, 170, 172, 178, 207–8, 539, 632; *see also* Moorleichen

peccary, 242

pediculosis, 499

Pekin Man (*Homo erectus*) *see Pithecanthropus*

pelicans, 363, 365; *Pelecanus crispus*, 363; *P. onocrotalus*, 363
Perca nilotica, 386
perch, 385, 386, 387
peridontal disease, 306, 310, 486
periostitis, 481, 483
periwinkle (*Littorina littorea*), 387, 392
perma-frost, 158, 163, 164
petrographic microscope, 597
petrological examination, 571–7; dating, 24
Phaseolus sp. 224, 225, 238; *P. coccineus*, 237; *P. vulgaris*, 237, 239
phosphate analysis, 120
Physalis (cape-gooseberry), 241
pigs, 261, 313, 389; ageing, 298–9; domestication, 257, 264, 265, 266, 270; X-ray, 516
pike, 379, 383, 384, 385, 387, 388
Piltdown man, 36, 39, 40, 41, 519, 530
pipi, 392
Pitahaya cactus, 249
Pithecanthropus (*Homo erectus*), 254, 255, 382; caries, 486; date, 99; stature, 466; X-ray, 520
pits, 681, 684, 687, 692–3, 696
plants, 167–250, 421, 566; diseases, 208, 209; husbandry, 169, 206–50; remains in caves, 157
pneumonia, 498, 499
Poa nemoralis, 209
poliomyelitis, 497
pollack, 385, 386
pollen analysis, 24, 129, 146, 167–77, 178, 322–3; coprolites, 224, 235, 248; climate, 129–30, 166, 176–7; fossil, 127; husks, 120; peats and muds, 127, 168, 170–2, 185; principles and uses, 167–8, 176–7; in normal soils, 172
populations: animal, 273–82; statistical approach to evolution of, 661–8; Carr-Saunders theory, 281–2; population equilibrium, 273; social organization as a regulator, 273–82; statistics, 676–9
Populus, 185
porpoise, 391
post-holes, 118, 119, 121, 189
Potamides semitrisulcatus, 390
potassium-argon dating, 24, 25, 58, 61, 88–105, 115, 252; analytical technique, 90–1; $^{40}Ar/^{39}Ar$ method, 103–4; comparison with other methods, 93; dating recent periods, 93–7; dating young samples, 97–9; errors, 99, 104; suitable minerals, 91–2; advances in technique, 101–5
potato, 225

Potentilla erecta, 209
pottery, 568, 569; archaeomagnetism, 80, 83, 84, 85, 87; dating, 138–9; grain imprints, 212–13; size of vessels, 676–7; thermoluminescent dating, 106–8, 568; wheels, 593–4
Pott's disease, 483, 497
prickly pear (*Opuntia*), 237, 238, 239, 240
prospecting, 681–707
proton gradiometer, 689–90, 694
proton magnetometer *see* magnetometers
Pulleniatina obliquiloculata, 112, 113
Pyrrhocorax pyrrhocorax, 366; *P. graculus*, 366

Quaternary dating, 58–61, 89, 97–9, 138, 162–6; 395, 397–400
querns, 132, 572, 575

rabbit, 261
radioactivity of fossils *see* autoradiography, uranium
radio-carbon dating, 24, 35–6, 39, 46–57, 58, 63, 64, 69, 72, 79, 116, 137, 139, 167, 170, 171, 179, 233, 248, 390, 392, 503, 506, 530; counting methods, 53–5; fundamental assumptions, 46–53; half life, 47, 53; marine mollusca, 407, 412–414; standards, 50
radiography, radiology *see* X-rays
radiometric assay, 24, 40–4; *see also* uranium
rays, 379, 384, 385, 392; eagle ray, 388
rectal prolapse, 498
reindeer, 260, 263, 312
relative dating, 35, 39, 45, 72
remanent magnetism *see* archaeomagnetism
reptiles, fossil, 534, 535
resistivity surveying, 695–707; alternative electrode arrangements, 704–6; improvement of results, 706–7; instruments, 698–700; principles, 696–8; probe spacing (separation), 701–2; suitability of conditions, 700–2; survey procedure, 702–4
Rh blood groups, 510, 511
rhinoceros, 37, 40, 530
rhizomes, 236
Rhodesian man, 518
river deposits, 125, 135
roach, 384, 385
roots, of trees, 184
rudd, 385
rye, 208

Salix, 185, 208

salmon, 379, 383, 384, 385, 387, 389
salmonella, 313
sarcoma *see* osteo-sarcoma
scallop (*Pecten maximus*), 387, 388
Scirpus (bulrush), 246, 247
scoliosis, 481
seals, 368, 387, 388, 391, 392, 417
sea-urchin, 236–7, 390
Setaria (foxtail grasses), 238, 240–2; *S. geniculata*, 237; *S. viridis*, 209
sex determination in man, 27, 429–39; methods, 432–7; sexual dimorphism, 430–1; sexual isolation, in domestication, 259; sex ratio, 26, 43
sharks, 377–8, 384, 391, 392
sheep, 257, 261–2; ageing, 287, 298, 313; domestication and breeding, 264, 265, 266, 270, 548; osteological differences from goat, 331–56; skins, 539–53, 626–7, 631; X-ray, 516
shellfish, 236–7, 383, 384, 387, 388, 389, 390–3, 407–14; and economy, 407–9; palaeotemperature analysis, 407, 408, 409–12; radiocarbon dating, 412–14
ship-worm (*Nausitora*), 392
Sieglingia decumbens, 209
silhouettes, soil, 118–23; skeletal, 120
silica skeletons, 120, 206, 211–12
silk, 539
silver, 559
Sinanthropus see Pithecanthropus
skate, 384, 385
skin, 539–54, 624, 627, 632; dating, 543; histology, 543–4; identification of ancient specimens, 545–551; preservation and tanning, 541–2, 545; staining reactions, 544–5, 548, 553, 527–8; structure, 540–1; survival, 120; *see also* fibre, leather, wool
slags, 132, 569, 575, 601
smallpox, 498
Smilodon californicus, 312
snails, 146, 399–400; shell, 235; shell in caves, 157
snow line, 146, 163–6
society, biological definition, 277–9
'soft-rot', 189
soft tissues, ancient, 27, 491–7, 523
soils, 118–66; and coprolites, 249; and cultivation, 232; Iron Age and later, 130–2; Mesolithic sites, 127; Mexican volcanic deposits, 126–7; Neolithic and Bronze Age sites, 128–30; and nitrogen analysis, 506, 508–9; Pleistocene deposits, 125–6; pollen analysis, 172–3; resis-

tivity measurement, 696–8; stratification and environment, 124–33; and wood preservation, 188, 568
soil formation, 126, 129–33, 158–9, 166, 172–3
Somerset trackways, 171, 178
spectrographic analysis, 597–8, 601, 604, 616
spectrometer, mass-, 49, 90, 102–3, 104; cycloidal, 91; glass sector, 90
spectrometry, X-ray fluorescent, 513–14, 599–600
spelt, 210
Sphaeroidinella dehiscens, 113
spider shell (*Pterocera lambis*), 389
spondylitis deformans, 481
sprat (*Clupea sprattus*), 387
squamous papilloma, 498
squash, 225, 236, 241
statistics, 28, 635–79; and archaeology, 635–48, 669–79; by computer, 649–60; and evolution, 661–8; history of application, 669–70; misinterpretations, 674; nomenclature, 670–2; problems and variables, 635–7
stature, 27, 453–67; estimates for earlier populations, 457–66; 'near giant' and 'near dwarf', 457; techniques for estimation, 455–7; variation, 453–66
steel, 554, 560–2
stomach contents, 206, 209
stone, 568, 571–7; axes, 571, 572–3, 576; axe factories, 571, 573–5
stratification, 124–33
stratigraphical dating, 24, 61, 96, 116, 138
stream channels, 139–40
sturgeon, 385, 389
sunflower (*Helianthus annuus*), 223, 225, 235, 237–238, 239, 241–2
surveying: magnetic 691–2; resistivity, 695–707
Swanscombe skull, 36, 38, 41, 126
sweet potato, 225
Swiss 'lake dwellings', 171, 365
symbiosis, 26, 259
syphilis, 483, 535
Sylvagus cunicularis, 242; *S. audubonii*, 242

Takahe (*Notoris*), 363
teeth, animal: ageing, 289–301; disease, 486; dogs, 304–7; electron microscopy, 565; evolutionary changes, 664–6; X-ray, 517, 519–20
teeth, human: ageing, 443–6, 473; cremation, 471, 473; disease, 482, 485–6; electron microscopy, 565; X-ray, 519–20; *see also* fossilization
Tellohm, 698

tench, 384

Tepexpan skeleton, 127, 431

textiles, 568, 624-5

thermoluminescent dating, 24, 106-8, 568; accuracy, 107; apparatus, 107-8; principles, 106-7

thermo-remanent magnetism *see* archaeomagnetism

thorium, 106, 107, 532

Thylodrias contractus (odd beetle), 240

Tilapia nilotica, 386

Tillandsia, 239, 242; *T. usneoides*, 239, 242

tin, 607, 608, 610, 611, 612

tobacco, 223, 225

tope, 385

torsk, 386

traumatic injury *see* fractures

travertine, 157, 159-60, 166

tree ring dating *see* dendrochronology

trephination, 484, 485

Trichuris see worms, intestinal

trout, 379, 383

tuberculosis, 482, 483, 497

tumours, 312-13, 484-5, 487, 497, 535

tunny, 384, 385, 386

turkey, 264, 367

turtles: green (*Chelonia nydas*), 389, 390, 391; loggerhead (*Caretta caretta*), 390

Typha latifolia (cattail), 236, 246, 247, 248

uranium, 37, 40-2, 44, 58-61, 88, 106, 107, 531-2

uranium lead dating, 93

Ursus see bears

Uta, 497

vascular disease, 499

vesicovaginal fistula, 499

vetchling, 213

volcanic deposits, 126-7

waterlogged remains, *see* lake deposits, Moorleichen, peat deposits, wood

watermelon seeds, 235

weapon testing effects, in radiocarbon dating, 50

whales, 368, 388, 391, 392; whalebone, 392

wheat, 206, 208, 213; *see* Emmer, Einkorn

whelk (*Buccinum undatum*), 387, 388

whitefish, 389

whiting, 385

willow *see* Salix

wolf (*Canis lupus*), 251, 257, 266, 303, 304-8, 310, 312, 661, 666, 667

wolverine (*Gulo gulo*), 253; *Gulo schlosseri*, 253

wood, 178-87, 568; dry, 183; silhouettes, 118, 119; structure, 179-81; survival, 188-90, 207; waterlogged, 119, 120, 178, 183-4, 189, 568

wool, 120, 121, 539, 544, 545-52, 553, 626, 629-630, 631, 632

worms, intestinal, 236, 248, 500; *Trichuris*, 208

wrasse, 384, 385, 386, 387

Würm Ice Age: caves, 162-6

X-rays, 513-25, 568-9; use in ageing, 287-8; animal bones, 516-18; diffraction analysis, 514-515; Egyptian mummies, 521-3; fluorescent analysis, 596, 599-600, 617-18; fossil man, 518-521; and human variation, 523; microscopy, 515; spectrography, 536

yak, 539

yams (*Dioscoreaceae*), domestication, 229-33; gardens, clearance for, 232; remains in cultivators' settlements, 232-3

yaws, 483, 484

Yucca, 238

zinc, 556, 559

Zinjanthropus, 383, 466